Anatomy, Physiology & Disease

Fourth Edition

Bruce J. Colbert
Director of Allied Health
University of Pittsburgh at Johnstown

Jeff Ankney
Director of Clinical Education,
Respiratory Care Program
University of Pittsburgh at Johnstown

Karen T. Lee
Associate Professor of Biology
University of Pittsburgh at Johnstown

Boston • Columbus • Indianapolis • New York • San Francisco
Amsterdam • Cape Town • Dubai • London • Madrid • Milan • Munich • Paris • Montréal • Toronto
Delhi • Mexico City • São Paulo • Sydney • Hong Kong • Seoul • Singapore • Taipei • Tokyo

Pearson

Pearson

330 Hudson Street, New York, NY 10013
Hardcover ISBN 10: 0-13-470947-0
Hardcover ISBN 13: 978-0-13-470947-5

BRIEF CONTENTS

Chapter 1   Anatomy, Physiology, and Disease: Learning the Language   1

Chapter 2   The Human Body: Reading the Map   31

Chapter 3   Biochemistry: The Basic Ingredients of Life   55

Chapter 4   The Cells: The Raw Materials and Building Blocks   75

Chapter 5   Tissues and Systems: The Inside Story   111

Chapter 6   The Skeletal System: The Framework   143

Chapter 7   The Muscular System: Movement for the Journey   181

Chapter 8   The Integumentary System: The Protective Covering   215

Chapter 9   The Nervous System: The Body's Control Center   251

Chapter 10   The Endocrine System: The Body's Other Control Center   311

Chapter 11   The Senses: The Sights and Sounds   345

Chapter 12   The Cardiovascular System: Transport and Supply   377

Chapter 13   The Respiratory System: It's a Gas   431

Chapter 14   The Lymphatic and Immune Systems: Your Defense Systems   479

Chapter 15   The Gastrointestinal System: Fuel for the Trip   519

Chapter 16   The Urinary System: Filtration and Fluid Balance   565

Chapter 17   The Reproductive System: Replacement and Repair   601

Chapter 18   Basic Diagnostic Tests: What Do the Tests Tell Us?   645

Chapter 19   Anatomy and Physiology and the Scientific Method   677

Chapter 20   The Journey's End: Now What?   699

Chapter 21   Health Care: Careers and Career Planning   731

The Study Success Companion: The Key to Your Successful Journey   759

Appendix A   Medical Terminology, Word Parts, and Singular and Plural Endings   779

Appendix B   Clinical Abbreviations and "Do Not Use" List   790

Appendix C   Infectious Diseases and Their Pathogens   800

Appendix D   Laboratory Reference Values   803

Appendix E   Multisystem Effects of Various Diseases and Conditions   807

Appendix F   Vitamins and Minerals: Sources, Function, and Effects of Deficiency and Toxicity   818

Appendix G   Standard and Transmission-Based Precautions   821

Glossary   826

Index   874

DEDICATIONS

To all the future health care professionals learning Anatomy, Physiology, and Disease. May your chosen professions be as personally rewarding as ours have been.

—*Your Travel Guides Bruce, Jeff, and Karen*

To those closest to me, who share this wonderful journey through life: my wife Patty, my sons Joshua and Jeremy, daughter-in-law Ali, and my brothers and sister. Finally, to the memory of my Mom and Dad, who taught me the importance of education.

—*Bruce*

To my wonderful family especially Mom and Dad, you both have always been there for the good and not so good times and to a very special son, Zack. I am so very proud of you! Patty, thanks for being so supportive throughout this project. And to all of my past teachers and professors; here's proof that underachievers sometimes do finally get it right!

—*Jeff*

I dedicate this book to my family who have always supported me, no matter where life has taken me; not only my "real" family—my late father, Ed, my mother Pat, brother Eddie, sister-in-law Sheila, my nephew Jimmy, and assorted aunts, uncles, and cousins, who really had no choice but to be part of my life—but also those members of my extended family who have inexplicably chosen to be part of my life, giving me the gift of their friendship. I couldn't have done it without them.

—*Karen*

CONTENTS

About the Authors xv

Preface xvi

Acknowledgments xvii

Reviewers xvii

Special In-Text Features Directory Listing xviii

A User's Guide to the Features of The Book xxi

Chapter 1 Anatomy, Physiology and Disease: Learning the Language 1

What Is Anatomy and Physiology? 2
Anatomy 2
Physiology 3
Putting It All Together 3

What Is Disease? 4

The Language 5
Medical Terminology 6
Abbreviations 9
The Metric System 11

Anatomy, Physiology, and Disease Concepts You Will Encounter on Your Journey 11
Metabolism 11
Homeostasis 12
Disease Concepts 15

The Body's Defense System 18
Body Barriers 18
Understanding Routes of Transmission 19
Standard Precautions 20

Summary 23

Case Study 24

Review Questions 26

Career Connections 28

Anatomy, Physiology, and Disease in Action 29

Chapter 2 The Human Body: Reading the Map 31

The Map of the Human Body 32
Body Positions 32

Pathology Connection: Body Positions and A&P Changes 34
Body Planes and Directional Terms 35
Additional Directional Terms 37
Body Cavities 40
Body Regions 41

Radiology: The Science of Viewing the Body 46
X-rays (Radiograph or Roentgenogram) 46
Computerized Tomography (CT or CAT Scan) 48
Magnetic Resonance Imaging (MRI) 48
Ultrasound (Sonography) 48

Summary 50

Case Study 51

Review Questions 52

Career Connections 54

Anatomy, Physiology, and Disease in Action 54

Chapter 3 Biochemistry: The Basic Ingredients of Life 55

Atoms, Elements, and Ions 56
Acids and Bases 58

Bonding 60

Water 61
Solutions 62
Biological Molecules 63
Metabolism 67
Enzymes: Making Reactions Happen 67

Summary 70

Case Study 71

Review Questions 71

Career Connections 73

Anatomy, Physiology, and Disease in Action 74

Chapter 4 The Cells: The Raw Materials and Building Blocks 75

Overview of Cells 76

Cell Structure 77
Cell Membrane 78

Transport Methods 79
Passive Transport 79

Pathology Connection: Cystic Fibrosis (CF): A Membrane Channel Abnormality 82

Pathology Connection: Diabetes Mellitus: A Disorder of Facilitated Diffusion 83
Active Transport 84

Pathology Connection: Familial Hypercholesterolemia: A Disorder of Endocytosis 86

Cellular Components 87
Cytoplasm 87
Nucleus and Nucleolus 87
Ribosomes 88
Centrosomes 89
Mitochondria 89
Endoplasmic Reticulum 90
Golgi Apparatus 90
Lysosomes 91
Other Interesting Parts 91

Pathology Connection: Organelle Disorders 92

Pathology Connection: Diabetes Mellitus (Revisited): A Disorder Tied to Cellular Respiration 93

Pathology Connection: PKU, an Enzyme Disorder 94
Mitosis 95

Cellular Reproduction 95
The Cell Cycle 96

Pathology Connection: Cancer: Mitosis Run Amok 98

Microorganisms 99
Bacteria 99
Viruses 100
Fungi 101
Protozoa 101

Pathology Connection: How Microorganisms Cause Disease 103

Summary 106

Case Study 107

Review Questions 108

Career Connections 110

Anatomy, Physiology, and Disease in Action 110

Chapter 5 Tissues and Systems: The Inside Story 111

Overview of Tissues 112
Tissue Types 112

Pathology Connection: Blood Sugar and Tissue Damage 120

Organs 121

Systems 122
Skeletal System 124
Muscular System 125
Integumentary System 126
Nervous System 127
Endocrine System 128
Cardiovascular System 129

Pathology Connection: Septicemia 130
Respiratory System 130
Lymphatic and Immune System 131
Gastrointestinal (Digestive) System 132

Pathology Connection: Body Image: Obesity and Anorexia 134
Urinary System 135
Reproductive System 136
Summary 138
Case Study 138
Review Questions 140
Career Connections 142
Anatomy, Physiology, and Disease in Action 142

Chapter 6 *The Skeletal System: The Framework 143*

System Overview: More Than the "Bare Bones" About Bones 144
General Bone Classification 144
Basic Bone Anatomy 145
Bone Tissue 147
Surface Structures of Bones 148
Bone Growth and Repair 149
Pathology Connection: Osteoporosis 151
Cartilage 153
Joints and Ligaments 154
Movement Classification 156
Pathology Connection: Common Joint Disorders 158
The Skeleton 160
Special Regions of the Skeletal System 160
Pathology Connection: Spinal Column Abnormalities 165
Pathology Connection: Bone Fractures and Healing 168
Maintaining Good Bone Health 169
A Quick Trip Through Some Diseases of the Skeletal System 171
Pharmacology Corner 175
Summary 176
Case Study 177
Review Questions 178
Career Connections 180
Anatomy, Physiology, and Disease in Action 180

Chapter 7 *The Muscular System: Movement for the Journey 181*

Overview of the Muscular System 182
Types of Muscles 182
Pathology Connection: Myopathy 184
Skeletal Muscles 185
Pathology Connection: Strains and Tears 185
Skeletal Muscle Injuries 188
Pathology Connection: Fibromyalgia Syndrome 192
Skeletal Muscle Movement 192
Contraction and Relaxation 192
Movement Terminology 194
Muscular Movement at the Cellular Level 196
The Functional Unit of the Muscle 196
Pathology Connection: Duchenne's Muscular Dystrophy (DMD) 199
Pathology Connection: Myasthenia Gravis (MG) 199
Pathology Connection: Tetanus 201
Muscular Fuel 202
Visceral or Smooth Muscle 203
Cardiac Muscle 204
A Quick Trip Through Diseases and Conditions of the Muscular System 205
Pharmacology Corner: Skeletal Muscle Drugs 207
Summary 208
Case Study 209
Review Questions 210
Career Connections 212
Anatomy, Physiology, and Disease in Action 213

Chapter 8 *The Integumentary System: The Protective Covering 215*

System Overview 216
Integumentary System Functions 216
The Skin 217
Pathology Connection: Skin Color and Disease 219
Pathology Connection: Infections of the Skin 221

How Skin Heals 225

Pathology Connection: Burns 227

Nails 230

Hair 232

Pathology Connection: Lice
and Scabies 234

Temperature Regulation 235

Pathology Connection: Skin Lesions 237

A Quick Trip Through Some Diseases
of the Integumentary System 238

Pharmacology Corner 244

Summary 244

Case Study 245

Review Questions 246

Career Connections 248

Anatomy, Physiology, and Disease
in Action 249

Chapter 9   The Nervous System: The Body's
Control Center 251

Overview 252
The Parts and Basic Operation
   of the Nervous System 252

Nervous Tissue 255
Neuroglia 255
Neurons 256

How Neurons Work 257
Excitable Cells 257
Action Potentials 258
Local Potentials 258
Impulse Conduction 259

Pathology Connection: Myelin
Disorders 261
How Synapses Work 262

Spinal Cord and Spinal Nerves 265
External Anatomy of the Spinal Cord 265
Internal Anatomy of the Spinal Cord 267

Pathology Connection: Polio and Post-
Polio Syndrome 271

Pathology Connection: Peripheral
Neuropathy and Spinal Cord Injury 272

The Brain and Cranial Nerves 276
The Brain's External Anatomy 276
Internal Anatomy of the Brain 279

Pathology Connection:
Brain Injury 280
Cerebrospinal Fluid and Ventricles 288
Cranial Nerves 288

Pathology Connection: Alzheimer's
Disease 288

Pathology Connection:
Hydrocephalus 291

The Big Picture: Integration of Brain,
Spinal Cord, and PNS 292
The Somatic Sensory System 292
The Motor System 294

Pathology Connection: Motor
Pathologies 296

The Autonomic Nervous
System 298
The Sympathetic Branch 299
The Parasympathetic Branch 300

A Quick Trip Through Diseases
of the Nervous System 302

Pharmacology Corner 304

Summary 305

Case Study 306

Review Questions 307

Career Connections 310

Anatomy, Physiology, and Disease
in Action 310

Chapter 10   The Endocrine System: The Body's
Other Control Center 311

Organization of the Endocrine
System 312
Endocrine Organs 312
Hormones 314

Control of Endocrine Activity 315
Homeostasis and Negative Feedback 315
Sources of Control of Hormone Levels 317

The Major Endocrine Organs 319
The Hypothalamus 319
The Pituitary 320

Pathology Connection: Posterior
Pituitary and Antidiuretic Hormone 322

Pathology Connection: Anterior
Pituitary 323
The Thyroid Gland 324

The Thymus Gland 325
The Pineal Gland 325
The Pancreas 325

Pathology Connection: The Thyroid Gland 326
The Adrenal Glands 329

Pathology Connection: Diabetes Mellitus 331

Pathology Connection: Steroid-Related Conditions 334
Cortisol and the Stress Response 335

The Gonads 336

Prostaglandins 337

A Quick Trip Through the Diseases of the Endocrine System 338

Pharmacology Corner 339

Summary 340

Case Study 341

Review Questions 342

Career Connections 344

Anatomy, Physiology, and Disease in Action 344

Chapter 11   The Senses: The Sights and Sounds 345

The Senses 346

Sense of Sight 347
The External Structures of the Eye 347
The Internal Structures of the Eye 348

Pathology Connection: Injuries and Disorders of the Eyes 350

The Sense of Hearing 356
Structures of the Ear 356

Pathology Connection: Diseases of the Ear 360

Other Senses 362
Taste 362
Smell 363
Touch 364

A Quick Trip Through Some Diseases of the Eye 368

A Quick Trip Through Some Diseases of the Ears 369

Pharmacology Corner 370

Summary 371

Case Study 372

Review Questions 372

Career Connections 374

Anatomy, Physiology, and Disease in Action 375

Chapter 12   The Cardiovascular System: Transport and Supply 377

System Overview 378

Incredible Pumps: The Heart 380
General Structure and Function 380
Cardiac Cycle 382

Pathology Connection: Problems with Cardiac Muscle and Cardiac Vasculature 387

Pathology Connection: Electrical Disturbances 397

Hematology 399
Blood Composition 399
Red Blood Cells 401
White Blood Cells 401
Inflammation 402
Thrombocytes 403
Blood Types and Transfusions 403

Pathology Connection: Assorted Blood Conditions 406

Blood Vessels: The Vascular System 407
Structure and Function 407
Capillaries and Veins 408
Blood Clotting 411

Pathology Connection: Clotting 413

Pathology Connection: Problems Associated with Systemic Blood Vessels 415

A Quick Trip Through Some Diseases of the Cardiovascular System 415

Pharmacology Corner 423

Summary 424

Case Study 425

Review Questions 425

Career Connections 428

Anatomy, Physiology, and Disease in Action 429

Chapter 13 The Respiratory System: It's a Gas 431

System Overview 432
Ventilation versus Respiration 434

The Respiratory System 436
The Airways and The Lungs 436
The Upper Airway of the Respiratory Tract 436

Pathology Connection: The Nose 439
The Sinuses 441
The Pharynx 442
The Larynx 443

Pathology Connection: The Upper Airway 444

The Lower Respiratory Tract 447
The Alveolar Capillary Membrane: Where the Action Is 450
Pulmonary Function Testing 452

Pathology Connection: The Lower Airways 454
The Housing of the Lungs and Related Structures 462

Pathology Connection: Pleural Space Problems 463
The Lungs 464
The Protective Bony Thorax 464
How We Breathe 465

A Quick Trip Through the Diseases of the Respiratory System 469

Pharmacology Corner 472

Summary 473

Case Study 474

Review Questions 474

Career Connections 476

Anatomy, Physiology, and Disease in Action 477

Chapter 14 The Lymphatic and Immune Systems: Your Defense Systems 479

The Defense Zone 480

The Lymphatic System 480

Pathology Connection: Tonsillitis 483
Lymph Organs 485

Pathology Connection: Lymphatic Disorders 486

Pathology Connection: Cancer Stages and the Lymphatic System 486

The Immune System 488
Antigens and Antibodies 488
Innate versus Adaptive Immunity 488
Components of the Immune System 489

Pathology Connection: Leukemia 491

Pathology Connection: Inflammation, a Two-Edged Sword 493

How the Immune System Works 495
Innate Immunity 495
Adaptive Immunity 496

Pathology Connection: Autoimmune Disorders 497

Pathology Connection: HIV and AIDS 502
B and T Cell Action 503

The Big Picture 507

Pathology Connection: Hypersensitivity Reactions 508

A Quick Trip Through Some Diseases of the Immune System 510

Pharmacology Corner 511

Summary 512

Case Study 515

Review Questions 516

Career Connections 518

Anatomy, Physiology, and Disease in Action 518

Chapter 15 The Gastrointestinal System: Fuel for the Trip 519

System Overview 520

The Mouth and Oral Cavity 522
Oral Cavity 522
Tongue 522
Salivary Glands 522
Teeth 524

Pathology Connection: Oral Disorders 527

Pharynx 527

Esophagus 528

The Walls of the Alimentary Canal 529

Stomach 531

Pathology Connection: Stomach Acid Disorders 535

Small Intestine 537

Large Intestine 541

Pathology Connection: Disorders of the Lower Gastrointestinal Tract 543

Accessory Organs 544
Liver 544
Gallbladder 545
Pancreas 546

Pathology Connection: Cholecystitis, Pancreatitis, and Hepatitis 547

Common Symptoms of Digestive System Disorders 548

A Quick Trip Through Some Diseases of the Gastrointestinal System 549

Pharmacology Corner 556

Summary 556

Case Study 558

Review Questions 558

Career Connections 562

Anatomy, Physiology, and Disease in Action 563

Chapter 16 *The Urinary System: Filtration and Fluid Balance 565*

System Overview 566

The Anatomy of the Kidney 567
External Anatomy 567
Internal Anatomy 568
Microscopic Anatomy of the Kidney: The Nephron 570

Pathology Connection: Kidney Stones and Polycystic Kidney Disease (PKD) 572

Urine Formation 576
Control of Filtration 576

Pathology Connection: Nephropathy 580
Control of Tubular Reabsorption and Secretion 582

Pathology Connection: Uremia and Renal Failure 585

Pathology Connection: Dialysis or Kidney Transplant Therapy 589
The Urinary Bladder and Urination Reflex 590

Pathology Connection: Incontinence and Urinary Tract Infection (UTI) 592

A Quick Trip Through Disorders of the Urinary System 593

Pharmacology Corner 595

Summary 596

Case Study 597

Review Questions 598

Career Connections 600

Anatomy, Physiology, and Disease in Action 600

Chapter 17 *The Reproductive System: Replacement and Repair 601*

Tissue Growth and Replacement 602
Mitosis 602

Sexual Reproduction 603
Reduction Division: Meiosis 603

The Human Life Cycle 605

The Human Reproductive System 607
Female Anatomy 607

Pathology Connection: Endometriosis 610

Reproductive Physiology: Female 613
The Menstrual Cycle 613

Pathology Connection: Menstrual Disorders 618
Male Anatomy 621

Pathology Connection: Male Reproductive Diseases 623

Reproductive Physiology: Male 625
Spermatogenesis 625

Pathology Connection: Erectile Dysfunction (ED) 627

Pregnancy 628

Pathology Connection: Infertility 629

Pathology Connection: Breast Health 632

A Quick Trip Through Some Diseases of the Reproductive System 634

Pharmacology Corner 636

Summary 637

Case Study 639

Review Questions 639

Career Connections 642

Anatomy, Physiology, and Disease in Action 643

Chapter 18   Basic Diagnostic Tests: What Do the Tests Tell Us? 645

Overview of Diagnostic Testing 646

Blood Testing 647
Blood Basics 647
General Blood Disorders 649
Specific Blood Tests 649
Blood Chemistry 655

Urine Testing 658
Dipsticks 659
Specific Urine Tests 660

Fecal Testing 665
Amount, Consistency, Form, and Shape 665
Stool pH 665
Stool Color 665
Blood in Stool 666
Mucus in Stool 666

Cerebral Spinal Fluid (CSF) Testing 667
CSF Color 667
CSF Cell Counts 668

Culture and Sensitivity (C&S) Testing 668

Cardiac Diagnostics 669
Electrocardiogram (ECG/EKG) 669
Holter Monitor 669
Stress Testing 670

"Scopes" 670

Pulmonary Function Testing (PFT) 671

Polysomnography 672

Summary 673

Case Study 674

Review Questions 674

Career Connections 676

Anatomy, Physiology, and Disease in Action 676

Chapter 19   Anatomy and Physiology and the Scientific Method 677

Overview of the Scientific Method 678
Patterns of Knowing 678
The Scientific Method 679
Formulating Questions 680
Hypotheses and Theories 680
Testing Hypotheses 682
Making Measurement 685
Presenting and Data 689
Drawing Inferences 692
Limitations of the Scientific Method 695

Summary 696

Review Questions 696

Anatomy, Physiology, and Disease in Action 698

Chapter 20   The Journey's End: Now What? 699

Forensic Science 700
Disease Detection 701
Primitive Surgery 701
Remains Identification 702
Murder Most Foul! 702
Fingerprints 703
DNA Fingerprinting 704

Geriatrics 705
General Body Changes 706
Gustatory Changes 707
The Brain and Nervous System 707
The Cardiovascular System 707
Genitourinary System 708
Integumentary System 708
Polypharmacy 708

Wellness 709
Nervous System 710
Skeletal System 710
Muscular System 711
Integumentary System 712
Cardiovascular System 712
Respiratory System 713

Gastrointestinal System 715
Endocrine System 717
Sensory System 717
Immune System 718
Reproductive System 718
Cancer Prevention and Treatment 720
More Amazing Facts 723
Some Things to Ponder and Some Things to Keep You Up at Night 724
Summary 725
Case Study 726
Review Questions 726
Anatomy, Physiology, and Disease in Action 729

Chapter 21   *Health Care: Careers and Career Planning 731*
Interests 732
Values 732
Abilities 732
Heath Care Education 733
Resources For Occupational Research 733
Jobs and Professions 734
Professional and Personal Characteristics 749
Ethical Roles and Responsibilities of a Health Care Worker 752
Meetings in the Workplace 753
Safety in the Workplace 753
Job-Seeking Skills 754
Your Career Plan 755
Volunteering 757
Suggested Activities 758

The Study Success Companion: The Key to Your Successful Journey 759
Study Skills 760
1. Select a Good Time and Place to Study 760
2. Use Good Study Habits 761
3. Take Care of Yourself 763
Stress Management 763
Stress Misconceptions 763
What Causes Physical and Emotional Stress? 764
A Stress Management System 766
Effective Coping Strategies 766
Effective Physical Strategies 767
The Mathematical Language of Medicine 769
Why Learn the Metric System? 769
Exponential Powers of 10 769
Systems of Measurement 770
Conversion of Units 774
Using the Factor Label Method for Conversion Between Systems 777

Appendix A   *Medical Terminology, Word Parts, and Singular and Plural Endings 780*
Word Parts Arranged Alphabetically and Defined 780
Endings in Medical Terminology 788

Appendix B   *Clinical Abbreviations and "Do Not Use" List 790*
Official "Do Not Use" List 798
Additional Abbreviations, Acronyms, and Symbols 799

Appendix C   Infectious Diseases and Their Pathogens 800

Viral Conditions 800

Bacterial Conditions 800

Mycotic (Fungal) Conditions 801

Conditions Caused by Protozoa 802

Appendix D   Laboratory Reference Values 803

Abbreviations Used in Reporting Laboratory Values 803

Hematology Tests: Normal Ranges 803

Hematology Tests: Coagulation Tests 804

Blood Chemistries: Normal Ranges 804

Urinalysis: Normal Ranges 805

Normal Values of Arterial Blood Gases 805

Common Blood Chemistries and Examples of Disorders They Indicate 805

Appendix E   Multisystem Effects of Various Diseases and Conditions 807

Appendix F   Vitamins and Minerals: Sources, Function, and Effects of Deficiency and Toxicity 818

Appendix G   Standard and Transmission-Based Precautions 821

Hand Hygiene 821

Respiratory Hygiene/Cough Etiquette 821

Personal Protective Equipment 821

Procedures 822

Gown 822

Mask 822

Goggles/Face Shield 822

Gloves 823

Removing Personal Protective Equipment 823

Mouthpieces, Resuscitation Bags, and Other Ventilation Devices 823

Caring for Soiled Linens 823

Disposing of Sharps 824

Communicable Diseases 824

HIV 824

MRSA (Methicillin-Resistant Staphylococcus Aureus) 824

SARS (Severe Acute Respiratory Syndrome) 825

Glossary 826

Index 874

Bruce Colbert is the Director of the Allied Health Department at the University of Pittsburgh at Johnstown. He holds a Master's in Health Education and Administration, has authored nine books, written several articles, and given over 250 invited lectures and workshops at both the regional and national level. Many of his workshops provide teacher training involving techniques to make the health sciences engaging and relevant to today's students. In addition, he does workshops on developing effective critical and creative thinking, stress and time management, and study skills. He is an avid basketball player, even after three knee surgeries, which may indicate he has some learning difficulties.

Jeff Ankney is the Director of Clinical Education for the University of Pittsburgh at Johnstown Respiratory Care program, where he is responsible for the development and evaluation of hospital clinical sites. In the past, Jeff has served as a public school teacher, Assistant Director of Cardiopulmonary Services, Program Coordinator of Pulmonary Rehabilitation, and a member of hospital utilization review, patient safety/strategic planning and hospital policy committees. He is a consultant on hospital management and pulmonary rehabilitation concerns. Jeff was also the recipient of the American Cancer Society Public Education Award. He is a pretty fair fly fisherman and wing shot, although his springer spaniel, Rusty, would probably disagree.

Karen Lee is an Associate Professor in the Biology Department at the University of Pittsburgh at Johnstown, where she teaches all the anatomy courses, including Anatomy and Physiology for Nursing and Allied Health students. She presents regularly at scientific conferences and has published several articles on crustacean physiology and behavior. Serving as the coordinator of undergraduate research on campus, she is also the chair of the University of Pittsburgh at Johnstown's annual undergraduate symposium. For the last twenty years she has sung bass in women's barbershop choruses and quartets and more recently has been harmonizing with any singer or guitar player who will let her near the microphone.

PREFACE

We have made every effort to put together an Anatomy, Physiology and Disease book that students would actually enjoy reading.

Anatomy, physiology, and *pathology* are critical concepts you must master to succeed in the health professions. *Anatomy, Physiology and Disease: An Interactive Journey for Health Professionals,* Fourth Edition, along with the accompanying *Study Success Companion,* are written in a manner that will enhance learning of the material versus mass memorization of facts. Too often students adopt the strategy of memorizing massive amounts of information and simply storing it in their short-term memories. Then they literally repeat this information during their exams. However, memorization alone does not help learners master the material and make the lasting connections that will help them *thrive* as a health care practitioner.

In the course of a day as a health professional, you will be exposed to a variety of diseases involving all parts of the body, and therefore you must truly *learn* the workings and interrelatedness of all the body systems and functions.

So what have we done to facilitate learning the material? First, we have placed study skills and stress management tips in a *Study Success Companion* in the back of your book to help you along your journey through this class and beyond. Second, we have strived to make anatomy, physiology, and pathology "come alive" by using an engaging writing style to make it seem as if we are sitting next to you talking about the concepts. We hope you consider us assistants to the most important guide through this journey: your teacher.

Humor, where appropriate, and analogies that compare the human body to everyday things to which you can relate, have been interwoven throughout the text. Finally, we have added special features in a unique fashion tailored to the visual learning styles and relevant learning that today's students require.

We have worked hard and sincerely hope these features will help make studying *Anatomy, Physiology and Disease: An Interactive Journey for Health Professionals,* Fourth Edition a positive experience. Have a safe and happy journey!

To Jill Rembetski, who acted as our guide through the development and completion of this textbook. To all those at Pearson who were so helpful and friendly in this monumental process. A special thanks goes to Marlene Pratt, Mark Cohen, and Melissa Kerian for their enthusiastic belief and support in the vision and execution of this unique project. Thank you to a great group of reviewers and contributors who helped shape this project with their thoughtful insights.

A thank you to the authors' sons, Jeremy Colbert and Zack Ankney, who helped with review and revisions for this edition from a student's perspective. Special thanks to Jan Snyder for putting up with two quirky authors and helping in so many ways. Thanks to Emergent Learning, LLC, and Jen Frew for her hard work and professionalism. Finally, thanks to Clarice Morris for creating the new Anatomy, Physiology, and Disease in Action activities.

REVIEWERS

Beverly Campbell, President
BECGroup Consulting

Shari Buffum Cloud, RN, BSN, NBCT
Medical Sciences/PLTW-Principles of Biomedical
    Sciences Instructor
South Mecklenburg High School
Charlotte, NC

Clarice K.W. Morris, PhD
Coordinator, Academy of Medical Professions
Charles E. Gorton High School

Matthew Rice
Charlotte-Mecklenburg Schools

SPECIAL IN-TEXT FEATURES DIRECTORY LISTING

Chapter 1

In-Text Features

Learning Hint: General Hints on Forming Medical Terms   6
Learning Hint: Combining and Forming Medical Terms   6
Learning Hint: The Longest Medical Term   10
Clinical Application: Metabolic Syndrome, or Syndrome X   12
Clinical Application: "Breaking" a Fever   14
Amazing Body Facts: Bizarre Signs and Symptoms   15
Clinical Application: The Vital Sign of Pulse   16
Clinical Application: The Geriatric Patient   19

Chapter 2

In-Text Features

Clinical Application: Do You Know Your Left from Your Right?   38
Clinical Application: Central versus Peripheral Cyanosis   39
Clinical Application: Hernias   42
Clinical Application: The Central Landmark: The Spinal Column   43
Amazing Body Facts: Psoas Test   44

Chapter 3

In-Text Features

Learning Hint: Negative Electrons   57
Amazing Facts: An Interesting Paradox   59

Chapter 4

In-Text Features

Applied Science: Atoms and Molecules   76
Learning Hint: Concentration Gradient   80
Applied Science: Cell Energy and ATP: The Energy Molecule   92
Clinical Application: Enzymes: Making Reactions Happen   94
Amazing Body Facts: Bacterial Reproduction   96
Learning Hint: Mitosis versus Meiosis   99
Clinical Application: Bacteria's Resistance to Antibiotics   105

Chapter 5

In-Text Features

Amazing Body Facts: Skin and Vitamin Production   113
Learning Hint: Serous Fluid   114
Amazing Body Facts: Blood and Lymph as Connective Tissues   115
Learning Hint: Mucous Isn't Always Mucus   116
Clinical Application: Melanoma   121

Chapter 6

In-Text Features

Amazing Body Facts: Bone Composition   145
Amazing Body Facts: Red Bone Marrow and Red Blood Cells   146
Amazing Body Facts: Aging and Bone Building   150
Amazing Body Facts: The Flexibility of Cartilage   154
Amazing Body Facts: Wear and Tear and Disease   155
Learning Hint: Number of Vertebrae   165
Clinical Application: When to See a Doctor   170

Chapter 7

In-Text Features

Clinical Application: Muscle Tone   184
Amazing Body Facts: Muscles   185
Amazing Body Facts: When Is a Muscle Tear Good?   188
Learning Hint: Muscle Names   189
Applied Sciences: Kinesiology   196
Learning Hint: Muscle Contraction Step-by-Step   200
Applied Sciences: Interrelatedness of Neuromuscular System   200
Amazing Body Facts: Rigor Mortis   201
Applied Science: Maintaining a Core Body Temperature   202
Learning Hint: Smooth Muscle Regulation of Blood Pressure   204
Applied Science: A Useful Application of a Deadly Toxin   205

Chapter 8
In-Text Features
Amazing Body Facts: A Bothersome Fact of Life 219
Amazing Body Facts: Keloids 227
Clinical Application: Medicine Delivery via the
    Integumentary System 230
Clinical Application: Assessing Peripheral
    Perfusion 231
Applied Science: Forensics and Hair 233

Chapter 9
In-Text Features
Amazing Body Facts: Faster Than a Speeding
    Bullet 254
Applied Science: Fugu 259
Clinical Application: Epilepsy 261
Clinical Application: Bioterrorism 264
Learning Hint: Directional Terms 266
Clinical Application: Spinal Blocks, Epidural
    Anesthesia, and Lumbar Punctures
    (Spinal Taps) 271
Clinical Application: Knee Jerk Reflex 274
Clinical Application: Carpal Tunnel Syndrome 275
Amazing Body Facts: Why Not a Smooth Brain? 278
Learning Hint: Mnemonic Devices 290
Clinical Application: Spastic versus Flaccid
    Paralysis 297

Chapter 10
In-Text Features
Amazing Body Fact: Lesser-Known Endocrine
    Glands 312
Clinical Application: Childbirth and Positive
    Feedback 318
Learning Hint: Hormone Names 319
Clinical Application: Cortisol Busters and Weight
    Loss 336

Chapter 11
In-Text Features
Amazing Body Fact: Why We Can See in the Dark 354
Clinical Application: Snellen Charts 355
Amazing Body Facts: Eye Dominance 355
Clinical Application: Life without Glasses 355

Applied Science: Sound Conduction 357
Clinical Application: Heat and Cold Therapy 365
Clinical Application: Cataract Surgery 367

Chapter 12
In-Text Features
Applied Science: Color Coded Blood 380
Learning Hint: Arteries or Veins? 380
Learning Hint: The Tricuspid Valve 382
Amazing Body Facts: Pulmonary Arteries and Veins 382
Clinical Application: Angiography 384
Amazing Body Facts: How Does It Keep Going and Going
    and Going? 385
Clinical Application: Osmotic versus Hydrostatic Pressure:
    The Great Balancing Act 392
Clinical Application: Cardiac Enzymes 392
Clinical Application: ECG/EKG 395
Clinical Application: CPR 396
Clinical Application: Heart Attacks 398
Amazing Body Facts: What's in a Drop of Blood? 399
Clinical Application: Umbilical Cord Blood and
    Leukemia 405
Amazing Body Facts: Coconut Juice Blood Transfusions
    and Artificial Blood 407
Clinical Application: Regulation of Blood Pressure 409
Clinical Application: Taking a Blood Pressure 410

Chapter 13
In-Text Features
Amazing Body Facts: Autocontrol of Cardiopulmonary
    System 432
Applied Science: Gas Exchange in Plants 435
Amazing Body Facts: Breath Test May Detect
    Cancer 437
Amazing Body Facts: Why Do We Breathe Through Our
    Mouth? 439
Clinical Application: Excessive Mucus Production 440
Clinical Application: Keeping the Vital Airway
    Open 443
Learning Hint: Epiglottitis 446
Clinical Application: The Angle Makes a Difference 448
Clinical Application: Therapeutic Oxygen 449
Clinical Application: What Can Go Wrong with Gas
    Exchange? 451
Applied Science: The Amazing Surfactant 453

Amazing Body Facts: Smoking Kills   459
Clinical Application: Family History and Asthma   459
Clinical Application: COPD Demographics   460
Clinical Application: Smoking History   460
Applied Science: Boyle's Law   466
Applied Science: pH and Ventilation   466
Amazing Body Facts: Exhaled CO_2 and Mosquitoes   467

Chapter 14
In-Text Features
Learning Hint: T Cells   500
Clinical Application: How You Acquire Immunity to
   Pathogens   506

Chapter 15
In-Text Features
Clinical Application: Sublingual Medication   525
Clinical Application: PEG Tube   534
Learning Hint: The Ending ASE   539
Learning Hint: Emulsifiers   540
Clinical Application: Lactose Intolerance   540
Clinical Application: Colostomy   543

Chapter 16
In-Text Features
Learning Hint: Visualizing the Peritubular System   570
Clinical Application: Trauma, Ischemia, and Kidney
   Damage   575
Clinical Application: Testing for Urinary Health   579
Amazing Body Facts: Urine   579
Amazing Body Facts: Glomerular Filtration   580
Amazing Body Facts: Tubular Reabsorption   585
Applied Science: Electrolytes and Acid Base Balance   585
Clinical Application: Kidney Disease and
   Hypertension   587

Chapter 17
In-Text Features
Learning Hint: Mitosis versus Meiosis   604
Clinical Application: Down Syndrome   604
Clinical Application: Pap Test   609
Amazing Body Facts: Boxers or Briefs?   623
Clinical Application: Androgen Insensitivity
   Syndrome   627
Amazing Body Facts: Hormones   627
Clinical Application: Contraception   629
Amazing Body Facts: A Million to One Shot   631

Chapter 18
In-Text Features
Amazing Body Facts: Blood Volume   649
Amazing Body Facts: RBCs and Blood Volume   651

Chapter 19
In-Text Features
Clinical Application   685
Amazing Body Facts   687

Chapter 20
In-Text Features
Applied Science: Forensics and History   701
Applied Science: Tomatoes Were Once Thought to be
   Poisonous   701
Applied Science: If Bones Could Speak   703
Amazing Body Facts: You're Not Getting Older, You're
   Getting Smarter   706
Clinical Application: Age- and Activity-Related Diets and
   Nutritional Needs   715
Applied Science: Antibiotics   718

Study Success Companion
In-Text Features
Clinical Application: Classical Conditioning   760
Applied Science: How We Learn   762
Clinical Application: Aiding Your Memory   762
Applied Science: Test Yourself—How Many Stress Signals
   Do You Have?   765
Clinical Application: Sadness versus Depression   765
Clinical Application: Preventive Medicine and Early
   Intervention   767
Learning Hint: Metric versus English   769
Applied Science: Scientific Notation—This Is Not the
   Scribblings of Albert Einstein   770
Applied Science: The Apothecary System   771
Learning Hint: Metric Prefixes   772
Learning Hint: Check Your Work   773
Clinical Application: Body Surface Area   776

A USER'S GUIDE TO THE FEATURES OF THE BOOK

We have designed this textbook to be fun, interesting, and rich in features to aid your understanding of this challenging topic. Here is a quick guide to what makes this text different from others. We hope that the special highlights of this book enhance your learning experience as the journey of your health care career unfolds.

SPECIAL FEATURES MAKE LEARNING FUN

Pronunciation Guides

Although this is not a medical terminology book, understanding and pronouncing medical words is critical to your success. The Terms to Know section in each chapter provides a phonetic pronunciation of the difficult terms.

Pronunciation Guide

Correct pronunciation is important in any journey so that you and others are completely understood. Here is a "see and say" Pronunciation Guide for the more difficult terms to pronounce in this chapter. In addition, the Audio Glossary includes an audio pronunciation and definition of each of these terms. Please note that pronunciations given are referenced to medical dictionaries, and regional variations may exist.

bacteria (back TEER ee ah)
benign (be NINE)
capsid (CAP sid)
centrioles (SEN tree olz)
centrosomes (SEN troh soams)
chemotherapy (KEE moh THAIR ah pee)
chromatin (CROW ma tin)
cilia (SIL ee ah)
cytokinesis (SIGH toe keh KNEE sis)
cytoplasm (SIGH toe plah zim)
cytoskeleton (SIGH toe SKEL eh ton)
deoxyribonucleic acid
  (dee AWK see RYE boe new KLEE ic)
diabetes mellitus (DIE uh BE teez meh LITE us)
endocytosis (en DOE sigh TOE sis)
endoplasmic reticulum
  (EN doh PLAZ mic ree TIH cue lum)
eukaryotic cell (you CARE ee AH tic)
exocytosis (EX oh sigh TOE sis)
flagella (flah GEL ah)
flora (FLOOR ah)
fungi (FUN jye)

Golgi apparatus (GOAL jee ap ah RA tus)
hypercholesterolemia
  (HI per koh LES tur ul EE me ah)
lysosomes (LIE soh soamz)
malignant (mah LIG nant)
meiosis (my OH sis)
metastasis (meh TAS tuh sis)
mitochondria (MITE oh KAHN dree ah)
mitotic (my TOT ick)
mitosis (my TOE sis)
mycelia (my SEE lee ah)
organelles (or ga NELZ)
osmosis (ahz MOE sis)
pathogen (PATH oh jen)
phagocytosis (FAG oh sigh TOH sis)
phenylketonuria (FIN ill KEE toe NEW ree ah)
pinocytosis (PIE no sigh TOE sis)
protozoa (pro toe ZOE ah)
ribonucleic acid (RYE boe new KLEE ic)
ribosomes (RYE boe soamz)
vesicle (VES ih kul)

Clinical Application

ANGIOGRAPHY

One way to get a good picture of the blood flow in a person's body (and any problems with it) is to perform an **angiogram**. An angiogram is an x-ray of the body after a **radio-contrast agent** (a dye that makes the blood contrast with its surroundings on an x-ray) has been injected into the blood. The angiographic x-ray shows shadows of the openings within the cardiovascular structures carrying blood; the blood vessels themselves do not appear. The most common use of an angiogram is to visualize the blood flow in the coronary arteries.

Clinical Applications

These highlight boxes show the relevance of what you are learning and how that knowledge is needed in clinical practice. This feature includes topics such as aging, major diagnostic studies, and therapeutics.

Pathology Connection

After discussions of Anatomy & Physiology concepts, a special section on related disease conditions will be presented. This will make the connection to why the understanding of the A&P concept discussed is so important to the pathologic process. This will aid the student in understanding abnormal diagnostic test results and why certain treatments are effective for a specific disease.

Pathology Connection

CYSTIC FIBROSIS (CF): A MEMBRANE CHANNEL ABNORMALITY

Cystic fibrosis is a relatively common (1 in 3,000 Caucasian births) incurable, fatal genetic disorder caused by the malformation of membrane channels for chloride and sodium ions. In people with CF, sodium and chloride do not diffuse across the cell membrane as they normally would because the channels are not normal. This makes the fluid around the cells extremely salty (excess sodium and chloride) and causes excessively thick mucus in the respiratory, digestive, and reproductive systems, clogging the organs. People with CF have difficulty breathing, nutritional deficits due to decreased absorption of nutrients, and increased risk of respiratory infections, diabetes, and infertility (especially males). Although CF cannot be cured, treatments are available, such as nutritional supplements, antibiotics to prevent pneumonia, and

APPLIED SCIENCE

Although cells are composed of small structures called organelles, these organelles are composed of even smaller substances. **Atoms**, which are the tiny building blocks of all matter, combine to form molecules such as water, sugar, and proteins, which are then used to build cellular structures and facilitate cellular functions. The four basic types of molecules found in cells are proteins, carbohydrates, lipids, and nucleic acids, which were covered in Chapter 3.

Applied Science

Instead of having a separate nonintegrated chemistry or physics chapter, the sciences are presented in context.

Amazing Body Facts

These are "that's awesome" kinds of facts to give an appreciation of just how wonderful the human design is. For example, nerve impulses can travel at speeds of up to 426 feet per *second!*

Amazing **Body Facts**

Bacterial Reproduction

Bacteria can reproduce so rapidly that they can double their population every half an hour! No wonder a bacterial infection can get out of hand so fast.

LEARNING HINT

Concentration Gradient

If a substance moves from higher concentration to lower concentration, it is said to be moving *with* the difference or concentration gradient. For example, if you are in a long grocery store check-out line "concentrated" with people and three new lanes open up, the people will quickly move from the highly concentrated line to the lower concentrated areas. Soon, you will notice, all lines will equalize, demonstrating that even people move with a concentration gradient and reach equilibrium.

Learning Hints

We present helpful hints to facilitate learning difficult concepts. These may sometimes be amusing stories or other learning aids.

Test Your Knowledge

After a concept is fully developed within a chapter, a "Test Your Knowledge" section will ensure you understand what was just covered before moving on and reducing the risk of getting really lost on your journey.

TEST YOUR KNOWLEDGE 4-1

Fill in the blanks:

1. This form of passive transportation is like combining drink mix and a pitcher of water: _____.

2. During osmosis, water travels across a semipermeable membrane from an area of _____ concentration of solute to an area of _____ concentration of solute.

3. _____ allows only certain sizes of particles to pass through.

4. The act of removing carbon dioxide from the blood to the lungs is achieved through _____.

5. Glucose is often transported by _____.

6. Diabetes mellitus may be caused by a deficiency in this hormone: _____.

7. Cystic fibrosis occurs when _____ are malformed.

Quick Trip Through the Diseases of . . .

This chart provides a valuable quick reference for diseases related to a given body system chapter. The chart includes the cause, signs and symptoms, diagnostic tests, and treatment for each disease.

A QUICK TRIP THROUGH SOME DISEASES OF THE REPRODUCTIVE SYSTEM

DISEASE	ETIOLOGY	SIGNS & SYMPTOMS	DIAGNOSITIC TEST(S)	TREATMENTS
Female				
Amenorrhea/ dysmenorrhea	Absent or painful menstruation; may be due to many different causes.	Lack of menstrual period/ pain during period.	Physical exam, hormone levels, imaging, exploratory surgery.	Hormones, NSAIDS, surgery, treat underlying conditions.
Premenstrual syndrome/ premenstrual dysphoric disorder	Exact cause not determined; may be due to irregular levels of estrogen or progesterone.	Constipation, nausea, headache, backache, edema, malaise, irritability, mental confusion, depression.	Currently, PMS is diagnosed if a woman has one affective (psychological) and one physical symptom. A woman is diagnosed with PMDD if she has five of the criteria.	Treat symptoms; proper nutrition, complex carbohydrates, anti-depressants, analgesics, and hormone therapy.

Pharmacology Corner

inflammation. More specific drugs that block cytokines are currently available, as are drugs that block the antibodies that mediate allergies. Experimental medications that block B cells, TNF, and complement are currently being tested. Steroids may often be effective in treating asthma and severe allergies, but long-term use of oral steroids can produce nasty side effects. Topical steroids, either inhaled or administered as nasal sprays, work well for many people. Patients with anaphylactic reactions to common allergens may be required to carry an EpiPen for emergencies. A shot of epinephrine constricts blood vessels, stimulates the heart, and opens air passages, decreasing the effects of anaphylactic reactions and giving a patient time to get to medical care.

Autoimmune disorders like RA and lupus used to be treated with NSAIDs and ste-

Pharmacology Corner

This section includes a variety of medications used in the treatment of diseases that are related to a given body system of the chapter.

SUMMARY

Snapshots from the Journey

- All living organisms are made of one or more cells. Cells are the fundamental units of living organisms.
- Even though cells are the fundamental units, they are composed of a variety of parts that are necessary for proper cellular function. These small parts are called organelles.
- Substances can cross the cell membrane via passive or active transport.
- Passive transport can occur through diffusion, facilitated diffusion, osmosis, or filtration.
- Active transport can occur through active transport pumps, endocytosis, or exocytosis.
- Problems with transport across cell membranes can cause serious disorders such as cystic fibrosis and diabetes.
- One form of cellular movement is through the use of flagella.
- Cilia found in the lungs aid in the removal of foreign particles in the airways through rhythmic movement.
- When organelles do not work properly, serious problems result, often in every cell of the body.

Snapshots from the Journey

This is a concise review summary of key points covered within each chapter.

RAY AND MARIA'S STORIES

Through the use of our two patients within each system chapter—Ray, a quadriplegic, and Maria, a diabetic—the text case studies pull together many of the points discussed within the chapter to show the interrelatedness of what you are learning. Getting to know these patients well will help you understand how a disease affects a variety of body systems.

RAY AND MARIA'S STORY

Now that we have followed Ray, a quadriplegic, and Maria, a diabetic's, trials and tribulations throughout this text, let's think about the systemic problems that may befall them as they age.

a. What research can you find that may help or reverse their initial medical conditions (spinal cord injuries and diabetes) in the near future?

_____

_____

b. What can be done proactively to prevent some of the potential problems that come with aging, especially in their individual cases?

_____

_____

CAREER CONNECTIONS

Exploration of career opportunities is integrated into each chapter.

CAREER CONNECTIONS

Now that you have read this chapter, here is a list of related professions you may be interested in investigating for a future career:

- Doula or Midwife

Research each profession and report on the following:

1. Profession description to include job responsibilities
2. Educational requirements
3. Job opportunities
4. Opportunities outside of the hospital setting
5. Salary range
6. Licensure and continuing education requirements

ANATOMY, PHYSIOLOGY, AND DISEASE IN ACTION

These new hands-on activities at the end of each chapter put what you are learning into play while supporting curriculum standards.

ANATOMY, PHYSIOLOGY, AND DISEASE IN ACTION

Materials:
Roles of bulletin board paper
Pencils
Different colored markers

Working in groups of twos or threes, trace one group member. Each group will need to have a frontal and a lateral tracing. Using different colored markers for each label, label the **planes:** transverse, frontal, and midsaggital planes; **directional** terms: proximal, distal, medial, lateral, anterior, posterior, ventral, dorsal, cranial, caudal, superior, and inferior; **cavities:** posterior, anterior, cranial, spinal, thoracic, abdominal, and pelvic; and **abdominal region and quadrants:** right hypochondriac, epigastric, left hypochondriac, right lumbar umbilical, left lumbar, right iliac, hypogastric, left iliac, and RUQ, RLQ, LUQ, and LLQ. Some of the terms will be found on one of the tracings; others will be found on both.

Using the tracing, fill in the following chart for the primary location of the following as it applies:

Organ	Cavity	Region	Quadrant
Appendix			
Liver			
Spleen			
Gall bladder			

ANCILLARIES GUIDE YOUR JOURNEY

Study Success Companion

Your Study Success Companion will help you establish a good foundation for your trip. This appendix includes study skills and stress management techniques to help you as you journey through Anatomy, Physiology and Disease. It also contains topics such as the Metric System in case you do not have this background and need a self-taught mini-refresher.

Student Workbook

This supplemental workbook contains even more practice and reinforcement opportunities and helps you prepare for quizzes and exams.

TEACHING ANCILLARIES BRING OUT THE BEST IN INSTRUCTORS

Perhaps the most gratifying part of an educator's work is the "aha" learning moment when the lightbulb goes on, and a student truly understands a concept—when a connection is made. Along these lines, Pearson is pleased to help instructors foster more of these educational connections by providing a complete battery of resources to support teaching and learning.

Teacher's Wraparound Edition

The Teacher's Wraparound Edition presents instructors with teaching tips and other relevant content directly alongside the full-page view of the student edition text. Instructors can see exactly what the student sees while referencing the information they need to manage the classroom and promote learning.

ONLINE RESOURCES

This program includes a digital companion piece designed to help enhance instruction, engage today's learning styles, and reinforce concepts. The teacher's online resources also include PowerPoint slides, Test Bank, and Answer Keys.

A COMMITMENT TO ACCURACY

It is vital that the content of this book and all ancillary resources be completely accurate, matching the need for precision in today's health care environment. To attain the highest level of accuracy possible throughout this educational program, we put an extensive development process into place. No fewer than a dozen content experts have read each page of chapter for accuracy, including all test questions, and all other ancillary resources.

Although our intent is for all books to be error-free, it is possible for some mistakes to get through our system. Pearson takes this issue seriously and therefore welcomes any and all feedback that you can provide along the lines of helping us enhance the accuracy of this book.

1

Anatomy, Physiology, and Disease
Learning the Language

Imagine the many potential problems you would encounter traveling to a foreign country where you do not speak the language. To maximize success and safety during your journey, one of the most important preparatory steps is to develop a basic understanding of the native language before you actually arrive. Every profession seems to have a language all its own. The health care profession is no exception. It has a highly specialized language complete with numerous medical abbreviations.

The language on which health professions and the study of anatomy, physiology, and disease is based is medical terminology. Therefore, this chapter lays the foundation of learning the native language (medical terminology) of medicine. In addition, this chapter introduces the key concepts of anatomy, physiology, and disease so future chapters can build on this foundation. Finally, as in all journeys, road signs can make your trip easier.

LEARNING OUTCOMES

At the end of your journey through this chapter, you will be able to:

- Understand the terms anatomy, physiology, and disease and their various related areas
- Relate the importance and purpose of medical terminology to anatomy, physiology, and disease
- Construct and define medical terms using word roots, prefixes, and suffixes
- Explain the concept and importance of homeostasis
- Contrast the metabolic processes of anabolism and catabolism
- Relate signs and symptoms to the disease process
- Discuss disease concepts related to the body's defense mechanism
- Contrast routes of transmission of disease and appropriate preventative measures

Pronunciation Guide

Correct pronunciation is important in any journey so that you and others are completely understood. Here is a "see and say" Pronunciation Guide for the more difficult terms to pronounce in this chapter. Please note that pronunciations given are referenced to medical dictionaries and regional variations may exist.

anabolism (ah NAB oh lizm)
anatomy (ah NA tom ee)
catabolism (ka TAB oh lizm)
diagnosis (DYE ahg NOH sis)
disease (dih ZEEZ)
epidemiology (EP uh dee me ALL oh jee)
etiology (EE tee ALL oh jee)
exacerbation (ecks ASS er BAY shun)
homeostasis (HOH me oh STAY sis)
idiopathic (ID ee oh PATH ick)
macroscopic anatomy
　(MAK roh SCOP ic ah NA tom ee)

microscopic anatomy
　(MY kroh SCOP ic ah NA tom ee)
metabolism (meh TAB oh lizm)
morphology (more FOL oh jee)
nosocomial (NOHS oh KOH me al)
pathogenic (PATH oh JEN ick)
pathology (path ALL oh jee)
physiology (fiz ee ALL oh jee)
prognosis (prog NOH sis)
rhinoplasty (RYE noh PLASS tee)
syndrome (SIN drohm)

WHAT IS ANATOMY AND PHYSIOLOGY?

You're probably so accustomed to hearing the words *anatomy* and *physiology* (A&P) used together that you may not have given much thought to what each one means and how they differ. They each have unique meanings. Let's take a closer look.

Anatomy

anatomy *(ah NAT oh mee)* The study of the structures of the human body.

Anatomy is the study of the internal and external structures of plants, animals, and, for our focus, the human body. The human body is an amazing and complex structure that can perform an almost limitless number of tasks. To truly understand how something works, it is important to know how it is put together. Leonardo da Vinci, in the 1400s, correctly drew the human skeleton and could be considered one of the earliest anatomists (one who studies anatomy). The word *anatomy* is from the Greek language and literally means "to cut apart," which is exactly what you must do to see how something is put together. For example, the study of the arrangement of the bones that comprise the human skeleton, which is the *anatomical* framework for our bodies, is considered skeletal anatomy.

Just as we can subdivide biology into more specific concentrations, such as cell biology, plant biology, and animal biology, we can also broadly divide anatomy into **microscopic anatomy (fine anatomy)** and **macroscopic anatomy (gross anatomy)**. Microscopic anatomy is the study of structures that can be seen and examined only with magnification aids such as a microscope. The study of cellular structures (cytology) and tissue samples (histology) are examples of microscopic anatomy.

microscopic anatomy (fine anatomy) Study of structures that require the aid of magnification.

macroscopic anatomy (gross anatomy) *(MAK roh SCOP ick ah NAH toh mee)* Study of large structures of the body.

Gross or macroscopic anatomy represents the study of the structures visible to the unaided or naked eye. For example, the study of the various bones that make up the human body is gross anatomy. Viewing an x-ray of the arm to determine the type and location of a broken bone is considered an examination of gross anatomy.

Physiology

Physiology focuses on the function and vital processes of the various structures making up the human body. These physiological processes include muscle contraction, our sense of smell and sight, how we breathe, and so on. We will focus on each of these processes in its respective chapter. Physiology is closely related to anatomy because it is the study of how an anatomical structure such as a cell or bone actually functions. Physiology deals with all the vital processes of life and has many subspecialties. Human physiology, animal physiology, cellular physiology, and neurophysiology are just some of the specific branches of physiology.

physiology *(FIZ ee ALL oh jee)* The study of the function of the body's structures.

Putting It All Together

In summary, anatomy focuses on structure and how something is put together, whereas physiology is the study of how those different structures *work* together to make the body function as a whole. For example, anatomy would be the study of the structure of the red blood cells (RBCs), and physiology would be the study of how the RBCs carry vital oxygen throughout our body. Closely related to anatomy is **morphology,** which is a science that deals with the form and structure of organisms (that is, individual living systems, such as people, animals, and plants). For example, the morphology of cells would be a description of the various shapes of cells. FIGURE 1-1 ▲ shows the morphology of deformed RBCs (sickle shaped) that are present in the disease sickle cell anemia. Because of the *anatomical* deformity, the *physiological* process of effectively carrying oxygen is adversely affected.

morphology *(more FOL oh jee)* The science of structure and form of organisms.

A   **B**

FIGURE 1-1 ▲ **A.** Normal red blood cells (RBCs) are flexible and donut shaped and move with ease through blood vessels. (Photo source: Sebastian Kaulitzki/Shutterstock.com.) **B.** The anatomical distortion of the *structure* of RBCs in sickle cell anemia affects its normal *function* to carry oxygen. In addition, the sickle cells lose their ability to bend and pass through the small blood vessels, thereby causing blockages to blood flow. (Photo source: CDC/Sickle Cell Foundation of Georgia: Janice Haney Carr.)

You will notice on your journey that the design of a structure is often related to its function. For example, as you will learn in Chapter 6, the type of joint located between bones dictates the functions and movements of those bones: hinge joints are located at the knees where back and forth bending movement is required, whereas a ball-and-socket joint of the hip provides for a greater range of motion.

Therefore, it makes sense to combine these two sciences into anatomy and physiology (A&P). Understanding human anatomy and physiology forms the foundation for all medical practice because medical treatment attempts to bring the body's structure and function back toward normal A&P.

WHAT IS DISEASE?

Disease, simply put, is a condition in which the body fails to function normally. The word **disease** literally means not (dis) at ease. If we consider the body at ease when normal anatomy and physiology exists, anything that upsets the normal structure or function could be called disease. The official medical term for the study of disease is **pathology**. Pathology is the branch of medicine that studies the characteristics, causes, and effects of disease. Another closely related term is *pathophysiology*, which is the science that investigates abnormal body function.

To effectively treat a disease, the cause (or **etiology**) of the illness must be determined. If the cause of a disease cannot be determined, it is called an **idiopathic** disease. A **nosocomial** infection is an infectious disease you acquire while in a medical facility. The study of the transmission, frequency of occurrence, distribution, and control of a disease is called **epidemiology**. For example, an epidemiologist determined that nearly 62 million cases of the common cold occur each year in the United States.

Although *communicable* and *contagious* may sound like the same thing, there is a fine difference. A **communicable disease** can be spread in a variety of ways, such as person-to-person or insect-to-person. In contrast, a **contagious disease** is one that is *readily* transmitted from one person to another, such as the common cold.

The Centers for Disease Control and Prevention (CDC) tracks disease worldwide. If a disease is continually present within a specific population or region, it is called **endemic**. If the disease occurs suddenly in large numbers over a specific region, it is called an **epidemic**. If the disease spreads country- or worldwide, it is called a **pandemic**. You will learn more terms associated with disease as you further explore this chapter.

---

disease *(dih ZEEZ)* Any change in the normal structure or function of the body.

pathology *(path ALL oh jee)* The study of disease.

etiology *(ee tee ALL oh jee)* The cause or origin of a disease.

idiopathic A condition with an uncertain or not yet determined cause.

nosocomial *(NO suh KOH mee all)* An infection acquired by a patient while at a hospital, nursing home, or any health care facility. Nosocome was a 17th-century word for "hospital." Newer term is HAI (hospital acquired infection).

epidemiology *(EP ih dee mee OL oh jee)* The study of the origin, distribution, and determinants of diseases.

communicable disease A disease that has the potential to be spread by a variety of ways such as person to person or insect to person.

contagious disease Any disease readily transmitted from one person to another.

endemic A condition or disease related to a specific population or region of the world.

epidemic An outbreak of a disease that suddenly affects a large group of people in a geographical region or a large defined population group.

pandemic Disease or condition that affects many people worldwide.

TEST YOUR KNOWLEDGE 1-1

Indicate whether the following examples are gross anatomy or microscopic anatomy by putting a G or an M in the space provided.

1. ____ Viewing an x-ray to determine the type of bone break

2. ____ Classifying a tumor to be cancerous by cell type

3. ____ Viewing bacteria to determine what disease is present

4. ____ Examining the chest for any obvious deformities

5. ____ The type of anatomy studied by a histotechnologist or cytotechnologist

Complete the following or choose the best answer:

6. John was diagnosed with idiopathic respiratory disease. What does this mean?

_____

_____

7. A study was conducted on the frequency of occurrence of a particular infection in South America. The scientists performing the study were called _____. The cause or _____ of the infection was determined to be a type of bacteria.

8. The spread of avian flu throughout the world would lead to a(an):
   a. endemic
   b. epidemic
   c. birdemic
   d. pandemic

9. An infection can cause you to have a fever. Discuss how fever influences homeostasis in the body.

THE LANGUAGE

Even if you're traveling to another city within your home country, you will most likely need to learn a few things about the language its citizens speak. For example, think of the many different names people use to identify a sandwich made on a long skinny roll. Your "sub" might be someone else's "grinder" or "hoagie." Keep in mind that there may also be small regional differences in language and abbreviations.

Medical Terminology

As stated earlier, the language of A&P and disease is based primarily on medical terminology. Understanding medical terminology may seem like an overwhelming task because, on the surface, there appears to be so many terms. In reality, there are only a relatively few word roots, prefixes, and suffixes, but they can be put together in a host of ways to form numerous terms.

Each medical term has a basic structure on which to build, and this is called the word root. For example, *cardi* is the word root for terms pertaining to the heart. Rarely is the word root used alone. Instead, it is combined with prefixes and suffixes that can change its meaning. Prefixes come before the word root, whereas suffixes come after the word root. The suffix *ology* means "study of," and therefore, we can combine *cardi* and *ology* to form **cardiology,** which is the study of the heart. The prefix *tachy* means "fast" and can be placed in front of the word root to form **tachycardia,** which means a fast heart rate.

Often you will be given a *combining form,* which is the word root and a connecting vowel (usually *o*), to make it easier to pronounce and link with possible suffixes. For example, the combining form for heart is cardi/o. FIGURE 1-2 ▲ shows the components of a medical term.

cardiology Study of the structure, function, and pathology of the cardiac system.

tachycardia *(TAK ih KAR dee ah)* A more rapid than normal heart rate (greater than 100 beats per minute in adults).

LEARNING HINT

General Hints on Forming Medical Terms

Although you can learn the various word roots, prefixes, and suffixes, it gets confusing trying to put them together correctly. In most instances, the medical definition as stated in plain English may seem backward as we combine the technical terms, especially when suffixes are used. For example, an inflammation of the stomach is gastritis, not itisgastro, and one who studies the stomach is a gastrologist, not an ologistgastro. When using prefixes, you usually put the parts together in the order you say the definition. For example, slow heart rate is bradycardia, not cardiabrady. As with general rules, there are exceptions, but with practice it will become familiar to you.

LEARNING HINT

Combining and Forming Medical Terms

If a suffix begins with a vowel, drop the vowel of the root in the combining form. For example, the combining form for stomach is gastr/o, and if we add the suffix for inflammation, *itis,* the medical term becomes *gastritis.*

FIGURE 1-2 ▲ How prefixes and suffixes can be combined with a word root to form many medical terms.

Using Tables 1-1, 1-2, and 1-3, look at all the terms you can make from just the one word root, cardi/o. *Cardiology* is the study of the heart, and a *cardiologist* is a specialist who studies the heart. *Bradycardia* is a slow heart, *tachycardia* is a fast heart, and an *electrocardiogram* is an electrical recording of the heart. If your heart were enlarged due to inflammation (*carditis*), you may develop *cardiomegaly,* which would mean you have a disease of the heart (*cardiopathy*). The Tin Man from *The Wizard of Oz* thought he had no heart (*acardia*), but later realized that he had a big heart (*cardiomegaly*) all along.

TABLE 1-1 ■ presents some common combining forms to get you started. Then let's add some common prefixes that can be placed before the word roots to alter their meaning (see TABLE 1-2 ■).

Finally, let's add some common suffixes (TABLE 1-3 ■) and then see what kinds of words we can form with just these few parts.

TABLE 1-1 ■ COMMON COMBINING TERMS

WORD ROOT/ COMBINING FORM	MEANING
abdomin/o	abdomen
aden/o	gland
angi/o	vessel
arthr/o	joint
cardi/o	heart
col/o	colon
cyan/o	blue
cyt/o	cell
derm/o	skin
erythr/o	red
gastr/o	stomach
glyc/o	sugar
hemat/o, hem/o	blood
hepat/o	liver
hist/o	tissue
hydr/o	water
leuk/o	white
mamm/o	breast
nephr/o	kidney
neur/o	nerve
oste/o	bone
path/o	disease
phag/o	to swallow
phleb/o, ven/o	vein
pne/o or pnea	to breathe
pneumon/o	air or lung
rhin/o	nose

TABLE 1-2 ■ COMMON PREFIXES

PREFIX	MEANING
a- or an-	without
acro-	extremities
brady-	slow
dia-	through
dys-	difficult
electro-	electric
endo-	within
epi-	upon or over
hyper-	above normal
hypo-	below normal
macro-	large
micro-	small
peri-	around
sub-	under, below
tachy-	fast

TABLE 1-3 ■ COMMON SUFFIXES

SUFFIX	MEANING
-al, ic	pertaining to or related to
-algia	pain
-cyte	cell
-ectomy	surgical removal of, or excision
-gram	actual record
-graphy	process of recording
-ist	one who specializes
-itis	inflammation of
-megaly	enlargement of
-ologist or logist	one who studies
-ology or logy	study of
-oma	tumor
-osis	condition of
-otomy	cutting into
-ostomy	surgically forming an opening
-pathy	disease
-penia	decrease or lack of
-phobia	fear of
-plasty	surgical repair
-scope	instrument to view or examine

Abbreviations

Abbreviations are used extensively in the medical professions. They are useful in simplifying long, complicated terms for disease, diagnostic procedures, and therapies that require extensive documentation. For now, review TABLE 1-4 ■ for some common abbreviations you may have heard in a health care setting or on television.

Of course you will learn many more terms and abbreviations as we explore the upcoming chapters and become fluent in conversational medical language. This will help you to avoid using lay terms (common, everyday terms) to describe medical and anatomical concepts. Now you know that the correct term for "getting a nose job" is **rhinoplasty** (surgical repair of the nose).

rhinoplasty *(RYE noh plass tee)* Surgical procedure that uses plastic surgery to change the size or shape of the nose.

TABLE 1-4 ■ COMMON MEDICAL ABBREVIATIONS

ABBREVIATION	MEANING
A&P	anatomy and physiology
ACLS	advanced cardiac life support
b.i.d.	twice a day
BM	bowel movement
BP	blood pressure
CA	cancer
CAD	coronary artery disease
CBC	complete blood count
CPR	cardiopulmonary resuscitation
CVA	cerebral vascular accident (stroke)
CXR	chest x-ray
Dx	diagnosis
GI	gastrointestinal
ICU	intensive care unit
IM	intramuscular
IV	intravenous
MI	myocardial infarction (heart attack)
NPO or n.p.o.	Latin *nil per os*, which means "nothing by mouth"
p.o.	orally
prn	when needed; from the Latin *pro re nata* meaning for an occasion that has arisen
q	every; for example q2h would be every 2 hours
	Note: q.d. and q.o.d., which means once daily and every other day, are on The Joint Commission "Do Not Use" List of medical abbreviations, as they can be mistaken for each other. The full "do not use" list is in Appendix B.
SOB	shortness of breath
STAT	Latin *statim*, which means "immediately"
t.i.d.	three times a day
ER/ED	emergency room/emergency department

Note: ER was popularized by the television show of the same name. However, in actuality it is really a whole department and not just a room, so most prefer the abbreviation ED, which stands for Emergency Department.

LEARNING HINT

The longest medical term is *Pneumonoultramicroscopicsilicovolcanoconiosis* of 45 letters, which is a form of pneumoconiosis (condition of the lung) caused by very fine (ultramicro) silicate or quartz dust.

TEST YOUR KNOWLEDGE 1-2

Define the medical terms:

1. acrocyanosis

_____

2. gastritis

_____

3. rhinoplasty

_____

4. bradycardia

_____

5. mammogram

_____

6. cytomegaly

_____

Give the correct medical term:

7. inflammation of the kidneys

_____

8. removal of the stomach

_____

9. enlarged heart

_____

10. disease of the bones

_____

11. specialist who studies the nerves

_____

The Metric System

Whereas medical terminology represents the written and spoken language for understanding anatomy and physiology, the metric system is the "mathematical language" of medicine. For example, blood pressure is measured in millimeters of mercury (mm Hg), and organ size is usually measured in centimeters (cm). Medications and fluids are given in milliliters (mL), and weight is often measured in kilograms (kg). What exactly does it mean when you are taught that normal cardiac output is six liters per minute? You can now see why you must be familiar with the metric system to truly understand anatomy and physiology and medicine. Although the metric system may seem complicated if you are not familiar with it, it really isn't if you have a basic understanding of math.

There are two major systems of measurement in our world today. The U.S. Customary System (USCS) is used by the general population of the United States. The International System of Units (SI) is used almost everywhere else, as well as by U.S. health care professionals. The SI system is also known as the **metric system** and is based on the power of ten. The metric system is also the system used by drug manufacturers.

metric system System of measurement based on the power of 10.

The USCS system is based on the British Imperial System and uses several different designations for the basic units of length, weight, and volume. We commonly call this the **English system**. For example, in the English system, volumes can be expressed as ounces, pints, quarts, gallons, pecks, bushels, or cubic feet. Distance can be expressed in inches, feet, yards, and miles. Weights are measured in ounces, pounds, and tons. This may be the system most Americans are familiar with, but it is not the system of choice used throughout the world and within the medical profession because the English system has no common base and is therefore very cumbersome to use. It is difficult to know the relationship between each unit of measure because they are not based in an orderly fashion according to the powers of ten as in the metric system. For example, how many pecks are in a gallon? Just what is a peck? How many inches are in a mile? These all require extensive calculations and memorization of certain equivalent values, whereas in the metric system, you simply move the decimal point the appropriate power of ten.

English system The weights and measuring system commonly used in the United States.

If you want to learn more about the metric system, please refer to the student *Study Success Companion* at the end of this text for a detailed explanation on how to use the metric system in the health care setting.

ANATOMY, PHYSIOLOGY, AND DISEASE CONCEPTS YOU WILL ENCOUNTER ON YOUR JOURNEY

In this section, we take a closer look at some additional concepts related to the study of A&P and pathology. You will learn more about these topics as you journey through the chapters in this text.

Metabolism

If you travel to other countries, you will see many different cultures and customs. Even though each culture is unique, they all share certain similarities. The same can be said in anatomy, physiology, and disease. We all share certain functions that are vital to

metabolism *(meh TAB oh lizm)*
Process of using oxygen and glucose to produce energy for cells. Metabolism also produces by-products like carbon dioxide and other waste products. The ongoing cycle of anabolism and catabolism.

anabolism *(ah NAB oh lizm)*
Assembly of new molecules in the body.

catabolism *(ka TAB oh lizm)*
Breaking down of molecules in the body.

homeostasis *(HOH mee oh STAY sis)*
State of equilibrium of the internal environment of the body, including fluid balance, acid-base balance, temperature, metabolism, and so forth, to keep all the body systems functioning optimally.

negative feedback loop
Physiological process that works against the trend. Most often brings a variable back to set point. For example, as blood pressure rises, heart rate may decrease to bring blood pressure back to "normal."

survival. All humans, for example, need food to produce complex chemical reactions necessary for growth, reproduction, movement, and so on. **Metabolism** refers to all the chemical operations going on within our bodies. Metabolism requires various nutrients or fuel to function and produces waste products much like a car consumes gas for power and produces waste, or exhaust. Metabolism, for now, can be thought of as "all the life-sustaining reactions within the body." Fever is a common disease process that will speed up metabolism.

Metabolism is further subdivided into two opposite processes. **Anabolism** is the process by which simpler compounds are built up and used to manufacture materials for growth, repair, and reproduction, such as the assembly of simple amino acids to form complex proteins. This is the building phase of metabolism. **Catabolism** is the process by which complex substances are broken down into simpler substances. For example, the breakdown of food into simpler chemical building blocks for energy use is a catabolic process. An abnormal and extreme example of catabolism is a starvation victim whose body "feeds on itself," actually consuming the body's own tissues.

Homeostasis

For the body to remain alive, it must constantly monitor both its internal and external environments and make the appropriate adjustments. For cells to thrive, they must be maintained in an environment that provides a proper temperature range, balanced oxygen levels, and adequate nutrients. Heart rate and blood pressure must also be monitored and maintained within a certain range or set point for optimal functioning depending on the body activity. **Homeostasis** is a state of being utilizing physiological processes that monitor and maintain a stable internal environment or equilibrium. Survival depends on the body's ability to maintain homeostasis. Homeostatic regulation refers to the adjustments made in the human organism to maintain this stable internal environment. Homeostasis can be maintained through biofeedback, which is the body's ability to sense and make changes. These adjustments can include both physical and chemical processes. An example of a physical processes is the perspiration that occurs to help cool the body to maintain a stable temperature in hot environments. Chemical processes can include active and passive cellular transport mechanisms to regulate the electrolyte balance within the bloodstream. The measure of acidity or alkalinity known as pH in the blood can be regulated by your respiratory rate and depth and you will learn more about this in the respiratory system chapter.

The thermostat in your house functions like a homeostatic mechanism. A temperature is set and then maintained by a sensor that monitors the internal environmental temperature and either heats the house if the sensor registers too cold or cools the

Clinical Application

METABOLIC SYNDROME, OR SYNDROME X

A disturbing syndrome is affecting nearly one quarter of the U.S. adult population, known as Metabolic Syndrome, or Syndrome X. A patient with this syndrome exhibits at least three of the following five common conditions: high blood sugar levels (hyperglycemia), high blood pressure (hypertension), abdominal obesity, high triglycerides (a lipid substance in the blood), and low level of HDL (which is sometimes referred to as "good cholesterol"). Individuals who exhibit this syndrome are at an increased risk for diabetes, heart attacks, and/or strokes. The main causes of the syndrome are poor diet and lack of exercise.

house if the sensor registers too hot. A continuous feedback loop from the sensor to the thermostat determines what action is needed. Because the feedback loop opposes the stimulus (cools down if too hot, heats up if too cold), it is referred to as a **negative feedback loop**.

The body also relies on negative feedback loops that continually sense the internal and external environment and signal the body to make adjustments to maintain homeostasis (see **FIGURE 1-3** ▲). For example, the hypothalamus in the brain represents the body's thermostatic control. If the hypothalamus receives sensory input indicating a very cold environment, it opposes this cold stimulus (negative feedback loop) and requests physiological processes to create or conserve heat within the body to maintain an internal temperature near 98.6°F. For example, the body begins to shiver, and this increased muscular activity generates heat. In addition, because most heat loss is through peripheral areas (head, arms, and legs), the body decreases the diameter of

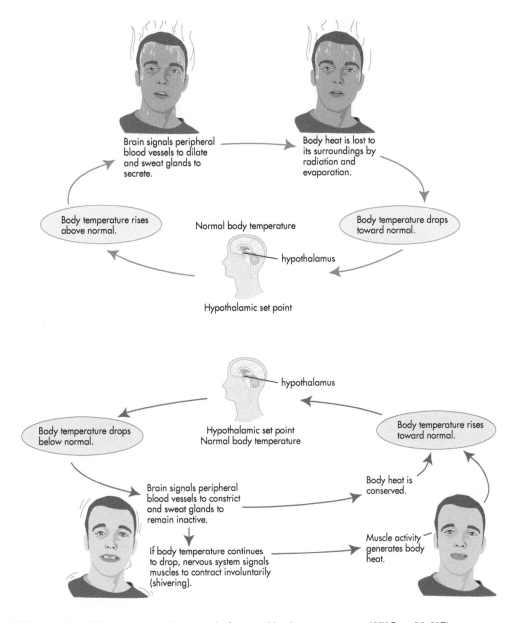

FIGURE 1-3 ▲ The homeostatic control of normal body temperature (37°C or 98.6°F).

the peripheral blood vessels (vasoconstriction), causing the blood to be farther away from the skin surface where the heat would be lost to the cold environment. This keeps the blood closer to the core of the body, where it is warmer. Of course, we can assist the body by wearing a heavy coat and hat, which would remove much of the stress of the cold environment, or simply by getting out of the cold and into a warmer environment.

Conversely, if you are in the desert and the temperature is 120°F, the body senses this as too hot and stimulates physiological processes to cool you down. These processes include sweating (because evaporation is a cooling process) and enlarging the peripheral vessels (peripheral vasodilation) in order to dissipate the body heat into the external environment.

In health care practice, if a patient presents with a very high temperature, he or she may need to be rapidly cooled with ice packs or baths to reduce the body temperature. Much of health care practice is just that—assisting the body through therapy and treatments so it can return to homeostasis.

positive feedback "Vicious cycle." During positive feedback, physiological processes send body chemistry or other attributes further and further away from equilibrium (set point). The trend will continue until something breaks the cycle.

Your body is also capable of **positive feedback,** which increases the magnitude of a change. This process is also known as a "vicious cycle." Positive feedback is not a way to regulate your body because it increases a change away from the ideal set point. In most cases, positive feedback is harmful if the vicious cycle cannot be broken, but sometimes positive feedback is necessary for a process to run to completion.

A good example of necessary positive feedback is the continued contraction of the uterus during childbirth. When a baby is ready to be born, a signal, not well understood at this time, tells the hypothalamus to release the hormone oxytocin from the posterior pituitary. Oxytocin increases the intensity of uterine contractions. As the uterus contracts, the pressure inside the uterus caused by the baby moving down the birth canal increases the signal to the hypothalamus. More oxytocin is released, and the uterus contracts harder. Pressure gets higher inside the uterus, the hypothalamus is signaled to release more oxytocin, and the uterus contracts yet harder. This cycle of ever-increasing uterine contractions due to ever-increasing release of oxytocin from the hypothalamus continues until the pressure inside the uterus decreases—that is, until the baby is born..

Clinical Application

"BREAKING" A FEVER

It is believed that most fevers are the body's way of making an inhospitable environment for a pathogen to survive. Why is it that when someone begins sweating after a prolonged fever, the fever is said to be "breaking"? A fever sets the hypothalamus to a higher set point temperature. The body increases metabolism to generate more heat to reach this now-higher set temperature. Once whatever is causing the fever is gone, the hypothalamus set temperature is turned back down to the true normal. The body must now rapidly get rid of the excess heat by the cooling process of evaporation through sweating.

Disease Concepts

Ideally, the body works to make things function smoothly and in balance. However, sometimes things happen to alter those functions. Eating habits, smoking, inherited traits, trauma, and aging can alter the body's balance and lead to disease. Environmental factors such as climate, pollution, radioactivity, chemical, electromagnetic fields, pathogens, carcinogens, and drugs can all have significant effects on body systems. For example, temperature impacts the muscular system as heat can cause cramping and induce fatigue. Chemicals and minerals such as lead can impact the nervous system. Again, in general terms, disease is a condition in which the body fails to function normally.

Think back to a time when you were sick. You may have had a fever, cough, nausea, dizziness, joint aches, or a generalized weakness. These are examples of **signs** and **symptoms** of disease. Although the terms *signs* and *symptoms* are often used interchangeably, each has its own specific definition. Signs are more definitive, objective, measurable indicators of an illness. Fever and change in the size or color of a mole are examples of signs. **Vital signs** are the signs vital to life and include pulse (heart rate), blood pressure, body temperature, and respiratory rate. The vital sign standard values can change according to the patient's age and sex. In some health care settings, weight is now being added to the list of vital signs. Because of variations in people, we often use a clinical range of acceptable values when measuring vital signs.

Symptoms, on the other hand, are perceived by the patient and are therefore more subjective and difficult to measure. A perfect example of a symptom is pain. Tolerance to pain varies among individuals, so an equal amount of pain such as a controlled pinprick applied to a number of people could be perceived as a light, moderate, or intense level of pain depending on each individual's perception. Other symptoms can include dizziness and itchiness. Despite the fact that symptoms are hard to measure, they are still very

sign A measurable, quantifiable indicator of body function.

symptom Any change in the body or its function as subjectively perceived by the patient.

vital signs Medical assessment during a physical examination in which the temperature, pulse, and respirations (TPR), as well as the blood pressure, are measured.

Amazing Body Facts

Bizarre Signs and Symptoms!

Here are some strange signs and symptoms that may be indications of diseases. To keep lawyers from making a ton of money on this book, please note that there are other signs, symptoms, and tests to determine specific diseases. Please do not use this list of oddities as a sole diagnostic tool! Void where prohibited, you must be 18 years of age to play, cannot be used with other coupons, and all other restrictions apply.

1. Generalized itching skin can be an indication of Hodgkin's disease.
2. Sweating at night may indicate tuberculosis.
3. A desire to eat clay or starchy paste may indicate an iron deficiency in the body.
4. Breath that smells like fruit-flavored chewing gum may be an indication of diabetes.
5. A magenta colored tongue may be indicative of a riboflavin deficiency.
6. A patient with profound kidney disease often doesn't have moons on his or her fingernails.
7. A "hairy" tongue may mean that a patient's normal mouth flora has died from improper use of antibiotics.
8. Spoon-shaped fingernails may point to an iron deficiency in the body.
9. Brown linear streaks on the fingernails of fair-skinned people may indicate melanoma (a form of skin cancer).

syndrome *(SIN drohm)* A set of symptoms and signs associated with, and characteristic of, one particular disease.

diagnosis *(dye egg NOH sis)* A determination as to the cause of the patient's symptoms and signs.

chief complaint or chief concern (CC) The main sign or symptom that caused an individual to seek healthcare.

important in the diagnosis of disease. Sometimes a disease exhibits a set group of signs and symptoms that may occur at about the same time. This specific grouping of signs and symptoms related to a specific disease is known as a **syndrome**. For example, the signs and symptoms of Down syndrome would include mild to moderate mental retardation, sloping forehead, low set ears, short broad hands, and often, cardiac valvular disease. Signs, symptoms, and syndromes are further explained throughout the rest of the textbook as they relate to the pathology of the various body systems.

The word *gnosis* is Greek for knowledge. *Dia* means through or complete, and therefore, *diagnosis* literally means "know through or completely." *Pro* is a prefix meaning before or in front of, and *prognosis* literally means the foreknowledge or predicting of the outcome of a disease.

Discovering as many signs and symptoms as possible can help to **diagnose** a disease. A diagnosis is an identification of a disease determined by studying the patient's signs, symptoms, history, and results of diagnostic tests. The diagnostic procedure is begun by first determining why the individual is seeking medical help. This is known as determining their **chief complaint or chief concern (CC)**.

Clinical Application

THE VITAL SIGN OF PULSE

The pulse is commonly taken by applying slight finger pressure over the radial artery located in either wrist (on the thumb side) and counting the number of beats in a 60-second period (please see **FIGURE 1-4** ▲). The normal heart rate for an adult is 60 to 100 beats per minute, the child rate is approximately 70 to 120, and a newborn's rate is 90 to 170 beats per minute. If an adult has a heart rate of 165 beats per minute, what medical term would you use to describe that condition?

Temporal artery

Common carotid artery

Brachial artery

Radial artery

Femoral artery

Popliteal artery

Posterior tibial artery

Dorsalis pedis artery

FIGURE 1-4 ▲ A health care professional taking a radial pulse and common pulse points.

Although the individual may have several medical problems, which may be of equal or more importance, the chief complaint is what brought that person to now seek help. It may be something as simple as a sore throat or as involved as shortness of breath with concurrent radiating chest pain. Regardless, it is important to accurately record their chief complaint. Expanding on this, the next step is to discuss and document the history of the present illness. Ask open-ended questions that allow the patient to fully explain what they feel. When did the symptoms first appear? What did you do to cause them? How long do they last? What makes them go away?

Getting the patient's medical history can help in determining the **etiology**, or cause, of the disease. The **prognosis** is the prediction of the outcome of a disease. For example, a 47-year-old female may be diagnosed with allergic asthma with an etiology of pollen exposure. This person's prognosis is good if she can avoid the pollen and take medication to decrease her allergic response. Hopefully, your prognosis for doing well in this course is excellent.

It is also helpful to determine if the chief complaint was gradual or of a sudden onset. Quite often, symptoms gradually develop from a disease process that may have been there for some time. These often are *chronic* conditions as opposed to *acute* conditions that exhibit a rapid onset of signs and symptoms. One of the problems with chronic conditions is that due to their usually gradual onset, older patients often attribute them to "just getting older" and often ignore them as an indicator of disease. As these conditions worsen, these people can no longer ignore these conditions, and they seek help. By that time, treating the disease may be more complicated or difficult due to its severity.

The signs and symptoms of a chronic disease may disappear at times, and this period is known as **remission** of the disease. **Relapses** are recurrences of the disease. If the signs and symptoms acutely "flare up," this is known as an **exacerbation** of the disease. Diseases that have a prognosis of death are referred to as **terminal** diseases. **Mortality** is the measure of the number of deaths that can be attributed to a certain disease in a given population over a specific period of time. **Morbidity** is the measure of disabilities and the extent of illness that is caused by a specific disease. For example, pancreatic cancer has a high mortality rate. Although polio historically has a low mortality rate, it has high morbidity due to paralysis, limb deformity, and decreased breathing abilities later in life.

etiology *(EE tee all oh jee)* The cause of the disease.

prognosis *(prog NOH sis)* The predicted outcome of a disease.

remission A lessening of severity or disappearance of symptoms.

relapse A reoccurrence of a disease or symptoms after an apparent recovery.

exacerbation *(eks AS er BAY shun)* A worsening or flare up of a disease process.

terminal illness A fatal illness.

mortality The number of deaths in a given population.

morbidity The level of disability/dysfunction caused by a specific disease.

TEST YOUR KNOWLEDGE 1-3

Answer the following questions:

1. Check which of the following are vital signs:
   a. _____ pulse
   b. _____ pain
   c. _____ blood pressure
   d. _____ age
   e. _____ indigestion
   f. _____ respiratory rate
   g. _____ body temperature

2. Which of the following is the medical term for the cause of a disease?
   a. prognosis
   b. diagnosis
   c. etiology
   d. syndrome

3. Which of the following is the medical term for the outcome of a disease?
   a. prognosis
   b. diagnosis
   c. etiology
   d. syndrome

THE BODY'S DEFENSE SYSTEM

pathogen *(PATH oh jenn)*
Microorganism that causes a disease. Pathogens include bacteria, viruses, protozoa, and other microorganisms, as well as plant cells like fungi or yeast.

Most microorganisms that enter the body are harmless, but some can be **pathogenic** (disease producing). Some microorganisms are pathogenic only when they enter through openings known as *portals of entry* or grow in an uncontrolled manner. For example *Escherichia coli (E. coli)* exists normally in your intestinal tract. It breaks down waste products and helps with the production of vitamin K. However, if *E. coli* enters your bloodstream, it can cause a severe and potentially fatal infection.

Body Barriers

Your body has a series of barriers and defenses to protect itself from infection. The first defense is your skin. As long as your skin is unbroken, it provides a shield from penetration by harmful organisms. Your skin is somewhat acidic in nature, so it provides an environment that many harmful organisms don't like.

immune response The series of body reactions to a pathogenic organism.

inflammatory response The defensive series of actions/events that the body performs in reaction to trauma or infection.

Sometimes an opening occurs on the skin's surface, allowing germs through that first barrier. Then the second barrier comes into action, and the **immune response** is triggered in the form of microscopic cells that either attack and "eat" those harmful invaders or release powerful chemicals that disintegrate parts of the invading germ.

An **inflammatory response** occurs whenever the tissues in your body are injured. This response can occur as a result of physical injury, intense heat, irritation from certain types of chemicals, or a bee sting. In addition, the inflammatory response can also occur as a reaction to the invasion of germs as in an infection. See **FIGURE 1-5** ▲. The four general signs/symptoms of an inflammatory response are: redness, increased temperature at the affected site, swelling (edema), and pain. The inflammatory response is normally protective and attempts to isolate the injured area and increase blood flow to restore normal function.

If you have been attacked by a certain pathogen before, a specific immune response is activated, and your body creates substances to specifically target and destroy the pathogen that had previously been in your body and caused problems. Closely related to the immune response is an **allergic** or **hypersensitivity reaction**. During an allergic reaction, the immune system response goes too far, causing tissue damage and impairing normal function.

allergic reaction or hypersensitivity Relating to any body response stimulated by an allergen.

FIGURE 1-5 ▲ Agents capable of stimulating an inflammatory response.

Clinical Application

THE GERIATRIC PATIENT

The "senior citizen" population continues to grow rapidly, but just because people are living longer, it doesn't mean that they are necessarily living better. Throughout this text you will learn that there are many differences between the various age groups of patients that you will deal with. For example, as people age, their bodies undergo changes in body composition and function, nutritional and drug dosage requirements, and mental functions. A role reversal may also occur, in which a parent gradually becomes dependent on an adult child. This change may create relationship problems among family members, with the health care professional often being pulled into the situation. There is the potential for you to make a difference in these situations by educating patients and family members or directing them to the proper professionals or organizations.

Understanding Routes of Transmission

Pathogens can gain entrance to your body in a variety of ways. The four main routes of transmission are: vectors, contact transmission, common vehicle, and airborne spread. Let's look at each one individually.

Although rarely occurring in hospitals, the vector route of transmission is quite common in the community. A **vector borne** transmission is one in which the organism is carried by an insect or other animal. This can occur in one of two ways. The insect may have the pathogen living inside it, and when it bites you, it infects your blood with that organism. This is known as a **biological vector**. An example of a biological vector is the spread of malaria through the bite of an infected *Anopheles* mosquito. Alternatively, the insect may have that organism *on* its body and spread it to you by landing on an open wound. This is known as a **mechanical vector**. If a fly walks over cow feces and then lands on an open bowl of potato salad sitting in the warm sun at your picnic, that would be considered disease spreading via mechanical vector.

Contact transmission can also happen in two ways: direct or indirect contact. An example of **direct contact** is when a patient has a bowel movement in bed, and the feces come into contact with an open wound on the patient's buttocks. Direct contact can also occur when a health care provider doesn't wash his or her hands or "glove up" before tending to an open wound. An example of **indirect contact** is when medical equipment is not properly sterilized before it is used on the next patient, and pathogens from the previous patient are transferred to the next. An example at home would be touching a door knob that had been previously handled by someone with the flu.

Common vehicle transmission is one you may hear about in the news. This occurs when consumable goods (such as blood or blood products, IV fluids, or food such as ground meat, vegetables, or seafood) become contaminated. This sets up the potential for a major epidemic and is readily recognizable by the sudden occurrence of many infections caused by the same pathogen.

Airborne transmission is a result of the spread of droplets that contain the pathogen. Examples include the spread of tuberculosis by sneezing or even laughing, or pathogens growing in an air conditioner and being spread when the air conditioner is turned on, as happened in the case of the outbreak of Legionnaires' disease in 1976 in Philadelphia.

vector borne An infective agent or disease carried by an insect or arthropod.

biological vector An animal vector which carries internally a disease-causing organism.

mechanical vector A vector where the infectious agent exists on the exterior of the insect or arthropod.

contact transmission General term for the spread of infectious agents by touch.

direct contact The spread of infectious agents by directly touching a contaminated surface.

indirect contact Spread of an infectious agent by touching a contaminated surface and then transmitting it to another individual.

common vehicle transmission The transmission of infectious agents via consumable goods such as blood or ground meat.

airborne transmission The spread of infectious agents through the air, often the result of sneezing or coughing.

chain of infection A process of infection that must have the following links in sequential order for an infection to occur: infecting agent, reservoir, route of transmission, portal of entry, susceptible host.

Standard Precautions Guidelines recommended by the Centers for Disease Control and Prevention to reduce the risk of the spread of infection in hospitals. These precautions (e.g., handwashing and wearing personal protective equipment such as gloves, mask, eye protection, gown) apply to blood, all body fluids, secretions, excretions (except sweat), nonintact skin, and mucous membranes of all patients and are the primary strategy for successful hospital acquired (nosocomial) infection control.

personal protective equipment (PPE) Items such as gowns, gloves, and masks used to prevent the spread of infectious agents.

Standard Precautions

The cycle of the infection, beginning with the creation of a source of infection, continuing with the transportation of the pathogen, and then ending with the entry into the body, is called the **chain of infection**. We can stop the spread of infectious disease simply by breaking this chain at some point. This can be done by something as simple as properly washing your hands.

Tracing the history of health care practices over time illustrates our attempts to improve our ability to prevent the spread of infection. However, in the not so distant past, our focus was very disease specific and not generalized to the health care provider and his or her interaction with each patient. The realization has come that infectious agents are not always recognized and labeled as such and that they may be present and can be spread without our awareness.

Because of this fact, **Standard Precautions** have been developed. These provide the most basic protection for both the health care provider and the patient. Standard Precautions assume that everyone, including the provider and receiver of health care, family members, and visitors, could be carrying a communicable disease.

The single most important practice to reduce the transmission of infectious agents in health care settings is hand hygiene. Hand hygiene includes effective handwashing with plain or antiseptic-containing soap and water, or the use of alcohol-based products that do not require the use of water.

Personal protective equipment (PPE) includes a variety of barriers and respirators used alone or in combination to protect mucous membranes, airways, skin, and clothing from contact with infectious agents. These items include gloves, isolation gowns, face protection (masks, goggles, and face shields), and respiratory protection with specialty masks. These items are specific to different types of communicable disease and their methods of spreading.

Another important measure that prevents transmission of hepatitis and human immunodeficiency virus is the prevention of needlesticks and other sharps-related injuries. These include measures to handle needles and other sharp devices in a manner that will prevent injury to the user and to others who may encounter the device during and after a procedure.

See FIGURE 1-6 ▲ for a Standard Precautions guide. As you can see by the chart, there are a variety of ways to stop the spread of infection. Once again, the single most important thing that you can do to stop the chain of infection is to wash your hands before and after working with each patient! See Appendix G for more information on Standard Precautions and for a list of procedures.

Standard Precautions Guidelines

Procedure	Wash Hands	Gloves	Gown	Mask	Eyewear
Talking to patient					
Adjusting IV fluid rate or noninvasive equipment	●				
Assess patient without touching blood, body, fluids, mucous membranes	●				
Assess patient including contact with blood, body fluids, mucous membranes	●	●			
Drawing blood	●	●			
Inserting venous access	●	●			
Suctioning	●	●	If splattering is likely	If splattering is likely	If splattering is likely
Handling soiled waste, linen, other materials	●	●	If they are extensively soiled or splattering is likely	If they are extensively soiled or splattering is likely	If they are extensively soiled or splattering is likely
Intubation	●	●	●	●	●
Inserting arterial access	●	●	●	●	●
Endoscopy	●	●	●	●	●
Operating and other procedures producing extensive splattering of blood or body fluids	●	●	●	●	●

FIGURE 1-6 ▲ Standard Precautions Guidelines.

TEST YOUR KNOWLEDGE 1-4

Choose the best answer:

1. A region of a state had an outbreak of hepatitis. When reviewing the histories of the victims, it was noted that they had received either whole blood or blood products within the past 9 months. On further investigation, it was determined that all the blood and blood products had come from one organization's blood lab that had failed to test their donors for hepatitis. This transmission of infection to others is known as:

   a. direct contact   c. common vehicle

   b. indirect contact   d. vector

Complete the following:

2. A 27-year-old female presents to the Emergency Department of a local hospital. She has a cough and complains of shortness of breath. An elevated temperature is noted along with an increased pulse rate. She states that her daughter had stayed home from school for the past few days and was diagnosed with an upper respiratory viral infection.

   a. What is her chief complaint?

   _____

   b. What is the etiology of her chief complaint?

   _____

   c. What follow-up questions would you ask about her chief complaint?

   _____

   d. Are there any possible routes of transmission involved? Which one(s)?

   _____

   e. What would you do to keep from spreading this infection to other patients?

   _____

SUMMARY

Snapshots from the Journey

■ Anatomy is the study of the actual internal and external structures of the body, and physiology is the study of how these structures normally function. Pathology is the study of the disease processes which can cause disruptions of normal body structures and functions.

■ Medical terminology is the language of medicine and combines word roots, prefixes, and suffixes to construct numerous medical terms to describe conditions, locations, diagnostic tools, and so on.

■ The metric system is the mathematical language of medicine based on the powers of ten. If you require more practice with this system, please go to your student *Study Companion Guide* at the end of this text for a simplified review.

■ Metabolism refers to all the chemical operations going on within the body and can be broken down into two opposite processes. The building phase of metabolism is anabolism, in which simpler compounds are built up and used to manufacture materials for growth, reproduction, and repairs. The tearing down phase is catabolism, in which complex substances are broken down into simpler substances, such as food broken down for energy use.

■ The body tries to maintain a balanced or stable environment called homeostasis. The body must constantly monitor the environment and make changes to maintain this balance, often through the use of negative feedback loops.

■ A change in objective measurable values such as temperature (signs) and subjective patient perceptions (symptoms) can indicate a disease is present. Vital signs are pulse, respirations, temperature, and blood pressure.

■ The body's defenses are set up to guard against pathogenic organisms invading through portals of entry. There are various routes of transmission for pathogens to gain entry, and these include vectors, contact transmission, common vehicle, and airborne spread.

CASE STUDY

A 66-year-old Asian male involved in a vehicular accident is taken to the ICU with dyspnea and abdominal pain. He has acrocyanosis, tachycardia, and a past medical history of cardiopathy. He weighs 150 pounds and is five feet six inches tall. His chest x-ray shows an enlarged heart. His facial injuries will require future rhinoplastic surgery. An electrocardiogram and lower GI series is ordered.

a. Where exactly in the hospital was the patient taken?

_____

_____

b. Describe the patient's color, heart rate, and breathing.

_____

_____

c. What is the medical term for what the x-ray showed?

_____

_____

d. What future facial surgery will he need?

_____

_____

RAY'S AND MARIA'S STORIES

As you journey through the chapters, you will meet two common cases that will demonstrate the interrelatedness of the various systems. Ray suffered a high cervical injury and is a ventilator-dependent quadriplegic. Ray's treatment will require a solid knowledge of the body's various systems to give him the best possible care. Maria is a diabetic and will also have multisystem involvement. You will be responsible for Ray's and Maria's care throughout the book by utilizing the knowledge you gain from each new chapter.

RAY'S STORY

Divide into groups of three students. Choose one group member for each role: Reader, Recorder, Presenter. The Reader should read Ray's story aloud to the group. The Recorder should read Questions a, b, and c that follow the story aloud to the group. All group members should discuss appropriate responses, citing examples from Ray's Story. The Recorder should write the group's responses to each question in the class notebook, making sure to use complete sentences and listing examples used during the group discussion. Then, the Recorder should read each aloud to the group to check for consensus.

Ray glanced at the strategically placed clock and calendar on the wall. It was 3:00 p.m., September 15. His buddies were on their way to the Caribbean for a week of cave diving. He was supposed to be on that plane with them. Instead, he was lying in a hospital bed. Since high school the four of them had been inseparable. Every spare dime they made went into their annual extreme vacation. They had been hang gliding over the Grand Canyon, rafting on the Amazon, sky diving and parasailing in Florida, and snowboarding down a glacier in Alaska. How ironic that a dip in a backyard swimming pool would put an end to all that. Not only wouldn't he be skiing or hang gliding any time soon, he couldn't even mark the red Xs on the calendar to keep track of the passing days. A nurse did that for him. In fact, nurses or his mom or his brother did everything for him. He couldn't even scratch his own nose, or even tell anybody when it itched.

He was just fooling around with his six-year-old cousin at the end of the summer, one last swim before his aunt and uncle closed their pool. He had done a back flip off the diving board dozens of times, but this time he miscalculated. He knew as soon as he hit the water that he was sinking too fast and tried desperately to correct, but he couldn't get his head around fast enough. His last thought as the bottom of the pool rose to meet him was that he was going to mess up his face.

When he regained consciousness several days later, his mother and the doctor gently explained what had happened to him. He had struck the bottom of the pool on the point of his chin, jamming and twisting his neck. His neck was broken, the first two vertebrae shattered, and his spinal cord irreversibly damaged. He was paralyzed from the neck down and would be dependent on a ventilator for the rest of his life.

a. Explain how the relationship of anatomy to physiology has worked against Ray.

_____

b. What is the etiology of Ray's current condition and his diagnosis?

_____

c. How would you state his prognosis? What future complications do you expect to see?

_____

The Presenter from each group should share their group's responses to Questions a, b, and c, with supporting examples, aloud to the class.

REVIEW QUESTIONS

Multiple Choice

1. Which of the following is an example of microscopic anatomy?
   a. viewing an x-ray
   b. examining the shape of an organ during an autopsy
   c. classifying a type of bacterial cell
   d. watching how the pupils in the eyes react to light

2. Acromegaly means which of the following?
   a. a large stomach
   b. enlarged extremities
   c. an inflamed stomach lining
   d. a large acrobat

3. The breakdown of sugar in the body for energy is called:
   a. anabolism
   b. catabolism
   c. dogabolism
   d. hyperbolism

4. Which of the following is a measurement system based on the power of ten?
   a. English system
   b. British Imperial system
   c. metric system
   d. weights and measures system

5. The cause of a disease is referred to as the:
   a. prognosis
   b. diagnosis
   c. pathology
   d. etiology

Fill in the Blank

1. Ted's knee injury occurred at last night's football game. Today his doctor wants to make a small incision and use a device to "view or examine the joint" to assess the damage. What is the term for this device? _____

2. _____ is the study of the structures of the body, and _____ is the study of the functions of these structures.

3. For years, Ali never learned to swim because of her unnatural fear of the water, which is called _____.

4. Pulse and temperature represent two _____ signs of the body.

5. Raheem had blood work done that showed a normal number of white blood cells (WBCs) and red blood cells (RBCs). What are the respective medical terms for these cell types? _____ and _____.

6. If a cause of a disease cannot be determined, it is referred to as a(n) _____ disease.

REVIEW QUESTIONS

Short Answer

1. Explain the difference between diagnosis and prognosis.

_____

_____

_____

2. Knowing that difficulty swallowing is called dysphagia, what do you think the function of a phagocyte is?

_____

_____

_____

3. Contrast negative and positive feedback loops.

_____

_____

_____

4. Describe one example of homeostasis in your body.

_____

_____

_____

5. Contrast the terms endemic, epidemic, and pandemic.

_____

_____

_____

Suggested Activities

1. Investigate how the chemical and physical process of biofeedback contributes to homeostasis. Report your findings to the class.

2. Make up 3 × 5 inch note cards with five word roots discussed in this chapter and see how many medical words you can make using either prefixes or suffixes in the tables. For example, the word root *arthr/o* can be used to make the following: arthritis, arthralgia, arthroscope, and arthroplasty. Confirm that you made a real word by looking it up in a medical dictionary.

3. Choose a body system. Research and develop a presentation identifying the effects of environmental factors, such as climate, pollution, radioactivity, chemicals, electromagnetic fields, pathogens, carcinogens, and drugs on that system. Present your findings to the class.

4. Working in pairs, select one of the body parameters (blood pH, body temperature, electrolyte balance, or blood pressure), and explain its homeostatic regulation.

CAREER CONNECTIONS

Now that you have read this chapter, here is a list of related professions you may be interested in investigating for a future career:

- Medical Assisting

- Medical Records and Health Information Technician

- Medical Transcriptionist

Research each profession and report on the following:

1. Profession description to include job responsibilities
2. Educational requirements
3. Job opportunities
4. Opportunities outside of the hospital setting
5. Salary range
6. Licensure and continuing education requirements

ANATOMY, PHYSIOLOGY, AND DISEASE IN ACTION

I. Case History

A 17-year-old boy and his brother, 7 years old, living in Michigan, go to the doctor. The patients were recently on a camping trip in August that covered several states in the northeast including New York, Connecticut, New Jersey, Massachusetts, Maine, and New Hampshire.

Chief Complaint:
After returning from the camping trip two weeks ago, the patients started feeling ill and are having a difficult time recovering from the trip. Nothing in the home or school environment has changed or is unusual.

Signs and Symptoms:
Myalgia, arthralgia, febrile, lymph adenomegaly

Diagnostic Tests:
Initial BP, TPR, CXR, CBC, EKG
Subsequent ELISA

Treatment:
Doxycycline 100mg 3 times daily for the seventeen-year-old
Amoxicillin for the seven-year-old, 50 mg/kg per day divided in 3 doses not to exceed 500 mg. (The child weighs 50 lb.)

Subsequent Symptom:
4 weeks post camping trip, erythema migrans

Assignment:
1. Translate all medical terms and abbreviations.
2. Were the initial diagnostic tests necessary?
3. If the 17-year-old took doxycyline for 21 days, what was the total amount of the antibiotic ingested?
4. How much amoxicillin would be given in one dose?
5. What personal protective equipment is necessary for the healthcare workers: physician/ laboratory personnel? What is the rationale?
6. What is the diagnosis? What is the definitive clue? What is the causative agent?
7. What are diseases/agents that may be associated with this disease?

ANATOMY, PHYSIOLOGY, AND DISEASE IN ACTION

II. Vital Signs

Materials:
Stethoscope
Aneroid sphygmomanometer
Thermometer (tympanic, oral)
Clock

Form groups of four. Each member will choose one of the following to teach the others in the group to measure vital signs: blood pressure, respiration rate, pulse, and temperature. Construct a chart to record the data for each member of the group along with the normal range for each vital sign including spaces. Take and record each measurement under the following conditions:
• After resting for five minutes, preferably horizontal
• Sitting for five minutes
• Performing 50 jumping jacks.

Develop a hypothesis for the expected results. Incorporate the following questions in a scientific lab report for each group.
1. Did the results support your initial hypothesis? What is the control? Variable?
2. Is each of the measurements in the normal range? Why or why not? What could account for the differences?
3. What is the average for the group? How does it compare with the other groups?
4. Compute the mean, median, and range for the class data.
5. How could disease, age, and gender affect the results?
6. Each member of the group should choose one item from the materials list, and verbally explain to other members how the item was used and why it was significant. If one of your group members is unsure, others can help by offering ideas and terminology.

III. Service Learning or Community Service Project

Research and construct a pictorial pain rating scale with descriptors for children or people who do not speak English. Present to various day care facilities in local area for consideration of use.

Materials:
Art supplies, tag board, computers

What are the positives and negatives of using this scale?

The Human Body
Reading the Map

Now that we have a basic understanding of the native language and some basic anatomy, physiology, and disease concepts, how will we successfully navigate through an unfamiliar city or country? We must, of course, study maps to plan our visit and know where we are going. The same effort is required to learn the "terrain" of the human body. This chapter provides the major *external* map of the human body that serves as a guide for future chapters, which map in detail the *internal* regions. We'll use medical directional terms and body locations as our foundation as we journey together through the human organism. If there is one thing we should know better than anything else, shouldn't it be our own bodies? Just as the old saying goes, by the end of our journey through this textbook, you will know your entire body like the back of your hand.

LEARNING OUTCOMES

At the end of your journey through this chapter, you will be able to:

- List and describe the various body positions
- Define the body planes and associated directional terms
- Locate and describe the body cavities and their respective organs
- List and describe the anatomical divisions of the abdominal region
- Identify and locate the various body regions
- Explain the various imaging techniques to view the body
- Describe situations in which body position can help or hinder the disease process

Pronunciation Guide

Correct pronunciation is important in any journey so that you and others are completely understood. Here is a "see and say" Pronunciation Guide for the more difficult terms to pronounce in this chapter. Please note that pronunciations given are referenced to medical dictionaries, and regional variations may exist.

abdominopelvic (ab DOM ih noh PELL vik)
anatomical (an ah TOM ih kal)
antecubital (an tee CUE bi tal)
buccal (BUCK al)
caudal (KAWD al)
cephalic (seh FAL ik)
coronal (koh ROH nal)
cranial (KRAY nee al)
crural (KROO ral)
distal (DISS tal)
dorsal (DOR sal)
embolism (EM bow lizm)
epigastric (ep ih GAS trik)
gluteal (GLOO tee al)

hypochondriac (HIGH poh KON dree ak)
hypogastric (HIGH poh GAS trik)
lateral (LAT er al)
medial (ME dee al)
mediastinum (ME dee ass TYE num)
midsagittal plane (mid SAJ ih tal)
orthopnea (or THOP nee ah)
pleural cavities (PLOO ral)
proximal (PROK sim al)
superficial (SOO per FISH al)
supine (sue PINE)
thoracic (thoh RASS ik)
transverse (tranz VERS)
Trendelenburg (tren DELL in berg)

anatomical position *(an ah TOM ih kal)* This is a standard position in which the body is standing erect, the head is up with the eyes looking forward, the arms are by the sides with the palms facing forward, and the legs are straight with the toes pointing forward.

THE MAP OF THE HUMAN BODY

When reading a map, you need certain universal directional terms, such as north, east, south and west. Maps of specific regions can include more details about that region, making it easier to explore. Likewise, scientists have created standardized body directional terms and split the body into distinct regions, sections, and cavities so that we can more clearly and rapidly locate and discuss anatomical features. Having certain anatomical landmarks on the body also provides needed points of reference for assessment and surgical procedures. For example, the spinal cord is a major anatomical landmark for many structures in the center of our bodies.

If a patient states, "I have pain in my stomach," what does that really tell you? Location of pain can help in determining what is wrong with a patient. It is helpful to know the type of pain (dull, sharp, or stabbing) and *exactly* where in that region the pain is located to help determine its cause. For example, pain in the general stomach area can indicate a variety of problems, such as an ulcer, heart attack, appendicitis, indigestion, or liver problems. Knowing the exact region can help a clinician better determine the problem with precision.

Body Positions

The body can assume many positions and therefore have different orientations. To standardize the orientation for the study of anatomy, scientists developed the **anatomical position**. The anatomical position, as shown in FIGURE 2-1 ▲, is a human standing erect, face forward, with feet parallel and arms hanging at the side, and with palms facing forward.

FIGURE 2-1 ▲ The anatomical position.

Other body positions that are important to discuss because of clinical assessments and treatments in health care are the **supine, prone, Trendelenburg,** and **Fowler's** positions. The supine position is lying face *upward,* or on your back. An easy way to remember is supine is lying on your spine. The prone position is lying face *downward,* or on your stomach. When a patient is in the Trendelenburg position, the head of the bed is lower than the feet. Fowler's position is sitting in bed with the head of the bed elevated 45 to 60 degrees. This position is often used in the hospital to facilitate breathing and for comfort of the bedridden patient while eating or talking. See FIGURE 2-2 ▲ for these body positions.

supine position *(sue PINE)* Position of lying on the posterior part of the body. Also known as the dorsal supine position.

prone position Lying with the anterior section of the body down.

Trendelenburg *(trin DELL in berg)* A patient position in which the head is lower than the body and legs.

Fowler's position A semi-sitting position with the torso at a 45- to 60-degree angle.

FIGURE 2-2 ▲ Common patient positions.

Pathology Connection

BODY POSITION AND A&P CHANGES

A patient may be placed in certain positions for treatment. For example, placing patients with secretions in the bases of their lungs in the Trendelenburg position helps drain those segments of the lungs. Although this is therapeutic, certain precautions must be taken. Because the head is lower than the heart, gravity increases the blood flow and therefore the intracranial pressure; note that "intra" means within. This position may be contraindicated in patients with cerebral injury or bleeding. Also, patients are more prone to aspirate (take in) vomitus into their lungs, and therefore patients should not eat within two to four hours of being placed in the Trendelenburg postion.

Another example of how body position can affect function involves cardiac patients. When a patient experiences severe heart failure, the neck veins become filled with extra blood due to the backup of fluid into the venous system. This is called **jugular venous distension** (JVD). If the patient experiences engorged, or swollen, neck veins while in the upright sitting position, this indicates severe heart failure. The physiologic reason is that the pressure of the "backed-up" venous blood has become greater than the effects of gravity.

Sometimes when a person quickly arises from a seated position he or she becomes weak and dizzy. This may be a sign of **orthostatic hypotension;** note that "ortho-" means to straighten. When the person is seated, the blood pressure may be low, but the brain is still receiving adequate blood flow (perfusion) for normal functioning. When the person stands, however, the heart has to pump harder against gravity to send the blood to the brain. If the heart cannot compensate, the pressure becomes even lower, and the person experiences weakness and/or dizziness due to lack of cerebral perfusion. These kinds of postural changes in blood pressure will be a problem for Ray, our spinal cord patient introduced to you in the Common Case Study at the end of Chapter 1, due to a dysfunction of his nervous system when propped up in his wheelchair.

Some people with breathing problems sometimes sleep better when they prop themselves up with several pillows in bed. Such patients are experiencing **orthopnea,** in which it is easier to breathe in a more upright position than lying flat. This is because when a person sits upright, gravity assists the diaphragm in the downward movement needed for inspiration. You'll learn more on how the diaphragm functions in Chapter 13 on the respiratory system.

jugular venous distension (JVD) The enlargement of the jugular veins due to venous engorgement.

orthostatic hypotension *(OR thoh STAT ick HIGH poh TEN shun)* An abnormal decrease in blood pressure as a result of changing position (such as quickly standing up).

orthopnea *(or THOP nee uh)* Labored breathing when lying flat and which improves when sitting up or standing.

TEST YOUR KNOWLEDGE 2-1

Complete the following:

1. Try standing in the anatomical position.

2. List the best body position (prone, supine, or Fowler's position) for the following circumstances:
   a. Getting a back massage _____
   b. Eating in a hospital bed _____
   c. Watching television in bed _____
   d. Watching the stars at night _____

3. A person experiencing orthopnea would breathe better in which position?

_____

4. What position would be contraindicated for someone who just had eye surgery?

_____

Body Planes and Directional Terms

Sometimes it is necessary to divide the body or even an organ or tissue sample into specific sections to further examine it. A **plane** is an imaginary line drawn through the body or organ to separate it into specific sections. For example, in **FIGURE 2-3** ▲, we see the **transverse plane** or **horizontal plane**, dividing the body into top (**superior**) and bottom (**inferior**) sections. This can also be called **cross-sectioning** the body. Cross-sectioning is often done with tissue and organ samples to further examine internal structures.

Notice in Figure 2-3 that certain directional terms can be used to describe areas divided by the transverse plane. One more analogy that relates to a map is the concept

plane A flat surface formed by making an imaginary cut through the body or a portion of it.

transverse plane *(tranz VERS)* Plane that divides the body into top and bottom sections, superior and inferior.

horizontal plane Another name for the transverse plane.

superior Pertaining to the upper half of the body or a position above an organ or structure.

inferior Pertaining to the lower half of the body or a position below an organ or structure.

cross-sectioning Making slices of a sample for examination purposes.

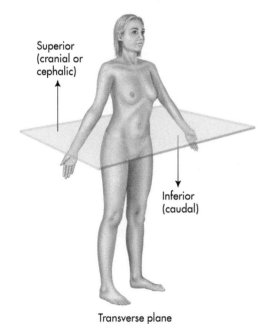

Superior (cranial or cephalic)

Inferior (caudal)

Transverse plane

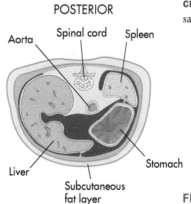

POSTERIOR

Aorta   Spinal cord   Spleen

Liver

Subcutaneous fat layer

ANTERIOR

Stomach

FIGURE 2-3 ▲ Transverse plane and a cross-sectional view of the upper abdominal region.

cranial *(KRAY nee al)* Pertaining to the skull.

cephalic *(seh FAL ik)* Toward the head of the body.

caudal *(KAWD al)* Toward the tailbone, feet, or lower part of the body.

median plane Imaginary division of the body from top to bottom dividing it into right and left sections.

midsagittal plane *(mid SAJ ih tal)* An imaginary vertical plane that divides the entire body into right and left sides and creates a midline. The midsagittal plane is named for the sagittal suture of the skull.

medial *(MEE dee al)* Pertaining to the middle of the body or the middle of an organ or structure.

lateral Pertaining to the side of the body or the side of an organ or structure.

frontal plane An imaginary plane parallel with the long axis of the body that divides the body into an anterior and posterior section.

coronal plane *(kor ROW nal)* Also called frontal plane; an imaginary vertical plane that divides the entire body into front and back sections. The coronal plane is named for the coronal suture where the anterior and posterior skull bones meet.

anterior The front of the body.

ventral Pertaining to the anterior of the body, particularly the abdomen.

of a reference point. If you were traveling from Colorado to Florida, you would have to travel in a southeasterly direction. Colorado is your starting point and serves as your reference point. However, if you were traveling from Florida to Colorado, you would travel in a northwesterly direction because Florida is now your point of reference. In Figure 2-3, you can see that superior (**cranial** or **cephalic**) means toward the head or upper body, and inferior (**caudal**) means away from the head or toward the lower part of the body. Any body part can be either superior or inferior depending on your reference point. For example, the knee is superior to the ankle if the ankle is the reference point. However, the knee is inferior when the thigh is used as the reference point. Two other terms from this illustration are cranial, which refers to the skull, and caucal, which refers to body parts near the tail (tailbone).

The **median plane,** or **midsagittal plane,** divides the body into right and left halves. FIGURE 2-4 ▲ shows this plane and the directional terms associated with it. **Medial** refers to body parts located near the middle or midline of the body. **Lateral** refers to body parts located away from midline (or on the side). If a technician were to section and examine an organ for disease, he or she might make a midsagittal cut (cut the organ into equal right and left halves) in order to examine the internal parts of the organ or might simply make several sagittal (vertical or lengthwise) cuts to slice the organ into smaller sections for closer examination.

The **frontal plane,** or **coronal plane,** divides the body into front and back sections. **Anterior** and **ventral** refer to body parts toward or on the front of the body, and

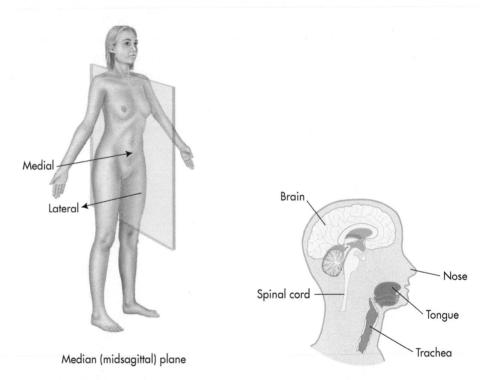

Median (midsagittal) plane

FIGURE 2-4 ▲ Midsagittal or median plane along with a mid-sagittal view of the head.

posterior and **dorsal** refer to body parts toward or on the back of the body. **FIGURE 2-5** ▲ demonstrates the coronal plane and associated directional terms. Remember, if during your trip you stop at the beach, you will know it is not safe to swim if you see a shark's *dorsal* fin sticking out of the water.

Additional Directional Terms

There are some additional directional terms that are important in health care. **Proximal** refers to body parts close to a point of reference or origin of the body. This is contrasted by **distal,** which refers to body parts away from a point of reference or origin. For example, using your shoulder as a reference point, your elbow is proximal to your shoulder, whereas your fingers are distal to your shoulder. **External** means on the outside, and **internal** refers to structures on the inside. Did you know that your externally located skin is actually the body's largest organ? Most other organs are located internally within body cavities.

Superficial means toward or at the body surface. When a clinician draws blood from you, he or she looks for superficial veins that are easy to see and easy to access with the needle. **Deep** means away from the body surface. The large veins in your legs are deep veins and are more protected than superficial veins because injury to them can be more critical to survival than can injury to a smaller, superficial blood vessel. These deep leg veins are a common site for blood clots (thrombi) to form that can then break away and travel to areas such as the lungs (pulmonary emboli) or brain (cerebral emboli) and block vital blood flow. An **embolism** is a sudden obstruction of a blood vessel by debris that can include blood clots (thrombi), plaques, bacteria, cancer cells, fat from bone marrow, and air bubbles.

Central refers to locations around the center of the body (torso and head), and **peripheral** refers to the extremities (arms and legs) or surrounding or outer regions. **TABLE 2-1** ■ provides a summary of directional terms.

posterior The back of the body.

dorsal *(DOR sal)* Pertaining to the posterior of the body, particularly the back.

proximal *(PROK sim al)* Referring to "near" a reference point.

distal *(DISS tall)* Moving from the body toward the end of a limb (arm or leg).

external Near or on the outside surface of the body or an organ.

internal Structures deep within the body or an organ.

superficial Related to, or located near, the surface.

deep Located underneath or further from a surface.

embolism A sudden obstruction of a blood vessel by debris.

central Located in the middle or equidistant from multiple points.

peripheral *(per IF er uhl)* Referring to "away from center" or the extremities.

Posterior or Dorsal

Anterior or Ventral

Frontal (coronal) plane

FIGURE 2-5 ▲ Frontal or coronal plane along with a coronal view of the chest and abdominal region.

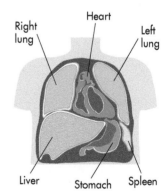

Right lung

Heart

Left lung

Liver

Stomach

Spleen

TABLE 2-1 ■ DIRECTIONAL TERMS

DIRECTIONAL TERM	MEANING	USE IN A SENTENCE
Proximal	Near point of reference	The recovery room is *proximal* to the operating room.
Distal	Away from point of reference	The fingers are *distal* to the shoulders.
External	On the outside	The *external* defibrillator is used on the outside of the chest.
Internal	On the inside	He received *internal* injuries from the accident.
Superficial	At the body surface	The cut was only *superficial*.
Deep	Under the body surface	The patient had *deep* wounds from the chainsaw.
Central	Locations around center of body	The patient had *central* chest pain.
Peripheral	Surrounding or outer regions	The patient had *peripheral* swelling of the feet.
Medial	Toward the midline	The nose is *medial* to the face.
Lateral	Toward the sides	The ears are *lateral* to the nose.

Clinical Application

DO YOU KNOW YOUR LEFT FROM YOUR RIGHT?

By now, it should be clear that you need a precise, standardized language with directional terms to study anatomy and physiology and apply it in a health care setting. Something as simple as left and right can become critical. For example, suppose you are a surgical technologist and are ordered to put a tag around a patient's right leg to designate it as the leg to be amputated in an upcoming surgery. If you approach the patient from the bottom of the bed and place the tag on the leg on your right side, you have erroneously placed it on the patient's left leg, and this could have disastrous results. Left and right always refer to the *patient's* left and right, not yours. See **FIGURE 2-6** ▲.

FIGURE 2-6 ▲ Body location terms.

Clinical Application

CENTRAL VERSUS PERIPHERAL CYANOSIS

Cyanosis is a condition of bluish-colored skin that is usually the result of low levels of oxygen in the blood. Peripheral cyanosis presents as bluish fingers and toes and may indicate the need for oxygen therapy, depending on the condition of the patient. Peripheral cyanosis is sometimes difficult to detect in people with dark skin. Central cyanosis is much more serious and presents as bluish discoloration of the torso and inside the mouth. See **FIGURE 2-7** ▲, which illustrates central and peripheral cyanosis.

CENTRAL CYANOSIS

PERIPHERAL CYANOSIS

FIGURE 2-7 ▲ Contrast of central versus peripheral cyanosis.

TEST YOUR KNOWLEDGE 2-2

Answer the following questions:

1. Give the opposite directional term:
   a. superior _____
   b. posterior _____
   c. caudal _____
   d. ventral _____
   e. distal _____
   f. external _____
   g. superficial _____
   h. peripheral _____
   i. medial _____

2. A spinal tap is performed at the _____ region of the body.

3. The plane that divides the body into upper and lower regions is called the _____ plane.

4. Cutting an organ into two equal halves (right and left) requires a(n) _____ incision.

5. A scratch on the surface of the skin is called a(n) _____ wound.

6. The wrist is _____ to the hand, whereas the elbow is _____ to the hand.

7. The nose is _____ to the mouth.

8. A pain in your side can also be referred to as _____ pain.

9. If your hands and feet are swollen with fluid (edema), you are said to have _____ edema.

10. A cerebral embolus can often originate in the _____ veins of the legs.

Body Cavities

The body has two large spaces or cavities that house and protect organs. Located in the back of the body are the dorsal cavities and in the front, the ventral cavities. FIGURE 2-8 ▲ illustrates these cavities.

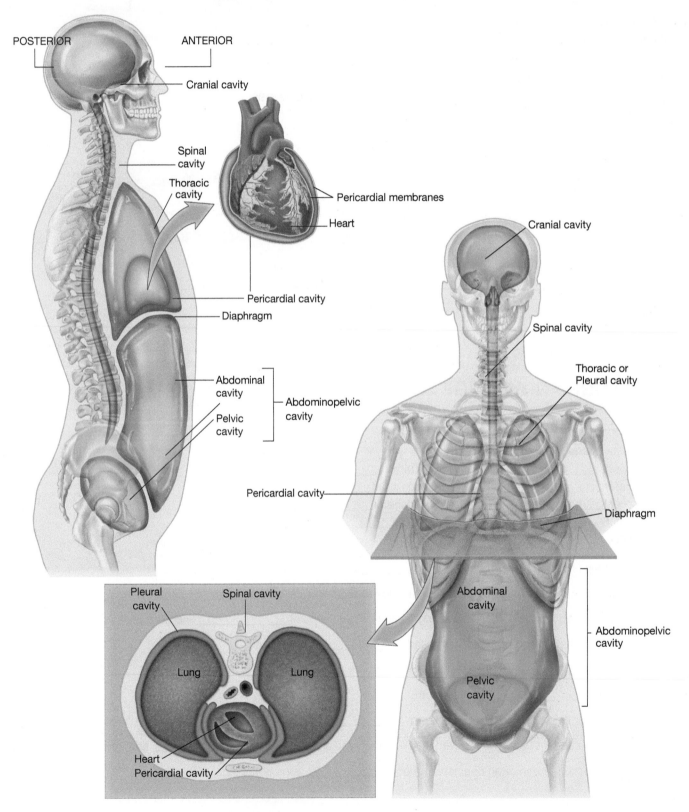

FIGURE 2-8 ▲ Various views of the main body cavities.

The larger anterior cavity is subdivided into two main cavities called the **thoracic cavity** and the **abdominopelvic cavity**. These cavities are physically separated by the large, dome-shaped muscle called the diaphragm, which is used for breathing. The thoracic cavity contains the heart, lungs, and large blood vessels. The heart has its own small cavity called the **pericardial cavity**. The abdominopelvic cavity contains the digestive organs, such as the stomach, intestines, liver, gallbladder, pancreas, and spleen in the upper or abdominal portion. The lower portion, called the pelvic cavity, contains the urinary and reproductive organs and the last part of the large intestine. A posterior, or dorsal, cavity is located in the back of the body and consists of the **cranial cavity**, which houses the brain, and the **spinal cavity**, which contains the spinal cord.

There are also smaller body cavities that designate specific areas, and these are further explored in upcoming chapters. For example, the nasal cavity is the space behind the nose, the oral or **buccal** cavity is the space within the mouth, and the orbital cavity houses the eyes.

thoracic cavity *(thoh RASS ick)* Hollow space within the thorax that is filled with the lungs, heart, and related structures in the mediastinum.

abdominopelvic cavity *(ab DOM ih noh PELL vik KAVih tee)* Continuous cavity within the abdomen and pelvis that contains the largest organs of the gastrointestinal system.

pericardial cavity The cavity that contains the heart.

cranial cavity Body cavity, located in the skull, that houses the brain.

spinal cavity *(SPY nal)* The spinal cavity lies within, and is protected by, the bones (vertebrae) of the spinal column. The spinal cavity contains the spinal cord, the spinal nerves, and spinal fluid.

buccal *(BUCK al)* Pertaining to cheek or mouth region.

TEST YOUR KNOWLEDGE 2-3

Identify the major body cavity in which the following organs are located:

1. heart _____

2. spinal cord _____

3. stomach _____

4. lungs _____

5. reproductive organs _____

6. brain _____

epigastric *(EP ih GAS trik)* Above the stomach.

hypochondriac Name of two of the abdominal regions left and right, under the ribs.

umbilical *(uhm BIL ih kuhl)* Pertaining to the umbilicus ("belly button").

Body Regions

The abdominal region houses a number of organs. Anatomists have divided this region as shown in **FIGURE 2-9** ▲. Understanding directional terms assists in locating the regions. For example, the **epigastric** region (*epi,* above; *gastric,* stomach) is located superior to the umbilical region. The right and left **hypochondriac** regions are located on either side of the epigastric region and contain the lower ribs. The centrally located **umbilical** region houses the navel or belly button. You may not remember your umbilical cord being cut as a newborn, but your belly button is a reminder that it occurred. Lateral to this region are the right and left lumbar regions at the level of the **lumbar** vertebrae. The **hypogastric** region lies inferior to the umbilical region and is flanked by the right and left iliac or inguinal regions. The **inguinal** region is where the thigh meets the trunk and is also called the groin region.

lumbar Two of the nine regions of the abdominopelvic area. The right and left lumbar regions are inferior to the right and left hypochondriac regions. Also refers to the lower back, spinal cord, and spinal column.

hypogastric Inferior to the stomach.

inguinal *(ING gwuh nal)* The groin; the term inguinal means referring to the groin.

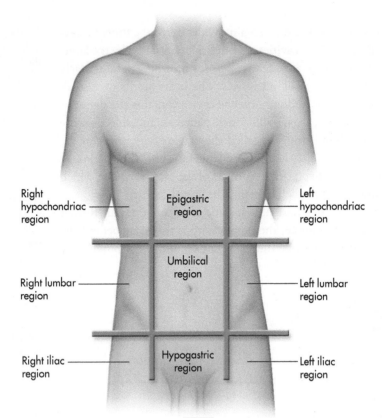

Right hypochondriac region

Epigastric region

Left hypochondriac region

Right lumbar region

Umbilical region

Left lumbar region

Right iliac region

Hypogastric region

Left iliac region

FIGURE 2-9 ▲ The nine divisions of the abdominal region.

Clinical Application

HERNIAS

You may have heard of an umbilical (belly button) hernia (bulge), or an inguinal hernia, and now you know exactly where such hernias are located. Just what is a hernia? A hernia is a tear in the muscle wall that allows a structure (usually an organ) to protrude through it. Sometimes this can be a minor nuisance, but a hernia can also be very dangerous if the blood flow is restricted to the portion of the organ that is protruding. Restricted blood flow can lead to death of the tissue and to serious consequences. Death of a tissue is called necrosis. **FIGURE 2-10** ▲ shows an inguinal and umbilical hernia with a protrusion of the intestines.

Small intestine

Inguinal ligament

Direct inguinal hernia

INFANT

Umbilical hernia

FIGURE 2-10 ▲ Illustrations of inguinal and umbilical hernias.

Clinical Application

THE CENTRAL LANDMARK: THE SPINAL COLUMN

The spinal, or vertebral, column is a major, centrally located anatomical landmark and has five sets of vertebrae (spinal bones) labeled for the body region (see **FIGURE 2-11** ▲). The seven cervical (C) vertebrae are located in the neck; the 12 thoracic (T) vertebrae are located in the chest; the five lumbar (L) vertebrae are located in the lower back; and the five fused sacral (S) vertebrae (sacrum) are located near the final coccyx vertebra (tailbone). For example, the T5 vertebra is used to help locate on a chest x-ray the area where the trachea bifurcates to the right and left lung. You'll learn even more about the spinal column and cord in Chapter 6, "The Skeletal System," and Chapter 9, "The Nervous System."

FIGURE 2-11 ▲ The spinal column.

A more practical way for health professionals to compartmentalize the abdominal region is to separate it into anatomical quadrants. **FIGURE 2-12** ▲ illustrates these quadrants, which are helpful in describing the location of abdominal pain. Knowing the organs located in the quadrant where the pain occurs can provide a clue to what type of problem the patient has. For example, tenderness in the right lower quadrant (RLQ) can be a symptom of appendicitis because that is where the appendix is located. RUQ (right upper quadrant) pain may mean a liver or gallbladder problem.

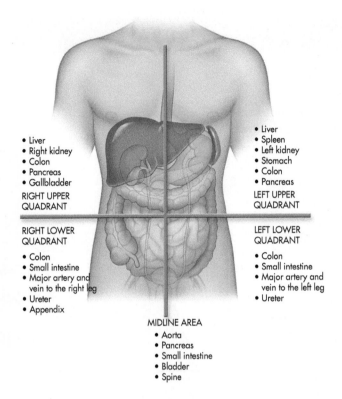

FIGURE 2-12 ▲ The clinical division of the abdominal region into quadrants with related organs and structures.

- Liver
- Right kidney
- Colon
- Pancreas
- Gallbladder

RIGHT UPPER QUADRANT

- Liver
- Spleen
- Left kidney
- Stomach
- Colon
- Pancreas

LEFT UPPER QUADRANT

RIGHT LOWER QUADRANT

- Colon
- Small intestine
- Major artery and vein to the right leg
- Ureter
- Appendix

LEFT LOWER QUADRANT

- Colon
- Small intestine
- Major artery and vein to the left leg
- Ureter

MIDLINE AREA
- Aorta
- Pancreas
- Small intestine
- Bladder
- Spine

Additional body regions further aid in locating areas and structures. For example, what if you were asked to obtain an axillary temperature on an infant? Just where is the brachial or femoral pulse? What part of the body does carpal tunnel syndrome affect? See **FIGURE 2-13** ▲ for other common body regions and parts that are discussed in later chapters. In addition, review **TABLE 2-2** ■ for further practical examples of the medical importance of the various body regions.

Amazing **Body Facts**

Psoas Test

The psoas (*SOH as*) test—with its strange name—is one way to help determine if a patient has appendicitis. The patient is placed in a supine position and instructed to raise his or her right leg while the practitioner places a hand on the patient's right thigh and gives a slight opposing downward force. If the patient has appendicitis, he or she will usually experience pain in the right lower quadrant.

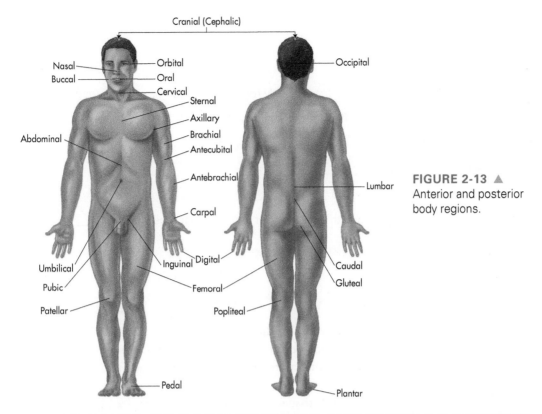

FIGURE 2-13 ▲
Anterior and posterior body regions.

TABLE 2-2 ■ EXAMPLES OF BODY REGIONS AND THEIR LOCATIONS

BODY REGION	LOCATION	MEDICAL EXAMPLE
Antebrachial	Forearm	Between the wrist and elbow
Antecubital	Depressed area in front of elbow	Area used to draw blood or start an IV
Axillary	Armpit	Can be used to take temperature
Brachial	Upper arm	Used to take blood pressure
Buccal	Cheek (inside)	Check buccal region for central cyanosis
Carpal	Wrist	Carpal tunnel syndrome
Cervical	Neck	Cervical collar needed for neck injuries
Digital	Fingers	Place digital oxygen sensors
Femoral	Upper inner thigh	Femoral pulse indicates adequate circulation to legs
Gluteal	Buttocks	The gluteal region is an injection site
Lumbar	Lower back	Lumbar pain often occurs on long car trips
Nasal	Nose	Medications can be given by nasal spray
Oral	Mouth	Oral route is the most common route for medications
Orbital	Eye area	Orbital injury can cause damage to sight
Patellar	Knee	Patellar injuries are very common in sports
Pedal	Foot	People with heart problems may have pedal edema (swelling)
Plantar	Sole of foot	Plantar warts can be painful
Pubic	Genital region	The pubic region is often checked for body lice
Scapular	Shoulder blades region	Pressure ulcers often form in the scapular region of bedridden patients
Sternal	Breastbone area	The sternal area is used for CPR
Thoracic	Chest	The thoracic area is used to listen to heart and lung sounds

TEST YOUR KNOWLEDGE 2-4

Fill in the blank with the appropriate medical term for the body region. These can have more than one answer.

1. People who chew smokeless tobacco or snuff are more susceptible to _____ cancer.

2. Antiperspirant sprays are usually used in the _____ region.

3. Belly button rings are usually found in the _____ region.

4. If you sit too long at your desk, you can develop _____ pain.

5. During physicals, your reflexes are checked with a little rubber hammer that taps your _____ region.

x-ray An electromagnetic radiation utilized to form a two dimensional image of the body for diagnostic purposes.

computed tomography (CT) Imaging diagnostic tool that combines a series of x-rays to give a three-dimensional view.

magnetic resonance imaging (MRI) Imaging technique utilizing high-intensity magnetism to produce high-quality body images for diagnostic purposes.

radiolucent *(RAY dee oh LOO sent)* Property of being partly or wholly penetrable by x-rays, giving a darker or black appearance.

radiopaque *(RAY dee oh PAYK)* Increased resistance to x-ray penetration making the image lighter or white.

RADIOLOGY: THE SCIENCE OF VIEWING THE BODY

Chapter 18 is devoted to diagnostic testing, but diagnostic imaging fits well within this chapter on body positions and locations. Positions are important in the radiologic sciences for obtaining a proper internal view of body structures. **X-rays** are a form of high-energy radiation that penetrates the body and gives a two-dimensional view of the bones, air, and tissues in the body. The standard x-ray (much like a photograph) can be computer-enhanced to give much greater detail and contrast and to allow for a more realistic three-dimensional view. For example, if a standard chest x-ray showed a golf ball–sized tumor in the lung, you would have no idea of its actual depth because it would look flat, like a quarter. **Computed tomography** (CT) scanning uses a narrowly focused x-ray beam that circles rapidly around the body. The computer constructs thin-slice images and combines them to give much greater detail and allow for a more three-dimensional view, much like a loaf of sliced bread gives a better idea of the total shape of the loaf than does a single slice. The CT scan reveals the true depth of the quarter-shaped tumor shown on the regular x-ray. A **magnetic resonance imager** (MRI) produces even greater detail of tissue structures, even down to individual nerve bundles. Another advantage of the MRI is the absence of radiation exposure.

X-rays (Radiograph or Roentgenogram)

The most common type of radiologic diagnostic modality is the x-ray. An x-ray is produced by passing x-ray beams through a specific area of the body and then exposing a photographic film to those rays that successfully pass through that area. As a result, the developed film or digital image will possess an image of varying degrees of dark and light, depending on the densities found in the body that the x-rays passed through. Less dense areas, such as the lungs, which contain a lot of air, allow the x-rays to pass through easily and show up on the film as a dark (**radiolucent**) region. Bones are much denser and allow fewer x-rays to pass through them. As a result, the denser bones appear as light (**radiopaque**) structures on the film. The densities of the other body parts are somewhere between these examples and vary in their lightness or darkness on the film. In general four densities can be found in the body:

1. *Air* is the least dense, and therefore the most radiolucent, showing up as black on an x-ray film.
2. *Tissue/fat* densities can depend on the thickness of the tissue and/or the amount of fat present. The thicker the layer, the more radiation is absorbed, and the lighter the image.
3. *Water* density can be represented by blood, or by edema as a result of tissue injury or inflammatory processes. Water density is a mid-range density: denser than air and less dense than bone.
4. *Bone/metal* is the highest density, absorbing the greatest amount of radiation. Because less radiation passes through and onto the film, the film image is white or lighter than the other densities.

One of the problems with an x-ray film is that it is a one-dimensional view of a specific area. As a result, the patient has to be positioned differently in relationship to the x-ray machine and film depending on what the physician is looking for. For example, it would be difficult to see a small lung tumor located right behind the heart if you were looking at a frontal view of the patient.

Every attempt should be made to position the patient's area to be x-rayed as close to the film as possible. This will help ensure that the structures appear as clear and as close to actual size as possible on the x-ray. The following are the three main views normally used in the clinical setting:

- **Posteroanterior (PA):** This standard position places the patient in an upright position with the chest placed in front of the x-ray film. The x-ray beam travels from the machine, through the patient's posterior region, out the patient's anterior, and onto the film. The shoulders are commonly rotated forward to move the shoulder blades away from the lungs if there is a question about any lung pathology. Generally, the distance between the x-ray machine and the film is six feet.
- **Anteroposterior (AP):** In this position, the patient's posterior is against the x-ray film. The x-ray beam travels through the patient's anterior region, out the posterior, and onto the film. The distance between the x-ray machine and the film is 48 inches. This is the position commonly seen in the hospital where a portable x-ray machine is brought to the patient's room if he or she is too ill to be taken to the radiology department. The patient is usually in a sitting position on the bed.
- **Lateral:** This position is often done as a complement to the PA image. The lateral view is done to eliminate interfering organs or structures in front of other structures of concern, such as a tumor. The object in question is placed as close to the film as possible. For example, if there is a suspected lesion in the left lung behind the heart, the left side of the patient is placed next to the film. This would be a left lateral view. This view prevents the heart from obstructing the view of the suspected tumor and, in conjunction with a PA x-ray, gives a more 3-D sense of the tumor.

Computerized Tomography (CT or CAT Scan)

As previously stated, one of the problems with an x-ray is that it provides a one-dimensional picture. The CT scan provides a high-resolution series of cross-sectional "slices" (much like a loaf of sliced bread) of the body. As a result, it creates a three-dimensional view of structures in the body as well as tissue structures within solid organs. This allows the clinician to determine the exact location, size, and shape of a suspected tumor in the body, which would not be possible with only an x-ray. The downside to a CT scan is the high level of radiation exposure required. A single CT scan is the equivalent of hundreds of chest x-rays in terms of radiation exposure.

Magnetic Resonance Imaging (MRI)

Instead of utilizing radiation, this diagnostic tool uses magnetic energy to produce cross-sectional images of body structures. The clarity of these images is generally much better than those from x-rays and is often better than a CT scan. However, there are some drawbacks. Because an intense magnetic field is used, certain steel aneurysm clips or prosthetic heart valves may be adversely affected, even to the point of shifting their position in the body. Patients must also be completely still, or there will be a loss in resolution. Open MRIs have been developed to decrease the feelings of claustrophobia experienced by some individuals in a closed MRI, which takes place inside a very small tunnel.

Ultrasound (Sonography)

Much more sensitive than a regular x-ray, ultrasound uses sound waves to distinguish structures in the body, much like SONAR or fish finders in fishing boats. Ultrasound studies also allow for body activities to be viewed in real time. Due to this feature, the actions of heart valves can be observed, or fetal development and movement can be monitored, for example. No radiation exposure is involved in these studies. In the past, there had been some concern about potential damage to a developing fetus due to the sound waves used during these studies, but no evidence has been found that this is a hazard. FIGURE 2-14 ▲ contrasts x-ray, CT, MRI, and ultrasound.

A

B

FIGURE 2-14 ▲ Contrasts of x-ray, CT, MRI, and ultrasound.
A. Abdominal region CT scan (Source: Hong xia/Shutterstock.com);
B. MRI image of the head (Source: CGinspiration/Shutterstock.com).

C

D

FIGURE 2-14 *(continued)* ▲ Contrasts of x-ray, CT, MRI, and ultrasound. **C.** x-ray showing typical joint replacement associated with osteoarthritis (Source: Santibhavank P/Shutterstock.com); **D.** Ultrasound (Source: Mikael Damkier/Shutterstock.com).

SUMMARY

Snapshots from the Journey

■ The body can assume many different positions, and to standardize the study of anatomy, scientists often reference the anatomical position. In the anatomical position, the person stands with face and toes forward, hands at sides, and palms facing forward. Other positions, such as the prone, supine, and Fowler's positions, are used in health care for assessment and treatment.

■ The body can be divided into different sections along different planes. For example, the transverse or horizontal plane divides the body into superior and inferior sections. The median or midsagittal plane divides the body into equal right and left halves. A sagittal section would divide a specimen into unequal right and left parts. The frontal or coronal plane divides the body into anterior and posterior sections.

■ Directional terms such as internal and external, proximal and distal, superficial and deep, central and peripheral help us to navigate the body.

■ It is important to remember that directions such as right and left are referenced from the patient's perspective and *not* yours.

■ The body has several cavities that house anatomical structures (mainly organs). For example, the cranial cavity houses the brain, the thoracic cavity houses the heart and lungs, the abdominopelvic cavity houses the digestive and female reproductive organs, and the spinal cavity houses the spinal cord.

■ The body has many specific regions. For example, the umbilical region is found around your navel, or belly button, and the femoral region is located in the upper inner thigh area.

■ The directional terms, anatomical landmarks, body regions, and body cavities are all important to know so that health care professionals can communicate in specific terms that leave no room for confusion.

■ Detailed images of the internal structures of the body can be obtained from imaging studies such as x-rays, CT scans, MRIs, and ultrasound.

CASE STUDY

A 50-year-old female patient presents with sternal pain radiating to the left brachial area. Peripheral cyanosis is noted in the digital areas, and she exhibits pedal edema. No epigastric pain is noted. She reports that she became dizzy and fell, bruising the right orbital region, and she received superficial cuts to the right patellar region. The physician orders an IV to be started in the left antecubital region. Please answer the following questions in common lay terms.

a. Where would you suggest placing a bandage?

_____

b. Where did her pain begin?

_____

c. Where does the pain move to?

_____

d. Does she have stomach pain?

_____

e. Where will the IV be started?

_____

f. What part of her body is swollen?

_____

RAY'S STORY

Ray's quadriplegia will require extensive radiologic studies throughout the rest of his life. Given the following scenarios, give your best diagnostic answer.

a. Because this was initially a neck injury, on what specific portion of the spinal column would you focus your studies?

_____

b. Due to being bedridden and inactive, Ray will be breathing in a monotonous shallow manner, even with the assistance of a mechanical ventilator and therefore not fully exercising his respiratory system. This can lead to lung collapse and pneumonia. On which body cavity would you focus your study?

_____

c. Ray will be more prone to accidental falls while being assisted in daily activities of living. What could happen that would require radiologic studies?

_____

REVIEW QUESTIONS

Multiple Choice

1. A massage therapist would ask you to assume which position for a back massage?
   a. prone
   b. supine
   c. Fowler's
   d. lotus

2. Which of the following is *not* in the abdominopelvic cavity?
   a. stomach
   b. liver
   c. reproductive organs
   d. heart

3. Carpal tunnel syndrome occurs in what region of the body?
   a. head
   b. cheek
   c. armpit
   d. wrist

4. The midsagittal plane divides the body into:
   a. top and bottom
   b. front and back
   c. upper and lower
   d. left and right

5. An organ contained in the RLQ would be:
   a. appendix
   b. heart
   c. lungs
   d. brain

6. The type of radiologic diagnostic tool that can give you real-time action images is:
   a. CT scan
   b. chest x-ray
   c. PET scan
   d. ultrasound

Fill in the Blank

1. A standard position in which a person stands erect, face forward, with feet parallel, arms at sides, and palms forward is called the _____ position.

2. The _____ position is lying face upward and on your back.

3. The mouth is located _____ to the nose, whereas the nose is located _____ to the mouth.

4. The organ found in the cranial cavity is the _____.

5. _____ indicates blueness of the extremities and therefore affects the peripheral areas of the body.

6. A person who gets weak and dizzy when he or she quickly stands may be suffering from _____.

REVIEW QUESTIONS

Short Answer

1. List the organs found in the abdominal cavity.

_____

_____

_____

_____

2. Contrast the differences between the prone, supine, and Fowler's positions.

_____

_____

_____

_____

3. List and describe two specific body regions that are found on the lower extremities.

_____

_____

_____

_____

4. List and describe the location of the nine abdominal regions using directional terms.

_____

_____

_____

_____

Suggested Activities

1. Using a white T-shirt, draw and label the abdominal quadrants and the related organs.

2. Play Pin the Tail on the Donkey by guiding the blindfolded person using only medical directional terms.

CAREER CONNECTIONS

Now that you have read this chapter, here is a list of related professions you may be interested in investigating for a future career:

- Radiologic Technology

- Surgical Technology

Research each profession and report on the following:

1. Profession description to include job responsibilities
2. Educational requirements
3. Job opportunities
4. Opportunities outside of the hospital setting
5. Salary range
6. Licensure and continuing education requirements

ANATOMY, PHYSIOLOGY, AND DISEASE IN ACTION

Materials:
Roles of bulletin board paper
Pencils
Different colored markers

Working in groups of twos or threes, trace one group member. Each group will need to have a frontal and a lateral tracing. Using different colored markers for each label, label the **planes**: transverse, frontal, and midsaggital planes; **directional** terms: proximal, distal, medial, lateral, anterior, posterior, ventral, dorsal, cranial, caudal, superior, and inferior; **cavities**: posterior, anterior, cranial, spinal, thoracic, abdominal, and pelvic; and **abdominal region and quadrants**: right hypochondriac, epigastric, left hypochrondriac, right lumbar umbilical, left lumbar, right iliac, hypogastric, left iliac, and RUQ, RLQ, LUQ, and LLQ. Some of the terms will be found on one of the tracings; others will be found on both.

Using the tracing, fill in the following chart for the primary location of the following as it applies:

Organ	Cavity	Region	Quadrant
Appendix			
Liver			
Spleen			
Gall bladder			

Biochemistry
The Basic Ingredients of Life

No journey would be complete without day trips to places off the beaten path that busy tourists often miss. In this chapter, we will take a day trip to chemistry. Why would we want to visit chemistry? Chemistry is the study of atoms and molecules and their interactions. Physiology, the study of how the body works, is largely about the interactions between molecules in our cells and tissues. Physiology, then, is mainly about chemistry or, more specifically, how chemistry relates to a living organism. This special division of chemistry is known as biochemistry. To understand how the body works and to lay a foundation for the upcoming cell chapter, Chapter 4, you need at least a basic understanding of biochemistry.

LEARNING OUTCOMES

At the end of your journey through this chapter, you will be able to:

- Differentiate between atoms, elements, and ions
- Define pH, acids, and bases and their role in the body
- Describe chemical bonding and the role of water
- Describe the properties of a solution
- Distinguish among the types of biological molecules
- Explain metabolism
- Explain cellular respiration
- Explain the role of enzymes in physiology

Pronunciation Guide

Correct pronunciation is important in any journey so that you and others are completely understood. Here is a "see and say" Pronunciation Guide for the more difficult terms to pronounce in this chapter. Please note that pronunciations given are referenced to medical dictionaries, and regional variations may exist.

adenosine triphosphate
   (uh DEN oh seen try FOSS fate)
amino (ah MEAN oh)
anabolism (ah NAB oh lizm)
catabolism (ka TAB oh lizm)
covalent (co VAY lent)
disaccharide (die SACK eh ride)

glycerol (GLIS er oll)
glycogen (GLIE koh jen)
metabolism (meh TAB oh lizm)
monosaccharide (mon oh SACK eh ride)
organelles (OR guh NELLZ)
phospholipid (FOS foh LIP id)

ATOMS, ELEMENTS, AND IONS

element A substance that cannot be further divided without losing its unique properties.

molecule An electrically neutral collection of atoms held together and forming a unique substance.

All matter, whether living, like our bodies, or nonliving, like this textbook, is made of **elements**. An element is the smallest unit that retains the unique chemical properties of that specific type of matter. Elements cannot be broken into smaller pieces by routine chemical techniques. Elements are *usually* abbreviated using the beginning letters of their technical names. For example, the element sodium (Latin name *natrium*) is abbreviated Na, whereas the element chlorine is abbreviated Cl. Two or more elements joined together form a **molecule**. Molecules with more than one type of element are known as compounds. Using our previous examples, the molecule you know as table salt is sodium chloride, abbreviated NaCl. TABLE 3-1 ■ shows some important trace elements found in the body.

TABLE 3-1 ■ SOME IMPORTANT TRACE ELEMENTS IN THE BODY

ELEMENT	ADULT DAILY REQUIREMENT	MAJOR ACTIVITIES WITHIN THE BODY	DEFICIENCY SYMPTOMS	DIETARY SOURCES
Iron (Fe) (Ferrous)	10 mg (males) 18 mg (females)	Formation of hemoglobin for oxygen delivery; enzymes	Dry skin, spoon-shaped nails; decreased hemoglobin count; anemia	Liver and other organ meats, oysters, red or dark meat, green leafy vegetables, fortified breads and cereals, egg yolks
Copper (Cu) (Cupric)	2.0–5.0 mg	Necessary in many enzyme systems; aids formation of red blood cells and collagen	Uncommon; anemia; decreased white cell count; bone demineralization	Nuts, organ meats, whole grains, shellfish, eggs, poultry, green leafy vegetables
Zinc (Zn)	15 mg	Amino acid metabolism; growth; maintain enzyme systems; energy production; collagen	Retarded growth and bone formation; dwarfism; skin inflammation; impaired taste; poor healing	Oysters, crab, lamb, beef, organ meats, whole grains

ELEMENT	ADULT DAILY REQUIREMENT	MAJOR ACTIVITIES WITHIN THE BODY	DEFICIENCY SYMPTOMS	DIETARY SOURCES
Manganese (Mn)	2.5–5.0 mg	Necessary for some enzyme systems; collagen formation; central nervous system function; fat and carbohydrate metabolism; blood clotting	Abnormal skeletal growth; impairment of central nervous system	Whole grains, wheat germ, legumes, pineapple, figs
Iodine (I)	150 mcg	Necessary for activity of thyroid gland	Hypothyroidism; goiter; cretinism	Seafood, iodized salt
Fluorine (F)	1.5–4.0 mg	Necessary for solid tooth formation and retention of calcium in bones with aging	Dental cavities	Tea, fish, water in some areas, supplementary drops, toothpaste

The smallest recognizable unit of an element is called an **atom** (see **FIGURE 3-1** ▲). Atoms consist of a nucleus, containing **protons** (positively charged particles) and **neutrons** (neutral particles). The nucleus is surrounded by **electrons** (negatively charged particles). In the periodic table, all the known elements are arranged based on the number of protons in their nucleus (see **FIGURE 3-2** ▲).

In a typical atom, the number of positively charged protons (+) equals the number of negatively charged electrons (−). This balance of electrons and protons results in an atom with a neutral charge. However, under certain conditions, atoms can gain or lose electrons. These atoms are called **ions** and have either a positive or negative charge. Atoms that have lost an electron will be positively charged, whereas atoms that have gained an electron will be negatively charged. Again, we can use sodium and chlorine as examples. When NaCl (salt) is formed, it is neutral and, therefore, has no charge. However, if the elements are separated (ionization), sodium loses an electron, becoming Na^+, sodium ion, whereas chlorine gains an electron, thus becoming Cl^-, chloride ion.

atom Smallest part of an element that still retains its properties.

proton Positively charged particle in the nucleus of the atom.

neutron A noncharged or neutral particle of the atom.

electron Negatively charged particle that circles the nucleus of the atom.

ion An atom or group of atoms that have lost one or more electrons giving it a positive charge or has gained one or more electrons giving it a negative charge.

LEARNING HINT

Negative Electrons

Electrons have a negative charge, so adding one makes an atom more negative (−). The minus sign is not an indication that the atom is smaller, but that is has gained an electron and, therefore, a negative charge.

Key:
⊕ = Proton
◯ = Neutron
● = Electron

A. Hydrogen (H)
($1p^+$; $0n^0$; $1e^-$)

B. Helium (He)
($2p^+$; $2n^0$; $2e^-$)

C. Lithium (Li)
($3p^+$; $4n^0$; $3e^-$)

FIGURE 3-1 ▲ The atom.

Representative [main group] elements

Representative [main group] elements

	IA	IIA		IIIB	IVB	VB	VIB	VIIB	VIIIB			IB	IIB	IIIA	IVA	VA	VIA	VIIA	VIIIA
1	1 H 1.0079																		2 He 4.003
2	3 Li 6.941	4 Be 9.012												5 B 10.813	6 C 12.011	7 N 14.007	8 O 15.999	9 F 18.998	10 Ne 20.180
3	11 Na 22.990	12 Mg 24.305												13 Al 26.982	14 Si 28.086	15 P 30.974	16 S 32.066	17 Cl 35.453	18 Ar 39.948
4	19 K 39.098	20 Ca 40.078	21 Sc 44.956	22 Ti 47.88	23 V 50.942	24 Cr 51.996	25 Mn 54.938	26 Fe 55.845	27 Co 58.933	28 Ni 58.933	29 Cu 63.566	30 Zn 65.39	31 Ga 69.723	32 Ge 72.61	33 As 74.922	34 Se 78.96	35 Br 79.904	36 Kr 83.8
5	37 Rb 85.468	38 Sr 87.62	39 Y 88.906	40 Zr 91.224	41 Nb 92.906	42 Mo 95.94	43 Tc 98	44 Ru 101.07	45 Rh 102.906	46 Pd 106.42	47 Ag 107.868	48 Cd 112.411	49 In 114.82	50 Sn 118.71	51 Sb 121.76	52 Te 127.60	53 I 126.905	54 Xe 131.29
6	55 Cs 132.905	56 Ba 137.327	57 La 138.906	72 Hf 178.49	73 Ta 180.948	74 W 183.84	75 Re 178.49	76 Os 190.23	77 Ir 192.22	78 Pt 195.08	79 Au 196.907	80 Ag 200.59	81 Tl 204.383	82 Pb 207.2	83 Bi 208.980	84 Po 209	85 At 210	86 Rn 222
7	87 Fr 223	88 Ra 226.025	89 Ac 227.028	104 Rf 261	105 Db 262	106 Sg 263	107 Bh 264	108 Hs 265	109 Mt 266	110 Uun 268	111 Uuu 272	112 Uub 227		114		116		118

Transition metals

Rare earth elements

Lanthanides	58 Ce 140.115	59 Pr 140.908	60 Nd 144.24	61 Pm 143	62 Sm 150.36	63 Eu 151.964	64 Gd 157.25	65 Tb 158.925	66 Dy 162.5	67 Ho 164.93	68 Er 167.26	69 Tm 168.934	70 Yb 173.04	71 Lu 174.967
Actinides	90 Th 232.038	91 Pa 231.038	92 U 230.029	93 Np 237.048	94 Pu 244	95 Am 243	96 Cm 247	97 Bk 247	98 Cf 251	99 Es 252	100 Fm 257	101 Md 258	102 No 259	103 Lr 262

FIGURE 3-2 ▲ The periodic table.

polar Having a charge at one end of a molecule.

electrolyte *(ee LEK troh lite)* Chemical element that carries a positive or negative charge and conducts electricity when dissolved in a solution: Examples include sodium (Na^+), potassium (K^+), chloride (Cl^-), calcium (Ca^{++}), and bicarbonate ($HCO3^-$). Electrolytes are carried in the plasma. Excess amounts in the blood are removed by the kidneys.

Please see **FIGURE 3-3 ▲**. Ions are also said to be **polar** because they have charges, like the poles on a battery. The positively charged atom is attracted to the negatively charged one. Conversely, negative charges repel negative charges and positive repel positive. Just remember, opposite charges attract, and like charges repel.

The reason why this is important is that **electrolytes** are charged ions found within the body, and they influence the nervous system, muscle activity, and fluid balance. Important electrolytes include sodium (Na^+), potassium (K^+), calcium (Ca^{2+}), magnesium (Mg^{2+}), chloride (Cl^-), hydrogen phosphate (HPO_4^-), and bicarbonate (HCO_3^-). One of the main functions of the urinary system is to regulate electrolyte balance to maintain cardiovascular health. For example, if potassium levels get too low or too high due to improper urinary regulation, the heart rhythm can become dangerously irregular.

Acids and Bases

Acids and bases are also electrolytes because they can conduct electricity and break down (dissociate) in water. You are probably familiar with the term *acid* and know that it can be quite harmful to other substances. Acids can dissolve metals and literally burn a hole

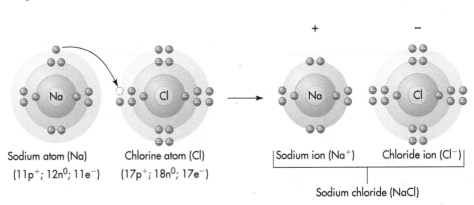

FIGURE 3-3 ▲ Formation of sodium chloride ions.

Sodium atom (Na) ($11p^+$; $12n^0$; $11e^-$)

Chlorine atom (Cl) ($17p^+$; $18n^0$; $17e^-$)

Sodium ion (Na^+)

Chloride ion (Cl^-)

Sodium chloride (NaCl)

through material (don't try this at home!). The definition of an acid is a chemical substance that can release hydrogen ions. Acids dissolved in water release hydrogen ions that can easily react with other atoms. For example, the chemical formula for hydrochloric acid, which is found in the stomach, is HCl, meaning one hydrogen atom combined with one chloride atom. If we break the compound HCl apart (dissociation), the released hydrogen atom can react with other atoms and potentially harm the body. Acids, such as lemon juice, taste sour.

Bases, which have a bitter taste, can accept hydrogen ions; for example, bicarbonate (HCO_3^-) can accept hydrogen ions (H^+), forming carbonic acid (H_2CO_3), which is a weak acid. Hydroxides (OH^-) are common bases, which accept spare hydrogen ions.

The concentration or amount of hydrogen and hydroxides are measured using the pH (potential of hydrogen) scale. The pH scale ranges from 0 to 14, where a value between 0 and 6.9 means there are more hydrogen ions compared to hydroxide or hydroxyl ions, and so it is said to be acidic. Neutral pH, in which there are the same number of hydrogen and hydroxyl ions, is 7. A pH greater than (>) 7 indicates that there are more hydroxyl ions, and therefore it is said to be more basic or alkalotic. To give some examples, the pH of blood is between 7.35 and 7.45, bleach has a pH of 9.5, and grapefruit juice has a pH of 3. Because our bodies can be exposed to potentially harmful substances, we must have systems to protect the body as much as possible from changes in pH. FIGURE 3-4 ▲ shows the pH of common substances.

Amazing **Body Facts**

An Interesting Paradox
It is interesting to note that hydrogen (H), a highly flammable gas, and oxygen (O_2), a gas that supports combustion, can combine to form H_2O (water) that can be used to extinguish fires.

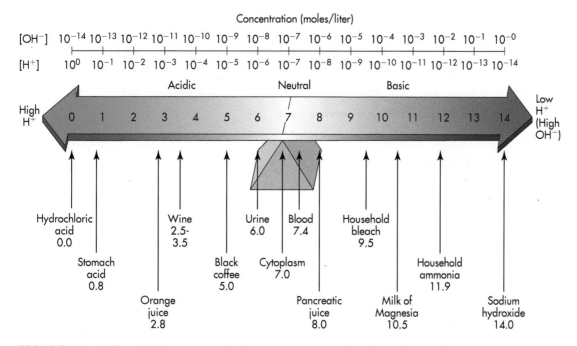

FIGURE 3-4 ▲ The pH of common substances.

The systems that help regulate the acid/base balance include the respiratory and renal systems. The role of the respiratory system (discussed in more detail in the Respiratory chapter) is to take in air and get rid of carbon dioxide (CO_2). Carbon dioxide is a weak acid. If we stop breathing, there is a buildup of CO_2 in the body, and this buildup of acid is detected in the brain, which gives a person an overwhelming desire to breathe. This is the simplest way of getting rid of excess acid, but if there is a problem with the respiratory system, the kidneys come to the rescue and enable the excretion of excess acid in the urine.

BONDING

Elements can be joined together to form molecules. The individual elements in molecules are held together by bonds between electrons in the atoms. If one atom *donates* electrons to the other atom, an **ionic bond** results (again see Figure 3-3). Because one atom has lost electrons and the other has gained them, the atoms involved in an ionic bond are ions and carry a positive or negative charge. Using our previous example, the bond between sodium and chlorine in table salt (NaCl) is an ionic bond, and if NaCl were to dissociate (break apart), it would form Na⁺ ions and Cl⁻ ions, respectively.

If the electrons are *shared* by the atoms involved in the bond, a **covalent bond** results (see **FIGURE 3-5** ▲). Covalent bonds may sometimes be unequal because one atom takes more than its share of the shared electrons. This type of covalent bond, a **polar covalent bond**, results in weak charges on the elements in the molecule. Polar covalent bonds are

ionic bond Bond formed by transfer of electrons.

covalent bond Bond formed by sharing of electrons in the outer shells.

polar covalent bond Unequal sharing of one or more electrons that result in a slight charge as in the water molecule.

A Formation of a single covalent bond

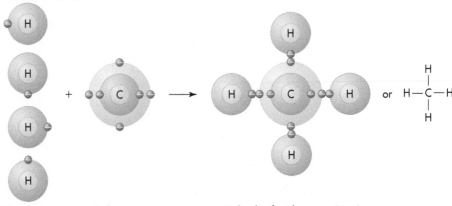

B Formation of a double covalent bond

C Formation of four single covalent bonds

FIGURE 3-5 ▲ Covalent bonding.

more polar (slight charge) than covalent bonds, but less polar than the higher charged ionic bonds. For a summary of bonds and their properties, see TABLE 3-2 ■.

TABLE 3-2 ■ SUMMARY OF BONDS AND THEIR PROPERTIES

TYPE OF BOND	ELECTRONS SHARED?	CHARGE?	EXAMPLE
Ionic	No, electrons donated	Yes, ions formed	NaCl
Polar covalent	Unequal sharing	Yes, molecule polar	H_2O
Covalent	Yes	No	CO_2

WATER

Water (H_2O) is the chief liquid in biological systems. All the fluid in your body is water based. Water is a polar solvent because the bonds between the H and O in water are polar covalent. Oxygen takes more than its share of electrons. (See FIGURE 3-6 ▲ for a comparison of carbon dioxide and water with a contrasting of the various bonds.) Thus, charged molecules will be attracted to one end or the other of a water molecule. Charged molecules containing elements like oxygen, phosphorus, and nitrogen mix easily with water. Such molecules are called **hydrophilic** (water loving). Other molecules that do not

hydrophilic Water loving.

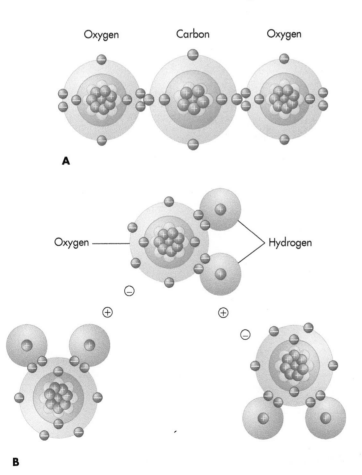

FIGURE 3-6 ▲ A. Carbon Dioxide. This molecule exhibits a non-polar bond and results in a linear and symmetrical molecule. **B.** Attraction between water molecules showing polar covalent bonding.

hydrophobic Water fearing.

hydrogen bond The bond between hydrogen molecules.

solution The combination of one or more substances dissolved in another.

solute The substance dissolved in a solution.

solvent The substance that dissolves the solute, usually water.

concentration The amount of solute dissolved in a solvent.

carry a charge, like fats and oils, do not mix well with water. They are called **hydrophobic** (water fearing). In the cellular chapter, we'll see how important hydrophobic and hydrophilic molecules are in regulating movement of substances across cell membranes.

In addition, the polarity of water causes the development of **hydrogen bonds** between water molecules. The hydrogen on one water molecule binds weakly to the oxygen on another water molecule. The bonds between the water molecules increase water's heat capacity. Water can *store* heat, meaning water heats up and cools down more slowly than air.

Solutions

When one substance is dissolved in another the combination is called a **solution**. The substance dissolved is called the **solute**. The substance doing the dissolving, usually water in living things, is called the **solvent** (see FIGURE 3-7 ▲). Electrolytes, those important ions necessary for fluid balance, are the solutes dissolved in your water-based body fluids. The amount of solute dissolved in a solvent is called the solute **concentration**.

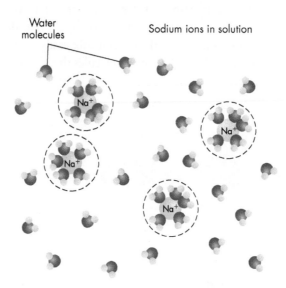

Water molecules

Sodium ions in solution

Na⁺ Na⁺ Na⁺ Na⁺

FIGURE 3-7 ▲ Solutions.

TEST YOUR KNOWLEDGE 3-1

Answer the following questions:

1. The most basic unit of matter is the _____.

2. Atoms that can gain or lose electrons are called _____.

3. Physiologically important ions are known as _____.

4. A solution is a(n) _____ dissolved in a(n) _____.

5. An increase in hydrogen ions would lead to a more _____ solution, and the pH would _____.

Biological Molecules

Most of your anatomy (bones, muscles, skin, hair, etc.) is made of molecules called **biological molecules**. Biological molecules are molecules found in living systems that contain mainly the elements carbon (C) and hydrogen (H), with lesser amounts of oxygen (O), nitrogen (N), sulfur (S), phosphorous (P), and other elements. These molecules fall into four broad categories: **carbohydrates, lipids, proteins,** and **nucleic acids.**

Carbohydrates

Carbohydrates are sugars and starches. They are used as energy sources for the body to function and as structural, or building, molecules. The name carbohydrate literally means "watered carbon." Carbohydrate molecules all have carbon, hydrogen, and oxygen in the ratio of 1 carbon to 2 hydrogens to 1 oxygen (CH_2O; see FIGURE 3-8 ▲).

Monosaccharides, or simple sugars, have five or six carbons. Glucose ($C_6H_{12}O_6$), your body's chief fuel, is a monosaccharide that is discussed in the upcoming cell chapter. If two monosaccharides are hooked together, a **disaccharide** is formed. Sucrose, or table sugar, consists of a glucose molecule and a fructose molecule hooked together. Polysaccharides are made when many monosaccharides are hooked together. **Glycogen,** a molecule in your liver that is used to store energy, consists of many, many glucose molecules in a long chain and therefore can be called on to break down and release more glucose into the blood when needed.

biological molecules Molecules that make up the composition of your body and contain mainly carbon, hydrogen, oxygen, nitrogen, sulfur, and phosphorous.

carbohydrates Sugars and starches used as energy sources and to provide structure.

lipids Biological molecules consisting mostly of carbon and hydrogen.

proteins Versatile molecules made of long chains of amino acids.

nucleic acids RNA and DNA that control activities of cells and contain genetic codes for reproduction.

monosaccharides *(MON oh SACK uh ridez)* Simple sugars with five or six carbons.

disaccharides *(die SAK uh rides)* Two monosaccharides linked together.

glycogen *(GLIE coh jin)* The form that glucose (sugar) takes when it is stored in the liver and skeletal muscles.

FIGURE 3-8 ▲ Carbohydrates: The combining of the monosaccharides glucose and fructose to form the disaccharide sucrose.

Lipids

Lipids consist of mainly carbon and hydrogen. They have very little oxygen. Because they have little oxygen or any other ions in them, lipids are hydrophobic. Lipids are used for energy storage, communication, and protection. There are many types of lipids (see FIGURE 3-9 ▲).

Fats and oils are probably the lipids most familiar to you. Fats and oils consist of three fatty acid chains and a **glycerol** molecule. They are energy storage molecules and can be broken down when needed by the body.

Waxes are lipids that consist of a fatty acid chain with an alcohol molecule. They are some of the most hydrophobic substances known and are used mainly for protection, particularly waterproofing. (Why do you wax your car?)

A **phospholipid** molecule has two fatty acid "tails" and a phosphate (PO_4^-) "head." The tails are hydrophobic, but the head is hydrophilic. Phospholipids are key molecules in the structure and function of cell membranes. The last category of lipids is steroids. Steroids are lipids with the carbon atoms arranged in rings. They are structural molecules or are used for communication between cells. Examples of steroids are cholesterol, estrogen, and testosterone. Anabolic steroids, which have been abused by many amateur and professional athletes, are also lipids. (More will be covered on steroids in Chapter 10.)

glycerol *(GLIS uh rall)* Portion of the fat molecule.

phospholipid *(FOSS foh LIP id)* Key molecules for structure and function of cell membranes composed of two fatty acid tails and a phosphate head.

A. Formation of a triglyceride (fat)

B. Phospholipid molecule (phosphatidyl choline)

C. Cholesterol (steroid)

FIGURE 3-9 ▲ Lipids.

Proteins

Proteins are molecules made of long chains of **amino acids** (see FIGURE 3-10 ▲). Because amino acids have nitrogen in them, proteins are always recognizable by the nitrogen molecules in the backbone of the molecule. A special linkage called a peptide bond ties the amino acids together and is unique to protein molecules. Proteins are the most versatile of all biological molecules, acting as structural molecules (collagen in tendons and ligaments), speeding up biological reactions (enzymes), storing energy (egg white albumin), moving your body (muscle protein), protecting against infection (antibodies), and allowing cells to communicate (the hormone insulin), to name just a few functions of proteins. The structure of a protein is determined by the order of amino acids in the molecule.

amino acids Building blocks of proteins.

Nucleic Acids

The last category of biological molecules is nucleic acids. The only two nucleic acids in nature are RNA and DNA. They are involved in controlling the activities of cells and are the molecules that contain your genetic code. You will learn more about nucleic acids when we discuss cellular reproduction (see FIGURE 3-11 ▲).

FIGURE 3-10 ▲ Various amino acids along with chemical equation demonstrating dehydration synthesis and hydrolysis.

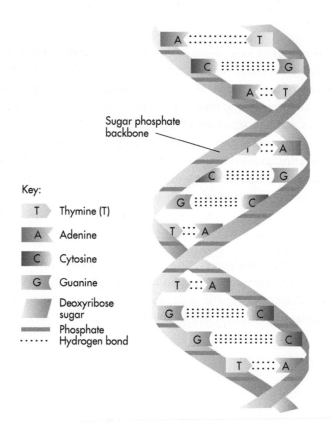

Sugar phosphate
backbone

Key:

T	Thymine (T)
A	Adenine
C	Cytosine
G	Guanine
	Deoxyribose sugar
	Phosphate
......	Hydrogen bond

FIGURE 3-11 ▲ Nucleic acids.

TEST YOUR KNOWLEDGE 3-2

Answer the following questions:

1. _____ molecules are found in living systems.

2. The building blocks of proteins are _____.

3. $C_{27}H_{45}OH$ belongs to the _____ category of biological molecules.

4. Label each of the following molecules as hydrophobic or hydrophilic.
   a. _____ $C_6H_{12}O_6$
   b. _____ wax
   c. _____ lipids

5. Carbohydrates are generally used for _____.

Metabolism

If you travel to other countries, you will see many different cultures and customs. Even though each culture is unique, they all share certain similarities. The same can be said in anatomy and physiology. We all share certain functions that are vital to survival. All humans, for example, need food to produce complex chemical reactions necessary for growth, reproduction, movement, and so on. **Metabolism** refers to all the chemical operations going on within our bodies. Metabolism requires various nutrients or fuel to function and produces waste products much like a car consumes gas for power and produces waste, or exhaust. Metabolism, for now, can be thought of as "all the life-sustaining reactions within the body."

Metabolism is further subdivided into two opposite processes. **Anabolism** is the process by which simpler compounds are *built up* and used to manufacture materials for growth, repair, and reproduction, such as the assembly of amino acids to form proteins. This is the *building* phase of metabolism. Many anabolic reactions are **dehydration synthesis** reactions in which water is removed and biological molecules are hitched together to form larger molecules. **Catabolism** is the process by which complex substances are *broken down* into simpler substances. For example, the breakdown of food into simpler chemical building blocks for energy use is a catabolic process. An abnormal and extreme example of catabolism is seen in a starvation victim, whose body "feeds on itself," actually consuming the body's own tissues. Many catabolic reactions are **hydrolysis reactions** in which water is added to break apart large molecules (see FIGURE 3-12 ▲).

metabolism *(meh TAB oh lizm)* Process of using oxygen and glucose to produce energy for cells. Metabolism also produces by-products like carbon dioxide and other waste products. The ongoing cycle of anabolism and catabolism.

anabolism *(ah NAB oh lizm)* Assembly of new molecules in the body.

dehydration synthesis *(dee high DREY shuhn SIN thuh siss)* An anabolic reaction that involves the removal of water to combine larger biological molecules.

catabolism *(ka TAB oh lizm)* Breaking down of molecules in the body.

hydrolysis A catabolic reaction in which water is added to break apart large molecules.

FIGURE 3-12 ▲ Metabolic reactions: Dehydration synthesis removes water and builds new compounds while hydrolysis breaks down compounds.

Enzymes: Making Reactions Happen

For your cells to be able to do anything, some chemicals must be broken down, and others must be made. You need building materials to build the small cell parts called **organelles** and to make energy. Any of these processes require chemical reactions to occur in the cell. The problem is that these reactions are usually very slow. So slow that by the time the reaction would happen, it would be too late for your cells to use the building materials. The hydrolysis and dehydration synthesis reactions used in cellular metabolism cannot happen without help. (You can't break down a piece of steak by just pouring water on it!) To solve this problem, cells have special proteins called **enzymes.**

Enzymes speed up the rate of chemical reactions, making them fast enough for your cells to use the materials. Enzymes are protein molecules that have special binding sites on them. Biological molecules bind to the enzymes and are carried through the reaction,

organelles *(OR guh NELLZ)* Small structures in the cytoplasm that have various specialized functions. Organelles include mitochondria, ribosomes, the endoplasmic reticulum, the Golgi apparatus, and lysosomes.

enzyme *(IN zyme)* Molecules that speed up the rate of chemical reactions in cells. Enzymes are particularly important in the breakdown and synthesis of biological molecules.

substrate The substance upon which an enzyme acts.

much like riders on a roller coaster (see FIGURE 3-13 ▲). When the reaction is finished, the enzyme goes back to get more molecules, called **substrates**. Because enzymes are a binding system, they are *specific*. Only certain molecules can be carried by certain enzymes. Substrates can *compete* for binding sites. If all the binding sites are full, the enzymes are said to be *saturated,* and molecules must wait for an empty enzyme before going through the reaction. The enzymes can also be blocked or *inhibited,* preventing the substrate from binding. Think again about the cars on a roller coaster. They can be filled. If there are lots of people waiting in line, the people compete for seats. If one car is broken, it will be blocked, perhaps by yellow tape, and people will not be able to ride on it. Like the roller coaster cars, enzymes are unchanged by their participation in the reaction.

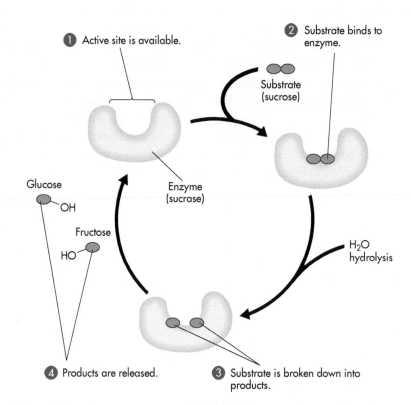

FIGURE 3-13 ▲ Enzymes: Note that the enzyme has the ending *ase* as in sucrase, and the actual substrate is sucrose.

cellular respiration The cellular process in which oxygen is used to break down glucose and other nutrients for energy needed for cellular activity.

adenosine triphosphate (ATP)
(ah DEN oh seen try FOSS fate)
Energy storage molecule used to power muscle contraction and other cellular reactions.

adenosine diphosphate (ADP)
(ah DEN oh seen die FOSS fate)
The compound that can be converted to ATP for energy storage. When ATP is broken down to ADP, energy is released that can be used for cellular energy.

Cell Energy and ATP: The Energy Molecule

We all know that we need to eat to obtain energy, but how does energy get from food to cells? In simple terms, the body takes in food and breaks it down (digestion). During this process, energy is released from the food. The problem is that cells can't use this energy directly. Only food converted to glucose can be used to make energy. Glucose can be used by your cells during a series of chemical reactions called **cellular respiration**. During cellular respiration, glucose is combined with oxygen and is transformed in your mitochondria into the high-energy molecule called **adenosine triphosphate (ATP)**. ATP is made of a base, a sugar, and three phosphate groups (hence, *triphosphate*). The phosphate groups are held together by high-energy bonds. When a bond is broken, a high level of energy is released. Energy in this form can be used by the cells. When a bond is used, ATP becomes **ADP (adenosine diphosphate),** which has only two phosphate groups. ADP now is able to pick up another phosphate and form a high-energy bond so energy is stored and the process can begin again! Life is good (see FIGURE 3-14 ▲).

FIGURE 3-14 ▲ Energy is released from the breaking of the phosphate bond in ATP when converting to ADP.

TEST YOUR KNOWLEDGE 3-3

Choose the best answer:

1. What molecule is broken down to make energy during cellular respiration?
   a. water
   b. glucose
   c. carbon dioxide
   d. citric acid

2. Why are enzymes necessary for cell metabolism?
   a. Cell metabolism would be too slow without them.
   b. They are necessary for active transport.
   c. They are cellular fuel.
   d. Our cells don't need enzymes.

3. Which of the following is true of enzymes?
   a. They slow down biological reactions.
   b. They are carbohydrates.
   c. They are not used up in the reactions.
   d. They are poisons.

4. During anabolic reactions, water is _____, and molecules are combined together to make a larger molecule.

SUMMARY

Snapshots from the Journey

- The smallest unit that is recognizable chemically is an element. Elements are made of atoms. Atoms consist of a nucleus (neutrons and protons) surrounded by electrons. Elements can be joined together to make molecules. All living matter is composed of elements.

- Atoms may gain or lose electrons, causing them to have a charge. These atoms are called ions. Physiologically important ions are called electrolytes.

- pH is the measure of acidity or alkalinity of the body. Carbon dioxide is a weak acid and must be appropriately removed to maintain a normal pH in the blood. This is accomplished by a balance between the renal and respiratory systems function.

- Atoms are bound together to form molecules. If electrons are shared by the atoms, the bond is covalent. If one atom gains electrons while the other loses them, the bond is ionic, and the molecule is polar.

- Water is a polar covalent molecule that is the basis of all body fluids. Molecules that mix with water are polar and are called hydrophilic. Molecules that will not mix with water are called hydrophobic. A solution consists of a substance dissolved (the solute) in a liquid (the solvent). The solvent in biological systems is usually water.

- Living things are made of biological molecules. Biological molecules fall into four categories based on physical and chemical characteristics: proteins, carbohydrates, lipids, and nucleic acids.

- For cells to carry out metabolism, they must have energy in the form of ATP. ATP is made via a complex series of reactions called cellular respiration. Enzymes, biological catalysts, are also necessary for cellular metabolism. ATP is broken down to ADP, and energy is released.

- Metabolism is dependent on the breakdown and manufacture of molecules called biological molecules. Each type, carbohydrates, lipids, proteins, and nucleic acids, have unique characteristics. Electrolytes are charged ions that have important roles in body functions.

CASE STUDY

Juanita has always been overly concerned about her weight, even though she is considered physically attractive and fit by her peers. However, the prom is approaching, and she has resorted to the dangerous practice of using diuretics to "slim down" to fit in her gown. During gym class she suddenly became light-headed, had heart palpitations, and was taken to the hospital. Her blood studies showed an electrolyte imbalance. Research diuretics and their connection to this case.

a. What electrolyte imbalance do you suspect from your research on diuretics?

_____

_____

b. What treatments would you recommend?

_____

_____

c. Do diuretics truly make you lose weight, and how would you counsel Juanita on the dangers of her actions?

_____

_____

REVIEW QUESTIONS

Multiple Choice

1. The nucleus of an atom consists of
   a. protons
   b. neutrons
   c. electrons
   d. a & b
   e. a, b, & c

2. A person loses body temperature faster in water than in air because water
   a. is hydrophilic
   b. has a high heat capacity
   c. is our major body fluid
   d. is heavier than air

3. Which of the following is not a property of enzymes?
   a. specificity
   b. saturation
   c. polarity
   d. inhibition

4. These biological molecules will not mix with water.
   a. proteins
   b. carbohydrates
   c. lipids
   d. amino acids

5. A new molecule is discovered in a deep sea cave fish. It has the following properties: hydrophilic, very large, and used for energy storage. What kind of molecule is it?
   a. lipid
   b. protein
   c. nucleic acid
   d. carbohydrate

REVIEW QUESTIONS

Fill in the Blank

1. Atoms or molecules that can gain or lose an electron are called _____.

2. Unequal sharing of electrons in a bond results in a(n) _____ bond.

3. Sodium, potassium, and chloride in body fluids are known as _____.

4. NaCl can be in solution in your body. What is the solvent? _____.

5. All the chemical reactions in your body are collectively known as _____.

6. Your cells need glucose to make this high-energy molecule. _____.

Short Answers

1. Explain the relationship between atoms, elements, molecules, and ions.

_____

_____

_____

2. List and explain the types of bonds between atoms.

_____

_____

_____

3. Distinguish among the four classes of biological molecules.

_____

_____

_____

_____

4. Explain the chemistry of water. Why is water important in biological systems?

_____

_____

_____

_____

5. Explain the functions of enzymes.

_____

_____

_____

_____

CAREER CONNECTIONS

Now that you have read this chapter, here is a list of related professions you may be interested in investigating for a future career:

- Forensics

- Immunology

Research each profession and report on the following:

1. Profession description to include job responsibilities
2. Educational requirements
3. Job opportunities
4. Opportunities outside of the hospital setting
5. Salary range
6. Licensure and continuing education requirements

ANATOMY, PHYSIOLOGY, AND DISEASE IN ACTION

I. Chemistry and Physical Health

The information in this chapter shows how chemistry has an influence on physical health, which in turn determines the quality of our life. This activity will focus on the important trace elements that are needed to sustain a healthy lifestyle. Use Table 3-1 as the guide complete the following activity.

Step 1: Locate a food product in your home to meet each of the trace elements listed in Table 3-1.

Step 2: Prepare a chart with the trace elements listed in Table 3-1 and list those food products that fulfill the adult daily requirements for each.

Step 3: Note any that are not found in your home.

Step 4: Create a 3-day menu that will meet the Adult Daily Requirement (ADR) for each trace element include in your menu the source of the trace element (example: Iron—Grape Nuts cereal) and the quantity (1/2 cup = 90% ADR).

Step 5: Note the additional food products you would need to purchase for your menu to meet all of the trace elements ADR.

Step 6: Describe how a multi-vitamin might help meet the trace elements ADR.

II. Disease and Organic Molecules

The following diseases are associated with the build-up or lack of certain organic molecules. For each case identify:

* cause
* signs and symptoms
* diagnosis
* treatment
* prognosis

Chose one of the following diseases and present the findings in class using a brochure or poster.

Newman Pick Disease
Gout
Porphyria
Maple Syrup Urine Disease
Tyrosinemia
Fabry's Disease
Phenylketonuria

Sickle Cell Anemia
Cystic Fibrosis
Guacher's Disease
Wolman's Disease
Cerebrotendinous xanthomatosis
Propionic academia

The Cells
The Raw Materials and Building Blocks

As you continue your journey, chances are that you will visit a city. A city is a complex combination of structures and systems. A brick or cement block is a basic structure on which many of the buildings of the city are constructed. The human body is also a complex combination of structures and systems, and a cell is the basic building block on which the body is built. Just as there are different types, shapes, and sizes of building blocks, there are different types, shapes, and sizes of cells. Blood cells, skin cells, nerve cells, and so on, are all different. You will learn more about each kind of cell in later chapters.

Although a cement block is a basic building block, it could not exist without sand, lime, and water, the components necessary to make cement. As this chapter explains, cells also consist of component parts, tiny cell structures called **organelles** that are needed to perform specific functions to keep the cell alive and properly functioning.

On a more involved level, cells of a similar type form tissue that works together in an organ, whereas organs perform specific functions to create a system. For example, cardiac cells form heart tissues, which form the heart organ, which is part of the circulatory system. Finally, systems work together to form a functioning organism, such as the amazing human body! When you think about it, we are very much like a city. A city, like the human body, needs transportation systems, control systems, systems to import food and water and export waste, and heating and cooling systems. A breakdown at any level (cellular, tissue, organ, or system) can have dire pathological consequences.

organelles *(OR guh NELLZ)* Small structures in the cytoplasm that have various specialized functions. Organelles include mitochondria, ribosomes, the endoplasmic reticulum, the Golgi apparatus, and lysosomes.

LEARNING OUTCOMES

At the end of your journey through this chapter, you will be able to:

- List and describe the various parts of a cell and explain their function and pathology
- Explain the process of cellular mitosis
- Describe cancer growth and staging
- Describe the types of active and passive transport within cells
- Explain cellular respiration and enzyme function and dysfunction
- Differentiate between bacteria, viruses, fungi, and protozoa and understand how these pathogens cause disease

Pronunciation Guide

Correct pronunciation is important in any journey so that you and others are completely understood. Here is a "see and say" Pronunciation Guide for the more difficult terms to pronounce in this chapter. Please note that pronunciations given are referenced to medical dictionaries, and regional variations may exist.

bacteria (back TEER ee ah)
benign (be NINE)
capsid (CAP sid)
centrioles (SEN tree olz)
centrosomes (SEN troh soams)
chemotherapy (KEE moh THAIR ah pee)
chromatin (CROW ma tin)
cilia (SIL ee ah)
cytokinesis (SIGH toe keh KNEE sis)
cytoplasm (SIGH toe plah zim)
cytoskeleton (SIGH toe SKEL eh ton)
deoxyribonucleic acid
  (dee AWK see RYE boe new KLEE ic)
diabetes mellitus (DIE uh BE teez meh LITE us)
endocytosis (en DOE sigh TOE sis)
endoplasmic reticulum
  (EN doh PLAZ mic ree TIH cue lum)
eukaryotic cell (you CARE ee AH tic)
exocytosis (EX oh sigh TOE sis)
flagella (flah GEL ah)
flora (FLOOR ah)
fungi (FUN jye)

Golgi apparatus (GOAL jee ap ah RA tus)
hypercholesterolemia
  (HI per koh LES tur ul EE me ah)
lysosomes (LIE soh soamz)
malignant (mah LIG nant)
meiosis (my OH sis)
metastasis (meh TAS tuh sis)
mitochondria (MITE oh KAHN dree ah)
mitotic (my TOT ick)
mitosis (my TOE sis)
mycelia (my SEE lee ah)
organelles (or ga NELZ)
osmosis (ahz MOE sis)
pathogen (PATH oh jen)
phagocytosis (FAG oh sigh TOH sis)
phenylketonuria (FIN ill KEE toe NEW ree ah)
pinocytosis (PIE no sigh TOE sis)
protozoa (pro toe ZOE ah)
ribonucleic acid (RYE boe new KLEE ic)
ribosomes (RYE boe soamz)
vesicle (VES ih kul)

OVERVIEW OF CELLS

cells The basic unit of life.

atom Smallest part of an element that still retains its properties.

Composed of chemicals and structures, **cells** make up all living things. Some organisms are composed of only a single cell. Practically all the cells in our body are microscopic in size, ranging from about one third to one thirteenth the size of the dot on this exclamation point! Equally amazing is that certain nerve cells can be two feet in length or longer! When we refer to cells as the "building blocks" of our bodies, we immediately think of brick-shaped objects. However, cells can be flat, round, threadlike, or irregularly shaped. Although the approximately *7.5 trillion* cells found in the human body vary in size, shape, and purpose, they normally work together to allow for proper functioning of processes necessary for life, such as digestion, respiration, reproduction, movement, and production of heat and energy. FIGURE 4-1 ▲ shows examples of various cell types found within the human body.

APPLIED SCIENCE

Although cells are composed of small structures called organelles, these organelles are composed of even smaller substances. **Atoms,** which are the tiny building blocks of all matter, combine to form molecules such as water, sugar, and proteins, which are then used to build cellular structures and facilitate cellular functions. The four basic types of molecules found in cells are proteins, carbohydrates, lipids, and nucleic acids, which were covered in Chapter 3.

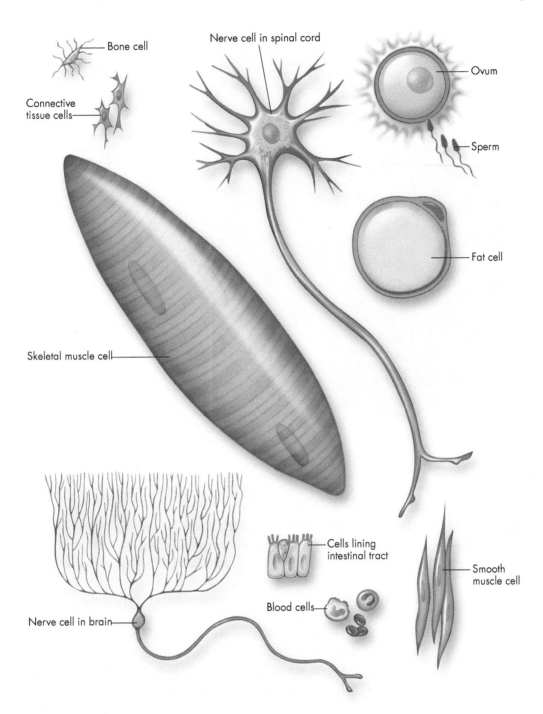

FIGURE 4-1 ▲ Various types of cells within the human body.

CELL STRUCTURE

Even though cells in our bodies can vary greatly in size, shape, and function, they share certain common traits. To better understand them, let's look at cells as miniature cities with a variety of systems, structures, and organizations that are necessary for proper function. Almost all human cells possess a nucleus (except mature red blood cells), organelles, cytoplasm, and a cell membrane. Each component of a cell has a special purpose. See **FIGURE 4-2** ▲, which represents a typical cell with its major components. We will now discuss the individual components.

FIGURE 4-2 ▲ Cellular components.

Cell Membrane

cell membrane Semipermeable barrier that surrounds a cell and holds in the cytoplasm. It allows water and some nutrients to enter and waste products to leave the cell.

The **cell membrane** is also called a *plasma membrane* because it surrounds the cytoplasm of the cell and acts as a protective covering. We can think of the cell membrane as the city limits. This is a defined boundary that possesses a definite shape and actually holds the cell contents together. Each cell, regardless of its shape or function, must have a cell membrane to maintain its integrity and survive.

For a city to thrive, people and materials must be able to travel into and out of the city. A cell membrane is responsible for allowing materials into and out of the cell. The membrane allows only certain things in or out. Because it chooses what may pass through, we call it a *selectively permeable* (formerly called *semipermeable*) membrane. In fact, cell membranes have specialized structures to help regulate the movement of some substances into and out of the cell. These structures (either channels, tunnels through the membrane, or carriers, which carry substances across the membrane) are essential for the health of cells. We will describe them in more detail later in this chapter.

In addition, the cell membrane has identification markers on it to show that it comes from a certain person, much like *PA* is an "identification marker" that tells us Pittsburgh, PA, is in Pennsylvania. If a foreign cell shows up in an individual (such as in a transplanted organ), the body signals an attack on that cell or group of cells. For all that it is responsible for, the cell membrane is only 3/10,000,000 of an inch thick. Please see **FIGURE 4-3** ▲ which depicts components of a cell membrane.

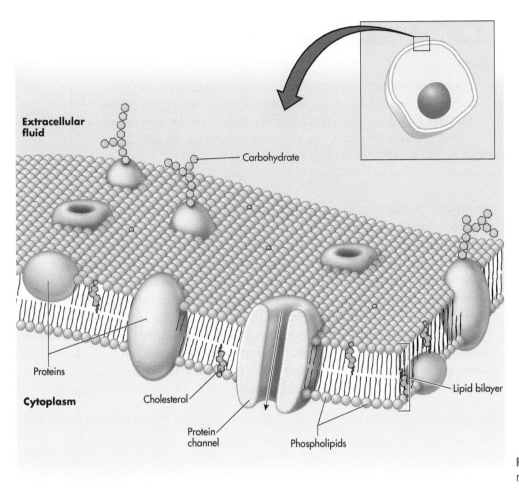

Extracellular
fluid

Carbohydrate

Proteins

Cytoplasm

Cholesterol

Protein
channel

Phospholipids

Lipid bilayer

FIGURE 4-3 ▲ The cell
membrane.

TRANSPORT METHODS

If we think of the cell membrane as the city limits or a boundary, how then do things get across this boundary? It can be done in two broad ways. **Passive transport** and **active transport** describe the movement of materials across the cell membrane. Both active and passive transport methods help the body to maintain homeostasis by regulating the movement of water and materials such as ions.

Passive Transport

Passive transport, as the words suggest, requires no extra form of energy to complete. It is similar to having a yo-yo in your hand and letting go. The yo-yo simply falls as it unwinds from the string. No input of energy is needed. Active transport requires some addition of energy to make it happen. Throwing your yo-yo requires an addition of energy from your arm. Passive transport can be further divided into four types:

* Diffusion
* Osmosis
* Filtration
* Facilitated diffusion

Diffusion is our most common means of passive transport by which a substance of higher concentration travels to an area of lesser concentration. The difference between these two concentrations is called the **concentration gradient.** This is like

passive transport The general term for the transportation of cellular material without the use of energy.

active transport The movement of cellular material that requires energy.

diffusion Process of movement of a substance from high concentration to low concentration.

concentration gradient The difference between solute concentrations of two solutions.

LEARNING HINT

Concentration Gradient

If a substance moves from higher concentration to lower concentration, it is said to be moving *with* the difference or concentration gradient. For example, if you are in a long grocery store check-out line "concentrated" with people and three new lanes open up, the people will quickly move from the highly concentrated line to the lower concentrated areas. Soon, you will notice, all lines will equalize, demonstrating that even people move with a concentration gradient and reach equilibrium.

dumping a packet of powdered drink mix into a pitcher of water. The water gradually assumes the color and flavor of the powder until the entire contents of the container are the same color and taste (nature likes a nice, equal balance!). Another example may be one of your classmates overusing perfume or cologne. Once in the classroom, the smell diffuses from high concentration on the individual to low concentration throughout the classroom. He or she may need to be reminded of the old saying that perfume should never announce your presence before your arrival.

Diffusion is necessary in the transportation of oxygen from the lungs and into the blood. It is also needed to transport the waste (carbon dioxide) from the blood to the lungs and eventually out into the air. This vital process is further discussed in Chapter 13, "The Respiratory System." See **FIGURE 4-4** ▲ for examples of diffusion.

A

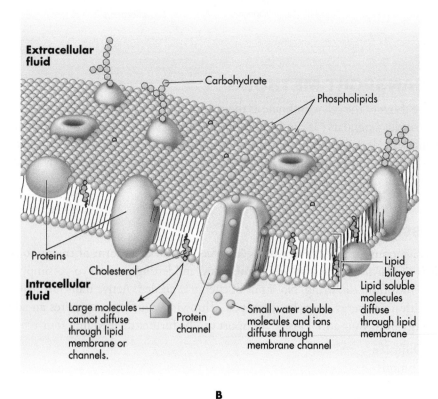

Extracellular fluid

Carbohydrate

Phospholipids

Proteins

Cholesterol

Intracellular fluid

Large molecules cannot diffuse through lipid membrane or channels.

Protein channel

Small water soluble molecules and ions diffuse through membrane channel

Lipid bilayer

Lipid soluble molecules diffuse through lipid membrane

B

FIGURE 4-4 ▲ Two examples of diffusion.

Osmosis is another form of passive transport, in which water travels through a selectively permeable membrane until concentrations of a substance are equalized. The **solute** is the substance that is dissolved in the water. Remember that nature likes things balanced and equal. Water tends to travel across a membrane from areas that have a low concentration of a solute to areas that have a higher concentration of the solute until the concentration is the same on both sides of the membrane. Keep in mind that the water is moving with *its* concentration gradient. See FIGURE 4-5 ▲ for a visual description. This ability of a substance to "pull" water toward an area of higher concentration of the solute is called **osmotic pressure**. The greater the concentration of the solute, the greater the osmotic pressure it exerts to bring in water.

Filtration differs from osmosis in that pressure is applied to force water and its dissolved materials across a membrane. Filtration caused by pressure is similar to a crowd of people being pushed through the turnstiles during rush hour, or the effect you get when you squeeze the trigger on a squirt gun. The major supplier of force in the body is the pumping of the heart, which forces blood flow into the kidneys,

osmosis The passage of the solvent through a semipermeable membrane to equalize concentrations.

solute The substance dissolved in a solution.

osmotic pressure The pressure that develops when there are two solutions of varying concentrations that are separated by a semipermeable membrane.

filtration Process in which water and substances in the blood are pushed through the pores of the glomerulus. The resulting fluid is known as filtrate.

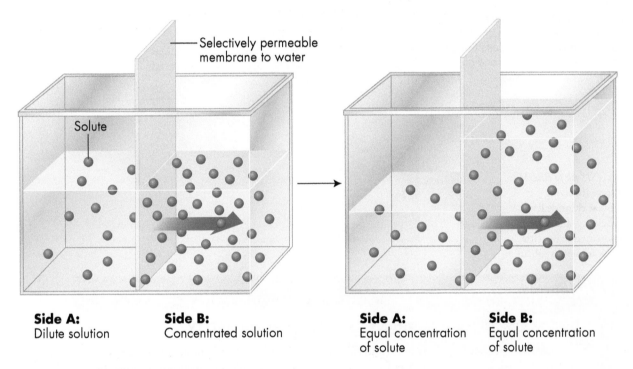

Side A:
Dilute solution

Side B:
Concentrated solution

Side A:
Equal concentration of solute

Side B:
Equal concentration of solute

FIGURE 4-5 ▲ During osmosis, water moves from an area of low solute concentration to an area of higher solute concentration.

where filtration takes place. This concept is expanded in Chapter 16, "The Urinary System." For now, see FIGURE 4-6 ▲, which illustrates the process of filtration.

Facilitated diffusion (also called carrier mediated passive transport) is a variation of diffusion in which a substance is helped in moving across the membrane, like an usher helping you to your seat at a ball game. The "usher" in this case is a carrier protein. Glucose is one substance that is often helped across the cell in this way. These carriers are very specific. Only glucose, for example, can be carried by its special carrier. You may wonder, if it is helped, how can it be considered *passive* transport? Think of it as a situation in which the glucose was already moving in an attempt to cross the membrane, and it conveniently encounters an already revolving door. Once it steps into the door, it is quickly "pushed" along until it comes out on the other side of the membrane. See FIGURE 4-7 ▲, which illustrates facilitated diffusion.

facilitated diffusion Also known as carrier mediated passive transport; the movement of substances into cells via carrier proteins.

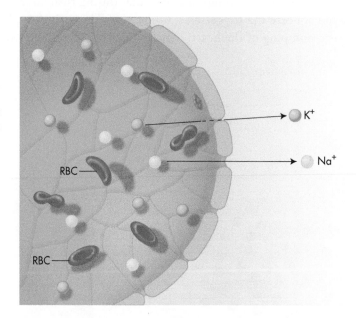

FIGURE 4-6 ▲ The process of filtration in the kidneys, where smaller solutes such as the electrolytes sodium and potassium pass through the membrane, whereas the larger blood protein and cells normally do not.

cystic fibrosis *(SIS tik fy BROH sis)* An inherited disease involving abnormal high sweat chloride levels, pancreatic insufficiency, and pus-producing pulmonary disease with high levels of thick tenacious mucus.

Pathology Connection

CYSTIC FIBROSIS (CF): A MEMBRANE CHANNEL ABNORMALITY

Cystic fibrosis is a relatively common (1 in 3,000 Caucasian births) incurable, fatal genetic disorder caused by the malformation of membrane channels for chloride and sodium ions. In people with CF, sodium and chloride do not diffuse across the cell membrane as they normally would because the channels are not normal. This makes the fluid around the cells extremely salty (excess sodium and chloride) and causes excessively thick mucus in the respiratory, digestive, and reproductive systems, clogging the organs. People with CF have difficulty breathing, nutritional deficits due to decreased absorption of nutrients, and increased risk of respiratory infections, diabetes, and infertility (especially males). Although CF cannot be cured, treatments are available, such as nutritional supplements, antibiotics to prevent pneumonia, and mucus-thinning drugs. Until recently, many CF patients did not survive into their 20s. With treatment available today, the average life span of a CF patient is longer than 35 years. CF can be diagnosed by prenatal or postnatal genetic testing or less accurately by testing the amount of sodium in sweat.

Cell Lobby

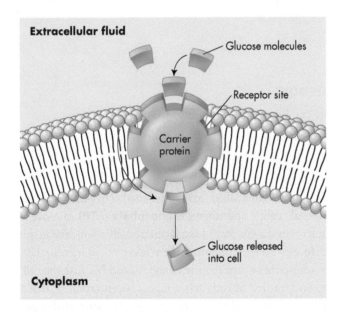

Extracellular fluid

Glucose molecules

Receptor site

Carrier protein

Glucose released into cell

Cytoplasm

FIGURE 4-7 ▲ Facilitated diffusion.

diabetes mellitus (DM)
Condition resulting from too little secretion of insulin, or a resistance to insulin, leading to increased levels of blood glucose.

diabetes *(DYE eh BEE teez)*
A general term for a group of diseases that are marked by the inability to regulate blood glucose.

insulin Hormone secreted by the pancreas that allows for glucose to be utilized for cellular respiration.

Pathology Connection

DIABETES MELLITUS: A DISORDER OF FACILITATED DIFFUSION

Diabetes mellitus (DM), usually known simply as **diabetes,** is a common health problem. The chief sign of diabetes, high blood sugar, is caused by a problem with facilitated diffusion. Remember when we discussed facilitated diffusion, we used glucose as an example. Glucose can't get into cells without facilitated diffusion. For glucose to get into cells by facilitated diffusion, a hormone, **insulin,** must be present. In DM, either insulin is absent or the cells are insensitive to insulin, so glucose doesn't get into cells like it should. This causes two problems. First, lots of glucose hangs around in the bloodstream, causing big osmotic problems for cells. Second, cells need glucose to make energy, so cells can't make as much energy as they need. This causes tremendous health problems. There will be a more detailed description of diabetes mellitus in the section on cellular respiration later in this chapter and more information on diabetes throughout the book.

TEST YOUR KNOWLEDGE 4-1

Fill in the blanks:

1. This form of passive transportation is like combining drink mix and a pitcher of water: _____.

2. During osmosis, water travels across a semipermeable membrane from an area of _____ concentration of solute to an area of _____ concentration of solute.

3. _____ allows only certain sizes of particles to pass through.

4. The act of removing carbon dioxide from the blood to the lungs is achieved through _____.

5. Glucose is often transported by _____.

6. Diabetes mellitus may be caused by a deficiency in this hormone: _____.

7. Cystic fibrosis occurs when _____ are malformed.

Active Transport

Active transport can be broken down into three types:

- Active transport pumps
- Endocytosis
- Exocytosis

active transport pumps (also called carrier mediated active transport) The movement of substances across cell membranes at the expense of adenosine triphosphate.

adenosine triphosphate (ATP) *(ah DEN oh seen try FOSS fate)* Energy storage molecule used to power muscle contraction and other cellular reactions.

endocytosis *(IN doh sigh TOH sis)* Ingestion of substances by a cell. Substances are taken into the cells after being surrounded by vesicles.

vesicle *(VESS ih kul)* A membrane-bound storage sac inside a cell.

phagocytosis *(FAG oh sigh TOH sis)* The process by which a phagocyte destroys a foreign cell or cellular debris; a type of endocytosis.

pinocytosis *(PIE noh sigh TOH sis)* Process in which a cell absorbs fluid material.

Active transport pumps (also called carrier mediated active transport) require the addition of an energy molecule called **adenosine triphosphate (ATP)** to move a substance. (We'll meet ATP again later in the chapter.) Like facilitated diffusion, active transport pumps use a protein carrier to move a specific substance across the cell membrane. Unlike facilitated diffusion, active transport pumps require energy to run because the cell is trying to move a substance into an area that already has a high concentration of that substance (up the concentration gradient). It's kind of like trying to put six pounds of sugar into a five-pound bag! It can be done, but you have to apply a lot of energy. A common example in our cells is the need to transport potassium (K^+). Cells contain a good amount of potassium. The only way to get more into a cell is to apply energy to "push" it in. Sodium (Na^+) is also part of this active transport pump and is needed to transmit an impulse, which will be explained further in the Chapter 9, "The Nervous System."

Endocytosis is utilized by the cells for the *intake* of liquid and food when the substance is too large to diffuse across the cell membrane. The cell membrane actually surrounds the substance with a small portion of its membrane, forming a chamber, or **vesicle**, which then separates from the membrane and moves into the cell. If a solid particle is being engulfed by a cell, we call it **phagocytosis**. White blood cells engulf bacteria to prevent infections in our bodies. If the intake involves liquid, it is called **pinocytosis**.

Exocytosis occurs when the cell needs to transport substances out of itself. Some cells may internally produce a substance needed outside the cell. Once this substance is made, it is surrounded by a membrane forming a vesicle (sac) and moves to the cell membrane. This vesicle becomes a part of the cell membrane and expels its load out of the cell. For further explanation of active transport, see **FIGURE 4-8** ▲.

exocytosis The expulsion of material from a cell using vesicles.

ACTIVE TRANSPORT PUMP

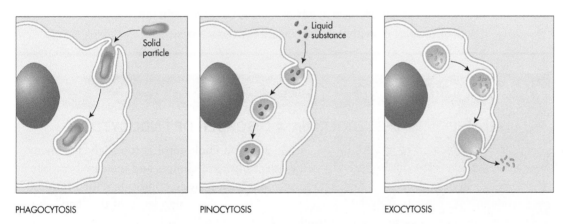

PHAGOCYTOSIS   PINOCYTOSIS   EXOCYTOSIS

FIGURE 4-8 ▲ Types of active transport in and out of cells.

TABLE 4-1 ■ summarizes all the methods of transport.

TABLE 4-1 ■ METHODS OF CELLULAR TRANSPORTATION

CELLULAR TRANSPORTATION METHODS	DESCRIPTION
Passive transportation (no energy required)	
Diffusion	Moving a substance from an area of high concentration to an area of low concentration
Filtration	Pressure is applied to force water and dissolved materials across a membrane
Osmosis	Water travels across a membrane from areas that have a low concentration of a solute to areas that have a higher concentration of solute until the concentration is the same on both sides of the membrane
Facilitated diffusion	Substance is assisted via carrier in a direction it was already traveling from an area of high concentration to an area of low concentration
Active transport (energy required)	
Active transport pumps	Require additional energy in the form of ATP to move substances against the concentration gradient (from low concentration to high concentration) using a carrier molecule
Endocytosis	Ingesting substances that are too large to diffuse across the cell membrane via vesicles
Phagocytosis	Form of endocytosis in which solid particles are being brought into the cell
Pinocytosis	Form of endocytosis in which liquid is being brought into the cell
Exocytosis	Transportation of material outside the cell via vesicles

Pathology Connection

FAMILIAL HYPERCHOLESTEROLEMIA: A DISORDER OF ENDOCYTOSIS

Hypercholesterolemia is a condition in which blood cholesterol is too high. For many people the condition can be cured by more nutritious food choices and increased exercise. However, some people have high cholesterol due to a genetic condition called **familial hypercholesterolemia**. Familial hypercholesterolemia causes high levels of the "bad" cholesterol known as low-density lipoprotein (LDL) in blood. Cholesterol moves into cells via **endocytosis**. Once inside, the cell uses the cholesterol to make other lipids. In people with familial hypercholesterolemia, excessive LDL doesn't move into cells and instead stays in the blood. This causes two problems. First, too little cholesterol is getting into the cells, so cells must make more cholesterol. In addition, the LDL that should be going into cells instead remains around in the blood causing plaques in blood vessels, like a buildup of rust in pipes. These plaques lead to clots, strokes, and heart attacks. The two forms of familial hypercholesterolemia are severe and moderate. People with severe familial hypercholesterolemia often have heart attacks or strokes as children, and this form is often fatal in children or teenagers. There is no effective treatment for the severe form. The moderate form also leads to heart attacks and strokes, but usually not until midlife. Moderate familial hypercholesterolemia can be treated with diet modifications and cholesterol-lowering drugs such as the statin group of drugs. It is estimated that 1 in 500 Americans has the moderate form.

hypercholesterolemia
(HIGH per koh LESS tur ul EE me ah) High levels of cholesterol in the blood.

familial hypercholesterolemia
(HIGH per koh LESS ter ol EE mee uh) A hereditary condition in which the low-density lipoproteins are not being removed from the blood properly by the lipoprotein receptors in the liver.

endocytosis *(IN doh sigh TOH sis)* Ingestion of substances by a cell. Substances are taken into the cells after being surrounded by vesicles.

TEST YOUR KNOWLEDGE 4-2

Complete the following:

1. Differentiate between phagocytosis and pinocytosis.

_____

_____

_____

2. Explain how familial hypercholesterolemia causes heart problems.

_____

_____

_____

3. Tell whether the following processes are active or passive:
   a. endocytosis _____
   b. facilitated diffusion _____
   c. osmosis _____
   d. phagocytosis _____
   e. filtration _____

CELLULAR COMPONENTS

Cytoplasm

Living organisms require balanced environments in which to thrive. Humans require the right mixture of oxygen and nitrogen; sea creatures require the right balance of salt and water; a chick embryo requires albumen, or "egg white," in which to develop. Likewise, the internal parts of a cell require a special environment, called **cytoplasm,** in order to survive. Cytoplasm is a watery solution of organic (proteins, carbohydrates, and lipids) and inorganic (minerals and gases) chemicals that is enclosed in the cell membrane. This solution helps to regulate the exchange of materials within the cellular environment.

cytoplasm Gel-like intracellular substance. Organelles are embedded in it.

Nucleus and Nucleolus

The **nucleus** has been described as the "brain of the cell." In our case, we will consider it to be City Hall: a control center. City Hall dictates the activity of the city departments much as the nucleus dictates the activities of the organelles in the cell. Because City Hall is crucial to the city's function, security is important to protect it from attack or damage. That is why metal detectors are installed at the doors. The nucleus of a cell is similar. It is surrounded by a double-walled nuclear membrane. Even though this membrane is composed of two layers, it has large pores that allow certain materials to pass into and out of the nucleus.

nucleus The control center or "brain" of the cell.

chromatin Genetic material found in the nucleus of a cell.

deoxyribonucleic acid (DNA) *(dee AWK see RYE boh new KLEE ick)* Sequenced pairs of nucleotides that form a double helix. A segment of DNA makes up a gene.

gene An area on a chromosome that contains all the DNA information needed to produce one type of protein molecule.

nucleolus Round, central region within the nucleus. It makes ribosomes.

ribonucleic acid (RNA) Molecule contained in ribosomes and necessary for making proteins.

ribosome Granular organelle located throughout the cytoplasm and on the endoplasmic reticulum. Ribosomes contain RNA and proteins and are the site of protein synthesis.

centrosome *(SEN truh sohm)* Region of cytoplasm usually near the nucleus that contains 1–2 centrioles.

Somewhere in City Hall are blueprints of the city showing the buildings, streets, water and gas lines, and so on. The nucleus also contains "blueprints"—and "building codes" too. **Chromatin** is the material found in the nucleus that contains **DNA (deoxyribonucleic acid)**. DNA contains the specifications (blueprints) for the creation of new cells. Chromatin eventually forms chromosomes, which contain **genes**. Genes determine our inherited characteristics. (Remember Aunt Pearl saying how much you look like your Uncle Elmer?)

A spherical body called the **nucleolus**, made up of dense fibers, is found within the cell nucleus. Its major function is to synthesize the **ribonucleic acid (RNA)** that decodes the DNA and forms ribosomes. Now we have the blueprints read, but what about the materials that we need? Who's in charge of getting these materials together? That's where ribosomes and **centrosomes** come into play. FIGURE 4-9 ▲ shows the cell membrane, cytoplasm, nucleus, and nucleolus. We will continue to build the cell's infrastructures as we discuss their specific functions.

Ribosomes

Ribosomes are organelles that are found on the endoplasmic reticulum (which will be discussed shortly) or floating around in the cytoplasm. Ribosomes are made of RNA and are the site for production of enzymes and other proteins that are needed for cell repair and reproduction. Following our analogy, consider ribosomes the manufacturing plant for building materials used for remodeling and repair.

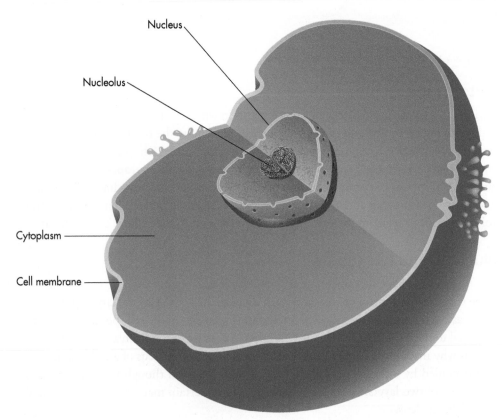

FIGURE 4-9 ▲ The cell membrane, cytoplasm, nucleus, and nucleolus.

Centrosomes

In a city, completely new structures often are needed to replace old ones. Therefore, the cell needs a building contractor to build new structures. The centrosomes are specialized regions that fill this need. Centrosomes contain **centrioles** that are involved in the division of the cell. Cellular division, or reproduction, will be discussed once we cover all the cell parts. Centrioles are tubular shaped and usually found in pairs. See FIGURE 4-10 ▲, which now adds the nucleus, nucleolus, ribosomes, and centrosomes to the cell.

centriole *(SEN tree ohl)* An organelle that precedes mitosis.

Mitochondria

Imagine what it would be like if we had no electricity in our city. Things would come to a standstill. The **mitochondria,** tiny bean-shaped organelles, act as power plants to provide up to 95% of the body's energy needs for cellular repair, movement, and reproduction. As a city's need for power increases, more power plants are built. Similarly, if a given cell type is very active and needs more power, there are a larger number of mitochondria in that cell. For example, liver cells, which are quite active, can have up to 2,000 mitochondria in each cell. In contrast, sperm cells "swim" with a tail (flagellum), so they need only a single mitochondrion coiled around the tail for energy. Special enzymes in the mitochondria help to take in oxygen and use it to produce energy. Whereas our city uses electricity for most of its power, the cell uses adenosine triphosphate (ATP), which is created by the mitochondria (shown in Figure 4-10).

mitochondria *(MYE toh KON dree uh)* The energy organelle of the cell.

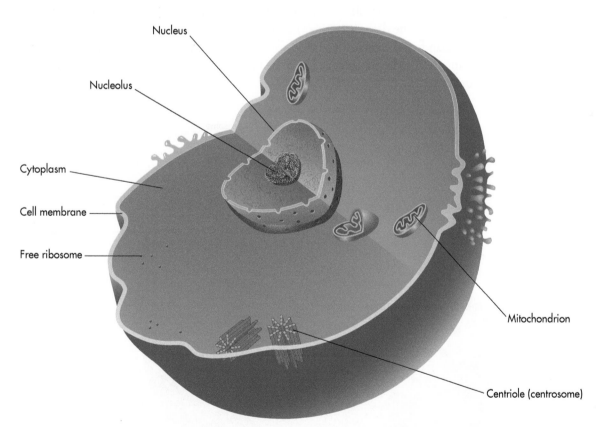

FIGURE 4-10 ▲ The cell membrane, cytoplasm, nucleus, nucleolus, ribosomes, centriole structure (centrosome region), and mitochondria.

Endoplasmic Reticulum

endoplasmic reticulum *(IN doh PLAS mik reh TIK yoo lum)* Organelle that consists of a network of channels that transport materials within the cell. Also the site of protein, fat, and glycogen synthesis.

Although there are paths, walkways, and sidewalks in our city, the main structure for travel is a road system. The **endoplasmic reticulum** is a series of channels set up in the cytoplasm that are formed from folded membranes. The endoplasmic reticulum has two distinct forms. One has a sandpaper-like surface, the result of ribosomes on its surface, which we call the *rough* endoplasmic reticulum, and it is responsible for the synthesis of protein. Once the protein is synthesized, it is sent to the Golgi apparatus for processing. The second form has no ribosomes on its surface, making it appear smooth, so we call it the *smooth* endoplasmic reticulum. (Complex stuff, huh?) The smooth endoplasmic reticulum synthesizes lipids (fats) and steroids. Think of this as a series of dirt and paved roads with butcher shops and food processing plants along the way (see **FIGURE 4-11** ▲).

Golgi Apparatus

Golgi apparatus *(GOAL jee ap uh RAT uhs)* Organelle of the cell that packages cellular material for transport.

Cities have factories with their own fleets of trucks. The **Golgi apparatus** is very similar to these factories. This organelle looks like a bunch of flattened, membranous sacs. Once the Golgi apparatus receives protein from the endoplasmic reticulum, it further processes and stores it as a shippable product, much like a packaging plant does. Not only does it prepare the protein for shipping, but also a part of the Golgi apparatus surrounds the protein with a vesicle that then separates itself from the main body of this organelle. That portion, with its load, then travels to the cell membrane, where it releases (secretes) the protein! This is an example of exocytosis. Cells in organs with a high level of secretion or storage (like the digestive system) contain higher numbers of the Golgi apparatus. Salivary glands and pancreatic glands, for example, are made of cells containing many Golgi apparati. Some proteins made in the Golgi apparatus stay in the cell and become lysosomes.

FIGURE 4-11 ▲
The cell membrane, cytoplasm, nucleus, nucleolus, ribosomes, centriole structure (centrosome region), mitochondria, endoplasmic reticulum, Golgi apparatus, and lysosomes.

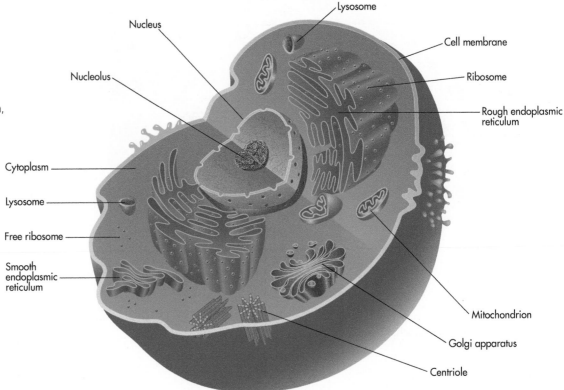

Lysosomes

All cities create waste that must be removed. Cells are no different. **Lysosomes** are vesicles containing powerful enzymes that take care of cleaning up intracellular debris and other waste. Lysosomes are multitalented. They also aid in maintaining health by destroying unwanted bacteria through the process of phagocytosis. Again, see Figure 4-11, which contains all the organelles.

lysosome *(LIE so soam)* Organelle that consists of a small sac with digestive enzymes in it. These destroy pathogens that invade the cell.

Other Interesting Parts

Cells need a way to move things around or move themselves from place to place. Vesicles, or chambers, often created by the Golgi apparatus, can be thought of as little trucks. They can be loaded up with substances, travel to another site in the cell or cell membrane, and then drop off their loads. Similar in some ways to the skeleton, the **cytoskeleton** is a network of microtubules and interconnected filaments that provide shape to the cell and allow the cell and its contents to be mobile. Suppose we could build cities that float on large bodies of water. How would we propel them to new locations? Certain cells can solve this problem through the use of **flagella,** or whip-shaped tails that move some cells in a fashion similar to that of a tadpole.

cytoskeleton *(SIGH toe SKEL ih ten)* The framework of a cell.

The future may offer new ways of transporting people and materials. For example, perhaps cities will install moving sidewalks, similar to those in some airports. Certain cells have solved such transport problems already through the use of **cilia**. Cilia are short, microscopic, hairlike projections located on the outer surface of some cells. They begin a wavelike motion that carries particles in a given direction. This is one way our lungs stay clean from the dust particles and germs that we inhale every day. The action is comparable to when a band member jumps into a crowd and is moved by the wave action of the audience's arms. This behavior is NOT recommended by the authors.

flagella *(fluh JEL uh)* Hairlike processes on bacteria or protozoa that cause movement.

cilia *(SILL ee ah)* Small hairs that flow in waves to move foreign particles away from the lungs toward the nose and the throat where they can be expelled. Also found inside the fallopian tube to propel an ovum toward the uterus.

Pathology Connection

ORGANELLE DISORDERS

All organelles can malfunction. Therefore, many disorders are caused by abnormalities in organelles. Many are widespread, affecting some or all the cells in the body. Here are just a few examples of organelle disorders.

- **Tay-Sachs, a disorder of lysosomes:** Lysosomal storage disorders occur when lysosomes are missing one of their enzymes. With the enzyme missing or broken, some molecules will not break down and will accumulate in cells. There are 40 different kinds of lysosomal storage disorders, all are genetic, and most lack effective therapies. Tay-Sachs disease is the best known of the lysosmal storage diseases. It was, until recently, most common in Jews of central and eastern European descent. Tay-Sachs is caused by a missing enzyme in the lysosomes of cells in the nervous system. Because of the missing enzyme, glycoproteins accumulate in cells in the nervous system, causing inflammation and eventually destroying the cells. The symptoms of Tay-Sachs—mental regression, dementia, and paralysis—appear during the first year of a patient's life. There is no treatment, so the disease is generally fatal within two or three years of onset. Tay-Sachs is diagnosed by the appearance of a cherry red spot on the back of patient's eyes and by abnormality in the startle reflex. The availability of a genetic test has decreased the incidence of Tay-Sachs in recent years.

- **Cigarettes and paralyzed cilia:** As you learned earlier, your lungs stay clean because of the action of cilia. One of the side effects of smoking is to paralyze cilia. If cilia cannot move, they cannot keep the lungs clean. This condition may lead to many of the lung problems seen in smokers and is the primary etiology for chronic obstructive pulmonary disease (COPD), which affects more than 12 million people in the United States. Passive smoking (the exposure of nonsmokers to cigarette smoke) also increases the risk of COPD-related diseases.

cellular respiration The cellular process in which oxygen is used to break down glucose and other nutrients for energy needed for cellular activity.

adenosine triphosphate (ATP) *(ah DEN oh seen try FOSS fate)* Energy storage molecule used to power muscle contraction and other cellular reactions.

adenosine diphosphate (ADP) *(ah DEN oh seen die FOSS fate)* The compound that can be converted to ATP for energy storage. When ATP is broken down to ADP, energy is released that can be used for cellular energy.

APPLIED SCIENCE

Cell Energy and ATP: The Energy Molecule

We all know that we need to eat to obtain energy, but how does energy get from food to cells? In simple terms, the body takes in food and breaks it down (digestion). During this process, energy is released from the food. Now, cells can't use this energy directly; only food converted to glucose (simple sugar) can be used to make energy. Your cells use glucose during a series of chemical reactions called **cellular respiration.** During cellular respiration, glucose is combined with oxygen and is transformed in your mitochondria into the high-energy molecule called **adenosine triphosphate (ATP).** During cellular respiration, glucose is "burned" in the presence of oxygen, making water, carbon dioxide, and lots of energy. The equation

$$C_6H_{12}O_6 + 6O_2 \longrightarrow 6CO_2 + 6H_2O + ATP \text{ (lots)}$$
Glucose + oxygen (Yields) carbon dioxide + water + energy

can be used to represent cellular respiration. Once the glucose is used up and energy is made, carbon dioxide and water are produced as waste products. To make energy for your cells, you must have glucose (from food) and abundant oxygen. Now you know why you breathe! You need to bring in oxygen to make energy, and you to need to exhale to get rid of the waste product carbon dioxide.

The point of cellular respiration is to make energy in the form of ATP. ATP is made up of a base, a sugar, and three (hence, *tri*phosphate) phosphate groups. The phosphate groups are held together by high-energy bonds. When a bond is broken, a high level of energy is released. Energy in this form can be used by the cells. When a bond is used, ATP becomes **ADP (adenosine diphosphate),** which has only two phosphate groups. ADP now is able to pick up another phosphate and form a high-energy bond so energy is stored and the process can begin again! Life is good.

Pathology Connection

DIABETES MELLITUS (REVISITED): A DISORDER TIED TO CELLULAR RESPIRATION

Diabetes mellitus (DM) is a disorder characterized by blood glucose levels that are much higher than normal because the glucose cannot get into cells from the bloodstream as a result of either an insulin deficit in the body or a cellular insensitivity to insulin. Insulin, a hormone secreted by the pancreas, is necessary for facilitated diffusion to carry glucose into cells. There are two types of DM: type I, which is also known as insulin-dependent diabetes mellitus (IDDM), juvenile, or early-onset diabetes, and type II, which is also known as non-insulin-dependent diabetes mellitus (NIDDM), or late-onset diabetes.

The two types of diabetes are very different diseases. Type I is an autoimmune disorder. For some reason, the immune system attacks the cells in the pancreas, the beta cells, which make insulin. They are destroyed and stop making insulin and hence the need for taking insulin. Type II is due to insulin resistance. That is, the pancreas makes plenty of insulin, but for some reason, your body's cells stop responding to it. The cells act as if there isn't enough insulin, even when there is enough. Type II is caused by obesity and is usually associated with high cholesterol, high lipids, and high blood pressure. Whether you have type I or type II diabetes, the ultimate problem is the same: too much glucose in the blood and too little glucose in cells.

The symptoms of diabetes—weight loss, excessive thirst and excessive urination, and chronic long-term problems like heart disease and kidney failure—are caused by the glucose abnormalities. For cells to make ATP in the mitochondria, glucose must be able to get into cells. If glucose doesn't get into cells, the cells will look for other sources of glucose in order to make enough ATP to survive. Cells will begin to sacrifice body tissues like muscles to get energy from alternate sources, such as fats and proteins. Body chemistry will be abnormal due to the breakdown of body tissues caused by the cells' desperate attempts to get fuel.

The extra glucose in the blood causes an abnormal concentration gradient between the inside and outside of cells. Your body desperately tries to get rid of the extra glucose by filtering extra blood through your kidneys. Your kidneys produce excessive amounts of urine. This causes water loss, which can lead to dehydration. People with untreated diabetes are often thirsty, driven to drink water to replace the water lost during urination.

Both types of diabetes are treatable. Type I is treated with daily insulin injections, but there is no cure. Patients should stick to a strict diet to help keep blood glucose at healthy levels. Type II is often treatable and even reversible. The most important treatments are adoption of a healthy diet, good exercise habits, and weight loss. Some patients with type II can treat their disease with diet and exercise alone. Drugs that stimulate the pancreas may also treat the disease, as can cholesterol-lowering medications. Some patients with type II may eventually become insulin dependent, but some can keep their disease from progressing to that point. We will discuss many more details of diabetes in later chapters as we continue our journey through the body.

Pathology Connection

PKU, AN ENZYME DISORDER

Phenylketonuria (PKU) is a genetic condition most common in Caucasians descended from Ireland, Scotland, and some Scandinavian countries. People with PKU are missing an enzyme called phenylalanine hydroxylase. Without this enzyme, the amino acid phenylalanine builds up in cells, especially in the nervous system, leading to progressive mental retardation in untreated individuals. In addition, individuals with PKU have light pigmentation of skin, hair, and eyes; abnormalities of posture and gait; and epilepsy.

The primary treatment for PKU is a low phenylalanine diet, typically avoiding high-protein foods. Recently, however, adhering to this diet has become a bit more complicated. Next time you pick up a can or bottle of diet soda, read the warning on the side of the can. Aspartame, the sweetener in NutraSweet, is made of two amino acids. One of them is phenylalanine! People with PKU must avoid consuming products containing Aspartame.

Children not following this prescribed diet can develop cognitive deficits. In adults, a significant percentage of patients "off diet" report depression or anxiety and other neurological changes. PKU is diagnosed by blood tests and genetic tests. Untreated PKU is rare in the United States because all states currently screen every newborn for PKU.

Clinical Application

ENZYMES: MAKING REACTIONS HAPPEN

For your cells to be able to do anything, some chemicals must be broken down and others must be made. You need building materials to build organelles and to make energy. Any of these processes require chemical reactions to take place in the cell. The problem is that these reactions are usually very slow—so slow that by the time the reaction happens, it would be too late for your cells to use the building materials. To solve this problem, cells have special proteins called **enzymes.** Enzymes speed up the rate of chemical reactions, making them fast enough for your cells to use the materials. Enzymes are like carrier molecules, in that they are not used up and they are very specific. Only certain reactions can be sped up (catalyzed) by certain enzymes.

phenylketonuria (PKU) *(FIN ill KEY toh NEW ree uh)* Inherited disease characterized by the excess of phenylketone in the urine due to an accumulation of phenylalanine in the tissues that may lead to brain injury or death.

enzyme *(IN zyme)* Molecules that speed up the rate of chemical reactions in cells. Enzymes are particularly important in the breakdown and synthesis of biological molecules.

Mitosis

Cellular reproduction is the process of making a new cell. Cellular reproduction is also known as **cell division** because one cell divides into two cells when it reproduces. Cells can only come from other cells. When cells make identical copies of themselves without the involvement of another cell, that is called **asexual reproduction**. Most cells are able to reproduce themselves asexually, whether they are animal cells, plant cells, or bacteria.

cell division The process of cellular replication.

asexual reproduction Reproduction in which sex cells are not utilized.

TEST YOUR KNOWLEDGE 4-3

Choose the best answer:

1. What organelle most closely follows the given analogy?
   a. City Hall _____
   b. road system _____
   c. power plant _____
   d. packing and shipping plant _____
   e. the "cell propeller" _____

Answer the following:

2. What is a lysosomal storage disorder?

_____

_____

3. Explain why enzymes are important.

_____

_____

4. Why is it so important for glucose to get into cells?

_____

_____

CELLULAR REPRODUCTION

The cells that make up the human body are a type of cell known as a **eukaryotic cell**. Eukaryotic cells have a nucleus, cellular organelles, and usually, several chromosomes in the nucleus. (Reminder: the genetic material of the cell, DNA, is bundled into "packages" of chromatin known as chromosomes.) Because chromosomes carry all the instructions for the cells, all cells must have a complete set after reproduction. These instructions include how the cell is to function within the body and blueprints for reproduction. No matter whether a cell has one chromosome, like bacteria, or 46 chromosomes, like humans, all the chromosomes must be copied before the cell can divide.

Let's start off with the simple cellular division of a bacterium. Bacterial cells, which do not have a nucleus or organelles, are called **prokaryotic cells** and reproduce very easily through a process known as **binary fission**. Bacterial cells simply copy their DNA, divide up the cytoplasm, and split in half.

Now let's go to the more complex cellular reproduction. Eukaryotic cells, like yours, must go through a more complicated set of maneuvers in order to reproduce. Not only do your cells have to duplicate all 46 of their chromosomes, but they also have to make sure that each cell gets all the chromosomes and all the right organelles. The process of sorting the chromosomes, so that each new cell gets the right number of copies of all of the genetic material, is called **mitosis**. Mitosis is the only way that eukaryotic cells can reproduce asexually.

eukaryotic cell *(yoo CARE ee awt ick)* The cells that make up the human body, possessing a nucleus, organelles, and several chromosomes.

prokaryotic Cells that do not have a nucleus or organelles as in bacterial cells.

binary fission Asexual reproduction in prokaryotic cells in which the cell enlarges, duplicates its chromosomes, and creates a transverse septum, forming two identical daughter cells.

mitosis Asexual cellular reproduction that produces exact copies of the original cell.

The Cell Cycle

cell cycle The life cycle of the cell, including normal activity (interphase) and cell division (mitotic phase).

interphase The stage of a cell between mitotic divisions during which DNA replication takes place.

mitotic phase The phase devoted to actual cell division.

cytokinesis *(SIGH tow ki NEE sis)* The division of cytoplasm during cellular division.

prophase The first step in mitosis where the nucleus disappears, chromosomes become visible and act as anchor lines, and centrioles move toward the sides of the cell.

metaphase Second step in mitosis where chromosomes line up in the center of the cell.

anaphase Third step in mitosis in which chromosomes split and spindles pull them apart.

telophase Fourth step in mitosis in which chromosomes migrate to ends of cell, spindles disappear, and the nuclei reappear.

The total life of a eukaryotic cell can be divided into two major phases known as the **cell cycle**. Most of the cell cycle is devoted to a phase known as **interphase**. During interphase, a cell is not dividing but is performing its normal functions along with stockpiling needed materials and preparing for division by also copying DNA and making new organelles. Only a brief portion of the cell cycle, the **mitotic phase,** is devoted to actual cell division. The mitotic phase is divided into two major portions. Mitosis is the division and sorting of the *genetic material,* whereas **cytokinesis** is the division of the *cytoplasm.*

As you might imagine, the cell cycle is very tightly controlled to avoid overproduction of cells. (The overproduction of cells can sometimes lead to cancer, which will be discussed later in the chapter.) At several places in the cell cycle there are checkpoints, spots where cells must wait for a signal to tell them to keep dividing. If something is wrong with the cell or there is some reason the cell should not reproduce, the cell will not get a signal and will stop dividing. If the timing is good, the cell will get the go-ahead signal and will divide without interruption.

Mitosis, the division of the genetic material, is the most complicated part of cell division for a eukaryotic cell. What further complicates mitosis is that the process is further divided into four specific phases. As you'll soon see, the four phases are based on the position of the chromosomes relative to the new cells. They are **prophase, metaphase, anaphase,** and **telophase.** To put all these processes and phases in perspective, please refer to the flowchart in FIGURE 4-12 ▲.

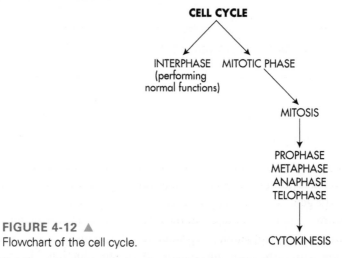

FIGURE 4-12 ▲
Flowchart of the cell cycle.

Amazing **Body Facts**

Bacterial Reproduction
Bacteria can reproduce so rapidly that they can double their population every half an hour! No wonder a bacterial infection can get out of hand so fast.

The Phases of Mitosis

Let's proceed step-by-step through the four phases of mitosis using FIGURE 4-13 ▲ as a reference.

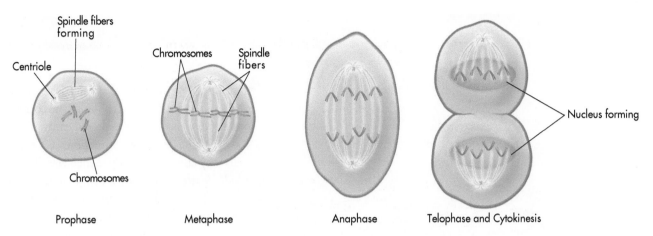

FIGURE 4-13 ▲ Phases of mitosis.

1. **Prophase (pro = *before*):** The nucleus disappears, the chromosomes become visible, and the centrioles move toward the sides of the cell; a set of chromosomal anchor lines or guide wires (the spindle) forms.
2. **Metaphase (meta = *between*):** The chromosomes line up in the center of the cell.
3. **Anaphase (an = *without*):** The chromosomes split, and the spindles pull them apart.
4. **Telophase (telo = *end*):** The chromosomes go to the far end of the cell, the spindle disappears, and the nuclei reappear.

During or directly after telophase, cytokinesis happens, and the cell divides in half. The original cell was the mother cell that has now formed into two new identical daughter cells. Thus mitosis, asexual reproduction in eukaryotic cells, results in two new daughter cells identical to the original mother cell.

Mitosis in Your Body

Mitosis (asexual cellular reproduction) serves many purposes in your body. First, your body uses mitosis any time your cells need to be replaced. Many tissues, like bone, epithelium, skin, and blood cells, all replace themselves on a regular basis. Mitosis also accomplishes repair and regeneration of damaged tissue. If you cut your hand, the skin is replaced, first by collagen, but eventually by the original type of tissue. Mitosis increases in cells near the injury so that the damaged or destroyed cells can be replaced. A broken bone is replaced in much the same way.

Growth is also accomplished by mitosis. Lengthening of bones as you grow, increases in muscle mass due to exercise, and most other ways that tissue gets bigger are all due to mitosis of cells in the tissues or organs. Without mitosis, your body would not be able to grow or replace old or damaged cells.

Sexual reproduction is different from mitosis. **Meiosis** is the term for the division of cells for human reproduction to occur. During meiosis, four cells are produced from one cell. These cells are not identical to the mother because they have half as many chromosomes. These cells are the eggs and sperm that will be used for reproduction. This process will be discussed in detail in Chapter 17, "The Reproductive System."

meiosis *(mye OH sis)* Form of cellular division that produces gametes.

atrophy *(AT roh fee)* Loss of muscle bulk in one or more muscles. It can be caused by malnutrition or can occur in any part of the body that is paralyzed and the muscles receive no electrical impulse from the nerves.

hypertrophy *(high PER troh fee)* Greater than normal growth.

hyperplasia *(HIGH per PLAY zee uh)* Excessive growth of normal cells.

metaplasia Conversion of one kind of tissue into a form that is not normal for that tissue.

dysplasia *(dis FAY jee ah)* Abnormal development of tissue.

benign *(bee NINE)* Not progressive, nonmalignant.

malignant *(mah LIG nant)* Cancerous, able to spread to distant parts of the body.

metastasis *(meh TASS tah siss)* Process by which cancerous cells break off from a tumor and move through the blood vessels or lymphatic vessels to other sites in the body.

metastasize To spread throughout the body to distant sites.

biopsy Obtaining of tissue samples for microscopic examination to help determine a diagnosis.

chemotherapy The use of chemical substances or drugs to treat a disease, usually used in reference to cancer treatment.

radiation therapy The use of energy from man-made ionizing radiation or from the radioactive decay of atomic nuclei to destroy diseased tissues, especially cancers.

surgery The branch of medicine dealing with manual and operative procedures to correct deformities and defects, repair injuries, and diagnose and cure certain diseases.

biological An agent derived from or made of living tissues or cells and used in health care.

immunotherapy The use of natural and synthetic substances to stimulate or suppress the immune response (as in patients with anaphylaxis or severe allergies), to treat deficits, or to interfere with the growth of malignant neoplasms.

Pathology Connection

CANCER: MITOSIS RUN AMOK

When the body is healthy, cells grow in an orderly fashion; they grow at the appropriate rate in the appropriate number, shape, and alignment. If everything is working as it should, the control system prevents cells from reproducing too fast. Sometimes conditions are altered in the body (either internally or externally) that trigger changes in the way the cells grow. Sometimes as a result of disuse or insufficient blood flow or malnutrition, cells may abnormally reduce their size. This is known as cellular **atrophy**. Think how your arm would look after months in a cast. Conversely, if you increase the workload on a cell, it will increase in size, and this is known as celluar **hypertrophy**. Imagine what your arm looks like when you work out with weights. Another way the body responds to increased workloads (or hormonal stimulation) is to increase the number of cells, and this is called **hyperplasia**. Sometimes during chronic periods of stress or stimulation the body will change one type of cell for another, as in cases of chronic inflammation. This process is called **metaplasia**. If these stressors or stimuli continue, it may cause cells to grow erratically, giving them an abnormal size, appearance, and shape. This is termed **dysplasia**. If the stimulus is removed soon enough, there is a potential for these cells to return to normal over time. However, if the stimulus continues, cell growth can become wild and uncontrolled, leading to too many cells being produced and resulting in a lump, or tumor. Generally, tumors are classified as either benign or malignant. **Benign** tumors typically grow slowly and push healthy cells out of the way. Usually, benign tumors are not life threatening. **Malignant,** or cancerous, tumors grow rapidly and invade rather than push aside healthy cell tissue.

Cancer actually means "crab" (remember your zodiac signs?) and is a good description of cancer cells in that they spread out into healthy tissue like the legs and pincers of a crab. Cancerous tumors also differ from benign tumors in that parts of a cancerous tumor can separate and travel through the blood system or the lymphatic network and start new tumors in other parts of the body. This breaking off and spreading of malignant cells is called **metastasis**. One reason that lung cancer is so deadly (more women die from it than from breast cancer) is that it can **metastasize** for a fairly long time before it is even diagnosed in the lungs. By the time it is discovered, tumors may be growing in the liver, brain, and other parts of the body, making survival very difficult.

Cancer prognosis and treatment options are often determined by the stage of the cancer at diagnosis. The most general cancer stages are determined by the amount of metastasis. Stage I cancer has not spread, stage II cancer has spread to nearby tissues, stage III cancer has spread to the lymphatic system, and stage IV cancer has spread to distant organs. Staging can also be done using the T, N, M classification system, which takes into account the extent of the primary *T*umor, the number of lymph *N*odes invaded by the cancer, and the extent of tumor *M*etastasis. More recently, scientists have begun to develop specific staging systems for specific cancers. These systems are developed after examination of the outcomes of thousands of cases looking for specific characteristics of tumors that better predict outcome.

Cancer is diagnosed by a variety of techniques, including imaging (MRI, CT scan, and x-ray), blood tests, and **biopsy,** which is the surgical examination of the abnormal tissue.

Cancer can be treated by any method that attacks cancer cells. The most common treatments are **chemotherapy**, which uses chemicals to kill rapidly dividing cells; **radiation therapy,** which uses energy to target cancer cells; **surgery,** which removes cancer cells from the body; and **biological** or **immunotherapy**, which trains the body's natural defenses to fight the cancer cells. Typically more than one treatment will be used to attack a cancer. Success of treatment type depends on stage at diagnosis and specific characteristics of the cancer itself. Some cancers are more responsive to treatment than others.

LEARNING HINT

Mitosis versus Meiosis

These words sound and look alike and are therefore often confused. Remember, m<u>ei</u>osis produces ga<u>me</u>tes or sexual cells, which contain half of the chromosomes because the sexual union of male and female will contribute the other half. M<u>i</u>tosis (*I reproduce myself*) is asexual and produces exact copies of the cell and the full complement of chromosomes because no union is needed.

TEST YOUR KNOWLEDGE 4-4

Choose the best answer:

1. Cells are reproducing themselves during this portion of the cell cycle:
   a. metaphase
   b. mitotic phase
   c. meiotic phase
   d. manic phase

2. During this phase of mitosis the nucleus disappears and the spindle appears:
   a. prophase
   b. metaphase
   c. anaphase
   d. telophase

3. During this phase of mitosis the chromosomes begin to pull apart:
   a. prophase
   b. metaphase
   c. anaphase
   d. telophase

4. Which of the following is not a function of asexual reproduction?
   a. tissue repair
   b. replacement of cells
   c. tissue growth
   d. cloning humans

MICROORGANISMS

As in any city, you have a large and diverse population. Although the vast majority of the population are good citizens who provide positive contributions to the city, some can cause problems. The same can be said for the world of microorganisms. The following are the main "microcitizens" of our city:

- Bacteria
- Viruses
- Fungi
- Protozoa

Bacteria

When you hear the word **bacteria,** you probably first think of an organism that produces disease, called a **pathogen.** You are somewhat correct in assuming so because bacteria make up the largest group of pathogens. Some bacterial pathogens even release toxic substances in your body. Bacteria, which are prokaryotes, grow rapidly and reproduce by splitting in half, sometimes doubling as rapidly as every 30 minutes.

bacteria Asexually reproducing cell capable of creating an infection.

pathogen *(PATH oh jenn)* Microorganism that causes a disease. Pathogens include bacteria, viruses, protozoa, and other microorganisms, as well as plant cells like fungi or yeast.

normal flora *(FLOOR ah)* The normal microorganisms found in a particular body region.

You will learn throughout this book that bacteria are often harmless and, in fact, essential for life. These bacteria live within or on us and are part of what is called our **normal flora**. For example, certain bacteria in your intestine help to digest food, and some help to synthesize vitamin K, which helps clot blood so you don't bleed to death when you get a cut or scrape. See **FIGURE 4-14** ▲, which shows examples of various types of bacteria.

Viruses

virus A parasitic microorganism that depends on other cells for its metabolic and reproductive needs.

capsid *(KAP sid)* The protein covering around a virus particle.

An even more basic pathogen is a **virus** (see **FIGURE 4-15** ▲). Viruses (from a Latin term meaning "poison") are infectious particles that have a core containing genetic material (codes to replicate) surrounded by a protective protein coat called a **capsid**. Some viruses have an additional layer, or membrane, surrounding the capsid. Viruses are interesting because they cannot grow, "eat," or reproduce by themselves. They must enter another cell (host cell) and hijack that cell's parts, energy supply, and materials to do all cellular activities! In addition, each virus must target specific cells in the body to claim as hosts. For example, the viruses that cause a cold target the cells found in the respiratory system, and the viruses that cause herpes target cells that are found in the tissues of our nervous system. Most of the upper respiratory infections that people get are caused by viruses, and like all viral infections, *they do not respond to antibiotics.*

It is interesting to note (or disturbing for those of you who worry about everything) that viruses can stay dormant in the body and become active once again later in life.

BACILLUS (ROD-SHAPED)

Diplococci
(cocci in pairs)
Di = two

Streptococci
(cocci in chains)
Strept(o) = chain

Staphylococci
(cocci in clusters)
Staphyl(o) = bunch

COCCI (SPHERICAL)

FIGURE 4-14 ▲ Types of bacteria.

Membranous envelope

Capsid (protein coat)

Nucleic acid (DNA or RNA)

Spikes (protein)

FIGURE 4-15 ▲ A virus.

This is true for people who have had chicken pox. Those viruses stay in the body and may later become active and cause a potentially painful skin condition called *shingles,* caused by the *herpes zoster* virus. It is also interesting to note that the actual virus is relatively easy to kill by itself, but once it becomes part of a cell, it is hard to kill without harming the host cell.

Fungi

Fungi, the plural form of fungus, can be either a one-celled or multicelled organism. These plantlike organisms have tiny filaments, called **mycelia,** that travel out from the cell to find and absorb nutrients. Like bacteria, fungi, such as edible mushrooms, can be good, but in certain situations they can also cause problems (see **FIGURE 4-16** ▲).

Fungi also can spread through the release of **spores.** Normally, people are not affected by fungi, but if the body has a problem with its immune system, then fungi have a chance to cause an opportunistic infection. If tissue becomes damaged, fungi can more easily create an infection. Fungal infections are often difficult to treat. Some antifungal drugs are highly toxic, and many fungal infections are resistant to treatment. Wind can pick up and carry spores that can be inhaled, potentially causing lung infections. Interestingly, you can inhale fungi spores and still not develop an infection. It is estimated that up to 80% of the population in certain regions of the United States have tested positive for the inhalation of certain fungi! Examples of fungal infections are athlete's foot and a mouth fungus called thrush or *candidiasis.*

fungi *(FUN jie)* A plantlike organism (includes mold and yeasts).

mycelia *(my SEE lee uh)* Cellular filaments as seen in fungal bodies.

spores Cells that have a protective barrier to allow for future reproduction in a hostile environment.

Protozoa

Protozoa are one-celled animal-like organisms that can be found in water, such as ponds, and in soil. Disease caused by these microorganisms can result from swallowing them (such as by drinking contaminated water) or from being bitten by insects that carry them in their bodies (such as malaria-carrying mosquitoes). See **FIGURE 4-17** ▲.

protozoa *(PROH teh ZOH uh)* Unicellular organisms.

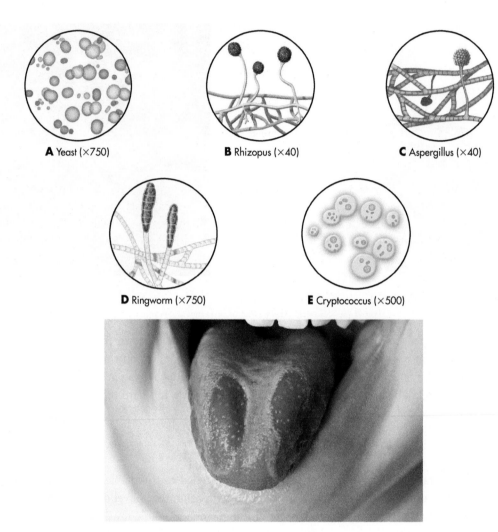

A Yeast (×750)   **B** Rhizopus (×40)   **C** Aspergillus (×40)

D Ringworm (×750)   **E** Cryptococcus (×500)

FIGURE 4-16 ▲ Types of fungi and a fungal infection of the tongue. (Photo Source: Angel Simon/ Fotolia.com)

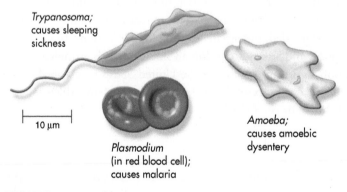

Trypanosoma; causes sleeping sickness

10 μm

Plasmodium (in red blood cell); causes malaria

Amoeba; causes amoebic dysentery

FIGURE 4-17 ▲ Protozoa.

Pathology Connection

HOW MICROORGANISMS CAUSE DISEASE

All microorganisms—bacteria, viruses, fungi, and protozoa—can cause disease, but the disease mechanism and treatments are different for each type of organism. Any microorganism that causes disease is called a pathogen. The treatment and course of any infection is determined by the type of pathogen involved.

Bacteria and Disease

Although bacteria can cause disease directly by destroying infected tissue, many bacteria cause disease due to the release of toxins into the host body. Toxins can cause many problems, including destruction of body tissues, destruction of blood cells, inhibition of ribosomes, fluid loss, high fever, decreased blood pressure, increased blood clotting, fluid in lungs, and paralysis. Signs and symptoms of bacterial infection may include high fever; rapid pulse and breathing; abnormal, often foul-smelling discharge from infected area; and pain and swelling at the site of infection. Other symptoms depend on the location of the infection. Bacterial infections are treated with **antibiotics,** chemicals that can kill the prokaryotic bacteria without harming eukaryotic cells. Most antibiotics are produced naturally by other microorganisms. See TABLE 4-2 ■ for common bacterial pathogens and their associated diseases.

antibiotics *(AN teh by OT icks)* Natural or synthetic substances that either destroy a bacterial microorganism or inhibit its growth.

Viruses and Disease

Viruses are not cells at all, but intracellular parasites composed of a nucleic acid (either DNA or RNA) with a lipid or protein coat. Viruses must use the materials of a cell to make more viruses. Viruses cause disease in two ways: directly, by shutting down a cell or destroying the cell outright (cell ruptures to release viruses), or indirectly, by making a good environment for the development of secondary bacterial or fungal infections. For example, influenza rarely kills people. The leading cause of death due to the flu is bacterial pneumonia, which can easily infect lung tissue damaged by the flu virus.

Signs and symptoms of viral infection include low-grade fever (although it may also be high sometimes), muscle aches, and general fatigue, though some viral infections may cause no symptoms. Viral infections are complicated in that they may be latent, hiding in the body without causing symptoms and then activating years after the infection. Some viral infections may also become chronic, causing low-level symptoms for weeks, months, or even years. There are very few treatments for viral infections. Viruses are not prokaryotes, so antibiotics do not kill viruses. In fact, because viruses are using the eukaryotic cell's machinery, antiviral drugs usually have side effects because they affect the host cell. Most viruses are destroyed by the immune system within a few days of infection. Although more antiviral drugs are becoming available, the most common treatments for most viral infections are rest, fluids, and management of symptoms to keep the patient comfortable. Please see TABLE 4-3 ■ for common pathogenic viruses and their associated diseases.

Fungi and Disease

Most fungal infections are caused by the inhalation or ingestion of fungal spores or the entrance of spores through open wounds. Spores are tiny bodies resistant to environmental changes, meaning they can stay dormant until conditions are just right. Most fungal spores do not cause disease in otherwise healthy individuals, though fungal infections of the skin, such as athlete's foot and jock itch, are common. Many fungal infections are opportunistic, causing disease in individuals with compromised immune systems or other underlying disease.

Pathology Connection

Symptoms of fungal infection vary widely depending on the location of the infection. Fungal infections are often difficult to treat. Some antifungal drugs are highly toxic, and many fungal infections are resistant to treatment.

Protozoans and Disease

Most protozoan infections are caused by ingestion of contaminated water or by insect bites. Many of these protozoans are parasites, actually taking up residence in the human body and living off its cells. Most protozoans that infect humans cause disease. Symptoms of protozoan infections vary widely depending on the type of protozoan infection. Many are very serious diseases that cause long-term debilitating illness, such as malaria, which is transmitted by *Anopheles* mosquitoes. Others are relatively mild illnesses, like "beaver fever" caused by *Giardia,* a protozoan that lives in streams and water supplies contaminated by fecal matter.

TABLE 4-2 ■ COMMON BACTERIAL PATHOGENS AND ASSOCIATED DISEASES

BACTERIAL PATHOGENS	DISEASES
Gram-positive cocci (purple stained spheres)	
Staphylococcus aureus	Skin infections, food poisoning
Streptococcus pyogenes	Pharyngitis (strep throat)
Streptococcus pneumoniae	Lobar pneumonia
Gram-positive bacilli (purple stained rods)	
Clostridium tetani	Tetanus
Clostridium botulinum	Botulism
Bacillus anthracis	Anthrax
Gram-negative cocci (red stained spheres)	
Neisseria gonorrhoeae	Gonorrhea
Gram-negative bacilli (red stained rods)	
Salmonella typhimurium	Salmonellosis
Legionella pneumophila	Legionellosis (Legionnaires' disease)
Pseudomonas aeurginosa	Urinary tract infections, burn infections

Clinical Application

BACTERIA'S RESISTANCE TO ANTIBIOTICS

Prior to the discovery of antibiotics in the 1930s, most people who got bacterial infections died of their infections. Those who did survive were often left with long-term effects. Diseases that are easy to deal with today, like strep throat or simple wound infections, once killed thousands of people every year. Many deaths during wars were caused by the bacterial infections of the wounds rather than the wounds themselves. When antibiotics were discovered they were considered a miracle cure and were used carelessly. As the drugs became readily available, doctors began to prescribe them whenever a patient wanted them, whether they had a bacterial infection or a viral infection. Farmers began to add antibiotics to livestock feed. At the time these practices seemed harmless. Now we know that overuse of antibiotics was a big mistake. Today, many bacteria cannot be killed by antibiotics that used to work without fail. Many bacteria have evolved resistance to the drugs. Some bacteria are even resistant to many different antibiotics. Bacterial infections, like strep pneumonia and tuberculosis, are not always killed by antibiotics that used to work on them in the past. Many bacterial infections must be treated by several antibiotics before the infection is killed. Think about the last time you or someone you know had to take an antibiotic. Did the first one work? Did the second? Thirty years ago, penicillin was the drug of choice for strep infections. Now doctors rarely prescribe penicillin because most bacteria are no longer sensitive. Sensible use of antibiotics and the development of new antibiotics is the only way to combat this important public health problem.

TABLE 4-3 ■ VIRAL PATHOGENS AND THEIR DISEASES

VIRUSES	DISEASES
DNA viruses	
Herpes viruses	
Herpes simplex 1	Cold sores and fever blisters
Herpes simplex 2	Genital herpes
Varicella-Zoster	Chicken pox and shingles
Hepatitis B	Hepatitis ("serum hepatitis")
Epstein-Barr	Infectious mononucleosis
RNA viruses	
Influenza A, B, C	Influenza ("flu")
Hepatitis A, C, D	Infectious hepatitis
Rhinovirus	Common cold
Human immunodeficiency virus	HIV infection/AIDS

SUMMARY

Snapshots from the Journey

- All living organisms are made of one or more cells. Cells are the fundamental units of living organisms.

- Even though cells are the fundamental units, they are composed of a variety of parts that are necessary for proper cellular function. These small parts are called organelles.

- Substances can cross the cell membrane via passive or active transport.

- Passive transport can occur through diffusion, facilitated diffusion, osmosis, or filtration.

- Active transport can occur through active transport pumps, endocytosis, or exocytosis.

- Problems with transport across cell membranes can cause serious disorders such as cystic fibrosis and diabetes.

- One form of cellular movement is through the use of flagella.

- Cilia found in the lungs aid in the removal of foreign particles in the airways through rhythmic movement.

- When organelles do not work properly, serious problems result, often in every cell of the body.

- Cells must have the energy molecule ATP to power the cell. ATP is made in the mitochondria by a process called cellular respiration. To make ATP, cells must have glucose and oxygen.

- Diabetes mellitus (DM) results when glucose cannot get into cells. Cells cannot make energy and excess glucose builds up in the blood causing many problems.

- Most chemical reactions in the body could not happen without the help of proteins called enzymes. Missing enzymes usually cause major problems.

- Cells and tissues grow, are replaced, and are repaired by asexual reproduction. Cells make identical copies of themselves. This takes place all over your body whenever tissues grow or are repaired.

- Some tissues, like epidermis, blood, and bone, replace themselves continually, always by asexual reproduction.

- The life of the cell can be depicted as a cell cycle. Only about 10% of the cell cycle is devoted to mitosis. The rest of the time the cell is in interphase, preparing to divide and carrying on day-to-day cellular activities.

- Asexual reproduction in eukaryotic cells is accomplished by a relatively complex process called mitosis and cytokinesis. Mitosis, the division of the genetic material, takes place in four phases: prophase, metaphase, anaphase, and telophase. Cytokinesis is the division of the cytoplasm and organelles. Mitosis produces two daughter cells, identical to each other.

- Meiosis is the sexual reproduction of cells. If an organism is going to reproduce sexually it must use specialized cells called gametes with only half the typical number of chromosomes for that organism. The chief difference between mitosis and meiosis is that mitosis is asexual and produces the exact number of chromosomes, whereas meiosis is sexual and combines two cells with half of the needed chromosomes.

- Cancer results when mitosis is not regulated and cells divide out of control, spreading to other tissues.

- Not all bacteria are bad. In fact, the body needs bacteria to survive.

- A virus is not technically a one-celled organism; it needs another cell to replicate.

- Fungi can be single-celled or multicelled organisms and can cause infections in the body. Spores can be immune to a harsh environment, thus allowing fungi to spread.

- Protozoa are one celled and can cause disease through ingestion or through insect bites.

- Many microorganisms cause disease. Each has unique characteristics and treatments. Antibiotics can be used *only* to treat illnesses caused by bacteria.

CASE STUDY

Given the following miniscenarios, identify what type of microorganism may be the causative agent.

a. Two young boys complain of a stomach ache and severe diarrhea after drinking pond water.

_____

_____

b. Julia is a 13-year-old with a compromised immune system due to an inherited disease. Ten days after returning home from a school field trip to a mushroom factory, Julia complains of shortness of breath and is diagnosed with a respiratory infection.

_____

_____

c. Bob has had a stubborn cold for three days and is given an antibacterial agent. However, he doesn't respond to the treatment, and the cold persists.

_____

_____

MARIA'S STORY

Maria is a 35-year-old diabetic who now takes good care of herself. Diagnosed with autoimmune type I at 12 years old, Maria rebelled against the dietary restrictions, daily insulin injections, and blood monitoring. During adolescence she had wild blood sugar swings, hypoglycemic episodes that would cause her to black out one day and be off the chart with hyperglycemia the next. She ignored all the "scare tactics" her doctors and parents tried to lay on her. She figured it was no big deal. She'd deal with her diabetes when she was good and ready.

In early 20s, Maria's retinas began to hemorrhage. Luckily the problem was caught early enough to save her eyesight. Then a minor cut on her leg turned into an ulcer that had to be treated surgically. Alarmed, she did some Web surfing and realized that she was flirting with disaster. She talked to her doctor and a nutritionist and began to stick to her diet and exercise program and to monitor her blood glucose level daily.

For several years her blood glucose was relatively stable, marked by occasional periods of hyperglycemia or hypoglycemia. When she turned 30, things began to unravel. Even when she followed her treatment plan rigorously, her blood sugar was sometimes difficult to control. She tried an insulin pump to stabilize her blood sugar. Nothing worked. She passed out several times in public and then began to have other problems. She had several skin infections and began to have sharp pain in her hands and feet. Her kidneys began to fail. In an attempt to control her diabetes, her doctor suggested a pancreas transplant.

a. List and explain two problems the lack of insulin causes for cells.

_____

_____

b. In what future system chapters will you expect to see Maria discussed?

_____

_____

REVIEW QUESTIONS

Multiple Choice

1. The cell membrane can best be described as:
   a. permeable to all materials
   b. nonpermeable
   c. rigid
   d. semipermeable

2. All the following are passive forms of transport *except:*
   a. facilitated diffusion
   b. exocytosis
   c. osmosis
   d. filtration

3. With a greater concentration of a solute, what will happen to osmotic pressure?
   a. It will become less.
   b. It will become greater.
   c. It will remain the same.
   d. There is no relation between osmotic pressure and the concentration of solute.

4. Cystic fibrosis is caused by:
   a. a missing carrier protein
   b. a malformed membrane channel
   c. a hole in the cell membrane
   d. too little insulin

5. Where are the specifications for the creation of new cells found?
   a. DNA
   b. RNA
   c. ATP
   d. ADP

6. Which microorganism can cause disease?
   a. bacteria
   b. fungi
   c. virus
   d. all of the above

7. Antibiotics are used to treat illness caused *only* by this type of pathogen:
   a. virus
   b. bacteria
   c. fungus
   d. protozoa

Matching

1. Match the following organelles with their function:

   _____ nucleus   a. the "powerhouse" of the cell
   _____ cell membrane   b. processing, packaging, and shipping of materials
   _____ Golgi apparatus   c. the gatekeeper of the cell
   _____ mitochondria   d. the "brain" of the cell
   _____ cytoplasm   e. the internal environment
   _____ lysosome   f. sanitation engineers

2. Match the disorder with its cause:

   _____ diabetes mellitus   a. uncontrolled mitosis
   _____ cystic fibrosis   b. missing lysosomal enzyme
   _____ cancer   c. missing cellular enzyme
   _____ Tay-Sachs disease   d. malformed membrane channel
   _____ PKU   e. failed facilitated diffusion

REVIEW QUESTIONS

Short Answer

1. List and describe the four methods of passive transport.

_____

_____

2. Why do viruses need cells?

_____

_____

3. How does passive transport differ from active transport?

_____

_____

4. Discuss how cells can provide motility for themselves.

_____

_____

5. Explain the importance of enzymes to cells.

_____

_____

6. Explain the stages of cancer.

_____

_____

7. Compare and contrast bacterial, viral, and fungal diseases.

_____

_____

Suggested Activities

1. Research the various cell types within the body, and see how many you can list.

2. Research five sexually transmitted diseases (STDs), and list the causative microorganism for each.

3. List the ways that we abuse antibiotics and ways that we could slow down antibiotics resistance in bacteria.

4. Working together in groups, develop specific examples of how active and passive transport systems help maintain homeostasis. Include an investigation into biofeedback methods and its relationship to homeostasis. Share your findings with the class.

5. Working together in small groups, develop several examples of the consequences when homeostasis is not maintained. Present your findings to the class.

CAREER CONNECTIONS

Now that you have read this chapter, here is a list of related professions you may be interested in investigating for a future career:

- Cytology

- Lab Technician

Research each profession and report on the following:

1. Profession description to include job responsibilities
2. Educational requirements
3. Job opportunities
4. Opportunities outside of the hospital setting
5. Salary range
6. Licensure and continuing education requirements

ANATOMY, PHYSIOLOGY, AND DISEASE IN ACTION

Materials:
Ziploc or Baggies plastic bags
Varieties of candy

Students will be asked to build a cell from candies they have chosen to represent the cell and the organelles of the cell. The students are asked to provide a rationale for their choices.

All participants will wash their hands before beginning this activity.

Suggestions: Mini Twizzlers for centrioles; Life Savers for vesicles; jelly beans for mitochondria; gummy worms for smooth and rough endoplasmic reticulum (sugar coated or not); orange slices for golgi bodies; M & M's for ribosomes; sugar-coated gum drops for lysosomes; and wrapped caramel swirls for the nuclei. After each student has presented their cell, celebrate by eating them!

Tissues and Systems
The Inside Story

5

Previously, we discussed cells as the basic building blocks of the body. In this chapter, we explore tissues, which are collections of similar cells. We can consider cells to be individual employees. At the next level, we can think of tissue as a group of these employees who have the same or similar educational background, such as radiologic technicians, at a hospital. A combination of tissues designed to perform a specific function or several functions is called an organ. This could be compared to an x-ray department in the hospital, where specific functions such as x-rays, CT scans, MRIs, and barium swallows (a procedure, not a bird!) are performed. Organs that work together to perform specific activities, often with the help of accessory structures, form what we call systems. We can compare a system to a hospital that provides a service (health care) to the citizens of our city through the combination of all the departments: laboratory, nursing, respiratory care, physical therapy, dietetics, housekeeping, and so on. Of course, all those systems combine to make a living organism, in this case the wondrous human body. This chapter provides an overview of tissues, organs, and systems, which will be expanded on in later chapters.

LEARNING OUTCOMES

At the end of your journey through this chapter, you will be able to:

- Explain the relationship between cells, tissues, organs, and systems
- List and describe the four main types of tissues
- Identify and describe the various body membranes
- Differentiate the three main types of muscle tissues
- Describe the main components of nervous tissue
- List and describe the main functions of the body systems
- Provide general examples of how pathologic conditions can have an impact on cells, tissues, organs, and body systems

Pronunciation Guide

Correct pronunciation is important in any journey so that you and others are completely understood. Here is a "see and say" Pronunciation Guide for the more difficult terms to pronounce in this chapter. Please note that pronunciations given are referenced to medical dictionaries, and regional variations may exist.

anorexia (an oh REX ee ah)
atherosclerosis (ATH ur oh skleah ROH sis)
cuboidal (cue BOYD al)
cutaneous membranes (cue TAY nee us)
epithelial tissue (ep ih THEE lee al)
genitourinary (JEN ih toe YUR ih NAIR ee)
glia (GLEE ah)
lymphocytes (LIMF oh sights)
meninges (men IN jeez)
neuroglia (noo ROG lee uh)

neuron (NOO ron)
parietal (pah RYE eh tal)
serous (SEER us)
skeletal muscle (SKEL eh tal)
squamous (SKWAY mus)
stratified (STRAT ih fied)
striated (STRY ate ed)
synovial (sin OH vee al)
transitional (tran ZISH uhn al)
visceral (VISS er al)

OVERVIEW OF TISSUES

Just as there are many different types of cells with various functions and responsibilities, tissues come in different shapes and sizes, again with the structure dependent on the function. Let's begin to explore the different tissue types.

Tissue Types

tissue Collection of similar cells that form a particular function.

squamous cells (*SKWAY mus*) Flat, scaly epithelial cells.

cuboidal cells (*KYOO boid al*) Cube-shaped epithelial cells.

columnar cells Column-shaped epithelial cells.

transitional cells (*tran ZISH on al*) Stretchable epithelial cells.

simple cells Epithelial cells that are arranged in a single layer and are of the same type.

stratified (*STRAT eh fied*) Having more than one layer.

pseudostratified Apparently composed of layers.

Tissue is a collection of similar cells that act together to perform a function. Imagine individual cells as bricks. Placing these bricks (cells) in a specific pattern creates the functional wall (tissue) of a building. There are many different types of tissues depending on the required function. The four main types of tissues are

- Epithelial
- Connective
- Muscle
- Nervous

Let's look at these major types of tissue and their subdivisions.

Epithelial Tissue

Similar in purpose to the plastic wrap we use to keep food fresh, epithelial tissue not only covers and lines much of the body but also covers many of the parts found in the body. The cells in this form of tissue are packed tightly together, forming a sheet that usually has no blood vessels in it.

We can further classify epithelial cells by their shape and arrangement. These cells can be flat or scalelike (**squamous**), cube-shaped (**cuboidal**), columnlike (**columnar**), or stretchy and variably shaped (**transitional**). If these cells are arranged in a single layer and are all the same type of cell, we classify them as **simple**. If they are arranged in several layers, we say they are **stratified,** and they are named by the type of cell that is on the outer layer (such as stratified columnar). An exception to that rule is **pseudostratified** columnar epithelium, which looks stratified but is not. The function required of the cell dictates which type of cell formation is utilized. For example, simple squamous cells are utilized in the lungs because of their flat, thin design, which makes for easy transfer of oxygen from the lungs to the blood. FIGURE 5-1 ▲ shows the types and locations of epithelial tissues. These are further discussed in later chapters.

Stratified squamous

Simple squamous

Stratified cuboidal

Simple cuboidal

Pseudostratified columnar

Simple columnar

FIGURE 5-1 ▲ Types and locations of epithelial tissues.

Membranes Generally, **membranes** are sheetlike structures found throughout the body that perform special functions. Although membranes can be classified as organs, we will discuss them along with tissues for ease of explanation.

   Epithelial membranes possess a layer of epithelial tissue and a bottom layer of a specialized connective tissue. Epithelial membranes are classified into three general categories, as you can see in TABLE 5-1 ■.

   FIGURE 5-2 ▲ shows the location of the serous and mucous membranes in the body.

membrane A thin soft pliable layer of tissue that can line a cavity or cover an organ or structure.

epithelial membrane *(EP ih THEE lee al)* Comprised of epithelial and connective tissues that serves as linings and coverings for various body structures.

Amazing **Body Facts**

Skin and Vitamin Production
You know that you get vitamins and minerals from the foods you eat and the supplements you take, but did you know that your skin produces vitamin D when you are exposed to sunlight?

TABLE 5-1 ■ TYPES OF EPITHELIAL MEMBRANES

1. Cutaneous	Functions like a tarp placed over a boat.
	The main organ of the integumentary system, commonly known as your skin.
	Makes up approximately 16% of the total body weight.
	Skin is your largest organ.
2. Serous	A two-layered membrane composed of the parietal and visceral layers with a potential space in between.
Parietal	Lines the wall of the cavities in which organs reside.
	Produces serous fluid, which reduces friction between different tissues and organs.
Visceral	Wraps around the individual organs.
	Also produces serous fluid, which reduces friction between different tissues and organs.
3. Mucous	Lines openings to the outside world, such as your digestive tract, respiratory system, urinary and reproductive tracts.
	Called mucous membranes because they contain specialized cells that produce mucus. Mucus can act as a lubricant like the oil in a car. Mucus also serves several other important purposes, as you will see in future chapters.

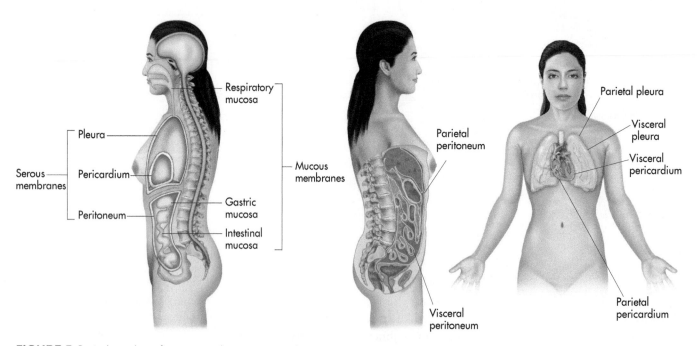

FIGURE 5-2 ▲ Location of serous and mucous membranes.

LEARNING HINT

To get a visualization of the importance of serous fluid consider the following: Without this friction-reducing fluid, each beat of your heart and every breath you take would be uncomfortable. The effect is similar to running water over a sheet of plastic placed on the grass. You can run, jump onto the plastic, and slide. Imagine how it would feel trying to do a body slide without the water running over the plastic!

Connective Tissue

Connective tissue is the most common tissue and is found throughout the body more than any other form. That is because it is found in organs, bones, nerves, muscles, membranes, and skin. Connective tissue's job is to hold things together and provide structure and support. Fine, delicate webs of loosely connected tissue (**areolar tissue**) hold organs together and help to hold other connective tissues together. Fat (**adipose tissue**) is also a connective tissue. Although we always seem to want to lose fat, we truly need some fat in our bodies for proper functioning. Connective tissue can also be more densely packed and form strong cordlike structures similar to wire cables on suspension bridges. *Tendons* and *ligaments* are composed of dense connective tissue. The skin also needs to be densely packed to form a protective barrier, and it therefore uses dense connective tissue. Because connective tissue is so versatile and found throughout the body, we will discuss it in more depth in the relevant chapters. Please see FIGURE 5-3 ▲, which illustrates the various types of connective tissues and shows some of the places where they are found.

areolar tissue Delicate webs of loosely connected tissue.

adipose tissue *(AD ih pose)* Fatty tissue.

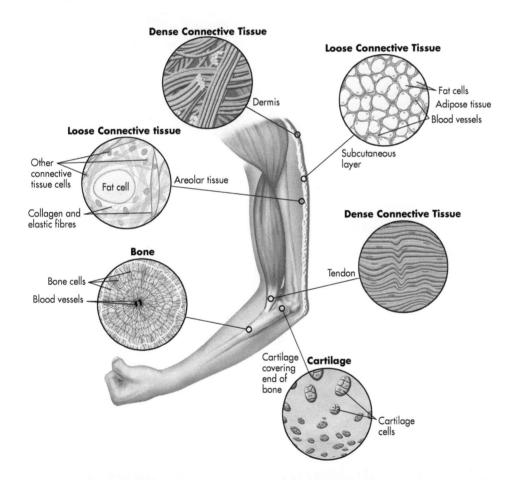

FIGURE 5-3 ▲ Types and locations of connective tissues.

Amazing Body Facts

Blood and Lymph as Connective Tissues

Even though blood and lymph are fluid, they are considered to be connective tissue because they are a liquid mixture composed of a group of cells that have specialized functions. These fluid connective tissues contain specialized cells and dissolved proteins suspended in a watery substance. We expand on these two very important tissues in later chapters.

synovial membrane *(sin OH vee al)* The membrane lining a capsule of the joint.

A membrane associated with connective tissue is the **synovial membrane**. This important membrane type is found in the spaces between joints and produces a thick, colorless, and slippery substance called synovial fluid, which greatly reduces friction when joints move. Imagine runners without synovial membranes: their knees just might burst into flames during track meets! FIGURE 5-4 ▲ shows a synovial joint and membrane.

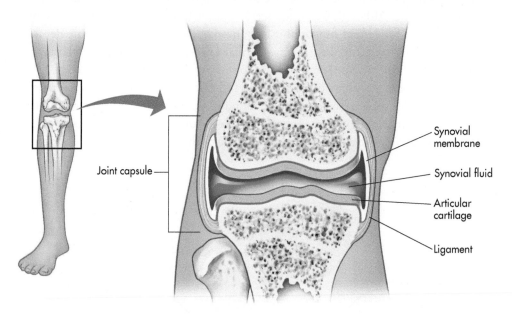

Joint capsule

Synovial membrane

Synovial fluid

Articular cartilage

Ligament

FIGURE 5-4 ▲ The synovial joint.

skeletal muscle *(SKELL eh tal)* One of three types of muscle in the body, but the only muscle that is under voluntary, conscious control. Under the microscope, skeletal muscle has a striated appearance.

cardiac muscle One of three types of muscle in the body. It is found only in the heart and cannot be controlled consciously.

smooth muscle One of three types of body muscles that is involuntarily controlled and found in the lining of the airways, blood vessels, and uterus.

striated *(STRY ate ed)* Striped.

Muscle Tissue

Muscle tissue provides the means for movement by and in the body. This form of tissue has the ability to shorten itself (contractility). There are three types of muscle tissue: **skeletal, cardiac,** and **smooth**.

Skeletal Muscle Skeletal muscle (often described as **striated** because of its striped appearance) is attached to bones and causes movement by contracting and relaxing. It also surrounds certain openings of the body, such as the mouth, and controls the size of the opening. Unless you are a ventriloquist, it is very hard to speak clearly without moving your lips. The cells that make up this tissue type are long and fiberlike with many nuclei in each cell. Our brain thinks about moving or speaking and causes the correct muscle to contract as necessary. Because this is a conscious effort, we call these muscles *voluntary* muscles.

Cardiac Muscle Cardiac muscle is found in the walls of the heart. Our hearts beat without our conscious control. Because the heart contracts and relaxes without conscious thought, this muscle type is considered *involuntary* muscle tissue. The cells in this tissue type interlock with one another, promoting more efficient contraction, as you will learn in Chapter 12, "The Cardiovascular System."

Smooth Muscle Smooth muscle tissue forms the walls of hollow organs, such as in our digestive system (which is why it is often called *visceral* tissue) and blood vessels. Because we don't have to consciously think about digesting food, we consider this muscle type to also be *involuntary* muscle tissue. Cells forming this tissue are not as long and fibrous as skeletal muscle, and each cell has only one nucleus. FIGURE 5-5 ▲ shows the various types of muscle tissue.

Nervous Tissue

Nervous tissue acts as a rapid messenger service for the body, and its messages can cause actions to occur. There are two types of nerve cells. **Neurons** are the conductors of information, and **glia** (sometimes called **neuroglia**) cells function as support by helping to hold the neurons in place. The branchlike formations that make up part of the neuron, called **dendrites,** receive sensory information. The trunk-shaped structure, called the **axon,** transports information *away* from the cell body. Ray, our spinal cord injury patient and common case study, has permanently damaged the axons running up and down his spinal cord, which carry information between the

neuron *(NEW ron)* An individual nerve cell. The functional part of the nervous system.

glia *(GLEE ah)* Nonnervous or supporting tissue found in the brain and spinal cord; made of glial cells.

neuroglia *(new ROG lee ah)* Cells that hold neurons in place and perform specialized tasks. Includes astrocytes, ependymal cells, microglia, oligodendrocytes, satellite cells, and Schwann cells. Also called glial cells.

dendrite *(DEN dright)* Multiple branches at the end of a neuron that carry information to the cell body.

axon *(AK son)* Part of the neuron that is a single, elongated branch at the opposite end from the dendrites. It receives an electrical impulse and releases neurotransmitters into the synapse. Axons are covered by an insulating layer of myelin.

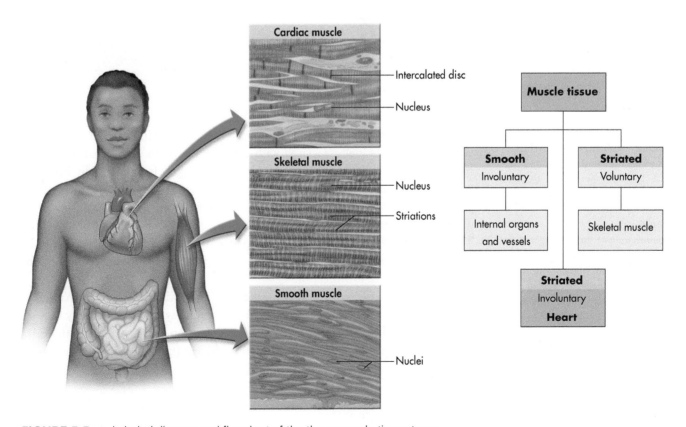

FIGURE 5-5 ▲ Labeled diagram and flowchart of the three muscle tissue types.

myelin sheath Layers of the cell membrane of Schwann cells (peripheral nervous system) or oligodendrocytes (central nervous system) that wrap nerve fibers, providing electrical insulation and increasing the velocity of impulse transmission.

body and the brain. Many nerves have an insulating layer called the **myelin sheath,** which is further discussed in Chapter 9, "The Nervous System." FIGURE 5-6 ▲ shows the two types of nerve cells.

Cell body

NEURON

Nucleus

Dendrites

Axon

Myelin sheath

NEUROGLIA (Glia)

FIGURE 5-6 ▲ The two main types of nerve cells.

meninges *(men IN jeez)* Three separate membranes that envelope and protect the entire brain and spinal cord. The meninges include the dura mater, arachnoid, and pia mater.

meninigitis *(men in JYE tiss)* Inflammation of the meninges of the brain or spinal cord by a bacterial or viral infection. Initial symptoms include fever, headache, nuchal rigidity (stiff neck) lethargy, vomiting, irritability, and photophobia.

carrier An individual who is infected by a disease and can potentially spread the disease.

Meningitis and Vaccinations Even membranes can be involved in pathologic processes. The membranes associated with covering the brain and spinal cord are called **meninges. Meningitis** (inflammation of the meninges) is a potentially life-threatening condition that can be caused by bacteria or viruses. The bacterial form of meningitis (for which *meningococcus* is one of the main causative agents) can be spread via droplets as a result of sneezing or coughing or by saliva contact of an infected person. This is why college students or military personnel in crowded situations are at higher risk. It is also believed that stressful situations and alcohol/tobacco consumption may increase the chance for infection.

Once you are infected, you become a **carrier** of the disease. That doesn't necessarily mean that you will develop the disease. Your immune system may actually destroy and remove that pathogen. Some individuals may develop the disease once the infecting agent gets into the bloodstream or the nervous system (meninges). Symptoms can range from nonspecific headaches or fever, nausea, neck stiffness, and a skin rash to hearing loss, neurologic/brain damage, kidney failure, and loss of limbs through necessary surgical removal. There is approximately a 10% fatality rate in bacterial meningitis. Although most of the media attention seems to focus on events on college campuses, those occurrences represent less than 3% of the cases in this country.

Enter the vaccine and the controversy. There has been some major debate about mandatory vaccination of individuals in the higher risk groups such as college students. Only about 25% of the cases in the United States are caused by a pathogen covered by the vaccine; approximately 75% of the U.S. cases are caused by pathogens it does not cover. Although the chances for getting bacterial meningitis is low (1–3 people per 100,000) and the chance of developing severe disability from the disease or dying is even less, that is of little consolation to patients with amputated legs and fingers or families of deceased patients.

So just get a vaccination and be done with it, right? Well, it's not that simple. Receiving a vaccination may expose you to potential adverse reactions. These reactions can include headaches, dizziness, vomiting, convulsions, and even death. In one United Kingdom study, it was found that one adverse reaction occurred for every 907 vaccinations given.

And now the question becomes, "What should I do?" The decision to use certain vaccines not required by law should be weighed by their benefits versus their potential danger. The choice is yours; choose wisely. You alone must make that decision, but base it on sound scientific evidence, not media hype or political musings. Are you a member of a higher risk group? Please see TABLE 5-2 ■, which lists universally recommended vaccinations.

TABLE 5-2 ■ UNIVERSALLY RECOMMENDED VACCINATIONS

POPULATION	VACCINES
All young children	Measles, mumps, and rubella Diphtheria-tetanus toxoid and pertussis Poliomyelitis Haemophilus influenzae type B Hepatitis B Varicella
Previously unvaccinated or partially vaccinated adolescents	Hepatitis B Varicella Measles, mumps, and rubella Tetanus-diphtheria and pertussis toxoid
All adults	Tetanus-diphtheria and pertussis toxoid
All adults aged > 65 years	Influenza Pneumococcal Tetanus-diphtheria and pertussis toxoid (those who have contact with infants and children)

Pathology Connection

BLOOD SUGAR AND TISSUE DAMAGE

You've probably listened to people talking about diabetes and the high levels of "sugar" in their blood or urine. But did you know that diabetes also affects tissues in the body? As you learned in the Common Case Study, Maria, a diabetic, doesn't produce enough insulin to allow glucose (the principal nutrient) into the body's cells. Because the cells don't have their main source of food, they resort to "eating" fats first and, later, the proteins found in the body. As the body uses up its protein, it is harder for the body to create more, and as a result tissues start to break down. It is more difficult and sometimes almost impossible for wounds to heal, and infections are harder to fight. That is why Maria developed a leg ulcer after a minor injury. In addition, blood circulation to tissue is decreased as lipids are released from fat tissues and are deposited around the inside wall of the blood vessels, impairing blood flow. This is a condition called **atherosclerosis.**

Tissue destruction and blood flow occlusion can cause diabetics to become susceptible to tissue death and gangrene, thus potentially leading to the loss of toes, feet, and even legs as their condition worsens. More life-altering effects of diabetes can be found in Chapter 10 and throughout the chapters in which we follow Maria's common case study.

atherosclerosis *(ATH er oh skleh ROH sis)* Hardening of the arteries as a result of plaque buildup in the lumen of the arteries.

TEST YOUR KNOWLEDGE 5-1

Complete the following:

1. List and describe the four types of epithelial cells.

   _____

   _____

2. Lubrication for joints is produced by which type of membrane?

   _____

   _____

3. Why is connective tissue so prominent in the body?

   _____

   _____

4. Explain the difference between the terms *mucous* and *mucus.*

   _____

   _____

5. When considering diabetes, which substance is prohibited from entering cells of the body? How can this potentially lead to tissue damage?

   _____

   _____

Clinical Application

MELANOMA

Melanoma, a skin cancer that affects the epithelial membrane, has had a rapid increase in the rate of incidence in the past several decades. Melanoma typically appears as a brown or black irregular patch on the skin or a change in an existing wart or mole. Treatment consists of surgical removal of the melanoma and the surrounding area and a possible follow-up with chemotherapy.

Melanoma is significant for two main reasons. First, it has a very high mortality rate, and in fact it is the cancer with the most rapidly increasing mortality rate. While causing only 3% of all skin cancers, it accounts for approximately 75% of all skin cancer deaths. It is the most common form of cancer in people ages 25 to 29. About 60,000 new cases are reported annually. Second, it is one of the more preventable cancers. The culprit? Excessive sun exposure and tanning! Although the classic patient has fair skin, blue eyes, and blonde or red hair, more darkly pigmented individuals are also at risk, but at a somewhat lower rate. The effects of blistering sunburns have an additive effect. This means that each childhood sunburn you had increases your chance of developing melanoma in adulthood. Protection from excessive sun and early detection are keys to survival.

melanoma A malignant pigmented mole or tumor.

Clinical Application

TECHNICAL ADVANCES AND LIMITATIONS

The rapid rate of technological advancement in society in general has had a major impact on the treatment of system disorders. Technology research and development has resulted in many life-saving devices—such as portable defibrillators—and pharmaceuticals that treat and control everything from diabetes to high cholesterol. However, there are still limitations to what technology can treat. For example, despite progress, there are no cures for cancer or Alzheimer's disease.

Researchers working for industry and the government are constantly exploring ways to overcome these limitations by developing new technologies for treating system disorders and to make existing technologies more efficient. For instance, there have been huge strides made in the treatment of many cancers, leading to longer patient survival and improved quality of life. These include advances in immunotherapy, targeted therapies, and combined chemotherapy and hormone therapy techniques.

ORGANS

As mentioned earlier, a hospital department is made up of employees who work together to perform specific functions. Similarly, an **organ** is the result of two or more types of tissues organizing in such a way as to accomplish a task that the tissues cannot do on their own. Your heart, lungs, stomach, liver, and kidneys are all examples of organs found in your body. Some organs occur singly, such as the heart, and some occur in pairs, such as the lungs.

It is important to understand that there are *vital* organs and organs that are not vital. Vital organs are the ones that you can't live without. Your heart, brain, and lungs are vital organs. Organs that you can live without include your appendix, spleen, and gallbladder.

organ A part of the body, comprised of tissues, that has a specialized function.

Some vital organs come in pairs, so if one is damaged or removed, you can still survive. Lungs and kidneys are a good example. TABLE 5-3 ■ provides a quick reference to the various organs of the body, their medical terminology combining form, and related medical specialty.

SYSTEMS

system An organized grouping of related structures or parts that perform specific functions.

A body **system** is formed by organs that work together to accomplish something more complex than what a single organ can do on its own. Take the heart, for example. Even if your heart is functioning perfectly, you would die without all the other parts that make up the cardiovascular system. Much like a road system in the city, you need the arteries, veins, and blood to get vital oxygen and nutrients to the cells and to remove the waste products produced by those cells.

Although we discuss the body systems separately, it is extremely important that you understand that all the body systems are interrelated, often depending on one another for proper functioning.

TABLE 5-3 ■ SYSTEMS AND ORGANS OF THE HUMAN BODY

BODY SYSTEM	ORGANS IN THE SYSTEM	COMBINING FORM	MEDICAL SPECIALTY
Integumentary	Skin	dermat/o, cutane/o	Dermatology (*DUR mah TAL oh jee*)
	Hair	trich/o	
	Nails	ung/o	
	Sweat glands	sud/o, hidr/o	
	Sebaceous glands	seb/o	
Musculoskeletal	Muscles	my/o, muscul/o	Orthopedics (*OR thoh PEE dik*s)
	Bones	oste/o	
	Joints	arthr/o	Rheumatology (*ROO mah TALL oh jee*)
Endocrine	Thyroid gland	thyr/o	Endocrinology (*EN doh krin ALL oh jee*)
	Pituitary gland	pituit/o	Internal medicine
	Testes	test/o, orchid/o	
	Ovaries	ovari/o, oophor/o	Gynecology (*GUY neh KOL oh jee*)
	Adrenal glands	adren/o	
	Pancreas	pancreat/o	
	Parathyroid glands	parathyroid/o	
	Pineal gland	pineal/o	
	Thymus gland	thym/o	
Cardiovascular	Heart	cardi/o	Cardiology (*car dee ALL oh jee*)
	Blood	hemat/o, hem/o	Hematology (*HEE mah TALL oh jee*)
	Arteries	arteri/o	Internal medicine
	Veins	phleb/o, ven/o, veni/o	

(continued)

TABLE 5-3 ■ SYSTEMS AND ORGANS OF THE HUMAN BODY *(continued)*

BODY SYSTEM	ORGANS IN THE SYSTEM	COMBINING FORM	MEDICAL SPECIALTY
Lymphatic and Immune	Spleen	splen/o	Immunology (*IM yoo NALL oh jee*)
	Lymph	lymph/o	
	Thymus gland	thym/o	
Respiratory	Nose	nas/o, rhin/o	Otorhinolaryngology (*OH toh RYE noh LAIR in GALL oh jee*)
	Pharynx	pharyng/o	Thoracic (*tho RASS ik*) surgery
	Larynx	laryng/o	
	Trachea	trache/o	
	Lungs	pneum/o	Pulmonology (*pull mon ALL oh jee*)
	Bronchial tubes	bronch/o	Internal medicine
Gastrointestinal	Mouth	or/o	Gastroenterology (*GAS troh EN ter ALL oh jee*)
	Pharynx	pharyng/o	Internal medicine
	Esophagus	esophag/o	
	Stomach	gastr/o	
	Small intestine	enter/o	
	Colon	col/o colon/o	Proctology (*prok TOL oh jee*)
	Liver	hepat/o	procto = anus
	Gallbladder	cholecyst/o	
	Pancreas	pancreat/o	
Urinary	Kidneys	nephr/o, ren/o	Nephrology (*neh FROL oh jee*)
	Ureters	ureter/o	Urology (*yoo RALL oh jee*)
	Bladder	cyst/o, vesic/o	uro = urine
	Urethra	urethr/o	
Reproductive	Ovaries	oophor/o	Gynecology
	Uterus	uter/o, hyster/o	gynec/o = woman
	Fallopian tubes	salping/o	Obstetrics (*ob STEH triks*)
	Vagina	vagin/o	
	Mammary glands	mamm/o, aden/o	
	Testes	orchid/o	
	Prostate	prostat/o	
	Urethra	urethr/o	
Nervous	Brain	encephal/o	Neurology (*noo RAL oh jee*)
	Spinal cord	myel/o, spin/o	Neurosurgery (*noo roh SIR jer ee*)
	Nerves	neur/o	
Senses	Eyes	ocul/o, ophthalm/o	Ophthalmology (*off thal MALL oh jee*)
	Ears	ot/o	Otolaryngology (*OH toh LAIR in GALL oh jee*)

Skeletal System

Throughout your journey, you will see many different kinds of buildings. The one thing all the buildings have in common is some sort of skeletal structure for support. Most people think that the skeleton's only job is to provide support and structure to the body, much like the framework of a house, but it does much more. The skeleton protects organs such as the brain; in combination with muscles, it provides movement; it acts as a storage vault for a variety of minerals, such as calcium and phosphorus; *and* it also produces blood cells! That's pretty impressive stuff! The main components of this system are bones, joints, ligaments, and cartilage. FIGURE 5-7 ▲ shows the main components of the skeletal system.

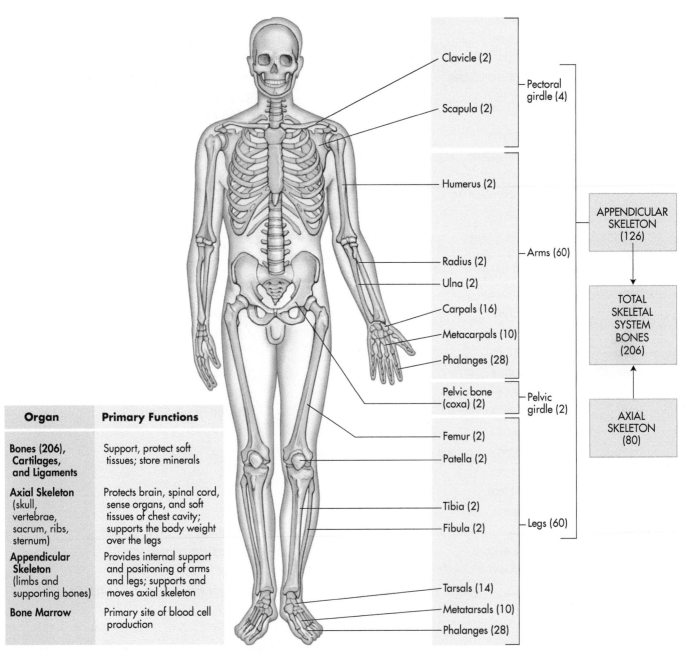

Organ	Primary Functions
Bones (206), Cartilages, and Ligaments	Support, protect soft tissues; store minerals
Axial Skeleton (skull, vertebrae, sacrum, ribs, sternum)	Protects brain, spinal cord, sense organs, and soft tissues of chest cavity; supports the body weight over the legs
Appendicular Skeleton (limbs and supporting bones)	Provides internal support and positioning of arms and legs; supports and moves axial skeleton
Bone Marrow	Primary site of blood cell production

Clavicle (2)
Scapula (2)
Pectoral girdle (4)
Humerus (2)
Radius (2)
Ulna (2)
Carpals (16)
Metacarpals (10)
Phalanges (28)
Arms (60)
Pelvic bone (coxa) (2)
Pelvic girdle (2)
Femur (2)
Patella (2)
Tibia (2)
Fibula (2)
Legs (60)
Tarsals (14)
Metatarsals (10)
Phalanges (28)

APPENDICULAR SKELETON (126)
TOTAL SKELETAL SYSTEM BONES (206)
AXIAL SKELETON (80)

FIGURE 5-7 ▲ The skeletal system.

Muscular System

"All of this dry reading makes me thirsty. I think I'll go get something to drink." The muscular system is responsible for getting you up and over to that refrigerator (see FIGURE 5-8 ▲). This voluntary action is made possible by skeletal muscles that are attached to your bones. Two general classifications of muscle are *voluntary* (of which we just had an example) and *involuntary*. Involuntary muscles perform without consciously being told to do so. The smooth muscle found in the walls of organs, often called *visceral muscle*, and the muscle found in the heart, called cardiac muscle, are examples of involuntary muscles. Smooth muscle is also found in blood vessels and airways, where it helps control the diameter of these passageways. So, the main parts of the muscle system are skeletal, smooth, and cardiac muscles.

Trapezius
Sternocleidomastoid
Deltoid
Pectoralis major
Biceps brachii
Rectus abdominis
Rectus femoris
Sartorius
Tibilias anterior
Gastrocnemius
Soleus

Organ	Primary Functions
Skeletal muscles (700)	Provide skeletal movement; control openings of digestive tract; produce heat; support skeletal position; protect soft tissues

FIGURE 5-8 ▲ The muscular system.

Integumentary System

All cities must have first responders, such as paramedics, police, firefighters, and safety inspectors, who cover and protect the city and its inhabitants. The body's first line of protection is your skin. Skin is the main part of the integumentary system. Besides protecting your body from invasion, the integumentary system also helps to regulate body temperature through sweating, shivering, and changes in the diameter of blood vessels in the skin. Much of the sensory information received from the outside world (heat, cold, pain, pressure, etc.) comes from sensors in the skin. Glands in the skin help to lubricate and waterproof the skin and also inhibit the growth of unwanted bacteria. The main components of this system include skin, hair, sweat glands, sebaceous glands, and nails (see **FIGURE 5-9** ▲).

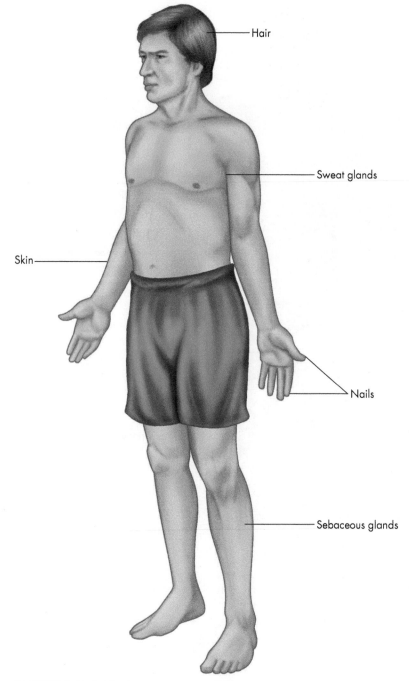

Organ	Primary Functions
Skin	Largest organ of the body
Epidermis	Covers surface, protects underlying tissues
Dermis	Nourishes epidermis; provides strength, contains glands
Hair Follicles	Produce hair
Hair	Provides sensation; provides some protection for head
Sebaceous glands	Secrete oil that lubricates hair
Sweat Glands	Produce perspiration for evaporative cooling
Nails	Protect tips of fingers and toes
Sensory Receptors	Provide sensations of touch, pressure, temperature, pain

FIGURE 5-9 ▲ The integumentary system.

Nervous System

Much like the activities of City Hall, the nervous system is the rapid messenger system of the body that both receives and sends messages for activities to occur. The messages conducted by the nervous system are stimulated by the body's internal and external environments. This is important not only so we may experience the world around us, but to also protect us from harm. The nervous system also monitors what is going on inside the body. How do we know when we are hungry or when we have had enough to eat? This information is obtained through **sensations,** which are conscious (and unconscious) feelings or an awareness of conditions that occur inside and outside of the body. These sensations are caused by stimulation of our sensory receptors. So, then, the three main functions of the nervous system are *sensory* (receiving messages*), processing/interpreting* messages, and *motor* (acting on those messages). The main parts of the nervous system are the nerve cells (glial cells and neurons), the spinal cord (damaged in Ray) along with its spinal fluid, peripheral nerves, and of course, the brain. The sensory organs include the eyes (sight), nose (smell), tongue (taste), skin (touch), and ears (hearing *and* balance). Chapter 11 covers the special senses in more detail. See **FIGURE 5-10** ▲, which depicts the nervous system.

sensation A feeling or awareness as a result of the stimulation of sensory receptors.

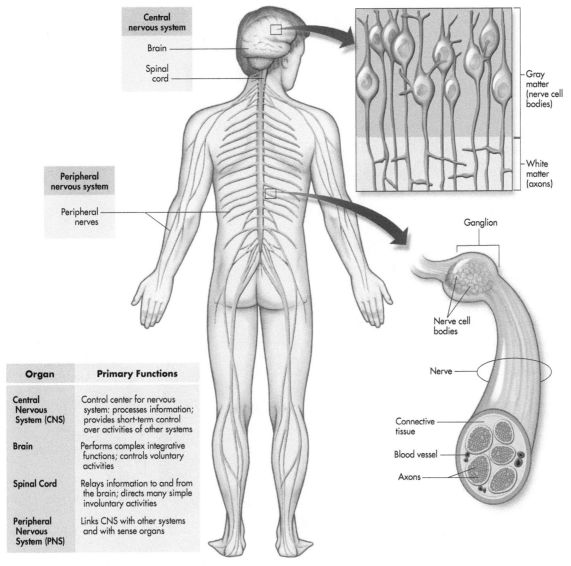

Organ	Primary Functions
Central Nervous System (CNS)	Control center for nervous system: processes information; provides short-term control over activities of other systems
Brain	Performs complex integrative functions; controls voluntary activities
Spinal Cord	Relays information to and from the brain; directs many simple involuntary activities
Peripheral Nervous System (PNS)	Links CNS with other systems and with sense organs

FIGURE 5-10 ▲ The nervous system.

endocrine glands Ductless glands that secrete macromolecules, called hormones, directly into the bloodstream, and such glands are richly supplied by blood capillaries. The endocrine glands include the adrenals, the parathyroids, the pineal, the pituitary, and the thyroid.

hormone *(HOR mohn)* Chemical messenger of the endocrine system that is released by a gland or organ and travels through the blood.

Endocrine System

Although not as quick acting as the nervous system, the endocrine system also acts as a control center for virtually all the body's organs (see **FIGURE 5-11** ▲). This control is accomplished through **endocrine glands** that release chemical substances called **hormones** that are circulated through the cardiovascular system. The endocrine system helps to regulate the body's metabolic processes that utilize carbohydrates, fats, and proteins, and it plays an important role in the rate of growth and reproduction.

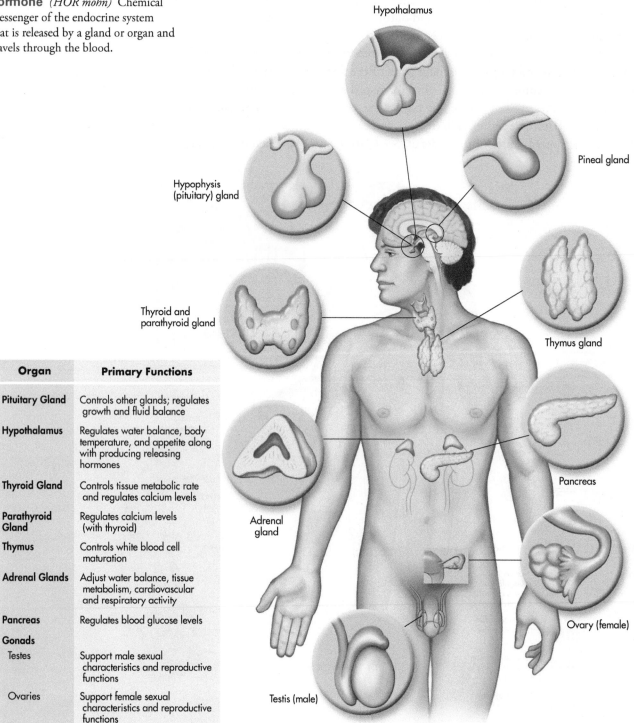

Organ	Primary Functions
Pituitary Gland	Controls other glands; regulates growth and fluid balance
Hypothalamus	Regulates water balance, body temperature, and appetite along with producing releasing hormones
Thyroid Gland	Controls tissue metabolic rate and regulates calcium levels
Parathyroid Gland	Regulates calcium levels (with thyroid)
Thymus	Controls white blood cell maturation
Adrenal Glands	Adjust water balance, tissue metabolism, cardiovascular and respiratory activity
Pancreas	Regulates blood glucose levels
Gonads	
Testes	Support male sexual characteristics and reproductive functions
Ovaries	Support female sexual characteristics and reproductive functions

FIGURE 5-11 ▲ The endocrine system.

In addition, the endocrine system helps to regulate the fluid and electrolyte balances of the body. If that weren't enough, the hormones produced by the endocrine system help you to deal with general stress and the stresses produced by infection and trauma! The main parts of the endocrine system are the hypothalamus; the pineal, pituitary, thyroid, parathyroid, thymus, and adrenal glands; the pancreas; and the gonads (testes in males and ovaries in females); plus a variety of hormones. In our Common Case Study, Maria's diabetes is caused by a dysfunctional pancreas, which does not produce enough of the hormone insulin.

Cardiovascular System

Often referred to as the circulatory system, the cardiovascular system, shown in FIGURE 5-12 ▲, is the main transportation system to each cell of our body, much like the

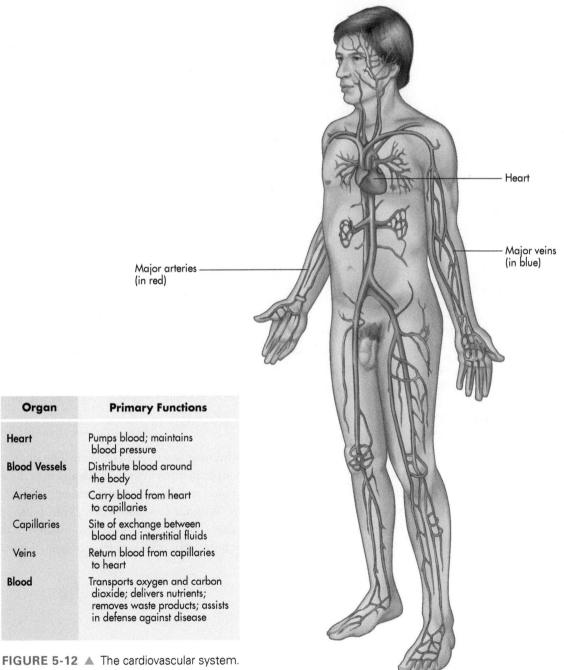

Heart

Major veins (in blue)

Major arteries (in red)

Organ	Primary Functions
Heart	Pumps blood; maintains blood pressure
Blood Vessels	Distribute blood around the body
Arteries	Carry blood from heart to capillaries
Capillaries	Site of exchange between blood and interstitial fluids
Veins	Return blood from capillaries to heart
Blood	Transports oxygen and carbon dioxide; delivers nutrients; removes waste products; assists in defense against disease

FIGURE 5-12 ▲ The cardiovascular system.

streets, sidewalks, and subways of our city. Through this system, water, oxygen, and a variety of nutrients and other substances necessary for life are transported to the cells, and waste products are transported away from the cells. Also like our city, these routes can become clogged or blocked, causing major problems. Imagine what happens to a busy four-lane highway if two of the lanes are shut down because of construction or an accident. The traffic slows and pressure builds up due to the congestion, much like the blood flow does when the arteries become partially obstructed. The buildup of pressure (hypertension) can be very dangerous. The main components of this system are the heart, arteries, veins, capillaries, and—of course—blood.

Pathology Connection

SEPTICEMIA

Many pathologic conditions involve only one body system. However, as you journey through this text, you will begin to visualize the interrelatedness of the systems and how a disease in one system will affect one or more of the other systems.

Septicemia (also called **sepsis** or **blood poisoning**) is a condition in which a pathogen is present in the blood. Because blood is needed throughout all the body's systems, the potential for a multisystem infection is a very real danger. For example, a perforation in the stomach or intestine (as caused by surgical procedures, trauma, knife wound, etc.) can allow gastric contents to spill into the abdominal cavity, which can lead to infection of that region. Blood that is perfusing (flowing through) that area may pick up some of the bacteria and spread it to other organs. Once in other organs, the bacteria can continue to colonize, thus potentially affecting function(s) of that organ. The term *sepsis syndrome* is often used when there is a decrease in blood perfusion to organs, with other systemic signs. "Septic shock" occurs when there is a drop in blood pressure due to the decrease in organ perfusion. If not quickly and effectively treated, the patient can die from multisystem failure, often referred to as **MODS** (multiple organ dysfunction syndrome). The mortality rates in these cases increase as the number of involved organ systems increases and can approach 100% if MODS continues for more than four days, depending on the patient.

Some signs/symptoms that can be related to sepsis/sepsis syndrome include fever, chills, tachypnea, tachycardia, skin lesions, diffused redness over areas of the skin (erythema), widespread erythema (erythroderma), hypoxemia, and changes in mental status. Both Ray and Maria are at increased risk for sepsis due to their chronic conditions.

septicemia *(SEP teh SEE me uh)* (also called **sepsis** or **blood poisoning**) Infection by pathogenic organisms in the blood.

MODS Multiple organ dysfunction syndrome.

Respiratory System

Think about a time you went swimming and stayed a little too long underwater, and you will remember how important our respiratory system is! We all know the old concept of being able to live weeks without food and days without water, but think about how long you would last without oxygen. Without conscious effort, your lungs move approximately 12,000 quarts of air a day! Our respiratory system, much like the ventilation system in an office building, not only supplies us with fresh oxygen, but performs several other important functions as well. Our lungs eliminate the carbon dioxide created as a result of cellular metabolism. The respiratory system filters, warms, and moistens air as it is inhaled. The mucous lining of the airway helps trap foreign particles and germs. This system also helps to maintain the proper acid–base balance of the blood and aids in the elimination of ingested alcohol. The main parts of the respiratory system are the pharynx, larynx, trachea, bronchial tubes, and lungs (see FIGURE 5-13 ▲).

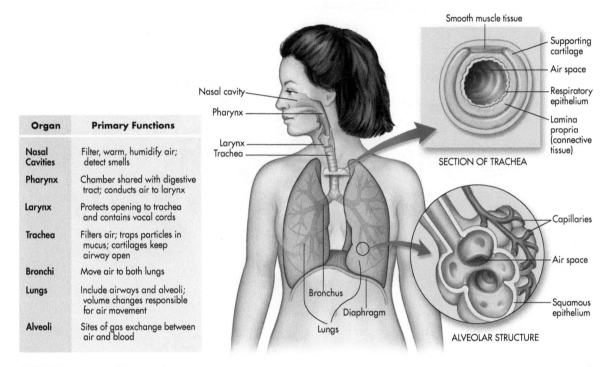

Organ	Primary Functions
Nasal Cavities	Filter, warm, humidify air; detect smells
Pharynx	Chamber shared with digestive tract; conducts air to larynx
Larynx	Protects opening to trachea and contains vocal cords
Trachea	Filters air; traps particles in mucus; cartilages keep airway open
Bronchi	Move air to both lungs
Lungs	Include airways and alveoli; volume changes responsible for air movement
Alveoli	Sites of gas exchange between air and blood

FIGURE 5-13 ▲ The respiratory system.

Lymphatic and Immune System

Much like the storm drain system of our city, this very important—but often forgotten—system is responsible for helping to maintain proper fluid balance in our body and to protect it from infection. Excess fluid that may collect in places it shouldn't in the body is brought back into the lymphatic system, cleaned and processed, and then recirculated. Special structures called **lymph nodes** act as filters to capture unwanted infective agents. Lymph vessels and ducts, lymph nodes, the thymus gland, tonsils, and the spleen are the major parts of the immune system. In addition, the immune portion of the lymphatic system produces specialized infection-fighting white blood cells called **lymphocytes.** The immune system is the police force of the human body, patrolling for harmful invaders (see FIGURE 5-14 ▲).

lymph nodes Small, encapsulated pieces of lymphoid tissue located along the lymphatic vessels. Lymph nodes filter and destroy invading microorganisms and cancerous cells present in the lymph.

lymphocytes *(LIM foh SIGHTS)* Specialized, infection-fighting white blood cells produced by the lymphatic system.

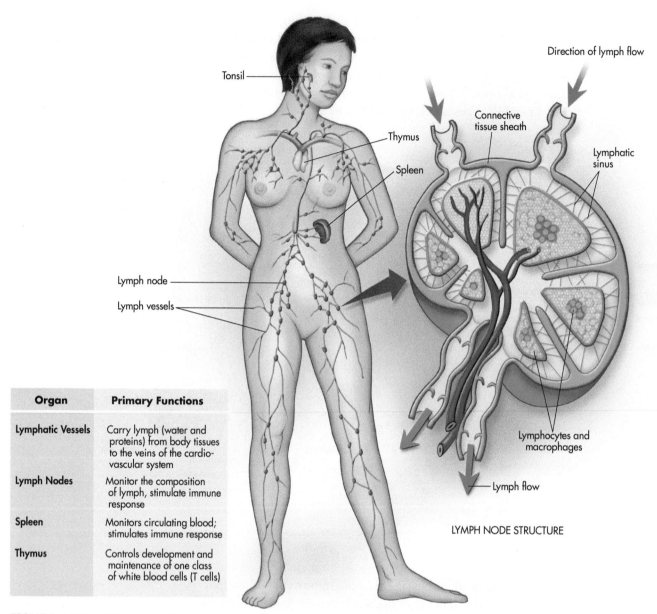

Tonsil

Thymus

Spleen

Direction of lymph flow

Connective
tissue sheath

Lymphatic
sinus

Lymph node

Lymph vessels

Lymphocytes and
macrophages

Lymph flow

LYMPH NODE STRUCTURE

Organ	Primary Functions
Lymphatic Vessels	Carry lymph (water and proteins) from body tissues to the veins of the cardio-vascular system
Lymph Nodes	Monitor the composition of lymph, stimulate immune response
Spleen	Monitors circulating blood; stimulates immune response
Thymus	Controls development and maintenance of one class of white blood cells (T cells)

FIGURE 5-14 ▲ The lymphatic system.

digestive system The alimentary canal (oral cavity, pharynx, esophagus, stomach, small and large intestines) and the accessory organs (teeth, tongue, salivary glands, liver, and pancreas).

Gastrointestinal (Digestive) System

The **digestive system** (often called the GI system, short for *gastrointestinal*) breaks down raw materials (food), both mechanically and chemically, into usable substances. Please see **FIGURE 5-15** ▲. Once these usable substances are created, this system absorbs them for transportation to the cells of the body. Materials that aren't used, as well as cellular waste, are transported out of the body by this system, much like the waste disposal and sewage system of our city. The main parts of the digestive system are the mouth, pharynx, esophagus, stomach, intestines, accessory organs, and anal canal.

Organ	Primary Functions
Salivary Glands	Provide lubrication; produce buffers and the enzymes that begin digestion
Pharynx	Passageway connected to esophagus
Esophagus	Delivers food to stomach
Stomach	Secretes acids and enzymes
Small Intestine	Secretes digestive enzymes; absorbs nutrients
Liver	Secretes bile; regulates blood chemistry
Gallbladder	Stores bile for release into small intestine
Pancreas	Secretes digestive enzymes and buffers; contains endocrine cells
Large Intestine	Removes water from fecal material; stores waste

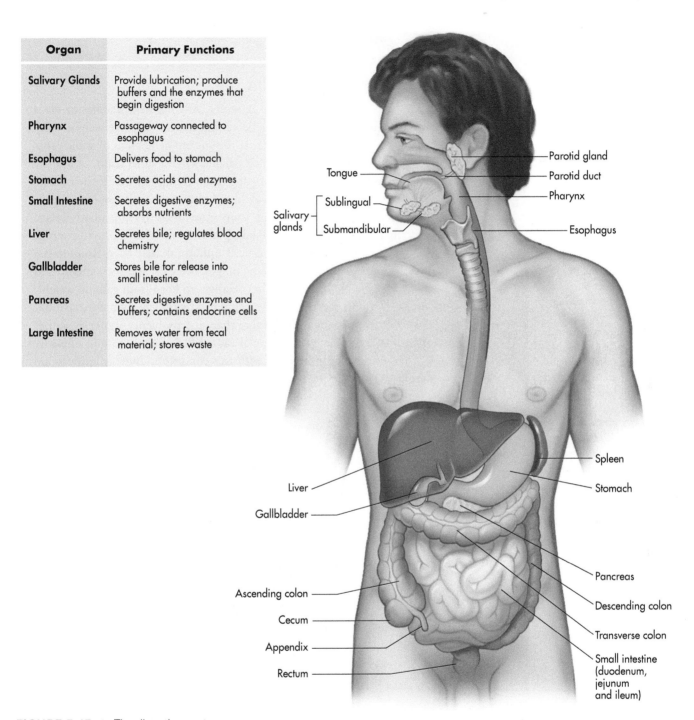

FIGURE 5-15 ▲ The digestive system.

Pathology Connection

BODY IMAGE: OBESITY AND ANOREXIA

It seems, at times, that we are a country of extremes. Anyone who watches or reads the news knows that the U.S. population is becoming increasingly overweight every year. The situation is so pervasive and severe that the current generation of adolescents potentially will have a shorter life span than their parents. On the other hand, we also are facing an epidemic of individuals trying to be super thin, trying to emulate their image of what a supermodel or movie star should look like. Although there is absolutely nothing wrong with proper dieting and exercising, some individuals develop a body image that is unrealistic. These individuals starve themselves or vomit after eating to attempt to keep from forming body fat, which they usually only think they have. **Bulimia** is a condition in which an individual goes on eating binges, overeats, and then attempts to get rid of the food by either vomiting or using laxatives to keep from gaining weight. **Anorexia nervosa** is the term used for the condition in which there is a progressive and severe weight loss even as the patient denies that there is a problem. Anorexics, rather than purging what they eat, often avoid eating or eat too little food to sustain a healthy weight. FIGURE 5-16 ▲ shows an individual with this condition. These conditions are both a mental and a physical health issue.

bulimia *(boo LIM ee uh)* An eating disorder marked by recurring episodes of binge eating, self-induced vomiting and diarrhea, and other attempts to reduce weight such as excessive exercising, dieting, and/or fasting; individual exhibits excessive and unrealistic concerns about body image.

anorexia nervosa *(an oh REK see ah ner VOH sah)* An eating disorder exhibiting an unrealistic body image, fear of weight gain, weight loss, and emaciation.

FIGURE 5-16 ▲ This is an example of an individual with a body image problem in which her self-perception is of being overweight. (Source: Mike Heywood/Shutterstock.com.)

Urinary System

While the digestive system plays a large role in the elimination of certain digested waste, the **urinary system** plays an important role in the elimination of waste products such as forms of nitrogen. In addition, electrolytes, drugs and other toxins, and excessive water are removed. This system is crucial for maintaining the proper balance of water you have in your body and regulating your blood pressure. The urinary system helps regulate the number of red blood cells and the acid–base and electrolyte balance of blood. The main parts of the urinary system are the kidneys, ureters, urinary bladder, and urethra (see FIGURE 5-17 ▲).

urinary system The organ system that includes the kidneys, ureters, bladder, and urethra. The kidneys form urine from blood plasma by filtration, reabsorption, and secretion. The formation of urine includes the excretion of waste products, but the kidneys also regulate the water and mineral content and the acid-base balance of the blood and all other body fluids. The other organs of the system are concerned with the elimination of urine after it has been formed.

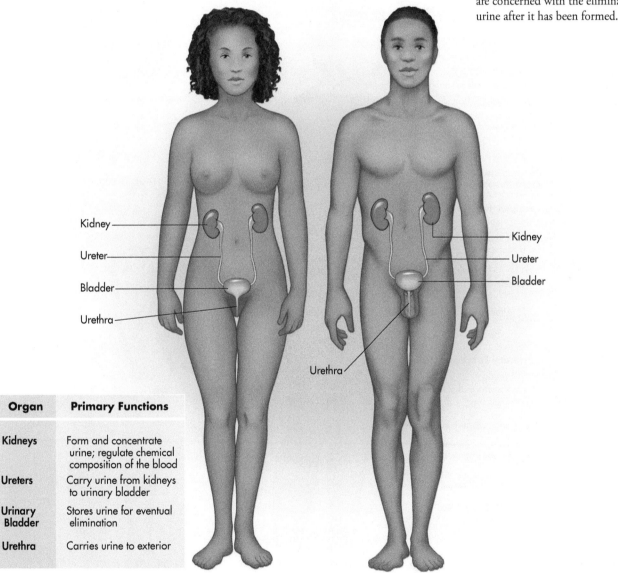

Organ	Primary Functions
Kidneys	Form and concentrate urine; regulate chemical composition of the blood
Ureters	Carry urine from kidneys to urinary bladder
Urinary Bladder	Stores urine for eventual elimination
Urethra	Carries urine to exterior

FIGURE 5-17 ▲ The male and female urinary systems.

Reproductive System

We build new cities or new buildings to accommodate growing needs or to replace wornout structures. The reproductive system does the same thing. Quite simply, without this system, we would not exist. The reproductive system is often combined with the urinary system to create the **genitourinary,** or **GU,** system. Humans require a male and female to produce offspring. The male is needed to provide sperm that contains certain genetic traits of that individual, whereas the female provides an egg with her traits and a place for the fertilized egg to grow to maturity. The main female parts of this system are the ovaries, eggs, fallopian tubes, uterus, and vagina. For men, the main parts are the testes, sperm, and penis (see FIGURE 5-18 ▲).

genitourinary system *(JEN ih toe YOUR ih nair ee)* Combination of two closely related body systems: the female and male genitalia and the urinary system. Also known as the urogenital system.

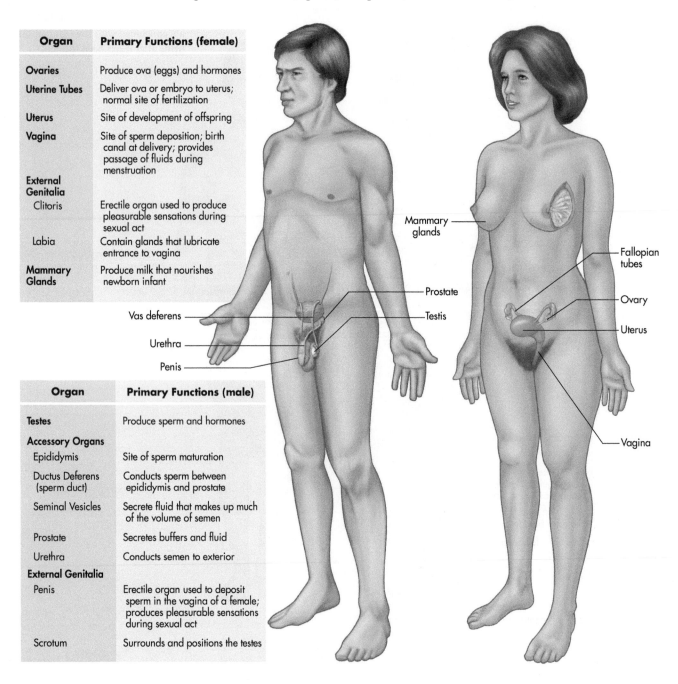

Organ	Primary Functions (female)
Ovaries	Produce ova (eggs) and hormones
Uterine Tubes	Deliver ova or embryo to uterus; normal site of fertilization
Uterus	Site of development of offspring
Vagina	Site of sperm deposition; birth canal at delivery; provides passage of fluids during menstruation
External Genitalia	
Clitoris	Erectile organ used to produce pleasurable sensations during sexual act
Labia	Contain glands that lubricate entrance to vagina
Mammary Glands	Produce milk that nourishes newborn infant

Organ	Primary Functions (male)
Testes	Produce sperm and hormones
Accessory Organs	
Epididymis	Site of sperm maturation
Ductus Deferens (sperm duct)	Conducts sperm between epididymis and prostate
Seminal Vesicles	Secrete fluid that makes up much of the volume of semen
Prostate	Secretes buffers and fluid
Urethra	Conducts semen to exterior
External Genitalia	
Penis	Erectile organ used to deposit sperm in the vagina of a female; produces pleasurable sensations during sexual act
Scrotum	Surrounds and positions the testes

FIGURE 5-18 ▲ The male and female reproductive systems.

TEST YOUR KNOWLEDGE 5-2

List the correct system for the following activities:

1. Exchanges carbon dioxide for oxygen

    _____

2. Eliminates nitrogen, drugs, and excessive water from the body

    _____

3. Main storage for calcium

    _____

4. Maintains body temperature and provides much of the sensory information from the external world

    _____

5. Protects the body from invading pathogens

    _____

6. Moves blood through the body

    _____

7. Converts food to energy

    _____

8. With the help of the sun, produces vitamin D

    _____

9. Maintains water homeostasis in the cardiovascular system which allows regulation of blood pressure

    _____

10. Collects fluid from tissues, cleans the fluid and returns it to the cardiovascular system.

    _____

11. These two systems are involved with removal of excess fluid in the body.

    _____

SUMMARY

Snapshots from the Journey

■ Cells are the basic building blocks of the body.

■ Tissues are collections of similar cells that act together to perform a function. The four main types of tissues are epithelial, connective, muscle, and nervous.

■ Membranes are sheetlike structures found throughout the body; they perform specific functions.

■ The four major membrane types are cutaneous, serous, mucous, and synovial.

■ Tissues that combine to perform a specific function or functions are called an organ.

■ Organs that work together, often with the help of accessory structures, to perform specific activities, are called a system.

■ There are 11 major body systems: skeletal, muscular, integumentary, nervous, endocrine, cardiovascular, respiratory, lymphatic/immune, gastrointestinal, urinary, and reproductive. Even though these are distinct systems, they are interrelated and their relationships are highlighted in upcoming chapters.

■ A disease process can affect more than one body system at a time, often making it more difficult to treat. Septicemia is one such example. If left unchecked, it can lead to multiple organ dysfunction syndrome (MODS).

CASE STUDY

A 73-year-old male presents to an emergency department of a local hospital. Initial assessment reveals the following:

- Afebrile
- Mild tachypnea with mild shortness of breath
- Acrocyanosis
- Mild tachycardia
- History of smoking
- History of diabetes
- Moderately overweight

Based on the information given, have members of the group identify which system or systems of the body they would want to further investigate to determine why this individual has come to the emergency department. You have had some medical terminology already but may need additional help from the text, medical dictionary, or Website. Compile a list of specialists or health care professionals to whom you might refer this patient and explain why.

RAY'S STORY

Ray is unable to move on his own due to his spinal cord injury. This condition presents many problems for the health care professional. Most tissues can repair themselves over time, but what about nervous tissue? Can nerve cells regenerate? Take the time to research new theories and ways to promote the repair and growth of nerve cells.

a. List the results of your research.

_____

_____

_____

_____

_____

_____

_____

_____

b. What are some other areas that relate to tissue care that we must consider for an individual who cannot move unassisted and will be bedridden for most of his or her life?

_____

_____

_____

_____

_____

_____

_____

_____

REVIEW QUESTIONS

Multiple Choice

1. Blood can be classified as which type of tissue?
   a. connective
   b. cardiac
   c. nerve
   d. muscle

2. This membrane lines body cavities and covers the organs found in those cavities:
   a. cutaneous
   b. serous
   c. mucous
   d. mucus

3. This muscle type has interlocking cells for more efficient contraction:
   a. skeletal
   b. neuroglial
   c. cardiac
   d. smooth

4. The acid–base balance found in your body is mainly controlled by the following system:
   a. skeletal
   b. urinary
   c. endocrine
   d. none of the above

5. Which of the following organs belong to the digestive system?
   I. urethra
   II. gallbladder
   III. spleen
   IV. small intestine
   a. I, II
   b. I, III, IV
   c. III, IV
   d. II, IV

6. This term refers to the drop in systemic blood pressure as a result of decreased blood perfusion to the organs due to widespread infection:
   a. MODS
   b. sepsis syndrome
   c. Downs BP
   d. septic shock

Fill in the Blank

1. The two systems that coordinate all the body's functions are the _____ and _____ systems.

2. The _____ system is the "motion" system.

3. Cartilage is a specific type of _____ tissue.

4. The layer of serous membrane that covers specific organs is called the _____ layer.

5. The largest organ of our body is _____.

6. MODS stands for _____.

REVIEW QUESTIONS

Short Answer

1. List in order from simplest to most complex the following: organs, cells, systems, tissues.

_____

_____

_____

_____

2. What is the purpose of dendrites?

_____

_____

_____

_____

3. What is the purpose of synovial fluid?

_____

_____

_____

_____

4. Contrast the three types of muscle tissues and identify where they are found.

_____

_____

_____

_____

Suggested Activities

1. Choose one system to research. Identify all the tissue types and membranes found within that system and describe the individual tissue and membrane functions.

2. Create five to ten multiple-choice quiz questions related to this chapter and have a quiz show contest.

3. Working with a partner, choose a body system. Research the technological advances and limitations in the treatment of disorders of that system. Write a report or create a presentation and present your findings to the class.

CAREER CONNECTIONS

Now that you have read this chapter, here is a list of related professions you may be interested in investigating for a future career:

- Histotechnology

Research each profession and report on the following:

1. Profession description to include job responsibilities
2. Educational requirements
3. Job opportunities
4. Opportunities outside of the hospital setting
5. Salary range
6. Licensure and continuing education requirements

ANATOMY, PHYSIOLOGY, AND DISEASE IN ACTION

For the following diseases, determine the system, organ, and etiology for the condition.

Disease	System	Organ	Etiology
Gout			
Keloids			
Guillain-Barré Syndrome			
Acromegaly			
Macular Degeneration			
Cystic Fibrosis			
Tinea barbae			
Glomerulonephritis			
Ricketts			
Ectopic pregnancy			
Beta-thalassemia			
Goiter			
Lou Gehrig's Disease (Amyotrophic lateral sclerosis)			
Multiple sclerosis			
Celiac Disease			
SCID (Severe Combined Immunodeficiency Deficiency)			
Polio			

Work in groups to present your findings. Additional materials may be used to enhance your presentation.

The Skeletal System
The Framework

As we continue our journey, we may stop to visit friends or relatives and perhaps stay overnight. Their house will protect us from the elements and provide a safe place to sleep. Our hosts will offer us a good breakfast in the morning from the stored goods within. Although we cannot see the framework that holds up the house, without it everything would collapse. We can think of the human body as a house. The wood framework is the skeleton, composed of bones that provide shape and strength. That is why we are beginning the system chapters with the body's own framework, on which the muscles and skin are layered, much like a house's walls and siding. Mounted on the framework are hinges that allow doors to swing open and shut and windows that glide open or close. These are analogous to the joints and muscles attached to the skeleton that allow for body movement.

What's the first thing you think of when someone asks about the function of the skeleton? From our analogy, you would probably say, "to provide support and allow us to move." But the skeleton does so much more. As explained in this chapter, the bones that make up your skeleton also protect the soft body parts, produce blood cells, and act as a storage unit for minerals and fat—much like our hosts' home, which has stored goods within for that scrumptious breakfast! In this chapter, we will also discuss the makeup and importance of the 206 bones in the adult skeleton, as well as cartilage, ligaments, and joints. And now it's time to "bone up" on the skeletal system.

LEARNING OUTCOMES

At the end of your journey through this chapter, you will be able to:

- Describe the functions of the skeletal system
- Identify and describe the anatomy and physiology of bone
- Locate and describe the various bones within the body
- Differentiate between bone, cartilage, ligaments, and tendons
- Locate and describe the various joints and types of movement of the body
- Explain common diseases and disorders of the skeletal system

Pronunciation Guide

Correct pronunciation is important in any journey so that you and others are completely understood. Here is a "see and say" Pronunciation Guide for the more difficult terms to pronounce in this chapter. Please note that pronunciations given are referenced to medical dictionaries, and regional variations may exist.

appendicular skeleton (app en DIK yoo lahr)
arthritis (are THRYE tiss)
arthroscopy (are THROSS koh pee)
articulation (are TICK you LAY shun)
axial (AK see al)
bursa (BURR suh)
cancellous bone (CAN cell us)
cartilage (KAR tih lij)
chondrosarcoma (KON droh sar KOE ma)
diaphysis (dye AFF ih sis)
endosteum (in DAWS tee um)
epiphyseal (eh PIFF ih SEE al)
epiphysis (eh PIFF ih sis)
fontanel (FAWN teh NELL)
Haversian canal (hah VER zhin)

hemopoiesis (HEE moh poy EE sus)
medullary cavity (MED you lair ee)
osseous tissue (OSS see us)
ossification (OSS ih fih KAY shun)
osteoarthritis (OSS tee oh are THRYE tiss)
osteocytes (OSS tee oh sites)
osteomalacia (OSS tee oh mah LAY she ah)
osteons (OSS tee onz)
osteoporosis (OSS tee oh poor OH sis)
periosteum (pair ee OSS tee um)
sternum (STUR num)
synovial (sin OH vee al)
trabeculae (tra BECK you lay)
vertebrae (VER teh bray)

SYSTEM OVERVIEW: MORE THAN THE "BARE BONES" ABOUT BONES

The skeleton has many more uses than just scaring people on Halloween. It is a wondrous structure that serves more functions than simply providing a framework for the human body. It also produces blood cells, provides protection for organs, helps us to breathe, acts as a warehouse for mineral storage, and, along with the muscular system, allows for movement.

General Bone Classification

The primary components of the skeleton are bones. Although they may seem lifeless and are composed of some nonliving minerals such as calcium and phosphorus, they are very much alive and are constantly building and repairing themselves. This is somewhat ironic because the word *skeleton* is derived from the Greek word meaning "dried-up body."

We can classify bone types according to their shape:

* Long bones
* Short bones
* Flat bones
* Irregular bones

Long bones are longer than they are wide and are found in your arms and legs. The femur, for example, is the longest and strongest bone in the body. *Short bones* are fairly equal in width and length, similar to a cube, and are mostly found in your wrists and ankles. *Flat bones* are thinner bones that can be either flat or curved and are platelike in nature. Examples of flat bones are the skull, ribs, and breastbone (**sternum**). *Irregular bones* are like the parts of a jigsaw puzzle. These are the odd-shaped bones needed to

sternum *(STER num)* Vertical bone of the anterior thorax to which the clavicle and ribs are attached. Also known as the breastbone.

connect to other bones. Some examples of irregular bones are the hip bones and the **vertebrae** that make up your spine. See FIGURE 6-1 ▲ for a view of the various bone shapes.

Basic Bone Anatomy

Let's look at the overall construction of a bone by examining a long bone in FIGURE 6-2 ▲. Bone is covered with **periosteum,** which is a tough and fibrous connective tissue. This cover contains blood vessels, which transport blood and nutrients into the bone to nurture the bone cells. It also contains lymph vessels and nerves. In addition, the periosteum provides anchor points for ligaments and tendons, which we discuss later. Note in Figure 6-2 that both ends of the long bone are larger than the middle portion. Each bone end is called an **epiphysis.** The region between or "running through" the two ends is called the **diaphysis,** or shaft.

The hollow region in the diaphysis is called the **medullary cavity** (sometimes called the **medullary canal**) and acts as a storage area for bone marrow, like a well-stocked kitchen cabinet. There are two kinds of bone marrow: red and yellow. **Red marrow** makes blood cells. **Yellow marrow** has a high fat content. In emergencies—for instance, in the event of massive blood loss—when you need more red blood cells, some of the yellow marrow can convert to red bone marrow to help in the production of red blood cells.

vertebrae *(VER teh bray)* One of 33 irregularly shaped bony segments of the spinal column.

periosteum *(per ee OSS tee um)* Thick, fibrous membrane that goes around and covers the outside of a bone.

epiphysis *(eh PIFF ih sis)* The widened ends of a long bone. Each end contains the epiphysial plate where bone growth takes place.

diaphysis *(dye AFF ih sis)* The straight shaft of a long bone.

medullary cavity Hollow region in the bone that stores bone marrow.

medullary canal See medullary cavity.

red marrow A form of bone marrow that creates blood cells.

yellow marrow A form of marrow that has high fat content and can produce blood cells.

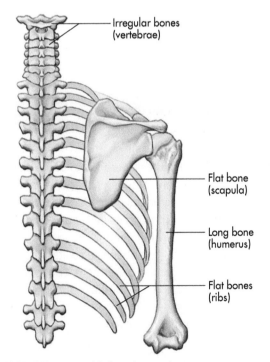

Irregular bones (vertebrae)

Flat bone (scapula)

Long bone (humerus)

Flat bones (ribs)

Short bones (tarsals)

FIGURE 6-1 ▲ Various bone shapes.

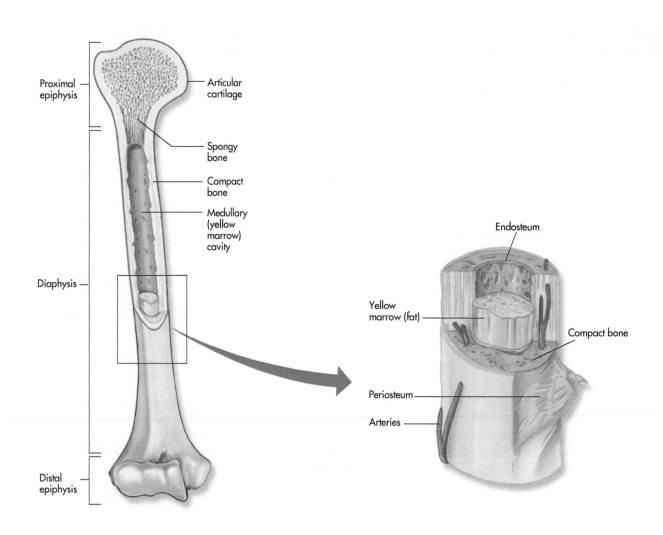

FIGURE 6-2 ▲ Basic bone anatomy.

hemopoiesis
(HEE moh poy EE sus)
Formation of blood
cells.

Amazing **Body Facts**

Red Bone Marrow and Red Blood Cells

The areas of bone with red bone marrow, which produces red blood cells, are found in the skull, clavicles (collar bones), vertebrae of the spinal column, sternum (breastbone), ribs, pelvis, and the spongy bone that makes up the epiphysis of the long bones. The production of red blood cells, known as **hemopoiesis,** is truly an incredible process. Because red blood cells last only about 120 days, red blood cell production is a constant job in order to maintain the trillions (give or take a few) of red blood cells contained in the human body. As a result, it has been calculated that approximately 3 million new red blood cells are created every second. Furthermore, your body can step up production to 10 times that rate in cases of severe blood loss. If the red marrow can't maintain the needed production, some of the yellow marrow can be converted to red marrow to assist. White blood cells, which fight infection, are also made in the marrow, but can be made in both red and yellow marrow.

Bone Tissue

There are two types of bone tissue: compact and spongy. **Compact bone** is a dense, hard tissue that normally forms the shafts of long bones and the outer layer of other bones. Microscopic examination reveals that the material of compact bone is tightly packed, making for a dense and strong structure. This material forms microscopic cylindrical-shaped units called **osteons,** or **Haversian systems.** Each unit has mature bone cells (**osteocytes**) forming concentric circles around blood vessels. The area around the osteocytes is filled with protein fibers, calcium, and other minerals. The osteons run parallel to each other, whereas blood vessels laterally connect with them to ensure that there is sufficient oxygen and nutrients for the bone cells.

Spongy (or **cancellous**) bone is different than compact bone. Instead of Haversian systems, spongy bone tissue has bars and plates called **trabeculae.** Irregular holes between the trabeculae give the bone a spongy appearance (porous). Spongy bone is lined with **endosteum,** a tissue similar to periosteum. Spongy bone serves two purposes: it helps make the bones lighter in weight, and it provides a space for red bone marrow, which produces red blood cells (see FIGURE 6-3 ▲).

compact bone Hard or dense bone forming the superficial layer of all bones.

osteons *(OSS tee ons)* Microscopic unit of compact bone.

Haversian systems See osteons.

osteocytes *(OSS tee oh sites)* Mature bone cells surrounded by bone matrix. They maintain the matrix in mature bone.

spongy bone A form of bone that makes bones lighter and provides a space for red bone marrow.

cancellous bone *(CAN cell us)* Spongy bone found in the epiphyses of long bones. Its spaces are filled with red bone marrow that makes blood cells.

trabecula *(tra BECK you la)* A thin bone strip used as a support structure in spongy bone.

endosteum *(in DOS tee uhm)* Lining of the spongy bone similar to periosteum.

FIGURE 6-3 ▲ Comparison of compact and spongy bone.

Surface Structures of Bones

Bone is not perfectly smooth but includes a variety of projections, bumps, and depressions. Generally, projecting structures act as points of attachment for muscles, ligaments, or tendons, whereas grooves and depressions act as pathways for nerves and blood vessels. Both projecting structures and depressions can work together as joining or articulation points to form joints, such as the ball-and-socket joint in the hip. TABLE 6-1 ■ lists many of these bone features.

TABLE 6-1 ■ BONE FEATURES

BONE SURFACE STRUCTURES	DESCRIPTIONS
Projecting Structures and Processes	
Condyle	A large, rounded knob, usually articulating with another bone
Crest	A narrow ridge
Epicondyle	An enlargement near or superior to a condyle
Facet	A small, flattened area
Head	An articulating end of a bone that is rounded and enlarged
Process	A prominent projection
Spine	A sharp projection
Trochanter	Located only on the femur; a larger version of a tubercle
Tubercle	A small, knoblike projection
Depressions and Openings	
Foramen	A passageway through a bone for blood vessels, nerves, and ligaments; a hole
Fossa	Either a groove or shallow depression
Meatus	A tube or tunnel-like passageway through bone
Sinus	A hollow area

Bone Growth and Repair

Ossification, or **osteogenesis**, is the formation of bone in the body. Bones grow *longitudinally* in order to lengthen (which makes you taller), and they grow *horizontally* (wider and thicker) so they can more efficiently support body weight and any other weight we support when we work or play. There are four types of cells involved in the formation and growth of bone:

- Osteoprogenitor cells
- Osteoblasts
- Osteocytes
- Osteoclasts

Osteoprogenitor cells are nonspecialized cells found in the periosteum, endosteum, and central canal of compact bones. Nonspecialized cells (bone stem cells) can turn into other types of cells as needed. **Osteoblasts** are the cells that actually form bones. They arise from the nonspecialized osteoprogenitor cells and are the bone cells that secrete a matrix of calcium and other minerals, such as phosphorus, that give bone its typical characteristics. **Osteocytes** are mature bone cells that were originally osteoblasts. In other words, osteoblasts surround themselves with a matrix of calcium that helps them become mature osteocytes. Bone is built up or formed by osteoprogenitor cells becoming osteoblasts, which in turn surround themselves with a mineral matrix to become fully developed osteocytes or bone cells.

Not only does the body constantly build new bone, but it also constantly tears down old bone. Deconstruction is the job of the **osteoclasts**. It is believed that osteoclasts originate from a type of white blood cell called a **monocyte** that is found in red bone marrow. As we have already learned, the bones of the body store both calcium and phosphorus in the osteoblasts. However, if the body suddenly needs more of these minerals for other functions, the osteoclasts will return the stored minerals back to the bloodstream. The osteoclasts' two jobs are to tear down bone material and help move calcium and phosphate into the blood. You can think of osteoblasts and osteoclasts as employees of a house remodeling company: the osteo**b**lasts ("b" as in builder) are masons laying down brickwork to make new exterior walls, and the osteo**c**lasts ("c" as in clearing away) are tearing out the inside to remodel. As will be explained shortly, the job the osteoclasts do is very important for bone growth and repair.

Bone development and growth begins in the womb through intramembranous and endochondral ossification. The process starts at 8 weeks after conception, when bone begins to replace cartilage. **Intramembranous ossification** occurs when bone develops between two sheets composed of fibrous connective tissue, such as in the development of your skull. Cells from connective tissue turn into osteoblasts and form a matrix similar to the trabeculae of spongy bone, whereas other osteoblasts create compact bone over the surface of the spongy bone. As discussed previously, once the matrix surrounds the osteoblasts, they become osteocytes. This is how the bones of the skull develop.

---

ossification *(AH siff ih KAY shun)* Process by which cartilaginous tissue is changed into bone from infancy through puberty. Also known as osteogenesis.

osteogenesis See ossification.

osteoprogenitor *(OSS tee oh proh JEN ih ter)* Nonspecialized cells that can become specialized (differentiate) when needed.

osteoblasts *(OSS tee oh blasts)* Osteocytes that form new bone.

osteocytes *(OSS tee oh sites)* Mature bone cells surrounded by bone matrix. They maintain the matrix in mature bone.

osteoclasts *(OSS tee oh klasts)* Osteocytes that break down old or damaged areas of bone.

monocytes Mononuclear white blood cells commonly found in high numbers in chronic infections.

intramembranous ossification *(os uh fih KAY shun)* Bone development between two sheets composed of fibrous connective tissue such as found in the skull.

Aging and Bone Building

Even in adults, bone continues to be broken down and rebuilt. In fact, about 10% of the body's bone is torn down and rebuilt each year! Your bones continue to increase in mass well into your 20s. The osteoclasts break down and remove worn-out bone cells and deposit calcium into the blood. They last for approximately three weeks. Osteoblasts then pull the calcium out of the blood, surround themselves with that mineralized matrix we talked about, and mature into osteocytes. Because of this continual breakdown of old and creation of new bone, adults actually need more calcium in their diets than children do! The process of breaking down and rebuilding bone continues well into a person's 40s, so there normally is no net gain or loss of bone mass.

This continuing process allows your body to sculpt bone into shapes that accommodate the body's activity. For example, exercise, such as running or weight lifting, causes calcium to stay in the bone, making it thicker, denser, and stronger than those of a sedentary person (couch potato) or an individual who experiences extended weightlessness, such as an astronaut. Continuous or repeated actions or postures tend to cause bone to be resculpted. For example, due to constant squatting, a certain pattern of bumps forms on the bones of the hips, shins, and knees. As a result of this pattern, it was determined that Neanderthal man squatted rather than sat.

endochondral ossification *(IN doh KON druhl)* Within a cartilage.

primary ossification center *(oss ih fih KAY shun)* A region where osteoblasts congregate to create spongy bone.

epiphyseal plate *(eh piff ih SEE al)* The growth plate

growth plate See epiphyseal plate.

The majority of your skeletal bones are created through **endochondral ossification**, in which shaped cartilage is replaced by bone, as shown in FIGURE 6-4 ▲. In this situation, which begins several months before birth, periosteum surrounds the diaphysis of the cartilage "bone" as the cartilage itself begins to break down. Osteoblasts come into this region and create spongy bone in an area that is then called the **primary ossification center**. Meanwhile, other osteoblasts begin to form compact bone under the periosteum. Here is where the osteoclasts come into play. Their job is to break down the spongy bone of the diaphysis to create the medullary cavity. After birth, the epiphyses on your long bones continue to grow. However, around the time of birth, secondary ossification of this area begins, with spongy bone forming and not breaking down. A thin band of cartilage forms an **epiphyseal plate** (often called the **growth plate**) between the primary and secondary ossification centers. This is the growth zone of your bones. The plate is important because, as long as it exists, the length and width of the bone will increase. As explained in Chapter 10, "The Endocrine System," hormones control the growth of bones. Eventually the plates become ossified, thereby stopping bone growth, usually at the end of puberty.

Initial foundation

Beginning of compact bone formation

Blood vessel development

Developing periosteum

Primary ossification region

1 2 3

FIGURE 6-4 ▲ Endochondral ossification of long bone.

Spongy bone

Secondary ossification region

Compact bone

Medullary cavity

Marrow

Secondary ossification region

Epiphyseal growth plate

Spongy bone

4 5 6

Articular cartilage

Pathology Connection

OSTEOPOROSIS

As time goes on, bone mass also changes with age. In our 50s, the skeleton begins to change as the breakdown of bone becomes greater than the formation of new bone. At the cellular level, the osteoclasts are tearing down more bone than the osteoblasts are forming. As a result, we see total bone mass beginning to gradually decrease. See **FIGURE 6-5** ▲ for an illustration contrasting a normal bone to an osteoporotic bone. A microscopic examination of bones going through this process reveals increasing holes in the bone. This bone is lighter in weight and weaker than healthy bone, thereby making it more prone to breakage. Men appear to lose less than 25% of their bone mass, whereas women can experience a 35% loss on average. Hormonal changes during menopause increase the risk and rate of bone loss in many women. Thin Caucasian and Asian women are at the highest risk. For both men and women, the risk of developing thin bones may be influenced by hereditary. This condition of decreasing bone density, known as **osteoporosis,** is a serious problem. It is estimated that more than 4 million Americans suffer with this disease, and 6 million related doctor visits are made each year.

    Is there any way to stop or at least slow down the loss of bone mass? The early intervention of preventative practices is crucial for all people. Simple dietary changes such as adding more calcium, fluoride, and vitamin D may help in maintaining bone density, as will the elimination of smoking and decrease of caffeine consumption. Smoking and caffeine are believed to aid in the depletion of calcium. Research is showing that exercise, especially weight-bearing and impact forms, improve bone density. This helps people of all ages, even those in their 80s and 90s. The use of medications that increase bone mass, such as alendronate, may also be considered. For some postmenopausal women, hormone replacement therapy (HRT) may be appropriate, but the use of HRT is controversial.

osteoporosis *(OSS tee oh por OH sis)* Condition of increased bone porosity that weakens the bones, usually seen in the elderly.

Osteoporosis

FIGURE 6-5 ▲ A normal bone compared to an osteoporotic bone. (Source: Alila Sao Mai/Shutterstock.com.)

Healthy bone   Osteoporosis

TEST YOUR KNOWLEDGE 6-1

Complete the following:

1. Label the diagram:
   a. diaphysis
   b. proximal and distal epiphysis
   c. periosteum
   d. spongy bone
   e. compact bone
   f. medullary cavity
   g. epiphyseal plate

2. Where are the locations and what is the purpose of red bone marrow?

   _____

   _____

   _____

3. Discuss three functions of bone in your body.

   _____

   _____

   _____

Choose the best answer:

4. Mature bone cells in compact bone are called:
   a. marrowcytes
   b. osteocytes
   c. riflecytes
   d. monocytes

5. The end of a long bone is called the:
   a. epiphysis
   b. periosteum
   c. diaphysis
   d. knob

Cartilage

Cartilage is a special form of dense connective tissue that can withstand a fair amount of flexing, tension, and pressure. Cartilage plays many roles throughout the body. The flexible parts of your nose and ears are cartilage. (Imagine how many people would have broken off ears and noses if it weren't for cartilage!) When you were born, two areas in the middle of your skull were made of membranes somewhat similar to cartilage. These "soft spots," called **fontanels,** slowly became bone during your first 2 years of life.

Cartilage also makes a flexible connection between bones. For example, the cartilage between the breastbone and ribs allows your chest to flex and give so you don't break your ribs when you run into things or collide with another player during a football game. Something as simple as taking a deep breath could become a major struggle if it weren't for this flexibility.

This amazing tissue also acts as a cushion between the bones. As you can see in FIGURE 6-6 ▲, **articular cartilage** is located on the ends of bones and acts as a shock

cartilage *(KAR tih lij)* Smooth, firm, but flexible connective tissue.

fontanels *(FAWN tah NELZ)* "Soft spots" found in newborn skulls.

articular cartilage Cartilage located on the ends of bones that acts as a shock absorber.

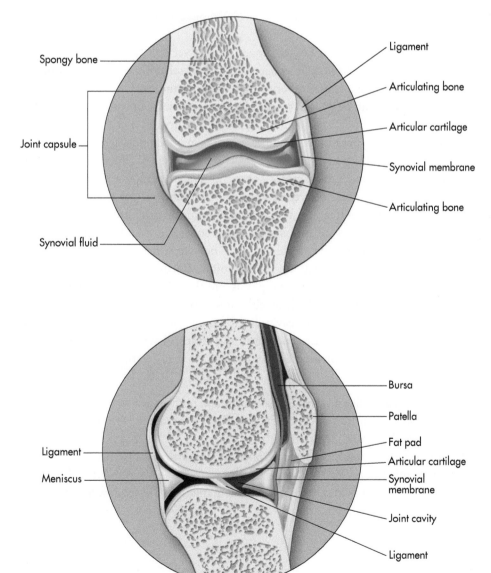

FIGURE 6-6 ▲ Articular cartilage and synovial joint.

Amazing Body Facts

The Flexibility of Cartilage

Did you know that before you were born your skeleton was entirely made of cartilage but through development most of it became bone? Your ears and nose will always remain cartilage, and therefore are called permanent cartilage. In some cases, our ears and nose may get larger as we get older because permanent cartilage can continue to grow.

bursa *(BUR sah)* Fluid-filled sac that decreases friction where a tendon rubs against a bone near a synovial joint.

synovial fluids *(sin OH vee al)* Clear, lubricating fluid that is secreted by the synovial membrane.

arthritis *(ahr THRYE tiss)* Inflammation of the joints.

osteoarthritis *(OSS tee oh ahr THRYE tiss)* Chronic inflammatory disease of the joints, particularly the large weight-bearing joints of the knees and hips, although it often occurs in the joints that move repeatedly like the shoulders, neck, and hands.

joint Area where two bones come together.

articulation *(AHR tick you LAY shun)* A joint where two bones come together and join or articulate.

ligament Fibrous band that holds two bones together.

tendons Cordlike, white band of nonelastic fibrous connective tissue that attaches a muscle to a bone.

fibrous joints *(FYE brus)* Joints located on your skull that allow for minimal flexing.

cartilaginous joint A joint with cartilage between the bones.

synovial joints *(sin OH vee al)* Joints, such as the knee, that have synovial fluid as a lubricant.

absorber, preventing the bone ends from grinding together as they move. Also at this location, a small sac, called the **bursa,** contains a lubricant called **synovial fluid.** Even with cartilage and synovial fluid protecting the area between bones, joints can wear out and become inflamed, resulting in a condition called **arthritis,** or **osteoarthritis.**

Joints and Ligaments

Without **joints,** the body could not move. Two or more bones joined together form a joint, or an **articulation**.

Freely moving joints have to be held together and yet still be moveable. This is accomplished through the use of another specialized connective tissue called a **ligament**. (Again, see Figure 6-6.) Ligaments are very tough, whitish bands that connect from bone to bone and can withstand fairly heavy stress. Do not confuse ligaments with **tendons**. Ligaments hold bone to bone, and tendons are cordlike structures that attach muscle to bone. There are several types of joints, and each works in a specific way.

Joints are classified either by function or structure. In terms of function, joints can be immobile, move a little, or move freely. For example, skull sutures are immobile, the pubic symphysis (line of fusion between two bones) between your pelvic bones moves a little, and your elbow moves freely. If we characterize joints by structure, we divide them based on the type of connective tissue that links the bones together. **Fibrous joints** are held together by short connective tissue strands. They are either immobile or slightly movable. The sutures in your skull are fibrous joints. **Cartilaginous joints** are held together by cartilage disks. The pubic symphysis and the joints between your ribs and sternum are cartilaginous joints, which are either immobile or slightly movable. Finally, **synovial joints** are joined by a joint cavity lined with a synovial membrane and filled with synovial fluid, which decreases friction in the joint. All synovial joints are freely moving. Synovial joints are constructed in various ways that determine how they can move:

- *Pivot joints* (which act like a turnstile) have a circular portion of one bone that rotates inside a ring-shaped portion of the other bone. Pivot joints are the type of joint found in your neck and forearm. They can only rotate.
- *Ball-and-socket joints* usually consist of a spherical bone articulating with a cup-shaped socket on the other bone. Ball-and-socket joints are found in your hips and shoulders and can perform all types of movement, including rotation. These allow for the greatest movement.

- *Hinge joints* are found in your knees and elbows. Typically, one bone is in the shape of a cylinder and the other a trough. They can either open or close.
- *Gliding joints* are the flat, or slightly curved, platelike bones found in your wrists and ankles. Gliding joints slide back and forth.
- *Saddle joints* have a bone shaped just like a saddle and another bone similar to a horse's back. This joint type is found in the base of your thumb. Saddle joints rock up and down and side to side.
- *Ellipsoidal joints* (also called *condyloid joints*) provide two axes of movement through the same bone, like the joint formed at the wrist with both the radius and ulna. The knuckles of your fingers are also ellipsoidal joints.

To better visualize these various joints, look at **FIGURE 6-7** ▲.

Amazing **Body Facts**

Wear and Tear and Disease

When considering chronic disorders of the skeletal system, most involve the joints and not the shafts of the bones. This is due to the wear and tear of contact areas over time. One major exception to this is osteoporosis, which affects actual bone integrity.

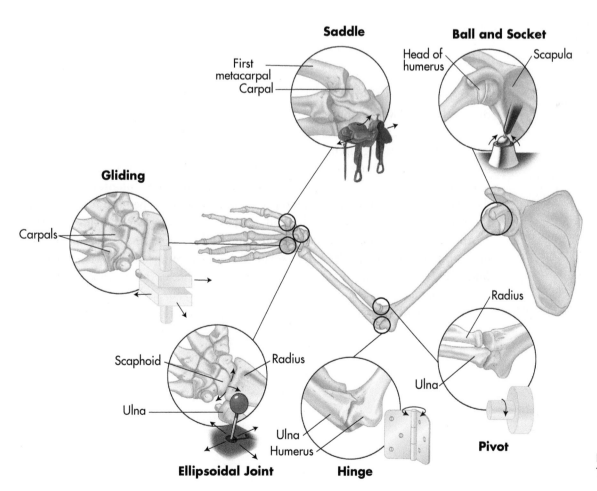

FIGURE 6-7 ▲
Types of joints.

TEST YOUR KNOWLEDGE 6-2

Choose the best answer:

1. A term that can be used to describe the formation of bone is:
   a. ossification
   b. periosteum
   c. bonafide
   d. osteoclasts

2. These cells actually form bones:
   a. osteoclasts
   b. osteons
   c. generator cells
   d. osteoblasts

3. Another name for the "growth plate" is:
   a. tectonic plate
   b. epiphyseal plate
   c. diaphysis plate
   d. periosteum plate

4. This special connective tissue composes your ears and nose:
   a. tendons
   b. ligaments
   c. cartilage
   d. cartridge

5. This lubricant helps to prevent wear between the joints:
   a. pleural fluid
   b. synovial fluid
   c. mucus
   d. petroleum jelly

6. These structures attach bone to bone:
   a. ligaments
   b. tendons
   c. cords
   d. articulations

---

flexion *(FLEK shun)* Bending of a joint to decrease the angle between two bones or body parts. Opposite of extension.

extension *(eks TEN shun)* Straightening a joint to increase the angle between two bones or body parts.

plantar flexion Movement of the foot away from the leg as a ballerina who dances on her toes.

dorsiflexion *(DOR seh FLEK shun)* Movement occurring when the foot is bent up toward the leg.

hyperextension The forced straightening of a joint beyond its normal limits.

abduction *(ahb DUK shun)* Moving a body part away from the midline of the body.

adduction *(ah DUCK shun)* Moving a body part toward the midline of the body.

Movement Classification

Because joints allow for various types of movement, these individualized movements can also be classified, as you can see in the examples in FIGURE 6-8 ▲. **Flexion** occurs when a joint is bent, decreasing the angle between the involved bones, as when the leg is bent at the knee. **Extension** is a result of straightening a joint so the angle between the involved bones increases, as occurs with a kicking motion. Ballerinas utilize **plantar flexion** when they dance on their toes. **Dorsiflexion** occurs when the foot is bent up toward the leg. If the joint is forced to straighten beyond its normal limits, **hyperextension** occurs.

Abduction and **adduction** can be confusing. A**b**duction means to move *away* from the body's midline (think, "**Be** gone!" as you move your arm up and away to swat a **b**ee). **Add**uction means to move *toward* the midline of the body. To remember **add**uction, think of your **add**ress, where packages and mail come *to* you. Then when you move your arm back toward yourself after swatting at a bee, you are **add**ucting your arm.

FIGURE 6-8 ▲ Classification of joint movements.

Inversion results when the sole of one foot is turned inward so it points to the other foot, whereas **eversion** is the opposite: the foot is turned outward, pointing away from the opposite foot. **Supination** occurs when the hand is turned to the point where the palm faces upward; **pronation** turns the palm downward. Although you may not have heard of **circumduction**, you have seen this combination of movements in the circular arm movement that a softball pitcher utilizes.

Protraction is the movement of a part forward. **Retraction** is the motion of drawing a part backward. Figure 6-8 shows the protraction and retraction of the jaw. The movements are analogous to a turtle sticking his head out (protracting) and drawing it back (retracting) into the shell.

Finally, **rotation** is when a bone "turns" on its axis. An example is when your head rotates (looking left and right) before you cross the street.

inversion The movement of the sole of a foot toward the other foot.

eversion Turning outward of the feet so the toes point away.

supination The turning of the hand so the palm faces upward.

pronation Turning of the hand so the palm faces downward.

circumduction The combination of movements to create a circular arm movement similar to a softball pitch.

protraction Movement of a body part forward.

retraction Drawing backward of a body part.

rotation Occurs when a bone turns on its axis.

Pathology Connection

COMMON JOINT DISORDERS

All good things must come to an end, and the same can be said about the health of your skeletal system. In general, as the body ages, the cartilage and bones deteriorate. Although this is a natural process that we will all encounter, we can slow the process down in many cases.

As the body ages, the chemical composition of cartilage changes. The bluish tint and flexibility of young skeletal cartilage changes to a more brittle, opaque yellow form. Calcification, or hardening, of cartilage leads to brittleness. Articular cartilage, once it becomes brittle, doesn't function as well as young, healthy cartilage. **Arthritis** is a general term used to describe an inflammatory process of a joint or joints. There are literally dozens of disorders that cause swollen, painful, and stiff joints that are classified as arthritis. The related tendons and ligaments also become less flexible, causing a decrease in the range of motion in joints. **Osteoarthritis** is a degenerative condition that is a result of simple "wearing out" of a joint from a sports injury, trauma, repetitive motion, obesity, or just the aging process. **Rheumatoid arthritis** is a chronic, systemic disease that is believed to be an autoimmune condition affecting the connective tissue of the body. This condition appears to affect mostly the small joints of the hands and feet, but it can also affect the elbows and knees. A third form of arthritis is **septic arthritis,** the result of the infective process of a pathogen that was introduced to a joint from a penetrating wound, or a blood-borne pathogen. For a list of the various treatments for these forms of arthritis, please go to the Quick Trip table at the end of the chapter.

Once considered a disease of royalty due to the belief that it was caused by excessive amounts of alcohol and rich foods, **gout** is a form of arthritis. Gout is a result of the body's decreased ability to control uric acid production or its excretion, thus causing high uric acid levels in the blood. Once the uric acid levels increase sufficiently, it crystallizes and is deposited in the connective tissue found throughout the body. If these crystals wind up in synovial fluid, sharp joint pain can occur. Primary gout may be an inherited disease due to a metabolic defect. Excessive ingestion of protein (as in meats) can lead to high uric acid levels. Secondary gout may be a result of chronic renal disease, drugs such as chlorothiazide (used to treat hypertension), lead poisoning, or leukemia. Although any joint may be affected, gout commonly affects the big toe! If not treated (sometimes by simply reducing protein intake), gout can lead to a chronic disability.

Although bursitis and tendonitis (tendinitis) are different disorders, they are similar due to their predisposing factors, symptoms, and treatment regimens. **Bursitis** is an inflammation of one or more bursae (the fluid-filled sacs that "oil" up your joints for friction-free movement). **Tendonitis** is an often-painful inflammation of the tendon itself or the tendon–muscle attachment. Even though bursitis can be caused by an infection of the bursae, both bursitis and tendonitis can be commonly caused by congenital defects, skeletal misalignment, repetitive movements, rheumatic (inflammatory) diseases, sports activities, and even our old friend, gout! Bursitis's resulting pain can present gradually or suddenly and often limits joint movement. Tendonitis commonly presents in the shoulder, producing joint pain during movement and also at night, when it can be severe enough to disturb sleep. The best "treatment" for both of these conditions is prevention through improving your strength and flexibility, warming up properly before exercise, and avoiding repeated stress and strain in sporting activities. Treatment for both includes rest of the affected joint(s), analgesics, and application of cold and moist heat. (Watch out for potential skin damage when using extreme temperatures.) The injection of corticosteroids into the affected joint may also be beneficial in reducing inflammation.

arthritis *(ahr THRYE tiss)* Inflammation of the joints.

osteoarthritis *(OSS tee oh ahr THRYE tiss)* Chronic inflammatory disease of the joints, particularly the large weight-bearing joints of the knees and hips, although it often occurs in the joints that move repeatedly like the shoulders, neck, and hands.

rheumatoid arthritis *(ROO meh toyd awr THRIGH tiss)* A chronic, systemic condition affecting synovial joints. Women are three times more affected than men. A common complaint is morning joint stiffness rather than after physical activities.

septic arthritis A form of joint inflammation due to infection.

gout Disease caused by excessive uric acid in the blood that is deposited in the joints, producing inflammation and pain.

bursitis *(bur SIGH tiss)* Inflammation of the bursa, resulting in joint swelling and pain.

tendonitis Inflammation of any tendon from injury or overuse.

Pathology Connection (continued)

A common sport injury involving the shoulder is a **torn rotator cuff**. The group of muscles that hold the head of the humerus into the shoulder socket is known as the rotator cuff. Sports such as tennis, baseball, and basketball tend to stress this region, and as a result, tears can occur in the tendons that hold those muscles in place. When these tears happen, there is a snapping sound and acute pain radiating from that area. In addition, there is difficulty abducting (raising) the affected arm. Surgery is often required to correct the tears, with rest and immobilization needed for 3 to 4 weeks. Active rehabilitation is often needed to restore full shoulder mobility and function.

Sudden and unusual movements during exercise, such as twisting an ankle, can cause a sprain. A **sprain** is an injury to the ligaments in a joint. A grade I sprain is mild. The ligaments swell and feel tender, but they are not torn. You can treat a grade I sprain at home. Pain medications, such as ibuprofen or acetaminophen, can help to reduce swelling and pain. The following steps (called RICE) should also be followed to treat a grade I sprain:

Rest
Ice for 48 hours
Compression of the injury with an elastic wrap
Elevation of the sprained area above the heart

A grade II sprain is more serious. A ligament is partially torn, so the joint swells and becomes very painful. When a grade II sprain happens, bruising occurs around the sprained joint, and it becomes difficult to move the joint without severe pain. RICE may help a grade II sprain, but it may also need additional medical treatment. A grade III sprain is even more serious. A ligament is completely torn, so the joint becomes impossible to move without severe pain. A grade III sprain may require a cast and physical therapy.

A hard fall or sudden blow to a joint can cause **joint dislocation**. When a joint becomes dislocated, its bones no longer line up properly. Dislocation to a joint can also damage the ligaments and nerves within the joint. It may be swollen, bruised, and very painful. A dislocated joint is an emergency that should always be treated by trained medical professionals. During treatment, a doctor may use **closed reduction,** a process of applying gentle pressure to move the joint back into place. The doctor may then use a splint or sling to immobilize the joint and allow it to heal.

Arthroscopy is a procedure used to diagnose and treat many joint injuries. Knee injuries are commonly treated with arthroscopy. An **arthroscope** is a snakelike instrument that contains a long tube, a fiber-optic light source, and an eyepiece. During arthroscopy, the tube of the arthroscope is inserted into the joint through a small incision in the skin. The light shines through the tube into the joint. A small television camera attached to the eyepiece projects images from within the joint onto a television screen. The projected images can help a physician diagnose any injuries to the joint. These images can also be used to assist the surgeon during joint repair surgery.

torn rotator cuff Tear or inflammation of the rotator cuff tendons in the shoulder.

sprain Overstretching or tearing of a ligament.

joint dislocation The movement of the joint out of its normal position.

closed reduction The setting of a bone into proper alignment without opening the skin.

arthroscopy *(ar THROSS koh pee)* The endoscopic examination of the interior region of the joint.

arthroscope An instrument used to view a joint.

TEST YOUR KNOWLEDGE 6-3

Choose the best answer:

1. A movement that increases the angle of a joint is known as:
   a. flexion
   b. abduction
   c. rotation
   d. extension

2. A joint in which bones are connected by short connective tissue strands is known as a:
   a. cartilaginous joint
   b. fibrous joint
   c. synovial joint
   d. freely moving joint

3. A joint in which flat bone surfaces move side to side past each other is known as a:
   a. condyloid joint
   b. hinge joint
   c. saddle joint
   d. gliding joint

4. This lubricant helps to prevent wear in joints:
   a. pleural fluid
   b. synovial fluid
   c. mucus
   d. petroleum jelly

5. These structures attach bone to muscle:
   a. tendons
   b. ligaments
   c. cords
   d. articulations

6. A young gymnast falls from the balance beam, rotating her knee. This is a problem because:
   a. the knee is a hinge joint and should not rotate
   b. the knee should only rotate when standing
   c. the knee joint is not a freely moving joint
   d. there is no problem, knees are supposed to rotate

---

axial skeleton *(AK see al)* The bones of the head, chest, and back.

appendicular skeleton *(app en DIK yoo lahr SKELL eh ton)* The bones of the shoulders, arms, hips, and legs.

phalanges *(fuh LAN jeez)* Bones of the fingers.

THE SKELETON

Anatomically, the skeleton can be divided into two main sections. The **axial skeleton** includes bones of the bony thorax, spinal column, hyoid bone (suspended approximately 2 cm above the larynx), bones of the middle ear, and skull. This part of the skeletal system protects the organs of the body and is composed of 80 bones. The **appendicular skeleton** is, as its name implies, the region of your appendages (arms and legs), as well as the connecting bone structures of the hip and shoulder girdles, and contains 126 bones (see FIGURE 6-9 ▲). Interestingly, nearly half the total number of your bones can be found in your hands and feet. Your ten fingers are made up of 28 bones called **phalanges**. Two phalanges are found in each thumb. Three phalanges are found in each finger.

Special Regions of the Skeletal System

The skeleton consists of many different special regions. These distinctions make it easier to locate and discuss the hundreds of bones and associated components in this system. In this section, we make a quick tour of each region, beginning at the top.

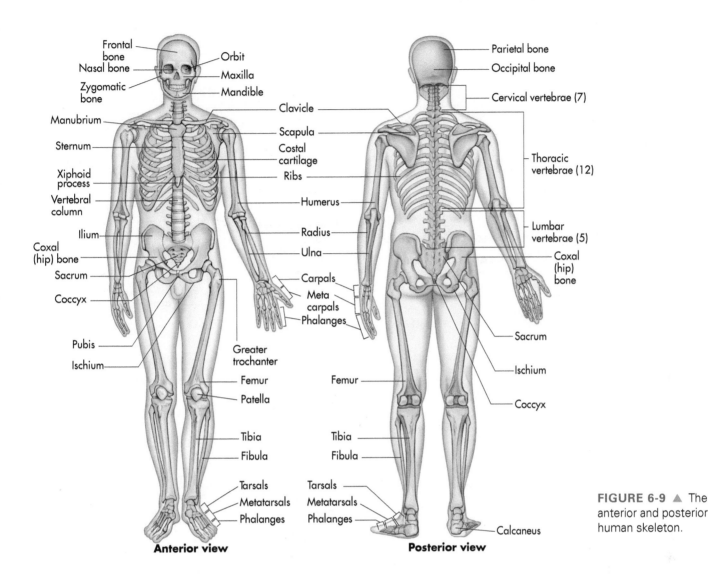

FIGURE 6-9 ▲ The anterior and posterior human skeleton.

The Skull

The cranial portion of the skull protects and houses the brain and has openings needed for our sensory organs, such as the eyes, nose, and ears. The skull also contains the **oral cavity** or **mouth,** which is a common passageway for both the digestive and respiratory systems. The mandible (moveable bone) and maxilla are the bones of the mouth. The skull contains fibrous connective tissue joints called **suture lines** that hold the bony plates of the skull together. Although these joints are not actually moveable, they do provide some degree of flexibility, which is important for absorbing shock from a blow to the head, thus decreasing the chance of a skull fracture. FIGURE 6-10 ▲ shows the bones of the skull in greater detail.

oral cavity The space inside the teeth and gums that is filled by the tongue when the mouth is closed and relaxed.

mouth The cavity within the cheeks, containing the tongue and teeth, and communicating with the pharynx.

suture lines Fibrous connective tissue joints of the skull.

Cranium
Suture
FRONTAL
PARIETAL
Sphenoid
TEMPORAL
ETHMOID
OCCIPITAL
Nasal
Lacrimal
Zygomatic
Vomer
Mastoid process
MAXILLA
External auditory canal
Styloid process
MANDIBLE

Skull

Face

Associated Bones
Auditory ossicles
Hyoid bone

Frontal bone
Zygomatic bone
Vomer
Sphenoid bone
Styloid process
External auditory canal
Jugular foramen
Occipital bone

Maxillary bone
Palatine bone
Zygomatic arch
Temporal bone
Mastoid process
Occipital condyle
Foramen magnum

Inferior view

Cranium
Parietal bone
Coronal suture
Temporal bone
Sphenoid bone
Zygomatic bone
Mastoid process
Temporomandibular joint

Frontal bone
Orbit
Nasal bone
Lacrimal bone
Vomer
Maxilla
Alveolar margins
Mandible (jaw)

FIGURE 6-10 ▲ Bones of the skull.

The Bony Thorax

The bones of the chest form a thoracic "cage" that provides support and protection for the heart, lungs, and great blood vessels (see **FIGURE 6-11** ▲). This cage is flexible because of cartilaginous connections that allow for movement during the process of breathing. The **sternum,** or **breastbone,** is the anatomical structure for performing compressions of the heart during cardiopulmonary resuscitation (CPR). The sternum is composed of three distinct areas. The **manubrium** is the superior portion, and the **body,** which is centrally located, is the largest portion. The **xiphoid** is the final and inferior portion that ossifies (hardens) by age 25 and can be broken off if CPR is improperly performed. During cardiac compressions, the heart is compressed anteriorly by the body of the sternum and posteriorly by the bones of the vertebral column.

The thoracic cage consists of 12 pairs of elastic arches of bone called ribs. The ribs are attached by cartilage to allow for their movement when we breathe. The true ribs are pairs 1 to 7 and are called **vertebrosternal** because they connect anteriorly to the sternum and posteriorly to the thoracic vertebrae of the spinal column. Pairs 8 to 10 are called the false ribs, or **vertebrocostal ribs,** because they connect to the costal cartilage of the superior rib and again posteriorly to the thoracic vertebrae. Rib pairs 11 and 12 are called the **floating ribs** because although they are connected posteriorly to the vertebrae, they have no anterior attachment.

sternum *(STER num)* Vertical bone of the anterior thorax to which the clavicle and ribs are attached. Also known as the breastbone.

breastbone Lay term for sternum.

manubrium *(mah NOO bree um)* The superior portion of the sternum.

body The centrally located and the largest portion of the sternum.

xiphoid *(ZYE foyd)* The inferior portion of the sternum.

vertebrosternal *(VER teh broh STIR null)* Referring to the true rib pairs 1–7 and their points of attachment.

vertebrocostal *(VER teh broh KOSS tul)* referring to the false rib pairs 8–10 and their points of attachment.

floating ribs Rib pairs 11 and 12 that have no anterior attachment.

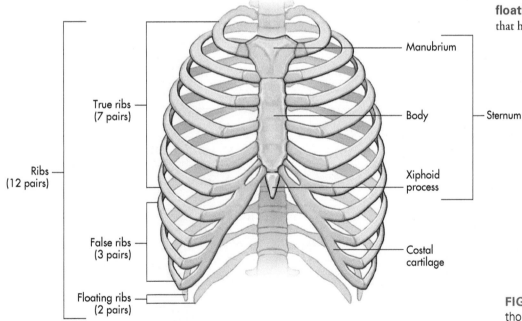

FIGURE 6-11 ▲ The bony thorax.

spinal column (vertebral column) A series of connected vertebrae that protect the spinal cord.

cervical Pertaining to the region of the neck and the cervix.

thoracic Pertaining to the chest or thorax.

lumbar Pertaining to the loins (the part of the back between the thorax and pelvis).

sacral *(SEY kral)* Referring to the five fused vertebra in the mid-buttock region.

tailbone See coccyx.

coccyx *(KAWK siks)* The final 3–5 small bones at the inferior end of the spinal column; also called tailbone.

The Spinal Column

The **spinal column (vertebral column)** protects the spinal cord, which is the super highway for information coming to and from the central nervous system. The individual bones, or vertebrae, are numbered and classified according to the body region where they are located (see **FIGURE 6-12** ▲). For example, seven vertebrae are found in the cervical or neck region, and they are numbered C-1 though C-7 respectively.

As seen in Figure 6-12, 7 vertebrae are in the neck region (**cervical**) where Ray, our quadriplegic, was injured, 12 are in the upper back (**thoracic**), 5 are in the lower back (**lumbar**), 5 fused vertebrae are in the midbuttock region (**sacral**), and 3 to 5 small bones are at the very end (**tailbone** or **coccyx**). At birth, the vertebral column is concave to the front, like a fetal position (primary curvature). The vertebral column later bends in the opposite direction as the infant starts to raise and hold its head up, as well as starts to walk. In other words, there will be secondary (anterior) curvatures by the time a child is age 2. From 2 years onward, the vertebral column develops a secondary curvature in the neck, a primary (posterior) curvature in the upper back, a secondary curvature in the lower back, and a primary curvature in the midbuttocks and tailbone regions.

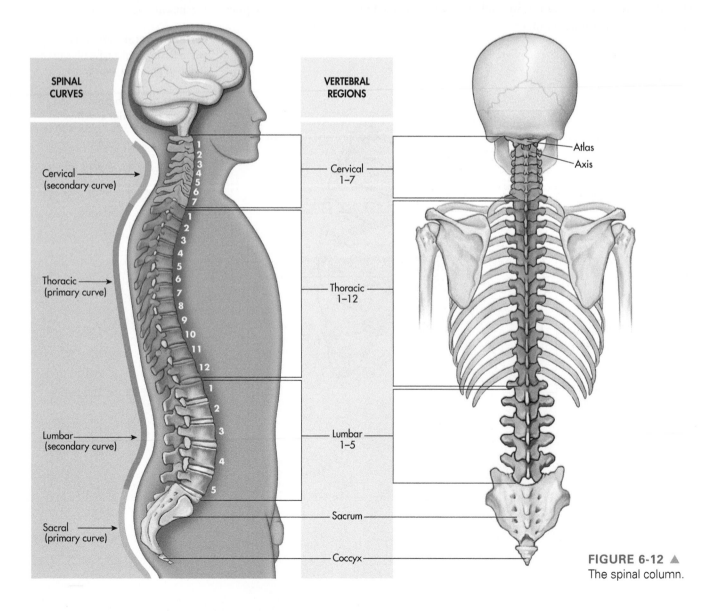

FIGURE 6-12 ▲
The spinal column.

Pathology Connection

SPINAL COLUMN ABNORMALITIES

A "slipped disk," or more correctly, a **herniated disk,** is a common disorder found in individuals younger than 45 years of age due to poor posture and/or poor lifting techniques, and in the geriatric population due to degenerative joint disease. The vertebral column is separated by pads of cartilage called **intervertebral disks.** Herniation occurs when the soft central part of the intervertebral disk is forced and protruded through the outer covering. The herniated portion then may press on a spinal nerve root, causing lower back pain. Sometimes this pain will radiate down the sciatic nerve to the buttock, leg, and foot on one side of the body. Although this condition can occur anywhere along the spine, such as the cervical area, which produces a tingling of the arm on the affected side, the lower back region appears to be the most common region. Treatment for this condition can include rest, application of heat, special exercises, analgesics, muscle relaxants, utilization of proper lifting techniques, and in severe cases, surgery.

Another potential spinal problem involves the spine's curvature. If the body is not in balance, whether due to congenital deformity, trauma, poor posture, or disease, these curvatures may be exaggerated, leading to a number of curvature abnormalities. **Kyphosis** is a condition in which the upper portion of the spine exhibits a posterior curve, producing what is commonly called a humpback or a hunchback. **Scoliosis** is a lateral (left or right) curvature of the spine. **Lordosis** is an anterior curve of the lower back and is commonly called swayback. FIGURE 6-13 ▲ illustrates these conditions. It is important to note that these conditions present at various levels of severity; some individuals may go through life never knowing that they have an abnormal curvature of the spine. The key to successful treatment is early detection. Spinal corrections can be accomplished through exercise, good nutrition with weight control, bracing, corrective shoes (so legs are of equal length), or surgery.

herniated disk
Common disorder in older patients where the soft central portion of the invertebral disk is forced through its outer covering.

intervertebral disks
Cartilage pads that separate vertebrae.

kyphosis *(kigh FOH sis)*
An exaggerated posterior curvature of the thoracic spine, also known as humpback, hunchback, or Pott's curvature.

scoliosis *(SKOH lee OH sis)* Lateral curvature of the spine.

lordosis *(lore DOH sis)*
An anteroposterior curvature of the spine (backward bending).

Upper and Lower Extremities

The appendicular region consists of the arms and legs. Because these areas perform most of the body movement, the greatest number of sport-related injuries occur here. Please see FIGURE 6-14 ▲, which shows the bones of the upper and lower extremities. These figures show the bony landmarks of the limbs and girdles, which will be beneficial in learning and understanding where the muscles discussed in Chapter 7 will attach.

Notice in Figure 6-14 that the pelvic girdle in women is different than in men. Women have a greater pubic angle, which facilitates childbirth, and also a relatively broad girdle to support the extra weight of the child. This difference can be used to identify the sex of a skeleton, such as in a murder case or an archeological find. The pelvis consists of several parts, including the ilium, ischium, and pubis.

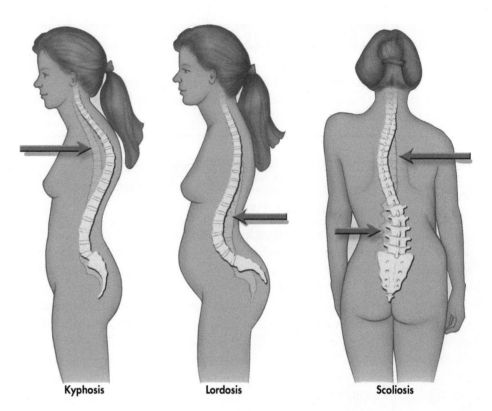

FIGURE 6-13 ▲ Spinal disfigurements compared to healthy spinal curves.

Kyphosis

Lordosis

Scoliosis

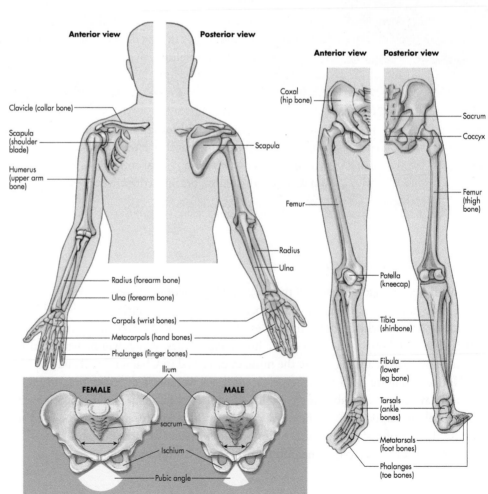

FIGURE 6-14 ▲ Bones of the upper and lower extremities.

Anterior view

Posterior view

Clavicle (collar bone)

Scapula (shoulder blade)

Humerus (upper arm bone)

Scapula

Radius (forearm bone)

Ulna (forearm bone)

Carpals (wrist bones)

Metacarpals (hand bones)

Phalanges (finger bones)

Radius

Ulna

Ilium

FEMALE

MALE

sacrum

Ischium

Pubic angle

Anterior view

Posterior view

Coxal (hip bone)

Sacrum

Coccyx

Femur

Femur (thigh bone)

Patella (kneecap)

Tibia (shinbone)

Fibula (lower leg bone)

Tarsals (ankle bones)

Metatarsals (foot bones)

Phalanges (toe bones)

TEST YOUR KNOWLEDGE 6-4

Answer the following:

1. What is the difference between the axial skeleton and the appendicular skeleton?

_____

_____

Choose the best answer:

2. Which of the following bones is considered to be part of the axial skeleton?
   a. humerus
   b. patella
   c. femur
   d. sternum

3. The number of vertebrae in the thoracic region is:
   a. 5
   b. 7
   c. 12
   d. 120

Answer the following:

4. Describe the difference between flexion and extension.

_____

_____

_____

5. This form of arthritis is a result of an excessive buildup of uric acid.

_____

fracture A break in the bone.

hairline fracture A fine bone fracture that resembles a hair on the x-ray.

simple fracture Also called a closed fracture; it is a bone break without a puncture to the skin.

closed fracture See simple fracture.

spiral fracture Bone break caused by a severe twist.

greenstick fracture An incomplete bone break, usually found in children who have softer more pliable bones.

comminuted fracture *(KOM uh noot ed)* Fracture that is a result of a bone being crushed.

compound fracture Also called an open fracture, where the bone is pushed through the skin.

open fracture See compound fracture.

set (reduced) The act of putting fractured bones in alignment so the ends meet.

closed reduction The setting of a bone into proper alignment without opening the skin.

surgical or open reduction A more complex setting of bone that may require pins, screws, plates, or other hardware to fix the bone fragments in place.

traction Use of weights to hold broken bones in place for proper healing.

hematoma *(HEE mah TOH mah)* A swelling as a result of a break in a blood vessel(s) usually confined to a specific area (tissue, organ, or space) in the body.

blood clot See hematoma.

Pathology Connection

BONE FRACTURES AND HEALING

Chances are that you have broken a bone or know someone who has broken a bone in the past, but did you know that not all breaks are the same? A **fracture** is any break in a bone. Although there are a variety of fractures, the following are the more common ones. Please refer to FIGURE 6-15 ▲ for further clarification.

A **hairline** fracture, which looks like a piece of hair on the x-ray, is a fine fracture that does not completely break or displace the bone. A **simple** or **closed** fracture is a break without a puncture to the skin. An individual in an accident who has a bone that is severely twisted may receive a **spiral** fracture. **Greenstick** fractures are incomplete breaks, which more often occur in children because they have softer, more pliable bones (like sapling branches) than adults (like seasoned twigs). If a bone is crushed to the point that it becomes fragmented or splintered, that is classified as a **comminuted** fracture. A fracture in which the bone is pushed through the skin is referred to as a **compound** or **open** fracture. These fractures are particularly nasty because deep tissue has the potential to be exposed to bacteria once the bone is set into place, and, hence, the chance for infection in addition to the break is increased. Again, see Figure 6-15 for examples of common fractures.

Bones take several weeks to heal. They can heal normally only if the ends of the bones are touching. If the bones are not touching (are poorly aligned), the bone must be **set (reduced)**. If the misalignment is slight, **closed reduction** may be sufficient. During a closed reduction, force is exerted on the broken bone to bring the bones into alignment. **Surgical** or **open reduction** is necessary for the treatment of more severe fractures. During a surgical reduction, pins, screws, plates, or other hardware are used to fix the bones in place. With either type of reduction, the broken bone must often be immobilized to keep the ends of the bone in proper alignment. A cast or splint is applied to immobilize the bone.

Traction may be used to treat fractures of long bones. Traction aligns broken bones and holds them in place. It uses heavy weights to exert a pulling force on the injured bones. The force from the weights keeps the broken bones in the correct position and allows them to heal normally.

In the first few hours after the injury, a **hematoma**, or **blood clot**, forms around the broken bone and inflammation sets in. For the next 3 to 4 weeks, a soft callus forms, replacing the hematoma and bridging the gap between the broken ends of the bone. The soft callus starts as hyaline cartilage, similar to the connecting cartilage that attaches the ribs to the sternum, which eventually contains some bone cells within it. Capillaries invade the site, ready to vascularize the healing bone. From week 4 to week 12 after the injury, a bony callus forms, replacing the soft callus via endochondral ossification. (Remember endochondral ossification? It's the same process that causes bone development in embryos and allows your long bones to get longer after birth.) Usually, the bony callus will contain excess bone. Remodeling is necessary after bony callus formation to make the repaired bone match the rest of the bone. See FIGURE 6-16 ▲, which illustrates the healing process of a bone.

Recent research shows that individuals with energy excess disorders like diabetes, where the individual has too much sugar in the blood, can lead to problems with skeletal system homeostasis. Individuals with these types of disorders are at a much greater risk for bone fracture and upon fracture, healing takes considerably longer.

FIGURE 6-15 ▲ **A.** Femur, AP view, comminuted fracture. (Source: Praisaeng/Shutterstock.com.) **B.** Tibia, simple, transverse fracture. (Source: itsmejust/Shutterstock.com.) **C.** Open fracture of the wrist. **D.** X-ray views of displaced fracture of the distal radius with wires showing internal fixation. (Source: Santibhavank P/Shutterstock.com)

1. Hematoma forms around the site of the injury
2. A soft callus of fibrous tissue and cartilage forms
3. Bony callus forms as a result of endochondral ossification
4. Bone remodeling occurs to reshape to original contour

FIGURE 6-16 ▲ The healing process of a bone.

MAINTAINING GOOD BONE HEALTH

Even though the loss of bone mass is a natural process of aging, it can be slowed by a healthy lifestyle. It is important to consume the proper amount of dietary calcium to build strong bones early in life. Proper calcium intake during the formative years, including the teenage years, and continued calcium consumption as the body ages, is crucial. Vitamin D is important because it allows your body to absorb ingested calcium from the digestive tract. As previously discussed, exercise (especially weight-bearing forms) also plays a vital role in developing and maintaining bones, so stay active. Conversely, the excessive use of caffeine and cigarette smoking can reduce bone density. Individuals who, for a lifetime, consume two cups of black caffeinated coffee per day tend to show an increase in bone loss. Cigarette smokers have shown a loss of 5% to 8% bone mineral density.

Although osteoporosis and arthritis are big concerns, there are many more potential disorders of bones and joints. As you can see in TABLES 6-2 ■ and 6-3 ■, these disorders can generally be classified by the following causative agents: congenital, degenerative, nutritional, secondary disorders, infection, inflammation, trauma, and tumors.

See the Quick Trip table for information on the different forms of arthritis and other diseases of the skeletal system.

Clinical Application

WHEN TO SEE A DOCTOR

We have discussed many pathological conditions relating to bones and the skeleton in this chapter, but when do you need to see a doctor, and when do you take care of things yourself? Anyone who has been involved in sports or physical labor knows all about the bumps, bruises, and strains that go along with those activities. So, in general, when should you see a doctor? Here are a few general guidelines:

- Any obvious bone deformity or misalignment of a joint
- Pain that continues beyond 10 days
- An injury that does not improve after 5 to 7 days
- Continued swelling and/or inflammation of a joint or injury
- Any indication of an infection such as a fever, pus, red streaks visible in tissue, or the swelling of lymph glands

Of course, these are guidelines, always use common sense to stay on the safe side.

TABLE 6-2 ■ BONE DISORDERS

CLASSIFICATION	EXAMPLE(S)
Congenital disorders	Abnormal curvature of the spine (kyphosis, lordosis, scoliosis), cleft palate, clubfoot, osteogenesis imperfecta, achondroplasia
Degenerative disorders	Osteoporosis
Infection	Osteomyelitis
Nutritional disorders	Osteomalacia (vitamin D deficiency), rickets (vitamin D deficiency), scurvy (vitamin C deficiency)
Secondary disorders	Endocrine system dysfunction: gigantism, pituitary dwarfism
Trauma	Bruises, fractures
Tumors	Chondrosarcomas, myelomas, osteosarcomas

TABLE 6-3 ■ JOINT DISORDERS

CLASSIFICATION	EXAMPLE(S)
Degenerative disorders	Osteoarthritis
Infection	Gonococcal arthritis, rheumatic fever, septic arthritis, viral arthritis
Inflammation	Bursitis, arthritis
Secondary disorders	Immune system dysfunction: rheumatoid arthritis; metabolic dysfunction: gout
Trauma	Ankle and foot injuries, dislocations, hip fractures, knee injuries

A QUICK TRIP THROUGH SOME DISEASES OF THE SKELETAL SYSTEM

DISEASE	ETIOLOGY	SIGNS AND SYMPTOMS	DIAGNOSTIC TEST(S)	TREATMENT
Arthritis	A general term for the inflammation of a joint/synovial membrane.			
Osteoarthritis	A degenerative condition in which a joint wears out, often a result of simple aging, sports injuries, trauma, obesity, or a family history of the disease.	Painful swelling of the affected joint, wearing away of the cartilage, develops a deformed joint.	Visual and radiologic examination, fluid culture for infective agents, patient history.	Rest, exercises (non-weight-bearing), analgesics, anti-inflammatories, steroid injections into affected site, surgical intervention/joint replacement.
Rheumatoid arthritis	An insidious, chronic, systemic, autoimmune disease affecting connective tissue in the body, and mostly the small joints of the hands and feet, can also affect the elbows and knees. Three times as many women as men develop this condition.	Stiffness, swelling, and fluctuating pain of multiple joints (usually symmetrical), pronounced joint deformities and destruction, synovial membrane inflammation, fibrous adhesions obliterate the joint spaces, other systemic effects involving connective tissue.	Visual and radiologic examination, fluid culture for infective agents, patient history, antibody screening (rheumatoid factor).	Aspirin (effective only for patients with mild disease) nonsteroidal anti-inflammatory drugs, corticosteroids, the cancer drug methotrexate in low doses, drugs that suppress the immune system specifically for autoimmune disorders (such as Humira™ and Enbrel™) rest, range-of-motion exercises, surgical intervention (in advanced cases).
Septic arthritis	Originates from an infective organism either from a penetrating joint wound or blood-borne pathogen.	Pain, swelling of affected joint, filling of the joint space with an inflammatory exudate that destroys the joint prior to replacing the space with fibrous tissue and then bone.	Visual examination and imaging, fluid culture for infective agents, patient history.	Preventative aseptic techniques and early, aggressive treatment with antibiotics.

A QUICK TRIP *(continued)*

DISEASE	ETIOLOGY	SIGNS AND SYMPTOMS	DIAGNOSTIC TEST(S)	TREATMENT
Bursitis	Repetitive movement, strain, congenital defect, rheumatic diseases.	Pain on movement, painful inflammation of affected site, swelling, limited range of motion due to pain.	Visual examination and imaging, patient history.	Joint rest, moist heat/cold therapy (although cold may aggravate the situation), analgesics, anti-inflammatory medications, corticosteroid injection at the affected site, draining if severe. Range-of-motion exercises once pain subsides to restore full joint function.
Cruciate ligament tears	Trauma involving the twisting of the leg, anterior or posterior blow when leg is planted or bearing weight. A common contact sport injury.	Pain, limited stability, and restricted mobility.	Physical examination and imaging, joint stability testing.	Rest, immobilization, surgical intervention.
Gout	A metabolic disease with joint involvement. Overproduction of uric acid, leading to crystallization and deposition of the excessive uric acid in synovial fluid. Excessive protein ingestion precipitates the condition. Possibly an inherited disease. 95% of cases are male; onset is usually after 30 years of age. Secondary gout may be caused by leukemia, lead poisoning, chronic renal diseases, or drug ingestion such as chlorothiazide. Considered by some to be a form of arthritis.	Excruciating pain in a joint, commonly the big toe. Involved joint is inflamed, hot, tender, and, in more severe cases, swollen. In advanced stages: hypertension, kidney stones, renal dysfunction, severe back pain, disability, ulceration, and unremitting pain.	Visual examination, blood testing for excessive uric acid.	Protein consumption restrictions, especially organ meats such as liver and seafood (high in purines that are precursors to uric acid). Rest and immobilization of the affected joint, blood uric acid monitoring, analgesics, anti-inflammatory medications, and drugs designed specifically for gout management, such as colchicine (utilized for the past 1,500 years), probenecid, and allopurinol. Low-fat dairy products seem to help prevent occurences.

DISEASE	ETIOLOGY	SIGNS AND SYMPTOMS	DIAGNOSTIC TEST(S)	TREATMENT
Kyphosis	Causative agents include congenital defect, trauma, diseases (e.g., polio). In adults: aging process, osteoporosis, tuberculosis, steroid therapy, arthritis, and tumor growth.	An exaggerated curve of the upper back (commonly called "humpback"). May lead to backache, fatigue, dyspnea, tenderness, muscle weakness, pulmonary insufficiency.	Visual examination and imaging.	Age and severity dependant: exercise, bracing, surgery, electrical stimulation, weight control.
Osteomalacia	Decreased or impaired mineralization of bone material due to insufficient vitamin D. May be due to improper diet, lack of sufficient sunlight, or a malabsorption condition.	Bone pain, loss of height, deformity of weight-bearing bones.	Bone scan, visual examination.	Correct the nutritional deficiency.
Osteomyelitis	An acute or chronic inflammatory condition of the bone, commonly caused by the bacteria *Staphylococcus aureus*. The infection usually originates from a wound, the skin, or throat. More common in children than adults, more common in boys than girls. In adults, may be a result of trauma, surgery, especially if any bone had been manipulated.	In children: most commonly occurs in the long bones and may affect the growth plates. In adults: most commonly occurs in the vertebrae and pelvis. Begins with sudden pain, swelling, heat, and tenderness of the affected site, high fever, chills. Nausea and malaise are also possible.	Visual examination, culture for suspected infecting agent.	Preventive therapy by decreasing the possibility of infection. Maintain a healthy immune system. Antibiotics (aggressive therapy), possible surgical debridement.

(continued)

A QUICK TRIP (continued)

DISEASE	ETIOLOGY	SIGNS AND SYMPTOMS	DIAGNOSTIC TEST(S)	TREATMENT
Osteoporosis	A metabolic problem with slow, progressive implications that lead to decreased bone mass. Usually a condition related to aging but may be related to diseases that decrease mobility. Also found in postmenopausal and estrogen-deficient women, regardless of age.	Decreasing bone density, compression fractures of the spine, wrist fractures, height loss up to 4–5 inches, thoracic and lumbar spine pain radiating around the trunk, kyphosis, decreased thoracic cavity size with decreasing exercise tolerance. In some cases, bone fractures that were attributed to falls actually occurred first and then the fall.	Imaging, bone densitometry.	Early initiation of preventative practices such as diet with sufficient calcium. Smoking and caffeine may aid in depleting calcium. Regular (daily is ideal) exercise, especially weight-bearing and impact sports/exercises. Supplements (calcium, vitamin D, fluoride), drugs that increase bone mass such as alendronate may also help. Estrogen replacement is somewhat controversial but may be beneficial.
Plantar fasciitis (runner's heel)	Repetitive impact trauma to the heel affecting the thick and fibrous connective tissue that extends the length of the foot beginning at the heel. Additional pain if pre-existing heel spur is involved. Predisposing factors can include sudden increases in activity, increase in body weight, high arches, poor supportive shoes, and flat feet.	Intermittent pain that worsens as one walks following sitting or standing for a considerable period of time.	Radiologic examination.	Rest, analgesics, anti-inflammatories, application of ice, utilization of padding for the heel, surgical intervention in some cases.
Rickets	A pediatric condition caused by the lack of vitamin D, leading to impaired calcium absorption and bone calcification. In adults, a deficiency of vitamin D may lead to bone softening (osteomalacia).	Weak, deformed bones.	Visual and radiological examination, patient history.	Dietary correction to increase vitamin D, supplemental vitamin D, sunlight exposure (which increases vitamin D production).

DISEASE	ETIOLOGY	SIGNS AND SYMPTOMS	DIAGNOSTIC TEST(S)	TREATMENT
Scoliosis	Congenital defect, trauma, poor posture, obesity.	A lateral curvature of the spine, usually affecting the chest or lower back regions. Symptoms include backache, fatigue, dyspnea, pulmonary insufficiency, and sciatica. Symptoms are dependent on the age of the patient, severity of the condition, and timeliness of the treatment.	Visual and radiologic examination.	Age and severity dependant. Options: exercise, bracing, surgery, electrical stimulation, weight control.
Tendonitis (tendinitis)	Repetitive movement or calcium deposits at the affected site, rheumatic diseases, congenital defects. Often occurs in conjunction with bursitis.	Inflammation of the involved tendon and/ or the connective tissue that attaches that tendon to the muscle or bone. Pain on movement and localized pain, especially at night.	Patient history, visual and radiologic examination.	Analgesics, joint rest, cold/moist heat therapy, corticosteroid injection at affected site, other anti-inflammatory medications.

Pharmacology Corner

There are several medication options when treating joint pain. Analgesic creams, often containing capsaicin, can help to ease minor joint pain. For more severe cases, corticosteroids are injected directly into the joints. Pain medication can include nonsteroidal anti-inflammatory drugs (NSAIDs), such as naproxen and ibuprofen, that reduce the inflammation and thus reduce the pain and swelling. Pain medication, including acetaminophen and aspirin, can help to ease pain in general. The cancer drug methotrexate in smaller doses has been used to treat rheumatoid arthritis, as has cyclosporine (an antirejection drug) and several new classes of immunosuppressants such as Remicade™, Humira™, and Enbrel™ (see Chapter 14 for more details).

In addition to proper diet and exercise, bone density in diseases such as osteoporosis can also be improved with calcium supplements. Interestingly, some calcium-based antacids used for heartburn can help improve bone density. Alendronate is a more powerful prescribed calcium medication that can be taken once a month. Vitamin D supplements help bone health by improving the body's ability to absorb calcium. Because vitamin D is a fat-soluble vitamin, care must be taken to avoid an overdose that may cause liver damage. Estrogen replacement therapy, although controversial, does seem to improve bone density in women.

SUMMARY

Snapshots from the Journey

- In addition to providing support and protection for the body, the skeleton also produces blood cells and acts as a storage unit for minerals and fat.

- The 206 bones of the skeleton can be classified according to their shapes: long bones, short bones, flat bones, and irregular bones.

- Bone is covered with periosteum, which is a tough, fibrous connective tissue. In long bones, each bone end is called an epiphysis, and the shaft is called the diaphysis. The hollow region within the diaphysis is called the medullary cavity and stores yellow marrow.

- Compact bone is a dense, hard tissue that normally forms the shafts of long bones or is found as the outer layer of the other bone types. Spongy bone is different in that it contains irregular holes that make it lighter in weight and provides a space for red bone marrow, which produces red blood cells.

- Ossification is the formation of bone in the body. Osteoprogenitor cells are nonspecialized cells that can turn into osteoblasts, which are the cells that actually form bones. Osteocytes are mature bone cells that were originally osteoblasts. Osteoclasts originate from a type of white blood cell called a monocyte, found in red bone marrow. Osteoclasts break down bone material and help move calcium and phosphate into the blood.

- A thin band of cartilage forms an epiphyseal plate (often referred to as the growth plate), and as long as it exists, the length and width of the bone will increase.

- Cartilage is a special form of dense connective tissue that can withstand a fair amount of flexing, tension, and pressure and makes a flexible connection between bones, as seen between the breastbone and ribs. It also acts as a cushion between bones.

- Various types of joints join two or more bones and allow various types of movement. The point at which they join is called an articulation. Ligaments are very tough, whitish bands of connective tissue that connect from bone to bone to hold the joint together and can withstand heavy stress.

- With the exception of osteoporosis, most chronic diseases of the skeleton involve the joints.

- The skeleton can be divided into two main sections. The axial skeleton includes the bones of the bony thorax, spinal column, hyoid bone, bones of the middle ear, and skull. The appendicular skeleton is composed of your appendages (arms and legs) and the connecting bone structures of the pelvic and shoulder girdles.

- Although they are different diseases, bursitis and tendonitis have similar treatment regimens that include rest of the affected joint(s), analgesics, and application of cold and moist heat. (Watch out for potential skin damage when using extreme temperatures.) The injection of corticosteroids into the affected joint may be beneficial in reducing inflammation.

- As we age, the chemical composition of cartilage changes, causing it to become more brittle. Articular cartilage that ages or becomes injured can lead to arthritis, which is an inflammatory process of the joint or joints. Gout is a form of arthritis and is a result of higher than normal levels of urea in the body. Bone mass also gradually decreases with age, beginning in a person's 50s. Even though this is a natural process of aging, it can be slowed by a healthy lifestyle.

- Although bumps and bruises are a fact of life and often not a big problem, the general guidelines concerning when to see a doctor include any obvious bone deformity or misalignment of a joint, pain that continues beyond 10 days, an injury that does not improve after 5 to 7 days, continued swelling and/or inflammation of a joint or injury, any indication of an infection (such as a fever, pus, red streaks visible in tissue), or the swelling of lymph glands. Finally, just use common sense to determine when to seek medical assistance.

CASE STUDY

A somewhat frail 76-year-old female visits her physician's office for an annual checkup. Her social history shows that she smokes a pack of cigarettes a day and is a heavy coffee drinker. She has had several fractured bones in the last 5 years that have required medical attention. During the initial examination, measurements show that the patient has lost approximately an inch of height over the past year. She has also lost several pounds but states that she still wears the same size clothes.

a. What possible bone disease do you think she is exhibiting?

_____

_____

_____

b. Describe the bone changes associated with this condition on a macro and cellular level.

_____

_____

_____

c. What treatments and/or lifestyle changes would you suggest?

_____

_____

_____

RAY'S STORY

You are a member of the discharge planning team responsible for developing a home care plan for Ray, a quadriplegic. Because of his condition, Ray can only breathe with mechanical assistance, cannot move himself without help from others, needs assistance eating, and spends most of his time lying in a bed. What suggestions would you make for his skeletal, bone, and joint health? Which professional(s) should be involved in maintaining or improving his "skeletal health"?

_____

_____

_____

_____

_____

REVIEW QUESTIONS

Multiple Choice

1. Your elbow is an example of which type of joint?
   a. hinge joint
   b. ball-and-socket joint
   c. gliding joint
   d. fibrous joint

2. The sternum is the correct medical term for which bone?
   a. shin bone
   b. breastbone
   c. shoulder blade
   d. collar bone

3. The end of a long bone is the:
   a. diplodicus
   b. epiphysis
   c. condylcorn
   d. perla

4. As long as this exists, your bones will increase in length and width:
   a. Torger center
   b. ossifier
   c. Mantoux membrane
   d. epiphyseal plate

5. The aging process, excessive caffeine, and cigarette smoking can each contribute to this bone disease:
   a. rheumatoid arthritis
   b. osteoporosis
   c. scoliosis
   d. de-ossification

6. This group of muscles is responsible for holding the head of the humerus in the shoulder joint socket:
   a. bundle branch
   b. rotator cuff
   c. ball flexor
   d. ossiforator

7. A "slipped disk" is more correctly called a:
   a. displaced disk
   b. degenerated disk
   c. herniated disk
   d. infarcted disk

Fill in the Blank

1. Name three large appendicular bones: _____, _____, and _____.

2. List three places where cartilage is found in the body: _____, _____, and _____.

3. _____ is a liquid found in joints that keeps them lubricated.

4. The specialized cells that constantly rebuild bone are called _____.

5. These specialized cells are needed to tear down bone: _____.

6. The condition of a lateral curvature of the spine is called _____.

7. _____ is an inflammation of the sac(s) that provide(s) the lubricating fluid for the joints in the body.

REVIEW QUESTIONS

Short Answer

1. Describe the difference in function between tendons and ligaments.

_____

_____

_____

_____

2. List three functions of the skeletal system.

_____

_____

_____

_____

3. What happens to our skeletal system as we age?

_____

_____

_____

4. What are the functions of cartilage?

_____

_____

_____

5. Discuss the general guidelines used to help determine when you should see a doctor following a bone or joint injury.

_____

_____

_____

Suggested Activities

1. Using art paper, cut out, label, and assemble bones to create a full-size skeleton.

2. Act out various range-of-motion exercises and perform and identify different joint movements.

3. Visit the library and research how the human skeleton has evolved, also noting the differences between male and female skeletons, posture changes, and changing shapes of various bones.

4. With a partner, research and analyze the effects of elasticity on the human body. Select three elastic body parts and list the effects that these body parts have on the body. Describe and analyze these effects in a report or oral presentation to the class.

CAREER CONNECTIONS

Now that you have read this chapter, here is a list of related professions you may be interested in investigating for a future career:

- Radiologic Technologists

Research each profession and report on the following:

1. Profession description to include job responsibilities
2. Educational requirements
3. Job opportunities
4. Opportunities outside of the hospital setting
5. Salary range
6. Licensure and continuing education requirements

ANATOMY, PHYSIOLOGY, AND DISEASE IN ACTION

I. Labeling Bones and Joints
Materials:

Skeleton and two colors of post-its or labels

Students need to purchase a Halloween skeleton, or have students draw their own skeletons. The skeletons and detail will vary. Have students label the bones with labels or post-its of one color. Using another color, students should label the type of joints. Some of the joints will be fused such that there is no movement. For those joints fill in the following chart:

Location	Type of Joint	Motion Prohibited

II. Move to the Beat
Materials:

Musically inclined students to establish a strong beat

Have a student call out movement descriptors in opposition pairs such as "Flex, Extend," "Inversion, Eversion." Students perform the movement in time with the beat.

The Muscular System
Movement for the Journey

7

As we continue our journey of exploration, we obviously need a transportation method to reach our destination. We can go by a plane, train, or automobile. However, no matter what transportation system we use, we must utilize the body's muscular system to get to the vehicle. Although the skeletal system provides the framework for the human body, the body also needs a system that allows movement, or locomotion, which is the job of the muscular system. We are most familiar with external movements that use our skeletal muscles to walk, run, or lift objects. However, internal movement within the body is necessary to transport food, air, waste products, and body fluids such as blood. For example, if you drink some bad water on our journey, the smooth muscles in your digestive tract will rapidly pass it through your system to be expelled in the form of urgent diarrhea. Different types of specialized muscles within the muscular system allow for both external and internal movement. This chapter defines and contrasts the different muscle types needed for external and internal body movement.

LEARNING OUTCOMES

At the completion of your journey through this chapter, you will be able to:

- Differentiate the three major muscle types
- Discuss the functions of tendons
- Explain the difference between voluntary and involuntary muscles
- Describe the various types of skeletal muscle movement
- Identify and explain the components of a muscle cell
- Describe the chemical activities required for muscle movement
- Describe the process of neuromuscular transmission
- Contrast the activity of cardiac, smooth, and skeletal muscles
- Discuss disorders of the muscular system

Pronunciation Guide

Correct pronunciation is important in any journey so that you and others are completely understood. Here is a "see and say" Pronunciation Guide for the more difficult terms to pronounce in this chapter. Please note that pronunciations given are referenced to medical dictionaries, and regional variations may exist.

abduction (ab DUK shun)
acetylcholine (ah SEET ul KOE leen)
actin (ak TIN)
adenosine triphosphate (ah DEN oh sin)
agonist (AG on ist)
aponeurosis (AP oh new ROH sis)
ataxia (ah TAK see ah)
atrophy (AT roh fee)
diaphragm (DYE ah fram)
electromyography (ee LEK troh my OG rah fee)
extension (eks TEN shun)
fibromyalgia (FIE bro my AL jee uh)
flaccid (FLAS sid)
flexion (FLEK shun)
glucose (GLOO kohs)

glycogen (GLIE co jin)
hypertrophy (high PER troh fee)
intercalated discs (in TER kuh LATE ed)
muscular dystrophy (MUS kyoo lahr DIS troh fee)
myalgia (my AL jee ah)
myasthenia gravis (my as THEE nee ah)
myofibril (my oh FIE bril)
myosin (MY oh sin)
rigor mortis (RIG or MORE tiss)
sarcomeres (SAR koh mearz)
sphincters (SFING terz)
synergistic (SIN er GIS tic)
tetanus (TET ah nus)
tonus (TONE us)
vasodilate (VASE oh DIE late)

OVERVIEW OF THE MUSCULAR SYSTEM

Because of the numerous functions they must perform, muscles come in many shapes and sizes. The structure of the muscle matches its function, as you will shortly see.

Types of Muscles

Muscle is a general term for all **contractile tissue**. The term *muscle* comes from the Latin word *mus,* which means "mouse," because the movement of muscles looks like mice running around under our skin. The contractile property of muscle tissue allows it to become short and thick in response to a nerve impulse and then to relax back to its original length once that impulse is removed. This alternate contraction and relaxation is what causes movement. Muscle cells are elongated and resemble fibers such as those in rope. Muscle tissue is constructed of bundles of these muscle fibers. Each fiber is approximately the diameter of a human hair. Under the direction of the nervous system, all the muscles provide for motion of some type for your body.

The body has three major types of muscles: **skeletal, smooth,** and **cardiac.** Let's begin with a general description and comparison of these three muscle types and then get more specific about each type.

Skeletal muscles are **voluntary** muscles, under conscious control, and derive their name from the attachment of the muscle to the skeletal system. The fibers in skeletal muscles appear to be striped and are therefore called **striated** (striped) muscle. These muscles allow us to perform external movements—running, lifting, or scratching, for example. These are the muscles we try to develop through exercise and sports and also so we look good at the beach.

muscle Many muscle fascicles grouped together and surrounded by fascia.

contractile tissue Tissue that can shorten in response to a stimuli.

skeletal muscle *(SKELL eh tal)* One of three types of muscles in the body, but the only muscle that is under voluntary, conscious control. Under the microscope, skeletal muscle has a striated appearance.

smooth muscle One of three types of body muscles and it is involuntarily controlled and found in the lining of the airways, blood vessels, and uterus.

cardiac muscle One of three types of muscle in the body. It is found only in the heart and cannot be controlled consciously.

voluntary muscle Muscle under conscious control.

striated *(STRY ate ed)* Striped.

Unlike skeletal muscle, smooth muscle is **involuntary** and not under our conscious control. It is also called smooth muscle because it does not have the striped appearance of skeletal muscles. This involuntary muscle is found within certain organs, blood vessels, and airways. Because it is the muscle of organs, it is sometimes called visceral muscle. Smooth muscle allows for the internal movement of food (peristalsis) in the case of the stomach and other digestive organs. Smooth muscle also facilitates the movement of blood by changing the diameter of the blood vessels (vasoconstriction and vasodilation) and also the movement of air by changing the diameter of the airways found in our lungs.

The third type of muscle is cardiac muscle, which has a striated appearance. This muscle type is found solely in the heart. It makes up the walls of the heart and causes the heart to contract. These contractions cause the internal movement (circulation) of blood within the body. Fortunately, cardiac muscle, like smooth muscle, is an involuntary muscle. Imagine if we had to think each time in order for our heart to beat. FIGURE 7-1 ▲ contrasts the three types of muscles found within the body.

All muscle has certain characteristics in common. One of these is the ability to be stretched. This is called *extensibility*. Think of yoga instructors and how flexible they can be to pose in yoga positions. It is fortunate for muscles to have extensibility to some degree. For example, if you swallow a large piece of food by accident, your visceral or smooth muscle in your esophagus and the sphincter muscle at the top of your stomach will stretch to let it pass.

We will now explore each of these types of muscles in further depth.

involuntary muscle Muscle that is not under conscious control.

Skeletal muscle

These voluntary muscles are attached to bones and are characterized by being long and cylindrical and have a pronounced striated appearance.

Cardiac muscle

This involuntary muscle is found in the walls of the heart. These lightly striated muscles function more efficiently through the use of intercalated discs.

Smooth muscle

This involuntary muscle type is found in the walls of hollow organs and vessels as well as respiratory airways. These nonstriated muscles contract and relax and help perform peristalsis and maintain the diameter of blood vessels and airways.

FIGURE 7-1 ▲ The three types of muscle: skeletal, cardiac, and smooth.

Clinical Application

tonus *(TONE us)*
A partial, steady contraction of a muscle; firmness.

hypertrophy *(high PER troh fee)* Greater than normal growth.

flaccid *(FLAH sid)* Limp or without muscle tone.

atrophy *(AT roh fee)* Loss of muscle bulk in one or more muscles. It can be caused by malnutrition or can occur in any part of the body that is paralyzed and the muscles receive no electrical impulse from the nerves.

myopathy *(my OP uh thee)* A general term for muscle disease.

MUSCLE TONE

Have you or someone you know ever had a cast on for an extended period of time? When it is removed, the arm or leg is much smaller and weaker than the limb without the cast. Why does this occur? Normally, all muscles exhibit muscle tone (**tonus**). Tonus is the partial contraction of a muscle with a resistance to stretching. Athletes who exercise regularly have increased muscle tone, making their muscles more pronounced, and also increased flexibility due to muscle stretching. The muscle fibers in an athlete increase in diameter (**hypertrophy**) and become stronger. Hypertrophy refers to increased growth or development. When muscles are not used, they begin to lose their tone and become **flaccid** (soft and flabby). For example, if a patient is required to remain in bed (bedfast) for an extended period of time, his or her muscles waste away (**atrophy**) from the lack of use. One of the reasons patients get out of bed as soon as possible is to prevent atrophy from occurring. Patients who are confined to bed, like our quadriplegic patient Ray, often have problems with muscle atrophy. If skeletal muscle is damaged, it can regenerate. However, if the damage is extensive, then a scar forms.

Pathology Connection

MYOPATHY

Myopathy is the general term for muscle disease or disorder. There are many causes of myopathy, including injury, genetics, nervous system disorders, medication, and cellular abnormalities. Symptoms of myopathy include weakness, cramping, stiffness, and spasm. Treatment for myopathy depends on the cause. Specific myopathies will be discussed at appropriate places in the chapter.

TEST YOUR KNOWLEDGE 7-1

Choose the best answer:

1. The biceps muscle is an example of a:
   a. smooth muscle
   b. cardiac muscle
   c. skeletal muscle
   d. dinosaur muscle

2. Smooth muscle is found in all the following *except:*
   a. airways
   b. digestive system
   c. blood vessels
   d. heart

3. Which types of muscles are striated?
   a. smooth and cardiac
   b. cardiac and skeletal
   c. skeletal and smooth
   d. smooth only

4. A decrease in the size of a muscle due to disuse or disease is called:
   a. myopathy
   b. hypertrophy
   c. atrophy
   d. amyotrophy

Skeletal Muscles

Skeletal muscles are attached to bones of the skeleton and provide movement for your body. As you learned in Chapter 6, "The Skeletal System," **tendons** are fibrous tissues that attach skeletal muscle to bones, and **ligaments** attach bone to bone. Some muscles can attach to a bone or soft tissue *without* a tendon. Such muscles use a broad sheet of connective tissue called an **aponeurosis**. This type of connection is found, for example, in some facial muscles.

Skeletal muscle is also known as voluntary muscle because we can control its movement by conscious thought. The numerous skeletal muscles found throughout the body are responsible for movement, giving the body its shape and form, maintaining our body posture, and heat generation. See FIGURE 7-2 ▲, which shows some of the major muscles found in the human body.

skeletal muscle *(SKELL eh tal)* One of three types of muscles in the body, but the only muscle that is under voluntary, conscious control. Under the microscope, skeletal muscle has a striated appearance.

tendon Cordlike, white band of nonelastic fibrous connective tissue that attaches a muscle to a bone.

ligament Fibrous band that holds two bones together.

aponeurosis *(AP oh nyoo ROH sis)* Broad sheet of connective tissue that serves as a muscle attachment.

Pathology Connection

STRAINS AND TEARS

Muscle **strains** are injuries caused by overstretching the tendons or the muscles themselves. Injuries can range from slight overstretch (a *pulled muscle*) to complete muscle tear or tendon rupture. Injuries may be acute, resulting from trauma, or chronic, typically resulting from overuse or disease. Symptoms of muscle or tendon injuries vary with severity. A mild strain, with no tear of tendon or muscle fibers, results in mild pain and perhaps some stiffness. A moderate strain, with some tearing of muscle or tendon fibers, will cause more severe pain as well as bruising and obvious weakness. A severe strain, usually a complete muscle or tendon tear, will result in severe pain, swelling, extensive bruising, and often complete loss of movement.

strain Overstretching of a muscle or tendon, often due to physical overexertion. This causes inflammation, pain, swelling, and bruising as the capillaries in the muscle tear. There can be small tears in the muscle itself. Also known as a pulled muscle.

Amazing **Body Facts**

Muscles

- Muscles make up almost half the weight of the entire body.
- There are 650 different muscles in the human body.
- The size of your muscles depends on how much you use them and how big you are. Ice skaters, for example, have large leg muscles.
- The little muscles around the eye can contract 100,000 times a day.
- Individual elongated muscle cells can be up to 12 inches, or 30 centimeters, in length.
- At about the age of 40, the number and diameter of muscle fibers begin to decrease, and by age 80, 50% of the muscle mass may be lost. Exercise and good nutrition help to minimize this loss.

Temporalis
Frontalis
Orbicularis oculi
Zygomaticus
Orbicularis oris
Masseter — Facial

Sternohyoid
Sternocleidomastoid — Neck

Platysma

Shoulder — Trapezius
Deltoid

Biceps brachii — Arm
Brachialis

Thorax — Pectoralis major
Latisimus dorsi
Serratus anterior

Rectus abdominis
External oblique — Abdomen

Brachioradialis
Extensor carpi radialis longus
Extensor carpi radialis brevis
Forearm — Extensor digitorum
Abductor pollicis longus
Extensor pollicis brevis

Tensor fasciae latae
Iliopsoas
Pectineus

Adductor longus
Sartorius
Gracilis — Thigh
Rectus femoris
Vastus medialis
Vastus lateralis

Peroneus longus
Gastrocnemius
Tibialis anterior — Leg
Soleus

Extensor digitorum longus

Anterior View

FIGURE 7-2 ▲ Anterior and posterior view of major muscles.

Neck
- Occipitalis
- Sternocleidomastoid
- Trapezius

Shoulder
- Deltoid
- Infraspinatus
- Teres major
- Rhomboid major

Latissimus dorsi

Arm
- Triceps brachii
- Brachialis

Forearm
- Brachioradialis
- Anconeus
- Extensor carpi radialis longus
- Extensor carpi radialis brevis
- Extensor digitorum
- Extensor carpi ulnaris
- Flexor carpi ulnaris
- Abductor pollicis longus
- Extensor pollicis brevis

Hip
- Gluteus medius
- Gluteus maximus

Thigh
- Adductor magnus
- Gracilis

Hamstrings
- Biceps femoris
- Semitendinosus
- Semimembranosus

Iliotibial tract

Leg
- Gastrocnemius
- Soleus
- Peroneus longus
- Peroneus brevis
- Calcaneal (Achilles) tendon

Posterior View

FIGURE 7-2 ▲ *(continued)*

Skeletal Muscle Injuries

Diagnosis of muscle or tendon injuries is accomplished by physical examination, imaging (MRI, x-ray), and medical history. Treatment of acute tendon or muscle strains varies with severity. Moderate and severe strains should be treated by a physician. In the early stages of the injury (during the first 72 hours) the standard treatment is *r*est, *i*ce, *c*ompression, and *e*levation (abbreviated RICE). Sometimes another letter is added to form PRICE, where *P* stands for *protection.* Acetaminophen (such as Tylenol™)or one of the NSAIDs (nonsteroidal anti-inflammatory drugs, ibuprophen, such as Advil™) may be given for pain relief, though their efficacy for promoting healing is questionable. After the first 72 hours, the injury should be rehabilitated, either by gradual increase in activity or by physical therapy. Heat may be applied at this stage. If after several weeks therapy has not shown any improvement, surgery may be necessary. Muscles or tendons that are obviously torn may be treated surgically at the time of diagnosis. Strains are often slow to heal, particularly tendon injuries. Keep in mind that skeletal muscle and dense regular connective tissue have only moderate ability to repair themselves.

tendonitis (or **tendinitis**) Inflammation of any tendon from injury or overuse.

Chronic tendon injuries are typically called **tendinitis** (or **tendonitis**). This name is incorrect, however, because there is rarely inflammation present in patients who present with symptoms of chronic tendon damage. More physicians are referring to these chronic injuries, often due to overuse (repetitive motion) or to untreated acute injuries, as tendin*osis*. However, the term *tendinitis* is so ingrained that it will probably continue to be used. For patients who do not have inflammation of the tendons but are still experiencing discomfort, treatment usually includes (P)RICE and the use of pain medications. Physical therapy may also be prescribed to improve and strengthen the muscles around the affected tendon, and the patient will likely be monitored to make sure the condition does not get worse.

tendinosis Chronic tendon injury.

Tendinosis is a degenerative disease leading to breakdown and scarring of tendons that appears to be caused by the failure of tendons to repair themselves after injury. Symptoms of tendinosis include pain, tenderness, and stiffness and often do not appear until the disease is advanced. Several tendons seem more susceptible to tendinosis than others, including the rotator cuff, Achilles tendon, tibialis posterior tendon, patellar tendon, and tendons of the lateral elbow. Several factors affect the development of tendinosis, including age, gender, skeletal anatomy, types of occupational equipment used, and systemic disease (like rheumatoid arthritis or diabetes mellitus). Maria, our diabetes patient, is at a slightly higher risk of tendon damage because of impaired wound healing. Treatment includes (P)RICE, rehabilitation, physical therapy, steroids (short term only), lasers, ultrasound, and extracorporeal shock wave therapy. Surgery may be used as a last resort. Unfortunately, none of these treatments have proven to be very effective. Long-term prognosis for chronic tendon injuries is not as good as for acute injuries.

shin splints A common running-induced injury of the extensor muscles and surrounding tissues of the lower leg.

A common running-related inflammatory injury of the extensor muscles and surrounding tissues of the lower legs is called **shin splints**. This condition can be treated

Amazing Body Facts

When is a Muscle Tear Good?

Some muscle tears are actually good for you. When muscle groups are exercised, they develop microscopic tears. The healing process actually leads to increased muscle growth and mass. This is most efficiently accomplished if you give that muscle group a rest after exercise.

with rest or reduction of intensity of the exercise along with ice, anti-inflammatory medication, and modification of footwear.

Skeletal Muscles of Specific Body Regions

Many times on a journey, we need a roadmap for reference. These roadmaps are often big maps of an entire state. However, there are also inserts of specific cities that give much greater detail. Think of Figure 7-2 as our "state map" of the anterior and posterior major muscles. The following series of "city maps" will provide you with greater detail.

Facial Skeletal Muscles Please see **FIGURE 7-3** ▲, which shows the facial skeletal muscles.

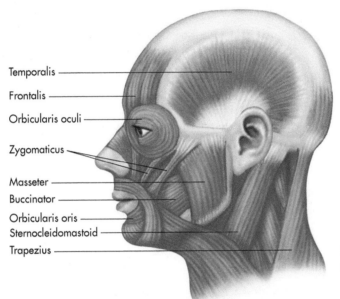

FIGURE 7-3 ▲ Skeletal facial muscles.

Labels (top to bottom):
Temporalis
Frontalis
Orbicularis oculi
Zygomaticus
Masseter
Buccinator
Orbicularis oris
Sternocleidomastoid
Trapezius

LEARNING HINT

Muscle Names

Muscles can be named based on any of the following criteria:

- Muscle location (Example: *biceps brachii* is in the arm. Brachii = *arm*.)
- Number of origins (Example: *biceps brachii* has two origins. Biceps = *two heads*.)
- Action (Example: *adductor longus* adducts the thigh.)
- Size (Example: *gluteus maximus*. Maxiumus = *biggest*.)
- Location of attachments (Example: *brachioradialis; radialis* refers to the radius.)
- Shape (Example: deltoid is triangular. Delta = *triangle*.)
- Combination (Example: *pectoralis major*. Pectoral = *chest*, major = *big*.)

Anterior and Posterior Trunk Skeletal Muscles Now take an in-depth look at the muscles of the anterior and posterior trunk of the body in FIGURE 7-4 ▲.

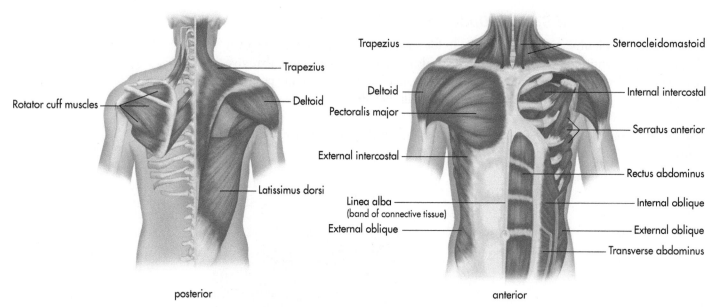

posterior   anterior

FIGURE 7-4 ▲ Skeletal muscles of the anterior and posterior trunk.

Skeletal Muscles of the Arm and Shoulder Moving out to the peripheral area of the body, we now zoom in on the skeletal muscles of the hand, arm, and shoulder in FIGURE 7-5 ▲.

FIGURE 7-5 ▲ Skeletal muscles of the shoulder, arm, and hand.

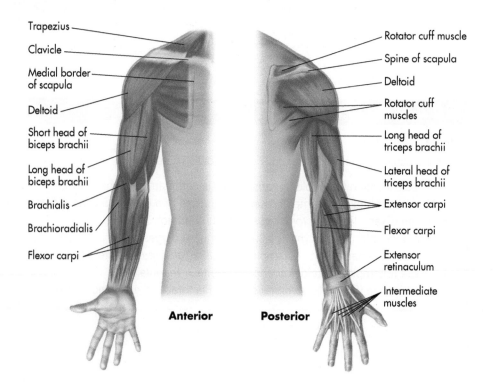

Anterior   Posterior

Skeletal Muscles of the Legs We finish our tour with the skeletal muscles of the hip and leg in FIGURE 7-6 ▲.

Muscles of the posterior left hip and thigh

Gluteus medius

Vastus lateralis (covered by fascia)

Gluteus maximus

Adductor magnus

Semi tendinosus

Gracilis

Hamstring group

Biceps femoris

Sartorius

Semimembranosus

Gastrocnemius

Muscles of the anterior left hip and thigh

Psoas major — Iliopsoas

Iliacus

Sartorius

Pectineus

Adductor longus

Adductor group

Adductor magnus

Gracilis

Rectus femoris

Vastus lateralis

Quadriceps femoris group

Vastus medialis

Patella

Patellar ligament

Gastrocnemius

Peroneus longus

Tibialis anterior

Tibia

Peroneus brevis

Extensor digitorum longus

Muscles of the lateral left leg

Vastus lateralis

Biceps femoris

Tibialis anterior

Head of fibula

Extensor digitorum longus

Gastrocnemius

Peroneus brevis

Peroneus longus

Calcaneal tendon

Peroneus tertius

FIGURE 7-6 ▲ Skeletal muscles of the hip and leg.

Pathology Connection

FIBROMYALGIA SYNDROME

Myalgia means pain or tenderness in a muscle. Myalgia is a symptom of many disorders, including acute injury and viral infection. This type of myalgia is usually treated using RICE and over-the-counter or prescription pain medication or by treating the viral infection that is causing the myalgia. **Fibromyalgia syndrome (FMS)** is a chronic pain syndrome characterized by pain of at least 3 months' duration, bilateral tenderness, fatigue, sleep disorders, depression, anxiety, and exercise intolerance. It is found in about 2% of the population of the United States and Canada. The majority of fibromyalgia patients are women. FMS is also common in patients with rheumatological disorders. FMS may be either primary, with FMS only, or secondary, with pain related to another disorder. The cause is unknown, but there is no inflammation involved. Evidence suggests that FMS may be caused by hyperactive stress response or by a sensory or neurological problem that leads to increased sensitivity to pain. FMS can be distinguished from other types of chronic pain by the location of pain in 11 of 18 designated tender points. Other disorders that cause chronic pain should always be ruled out. There is no definitive treatment for FMS. Symptom management is often inadequate. Some patients are helped by antidepressants (even without evident depression), antiepileptic medications, exercise, or pain relievers.

myalgia *(my AL jee ah)* Pain in one or more muscles due to injury or muscle disease. Polymyalgia is pain in several muscle groups.

fibromyalgia *(FYE bro my AL je uh)* Pain located at specific, small trigger points along the neck, back, and hips. The trigger points are very tender to the touch and feel firm.

agonist *(AG on ist)* The most important muscle that causes a movement, the prime mover.

primary movers Muscles or muscle groups that cause movement. Also known as agonists.

point of origin End of the muscle that is attached to stationary bone.

point of insertion Muscle end that is attached to a moving bone.

SKELETAL MUSCLE MOVEMENT

The body requires several different types of movement for various tasks. This movement is accomplished through the coordination of the contraction and relaxation of various muscles. All muscles have four common characteristics. They are *contractility, excitability* or *irritability, extensibility,* and *elasticity.* Contractility is the ability to shorten or contract. Excitability or irritability is the ability to respond to certain stimuli by producing electric signals called impulses. Extensibility is the muscle's ability to be stretched. Elasticity is the muscle's ability to return to its original length when relaxing.

Contraction and Relaxation

Movement of the body is a result of the contraction (shortening of the muscle fibers) of certain muscles. Consider the act of bending your arm so your fingers touch your shoulder. To really learn the concept, actually bend your arm and touch your fingers to your shoulder while resting your other hand on your biceps brachii muscle. In order to do this, your forearm is drawn to your shoulder as a result of the contraction of your biceps brachii. Did you feel the shortening and bulging of the biceps? Muscles, either by themselves or in muscle groups that cause movement, are known as **agonists** or **primary movers**.

The chief muscle causing the movement is the primary mover, and in this example it is the biceps muscle. Typically, as your muscle contracts, one of the bones will move (lower forearm) while the other (humerus) will remain stationary. The end of the muscle that is attached to the stationary bone is the **point of origin,** and in this example, it is at the shoulder area. The muscle end that is attached to the moving bone is the **point of insertion;** in this example, it is near the elbow (see FIGURE 7-7 ▲). So the action of a muscle is to move the insertion toward the origin. Also see TABLE 7-1 ■, which describes some of the major skeletal muscles along with their location and function.

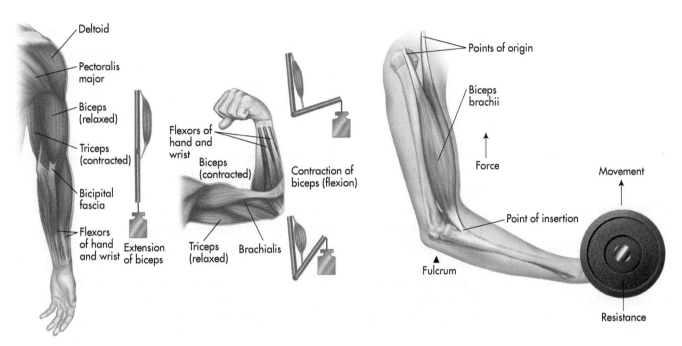

FIGURE 7-7 ▲ Coordination of antagonistic muscles to perform movement.

TABLE 7-1 ■ MAJOR MUSCLES, ORIGINS, INSERTIONS, AND ACTIONS

MUSCLE NAME	MUSCLE LOCATION	MUSCLE ORIGIN	MUSCLE INSERTION	MUSCLE ACTION
Biceps brachii	Anterior upper arm	Scapula	Radius	Flexes arm
Triceps brachii	Posterior upper arm	Proximal humerus and scapula	Posterior ulna (proximal)	Extends arm
Orbicularis oculi	Encircles eye	Frontal, maxilla and orbit	Eyelid	Closes eyelid
Masseter	Jaw or mandible	Zygomatic arch	Mandible	Closes jaw
Sternocleidomastoid	Anterolateral neck	Sternum and clavicle	Mastoid process	Flexes and rotates head
Pectoralis major	Chest	Clavicle, ribs, sternum	Proximal humerus	Flexes, rotates, and adducts arm
Deltoid	Shoulder	Clavicle and scapula	Proximal humerus	Adducts arm
Intercostals:	Between ribs			Assist in ventilation
External		Inferior rib	Superior rib	Elevate rib cage
Internal		Superior rib	Inferior rib	Depress rib cage
Diaphragm	Floor of thoracic cavity	Inferior rib cage and sternum	Central tendon	Prime mover of inspiration
Gluteus maximus	Buttocks	Ilium, sacrum, and coccyx	Proximal femur	Extends thigh
Hamstrings	Posterior portion of thigh	Ischium	Tibia	Flexes lower leg
Quadriceps	Anterior portion of thigh	Pelvis	Patella and tibia	Extends lower leg
Tibialis anterior	Anterior of lower leg	Proximal tibia	Metatarsals	Dorsiflexes foot
Gastrocnemius	Main muscle of calf (posterior lower leg)	Distal femur	Calcaneus via calcaneal (Achilles) tendon	Plantar flexes foot

synergistic *(sin er GIS tick)* A cooperating action of certain muscles.

antagonist The muscle that does the opposite of the agonist.

diaphragm *(DYE ah fram)* Muscular sheet that divides the thoracic cavity from the abdominal cavity. Most important ventilation muscle.

rotation Occurs when a bone spins on its axis.

abduction *(ahb DUK shun)* Moving a body part away from the midline of the body.

adduction *(ah DUCK shun)* Moving a body part toward the midline of the body.

extension *(eks TEN shun)* Straightening a joint to increase the angle between two bones or body parts.

extensor muscle Muscle that produces extension when it contracts.

flexion *(FLEK shun)* Bending of a joint to decrease the angle between two bones or body parts. Opposite of extension.

flexor muscle Muscle that produces flexion when it contracts.

ataxia *(ah TAK see ah)* Lack of coordination of the muscles during movement, particularly the gait. Caused by diseases of the brain or spinal cord, cerebral palsy, or an adverse reaction to a drug.

Other muscles can assist this movement, such as some of the muscles in the hands and wrist. These are called **synergistic** muscles because they assist the primary mover. To straighten out that same arm requires you to contract the triceps muscles. Your biceps must also relax, but this is a passive process. You do not relax your biceps, but simply stop contracting it, and it relaxes. Because these muscles cause movement in the opposite direction when they contract, they are called **antagonists**. This brings us to an important concept. All movement is a result of contraction of primary movers and relaxation of *opposing* muscles. In our example, you cannot forcefully contract the biceps muscles and straighten out your arm. Try it. Again, see Figure 7-7 for the illustration of the antagonistic muscles of the biceps and triceps.

One very important skeletal muscle that controls our breathing is the **diaphragm**. This dome-shaped muscle separates the abdominal and thoracic cavities and is responsible for performing the major work of bringing atmospheric air into our lungs. Exactly how this process occurs is discussed in detail in Chapter 13, "The Respiratory System." The diaphragm is unique in that it is under both voluntary and involuntary control. You don't have to think each time you breathe, but you can voluntarily change the way you breathe. FIGURE 7-8 ▲ shows the major muscles of breathing.

Movement Terminology

Certain terms are utilized to describe the direction of body movement. In Chapter 6, we discussed movement as it relates to joints in the skeletal system. In this chapter, we briefly discuss movement as it relates to muscles. **Rotation** describes circular movement that occurs around an axis. Rotation occurs, for example, when you turn your head from left to right or right to left. **Abduction** means to move *away* from the midline of the body. (If somebody is abducted, they are kidnapped or taken away from their family.) When you raise your arm to point when giving directions, you are performing abduction. **Adduction** occurs when you produce a movement that moves *toward* the midline of the body. When you bring your arm back down to your side from pointing, you are performing adduction.

Extension is a term used for *increasing* the angle between two bones connected at a joint. Extension is needed when you kick a football. In this situation, extension occurs when your leg straightens out during the kick. The muscle that straightens the joint is called the **extensor muscle**. **Flexion** is the opposite of extension. In this situation, you *decrease* the angle between two bones. Flexion occurs when you bend your legs to sit down. Flexion and rotation occur when you get your arm into position to arm wrestle. The muscle that bends the joint is called the **flexor muscle**. In this case a picture is worth a thousand words or at least the 124 words used to explain these concepts. FIGURE 7-9 ▲ illustrates these movements. Some muscular diseases can cause **ataxia**, which is a condition of irregular muscle movement and lack of muscle coordination.

Amazing Body Facts

Biomechanics

Biomechanics = Life + machine. Did you know that your body can be thought of as a machine? Individuals who work to aid those who have been injured on the job, occupational therapists, use biomechanics to determine how best to instruct an injured person to lift objects. These occupational therapists apply the principles of mechanics and lever systems to the human body. This application requires the use of anthropometric data, critical data being the distance/length of body levers (bones) between joints. Think of your body in terms of levers. If you want to know how much effort it will take to stand on your tip toes like a ballerina, think of your body as a second class lever. Your foot is the fulcrum, the resistance is in the middle and the effort comes from the calf. These principles can be applied to understand force in all areas of the body.

Intercostal muscles

Ribs

Diaphragm

FIGURE 7-8 ▲ The diaphragm: the major muscle of breathing.

Flexion

Biceps brachii (contracted)

Triceps brachii (relaxed)

FIGURE 7-9 ▲ The types of skeletal movement. **A.** Flexion and extension of left forearm. **B.** Flexion and extension of the leg.

Extension

Biceps brachii (relaxed)

Triceps brachii (contracted)

A

Quadriceps femoris group (relaxed)

Hamstring group (contracted)

Flexion

Quadriceps femoris group (contracted)

Hamstring group (relaxed)

Extension

B

TEST YOUR KNOWLEDGE 7-2

Give the correct body movement term for the following activities:

1. Looking right and left at a stop sign _____

2. Doing a split _____

3. Patting yourself on the back for labeling all these activities correctly _____

4. The first movement in curling a weight _____

5. Returning the weight from the curled position to your side _____

Fill in the blank:

1. Overstretch of a muscle or tendon is called a(n) _____.

2. Chronic tendon injury is properly called _____.

3. Fibromyalgia is a chronic inflammatory condition. True or false? _____

4. Muscles may be named by the location of their _____.

APPLIED SCIENCE

Kinesiology

Kinesiology is the study of muscles and movement. A kinesiologist is one who studies movement and can employ therapeutic treatment (kinesiotherapy) by specific movements or exercises.

epimysium *(EP ih MIZ ee uhm)* The outermost sheath of connective tissue that surrounds skeletal muscle.

perimysium *(per ih MISS ee uhm)* The connective tissue sheath that surrounds each primary bundle of muscle fibers.

endomysium A thin sheath of connective tissue, consisting principally of reticular fibers, that invests each striated muscle fiber and binds the fibers together within a fasciculus.

myofibril *(my oh FYE bril)* Cylinder containing the thin filament (actin) and thick filament (myosin) within the muscle fiber that give it its characteristic striated appearance.

MUSCULAR MOVEMENT AT THE CELLULAR LEVEL

Exactly how is skeletal muscular contraction and relaxation accomplished? How does the muscle tissue cause a coordinated and smooth contraction? Let's look in more detail at how muscles work.

The Functional Unit of the Muscle

Skeletal muscles look very simple if you examine only their macroanatomy. However, if you look deep into a skeletal muscle, it is divided up into several layers of cylinders packed inside each other. The typical muscle, like the biceps brachii, is surrounded by connective tissue, continuous with the tendon, called **epimysium**. Inside the muscle are bundles of muscle fibers surrounded by **perimysium**. These bundles are called fascicles. The muscle fibers themselves are elongated cells up to 12 inches, or 30 centimeters, in length. Each muscle fiber is encased in a connective tissue sheath called **endomysium** and is filled with cylinders called **myofibrils**. The muscle myofibril is sort of like a strand of metal, and these strands of metal can be bundled together to form a cable (see **FIGURE 7-10A** ▲).

Each myofibril is made of protein threads arranged in contractile units called **sarcomeres.** Each fiber has the ability to contract because of the makeup of the sarcomere. Each sarcomere has two types of protein threads called thick and thin **myofilaments.** The thick myofilaments are made up of the protein **myosin,** and the thin ones are primarily made up of the protein **actin.** The sarcomere has the actin and myosin filaments arranged in repeating units (sarcomeres) separated from each other by dark bands called **Z lines,** which give the striated appearance to skeletal muscle (see FIGURE 7-10A ▲ and B ▲). Each myofibril is made up of several sarcomeres.

Note in FIGURE 7-10C ▲ that the contraction of a muscle causes the two types of myofilaments to slide toward each other, shortening each sarcomere and therefore the entire muscle.

sarcomeres *(SAR koh meerz)* Portion of striated muscle fibril that lies between the two adjacent dark lines.

myofilament *(MY oh FILL uh mints)* A filament within the myofibril of muscle cells.

myosin *(MY oh sin)* The thick protein filament found in muscle fibers.

actin *(ak TIN)* One of the two proteins in muscle fibers needed for contraction.

Z lines Lines visible on the surface of skeletal muscle that mark the ends of each sarcomere.

A MUSCLE SEGMENT

C SARCOMERE

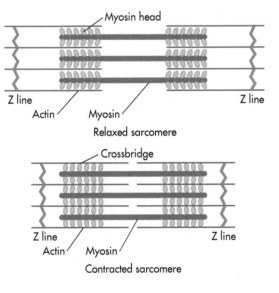

B MUSCLE SEGMENT WITH SARCOMERE

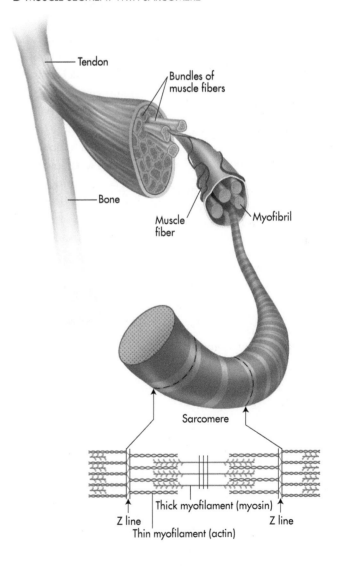

FIGURE 7-10 ▲ **A.** The muscle segment; **B.** The muscle segment with sarcomere; and **C.** Relaxed and contracted sarcomeres.

Picture a tube sliding within a tube, such as on a trombone. This sliding filament action and corresponding contraction requires that temporary connections, or crossbridges, be formed between the thick filament heads (myosin heads) and the thin filaments (actin) to pull the sarcomere together. Once the crossbridges form, the myosin heads rotate and pull the actin toward the center of the sarcomere. When the sarcomere relaxes, the filaments return to their resting or relaxed position. Visualize a raised drawbridge, where cars cannot pass. In order to be functional, the cross-connection—or lowering of the drawbridge—must occur, similar to the crossbridges needed to be formed for a muscle contraction. This model of muscle contraction is called the sliding filament-cross bridge model.

Important Ingredients: ATP and Calcium

In the previous analogy of the drawbridge, consider that a toll must be paid for the bridge to lower and connect. The body's tolls are the energy molecule **adenosine triphosphate (ATP)** and **calcium (Ca)**, which are needed for contraction and relaxation. ATP provides the energy to help the myosin heads form and break the crossbridges with actin. When the muscle is relaxed, calcium is stored away from the actin and myosin in the **sarcoplasmic reticulum (SR)**, a modified endoplasmic reticulum. When the muscle is stimulated, calcium is released from the SR and allows actin, myosin, and ATP to interact, which causes the contraction. When calcium returns to the SR, the crossbridges are broken, and the muscle relaxes.

When the nervous system tells the muscle to contract by releasing the neurotransmitter acetylcholine (ACh), the signal causes the **sodium ion channels** on the muscle fiber membrane to open. The cell membrane of each muscle fiber is called the **sarcolemma**. Sodium ions flow through these channels into the muscle fibers. This causes the muscle fibers to become excited, and calcium is released from the sarcoplasmic reticulum. The calcium, now free in the cytoplasm of the muscle fiber, helps myosin bind with actin in the presence of ATP. The calcium is then pumped back into the sarcoplasmic reticulum for storage, and the muscle relaxes.

adenosine triphosphate (ATP)
(ah DEN oh seen try FOSS fate)
Energy storage molecule used to power muscle contraction and other cellular reactions.

calcium (Ca) Important for blood clotting, enzyme activation, and acid-base balance. It gives firmness and rigidity to bones and teeth. It is essential for lactation, the function of nerves and muscles (including heart muscle), and maintenance of membrane permeability.

sarcoplasmic reticulum (SR)
(SAR koh PLAZZ mic re TICK you lum) Storage space within muscle for calcium.

sodium ion channels Pathways for sodium ions to exist and enter the cell.

sarcolemma *(sahr kuh LEM uh)* The cell membrane of a muscle cell.

Pathology Connection

DUCHENNE'S MUSCULAR DYSTROPHY (DMD)

Duchenne's muscular dystrophy (DMD) is a genetic, incurable myopathy. It is the most common childhood form of muscular dystrophy. Because the gene for DMD is carried on the X chromosome, the disease is seen overwhelmingly in boys. It is relatively common, with an incidence of 1 in 3,500 live male births. The disease is caused by a mistake in the gene for a protein called dystrophin. Scientists think dystrophin's function is to hold muscle fibers together during contraction. Without functional dystrophin, muscle fibers degenerate. All types of muscle—smooth, cardiac, and skeletal—are affected.

Symptoms are typical of myopathy, mainly muscle weakness, in the early stages of the disease. As the disease progresses, muscles become progressively weaker, scarred, and filled with fatty deposits as the muscle fibers disappear. DMD is progressive. Most boys are diagnosed around age 4 and are wheelchair-bound by age 10. Average life span is 17 years. Many DMD patients have significant cardiac and smooth muscle abnormalities as well. Death is usually due to respiratory or cardiac failure. A milder, late-onset form of muscular dystrophy, called Becker's muscular dystrophy (BMD), is diagnosed in patients in their 20s and 30s. It leads to debilitating myopathy, but progresses more slowly.

DMD is diagnosed by physical examination. Its diagnostic symptoms include gait abnormality in toddlers, progressive myopathy, and pseudohypertrophy in the calves. Biochemical tests for muscle enzymes, genetic testing, muscle biopsy, and an **electromyogram (EMG)** can confirm diagnosis based on physical exam. An electromyogram is a test in which a muscle group is stimulated with an electrical impulse that causes a contraction. The strength of the contraction can then be recorded. There is no effective treatment for DMD, so treatment is mainly symptom management, including assistive devices and palliative care. Physical therapy should not be used because it increases the breakdown of muscle fibers. Some treatments in the experimental stage may offer hope for decreasing progression of the disease, including steroids, immunosuppressants, nutritional supplements, gene therapy, and stem cells. Research is focusing on increasing muscle repair to keep pace with muscle damage.

Pathology Connection

MYASTHENIA GRAVIS (MG)

Myasthenia gravis (MG), which literally means *grave muscle weakness,* is an autoimmune disorder in which the immune system attacks and destroys a large number of acetylcholine receptors at the neuromuscular junction. The remaining receptors are blocked, and there are also modifications of the muscle fiber at the neuromuscular junction. Motor neurons (nerve cells that cause movement) continue to release acetylcholine, but because of the damage, the muscle cannot respond. Eye muscles are typically the first muscles affected, but some patients initially experience difficulty chewing, swallowing, or talking. This disorder, like most autoimmune disorders, is progressive, though the course of the disease varies widely among patients. The muscle weakness fluctuates, worsening with activity and improving with rest.

MG is a rare disorder, but is most common in women under 40 years old and in men over 50. Because it is rare, MG is hard to diagnose and is often not diagnosed during the first year of the disease. Many disorders cause muscle weakness, but the fluctuating weakness seen in MG is unique. Blood tests for acetylcholine receptor antibodies (molecules that attack the receptors), and electromyography (muscle recordings) are the best way to diagnose MG. There is no specific definitive treatment for MG. Treatment typically includes acetylcholinesterase (AChE) inhibitors (allows for more ACh to be available), corticosteroids, immunosuppressants, and plasma exchange.

Duchenne's muscular dystrophy (DMD) Pseudohypertrophic muscular dystrophy marked by weakness and pseudohypertrophy of the affected muscles. It is caused by mutation of the gene responsible for producing the protein dystrophin. The disease begins in childhood, is progressive, and affects the shoulder and pelvic girdle muscles. The disease, mostly affecting males, is transmitted as a sex-linked recessive trait.

electromyogram (EMG) *(ee LEC troh MY oh gram)* A recording or tracing of the muscular activity as a result of electrical stimulation.

myasthenia gravis (MG) *(MY ass THEE nee ah)* Abnormal and rapid fatigue of the muscles, particularly evident in the muscles of the face; there is ptosis of the eyelids. Symptoms worsen during the day and can be relieved by rest. The body produces antibodies against its own acetylcholine receptors located on muscle fibers. The antibodies destroy many of the receptors. There are normal levels of acetylcholine, but too few receptors remain to produce sustained muscle contractions.

Muscle Contraction Step-by-Step

1. Acetylcholine (ACh), a neurotransmitter, is released from a neuron.
2. ACh binds to the muscle and causes sodium channels to open. Sodium flows into the muscle fiber, and the fiber becomes excited.
3. The excitement of the muscle fibers causes calcium to be released into the cytoplasm from the sarcoplasmic reticulum.
4. The calcium allows the forming of cross bridges between myosin heads and actin myofilaments.
5. ATP is used up, allowing cross bridges to break and reform, pulling the actin myofilaments closer together as they slide along the myosin filaments. The sarcomere shortens.
6. Many shortened sarcomeres results in shortening of many muscle fibers. This is muscle contraction.

Interrelatedness of Neuromuscular System

As you will discover in Chapter 9, contraction of a skeletal muscle requires the coordination of both the muscular and nervous systems. A **motor unit** is a motor neuron plus all the muscle fibers it stimulates. The initiation of a skeletal muscular contraction requires an impulse from a motor neuron of the nervous system to trigger a release of a neurotransmitter, a chemical signal, called **acetylcholine (ACh),** which opens the sodium ion channels and sets the process of muscle contraction into motion. Acetylcholine is a neurotransmitter that diffuses across the synaptic cleft. This all occurs at the neuromuscular junction. This is the junction between the motor neuron's fiber that transmits the impulse and the sarcolemma (the muscle cell membrane). The surface of the muscle is studded with sodium channels that are **ligand gated** (requiring a "special key" to open). A ligand-gated channel opens or closes when a molecule binds to a receptor that is part of the channel, like a key fitting into a lock. In the case of skeletal muscles, the ligand (key) is the neurotransmitter acetylcholine (ACh). Acetylcholine is released from the terminal end of a motor neuron, diffuses across the synaptic cleft, and binds to the surface of the skeletal muscle, opening sodium channels and causing sodium to flow into the cell. The sodium flowing in leads to calcium release, and the muscle contracts. Like all chemical synapses, the neuromuscular junction must be cleaned up at the terminal end of transmission. The enzyme responsible for cleaning up the synapse is called **acetylcholinesterase.** Note that "ase" at the end of the word means to "break down."

motor unit Motor neuron and all the muscle fibers it stimulates.

acetylcholine (ACh) *(AS eh till KOH leen)* Neurotransmitter between neurons in the brain and spinal cord or between a neuron and a voluntary skeletal muscle.

ligand gated The opening and closing of a cellular channel when a molecule binds to a receptor.

acetylcholinesterase *(AS eh till KOH lin ehs tur ace)* The enzyme that stops the action of acetylcholine.

Pathology Connection

TETANUS

Tetanus (also known as lockjaw) is a muscle disorder caused by an untreated bacterial infection of a wound. It was long thought that you got tetanus from stepping on a rusty nail, but actually the bacteria reside in the soil, and the puncture allows for their entry. Therefore, a new clean nail is just as dangerous. The bacteria (*Clostridium tetani*) release a toxin that keeps muscle constantly contracted such as the jaw being "locked" tight. Only a tiny amount of toxin, less than a milligram, is needed to cause the disease. (Remember our discussion of bacterial pathology in Chapter 4.) Tetanus symptoms include muscle spasm, rigid paralysis, stiffness, and pain. Spasm can be initiated with minimal stimuli, such as loud noises or even turning on a light. Patients may also have a fever. Symptoms appear 3 days to 3 weeks postinjury. Symptoms are usually progressive and can eventually paralyze the diaphragm. Diagnosis of tetanus is by physical examination and laboratory testing to rule out other disorders. Treatment includes cleaning of the wound that is the source of the bacteria, injection or IV tetanus antitoxin, sedation, ventilator support, and pain management. Most patients must be treated in the intensive care unit (ICU). Recovery takes several weeks, and many patients have long-term problems.

Because of widespread vaccination against tetanus, most clinicians in the United States and other developed countries will never see a case of tetanus. Tetanus would otherwise be rather common, as its infectious bacteria is widespread in soil around the world. Prior to vaccination, there were 500 cases per year in the United States. Today there are 800,000 tetanus cases per year worldwide, mainly in countries without vaccination programs. Current recommendations are that children be vaccinated several times for tetanus and that adults be vaccinated every 10 years.

Several other disorders, classified as neuromuscular disorders, also cause paralysis of skeletal muscle, due to abnormalities of the nervous system. These include Guillain-Barré syndrome, postpolio syndrome, and Lou Gehrig's disease. These will be described in Chapter 9.

tetanus *(TET ah nus)* An acute, infectious disease caused by a bacterium that can lead to severe spasms of voluntary muscles.

Amazing Body Facts

Rigor Mortis

Have you ever heard of a dead body rising from a table or showing signs of movement? This may sound like the opening for a movie about zombies or the "undead." Actually, it is a normal physiological process called **rigor mortis** that can be explained by science and not by science fiction.

When a body dies, all the stored calcium cannot be pumped back into the sarcoplasmic reticulum. Therefore, excess calcium remains in the muscles throughout the body and causes the muscle fibers to shorten (contract) and stiffen the whole body. In addition, ATP is not present in a dead body to break the cross bridges. This stiffening process of the entire body is termed rigor mortis.

rigor mortis *(RIG er MORE tiss)* A stiffness that occurs in dead bodies as a result of retained calcium and decreased ATP.

MUSCULAR FUEL

glycogen *(GLIE coh jin)* The form that glucose (sugar) takes when it is stored in the liver and skeletal muscles

glucose *(GLOO kohs)* A simple sugar found in foods and also the sugar in the blood.

fermentation The oxidative decomposition, under anaerobic conditions, of complex substances through the action of enzymes or ferments, produced by microorganisms. Bacteria, molds, and yeasts are the principal groups of organisms involved.

lactic acid Acid that builds up due to anaerobic metabolism.

oxygen debt The amount of extra oxygen that is required by muscle tissue during its recovery from strenuous exercise.

Muscle, like all tissue, needs fuel in the form of nutrients and oxygen in order to survive and function. The body stores a carbohydrate called **glycogen** in the muscle. Glycogen is always on reserve waiting to be converted to a usable energy source. When needed, the muscle can convert glycogen to **glucose**. During cellular respiration, which requires oxygen, energy is released from the glucose and converted to ATP, which powers the muscle. For very intense exercise, the body uses the process of **fermentation** to break down glucose and provide ATP. This process is less efficient than using glucose and can provide energy for only a short time, but it does not require oxygen. A by-product of this process is **lactic acid,** which builds up in the muscles, causing temporary muscle fatigue, or weakness. After exercise is completed, more oxygen is needed to convert the lactic acid back to glucose. This additional oxygen is known as the body's **oxygen debt.** The body overcomes this debt by increasing the rate of breathing and heart rate until it has returned to normal.

Muscles with very high demands (such as leg muscles) also store fat and use it as energy. The release of energy also produces heat, and this is why strenuous or prolonged exercises can overheat our bodies.

The higher-demand muscles not only use fat as an energy source, but also have a much richer blood supply than do less-demanding muscles. These muscles are needed for endurance, such as required by long-distance running. The richer blood supply carries extra oxygen to hardworking muscles, giving those muscles a darker color. In addition, the presence of a molecule, myoglobin, capable of storing oxygen, also causes the darker color of these muscles.

Some muscles, such as those in the hand, have fewer heavy demands placed on them and need only a small supply of blood. These muscles utilize the local blood supply for glucose and the glycogen stored within. They therefore have a lighter color. These muscles are faster but do not have the endurance capabilities that heavily used muscles have. Next time you take a long walk, keep pumping your hand. Although the hand can move faster than the leg muscles, it will tire more quickly.

Another example can be found in a chicken. Because its breast and wing muscles are not heavily used, those parts contain white meat. Its legs, however, endure constant use, and the meat is therefore dark. By contrast, a goose, a migratory bird that must fly long distances (endurance), has dark breast meat. Now you know why a chicken's breast meat is white. When was the last time you saw a chicken flying overhead?

APPLIED SCIENCE

Maintaining a Core Body Temperature

Not only do muscles produce movement, but they also help maintain posture, stabilize joints, and produce body heat. Producing heat is important in maintaining the body core temperature. As the energy-rich ATP is used for muscle contraction, three-fourths of its energy escapes as heat. This process helps to maintain body temperature by producing heat when muscles are utilized. This is why your temperature rises when exercising and also why you shiver when you are very cold. Shivering is your body's way of saying it is too cold and it needs to generate a lot of heat via many muscle contractions (shivering). In turn, this increases the body temperature.

TEST YOUR KNOWLEDGE 7-3

Fill in the blank:

1. The region between two Z lines is called a(n) _____.

2. The thick myofilament needed for muscle contraction is composed of _____.

3. The thin myofilament needed for muscle contraction is composed of _____.

4. The two ingredients needed for cross bridges to form and break are _____ and _____.

5. Muscular dystrophy causes fragile muscle fibers due to this missing or damaged protein _____.

6. _____ is caused by a toxin created by bacteria found in the soil.

VISCERAL OR SMOOTH MUSCLE

We introduced the concept of smooth muscle earlier in this chapter; now let's take a closer look. **Visceral muscle,** or **smooth muscle,** is found in organs (except the heart) such as the stomach and other digestive organs, and in the blood vessels and bronchial airways. The ability of smooth muscle to expand and contract plays a vital role in many of the body's internal workings. For example, blood pressure can be affected by whether the blood vessels get larger in diameter (**vasodilate**) or get smaller in diameter (**vaso-constrict**). Vasodilation can lead to decreases in blood pressure due to smooth muscle relaxation in the vessel that allows it to enlarge. The enlarged vessel has less resistance to flow, and the blood pressure therefore goes down. Conversely, vasoconstriction can cause increased blood pressure due to the smooth muscle contraction that restricts the blood vessel.

As another example, during an asthma attack, smooth muscles in the airways of the lungs constrict, making it difficult to get air into and out of the lungs. This is what causes the wheezing sound heard during an attack.

A special type of smooth muscle, called a **sphincter,** is found throughout your digestive system. Sphincters usually occur between major digestive organs, such as between the esophagus and stomach. These donut-shaped muscles act as doorways to let materials in and out by alternately contracting and relaxing. For example, the sphincters of the stomach act like doors that open up to allow food in from the esophagus and also to allow partially digested food out into the small intestine. Have you ever swallowed a large amount of bread or stuffing and had it get stuck on the way down to your stomach? This is a painful reminder that there is a sphincter that must relax and open to allow food to

Visceral muscle See smooth muscle.

smooth muscle One of three types of body muscles that is involuntarily controlled and found in the lining of the airways, blood vessels, and uterus.

vasodilation *(VAY zoh dye LAY shun)* Relaxation of the smooth muscle in the artery wall, causing the artery to become larger in diameter

vasoconstriction *(VAY zoh kon STRIK shun)* Constriction of the smooth muscle in the artery wall which causes the artery to become smaller in diameter.

sphincter *(SFINGK ter)* Muscular ring around a tube; a valve.

LEARNING HINT

Smooth Muscle Regulation of Blood Pressure

In considering blood pressure, visualize a large highway. If one lane is taken away (vasoconstriction), the same number of cars must now fit through one less lane, leading to traffic congestion (increase in pressure). If you open up another lane (vasodilate), you relieve some of this pressure.

enter your stomach. The muscles of the digestive system are discussed in greater depth in Chapter 15, "The Gastrointestinal System."

Smooth (visceral) muscles are involuntary muscles and do not contract as rapidly as skeletal muscles. Skeletal muscles, once stimulated, can contract 50 times faster than smooth muscle. Because of their slower activity and lower metabolic rate, smooth muscles receive only moderate amounts of blood. Once injured, smooth muscle rarely repairs itself; instead it forms a scar.

CARDIAC MUSCLE

cardiac muscle One of three types of muscle in the body. It is found only in the heart and cannot be controlled consciously.

Cardiac muscle forms the walls of the heart. The contraction of cardiac muscle squeezes blood out of the chambers of the heart, causing the blood to circulate through your body. Cardiac muscle is involuntary muscle. Cardiac muscle fibers are somewhat shorter than the other muscle types. Because the heart must work constantly, the cardiac muscles must receive a generous blood supply to get enough oxygen and nutrition, as well as to get rid of waste. In fact, cardiac muscle has a richer supply of blood than any other muscle in the body. The cardiac muscle fibers are connected to each other by **intercalated discs**. Because of this connection, as one fiber contracts, the adjacent one contracts, and so on. This is similar to the domino effect or the human wave at a football stadium if done correctly. A wave of contraction occurs, allowing blood to be squeezed out of the heart and into the body. This directed wave is important for a full and effective emptying of the blood within the heart. Imagine if everyone squeezed the tube of toothpaste in the middle: think of all the wasted toothpaste that would be left in the tube and how happy the toothpaste manufacturers would be. See FIGURE 7-11 ▲.

intercalated discs *(in ter KUH late ed)* Structures that connect heart tissue cells to facilitate a smooth contraction.

Cardiac muscle does not regenerate after severe damage, and this damage often leads to tissue death, such as occurs in a severe heart attack. If the blood supply going to the heart from the coronary arteries is blocked, cardiac muscle damage can occur, causing scarring of the heart. Scar tissue does not help the healthy muscles of the heart to contract. If the scarred area is extensive, the remaining cardiac muscle may not be sufficient to pump blood efficiently. An individual with scarred cardiac muscle may have a severely diminished cardiac output, which could lead to severe disability or even death.

Cardiac Muscle

Intercalated disc

Nucleus

FIGURE 7-11 ▲ Heart and intercalated discs.

APPLIED SCIENCE

A Useful Application of a Deadly Toxin

Botulism is a potentially deadly disease caused by food poisoning with the *Clostridium botulinum* bacteria. Science has found a way to utilize the poison generated by this bacterium for medical and cosmetic treatment. Small amounts of *botulinus* toxin are injected into facial muscles to stop previously untreatable facial twitching. The toxin basically paralyzes the muscles. The same toxin is used to treat wrinkles without the use of surgery and is known as Botox injection.

A QUICK TRIP THROUGH DISEASES AND CONDITIONS OF THE MUSCULAR SYSTEM

DISEASE	ETIOLOGY	SIGNS AND SYMPTOMS	DIAGNOSTIC TEST(S)	TREATMENT
Strains (tears)	Acute injury.	Varies with severity; may include pain, stiffness, bruising, weakness, loss of function.	Examination, radiologic studies, patient history.	Depends on severity, (P) RICE, pain relievers, heat, physical therapy, surgery.
Tendinosis (tendinitis)	Chronic overuse or disease.	Varies with severity; may include pain, stiffness, weakness.	Examination, radiologic studies, patient history.	(P)RICE, physical therapy, anti-inflammatory drugs, lasers, ultrasound, shock waves.

DISEASE	ETIOLOGY	SIGNS AND SYMPTOMS	DIAGNOSTIC TEST(S)	TREATMENT
Shin splints	Repetitive lower body exercise such as running; can be due to faulty foot mechanics or footwear.	Pain in the tibia region.	Patient history and physical exam.	Ice packs, anti-inflammatory medications, decrease of exercise intensity, avoidance of hills and hard surfaces, change in footwear.
Cramps/spasms	Sudden, severe involuntary muscle contraction.	Can be result of prolonged physical activity, excessive fluid/electrolyte loss, menstruation.	Patient history and physical exam; blood work for electrolyte levels.	Rest from specific task, rehydration, passive stretching, dietary electrolyte replacement.
Fibromyalgia syndrome	Unknown, but may be neurological.	Chronic pain, bilateral tenderness, fatigue, sleep disorders, depression, exercise intolerance.	Location of pain confined to "tender points".	Symptom management not very effective, some helped by antidepressants, exercise, pain relievers, anti-epileptic medications.
Duchenne's muscular dystrophy (DMD)	Genetic defect in muscle protein, causes disintegration of muscle fibers.	Muscle weakness in early stages; later, significant progressive muscle weakness including skeletal, cardiac, and smooth muscles.	Physical exam, biochemical and genetic tests, electromyogram (EMG), muscle biopsy.	No real treatment, disease is invariably fatal in adolescence or young adulthood; symptom management and palliative care; some experimental treatments in development.
Mitochondrial myopathy	Defect in ATP production in mitochondria.	Progressive muscle weakness, often accompanied by hearing loss, diabetes mellitus, heart problems, nervous system disorders, and other biochemical abnormalities.	Genetic tests, biochemical tests, EMG, muscle biopsy (for ragged red fibers).	No consensus on treatment, some drugs can decrease symptoms but nothing can stop progression.
Myasthemia gravis	Autoimmune attack at neuromuscular junction.	Progessive, flucuating muscle weakness, often starting with facial or eye muscles.	Blood tests, EMG.	Steroids, immunosuppressant drugs, plasma exchange, acetlycholinesterase inhibitors.
Tetanus (lockjaw)	Bacterial infection; Clostridium tetani.	Progressive muscle spasm, paralysis, stiffness and pain, especially in jaw.	Physical exam, lab tests to rule out other disorders, history of wound.	Wound hygiene, antibiotics, tetanus antitoxin, sedation, ventilator support, pain management.

Pharmacology Corner

SKELETAL MUSCLE DRUGS

Although there are many types of muscles, this corner will focus on drugs related to skeletal muscles. Cardiac and smooth muscles will be discussed in their respective chapters. At some times in our lives, we have all pulled or strained muscles. The most common drugs prescribed to treat the pain and resulting discomfort are anti-inflammatories and pain medication. The anti-inflammatories are of the nonsteroidal type due to the many potential side effects of steroid use and are known generally as nonsteroidal anti-inflammatory drugs (NSAIDs). Examples include ibuprofen (Advil™) and naproxen (Alleve™). Common pain medications include aspirin and acetaminophen (Tylenol).

Sometimes the actual muscle itself must be rested in order to heal. This mild relaxation can be achieved by a muscle relaxant. Skeletal muscle relaxants also help to relieve musculoskeletal pain or spasm. They are used to treat spasticity in stroke patients and in patients with multiple sclerosis or spinal cord injuries. Examples include Flexeril™ and Parafon Forte™, both of which tell the brain to decrease muscle tone.

There are certain situations when we want to clinically induce paralysis. For example, during surgery we don't want to have the patient moving all around the table! Here, neuromuscular blocking drugs actually cut off the communication between the brain and muscles. Examples include succinlycholine (Anectine™) and pancuronium (Pauvulon™).

Clinical paralysis is a very precise science because an overdose of these medications can stop the heart or breathing. Even though the patient is completely paralyzed, he or she can still feel pain and be conscious and aware. This is why it is imperative to give other drugs that sedate the patient.

SUMMARY

Snapshots from the Journey

- The three main types of muscles are skeletal, smooth, and cardiac.

- Skeletal muscle is striated (striped) voluntary muscle that allows movement, stabilizes joints, and helps maintain body temperature.

- Smooth muscle is nonstriated involuntary muscle found in the organs of the body and linings of vessels; it facilitates internal movement within the body.

- Cardiac muscle is involuntary, striated muscle found only in the heart.

- All movement is a result of contraction of primary movers and relaxation of opposing muscles.

- Muscles usually attach to bones via tendons.

- Large muscles consist of many single muscle fibers comprised of myofibrils. The smallest functional contractile unit is called a sarcomere.

- Each sarcomere unit contains the two threadlike contractile proteins: myosin and actin.

- Muscles contract as the actin and myosin protein filaments, in the presence of ATP and calcium, form cross bridges that cause the filaments to slide past each other, thereby causing the muscle to contract or shorten.

- There is an interrelation between the nervous and muscular systems in which the motor neuron of the nervous system initiates the activity of muscle contraction through the release of a neurotransmitter transmitter chemical called acetylcholine (ACh).

- There are many common diseases and conditions of the muscles, and because the nervous system is so closely related, there are also many common neuromuscular diseases.

MARIA'S STORY

You may remember Maria, who is an insulin-dependent diabetic. Recently, on the advice of her doctor, she began an exercise program. She started slowly, walking for 20 minutes per day. After a month of walking she decided to take an aerobics class. Two weeks into the class, one of her knees became painful and stiff. Her doctor explained to her that, as a diabetic, she is at a risk for tendinosis.

a. Do Maria's symptoms fit the symptoms of tendinosis?

_____

b. Why might diabetics be at higher risk for tendinosis?

_____

c. Is this a new injury or a more long-standing problem?

_____

RAY'S STORY

Ray is devastated. His mother finally brought him a mirror so he could look at his body. He couldn't believe his eyes. He had been injured for a few months and now looked like a skeleton. He had always taken pride in his appearance, working out regularly. He had even entered a Mr. Muscles contest once on a dare from his buddies.

How would you explain to Ray what happened to his body (or appearance)?

_____

_____

_____

_____

REVIEW QUESTIONS

Multiple Choice

1. Another name for voluntary muscle is:
   a. skeletal
   b. smooth
   c. cardiac
   d. nonstriated

2. Which structure does *not* contain smooth muscle?
   a. blood vessels
   b. heart
   c. digestive tract
   d. bronchi

3. Most skeletal muscles attach to bones via:
   a. ligaments
   b. joints
   c. flexors
   d. tendons

4. The state of partial skeletal muscle contraction is known as:
   a. homeostasis
   b. muscle tone
   c. partialus contractus
   d. flexerus

5. Cardiac muscle:
   I. is a voluntary muscle
   II. has intercalated disks to assist contraction
   III. regenerates after injury
   IV. lines the blood vessels
   a. I only
   b. I and II
   c. II only
   d. I, II, III, and VI

6. A disorder characterized by multiple points of tenderness and fatigue is:
   a. pompe disease
   b. fibromyalgia
   c. tendinosis
   d. Duchenne muscular dystrophy

Fill in the Blank

1. A sudden or violent muscle contraction is a(n) _____.

2. Partial or total loss of voluntary muscle use is _____.

3. The neurotransmitter that is necessary for skeletal muscle contraction is _____.

4. The body stores a carbohydrate called _____ in the muscle; it can be converted to a usable energy source.

5. _____ means pain or tenderness in the muscle.

6. Chronic injury to a tendon is known as _____.

7. This molecule is missing or defective in people with Duchenne muscular dystrophy: _____.

8. Which neuromuscular disorder is caused by a bacterial toxin? _____.

REVIEW QUESTIONS

Short Answer

1. List the three major muscle types and give an example of each.

_____

_____

_____

2. Contrast the terms *hypertrophy* and *atrophy*, and give an example of how each situation could occur.

_____

_____

_____

3. Explain how vasoconstriction and vasodilation affect blood pressure.

_____

_____

_____

4. Explain the steps needed in a skeletal muscle contraction.

_____

_____

_____

_____

5. Define myopathy and explain two disorders that cause myopathy.

_____

_____

_____

6. Muscle disorders may be caused by malfunction of organelles or structural breakdown of muscle fibers. List and briefly explain these disorders.

_____

_____

_____

Suggested Activities

1. Pick a major muscle group and discuss how your life would be different if that group could not function properly due to a disease or accident.

2. Bodybuilding requires an extensive knowledge of muscles and muscle groups. Demonstrate five different exercises and the different muscles they would develop.

3. Pair off with a partner and perform various muscle movements showing rotation, abduction, adduction, extension, and flexion. See if your partner can accurately classify each motion.

CAREER CONNECTIONS

Now that you have read this chapter, here is a list of related professions you may be interested in investigating for a future career:

- Kinesiology

- Physical Therapy

- Occupational Therapy

- Massage Therapy

Research each profession and report on the following:

1. Profession description to include job responsibilities
2. Educational requirements
3. Job opportunities
4. Opportunities outside of the hospital setting
5. Salary range
6. Licensure and continuing education requirements

ANATOMY, PHYSIOLOGY, AND DISEASE IN ACTION

I. Building Muscles

Materials:
Two strips of cardboard 2 inches by 6 inches
Hole puncher
Paper fasteners
Wide strip Scotch tape
Two 3 inch rubber bands

1. Tape cardboard strips together end-to-end (humerus and radius/ulna). Mark one of the strips as the top (biceps) and the other side of the strip bottom (triceps).
2. Punch holes in each of the strips approximately 1 1/2 inches from the tape.
3. Place one rubber band on top and one below each hole and attach them with a fastener.
4. This represents the elbow joint.
5. Observe what happens to the top rubber band (biceps) of the strip when the elbow bends and what happens to the bottom rubber band (triceps) at the same time.
6. From these observations, explain what actually happens within the muscle to make a muscle contract and relax.
7. From the diagrams below, identify which would occur during contraction of the bicep.

8. Each of these divisions represents a sarcomere, label the protein components in the following diagram.

9. What happens to the filaments during the contraction process? Notice that the thin filaments are attached to the ends of the sarcomere? How might this aid in the contraction of the muscle?

ANATOMY, PHYSIOLOGY, AND DISEASE IN ACTION

II. Effect of Fatigue on Muscle Action

1. Count how many times a fist can be clenched in 20 seconds. Record in the table below.

2. Repeat nine more times and record results. Do not rest between trials.

Trial	# of Clenches in 20 seconds
1	
2	
3	
4	
5	
6	
7	
8	
9	
10	

3. What are the three changes you observed in a muscle while it is working (contracted)?

4. Make a line graph of your results of the fatigue experiment. Be sure to label and fill in the values on the vertical axis.

5. What effect did fatigue have on the action of the hand muscles? Explain.

_____

_____

_____

The Integumentary System
The Protective Covering

You learned in Chapter 6 that the skeletal system is like the framework of a building or house. But the framework is just one part of a building; the integrity of a house wouldn't last very long without shingles on its roof, siding of some sort, and windows, all of which help prevent the environment from damaging the main structures and inner workings. Like a house, the human body must be sheltered from the environment, and that is the job of the integumentary system. Your skin forms a protective barrier to shield your body from the elements, guard against pathogens, and perform several other vital functions.

Think how important your skin is to your well-being and your ability to fully enjoy your journey. Without your skin, you would be unable to regulate your body temperature and would be uncomfortable in any environment. We paint our houses to protect them from the elements; likewise, we apply sunscreen when we spend a day at the beach. Although your skin is an important organ, there are also several other accessory components such as nails, hair, and glands—hence the name integumentary *system*.

LEARNING OUTCOMES

At the end of your journey through this chapter, you will be able to:

- Discuss the functions of the integumentary system
- List and describe the layers of the skin
- Explain the healing process of skin
- Describe the structure and growth of hair and nails
- Explain how the body regulates temperature through the integumentary system
- Describe various skin diseases, causative agents, and their related treatments

Pronunciation Guide

Pro·nun·ci·a·tion
Definitions/Parts

Correct pronunciation is important in any journey so that you and others are completely understood. Here is a "see and say" Pronunciation Guide for the more difficult terms to pronounce in this chapter. Please note that pronunciations given are referenced to medical dictionaries, and regional variations may exist.

alopecia (al oh PEE she ah)
apocrine (APP oh krine)
avascular (ay VASS cue ler)
carotene (CARE eh teen)
corium (CORE ee um)
ecchymosis (ek ee MOH sis)
eccrine (EKK rin)
epidermis (ep ih DER miss)
epithelial cells (ep ih THEE lee al)
follicle (FALL ih kul)
hypodermis (high poh DER miss)
keratin (KAIR eh tin)
keratinization (KER eh tin eye ZAY shun)
keratinized (KER eh tin ized)
lesion (LEE zhun)
lipocyte (lip OH site)

lunula (LOO nu la)
meibomiam gland (my BOH me am)
melanin (MELL an in)
melanocytes (mell AN oh sights)
pustule (PUS tyool)
sebaceous (see BAY shus)
seborrheic keratosis (SEB oh REE ik KERR ah TOH sis)
sebum (SEE bum)
scabies (SKAY beez)
stratum corneum (STRAY tum core NEE um)
subcutaneous fascia (sub cue TAY nee us FASH ee ah)
tinea (TIN ee ah)
vasoconstriction (VAZE oh kon STRIKT shun)
vasodilation (VAZE oh dye LAY shun)
vesicles (VES ih koolz)

SYSTEM OVERVIEW

In this section, we will look at the functions and parts of the **integumentary system**. This system is the protective covering of the body and is the most exposed system. Get ready for this chapter to "get under your skin."

Integumentary System Functions

The integumentary system includes the skin and its accessory components of hair, nails, and associated glands. The skin is your first line of defense protecting you from disease, and intact skin is the best protection from most infections. Surprisingly, some diseases of the integumentary system are actually caused by diseases from other body systems! Measles would be a perfect example. This is a viral disease of the respiratory system that causes a rash on your skin.

Your integumentary system also performs several vital functions besides protecting you from an invasion of disease-producing pathogens. This system helps keep the body from drying out, provides a natural sunscreen, and acts as storage for fatty tissue necessary for energy. Importantly, with the aid of some sunshine, the integumentary system produces vitamin D (needed to help your body utilize phosphorus and calcium for proper bone and tooth formation and growth). Finally, the skin allows for sensory input (pleasant and unpleasant sensations involving pressure and temperature, for example) to your brain and helps regulate your body temperature.

integumentary system *(in TEG you men tah ree)* The skin and its accessory components of hair, nails, and associated glands.

The Skin

Easily weighing twice as much as your brain, your skin is quite a large organ, approaching 20 pounds in an average adult. In fact, the skin is your largest organ. It covers an area of about 20.83 square feet on an adult-sized body. A closer examination of a cross section of skin reveals three main layers of tissue:

* **Epidermis**
* **Dermis**
* **Subcutaneous fascia** (also called the **hypodermis** layer because it lies *under* the dermis)

As we discuss these three layers, please refer to **FIGURE 8-1** ▲ for further clarification.

Epidermis

The epidermis is the layer of skin that we normally see. It is made up of several even smaller layers of stratified squamous epithelium. The epidermis is interesting for several reasons. First, it is **avascular** and contains no nerve cells (note that *a* means "without" and *vascular* means "blood vessels"). Second, the cells on the surface of this layer are constantly shedding, being replaced with new cells that arise from the deeper region called the **stratum basale** or basal layer of the epidermis in a process that takes 2 to 4 weeks. Cells are born in the basal layer. This layer is also called the

epidermis *(EP ih DER miss)* Thin, outermost layer of skin. The most superficial part of the epidermis consists of dead cells filled with keratin. The deepest part (basal layer) contains constantly dividing cells and melanocytes.

dermis *(DER miss)* Layer of skin under the epidermis. It is composed of collagen and elastic fibers. It contains arteries, veins, nerves, sebaceous glands, sweat glands, and hair follicles.

subcutaneous fascia (also called the **hypodermis layer**) *(sub kyoo TAY nee us FAY she ah)* Connective tissue layer beneath the skin.

avascular *(ay VASS cue ler)* Without blood vessels.

stratum basale The stem cell layer of the epidermis.

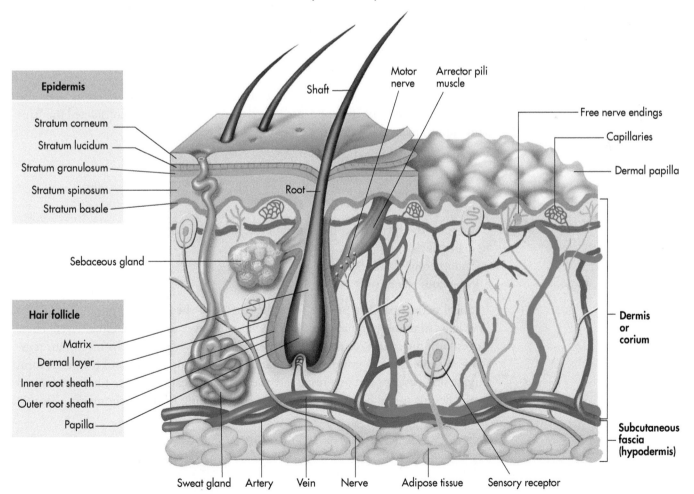

FIGURE 8-1 ▲ The three layers of the skin.

keratin *(KER ah tin)* Hard protein found in the cells of the outermost part of the epidermis and in the nails.

stratum corneum *(STRAY tum CORE nee um)* The outermost, horny layer of the epidermis.

melanocytes *(mell AN oh sights)* Cells that produce melanin.

melanin *(MELL an in)* Dark brown or black pigment that gives color to the skin and hair.

carotene *(CARE eh teen)* A yellow pigment found in plant and animal tissue.

corium *(CORE ee um)* Layer of skin immediately under the epidermis. Also known as the true skin or dermis.

stratum germinativum. As cells are pushed toward the surface, they die and fill up with the protein, **keratin.** In fact, the outermost surface of skin is actually a layer of dead cells called the **stratum corneum,** which are characteristically flat, scaly, keratinized (hardened) epithelial cells. Through everyday activities, such as bathing, drying off, and moving around, the body sloughs off *500 million* cells a day, equaling about *one and a half pounds* of dead skin a year! This continuous replacement of cells is very important because it allows your skin to quickly repair itself in case of injury.

Specialized cells called **melanocytes** are located deep in the epidermis and are responsible for skin color. Melanocytes produce **melanin,** which is the actual substance that affects skin color. An interesting note is that all people possess about the same number of melanocytes. The variations of skin color are a result of the amount of melanin that is produced and how it is distributed. This is obvious when you are exposed to the ultraviolet rays of the sun. In order to protect your skin, melanocytes produce more melanin, and voila!, you've got a tan. You will also note that in time you will develop a tan line demonstrating that the production of melanin occurs only as needed, in the areas where needed. Regardless of an individual's skin tone or color, all skin types respond to sun exposure. For some of us, the melanin locates in patches on the skin, forming *freckles.* **Carotene,** which is another form of skin pigment, gives a yellowish hue to skin. Individuals with a pinkish hue derive that color from the hemoglobin in their blood.

People with a condition called *albinism* have very little pigment in their skin, hair, or eyes. This is because they have inherited genes that do not allow their body cells to produce the usual amounts of melanin. People with albinism may have vision problems due to the lack of pigment in their eyes. They may also be at a greater risk for skin cancer.

Dermis

The layer right below, or inferior to, the epidermis layer is the thicker dermis layer, also called the **corium.** This layer of dense irregular connective tissue is considered the "true skin" and contains the following:

- Capillaries (tiny blood vessels)
- Collagenous and elastic fibers
- Involuntary muscles
- Nerve endings
- Lymph vessels (transport fluids from tissue to the blood system)
- Hair follicles
- Sudoriferous glands (sweat)
- Sebaceous glands (oil)

Small dermal papillae project from the surface of the dermis (stratum basale, also known as stratum germinativum) and anchor this layer to the epidermal layer. These ridges form finger and toe prints and are arranged so they provide the maximum resistance to slipping when gripping and holding objects. Fingerprints and toe prints form unique skin patterns and as a result, are used in identification. Nerve fibers are located in the dermis so the body can sense what is happening in the environment. Because this layer also possesses blood vessels, this is where your blush comes from when you get embarrassed!

The collagenous and elastic fibers of this layer help your skin flex with the movements that you make. Without that ability, your skin would eventually tear from all your moving around. In addition to flexing, these fibers allow your skin to quickly return to its normal shape when at rest. In older people and people regularly exposed to high levels of sunlight, the skin's firmness and ability to rapidly recoil to the normal state decreases. To better understand this process, try this experiment. With one of your hands resting palm down, take the thumb and index finger of your other hand and gently pinch and pull up the skin on the back of your resting hand. Let go and observe how quickly the skin recoils to normal. Try this experiment with an older person and observe how much slower his or her skin returns to normal. Remember to ask them first! Another example of the skin's resilience due to the collagenous and elastic fibers is when it returns to normal after an injury that caused swelling.

bilirubin *(bill ih ROO bin)* A yellow bile pigment formed from the breakdown of old worn out red blood cells.

jaundice *(JAWN dis)* A general term for the yellow staining of body tissues and fluids due to an excessive amount of bilirubin in the blood. There are various causes of jaundice

ecchymosis *(eck ih MOH sis)* Superficial bruising under the skin or mucous membrane due to bleeding.

Pathology Connection

SKIN COLOR AND DISEASE

At times skin color can indicate an underlying disease. Although carotene gives a yellowish hue to skin, that is normal. In a situation where liver disease exists, the body can't excrete a substance call **bilirubin**. As bilirubin builds up in the body, **jaundice** occurs, giving the skin a deeper yellow color. The changes in color are not as apparent on individuals with darker skin, but the yellowish color is easily seen in the whites of the eyes. Although bronze skin is associated with healthy outdoor living, individuals with a malfunctioning adrenal gland may have the same color due to excessive melanin deposits in the skin. Excessive bruising (black and blue marks called **ecchymosis**) could indicate skin, blood, or circulatory problems as well as possible physical abuse.

Amazing **Body Facts**

A Bothersome Fact of Life

Sometimes the sebaceous glands within the skin become blocked. As a result, sebum, the skin's oil produced by these glands, stagnates and is exposed to air, drying it out. When this occurs, the sebum turns black, creating the infamous *blackhead!* To make matters worse, if that blackhead becomes infected, a *pimple* is formed (medically known as a *pustule*). The best thing to do is keep those areas clean through gentle washing with soap and water and let nature take its course.

A somewhat related condition is folliculitis, which is usually a staphylococcus bacterial infection and inflammation of hair follicles. This condition presents with the formation of small pustules that surround the follicle.

This brings us to the topic of cleaning your skin. The skin is generally too dry for microbial growth, except for certain areas. Most skin bacteria is associated with hair follicles or sweat glands, so cleaning the areas of your skin that are hair covered and/or contain a high concentration of sweat glands is especially important. In addition, washing your hands frequently is the best way to prevent spread of disease. However, be careful not to wash too frequently with too hot water and/or too harsh soap, and avoid aggressive drying. This is important because excessive cleaning has the potential to dry out your skin and remove the antibacterial layer of sebum. In fact, aggressive washing with a soap that isn't pH balanced (the same acidity as your skin) can cause skin to lose its antibacterial abilities for up to 45 minutes after washing. As with most things in life, moderation is the key.

apocrine glands *(APP oh krin)* Sweat glands found in the pubic and axillary regions which open into the hair follicles.

eccrine glands *(ECK rin)* Sweat glands that cover the entire skin surface.

sebaceous glands *(seh BAY shus)* An exocrine gland of the skin that secretes sebum. Sebaceous glands are located in the dermis. Their ducts join with a hair and sebum coats the hair shaft as it moves toward the surface of the skin. Also known as oil glands.

sebum *(SEE bum)* Oily substance secreted by sebaceous glands.

Sweat and Sebaceous Glands

Sweat and sebaceous glands are part of the dermis. Sweat glands are distributed over the entire skin surface, with large numbers under the arms, in the palms, on the soles of the feet, and on the forehead. The perspiration they generate is excreted through pores. There are two main types of sudoriferous, or sweat, glands: apocrine and eccrine glands (see FIGURE 8-2 ▲). **Apocrine** sweat glands secrete at the hair follicles in the groin, anal region, and the armpits. These axillary sweat glands become active around puberty and are believed to act as a sexual attractant. Located all over your skin, and in people of all ages, **eccrine glands** are important in the regulation of body temperature. Eccrine glands are found in greater numbers on your palms, feet, forehead, and upper lip. Sweat glands can be activated by heat, pain, fever, or nervousness. Your body has approximately 3,000,000 sweat glands, generating an average fluid loss via sweating of 500 mL per day. It is interesting to note that sweat is 99% water and by itself does not have a strong odor. However, if it is left on the skin, bacteria degrade substances in the sweat into chemicals that give off strong smells, commonly called body odors. Ingestion of certain foods, like garlic, can also affect the odor of sweat.

Sebaceous glands play an important role by secreting oil, or **sebum,** that keeps the skin from drying out. Because sebum is somewhat acidic in nature, it also helps destroy

FIGURE 8-2 ▲ Sweat and sebaceous glands.

some pathogens on the skin's surface. Sebaceous glands are usually found in hair-covered areas, where they are connected to hair follicles. The glands deposit sebum on the hairs and bring it to the skin surface along the hair shaft. Sebaceous glands are also found in areas that do not have hair follicles, such as eyelids, penis, labia minora, and nipples. In these areas the sebum transverses ducts that terminate in sweat pores on the surface of the skin. A specialized form of sebaceous gland located at the rim of the eyelids called **meibomian glands** (or tarsal glands) secrete sebum into the tears that coat the eye, slowing evaporation.

Subcutaneous Fascia

Finally, the innermost layer is the **subcutaneous fascia,** or **hypodermis,** which is composed of elastic and fibrous connective tissue and fatty tissue. Within this layer, **lipocytes,** or fat cells, produce the fat needed to provide padding to protect the deeper tissues of the body and act as insulation for temperature regulation. Fat is also necessary as an efficient store for energy. The hypodermis is also the layer of skin that is attached to the muscles of your body.

meibomian glands *(mye BOH me an)* Also known as tarsal glands; specialized form of sebaceous glands located at the rim of the eyelids.

subcutaneous fascia *(sub kyoo TAY nee us FAY she ah)* Connective tissue layer beneath the skin.

hypodermis See subcutaneous fascia.

lipocyte Cell in the subcutaneous layer that stores fat.

herpes Viral infection that can cause a variety of skin conditions to include cold sores and shingles.

vesicle *(VESS ih kul)* A small bladder or blister.

Herpes varicella See chickenpox.

chickenpox *(Varicella)* An acute, contagious disease found usually in children, caused by the Varicella Zoster virus, exhibiting papules that become vesicles, and then pustules.

Pathology Connection

INFECTIONS OF THE SKIN

In this section we will discuss a variety of additional skin conditions that are caused by infection. **Herpes** is a lifelong viral infection that produces an inflammation of the skin in the form of clusters of small, fluid filled blisterlike sacs called **vesicles.** Although this is a lifelong infection, there are periods of remission (periods where there are no noticeable signs of infection) and exacerbation (periods of "flare-ups"). Exacerbation is usually caused by decreased immunity as a result of stress or other diseases. See FIGURE 8-3 ▲ for an example of herpes.

Herpes varicella is also called **chickenpox** and is a highly contagious common childhood infection that can be spread by airborne particles or direct contact. Vesicles produced by herpes varicella can be found on the face, trunk, and extremities. It can be widespread or limited in nature and can cause intense itching. A vaccine can now be given to children for chickenpox. This vaccine decreases the risk of contracting the disease, and if it is contracted, the disease is less

A

B

FIGURE 8-3 ▲ Types of Herpes. **A.** Shingles. (Courtesy of CDC/ Dr. K.L. Hermann.) **B.** Typical cold sores or fever blisters. (Courtesy of CDC/ Robert E. Sumpter.)

(continued)

Pathology Connection (continued)

severe without possible deadly complications. For those who reach adulthood without having the disease and have a negative titer, which means bloodwork shows the person has never been exposed to chickenpox, the vaccine may be worth consideration, even in older patients.

Herpes zoster is commonly known as **shingles** and is a painful condition that creates lesions that appear to follow a spinal nerve pathway. It is believed that shingles is the dormant, adult version of chickenpox that the patient initially had exhibited in childhood. Shingles develop in the adult when the immune system cannot keep herpes zoster in check as a result of stress, disease, trauma, or the ordinary aging process. Approximately 50% of individuals over 80 have had at least one episode of shingles. Although the blisters and rashes are usually found on the trunk in a midline fashion, following the course of a sensory nerve, they are often located on the face and can cause conjunctivitis. In either case, these lesions are extremely painful, producing sharp, stabbing sensations that may last from 10 days to several weeks.

Herpes simplex type 1 forms the cold sore (fever blister) that is found around the mouth or nose following the common cold or febrile situations. **Herpes simplex type 2** is the causative agent of genital herpes. In its active stage, this virus produces blisters in the genital area. The lesions created by herpes simplex type 1 and type 2 are the same and clinically indistinguishable. Herpes simplex type 2 is highly contagious when in its active stage, although it can also be spread in its remission stage. It is spread by direct contact. Although it is mainly spread by sexual contact, it is not limited only to sexual transmission. *Herpes simplex type 2* can also be transmitted from infected mother to newborn child during vaginal delivery.

The drug acyclovir may be used to prevent outbreaks by people who have genital herpes. It can also be used to treat the symptoms of chickenpox and shingles. However, it cannot cure herpes.

Warts, or **verruca,** are caused by the papillomavirus, which causes a hypertrophy of the keratin cells in the skin. Warts present in a variety of shapes, sizes, numbers, and appearances. See FIGURE 8-4 ▲ for examples of warts

Common warts are normally found on children's hands and fingers. These normally painless and harmless warts are spread as a result of scratching and direct contact with the affected area. Often they will disappear on their own. Adults should be concerned with wart-like lesions that form on their skin that could possibly be a form of skin cancer. These should be watched for any change in character such as size, shape, or color.

(continued)

herpes zoster (shingles) The common name for the skin rash caused by herpes zoster.

herpes simplex type 1 Herpes caused by herpes simplex virus 1. The infections are categorized by the site of infection.

herpes simplex type 2 Herpes caused by herpes simplex virus 2. The infections are categorized by the site of infection.

warts Raised, cutaneous elevations. Also called verruca.

verruca *(vur ROO kuh)* A wart.

common wart Also known as verruca vulgaris, usually found on the backs of the hands and fingers; however, it may occur on any area of the skin.

FIGURE 8-4 ▲ Examples of warts.
A. Plantar wart. (Source: Dr. P. Marazzi/Photo Researchers, Inc.) **B.** Common wart. (Source: Dr. P. Marazzi/Photo Researchers, Inc.)

Pathology Connection (continued)

Plantar warts are found on the soles of the foot and tend to grow inward, exhibiting a smooth surface. The fact that this type of wart grows inward tends to make walking painful if the wart is located on a pressure point. The first line of treatment is with a topical application of salicylic acid, but this usually provides only temporary relief and they come back. These warts can be removed surgically or cryogenically (frozen).

Genital warts are highly contagious and sexually transmitted. Evidence indicates a strong correlation between genital warts and cervical cancer. The evidence is strong enough that there currently is a controversy over requiring a papillomavirus vaccine for teenage girls and boys.

Fungi can also cause various skin disorders. **Tinea** is a general term relating to fungal skin infections that are usually located in warm, moist regions of the body. Fungal infections exhibit cracking and weeping (secreting fluid) skin with an itch. Often fungal infections can reoccur to the point of being a chronic condition. There are many fungal infections, usually named for the region in which they are found. See **FIGURE 8-5** ▲ for examples of fungal infections.

Tinea pedis, or athlete's foot, is the most common fungal skin infection. It is highly contagious, spreading by direct contact with contaminated surfaces, such as shower and locker room floors and towels. Because the areas between the toes are warm and maintain moisture, this is the most common location for tinea infections (see Figure 8-5A). If left untreated, the fungus can spread over the entire foot.

Tinea cruris, also known as jock itch, mainly affects men. It is a fungal infection of the groin and scrotal areas. Warm weather with increased perspiration, increased physical activity, and tight-fitting shorts, pants, or undergarments tend to aggravate this condition.

plantar wart A wart on a pressure-bearing area, especially the sole of the foot.

genital wart A wart of the genitalia, caused by strains of human papillomavirus (HPV), some of which are transmitted by sexual contact.

tinea Any fungal infection found on the body.

tinea pedis Also known as athlete's foot. A scaling, cracked, or macerated rash typically found between the toes and occasionally on the sole of the foot or the heels.

tinea cruris A fungal skin disease of surfaces of contact in the scrotal, crural, anal, and genital areas.

A

B

C

FIGURE 8-5 ▲ Examples of fungal infections. **A.** Athlete's foot (*tinea pedis*). (Courtesy of CDC.) **B.** Fungal infection of the fingernail (*tinea unguium*). (Courtesy of the CDC/Sherry Brinkman.) **C.** Ring worm (*tinea corporis*). (Courtesy of CDC/ K. Mae Lennon, Tulane Medical School; Clement Benjamin.)

(continued)

Pathology Connection (continued)

tinea corporis
Tinea of the body.
It begins with red,
slightly elevated
scaly patches that on
examination reveal
minute vesicles
or papules. New
patches spring from
the periphery while
the central portion
clears. There is often
considerable itching.

tinea unguium
Also known as
onychomycosis. A
fungal infection of the
nails usually caused
by Trichophyton
and Tinea species
and occasionally by
Candida or other
fungi. The hallmarks
of the disease are
thickening, scaling,
and discoloration of
the nailbed.

cellulitis *(SELL
you LIE tis)* Bacterial
infection of skin and
subcutaneous tissues.

Lyme disease
Named after the town
of Lyme, Connecticut,
it is the number
one vector-borne
disease in the United
States. A multisystem
disorder caused by the
spirochete, Borrelia
burgdorferi, it is
spread by deer tick
bites causing a bull's
eye rash at the bite
site.

Tinea corporis is somewhat misleadingly known as ringworm (see Figure 8-5B). This condition presents on the smooth skin of the legs, arms, and body as red, ring-shaped structures with a pale center. This can resemble the shape of a worm under the skin, but no worm is involved; a parasitic fungus is responsible for the infection.

Tinea unguium is a condition in which a fungal infection is involved with either fingernails or toenails (see Figure 8-5C). These infections can be difficult to treat due to the infection's location under the affected nail. If this disease is left untreated, the nail will become overgrown and thickened with a white and brittle appearance.

Cellulitis, which is caused by the bacterium *Staphylococcus,* is an inflammatory condition of the skin and subcutaneous tissue, producing a red, swollen, and painful area. Often the source of this infection is a bedsore, ulcer, or wound. If left untreated, cellulitis can lead to life-threatening situations such as endocarditis or even septicemia.

You probably have heard a lot about this next condition if you listen to the news or spend a fair amount of time outdoors. Named after the town of Lyme, Connecticut, **Lyme disease** involves multiple systems of the body as a result of a bacterial infection that is spread via the bite of the deer tick. Flulike symptoms, malaise, joint inflammation, fever, and chills are some of the symptoms of this disease. If left untreated, Lyme disease can lead to neurologic problems, cardiovascular complications, and even arthritis. So why are we discussing this disease in the integumentary section of this book? A common early sign of this condition is a rash that looks like a red circle with a lighter center resembling a bull's eye. This rash appears between a few days and several weeks following the tick bite (see FIGURE 8-6 ▲). A blood test will confirm the actual infection.

A **B**

FIGURE 8-6 ▲ **A.** Bull's eye rash caused by Lyme disease. (Courtesy of the CDC/James Gathany) **B.** The bite of the female western blacklegged tick, *Ixodes pacificus,* may cause Lyme disease. (Courtesy of the CDC/Dr. Amanda Loftis, Dr. William Nicholson, Dr. Will Reeves, Dr. Chris Paddock.)

TEST YOUR KNOWLEDGE 8-1

Complete the following:

1. List the three main layers of skin.

_____

_____

_____

2. List four of the functions of your integumentary system.

_____

_____

_____

_____

Choose the best answer:

3. Which cells are responsible for your normal skin color?
   a. monocytes
   b. jandicytes
   c. eyecytes
   d. melanocytes

4. The two main types of sudoriferous glands are:
   a. apocrine and pelicine
   b. appeltine and eccrine
   c. eccrine and apocrine
   d. sudacrine and melocrine

5. This form of herpes causes the painful condition known as shingles:
   a. varicella
   b. zoster
   c. simplex type 1
   d. simplex type 2

6. This form of wart can make walking painful due to its inward growth and position over a pressure point:
   a. plantar
   b. common
   c. genital
   d. cruris

HOW SKIN HEALS

Just as storms can damage the exterior of a house by high winds tearing off shingles or siding, lightning burning portions of the exterior, or ice causing damage to the roof, many ordinary objects can damage skin. As a result, the body has developed ways to repair itself when injury threatens its first line of defense—the skin.

If skin is punctured and the wound damages blood vessels in the skin, as shown in **FIGURE 8-7** ▲, the wound fills with blood. Blood contains substances that cause it to clot. (For more information about clotting, see Chapter 12.) The top part of the clot, which is exposed to air, hardens to form a scab. This is nature's bandage, forming a barrier between the wound and the outer environment to prevent pathogens from entering. So don't pick your scabs.

Next, the inflammatory response occurs, with the migration of white blood cells (WBCs) to the damaged area to destroy any pathogens that may have entered when the wound

fibroblasts Any cell from which connective tissue is created.

occurred. At about the same time, cells called **fibroblasts** (cells that can develop into connective tissue) come in and begin pulling the edges of the wound together. The basal layer of the epidermis begins to hyperproduce new cells for the repair of the wound. If the wound is severe enough, a tough scar composed of collagen fibers may form. Scars usually don't contain any accessory organs of the skin or any sense of feeling. Scar production can be greatly minimized if stitches, adhesive strips, or a specialized glue are used to draw the margins of the wound together before the healing process begins. Ideally, the wound starts to heal from the inside before healing toward the outside. This aids in preventing pathogens from becoming trapped between a healed surface and the deeper layers of skin, where they could develop into a major pocket of infection. Diabetic patients like Maria often have difficulty with wound healing due to a decrease in both blood flow and WBC activity to the damaged area.

FIGURE 8-7 ▲ Wound repair.

Amazing **Body Facts**

Keloids

A **keloid** can be considered a "scar gone wild." It is a mass of scar tissue that has a raised, firm, irregular shape (see **FIGURE 8-8** ▲). A keloid often occurs as a result of trauma or surgical incision and can even form following an ear piercing. The formation of this mass is a result of an overproduction of connective tissue at the affected site. The formation of keloids appears to be more prominent in the black population. Surgical removal would not make sense (because more keloids would form), so treatment usually consists of steroid injection at the lesion site and cryotherapy (freezing).

A

B

keloid *(KEE loid)*
An unusually thick and fibrous scar on the skin.

**FIGURE
8-8** ▲ Examples of keloids. (Source: A. Custom Medical Stock Photo, Inc.; B. Fedorov Oleksiy/Shutterstock.com.)

Pathology Connection

BURNS

Skin burns present special problems for healing. We naturally think that burns are caused by heat, and that is true. However, burns can also be caused by chemicals, electricity, or radiation. When assessing the damage caused by burns, there are two factors to consider: the depth of the burn and the size of the area damaged by the burn.

The depth of a burn relates to the layer or layers of skin affected by the burn. A **first-degree burn** has damaged only the epidermis and is classified as a **partial-thickness burn** (that is, a burn that does not affect the entire depth of the skin). With a first-degree burn there is skin redness and pain but no blistering. The pain usually subsides in 2 to 3 days with no scarring. The damaged layer of skin usually sloughs off in about a week or so. A sunburn is a classic example of a first-degree burn.

Second-degree burns involve the entire depth of the epidermis and a portion of the dermis. These burns are still considered partial-thickness burns because they do not go all the way through the skin. Such burns cause pain, redness, and blistering. The extent of blistering is directly proportional to the depth of the burn. Blisters continue to enlarge even after the initial burn. Excluding any additional complications, such as infection, these blisters usually heal within 10 to 14 days, but burns reaching deeper into the dermis require anywhere from 4 to 14 weeks to heal. Scarring in second-degree burn cases is common.

first-degree burn
A superficial burn in which damage is limited to the outer layer of the epidermis and is marked by redness, tenderness, and mild pain. Blisters do not form, and the burn heals without scar formation. A common example is sunburn.

partial-thickness burn A classification of the severity of a burn. This level of burn damage includes the entire depth of the epidermis and a portion of the dermis.

second-degree burn A partial thickness burn that involves the entire depth of the epidermis and a portion of the dermis.

(continued)

Pathology Connection (continued)

Small second-degree burns may be treated at home. For a burn without open blisters, the patient should run cool water over the burn. They should dry the burn carefully, in order to avoid breaking the blisters and apply a dry, sterile dressing to the burn. They may take ibuprofen to help with the pain. A burn with open blisters should be covered with a dry, sterile bandage. Larger second-degree burns or burns with open blisters may need to be treated by a doctor. The doctor may prescribe intravenous fluids to replace those lost by your body and antibiotics to fight infection. Stronger pain medicine may also be prescribed.

Third-degree burns affect all three of the skin layers and are therefore classified as **full-thickness burns**. Here the surface of the skin has a leathery feel to it and varies in color: black, brown, tan, red, or white. Initially, the victim will feel no pain at the affected site because pain receptors are destroyed by third-degree burns. Also destroyed are the sweat and sebaceous glands, hair follicles, and blood vessels. Third-degree burns can be life threatening, but improvements in burn care have reduced the number of mortalities. A doctor may prescribe antibiotics to fight infection and intravenous fluids for rehydration. Skin grafting may be necessary.

Fourth-degree burns are burns that penetrate to the bone. These burns are full-thickness burns that also destroy tendons and muscle. The victim feels no pain at the affected site. Fourth-degree burns on arms or legs may require amputation of the affected area.

A clinician can estimate the extent of the area covered by the burn by using the "rule of nines." As you can see in FIGURE 8-9 ▲, the body is divided into the following regions and given a percentage of body surface area value: head and neck, 9%; *each* upper limb, 9%; *each* lower limb, 18%; front of trunk, 18%; back of trunk and buttocks, 18%; perineum (including the anal and urogenital region), 1%. These region can also be further divided for smaller burn areas, as you can see in Figure 8-9.

The clinical concerns for burn patients relate to the functions of the skin already discussed:

- Bacterial infection
- Fluid loss
- Heat loss

Patients with third-degree burns need prompt medical treatment. The patient should be taken to a burn center or hospital emergency room. Burn patients generally receive intravenous therapy, which provides replacement fluids, antibiotics, and pain medications. Burns are cleaned, treated with antibiotic cream, and covered with dry, sterile dressings. The burn patient may also be given a tetanus shot. The patient may also be placed in a hyperbaric chamber—a sealed structure in which pure oxygen is supplied at a higher-than-normal atmospheric pressure. Exposure to increased levels of oxygen helps to speed healing.

Severe burns, such as third-degree burns, require healing at an intensity that the body can't normally achieve on its own. Damaged skin must be removed as soon as possible to allow the process of skin grafting to begin. In this process, healthy skin is placed over damaged areas so it may begin to grow. Ideally, it is best to use the patient's own skin, known as **autografting,** because it generally eliminates the chances of tissue rejection. However, the destruction may be severe enough to require tissue from a donor (**heterografting**). Grafting usually requires repeat surgeries because large areas cannot be done all at once, and often the grafts don't "take." Other options may include growing sheets of skin in a laboratory from the patient's cells or utilizing synthetic materials that act as skin.

third-degree burn A burn that extends through the full thickness of the skin and subcutaneous tissues beneath the dermis. The burn leaves skin with a pale, brown, gray, or blackened appearance. The burn is painless because it destroys nerves in the skin. Scar formation and contractures are likely complications.

full-thickness burn An assessment of the severity of a burn in which the burn has penetrated through all three of the skin layers.

fourth-degree burn A full thickness burn that penetrates to the bone.

autografting The use of one's own skin to replace burnt tissue.

heterografting The use of donor tissue to repair burnt skin.

Pathology Connection

FIGURE 8-9 △ Assessing the degree of the burn. (Source: A. Suzanne Tucker/Shutterstock.com. B. St. Stephen's Hospital, London/Photo Researchers, Inc.)

Clinical Application

MEDICINE DELIVERY VIA THE INTEGUMENTARY SYSTEM

A variety of medicines can be delivered via the integumentary system. Medicines can be applied to adhesive patches that are placed on the skin where it is slowly absorbed into the bloodstream. These are called **transdermal patches.** Nicotine (for smoking cessation), nitroglycerin (for vasodilation in the heart), birth control compounds, and pain medication, for example, can be delivered in this manner. If a more rapid response is required, the cardiac drug nitroglycerin can be placed under the tongue (**sublingually**), where it is rapidly absorbed into the bloodstream because of the high vascularization of the mucosa in that area.

Of course, the other method of drug delivery via the integumentary system is a little more painful but very effective. Injection is used when a drug can't be taken by mouth or the digestive system may alter the desired effects of the drug. Medication can be injected utilizing a syringe and needle to deliver the medication either **subcutaneously** (under the skin) or **intradermally** (into the skin). Other routes of injection also include intramuscular (IM), intraspinal, and intravenous (IV) routes.

transdermal patches A form of drug delivery that allows drug absorption through the skin from a patch, containing the medication, that adheres to the skin.

sublingually Under the tongue.

subcutaneously *(sub kyoo TAY nee us lee)* Under the skin.

intradermally Into the skin.

nail root Also known as the germinal matrix; where nails begin their growth.

germinal matrix See nail root.

nail bed Pink portion under the fingernail that is part of the epidermis.

keratinized To become hard.

cuticle Layer of dead skin that arises from the epidermis around the proximal end of the nail. It keeps microorganisms from the nail root.

nail body The visible portion of the nail.

sterile matrix The proximal layer of cells that help the nail body stick to the nail bed.

lunula *(LOO new lah)* Whitish half-moon visible under the proximal portion of the nail plate. It is the visible tip of the nail root.

NAILS

Specialized epithelial cells originating from the **nail root** form your nails (see **FIGURE 8-10** ▲). The nail root is also called the **germinal matrix**. As these cells grow out and over the **nail bed** (actually a part of the epidermis), they become **keratinized,** forming a substance similar to the horns on a bull that is the same protein that fills the cells of the stratum corneum. This process occurs as cells dry and shrink, are pushed to the surface, and become filled with a hard protein called keratin. The **cuticle** is a fold of tissue that covers the nail root. The portion that we see is called the **nail body**. The **sterile (nail) matrix** is a proximal layer of cells that helps the nail body to stick to the nail bed. Nails normally grow about 1 millimeter in length every week. The pink color of your nails comes from the vascularization of the tissue under the nails, whereas the white half-moon shaped area, or **lunula,** is a result of the thicker layer of cells at the base.

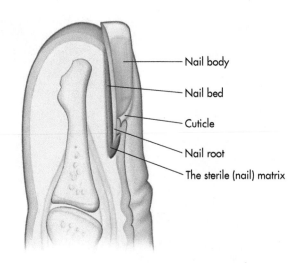

Free edge of nail
Nail bed
Lunula
Cuticle

Nail body
Nail bed
Cuticle
Nail root
The sterile (nail) matrix

FIGURE 8-10 ▲
Structures of the fingernail.

Clinical Application

ASSESSING PERIPHERAL PERFUSION

The pink color of the nail bed is clinically significant in that it can aid in the assessment of perfusion (blood flow) to the extremities and can be a determinant of oxygenation. If you pinch one of your fingernails straight down with the thumb and index finger of your other hand for 5 seconds and release that pinch, you will note that the nail bed changes from a blanched white color back to pink in a matter of seconds. This shows good perfusion as a result of the blood rushing back into the nail bed. In cases of poor perfusion, it takes longer for the nail bed to "pink up." Normally, it takes less than 3 seconds for the nail to return to pink from the blanched white state. If that time is greater than 3 seconds, perfusion to the extremities is considered sluggish. If the refill time is greater than 5 seconds, there is clearly an abnormal situation occurring. This test is called capillary refill time (see FIGURE 8-11 ▲).

Diabetes is a disease that may cause a condition of reduced blood flow to the extremities known as **peripheral vascular disease** (PVD). An increase in the time required to reperfuse the nail bed may be an indication of PVD. Blood clots or vascular spasms can decrease blood flow and thereby extend refill time, as can hypothermia, which naturally constricts blood vessels in the periphery to conserve heat.

In addition, nail beds can change colors under certain conditions. For example, as the level of oxygen decreases in the tissue, the nail beds become bluish in tint. Of course, one can always paint their nails different colors!

peripheral vascular disease (PVD)
Condition of reduced blood flow to the extremities.

FIGURE 8-11 ▲ Clinician performing capillary refill assessment.

HAIR

Body hair is normal and served important purposes in our evolutionary past as well as today. Hair helps to regulate body temperature, as you will see in the next section, and it functions as a sensor to help detect things on your skin, such as bugs or cobwebs. Eyelashes help to protect your eyes from foreign objects, and hair in the nose helps to filter out particulate matter.

Hair is composed of a fibrous protein called **keratin**, just like your fingernails and toenails. This is also the same protein that fills the dead cells on the surface of the epidermis. The hair that you see is called the shaft. The shaft is covered by a protective layer of flat cells called the **cuticle**. The **cortex** layer lies beneath the cuticle (see FIGURE 8-12 ▲). The cortex is made of twisted proteins and the melanin pigments that give hair its color. Coarse hair has another layer of cells beneath the cortex, called the **medulla**. Each hair has a root that extends down into the dermis to the **follicle**. The follicle is formed by epithelial cells, which have a rich source of blood provided by the dermal blood vessels. As a result, cells divide and grow in the base of the follicle. As new cells continually form, the older cells are crowded out and pushed upward toward the skin's

keratin *(KER ah tin)* Hard protein found in the cells of the outermost part of the epidermis and in the nails.

cuticle A layer of solid or semisolid tissue that covers the free surface of a layer of epithelial cells. It may be horny or chitinous and sometimes is calcified.

cortex The outer layer of a structure, as a hair or the lens of the eye.

medulla The central axis of a hair.

follicle *(FALL ih kul)* A site where a hair is formed. The follicle is located in the dermis.

FIGURE 8-12 ▲ Diagram of a hair follicle.

surface. As these old cells are pushed away from the blood source (which provides their nourishment), they die, becoming keratinized in the process. So basically, the hair you see on the individual next to you is a bunch of dead cells. This isn't so bad considering that if your hairs were alive, your haircuts would be extremely painful, with a good chance of you bleeding to death if you got more than a light trim! The old, popular belief that shaving or frequent cutting of hair makes it grow quicker or thicker is wrong. Neither shaving nor cutting hair does anything to affect the rate of cell growth at the base of those hair follicles. On average, each hair on your head lasts about 3 to 4 years and grows approximately one half an inch each month.

If you look at Figure 8-12, you will note that there is a **sebaceous gland** associated with the hair follicle. The sebaceous gland secretes **sebum,** an oily substance that coats the follicle and works its way to the skin's surface to waterproof and lubricate the skin and hair. Sebum is somewhat antibacterial, so it aids in decreasing infections on your skin. Sebum production decreases with age. As a result, older individuals exhibit drier skin and more brittle hair.

Like skin color, your hair color is dependent on the amount and type of melanin you produce. Generally, the more melanin, the darker the hair. White hair occurs in the absence of melanin. Red hair is a result of an altered melanin that contains iron. Gray hair is usually due to age-related decreases in melanin production.

You may be extremely envious of someone with a head full of curly hair or of someone with absolutely straight hair. Don't be envious of the person—just envy his or her hair shafts! Flat hair shafts produce curly hair, and round hair shafts produce straight hair.

Alopecia is the term for any type of hair loss and can be acute or chronic. Some forms of alopecia, such as male-pattern baldness, do not represent a disease, but are inherited traits. Hair loss can also be a result of chemotherapy for cancer treatments, hormonal imbalance, infections, severe emotional or physical stress, or side effects of some other medications.

sebaceous glands *(seh BAY shus)* An exocrine gland of the skin that secretes sebum. Sebaceous glands are located in the dermis. Their ducts join with a hair and sebum coats the hair shaft as it moves toward the surface of the skin. Also known as oil glands.

sebum *(SEE bum)* Oily substance secreted by sebaceous glands.

alopecia *(AL oh PEE she ah)* Absence or loss of hair.

APPLIED SCIENCE

Forensics and Hair

An interesting characteristic concerning hair is its ability to tell a pathologist if an individual ingested certain drugs or other substances, such as lead or arsenic. Trace amounts of ingested substances can become a part of the hair's composition. As a result, analysis of a hair sample can reveal what and how long ago something was ingested. The longer the length of hair, the longer the record of what that individual consumed.

The life span of hair is dependent on location. Eyelashes last around 3 to 4 months, whereas the hair on the scalp lasts for about 3 to 4 years. Teachers with difficult classes usually pull their hair out sooner!

Pathology Connection

LICE AND SCABIES

One of the "rites of passage" in school used to be having your scalp checked for head lice. Lice are tiny insect parasites. **Pediculosis** is the term for an infestation with lice that is a result of direct contact with a person infested with lice or sharing objects that may be infested. Please note that lice know nothing about the socioeconomic status of their victims. *Anyone* can become infested.

There are several types of lice infestations. **Head lice** is the common type that you are checked for in school. **Body lice** infestations are often a result of poor personal hygiene. These lice can be carriers of disease such as typhus. **Pubic lice,** commonly called "crabs," are spread through sexual contact.

Treatment for all forms of lice is the same: bathing or shampooing with a medicated shampoo specifically designed to eliminate lice and their eggs (known as "nits"). All bedding, towels, clothing, hats, combs, and hairbrushes must be thoroughly cleaned or discarded to prevent re-infestation.

Another little fellow that can cause problems is a tiny mite that burrows into the skin to lay eggs, causing a condition known as **scabies.** These mites are transmitted via direct contact from an infected individual and usually lodge themselves in the folds of the skin (wrist, underarms, groin, under breasts, etc.). Symptoms of scabies include vesicles, **pustules,** and intense itching of the affected area. The eggs usually hatch within 3 to 5 days. The young mature on the skin surface within 2 to 3 weeks, and if not destroyed, they mate and start the whole process over again. A specially formulated cream is used on the skin to kill these mites. All infected individuals must be treated for the cycle of infestation to be broken. For examples of lice and scabies, see **FIGURE 8-13** ▲.

A   **B**

FIGURE 8-13 ▲ **A.** A lateral view of a female body louse, *Pediculus Humanus Var. Corporis* and **B.** A rash composed of pimplelike irritations on the abdomen and thorax due to canine scabies. (Courtesy CDC/ Frank Collins, PhD.)

---

pediculosis
(pee DICK you LOH sis) A condition of lice infestation.

head lice Lives in the fine hair of the head, including the beard and eyebrows. Its eggs, commonly called nits, may be found glued to hairs. They form nests in the vicinity of the ears. This organism is the cause of pediculosis capitis.

body lice Inhabits the seams of clothing worn next to the body and feeds on regions of the body covered by that clothing. Eggs are attached to fibers of the clothing. This organism causes human illnesses including pediculosis corporis and trench fever.

pubic lice Also known as crab lice, which infests human pubic hair. It is transmitted by direct contact and through bedding or shared towels.

scabies A contagious skin condition caused by the itch mite, Sarcoptes scabiei.

pustule *(PUS tyool)* A small elevation of skin filled with lymph or pus.

TEST YOUR KNOWLEDGE 8-2

Choose the best answer:

1. The blood clot that forms in a wound that is exposed to air becomes a:
   a. scar
   b. scab
   c. hematoma
   d. keloid

2. When assessing the skin damage caused by a burn, the two main factors to assess are:
   a. temperature and depth
   b. depth and odor
   c. area of damage and depth
   d. odor and color

3. The white, half-moon-shaped area of your fingernail is called:
   a. cuticle
   b. lunula
   c. keratin
   d. lingula

4. The medical term for hair loss is:
   a. heterografting
   b. pediculosis
   c. rediculosis
   d. alopecia

5. A skin formation that can be considered a "scar gone wild" is a:
   a. scab
   b. hematoma
   c. keloid
   d. lunula

TEMPERATURE REGULATION

The integumentary system plays a major role in the regulation of body temperature. It is amazing how we can stay in a relatively "tight" range of body temperature while we do a variety of things in a variety of environments. Of course, clothes do help tremendously, but still it is critical to have a properly functioning temperature regulator like our integumentary system. This is accomplished through a complex series of activities.

Part of temperature regulation is accomplished by changes in the size of blood vessels in your skin. As your temperature rises, your body signals the blood vessels in your skin to get larger in diameter. This is called **vasodilation**. It is the body's attempt to get as much "hot" blood as possible exposed to a cooler surrounding environment, so the heat radiates away from the body. In addition, sweat glands excrete water, as well as substances such as nitrogenous wastes and sodium chloride, onto the skin's surface. As the water evaporates, cooling occurs. As long as you stay hydrated and are able to produce sweat, this system works pretty well. Hydration is especially important before and during activities to avoid feeling thirsty. Thirst indicates that the body has already reached a level of dehydration. It's pretty easy to dehydrate, especially when you take into consideration that you can have up to 3,000 sweat glands on a square inch of skin on your hands and feet, and you can potentially excrete up to 12 liters of sweat in a 24-hour period! The risk of dehydration can be serious.

Conversely, if you were in a cold environment and needed to warm up, your blood vessels would become smaller in diameter, or vasoconstrict. **Vasoconstriction** forces

vasodilation *(VAY zoh dye LAY shun)* Relaxation of the smooth muscle in the artery wall, causing the artery to become larger in diameter.

vasoconstriction *(VAY zoh kon STRIK shun)* Constriction of the smooth muscle in the artery wall which causes the artery to become smaller in diameter.

blood *away* from the skin and back toward the core of the body where the heat is. The perfect visual explanation of vasoconstriction is a skinny little kid running around a pool on a chilly summer day, shivering, with blue lips. The lips are blue because of vasoconstriction. Rings have a tendency to slide off your fingers in cold weather more readily than in hot weather because of vasoconstriction.

arrector pili *(ah REK tor PILL eye)* Muscle used to straighten hair when one becomes chilled or frightened.

Body temperature regulation is also aided by the hairs on your skin. Muscles in your skin called **arrector pili** are attached to your hairs. When those muscles contract, they make your hairs stand erect. The constriction of those muscles shows up as gooseflesh or goose bumps when you are chilled. When the hair stands up, pockets of still air are formed right above the skin, creating a dead air space that insulates the skin from the cooler surrounding environment. This is also how goose down (feather) clothing works in protecting against winter's cold. Interestingly, older homes, built before the now-common and effective practice of placing insulation in the walls and ceilings, actually insulated the homes through the creation of dead air (nonmoving) spaces between the outer and inner walls. See **FIGURE 8-14** ▲, which illustrates how your integumentary system regulates body temperature with the aid of your nervous system. Patients with spinal cord injuries such as Ray have poor control of their body temperatures. This is because their nervous systems can't communicate well with their bodies to control vasoconstriction and vasodilation in response to temperature change.

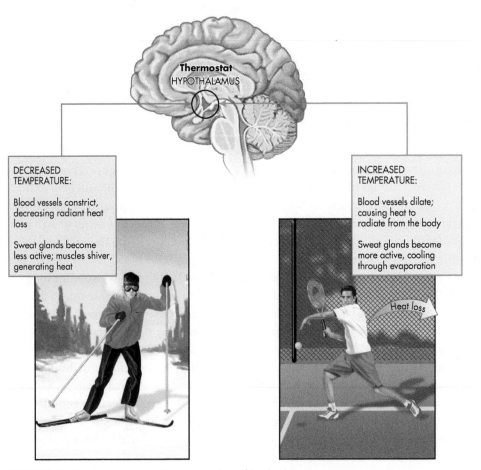

FIGURE 8-14 ▲ Integumentary regulation of body temperature.

Pathology Connection

SKIN LESIONS

A **lesion** is a pathologically altered piece of tissue that can include a wound, an injury, or a single infected patch of skin. The color of a lesion is usually different than that of normal skin. FIGURE 8-15 ▲ shows a variety of lesion types.

lesion *(LEE zhun)*
General category for any area of visible damage on the skin, whether it is from disease or injury.

A **macule** is a discolored spot on the skin; freckle

A **pustule** is a small, elevated, circumscribed lesion of the skin that is filled with pus; whitehead

A **wheal** is a localized, elevation of the skin that is often accompanied by itching; urticaria

An **erosion** or ulcer is an eating or gnawing away of tissue; decubitus ulcer

A **papule** is a solid, circumscribed, elevated area on the skin; pimple

A **crust** is a dry, serous or seropurulent, brown, yellow, red, or green exudation that is seen in secondary lesions; eczema

A **nodule** is a larger papule; acne vulgaris

A **scale** is a thin, dry flake of cornified epithelial cells such as psoriasis

A **vesicle** is a small fluid filled sac; blister. A bulla is a large vesicle; varicella (chickenpox)

A **fissure** is a crack-like sore or slit that extends through the epidermis into the dermis; athlete's foot

FIGURE 8-15 ▲ Various types of skin lesions.

A QUICK TRIP THROUGH SOME DISEASES OF THE INTEGUMENTARY SYSTEM

DISEASE	ETIOLOGY	SIGNS AND SYMPTOMS	DIAGNOSTIC TESTS	TREATMENT
Abrasion	Mechanical removal of skin.	Loss of skin surface integrity, redness, swelling, inflammation.	Visual examination.	Proper cleansing technique, removal of any foreign matter, antiseptic, bandage if necessary.
Acne	A metabolic condition, allergies, various drugs or endocrine disorders are possible causative agents.	Inflammation of hair follicles/sebaceous glands especially on the face, neck, chest, upper back/shoulders; can form blackheads, cysts, nodules, pustules, and pimples.	Visual examination.	Mild: proper cleansing techniques and OTC treatments; Severe: proper cleansing techniques including prescribed medications, antibiotics, steroids and/or all-trans retinoic acid (tretinoin).
Basal cell carcinoma	New growth or malignant tumor.	Begins as small, shiny papule, enlarges to form a whitish border around a central depression or ulcer that may bleed.	Biopsy.	Surgical removal, radiation, or cryosurgery.
Bed sores (decubitus or pressure ulcer)	Tissue injury (resultant of unrelieved pressure placed on a specific area).	A red, inflamed, craterlike lesion usually located over a bony prominence; classified in stages 1–4, with 4 being to the bone.	Visual inspection, culturing of site for infection.	Preventative measures such as turning at least every 2 hours and padding. Treat infection of the sore.
Boil (furuncle)	Bacteria (*Staphylococcus*).	Inflammation, a localized encapsulated pus filled lesion, painful affected site. Carbuncles are large abscesses composed of several furuncles.	Visual examination, site culture.	Proper antiseptic cleansing techniques, antibiotics, application of warm moist heat; depending on severity, may require draining.

(continued)

A QUICK TRIP *(continued)*

DISEASE	ETIOLOGY	SIGNS AND SYMPTOMS	DIAGNOSTIC TESTS	TREATMENT
Burns (thermal)	Heat or radiation of varying intensities and duration.	Depending on the intensity and duration: reddening of the affected surface, penetrating additional skin layers as the severity increases; color dependent on the severity, with a deepening red to black.	Visual examination.	Dependent on the severity.
Cellulitis	Bacteria (*Streptococcus* and *Staphylococcus*).	Inflammation of skin and subcutaneous tissue, red and swollen, painful.	Visual examination, site culture.	Antibiotics (oral or intravenously, dependant on the severity).
Contusion (bruise)	Blunt force or some form of skin injury without the skin surface breaking.	Pain, swelling, discoloration.	Visual inspection; imaging may be needed to check for more severe injury.	Cold applications, firm bandage to impede swelling, elevation when possible, heat application, massage.
Dermatitis (contact)	Contact with an allergen (extreme range of potential agents including, soaps, cosmetics, metals, drugs, plastics, etc.).	Small, reddish lesions to larger vesicles, weepy and crusted areas, itching possible.	Visual examination.	Avoidance of the causative agent; medication to decrease inflammatory process.
Dermatitis (general)	Stress, habitual scratching, dry skin such as winter itch.	Skin blotches, rash with itching and redness.	Patient history, visual examination.	Removal from stressful situation or moisturize the skin; topical steroid ointments can be used for itchiness.

(continued)

DISEASE	ETIOLOGY	SIGNS AND SYMPTOMS	DIAGNOSTIC TESTS	TREATMENT
Eczema	Genetic predisposition to allergies (in infants it may include reaction to milk/dairy products, other foods), stress.	Skin inflammation, redness, vesicles, scales, crusting, pustules.	Visual examination, history.	No true cure; treat symptoms; eliminate offending food, reduce stress, topical cortiosteroidal creams, skin moisturizers, antihistamines.
Folliculitis	Bacteria (usually *Staphylococcus*).	Small pustules that form around the base of the hair follicle.	Visual examination, site culture.	Proper daily cleansing with an antiseptic cleanser, oral antibiotics (chronic or severe cases).
Herpes	Herpes family of viruses.	Clusters of fluid-filled vesicles in patterns specific to the condition, skin inflammation, rash, pain related to the involved sensory nerve; remains dormant until immunosuppression.	Visual examination, site culture.	Antiviral drugs, usually self-limiting.
Hives (urticaria)	Allergic reaction to an external agent such as bee stings, plants, temperature extremes, sunlight, or internal agents such as foods, food additives, medication, antibiotics, or specific disease conditions.	Itchy wheals surrounded by a red inflamed area; can cover most of body.	Visual examination, patient history.	Antihistamines, allergen avoidance.
Keloid	Tissue trauma or surgical incision.	Overproduction of collagen during tissue repair often creating a larger structure than the original scar/traumatized area.	Visual inspection.	Surgical removal; however, great potential for keloids to grow back.

(continued)

A QUICK TRIP *(continued)*

DISEASE	ETIOLOGY	SIGNS AND SYMPTOMS	DIAGNOSTIC TESTS	TREATMENT
Lyme disease	Tick bite containing a specific spirochetal bacterium.	Bull's-eye macule/ papule at the site of the tick bite, flulike symptoms, stiff neck, swollen lymph node(s), joint aches, fever, headache, persistent sore throat, dry cough. Possible neurologic, cardiac, and arthritic complications if left undiagnosed/ untreated.	Visual examination, blood test, patient history.	Vaccine, antibiotics, treat secondary conditions; repeat infection is a possibility.
Malignant melanoma	Occurs in melanocytes, excessive exposure to the sun.	May appear as a brown or black irregular patch that appears suddenly. A color or size change in a preexisting wart or mole may also indicate melanoma. Metastasizes to other areas quickly.	Biopsy.	Surgical removal of the melanoma and the surrounding area and chemotherapy.
Pediculosis	Lice.	Lice and nits (egg deposits).	Visual inspection.	Proper cleansing techniques with medicated soap/ shampoo, cleaning of all clothing, bedding, towels, combs, etc. to remove the infestation.
Psoriasis	Possible genetic basis with attacks triggered by emotional stress, illness, sunlight, or skin damage.	Red skin with silvery patches, rapid replacement of the epidermal cells, dry cracking skin with crusting, can be painful; common to have periods of remission then exacerbation; may be an arthritic component.	Visual examination, patient history.	Supportive, skin applications to deal with the symptoms; medications: steroids, ultraviolet light.

A QUICK TRIP *(continued)*

DISEASE	ETIOLOGY	SIGNS AND SYMPTOMS	DIAGNOSTIC TESTS	TREATMENT
Scabies	Mites.	Elevated, grayish-white lines (burrows), vesicle and pustule formation (due to bite, feces, ova of the offending mite), intense itching.	Visual inspection.	Proper cleaning technique, application of medicated cream, all infected individuals must be treated to prevent reinfection.
Seborrheic keratosis	Unknown agent(s) causing the benign overgrowth of epithelial cells.	A well-defined, warty-scaled lesion that can present in a variety of colors from yellow to brown.	Visual inspection, laboratory examination.	Scraping (curettage), or freezing.
Squamous carcinoma	Abnormal cell growth, arising from the epidermis and occurs most often on the scalp and lower lip.	Abnormal appearance of skin, ulcer, pimple, or mole.	Biopsy.	Surgical removal or radiation.
Tinea barbae (barber's itch) *Tinea capitis* (scalp) *Tinea corporis* (ringworm) *Tinea cruris* (jock itch) *Tinea pedis* (athlete's foot) *Tinea unguium* (nails)	Fungi.	Case dependent; red ring-shaped patches (mimicking a worm), red inflamed skin, cracked and weeping area(s), itch, discoloration of affected nails.	Visual examination, microscopic examination, site culture.	Maintain clean dry condition of affected area, antifungal medication (topical or systemic).
Warts: common, plantar, or genital	Viruses.	Raised, rubbery, scaly growths of varying sizes and colors.	Visual examination.	Chemical or physical removal.

There are so many common pathological conditions of the integumentary system that a picture truly is worth a thousand words. Please see **FIGURE 8-16** ▲ to view additional photos of types of integumentary conditions.

FIGURE 8-16 ▲ Various types of integumentary conditions. **A.** Urticaria (hives). (Source: konmesa/Shutterstock.com)
B. Malignant melanoma. (Australis Photography/Shutterstock.com) **C.** Acne. (Source: Bad Man Production/Shutterstock.com) **D.** Poison ivy
(contact dermatitis). (Source: carroteater/Shutterstock.com) **E.** Herpes simplex. (Source: CLS Design/Shutterstock.com) **F.** Burn, second
degree. (Source: ittipon/Shutterstock.com)

Pharmacology Corner

Although medications are often delivered orally in the form of pills or injected into the body, they can also be delivered through the skin. Transdermal patches allow medication to be slowly and uniformly absorbed over time. These patches are convenient because they only have to be placed on the skin usually in the morning and then forgotten about until the next morning. Examples of medication delivered in this fashion include heart medication (nitroglycerin), smoking cessation aids (nicotine patches), and birth control. Another advantage of the nicotine patch is that the craving for nicotine is satisfied without all the other thousands of toxic and cancer-causing chemicals found in cigarettes.

The treatment of skin irritations and inflammatory reactions may require the use of topical creams. Mild creams can be used to stop the itching associated with many conditions. More powerful creams containing corticosteroids can provide anti-inflammatory relief without the systemic side effects associated with steroids that are fully absorbed into the bloodstream.

A variety of medicated shampoos can be used to treat lice and dandruff (excessive dry scalp with sloughing skin). Antifungal preparations can be effective on skin fungal diseases such as ringworm and athlete's foot. Antiviral creams can be used to treat herpes and other viral skin conditions. Finally, antibiotics can be used to treat bacterial skin infections and also as a prophylactic (preventative) treatment of wounds to prevent opportunistic infection.

SUMMARY

Snapshots from the Journey

- Your skin is your largest organ covering a little less than 21 square feet.
- Your skin is an amazing organ that does the following:
  a. Acts as a barrier to infection both as a physical shield and through the secretion of an antibacterial substance
  b. Acts as a physical barrier to injury
  c. Helps to keep the body from dehydrating
  d. Stores fat (yes, you do need some fat!)
  e. Synthesizes and secretes vitamin D with the help of sunshine
  f. Regulates body temperature
  g. Provides a minor excretory function in the elimination of water, salts, and urea
  h. Provides sensory input
- The skin is composed of three layers: epidermis, dermis, and subcutaneous fascia.
- Skin is not static; it constantly recreates itself.
- Various glands in the skin help moisturize, waterproof, and control body temperature as well as excrete some waste products.
- The severity of burns to the skin is evaluated by the depth of the burn and the area that the burn covers.
- Nails are protective devices composed of dead material.
- Hair (also dead material) aids in controlling body temperature.

CASE STUDY

A 27-year-old female presents to her doctor's office with complaints of red, itching, and oozing skin for the past two days. Physical examination and history reveal the following: a well-nourished white female who is in otherwise good health, no known allergies, normal vital signs, pupils normal and reactive, reflexes good, breath sounds normal, liquid-filled vesicles and scabbing on both legs from the top of her sock lines to the bottom of her shorts, and new vesicles have formed around her eyes. The patient stated that she returned from a primitive camping and hiking vacation in Virginia 2 days ago.

1. Based on this information, what do you think is the diagnosis?

_____

_____

_____

2. What caused the vesicles to begin to form around her eyes?

_____

_____

_____

RAY'S STORY

Family education will play an important role for Ray, our quadriplegic, once he gets home. Although proper ventilator care will be crucial for his survival, why do you think skin care is so important? How will Ray's inability to move potentially cause skin problems? Discuss areas of concern and potential problems involving Ray's integumentary system. What education/training might be important for members of Ray's family?

_____

_____

_____

MARIA'S STORY

Maria, our 35-year-old diabetic, has been developing a series of integumentary system problems over the past several years. Diabetes can, in some ways, be considered a vascular disease. Research the effects of diabetes as it relates to the integumentary system. How and why does diabetes affect wound healing? Why is there a high incidence of toe and leg amputations in the diabetic population? What preventative care measures can be taken to ensure good health of the diabetic's integumentary system?

_____

_____

_____

REVIEW QUESTIONS

Multiple Choice

1. The substance that is mainly responsible for skin color is:
   a. melanin
   b. pigmentin
   c. carrots
   d. luna

2. Whether you have naturally curly or straight hair is dependent on the shape of your:
   a. hair follicle
   b. hair shaft
   c. sebum
   d. melanin

3. The fibrous protein that makes up your hair and nails and fills your epidermal cells is called:
   a. carotene
   b. myelin
   c. keratin
   d. dermasene

4. In a cold environment, to maintain a core body temperature, peripheral blood vessels:
   a. vasodilate
   b. venospasm
   c. shiver
   d. vasoconstrict

5. The hair on your scalp can last:
   a. 3 to 4 months
   b. until your 40s
   c. 3 to 4 years
   d. until you have kids

6. Athlete's foot is caused by a:
   a. virus
   b. bacterium
   c. fungus
   d. prion

7. Ringworm is also known as:
   a. *Tinea pedis*
   b. *Tinea cruris*
   c. *Tinea corporis*
   d. *Tinea pennia*

Fill in the Blank

1. The three main layers of skin are the _____, _____, and _____.

2. The two main types of sweat glands are the _____ and the _____ glands.

3. Sebaceous glands secrete an oily substance called _____.

4. For some individuals, melanin locates in small patches called _____.

5. Jaundice, a condition associated with liver disease, occurs as a result of the build-up of _____.

6. _____ is an inflammatory condition of the skin and subcutaneous tissue that produces a red, swollen, painful area. It is caused by the *Staphylococcus* bacterium, and if left untreated it may lead to endocarditis or septicemia.

7. Cold sores, or fever blisters, are caused by the virus_____.

8. Tiny mites called_____ burrow into the skin to lay eggs, causing the formation of vesicles and pustules with intense itching of the skin.

REVIEW QUESTIONS

Short Answer

1. Discuss three functions of the integumentary system.

_____

_____

_____

2. Discuss the functions of sebum.

_____

_____

_____

3. Why is there an increased production of melanin when there is increased sun exposure?

_____

_____

_____

4. How does the integumentary system assist in the regulation of body temperature?

_____

_____

_____

5. Discuss the three forms of pediculosis found in this chapter. How is this condition treated?

_____

_____

_____

6. Although Lyme disease produces symptoms that are flulike in nature as well as having the potential to create neurological and cardiovascular problems, why have we discussed it in the integumentary chapter?

_____

_____

_____

Suggested Activities

1. Contact a local dermatologist to speak to your class on diagnosing and treating skin diseases.

2. Research the variety of medications used to treat acne. Focus on the mode of action, benefits, and side effects of each medication.

3. Working in groups, perform peripheral perfusion assessments and record times. Then, place hands in ice water bath for 30 seconds, and record and discuss differences in reperfusion times. Report your findings to the class.

CAREER CONNECTIONS

Now that you have read this chapter, here is a list of related professions you may be interested in investigating for a future career:

- EMT-Paramedic

- Nursing

Research each profession and report on the following:

1. Profession description to include job responsibilities
2. Educational requirements
3. Job opportunities
4. Opportunities outside of the hospital setting
5. Salary range
6. Licensure and continuing education requirements

I. Physiology of Temperature Regulation

One of the major functions of the integumentary system is temperature regulation. In a cold environment, individuals tend to have a bluish color. Several physiological events occur that involve the nervous and muscular systems that serve to increase the temperature of the body. Give at least three events/examples and explain how they serve to increase the body temperature.

Physiological Event	Result

In extreme conditions individuals my lose fingers and toes. Explain how this is really an adaptive mechanism for the individual.

On the other hand, when individuals are placed in an extremely warm environment, the nervous, muscular, and chemical processes are involved. In the table below, list and explain these actions

Physiological Event	Result

Using your knowledge from your chemistry class, explain how the heating curve shown below helps to lower the body temperature.

(continued)

ANATOMY, PHYSIOLOGY, AND DISEASE IN ACTION

II. Anatomy and Art

Materials:
½ inch mosaic tiles in various colors
Tile cutter
Adhesive
Grout
Melanite board

Students can make a mosaic of a diagram to show the layers of the skin, the blood vessels, hair follicle and shaft, sebaceous gland, and sweat glands. The mosaic can be hung in the classroom.

The Nervous System
The Body's Control Center

To pass the time, it's a good idea to take an interesting novel along when we travel. The nervous system, due to its complexity and importance, is our novel for this journey! Don't be dismayed by its length, because Chapter 10, "The Endocrine System," the related control system, will be a "short story" by comparison. So far on our journey, we have seen infrastructure, the building blocks and support systems of the city. Soon we will visit transportation, protection, and energy delivery systems. Like any efficient city, the body must have a control system, a system to monitor conditions, take corrective action when necessary, and keep everything running smoothly. Imagine what would happen if a traffic light network in a city suddenly failed.

The control systems of the body are the nervous and endocrine systems, which receive help from your various senses. Like any control system, they have a large, complex job that is sometimes difficult to understand. They must keep track of everything that is happening in the body. Therefore, the nervous and endocrine systems are perhaps the most complex and vital systems we will visit. In this chapter, we start at the bottom of the control hierarchy, with the cells and the spinal cord. Then we focus on the higher-level control at the brain, and finally we pull everything together to see how all the pieces of the puzzle form the big picture.

LEARNING OUTCOMES

Upon completion of your journey through this chapter, you will be able to:

- List and describe the components and basic operation of the nervous system
- Contrast the central and peripheral nervous systems
- Define the parts and functions of nervous tissue
- Discuss the anatomy and physiology of the spinal cord
- Organize the hierarchy of the nervous system
- Locate and define the external and internal structures of the brain and their corresponding functions
- Describe the sensory and motor functions of the brain with related structures
- Contrast the parasympathetic and sympathetic branches of the autonomic nervous system
- Discuss some representative diseases of the nervous system

Pronunciation Guide

Correct pronunciation is important in any journey so that you and others are completely understood. Here is a "see and say" Pronunciation Guide for the more difficult terms to pronounce in this chapter. Please note that pronunciations given are referenced to medical dictionaries, and regional variations may exist.

acetylcholine (ACh) (AS eh till KOH leen)
acetylcholinesterase (AChE)
  (AS eh till KOH lin ehs tur ace)
amyotrophic (AY my oh TROF ick)
arachnoid mater (ah RAK noyd MAY ter)
astrocytes (ASS troh SITES)
axon (AK son)
basal nuclei (BAY sal noo KLEE ie)
cauda equina (KAW duh EE kwine ah)
cerebellum (ser EE BELL um)
cerebrospinal fluid (ser EE broh SPY nal)
cerebrum (ser EE brum)
commissures (KAH mih shurz)
corpus callosum (KOR pus kah LOH sum)
corticobulbar tract (KOR ti coe BUL bar)
corticospinal tract (KOR ti coe SPY nal)
dendrites (DEN drights)
diencephalon (dye en SEFF ah lon)
dorsal root ganglion (GANG lee on)
dura mater (DOO rah MAY ter)
ependymal cells (ep PEN deh mall)
epidural space (EP ih DURE all)
fissure (FISH er)
fornix (FOR niks)
ganglia (GANG lee ah)
ganglion (GANG lee on)
glial cells (GLEE all)
Guillain Barré (Gey YAHN bar RAY)
gyri (JIE rie)
hydrocephalus (HIGH droh SEF ah lus)
hypothalamus (HIGH poh THAL ah mus)

interneurons (in ter NOO rons)
limbic system (LIM bick)
medulla oblongata (meh DULL lah ob long GAH ta)
meninges (men IN jeez)
meningitis (men in JYE tiss)
microglia (mie crow GLEE ah)
myelin (MY eh lin)
neuroglia (noo ROH glee ah)
neurotransmitter (noo roh TRANS mit ter)
nodes of Ranvier (ron vee AYE)
occipital lobe (ok SIP eh tal)
oligodendrocytes (AH li go DEN droe sites)
parietal lobe (pah RYE eh tal)
pia mater (PEE ah MAY ter)
pineal body (pih NEE al)
plexus (PLECK sus)
reticulospinal (reh TICK you low)
Schwann cells (SHWAN)
sclerosis (skluh ROH sis)
somatic nervous system (so MAH tick)
spinocerebellar tract (SPY no ser eh BELL ar)
spinothalamic tract (SPY no THAL ah mick)
subarachnoid space (SUB ah RACK noyd)
subdural space (sub DOO ral)
sulcus (SULL cus)
sulci (SULL kie)
synapse (SIN aps)
thalamus (THAL ah mus)
ventricles (VEN trik kulz)
vesicles (VESS ih kulz)

OVERVIEW

We begin this journey with an overview of the entire system to show how all the components are interrelated. Let's start with the basic operations.

The Parts and Basic Operation of the Nervous System

The organization of the nervous system can be compared to a computer. Information is entered into the computer by various "senses": keyboard, mouse, microphone, Internet connection, and so on. The main components of the computer's "brain" are the hard drive (long-term memory), random access memory (short-term memory), and central processing unit (thinking and decision making). The computer's output—its interaction with the world—exits via ports and cables to printers, displays, speakers, and other devices.

Typically, we refer to the brain and spinal cord as the **central nervous system (CNS)** and everything outside the brain and spinal cord, which represents the input and output pathways, as the **peripheral nervous system (PNS)**. FIGURE 9-1 ▲ is a schematic of the organization of the branches of the nervous system that will be discussed as we journey through this chapter.

The nervous system's "input devices" comprise the **sensory system**. Your senses sample the environment and bring the information to the nervous system, as will be explored further in Chapter 11. Your sensory system receives and measures information about everything and anything, both within your body and in the outside environment. This sensory information then goes into the nervous system, where it is

central nervous system (CNs) Division of the nervous system that includes the brain and the spinal cord.

peripheral nervous system (PNs) Division of the nervous system that includes the cranial nerves and the spinal nerves.

sensory system Portion of nervous system that receives input.

FIGURE 9-1 ▲ Organization of the nervous system.

motor system The system responsible for movement.

somatic sensory system The portion of the nervous system that provides sensory input for the sense of touch.

autonomic nervous system Division of the peripheral nervous system that carries nerve impulses to the heart, involuntary smooth muscles, and glands. It includes the parasympathetic nervous system (active during sleep and light activity) and the sympathetic nervous system (active during increased activity, danger, and stress).

parasympathetic nervous system (PAIR uh SIM peh THET ik) Division of the autonomic nervous system that uses the neurotransmitter acetylcholine and carries nerve impulses to the heart, involuntary smooth muscles, and glands while the body is at rest.

sympathetic Division of the autonomic nervous system that uses the neurotransmitter norepinephrine and carries nerve impulses to the heart, involuntary muscles, and glands during times of increased activity, danger, or stress.

handled by the brain and spinal cord. The brain and spinal cord combine the input with other kinds of information, compare it to information from past experiences, and make decisions about how to respond to the information.

Once the brain and spinal cord determine an appropriate response to manage the new information, the output side is activated. The output side carries out the orders from the brain and spinal cord. The output side, often called the **motor system**, carries orders to all three types of muscles and to the body's glands, telling them how to respond to the new information. The motor system is divided into two branches: the **somatic nervous system**, which controls skeletal muscle and voluntary movements, and the **autonomic nervous system**, which controls smooth and cardiac muscle in your organs and also several glands. Autonomic output is involuntary and not under conscious control. The autonomic nervous system is further divided into two branches: **parasympathetic** and **sympathetic**. The parasympathetic branch, often called "resting and digesting," controls normal body functions, whereas the sympathetic branch is the body's alert system, commonly known as the "fight-or-flight" response system. Again, please refer to Figure 9-1.

The organization of the nervous system is easier to understand if we look at a real-life event. Imagine that you drive over to your friend's house. As you step onto her walkway, a large dog bounds down the front steps barking and snarling at you. Your sensory system gathers the following information about the new stimulus: large unfriendly dog; distance from your car; lack of immediate help. The information goes into your spinal cord and brain, which makes several decisions. You are in danger; something must be done. To gear up for action, your brain and spinal cord send directions via your autonomic nervous system to your organs. Your heart rate, blood pressure, and respiration rate rise. More blood is delivered to your skeletal muscles and heart to get you fully ready to respond. This is all involuntary, meaning you cannot consciously control it. Your nervous system readies your skeletal muscles to get you out of there. This fight-or-flight response is discussed later in further depth. If you can control your fear, you back slowly away from the situation. If you are scared witless, you run from the yard as fast as you can. Either way, you can hopefully escape the danger with your skin and your pride intact.

Each part of the nervous system has a separate but unmistakably connected role to play in assessing a situation and responding to it. The nervous system is active 24 hours a day, seven days a week, for your entire life. Some situations, like the unfriendly dog, a sudden drop in blood pressure, or a terrible car accident, may be life threatening. Others, like an ant crawling across your foot or a pencil rolling under the desk just out of reach, are simply annoying. Everything that happens in your world is monitored and responded to by your nervous system. It's a truly Herculean task!

Amazing Body Facts

Faster Than a Speeding Bullet

Well, not literally! Your nervous system must respond very quickly to stimuli. Think about how fast you pull your hand away from a hot stove or step on the brake when something runs in front of your car. Nerve impulses can move very quickly. Some neurons have speeds as fast as 100 meters per second. That's in the neighborhood of 200 miles per hour. Bullets, on the other hand, can travel thousands of miles per hour!

NERVOUS TISSUE

Like all organs, the components of the nervous system are made up of tissue. But unlike other systems, the nervous system contains no epithelium, connective tissue, or muscle tissue. Nervous tissue is made up of two different types of cells: neuroglia and neurons.

Neuroglia

The **neuroglia** or **glial cells** are specialized cells in nervous tissue that allow it to perform nervous system functions. In the CNS, there are four types of glial cells:

- **Astrocytes** are metabolic and structural support cells that hold the neurons and blood vessels close together and form part of blood–brain barrier.
- **Microglia** can attack microbes and remove debris.
- **Ependymal cells** do the job of epithelial cells, covering surfaces and lining cavities.
- **Oligodendrocytes** hold nerve fibers together and make a lipid insulation called **myelin,** described in more detail a bit later.

In the PNS, there are only two types of glial cells: **Schwann cells,** which make myelin for the PNS, and **satellite cells,** which are support cells. Please see **FIGURE 9-2 ▲**, which shows a cutaway view of the spinal cord of the CNS showing the four types of neuroglial cells found there and a peripheral neuron with its glial cells.

neuroglia *(new ROG lee ah)* Cells that hold neurons in place and perform specialized tasks. Includes astrocytes, ependymal cells, microglia, oligodendrocytes, satellite cells, and Schwann cells. Also called glial cells.

glial cells *(GLEE all)* Cells that include astrocytes, oligo- dendrocytes, ependymal cells, microglia cells, Schwann cells, and satellite cells

astrocyte *(ASS troh SITE)* Star-shaped cell that provides structural support for neurons, connects them to capillaries, and forms the blood–brain barrier.

microglia *(MYE crow GLEE ah)* Cells that move, engulf, and destroy pathogens anywhere in the central nervous system.

ependymal cells *(ep IN dih mal)* Specialized cells that line the walls of the ventricles and spinal canal and produce cerebrospinal fluid.

oligodendrocytes *(ALL ih go DEN droh sites)* Neuroglial cells, which produce myelin in the CNS.

myelin *(MY eh lin)* Fatty sheath around the axon of a neuron. It speeds up impulse conduction. Myelin around the axons of the brain and spinal cord is produced by oligo-dendrocytes. Myelin around axons of the cranial and spinal nerves is produced by Schwann cells. An axon with myelin is said to be myelinated.

Schwann cells *(SHWAN sell)* Cell that forms the myelin sheaths around axons of the cranial and spinal nerves.

satellite cells Neuroglia cells that enclose the cell bodies of neurons in the spinal ganglia.

CNS Glial Cells	PNS Glial Cells
Astrocyte—Metabolic and structural support	Schwann cells—Produce myelin
Microglia—Remove debris	Satellite cells—Support cells
Oligodendrocytes—Make lipid insulation (Myelin)	
Ependymal cells—Cover and line cavities	

FIGURE 9-2 ▲ Glial cells and their functions.

neurons *(NEW ron)* An individual nerve cell. The functional part of the nervous system.

neuron cell body The part of cell containing the nucleus but not the axon or dendrite.

dendrite *(DEN dright)* Multiple branches at the end of a neuron that carry information to the cell body.

axon *(AK son)* Part of the neuron that is a single, elongated branch at the opposite end from the dendrites. It receives an electrical impulse and releases neurotransmitters into the synapse. Axons are covered by an insulating layer of myelin.

Neurons

The glial cells do all the support activities for the nervous system, such as lining and covering cavities and supporting and protecting structures. None of the glial cells, however, are capable of measuring the environment, making decisions, or sending orders. All the control functions of the nervous system must be carried out by a second group of cells called **neurons**.

Neurons are rather bizarre-looking cells, often with many branches and what appears to be a tail (see **FIGURE 9-3** ▲). The main function of a neuron is to transmit messages from one cell to another. Each part of a neuron has a specific function. The **neuron cell body**'s main function is that of cell metabolism. Its **dendrites** receive information from the environment or from other cells and carry that information to the cell body. The **axon** generates and sends signals to other cells. Those signals

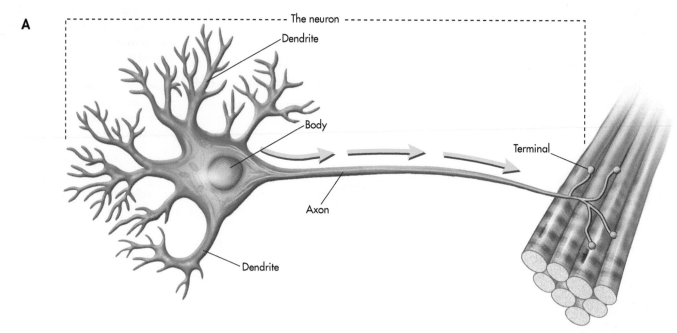

A

The neuron

Dendrite

Body

Terminal

Axon

Dendrite

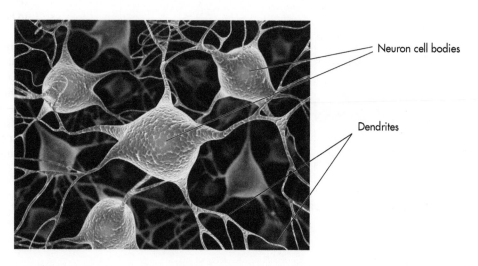

B

Neuron cell bodies

Dendrites

FIGURE 9-3 ▲
A. neuron connection to a skeletal muscle.
B. An association neuron.
(Source: Ktsdesign/ Shutterstock.com.)

travel down the axon until they reach the **axon terminal,** which then connects to a receiving cell. This space between the axon terminal and receiving cell is called a **synapse.** If the receiving cell is a skeletal muscle cell, then this particular synapse is called the **neuromuscular synapse** or **junction** (see Chapter 7).

Neurons can be classified by how they look (structure) or what they do (function). From a structural point of view, they can be classified as follows:

* Neurons that have one axon and one dendrite (bipolar)
* Neurons that have one axon and many dendrites or branches (multipolar), as in Figure 9-3A
* Neurons that have one process that splits into a central and a peripheral projection (unipolar)

Classified by function, input neurons are known as **sensory neurons** (afferent neurons). They carry impulses from the skin and sensory organs to the spinal cord and the brain. Output neurons are known as **motor neurons** (efferent neurons). They carry messages from the brain and spinal cord to muscles and glands. Neurons that carry information between neurons are called **interneurons** (*inter* means between) or **association neurons.** See FIGURE 9-3B ▲.

axon terminal The end point of a neuron.

synapse *(SIN aps)* Space between the axon of one neuron and the dendrites of the next neuron.

neuromuscular synapse or **junction** *(noor oh MUHS kyuh ler JUHNGK shuhn)* Area on a single muscle fiber where a nerve connects.

sensory neurons Portion of nervous system that receives input.

motor neurons Neuron that innervates muscle tissue.

interneurons *(in ter NEW ronz)* Neurons that facilitate communication between neurons.

TEST YOUR KNOWLEDGE 9-1

Choose the best answer:

1. Which cells are the support cells in the nervous system?
   a. neurons
   b. neuroglia
   c. epithelium
   d. all of the above

2. The output side of your nervous system is called:
   a. sensory
   b. motor
   c. central
   d. exit

3. The part of the nervous system that integrates and processes information is known as the:
   a. PNS
   b. PBS
   c. CNS
   d. CIA

4. The lipid insulation of nervous tissue is called:
   a. glia
   b. myelin
   c. Schwann cells
   d. astrocytes

---

association neuron Neurons that mediate impulses between a sensory and motor neuron.

HOW NEURONS WORK

Now that we know the basic structure of neurons, let's take a closer look at how they function.

Excitable Cells

A neuron is an **excitable cell.** An excitable cell carries a small electrical charge when stimulated. Each time charged particles flow across a cell membrane, their movement generates a tiny electrical current. (Electricity is just the movement of charges from one place to the other.) All three types of muscle cells are excitable cells, as are many gland cells. Because neurons are excitable cells, it makes sense that the way neurons send and receive signals is via tiny electrical currents.

excitable cell Cell that carries an electrical charge when stimulated.

How, you might ask, can cells carry electricity? It seems hard to believe, but cells are like miniature batteries, able to generate tiny currents simply by changing the permeability of their membranes. Perhaps the plot of the *Matrix* movies in which humans are used by machines as batteries is not so far-fetched.

Action Potentials

resting cell Nervous cell that is neither stimulated nor excited.

polarized Cell that has a difference in charge across its membrane so it is more negative on the inside than on the outside of the membrane.

depolarization Changing of the permeability of the cell membrane of any excitable cell, for example cardiac muscle or a neuron, that leads to a change in charge across the cell membrane.

repolarization The return of membrane potential toward resting.

hyperpolarized The charge across the cell membrane is more negative than resting.

refractory period Short period of time when an excitable cell, like a neuron or cardiac muscle cell, is resting and unresponsive to electrical impulses.

action potential The change of the electrical charge of a nerve or muscle fiber when stimulated. Action potentials are all or none.

local potential Change in the electrical charge across a cell membrane that is proportional to the size of the stimulus.

impulse conduction The propagation of an electrical impulse through the nervous system.

A cell that is not stimulated or excited is called a **resting cell** and is said to be **polarized**. It has a difference in charge across its membrane so that it is more negative on the inside than on the outside. When that cell gets stimulated (excited), sodium gates in the cell membrane spring open. When these sodium gates open, they allow sodium ions (Na^+) to travel across the cell membrane. These sodium ions are positively charged, so when they go into the cell, the cell becomes more positive. A cell that is more positive than resting becomes **depolarized**. In less than a millisecond, the gates on the sodium channels shut, just like the automatic doors at the supermarket. Then other gates open for potassium channels. Potassium (K^+), which is also positive, leaves the cell, taking its positive charges with it. The inside of the cell becomes more negative again, eventually returning to rest. This is **repolarization** (see FIGURE 9-4 ▲).

Sometimes a cell overshoots its charge and becomes more negative than when it is at rest. Then the cell is **hyperpolarized**. Eventually, the cell will return to resting. A cell is unable to accept another stimulus until it repolarizes (returns to its resting state), and the period during which it cannot accept another stimulus is called the **refractory period**. This whole series of permeability changes within the cell, and the resultant changes in charge across the cell membrane is called the **action potential**.

Action potentials are "all-or-none," which means that the action potential, once it starts, will always finish and will always be the same size. Either a cell has one or it doesn't. There are no small or large action potentials.

Local Potentials

Neurons can use their ability to generate electricity to send, receive, and interpret signals. Some neurons can signal the level of a stimulus. This phenomenon, known as a **local potential**, is different from the action potential previously discussed. In a local potential, the *size or amount* of the stimulus determines the excitement of the cell. A big stimulus causes a bigger depolarization than a small stimulus. Several local potentials can add together to form an action potential. (Local potentials, then, are not all-or-none but vary, depending on the degree of stimulation.)

Once several local potentials reach a threshold level, an action potential is triggered. The various dendrites carry the depolarization to the sensory neuron cell body. The cell body takes that information and generates an action potential, if the stimulus is big enough. Once an action potential is formed, it travels down the axon from the cell body to the terminal. This movement is called **impulse conduction**.

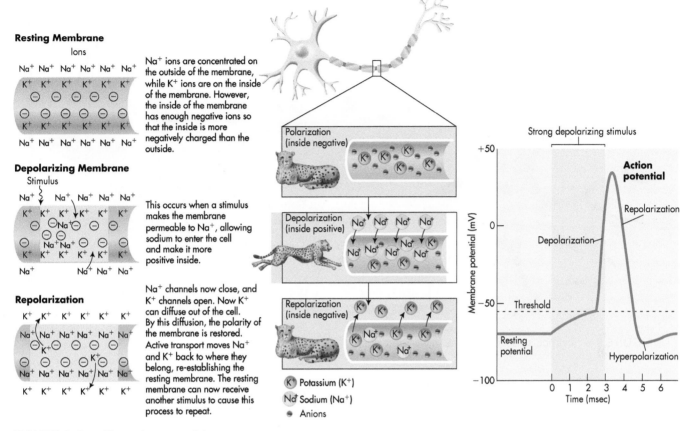

Resting Membrane

Ions

Na^+ ions are concentrated on the outside of the membrane, while K^+ ions are on the inside of the membrane. However, the inside of the membrane has enough negative ions so that the inside is more negatively charged than the outside.

Depolarizing Membrane

Stimulus

This occurs when a stimulus makes the membrane permeable to Na^+, allowing sodium to enter the cell and make it more positive inside.

Repolarization

Na^+ channels now close, and K^+ channels open. Now K^+ can diffuse out of the cell. By this diffusion, the polarity of the membrane is restored. Active transport moves Na^+ and K^+ back to where they belong, re-establishing the resting membrane. The resting membrane can now receive another stimulus to cause this process to repeat.

Polarization (inside negative)

Depolarization (inside positive)

Repolarization (inside negative)

K^+ Potassium (K^+)

Na^+ Sodium (Na^+)

Anions

Strong depolarizing stimulus

Action potential

Repolarization

Depolarization

Threshold

Resting potential

Hyperpolarization

Membrane potential (mV)

Time (msec)

FIGURE 9-4 ▲ The action potential.

APPLIED SCIENCE

Fugu

The puffer fish, fugu, is considered a dangerous delicacy in Japan because if you eat it, you could die! Fugu can be served only by specially certified chefs trained to prepare the fish so it is safe to eat. Puffer fish contain a poison, tetrodotoxin (TTX), in their tissues that blocks sodium channels, preventing sodium from entering cells. Cells exposed to TTX cannot depolarize. Thus, neurons cannot fire action potentials. People who consume improperly prepared fugu become paralyzed. Symptoms develop as headache, dizziness, vomiting, and chest tightness within 15 minutes to 20 hours post-ingestion. Eventually, victims develop paralysis. If untreated, death can result in as little as 4 hours, usually from respiratory paralysis.

Impulse Conduction

The speed of impulse conduction along an axon is determined by two characteristics: the presence of a myelin sheath and the diameter of the axon. Myelin is a lipid insulation or sheath formed by the **oligodendrocytes** in the CNS and the **Schwann cells** in the PNS. In preserved brains, the myelinated axons look white. Unmyelinated parts of the CNS, like cell bodies, look gray. Therefore, what we call "white matter" is typically made of axons, and what we call "gray matter" is made of cell bodies. The cell membranes of oligodendrocytes or entire Schwann cells are wrapped around an axon like a bandage. Between adjacent glial cells are tiny bare spots called **nodes of Ranvier** (see FIGURE 9-5 ▲). When an axon is wrapped in myelin, we call the axon myelinated. Myelin is essential for the speedy flow of action

oligodendrocytes *(ALL ih go DEN droh sites)* Neuroglial cells, which produce myelin in the CNS.

Schwann cells *(SHWAN sell)* Cell that forms the myelin sheaths around axons of the cranial and spinal nerves.

nodes of Ranvier Constriction of the myelin sheath on a myelinated nerve fiber that facilitates nodal transmission of the impulse.

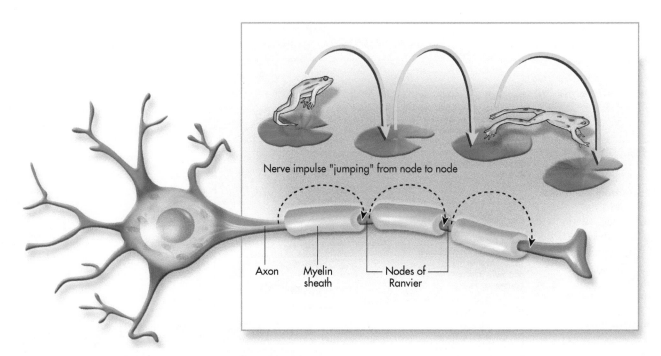

Nerve impulse "jumping" from node to node

Axon   Myelin   Nodes of
        sheath   Ranvier

FIGURE 9-5 ▲ Impulse conduction via myelinated axon.

potentials down axons. In an unmyelinated axon, the action potential can only flow down the axon by depolarizing each and every millimeter of the axon. Every single sodium channel must open, and every single potassium channel must open. It is a relatively slow process. In a myelinated axon, only the channels at the nodes must open for the action potential to flow down the axon. Myelin prevents ions from passing through channels because ions are water soluble, and myelin is a lipid. (Remember, charged particles cannot get through lipids.) The action potential therefore "skips" down the axon from node to node (nodal transmission) rather than creeping along the entire length of the axon. It works the same way as if you try to walk across the floor heel to toe, never missing a spot and then skip across the floor in large leaps. Which is faster?

The diameter of the axon also affects the speed of action potential flow. Think about moving through two different pipes, say on a playground or obstacle course. One pipe is one-half meter in diameter (less than 2 feet). To move through the pipe, you must crawl. The other pipe is 2 meters in diameter (more than 6 feet). Most of you can stand in this pipe with room to spare. Which trip would be faster? Obviously, it's the one through the larger-diameter pipe. You don't have to crawl, so you don't get hung up on the side. Heck, you could even run through the big pipe! For ions, the axon is essentially a pipe. The wider the axon, the faster the ions flow. The combination of myelination and large diameter makes a huge difference in speed. Small, unmyelinated axons have speeds as low as 0.5 meters per second, whereas large-diameter, myelinated axons may be as fast as 100 meters per second. That's 200 times faster!

Clinical Application

EPILEPSY

Epilepsy is a disorder in which irregular electrical signals are suddenly discharged from neurons, causing the brain to become overloaded with impulses, causing a seizure. A mild seizure, or petit mal seizure, can cause a drop in awareness or muscle coordination. The person experiencing a petit mal seizure may seem to be daydreaming or just staring into space. A severe seizure, or grand mal seizure, can cause convulsions. The person experiencing a grand mal seizure may drop to the floor, shake, and twitch. Epilepsy may be caused by earlier brain damage due to trauma, stroke, exposure to toxins, or lack of oxygen during childbirth. In most cases, the cause of epilepsy is never identified. However, diagnosis of epilepsy and evaluation of the severity of the seizures can be done. An electroencephalogram, EEG, can be utilized to detect the action potentials in the brain with the use of electrodes, small flat discs which are attached to the scalp. The read out of an EEG shows up as waves of electrical activity.

multiple sclerosis (MS) *(sklih ROH sis)* A chronic disease of the central nervous system involving the destruction of myelin and the nerve axons in various regions of the brain and the spinal cord at different times.

Pathology Connection

MYELIN DISORDERS

Multiple Sclerosis

Multiple sclerosis (MS) is a disorder of the myelin in the CNS, which affects 200,000 to 400,000 people in the United States alone. Patients with multiple sclerosis have many areas in their nervous system where the myelin has been destroyed, probably by autoimmune attacks. In some patients, axons and cell bodies are also destroyed. The brain, spinal cord, and optic nerves are often involved. In areas without myelin, impulse conduction is slow or impossible. Imagine an electrical wire with many bare spots or with no insulation. These bare or exposed parts can "short out" and prevent the current from passing further down the wire. These areas of damaged myelin often have plaques, or scarred areas, that give MS its name. (Note that *scleros* means "to harden.") Symptoms of multiple sclerosis differ from patient to patient depending on where the myelin damage occurs. Patients may have disturbances in vision, balance, speech, or movement.

MS can be grouped into two types based on the pattern of the disease. Relapsing-remitting MS is characterized by flare-ups, with obvious symptoms, and periods in which the patients have no symptoms, called remissions. Chronic progressive MS has no remission periods, and patients become steadily more disabled. Most patients are initially diagnosed with relapsing-remitting MS, but at least 50% of them will progress to the chronic progressive form. MS is more common in women than in men and is diagnosed most often in people younger than the age of 50.

There is no definitive diagnosis for MS. Patient history suggesting flare-ups and remissions, visual disturbances along with muscle weakness, and the presence of plaques in an MRI, all can aid in the diagnosis of MS. As with most other progressive neurological disorders, there is no cure for MS. Especially during acute flare-ups, some patients are helped by steroids, plasma exchange, or intravenous Immunglobin G. Several immunosuppressant drugs have been shown to decrease the number of relapses and prevent conversion from relapsing-remitting to chronic progressive and may slow progression in some patients. Symptom management, decreasing fatigue, and treating depression are important for many people living with MS.

(continued)

Pathology Connection (continued)

Guillain-Barré Syndrome

Guillain-Barré syndrome (GBS) is a paralysis caused by an autoimmune attack on peripheral myelin, Schwann cells, or peripheral axons. There are 1 to 2 cases of GBS/100,000 people in the United States each year. Patients develop, over variable periods of time, weakness and usually ascending paralysis of a limb, face, and diaphragm. The course of the disease can be divided into three phases. The acute phase is the initial onset of the disease, during which the patient gets steadily worse. The plateau phase is a period of days to weeks in which the patient's condition is stable. During the recovery phase, which may last up to 2 years, patients recover function. Some patients may have a mild form of Guillain-Barré syndrome, but many with severe disease must be kept on a ventilator until the paralysis resolves. Patients may recover full function, but a significant portion of those with severe GBS still have measurable disability 2 years after recovery. The cause of the disease is not known, though many patients develop Guillain-Barré syndrome after a viral infection.

Diagnosis of GBS is difficult because its chief symptom, weakness, may be caused by many different disorders. Patient history is the best way to diagnose the disorder. Rapid-onset ascending paralysis after an infection could indicate GBS. Nerve conduction and EMG (muscle recordings) can be used to help confirm diagnosis. Often there are high protein levels in the cerebrospinal fluid (CSF) but no white blood cells. There is no effective treatment for GBS except supportive care to treat the symptoms, including ventilation support, prevention of blood clots and bed sores, and pain medication. Some patients improve more rapidly with plasma exchange, which decreases immune function. Fortunately, the disorder is usually temporary. Many patients need rehabilitation after their PNS recovers.

Guillain-Barré syndrome (GBs) *(gee YAH bar RAY)* A neuromuscular disease that usually leads to ascending flaccid paralysis.

vesicles Membrane-bound storage sac inside a cell.

neurotransmitters *(NEW roh TRANS mitt er)* Chemical messenger that travels across the synapse between a neuron and another neuron, muscle fiber, or gland.

How Synapses Work

For neurons to communicate, there must be some way for a message to be sent from one neuron to the other. This communication occurs at the synapse. Before synaptic transmission occurs, an action potential is generated and flows toward the axon terminal.

Chemical Synapses

When an impulse arrives at the axon terminal, the terminal depolarizes and calcium gates open. Calcium ions flow into the cell, which causes more depolarization, which causes more calcium to come in, and so on. In addition, when calcium flows in, it triggers a change in the terminal. Tiny sacs in the terminal called **vesicles** release their contents from the cell via exocytosis (to expel) when calcium flows in. These vesicles are filled with molecules called **neurotransmitters**.

These neurotransmitters are used to send the signal from the neuron across the synapse to the next cell in line. The neurotransmitter binds to the cell receiving the signal and causes gates to open or close. Some neurotransmitters excite the receiving cell, and some calm it down. In the case of the hammered thumb, the neurotransmitter would be released in your spinal cord and would excite a pain neuron. The receiving neuron would be stimulated and take the information about your thumb to your brain, where you would register the pain. You have already learned about a very common chemical synapse: the neuromuscular junction.

The last step in the transfer of information is cleanup. The neurotransmitter must be taken away from the synapse or it will continually bind to the receiving cell. This cleanup is accomplished through an inactivator, usually an enzyme. For example, if the neurotransmitter chemical is **acetylcholine (ACh),** like in the neuromuscular junction, it will be inactivated by **acetylcholinesterase (AChase),** an enzyme that breaks down ACh. Note that the ending *ase* means enzymes which "break down" the substance, in this case acetylcholine. This type of information flow, using neurotransmitters, is called a **chemical synapse** because chemicals (neurotransmitters) are used to carry the information from one cell to another. See **FIGURE 9-6** ▲ for the steps in chemical synaptic transmission.

Our understanding of chemical synapses has led to several breakthroughs for treating mental illness. Many current medications are designed to modify synapses. Selective serotonin reuptake inhibitors (SSRIs) are good examples. These medications prevent the cleanup of the neurotransmitter serotonin from synapses, thereby increasing the effects of serotonin on the receiving cell. Many antidepressants and antianxiety medications are SSRIs. **TABLE 9-1** ■ contains other examples of clinically important neurotransmitters. Remember the neuromuscular junction from Chapter 7? That is perhaps the best understood chemical synapse in the human body. The transmitting neuron is a motor neuron, the receiving cell is a skeletal muscle fiber, and the neurotransmitter is acetylcholine.

acetylcholine *(AS eh till KOH leen)* Neurotransmitter between neurons in the brain and spinal cord or between a neuron and a voluntary skeletal muscle.

acetylcholinesterase *(AS eh till KOH lin ehs tur ace)* The enzyme that stops the action of acetylcholine.

chemical synapse *(SIN aps)* Site of communication between neurons and other excitable cells. Neurotransmitters are released from the neuron (presynaptic cell) and travel to a muscle or gland cell (the postsynaptic cell), allowing communication between the two cells.

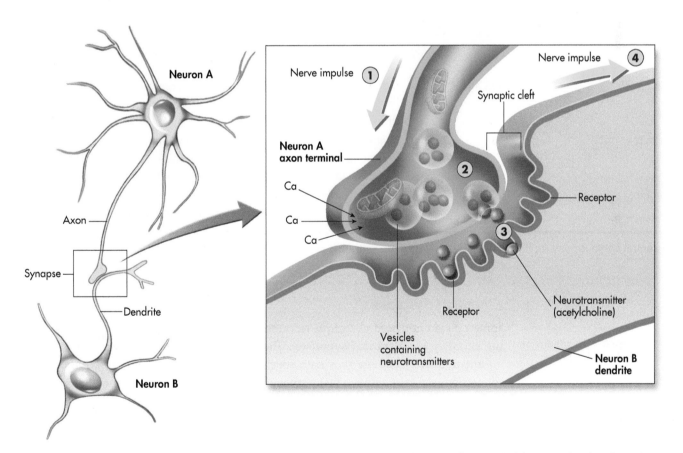

FIGURE 9-6 ▲ The chemical synapse. Step 1: The impulse travels down the axon. Step 2: Vesicles are stimulated to release a neurotransmitter (exocytosis). Step 3: The neurotransmitter travels across the synapse and binds with the receptor site of post synaptic cell. Step 4: The impulse continues down the dendrite.

Clinical Application

BIOTERRORISM

If acetylcholinesterase activity is prevented, acetylcholine continually stimulates the muscle, eventually paralyzing it. Some insecticides and the nerve gas Sarin, which killed 12 people and injured hundreds of others during a terrorist attack in a Tokyo subway tunnel in 1995, are acetylcholinesterase inhibitors. They kill by causing paralysis of skeletal muscles, including the diaphragm, the most important respiratory muscle. Victims of Sarin or overexposure to organophosphate insecticides can die from respiratory arrest.

TABLE 9-1 ■ SELECTED COMMON NEUROTRANSMITTERS

NEUROTRANSMITTER	LOCATION	FUNCTION	COMMENTS
Acetylcholine	CNS* and PNS*	Generally excitatory but is inhibitory to some organs and glands	Found in skeletal neuromuscular junctions and in many ANS* synapses
Norepinephrine	CNS and PNS	May be excitatory or inhibitory, depending on the receptors	Found at visceral and cardiac muscle synapses, ANS
Epinephrine	CNS and PNS	May be excitatory or inhibitory, depending on the receptors	Found in pathways concerned with behavior and mood
Serotonin	CNS	Generally inhibitory in hormones that cause depression	Found in pathways that regulate temperature, sensory perception, mood, onset of sleep
Endorphins	CNS	Generally inhibitory	Inhibit release of pain neurotransmitters

*CNS = central nervous system; PNS = peripheral nervous system; ANS = autonomic nervous system.

Electrical Synapses

electrical synapse Gap or junction between two neurons involving electrical charges.

gap junction A special connection found in electrical synapses.

Some cells do not need chemicals to transmit information from one cell to another. Instead, they use **electrical synapses**. The cells in an electrical synapse can transfer information freely because they have special connections called **gap junctions**. Such connections can exist between many types of excitable cells. They are found, for example, in the intercalated discs between cardiac muscle fibers.

TEST YOUR KNOWLEDGE 9-2

Choose the best answer:

1. Which ions move *into* neurons during the action potential?
   a. potassium
   b. calcium
   c. sodium
   d. acetylcholine

2. Which of the following is all-or-none?
   a. local potential
   b. action potential
   c. chemical synapse
   d. impulse conduction

3. The molecules used to send signals across synapses are called:
   a. hormones
   b. ions
   c. neurotransmitters
   d. messengers

4. What is another name for myelinated axons?
   a. gray matter
   b. dura mater
   c. white matter
   d. duzitmater

5. Multiple sclerosis symptoms are caused by:
   a. destruction of CNS myelin
   b. destruction of PNS myelin
   c. neuron death
   d. damage to the spinal cord

6. Which of the following is true of Guillain-Barré syndrome?
   a. It is genetic.
   b. It is always permanently disabling.
   c. It causes brain damage.
   d. It may be associated with a virus.

SPINAL CORD AND SPINAL NERVES

So far we've discussed the nervous system at the cellular and tissue level. In addition, we've described how impulses are transmitted in the nervous system. Now let's focus on the main highway that these impulses travel.

External Anatomy of the Spinal Cord

The **spinal cord** is located in a hollow tube running inside the vertebral column from the foramen magnum of the skull to the second lumbar (L2) vertebrae. You can think of your spinal cord as a very sophisticated neural information superhighway that allows nerve impulses to travel to and from the brain. You can also think of the spinal cord as a nerve center that controls many reflexes. The spinal cord is divided into 31 segments, each with a pair of **spinal nerves**. Both the spinal cord segments and the spinal nerves are named for their corresponding vertebrae. The spinal cord ends at L2 in a pointed structure called the **conus medullaris**. Hanging from the conus medullaris is the **cauda equina**. The cauda equina is the bunch of spinal nerves, L2 through the coccygeal (Co) nerves, dangling loosely in a bath of **cerebrospinal fluid (CSF)**, which acts as a shock absorber for both the brain and spinal cord. The spinal cord has two widened areas, the cervical and lumbar enlargements, which contain the neurons for the limbs. See FIGURE 9-7 ▲.

spinal cord Part of the central nervous system. Continuous with the medulla oblongata of the brain and extends down the back in the spinal cavity. Ends at L2 and separates into individual nerves (cauda equina).

spinal nerves Thirty-one pairs of nerves. Each pair comes out from the spinal cord between two vertebrae. An individual spinal nerve consists of dorsal nerve roots and ventral nerve roots.

conus medullaris *(KOH nus med you LAIR iss)* A pointed structure at the posterior end of the spinal cord.

cauda equina *(KAW dah ee KWYE nah)* A bunch of spinal nerves dangling at the end of the spinal cord similar to a horse's tail.

cerebrospinal fluid (CSF) *(SER eh broh SPY nal FLOO id* The fluid cushion that protects the brain and spinal cord from shock.

LEARNING HINT

Directional Terms

In the spinal cord, directional terms—anterior, posterior, dorsal, and ventral—are very important because function is linked to location. It is easy to get confused by the use of anterior and posterior for some structures and dorsal and ventral for others. Just keep in mind that in humans, anterior is ventral and posterior is dorsal. The names are interchangeable for all the structures except the spinal roots. The spinal roots are *always* called dorsal or ventral.

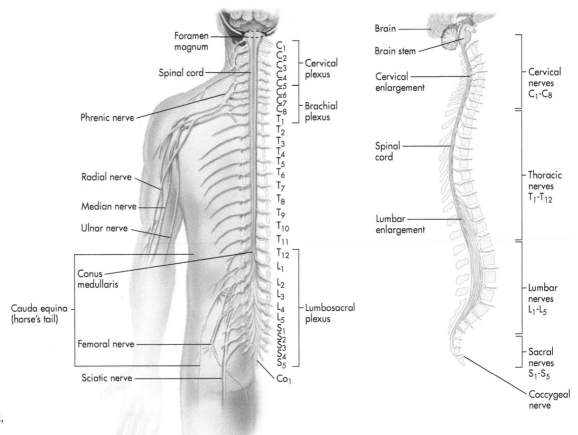

FIGURE 9-7 ▲ The spinal cord. Please note that although there are seven cervical vertebrae, there are eight pairs of cervical spinal nerves.

meninges
(men IN jeez)
Three separate membranes that envelope and protect the entire brain and spinal cord. The meninges include the dura mater, arachnoid, and pia mater.

dura mater *(DOO ra MAY ter)* Tough, outermost layer of the meninges. The dura mater lies just under the bones of the cranium and vertebrae.

arachnoid mater *(ah RAK noyd MAY ter)* Weblike connective tissues that attach to the pia mater. The space under the arachnoid mater (subarachnoid space) contains cerebral spinal fluid.

pia mater *(PEE ah MAY ter)* Thin, delicate, innermost layer of the meninges that covers the surface of the brain and spinal cord. It contains many small blood vessels.

Meninges

The CNS, both brain and spinal cord, are surrounded by a series of protective membranes called the **meninges**. The purpose of the meninges is to cover the delicate structures of the brain and spinal cord. In essence, they help to set up layers that act as cushions and shock absorbers for the brain and spinal cord. The meninges form three distinct layers. The outer layer of thick, fibrous tissue is called the **dura mater**. The middle layer, a wispy, delicate layer resembling spider webs, is the **arachnoid mater**, which is composed of collagen and elastic fibers. The third, innermost layer, which is fused to the neural tissue of the CNS, is the **pia mater**. This layer contains blood vessels that serve the brain and spinal cord.

A series of spaces are associated with the meninges. Between the dura and the vertebral column is a space filled with fat and blood vessels called the **epidural space**. Between the dura mater and the arachnoid mater, under the dura mater, is the **subdural space,** which is filled with a tiny bit of fluid. Between the arachnoid mater and the pia mater is the large **subarachnoid space,** filled with cerebrospinal fluid, acting as a fluid cushion for the CNS. In addition, CSF can also transport dissolved gases and nutrients, as well as chemical messengers and waste products, because there is no blood in the CNS itself. These three membranes and their fluid-filled spaces, together with the bones of the skull and vertebral column, form a strong protection system against CNS injury. Please see FIGURE 9-8 ▲.

epidural space *(ep ih DURE all)* Area between the dura mater and the vertebral body.

subdural space *(sub DOO ral)* The space between the arachnoid and dura mater.

subarachnoid space *(SUB ah RACK noyd)* Space beneath the arachnoid layer of the meninges. It is filled with cerebrospinal fluid.

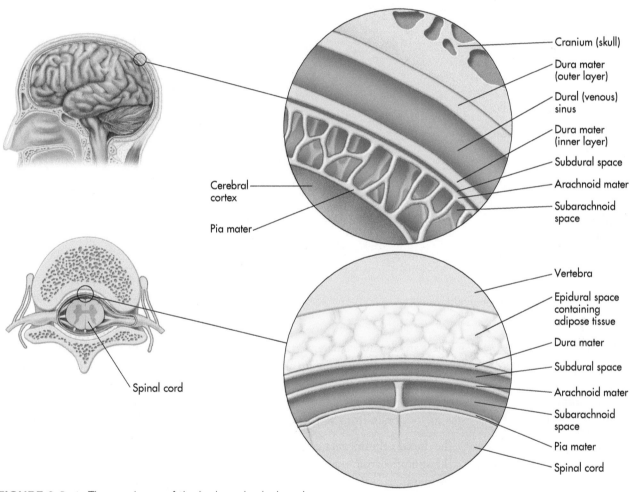

Cranium (skull)
Dura mater (outer layer)
Dural (venous) sinus
Dura mater (inner layer)
Subdural space
Arachnoid mater
Subarachnoid space

Cerebral cortex
Pia mater

Spinal cord

Vertebra
Epidural space containing adipose tissue
Dura mater
Subdural space
Arachnoid mater
Subarachnoid space
Pia mater
Spinal cord

FIGURE 9-8 ▲ The meninges of the brain and spinal cord.

fissure *(FISH er)* Deep division on the surface of the brain and spinal cord.

sulcus *(SULL cuss)* One of many shallow grooves between the gyri in the cerebrum and cerebellum. Plural: sulci.

column The white matter found in the spinal cord that acts as nerve tracts and pathways.

horns Grey matter in spinal cord that contain neuron cell bodies and are involved in sensory, motor, and autonomic functions.

Internal Anatomy of the Spinal Cord

The spinal cord is divided by an anterior median fissure and a posterior median sulcus. A **fissure** is a deep groove on the CNS surface; a **sulcus** is a shallow groove on the CNS surface. Please see FIGURE 9-9 ▲. The interior of the spinal cord is then divided into a series of sections of white matter **columns** and gray matter **horns**. The horns are the regions that contain neuron cell bodies. There are three types of horns. The *posterior or dorsal horn* is involved in sensory functions, the *anterior or ventral horn* in motor functions, and the *lateral horn* in autonomic functions.

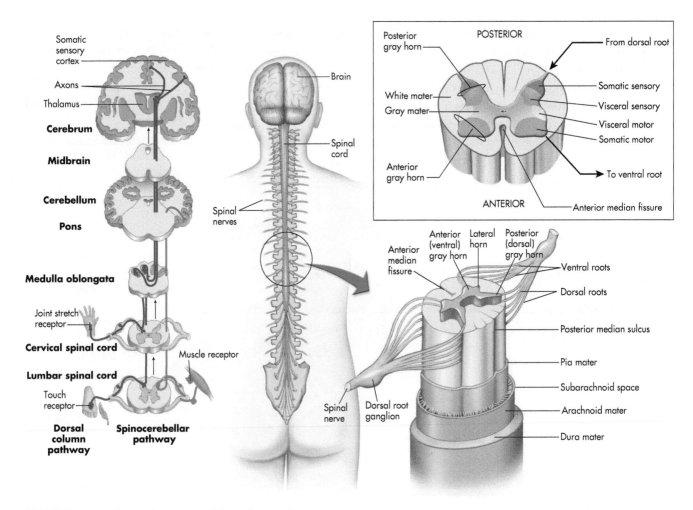

FIGURE 9-9 ▲ Internal anatomy of the spinal cord.

dorsal column tract Spinal cord pathway that carries fine touch sensation from the spinal cord to the brain.

spinothalamic tract *(SPY no THAL ah mick)* Sensory pathway from the spinal cord to the thalamus and eventually the primary somatic sensory cortex. Contains pain and crude touch information.

spinocerebellar tract *(SPY no SAIR eh BELL ar)* Sensory pathway from the spinal cord to the cerebellum.

corticospinal tract *(CORE tih coh SPY nal)* Pertaining to the tract between the cerebral cortex and spinal cord. Carries orders for voluntary movements.

corticobulbar tract *(CORE tih coh BUL bar)* Spinal cord tract that carries impulses to the brainstem from the motor cortex. Carries orders for voluntary movements.

There are also dorsal, lateral, and ventral columns. These columns act as nerve tracts, pathways, or axons, running up and down the spinal cord to and from the brain. Three ascending pathways, the **dorsal column tract**, the **spinothalamic tract**, and the **spinocerebellar tract**, carry information from your sense of touch to the spinal cord and then to your brain from all parts of the skin, joints, and tendons. Again see Figure 9-9.

- The dorsal column tract carries fine-touch and vibration information to the brain.
- The spinothalamic tract carries temperature, pain, and crude touch information to the brain.
- The spinocerebellar tract carries information about posture and position to the brain.

Several descending pathways carry motor information (orders for voluntary movements) from the brain to the spinal cord, including the **corticospinal tract, corticobulbar tract, reticulospinal tract,** and **rubrospinal tract.** The axons from all pathways synapse on motor neurons in the ventral horn.

- The corticospinal tract carries orders from the brain to the motor neurons in the ventral horn of the spinal cord.

- The corticobulbar tract carries orders from the brain to motor neurons in the brain stem (more details later).
- The reticulospinal and rubrospinal tracts (along with several other tracts) carry information from higher brain structures to the brain stem and ventral horn, which helps to coordinate movements.

Whether the tracts are ascending or descending, it helps to think of the columns as individual communication wires, part of a vast network of wires, transporting information to the appropriate parts of the system. This is the neural information superhighway.

In addition, the spinal cord has several other features. The **commissures,** gray and white, connect left and right halves of the cord so the two sides of the CNS can communicate. (See, the right hand *does* usually know what the left hand is doing, even if it doesn't always seem like it!) The central canal is a cavity in the center of the spinal cord that is filled with cerebrospinal fluid. The **spinal roots,** projecting from both sides of the spinal cord in pairs, fuse to form spinal nerves. (The roots are the on-ramps and off-ramps of the neural superhighway.) The **dorsal root,** with the embedded **dorsal root ganglion,** a collection of sensory neurons, carries sensory information, whereas the **ventral root** carries motor information. Again, please refer to Figure 9-9.

Spinal Nerves

Nerves are the connection between the CNS (brain and spinal cord) and the world outside the CNS. Nerves are therefore part of the PNS. Isn't it amazing that the brain, which is totally encased in darkness, can receive and interpret the nerve messages from the PNS to allow us to see the wonderful world around us? All nerves consist of bundles of axons, blood vessels, and connective tissue. Nerves run between the CNS and organs or tissues, carrying information into and out of the CNS. The nerves connected to the spinal cord are called **spinal nerves.** There are 31 pairs of spinal nerves, each named for the spinal cord segment to which they are attached. Because each spinal nerve is a fusion of dorsal and ventral roots, spinal nerves carry both sensory and motor information. A nerve that carries *both* types of information is called a **mixed nerve.** All spinal nerves are mixed. When spinal nerves leave the vertebral column, they can go through a number of different pathways to reach the peripheral tissues. Spinal nerves from the thoracic spinal nerves project directly to the thoracic body wall without branching. Spinal nerves from the cervical, lumbar, and sacral regions of the spinal cord go through complex branching patterns, recombining with nerves from other spinal cord segments before projecting to peripheral structures. These complex branching patterns are called **plexuses.** See FIGURE 9-10 ▲.

reticulospinal tract *(reh TIK yoo loh SPY nal)* One of several descending spinal motor pathways that carry information to help coordinate movements.

rubrospinal tract One of several descending spinal motor pathways that carry information to help coordinate movements.

commissures *(KAHM ih shurz)* Transverse bands of nerve fibers; carry information from one side of the nervous system to the other.

spinal roots Axon bundles attached to each spinal cord segment. The dorsal roots are sensory, and the ventral roots are motor. The dorsal and ventral roots join to form the spinal nerves.

dorsal root The radix dorsalis or sensory root of each spinal nerve.

dorsal root ganglion *(DOR sal ROOT GANG lee on)* A collection of sensory neurons on the dorsal roots of the spinal cord.

ventral root Spinal root that carries motor information.

nerves Bundles of individual axons.

spinal nerves Thirty one pairs of nerves. Each pair comes out from the spinal cord between two vertebrae. An individual spinal nerve consists of dorsal nerve roots and ventral nerve roots.

mixed nerve A nerve that carries both sensory and motor information.

plexuses *(PLECK sus)* A network of nerves or vessels.

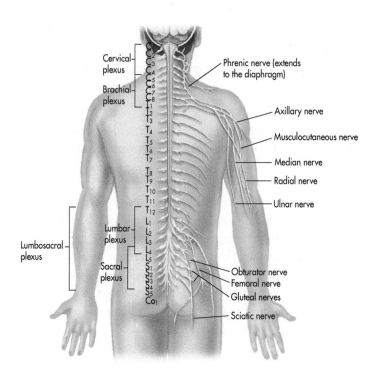

SPINAL NERVE PLEXUSES

PLEXUS	LOCATION	SPINAL NERVES INVOLVED	REGION SUPPLIED	MAJOR NERVES LEAVING PLEXUS
Cervical	Deep in the neck, under the sternocleidomastoid muscle	C_1-C_4	Skin and muscles of neck and shoulder; diaphragm	Phrenic (Diaphragm)
Brachial	Deep to the clavicle, between the neck and the axilla	C_5-C_8, T_1	Skin and muscles of upper extremity	Musculocutaneous Ulnar Median Radial Axillary
Lumbosacral	Lumbar region of the back	T_{12}, L_1-L_5, S_1-S_4	Skin and muscles of lower abdominal wall, lower extremity, buttocks, external genitalia	Obturator Femoral Sciatic Pudendal

FIGURE 9-10 ▲ Spinal cord plexuses.

reflex Involuntary muscle reaction that is controlled by the spinal cord. In response to pain, the spinal cord immediately sends a command to the muscles of the body to move. All of this takes place without conscious thought or processing by the brain. The entire circuit is also known as a *reflex arc.*

withdrawal reflex Flexion of a body part in response to a painful stimulus.

vestibular reflex A reaction that stabilizes the position of the head according to sensory information from the labyrinth of the ear and the nerves in the neck.

startle reflex A reflex seen in infants in response to stimuli, such as that produced by suddenly striking the surface on which the infant rests. The infant responds by rapid abduction and extension of the arms followed by an embracing motion (adduction) of the arms.

Reflexes

Reflexes are the simplest form of motor output. Reflexes are generally protective, keeping you from harm without thought. They are involuntary, and usually the response is proportional to the stimulus. Some familiar reflexes are the **withdrawal reflex,** activated for example, when you pound yo ur thumb with a hammer or touch a hot stove; the **vestibular reflex,** which keeps you vertical; and the **startle reflex,** which causes you to jump at loud sounds. The amazing thing about reflexes is that they can often occur without your brain being involved. For many reflexes, the spinal cord serves as the reflex center, and no impulses need to go to the brain.

Pathology Connection

POLIO AND POST-POLIO SYNDROME

Polio is a form of paralysis caused by the poliomyelitis virus. Polio was a rather common virus prior to the start of large-scale vaccinations in the 1950s. Today polio has nearly been wiped off the face of the earth. The last naturally acquired case of polio in the United States was in 1979. Even before vaccinations, most people (99%) who caught polio only had a mild upper respiratory or digestive illness, lasting for a few days. It would hardly seem worth ridding the world of the virus. However, the other 1% of the polio patients develop the paralytic form. In paralytic polio, the virus somehow gets into and kills the neurons in the ventral horn (motor pathways) of the spinal cord. Sensory neurons are spared, so patients with polio can feel, but they cannot move the affected body parts. Of these patients, 25% suffer permanent disability. In 1952 there were 21,000 cases of the paralytic form of polio in the United States alone. There is no treatment for polio. Patients are kept alive during the acute phase and, if they survive, undergo extensive rehabilitation (if available). Polio is very rare today. It was eradicated from the Western Hemisphere in 1994 and should be destroyed completely in our lifetime. Clinicians in the United States are unlikely to ever see a case of polio.

Polio, however, is coming back to haunt many patients who thought they had put the disease behind them. Post-polio syndrome (PPS) is a progressive weakness appearing several decades after the polio infection. It is estimated that 25% to 40% of all people who had paralytic polio will develop PPS. The cause of PPS is not known. However, it appears to be directly related to the damage left by the polio virus. In the parts of the spinal cord damaged by polio, neurons are actually destroyed. Patients recover by using the few surviving motor neurons to power the muscles. For example, a normal motor neuron might communicate with 1,000 muscle fibers. In a recovered polio patient that same neuron might need to communicate with 5,000 or 10,000 muscle fibers. Current thinking is that these surviving neurons become severely overworked and eventually begin to die themselves, causing muscle weakness. This may seem like a minor disorder, but keep in mind that there are approximately 500,000 paralytic polio survivors in the United States today. (We aren't really sure of the number because the past records aren't great.) Worldwide there are millions of paralytic polio patients who have recovered and are at risk for PPS. As you might imagine, diagnosis is difficult and consists mainly of ruling out other causes for progressive muscle weakness in polio survivors. There are no treatments to stop the progression of PPS, but an individually designed and supervised exercise program has been shown to improve muscle function in some patients.

spinal block An obstruction of the flow of cerebrospinal fluid through the spinal subarachnoid space. This term is commonly (though inaccurately) used to refer to spinal anesthesia.

Clinical Application

SPINAL BLOCKS, EPIDURAL ANESTHESIA, AND LUMBAR PUNCTURES (SPINAL TAPS)

The anatomy of the spinal cord, particularly in the lumbar region, makes for easy access to the nervous system for pain relief and testing of CSF.

During labor or in preparation for a Cesarean section, women often receive pain relief by drugs delivered to the spinal cord. Surgeries on body parts below the waist are now being performed under spinal anesthesia instead of general anesthesia, allowing the patient to be awake during the procedure and decreasing complications due to general anesthesia. A **spinal block** is the injection of an anesthetic into the subarachnoid space via a needle. It is a one-time injection that wears off after a couple of hours, but

Clinical Application (continued)

gives rapid, total anesthesia. Patients lose both sensory and motor activity below the injection. An **epidural** is the delivery of local anesthetic into the epidural space by a catheter (a small tube). The catheter allows continuous injection of the anesthetic. Ideally, epidural anesthesia allows a woman to continue to participate actively in the birth without severe labor pains. Epidural injections of steroids are sometimes prescribed for patients with chronic lower back injuries to relieve pain and inflammation.

During a neurological exam, a physician may want to sample CSF. The best place to sample CSF is in the lumbar region because of the loose nerves of the cauda equina. Taking the sample in the lumbar region decreases the likelihood of damage to the spinal cord. Thus, the technique for sampling CSF most often used is the **lumbar puncture,** also known as the **spinal tap.** CSF can be removed by inserting a needle between L3 and L4 or L4 and L5. Then the fluid can be examined for pathogens, chemical abnormalities, or the presence of blood.

Pathology Connection

PERIPHERAL NEUROPATHY AND SPINAL CORD INJURY

Peripheral neuropathy encompasses a number of disorders involving damage to peripheral nerves. Because peripheral nerves are involved in sensory, motor, and autonomic function, the symptoms of peripheral neuropathy vary greatly among patients. Symptoms include muscle weakness and decreased reflexes, numbness, tingling, paralysis, pain, difficulty controlling blood pressure, abnormal sweating, and digestive abnormalities. Nongenetic causes of neuropathy can be grouped into three broad categories: systemic disease, trauma, and infection or autoimmune disorders. Trauma, such as falls or automobile accidents, causes mechanical injury to nerves and is the most common cause of peripheral neuropathy. Nerves may be severed, crushed, or bruised. Systemic disorders that cause peripheral neuropathy include kidney disorders, hormonal imbalance, alcoholism, vascular damage, repetitive stress, chronic inflammation, diabetes, toxins, and tumors. The most common of these is diabetes. Infections such as shingles, Epstein-Barr virus, herpes, HIV, Lyme disease, and polio cause peripheral neuropathy. Guillain-Barré syndrome is an acute form of peripheral neuropathy. Some forms of neuropathy, like Charcot Marie Tooth disease, are inherited. The pain that Maria, our diabetes patient, has been feeling may be the early stages of peripheral neuropathy.

Diagnosis of peripheral neuropathy is not easy. History of symptoms, presence of other conditions that cause neuropathy, CT, MRI, electromyogram (EMG), and biopsy can all aid in the diagnosis. Treatment consists of treating the underlying cause of the neuropathy and using medication and therapy to treat the symptoms.

Even though the spinal cord is well protected by the bones and meninges, trauma can cause damage to the delicate neural tissue. The most common cause of spinal cord injuries is car accidents, followed by violence, falls, work injuries, and disease. More than half of all spinal cord injuries occur in people between 16 and 30 years old. The overwhelming majority of spinal cord injuries are in

(continued)

epidural An injection of anesthetic into the peridural space to produce epidural anesthesia.

lumbar puncture Technique used to sample cerebral spinal fluid (CSF); also known as a spinal tap.

spinal tap See lumbar puncture.

peripheral neuropathy Condition of the peripheral nerves resulting in pain and dysfunction of these nerves. Often related to diabetes.

quadriplegic *(kwad reh PLEE jik)* One who has paralysis of all four limbs.

paraplegia *(par uh PLEE jee ah)* Paralysis of the lower body and of both legs.

phrenic nerve *(FRIN ick)* Nerve that innervates the diaphragm that controls breathing.

Pathology Connection (continued)

males. There are 10,000 spinal cord injuries per year that leave patients with some paralysis and a quarter of a million spinal cord injury survivors currently living in the United States. The spinal cord may be partially or completely severed, crushed, or bruised. Bruises to the spinal cord may resolve with time and rehabilitation, but a severed or crushed spinal cord is usually a permanent injury.

The initial injury to the spinal cord is often not the biggest problem. After the injury, the body's response to the injury often does more damage to the already injured tissue. The spinal cord swells, blood flow decreases, the immune system removes tissue and demyelinates the surviving tissue, release of excess neurotransmitters kills cells, and damaged neurons self-destruct.

Spinal cord injury usually results in paralysis and sensory loss below the injury, and the extent of the paralysis is related to the location of the spinal cord injury. Patients with injuries to the cervical spinal cord are **quadriplegics,** paralyzed in all four limbs. Some quadriplegics, with damage very high in the cervical spinal cord, have paralyzed diaphragms and cannot breathe on their own. Patients with injuries in the thoracic spinal cord and lower have **paraplegia.** They can move their arms but their legs are paralyzed.

The difference between being able to breathe on your own after a spinal cord injury and being dependent on a ventilator is literally a matter of centimeters. One of the nerves that projects from the cervical plexus is called the **phrenic nerve.** This nerve is the motor nerve for your diaphragm, your main breathing muscle. If the spinal cord is damaged below the cervical plexus, such as in the high thoracic region, the phrenic nerve can receive signals from the brain and send them to the diaphragm, and the injured person is able to breathe. On the other hand, if the damage to the spinal cord is between the brain and the cervical plexus, the path from the brain to the phrenic nerve is blocked, and the signals can't get to the diaphragm from the brain. The diaphragm is paralyzed, and the person cannot breathe on his or her own. However, even patients with thoracic or low cervical injuries may have difficulty coughing or breathing deeply due to paralysis of abdominal muscles.

In an interesting side note, sexual function is often preserved in patients with spinal cord injuries. Many men with spinal cord injuries can still have an erection. Penile erection is a reflex, so damage to spinal cord pathways doesn't prevent the penis from becoming erect under the right circumstances. Though ejaculation (sperm leaving the penis) is often impaired, sperm are normal and can be used for conception with medical intervention. Even men who are quadriplegic may be able to father a child. In women, the menstrual cycle may be abnormal due to post-injury hormonal changes, but many women with spinal cord injuries remain fertile and may be able to carry a child, with adequate medical supervision.

Sensory information below the injury is also lost. Patients with spinal cord injuries have no sense of touch—including pain, temperature, pressure or position—below their injury. Remember Ray, who was injured in the swimming pool accident? His injury is above C3, so he has no sense of touch below his chin, including heat, cold, or pain.

Diagnosis of a spinal cord injury is accomplished by a neurological exam that tests sensory and motor function and by any of several different types of imaging studies including MRI, x-ray, CT scans, and myelography (a special x-ray using contrast dye).

Treatment for spinal cord injury in the acute stage, right after injury, consists of attempts to prevent further damage. The injury is immobilized, respiration is aided, low blood pressure or cardiac problems are treated, drugs may be given to reduce the damage caused by inflammation and cell death, and the injury is permanently stabilized using a variety of surgical techniques. After the acute phase, the focus of treatment changes. Long-term problems caused by the injury must be treated or prevented, including respiratory difficulties, blood pressure abnormalities, pneumonia, blood clots, organ dysfunction, pressure sores, pain, and bladder and bowel dysfunction. Once stabilized, patients receive lengthy rehabilitation. In the past, rehabilitation focused on teaching patients to live with their disabilities. More recent evidence suggests that extensive and vigorous rehabilitation may allow spinal cord injury patients to recover more function than initially anticipated after their injury. Thus, rehabilitation often includes both coping skills and exercises designed to aid recovery of as much function as possible.

Clinical Application

KNEE-JERK REFLEX

The most common example of a reflex is the patellar tendon (knee-jerk) reflex. You may have experienced this reflex at the doctor's office. The doctor taps your knee with a hammer, and your leg kicks, seemingly against your will. What exactly is going on? When the doctor taps your knee, the hammer gently tugs on a tendon that is connected to your quadriceps muscles. The quads are gently tugged. This causes them to lengthen slightly. This length change is received by a sensory neuron and transmitted back to the spinal cord. The sensory neuron synapses with a motor neuron in the ventral horn. The motor neuron sends a signal to the quadriceps to stop the stretch. How do the quads stop the stretch? They shorten (contract). When a muscle shortens, it causes a movement. The shortening of the quadriceps muscles extends your knee, causing your leg to kick (see **FIGURE 9-11** ▲.)

This action is totally reflexive (no pun intended). You can't stop yourself from kicking, even if you try. You do not have to think about kicking. The action happens without your brain. Only the spinal cord is necessary. The real purpose of this reflex is obviously not to react to being hit with a rubber hammer. The reflex actually prevents your knees from collapsing while you are standing up. Any time your knees bend, even a little bit, the reflex kicks in (pun intended) and straightens your knees. The reflex is so small that you don't even notice.

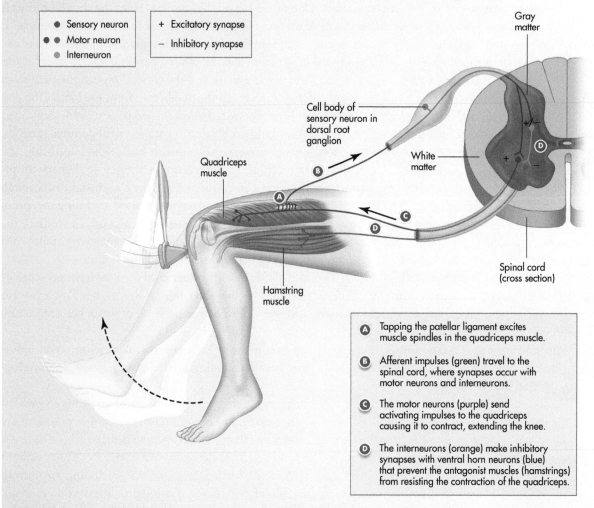

FIGURE 9-11 ▲ The patellar reflex. **A.** Striking the patellar ligament excites the quadriceps muscle spindles. **B.** Sensory input travels to spinal cord and synapses with motor neurons and interneurons. **C.** Motor neurons send impulses to contract the quadriceps, thus extending the lower leg. **D.** Interneurons make inhibitory connections in the ventral horn of the spinal column to prevent hamstrings (antagonist muscles) from contracting so they do not resist the movement.

Clinical Application

CARPAL TUNNEL SYNDROME

A very common form of peripheral neuropathy caused by repetitive motion is **carpal tunnel syndrome (CTS),** an inflammation and swelling of the tendon sheaths surrounding the flexor tendon of the palm. This is usually a result of repetitive motion such as typing on a keyboard. As a result of this inflammation and swelling, the median nerve is compressed, producing a tingling sensation or numbness of the palm, thumb and first three fingers. Carpal tunnel syndrome is often corrected surgically.

carpal tunnel syndrome (CTS)
A condition affecting the median nerve distribution of the hand leading to pain and/or numbness. Repetitive motion is the most common cause of this condition.

TEST YOUR KNOWLEDGE 9-3

Choose the best answer:

1. The segments of the spinal cord are named for:
   a. the bones of the skull
   b. the vertebrae
   c. their function
   d. none of the above

2. This layer of the meninges is fused to the surface of the CNS:
   a. dura mater
   b. pia mater
   c. arachnoid mater
   d. whatsa mater

3. The ventral root carries _____ information, and the dorsal root carries _____ information.
   a. motor; motor
   b. motor; sensory
   c. sensory; sensory
   d. sensory; motor

4. What is the term for axon pathways carrying information up and down the spinal cord?
   a. horns
   b. roots
   c. columns
   d. ganglia

5. How is spinal cord injury treated initially?
   a. stabilization of injury
   b. drugs to prevent tissue damage
   c. cardiovascular and respiratory support if needed
   d. all of the above

6. A patient complains of progressive weakness in the muscles of her legs. You begin a patient history. During your conversation she relates to you that she had some kind of virus as a child that left her with a temporary limp. Apparently she was really sick for a while, but she doesn't remember much about it. What is the most obvious possible diagnosis?
   a. Multiple sclerosis
   b. Charcot Marie Tooth
   c. Post-polio syndrome
   d. Spinal cord injury

THE BRAIN AND CRANIAL NERVES

The brain lies at the top of the spinal cord, beginning at the level of the foramen magnum and filling the cranial cavity. It acts as the main processor and director of the nervous system. The cranial nerves leave the brain and go to specific body areas, where they receive information and send it back to the brain (sensory), and the brain then sends back instructions as to the appropriate response (motor).

Just like a grocery store needs to be organized into sections such as produce, meats, and deli, the brain can be divided into several anatomical and functional sections. We will talk about each section separately and then describe the interactions between the brain parts and the spinal cord.

The Brain's External Anatomy

Let's start our journey looking at the outside of the brain, and then we will zoom in on the internal structures. From the outside, you can see that the brain consists of a **cerebrum, cerebellum,** and **brain stem.** Please see FIGURE 9-12 ▲.

cerebrum *(SER eh brum)* The largest and most visible part of the brain. Its surface contains gyri and sulci and is divided into two hemispheres.

cerebellum *(ser eh BELL um)* Small rounded section that is the most posterior part of the brain. Monitors muscle tone and position and coordinates new muscle movements.

brain stem Most inferior part of the brain that joins with the spinal cord. It is composed of the midbrain, pons, and medulla oblongata.

FIGURE 9-12 ▲ External brain anatomy and lobes.

Cerebrum

The cerebrum, the largest part of the brain, is divided into two **hemispheres,** a right and left, by the longitudinal fissure, and divided from the cerebellum ("little brain") by the transverse fissure. The surface of the cerebrum is not smooth, but broken by ridges (**gyri**) and grooves (**sulci**) collectively known as **convolutions**. These convolutions serve a very important purpose by increasing the surface area of the brain, yet allowing it to be "folded" into a smaller space. Most of the sulci are extremely variable in their locations among humans, but a few are in basically the same place in every brain. These less variable sulci are used to divide the brain into four large sections called **lobes,** much like the major departments in a grocery store are separated by aisles.

The lobes (see **TABLE 9-2** ■) are named for the skull bones that cover them, and they occur in pairs, one in each hemisphere. The most anterior lobes, separated from the rest of the brain by the central sulci, are the **frontal lobes**. Posterior to the frontal lobes are the **parietal lobes**. Posterior to the parietal lobes are the **occipital lobes**. (There is no obvious dividing line between the parietal and occipital lobes, and these represent the most posterior lobes at the back of the skull.) The most inferior lobes, separated by the lateral fissures, are the **temporal lobes**. Again, please see Figure 9-12, which shows the lobes of the brain and the sulci that separate them. There is a section of the brain, the **insula,** deep inside the temporal lobes, which is often listed as a fifth lobe, but it is not visible on the surface of the cerebrum.

Much of the information coming into and leaving your brain is **contralateral**. That is, the left side of the body is controlled by the right side of your cerebrum, and the right side of the body is controlled by your left brain.

Cerebellum

The cerebellum is posterior to the brain stem and plays an important role in sensory and motor coordination and balance. Its surface is also convoluted like that of the cerebrum. From its external appearance, it is easy to see why anatomists consider the cerebellum the "little brain."

hemisphere One-half of the cerebrum, either the right hemisphere or the left hemisphere.

gyri *(JYE rye)* Convolutions of the cerebral hemispheres of the brain.

sulcus *(SULL cuss)* One of many shallow grooves between the gyri in the cerebrum and cerebellum. Plural: sulci.

convolutions Folds found on the surface of the cerebrum

lobes Large area of the hemisphere of the cerebrum. Each lobe is named for the bone of the skull that is next to it: frontal lobe, parietal lobe, temporal lobe, and occipital lobe.

frontal lobe Lobe of the cerebrum that is responsible for motor activities, conscious thought, and speech.

parietal lobes *(pah RYE eh tal)* Lobe of the cerebrum that receives sensory information about temperature, touch, pressure, vibration, and pain from the skin and internal organs.

occipital lobes *(awk SIP eh tal)* Lobe of the cerebrum that receives sensory information from the eyes. Contains the visual cortex for the sense of sight.

temporal lobes Lobe in the cerebrum that contains neurons for processing auditory and olfactory information.

insula *(IN soo luh)* The deep lobes of the cerebral hemispheres.

contralateral Term describing the left side of the body being controlled by the right side of the brain and vice versa.

TABLE 9-2 ■ CEREBRAL LOBES AND CEREBELLUM

STRUCTURE	MAJOR FUNCTIONS
Cerebral Lobes	
Frontal lobe	Motor function, behavior, judgment and emotions, memory storage, thinking, smell, speech
Parietal lobe	Body sense, perception, and language
Occipital lobe	Interprets vision
Temporal lobe	Hearing, taste, language comprehension, integration of emotions
Insula	Autonomic functions
Cerebellum	Sensory and motor coordination and balance

medulla oblongata *(meh DULL lah ob long GAW tah)* Most inferior part of the brain stem that joins to the spinal cord. It relays nerve impulses from the cerebrum to the cerebellum. It contains the respiratory center. Cranial nerves IX through XII originate there.

pons Area of the brain stem that relays nerve impulses from the body to the cerebellum and back to the body. Area where nerve tracts cross from one side of the body to the opposite side of the cerebrum. Cranial nerves V through VIII originate there.

midbrain An area that connects the pons and the cerebellum with the hemispheres of the cerebrum.

reticular system Diffuse network of neurons in the brainstem that "wakes up" the cerebral cortex thus providing awareness of one's surroundings.

persistent vegetative state (PVS) A continuous condition of complete unawareness of the environment with either complete or partial hypothalamic and autonomic brain stem functions. Sleep–wake cycles also exist. This condition may be caused by brain trauma, degenerative disease, metabolic disorders, or developmental defects.

minimally conscious state (MCS) See persistent vegetative state (PVS).

meninges *(men IN jeez)* Three separate membranes that envelope and protect the entire brain and spinal cord. The meninges include the dura mater, arachnoid, and pia mater.

The Brain Stem

The brain stem (see **TABLE 9-3 ■**) is a stalklike structure inferior to and partially covered by the cerebrum. It is divided into three sections. The **medulla oblongata** is continuous with the spinal cord. The **pons** is just superior to the medulla oblongata and connects the medulla oblongata and the cerebellum with the upper portions of the brain. The **midbrain** is the most superior portion of the brain stem (see **FIGURE 9-13 ▲**).

The **reticular system** is a diffuse network of neurons in the brain stem that is responsible for "waking up" your cerebral cortex as part of a larger network of nuclei known as the reticular activating system. Reticular system activity is vital for maintaining conscious awareness of your surroundings. When your alarm clock wakes you in the morning, your reticular system is responsible for nudging your cortex out of slumber. General anesthesia inhibits the reticular system, rendering surgery patients unconscious. Injury due to ischemia, mechanical damage, or drugs can damage the reticular system and lead to persistent unconsciousness.

Amazing **Body Facts**

Why Not a Smooth Brain?

The surface of the brain is folded and rippled into a series of convolutions. These convolutions allow lots of brain surface area to fit into a very small space. If you could lay the convolutions flat, they would be the size of a pillow case. Talk about your big heads! Another fact to keep in "mind" is that the vital brain can die if deprived of oxygen in as little as 4 to 8 minutes.

The brain stem receives sensory information and contains control systems for vital functions such as blood pressure, heart rate, and breathing. The brainstem controls the vital functions of life, and patients with severe brain injuries but with an intact brain stem can continue in a vegetative state as long as they are nutritionally supported. This condition is called a **persistent vegetative state (PVS)** or **minimally conscious state (MCS)**.

The brain, like the spinal cord, is covered with protective membranes called **meninges**. Again, please see Figure 9-13. The meninges of the brain are continuous with the spinal cord meninges. A potentially fatal condition is an infection of the meninges called

TABLE 9-3 ■ THE BRAIN STEM

STRUCTURE	FUNCTION
Midbrain	Relays sensory and motor information
Pons	Relays sensory and motor information; role in breathing
Medulla oblongata	Regulates vital functions of heart rate, blood pressure, breathing, and reflex center for coughing, sneezing, swallowing, and vomiting

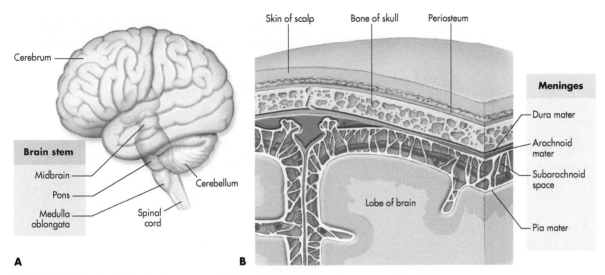

FIGURE 9-13 ▲ **A.** The brain stem and **B.** meninges.

meningitis, which can rapidly spread and affect the brain and spinal cord through this common covering.

Meningitis causes inflammation of the meninges. Its symptoms include headache, fever, and stiff neck. Most cases of meningitis are caused by viral infection, but very serious cases can be caused by bacterial infection. If untreated, bacterial meningitis can cause seizures, coma, or death.

Meningitis can be diagnosed by a spinal tap or lumbar puncture. In this procedure, the physician collects a sample of cerebrospinal fluid. Fluid from a patient with meningitis generally has low glucose levels and elevated white blood cell and protein levels. The fluid may show signs of specific bacteria. If the patient has viral meningitis, genetic material from viruses will show up in the fluid.

If bacterial meningitis is diagnosed, the patient is immediately given intravenous antibiotics. Fluids may also be drained from around the brain. If viral meningitis is diagnosed, the patient is prescribed bed rest, fluids, and medication to relieve pain and swelling. Viral meningitis usually resolves in about 1 to 2 weeks.

Bacterial meningitis may be difficult to treat due to the *blood–brain barrier.* The blood–brain barrier prevents the entry of various drugs and other substances into brain tissue. This barrier is normally protective of the brain, but it can allow damage to brain tissue when it blocks lifesaving medicines. Large concentrations of intravenous drugs are used to deliver drugs to infection around brain tissue.

Internal Anatomy of the Brain

The inside of the brain has, like the spinal cord, white matter, gray matter, and hollow cavities containing cerebrospinal fluid. (See! We really do have holes in our heads.) Unlike the spinal cord, however, the white matter is surrounded by the gray matter in the brain. (Remember, in the spinal cord, the white matter surrounds the gray matter.) The layer of gray matter surrounding the white matter is called the **cortex.** In the cerebrum it is called the cerebral cortex, and in the cerebellum it is called the cerebellar cortex. Throughout the brain there are deep "islands" of gray matter surrounded by white matter. These islands are called **nuclei.** The nuclei in the cerebrum can be part of the **basal nuclei** (also known as the basal ganglia), which is a motor coordination system, or part of the **limbic system,** which controls emotion, mood, and memory.

meningitis *(men in JYE tiss)* Inflammation of the meninges of the brain or spinal cord by a bacterial or viral infection. Initial symptoms include fever, headache, nuchal rigidity (stiff neck) lethargy, vomiting, irritability, and photophobia.

cortex In the brain, a surface sheet of layered or laminated gray matter, as in the outermost sector of the cerebral and cerebellar hemispheres.

nuclei In the central nervous system, a group of neuronal cell bodies that are clustered together and form a coherent demarcated mass in stained brain sections.

basal nuclei *(BAY sal NOO klee eye)* Clusters of cells (nuclei) deep in the diencephalon, midbrain, and cerebrum that help fine-tune voluntary movements.

limbic system *(LIM bick)* Processes memories and controls emotions, mood, motivation, and behavior. Links the conscious to the unconscious mind. Limbic system consists of the thalamus, hypothalamus, hippocampus, amygdaloid bodies, and fornix.

traumatic brain injury (TBI) This refers to a severe brain injury that may leave residual impairment.

concussion A brain injury resulting from an impact with an object.

contusion A bruise.

stupor *(STOO per)* A brief period of impaired consciousness.

coma A state of unconsciousness in which the patient cannot be aroused, even following stimulation.

vegetative state Situation in which an individual has no response to surroundings.

persistent vegetative state A continuous condition of complete unawareness of the environment with either complete or partial hypothalamic and autonomic brain stem functions. Sleep–wake cycles also exist. This condition may be caused by brain trauma, degenerative disease, metabolic disorders, or developmental defects.

stroke A condition of sudden loss of neurological function brought about by vascular injury to the brain. Can be caused by a blood blockage due to a clot or by hemorrhage.

cerebrovascular accident (CVA) *(SER eh broh VAS kyuh ler)* A sudden loss of neurological function caused by some vascular injury to the brain, either through hemorrhage or blockage of blood flow to the brain.

Pathology Connection

BRAIN INJURY

Traumatic brain injury (TBI), or simply head injury, occurs when force is applied to the skull, causing damage to brain tissue. Injury to the brain can occur due to vehicle accidents (the most common cause), falls, violence, and sports injuries, and damage similar to TBI can be caused by lack of oxygen, strokes, or brain hemorrhage. Fifty percent of traumatic brain injuries caused by accidents or violence are alcohol related. One hundred cases of TBI occur per 100,000 people in the United States each year and there are between 2 and 6 million brain injury survivors in the United States today. The most likely ages for a traumatic brain injury are under the age of 5, between the ages of 15 and 24 (males), and over the age of 75. The severity of post-injury disability from TBI depends on the severity of the injury, the age and health of the patient, and the location of the injury. Brain injuries can be closed (the skull is not open) or penetrating (the skull is punctured by an object) and can range in severity from mild to moderate to severe. A mild brain injury is more commonly known as a **concussion**. A **contusion,** which is swelling and bleeding at the site of injury, is more serious. In more serious cases, a severe hemorrhage (hematoma) may result.

Symptoms of head injury include dizziness, confusion, headache, blurred vision, ringing ears, sleepiness, and mood or cognitive changes. More serious injuries have more severe symptoms, including vomiting, dilated pupils, convulsions, motor deficits, slurred speech, confusion or agitation, and perhaps prolonged unconsciousness. Motor and sensory deficits from head injuries are often confined to one side of the body. (Remember that the cerebrum is contralateral: the right side controls the left body and vice versa.) Patients with severe injuries may be in a **stupor** (brief period of impaired consciousness or arousal), a **coma** (no consciousness), a **vegetative state** (may have arousal and sleep–wake cycles but no response to surroundings), a *minimally conscious state* (MCS; evidence for periods of awareness), or a **persistent vegetative state** (often a permanent condition), depending on the severity of their injury.

The condition known as a **stroke,** or **cerebrovascular accident (CVA),** which can cause permanent brain injury, is caused by the disruption of blood flow to a portion of the brain due to either hemorrhage (10% of cases) or blood clot (90% of cases). If the oxygen is disrupted for long enough, brain tissue will die. The symptoms of stroke vary depending on the location of the stroke and can include sudden severe headache, dizziness, loss of vision in one eye, aphasia, dysphasia, coma, and possible death. Paralysis and hemiplegia

(continued)

Pathology Connection (continued)

are also possible. According to the Centers for Disease Control and Prevention, stroke is the third-leading cause of death in the United States and is the number one cause of serious long-term disability. Clots are the cause of the majority of strokes. Risk factors include smoking, hypertension, heart disease, and a family history of having the disease. Strokes can also rob patients of the ability to speak and can cause blindness and destroy memory. Symptoms of stroke usually appear suddenly. Some patients have a series of minor strokes (almost like tiny earthquakes before the big one) with minor, temporary symptoms before they have a major stroke. These mini-strokes are called **transient ischemic attacks,** or **TIAs.** Please see FIGURE 9-14 ▲, which shows a cerebral embolism and cross-section of a brain showing a cerebrovascular accident.

A **hematoma** is a pool of blood between any of the layers of meninges and the skull. The most common locations for hematomas are **epidural** (between the dura mater and the skull), **subdural** (between the dura mater and the arachnoid mater), and **subarachnoid** (in the subarachnoid space). A blow to the head can rupture tiny blood vessels in the skull, causing them to bleed into the space. A stoke or ruptured aneurysm (weak spot in a blood vessel inside the skull) can also cause a hematoma.

Several techniques are used to diagnose a brain injury. The Glasgow Coma Scale is a scale that is scored from 3 to 15, based on the patient's ability to open their eyes on command, respond verbally to questions, and move their limbs when requested. A lower number indicates a more severe injury. Imaging, CT, MRI, and PET scanning are used to pinpoint the location and severity of injury and to monitor any changes.

Treatment of head injury, like treatment of spinal cord injury, involves both prevention of further injury and treatment of existing injury. Remember that the spinal cord self-destructs after an injury, doing damage to itself. Like the spinal cord, the injured brain will self-destruct due to increased swelling and cell death caused by the tissue's attempt to repair the damage. In addition, in closed head injuries, if the brain tissue swells or if there is significant bleeding, pressure inside the skull (intracranial pressure) will rise. Because the fluid (blood or tissue fluid) can't be compressed and the skull will not expand to relieve the pressure, more brain tissue will be destroyed by the pressure. In addition, as the brain swells it presses the brain stem downward through the foramen magnum, actually causing a herniation (protrusion). The herniation causes damage to respiratory centers in the brainstem and decreases blood flow to the brain. The combination of abnormal ventilation and decreased blood flow causes more damage to brain tissue.

Acute care of head injury involves immobilization of the head, stabilization of cardiovascular and respiratory functions, monitoring of intracranial pressure, medication to decrease intracranial pressure, and surgery to remove clots,

(continued)

transient ischemic attacks (TIAs) *(is KEE mick)* A "mini-stroke" that causes minor symptoms that are temporary in nature.

hematoma *(HEE mah TOH mah)* A swelling as a result of a break in a blood vessel(s) usually confined to a specific area (tissue, organ, or space) in the body.

epidural Located either over or on the dura.

subdural *(sub DOO ral)* The space between the arachnoid and dura mater.

subarachnoid *(SUB ah RACK noyd)* Space beneath the arachnoid layer of the meninges. It is filled with cerebrospinal fluid.

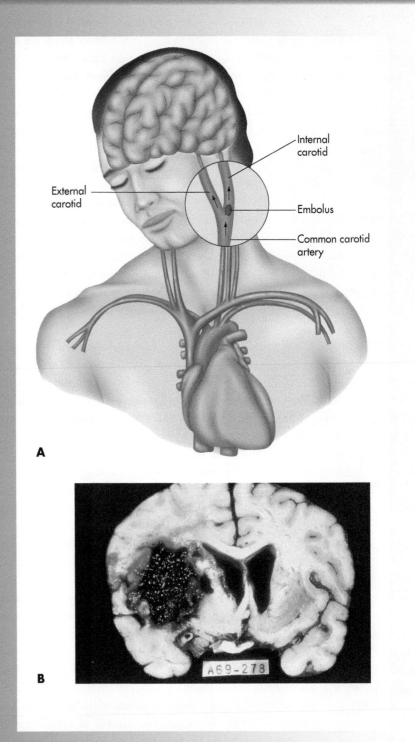

FIGURE 9-14 ▲ **A.** Embolus traveling to the brain and
B. cross-section of brain showing cerebrovascular accident (CVA).

Pathology Connection

blood, or foreign objects (for example, bullet or bone fragments) from the brain. Post-injury complications must also be treated, including hydrocephalus, infection, pain, bed sores, and multiple organ failure. In addition, many head injury patients, especially those injured in accidents, have other injuries that complicate their treatment and recovery.

After the acute period, many patients with brain injuries continue to have problems. Approximately 40% of brain-injured people, even with mild injuries, experience post-concussion syndrome. Several days or weeks after the injury, patients experience dizziness, headache, memory and concentration problems, irritability, disordered sleep, and anxiety and depression. The condition is usually temporary. Many patients with severe injury need lengthy rehabilitation to regain function. Patients with moderate or severe brain injuries are often left with permanent disabilities, including motor, sensory, and speech deficits; memory loss (the most common intellectual deficit); attention or problem-solving deficits; vision problems; and persistent pain. Recently, the seriousness of cumulative effects of minor brain injuries has been recognized, resulting in rule changes after concussion in major sports organizations, such as the NFL and NHL for example. Players who used to go back into the game after "getting their bell rung" now are required to sit out one or even several games until they are fully recovered. For many years, the medical community thought that injured brains could not recover functions, but new data suggests that the human brain is capable of some degree of rewiring. This ability to reroute information is probably responsible for the extraordinary recovery sometimes seen after brain injury. However, many people remain permanently disabled.

precentral gyrus *(JYE rus)* Ridge on the surface of the cerebrum anterior to the central sulcus in each hemisphere. The precentral gyrus contains the primary motor cortex for voluntary movements.

postcentral gyrus *(JYE rus)* Ridge on the surface of the cerebrum posterior to the central sulcus in each hemisphere. The postcentral gyrus contains the primary somatic sensory area for your sense of touch.

primary motor cortex Located in the precentral gyrus, this portion of the brain contains a map of the body to control motor function.

Broca's area *(BROH kas)* Area of brain that controls movements associated with speech.

primary somatic sensory cortex Area of the cerebral cortex that allows for understanding and interpretation of somatic sensory information.

somatic sensory association area An area of parietal lobe needed for understanding and interpretation of somatic sensory information.

Wernicke's area *(VER nih KEEZ)* Found in parietal lobe, this region controls the understanding of language.

Cerebrum

The inside of the cerebrum reflects its external anatomy (see FIGURE 9-15 ▲). The lobes—frontal, temporal, parietal, occipital, and insula—are clearly visible. On either side of the central sulcus are two gyri named for their locations: the **precentral gyrus**, anterior to the central sulcus (frontal lobe), and the **postcentral gyrus**, posterior to the central sulcus (parietal lobe). The structures in the cerebrum are responsible for conscious thought, judgment, reasoning, memory, and willpower.

A specialized area called the **primary motor cortex** is located in the precentral gyrus in the frontal lobe. The primary motor cortex has a map of the body with each area dedicated to motor function of a specific body area. Check out the size of the primary motor cortex dedicated to each body part in FIGURE 9-16 ▲. Do the sizes of the areas correspond to the sizes of the body parts? Not really: the hands, lips, and head have very large maps, whereas the legs and arms have very small maps compared to each body part's size. What do the hand and lips have in common that makes them different from the arms and legs? They are required to perform more finely coordinated movements, such as speaking and handwriting (or typing) and, therefore, have more motor output. If you aren't convinced, think about how much harder it would be to type with your feet than with your hands. This map can be drawn as a homunculus (little man) with huge hands, lips, and head (see Figure 9-16).

Also in the frontal lobe are the premotor and prefrontal areas, which *plan* movements. The plan from these two areas is sent to the primary motor cortex. The premotor and prefrontal areas are anterior to the primary motor cortex. In addition there is a motor speech area in the frontal lobe, called **Broca's area**, that controls movements associated with speech.

The brain must also have a specialized area for sensory input and processing. The parietal lobe contains the **primary somatic sensory cortex**, located in the postcentral gyrus. Like the primary motor cortex, primary somatic sensory cortex has a map. Please see FIGURE 9-17 ▲. In this case, however, the sizes of the body maps are proportional to the amount of the sensory input provided. For example, the hands provide much more sensory input due to touch than your neck would, and as a result the area devoted to the neck is much smaller.

Another area of the parietal lobe allows *understanding* and *interpretation* of somatic sensory information. It is located in the parietal lobe just posterior to somatic sensory cortex and is known as the **somatic sensory association area**. **Wernicke's area**, also in the parietal lobe, controls understanding of language. Wernicke's area is part of a much larger posterior association area, which integrates multiple sensory inputs.

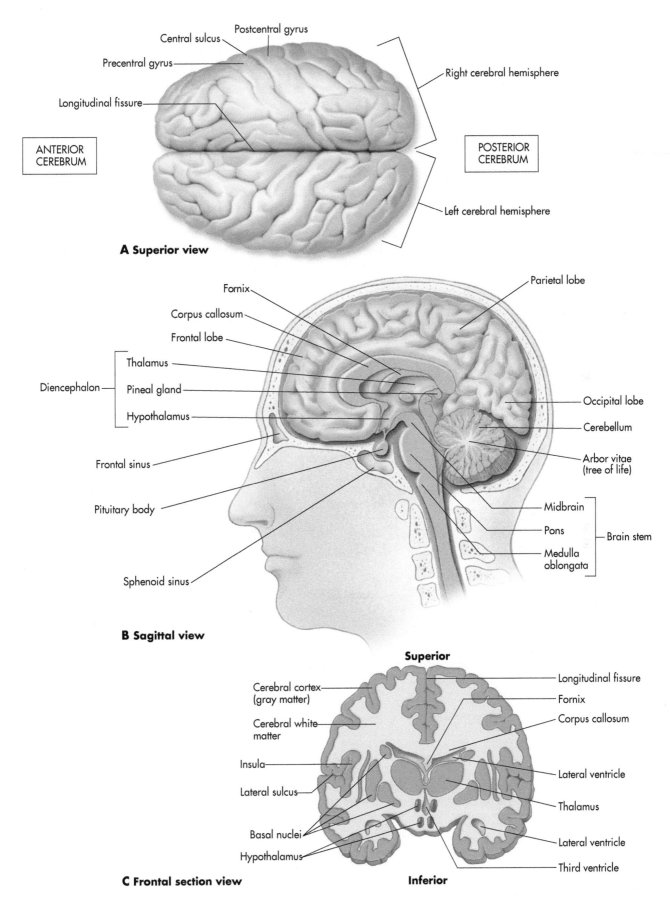

A Superior view

B Sagittal view

C Frontal section view

FIGURE 9-15 ▲ **A.** Superior, **B.** sagittal, and **C.** frontal section view of the brain.

MOTOR MAP IN PRE-CENTRAL GYRUS

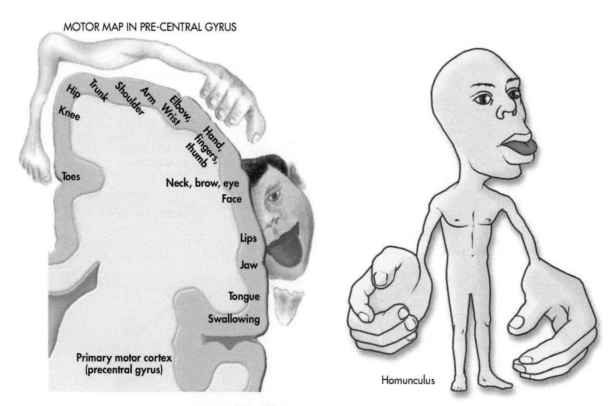

FIGURE 9-16 ▲ Motor areas of the brain, with homunculus. Notice the body parts that require a lot of motor movements are allotted a much larger region in the primary motor cortex.

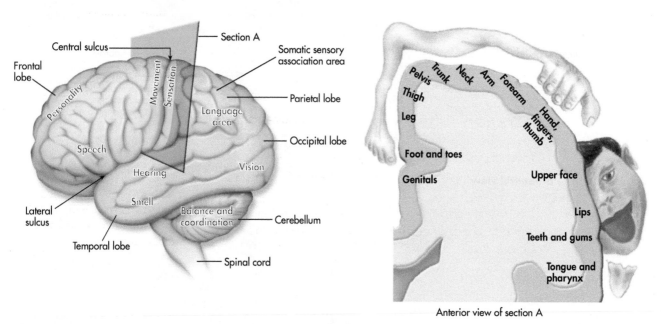

Anterior view of section A

FIGURE 9-17 ▲ Primary somatic sensory area. Notice the size of the body parts are proportional to the amount of the sensory input provided. For example, the hands provide much more sensory input due to touch than your neck would, and as a result the area devoted to the neck is much smaller.

The right and left hemispheres are connected by a collection of white matter surrounding the lateral ventricles, called the **corpus callosum**. This connection allows for cross-communication between the right and left sides of the brain. Many of our day-to-day activities, like walking or driving, require both sides of the body, and therefore both sides of the brain, to be well coordinated. Imagine walking if your legs were acting independently!

Diencephalon

Inferior to the cerebrum is a section of the brain that is not visible from the exterior, called the **diencephalon** (shown in Figure 9-15). The diencephalon can be divided into the **thalamus, hypothalamus, pineal body,** and **pituitary gland.** See TABLE 9-4 ■ for diencephalon structures and their corresponding functions. The hypothalamus, pituitary, and pineal represent an interface with the endocrine system (the other control system), covered in Chapter 10. The diencephalon contains a number of nuclei that are part of the basal nuclei and limbic system.

The Cerebellum

The external similarities between the cerebellum and cerebrum are also obvious internally (again see Figure 9-15). The cerebellum has a gray matter cortex and a white matter center, known as the **arbor vitae** (tree of life). The cerebellum also has nuclei that coordinate motor and sensory activity. Essentially, the cerebellum fine-tunes voluntary skeletal muscle activity and helps in the maintenance of balance by comparing planned movements to actual movements.

TABLE 9-4 ■ DIENCEPHALON

STRUCTURE	FUNCTION
Thalamus	Relays and processes information going to the cerebrum
Hypothalamus	Regulates hormone levels, temperature, water balance, thirst, appetite, and some emotions (pleasure and fear); regulates the pituitary gland and controls the endocrine system
Pineal body	Responsible for secretion of melatonin (body clock)
Pituitary gland	Secretes hormones for various functions (explained in Chapter 10)

corpus callosum *(CORE pus kah LOH sum)* Thick white band of nerve fibers that connects the two hemispheres of the cerebrum and allows them to communicate and coordinate their activities.

diencephalon *(dye en SEFF ah lon)* Central part of the brain that contains the thalamus and hypothalamus.

thalamus *(THAL ah mus)* Relay station in the brain that receives sensory nerve impulses from the optic nerves and sends them to the visual centers in the occipital lobes of the brain.

hypothalamus *(HGH poh THAL ah mus)* Endocrine gland located in the brain just below the thalamus. It produces (but does not secrete) antidiuretic hormone (ADH) and oxytocin. The hypothalamus is in the center of the brain and coordinates the activities of the pons and medulla oblongata. It also controls heart rate, blood pressure, respiratory rate, body temperature, sensations of hunger and thirst, and the circadian rhythm. It also produces hormones as part of the endocrine system. In addition, the hypothalamus helps control emotions (pleasure, excitement, fear, anger, sexual arousal) and bodily responses to emotions; regulates the sex drive; contains the feeding and satiety centers; and functions as part of the "fight-or-flight" response of the sympathetic nervous system.

pineal body *(PIN ee al)* Endocrine gland in the brain that lies posterior to the pituitary gland. It secretes the hormone melatonin.

pituitary gland *(pih TOO ih tair ee)* Endocrine gland in the brain that is connected by a stalk of tissue to the hypothalamus. Also known as the hypophysis. It is known as the master gland of the body. It consists of the anterior and the posterior pituitary gland.

arbor vitae *(ARE ber VAHY tee)* The white matter center of the cerebellum known as the "tree of life."

ventricles *(VEN trih kulz)* Four hollow chambers within the brain that contain cerebrospinal fluid. The two lateral ventricles are within the right and left hemispheres of the cerebrum. The third ventricle is small and connects the lateral ventricles to the fourth ventricle, which is at the level of the pons and medulla oblongata.

subarachnoid space *(sub DOO ral)* The space between the arachnoid and dura mater.

cerebrospinal fluid (CSF) *(SER eh broh SPY nal FLOO id)* The fluid cushion that protects the brain and spinal cord from shock.

choroid plexus Small, tufted projections into the third, fourth, and lateral ventricles of the brain that are made of blood vessels of the pia mater covered by a thin coat of ependymal cells. These projections secrete cerebrospinal fluid.

arachnoid villi Folds of the arachnoid layer of the cranial meninges that project through the inner layer of dura mater into the superior sagittal sinus and other venous sinuses of the brain. Through them, cerebrospinal fluid re-enters the bloodstream.

Cerebrospinal Fluid and Ventricles

As in the central canal in the spinal cord, there are fluid-filled cavities in the brain. The cavities in the brain are called **ventricles,** and they are continuous with the central canal of the spinal cord and the **subarachnoid space** of both the brain and the spinal cord. These ventricles, four in total, allow for the circulation of cerebrospinal fluid throughout the brain. The two lateral ventricles are in the cerebrum; the third ventricle is in the diencephalon, a region between the cerebrum and brain stem, and the fourth ventricle is in the inferior part of the brain between the medulla oblongata and the cerebellum (see FIGURE 9-18 ▲).

The ventricles of the brain, the central canal of the spinal cord, and the subarachnoid space, surrounding both parts of the CNS are all filled with **cerebrospinal fluid (CSF).** The CSF is filtered from blood in the ventricles by tissue called **choroid plexus.** Produced at the rate of 750 mL daily, CSF made in the lateral ventricles flows through a tiny opening into the third ventricle and then through another opening into the fourth ventricle. From the fourth ventricle, CSF flows into the central canal of the spinal cord and the subarachnoid space. CSF is returned to the blood via special "ports" (the **arachnoid villi**) between subarachnoid space and blood spaces in the dura mater (the **dural sinuses**).

Cranial Nerves

For the CNS to function, it must be connected to the outside world via nerves of the PNS. We have already seen that the spinal cord is connected to the outside via spinal

---

Pathology Connection

ALZHEIMER'S DISEASE

Alzheimer's disease is a progressive degenerative disease of the brain and is the most common cause of dementia among people 65 years or older. This disease may progress over 5 to 18 years and is characterized by memory loss and diminishing cognitive functions. As Alzheimer's disease progresses, tangles of fibers develop in nerve cells, and abnormal protein deposits surround the cells. Both the tangles and deposits interfere with brain function. The etiology of this disease is unknown. Age is the most important risk factor, but recent research suggests a link between the risk of Alzheimer's disease and cardiovascular disease risk factors.

Alzheimer's symptoms begin gradually with mild forgetfulness, such as difficulty remembering recent events or familiar names. In the first stage of the disease, patients experience confusion, anxiety, some memory loss, and poor judgment. During the second stage, patients experience more memory loss, have difficulty recognizing people, have trouble remembering words, experience sleeplessness and confusion, and start to experience motor problems and a loss of social skills. In the third stage, patients have difficulty speaking, reading and writing, and even maintaining personal hygiene. They become bedridden and develop conditions related to inactivity, such as bed sores and pneumonia. As the condition worsens, patients' personalities change to the point that they become anxious or aggressive and can become so confused that they get lost even in familiar locations. This has led to a classification of symptoms known as the four A's: anger, aggression, anxiety, and apathy.

There is no known cure for this disease. Certain medications may help to slow the progression of the early and middle stages of this disease. Recent research has focused on the use of preventative medications such as statins, which may reduce the buildup of plaque in the brain. Smoking appears to be a contributing factor.

nerves. The brain also has nerves to connect it to the outside, aptly named **cranial nerves** (see FIGURE 9-19 ▲). Cranial nerves are like spinal nerves in that they are the input and output pathways for the brain, just as the spinal nerves are the pathways for the spinal cord. However, that is really where the similarities end. You should remember that there are 31 pairs of spinal nerves and that all of them are mixed nerves: They carry both sensory and motor information because they are formed by a combination of dorsal and ventral roots. There are far fewer cranial nerves—only 12 pairs. All but the first two pairs arise from the brain stem. Cranial nerves are not all mixed. Some cranial nerves are mainly sensory nerves, providing input; some are mainly motor nerves, directing activity; and some are mixed. Cranial nerves are much more specialized than spinal nerves and are named based on their specialty. Some cranial nerves carry sensory and motor information for the head, face, and neck, whereas others carry visual, auditory, smell, or taste sensation. TABLE 9-5 ■ lists cranial nerves and their functions.

Peripheral neuropathy, damage to peripheral nerves, is not just about spinal nerves. Cranial nerves are also subject to peripheral neuropathy. The symptoms, however, would be seen on the face and head or in the special senses (vision, hearing, taste, and smell).

dural sinuses Any of several large endothelia-lined collecting channels into which veins of the brain and inner skull empty and which then empty into the internal jugular vein. These venous sinuses are found between the two layers (periosteal and meningeal) of the dura mater. Their walls have no muscle, and they have no valves to give direction to the blood flow. The venous sinuses in the skull include the superior sagittal, inferior sagittal, straight, transverse, and cavernous sinuses.

Alzheimer's disease *(ALTS high merz)* A progressive, degenerative disease of the brain that is the most common cause of dementia in individuals 65 or older.

cranial nerves Twelve pairs of nerves that originate in the brain. Carry sensory nerve impulses to the brain from the nose, eyes, ears, and tongue for the senses of smell, vision, hearing, and taste. Also carry sensory nerve impulses to the brain from the skin of the face. Also carry motor nerve impulses from the brain to the muscles of the face, mouth, and throat; eye; and salivary glands.

FIGURE 9-18 ▲ Cerebral spinal fluid (CSF) circulation and internal anatomy of brain. CSF flow: 1) CSF is produced by the choroid plexus in each of the four ventricles. 2) CSF flows from the ventricles to the central canal of the spinal cord. 3) CSF also flows from the ventricles into the subarachnoid space surrounding the brain. 4) CSF is absorbed into the dural venous sinuses via the arachnoid villi.

LEARNING HINT

Mnemonic Devices

A *mnemonic device* is a tool used to help you memorize long lists. It can be very useful in anatomy. To make a mnemonic device, take the first letter of each part of the list you are trying to memorize and make it into a sentence. An example for the cranial nerves is this one: **O**n **O**ld **O**lympus **T**owering **T**ops **A** **F**inn **V**ith **G**erman **V**alked **A**nd **H**opped. Then when you know the nerves in order, their names will often help you remember their functions.

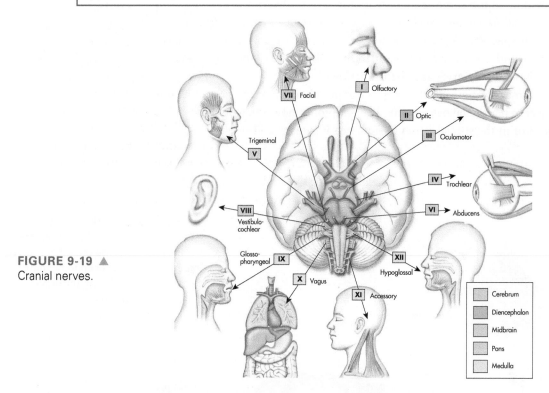

FIGURE 9-19 ▲ Cranial nerves.

TABLE 9-5 ■ CRANIAL NERVES AND FUNCTIONS

NERVE	FUNCTION
Olfactory (I)	Sensory (smell)
Optic (II)	Sensory (vision)
Oculomotor (III)	Mixed, chiefly motor for eye movements
Trochlear (IV)	Mixed, chiefly motor for eye movements
Trigeminal (V)	Mixed, sensory for face, motor for chewing
Abducens (VI)	Mixed, chiefly motor for eye movements
Facial (VII)	Motor for facial expression
Vestibulocochlear (VIII)	Sensory, hearing, and balance
Glossopharyngeal (IX)	Mixed, motor for throat muscles; sensory for taste
Vagus (X)	Mixed, motor for autonomic heart, lungs, viscera; sensory for viscera, taste
Accessory (XI)	Mixed, chiefly motor; motor and sensory for larynx, soft palate, trapezius, and sternocleidomastoid muscles
Hypoglossal (XII)	Chiefly motor for tongue muscles

Pathology Connection

HYDROCEPHALUS

The balance of CSF made and CSF reabsorbed by the blood is very important. The brain is a very delicate organ captured between the liquid CSF and the bones of the skull. If there is too much CSF, a condition called **hydrocephalus** (literally "water in the head") occurs, damaging brain tissue. See FIGURE 9-20 ▲. Hydrocephalus can be caused by blockage of the narrow passages between the ventricles due to trauma, birth defects or tumors, or decreased reabsorption of CSF due to subarachnoid bleeding. Hydrocephalus may be accompanied by increased intracranial pressure or may have no apparent rise in pressure (normal pressure hydrocephalus).

Symptoms of hydrocephalus vary depending on the age of the patient and the type of hydrocephalus. In infants, whose skulls have not completely hardened, the skull may expand. Patients may experience vomiting, irritability, and seizures. In older children and adults, the skull does not change size, but the rising pressure causes headache, nausea, blurred vision, balance and coordination problems, sleepiness, and personality changes. Normal pressure hydrocephalus, seen mainly in the elderly, causes dementia and motor problems. It is a chronic progressive disease often accompanied by or caused by other neurological problems.

Hydrocephalus is diagnosed using imaging including CT and MRI (looking for enlarged ventricles) and monitoring of intracranial pressure. Hydrocephalus may be treated by medication, but the most common treatment is insertion of a **shunt**, a tube that drains the extra CSF into the patient's heart or abdominal cavity (again see Figure 9-20). Long-term prognosis for patients with hydrocephalus is mixed. Many have long-term problems.

hydrocephalus *(HIGH droh SEF uh luhs)* A general term for the accumulation of excessive amounts of cerebrospinal fluid within the brain's ventricles.

shunt An anomalous passage or one artificially constructed to divert flow from one main route to another.

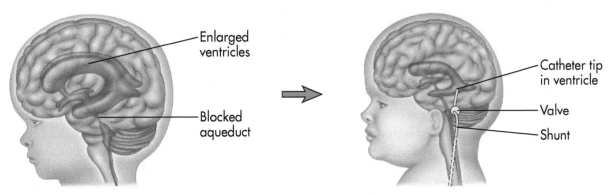

FIGURE 9-20 ▲ Hydrocephalus.

TEST YOUR KNOWLEDGE 9-4

Choose the best answer:

1. Which of the following is not part of the brain stem?
   a. pons
   b. medulla oblongata
   c. midbrain
   d. diencephalon

2. Deep islands of gray matter are known as:
   a. hemispheres
   b. gyri
   c. nuclei
   d. nerves

3. Which of the following is not found in the diencephalon?
   a. thalamus
   b. pineal
   c. postcentral gyrus
   d. hypothalamus

4. This lobe contains the primary visual cortex:
   a. frontal
   b. temporal
   c. occipital
   d. parietal

5. To prevent further brain injury after TBI, doctors must control:
   a. body temperature
   b. intracranial pressure
   c. demyelination
   d. peripheral neuropathy

THE BIG PICTURE: INTEGRATION OF BRAIN, SPINAL CORD, AND PNS

So how does the brain work with the spinal cord and peripheral nervous system (PNS)? Let's begin to put the pieces together by revisiting the overall organizational chart of the nervous system. FIGURE 9-21 ▲ will serve as our guide to keep our location clear.

The Somatic Sensory System

somatic sensory system The portion of the nervous system that provides sensory input for the sense of touch.

somatic sensation The sense of touch.

The **somatic sensory system** provides sensory input for your nervous system. We have already mentioned the parts of your brain that are dedicated to your special senses: vision (occipital lobe), hearing (temporal and parietal lobes), taste (temporal lobe), and smell (frontal lobe). We have not yet talked in detail about the sense of touch, called **somatic sensation**. Somatic sensation allows you to feel the world around you. Somatic sensation includes not just fine touch, which enables you to tell the difference between a peach and a nectarine or a golf ball and a Ping-Pong ball, but also crude touch, vibration, pain, temperature, and body position. Although your special senses are all carried on cranial nerves, information for somatic sensation comes into *both* the brain and the spinal cord. Ultimately, for you to attach meaning to the sensation, the sensory information must get to your brain. The pain that Maria, our diabetes patient, feels is due to damage to her peripheral nerves. Her somatic sensory system perceives their malfunction as pain.

Let's start with the spinal cord. When we talked about reflexes, we saw somatic sensory information come into the spinal cord via the dorsal root and synapse with a motor neuron in the ventral horn. Let's go back to hitting your thumb with a hammer. The pain neurons, with bodies in the dorsal root ganglion, are depolarized and send

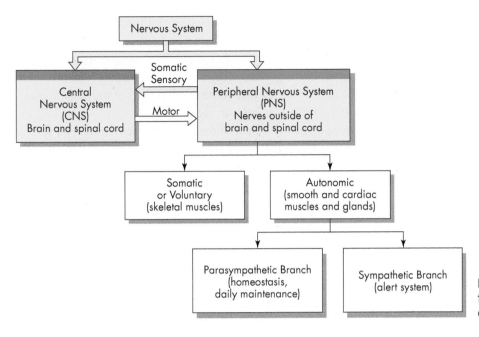

FIGURE 9-21 ▲ Nervous system flowchart highlighting the areas thus far explained.

signals to the spinal cord via the spinal nerve and dorsal root. The neurons synapse with motor neurons, causing you to pull your hand away from the stimulus. These same pain neurons join the spinothalamic tract in your spinal cord and simultaneously send a pain signal to your brain. The signal goes first to the thalamus and other parts of the diencephalon, causing physiological symptoms like sweating and increased heart rate. The pain then continues along the pathway to your somatic sensory cortex (in the postcentral gyrus). There, the exact location of the pain becomes apparent to you. Now you know *where* the pain is but still may not recognize it as pain. The *understanding* occurs when the information is integrated with sensation in the somatic sensory association area (in the parietal lobe). Now you know that you have hurt yourself! All the receiving and processing of information and associated actions happen almost instantaneously.

Because there are many variations of "touch" information that come in from all parts of the body, your body needs different neural highways to send that information to the brain effectively. See TABLE 9-6 ■ for a description of sensory spinal cord pathways.

TABLE 9-6 ■ SPINAL CORD PATHWAYS FOR SENSORY INFORMATION

PATHWAY	INFORMATION	FROM	TO
Spinothalamic		skin	somatic sensory cortex
Lateral	pain; temperature	skin	somatic sensory cortex
Anterior	itch; pressure; tickle	skin	somatic sensory cortex
Dorsal column	fine touch; limb position	skin; joints	somatic sensory cortex; cerebellum
Spinocerebellar	posture	joints; tendons	cerebellum

The sensory information coming into the brain must go to a specific area for processing. As you can see from Table 9-6, the dorsal column and spinothalamic tracts both transport sensory information from your skin to the primary somatic sensory cortex, located in the postcentral gyrus of the parietal lobe. The axons transport information to specific parts of the somatic sensory cortex that correspond to parts of the body as previously discussed in the sensory cortex map (refer to Figure 9-17).

The neurons in the somatic sensory cortex allow conscious sensation. You feel an insect crawling on your arm because the insect stimulates the "arm" neurons in your somatic sensory cortex. The somatic sensory system works on a kind of hierarchy, with the sensory neurons in the spinal cord and brain stem collecting information and passing it to areas in the thalamus, cerebellum, and cerebral cortex for processing. Your *actual* understanding of complex sensory input happens only *after* the information is passed to the somatic sensory cortex and somatic sensory association area.

The Motor System

The motor system is also a hierarchy, working in parallel with the somatic sensory system. Remember from earlier in the chapter that the output side carries out the orders from the brain and spinal cord. The motor system carries orders to all three types of muscles and to the body's glands, telling them how to respond to the new information. However, now information is moving in the opposite direction, from brain to spinal cord. See FIGURE 9-22 ▲ to show our current progress on the nervous system organizational chart.

Cerebral Cortex

The somatic motor system controls voluntary movements under orders from the cerebral cortex. When you decide to move, the movements are planned in the prefrontal cortex and premotor cortex in the frontal lobe. This plan is then sent to the primary motor cortex, in the precentral gyrus. The orders are then sent to the spinal cord directly and also to a number of coordination centers, including the thalamus, basal nuclei, and cerebellum.

FIGURE 9-22 ▲ Progress thus far on the nervous system flowchart.

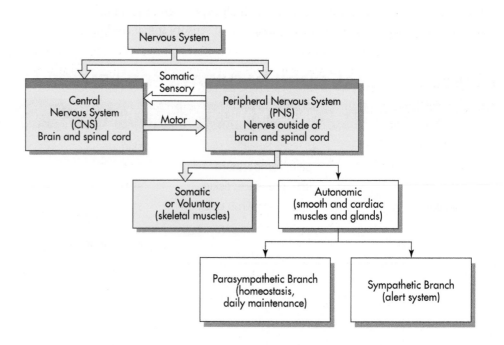

Subcortical Structures

The plan for movement leaves the motor cortex and connects with neurons in the thalamus, which is located in the diencephalon. The thalamus, basal nuclei, and cerebellum are part of a complicated **motor coordination loop**. Here, the movement is fine-tuned, posture and limb positions are taken into account, other movements are turned off, and movement and senses are integrated. This loop is fundamental. Without the coordination loop among the subcortical (under the cortex) structures, movements would be at the very least jerky and inaccurate.

Cerebellum So far we have glossed over the important function of the cerebellum. The cerebellum has both motor and sensory inputs and outputs from the cerebral cortex, the thalamus, the basal nuclei, and the spinal cord. The cerebellum gets information about the *planned* movement and the *actual* movement and compares the plan to the actual. If the plan and the actual do not match, the cerebellum can adjust the actual movement to fit the plan. The function of the cerebellum is subtle and still a bit of a mystery, but without the cerebellum, movements would be inaccurate at best.

Spinal Cord Pathways While the movement information plan is being processed by the thalamus, basal nuclei, and cerebellum, it moves direcly to the spinal cord and brain stem via the **corticospinal** and **corticobulbar tracts**. The corticospinal and corticobulbar tracts from your motor cortex are *direct* pathways, carrying orders to the neurons in the brain stem and ventral horn of the spinal cord. The pathways coming from subcortical structures are considered *indirect* pathways, which help coordinate movement.

The spinal cord pathways send orders from the brain to the motor neurons in the spinal cord and brain stem. The motor neurons in your spinal cord connect to skeletal muscles via the cranial nerves (in the brain stem) or spinal nerves (in the spinal cord), sending orders to the skeletal muscles to carry out the planned movement or coordinate ongoing movements. (Remember, these neurons communicate with the muscles via the neuromuscular junction, and therefore release the neurotransmitter acetylcholine across the synapse.) A second function of the motor tracts is to fine-tune reflexes. These tracts inhibit reflexes, making them softer than they would be if they had no influence from the brain.

Let's return to the hitting your thumb with the hammer example. After you hit your thumb, the first motor activity is a withdrawal reflex. You pull your thumb away from the painful stimulus. As we mentioned before, this is not a voluntary movement. It isn't planned. Only your spinal cord motor neurons are necessary for withdrawal. However, after the initial withdrawal, what do you do next? You look at your thumb. That is a planned movement. It requires coordination between your motor system, to uncover your thumb and move it into your visual field, and your visual system to look at your thumb. You walk to the kitchen, open the freezer, get out the ice, and make an ice pack. Then you grab a cold soda from the fridge and walk back into the living room, nursing your wounds. All this activity requires motor planning and coordination. You must reach for the freezer door and open it accurately. You must stay upright with respect to gravity. You must open a plastic bag and put ice in it. None of this happens without careful motor planning and coordination.

motor coordination loop A complicated relationship between the thalamus, basal nuclei, and the cerebellum that allows for fine tuned movement.

corticospinal tract *(CORE tih coh SPY nal)* Pertaining to the tract between the cerebral cortex and spinal cord. Carries orders for voluntary movements.

corticobulbar tract *(CORE tih coh BUL bar)* Spinal cord tract that carries impulses to the brainstem from the motor cortex. Carries orders for voluntary movements.

Pathology Connection

MOTOR PATHOLOGIES

Cerebral Palsy (CP) is a permanent, nonprogressive set of motor deficits diagnosed in infants and young children, generally thought to be due to damage to the motor cortex. No single cause has been identified for CP, but many risk factors are associated with the disorder, including low birth weight, premature birth, multiple births, infection during pregnancy, developmental abnormalities, brain hemorrhage, **perinatal** brain injury, lack of oxygen, and childhood illness. The symptoms of CP vary from mild foot drag and uncoordination to complete paralysis, including the inability to speak. Symptoms of CP include abnormally increased muscle tone, overactive reflexes, lack of coordination of voluntary movements, foot drag, drooling, speech difficulties, fine motor problems, and tremor or other uncontrollable movements.

Some people with CP are also mentally retarded, are autistic, or have seizures, but many CP patients are of average or above-average intelligence. Diagnosis of CP, especially mild cases, can be difficult. Observing childhood motor skills and developmental milestones, taking images such as CT scans or MRIs, and ruling out other causes of motor deficits are the best ways to diagnose CP. Treatment includes a variety of physical and occupational therapy, assistive devices, and drugs to control the symptoms. Stem cell usage shows promise.

Parkinson's disease (PD) is a chronic progressive motor disorder, common in elderly patients, characterized by resting tremor (rhythmic shaking), slow movement, impaired balance, rigidity, fatigue, and a number of cognitive and emotional disturbances. PD is caused by the disappearance of dopamine neurons in one of the basal nuclei, which later spreads to the cerebral cortex. The cause of PD is unknown, but toxins, mitochondrial malfunctions, TBI, or a virus may be involved. Some cases of PD are genetic. Most PD patients are elderly, but some younger people, like the actor Michael J. Fox, have an early-onset form of the disease.

Diagnosis of PD is easier than for some other progressive motor disorders. Patient history and a thorough physical exam are often enough to diagnose PD. PD patients have a characteristic shuffling gait, and their muscles pop or snap. The rigidity appears almost as if the muscles catch and then release. This type of rigidity is called "cogwheel" rigidity, and it is diagnostic for PD. Imaging studies are useful for ruling out other disorders because, unlike many other disorders, early-stage PD patients will have absolutely normal scans. Several numerical scales can be used to describe the severity of the disease.

Treatment of PD is generally with the use of dopamine-enhancing drugs. The most common and most effective of these is L-dopa. Unfortunately, L-dopa, when used long term, has nasty side effects, including hallucinations and excessive uncontrollable movement. PD patients on L-dopa also have "on" and "off" periods that are unpredictable. Other medications are used to control PD symptoms of tremor, depression, and blood pressure effects. Deep brain stimulation may also be used to treat the symptoms of PD. For example, deep brain stimulation of the thalamus decreases tremor.

Amyotrophic lateral sclerosis (ALS), also known as Lou Gehrig's disease, is a rapidly progressive, fatal degeneration of the motor system. On average, patients with ALS die within 5 years of diagnosis, though some patients, like the physicist Stephen Hawking, live much longer. Symptoms usually appear between the ages of 40 and 60 and begin with muscle weakness, twitching, and cramping, and then progress to complete paralysis, including difficulty speaking and swallowing and eventually to paralysis of the diaphragm. At that point, patients will become ventilator dependent. Eye movements and control of the bladder and bowels are usually retained. Death is usually due to respiratory failure.

The cause of ALS is unknown, but we do know that there is an increase in self-destruction of motor neurons in the cerebral cortex, brain stem, and spinal cord. There is evidence that toxins, damage from

(continued)

Pathology Connection (continued)

free radicals, or mitochondrial problems may be involved. Usually there is excess activity of neuroglia, including microglia and astrocytes, and excess production of the neurotransmitter glutamate, all of which increase neuron death.

There is no definitive diagnostic test for ALS, but it has one unique characteristic. ALS is the only motor disorder that exhibits both flaccid and spastic paralysis. Most other disorders affect either upper motor neurons (spastic paralysis) or lower motor neurons (flaccid paralysis). ALS affects both. In ALS, unlike some other forms of paralysis, sensation is normal. EMG, imaging, and blood and urine tests can help rule out other disorders. A neural biopsy may also be helpful.

As we have seen with many other neurological disorders, there is no cure for ALS. Only one drug, riluzole, has been approved for treatment. This drug decreases the neurotransmitter glutamate and decreases cell death, slowing the progression of the disease. There are other treatments to reduce symptoms and improve quality of life.

Clinical Application

SPASTIC VERSUS FLACCID PARALYSIS

A good illustration of the relationship between the brain, spinal cord pathways, and ventral horn motor neurons are the two types of paralysis. **Paralysis** is the inability to control voluntary movements. Paralysis can be either **spastic** or **flaccid**. Spastic paralysis is characterized by muscle rigidity or increased muscle tone and overactive reflexes. In spastic paralysis, the muscles are rigid and the reflexes are overactive because of decreased communication from the brain to the ventral horn motor neurons in the spinal cord and brain stem motor neurons. Muscles contract spontaneously, and reflexes do not have any control signals from the brain. Stroke, head injuries, cerebral palsy, multiple sclerosis, basal nuclei disorders (like Parkinson's disease), and spinal cord injuries can cause spastic paralysis.

Flaccid paralysis is characterized by floppy muscles (decreased muscle tone) and decreased reflexes. In flaccid paralysis, the damage is to the spinal nerves or ventral horn (or brain stem) motor neurons. Impulses cannot get to the muscles from the motor neurons. Therefore, the muscles are floppy and reflexes are absent. Flaccid paralysis can be caused by peripheral neuropathy or disorders like polio and Guillain-Barré syndrome. Maria, our diabetes patient, with the beginnings of peripheral neuropathy, may eventually experience localized flaccid paralysis.

cerebral palsy A general term for a nonprogressive motor impairment due to lesions or abnormalities of the brain that occurred during early stages of its development.

perinatal *(per ih NAY tall)* At or near the time of birth.

Parkinson's disease (PD) A chronic degenerative disease of the central nervous system that causes impaired movement and changes in mood and cognition. Usually found in individuals older than 65.

amyotrophic lateral sclerosis (ALS) *(AA my o TROF ic)* Neuromuscular disease that destroys both upper and lower motor neurons that leads to a loss of muscle control.

paralysis *(puh RAL uh sis)* Temporary or permanent loss of muscle function.

spastic Characterized by increased muscle tone and overactive reflexes.

flaccid *(FLAH sid)* Limp or without muscle tone.

TEST YOUR KNOWLEDGE 9-5

Choose the best answer:

1. The size of the map for a particular body part in the precentral gyrus is determined by:
   a. the amount of fine motor control
   b. the size of the body part
   c. the importance of the body part
   d. all of the above

2. The cerebellum compares:
   a. shapes of objects
   b. planned movement to actual movement
   c. textures
   d. position of objects in space

3. Which of the following spinal cord pathways carries pain and temperature information?
   a. dorsal column
   b. spinothalamic
   c. corticospinal
   d. thermostatic

4. The _____ sends direct messages to ventral horn motor neurons, whereas the _____ are involved in indirect pathways.
   a. thalamus; basal nuclei
   b. primary sensory cortex; thalamus
   c. cerebellum; primary motor cortex
   d. primary motor cortex; basal nuclei

5. This disorder is characterized by slow movements, resting tremor, and popping rigidity:
   a. ALS
   b. Huntington's disease
   c. spinal cord injury
   d. none of the above

6. This disorder has both upper and lower motor neurons signs:
   a. ALS
   b. Huntington's disease
   c. spinal cord injury
   d. none of the above

---

ganglion *(GANG lee on)* Mass of nervous tissue composed mostly of nerve cell bodies and lying outside the brain and spinal cord.

postganglionic neuron *(post GANG lee ON ick)* Autonomic neuron that connects to a smooth muscle or a gland.

sympathetic nervous system Division of the autonomic nervous system that uses the neurotransmitter norepinephrine and carries nerve impulses to the heart, involuntary muscles, and glands during times of increased activity, danger, or stress.

parasympathetic nervous system *(PAIR uh SIM peh THET ik)* Division of the autonomic nervous system that uses the neurotransmitter acetlycholine and carries nerve impulses to the heart, involuntary smooth muscles, and glands while the body is at rest.

THE AUTONOMIC NERVOUS SYSTEM

The peripheral nervous system is divided into two systems: the somatic system, which controls skeletal muscles, and the autonomic system, which controls involuntary muscles. These muscles are the smooth muscles found in structures such as the blood vessels and airways and cardiac muscle found in the heart. Glands are also controlled by this system. The autonomic system controls physiological characteristics such as blood pressure, heart rate, respiration rate, digestion, and sweating.

The neurons for the autonomic system, like the somatic motor neurons, are located in the spinal cord and brain stem and release the neurotransmitter acetylcholine. This is where the similarity ends. The autonomic motor neurons are all located in the lateral horn rather than the ventral horns, and unlike the somatic motor neurons, autonomic neurons do not connect directly to muscles. Instead, they make a synapse in a ganglion outside the CNS. A **ganglion** is a group of nerve cell bodies outside the CNS. You can think of this as a junction box where the signal can be passed on to the next part of the circuit. Then a second motor neuron, called a **postganglionic neuron,** connects to the smooth muscle or gland.

The autonomic nervous system is divided into two subdivisions, or branches: the **sympathetic** and the **parasympathetic.** Please see FIGURE 9-23 ▲.

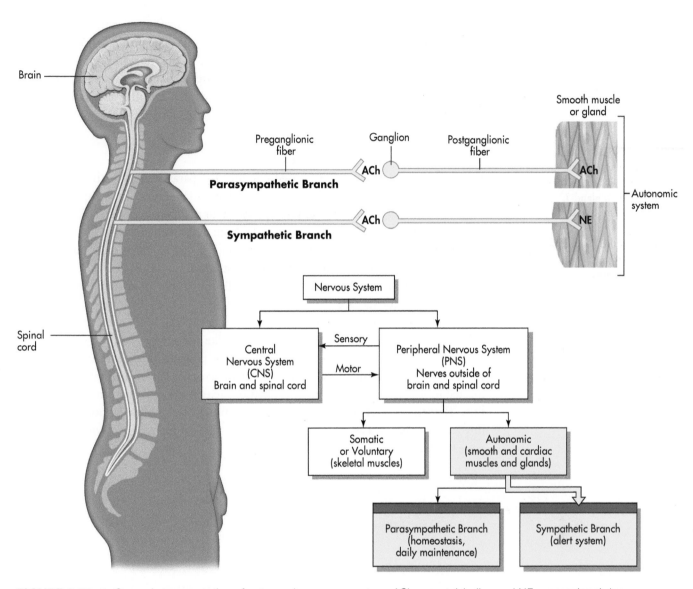

FIGURE 9-23 ▲ General representation of autonomic nervous system. ACh = acetylcholine and NE = norepinephrine.

The Sympathetic Branch

The sympathetic branch controls the fight-or-flight response. It is charged with getting your body ready to expend energy. Sympathetic effects include increased heart rate, increased blood pressure, sweating, and dry mouth—all the symptoms of an adrenaline rush. This part of the autonomic system was responsible for your racing heart, rapid breathing, and intense sweating when confronted in our earlier example of the snarling dog. Your heart pumped more blood to your muscles, and your lungs took in more oxygen, both of which got you "up" to either fight or, most likely, flee. Another sympathetic response is dilation of your pupils to help you see the situation at hand much better. Sympathetic output is pretty strong when you hit your thumb with the hammer too.

The **preganglionic neurons** for the sympathetic system are located in the thoracic and first two lumbar segments of the spinal cord. Due to their location, they are classified as **thoracolumbar.** The preganglionic neurons, which secrete acetylcholine, synapse with the **postganglionic neurons** in the sympathetic ganglia. The ganglia

preganglionic neuron *(pre GANG lee ON ick NEW ron)* Found in the autonomic system, it uses ACh as the neurotransmitter and junctions with post-ganglionic neurons.

thoracolumbar Pertaining to the thoracic and lumbar parts of the spinal cord; denoting their ganglia and the fibers of the sympathetic nervous system.

postganglionic neurons *(post GANG lee ON ick)* Autonomic neuron that connects to a smooth muscle or a gland.

paravertebral ganglia *(PAIR ah VUR teh brawl GANG glee uh)* Ganglia of the sympathetic nervous system that form a chain-like structure that runs parallel to the spinal cord.

norepinephrine *(NOR ep ih NEFF rinn)* Neurotransmitter for the sympathetic nervous system. It moves between neurons and an involuntary muscle, organ, or gland. Controls the fight-or-flight response.

epinephrine *(EP ih NEFF rinn)* Hormone secreted by the adrenal medulla in response to stimulation by nerves of the sympathetic nervous system.

craniosacral The brainstem and sacral spinal cord, origin of parasympathetic preganglionic neurons.

for the sympathetic division form a pair of chainlike structures that run parallel to the spinal cord. These are called **paravertebral ganglia**. The postganglionic neurons release the neurotransmitter **norepinephrine**. One of the most important effects of the sympathetic system is its stimulation of the adrenal gland to release the hormone **epinephrine** (adrenalin), the chemical that causes that familiar adrenalin rush by circulating in the blood stream. (Again, please refer to Figure 9-23.)

The Parasympathetic Branch

If you have a gas pedal, you also need a brake. The parasympathetic division is often called "resting and digesting" because it has the opposite effect of the sympathetic division. The parasympathetic division is responsible for maintenance of everyday activities. It also helps bring you back down to normal from a sympathetic response. Parasympathetic effects include decreased heart rate, respiration, and blood pressure and increased digestive activity, including salivation and even stomach rumbling. The parasympathetic system allows you to calm down after you get the ice pack on your thumb or the dog is safely locked inside its cage.

The neurons of the parasympathetic system are in the brain stem and the sacral spinal cord and thus are called **craniosacral**. Like the preganglionic synapses of the sympathetic system, they release acetylcholine. The preganglionic neurons synapse with postganglionic neurons in the parasympathetic ganglia. Parasympathetic ganglia are located near the organs. Postganglionic neurons release the neurotransmitter acetylcholine. (Remember, acetylcholine excites skeletal muscle, but inhibits smooth and cardiac muscle.) See **FIGURE 9-24** ▲, which contrasts the parasympathetic and sympathetic nervous systems.

A QUICK TRIP *(continued)*

DISORDER	ETIOLOGY	SIGNS AND SYMPTOMS	DIAGNOSTIC TEST(S)	TREATMENTS
Peripheral neuropathy	Damage to peripheral nerves due to injury or illness.	Motor and sensory abnormalities; including weakness, pain, numbness, and tingling.	Imaging, biopsy, patient history.	Symptom management, treatment of underlying disorder causing nerve damage.
Traumatic brain injury	Damage to brain tissue due to mechanical injury, lack of oxygen, or brain hemorrhage.	Depends on injury severity and location. Ranges from dizziness and nausea to severe cognitive disturbances, memory loss, seizures, and unconsciousness.	Glasgow Coma Scale, imaging.	Acute treatment to prevent further injury: immobilization, surgery, medication to relieve intracranial pressure. Long-term care: PT, OT, supportive care, and symptom management.
Hydrocephalus	Excess CSF in brain due to trauma, birth defects, tumors, etc.	Symptoms vary with age: skull expansion and irritability in babies; irritability, vomiting, seizures, sleepiness, and dementia in older patients.	Imaging, pressure monitoring.	Shunt insertion.
Cerebral palsy (CP)	Risk factors include premature birth, low birth weight, developmental abnormalities, perinatal brain injury.	Nonprogressive motor deficits in young children.	Observation of childhood motor skills, rule out other disorders.	No cure: PT, OT, assistive devices, symptom management.
Parkinson's disease (PD)	Progressive loss of dopamine neurons.	Resting tremor, slow movement, rigidity, cognitive and emotional disturbance.	History, imaging, neurological exam.	No cure: Dopamine-enhancing drugs, symptom management, deep brain stimulation.

(continued)

A QUICK TRIP (continued)

DISORDER	ETIOLOGY	SIGNS AND SYMPTOMS	DIAGNOSTIC TEST(S)	TREATMENTS
Huntington's disease	Genetic; progressive loss of neurons from basal nuclei and cerebral cortex.	Mid-life onset of chorea (excessive movement), mood swings and memory loss, progressing to dementia and paralysis.	Family history, imaging, genetic testing.	No cure; medication to control emotional and motor symptoms, no drug treatment for dementia.
Amyotrophic lateral sclerosis (ALS)	Progressive loss of motor neurons in CNS and PNS, cause unknown.	Progressive muscle weakness, twitching, and cramping, eventually leading to complete paralysis. Sensation is normal.	No definitive diagnosis, but presence of both flaccid and spastic paralysis indicates ALS. Rule out other disorders.	No cure; drug treatment may slow progression, symptom management.
Alzheimer's disease	Not fully known; believed to be a buildup of plaque in the brain and/or a defect in the neurotransmitter system in the brain.	Varying degrees of confusion, memory loss, cognitive defects, and personality changes.	History and physical exam, interview of family members, and various cognitive tests.	No cure; drug therapy can prevent or decrease some symptoms in early to middle stages of disease.

Pharmacology Corner

blood–brain barrier A structural and functional barrier that prevents some substances from diffusing from the blood to the brain tissue.

The **blood–brain barrier** is an anatomical/physiological protective structure of the brain believed to consist of walls of capillaries in the CNS and surrounding glial membranes. The blood–brain barrier functions to prevent or slow down the passage of a variety of chemical compounds and pathogens from the blood and into the central nervous system. Some beneficial drugs cannot pass through this barrier easily and as a result make it difficult to treat brain diseases such as meningitis.

Dozens of medications affect the nervous system. Most medications affect chemical synaptic transmission. Nicotine (in tobacco), opiates (like morphine and heroin), L-dopa (used to treat Parkinson's disease), and benzodiazepines (found in tranquilizers like Valium™) bind to the receptors for neurotransmitters, mimicking the effects of the neurotransmitter. Some of these drugs are stimulants and some are depressants, depending on the activity of the neurotransmitter they mimic. Monoamine oxide (MAO) inhibitors (like Selegiline™ for Parkinson's disease and Nardil™ for depression), selective serotonin reuptake inhibitors (SSRIs like Prozac™ for depression), and acetylcholinesterase inhibitors (like Neostigmine for myasthenia gravis or donepezil/Aricept™ for Alzheimer's disease) stop neurotransmitters from being removed from the synapse, prolonging their activity. Again, their effects depend on the effects of the neurotransmitter. Receptor inhibitors block receptors, preventing the neurotransmitter's effects. Examples include scopolamine (for motion sickness) and succinylcholine (a muscle paralyzer), which block acetylcholine receptors, and Lopressor™ and Zobeta™, beta-blockers that block norepinephrine receptors to treat cardiac problems.

SUMMARY

Snapshots from the Journey

- The nervous system is the body's computer, its information superhighway. It has a sensory (input) system, an integration center, the CNS, and a motor (output) system. The input and output nerves are in the PNS, and the brain and spinal cord are the CNS.

- The tissue of the nervous system is made up of two types of cells: neurons, which send, receive, and process information; and neuroglia, which support the neurons.

- Neurons are excitable cells. They do their jobs by carrying tiny electrical currents caused by changes in cell permeability to certain ions. These tiny electrical currents can be all-or-none (action potentials), can change depending on the size of the stimulus (local potentials), can travel down axons (impulse conduction), or can be used to transmit information from one cell to another (synapses).

- The CNS is composed of the brain and spinal cord.

- The CNS is surrounded by a three-layered membrane system: dura mater, arachnoid mater, and pia mater, collectively known as the meninges. Cerebrospinal fluid (CSF) is also contained in the space between the arachnoid and pia maters.

- The spinal cord has 31 segments, each with a pair of spinal nerves. The spinal nerves are a part of the peripheral nervous system and are made of a pair of spinal roots. The ventral root is integral to motor function, and the dorsal root is integral to sensory function. Spinal nerves are mixed: They carry both sensory and motor information.

- Tracts run up and down the spinal cord to and from the brain. The tracts going toward the brain carry sensory information to the brain. The tracts coming from the brain toward the spinal cord carry motor information from the brain.

- The brain is a hierarchical organ. It is divided into compartments (lobes), each with very specific functions. The nerves attached to the brain are called cranial nerves, which occur in 12 pairs. They can be sensory, motor, or mixed.

- The cerebrum controls your conscious movement and sensation. Beneath the cerebrum are the diencephalon, brain stem, and cerebellum. Each part plays an important role in coordinating sensory and motor information for the cerebrum.

- The cerebral cortex contains motor and sensory maps of the body. Orders for voluntary movements originate in the primary motor cortex, located in the precentral gyrus of the frontal lobe, and travel down the spinal cord via direct spinal cord tracts. Subcortical structures coordinate this information via indirect tracts.

- The somatic sensory cortex is in the postcentral gyrus of the parietal lobe. Sensory information from the spinal cord tracts eventually ends up in this part of the cortex. When the information

SUMMARY (continued)

arrives there, you become aware of your sense of touch. Other parts of the brain, called association areas, allow you to make connections between different types of sensory information and to compare current experience to memories.

■ Ventricles are the cavities in your brain. The spinal cord cavity is the central canal. These cavities are part of an elaborate protection system for your CNS and are filled with cerebrospinal fluid.

■ The nervous system also controls involuntary movement via a part of the system known as the autonomic nervous system. The sympathetic division controls the fight-or-flight response, and the parasympathetic division controls day-to-day activities.

■ The nervous system can have many disorders. Most are chronic, progressive, and incurable. In all cases, whether the disorder is central or peripheral, genetic, or caused by disease or trauma, the symptoms are often the same. Muscle weakness, loss of sensation, and respiratory difficulty often accompany problems in the nervous system. The subtle differences between the symptoms are the key to making these difficult diagnoses and finding the appropriate treatment. Treatment generally consists of symptom management and prevention of further deterioration.

RAY'S STORY

Let's visit with Ray again. This is the young man who hit his chin on the bottom of the swimming pool doing a back flip. He had struck the bottom of the pool on the point of his chin, jamming and twisting his neck. His neck is broken, the first two vertebrae are shattered, and his spinal cord is irreversibly damaged. He is paralyzed from the neck down and is ventilator dependent.

a. What is the level of Ray's injury? (Cervical, thoracic, lumbar, or sacral)

_____

b. Why can't he breathe? (Be specific.)

_____

c. What do you call the paralysis of all four limbs?

_____

d. What complications might be a problem for Ray?

_____

e. Does Ray have spastic or flaccid paralysis?

_____

REVIEW QUESTIONS

Multiple Choice

1. The input side of your nervous system is known as:
   a. motor
   b. sensory
   c. association
   d. all of the above

2. During depolarization, _____ ions move _____ a neuron.
   a. K⁺; out of
   b. K⁺; into
   c. Na⁺; out of
   d. Na⁺; into

3. Bob is stopped in a busy street intersection waiting to take a left turn when a drunk driver runs the light, T-boning Bob's Corvette. When the EMTs arrive, Bob is still pinned in the car and is in respiratory arrest. When he regains consciousness at the hospital, Bob is dismayed to discover that he cannot move or feel his body and that he is on a ventilator. Where is his injury?
   a. C1
   b. C8
   c. T10
   d. L1

4. One of the following brain parts is *not* subcortical. Which one?
   a. hypothalamus
   b. medulla oblongata
   c. precentral gyrus
   d. pineal body

5. The size of the map of each body part in the postcentral gyrus is determined by the:
   a. sensitivity of the body part
   b. size of the body part
   c. importance of the body part
   d. fine motor control of the body part

6. The sympathetic nervous system:
   a. causes decreased heart rate
   b. has ganglia near the organs
   c. has ganglia near the spinal cord
   d. all of the above

7. This part of the brain contains the body's set points and controls most of its physiology, including blood pressure and hunger level:
   a. thalamus
   b. hypothalamus
   c. amygdala
   d. hippocampus

8. Which of these disorders is caused by loss of neurons from the basal nuclei?
   a. multiple sclerosis
   b. amyotrophic lateral sclerosis
   c. cerebral palsy
   d. Parkinson's disease

9. Amyotrophic lateral sclerosis is different from the many other progressive neurological disorders because patients:
   a. have normal sensation
   b. are easy to diagnose
   c. have symptoms of both flaccid and spastic paralysis
   d. rarely die from the disease

10. Which of the following is *not* progressive?
    a. amyotrophic lateral sclerosis
    b. multiple sclerosis
    c. Parkinson's disease
    d. cerebral palsy

REVIEW QUESTIONS

Fill in the Blank

1. The speed of impulse conduction is determined by _____ and _____.

2. _____ fluid is contained in the _____ space between the arachnoid mater and pia mater.

3. Most of the symptoms of MS are caused by destruction of _____ in the brain and spinal cord.

4. The most common cause of spinal cord injuries is _____.

5. Rapid onset, ascending paralysis is a hallmark of this disorder _____.

6. The occipital lobe is responsible for this sensation: _____.

7. The white matter of the spinal cord contains _____ tracts, which are motor, and _____ tracts, which are sensory.

8. Emotion, mood, and memory are controlled by this collection of nuclei: _____.

9. _____ is characterized by tremor, rigidity, and slow movement.

10. What is one of the leading killers of patients with progressive neurological disorders? _____

Short Answer

1. Explain the changes in a neuron during an action potential.

_____

_____

_____

_____

2. List the steps in chemical synaptic transmission.

_____

_____

_____

_____

3. List the types of neuroglia and their functions.

_____

_____

_____

_____

REVIEW QUESTIONS

4. Explain what happens to spinal cord tissue after injury.

_____
_____
_____
_____

5. List the differences between the sympathetic and parasympathetic nervous systems.

_____
_____
_____
_____

6. Explain how the cerebral cortex and subcortical structures interact to produce motor output.

_____
_____
_____
_____

7. Explain how the location of a stroke or traumatic brain injury can determine the symptoms.

_____
_____
_____
_____

8. Discuss how the location of spinal cord trauma would effect a diagnosis of paraplegic vs quadriplegic.

Suggested Activities

1. With a partner, test your knee-jerk reflexes using reflex hammers. Try to control the reflex. Can you? Try it with your eyes closed. What does that say about reflexes?

2. Grab a friend and explain the action potential and chemical synapse to her or him. Can you do it?

3. Find the parts of the brain on a preserved brain, diagram, or model.

4. Select a partner and play nervous system jeopardy. Can you identify the function of all of the parts of the nervous system?

CAREER CONNECTIONS

Now that you have read this chapter, here is a list of related professions you may be interested in investigating for a future career:

- Pharmacy

- Electroneurodiagnostician

Research each profession and report on the following:

1. Profession description to include job responsibilities
2. Educational requirements
3. Job opportunities
4. Opportunities outside of the hospital setting
5. Salary range
6. Licensure and continuing education requirements

ANATOMY, PHYSIOLOGY, AND DISEASE IN ACTION

Materials:
White bathing cap
Permanent markers of various colors

Using one side of the bathing cap, outline the sections of the brain as shown in a sagittal view. Use different colors for the cerebrum, the cerebellum, and the brain stem. Label the cerebrum (pituitary gland, and diencephalon—thalamus, pineal gland, hypothalamus), frontal lobe, corpus callosum, fornix, parietal lobe, and occipital lobe; cerebellum and arbor vitae; and brain stem (midbrain, pons, and medulla oblongata). The primary function for each part should also be included.

The bathing cap can then be mounted on tag board as an additional activity. Braided thick yarn can be attached to the medulla oblongata to represent the spinal cord. The sympathetic and the parasympathetic branches of the autonomic nervous system can be incorporated into the diagram along with the regions of the spinal cord from which the neurons originate and their site of action.

The Endocrine System
The Body's Other Control Center

Here we are again, talking about control. We have already visited one of the control systems—the complex structure of cells and connections known as the nervous system. Now we visit yet another control system—the endocrine system. These two control systems may seem like separate systems, but they are interconnected and always monitor each other's activities. The nervous system collects information and sends orders with a speed that is truly mind-boggling. Whereas the endocrine system also collects information and sends orders, it's a slower, more subtle control system. The endocrine system's orders to the body also last much longer than those made by the nervous system. You might think of the endocrine system as sending "standing orders," or orders meant to be obeyed indefinitely unless changed by another set of orders. The orders change subtly on a regular basis, but their intention is constant. The nervous system, on the other hand, issues orders that are to be obeyed instantaneously but are used for short-term situations. The endocrine system demands organs to "carry on," whereas the nervous system expects them to respond immediately.

On our journey, suppose we stop at an amusement park to ride a roller coaster. Afterward, en route to our next destination, we are forced off the road because of a near miss with a truck. Even after the roller coaster ride is over or the truck is long gone, your legs still shake, your heart continues to race, and your blood pressure remains elevated, even though you are no longer in danger. We call such lingering effects the "adrenaline rush." These lingering effects are not due to continued activity of the nervous system, but rather to endocrine activity deliberately triggered by the autonomic nervous system.

LEARNING OUTCOMES

At the completion of your journey through this chapter, you will be able to:

- Discuss the functions of the various endocrine glands
- Describe the purpose and effects of hormones within the body
- Discuss the process of homeostatic control and feedback mechanisms of hormone levels
- Differentiate between hormonal control, humoral control, and neural control of hormones
- Explain common diseases of the endocrine system

Pronunciation Guide

Correct pronunciation is important in any journey so that you and others are completely understood. Here is a "see and say" Pronunciation Guide for the more difficult terms to pronounce in this chapter. Please note that pronunciations given are referenced to medical dictionaries, and regional variations may exist.

adrenal cortex (ah DREE nal KOR teks)
adrenal medulla (ah DREE nal meh DULL lah)
antidiuretic hormone (AN tye dye yoo RET ick)
endocrine (EHN doh krin)
epinephrine (EP ih NEFF rin)
homeostasis (HOH mee oh STAY sis)
hormone (HOR moan)
hypercholesterolemia
  (HIGH per koh LESS ter ohl EE me ah)
hyperpituitarism (HIGH per peh TOO eh tair izm)
hypopituitarism (HIGH poh peh TOO eh tair izm)
hypothalamus (HIGH poh THAL ah mus)

melatonin (MELL ah TOH nin)
norepinephrine (nor EP ih NEFF rin)
oxytocin (AHK see TOH sin)
pancreas (PAN kree ass)
parathyroid gland (PAIR ah THIGH royd)
pineal gland (PIN ee al)
pituitary (pih TOO ih tair ee)
prolactin (proh LAK tin)
testes (TESS teez)
thymus (THIGH mus)
thyroid (THIGH royd)

ORGANIZATION OF THE ENDOCRINE SYSTEM

The endocrine system has many organs that secrete a variety of chemical substances. Let's begin by looking at the basic organization of the system.

Endocrine Organs

endocrine system *(EHN doh krin)* Body system that includes the testes, ovaries, pancreas, adrenal glands, thymus, thyroid gland, parathyroid glands, pituitary gland, and pineal gland. It produces and releases hormones into the blood to direct the activities of other body organs.

hormones *(HOR moan)* Chemical messenger of the endocrine system that is released by a gland or organ and travels through the blood.

exocrine Glands and organs that excrete through a duct.

The **endocrine system** is a series of organs and ductless glands (see FIGURE 10-1 ▲) in your body that secrete chemical messengers called **hormones** *into* your bloodstream. (Note that endo means "into," and crine means "to secrete.") In contrast, **exocrine** glands and organs such as the pancreas and the sweat, salivary, and lacrimal glands produce secretions that must *exit* that particular gland through a duct.

We have already discussed some of the endocrine glands, such as the hypothalamus, pituitary, and pineal glands, because they are part of the nervous system and provide a link between the two control systems. We will visit some of the other endocrine glands later when we journey through the urinary, reproductive, and digestive systems. Many endocrine glands, like the hypothalamus and pancreas, have multiple functions.

It may seem like an overwhelming task to learn all the endocrine glands and their associated hormones. Therefore, we will begin our discussion with a concise overview to

Amazing Body Facts

Lesser-Known Endocrine-Like Glands

Did you know that many organs, such as the heart, small intestine, kidneys, stomach, and placenta, can also secrete hormones and therefore have endocrine-like functions? These and many other organs are not listed as endocrine glands because their primary jobs are focused on other tasks, like pumping blood, storing and digesting food, or nourishing an embryo. But the hormones secreted by other organs are still an important part of the body's control systems.

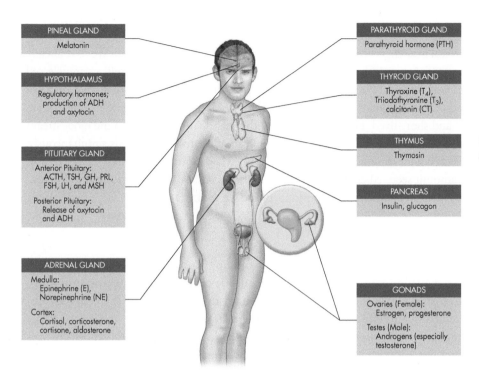

FIGURE 10-1 ▲ The endocrine glands and their hormones.

lay a foundation on which to build. As we journey through this chapter, these concepts are reinforced and expanded. For now, see **TABLE 10-1 ■**, which lists the wide variety of functions of endocrine organs.

TABLE 10-1 ■ ENDOCRINE ORGAN FUNCTIONS

ENDOCRINE ORGAN	HORMONE RELEASED	EFFECT
Hypothalamus	A variety of hormones; see Table 10-3	Controls pituitary hormone levels
Pineal	Melatonin	Believed to regulate sleep
Pituitary	A variety of hormones; see Table 10-3	Controls other endocrine organs
Thyroid	Thyroxine, triiodothyronine	Controls cellular metabolism
	Calcitonin	Decreases blood calcium
Parathyroid glands	Parathyroid hormone	Increases blood calcium
Pancreas	Insulin	Lowers blood sugar
	Glucagon	Raises blood sugar
Adrenal glands	Epinephrine, norepinephrine	Fight-or-flight response
	Adrenocorticosteroids	Many different effects
Ovaries	Estrogen, progesterone	Control sexual reproduction and secondary sexual characteristics, such as pubic hair and axillary hair
Testes	Testosterone	Control secondary sexual characteristics, such as growth of beard and other hair, deepening of voice, increase in musculature, production of sperm
Thymus	Thymosin	Immune system, causing maturation of white blood cells

Hormones

The chemical messengers released by endocrine glands are called hormones. We have already seen one type of chemical messenger: the neurotransmitter. Neurotransmitters are released by neurons at chemical synapses. They diffuse across the synapse (a very tiny space) to a cell on the other side, and they bind to that cell. They are cleaned up quickly, so their effects are localized and short-lived. Hormones, on the other hand, are released into the bloodstream and travel all over your body. Some hormones can affect millions of cells simultaneously. Their effects last for minutes or even hours or days. Many hormones are secreted constantly, and the amount secreted changes as needed. To help clarify the similarities and differences between a neurotransmitter and hormone, please see TABLE 10-2 ▪.

How Hormones Work

Like neurotransmitters, hormones work by binding to receptors on target cells. But hormones may bind not only to sites on the outside of the cell, like neurotransmitters, but also to sites inside the cell. If hormones bind to the outside of the cell, they can have several different effects, either changing cellular permeability or sending the target cell a message that changes enzyme activity inside the cell. Thus, the target cell changes what it has been doing, usually by making a new protein or turning off a protein it has been making.

TABLE 10-2 ▪ COMPARISON OF NEUROTRANSMITTERS AND HORMONES

NEUROTRANSMITTERS	HORMONES
Chemical messengers	Chemical messengers
Bind to receiving cell	Bind to receiving cell
Control cell excitation	Control cell activities
Released by neurons	Released by neurons, glands, or organs
Released at chemical synapse	Released into bloodstream
Intended target very close	Travel to distant target
Effects happen quickly (less than a second)	Effects take time (seconds or minutes)
Effects wear off quickly (few seconds)	Effects long lasting (minutes or hours)
Affect single cell	Can affect many cells

One special class of hormones, **steroids,** is particularly powerful because steroids can bind to sites inside cells. (Thyroid hormones also enter cells, but many other hormones do not.) Steroids are lipid molecules that can pass easily through the target cell membrane. These hormones can then interact directly with the cell's DNA, the genetic material, to change cell activity. These hormones are carefully regulated by the body because of their ability, even in very small amounts, to control target cells. See the section "The Adrenal Glands" for further discussion of steroid hormones and the dangers of taking steroids.

steroids One of the sex hormones and hormones of the adrenal cortex.

TEST YOUR KNOWLEDGE 10-1

Choose the best answer:

1. What chemical, when secreted into the bloodstream, controls the metabolic processes of target cells?
   a. neurotransmitter
   b. secretion
   c. hormone
   d. ligand

2. Steroid hormones are very powerful because they:
   a. are hormones
   b. are medicine
   c. interact directly with DNA
   d. are secreted outside the body

3. Which of the following is true of hormones?
   a. They last a short time.
   b. They are fast acting.
   c. They affect distant targets.
   d. They leave the body.

CONTROL OF ENDOCRINE ACTIVITY

Many endocrine glands and organs are active all the time. The amount of hormones they secrete changes as the situation demands, but unlike neurons, the cells in the endocrine glands often secrete hormones continuously. How is the activity controlled? How do these glands and organs know how much hormone to secrete?

Homeostasis and Negative Feedback

To understand how the endocrine system is controlled, we first have to revisit the concept of **homeostasis** discussed at the beginning of our journey in Chapter 1 (see FIGURE 10-2 ▲).

Recall that many of the chemical and physical characteristics of the body have a standard level, or **set point,** that is the ideal level for that particular value. Blood pressure, blood oxygen, heart rate, and blood sugar, for example, all have "normal" ranges. Your control systems, nervous and endocrine, work to keep the levels at or near ideal. There is a way for your body to measure the variable, a place where the "ideal" level is stored, and a way for the body to correct levels that are not near ideal. For example, neurons measure your body temperature. The hypothalamus stores the set point. If your temperature falls below the set point temperature, the hypothalamus causes shivering to produce additional heat. If body temperature rises above the set point, the hypothalamus causes sweating.

homeostasis *(HOH mee oh STAY sis)* State of equilibrium of the internal environment of the body, including fluid balance, acid–base balance, temperature, metabolism, and so forth, to keep all the body systems functioning optimally.

set point The normal physiologic range (as in body temperature and blood pressure) to maintain homeostasis.

negative feedback Physiological process that works against the trend. Most often brings a variable back to set point. For example, as blood pressure rises, heart rate may decrease to bring blood pressure back to "normal."

positive feedback "Vicious cycle." During positive feedback, physiological processes send body chemistry or other attributes further and further away from equilibrium (set point). The trend will continue until something breaks the cycle.

If any of the body's dozens of homeostatic values become seriously disrupted, the control systems work to bring them back to set point. This process is called **negative feedback** (see **FIGURE 10-3** ▲). Most of you are familiar with negative feedback in real life. When you pump gas, a sensor in the nozzle turns off the flow of gas when the tank is full. That is negative feedback. The gas is flowing, the tank is filling, and when the goal is reached, the gas stops flowing. In the body, negative feedback counteracts a change. As blood pressure rises, for example, your body works to bring it down to normal. If blood pressure falls, your body works to raise it back to the normal set point. Hormones work the same way. As hormone levels rise, negative feedback turns off the endocrine organ that is secreting the hormone.

The body is also capable of **positive feedback,** which increases the magnitude of a change. The flow of sodium into a neuron during depolarization is a real-life example we have already visited. The more depolarized a neuron becomes, the more sodium flows in, so it becomes more depolarized, so more flows in, and so on. Childbirth also involves an important positive feedback mechanism (see the Clinical Application in this chapter).

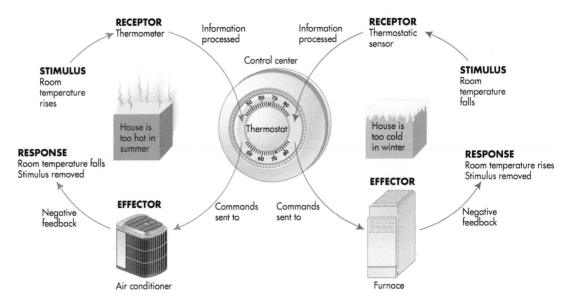

FIGURE 10-2 ▲ Homeostasis is analogous to regulation of temperature via a thermostat.

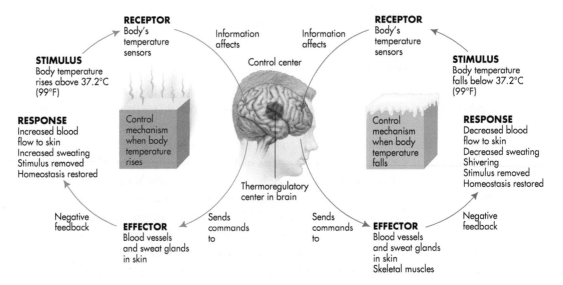

FIGURE 10-3 ▲ Homeostasis and negative feedback as related to control of body temperature.

Therefore, positive feedback is not a way to regulate your body because it increases a change away from set point. What if instead of shivering when you got cold to raise your body temperature, you got colder and colder and colder?

Sources of Control of Hormone Levels

Hormone levels can be controlled by the nervous system (**neural control**), by other hormones (**hormonal control**), or by body fluids such as the blood (**humoral control**).

neural control The nervous system control of hormone levels.

hormonal control Hormone levels controlled by other hormones.

humoral control Hormone levels controlled by body fluids such as blood.

Neural Control

Some hormones are directly controlled by the nervous system. For example, the adrenal glands receive signals from the sympathetic nervous system. When the sympathetic nervous system is active (remember the near-wreck), it sends signals to the adrenal glands to release epinephrine and norepinephrine as hormones, prolonging the effects of sympathetic activity (see FIGURE 10-4 ▲).

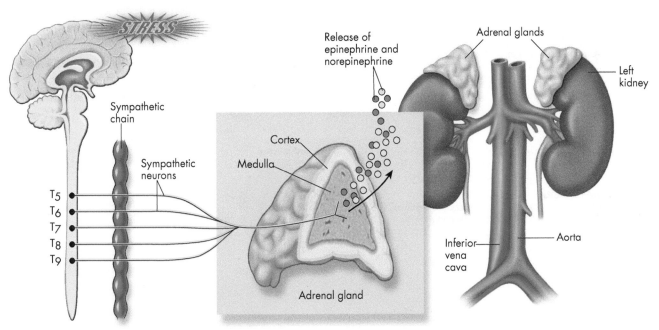

FIGURE 10-4 ▲ Sympathetic control of adrenal gland.

Hormonal Control

Other hormones are part of a hierarchy of hormonal control in which one gland is controlled by the release of hormones from another gland higher in the chain, which is controlled by another gland's release of hormones yet higher in the chain. Orders are sent from one organ to another. This is very similar to a relay race at a track meet where the baton is smoothly handed from one runner to the next to send the baton to the finish line. Negative feedback controls the flow of orders via hormones from one part of the "chain of command" to the other. For example, the hypothalamus has control over the pituitary, which has control over the adrenal gland, which secretes the hormone cortisol. Increased cortisol secretion is one way that the body copes with stress, and as cortisol levels rise in the blood, further release of hormones at the hypothalamus is depressed. This is an example of negative feedback. Please see FIGURE 10-5 ▲.

humoral control Hormone levels controlled by body fluids such as blood.

Humoral Control

Still other endocrine organs or glands can directly monitor the body's internal environment by monitoring the body fluids, such as the blood, and respond accordingly. *Humoral* pertains to body fluids or substances, and therefore control through body fluids is called **humoral control**. For example, the pancreas secretes insulin in response to rising blood sugar, as shown in FIGURE 10-6 ▲. In diabetics, like Maria, this response is impaired due to destruction of the pancreas by the immune system.

Clinical Application

CHILDBIRTH AND POSITIVE FEEDBACK

Positive feedback is often harmful if the cycle cannot be broken, but sometimes positive feedback is necessary for a process to run to completion. A good example of necessary positive feedback is the continued contraction of the uterus during childbirth. When a baby is ready to be born, a signal tells the hypothalamus to release the hormone **oxytocin** from the posterior pituitary. Oxytocin increases the intensity of uterine contractions. As the uterus contracts, the pressure inside the uterus caused by the baby moving down the birth canal increases the signal to the hypothalamus: More oxytocin is released, and the uterus contracts harder. As pressure gets higher inside the uterus, the hypothalamus is signaled to release more oxytocin, and the uterus contracts even harder. This cycle of ever-increasing uterine contractions due to ever-increasing release of oxytocin from the hypothalamus continues until the pressure inside the uterus decreases—that is, when the baby is born.

oxytocin *(AWK see TOH sin)* Hormone secreted by the posterior pituitary gland. It stimulates the uterus to contract and begin labor. It stimulates the "let-down reflex" to get milk flowing for breastfeeding.

FIGURE 10-5 ▲ Hormonal control of adrenal gland. CRH = corticotropin releasing hormone; ACTH = adrenocorticotropic hormone.

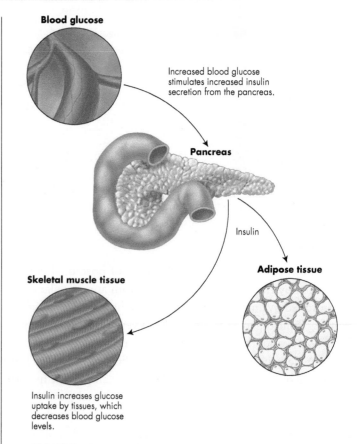

FIGURE 10-6 ▲ Humoral control of blood sugar levels.

TEST YOUR KNOWLEDGE 10-2

Choose the best answer:

1. Which of the following is the least common way that hormones are regulated?
   a. negative feedback
   b. chain of command
   c. positive feedback
   d. direct control by nervous system

2. The "ideal" value for a body characteristic is called the:
   a. set point
   b. average
   c. goal
   d. feedback point

3. _____ feedback enhances a change in body chemistry.
   a. Negative
   b. Positive
   c. Regular
   d. Cyclic

THE MAJOR ENDOCRINE ORGANS

The endocrine system has several organs, and each has specific tasks within the body. The messages to carry out these tasks are related to the hormones they release.

The Hypothalamus

We already visited the **hypothalamus** when we stopped at the central nervous system. Located in the diencephalon of the brain, this gland is an important link between the two control systems: nervous and endocrine (**FIGURE 10-7** ▲). (Remember from Chapter 9, the diencephalon is situated between the brainstem and cerebrum and acts as an important regulator of many body processes.) The hypothalamus controls much of the body's physiology, including hunger, thirst, fluid balance, and body temperature, to name only a few of its functions. The hypothalamus is also, in part, the "commander-in-chief" of the endocrine system because it controls the pituitary gland and therefore most of the other glands in the endocrine system. **TABLE 10-3** ■ lists the hypothalamic and pituitary hormones.

hypothalamus *(HGH poh THAL ah mus)* Endocrine gland located in the brain just below the thalamus. It produces (but does not secrete) antidiuretic hormone (ADH) and oxytocin. The hypothalamus is in the center of the brain and coordinates the activities of the pons and medulla oblongata. It also controls heart rate, blood pressure, respiratory rate, body temperature, sensations of hunger and thirst, and the circadian rhythm. It also produces hormones as part of the endocrine system. In addition, the hypothalamus helps control emotions (pleasure, excitement, fear, anger, sexual arousal) and bodily responses to emotions; regulates the sex drive; contains the feeding and satiety centers; and functions as part of the "fight-or-flight" response of the sympathetic nervous system.

prolactin *(proh LAK tinn)* Hormone secreted by the anterior pituitary gland. It stimulates milk glands of the breasts to develop during puberty and to produce milk during pregnancy.

LEARNING HINT

Hormone Names

Most hormones are named according to where they are secreted or what they do. If you learn the meanings of their names, you can usually tell something about the hormone. For example, growth hormone stimulates cells to grow. **Prolactin** increases milk production. (Note that *pro* means "for," and lactin means "milk.") Even a complicated hormone name like adrenocorticotropic hormone can be picked apart fairly easily. *Adreno* refers to the adrenal gland, and *cortico* refers to the cortex. Therefore, adrenocorticotropic hormone is a hormone that changes the activity (in this case increases) of the adrenal cortex. Also keep in mind that most hormones are known by their abbreviations, for obvious reasons. Adrenocorticotropic hormone, for example, is abbreviated ACTH, which is much easier to say and write.

The Pituitary

pituitary *(pih TOO ih tair ee)*
Endocrine gland in the brain that is connected by a stalk of tissue to the hypothalamus. Also known as the hypophysis. It is known as the master gland of the body. It consists of the anterior and the posterior pituitary gland.

The **pituitary,** also a part of the diencephalon, is a small gland, about the size of a grape, located at the base of the brain. The pituitary is commonly known as the "master gland," indicating its important role in control of other endocrine glands. However, that name is misleading because the pituitary gland rarely acts on its own. The pituitary acts only under orders from the hypothalamus. If the hypothalamus is the "commander-in-chief," the pituitary is a high-ranking soldier who carries out the orders.

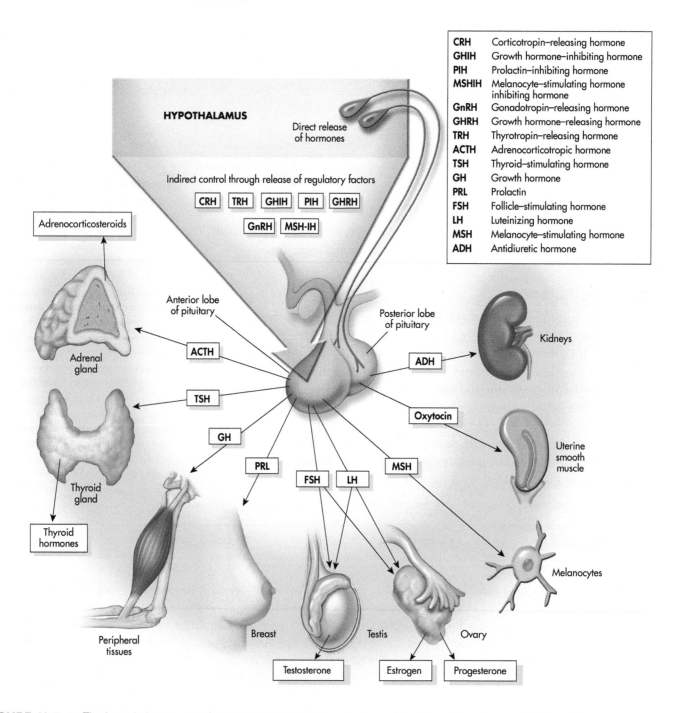

CRH	Corticotropin–releasing hormone
GHIH	Growth hormone–inhibiting hormone
PIH	Prolactin–inhibiting hormone
MSHIH	Melanocyte–stimulating hormone inhibiting hormone
GnRH	Gonadotropin–releasing hormone
GHRH	Growth hormone–releasing hormone
TRH	Thyrotropin–releasing hormone
ACTH	Adrenocorticotropic hormone
TSH	Thyroid–stimulating hormone
GH	Growth hormone
PRL	Prolactin
FSH	Follicle–stimulating hormone
LH	Luteinizing hormone
MSH	Melanocyte–stimulating hormone
ADH	Antidiuretic hormone

FIGURE 10-7 ▲ The hypothalamus, anterior and posterior pituitary glands, and their targets and associated hormones.

TABLE 10-3 ■ SELECTED HYPOTHALAMIC AND PITUITARY HORMONES

HORMONE	FUNCTION
Hypothalamus	
Growth hormone–releasing hormone (GHRH)	Increases the release of growth hormone from the pituitary gland
Growth hormone–inhibiting hormone (GHIH)	Decreases the release of growth hormone from the pituitary gland
Corticotropin-releasing hormone (CRH)	Increases the release of adrenocorticotropic hormone from the pituitary gland
Gonadotropin-releasing hormone (GRH)	Increases the release of luteinizing hormone and follicle-stimulating hormone from the pituitary gland
Thyrotropin-releasing hormone (TRH)	Increases the release of thyroid-stimulating hormone from pituitary gland
Posterior Pituitary	
Antidiuretic hormone (ADH), also known as vasopressin	Dilutes blood and increases fluid volume by increasing water reabsorption in the kidney
Oxytocin	Increases uterine contractions
Anterior Pituitary	
Growth hormone (GH)	Increases tissue growth
Thyroid-stimulating hormone (TSH)	Increases secretion of thyroid hormones
Adrenocorticotropic hormone (ACTH)	Increases steroid secretion from adrenal gland
Prolactin	Increases milk production
Luteinizing hormone (LH)	Stimulates ovaries and testes for ovulation and sperm production
Follicle-stimulating hormone (FSH)	Stimulates estrogen secretion and sperm production

The Posterior Pituitary (or Neurohypophysis)

The pituitary is split into two segments: the **posterior pituitary** and the **anterior pituitary**. The posterior pituitary is an extension of the hypothalamus. Hypothalamic neurons, specialized to secrete hormones instead of neurotransmitters, extend their axons through a stalk to the posterior pituitary. Using the posterior pituitary as a sort of launch pad, these neurons secrete two hormones: **antidiuretic hormone** (**ADH**; also called vasopressin) and **oxytocin**. Both of these hormones are secreted from the posterior pituitary, but they are made by the hypothalamus.

ADH does exactly what its name suggests: It is an antidiuretic. A diuretic is a chemical that increases urination, so an antidiuretic *decreases* urination. The effect of ADH, then, is to decrease fluid lost due to urination, increasing body fluid volume. ADH is secreted when the hypothalamus senses decreased blood volume or increased blood osmolarity (more solids suspended in blood). ADH circulates through the bloodstream and targets the kidneys specifically, causing them to absorb more water. It is very important in long-term control of blood pressure, especially during dehydration. (For more information on ADH, see Chapter 16, "The Urinary System.")

posterior pituitary *(poh STEER ee er pih TOO ih tair ee)* An extension of the hypothalamus that secretes oxytocin and ADH.

anterior pituitary *(an TEER ee or pih TOO eh TAIR ee)* A gland controlled by the hypothalamus but also secretes a number of hormones.

antidiuretic hormone (ADH) *(AN tye dye yoo RET ik)* Hormone secreted by the posterior pituitary gland. It stimulates the kidneys to move water back into the blood to increase the volume of blood.

oxytocin *(AWK see TOH sin)* Hormone secreted by the posterior pituitary gland. It stimulates the uterus to contract and begin labor. It stimulates the "let-down reflex" to get milk flowing for breastfeeding.

anterior pituitary *(an TEER ee or pih TOO eh TAIR ee)* A gland controlled by the hypothalamus but also secretes a number of hormones.

diabetes insipidus (DI) A condition with the primary symptoms of frequent urination and thirst caused either by inadequate amounts of circulating vasopressin (antidiuretic hormone) in the body (hypothalamic DI) or by failure of the kidney to respond to antidiuretic hormone (nephrogenic DI).

syndrome of inappropriate antidiuretic hormone (SIADH) A condition characterized by severe hyponatremia (low blood sodium), usually due to overproduction of ADH regardless of blood osmolarity.

As we discussed in the section on positive feedback, the second hypothalamic hormone released from the posterior pituitary is oxytocin. Oxytocin is important in maintaining uterine contractions during labor in women and is involved in milk ejection in nursing mothers. Oxytocin's function in males is unknown.

The Anterior Pituitary (or Adenohypophysis)

The **anterior pituitary** is also controlled by the hypothalamus, but is an endocrine gland in its own right. The anterior pituitary makes and secretes a number of hormones, under hormonal control by the hypothalamus, that control other endocrine glands. (Growth hormone and prolactin are exceptions to this rule.) Refer back to Table 10-3 and Figure 10-7 for a list of hypothalamic and pituitary hormones. We discussed this relationship previously when we talked about hormonal control. The hypothalamus secretes a hormone that controls hormone secretion by the anterior pituitary, which usually controls the secretion of hormones by another endocrine gland. The hormone levels are controlled by negative feedback to both the pituitary and the hypothalamus.

Pathology Connection

POSTERIOR PITUITARY AND ANTIDIURETIC HORMONE

Drinking too much alcohol can lead to several unpleasant consequences, not the least of which is the development of a hangover. The symptoms of a hangover are due to many side effects from alcohol consumption, but the most important may be that alcohol turns off ADH. The more alcohol you drink, the less ADH you secrete, and the more dehydrated you become. That makes you thirsty, so you drink some more alcohol, and you secrete even less ADH and become even more dehydrated. The more alcohol you drink, the more you urinate and the more dehydrated you are. This is part of the reason why consuming too much alcohol on Friday night can make you miserable on Saturday morning.

Diabetes Insipidus

Diabetes Insipidus (DI) is a condition characterized by the production of large amounts of very dilute urine. It is typically caused by underproduction of ADH due to noncancerous pituitary tumors. Generally, excessive urination is the only symptom of DI because thirst compensates for fluid loss. In severe cases, DI can be treated by taking medications which function like ADH.

Syndrome of Inappropriate Antidiuretic Hormone Secretion

Syndrome of inappropriate antidiuretic hormone (SIADH) is a condition characterized by severe hyponatremia (low blood sodium), usually due to overproduction of ADH regardless of blood osmolarity. It leads to fluid retention and very dilute plasma. The dilution of plasma leads to dangerously low sodium levels in the blood. Causes of SIADH include pulmonary disease, cancer, medications, and central nervous system disorders. One of the most common causes of SIADH is traumatic brain injury. Symptoms of SIADH include confusion, altered consciousness, fatigue, nausea, muscle cramps, and loss of appetite. Untreated hyponatremia can lead to brain herniation and coma and can be fatal. Given that the symptoms of SIADH overlap with those of TBI it is often difficult to diagnose SIADH. Also, since this is a disorder caused by too much water retention, giving IV fluids may exacerbate the problem. Current research is aimed at finding better ways to diagnose SIADH especially in brain injured patients.

Pathology Connection

ANTERIOR PITUITARY

Hypopituitarism

Hypopituitarism is a decrease in pituitary function caused by tumors, surgery, radiation, or head injury. Hypopituitarism is characterized by loss of any or all of the anterior pituitary hormones including ACTH, GH, LH, and TSH, causing a variety of symptoms. LH and GH are usually the most severely affected.

Hypopituitarism is difficult to diagnose and treat because symptoms are often vague or subtle. In one study, one quarter of patients with traumatic brain injuries had symptoms of hypopituitarism that were untreated one year after injury, even though they had recovered enough to be released from rehabilitation.

If hypopituitarism is caused by a pituitary tumor, the tumor may be removed. No matter the cause, hormone replacement is the treatment of choice. Effective replacement of pituitary hormones is difficult, and it often takes months to adjust the medication to appropriate therapeutic levels.

Hyperpituitarism

Hyperpituitarism, overproduction of pituitary hormones, is usually cased by benign pituitary tumors. Symptoms include reproductive abnormalities, acromegaly, cardiac dysfunction, sleep apnea, Cushing's syndrome (see section on the adrenal gland for detailed discussion), and hyperthyroidism.

Like many hormonal disorders, hyperpituitarism is difficult to diagnose due to the vagueness of symptoms. Imaging studies and hormone levels are generally used. Hyperpituitarism is treated by decreasing the size of the tumor or removing it.

Stature Disorders

Stature disorders are those disorders that result in well-below-average height (called **dwarfism**) or well-above-normal height (called **giantism** or **gigantism**). Some of these disorders are caused by abnormalities in skeletal development or nutritional deficiencies. However, growth hormone (GH) problems are often implicated. If GH secretion is insufficient during childhood, children do not grow to "standard" height. This type of dwarfism results in stunted adult height. However, if GH deficiency is diagnosed before closure of the growth zones of the long bones, it can be treated with GH injections. Children treated with GH injection may attain full height.

On the other end of the spectrum are those who secrete too much GH. If the oversecretion happens during childhood, people get extremely tall. (The current record in the Guinness Book of World Records is more than 8 feet tall.) Gigantism causes many health problems. The body gets so big that it cannot support itself. Most cases are caused by non-cancerous pituitary tumors. Treatment is often difficult. Surgery is the treatment of choice for this disorder, but must often be supplemented by radiation and drug therapies.

Oversecretion of GH in adults, after bones have stopped growing, causes **acromegaly**, a painful, often crippling disorder characterized by excess growth of body tissue, especially those of the face and extremities. Bones become deformed, and organs may malfunction due to excess growth. Like gigantism, acromegaly is usually caused by noncancerous pituitary tumors. Treatment for acromegaly is the same as for gigantism. Acromegaly is one of the potential side effects of using growth hormone for performance enhancement.

hypopituitarism The underproduction of thyroid hormones, resulting in low metabolism, excessive weight gain, lethargy, and depression

dwarfism A condition of being abnormally undersized. May be due to an endocrine condition, heredity, nutritional deficiency, diseases of the skeleton, or others.

gigantism *(jy GAN tizm)* An excessive development of a body or body part often as a result of an abnormal hormone level.

acromegaly *(ACK row MEG ah lee)* A hormonal condition of gradual coarsening and enlargement of bones and facial features.

TEST YOUR KNOWLEDGE 10-3

Choose the best answer:

1. Oxytocin:
   a. is secreted by the anterior pituitary
   b. decreases uterine contractions
   c. is secreted from the posterior pituitary
   d. is a way to get more oxygen to your toes

2. The _____ is controlled by hormones from the hypothalamus, whereas the _____ actually secretes hypothalamic hormones.
   a. posterior pituitary; posterior pituitary
   b. anterior pituitary; anterior pituitary
   c. anterior pituitary; posterior pituitary
   d. posterior pituitary; anterior pituitary

3. This gland, under orders from the hypothalamus, releases hormones that control other endocrine glands:
   a. adrenal gland
   b. anterior pituitary
   c. thyroid gland
   d. pancreas

4. Which gland does ACTH control?
   a. adrenal gland
   b. anterior pituitary
   c. thyroid gland
   d. pancreas

5. SIADH is caused by excess secretion of:
   a. cholesterol
   b. epinephrine
   c. growth hormone
   d. antidiuretic hormone

6. Alcohol inhibits secretion of ADH. This causes:
   a. headache
   b. lots of dilute urine
   c. decreased urination
   d. stupidity

The Thyroid Gland

thyroid *(THIGH royd)* Endocrine gland in the neck that produces and secretes the hormones T3, T4, and calcitonin. Its two lobes and narrow connecting bridge (isthmus) give it a shieldlike shape.

thyroxine Hormone T4 secreted by the thyroid gland.

triiodothyronine *(TRY eye oh doh THYE roh nine)* Hormone T3 secreted by the thyroid gland.

The **thyroid** gland, located in the anterior portion of your neck on either side of the larynx over the trachea, is a butterfly-shaped (H-shaped) organ. The thyroid gland is responsible for secreting the hormones **thyroxine** (T_4) and **triiodothyronine** (T_3), under orders from the pituitary gland (see **FIGURE 10-8** ▲). Thyroxine is controlled by secretion of TSH. The designations T_4 and T_3 refer to the number of iodine atoms in the hormone. The importance of these hormones is so great that in many countries, table salt contains added iodine to ensure that people get enough iodine in their diets to make adequate amounts of thyroid hormones.

T_4 and T_3 control cell metabolism and growth. Maintenance of these hormone levels takes place in a negative feedback loop. Control of T_4 and T_3 is an example of hormonal control. When blood levels of T_4 or T_3 drop, neurons in the hypothalamus sense the drop and produce thyrotropin-releasing hormone, or TRH. TRH stimulates the pituitary gland to produce TSH, or thyroid-stimulating hormone. TSH binds to cells on the thyroid gland and stimulates the thyroid to produce T_4 and T_3. Neurons in the hypothalamus sense when T_4 and T_3 blood levels are back to normal, and they produce less TRH. This decreases the secretion of TSH in the pituitary gland. With less TSH to trigger the thyroid gland, the production of T_4 and T_3 decreases. When levels of thyroid hormone get too low, the cycle starts again.

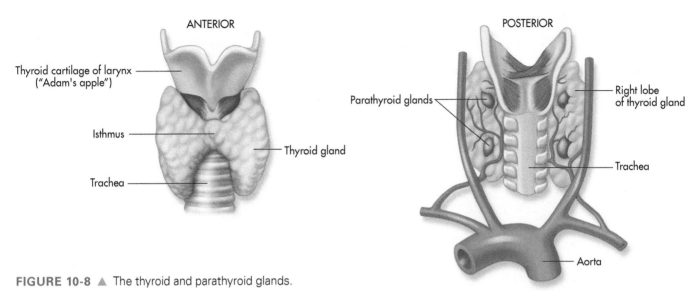

ANTERIOR

Thyroid cartilage of larynx
("Adam's apple")

Isthmus

Trachea

Thyroid gland

POSTERIOR

Parathyroid glands

Right lobe
of thyroid gland

Trachea

Aorta

FIGURE 10-8 ▲ The thyroid and parathyroid glands.

T_4 and T_3 are generally referred to as "thyroid hormones" and are of great clinical importance. Overproduction (hyperthyroidism) or underproduction (hypothyroidism) can cause a variety of clinical symptoms because the level of these hormones is essential in controlling growth and metabolism of body tissues, particularly in the nervous system.

The thyroid gland also secretes a third hormone, **calcitonin**, which decreases blood calcium by stimulating bone-building cells. This prevents hypercalcemia (high blood calcium levels), which can cause conditions such as arrhythmia, kidney stones, and osteoporosis.

The Thymus Gland

The **thymus gland** is both an endocrine gland and a lymphatic organ. It is located in the upper thorax behind the sternum and plays an important function in the immune system. It produces a hormone called **thymosin,** which helps with the maturation of white blood cells to fight infections. It begins to disappear during puberty. This gland is further discussed in Chapter 14, "The Lymphatic and Immune System."

The Pineal Gland

The tiny **pineal gland** is found in the brain, and its full function still remains unknown. However, it has been shown to produce the hormone **melatonin,** which rises and falls during the waking and sleeping hours. It is believed this hormone is what triggers our sleep by peaking at night and causing drowsiness.

The Pancreas

The **pancreas** is an accessory organ of the digestive system. It is located in the upper abdomen, near the stomach. Part of the pancreas acts as an exocrine organ. This part produces and secretes digestive enzymes that help to break down starches, fats, and proteins, and this will be further discussed in Chapter 15 on the gastrointestinal system. The other part of the pancreas acts as an endocrine organ. This part produces hormones that regulate blood sugar.

calcitonin A hormone produced by the human thyroid gland that is important for maintaining a dense, strong bone matrix and regulating the blood calcium level.

thymus gland *(THIGH mus)* Lymphoid organ in the thoracic cavity. As an endocrine gland, it releases hormones known as thymosins. Thymosin causes lymphoblasts in the thymus to mature into T lymphocytes.

thymosin *(thigh MOH sin)* Hormone secreted by the thymus gland that helps white blood cells mature during childhood.

pineal gland *(PIN ee al)* Endocrine gland in the brain that lies posterior to the pituitary gland. It secretes the hormone melatonin.

melatonin *(MELL ah TOH ninn)* Hormone secreted by the pineal body. It maintains the 24-hour wake–sleep cycle known as the circadian rhythm.

pancreas *(PAN kree ass)* A digestive and endocrine organ located in the abdominal cavity that produces digestive enzymes (amylase, lipase, protease, peptidase) and releases them into the duodenum. It also contains the islets of Langerhans (alpha, beta, and delta cells) that produce and secrete the hormones glucagon, insulin, and somatostatin.

hypothyroidism
The underproduction of thyroid hormones, resulting in low metabolism, excessive weight gain, lethargy, and depression.

hypercholesterolemia
(HIGH per koh LESS tur ul EE me ah) High levels of cholesterol in the blood.

Hashimoto's thyroiditis
(HAH shee MOH tohs THIGH roy DYE tiss) An autoimmune disease involving inflammation, then destruction and fibrosis of the thyroid gland, which leads to hypothyroidism.

congenital hypothyroidism
Hypothyroidism present at birth.

hyperthyroidism
The overproduction of thyroid hormones, often resulting in increased metabolic rate, weight loss, and nervous irritability.

Graves' disease
A distinct form of hyperthyroidism that includes an enlarged thyroid gland and various ocular findings such as stare and lid lag.

thyroid storm A rare but potentially life-threatening result of untreated hyperthyroidism that can cause cardiac arrhythmias, congestive heart failure, and shock.

Pathology Connection

THE THYROID GLAND

Hypothyroidism

Hypothyroidism occurs when too little thyroid hormone is produced. It can be caused by decreased production of hypothalamic (TRH), pituitary (TSH), or thyroid (T_4 or T_3) hormones. Symptoms of hypothyroidism include fatigue, feeling cold, brittle or thinning hair, constipation, brittle nails, bradycardia, leg cramps, muscle pain, weight gain, hyperlipidemia, **hypercholesterolemia**, forgetfulness, depression, sexual dysfunction, and dry, itchy skin.

Hashimoto's thyroiditis is the most common cause of hypothyroidism. It is caused by autoimmune attack on the thyroid gland. For unknown reasons, the immune system begins to attack the cells in the thyroid, causing inflammation and damage to the gland. This damage eventually leads to decreased production of thyroid hormones—hypothyroidism. In addition, the thyroid may swell, causing pain and difficulty swallowing. Hashimoto's thyroiditis, like many autoimmune disorders, is most common in women between 30 and 50 years old.

Hashimoto's thyroiditis can be distinguished from other kinds of thyroid disorders by blood tests. The disease is characterized by high TSH levels and low T_4 levels. It can be treated by daily doses of synthetic T_4.

Congenital hypothyroidism is hypothyroidism present at birth, occurring in about 1 in 4,000 live births. Congenital hypothyroidism is caused by anatomical thyroid abnormalities (no thyroid present in some cases), thyroid metabolism errors, or iodine deficiency. Untreated congenital hypothyroidism causes severe intellectual disabilities and short stature. It is the most common preventable cause of mental retardation. Newborn screening for congenital hypothyroidism is standard in developed countries. If treated early most babies with congenital hypothyroidism have the potential to grow up without learning problems.

Hyperthyroidism

Hyperthyroidism is the overproduction of thyroid hormone. Symptoms of hyperthyroidism include feeling hot, muscle tremors, sweating, muscle weakness, tachycardia, cardiac arrhythmia, loose bowels, infertility, nervousness, irritability, and enlarged, bulging eyes. Patients with hyperthyroidism are often hypersensitive to the effects of the sympathetic hormones norepinephrine and epinephrine. People with hyperthyroidism eat large quantities of food, but continue to lose weight. See FIGURE 10-9 ▲, which contrasts signs and symptoms of hypothyroidism and hyperthyroidism.

Graves' disease, the most common cause of hyperthyroidism, is also an autoimmune disorder. In this case, the immune system binds to TSH receptors, stimulating the thyroid to produce excess thyroid hormone. Like Hashimoto's thyroiditis, Graves' disease is more common in women of childbearing age. Acute Graves' disease can often result in a potentially fatal form of hyperthyroidism called a **thyroid storm.**

Diagnosis of Graves' disease is made by blood tests (low TSH levels with high T_4 levels) and increased levels of radioactive iodine uptake by the thyroid. Patients may also have a condition called exophthalmos, in which swelling of tissue behind the eyes makes the eyeballs bulge, giving the appearance of "bug eyes." There are three treatment options for Graves' disease: anti-thyroid medications to decrease thyroid activity or beta-blockers to decrease the activity of epinephrine and norepinephrine, treatment with radioactive iodine to kill thyroid cells, and removal of the

Pathology Connection (continued)

thyroid gland. If the thyroid gland is removed or destroyed, daily doses of thyroid hormones are required.

Goiter is the enlargement of the thyroid and can be the result of either hypothyroidism or hyperthyroidism. A goiter can interfere with swallowing or breathing and can produce tightness in the throat. The swelling itself may not be painful. Medications or radioactive iodine treatment may shrink a goiter. A goiter may also be removed surgically. A simple goiter is caused by lack of dietary intake of iodine. See FIGURE 10-10 ▲ for examples of goiter and Graves' disease.

Parathyroid Glands

The thyroid gland has two small pairs of glands embedded in its posterior surface. These glands are called the **parathyroid glands,** and they produce **parathyroid hormone (PTH),** which regulates the levels of calcium in the bloodstream. There are four parathyroid glands, and each is the size of a grain of rice. If calcium levels get too low, the parathyroid glands are stimulated to release PTH, which stimulates bone-dissolving cells and thereby releases needed calcium in the bloodstream. Again, see Figure 10-8.

Damage to the parathyroid glands (during surgery or, in rare instances, during radioactive iodine treatment for hyperthyroidism) can reduce the production of parathyroid hormone. Hypoparathyroidism, or insufficient production of parathyroid hormone, can lead to a drop in calcium levels in the blood. Low blood calcium can interfere with nerve function and cause the condition called **tetany.** Patients with tetany may experience muscle spasms, cramps, uncontrolled twitching, or seizures. Spasms of respiratory muscles, including those in the larynx, can cut off air supply and cause death. Tetany can be treated with calcium and vitamin D supplements. Parathyroid hormone treatment may also be used. If the tetany is severe, the patient may be treated with intravenous calcium to restore blood calcium levels.

goiter *(GOY ter)* Enlargement of the thyroid gland.

parathyroid glands *(PAIR ah THIGH royd)* Endocrine glands, four of them, on the posterior lobes of the thyroid gland. They produce and secrete parathyroid hormone.

parathyroid hormone (PTH) Hormone secreted by the parathyroid glands that regulates levels of calcium in the bloodstream.

tetany Rigid paralysis.

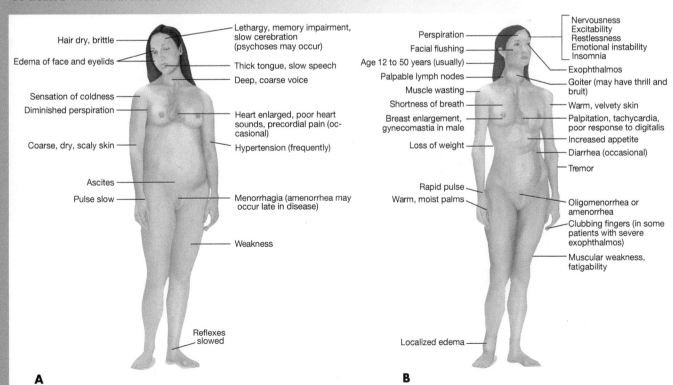

FIGURE 10-9 ▲ A comparison of the signs and symptoms of **A.** hypothyroidism and **B.** hyperthyroidism.

(continued)

Pathology Connection (continued)

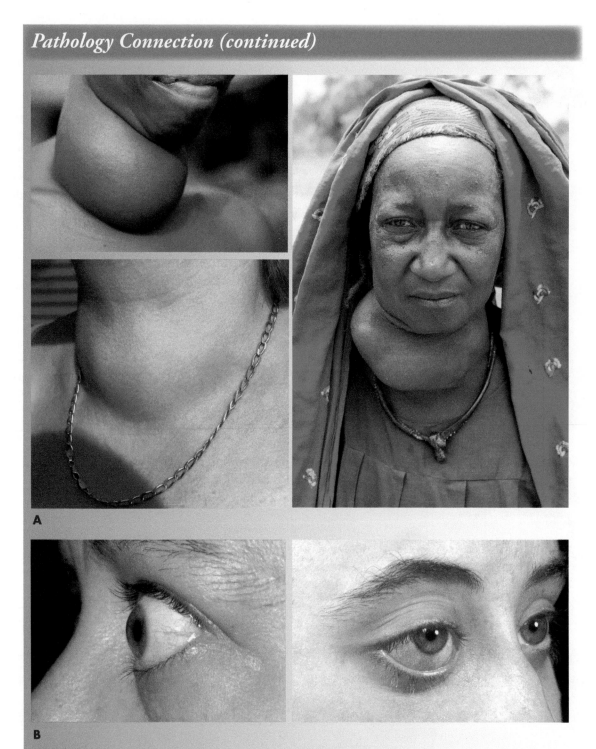

FIGURE 10-10 △ **A.** Examples of various goiters. (Sources: Carmazine Scott/Getty Images; Wellcome Image Library/Custom Medical Stock; Marka/Custom Medical Stock) **B.** Ocular changes in Grave's disease. (Sources: Dr. P. Marazzi/Photo Researchers/Science; Wellcome Image Library/Custom Medical Stock)

The pancreas is largely responsible for maintaining blood sugar (glucose) levels at or near a set point. The normal clinical range for blood glucose levels is 70 to 105 mg/dL (milligrams per deciliter). The pancreas can measure blood sugar, and if the blood glucose is high or low, the pancreas releases a hormone to correct the level. Control of blood sugar by the pancreas is perhaps the best example of humoral control of hormone levels.

To understand the importance of the pancreas, let's go back in your journey to the chapter on cells. Why does it matter how much glucose is in your blood? Why devote much of an organ, and a pretty big one at that, to controlling blood sugar? There are two reasons why blood glucose is important. Too much glucose floating around in your blood causes many problems with the fluid balance of your cells. Recall that if the concentration of the fluid outside a cell is high in solutes, the cell will lose water to its surroundings. If the solute concentration is low outside the cell, the cell will fill with water. Obviously, that's a serious problem. It does not matter if the solids are salts or glucose, the result is the same. Blood glucose must therefore be maintained at a certain level for cells to neither gain nor lose water. Why else is glucose important? Glucose is vital for cellular respiration. Cellular respiration is needed to get energy, by making adenosine triphosphate (ATP). Remember from Chapter 3 that the chief way most cells make ATP, the energy that powers cells, is by breaking down glucose during cellular respiration. Therefore, cells need to have enough glucose that they can make sufficient ATP to carry out their daily activities.

The pancreas makes two hormones that control blood glucose: **insulin**, which most of you have heard of before, and **glucagon**. These hormones are produced by two specialized groups of cells in pancreatic tissue called the **islets of Langerhans**. Beta cells in the islets secrete insulin, whereas alpha cells secrete glucagon. Insulin, the hormone that is missing or ineffective in diabetes mellitus (diabetes), removes glucose from the blood by directing the liver to store excess glucose and by helping glucose to get inside the cells (facilitated diffusion) so it can be used to make ATP. (Remember that glucose, a carbohydrate, is water soluble, so it cannot get into cells by itself.) When would insulin be secreted by the pancreas: when blood glucose is high or when blood glucose is low? Because insulin removes glucose from the blood, it *lowers* blood sugar, so it is released when blood sugar is high (hyperglycemia), like right after a meal.

Glucagon does the opposite of insulin. Glucagon puts glucose into the bloodstream mainly by directing the liver to release glucose that was stored in the form of **glycogen**. Glucagon is released typically several hours after a meal to prevent blood glucose from dropping too low (hypoglycemia). These two hormones control blood glucose very tightly in healthy humans (see FIGURE 10-11 ▲). Other hormones, like the adrenal hormone cortisol, also aid in the control of blood sugar.

The Adrenal Glands

The **adrenal** glands are a pair of small glands that sit on top of your kidneys like baseball hats. The adrenal glands are split into two regions: the **adrenal cortex**, an outer layer, and the **adrenal medulla**, the middle of the gland. (Note that it is best to be specific when talking about the *adrenal* cortex because your cerebrum has a cortex too.)

The Adrenal Medulla

The adrenal medulla releases two hormones: **epinephrine** (also known as **adrenaline**) and **norepinephrine**. These hormones increase the duration of the effects of your sympathetic nervous system. Remember your friend's snarling dog? Cells of the adrenal medulla receive

insulin Hormone secreted by the pancreas that allows for glucose to be utilized for cellular respiration.

glucagon *(GLOO kah gawn)* Hormone secreted by the pancreas that increases the blood glucose by stimulating the liver to change stored glycogen to glucose.

islets of Langerhans *(EYE let, LAN gur hanz)* Specialized group of cells in pancreatic tissue that produce insulin and glucagon.

glycogen *(GLIE coh jin)* The form that glucose (sugar) takes when it is stored in the liver and skeletal muscles.

adrenal *(ad REE nal)* Referring to the adrenal gland.

adrenal cortex *(ad REE nal KOR teks)* Outermost part of the adrenal gland. It produces and secretes three groups of hormones: mineralocorticoids (aldosterone), glucocorticoids (cortisol), and some androgens (male hormones).

adrenal medulla *(ad REE nal meh DULL lah)* Innermost part of the adrenal gland. It produces and secretes the hormones epinephrine and norepinephrine.

epinephrine *(EP ih NEFF rinn)* Hormone secreted by the adrenal medulla in response to stimulation by nerves of the sympathetic nervous system.

adrenaline *(ah DREN ah lin)* Also known as epinephrine, secreted by the adrenal medulla.

norepinephrine *(NOR ep ih NEFF rinn)* Hormone secreted by the adrenal medulla in response to stimulation by nerves of the sympathetic nervous system.

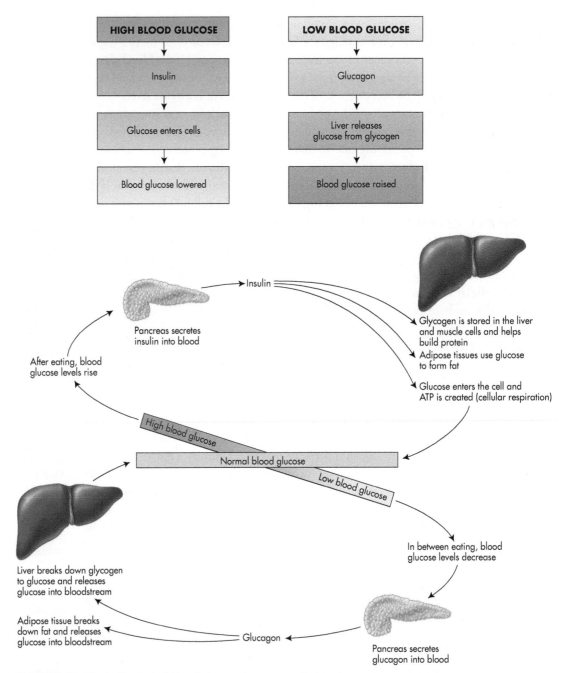

FIGURE 10-11 ▲ Control of blood glucose by pancreatic hormones.

adrenal cortex *(ad REE nal KOR teks)* Outermost part of the adrenal gland. It produces and secretes three groups of hormones: mineralocorticoids (aldosterone), glucocorticoids (cortisol), and some androgens (male hormones).

adrenocorticosteroids *(ad REE noh KORE tih koh STEER oydz)* Collective term for numerous hormones secreted by the adrenal cortex.

the neurotransmitter norepinephrine from the sympathetic nervous system. (It is both a hormone and a neurotransmitter, depending on where it is released.) The neurotransmitter triggers the release of norepinephrine and epinephrine into the bloodstream, increasing heart rate, blood pressure, and respiration rate and giving you sweaty palms and dry mouth. Again, the effects of the hormones last much longer than effects of the neurotransmitter.

The Adrenal Cortex

The **adrenal cortex** makes dozens of steroid hormones known collectively as **adrenocorticosteroids** (steroids in the adrenal cortex). The adrenal cortex releases steroid hormones under the direction of the anterior pituitary. Many of these steroid hormones are so important that a decrease in their production could be fatal relatively quickly. Some of these hormones, the **mineralocorticoids,** regulate electrolyte and fluid balance. The **glucocorticoids** regulate blood sugar. Others are in part responsible for regulation of reproduction and secondary sexual characteristics, and still others control cell metabolism, growth, and immune system function.

mineralocorticoids *(MIN er al CORE teh koydz)* Hormones secreted by the adrenal cortex that regulate electrolytes, salts, and fluid balance.

glucocorticoids *(GLOO koh CORE tih koidz)* Hormones produced by the adrenal cortex that regulate blood sugar.

Pathology Connection

DIABETES MELLITUS

Diabetes mellitus is a condition characterized by abnormally high blood glucose (hyperglycemia) because of the decreased secretion of insulin or the body's insensitivity to insulin. Type 1 or juvenile onset is caused by the immune system's destruction of the insulin-producing cells of the pancreas and is generally diagnosed in people under the age of 40. Patients with type 1 diabetes, such as our patient Maria, do not produce enough insulin. They are always dependent on daily doses of insulin.

Type 2 (sometimes called late onset) is caused by insensitivity of the body's tissues to insulin and has typically been diagnosed in patients over 50, particularly those with other complicating conditions like obesity. Currently there is a trend of seeing type 2 diabetes in children and becoming more common in adolescents and young adults. Patients in early stages of type 2 diabetes can often be treated with a carefully controlled diet and weight-loss regimen or antidiabetic drugs, which help maintain glucose levels. Some type 2 patients become insulin dependent as the disease progresses and evidence suggests that some type 2 patients may actually have delayed-onset autoimmune diabetes.

Diagnosis is usually accomplished using blood tests and urinalysis. Some blood substances, such as glucose, will "spill" over into the urine. This is why diabetics, like Maria, sometimes have glucose in their urine. Sugar (glucose) tests can be used to detect diabetes, confirm the diagnosis of diabetes, or determine the effectiveness of the treatment for diabetes. Note that sugar in urine, known as glucosuria or glycosuria, is not always abnormal. Situations of emotional stress, diet, or a low reabsorption rate by the kidneys with normal blood levels of glucose may cause high readings. However, you will find that in most cases, sugar in the urine of your patient is a result of diabetes mellitus. Normal urine glucose: < 0.5 mg/dL. See FIGURE 10-12 ▲, which shows various effects of diabetes mellitus.

In both types of diabetes, abnormally high blood glucose (hyperglycemia) must be resolved. If blood glucose remains high, the kidneys work overtime to excrete the excess sugar. Increased urination and dehydration are the most obvious symptoms. The stress of trying to get rid of the excess blood sugar eventually causes kidney damage. In addition, if insulin is not effective, glucose cannot get into cells. Cells must have glucose in order to make ATP. If cells can't get glucose and can't make ATP, they will look for other sources of energy. Untreated diabetics often lose weight as their body searches for other energy sources. Often, their blood becomes increasingly acidic due to their abnormal metabolism. There is often difficulty in wound healing and permanent damage to the peripheral nervous system. The changes in blood chemistry lead to tissue and organ damage. Left untreated, diabetes mellitus may lead to coma and death. Even diabetics who follow a strict treatment regimen often have poorly controlled blood glucose levels due to the complexity of our blood glucose control system. TABLE 10-4 ■ compares type 1 and type 2 diabetes.

diabetes mellitus (DM) Condition resulting from too little secretion of insulin leading to increased levels of blood glucose.

(continued)

Pathology Connection (continued)

Blood glucose that is too low, hypoglycemia, is actually a more acute problem than hyperglycemia for most diabetics and is the primary side effect of insulin therapy. Tight glucose control increases the risk of hypoglycemia. The early symptoms of hypoglycemia include hunger, nervousness, dizziness, anxiety, difficulty speaking, and weakness. If not resolved, hypoglycemia can progress to cause mental confusion, seizures, coma, and even death. Too little blood glucose causes fluid balance problems. In addition, too little blood glucose also means that cells, particularly those in the brain, cannot get the glucose they need to produce energy.

Therefore, the body has an elaborate defense mechanism against hypoglycemia. If blood glucose drops too low, the pancreas decreases its insulin secretion and increases secretion of glucagon. In addition, the adrenal medulla secretes epinephrine. The hypothalamus is involved in that it senses the decrease in blood sugar and triggers the action of the adrenal gland via sympathetic control. (Remember from our discussion of neural control of hormone levels that the hypothalamus has some control over the sympathetic nervous system, which controls epinephrine release by the adrenal gland.) The hypothalamus also triggers feelings of hunger during hypoglycemia, so patients will eat food, increasing glucose levels. For some diabetics, hypoglycemia becomes a recurrent problem. It is thought that damage to the autonomic nervous system or decreased CNS sensitivity caused by repeated hypoglycemic incidents makes it difficult for the body to defend against future hypoglycemic episodes and even decreases awareness of symptoms of hypoglycemia. In some patients this effect can be reversed or diminished by a proper diabetic-approved diet. The only way to treat acute hypoglycemia is to get sugar quickly into the bloodstream. For patients in early hypoglycemia, sugar consumption, sugar-sweetened sodas, orange juice, or hard candy are among the best ways to increase blood sugar. Severe hypoglycemia requires medical attention. People who are not diabetic may also experience symptoms of hypoglycemia if blood glucose drops too low. A person experiencing hypoglycemic symptoms must get medical treatment immediately.

TABLE 10-4 ■ COMPARISON OF TYPE 1 AND TYPE 2 DIABETES

	TYPE 1 DIABETES	TYPE 2 DIABETES
Cause	Autoimmune destruction of pancreas; not enough insulin is produced	Insulin resistance, obesity and sedentary lifestyle; insulin produced by pancreas does not work effectively
Age at onset	Typically before the age of 40	Typically later in life, though some obese and/or sedentary children are being diagnosed
Treatment	Insulin injections, insulin pump, pancreas transplant, stem cells	Diet and exercise, medications, insulin in later stages
Symptoms	Usually sudden and severe, excess urination, extreme thirst, weight loss	Often more subtle than type 1 symptoms, excess urination, thirst

(continued)

Pathology Connection (continued)

Diabetic retinopathy

Nonproliferative retinopathy
(early stage)

— Microaneurysms
— Cotton-wool spots

— Hemorrhages
— Narrowed arterioles

Proliferative retinopathy
(late stage)

Massive hemorrhage

Retinitis proliferans

Diabetic nephropathy

Diabetic glomerulo-sclerosis

Diabetes mellitus is the leading cause of end-stage renal disease in the Western world

Cerebrovascular disease

Stroke due to a ruptured plaque in an artery supplying the brain

Myocardial infarction

Heart disease, including heart attack, which accounts for 70% of the mortality in people with diabetes

Atheromatous aorta and branches

FIGURE 10-12 ▲ Various effects of diabetes mellitus.

Pathology Connection

STEROID-RELATED CONDITIONS

Addison's Disease

Addison's disease is caused by insufficient production of adrenocorticosteroids, particularly cortisol, a glucocorticoid, and aldosterone, a mineralocorticoid. The disease can be fatal if not treated. Symptoms include weight loss, muscle weakness, fatigue, low blood pressure, hypoglycemia, irritability, depression, and excessive skin pigmentation. (Compare these to the symptoms of Cushing's disease, which is characterized by the oversecretion of cortisol.) Many cases of Addison's disease are autoimmune (body attacking itself), but other causes may include infection and cancer. Abnormalities of the hypothalamus and pituitary may also cause Addison's disease. It is diagnosed with blood tests and imaging studies and is treated with hormone replacement.

Cushing's Syndrome

Cushing's syndrome is caused by oversecretion of cortisol. Symptoms include upper body obesity, round face, easy bruising, osteoporosis, fatigue, depression, hypertension, and hyperglycemia (high blood glucose). Women may have excess facial hair and irregular periods; men may have decreased fertility and decreased sex drive. Cushing's syndrome may be a side effect of medical use of steroids, like prednisone, or may be due to pituitary tumors, adrenal tumors, or one of several genetic disorders. New data suggests that some cases of metabolic syndrome (abdominal obesity occurring with high cholesterol, high blood pressure, and hyperglycemia or insulin resistance) may be minor or subtle cases of Cushing's syndrome.

Diagnosis of Cushing's, particularly telling pituitary causes of Cushing's apart from other causes, is relatively complicated. Techniques include MRI, blood cortisol levels, clinical profile, 24-hour urine cortisol testing, hormone levels, dexamethasone suppression tests, genetic testing, and pituitary sampling.

Treatment depends on the underlying cause of the disorder. Classic Cushing's is due to a pituitary tumor that produces too much ACTH, stimulating the adrenal gland to produce too much cortisol. There are no approved drug therapies for classic Cushing's, though several clinical trials are underway. The tumor must be removed, and in the case of a pituitary tumor, damage to the pituitary usually requires hormone replacement for the rest of the patient's life. Other cases of Cushing's are caused by overproduction of cortisol by the adrenal gland independent of what the pituitary and/or hypothalamus are doing. Surgery may be necessary, but in many cases the disease can be managed by drug therapy to decrease cortisol secretion.

Side Effects of Therapeutic Steroids

Prednisone is clinically important in the treatment of inflammation, organ transplant rejection, and immune disorders, but prescription steroids are a double-edged sword. These medications are so powerful that they can cause dangerous side effects, such as bone density loss, weight gain, fat deposits, and delayed wound healing, much like Cushing's syndrome. In addition, these drugs, even when taken for a short time, cannot be discontinued suddenly. Patients must be weaned off their medication slowly. Why? We aren't really sure. One hypothesis suggests that when a patient takes a steroid medication, the adrenal gland decreases steroid production in response. (Remember negative feedback: As hormone levels rise, hormone secretion decreases.) Other suggested mechanisms are biochemical changes, changes in the adrenal gland itself, and even changes in the immune system caused by steroid use. In any case, if the medication is

Addison's disease A rare illness marked by gradual, progressive failure of the adrenal glands and by insufficient production of steroid hormones.

Cushing's syndrome A condition usually the result of the usage of higher levels of corticosteroids in which the patient develops physical features that can include buffalo hump, a rounded face (moon face), weight gain, and increased fragility of the skin.

Pathology Connection (continued)

removed suddenly, patients are left with serious withdrawal symptoms. Steroids, even those used for a short time, must be tapered off slowly to avoid withdrawal.

Steroid Abuse

It is no surprise, then, that taking steroid medications for the purpose of increasing athletic performance is prohibited by amateur and professional sports organizations. **Anabolic steroids** are a class of steroid molecules that cause large increases in muscle mass when compared to working out without steroids. Some athletes use anabolic steroids to enhance performance or to get big muscles much faster than they would without steroids. Because steroid hormone levels are so tightly controlled by the body, anabolic steroids have a number of side effects. (Think back to the discussion of prednisone at therapeutic levels; abuse levels are much higher.) Men abusing steroids may experience changes in sperm production, enlarged breasts, and shrinking of their testicles. Women may experience deepening of the voice, decreased breast size, and excessive body hair growth. Steroid abuse may lead to cardiovascular diseases and increased cholesterol levels. Many steroids suppress immune function, and because steroid use is illegal, many abusers expose themselves to hepatitis B and HIV when sharing needles. Steroid abuse has also been linked to increased aggressive behavior. All major professional and amateur athletic organizations ban the use of steroids.

anabolic steroids *(an ah BALL ick)* A class of steroids that cause large increases in muscle mass with many side effects.

Cortisol and the Stress Response

The typical cortisol secretion pattern is peak cortisol levels just before waking with cortisol decreasing as the day goes on. During the day, there are peaks and valleys superimposed on the overall levels. Cortisol levels also peak during times of stress.

Your body has a set response to any stressor, whether physiological—such as hypothermia, decreased blood volume, or hyperglycemia—or psychological—such as a big exam or a near collision. When you are exposed to stressors, both the sympathetic nervous system and the adrenal cortex are activated. Epinephrine and norepinephrine are released from the adrenal medulla, raising blood pressure and heart rate, raising respiration rate, increasing blood glucose, and decreasing digestion and other nonessential physiological responses. The adrenal cortex, under orders from the hypothalamus and pituitary, releases cortisol, a glucocorticoid hormone, causing increased blood glucose, and changes in immune response. This initial stress response is appropriate and useful, allowing your body to be ready to expend energy. If the stress continues, this response also continues, entering a phase of adaptation in which there is a balance between stress response and homeostatic mechanisms, and homeostasis is maintained. This is still a useful and healthy response to stress. However, if stress becomes chronic, the secretion of epinephrine, and cortisol in particular, becomes pathological.

The response of the body to chronic stress is also influenced by many other factors, including psychological factors. Increased optimism, greater social support mechanisms, and lower perceived stress are all associated with lower cortisol levels, whereas depression and anxiety are associated with higher levels of cortisol.

In some overweight people, high cortisol levels are associated with increased risk of type 2 diabetes, heart disease, and stroke. However, these are only associations. That cortisol *causes* these conditions has not been shown. It is a "chicken versus egg" problem. Does high cortisol cause these problems or do these problems cause high cortisol? Results are complicated due to the complexity of hormonal regulation, studies are often conflicting, and age, gender, and the effects of other conditions complicate the picture. There is much more research to be done before we understand the complex relationship between cortisol levels and disease.

THE GONADS

The chief function of the gonads—the testes in males and the ovaries in females—is to produce and store gametes (reproductive cells), eggs, and sperm. However, the gonads also produce a number of sex hormones that control reproduction in both males and females, including testosterone in males and estrogen and progesterone in females. For more details on the sexual hormones produced by the gonads, see Chapter 17.

Estrogen, produced by the ovary in the female, is responsible for the development of both the reproductive organs and the secondary sex characteristics in females. Progesterone, also produced by the ovary, helps to regulate the menstrual cycle in females. In the male, the **testes** produce testosterone, which is responsible for development of the reproductive organs and secondary sex characteristics, such as the male's deep voice. For more details on these hormones, see Chapter 17.

testes *(TESS teez)* Small, egg-shaped glands in the scrotum. Also known as the testicles. They contain interstitial cells that secrete testosterone. They also contain the seminiferous tubules that produce spermatozoa.

Clinical Application

CORTISOL BUSTERS AND WEIGHT LOSS

It is clear that very high cortisol levels, such as in Cushing's disease, cause weight gain, and that very low cortisol, such as in Addison's disease, causes weight loss. There is evidence that chronic high cortisol is associated with risk factors for metabolic syndrome: abdominal obesity, hypercholesterolemia, hyperglycemia, and hypertension. However, this association is more apparent only in a subset of people who are overweight. Conversely some overweight people have low cortisol levels. Perhaps the combination of high body mass index and high cortisol is the culprit, but the interaction of hormone levels, blood chemistry, and body fat is also complicated by gender, age, and, no great surprise, stress levels. At this time there is no clear picture of how cortisol is related to obesity and risk factors for health problems associated with increased body weight, although high cortisol combined with obesity and other risk factors is often a sign of problems to come.

You may have all seen the advertisements for "cortisol busters," which claim to cause significant, rapid weight loss simply by decreasing blood cortisol levels. These products claim that abdominal fat is caused by high cortisol levels, regardless of what you are eating or how much you are exercising. (They do, however, suggest a sensible diet and exercise plan while taking their product.) Given the available scientific information, it seems unlikely that simply decreasing cortisol will cause rapid, healthy weight loss. You are better off exercising more and eating more nutritiously if you wish to lose weight, though it's probably not a bad idea to decrease your overall stress levels. Chronic secretion of cortisol has a number of effects on metabolism, including increased appetite, changes in the immune system that increase autoimmunity and decrease defense against infection, increased heart rate, hypertension, hyperglycemia, hypercholesterolemia, increased abdominal fat, anxiety, and depression. (Remember the symptoms of Cushing's syndrome?) So there appears to be a trade-off at work. A certain amount of stress is productive and useful, sharpening awareness and increasing energy levels, but chronic stress causes detrimental physiological and psychological changes.

PROSTAGLANDINS

Prostaglandins are molecules that act like hormones. Many different body tissues produce prostaglandins. These molecules have a variety of functions, depending on where they were produced. Some prostaglandins help to constrict and dilate smooth muscle—in the blood vessels, digestive tract, or the bronchial tubes of the lungs. Others help with contraction of the uterus during childbirth. Other prostaglandins respond to tissue inflammation. Each prostaglandin generally acts in a small area of the body—on the cells or tissues where it was produced. Prostaglandins have a short-term but powerful effect on these local tissues. FIGURE 10-13 ▲ shows examples of some common endocrine disorders.

A   B   C

FIGURE 10-13 ▲ Examples of Endocrine Disorders. **A.** An infant with congenital hypothyroidism. (Source: Bettina Cirrone/Photo Researchers, Inc.) **B.** A patient with Cushing's syndrome. (Source: Biophoto Associates/Photo Researchers, Inc.) **C.** A patient with gigantism. (Source: Bettina Cirrone/Photo Researchers, Inc.)

A QUICK TRIP THROUGH THE DISEASES OF THE ENDOCRINE SYSTEM

DISORDER	ETIOLOGY	SIGNS AND SYMPTOMS	DIAGNOSTIC TEST(S)	TREATMENTS
Diabetes insipidus	ADH deficiency.	Copious, dilute urine.	Rule out diabetes mellitus, ADH levels.	If caused by a medication, eliminate the medication. If low ADH, give synthetic vasopressin.
Syndrome of inappropriate antidiuretic hormone (SIADH)	Excess ADH production usually caused by pulmonary disease, cancer, medications, and central nervous system disorders leading to severe hyponatremia.	Confusion, altered consciousness, fatigue, nausea, muscle cramps and loss of appetite.	Rule out TBI, evaluate volume status.	Restrict water, infusion of hypertonic saline.
Gigantism/ acromegaly	Excess growth hormone from hyperfunction of pituitary, often due to pituitary tumor.	In children, overgrowth of long bones results in rapid growth to height in great excess of normal height, in adults, excess growth and deformity of body tissues.	Imaging, blood tests for hormone levels.	Removal of pituitary tumor, followed by hormone replacement therapy.
Dwarfism	Growth hormone deficiency from hypofunction of pituitary in childhood.	In children, failure to attain normal height, abnormally slow growth.	Blood tests, rule out other causes of dwarfism.	Early diagnosis, growth hormone injections.
Graves' disease	Hyperthyroidism due to autoimmune attack on thyroid.	Tremors, sweating, weakness, tachycardia, arrhythmia, irritability.	Blood tests—low TSH levels but high T_4 levels, radioactive iodine uptake.	Removal or destruction of thyroid or anti-thyroid medication, followed by daily thyroid hormone.
Congenital hypothyroidism	Hypothyroidism present at birth due to anatomical thyroid abnormalities, thyroid metabolism errors, or iodine deficiency.	Dull look, puffy face, thick tongue that sticks out; many newborns exhibit no symptoms.	Newborn screening, including x-ray, thyroid scan.	Early treatment is critical and includes daily thyroid hormone.
Hashimoto's thyroiditis	Hypothyroidism due to autoimmune attack on thyroid.	Fatigue, thinning hair, bradycardia, hypercholesterolemia, depression.	Blood tests—high TSH with low T_4.	Daily thyroid hormone.
Diabetes mellitus	Insulin deficiency caused by autoimmune attack on pancreas, or insulin resistance.	Excess urination and increased thirst due to high blood glucose.	Urine glucose, blood glucose, glucose tolerance testing.	Diet, exercise, antidiabetic medications, insulin injections.

(continued)

A QUICK TRIP *(continued)*

DISORDER	ETIOLOGY	SIGNS AND SYMPTOMS	DIAGNOSTIC TEST(S)	TREATMENTS
Addison's disease	Deficiency of adrenocorticosteroids due to autoimmune attack on adrenal cortex.	Weakness, fatigue, hypotension, hypoglycemia, depression.	Imaging and blood tests for corticosteroids.	Hormone replacement.
Cushing's disease	Excess cortisol usually due to benign pituitary tumor.	Abdominal obesity, easy bruising, hypertension, hyperglycemia, hypercholesterolemia, depression.	Imaging, blood cortisol levels, urine cortisol, CTH levels, dexamethasone suppression test, pituitary biopsy.	Tumor removal followed by hormone replacement. If caused by overuse of steroids, decrease or eliminate use.
Chronic stress	Excess cortisol in response to stressors.	Depression, anxiety, perhaps obesity, hypercholesterolemia, hypertension, increased susceptibility to infection.	No good test. Effects of stress vary widely among individuals.	Decrease stress, treatment of symptoms.

Pharmacology Corner

Many hormonal disorders can be treated with hormone replacement therapy. For example Synthroid™ (a synthetic hormone) is used in the treatment of hypothyroidism. Hydrocortisone, a steroid, is used to replace cortisol in the treatment of Addison's disease. Prednisone™, which acts like a corticosteroid, can be used to replace corticosteroids or as an anti-inflammatory drug (in patients with normal corticosteroid levels) and to treat severe allergies, rheumatoid arthritis, or other chronic conditions. Children with growth hormone deficiency are treated by growth hormone injections.

One of the most commonly used medications in the treatment of diabetes is insulin. There are various ways to administer insulin, including a recently introduced aerosol inhaler that replaces the more invasive daily injections. Often in late-onset diabetes the insulin is functioning but very poorly. Drugs such as Glucophage™ help to potentiate (make stronger) the effect of insulin, making it function more efficiently.

Sometimes hormones need to be inhibited rather than replaced. Mitotane™, a cortisol inhibitor, can be used to treat some kinds of Cushing's syndrome. Somatostatin™ analogs can be used to decrease growth hormone production in the treatment of acromegaly. In addition, disorders may be treated by blocking the receptors that receive the hormone at the target cell. For example, scientists are experimenting with specific aldosterone blockers to treat high blood pressure.

SUMMARY

Snapshots from the Journey

- The endocrine system works together with the nervous system to regulate the activities of all the body systems. The endocrine system secretes hormones that act very slowly on distant targets. Their effects are long lasting.

- Most hormones act on cells by binding to external receptors, causing changes in enzyme activity inside the target cell. Steroids, however, can enter cells and interact directly with DNA, which makes steroids very powerful.

- Hormone levels are controlled largely by negative feedback. When hormone levels rise, signals are transmitted to the endocrine organ releasing the hormone, telling the organ to decrease the amount of hormone released. Hormone levels will then decrease. The optimal level of the hormone is called the set point. If the signal brings a hormone back to set point, the action is called negative feedback. If the signal causes the hormone to get further away from set point, the action is positive feedback.

- Hormone levels can be regulated by three mechanisms: changes in the body's internal environment, control by hormones released by another endocrine gland, and direct control by the nervous system.

- The hypothalamus, a part of the diencephalon, controls much of the endocrine system by controlling the pituitary gland. The pituitary gland has two parts: the posterior pituitary, which is part of the hypothalamus and actually secretes hypothalamic hormones (ADH and oxytocin), and the anterior pituitary, which secretes several different hormones under the influence of hormones from the hypothalamus. The hormones secreted by the anterior pituitary typically control other endocrine glands. (Growth hormone is an exception.)

- Noncancerous pituitary tumors cause a number of different endocrine disorders, depending on whether hormones are oversecreted or undersecreted. Hyperpituitarism, acromegaly, gigantism, and Cushing's syndrome are caused by oversecretion of pituitary hormones.

- Several other endocrine glands have important control functions. The thyroid gland secretes the iodine-containing hormones triiodothyronine (T_3) and thyroxine (T_4), which control growth and cellular metabolism.

- Autoimmune attack on the thyroid can cause serious problems. Hashimoto's thyroiditis, the most common form of hypothyroidism, causes the typical symptoms of hypothyroidism, including bradycardia, thinning hair, leg cramps, fatigue, forgetfulness, and depression. Graves' disease, the most common cause of hyperthyroidism, causes tremors, anxiety, irritability, cardiac arrhythmia, and excessive sweating.

- The pancreas secretes two hormones: insulin, which lowers blood sugar, and glucagon, which raises blood sugar. Diabetes is caused by a decrease in insulin secretion or decreased sensitivity to insulin. Very high blood sugar is the result. Hypoglycemia (low blood sugar) is also a problem for diabetics and is the chief side effect of insulin therapy. Many diabetics have health problems due to the difficulty of effectively controlling blood glucose.

SUMMARY

- The adrenal glands are split into two parts. The adrenal medulla is an extension of the sympathetic nervous system, releasing epinephrine and norepinephrine as hormones during fight-or-flight response. The adrenal cortex releases many different adrenocorticosteroid hormones, which control reproduction, inflammation, tissue growth, and immunity.

- One of the most important hormones released by the adrenal cortex is cortisol, a glucocorticoid, but we do not really understand how it works. It is well known that too much cortisol (Cushing's) causes weight gain and that too little cortisol (Addison's) causes weight loss. But these are diseases. Our understanding of how cortisol is involved in obesity and its related conditions that make up metabolic syndrome—hypertension, hypercholesterolemia, and insulin resistance—is not complete.

MARIA'S STORY

Let's revisit Maria's case. She is a 35-year-old insulin-dependent diabetic who currently takes good care of herself. She did not take good care of herself as a teenager. She is on an insulin pump to try to control her blood sugar, but has recently passed out in public several times.

a. What condition causes her to pass out? (hyperglycemia or hypoglycemia)

_____

_____

b. Why does this condition develop?

_____

_____

c. What is the appropriate treatment for the early stages of this condition?

_____

_____

d. Given that she has been a diabetic for so long, why doesn't Maria realize she is in trouble before she passes out?

_____

_____

REVIEW QUESTIONS

Matching

1. Match the hormone on the left with its function on the right.

_____ ADH	a. decreases blood sugar
_____ insulin	b. increases thyroid hormone secretion
_____ glucagon	c. regulates cell metabolism
_____ oxytocin	d. increases steroid release
_____ epinephrine	e. increases uterine contractions
_____ thyroxine	f. decreases urination
_____ prolactin	g. prolongs sympathetic response
_____ ACTH (adrenocorticotropic hormone)	h. stimulates tissue growth
_____ TSH	i. increases blood sugar
_____ growth hormone	j. increases milk production in females

2. Match the hormone abnormality on the left with the disease on the right.

_____ too much ADH	a. gigantism
_____ too little insulin	b. Diabetes mellitus
_____ too little cortisol	c. Dwarfism
_____ too little thyroid hormone	d. SIADH
_____ too little growth hormone	e. Graves' disease
_____ too much thyroxine	f. Addison's disease
_____ too much cortisol	g. changes in sexual characteristics, immune suppression, rage
_____ too much growth hormone	h. Hashimoto's thyroiditis
_____ too many steroids	i. Cushing's disease

Multiple Choice

1. ADH stands for:
   a. vasodilate
   b. antidiuretic hormone
   c. androdoginin hormone
   d. all-diglyceride hormone

2. The "master gland" is the:
   a. adrenals
   b. pituitary
   c. thyroid
   d. pancreas

3. The thymus gland's main function is:
   a. reproduction
   b. growth
   c. immunity
   d. RBC levels

4. The pineal gland is located in/on the:
   a. kidneys
   b. brain
   c. thorax
   d. abdomen

5. Glucagon performs the opposite action of:
   a. glucose
   b. insulin
   c. ATP
   d. WBCs

6. Anxiety, rapid heartbeat, and sweating are symptoms of:
   a. Graves' disease
   b. Cushing's syndrome
   c. Hashimoto's thyroiditis
   d. all of the above

REVIEW QUESTIONS

7. Glucocorticoid hormones control:
   a. glucose
   b. insulin
   c. ATP
   d. WBCs

8. This hormone may be involved in metabolic syndrome:
   a. glucagon
   b. ADH
   c. TSH
   d. cortisol

Short Answer

1. Compare and contrast neurotransmitters and hormones.

_____

2. List the sources of control of hormone levels.

_____

3. Explain negative feedback and its role in controlling hormone levels.

_____

4. Discuss why the use of anabolic steroids should be outlawed for performance enhancement.

_____

5. What is the difference between neural control and humoral control of endocrine glands?

_____

6. Explain the difference between type 1 and type 2 diabetes.

_____

7. Why are hormone disorders so difficult to diagnose?

_____

8. Explain the difference between "good stress" and "bad stress."

_____

Suggested Activities

1. Review the hormones secreted by each endocrine organ and their functions. Make up 3 × 5 cards with the endocrine gland on the front and the hormones it produces on the back. Pick a partner and quiz each other. Once you and your partner can match the gland to the hormones, make up another set of cards with the hormone on the front and its activity or function on the back, and again quiz each other.

2. Review the endocrine diseases listed in this chapter. Make up 3 × 5 cards with the signs and symptoms on the front and the actual disease printed on the back. In a small group or with a partner, try to stump each other in determining the correct disease diagnosis.

CAREER CONNECTIONS

Now that you have read this chapter, here is a list of related professions you may be interested in investigating for a future career:

- Radiologic Technologists

Research each profession and report on the following:

1. Profession description to include job responsibilities

2. Educational requirements

3. Job opportunities

4. Opportunities outside of the hospital setting

5. Salary range

6. Licensure and continuing education requirements

ANATOMY, PHYSIOLOGY, AND DISEASE IN ACTION

Materials:
Particle Board
Hammer
Nails
Different Colored Yarn
3 x 5 and 5 x 7 index cards
Markers
File folder labels

Students will be divided into groups of ten. One student will act as the coordinator for the group. The coordinator will label the 5 x 7 index cards with the terms: hypothalamus, anterior pituitary, and posterior pituitary glands. The coordinator will then place them on the board at the appropriate location. The coordinator will also pound a nail into each location. Each of the other nine students will chose one of the target organs of the endocrine glands and trace the pathway from the hypothalamus/pituitary glands to the target organ, wrapping the yarn around the appropriate nails. Label the intermediary hormones using the folder labels and put on the yarn. On the 3 x 5 card label the hormone released and its effect below the target organ. Make sure to indicate if it is regulated by positive (+) or negative (-) feedback and the effect it produces. Determine a disease that is associated with that hormone and report it on a 3 x 5 card below the target organ.

The Senses
The Sights and Sounds

As we stroll through the city on our journey, we take in many sights, sounds, and smells. As you look around, you may see many different buildings and types of people. The city is also noisy, full of car horns honking, brakes squealing and people talking. You will smell delicious food wafting out restaurant windows or the stench of garbage overflowing dumpsters. Our senses receive all this input and send it to the brain for interpretation so we can understand and appreciate what is happening around us. These senses are highly integrated with the nervous system, enabling us to respond quickly and thereby protecting us from harm. For example, we need to *see* that oncoming speeding car as we step away from the curb and *hear* the blaring horn to respond by quickly stepping back to the safe confines of the sidewalk. See how sensory input can determine motor response?

LEARNING OUTCOMES

At the end of your journey through this chapter, you will be able to:

- Differentiate between general and special senses
- Describe the internal and external anatomy and functions of the eye
- Describe the internal and external anatomy and functions of the ear
- Discuss the process involved with the senses of taste, smell, and touch
- Contrast the types of pain and the pain response
- Explain several common disorders of the eye, ear, and senses

Pronunciation Guide

Correct pronunciation is important in any journey so that you and others are completely understood. Here is a "see and say" Pronunciation Guide for the more difficult terms to pronounce in this chapter. Please note that pronunciations given are referenced to medical dictionaries, and regional variations may exist.

amblyopia (am blee OH pee ah)
anesthesia (an ess THEE zee ah)
aqueous humor (AY kwee us HYOO mer)
auricle (AW rih kul)
cataract (KAT ah rakt)
cerumen (seh ROO men)
ceruminous glands (seh ROO men us)
choroid (KOH royd)
ciliary muscles (SILL ee air ee)
cochlea (KOHK lee ah)
conjunctiva (KON junk TIH vah)
conjunctivitis (kon JUNK tiv EYE tis)
endolymph (EN doe limf)
Eustachian tubes (yoo STAY she ehn)
external auditory meatus (AW dih tor ee mee AY tus)
glaucoma (glaw KOH mah)
gustatory sense (GUS ta TORE ee)
hyperopia (HIGH per OH pee ah)
incus (ING kus)
iris (EYE riss)
labyrinth (LAB ih rinth)
labyrinthitis (LAB ih rinn THYE tiss)
lacrimal apparatus (LAK rim al app ah RA tus)

malleus (MALL ee us)
Ménière's disease (MAIN ee AIRZ)
myopia (my OH pee ah)
nyctalopia (nik tah LOH pee ah)
ossicle (AH sih kel)
otitis media (oh TYE tiss ME dee ah)
perilymph (per ih LIMF)
photopigments (FOE toe PIG mints)
pinna (PINN ah)
presbycusis (prez be KYOO sus)
presbyopia (PRESS bee OH pee ah)
pupil (PYOO pill)
retina (RETT in ah)
sclera (SKLAIR ah)
stapes (STAY peez)
strabismus (strah BIZ mus)
tactile corpuscle (KOR pus el)
tinnitus (tinn EYE tus)
tympanic membrane (tihm PAN ick)
vestibule chamber (VESS tih byool)
vestibulocochlear (VESS tih byoo loh KOHK lee are)
vitreous humor (VITT ree us HYOO mer)

THE SENSES

Our body's senses enable us to experience all aspects of our journey. They are truly remarkable sensors through which we see, hear, smell, taste, and feel the world around us.

Our senses monitor and detect changes in the environment and send this information from the receptor to the brain via sensory (afferent) neurons. The brain interprets the information and in many circumstances makes the appropriate motor (efferent) response.

Traditionally, we are taught that we possess five senses: vision, hearing, smell, taste, and touch. However, there are more areas of sensory input into the brain. What about pain and pressure sensations? How do we "feel" hot and cold? How does our body sense position and balance (equilibrium)? What about feelings of hunger and thirst? These, too, are senses that are very important to our survival.

The senses of sight (eyes), hearing and balance (ears), taste (tongue), and smell (nose) are referred to as our **special senses**. These senses are found in well-defined regions of the head. However, other senses, called **general senses,** are scattered throughout various

special senses Senses that include sight, hearing and balance, taste, and smell.

general senses Senses that are scattered throughout the various regions of the body that include sensations of heat, cold, pain, nausea, hunger, thirst, and pressure or touch.

regions of the body. These include the sensations of heat, cold, pain, nausea, hunger, thirst, and pressure or touch.

The senses can be further broken down. For example, the receptors of the skin are called the **cutaneous senses** and include touch, heat, cold, and pain. The **visceral senses** include nausea, hunger, thirst, and the need to urinate and defecate.

Before finishing this discussion of the various senses, we should also mention a final, more controversial sense. By "reading your mind," we see you already identified it as extrasensory perception, or ESP. The phrase *extrasensory perception* literally means senses outside the normal sensory perceptions. Although there is still debate over whether this phenomenon exists, we just "know" this chapter will be an "eye-opening" experience for you. We hope the puns aren't stimulating your visceral senses and making you nauseous.

SENSE OF SIGHT

While on our journey, we see many amazing sights. To record these sights for later viewing, we may take along a camera and film. The eye has many similarities to a camera. The light rays from the images photographed with a camera pass through the small opening (comparable to the pupil) and through the transparent lens (lens of the eye), where the rays are then focused on a photoreceptive film (retina). The shutter of a camera opens and closes at various speeds to adjust the amount of light exposure on the film. The shutter (iris) must allow just the right amount of light to enter and focus properly on the film for a clear image. A camera may be packed away in a suitcase or thrown in a car and therefore needs protection from being dropped or exposed to a harsh environment. You will soon see how the external structures of the eye help protect it from injury, much like a camera case protects a camera. In addition, the camera lens must be kept clean to ensure a clear picture. The lacrimal glands secrete tears to help to perform this function for the eyes. Now that you have this analogy to give you the big picture, let's explore the specific structures and functions of the eye.

The External Structures of the Eye

The **orbit** (or **orbital cavity**) is a cone-shaped cavity formed by the skull that houses and protects the **eyeball**, a one-inch sphere. This cavity is padded with fatty tissue that cushions and protects the eyeball from injury and has several openings through which nerves and blood vessels can pass. The eyeball is connected to the orbital cavity by six short muscles that provide support and allow rotary movement so you can see in all directions. Also protecting the eye is a pair of movable folds of skin, commonly called **eyelids,** which contain **eyelashes** to help prevent large particles from entering. The eyelashes act as sensors to cause rapid closure as a foreign object approaches the eyeball. The eyelids close over the eye much like the lens cover of a camera to protect the eye from intense light, foreign particles, and impact injuries. The eyelids also contain sebaceous glands that secrete sebum onto the eyelids to keep them soft, pliable, and a little sticky to trap particles.

A protective membrane called the **conjunctiva** lines the inner eyelid and covers the exposed surface of the eyeball protecting the exposed eye surface. Each eye has a **lacrimal apparatus** that produces and stores tears. The lacrimal apparatus includes the **lacrimal gland** and its corresponding ducts or passageways that transport the tears. The lacrimal glands (*exocrine* because their secretions of tears go *outside* the body) produce tears, which are needed for constant cleansing and lubrication and which are

cutaneous senses Result from receptors in the skin that include touch, heat, cold, pressure, and pain.

visceral senses Senses that include nausea, hunger, thirst, and the need to urinate and defecate.

orbit Bony socket in the skull that surrounds all but the anterior part of the eyeball.

orbital cavity See orbit.

eyeball The globe of the eye.

eyelid One of two movable protective folds that cover the anterior surface of the eyeball when closed.

eyelash A stiff hair on the margin of the eyelid.

conjunctiva *(kon JUNK tih vah)* Delicate, transparent mucous membrane that covers the inside of the eyelids and the anterior surface of the eye.

lacrimal apparatus *(LACK rim al app ah RA tus)* Structures involved with the secretion and production of tears.

lacrimal gland The gland that secretes tears.

antiseptic A substance capable of destroying microorganisms.

aqueous humor *(AY kwee us HYOO mer)* Clear, watery fluid of the eye produced by the ciliary body. It circulates through the posterior and anterior chambers and takes nutrients and oxygen to the cornea and lens.

vitreous humor *(VITT ree us HYOO mer)* Clear, gel-like substance that fills the posterior cavity of the eye.

sclera *(SKLAIR ah)* White, tough, fibrous connective tissue that forms the outer layer around most of the eye. Also known as the white of the eye.

choroid *(KOH royd)* Spongy membrane of blood vessels that begins at the iris and continues around the eye. In the posterior cavity, it is the middle layer between the sclera and the retina.

retina *(RET ih nah)* The innermost membrane lining the eye. It contains rods and cones. Landmarks include the optic disk and macula.

cornea *(CORE nee uh)* Transparent layer over the anterior part of the eye. It is a continuation of the white sclera.

iris *(EYE riss)* Colored ring of tissue whose muscles contract or relax to change the size of the pupil in the center of the iris.

pupil *(PYOO pill)* Round opening in the iris that allows light rays to enter the internal eye.

lens Clear, hard disk in the internal eye. The muscles and ligaments of the ciliary body change its shape to focus light rays on the retina.

ciliary muscle *(SILL ee AIR ee)* Smooth muscle that alters the lens of the eye to accommodate for near vision.

accommodation The change in size of the pupil and lens curvature to allow for proper focusing on the retina.

spread over the eye surface by blinking. Our eyes are constantly tearing, but they do not overflow because excess tears drain into the nasal cavity via two small openings in the inner corner of the eye. However, when we cry, the excess runs down our cheeks and more drains into our nose, causing it to run. The tears also act as an **antiseptic** to keep the eyeballs free of germs. Please see FIGURE 11-1 ▲ for the external structures of the eye and the structures involved with tearing.

The Internal Structures of the Eye

The globe-shaped eyeball is the organ of vision and is separated into two chambers of fluid that help to protect the eye. These "fluids of the eye" are called *humors*. The **aqueous humor** ("watery" humor) bathes the iris, pupil, and lens and fills the anterior and posterior chambers, in the front of the eye. The **vitreous humor**, which maintains eye shape and refracts light rays, is a clear, jellylike fluid that occupies the entire eye cavity behind the lens.

The eyeball has three layers. Please see FIGURE 11-2 ▲ for the layers and internal structures of the eye. These layers are the **sclera, choroid,** and **retina**. The sclera is the outermost layer and is a tough, fibrous tissue that serves as the protective shield we commonly call the "white of the eye." The fluids within the eye exert pressure on the sclera, helping maintain the shape of the eye. The extrinsic muscles responsible for moving the eye are attached to the sclera. The sclera contains a specialized portion called the **cornea** (window of the eye), which contains no blood vessels and is transparent to allow light rays to pass into the eye. The cornea has a curved surface that enables it to bend the entering light waves to focus them on the surface of the retina.

The middle layer, or choroid (also called choroid coat or choroidea), is a highly vascularized and pigmented region that provides nourishment to the eye. This layer also contains the iris and the pupil. The **iris** is the colored portion of the eye that controls the size of the opening (**pupil**) where light passes into the eye. The iris is a *sphincter*, which means it has intrinsic muscles that can relax or contract depending on light conditions. In low light, the iris relaxes, causing the pupil to dilate and allowing more light into the eye for a better image. In bright light, the pupil constricts, causing less light into the eye.

The third and innermost layer is the retina. This area contains the nerve endings that receive and interpret the rays of light. Located behind the iris and pupil is an elastic, disc-shaped, biconvex crystalline structure called the **lens**. The lens lies between the anterior and posterior chambers of the eye. The lens is surrounded by **ciliary muscles**. When light enters the eye, it is refracted, or bent, by the lens. Ciliary muscles can alter the shape of the lens, making it thinner or thicker to change the angle of refraction, which allows the focusing of incoming light rays on the retinal area. This process, called **accommodation**, combines changes in the size of the pupil and the lens curvature to make sure the image converges in the same place on the retina and therefore is properly focused.

In summation, light rays enter the eye and pass through the conjunctival membrane, cornea, aqueous humor, pupil, lens, and vitreous humor and are focused on the retina. Here the photoreceptors in the retina cause an impulse to be sent to the optic nerve (cranial nerve II), which carries it to the brain for the interpretation we call vision. See if you can trace the pathway light takes in Figure 11-2. Refer to TABLE 11-1 ■, which summarizes the major structures and their corresponding functions of the eye.

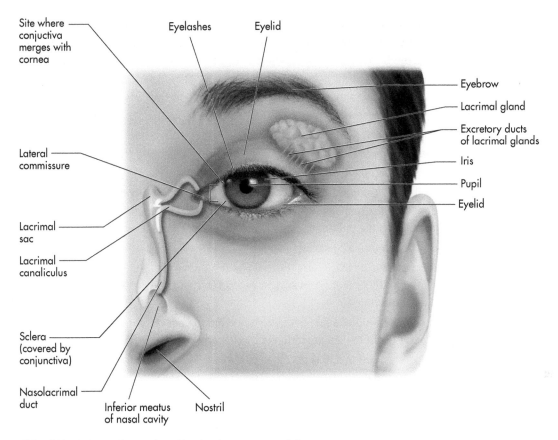

Site where conjuctiva merges with cornea

Eyelashes

Eyelid

Eyebrow

Lacrimal gland

Excretory ducts of lacrimal glands

Iris

Pupil

Eyelid

Lateral commissure

Lacrimal sac

Lacrimal canaliculus

Sclera (covered by conjunctiva)

Nasolacrimal duct

Inferior meatus of nasal cavity

Nostril

FIGURE 11-1 ▲ External and lacrimal structures of the eye.

Conjunctiva

Upper lid

Anterior chamber

Aqueous humor (liquid filling)

Cornea

Pupil

Lens

Iris

Eyelash

Lower lid

Posterior chamber

Suspensory ligament

Ciliary body

Vitreous humor (liquid filling)

Choroid layer

Retina

Sclera

Fovea centralis

Optic nerve

Central retinal artery and vein

FIGURE 11-2 ▲ The internal structures of the eye.

TABLE 11-1 ■ STRUCTURES AND FUNCTIONS OF THE EYE

ORGAN OR STRUCTURE	PRIMARY FUNCTION
Orbit	Cone-shaped cavity that contains the eyeball; padded with fatty tissues, the orbit has several openings for nerves and blood vessels to pass through
Eye muscles	Six short muscles that provide support and rotary movement
Eyelids	Moveable folds of skin containing eyelashes to protect eye from intense light, foreign particles, and impact injuries
Conjunctiva	Protective membrane that covers the exposed surface of eyeball
Lacrimal apparatus	Includes the lacrimal gland that produces tears that lubricate and cleanse the eye and the corresponding ducts or passageways to transport the tears
Eyeball	Globe-shaped organ of vision
Sclera	Outermost layer of the eyeball, known as the "white" of the eye; maintains shape of eye; contains the transparent curved cornea, which bends outside light rays to focus them on the surface of the retina
Choroid	Middle layer of the eyeball, containing rich blood vessels and pigmentation to prevent internal reflection of light rays; also contains the iris and pupil
Iris	Colored portion of eye, the part that controls the size of the opening (pupil) where light passes into the eye
Pupil	The opening through which light passes into the eye
Retina	Innermost layer of the eyeball, containing the nerve endings that receive and interpret the rays of light for vision
Optic disk	The area where the neurons of the optic nerve exit the retina
Lens	Located behind the pupil, the lens is controlled by ciliary muscles that shape the lens by thinning or thickening the lens to allow light to focus on the retinal surface; this process, called *accommodation*, combines changes in pupil size and the lens curvature to ensure the light rays focus properly on the retina.

Pathology Connection

INJURIES AND DISORDERS OF THE EYE

Eye injuries can result in permanent impairment or loss of sight. Injuries often result from exposure to chemicals, physical blows, and the insertion of foreign objects. Some chemicals, such as soaps, cause only mild irritation. Other chemicals, such as acids and cleaning products, can cause permanent damage. Symptoms include redness, swelling, and pain. Chemicals should be flushed from the eye using large amounts of water or saline solution. Medical care is required if exposure is persistent or involves a dangerous chemical. Physical blows may cause injuries such as retinal detachment, in which the retina separates partially or fully from the back of the eye. Symptoms include blurred vision or loss of vision in the injured eye. In addition to damaging the eye, physical blows can cause fractures in the orbital area, so medical care is required. Insertion of foreign objects, such as sand or broken glass, causes corneal abrasions and may puncture the eye. Such injuries are treated by covering the eye and immediately seeking medical help. The object should not be removed, as doing so may cause more damage.

A **stye,** which is also known as a **hordeolum,** is an abscess that forms at the base of an eyelash due to infection of a sebaceous gland. Often the result of bacterial infections, styes are red, swollen, and

stye Also known as hordeolum, this is an abscess that forms at the base of an eyelash due to infection of a sebaceous gland.

hordeolum See stye.

(continued)

Pathology Connection (continued)

painful. They resemble acne pimples. Styes are treated by applying warm compresses, which help relieve discomfort and speed the bursting of the stye.

Conjunctivitis is an inflammation of the membrane that lines the eye and is characterized by red swollen eyes. This condition can be either acute or chronic and can be caused by a variety of irritants such as fumes or onions. Pathogens such as viruses and bacteria can also be a culprit. The acute infective phase is commonly called pink eye; it is a highly contagious form caused by *Staphylococcus aureus* bacteria. In developing countries, chronic conjunctivitis is called trachoma and is caused by *Chlamydia trachomatis*. These cases are often highly contagious and can cause corneal damage and impair vision. They can be treated with antibiotics.

A cataract is a condition in which the lens loses its flexibility and transparency, and light cannot easily pass through the clouded lens. Although the exact cause of cataracts is unknown, it has been shown that increased exposure to sunlight may speed up the development of cataracts. Congenital defects, trauma, and aging are contributing factors to cataract formation. When untreated, this condition can lead to blindness. It is interesting to note that cataract surgery was one of the earliest recorded surgical procedures, dating back to ancient Greece.

Glaucoma is caused by increased pressure in the fluid of the eye; this high pressure causes compression and damage of the optic nerve. In addition, the pressure compresses the small capillaries in the eyes causing them to lose their elasticity and collapse leading to retinal damage. This increased pressure is due to overproduction of aqueous humor or lack of drainage. Most cases develop gradually, with symptoms that include aching and the appearance of a halo around sources of light. Peripheral vision is reduced, which eventually progresses to tunnel vision and then blindness. Glaucoma occurs in 20% of adults over 40 and accounts for 15% of the cases of blindness in America. This is a tragic loss because glaucoma can be readily diagnosed and treated with medication and surgery. Annual visits to an ophthalmologist can lead to early diagnosis and treatment. To identify the onset of glaucoma, an ophthalmologist uses a tool called a tonometer to measure pressure within an eye. The goal is to lower intraocular pressure.

Macular degeneration is the reduction or loss of central vision in which peripheral vision is unaffected. It is estimated to develop in 10% of the elderly. There are two forms of macular degeneration: atrophic (dry) and exudative (hemorrhagic). There is no cure for the atrophic form, but the exudative form can be improved slightly with argon laser therapy.

Retinopathy (irreversible damage to the retina) can be caused by hypertension or diabetes mellitus and can result in vision impairment or blindness. Smoking can further aggravate this condition. Maria is at risk for diabetic retinopathy and possible blindness as a result of her diabetes.

The eye can have several defects that impair vision. The eyes may have difficulty focusing on near or far objects because the light rays are not focusing properly on the retina. Hyperopia (farsightedness) occurs when the eye cannot focus properly on nearby objects. Hyperopia usually occurs because the eyeball is too short, and the focal point of the lens is beyond the retina. Glasses using convex lenses are used to correct hyperopia, refocusing the focal point forward and on the retina. As the ciliary muscles age, they weaken, and pupil size is decreased, reducing the amount of light coming into the retina. Presbyopia is farsightedness that occurs with age, usually between 40 and 45 years. The lens becomes stiff and yellowish. Such age-related changes make it difficult for older adults to focus and make them more sensitive to glare that

conjunctivitis
(konJUNK tiv EYE tiss) Inflamed, reddened, and swollen conjunctivae with dilated blood vessels on the sclera. Caused by a foreign substance in the eye or an infection.

pink eye Also known as conjunctivitis; it is an inflammation of the membrane that lines the eye.

trachoma *(tray KOH mah)* A chronic form of conjunctivitis that is highly contagious.

cataract *(KAT ah rakt)* Clouding of the lens. Protein molecules in the lens begin to clump together. Caused by aging, sun exposure, eye trauma, smoking, and some medications.

glaucoma *(glaw KOH mah)* Increased intraocular pressure (IOP) because aqueous humor cannot circulate freely. In open-angle glaucoma, the angle where the edges of the iris and cornea touch is normal and open, but the trabecular meshwork is blocked. Open-angle glaucoma is painless but destroys peripheral vision, leaving the patient with tunnel vision. In closed-angle glaucoma, the angle is too small and blocks the aqueous humor. Closed-angle glaucoma causes severe pain, blurred vision, and photophobia. Glaucoma can progress to blindness.

macular degeneration Progressive deterioration of the macula lutea of the retina leading to vision loss.

atrophic A decrease in size of an organ or tissue; wasting.

(continued)

exudative Pathological oozing of fluids, usually the result of inflammation.

retinopathy *(ret ih NAH path ee)* Disease of the retina caused by hypertension or diabetes.

hyperopia *(HIGH per OH pee ah)* Farsightedness. Light rays from a far object focus correctly on the retina, creating a sharp image. However, light rays from a near object come into focus posterior to the retina, creating a blurred image.

presbyopia *(PRESS bee OH pee ah)* Loss of flexibility of the lens with blurry near vision and loss of accommodation.

bifocals Corrective lenses with two points of focus, used to treat presbyopia.

myopia *(my OH pee ah)* Nearsightedness. Light rays from a near object focus correctly on the retina, creating a sharp image. However, light rays from a far object come into focus anterior to the retina, creating a blurred image.

amblyopia *(am blee OH pee ah)* Reduction of vision due to dominance of one eye. Also known as lazy eye.

diplopia Brain receives two images and the person has double vision.

strabismus *(struh BIZ muhs)* Condition of eyes crossing due to inability to coordinate muscles of both eyes.

nyctalopia *(nick tah LOW pee ah)* The inability to see in dim light, night blindness.

Pathology Connection (continued)

can impair their nighttime driving abilities. Corrective lenses called **bifocals** can be used to treat presbyopia. Bifocal lenses have two points of focus: an upper part for distance vision and a lower part for near vision. **Myopia** (nearsightedness) causes objects at a distance to appear blurred. In myopia, the eyeball is too long, so the focal point of the lens falls in front of the retina. Glasses that use concave lenses correct myopia by refocusing the focal point backward and onto the retina. Students with myopia may have trouble seeing the board at the front of the class. Please see FIGURE 11-3 ▲ for a comparison on near- and farsightedness. **Amblyopia,** or lazy eye, causes poor vision in one eye because of abnormal dominance of the other eye, which does most of the work. Lazy eye usually occurs in childhood. If not corrected, it can lead to blindness in the lazy eye. The treatment for amblyopia is to cover the dominant eye, forcing the weak eye to work. Corrective lenses and surgery may also be needed.

Normally, the brain perceives the images received by each eye as one image. In **diplopia,** the brain perceives two images, so a person affected by diplopia has double vision. Double vision occurs because one eye is not aligned with the other, so the image does not fall on a corresponding point on the retina of each eye. Diplopia may be the result of a nonocular disease, so the disease needs to be treated. Otherwise, diplopia treatment includes placing a temporary eye patch over the misaligned eye, using special corrective lenses, or realigning the misaligned eye surgically.

In **strabismus,** one eye is misaligned due to an inability of the muscles in one eye to coordinate movement with the other eye. The affected eye turns inward, outward, upward, or downward in relation to the other eye, often giving the affected person a cross-eyed appearance. Children usually suffer from strabismus, which often results from a congenital defect. Acquired strabismus may result from injury or disease. In some cases, strabismus can be treated with exercises or corrective lenses. For many people, strabismus must be treated surgically to modify the affected muscles in an effort to realign the eyes.

Degeneration of the retina can cause difficulty seeing at night or in dim light. **Nyctalopia** is the name for this condition, often caused by a vitamin A deficiency. Vitamin A is a vital ingredient needed to make photopigments in rod cells. Photopigment is a light-sensitive chemical that triggers the photoreceptors along the visual nerve pathway. As a child you might have been told to eat your carrots so you could see well. Of course, carrots are very high in vitamin A.

Retinal disorders can be inherited, such as red-green color blindness due to genes on the X chromosome that cause abnormal photopigments in the cones. People with this condition can see colors but can't distinguish the difference between red and green. Colored figures are used to screen for color blindness to see if patients can differentiate between green, blue, and red. Because red-green color blindness is an X-linked disorder, more men get the condition. See FIGURE 11-4 ▲ to determine if you have color blindness.

Annual eye exams diagnose many of the problems listed previously, and early diagnosis can improve treatment. Ophthalmologists and optometrists use various tools such as eye charts, tonometers for measuring ocular pressure, and ophthalmoscopes for viewing the interior of the eye to identify and assess eye problems.

In addition, the eyes can be used to help diagnose a variety of nonvisual diseases. For example, a yellow tint to the conjunctiva (jaundice) may indicate a liver disease. A neurological assessment called PERLA, which stands for *pupils equal, reactive to light and accommodation,* can be used to assess brain injury. The rapid eye movement, or REM, stage of sleep is measured during sleep studies and helps to diagnose sleep disorders.

Myopic eye

Lens

Myopic cornea

Focal point is in front of retina

Retina

Images on retina are blurry

Normal eye

Lens

Cornea

Retina

Hyperopic eye

Eye ball is too short

Lens

Retina

Hyperopic cornea

Focal point is behind retina

Images on retina are blurry

FIGURE 11-3 ▲ A comparison on near- and farsightedness.

Pathology Connection (continued)

FIGURE 11-4 ▲ Ishihara charts to determine color blindness. Can you see the number?

Amazing Body Facts

Why We Can See in the Dark

The retina is a delicate membrane that continues posteriorly and narrows to become the **optic nerve.** It contains two types of light-sensing receptors called rods and cones. The **rods** are active in dim light and do not perceive color, whereas the **cones** are active in bright light and do perceive color. The retina of each eye contains about 3 million cones and 100 million rods. Together they enable you to see in a variety of light conditions. Do you ever wonder why you have to look off to the side at night to see stars more clearly? That is because cones and rods are not evenly distributed throughout the eye. The center of your eye contains only cones while the perimeter is dense with rods. This means when you look directly at a star it disappears or becomes dim because "cones" can not "see" it. This is why you only see shooting stars in your peripheral vision.

The rods and cones contain **photopigments** that cause a chemical change when light hits them. This chemical change causes an impulse to be sent to the optic nerve, and then to the brain, where the impulse is interpreted and we "see" the object. This interpretation occurs in the visual part of the cerebral cortex, located in the occipital lobe. The area where the neurons of the optic nerve exit the retina is known as the **optic disk.** This area is called the **blind spot** because it lacks rods and cones, so it cannot sense light or color.

optic nerve Cranial nerve II which carries information to the brain for interpretation of vision.

rods Light-sensitive cells in the retina. They detect black and white and function in daytime and nighttime vision.

cones Light-sensitive cells in the retina that detect colored light. There are three types of cones, each of which responds to either red, green, or blue light.

photopigments *(FOE toe PIG mints)* Chemicals in retinal cells that have light sensitivity.

optic disk Area where neurons of the optic nerve exit the retina.

blind spot An area of the retina where no vision occurs due to a lack of rods and cones.

Clinical Application

SNELLEN CHARTS

Eye-care professionals and others often measure visual acuity using a Snellen chart. You have probably seen one of these if you have taken a vision test for a driver's license. A traditional Snellen chart has 11 lines of block letters, getting progressively smaller toward the bottom. The patient covers one eye and then reads aloud the letters of each row. The smallest row that the patient can read accurately indicates the visual acuity in that eye.

(Source: Radu Bercan/Shutterstock.com.)

Amazing **Body Facts**

Eye Dominance

Most people have a dominant eye. To find yours, look at a small, distant object with both eyes open. Extend both arms with both palms facing that object. Slowly bring your hands together so there is a small opening or window formed in the space between the thumbs and the index figure. Now locate your distant object in that opening with both eyes open. Now alternately close each eye to determine which eye still sees that object. This is your dominant eye. Generally speaking, right-handed people have right-dominant eyes.

Clinical Application

LIFE WITHOUT GLASSES

Traditionally people with eye problems had to resort to eyeglasses or contact lenses as their only options. Thanks to the development of modern techniques, eyes can be surgically altered to bring them back toward normal vision. These techniques are listed under the general term **refractive eye surgery** and can include **radial keratotomy (RK),** in which actual incisions are made around the cornea. Recently lasers have also been employed to reshape the corneal tissue, as **in situ keratomileusis (LASIK)** surgery.

refractive eye surgery A surgical procedure that alters the eye to improve vision.

radial keratotomy *(ker eh TOT oh mee)* Vision surgery that makes incision around the cornea to improve sight.

in situ keratomileusis (LASIK) surgery *(in SIT oo KER ah toh mih LOO sis)* The use of laser to reshape corneal tissue to improve vision.

TEST YOUR KNOWLEDGE 11-1

Choose the best answer:

1. Which of the following is *not* a layer of the eye?
   a. photo optic
   b. sclera
   c. choroid
   d. retina

2. Which layer of the eye contains the iris and the pupil?
   a. cornea
   b. sclera
   c. choroid
   d. retina

3. The _____ is the colored portion of the eye that controls the opening, or _____, where light passes through.
   a. retina; pupil
   b. pupil; iris
   c. sclera; pupil
   d. iris; pupil

Complete the following:

4. _____ is a disease caused by increased pressure in the fluid of the eye that can lead to blindness.

5. _____ is a condition in which the eye can't focus on nearby objects.

6. Glaucoma, a condition of the eye, is caused by _____ pressure in the fluid of the eye. This pressure increase results in _____ of the ocular capillaries leading to damage of the retina.

---

external ear A portion of the ear we see that includes the auricle (pinna), ear lobe, and external auditory canal.

middle ear Region of the ear that includes the ear drum, malleus, incus and stapes, oval window, and eustachian tubes.

tympanic cavity See middle ear.

inner ear Region of ear that contains the cochlea, vestibule chamber, and the semicircular canals.

labyrinth *(LAB ih rinth)* Intricate communicating passage of the inner ear essential for maintaining equilibrium.

THE SENSE OF HEARING

On our journey, we hear many interesting sounds. Without our ears, we would miss all the pleasant noises, and the not-so-pleasant ones, that add to the appreciation of the journey. Also, on our journey, we may walk over some rough and uneven terrain. Our ears are also responsible for our sense of balance so we don't fall and get hurt. We can "hear" your heart pounding with anticipation, so let's explore the specific structures and functions of the ear.

Structures of the Ear

The ear is responsible for hearing and for maintaining our equilibrium, or sense of balance. We hear by receiving sound vibrations usually via the air (unless we are underwater) and translating them into an interpretable sound via the vestibulocochlear nerve. The ear can be separated into three divisions: the **external ear,** the **middle ear** (also called the **tympanic cavity**), and the **inner ear** (also called the **labyrinth**). See FIGURE 11-5 ▲ for the structures of the ear.

APPLIED SCIENCE

Sound Conduction

Many people are under the false impression that sound travels best through air because air is the medium in which we are immersed. However, sound is transmitted due to molecular collisions and is *better* transmitted where the molecules are closer together, such as in a liquid or solid medium. This is why whales can communicate with each other up to two miles apart underwater. This is also why trapped underground miners tap on the wall instead of shouting for help.

The External (Outer) Ear

The external ear is the outer projection, the part we can see. It comes in all shapes and sizes. (Remember Dumbo the Elephant?) It also includes the canal (where people put cotton swabs, despite the warning label) leading into the middle ear. The projecting part is called the **pinna** or **auricle**, which collects and directs sound waves into the **auditory canal** or **external auditory meatus**. The canal contains earwax, called **cerumen**, which is secreted by the **ceruminous glands** to lubricate and protect the ear. At the end of the canal is the **eardrum**, or **tympanic membrane**, where the external ear ends and the middle ear begins. (Note that tympanon means "drum.") Don't you wish there was just *one* term everyone agreed on for these structures?

The Middle Ear

The middle ear, or tympanic cavity, is basically a space in the temporal bone that contains the three smallest bones of your body. The three bones, or **ossicles**, are joined so they can amplify the sound waves the tympanic membrane receives from the external ear. (Sound travels best through a solid.) Once amplified, the sound waves are transmitted

pinna *(PINN ah)* The auricle of the exterior ear that collects sound waves.

auricle *(AW rih kul)* The visible external ear. Also known as the pinna.

auditory canal One of two canals that lead to the ear.

external auditory meatus *(AW dih tor ee mee AY tus)* Opening at the entrance to the external auditory canal where sound waves enter.

cerumen *(seh ROO men)* Sticky wax that traps dirt in the external auditory canal.

ceruminous gland *(seh ROO men us)* Gland that produces the waxlike substance in the ear.

eardrum Also known as the tympanic membrane; found in the middle ear.

tympanic membrane *(tihm PAN ik)* Membrane that divides the external ear from the middle ear. Also known as the eardrum.

ossicles *(AH sih kulz)* Three tiny bones in the middle ear that function in the process of hearing: malleus, incus, and stapes.

FIGURE 11-5 ▲ Structures of the ear.

hammer One of the three small bones of the ear, also known as the malleus.

malleus *(MALL ee us)* First bone of the middle ear. It is attached to the tympanic membrane on one end and to the incus on the other end. Also known as the hammer.

anvil One of the three small bones in the ear.

incus *(ING cus)* Second bone of the middle ear. It is attached to the malleus on one end and the stapes on the other end. Also known as the anvil.

stirrup One of the three small bones in the ear, also known as the stapes.

stapes *(STAY peez)* Third bone of the middle ear. It is attached to the incus on one end and the oval window on the other end. Also known as the stirrup.

oval window Opening in the temporal bone between the middle ear and the vestibule of the inner ear. The opening is covered by the end of the stapes.

Eustachian tube *(yoo STAY she ehn)* Tube that connects the middle ear to the nasopharynx and equalizes the air pressure in the middle ear.

cochlea *(COCK lee ah)* Structure of the inner ear that is associated with the sense of hearing. It relays information to the brain via the cochlear branch of the vestibulocochlear nerve.

vestibule chamber *(VESS tih byool)* A small cavity or space at the beginning of a canal.

semicircular canals *(SEM ee SIR kyoo lar)* Three canals in the inner ear that are oriented in different planes (horizontally, vertically, obliquely) that help the body keep its balance. They relay information to the brain via the vestibular branch of the vestibulocochlear nerve.

perilymph *(per ih LIMF)* Pale lymph fluid found in the labyrinth of the inner ear.

to the fluid contained in the internal ear. Once again, this is another example of sound waves being transmitted more efficiently though a liquid medium than in air.

The bones of the ears are named according to their shapes. The first ossicle attached to the tympanic membrane is the **hammer**, or **malleus**. The **anvil**, or **incus**, is attached to the hammer. Finally, the **stirrup**, or **stapes**, connects to a membrane called the **oval window**. The oval window begins the inner ear and carries the amplified vibrations from the tympanic ossicles. During transmission, the sound or vibrations can be amplified as much as 22 times their original level.

Also contained within the middle ear are the **Eustachian tubes**, which connect the pharynx to the middle ear. This effectively equalizes the air pressure on either side of the eardrum. The Eustachian tubes act as a passageway to allow for equalization of pressure between the outside atmospheric pressure coming through the nose and throat openings and the inner ear. This allows for equalization of pressure between the atmosphere and the middle ear. This pressure equalization allows the eardrum to vibrate freely with incoming sound waves. Sudden pressure changes, such as those caused by flying in an airplane, can affect this area. This is why, when flying, you are instructed to chew gum or swallow so the inner ear can better sense and adjust to the rapidly changing outside atmosphere via the Eustachian tubes.

The Inner Ear

The oval window membrane is the portal into the inner ear. This area contains three separate, hollow, bony spaces that form a complex maze of winding and twisting channels. Because another name for a maze is labyrinth, this area can also be called the bony labyrinth. The three areas are the **cochlea**; the **vestibule chamber,** which houses the inner ear; and the **semicircular canals**.

The cochlea is the bony spiral or snail shell–shaped portion of the internal ear connected to the oval window membrane (see **FIGURE 11-6** ▲). The cochlea contains a membranous tube, the cochlear duct, filled with a fluid called **perilymph** that helps to transmit the sound through this area. The sound is then transmitted to the back of the

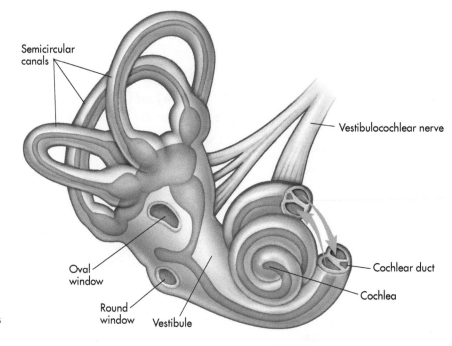

FIGURE 11-6 ▲ The internal structures of the cochlea.

cochlea, which contains another fluid called **endolymph**. Here the sound is carried to tiny hairlike receptors of the **organ of Corti** that pick up the vibrations of the fluid and conduct the signal to the brain via the **acoustic** (auditory), or **vestibulocochlear, nerve** (cranial nerve VIII). TABLE 11-2 ■ lists the major structures and functions of the ear.

Sound waves enter the external canal and vibrate the eardrum or tympanic membrane in a process called **sound conduction**. The middle ear then amplifies the sound through the respective ossicles. This process is called **bone conduction** of sound. The last ossicle (stapes) vibrates and causes a gentle pumping against the oval window membrane. This causes cochlear fluid to vibrate small hairlike nerve cells found in the organ of Corti. As a result of the vibrating sensory cells (hairlike nerves), a nerve impulse is sent to the temporal lobe of the brain, where it is interpreted as sound, a process called **sensorineural conduction**. Please see FIGURE 11-7 ▲ to better understand the process of hearing.

Low-intensity sound waves, similar to a clock ticking, send vibrations that cause the sensory cells to move in waves that are interpreted by the brain as that "ticktock" sound. In extreme cases where intense sound waves are produced, such as from a gun blast, it is believed that the vibrations are so great that they may knock over the hairlike cells much like an earthquake knocks over tall trees. Repeated assaults can lead to permanent hearing damage. Therefore, it is a "sound" investment to wear proper hearing protection around loud noises.

The ear is also responsible for your sense of balance or equilibrium. The semicircular canals process sensory input related to equilibrium. They contain nerve endings or

endolymph *(IN doe limf)* Fluid within the labyrinth of the ear.

organ of Corti Structure that possesses tiny hair-like receptors that pick up vibrations whose signals are sent to the brain for interpretation.

acoustic nerve See vestibulocochlear nerve.

vestibulocochlear nerve *(VESS tih byoo loh KOHK lee are)* The eighth cranial nerve responsible for hearing and balance. Sometimes called the acoustic nerve.

sound conduction The process in which sound waves enter the external canal and vibrate the eardrum.

bone conduction The process of the middle ear amplifying the sound through respective ossicles.

sensorineural conduction *(SEN soh ree NEW ral)* The process of sending nerve impulses to the temporal lobe of the brain where it is interpreted as sound.

TABLE 11-2 ■ STRUCTURES AND FUNCTIONS OF THE EAR

ORGAN OR STRUCTURE	FUNCTION
External Ear	
Auricle, or pinna	Cartilaginous projection that collects and directs sound waves into the auditory canal much like a satellite dish collects transmissions from space
Auditory canal, or external auditory meatus	Canal that contains earwax, or cerumen, secreted by the ceruminous glands that lubricate and trap foreign particles
Eardrum, or tympanic membrane	Membrane that separates the external and middle ear
Middle Ear	
Ossicles	Three small bones (hammer-, anvil-, and stirrup-shaped) that help amplify and transmit sound
Eustachian tubes	Allow for equalization of external (atmospheric) and internal (within the middle ear) pressure on the tympanic membrane so the eardrum can freely vibrate with incoming sound
Inner Ear, or Labyrinth	
Cochlea	Bony, snail-shaped portion of the internal ear containing perilymph fluid, which helps to transmit sound
Semicircular canals	Three canals containing endolymph fluid, which transmits positional changes to tiny, hairlike receptors that are stimulated and conduct the signal to the brain via the acoustic or vestibulocochlear nerve (eighth cranial nerve) to help maintain balance

receptors in the form of hair cells. The semicircular canals are three loops within the inner ear that help to maintain balance. Like the cochlea, they are filled with endolymphatic fluid, and each canal duct contains a sensory receptor. This fluid moves when you change body position. The movement is picked up by the sensory receptor, which triggers a nerve impulse to travel to the brain stem and the cerebellum via the vestibulocochlear nerve. Here the impulse is interpreted as body position to help maintain muscle coordination and body equilibrium.

FIGURE 11-7 ▲ The steps in the hearing process. 1) Sound waves enter the outer ear and travel through the ear canal. 2) Sound waves vibrate the ear drum. 3) The vibrations now vibrate the auditory ossicles in the middle ear. 4) Pressure waves created by stapes transfer to the oval window causing cochlea fluid to vibrate hairlike nerve cells. 5) Vibrations travel through the cochlear duct. 6) Signals travel to the brain's auditory center via the auditory nerves.

external otitis (oh TYE tiss) An inflammation of the outer ear.

otitis media (oh TYE tiss ME dee ah) Acute or chronic bacterial infection of the middle ear.

myringotomy (mir in GOT oh mee) A surgical procedure in which tiny tubes are inserted through the tympanic membrane to relieve pressure in cases of recurrent or chronic otitis media.

Pathology Connection

DISEASES OF THE EAR

Deafness can be either partial or complete and is caused by a variety of conditions, ranging from inflammation and scarring of the tympanic membrane to auditory nerve and brain damage. Hearing loss may also be caused by chronic exposure to loud sounds. Conductive hearing loss occurs when sound waves are prevented from reaching the inner ear. Excess earwax and otosclerosis cause conductive hearing loss. When the nerves of the ear are damaged, sensorineural hearing loss occurs.

External otitis, commonly called "swimmer's ear," is an infection caused by bacteria and fungi. Symptoms can include pain, fever, and temporary hearing loss. It is commonly contracted from contaminated swimming pools and beaches and can be prevented by cleaning and drying the external ear after swimming or wearing earplugs.

Otitis media is an acute infection of the middle ear, usually caused by a bacteria or virus, and is frequently found in infants and young children because of their immature Eustacian tubes. It is commonly associated with an upper respiratory infection (URI) such as a cold. Symptoms can include pain, edema, and pus. If left untreated, otitis media can perforate the tympanic membrane (eardrum). Otitis media is first treated with antibiotics. If the otis media is recurrent and chronic in nature, doctors perform a **myringotomy,** a surgical procedure during which tiny tubes are inserted

(continued)

Pathology Connection

through the tympanic membrane to relieve pressure. The tubes eventually fall out of the ear as the eardrum heals.

By examining the structure of the ear, can you see how a sinus infection (sinusitis) can spread to an ear infection and vice versa? There is also potential for invasion of the nearby honeycombed sinus area called the mastoid process. If colonized, it leads to **mastoiditis**. Mastoiditis can potentially lead to brain infections.

Labyrinthitis is an inflammation of the inner ear and is usually due to infection. Labyrinthitis can cause **vertigo**, which is a feeling of dizziness or whirling in space. If you are not sure what vertigo is, watch the Alfred Hitchcock classic movie of the same name. Not only does it clearly demonstrate vertigo, but it is also a great mystery movie. **Ménière's disease** is a chronic condition that affects the labyrinth (inner ear) and leads to progressive hearing loss and vertigo.

Otosclerosis is a chronic, progressive middle ear disorder that is characterized by excess bone growth in the middle ear. It primarily affects the stapes, or stirrup bone, causing excess growth of spongy bone tissue. The spongy bone tissue hardens and immobilizes the bone, causing a ringing in the ear(s) called tinnitus and deafness. A hereditary disease that eventually affects both ears, otosclerosis is treated by stapedectomy surgery. During a **stapedectomy,** the stapes is removed and replaced with a plastic or wire substitute.

Tinnitus is a symptom of sensorineural hearing loss. This condition affects approximately one in five individuals. It is a ringing, roaring, buzzing, hissing, or even clicking sound in the ears, which according to superstition, means someone is talking about you. Tinnitus occurs due to inner ear cell damage when the hairs of the inner ear are bent or broken, leading to a sending of random electrical impulses to the brain. The sound produced can occur in either one or both of your ears. Many specialists feel that the sound is produced by the brain to compensate for the lack of sounds no longer heard due to hearing loss. Clinically, it isn't a condition in itself, but rather, it can occur as a result of a variety of factors that can include chronic exposure to loud noises, old age, hearing loss called **presbycusis,** stress, depression, Ménière's disease, some medications (including certain antibiotics and cancer drugs), wax buildup, and various disturbances to the auditory nerve. In many cases, the exact cause of tinnitus is never discovered. Caffeine, alcohol, and chocolate can often intensify the sounds produced by tinnitus.

mastoiditis *(mass toy DYE tiss)* Inflammation of the mastoid sinuses, usually as a result of the spread of infection from acute otitis media.

labyrinthitis *(LAB ih rinn THIGH tiss)* Bacterial or viral infection of the semicircular canals of the inner ear, causing severe vertigo.

vertigo *(VER tih goh)* Sensation of being off balance when the body is not moving. Caused by upper respiratory infection, middle or inner ear infection, head trauma, or degenerative changes of the semicircular canals.

Ménière's disease *(MAIN ee AIRZ)* Recurring and progressive disease that includes progressive deafness, ringing ears, dizziness, and the feeling of fullness in the ears.

otosclerosis Chronic progressive deafness, especially for low tones. It is caused by the formation of spongy bone, especially around the oval window.

stapedectomy *(STAY pee DECK toh mee)* A surgical procedure in which the stapes of the ear is removed and replaced with a plastic or wire substitute.

tinnitus *(tinn EYE tus)* Sounds (buzzing, ringing, hissing, or roaring) that are heard constantly or intermittently in one or both ears, even in a quiet environment.

presbycusis Progressive loss of hearing with aging, typically resulting from sensorineural hearing loss.

TEST YOUR KNOWLEDGE 11-2

Choose the best answer:

1. The structure that marks the end of the external ear and the beginning of the middle ear is called the:
   a. pinna
   b. hammer
   c. tympanic membrane
   d. labyrinth

2. The structures of the ear that are important for balance are the:
   a. ceruminous glands
   b. incus, malleus, and stapes
   c. semicircular canals
   d. Eustachian tubes

Provide the synonymous terms for each of the following:

3. auricle _____

4. earwax _____

5. malleus _____

6. anvil _____

7. stirrups _____

Complete the following:

8. _____ is a condition of ringing in the ears.

9. _____ is an inflammation of the inner ear usually due to infection and causes vertigo.

OTHER SENSES

Other senses also help us to interpret the world around us. These include the senses of taste, smell, and touch.

Taste

gustatory sense *(GUS ta TORE ee)* Sense of taste.

taste buds Sensory end organs that provide us with a sense of taste.

umami *(oo MAM ee)* Japanese for savory or delicious and one of our tastes.

The sense of taste is referred to as the **gustatory sense**. The tongue is covered with tiny bumps called papillae, shown in FIGURE 11-8 ▲, each of which contains several taste receptors. These taste receptors are called **taste buds** and can also be found in other parts of the mouth, such as the soft palate and the back of the throat. Taste buds send signals to the brain by way of three distinct cranial nerves. One nerve innervates the anterior two-thirds of the tongue, a second innervates the posterior portion of the tongue, and a third nerve innervates the throat, but the taste buds do not have any distinct pattern on the tongue as was once thought. Taste buds detect five tastes: *sweet, sour, salty, bitter,* and **umami**. Umami has been recently added because it is the distinct

FIGURE 11-8 ▲ The sense of taste.

savory taste of glutamates often found in Asian cuisine, which cannot be duplicated by the combination of any of the other four tastes. Quite often, taste preferences change with the body's need, which is why, for example, pregnant women may crave a variety of foods throughout their pregnancy. The refinement of food taste is primarily dependent on the sense of smell.

Smell

The sense of smell arises from the receptors located in the olfactory region or the upper part of the nasal cavity (see **FIGURE 11-9** ▲). We "sniff" to bring smells up to this area, where they can be interpreted by tissues in the nose—olfactory epithelium—which contain specialized nerve cell receptors. Remember that taste and smell are closely related—and in fact smell accounts for 90% of taste—which is why we can't taste foods when we have a severe head cold. Pleasant food odors also initiate digestive enzymes, so when you smell that cinnamon apple pie baking, your mouth really may water in anticipation.

Smell is also closely linked to memory. Have you ever smelled cookies or cinnamon and automatically thought about a special holiday or family celebration? Smell has been shown to trigger memories. This may be useful someday with the treatment of dementia type diseases.

rhinitis *(rye NIGH tiss)* An acute, temporary, seasonal or year-round inflammation of the nasal mucosa with nasal congestion and increased mucus production.

histamine *(HISS tah meen)* A chemical released by basophils. Histamine dilates blood vessels and increases blood flow to damaged tissue. Allows protein molecules to leak out of blood vessels into the surrounding tissue. This produces redness and swelling.

tactile corpuscles *(TAK tile KOR pus elz)* Elongated bodies found in nerve ends that act as receptors for slight pressure or touch.

adaptation The adjustment of an organism to changing environments.

Viral and bacterial infections, allergies, harsh odors, and the use of certain illegal drugs, such as cocaine, all can contribute to a condition known as **rhinitis**. This condition causes inflammation of the mucous membranes that line the nasal passage and is characterized by congestion and drainage. Rhinitis develops in response to the body's release of **histamine,** a molecule released during an immune response. Rhinitis treatment includes removing the irritant causing the reaction and the use of antihistamine medications. In cases of chronic rhinitis, surgery may be performed to clear nasal obstructions.

Touch

Touch receptors are small, rounded bodies called **tactile corpuscles** located in skin and especially concentrated in the fingertips. They are also located on the tip of the tongue. It is interesting to note that even when a patient is locally anesthetized (and awake), there are no pain sensations, but the patient is still conscious of pressure through these deep touch sensors.

Temperature sensors are also found in the skin. The body has separate heat and cold receptors. These receptors may cause an interesting phenomenon called **adaptation** to occur. Continued sensory stimulation causes the sensors to desensitize or adapt. For example, if you are continually exposed to the cold, the receptors adjust so you won't feel so cold. That is why an outside temperature of 50 degrees seems warm after a long cold winter, but that same temperature seems cold after a long hot summer. Another example

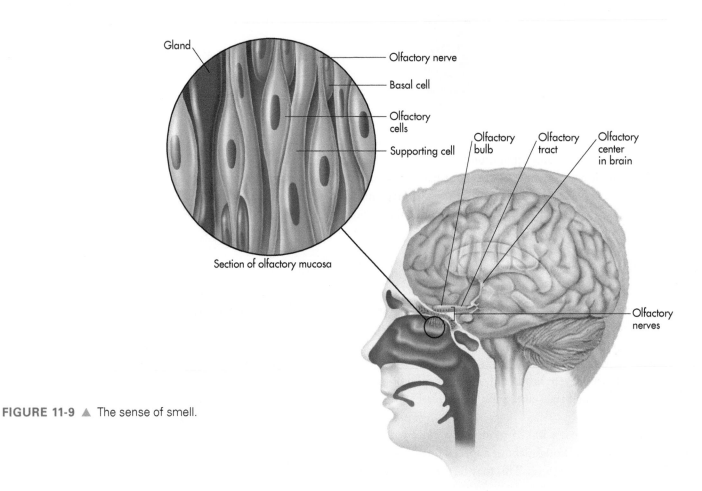

FIGURE 11-9 ▲ The sense of smell.

Clinical Application

HEAT AND COLD THERAPY

Heat and cold therapy are used for a variety of injuries. These therapies rely on physiological changes in the body in response to either heat or cold. For example, heat relaxes muscles and dilates blood vessels, thereby bringing more blood flow to the site of injury. Cold therapy constricts blood vessels and minimizes the amount of blood and swelling at a site.

is that when you first enter a hot bath, it may feel extremely hot. After a few seconds, it doesn't feel so hot, yet the actual temperature of the water has not yet changed.

Pain is a very important protective sense. It is the body's way of drawing attention to a particular danger, such as the "hitting your finger with a hammer" example used in the nervous system chapter. Pain is the most widely distributed sense, found in skin, muscle, joints, and internal organs. Pain receptors are merely branches of nerve fibers called **nociceptors** (free nerve endings).

There are even different types of pain. **Referred pain** originates in an internal organ yet is felt in another region of the skin because internal organs are not mapped on your somatic sensory cortex. For example, liver and gallbladder disease often cause pain in the right shoulder. See FIGURE 11-10 ▲ to view various sites of referred pain. **Phantom pain** can result from an amputated limb: An individual can feel pain in an arm or leg he or she no longer has.

nociceptors *(NOH see SEP torz)* Free nerve endings that are receptors of pain stimuli (pain receptors).

referred pain A perceived pain site other than the actual site of the trauma or disease.

phantom pain A sensation that an amputated limb is still present and is exhibiting pain.

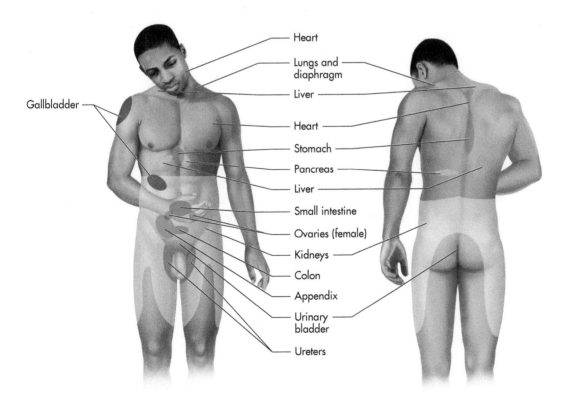

Gallbladder

Heart
Lungs and diaphragm
Liver
Heart
Stomach
Pancreas
Liver
Small intestine
Ovaries (female)
Kidneys
Colon
Appendix
Urinary bladder
Ureters

FIGURE 11-10 ▲ Various sites of referred pain.

anesthesia *(an ess THEE zee ah)* Condition in which sensation of any type, including touch, pressure, proprioception, or pain, has been completely lost.

Pain receptors do not adapt as heat and cold receptors do. Pain is felt for as long as the stimulus is there that is causing it or unless a person is under **anesthesia**. An interesting debate is whether or not some people have higher or lower thresholds of pain. See **FIGURE 11-11** ▲ for the senses of touch.

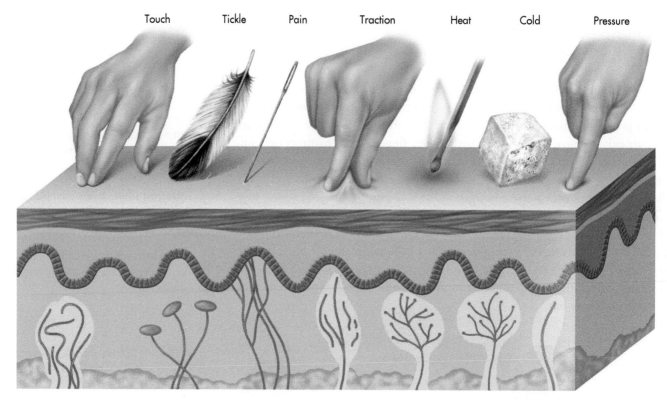

Touch   Tickle   Pain   Traction   Heat   Cold   Pressure

FIGURE 11-11 ▲ The sense of touch.

proprioception *(PROH pree oh SEP shun)* The sensation of movement and position of the body.

Proprioception is your body orientation sense that allows you for example to locate a body part with your eyes closed or know your arm is raised over your head without seeing it. Proprioreceptors are found in muscles, tendons, joints, and the inner ear, where they help with equilibrium. Motion sickness such as car sickness or sea sickness occurs in response to excessive stimulation of the equilibrium receptors in the ear.

FIGURE 11-12 ▲ shows some common eye disorders.

A

B

C

D

FIGURE 11-12 ▲ Some common eye disorders. **A.** Conjunctivitis ("pinkeye"). (Source: Levent Konuk/Shutterstock.com.) **B.** Cataract of right eye. **C.** Stye. (Source: Losevsky Pavel/Shutterstock.com.) **D.** A conjunctival hemorrhage of the right eye of this patient with infectious mononucleosis. (Courtesy: CDC/Dr. Thomas F. Sellers/Emory University.)

Clinical Application

CATARACT SURGERY

Cataract surgery is the most frequently performed surgery in the United States with a very high success rate. The clouded lens is removed and replaced with a clear plastic intraocular lens (IOL).

A QUICK TRIP THROUGH SOME DISEASES OF THE EYE

DISEASE	ETIOLOGY	SIGNS AND SYMPTOMS	DIAGNOSTIC TEST(S)	TREATMENT
Astigmatism	Alteration in the shape of the cornea in which it becomes more oblong or football shaped than spherical. Usually hereditary but can result from eye injury.	Blurred vision, eye strain and headaches.	Eye exam to view shape of cornea.	Unless extreme, it can be treated with eyeglasses or contact lenses. If extreme, refractive eye surgery.
Amblyopia (lazy eye)	Eye trauma or strong refractive error (nearsightedness or farsightedness); generally develops in young children.	Squinting or completely closing one eye to see, poor vision, eyestrain, and headaches.	History and eye exam.	Patching stronger eye to force weaker eye to function better, atropine eye drops, correcting refractive problems or surgery.
Blepharitis	Inflammation of eyelids, usually caused by bacterial infection.	Eye irritation, burning, tearing, dryness, and foreign body irritation.	History and eye exam.	Warm compresses, cleansing the eyes, antibiotics, artificial tears, and sometimes steroids.
Cataracts	Clouding of the lens, usually caused by protein clumping together as we age. Cause unknown but excessive UV light exposure suspected. Diabetics are at higher risk. Frequently occurs in people over 70.	Painful, gradual blurring and loss of vision.	Eye exam.	In early stages, glasses or magnification aids may help. Surgical correction of the lens is indicated when vision is seriously impaired.
Color blindness	Not really blindness at all but a genetic disorder that causes a deficiency in the way we see color. Red-green color deficiency is most common form. Caused by retinal cells inability to respond to certain colors. Usually hereditary via the mother, and more common in males. Aging and disease can also cause.	Difficulty distinguishing red from green or blue from yellow.	Ishihara plates (see Figure 11-4).	No cure but needs to be recognized early to prevent developmental issues.
Conjunctivitis (pinkeye)	Inflammation of the conjunctiva membrane caused by bacteria, viral or allergies.	Pinkish eye, discharge, excessive eye watering, pain, and itching.	History, eye exam and culture and sensitivity.	Avoidance of cause and infection precautions. Warm compresses. Antibiotic eye drops for bacterial infections and antihistamines for allergic forms.

DISEASE	ETIOLOGY	SIGNS AND SYMPTOMS	DIAGNOSTIC TEST(S)	TREATMENT
Diabetic Retinopathy	High blood sugar, damages the blood vessels in the eyes. Later stages can have new blood vessel growth over the retina, which can cause scar tissue and lead to retinal detachment. If untreated can cause blindness.	Floaters, double vision, fluid leakage, and swelling.	Fluorescein angiography. A contrast dye is injected and the blood flow to the retina is then assessed.	Laser photocoagulation to seal leaking blood vessels and destroy new growth. Some drugs helpful in early stages. May be prevented by good blood sugar control.
Dry eye syndrome	Chronic lack of eye lubrication and moisture due to lack of tear production. Can be part of aging process, side effect of medications, climate related (dry, dusty, or windy), long term contact use, lack of blinking or certain disease state. More common in women; smoking increases risk.	Dryness, scratchiness, and burning.	History and eye exam.	Avoid irritating cause. When prevention or cure not possible, artificial tears (lubricating eye drops) can be used to alleviate symptoms.

A QUICK TRIP THROUGH SOME DISEASES OF THE EARS

DISEASE	ETIOLOGY	SIGNS AND SYMPTOMS	DIAGNOSTIC TEST(S)	TREATMENT
External otitis, (Swimmer's ear)	Commonly caused by infection from water contaminated by bacteria or fungi.	Pain, fever, and temporary hearing impairment.	Visual ear exam.	Prevention by cleaning and drying external ear after swimming or by wearing earplugs.
Otitis media	Acute infection of the middle ear, usually caused by a bacteria or virus. Commonly associated with an upper respiratory infection, or URI, such as a cold.	Pain, edema, pus. If left untreated can perforate the tympanic membrane. There is potential for invasion of nearby mastoid process, leading to mastoiditis.	Otoscopic examination.	Treatment of underlying infection. Use of antibiotics if identified as bacterial infection.
Labyrinthitis	Inflammation of the inner ear usually caused by infection.	Vertigo; feeling of dizziness or whirling in space.	Patient history, radiologic studies.	Antivert class drugs, and in many cases Benadryl™ has been successful.

(continued)

A QUICK TRIP *(continued)*

DISEASE	ETIOLOGY	SIGNS AND SYMPTOMS	DIAGNOSTIC TEST(S)	TREATMENT
Ménière's disease	Chronic condition that affects the labyrinth.	Progressive hearing loss, tinnitus, and vertigo.	Patient history and exam; audiologic and radiologic exams.	Diuretics to "dry" out the labyrinth, decrease caffeine consumption.
Tinnitus	Can occur as a result of chronic exposure to loud noises, Ménière's disease, some medications, wax build-up, or various disturbances to the auditory nerve.	Ringing in ears.	History.	Eliminate loud noises.

Pharmacology Corner

mydriatic agents *(mid ree AT ik)* Drugs that dilate the pupil.

miotic agents Class of drugs that constrict the pupil.

There are times when the pupils of the eye should be dilated for an eye examination to allow for better visualization of the inner parts of the eye. The class of pupil dilating drugs is called **mydriatic agents**; atropine is an example. Patients are advised to wear sunglasses after an eye exam because the pupil cannot react to bright light until the drug wears off. On the other hand, certain drugs such as narcotics cause the pupils to constrict, sometimes so severely that the pupils look like pinpoints. The class of pupil constricting agents are called **miotic agents**.

Topical antibiotics (liquid drop and salve form) can be used for eye infections.

Ear medications can also consist of topically applied antibiotics applied for infections. In addition, topical anesthetics can be used for severe ear pain such as results from swimmer's ear. Antivert™ is a type of medication that affects the neural pathways that originate in the labyrinth and as a result inhibits nausea and vomiting caused by motion sickness.

SUMMARY

Snapshots from the Journey

- The senses of sight (eyes), sound and equilibrium (ears), taste (tongue), and smell (nose) are called special senses. The body feels other sensations, such as touch, heat, cold, and pain, which are called general senses.

- The eye is very similar to a camera, with lens cover (eyelids), opening (pupils), shutter (iris), lens (eye lens), and photoreceptive film (retina).

- Light rays enter the eye and pass through the conjunctival membrane, cornea, aqueous humor, pupil, lens, and vitreous humor and are focused on the retina. The photoreceptors in the retina cause a chemical impulse to be sent to the optic nerve, which carries it to the brain for the interpretation we call vision.

- The ear has three major divisions: the external, middle, and inner ear. The ear is the organ for hearing and maintaining our sense of balance.

- Sound waves enter the external canal and vibrate the eardrum, or tympanic membrane. The middle ear then amplifies the sound through the respective tiny bones, or ossicles. The last ossicle (stapes) vibrates and causes a gentle pumping against the oval window membrane. This causes cochlear fluid (perilymph) to move and vibrates tiny, hairlike neurons, which transmit an impulse to the hearing centers in the brain, where the sound is interpreted.

- The semicircular canals are responsible for maintaining body balance.

- Our sense of taste, or gustatory sense, has traditionally been thought to consist of sweet, sour, salty, and bitter. A fifth taste, umami, has recently been distinguished as its own category. The sense of taste originates on taste buds on the tongue and is closely associated with the sense of smell.

- The sense of smell arises from the olfactory region of the nose.

- The sense of touch allows perceptions of pain, temperature, pressure, traction, and the sensation of being "tickled."

MARIA'S STORY

Maria, a diabetic, has been going through a period of high stress and has been poorly monitoring her diabetes. She has noticed increasing visual problems and often sees specks floating in her visual field. Twice she had double vision episodes.

a. What should Maria's action plan include to get her back on track?

_____

_____

b. What could be the cause of the visual disturbances, and what should she do about them?

_____

_____

c. What structures of the eye are affected, and why?

_____

_____

d. Ultimately what eye disease(s) can Maria expect if she does not control her diabetes?

_____

_____

REVIEW QUESTIONS

Multiple Choice

1. The part of the eye that allows for varying amounts of light onto the retina is the:
   a. lens
   b. humor
   c. iris
   d. optic nerve

2. The photopigment structures responsible for the ability to see colors are:
   a. cones
   b. rods
   c. iris
   d. pupil

3. The incus is found in the:
   a. inner ear
   b. middle ear
   c. external ear
   d. region of South America

4. What is the correct descending order for the media through which sound travels, with the most efficient conductor of sound listed first:
   a. liquid, air, solid
   b. solid, liquid, air
   c. air, liquid, solid
   d. they are all equal

5. Another word for the sense of taste is:
   a. olfactory
   b. vertigo
   c. mastication
   d. gustatory

6. This highly contagious disease is also known as pinkeye:
   a. conjunctivitis
   b. myopia
   c. glaucoma
   d. contactitis

REVIEW QUESTIONS

Fill in the Blank

1. The two functions of the ear are _____ and _____.

2. The three ossicles of the ear are the _____, _____, and _____.

3. _____ is a chronic disease that affects the middle ear and includes progressive hearing loss, tinnitus, and vertigo.

Short Answer

1. Differentiate between special and general senses.

_____

2. What are the five basic tastes?

_____

3. Define *adaptation* in relation to temperature sensors.

_____

4. How does the body protect the eyes?

_____

5. How is an eye like a camera?

_____

Suggested Activities

1. Ask a local ophthalmologist to visit your class and explain the latest concepts and procedures in corrective vision surgery. In addition, have him or her bring an eye chart and explain 20/20 vision.

2. The sense of sight is also important to the interpretation of our sense of taste. Blindfold participants and have them identify similar products with varying tastes, such as different types of sodas or jelly beans, and see if they can correctly identify the flavor.

3. Hold this page about 15 inches from you face. Close your left eye and stare at the black dot while bringing the page slowly closer to your face. While staring at the dot, you will notice the X in the periphery disappear. You have just discovered your blind spot.

•

CAREER CONNECTIONS

Now that you have read this chapter, here is a list of related professions you may be interested in investigating for a future career:

- Ophthalmology and Opticians

- Audiologist

Research each profession and report on the following:

1. Profession description to include job responsibilities
2. Educational requirements
3. Job opportunities
4. Opportunities outside of the hospital setting
5. Salary range
6. Licensure and continuing education requirements

ANATOMY, PHYSIOLOGY, AND DISEASE IN ACTION

I. Visual Activity

Materials:
Stigmatism Chart, which can be downloaded from the Internet
Snellen Eye Chart perhaps from the nurse's office
Yard Stick or Tape Measure

Astigmatism is an alteration of the cornea in which it becomes more oblong. Light fails to come to a single focus on the retina to produce clear vision. Instead, multiple focus points occur, either in front of the retina or behind it (or both). To test for an astigmatism:

1. Remove prescription glasses
2. Cover one eye and look at the center circle in the diagram below. If the radiating lines appear equally dark, there is no astigmatism.
3. Test the other eye.
4. If glasses are worn, repeat the test with glasses.

II. Visual Acuity

1. Mount the Snellen Eye Chart on a wall. (The nurse's office may have one.)
2. Make a chalk line 20 feet from the chart.
3. Working in pairs, have one student cover the right eye (without glasses) and read the smallest letters on the chart correctly.
4. Record the rating. If the smallest letters that can be read are on line 5, the vision is recorded as 20/40 in the left eye, meaning that what should be seen at 40 feet is seen at 20 feet.
5. Repeat covering the left eye.

(continued)

ANATOMY, PHYSIOLOGY, AND DISEASE IN ACTION

III. Locating Sound

Materials:

Tuning fork (If not available, ticking clock or whispering may be substitutes)

The direction of sound is dependent on how fast it is detected by both or one ear. A difference in the hearing ability of the two ears can lead to a false direction of sound.

1. Work in pairs.
2. One of the partners should be seated with their eyes closed. With each test the subject should tell the location of the sound and record their perceptions. Strike the tuning fork:
   a. Directly below and behind the head
   b. Directly above the head
   c. Directly behind the head
   d. Directly in front of the face
   e. To the left and right side of the head
3. Note if there are any discrepancies. Additional studies could be inserted to see if there is a correlation with using earphones to listen to music or using tuning forks with different frequencies.

IV. Static Balance

Materials:

Graph chart paper
Tape

1. Mount the chart paper on the wall.
2. Working in pairs, have the subject remove their shoes and stand in front of the chart paper.
3. Record the number of divisions the subject has moved after 30 seconds under the following conditions:
   a. Standing on both feet, arms at side, eyes open
   b. Standing on both feet, arms at side, eyes closed
   c. Standing on one foot, arms at side, eyes closed
   d. Standing on both feet, arms extended, eyes open

What seems to be involved in the maintenance of equilibrium? Don't forget the obvious.

V. Relationship between Taste and Smell

All participants wash their hands before beginning this exercise.

Materials:

Individually wrapped lifesavers candy of different flavors

1. Working in groups of two, have the subject close their eyes and pinch their nose.
2. Unwrap one of the candies and drop it in the subject's hand.
3. The subject should then place the candy in their mouth and guess the flavor.
4. After guessing release the nose but with eyes closed. The subject should guess again.
5. Record the results for three different candies
6. Repeat the experiment with the experimenter becoming the subject. (Use different flavors that have not been seen.)

What are the senses that seem to be involved in taste?

12

The Cardiovascular System
Transport and Supply

On our cross-country journey, we will see a series of rivers and streams and perhaps some canals. Historically, these waterways have been used as a way of transporting food and supplies to people. These very same waterways also had by-products of industry dumped back into them. This is very similar to the *cardiovascular system,* also called the *circulatory system,* through which nutrients and oxygen are transported to the cells in the body and carbon dioxide and other waste products of cells' metabolism are removed. The cardiovascular system is also a lot like a hot water heating system in a house. The furnace has a pump (heart) to circulate the hot water (blood) through the piping system (vessels) to deliver the much-needed heat to every room throughout the building. So let's get right to the "heart" of the matter.

LEARNING OUTCOMES

Upon completion of your journey through this chapter, you will be able to:

- Identify structures and functions of the cardiovascular system
- Trace the blood flow through the vessels and chambers of the heart
- Explain the coronary circulation
- Describe the contraction of the heart and the conduction system
- Differentiate between arteries, veins, and capillaries
- List the major components of blood and their functions
- Discuss the importance of blood typing
- Explain the process of blood clotting
- Explain the importance of blood pressure regulation
- Describe various cardiovascular diseases

Pronunciation Guide

Correct pronunciation is important in any journey so that you and others are completely understood. Here is a "see and say" Pronunciation Guide for the more difficult terms to pronounce in this chapter. Please note that pronunciations given are referenced to medical dictionaries, and regional variations may exist.

agglutinate (ah GLUE tin ate)
albumin (al BYOO men)
anastomosis (ah NASS teh MOE sis)
anemia (ah NEE mee ah)
aneurysm (AN yoo rizm)
arterioles (ahr TEE ree ohlz)
arteriosclerosis (ar TEE ree oh skleh ROH sis)
atherosclerosis (ATH er oh skleh ROH sis)
atrioventricular (AY tree oh vehn TRIK yoo lahr)
atrium; atria (AY tree um; AY tree ah)
autorhythmicity (AW toe rith MIH sih tee)
basophils (BAY soh fillz)
bundle of His (HISS)
diastole (dye ASS toe lee)
embolus (EM boh lus)
endocardium (EHN doh KAR dee um)
eosinophils (EE oh SIN oh fillz)
epicardium (ep ih KAR dee um)
erythrocytes (eh RITH roh sights)
fibrinogen (fye BRINN oh jenn)
hemophilia (HEE moh FILL ee ah)
hemopoiesis (HEE moh poy EE sis)
hemostasis (HEE moh STAY sis)

homeostasis (HOE mee oh STAY sis)
infarct (IN farkt)
inotropism (EYE no TROPE izm)
ischemia (iss KEE mee ah)
leukocytes (LOO koh sights)
lysosomes (LIE so zoams)
myocardium (my oh KAR dee um)
neutrophils (NOO trow fillz)
phagocytosis (FAG oh sigh TOH sis)
polycythemia (PALL ee sigh THEE mee ah)
prothrombin (pro THROM bin)
septum (SEHP tum)
sinoatrial (SIGH noh AT tree al)
systole (SISS toh lee)
thrombin (THROM bin)
thrombocytes (THROM boh sights)
thrombocytopenia
  (THROM boh SIGH toh PEE nee ah)
thrombus (THROM bus)
tunica externa (TOO nick ah ex TERN ah)
tunica interna (TOO nick ah in TERN ah)
tunica media (TOO nick ah MEE dee ah)
venules (VEHN yulz)

SYSTEM OVERVIEW

cardiovascular system Body system that includes the heart, blood, arteries, veins, and capillaries. It distributes blood throughout the body.

heart A hollow, muscular organ, the pump of the circulatory system.

blood The cell-containing fluid that circulates through the heart, arteries, veins, and capillaries, carrying nourishment, electrolytes, hormones, vitamins, antibodies, heat, and oxygen to the tissues and taking away waste matter and carbon dioxide.

The major components of the **cardiovascular system** include the **heart** (which is the organ that pumps blood through the system), **blood** (a form of connective tissue that has a fluid component called **plasma** and a variety of cells and substances), and **blood vessels** (a network of passageways to transport the blood to and from the body's cells).

Blood vessels can be further classified. Vessels that carry blood away from the heart are called **arteries**. These main vessels branch out into ever-smaller vessels called **arterioles**, which eventually become **capillaries**. Capillaries are where the exchange of nutrients, gases, and waste products occurs at the cellular level. Capillaries are also the transition vessels where blood begins its trip back to the heart through ever-merging vessels that form larger **veins**. The tiniest of these veins are called **venules**. To view this transitional region along with the cardiovascular system, see FIGURE 12-1 ▲.

The cardiovascular system includes the heart, blood, and blood vessels. The circulatory system can technically include the cardiovascular system and the lymphatic system, which will be further covered in the immune system chapter. The cardiovascular system has four main functions. First, it functions to pump materials throughout the body. Second, it is designed specifically to transport blood to various parts of the body. Third, this movement of materials facilitates the delivery of vital materials, such as oxygen

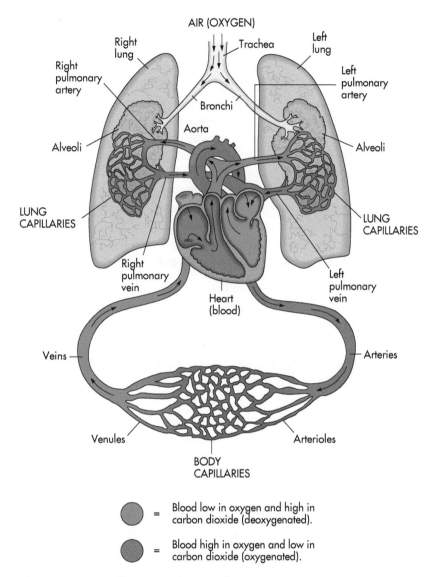

FIGURE 12-1 ▲ Overview of the cardiovascular system.

plasma *(PLAZ mah)* Clear, straw-colored fluid portion of the blood that carries blood cells and contains dissolved sub- stances like proteins, glucose, minerals, electrolytes, clotting factors, complement proteins, hormones, bilirubin, urea, and creatinine.

blood vessels The veins, arteries, and capillaries.

arteries Blood vessels that carry blood away from the heart.

arteriole *(ahr TEE ree ohl)* Smallest branch of an artery.

capillaries *(KAP ih LAIR eez)* The smallest blood vessels in the body, connecting blood vessels between arterioles and venules. The exchange of oxygen and carbon dioxide takes place in the capillaries.

vein Blood vessel that carries oxygen-poor blood as well as carbon dioxide and waste products of cellular metabolism away from the cells and back to the heart. Veins have one-way valves that keep blood from flowing backward, away from the heart. The exception is the pulmonary vein, which carries oxygenated blood from the lungs to the heart.

venules *(VIN yulz)* Smallest branches of a vein.

and nutrients, to the cells of the body and the removal of cellular wastes. Finally, the circulatory system functions to return excess tissue fluid, often in the form of lymph, to general circulation.

In general, veins differ from arteries not only because veins bring blood back to the heart but also because the blood now is *deoxygenated* (contains less than the normal arterial amount of oxygen) and has a higher level of carbon dioxide and other waste products of cellular metabolism. Arteries transport blood under higher pressure than do veins because the blood is being forcefully pushed out of the heart via arteries. In contrast, venous blood is passively returning to the heart, driven mainly by the pressure of the blood circulation. Veins also have thinner walls than arteries, are more numerous, and have a larger capacity to hold blood.

Color-Coded Blood

Notice in Figure 12-1 that blood is depicted as being "blue" or red depending on the area in which it is located. When the blood contains high amounts of oxygen (oxygenated), it causes a chemical change within the red blood cell. This occurs in the blood of most arteries. As a result of that change, the arterial blood turns a bright red color. As the oxygen is being delivered to the tissues in the body, the blood begins to turn a dark crimson color due to lower levels of oxygen saturation on the red blood cells. This occurs mostly in the veins that have lower levels of oxygen (deoxygenated) due to their delivery or dumping of oxygen to the tissues. You can see the darker veins within your wrists or arms. However, when you cut a vein, the blood is no longer darker red because it immediately comes into contact with the oxygen in the atmosphere and becomes bright red again.

INCREDIBLE PUMPS: THE HEART

Let's begin our journey with the main organ of the cardiovascular system: the heart. Although it is often described as the "pump" of the cardiovascular system, you will soon see that it is actually *two* pumps working together.

Arteries or Veins?

Remembering what arteries and veins do can be confusing. One easy way to remember is that arteries take blood *away* from the heart. Both words start with *a*. Obviously, then, veins have to bring blood back to the heart.

pericardium *(per ih CAR dee uhm)* The serous membrane that surrounds the heart.

serous pericardium A flattened sac formed of a single layer of cells and connective tissue.

parietal layer The middle layer of the pericardial sac, a serous membrane lining the fibrous pericardium.

visceral layer The side of the sac attached to the external surface of the heart.

pericardial cavity The potential cavity between the parietal and visceral layers of the pericardium.

epicardium *(EP ih KAR dee um)* Another name for the visceral pericardium.

myocardium *(MY oh CAR dee uhm)* Middle layer of the heart wall composed of cardiac muscle.

endocardium *(IN doh KAR dee um)* Innermost layer of the heart. It covers the inside of the heart chambers and valves.

General Structure and Function

The heart is a specially shaped muscle, about the size of your fist, containing a series of chambers that move blood throughout the body. The heart is surrounded by a serous membrane called the **pericardium.** The outer layer is a tough fibrous pericardium. Inside the fibrous pericardium is **serous pericardium,** a serous membrane with two layers, the **parietal layer** which lines the fibrous pericardium and the **visceral layer** is fused to the heart surface. There is a potential cavity between the layers called the **pericardial cavity.** The outer layer of the heart wall, the visceral pericardium, is also known as the **epicardium.** The middle layer of the heart wall, the **myocardium,** is made of cardiac muscle. The heart is lined by epithelium, called the **endocardium.** See FIGURE 12-2 ▲.

BASE

Superior vena cava
(from head and arms)

Aorta

Left pulmonary artery
(to lung)

Right
pulmonary
artery (to lung)

Pulmonary valve

Left pulmonary veins
(from lung)

Right
pulmonary
veins (from
lung)

Left atrium

Right atrium

Bicuspid (mitral) valve

Tricuspid valve

Aortic valve

Chordae tendineae

Myocardium
(heart muscle)

Epicardium
(outer layer)

Left ventricle

Inferior vena cava
(from trunk and legs)

Interventricular
septum

Endocardium

Right ventricle

APEX

FIGURE 12-2 ▲ The anatomy of the heart. Remember: The heart is labeled right and left based on the patient's perspective.

veins Blood vessesl that carry oxygen-poor blood as well as carbon dioxide and waste products of cellular metabolism away from the cells and back to the heart. Veins have one-way valves that keep blood from flowing backward, away from the heart. The exception is the pulmonary vein, which carries oxygenated blood from the lungs to the heart.

arteries Blood vessels that carry blood away from the heart.

atrium (atria) *(AY tree um, AY tree ah)* Two upper chambers of the heart. Intra-atrial structures are located within the atria.

ventricles *(VEN trih kulz)* Two lower chambers of the heart. Intraventricular structures are located in the ventricles.

interatrial septum *(IN ter AY tree al)* The wall that separates the right and left atria.

interventricular septum *(in TUR ven TRIK yuh ler SEP tum)* The wall that separates the right and left ventricles.

right atrium Chamber that collects blood that is returning from the venous system of the body.

superior vena cava *(VEE nah KAY vah)* Largest vein that drains venous blood from the upper portions of the body into the right atrium.

inferior vena cava The vena cava is the largest vein in the body. The inferior vena cava receives blood from the abdomen, pelvis, and lower extremities and takes it to the heart.

right ventricle Chamber of the heart that pumps blood to the lungs for gas exchange.

atrioventricular valve *(AY tree oh vehn TRIK yoo lahr)* The valve situated between the atrium and the ventricle.

AV valve See atrioventricular valve.

tricuspid *(try KUS pid)* Having three cusps or points as in the tricuspid valve of the right heart.

The heart is located in the thoracic cavity, slightly left of the center of your chest and above your diaphragm. As strange as it may initially appear, the *base* of the heart is proximal to (closer to) your head, whereas the *apex* of the heart is distal (further away from it).

Although the heart is a single organ, it is easier to understand its function if you think of it as two separate pumps working together. The right side of the heart is responsible for collecting blood from the body and sending it to the lungs to pick up oxygen and get rid of carbon dioxide. The left side of the heart collects blood from the lungs and pumps it through the body. Before we explore the heart, it's important to review that blood returning to the heart travels through **veins** (thus, venous blood), and blood traveling away from the heart travels through **arteries** (thus, arterial blood). You have probably already heard of some veins and arteries. For example, the carotid arteries are the large arteries on each side of the neck that deliver blood from the heart to the head. The jugular veins are large veins that take blood from the head to the heart.

Inside the heart are four chambers, two upper chambers called **atria,** and two lower chambers called **ventricles**. The chambers of the right side of the heart are separated from the chambers of the left side, so there is normally no mixing of blood from one side to the other. The wall that separates the two smaller chambers (atria) is called the **interatrial septum;** the wall between the two larger chambers (ventricles) is called the **interventricular septum**. (Septum means "wall.") When looking at Figure 12-2, you will notice the small chamber in the upper left quadrant of the picture. That is the **right atrium**. (Remember, locations are based on the *patient's* perspective). This is a collecting chamber where blood is returned to the heart after its trip through the body. The two large veins that bring the blood to the right atrium are the **superior vena cava** (blood from the head, neck, chest, and upper extremities) and **inferior vena cava** (blood from the trunk, organs, abdomen, pelvic region, and lower extremities). Once the blood is collected, it drains through a one-way valve to a larger chamber in the right side called the **right ventricle**. That one-way valve is called the right **atrioventricular valve,** or **AV valve**. This is also called the **tricuspid** valve because the valve is formed with three cusps. The opening and closing of these valves produces the "lubb dupp" sound characteristic of the heart.

Cardiac Cycle

cardiac cycle The movement of the heart in which it contracts to pump blood (systolic phase) and relaxes to allow the chambers to fill with blood (diastolic phase).

systole *(SISS toh lee)* Combined contractions of the atria and the ventricles.

diastole *(dye ASS toe lee)* Resting period between contractions. It is when the heart fills with blood.

pulmonary semi-lunar valve Valve located between the right ventricle and pulmonary trunk.

pulmonary artery Artery that carries blood from the heart to the lungs. The pulmonary artery is the only artery in the body that carries blood that has low levels of oxygen.

cardiopulmonary circulation The process of circulating blood through the lungs to pick up oxygen and drop off carbon dioxide to be exhaled into the atmosphere.

The movements of the heart, called the **cardiac cycle,** can be divided into two phases called **systole** and **diastole.** Usually when discussing heart movement we refer to ventricle activity.

When the right ventricle is full of blood, the heart contracts (systole). Because valves are one way, as the right ventricular pressure increases, the tricuspid valve shuts so blood doesn't squirt back into the right atrium. As the pressure increases, the blood has to go somewhere. The only way for the blood to travel is through the **pulmonary semi-lunar valve** to the pulmonary trunk, which divides into the left and right **pulmonary arteries.**

Cardiopulmonary circulation is the process of circulating blood through the lungs, picking up oxygen from the lungs, and depositing carbon dioxide there to be released from the body during an exhalation. Each pulmonary artery goes to its respective lung and branches out into ever-smaller vessels to the point where they become capillaries that form a network around each air sac in the lungs. This is where the blood gives up carbon dioxide, one of the waste products of metabolism by cells, and picks up a fresh supply of oxygen from the lungs. These capillaries containing freshly oxygenated blood converge into increasingly larger vessels until they form the left and right pulmonary veins. FIGURE 12-3 ▲ illustrates the blood flow through the heart.

The pulmonary veins meet and pour their contents into the **left atrium.** Once the left atrium is filled, blood flows through the left AV valve and into the **left ventricle.** When the left ventricle is full, the heart contracts again. The ventricular pressure increases, forcing the left AV valve shut and ejecting the blood out of the left ventricle through the aortic semilunar valve to the ascending aorta, sending it on its way throughout the body. Two more familiar names for the left AV valve are **bicuspid** (formed by only two leaves or cusps) or **mitral** valves. Now the ventricles and atria can rest (**diastole**) as the atria fill with blood before they squeeze another load of blood into the ventricles. It is important to note that the chambers of the heart fill during diastole, or the relaxation phase, and eject blood during systole, or the contraction phase.

LEARNING HINT

The Tricuspid Valve

Remember the T̲ricuspid valve is on the R̲ight side of the heart.

Amazing Body Facts

Pulmonary Arteries and Veins

Pulmonary veins and arteries are critical because they serve a unique function. The pulmonary arteries are the *only* arteries in the body that carry *deoxygenated* blood away from the right heart to travel to the lungs to become oxygenated. The pulmonary vein collects this oxygenated blood and returns it to the left side of the heart, and therefore it is the *only* vein to carry oxygenated blood.

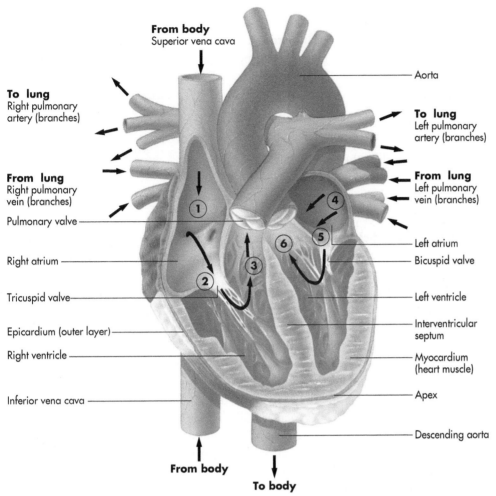

From body
Superior vena cava

Aorta

To lung
Right pulmonary
artery (branches)

To lung
Left pulmonary
artery (branches)

From lung
Right pulmonary
vein (branches)

From lung
Left pulmonary
vein (branches)

Pulmonary valve

Right atrium

Left atrium

Bicuspid valve

Tricuspid valve

Left ventricle

Epicardium (outer layer)

Interventricular
septum

Right ventricle

Myocardium
(heart muscle)

Apex

Inferior vena cava

Descending aorta

From body

To body

RIGHT HEART PUMP

1. Deoxygenated blood returns from the upper and lower body to fill the right atrium of the heart creating a pressure against the atrioventricular (AV) or tricuspid valve.

2. This pressure of the returning blood forces the AV valve open and begins filling the ventricle. The final filling of the ventricle is achieved by the contracting of the right atrium.

3. The right ventricle contracts increasing the internal pressure. This pressure closes the tricuspid valve and forces open the pulmonary valve thus sending blood toward the lung via the pulmonary artery. This blood will become oxygenated as it travels through the capillary beds of the lung and then returns to the left side of the heart.

LEFT HEART PUMP

4. Oxygenated blood returns from the lung via the pulmonary vein and fills the left atrium creating a pressure against the bicuspid valve.

5. This pressure of returning blood forces the bicuspid valve open and begins filling the left ventricle. The final filling of the left ventricle is achieved by the contracting of the left atrium.

6. The left ventricle contracts increasing internal pressure. This pressure closes the bicuspid valve and forces open the aortic valve causing oxygenated blood to flow through the aorta to deliver oxygen throughout the body.

FIGURE 12-3 ▲ The functioning of the heart valves and blood flow.

left atrium The chamber of the heart that receives oxygenated blood from the lungs.

left ventricle Chamber of the heart that pumps the oxygenated blood through the body.

bicuspid *(by KUS pid)* A two-leafed structure, as in the bicuspid valve of the heart.

mitral *(MYE tral)* Pertaining to the bicuspid or mitral valve of the heart.

diastole *(dye ASS toe lee)* Resting period between contractions. It is when the heart fills with blood.

pulse What is felt when an artery is palpated and the heart contracts.

Heart rate can be measured by counting the **pulse,** which is the rhythmic expansion and contraction of arteries due to the opening and closing of the aortic semilunar valve. Pulse can be measured in several places on the body:

• Brachial arteries: Pulse is checked by placing fingers on the anterior side of the elbow, where the arm flexes toward the body.

• Carotid arteries: Pulse is checked by placing fingers on the large arteries on either side of the neck.

- Femoral arteries: Pulse is taken by placing fingers on the anterior midline of the leg where the leg flexes in relation to the trunk.
- Pedal arteries: Pulse is taken by placing fingers on arteries on top of the foot.
- Popliteal arteries: Pulse is taken by placing fingers on arteries in the posterior knee.
- Radial pulse: Pulse is taken by placing fingers on arteries in the anterior wrist on the thumb side.

Some points to remember are that:

- Both atria fill at the same time.
- Both ventricles fill at the same time.
- Both ventricles eject blood at the same time when the heart contracts.

Do you ever get yelled at or get mad at the *other* person for squeezing the toothpaste tube in the middle? What's the big deal? When you eat a freeze pop, do you squeeze it in the middle or from the bottom and work the contents up to your mouth? These two examples are important to visualize because the heart has to contract in a certain way to make sure that all the blood is squeezed out during each contraction. In order to do this, the contraction begins at the apex and travels upward. As you trace the flow of blood in Figure 12-3, you will see how efficient this is. You should also notice that there is a semilunar valve located at the exit of both ventricles. Because your circulatory system is a pressurized system, these valves are necessary to prevent any ejected blood from leaking back in.

If you further examine the heart illustration, you will notice that the walls of the atria are thinner than the ventricular walls. This is because higher pressures are generated in the ventricles to move blood. You should also note that the walls of the left ventricle are thicker than the walls of the right ventricle. When you think about it, this makes total sense. The right ventricle has to pump blood only a short distance through the vasculature of the lungs and back to the heart. This is called the **pulmonary circulation**. The left ventricle, on the other hand, has to pump all the blood

pulmonary circulation Movement of blood from right ventricle to lungs and then back to left atrium.

angiogram *(AN jee oh gram)* A radiographic recording of the size, shape, and location of the heart and its blood vessels following the injection of a radiopaque medium.

radiocontrast agent A dye placed into the blood to make it contrast its surroundings on an x-ray.

Clinical Application

ANGIOGRAPHY

One way to get a good picture of the blood flow in a person's body (and any problems with it) is to perform an **angiogram.** An angiogram is an x-ray of the body after a **radiocontrast agent** (a dye that makes the blood contrast with its surroundings on an x-ray) has been injected into the blood. The angiographic x-ray shows shadows of the openings within the cardiovascular structures carrying blood; the blood vessels themselves do not appear. The most common use of an angiogram is to visualize the blood flow in the coronary arteries.

throughout the body and back to the right atrium! This is referred to as the **systemic circulation**. The resistance of all those blood vessels in the body (systemic) is six times greater than the resistance of the pulmonary vasculature.

In the Amazing Body Facts box, you learned that the heart muscles have a blood-rich environment. In FIGURE 12-4 ▲, you can see that a portion of the newly oxygen-enriched blood is diverted from the aorta by the right and left **coronary arteries**. These arteries continuously divide into smaller branches, forming a web of interconnections known as **anastomoses**, which enable the heart muscle to constantly and fairly consistently receive a rich supply of blood. It is interesting to note that regular aerobic exercise can increase the density of these blood vessels that supply the heart. The number of anastomoses also increases, as does their number of locations. This is important for people with blockage of a small coronary artery. This may lead to an increased survival rate during a heart attack because blood may have alternate routes to travel, which could help to prevent heart muscle damage.

The right coronary artery provides blood for the right ventricle, posterior portion of the interventricular septum, and inferior parts of the heart. The left coronary artery provides blood to the left lateral and anterior walls of the left ventricle and to portions of the right ventricle and interventricular septum.

systemic circulation Movement of blood from the left ventricle throughout the body and back to the right atrium.

coronary arteries Blood vessels that provide oxygen enriched blood to the heart.

anastomoses Interconnections of blood vessels.

intercalated discs *(in ter KUH late ed)* Structures that connect heart tissue cells to facilitate a smooth contraction.

Amazing Body Facts

How Does it Keep Going and Going and Going?

One of the amazing things about your heart is that it continues to beat day after day without you even thinking about it. Here is a neat experiment. Previously, we said that your heart is about the size of your fist. Let's pretend that your fist is your heart. To mimic the pumping action of your heart, open your fist with your fingers fully extended. Now make a tight fist. Continue this action of fully opening and tightly closing your hand for the next *60 seconds*. Chances are good that your hand will feel like it's ready to fall off of your arm! If this is how your hand feels after 60 seconds, how does your heart constantly beat approximately 100,000 times and move approximately 1,800 gallons of blood each day for decades and decades? Think back to Chapter 7 on muscles. Cardiac muscle cells have specialized connections called **intercalated discs**. These connections, along with associated pores, provide an efficient connection with adjacent muscle cells so electrical impulses, ions, and various small molecules can readily travel throughout the heart, allowing a smooth contraction from one area of the heart to another. The vasculature of the heart takes approximately 5% of oxygenated blood from each heartbeat to ensure there is a blood-rich environment so plenty of oxygen and nutrients are available.

FIGURE 12-4 ▲ Coronary circulation.

Pathology Connection

PROBLEMS WITH CARDIAC MUSCLE AND CARDIAC VASCULATURE

Pump Problems

So far, we have discussed how a healthy heart works. However, certain events can affect the efficiency of the heart's pumping action. Remember that this is a two-pump system. What may damage one pump may not always damage the other pump.

Let's look at the right side of the heart first. Right-side heart failure is a potentially serious condition in which the right-side pump can't move blood as efficiently as it should. This is a result of the heart muscle of the right pump *chronically* working harder than normal. As with any muscle that you exercise over time, heart muscle also becomes larger. In this case, the muscles on the right side of the heart become too large and can no longer efficiently pump blood. Remember that the left side is pumping normally, and we are working with a closed system, much like a water pump and cooling system in a car. As the healthy left side pumps blood through your body and back to the right side, the now-inefficient right side cannot take all the returning blood to pump it to the lungs. As a result, the blood begins to back up. The vessels in the body are flexible and can expand a little to take that extra volume of blood, so extended neck veins can be a sign of a right-side pumping problem. Certain organs can hold more blood than usual, so an engorged liver and spleen can also be a sign of right heart failure. Tissues in the periphery can hold extra fluid, so swollen ankles, feet, and/or hands can also be a sign of right-sided heart failure. Disease conditions such as **polycythemia,** in which the blood is thicker than normal and, therefore, is harder to pump, or blood vessels in the lungs that constrict more than normal, making it harder to push blood through them, can cause the right ventricle to work harder. Because these two conditions are often related to certain lung diseases, it is no surprise that 85% of patients with chronic obstructive pulmonary disease develop right-side heart failure.

Heart failure (in the past, often called *congestive* heart failure) is a potentially life-threatening condition that is usually a problem of the left pump of the heart and can be caused by decreased pumping efficiency of damaged muscle fibers of the left ventricle following a heart attack. This is a situation in which the pumping action of the heart cannot overcome an increased systemic blood pressure, or in which the systemic blood pressure is normal but the left ventricle is too weakened to effectively pump blood. As a result of this increasing vascular pressure, fluid begins to leak out of the vessels and into the tissues of the body. Now let's consider a left-sided heart failure scenario. The healthy right pump pushes blood through the vasculature of the lungs on its way to the left-side pump. If the left side can't keep up with the blood being delivered to it, the blood backs up into the lungs, increasing the pressure in those blood vessels. (Remember, this is a closed system!) Once that pressure reaches a certain point, fluid leaks out of the vessels and into the lung tissue and even the air spaces. **Pulmonary edema** is the term for fluid that forms in the lungs and causes difficulty breathing. See FIGURE 12-5 △. Heart failure can be treated with cardiotonic agents that increase the rate and force of contraction along with diuretics to rid the system of excess fluid.

Myocardial Infarction (MI) is a condition related to the upcoming "vessel problems" section in which there is too little or no blood flow to the myocardium (the heart muscles). At first, an inadequate flow of blood to the cardiac muscles known as **ischemia** will make the patient feel uncomfortable and anxious, and often they will have a pain or discomfort in their chest known as **angina pectoris,** which comes from the lack of O_2 to the heart. The chest pain may radiate to the left

---

polycythemia
(PAUL ee sigh THEE mee ah) Increased number of erythrocytes due to uncontrolled production by the red marrow. The viscosity of the blood increases; it becomes viscous (thick), and the total blood volume is increased.

heart failure (HF) Inability of the heart to pump sufficient amounts of blood. Caused by chronic coronary artery disease or hypertension.

pulmonary edema *(eh DEE mah)* A potentially life-threatening condition in which there is an accumulation of fluid in the interstitium and the alveoli of the lungs that can block the exchange of oxygen and carbon dioxide.

myocardial infarction (MI) The disruption of blood flow to the heart leading to cardiac tissue damage and decreased function, commonly referred to as a heart attack.

ischemia *(iss KEE mee ah)* Tissue injury due to a decrease in blood flow.

angina pectoris *(AN jih nah PEK tor iss)* A constricting pain or uncomfortable heaviness in the chest often radiating to the shoulder and down the left arm due to cardiac muscle ischemia related to coronary disease.

Pathology Connection (continued)

shoulder, arm, neck, and jaw; the patient may also experience nausea, diaphoresis, and dyspnea. Application of nitroglycerin commonly reduces or eliminates angina pectoris due to its ability to increase blood flow to the cardiac muscles by dilating coronary blood vessels. There is no permanent damage to cardiac muscle at this point; patients are typically prescribed bed rest and oxygen. If a situation occurs in which there is blockage of coronary blood flow due to a clot (**coronary thrombosis**), a heart attack occurs. If the blood supply is not quickly returned to that region, death (necrosis) of that heart tissue will occur. In this case, there is actual tissue damage and death known as an **infarct**—hence the term **myocardial infarction**. This type of damage is permanent. Remember, cardiac muscle cannot repair itself. Anticoagulant medications may be administered to prevent additional clots from forming. Surgery may be required to break up clots or to bypass a clogged artery.

Sometimes the heart muscle is fine, but there is a problem with one or more of the heart valves that seal off the chambers during contraction. There are two possible types of problems: either the passageway through the valve is too small (**stenotic**) and restricts sufficient blood flow, or the passageway is too large (**valvular insufficiency**), and blood squirts backward into the chamber on contraction.

A **murmur** is a heart sound that provides the clinician a potential clue to the presence of a valve problem. It is caused by the vibrations created by the flow of blood through the heart or

coronary thrombosis *(throm BOH sis)* A blood clot in the coronary artery, which is the most common cause of a myocardial infarction.

infarct *(IN farkt)* Cellular death due to lack of blood flow (perfusion).

myocardial infarction (MI) The disruption of blood flow to the heart leading to cardiac tissue damage and decreased function, commonly referred to as a heart attack.

stenotic The constriction or narrowing of a passage or orifice.

valvular insufficiency A pathologic condition in which the valve(s) of the heart do not function normally.

murmur An abnormal heart sound that may or may not be a result of heart disease.

FIGURE 12-5 ▲ Left-side and right-side heart failure.

(continued)

Pathology Connection (continued)

proximal great veins. This sound may also be indicative of an aortic aneurysm or aortic stenosis. A problem that can occur in either case is the increased tendency to form clots in the damaged valve area. Such clots can detach, flow through the blood vessels, and cause a pulmonary embolus in the lungs or a stroke in the brain.

There are also potential problems with the small, specialized muscles called the **papillary muscles** that attach to the undersides of the cusps and contract when the ventricles contract so the cusps don't flap back up into the atria. The failure of the papillary muscles to properly contract will allow blood to flow backward into the atrium instead of flowing forward. One of the classic causes of valvular damage is the streptococcal organism responsible for rheumatic fever. As the body fights this specific infection, antibodies are created that not only fight the infection, but unfortunately also attack the patient's own heart valves, especially the mitral valve. Even though we are now treating infections much more efficiently than in the past, this disease may still occur.

Often the effectiveness of valvular function can be determined clinically through the use of **echocardiography**. This is accomplished by a device that utilizes sound waves (ultrasound, which we can't hear) in a way similar to submarine sonar systems or "fish finders" used by sport fishermen. These sound waves bounce off the various structures of the heart and can give us a real-time view of how well everything is working in the heart.

Heart Vessel Problems

A common problem with blood vessels occurs to some degree for all of us as we age. **Arteriosclerosis,** also known as hardening of the arteries, is a result of the thickening of the inner layer, which causes the involved vessels to become less flexible or even brittle. Blood vessels in this condition have a tendency to rupture. Because these vessels are less flexible and can't readily accommodate increases in blood volume, the body is more susceptible to high blood pressure, or hypertension. Treatment begins with lifestyle changes that overcome at-risk behaviors such as lack of exercise, improper diet, and smoking. Medications and surgeries are used to treat specific types of arteriosclerosis.

Normally, blood vessels have a smooth inner lining, which promotes efficient blood flow by decreasing resistance. **Atherosclerosis** is a potentially life-threatening condition in which fatty deposits, called **plaque,** build up on the inner lining of blood vessels. As a result, blood flow can become greatly restricted or totally blocked. The fatty material that makes up plaque is composed mostly of **cholesterol**. Interestingly, all blood vessels are susceptible to atherosclerosis, but the aorta and coronary arteries seem particularly susceptible to developing this condition. Cerebral arteries can also be affected (see **FIGURE 12-6** ▲).

As with arteriosclerosis, treatment begins with lifestyle changes. In some cases, the patient may be prescribed medications that control cholesterol, antiplatelet medications, anticoagulants, and blood pressure medications. Surgeries, such as angioplasty and bypass surgery, can be used to open or bypass affected blood vessels.

(continued)

papillary muscles
(PAP uh LAIR ee)
Specialized muscles that are attached to the valves of the heart.

echocardiography
(ECK oh CAR dee AWG rah fee) A non-invasive diagnostic procedure using sound waves to visualize cardiac structure and function.

arteriosclerosis
(ar TEE ree oh skleh ROH sis) Progressive degenerative changes that produce a narrowed, hardened artery.

atherosclerosis
(ATH er oh skleh ROH sis) The most common form of arteriosclerosis, marked by cholesterol-lipid-calcium deposits in the walls of arteries that may restrict blood flow.

plaque *(plak)*
A patch on skin or mucous surface often caused by lipids or calcium. Can build up in atherosclerotic heart disease and block blood vessels.

cholesterol Lipid molecule that is a component of bile and is a precursor to steroid hormones.

Pathology Connection (continued)

Heredity seems to be one factor for atherosclerosis, and atherosclerosis is also a common complication of diabetes. It is interesting that many medical professionals feel that diabetes should be classified as a cardiovascular disease. Diet and lifestyle also seem to predispose some individuals to atherosclerosis.

There are several ways to improve blood flow to the heart's tissues. A coronary angioplasty (see FIGURE 12-7 ▲) is a procedure in which a balloon-tipped catheter is threaded to the coronary

FIGURE 12-6 ▲
Atherosclerosis.

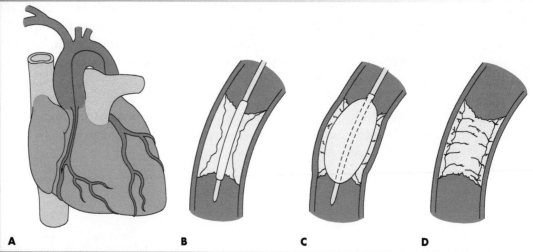

FIGURE 12-7 ▲ Balloon angioplasty. **A.** The balloon catheter is threaded into the affected coronary artery. **B.** The balloon is positioned in the area of obstruction. **C.** The balloon is inflated, flattening the plaque against the arterial wall. **D.** The balloon is deflated and the catheter is removed, blood flow improves.

Pathology Connection (continued)

artery with the aid of a fluoroscope to where plaque is reducing the blood flow to the heart tissues. Once in the proper position, the balloon is inflated to "open up" the lumen of the artery and thus increase the blood flow. As time goes on, these areas often start to occlude again. To help prevent this reoccurrence, wire **stents** are inserted via the catheter to hold those areas open. See **FIGURE 12-8** ▲ for an example of an intracoronary artery stent. These stents usually remain in the patient for the rest of his or her life. A new type of stent, a bioabsorbable stent, has recently been developed that will be absorbed by the body in approximately two years, thus allowing the involved blood vessel to return to a more natural state, becoming more flexible. As a result, less anticoagulant therapy may be needed over time.

A more involved surgical procedure to restore proper blood flow to the heart muscle is the coronary artery bypass graft, or CABG. In this situation, healthy blood vessels from other regions of the patient's body (such as leg veins or the mammary artery) are used as replacements for the clogged coronary arteries. As with any surgical procedure, there are risks, but this procedure has a low mortality rate, and with proper rehabilitation and lifestyle changes, these patients generally can expect a normal quality of life.

Contractility Issues

Did you know that other organs of the body can affect how the heart pumps? You are surely aware of the brain and how autonomic functions affect heart rate, but did you know that the thyroid can affect the heart as well. Individuals with hypothyroidism, a condition in which the thyroid does not produce enough hormones, can lead to an increase in peripheral vessel smooth muscle contraction. What this means for the heart is that the heart has to work harder to get the blood to the tissue because it must overcompensate for the resistance met in the vessels. This is one reason individuals with hypothyroidism report tiredness as one of the major symptoms; they aren't getting enough oxygen into the tissues!

stents Screen-like cylinders that are inserted into coronary vessels to hold them open, thus increasing blood flow.

A B C

FIGURE 12-8 ▲ Placement of an intracoronary stent. **A.** The stainless steel stent is fitted over a balloon-tipped catheter. **B.** The stent is positioned at the blockage and expanded. **C.** The balloon is deflated and removed, leaving the stent in place.

Clinical Application

OSMOTIC VERSUS HYDROSTATIC PRESSURE: THE GREAT BALANCING ACT

Knowing that your circulatory system is pressurized and that capillary walls are semipermeable, did you ever wonder why blood doesn't continually leak out of them or how swollen tissue from an injury, such as a contusion, finally "goes down"? These are normally a result of an amazing balancing act between hydrostatic pressure and osmotic pressure. Hydrostatic pressure is the force that the liquid portion of blood exerts on the inner wall of the blood vessel trying to "push" fluid through the wall and out into surrounding tissue. Normally, a hydrostatic pressure of 10 to 15 mmHg tends to push fluid out of the capillaries and into surrounding tissue. To counteract this "pushing" force, plasma proteins in the blood (albumin and globulin particles), which are too large to pass though the vessel wall, create what is called colloid osmotic pressure (also known as oncotic pressure). This "pulling" force, which is normally 25 to 30 mmHg, tends to draw fluid from the tissues back into the blood vessels because it is a greater force than the hydrostatic pressure. Whenever hydrostatic pressure is greater than oncotic pressure, fluid "leaks out." Whenever oncotic pressure is greater than hydrostatic pressure, fluid is drawn back into the blood vessels.

Clinical Application

CARDIAC ENZYMES

Because there is tissue damage and tissue death as a result of a heart attack, we can look for several enzymes that are released when cardiac muscle cells die. Although this enzyme is commonly found in the cells of skeletal muscles, creatine kinase (CK) in a special form, called CK-MB, is found in heart muscle cells. Once an MI occurs, this special cardiac enzyme is released and can be detected in a patient's blood within 2 to 6 hours. Lactate dehydrogenase, an enzyme found in many of the body's cells including cardiac muscle, will also increase in approximately 12 hours following a heart attack. Two proteins, troponin I and II, are also released when there is cardiac tissue death. Their blood levels begin to rise around 4 to 6 hours following an MI. These levels continue to stay elevated for up to 10 days. As you can surmise, it is important to monitor the blood levels for several days to note any changes in blood levels of these substances to aid you in determining if an MI did occur.

TEST YOUR KNOWLEDGE 12-1

Choose the best answer:

1. Which blood vessels carry blood away from the heart?
   a. capillaries
   b. venules
   c. veins
   d. arteries

2. How many chambers are found in the human heart?
   a. one
   b. two
   c. three
   d. four

3. Which blood vessel type is involved in the exchange of oxygen and nutrients with the tissues of the body?
   a. arterioles
   b. sphincters
   c. arteries
   d. capillaries

Complete the following:

4. The chamber responsible for pumping blood to the body's various organs is the _____.

5. Which side of the heart pumps blood to the lungs? _____.

6. Reduced blood flow to cardiac tissue that leads to injury is called _____.

7. _____ means death of cardiac tissue.

The Electric Pathway

Cardiac muscles don't rely on nerve impulses or hormones to contract. In fact, they contract on their own. This unique ability is known as **autorhythmicity**. The problem with this ability is that uncontrolled individual contractions would prohibit the heart from contracting effectively. This potential problem is solved through the use of specialized cardiac cells that create and distribute an electrical current that controls and directs heart contraction. Think of this as the electric company that supplies electricity to your home and to the fine educational institution you are attending.

Nodal cells (also called **pacemaker cells**) are specialized cells that not only create an electrical impulse but also create these impulses at a regular interval. These cells are connected to each other and to the conducting network, which we discuss soon. Nodal cells are divided into two groups. The main pacemaker cells are found in the wall of the right atrium, near the entrance of the superior vena cava. This collection of pacemaker cells forms the **sinoatrial node, or SA node.** The SA node generates an electric impulse at approximately 70 to 80 impulses per minute. There is a second collection of pacemaker cells located at the point where the atria and the ventricles meet. This collection forms what is called the **atrioventricular node, or AV node.** The cells in the AV node generate an electric impulse at a rate of 40 to 60 beats per minute.

autorhythmicity *(AW tow rith MIH sih tee)* The heart's ability to generate its own stimulus.

nodal cells Pacemaker cells that create an electrical impulse at a regular interval causing the heart to contract.

pacemaker cells Cells or groups of cells that automatically generate electrical impulses.

sinoatrial node *(sighn oh AY tree al)* Pacemaker of the heart. Small knot of tissue located in the posterior wall of the right atrium in a shallow channel near the entrance of the superior vena cava. The SA node dictates the heart rate at 70–80 beats per minute when the body is at rest. It generates the electrical impulse for the entire conduction system of the heart.

SA node See sinoatrial node.

atrioventricular node *(AY tree oh vehn TRIK yoo lahr)* Small knot of tissue located between the right atrium and right ventricle. The AV node is part of the conduction sys- tem of the heart and receives electrical impulses from the SA node.

AV node See atrioventricular node.

autonomic nervous system Division of the peripheral nervous system that carries nerve impulses to the heart, involuntary smooth muscles, and glands. It includes the parasympathetic nervous system (active during sleep and light activity) and the sympathetic nervous system (active during increased activity, danger, and stress).

sympathetic nervous system Division of the autonomic nervous system that uses the neurotransmitter norepinephrine and carries nerve impulses to the heart, involuntary muscles, and glands during times of increased activity, danger, or stress.

inotropism *(EYE no TROPE izm)* An influence on the force of muscular contraction.

parasympathetic nervous system Division of the autonomic nervous system that uses the neurotransmitter acetylcholine and carries nerve impulses to the heart, involuntary smooth muscles, and glands while the body is at rest.

vagus nerve *(VAY gus)* Cranial nerve X. Sensation and movement of the throat. Sensory and motor for thoracic and abdominal organs.

Which one dictates how fast the heart beats? Think of the SA node as the power station and the AV node as a substation that supplies electricity via an electrical grid for a small city. The SA node sends its impulse to the AV node for distribution before the AV node can send its own. However, if the SA node cannot generate an impulse, the AV node takes control and sends out impulses that result in a slower heartbeat, but a heartbeat nonetheless. FIGURE 12-9 ▲ shows the conduction system of the heart.

"How come my heart rate isn't always 70 to 80 beats per minute, like when I play sports or get scared?" you might ask. It's true that the SA node sets the heart rate when the body is at rest, but several influences can increase or decrease heart rate. The **autonomic nervous system** (both the sympathetic and parasympathetic divisions) has direct connections to the SA and AV nodes as well as to the myocardium. The **sympathetic division** can release neurotransmitters that increase heart rate and the force of the contraction (**inotropism**). To counteract this, the **parasympathetic division**, through the **vagus nerves** (cranial nerve X), can release a neurotransmitter that can decrease both the pulse and force of contraction.

In addition, ions, hormones, and body temperature can alter heart rate. For example, as body temperature increases, so does the rate and force of contractions because of the increased metabolic rate of cardiac muscle cells. Conversely, as the body cools down below normal temperature, the rate and force of cardiac contractions decrease.

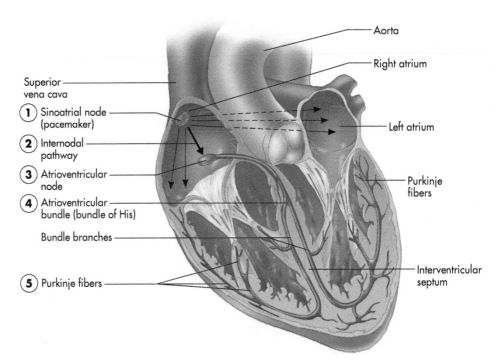

1. The sinoatrial (SA) node fires a stimulus across the walls of both left and right atria causing them to contract.

2. The stimulus arrives at the atrioventricular (AV) node.

3. The stimulus is directed to follow the AV bundle (bundle of His).

4. The stimulus now travels through the apex of the heart through the bundle branches.

5. The Purkinje fibers distribute the stimulus across both ventricles causing ventricular contraction.

FIGURE 12-9 ▲ Conduction system of the heart.

Clinical Application

ECG/EKG

Because the myocardial contraction is initiated and continues because of an electrical impulse, that charge can actually be detected on the surface of the body. This surface detection of the electric impulse traveling through the heart can be recorded by using an **electrocardiograph,** which records an **electrocardiogram** (ECG or, the German form EKG). See **FIGURE 12-10** ▲.

The normal ECG has three distinct waves that represent specific heart activities. The **P wave** is the first wave on the ECG and represents the impulse generated by the SA node and depolarization of the atria right before they contract. The next wave is called the **QRS complex** (a combination of Q, R, and S waves). It represents the depolarization of the ventricles that occurs right before the ventricles contract. The ventricles begin contracting right after the peak of the R wave. Due to the greater muscle mass of the ventricles compared to the atria, this wave is greater in size than the P wave. The final wave is the **T wave,** which represents the repolarization of the ventricles when they are at rest before the next contraction. "Aha," you say, "where is the repolarization of the atria?" It occurs during the QRS complex but is usually overshadowed by the ventricles' activity. In the recording of a healthy heart, there are set ranges for the height, depth, and length of time for each of the waves and wave complexes. Changes in those parameters, or the addition of other abnormal types of waves, known as **cardiac arrhythmias** or **dysrhythmias,** can indicate health problems that involve the heart.

electrocardiograph A device for recording changes in the electrical energy produced by the action of heart muscles.

electrocardiogram The graphic record created by electrocardiography.

P wave The first wave on an electrocardiogram and represents the depolarization of the atria, whose electrical changes in turn cause atrial contraction.

QRS complex Electrical tracing found on an electrocardiogram that represents the depolarization of the ventricles.

T wave The portion of the electrical activity of the heart that reflects repolarization of the ventricles.

cardiac arrhythmias *(ah RITH mee uhs)* Abnormal conductive and contraction rhythms of the heart.

dysrhythmia *(dis RITH mee ah)* See cardiac arrhythmia.

S-A node

P wave	QRS complex	T wave
Corresponds to contraction of the atria. Atrial repolarization normally occurs during the QRS complex and thus is not seen on the tracing.	Correlates to ventricles contracting	Represents preparation for next series of complexes (ventricular repolarization)

FIGURE 12-10 ▲ Typical ECG tracing.

Epinephrine is a hormonal substance that has the same effects as the sympathetic nerves, so it increases heart rate. Electrolytes are important players, especially when there is an imbalance of too many or too few specific ones. Low sodium or potassium can alter heart activity, as can abnormal levels of calcium. Low potassium can lead to a weak heartbeat, whereas high levels of calcium can prolong heart muscle contractions to the point where the heart can stop beating. These are just a few examples of what can happen when electrolyte levels are outside normal range. Age, gender, and a history of exercise or lack thereof can all affect your heart rate. Normally, the resting heart rate for a female is 72 to 80 beats per minute, and the average resting heart rate for males is 64 to 72 beats per minute. That's about 100,000 beats per day.

So far, we have our two generators and regulators of electricity. On our journey we can see how electricity is moved in the form of electric lines along the road. In the heart, the movement of the electric impulses is done by specialized conducting cells. This power grid of electric distribution has to be set up so the following actions can occur:

1. First, the right and left atria contract together and *before* the right and left ventricles.
2. Then, the two ventricles must contract together. But the direction of the wave of ventricular contraction has to be from the *apex* to the *base* of the heart. This ensures that all of the blood is squeezed out of the ventricles. (Remember the tube of toothpaste?)

So let's retrace the electrical "wiring," as was illustrated in Figure 12-9. Once an electric impulse is generated at the SA node, several pathways composed of conducting cells transmit that impulse to the AV node. A slight signal delay allows for the atria to fill with blood before contraction occurs. Once this charge reaches the AV node, it continues its journey through the **AV bundle**, also known as the **bundle of His** (which sounds like "hiss"). Traveling down the interventricular septum, the AV bundle eventually divides into the **right bundle branch** and the **left bundle branch**. These branches spread across the inner surfaces of both ventricles. Finally, another type of specialized cells called **Purkinje fibers** carry the impulse to the contractile muscle cells of the ventricles. And so the contraction begins at the apex, and the wave of contraction smoothly continues up the ventricles, squeezing out all the blood.

AV bundle See bundle of His.

bundle of His *(HISS)* Section of the conduction system of the heart after the AV node. It splits into the right and left bundle branches.

right bundle branch An atrioventricular bundle of "electrical wiring" that spreads across the inner surface of the right ventricle allowing for a smooth and effective heart contraction.

left bundle branch An atrioventricular bundle of "electrical wiring" that spreads across the inner surface of the left ventricle allowing for a smooth and effective heart contraction.

Purkinje fibers *(per KIN jee)* Specialized cells that carry the impulse to the contractile muscle cells of the ventricle.

cardiopulmonary resuscitation (CPR) The actions (both through cardiac compressions and assisted breathing) to create normal heart function in an individual who has cardiac arrest.

Clinical Application

CPR

If the patient's heart has stopped beating or the patient has stopped breathing, **cardiopulmonary resuscitation (CPR)** is performed. CPR consists of artificial blood circulation (chest compressions) and artificial respiration (lung ventilation). CPR is generally continued until the patient regains a heartbeat or is declared dead. CPR is unlikely to restart the heart; its purpose is to maintain a flow of oxygenated blood to the brain and heart, thereby delaying tissue death and extending the brief window of opportunity for a successful resuscitation without permanent brain damage. Defibrillation is usually needed to restart the heart. The newer CPR guidelines emphasize compressions over ventilation.

Pathology Connection

ELECTRICAL DISTURBANCES

Previously, we discussed problems with the pump and vessels of the heart. Those conditions can lead to a disruption of the normal generation of or the conduction of the electrical impulses in the heart, which can bring about an abnormal rhythm to the heartbeat (arrhythmia or dysrhythmia). For example, infarcted cardiac muscle does not conduct electrical impulses well because scar tissue does not function like normal cardiac muscle. There are also situations in which an area of cardiac tissue is injured and becomes excited to the point where it initiates contractions. Some of those abnormal heartbeats can be very rapid (up to 300 abnormal contractions per minute!) and are known as a **flutter** if those contractions are coordinated. If those rapid contractions are erratic, then they are called **fibrillations**. Both of these types are potentially life threatening, especially if they occur in the ventricular area. Rapid contractions such as those do not allow time for the ventricles to effectively fill with blood so it can be effectively pumped to where it needs to go.

Sometimes the electrical impulse is blocked so a smooth heart contraction can't occur. This is known as a **heart block** and can vary in the amount of electrical impulse that can pass through the heart. The problem with this situation is that the main electrical charge needed to get a smooth and effective heart contraction is delayed, and the heart muscle starts to contract out of synch with the other chambers.

An artificial pacemaker may need to be implanted to bring about a normal electrical impulse to the heart. This is accomplished by threading one or more leads into the heart chamber(s) that need a proper electrical impulse. By using dual leads, impulses between the atrium and ventricle can be properly coordinated. The pacemaker can then be set to provide the right impulse for the correct heartbeat. Some pacemakers are set up to provide impulses only when the heart can't do it on its own. For an example of a pacemaker and its leads, please look at **FIGURE 12-11** ▲.

flutter An abnormal, rapid heartbeat of up to 300 coordinated contractions per minute.

fibrillations *(FIB rih LAY shuns)* Rapid erratic abnormal heart beats.

heart block A blockage of the normal cardiac conduction system pathways.

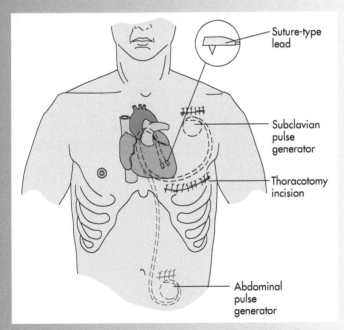

FIGURE 12-11 ▲ Placement of a permanent pacemaker.

(continued)

Pathology Connection (continued)

A **defibrillator** (with an automated external defibrillator, or AED, being one example of this device) is an "extreme pacemaker." A defibrillator is a device that is used to overpower ineffective electrical impulses and arrhythmias (such as ventricular fibrillation) by applying an electrical impulse to all the cardiac muscle at once so a normal rhythm can begin again.

defibrillator An external or internal electronic device used to shock the patient's heart in an attempt to bring it back to a normal rhythm.

silent MI A myocardial infarction that does not exhibit the classic signs of a heart attack, such as chest pain radiating from the left shoulder down the arm.

Clinical Application

HEART ATTACKS

You may think that the classic heart attack is when the victim clutches his or her chest in extreme pain and falls over. However, many heart attacks start out slowly with little or no pain (often called a **silent MI**) and may progress over a few hours, days, or even a week, showing only subtle signs.

Symptoms that can be indicative of an MI are centrally located chest pain, chest heaviness, or vague discomfort; pain in the left shoulder or shoulder blade, neck, and jaw (where it mimics a toothache) and radiating down the left arm; nausea; heartburn; generalized weakness; or a clammy, sweaty feeling. Shortness of breath and/or dizziness and anxiety can also be warning signs. Women often exhibit "nontraditional" signs and symptoms, such as pain in the shoulder blade or jaw, and such symptoms are missed as indicators of a heart attack, often with tragic results.

Another big problem is that the victim often goes into denial, trying to explain away the symptoms as the result of some other problem, such as indigestion from eating too much or food that "doesn't agree with me" or thinking that it's a gallbladder problem or a pulled muscle. This can cost the patient valuable time in the treatment for a heart attack. Indeed, the first hour is when much of the heart damage occurs.

Call 911 *immediately* if you even suspect a heart attack. Research shows that an individual who is experiencing a heart attack should also immediately chew and swallow an aspirin tablet, preferably a plain, nonenteric coated adult aspirin. The anticoagulating ability of aspirin helps to keep blood flowing through the coronary vasculature, hopefully decreasing the amount of damage to the heart muscle. Most heart attacks are survivable *if* you act quickly and seek treatment immediately.

HEMATOLOGY

Hematology is the branch of medicine that is concerned with the study of blood and blood diseases. Now that we understand the pump, let's talk about what exactly the heart pumps. Blood is a fluid form of connective tissue that is responsible for four very important functions, listed next. The body uses blood to:

1. Transport oxygen, nutrients, cellular waste products, and hormones throughout the body
2. Aid in distribution of heat
3. Regulate acid/base balance
4. Protect against infection

Blood transports oxygen from the lungs, nutrients and fat cells from the digestive system, and hormones from endocrine glands to the *trillions* of cells in the body. On the return trip from those cells, blood transports carbon dioxide and other waste products that were formed from metabolic activities of the cells to the kidneys, lungs, and other organs for removal from the body.

Blood helps to regulate body temperature by absorbing heat generated by skeletal muscles, then spreading it throughout the rest of the body. Conversely, blood can radiate excess heat out of the body through the skin. Blood can take in or give up more fluid to help regulate the fluid balance of the body.

Blood helps to regulate a variety of levels in the body to maintain **homeostasis** by ensuring that **pH** (levels of acidity or alkalinity) and **electrolyte** (ion) values are within normal parameters for proper cell functioning.

Finally, but no less important, blood helps to protect us from invasion and infection by pathogens and toxins. This is done by specialized **white blood cells** (often shortened to **WBCs**) and special proteins called **antibodies**.

The amount of blood in the body depends on an individual's size and gender. Normally, the body contains between 4 and 6 liters (8 to 12 pints) of blood, which accounts for 7 to 9% of total body weight.

Amazing Body Facts

What's in a Drop of Blood?

In one drop of blood, you will find 5 million red blood cells, 250,000 to 500,000 platelets, and 7,500 white blood cells. Don't forget that there are a lot of other substances, such as plasma proteins, nutrients, oxygen, carbon dioxide, hormones, and electrolytes, in there too. This helps to make blood five times thicker than water. With a life expectancy of approximately 120 days, new red blood cells are created to replace old ones broken down by the spleen and liver at the rate of 2 million each second! Even more amazing is that the total surface area of all the red blood cells in your body is greater than the surface area of a football field!

Blood Composition

Although we can classify blood as a connective tissue, it is important to understand all the components that make up blood. When blood is separated by a centrifuge, the major components are **plasma** and **formed elements** (the cells). The centrifuge is a machine that spins a test tube of blood at a very fast rate. Due to the spinning force of the centrifuge, the heavier components, like the formed elements, are forced to the

---

hematology *(hee mah TALL oh jee)* The study of blood-related diseases and conditions.

homeostasis *(HOH mee oh STAY sis)* State of equilibrium of the internal environment of the body, including fluid balance, acid–base balance, temperature, metabolism, and so forth, to keep all the body systems functioning optimally.

pH A test to determine how acidic or alkaline a substance is.

electrolyte *(ee LEK troh lite)* Chemical element that carries a positive or negative charge and conducts electricity when dissolved in a solution: Examples include sodium (Na^+), potassium (K^+), chloride (Cl^-), calcium (Ca^{++}), and bicarbonate (HCO^-). Electrolytes are carried in the plasma. Excess amounts in the blood are removed by the kidneys.

white blood cells (WBCs) Leukocytes; responsible for the immune response.

antibodies *(AN teh bahd ee)* Proteins secreted by B lymphocytes (plasma cells) that attack infected cells.

plasma *(PLAZ mah)* Clear, straw-colored fluid portion of the blood that carries blood cells and contains dissolved substances like proteins, glucose, minerals, electrolytes, clotting factors, complement proteins, hormones, bilirubin, urea, and creatinine.

formed elements Cellular parts of the blood including red and white blood cells and platelets.

plasma proteins *(PLAZ mah)* Protein molecules in the plasma. An important one is albumin.

albumin *(AL byoo men)* Most abundant plasma protein.

fibrinogen *(fye BRINN oh jenn)* Blood clotting factor.

globulins *(GLOB yuh linz)* Protein antibodies that protect against infection.

bottom of the tube, and the lighter component (plasma) is displaced to the top of the tube (see FIGURE 12-12 ▲).

Plasma is the yellowish, straw-colored liquid that comprises about 55% of the blood's volume and contains about 100 different substances dissolved within the liquid. So, if your total blood volume is 5 liters, you have about 2.6 liters of plasma. Although plasma is about 90% water; nutrients, salts, and a small amount of oxygen are also dissolved into the plasma for transport to the body's cells. Hormones and other cell activity–regulating substances are found in plasma. **Plasma proteins** are an important group of dissolved substances that include **albumin**, which aids in keeping the correct amount of water in the blood; **fibrinogen**, which is a substance needed for blood clotting; and **globulins**, which are antibodies that protect us from

FIGURE 12-12 ▲ Composition of blood.

infection. Another plasma protein is **prothrombin**, which helps the blood coagulate and is dependent on vitamin K for its production. Blood **serum** is the plasma without fibrinogen and the other blood clotting agents.

Formed or solid elements include the following:

- **Red blood cells (RBCs)** or **erythrocytes**
- **White blood cells (WBCs)**, or **leukocytes**, which can be further classified as neutrophils, basophils, eosinophils, lymphocytes, and monocytes
- **Thrombocytes** (also known as **platelets**), which aid in clotting

Red Blood Cells

RBCs, lacking a nucleus, and therefore unable to divide to form new cells, are created by the red bone marrow through a process called **erythropoiesis** and are similar in shape to a doughnut. The shape of the red blood cells is also sometimes described as a biconcave disk. RBCs perform two crucial functions. With the aid of an iron-containing red pigment called **hemoglobin** (which comes from the roots *heme*, meaning iron, and *globin*, meaning protein), RBCs transport oxygen from the lungs to the cells in the body. In addition, they help to transport carbon dioxide, a by-product of cellular respiration, from the cells to the lungs for removal from the body.

White Blood Cells

There are several types of WBCs (leukocytes). **Polymorphonuclear granulocytes** originate from red bone marrow. The **mononuclear agranulocytes** also originate from bone marrow but mature in lymphoid and myeloid tissues. WBCs are our guardians from invasion and infection. They may be granular, agranular, translucent, or ameboid in shape and are larger than red blood cells (erythrocytes). See **FIGURE 12-13** ▲.

The types of WBCs that compose the polymorphonuclear granulocyte group are neutrophils, eosinophils, and basophils. **Neutrophils** are the most aggressive WBCs in cases where bacteria attempt to destroy tissue. Neutrophils move through capillary walls into surrounding tissue to fight infection and help repair damaged tissue. By degrading the capillary wall in a process called **diapedesis**, neutrophils can escape into the surrounding tissue to perform the work of immune system response. **Phagocytosis** is the process in which neutrophils surround and ingest an invader, pathogenic, or disease-producing, microorganism and attempt to destroy it by utilizing cell particles called **lysosomes** that release powerful enzymes. As an infection occurs, the body produces a higher-than-normal number of neutrophils. **Eosinophils** are utilized to combat parasitic invasion and respond to allergic reactions in the body. **Basophils** are involved with allergic reactions by enhancing the body's response to irritants that cause allergies. In addition, basophils are important because they secrete the chemical **heparin**, which helps to keep blood from clotting as it courses through blood vessels.

The types of WBCs that comprise the mononuclear agranulocyte group are monocytes and lymphocytes. **Monocytes** are found in higher-than-normal amounts when a chronic (long-term) infection occurs in the body. Like neutrophils, monocytes destroy invaders through phagocytosis. Even though it takes longer for monocytes to arrive on the scene of infection, their numbers are greater than neutrophils, and therefore they destroy more pathogens. **Lymphocytes** are unique cells that protect us from infection. Instead of utilizing phagocytosis, they are involved in a process that produces antibodies that inhibit or directly attack invaders. Some lymphocytes kill pathogens directly.

prothrombin *(pro THROM bin)* Blood clotting factor that is activated just before the thrombus is formed.

serum Blood plasma without fibrinogen and other clotting agents.

red blood cells (RBCs) See erythrocytes.

erythrocytes *(eh RITH roh sight)* A red blood cell. Erythrocytes contain hemoglobin and carry oxygen and carbon dioxide to and from the lungs and cells of the body.

white blood cells (WBCs) Leukocytes; responsible for the immune response.

leukocytes *(LOO koh sights)* White blood cells. There are five different types of mature leukocytes: neutrophils, eosinophils, basophils, lymphocytes, and monocytes.

thrombocyte *(THROM boh sight)* Cell fragment that is flat and does not have a nucleus. It is active in the blood-clotting process. Thrombocytes are also known as blood platelets.

platelets *(PLATE lets)* Another term for thrombocytes which help blood to clot.

erythropoiesis *(eh RITH roh poy EE sis)* Formation of red blood cells.

hemoglobin *(HEE moh GLOH bin)* Substance in an erythrocyte that binds to oxygen and carbon dioxide. Its globin chains give it a round shape. When it is bound to oxygen, it forms the compound oxyhemoglobin.

polymorphonuclear granulocytes White blood cells with a nucleus made of two or more lobes, i.e., the granular leukocytes: neutrophils, eosinophils, or basophils, and whose cytoplasm contains granules.

mononuclear agranulocytes A nongranular white blood cell having one nucleus, (a lymphocyte or a monocyte).

neutrophil *(NOO troh fill)* A type of leukocyte that performs nonspecific phagocytosis.

diapedesis *(dahy uh pi DEE sis)* The degradation of a capillary wall that allows neutrophils to escape into surrounding tissue to provide an immune system response.

phagocytosis *(FAG oh sigh TOH siss)* The process by which a phagocyte destroys a foreign cell or cellular debris; a type of endocytosis.

lysosome *(LIE so soam)* Organelle that consists of a small sac with digestive enzymes in it. These destroy pathogens that invade the cell.

eosinophil *(EE oh SIN oh fill)* Type of leukocyte. It is classified as a granulocyte because it has granules in the cytoplasm. Eosinophils are involved in allergic reactions and defense against parasites.

basophil *(BAY soh fill)* Least numerous of the leukocytes. It is classified as a granulocyte because granules in its cytoplasm stain dark blue to purple with basic dye. It releases histamine and heparin at the site of tissue damage.

heparin Substance that inhibits coagulation of blood.

monocyte Mononuclear white blood cells commonly found in high numbers in chronic infections.

lymphocytes *(LIM foh SIGHTS)* Specialized, infection-fighting white blood cells produced by the lymphatic system.

inflammation *(in flah MAY shun)* Tissue reaction to injury that includes swelling and reddening due to increased blood flow to the area.

pus Yellow or whitish yellow substance that is a by-product of phagocytosis.

abscess *(AB ses)* A collection of pus in an enclosed body space.

pyrexia *(pie REK see uh)* Fever produced as part of the body's immune response to infection and disease.

FIGURE 12-13 ▲ Functions of white blood cells. (Photo Source: ggw1962/Shutterstock.com.)

Fighting infection and foreign invaders is discussed, along with the lymphatic system, in Chapter 14.

Inflammation

In the mad rush to fight infection, injury, or disease, blood cell action can cause several symptoms of the body's natural immune defense system. **Inflammation** is a complex system of responses by vascular tissues to pathogens, damaged cells, or other irritants. Inflammation can cause several visible symptoms, including redness, swelling, pain, and localized heat. These symptoms are due to the increased blood flow at the point of irritation or infection. This excess blood in the tissues is also known as edema. You will read more about inflammation in Chapter 14.

In some cases, inflammation is accompanied by **pus,** a yellow or whitish-yellow substance produced in the aftermath of phagocytosis. Pus is made up of a fluid that contains the dead neutrophils left over from the immune response and is therefore an indication of infection. When pus collects in an enclosed body space, it forms an **abscess.** Inflammation is often accompanied by **pyrexia,** or fever, a part of the body's immune response to infection and disease. Fever has been shown to increase the mobility of leukocytes and thereby enhance phagocytosis.

Thrombocytes

Thrombocytes, also known as **blood platelets,** are the smallest of the formed elements and are responsible for the blood's ability to clot. In addition, thrombocytes can release a substance called **serotonin,** which can cause smooth muscle contraction (vasoconstriction) and decreased blood flow.

Thrombocytes are actually cell fragments produced by budding off other cells called **megakaryocytes,** a type of bone marrow cell. Megakaryocytes exist in the body for approximately a week, producing between 5,000 and 10,000 platelets, and are then destroyed in the spleen or liver. Thrombocytes are synthesized in the red marrow.

blood platelets Blood cells responsible for clotting. Also known as thrombocytes.

serotonin A vasoconstrictor found in platelets.

megakaryocytes Large bone marrow cells with large or multiple nuclei from which platelets are derived.

TEST YOUR KNOWLEDGE 12-2

Choose the best answer:

1. Which cell type does not belong in this group?
   a. erythrocyte
   b. lymphocyte
   c. monocyte
   d. eosinophil

2. What substance found in red blood cells is responsible for oxygen transport?
   a. gobuloglobin
   b. hemoglobin
   c. gammaglobulin
   d. cytoplasm

3. Which portion of an ECG tracing represents ventricular depolarization?
   a. T wave
   b. QRS complex
   c. P wave
   d. SA node

Complete the following:

4. This important plasma protein helps to maintain fluid balance of your blood: _____.

5. The main pacemaker of the heart is the _____.

Blood Types and Transfusions

Not all human blood is the same. A person in need of a blood transfusion cannot be given blood from a randomly selected donor. Incompatibility of blood types is due in part to antigens. An **antigen** is a protein on cell surfaces that can stimulate the immune system to produce **antibodies,** which fight foreign invaders. Antigens are often foreign proteins introduced into the body through wounds, blood transfusions, and so on. Because they are not "native" to the body, they are called "non-self-antigens." They differ from our own "self-antigens" that exist on the cell membrane of every cell in the body. The chain of events that occurs between antigens and antibodies is called the antigen–antibody reaction, which is the basis for immune response, as you will see in Chapter 14. Antibodies often react with the antigens that caused them to form, and the

antigens *(AN tih jennz)* Substance that causes a formation of antibodies. Cell surface markers that help the immune system identify cells.

antibody *(AN teh bahd ee)* Proteins secreted by B lymphocytes (plasma cells) that attack infected cells.

agglutinate *(ah GLUE tin ate)* To clump.

antigens stick together, or **agglutinate,** in little clumps. Although there are at least 50 different antigen types found on the surface of a red blood cell, our main focus is on the A, B, and Rh antigens.

Everybody has only *one* of the following blood types, inherited from parents:

Type A   Type B   Type AB   Type O

Type A blood is very common. Approximately 41% of the American population has this type of blood. *A* represents a specific type of self-antigen that is found on the cell membrane of each red blood cell in the body of a person with type A blood. Because that person was born with type A blood, no antibodies were created to fight it, so there are no anti-A antibodies in his or her plasma. Type A blood *does* contain anti-B antibodies.

Type B red blood cells possess type B self-antigens and the plasma contains anti-A antibodies. Apparently, these two blood types don't like each other!

Type AB, however, tries to get along with both A and B. Its red blood cells contain *both* of the A and B self-antigens with neither A nor B antibodies in the plasma.

Not to be outdone, type O red blood cells contain *no* A or B antigens, but its plasma contains *both* A and B antibodies.

This information is important to know if there is a need to transfuse blood. If the donor's antigens and the antibodies in the blood recipient's plasma agglutinate, serious harm and even death can occur.

If a *donor* gives blood that contains no A or B antigens, agglutination by anti-A and/or anti-B antibodies in the *recipient's* blood is prevented. Because type O doesn't have A or B antigens, it can be given to anyone, so a donor with a form of type O blood (O negative) is a **universal donor.** Because type AB doesn't contain plasma anti-A antibodies or anti-B antibodies, it can't clump with any donated blood that contains A or B antigens. Because of this, a type AB person is labeled a **universal recipient.** FIGURE 12-14 ▲ shows blood types with matching antigen and antibodies and which recipient's blood would safely match the donor's blood.

Are you with us so far? Good. Now there is one more thing we need to add: the **Rh factor.** Based on a discovery of a special blood antigen first found in the blood of Rhesus monkeys, it was discovered that approximately 85% of the white and 88% of the African-American population of the United States possess the Rh antigen in their blood. Individuals with this antigen in their blood are said to be *Rh-positive.* Conversely, those without this antigen are *Rh-negative.* When typing an individual's blood, the term *Rh* is eliminated, so an individual would be O-positive or AB-negative, for example. A problem arises when there is an Rh-positive father and an Rh-negative mother. If their first baby inherits the father's Rh-positive blood trait, the mother will develop anti-Rh antibodies (remember the foreign invader scenario?). This baby will be okay, but any future baby born to these parents may be attacked by the anti-Rh antibodies of the mother *if* that baby has the Rh-positive trait in its blood.

universal donor A person who has a form of type O blood, which can be transfused to any individual of the ABO blood groups.

universal recipient A person who has type AB blood and therefore can receive blood from any of the ABO blood groups.

Rh factor A blood group discovered on the surface of erythrocytes of Rhesus monkeys and found to a variable degree in humans. Can be Rh-negative or Rh-positive.

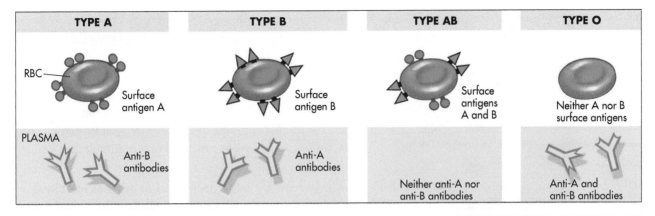

Recipient's blood		Reactions with donor's blood			
RBC antigens	Plasma antibodies	Donor type O	Donor type A	Donor type B	Donor type AB
None (Type O)	Anti-A Anti-B				
A (Type A)	Anti-B				
B (Type B)	Anti-A				
AB (Type AB)	(None)				

FIGURE 12-14 ▲ Blood types and results of donor and recipient combinations.

Clinical Application

UMBILICAL CORD BLOOD AND LEUKEMIA

Leukemia is most commonly treated via bone marrow transplant, but when a suitable donor is not available, umbilical cord blood, which is rich in stem cells, has been used as an alternative treatment. Special cord blood banks have been established, using umbilical cords that would otherwise be discarded after birth. Cord blood transplants are considered a "last resort" for leukemia patients because of the cost and the complications, but the procedure has saved many people who otherwise would have died.

secondary polycythemia Condition of abnormally high numbers of erythrocytes in the blood due to chronic low levels of oxygen.

primary polycythemia An abnormally high amount of erythrocytes in the blood that can be a result of bone cancer.

anemia *(ah NEE mee ah)* Any condition in which the number of erythrocytes in the blood is decreased.

leukemia *(loo KEE mee uh)* Cancer of leukocytes (white blood cells), including mature lymphocytes, immature lymphoblasts, as well as myeloblasts and myelocytes that mature into neutrophils, eosinophils, or basophils. The malignant leukocytes crowd out the production of other cells in the bone marrow. Leukemia is named according to the type of leukocyte that is the most prevalent and whether the onset of symptoms is acute or chronic. Types of leukemia include acute myelogenous leukemia (AML), chronic myelogenous leukemia (CML), acute lymphocytic leukemia (ALL), and chronic lymphocytic leukemia (CLL).

leukocytosis *(LOO koh sigh TOH sis)* Increase in the number of white blood cells above normal.

Pathology Connection

ASSORTED BLOOD CONDITIONS

Secondary polycythemia is a condition in which chronic low levels of oxygen (due to lung disease or living in high altitudes) cause the body to produce more than normal amounts of erythrocytes to transport more efficiently the smaller amounts of available oxygen. **Primary polycythemia** does the same thing but can be caused by bone marrow cancer stimulating overproduction.

Anemia is a blood condition in which there is a less than normal number of red blood cells or there is abnormal or deficient hemoglobin. Anemia can be a result of bone marrow dysfunction, low levels of iron or vitamins, or the improper formation of red blood cells. Individuals with anemia share these common symptoms:

- Pale skin tone (pallor)
- Pale mucous membrane and nail beds
- Fatigue and muscle weakness
- Shortness of breath
- Chest pains in some heart patients due to decreased levels of oxygen being supplied to the heart

Specific kinds of anemia are due to particular causes, affect different patient populations, and have different treatments. For example, *iron-deficiency anemia* is caused by a deficiency of dietary iron causing insufficient hemoglobin production. It typically affects women, children, and adolescents and is treated by prescribing iron supplement pills and boosting the amount of green, leafy vegetables in the diet. Another example is *aplastic anemia,* in which the bone marrow does not produce enough blood cells. This type of anemia is typically a side effect of drug or radiation therapy used to treat diseases such as cancer.

Sickle cell anemia is a chronic, inherited condition occurring primarily in African Americans in which red blood cells and hemoglobin molecules do not form properly. The resultant red blood cells are crescent or sickle-shaped and have a tendency to rupture. As they are destroyed, the body is stimulated to produce greater numbers of red blood cells to replace them. Unfortunately, at that high production rate, the blood cells cannot mature fast enough. The ruptured cells also clog up smaller blood vessels. Clogged vessels combined with the increased thickening of the blood from excess red blood cells and cell parts lead to increased clotting and an impaired ability to carry oxygen.

There are several blood problems involving white blood cells. **Leukemia,** usually due to bone marrow cancer (malignancy), is a condition in which a higher-than-normal number of white blood cells are produced. You might think this would be a good thing; however, the problem is that the white blood cells produced are immature and therefore ineffective in protecting the body from infection. **Leukocytosis** also exhibits as a situation in which there is a higher-than-normal number of white blood cells. In this case, the cause is often an infection that is being fought. **Leukopenia** is a condition in which the number of white blood cells is lower than normal. This can be a result of drugs that suppress their production, such as corticosteroids and anticancer agents. Chronic infections can also wear the body down to the point that it cannot produce the necessary numbers of white blood cells.

Amazing **Body Facts**

Coconut Juice Transfusions and Artificial Blood

There are reports that in the Pacific Theater during World War II, coconut juice was used on injured soldiers to bring their blood volumes up when there was a lack of real blood. The juice was supposedly sterile when taken directly from the coconut and transfused into their veins.

Currently, there is much research in the development of artificial blood or blood substitutes. The main objective is to develop a blood form that can be universally used for all humans without the need to match specific blood types. Other objectives include making a substitute that is free of bloodborne diseases, has the ability to be rapidly infused, has increased oxygen-carrying capacity, and has an extended shelf-life. Some artificial blood is made by chemically altering and refining natural blood components, and some artificial blood is synthetic in nature.

BLOOD VESSELS: THE VASCULAR SYSTEM

So far, we have a pump and some fluid. We now need a way to transport the blood away from and then back to the heart. The arteries and veins we discussed previously now come into play.

Structure and Function

Initially, blood leaves the heart through the aorta, which branches into large vessels called **arteries**. Arteries divide into smaller and smaller ones as they spread out through the body. The smallest forms of arteries are **arterioles**. Arterioles feed the capillaries that form the capillary beds in your body's tissues. Here is where fresh oxygen and nutrients are supplied to the cells of your body, and carbon dioxide, along with other waste products, is picked up by the blood for removal.

Blood from the capillary beds begins its return trip to the heart by draining into tiny veins called **venules**. Venules combine into **veins,** which eventually combine into the great veins (superior and inferior vena cavae) that empty back into your heart.

For most blood vessels, the walls are composed of three layers, often called coats or tunics. See FIGURE 12-15 ▲. The **tunica interna** is the innermost layer and is composed of a thin, tightly packed layer of squamous epithelial cells over a layer of loose connective tissue. The compacting of the epithelial cells provides a smooth surface so blood can easily pass through. The next layer is thicker and is composed mainly of smooth muscle and elastic tissue and collagen. This middle layer is called the **tunica media.** By contracting or relaxing those muscles, this layer actually controls the diameter of the vessels to meet certain blood flow needs of the body at a given time. Your sympathetic nervous system determines these needs and signals the vessels to **vasoconstrict** (decrease the inner diameter or lumen) or **vasodilate** (increase the inner diameter or lumen) as needed. This change in diameter changes blood pressure (**BP**); as the vessels dilate, BP decreases. Constriction leads to BP increases. The outermost, or external, coat is the **tunica externa.** Its job is to provide vessel support and protection, so it is composed of mostly fibrous tissue.

leukopenia Abnormal decrease of white blood cells.

arteries Blood vessels that carry blood away from the heart.

arteriole *(ahr TEE ree ohl)* Smallest branch of an artery.

venules *(VIN yulz)* Smallest branches of a vein.

vein Blood vessel that carries oxygen-poor blood as well as carbon dioxide and waste products of cellular metabolism away from the cells and back to the heart. Veins have one-way valves that keep blood from flowing backward, away from the heart. The exception is the pulmonary vein, which carries oxygenated blood from the lungs to the heart.

tunica interna *(TOO nee kah in TERN ah)* The inner lining of a blood vessel.

tunica media *(TOO nee kah mee DEE ah)* The middle muscular layer of a blood vessel.

vasoconstriction *(VAY zoh kon STRIK shun)* Constriction of the smooth muscle in the artery wall which causes the artery to become smaller in diameter.

vasodilation *(VAY zoh dye LAY shun)* Relaxation of the smooth muscle in the artery wall, causing the artery to become larger in diameter.

BP (blood pressure) The tension exerted on the walls of arteries by: the strength of the contraction of the heart; the resistance of arterioles and capillaries; the elasticity of blood vessels; the blood volume; and blood viscosity.

tunica externa *(TOO nee kah ex TERN ah)* The outer layer of a blood vessel.

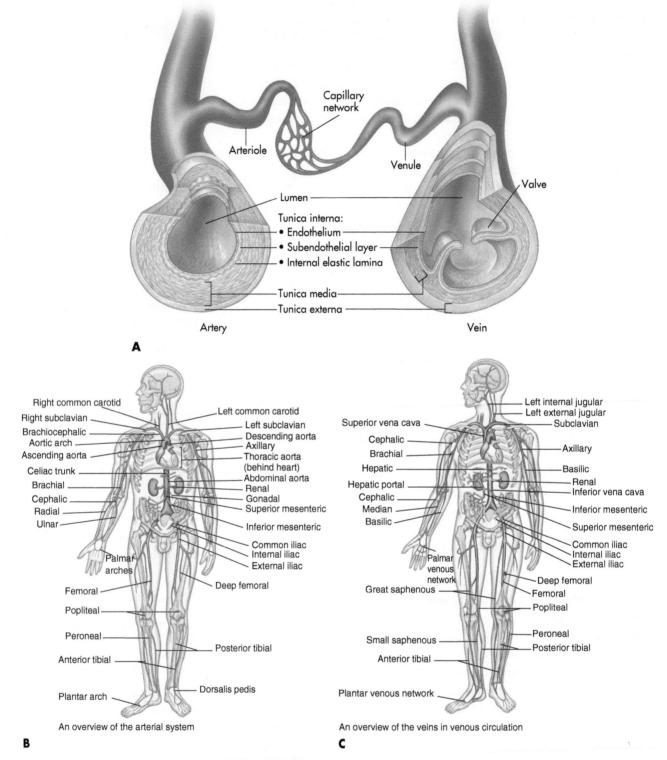

FIGURE 12-15 ▲ **A.** Blood vessels and the capillary connection. **B.** Locations of major arteries. **C.** Locations of the major veins.

Capillaries and Veins

The structure of a blood vessel varies depending on its job. Arteries possess much thicker walls than veins. As we said earlier, this makes sense because arteries are closer to the heart and have to deal with higher pressures. In fact, larger arteries contain complete sheets of elastic tissue, **elastic laminae,** in their middle walls to help deal with increased

elastic laminae *(LAM eh nee)*
Sheets of elastic tissue found in the middle walls of larger arteries.

pressure. Veins can possess thinner walls because the pressure on them is lower than in arteries, but the inside opening, known as the **lumen,** is larger than in arteries. In addition, the larger veins of the body, especially in the legs, contain valves that prevent blood from flowing backward. Remember, the venous side is lower in pressure. Another means the body has to help move venous blood toward the heart is through the use of skeletal muscle. The relaxation and contraction of skeletal muscles that surround veins help to "milk" the blood toward the heart.

Clinical Application

REGULATION OF BLOOD PRESSURE

Blood pressure, like many of your body's characteristics is controlled by homeostasis. As BP rises, homeostasis will bring it down back to normal, if BP falls, homeostasis will bring it back up to set point. Blood pressure can be controlled by blood vessel diameter (**peripheral resistance**), the amount of blood pumped by the heart (**cardiac output, or CO**), and by changes in fluid volume. Cardiac output is a function of heart rate (HR) and the amount of blood pumped with each contraction (**stroke volume, or SV**). Cardiac output can be calculated by the formula CO = HR × SV and is measured in ml/minute. Stroke volume is influenced mainly by blood volume. Peripheral resistance is controlled mainly by blood vessel diameter (vasoconstriction and vasodilation). For example, increased fluid volume, increased heart rate, and increased peripheral resistance (vasoconstriction increases peripheral resistance) would lead to increased blood pressure.

Heart rate, stroke volume, and peripheral resistance are regulated by the autonomic nervous system. We have already discussed the regulation of heart rate and force previously. Sympathetic output increases HR and SV while parasympathetic output decreses HR. Ions, temperature, and emotions also influence HR and SV.

Peripheral resistance is controlled by the sympathetic nervous system. When blood pressure drops, sympathetic signals to blood vessels cause **vasoconstriction** (decrease the inner diameter or lumen) increasing peripheral resistance and increasing BP. If BP increases, blood vessels **vasodilate** (increase the inner diameter or lumen) as needed to lower blood pressure.

Fluid volume is controlled by many hormones, including ADH. All of these hormones affect the kidney causing either increased or decreased urination. Decreased urination increases fluid volume thereby increasing BP. Thus, if you get dehydrated and BP falls, ADH will be secreted, decreasing urination and bringing BP back to normal. There is a complex relationship between kidney function and blood pressure regulation. For details of the role of kidney function on BP, see Chapter 16, "The Urinary System."

See TABLE 12-1 ■.

lumen *(LOO men)* Opening in the center of a large tube, for example the center of the tubes in the digestive and respiratory systems and the blood vessels.

peripheral resistance The resistance of the arterial vascular system, especially the arterioles and capillaries, to the flow of blood.

cardiac output (CO) The amount of blood discharged from the left or right ventricle per minute.

stroke volume (SV) The amount of blood ejected by the left ventricle at each heartbeat.

vasoconstriction *(VAY zoh kon STRIK shun)* Constriction of the smooth muscle in the artery wall which causes the artery to become smaller in diameter.

vasodilate *(VAY zoh dye LAY shun)* Relaxation of the smooth muscle in the artery wall, causing the artery to become larger in diameter.

Table 12-1 ■ Classifying Blood Pressure Readings

Clinical Application

TAKING A BLOOD PRESSURE

An important diagnostic test is the determination of arterial blood pressure (BP). This is done with a stethoscope and a sphygmomanometer. As shown in **FIGURE 12-16** ▲, an inflatable cuff is placed around the arm, above the elbow, so when the cuff is inflated, it squeezes the brachial artery shut. Your stethoscope is placed over the brachial artery in the proximity of the patient's elbow. The cuff can then be inflated by repeatedly squeezing the bulb while listening with the stethoscope. As you listen while you inflate the cuff, continue squeezing the bulb until you raise the pressure to about 30 millimeters of mercury (mm Hg) *beyond* the point that the pulse is no longer heard.

Once the pressure is 30 mm Hg above the point where pulse sound is lost, you open the release valve *slightly* so the cuff slowly deflates as you listen to the brachial artery. As the cuff pressure decreases to slightly below systolic pressure (pressure when the heart contracts), the sound of blood being pushed through the artery by the heart can be heard. That is the peak systolic pressure, or top number of the blood pressure (BP) reading.

As the cuff pressure decreases, the sound of the pulse decreases and then disappears. That point is where the cuff pressure is equal to the arterial pressure when the heart is at rest (diastole). This last muffled sound heard is the bottom number in the BP reading. One-twenty over eighty (120/80) has traditionally been accepted as a normal BP for healthy young adults. Recently, lower values are being considered as more in line with a healthy value. Time and continued study will tell which will be the accepted value.

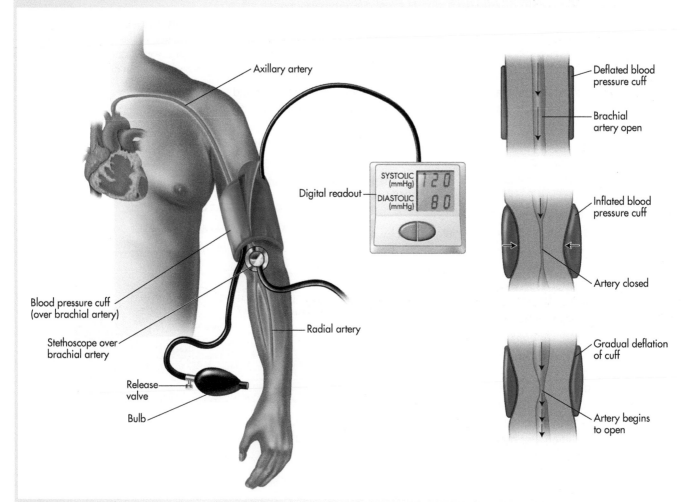

FIGURE 12-16 ▲ Blood pressure measurement.

Finally, we have the **capillaries,** which are composed of only the tunica interna. With a diameter of only 0.008 millimeters (slightly larger than the diameter of a single red blood cell), this microscopic wall is only one cell in thickness so oxygen and nutrients can easily move into the cells, whereas carbon dioxide and wastes can move into the blood. This is important because even at rest, metabolizing cells require approximately 250 milliliters of oxygen while producing almost 200 milliliters of carbon dioxide *every minute!* Dozens of capillaries form a web, or network, of vessels called a **capillary bed.** As you can see in FIGURE 12-17 ▲, capillary beds are composed of two types of blood vessels: a **vascular shunt,** which is a main road connecting the arteriole to the venule, and **true capillaries,** which make the actual exchanges with cells. True capillaries can be considered the on-ramps and off-ramps to and from the vascular shunt. In Figure 12-17, you will notice a group of structures called **pre-capillary sphincters.** These structures are composed of smooth muscle and act as tollbooths either allowing blood to flow through or stopping blood flow when they contract. If the blood flows through, it travels through the true capillaries and to cells of the tissue. If the blood is stopped at the precapillary sphincters, then the blood travels through the vascular shunt.

Blood Clotting

As we have discussed, the cardiovascular system is a closed and pressurized system. Imagine what could happen if a leak or a break in the system occurred. You have probably seen cars along the road with blown radiator hoses. The steam shoots out, and the car goes nowhere. A similar condition can occur in your body; no steam shoots out of

capillaries *(KAP ih LAIR eez)* The smallest blood vessels in the body, connecting blood vessels between arterioles and venules. The exchange of oxygen and carbon dioxide takes place in the capillaries.

capillary bed A network of capillaries.

vascular shunt *(VAS kyuh ler shuhnt)* In a capillary bed, it is the main pathway connecting the arteriole to the venule.

true capillaries The actual blood vessels where gas and nutrient exchange occurs.

pre-capillary sphincters Smooth muscle structures that direct the flow of blood before entering the capillary bed.

FIGURE 12-17 ▲ Capillary beds and sphincters.

hemostasis *(HEE moh STAY siss)* The cessation of bleeding after the formation of a blood clot.

prothrombin *(pro THROM bin)* Blood clotting factor that is activated just before the thrombus is formed.

thrombin *(THROM bin)* An enzyme that reacts with fibrinogen, converting it to fibrin, which forms a clot.

fibrinogen *(fye BRINN oh jenn)* Blood clotting factor.

fibrin *(FYE brin)* Fiber strands that are formed by the activation of clotting factors. Fibrin traps erythrocytes and this forms a blood clot.

your blood vessels, of course, but if enough blood is lost, you won't go anywhere and will die. Thanks to several substances in your blood, some leaks or breaks that occur can be stopped. **Hemostasis** (the stoppage of blood) is accomplished through a chain of events shown in **FIGURE 12-18** ▲.

Damage to the innermost wall of a vessel exposes the underlying collagen fibers. Platelets that are floating around in the blood begin attaching to the rough, damaged site. The attached platelets release several chemicals that draw more platelets to that site, creating a platelet plug. These platelets also release serotonin, which causes blood vessels to spasm, thereby decreasing blood flow to that area. Within approximately 15 seconds from the time of the initial injury, the actual coagulation (clotting) of blood begins. With the help of calcium ions and 11 different plasma proteins (clotting factors), a chain reaction starts. One of the clotting proteins, **prothrombin,** which is produced by the liver with the help of vitamin K, converts to **thrombin.** Thrombin transforms **fibrinogen,** which is dissolved in the blood, into its insoluble, hairlike form called **fibrin.** Fibrin forms a netlike patch at the injury site and snags more blood cells and platelets, and within 3 to 6 minutes, a clot is created. Once the clot is formed, it eventually begins to retract, and as a result, pulls the damaged edges of the blood vessel together. This allows the edges to regenerate the necessary epithelial tissue to make a permanent repair over time. Once the clot has outlived its usefulness, it is dissolved. Again, please see Figure 12-18.

FIGURE 12-18 ▲ The clotting process.

Pathology Connection

CLOTTING

Sometimes, there is a problem with the inability of blood to clot properly. **Hemophilia** is a general term used to describe inherited blood conditions that prohibit or slow down the blood's ability to clot. One type of hemophilia is a hereditary condition transmitted from mother to son that occurs because of a missing clotting factor. **Thrombocytopenia** is a type of hemophilia in which clotting is impaired because there are fewer-than-normal circulating platelets. If the platelet count is low enough, even normal movement can lead to bleeding. This condition can be caused by liver dysfunction, vitamin K deficiency, radiation exposure, or bone marrow cancer.

The chain reaction that causes a clot must be stopped when it has accomplished its purpose, or else clotting would continue throughout the vascular system. However, there are times when unwanted clotting occurs. A rough surface on an otherwise smooth lumen of a blood vessel may allow platelets to begin "sticking" there, forming a type of clot called a **thrombus** (or **thrombosis**). A thrombus that forms in the vascular system of the heart can partially or totally block blood flow to a portion of the heart, resulting in a coronary thrombosis, which can cause a heart attack. The degree of blockage along with the heart area affected determines the severity of the attack. If allowed to increase in size as more blood cells attach to it, total blockage of blood flow can happen.

Another scenario is the potential for a portion, or several portions, of the thrombus to break off and flow through the circulatory system like an iceberg at sea. This floating thrombus, called an **embolus,** is not a problem until it travels down too narrow a blood vessel and becomes lodged, partially or totally blocking downstream blood flow. A cerebral embolus would affect blood flow to the brain, causing a stroke; a pulmonary embolus would lodge in the lung region and affect your ability to get oxygen into your blood, as you will see in Chapter 13.

hemophilia *(HEE moh FILL ee ah)* Inherited genetic abnormality of a gene on the X chromosome that causes an absence or deficiency of a specific clotting factor. When injured, hemophiliac patients cannot easily form a blood clot and continue to bleed for long periods of time.

thrombocytopenia *(THROM boh SIGH toh PEE nee ah)* Deficiency in the number of thrombocytes. This can be due to exposure to radiation or toxic chemicals or drugs that damage the stem cells in the bone marrow.

thrombus *(THROM bus)* A blood clot.

thrombosis See thrombus.

TEST YOUR KNOWLEDGE 12-3

Choose the best answer:

1. The universal donor blood type is:
   a. O-negative
   b. AB-positive
   c. Rh-positive
   d. B-positive

2. The smallest form of arteries are:
   a. arterules
   b. capillaries
   c. arterioles
   d. vessicles

3. A type of unwanted blood clot is a:
   a. bolus
   b. thrombus
   c. omnibus
   d. skoolbus

Complete the following:

4. List the three layers commonly found in a blood vessel:

_____

5. Discuss how a sickle shaped red blood cell, as a result of an individual with sickle cell anemia (a congenital disorder), could disrupt blood flow in the capillaries.

embolus *(EM boh lus)* Mass of undissolved matter present in the blood or lymphatic vessels that was brought there by the blood or lymph current.

aneurysm *(AN yoo rizm)* Area of dilation and weakness in the wall of an artery. This can be congenital or where arteriosclerosis has damaged the artery. With each heartbeat, the weakened artery wall balloons outward. Aneurysms can rupture without warning. A dissecting aneurysm is one that is enlarging by tunneling between the layers of the artery wall.

hematoma *(HEE mah TOH mah)* A swelling as a result of a break in a blood vessel(s) usually confined to a specific area (tissue, organ, or space) in the body.

peripheral vascular disease (PVD) *(per IF er uhl VAS kyuhler)* Condition of reduced blood flow to the extremities.

When blood does not travel through the vessels at a fast enough rate, unwanted clots can form. People who are bedridden, on long plane flights or bus or car rides, or immobile for extended periods of time are susceptible to thrombus formation. This will be a continuing problem for Ray. It also appears that women who smoke and use oral contraceptives and individuals on some types of chemotherapy are at a higher risk for clot formation.

Substances that decrease the blood's ability to coagulate, such as aspirin or heparin, help prevent unwanted clotting. Once a clot forms, "clot busters" such as the drug streptokinase, are given to regain proper blood flow. The body's natural way of stopping bleeding is clot formation, but when that doesn't work, health care workers can stop bleeding by applying pressure to several pressure points. These are illustrated in FIGURE 12-19 ▲.

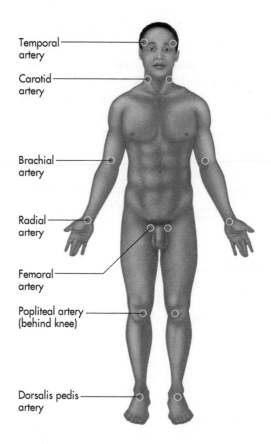

Temporal artery

Carotid artery

Brachial artery

Radial artery

Femoral artery

Popliteal artery (behind knee)

Dorsalis pedis artery

FIGURE 12-19 ▲ Pressure points.

Pathology Connection

PROBLEMS ASSOCIATED WITH SYSTEMIC BLOOD VESSELS

Arteries are designed to handle the increased pressures generated by a beating heart. In some individuals, arterial walls may not always be able to maintain their integrity. An **aneurysm** is a localized weakened area of blood vessel wall that may have been caused by a congenital defect, disease, or injury. This weakened area of the blood vessel may balloon. There also appears to be a familial tendency for abdominal aneurysms, which often present no warning symptoms. The danger is when the aneurysm expands to the point that it ruptures, causing hemorrhaging. If it is in a major artery, an individual can bleed out in a matter of minutes. If the aneurysm is detected on an x-ray or ultrasound, surgical intervention can remedy the situation. Early detection is important. Aneurysms require surgical treatment. In some cases, the damaged portion of the vessel is removed and replaced with an artificial blood vessel. In other cases, a stent is inserted to support the damaged blood vessel.

Visible **hematomas** are swollen areas that appear as purple, yellow, or greenish splotches in the tissue just under the skin. Hematomas are localized collections of blood in body tissues, internal organs, or body spaces caused by an injury that ruptures a blood vessel. You may know hematomas by their common name: a bruise. They can gradually move or diffuse to nearby tissue—for example, a sprained thumb may initially appear purple around the affected joint, but eventually the entire thumb may turn purple due to flow of the collected blood.

Peripheral vascular disease (PVD) is a condition that is caused by a plaque build-up (atherosclerosis) in the leg arteries. In this situation, there is often a sufficient blood flow to the legs during rest and minimal exertion; however, as activity increases, blood supply to the legs is less than the demand. As a result, cramping occurs that is relieved, upon rest. Treatment can be either cleaning out the plaque in the affected arteries or vessel replacement.

If smaller arteries are involved, the blood supply to the toes and feet may be insufficient. This may lead to their inability to heal if injured, tissue necrosis, and gangrene which is tissue death related to insufficient blood flow. This situation may require surgical amputation of the affected area.

A QUICK TRIP THROUGH SOME DISEASES OF THE CARDIOVASCULAR SYSTEM

DISEASE	ETIOLOGY	SIGNS AND SYMPTOMS	DIAGNOSTIC TEST(S)	TREATMENT
Pump Problems				
Cardiac tamponade (pericarditis)	Inflammatory process that produces a pericardial effusion, trauma, rupture of heart or aorta into pericardium.	Pain possible, tightness/fullness in chest, possible frank dyspnea, loss of consciousness if extreme.	Patient examination/history, radiologic studies.	Medical treatment, removal of the offending fluid if no rapid improvement.
Endocarditis	Inflammatory process/infection.	Anorexia, back pain, fever, murmur, night sweats, weight loss.	Echocardiography.	Antibiotics.
Heart failure: A general term for either right- or left-side heart failure. Formerly known as congestive heart failure. See FIGURE 12-20 ▲.	Pulmonary hypertension, high blood pressure, polycythemia, increased work of the heart, MI, valvular disease, cardiac infections.	(Right) peripheral edema, enlarged spleen, distended neck veins, (left) pulmonary edema, shortness of breath.	Patient history, physical examination, radiologic studies.	Treat causative condition, oxygen, medication to improve heart function, diuretics. Decrease the work of the heart.

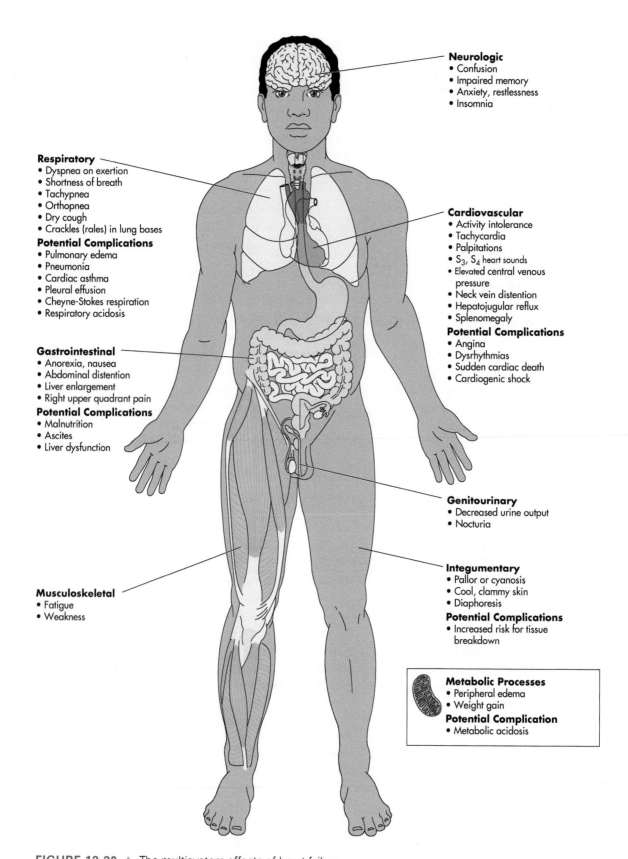

Neurologic
- Confusion
- Impaired memory
- Anxiety, restlessness
- Insomnia

Respiratory
- Dyspnea on exertion
- Shortness of breath
- Tachypnea
- Orthopnea
- Dry cough
- Crackles (rales) in lung bases

Potential Complications
- Pulmonary edema
- Pneumonia
- Cardiac asthma
- Pleural effusion
- Cheyne-Stokes respiration
- Respiratory acidosis

Gastrointestinal
- Anorexia, nausea
- Abdominal distention
- Liver enlargement
- Right upper quadrant pain

Potential Complications
- Malnutrition
- Ascites
- Liver dysfunction

Cardiovascular
- Activity intolerance
- Tachycardia
- Palpitations
- S_3, S_4 heart sounds
- Elevated central venous pressure
- Neck vein distention
- Hepatojugular reflux
- Splenomegaly

Potential Complications
- Angina
- Dysrhythmias
- Sudden cardiac death
- Cardiogenic shock

Genitourinary
- Decreased urine output
- Nocturia

Integumentary
- Pallor or cyanosis
- Cool, clammy skin
- Diaphoresis

Potential Complications
- Increased risk for tissue breakdown

Musculoskeletal
- Fatigue
- Weakness

Metabolic Processes
- Peripheral edema
- Weight gain

Potential Complication
- Metabolic acidosis

FIGURE 12-20 ▲ The multisystem effects of heart failure.

A QUICK TRIP *(continued)*

DISEASE	ETIOLOGY	SIGNS AND SYMPTOMS	DIAGNOSTIC TEST(S)	TREATMENT
Murmur	A result of blood leaking backward due to a faulty heart valve or a narrowed valve opening.	Abnormal sound of the blood flow in the heart.	Auscultation, with ultrasonic confirmation.	Correction of the condition creating the abnormal murmur.
Prolapse (valve)	Various connective disease disorders, sometimes coronary artery disease.	Possibly asymptomatic, murmur, fatigue, palpitations, dyspnea, increased chance for clot development.	Auscultation, echocardiography, radiologic studies, cardiac catheterization, stress testing.	Possible valve reconstruction/ replacement if severe, medication.
Stenosis (valve)	Rheumatic fever, congenital origin, aging process.	Murmur, possible fatigue, chest pain, dyspnea, lower PaO_2, pulmonary edema, syncope.	Auscultation, cardiac catheterization, echocardiography, radiologic studies, stress test.	Possible valve replacement, medication.

Blood Vessel Problems

DISEASE	ETIOLOGY	SIGNS AND SYMPTOMS	DIAGNOSTIC TEST(S)	TREATMENT
Aneurysm	Genetic predisposition, hypertension, trauma, atherosclerosis, tertiary syphilis (rare).	Pain, differences in right and left femoral pulses.	Radiologic studies.	Observation and, if severe or threatening enough, surgical repair.
Angina	Ischemia of the myocardium, as a result of poor blood perfusion of heart tissue (see *Atherosclerosis*).	Chest discomfort/pain.	Patient history, blood work to rule out acute MI.	Nitroglycerin, oxygen, procedures to reopen cardiac vasculature/ perfusion.
Arteriosclerosis	"Hardening of the arteries" due to age, materials deposited in the inner walls of arteries, or other degenerative conditions.	See atherosclerosis.	See atherosclerosis.	See atherosclerosis.

(continued)

A QUICK TRIP *(continued)*

DISEASE	ETIOLOGY	SIGNS AND SYMPTOMS	DIAGNOSTIC TEST(S)	TREATMENT
Atherosclerosis (a peripheral vascular disease, or PPD)	The most common form of arteriosclerosis ("hardening of the arteries") and is caused by the buildup of a yellow, fat-like substance called plaque. Caused by heredity, improper diet, smoking, sedentary lifestyle, stress.	Often no signs or symptoms for many years, then increased blood pressure, angina, transient ischemic accident (TIA).	Angiogram, blood tests, stress testing, MRI, ultrasound imaging.	Improved diet, exercise, smoking cessation, stress reduction, balloon angioplasty, surgical repair.
Coronary artery disease (CAD)	An insufficient blood flow to heart tissue usually due to atherosclerosis but may be due to clot(s) in coronary artery.	The classic symptom is angina but may include nausea, sweating, fainting, clammy hands, pulmonary edema, various locations of pain.	See atherosclerosis.	See atherosclerosis.
Embolism (traveling blood clot)	Thrombophlebitis, venous stasis, inflammation, smoking, hyper-coagulation disorders, contraceptives, varicose veins, foreign particles, trauma, tumor, pregnancy.	Dependent on location, size, and number of embolus.	Perfusion scan.	"Clot busting" medication/surgical removal, preventative measures that include: anticoagulant medications, physical activity, treating thrombophlebitis, smoking cessation.
Hypertension (high blood pressure)	Heredity, diet (high fat and salt intake), age (increases the older you are), obesity, smoking, stress, decreasing flexibility of the blood vessels.	Often not noticed until a heart attack or stroke occurs, easily determined with a blood pressure cuff, increased mass of left ventricle, ringing in ears, not "feeling right," agitated/short temper. May lead to strokes, heart attacks, and kidney failure.	Blood pressure cuff measurement.	Changes in diet, weight loss, exercise, relaxation techniques, decreased alcohol intake, smoking cessation, medications (that either are diuretics, promote increased blood flow to the periphery, or affect heart function).

(continued)

A QUICK TRIP (continued)

DISEASE	ETIOLOGY	SIGNS AND SYMPTOMS	DIAGNOSTIC TEST(S)	TREATMENT
Myocardial infarct (heart attack)	Conditions/situations that lead to a decreased blood flow to the heart tissue that leads to ischemia and necrosis.	Indigestion, heavy/crushing/squeezing discomfort or pain in the center of the chest, radiating pain to left shoulder/arm, jaw, shoulder blades, anxiety, inability to sleep, dyspnea, nausea/vomiting, sweating.	ECG, physical examination, patient history.	CPR, oxygen, cardiac drugs, cardioversion or pacemaker, surgery.
Peripheral vascular disease (PVD)	Atherosclerosis, plaque buildup, in arteries with a progressive narrowing of the lumen. Diabetes can be a causative factor.	Pain, cramping, decreased blood flow to affected areas, decreased ability to heal, sensitivity to cold temperatures, necrosis, gangrene.	Patient history, physical examination, vascular studies.	Treatment of underlying cause, surgical intervention (cleaning out plaque or grafting on a healthy artery).
Varicose veins	Swollen and distended blood veins normally found superficially in the legs but can be found in the rectal area (hemorrhoids). Caused by excessive blood pressure. Contributing factors: heredity, obesity, sitting or standing still for long periods of time, physical exertion, age, and pregnancy.	Symptoms vary in severity from none to extreme, including night cramps, dull aching, pain in feet and ankles, easily fatigued. Pain, itching and even bleeding for hemorrhoids.	Physical examination.	Weight loss, physical movement to prevent venous stasis (daily walking), support hose, elevation of legs, surgery, laser usage, sclerotherapy (saline injections). Stool softeners, surgery for hemorrhoids.

Electrical Conduction Problems

DISEASE	ETIOLOGY	SIGNS AND SYMPTOMS	DIAGNOSTIC TEST(S)	TREATMENT
Bradycardia	Heart damage, increased vagal stimulation, certain drugs, may be idiopathic.	Slower than normal heart rate, usually a rate less than 60 beats per minute or less than 50 beats per minute at rest or during sleep, lethargy.	ECG.	Possible pacemaker.
Fibrillation (atrial or ventricular)	Acute MI, electrolyte imbalances, hypertrophy, electrical shock.	If ventricular, decrease of blood flow—collapse with possible impending cardiac arrest. If atrial—palpitations.	ECG.	CPR, defibrillation, medication.

(continued)

A QUICK TRIP (continued)

DISEASE	ETIOLOGY	SIGNS AND SYMPTOMS	DIAGNOSTIC TEST(S)	TREATMENT
Flutter	Intrinsic heart disease, or extrinsic influences such as alcoholism.	An unstable rhythm that can revert to a sinus rhythm or to a fibrillation.	ECG.	Cardioversion, medication.
Heart block	Scar tissue in heart muscle may affect the smooth flow of the electrical impulse.	Irregular beat, palpitations, slower pulse.	ECG.	Pacemaker.
Palpitation	Structural abnormalities, irritation/inflammation/trauma to heart tissue, drugs, stress, various diseases of other body systems.	Irregular/abnormal heart rhythm.	ECG.	Correction of causative agent, medications.
Premature contraction	In healthy people: may be due to caffeine, nicotine, or stress. Often common in patients with heart disease.	Irregular rhythm.	ECG.	Eliminate the causative agent.
Tachycardia	Initial response to a decrease in oxygen to the tissues, a result of stress or physical demands, heart disease. May also be idiopathic or congenital.	A more rapid than normal heart rate (more than 100 beats per minute) in absence of exercise/stimulation.	ECG.	Medication, certain types may respond to carotid massage, cardioversion, vagal maneuvers.

Hematology Related Problems

Anemia	Cancer, radiation, or chemotherapy that alters bone marrow; too little amino acids, folic acid, iron, or vitamins B_6 or B_{12}; production of defective erythrocytes; excessive blood loss.	Pallor, fatigue, tissue hypoxia, muscle weakness, shortness of breath, palpitations, angina.	Blood tests, patient history, physical examination.	Treat condition creating anemia, stop bleeding, replace erythrocytes, correct dietary deficiencies.

(continued)

A QUICK TRIP *(continued)*

DISEASE	ETIOLOGY	SIGNS AND SYMPTOMS	DIAGNOSTIC TEST(S)	TREATMENT
Erythrocytopenia	Decreased RBC production, increased RBC lysis, hemorrhage, dietary insufficiency, Hodgkin's disease, multiple myeloma, leukemia, lupus erythematosus, Addison's disease, subacute endocarditis pregnancy, drugs.	Decreased number of blood cells for a given volume of blood, headache, fatigue, pallor, shortness of breath, or may be a life-threatening situation if severe.	Blood tests.	Treat causative agent, medications, blood transfusion.
Erythrocytosis	Polycythemia (vera and secondary), severe diarrhea, dehydration, pulmonary fibrosis, during and immediately after hemorrhaging, acute poisoning, high-altitude living, drugs such as gentamicin.	Increased number of red blood cells for a given volume of blood, reddened skin tone, increased blood pressure, increased cardiac workload, bloodshot eyes, splenomegaly, increased risk of clots.	Patient history, physical examination, blood tests, radiologic studies.	Correction of causative condition.
Hemophilia	Inherited bleeding disorder, although one-third of the cases exhibit no familial history of hemophilia.	Bleeding episodes often into joint and muscle areas. Pain often accompanies these episodes. Internal bleeding always a possibility.	Blood tests.	Infusions of clotting factor, development of a synthetic clotting factor a consideration.
Hyperlipidemia	An increasing problem in which there is an excessive amount of fatty substances in the blood, which include cholesterol, triglycerides, and fatty acids.	High levels of low density lipoprotiens (LDL) and triglercerides, lower than expected levels of high-density lipoproteins (HDL), fat deposits in arteries, Hypertension and coronary artery disease.	Patient history, physical examination, blood work.	Dietary changes, increased activity level, stress reduction, statin medications, niacin.

(continued)

A QUICK TRIP *(continued)*

DISEASE	ETIOLOGY	SIGNS AND SYMPTOMS	DIAGNOSTIC TEST(S)	TREATMENT
Leukemia	Unknown; possibly, inherited factors, radiation, viral causes.	Headache, fatigue, dyspnea, sore throat, fever, swollen lymph nodes, bleeding of mucosal membranes of the mouth and GI tract, bone and/or joint pain, enlarged, lymph nodes/ liver/ spleen, repeat infections, anemia.	Physical examination, blood work, radiologic exam.	Chemotherapy, bone marrow transplant.
Leukocytopenia	Viral infection, chronic infections, bone marrow depression, diabetes, alcoholism, acute leukemia, radiation, cancer chemotherapy.	Lower than normal white blood cell count for a given volume, decreased immunity.	Blood test.	Treat causative agent, medication.
Leukocytosis	Infection, leukemia, malignancy (esp. liver, bone, GI tract, metastasis), hemorrhage, trauma, tissue necrosis, certain drugs, toxins.	An increase in the number of white blood cells for a given blood volume.	Blood test.	Treat causative agent.
Polycythemia	Primary result of myeloid leukemia. Often secondary to chronic hypoxia, high-altitude living, congestive congenital heart disease. Can be a result of renal disease, liver cancer.	A higher-than-normal number of circulating red blood cells in relation to the normal blood volume—not to be confused with an increased red blood concentration due to a decrease in plasma volume such as in a burn patient.	Blood test, bone marrow biopsy.	Elimination of the causative agent.
Thrombocytopenia	Less-than-normal level of platelets, may be due to leukemia, bone marrow aplasia, hypersplenism, certain drugs, or following viral infection.	Spontaneous bleeding into tissue (including GI and urinary tracts), petechiae/purpura.	Blood tests, patient history.	Treat causative agent, platelet transfusions.

Pharmacology Corner

As previously stated, quick response time is necessary for the treatment of an MI. The main object is to rapidly get blood flow back to the heart muscle. Nitroglycerin increases blood flow to cardiac muscle through vasodilation of the coronary vasculature. Ischemic areas affected by coronary artery clots must have the blood vessels opened up to return the blood flow to that area. This is accomplished by administering some type of thrombolytic agent that actually dissolves the clot such as streptokinase. To prevent any future clot formations, anticoagulants such as heparin and Coumadin® can be administered.

Oxygen is provided to decrease the work of the heart. Even if the blood supply to the heart is still reduced, the blood that gets there will be enriched with oxygen, which is needed to sustain life. Other drugs may be given to improve heart function. Surgical intervention such as the previously discussed balloon catheter or CABG may be necessary.

Many groups are affected by high blood pressure, but postmenopausal women and African Americans are most frequently affected. Blood pressure medications can lower blood pressure in several ways: decrease blood volume (diuretics), vasodilate peripheral vessels (ACE, angiotensin-converting enzyme, inhibitors), or slow down the heart rate (beta-blockers or calcium channel blockers).

Although exercise and diet are critical for a healthy cardiovascular system, sometimes it is not enough. Drugs such as the statin class (Zocor®, Lipitor®) are prescribed to decrease total cholesterol levels in the blood to help prevent clogged arteries.

Extremely low blood pressure as in shock can affect perfusion to vital areas and lead to tissue damage and death. Drugs to treat shock would include agents that stimulate the heart to increase rate and force of contraction such as epinephrine and dopamine. In cases of blood loss, blood replacement and/or IV volume replacement therapy is needed.

Pathology Connection

If you look at the "quick trip through some of the diseases of the cardiovascular system" you will see a few commonalities associated with the diseases. A few that need to be addressed are adipose tissue deposition and high fat diets. Individuals who consume more calories per day than are required to operate their bodies are said to be in energy excess. Most individuals required 1500-2000 calories a day to maintain their weight. If an individual consumes more calories than needed the body will store that energy as adipose tissue, fat. When individuals store too much fat that can influence cardiovascular performance. Here's why…on average every extra pound of adipose tissue an individual has on their body requires approximately one mile of capillaries to maintain it. This makes the heart have to work harder to maintain blood supply to the tissues. Also if the calories consumed are from foods with high fat contents, this can lead to diseases like atherosclerosis, coronary artery disease and hypertension. It is of the upmost importance that individuals consider their food choices and how those choices can relate to physiology.

SUMMARY

Snapshots from the Journey

- Like a system of rivers and canals, the cardiovascular system is responsible for transportation of oxygen, hormones, and nutrients to the tissues of the body and for removing the by-products of metabolism by the cells.

- The cardiovascular system is a closed, pressurized system much like the engine cooling system of a car.

- The cardiovascular system also helps maintain proper fluid balance of the body and assists in the control of body temperature.

- The cardiovascular system is a major player in the body's defense from infection.

- The heart is an organ that is actually two pumps working together to move blood.

- The heart's right pump moves blood collected from the body to the lungs, where oxygen is loaded and carbon dioxide is removed to be exhaled by the lungs.

- The heart's left pump takes the freshly oxygenated blood and pushes it through the body so cells can be kept healthy.

- Arteries carry blood away from the heart.

- Veins carry blood to the heart.

- Capillaries are blood vessels with walls the thickness of only one cell, which readily allows for the transfer of oxygen and nutrients to the tissues in the body.

- This thinness of capillary walls also allows for waste products of the cells' metabolism to be picked up by the blood for removal.

- The major components of blood are plasma, erythrocytes (red blood cells, the main transporter of oxygen), leukocytes (white blood cells, protectors from infection), and platelets (aid in the clotting of blood).

- Blood pressure is regulated by a complex interaction between heart activity, fluid volume, and blood vessel diameter. The kidney is very important in regulation of BP.

MARIA'S STORY

Maria (our diabetic) may develop complications that may impair her wound-healing process. She is getting concerned as she gets older that this may become more of a problem and is aware of preventative measures. She is not exactly sure why the physicians are so worried about her cardiovascular status.

a. Explain how the cardiovascular system may be a contributing factor.

_____

_____

_____

b. What preventative measures can Maria take?

_____

_____

_____

c. Which specialist(s) would you consult to prevent these potential problems?

_____

_____

_____

REVIEW QUESTIONS

Multiple Choice

1. A condition in which one side or the other of the heart cannot pump efficiently enough to overcome vascular resistance, resulting in leakage from the vessels into tissues, is:
   a. heart failure
   b. cardiac tamponade
   c. vesiculitis
   d. atherosclerosis

2. Plaque deposits in blood vessels are composed mostly of:
   a. platelets
   b. cholesterol
   c. fibrin
   d. heme

3. A localized weakness in the walls of a blood vessel is called a(n):
   a. aneurysm
   b. altruism
   c. embolism
   d. stint

REVIEW QUESTIONS

4. Which of the following symptoms would *not* normally be related to anemia?
   a. shortness of breath
   b. fatigue
   c. increased urine output
   d. pallor

5. A general term to describe an inherited blood-clotting disorder is:
   a. hemorahgeia
   b. hemophilia
   c. hemoglobin
   d. polycythemia

Fill in the Blank

1. List the three ways that blood pressure can be controlled pharmacologically:

   _____

   _____

   _____

2. Decreased blood flow to cardiac muscle that only *injures* the tissue creates a condition known as _____.

3. The structures composed of smooth muscle that direct the flow through capillary beds are called _____.

4. _____ is an important vitamin that is needed for the proper clotting of blood.

5. _____ is a term used for the dividing wall between the ventricles.

Matching

1. _____ Angina
2. _____ Murmur
3. _____ Varicose veins
4. _____ Anemia
5. _____ Aneurysm
6. _____ Atherosclerosis
7. _____ Embolism

   a. The sound resulting from blood leaking backward due to a faulty heart valve or a narrowed valve opening
   b. Distortion of the walls of a blood vessel due to genetics, hypertension, or trauma that can potentially rupture
   c. Chest pain due to ischemia of the myocardium as a result of poor blood perfusion
   d. Most common form of arteriosclerosis, caused by the buildup of plaque in the blood vessels
   e. A blockage of blood flow due to a traveling clot caused by trauma, venous stasis, smoking, contraceptive use or inflammation
   f. Dilated and distorted blood veins normally found superficially in the legs
   g. Iron-poor blood due to radiation, chemotherapy, bone marrow disease, or dietary deficiencies

REVIEW QUESTIONS

Short Answer

1. Why is the direction of the wave of contraction so important in the heart?

_____

_____

2. Describe the flow of blood beginning at the right atrium and ending at the aorta.

_____

_____

3. Provide one reason the proper amount of iron is so important in your diet.

_____

_____

4. Why can polycythemia potentially cause a heart problem?

_____

_____

Suggested Activities

1. Make arrangements for a tour of a local blood bank to better understand the screening process for donors, how blood is typed, how it is stored, and how it is broken down into useful components.

2. Conventional wisdom dictates that a low-fat diet rich in fruits, vegetables, and grains keeps you "heart healthy," yet low-carbohydrate, high-fat diets are popular for weight loss (which increases heart health) and for reducing problems associated with diabetes. Research and discuss both sides of the argument.

3. Research and present to the class your findings on all of the useful components of a donated unit of blood.

4. Find a partner and take each other's blood pressure and pulse while sitting in a chair, while lying down, and right after walking up a flight of stairs. Compare your results with your classmates'. Discuss any similarities or differences.

5. Research the latest advances in bioengineering technology and stem cell research. Select a specific advance that interests you and develop a poster presentation to share with your class.

6. For an investigation into the therapeutic effects of external sources of electricity on the body system, research the uses of TENS therapy (transcutaneous electrical nerve stimulation). What are some of the conditions for which it is recommended? If you can, talk to a physical therapist or pain management specialist about their views on the therapy and the patients for whom it is best suited. Create a presentation explaining what you discovered from your investigation and deliver it to your class.

7. Research the latest advances in bioengineering technology and stem cell research. Select a specific advance that interests you and develop a poster presentation to share with your class.

CAREER CONNECTIONS

Now that you have read this chapter, here is a list of related professions you may be interested in investigating for a future career:

• Cardiovascular Technology

Research each profession and report on the following:

1. Profession description to include job responsibilities
2. Educational requirements
3. Job opportunities
4. Opportunities outside of the hospital setting
5. Salary range
6. Licensure and continuing education requirements

ANATOMY, PHYSIOLOGY, AND DISEASE IN ACTION

I. Cardiovascular Design

Materials:
Heavy walled, rubber tubing
Clear vinyl tubing
Tubing connector to fit tubing and micro-tubing
Micro tubing
One-way valve
Bi-directional valve

Students are divided into groups of four. They are asked to use the materials to construct a working cardiovascular system. Associate each of the materials with the component of the cardiovascular system and explain the rationale for the choice. Try the system with water.

How is the water used? Fill the bulb with water and reattach the tubing. Is it an effective, functioning circulatory system?

II. Steps of CPR

Develop an algorithm for the procedures of CPR/AED that incorporates the following conditions:

- No pulse, no breathing
- Unconscious, breathing and pulse
- No breathing, no pulse, AED indicates no electrical activity
- No breathing but a pulse
- No breathing, has a pulse, air does not go in
- No breathing, no pulse, AED indicates fibrillation

III. Metabolic Syndrome

Consuming too many calories with poor diets and little exercise leads to many energy excess conditions. Working in small groups, research Metabolic Syndrome and how it relates to energy excess conditions, childhood obesity, and adult disease/complications. Share your findings with the class.

The Respiratory System
It's a Gas

Without fuel, we wouldn't get very far on our trip. Our car wouldn't start without gasoline, our plane would be grounded without jet fuel, and our bodies would die without the fuel necessary for metabolism. The respiratory system's primary function is to transport the vital fuel, oxygen, from the atmosphere to the bloodstream to be utilized by cells, tissues, and organs for the process of cellular respiration, which is necessary to sustain life. This amazing system is often taken for granted. We don't even consciously realize that the respiratory system is moving 12,000 quarts of air a day into and out of our lungs. On our journey, the fuel for our means of transportation also produces waste by-products or exhaust. For example, our car produces waste gases that it eliminates through its exhaust system. The body also produces a waste gas, carbon dioxide, during metabolism that needs to be eliminated via the respiratory system so it does not build up in toxic levels. In this chapter, we explore the journey oxygen molecules must take from the outside atmosphere to our cells and tissues. In addition, we travel with carbon dioxide as it leaves the respiratory system and is placed back into the atmosphere. Hopefully, your journey through the respiratory system will be a "breathtaking" experience.

LEARNING OUTCOMES

At the end of the journey through this chapter, you will be able to:

- List and state the basic functions of the components of the respiratory system
- Differentiate between respiration and ventilation
- Explain how the respiratory system warms and humidifies inhaled air
- State the purpose and function of the mucociliary escalator
- Differentiate between the upper and lower airways and their functions
- Discuss the process of gas exchange at the alveolar level
- Describe the various skeletal structures related to the respiratory system
- Explain the actual process of breathing
- Discuss several common respiratory system diseases

Pronunciation Guide

Pro·nun·ci·a·tion
Definitions/Parts

Correct pronunciation is important in any journey so that you and others are completely understood. Here is a "see and say" Pronunciation Guide for the more difficult terms to pronounce in this chapter. Please note that pronunciations given are referenced to medical dictionaries, and regional variations may exist.

adenoid (AD eh noid)	**hilum** (HIGH lim)
alveoli (al VEE oh lye)	**hydrothorax** (HIGH dro THOH raks)
asthma (AZ mah)	**laryngitis** (lair in JYE tis)
atelectasis (at eh LEK tah sis)	**laryngopharynx** (lair IN goh FAIR inks)
bronchi (BRONG kye)	**larynx** (LAIR inks)
bronchioles (BRONG kee ohlz)	**lingula** (LING gu lah)
bronchitis (brong KYE tis)	**mediastinum** (MEE dee ah STY num)
capillaries (KAP ih LAIR eez)	**medulla oblongata** (meh DULL lah ob long GOT ah)
carina (kuh RINE uh)	**nasopharynx** (NAY zoh FAIR inks)
cilia (SIL ee ah)	**palatine** (PAL ah tine)
conchae (KONG kay)	**parietal pleura** (pah RYE eh tal PLOO rah)
diaphragm (DIE ah fram)	**pharyngitis** (FAIR in JYE tis)
dyspnea (DISP nee ah)	**pharynx** (FAIR inks)
emphysema (EM fih SEE mah)	**pleural effusion** (PLOO ral eh FYOO zhun)
empyema (EM pye EE mah)	**pneumothorax** (NOO moh THOH raks)
epiglottis (ep ih GLOT tiss)	**oropharynx** (OR oh FAIR inks)
erythrocytes (eh RITH roh sights)	**respiration** (res pir AY shun)
erythropoietin (eh RITH roh poy EE tin)	**sternum** (STER num)
erythropoiesis (eh RITH roh poy EE sis)	**surfactant** (sir FAC tent)
esophagus (eh SOFF ah gus)	**tuberculosis** (too BER kew LOH sis)
Eustachian tubes (yoo STAY she ehn)	**trachea** (TRAY kee ah)
glottis (GLOT iss)	**ventilation** (ven tih LAY shun)
hemoglobin (HEE moh GLOH binn)	**vibrissae** (vye BRISS ee)
hemothorax (HEE moh THOH raks)	**visceral pleura** (VISS er al PLOO rah)

oxygen (O$_2$) A colorless, odorless, tasteless, gaseous chemical element. It occurs free in the atmosphere and makes up approximately 21% of the volume of the atmosphere.

respiration *(ress pire AY shun)* The process of gas exchange at the lungs or tissue sites. Oxygen and carbon dioxide are exchanged in the alveoli during external respiration. Oxygen and carbon dioxide are exchanged at the cellular level during internal respiration. Also the use of glucose and oxygen by cells to produce ATP.

SYSTEM OVERVIEW

Along your journey, you will undoubtedly have plenty of exercise walking to see the sights. Have you ever wondered why you feel out of breath or why breathing faster and deeper helps you to recover from strenuous exercise? Our body uses energy from the food we eat, but cells can only obtain the energy in the form of glucose from food with the help of the vital gas **oxygen (O$_2$)**, which allows for cellular **respiration**. Luckily, oxygen is found in relative abundance in the atmosphere and therefore in the air we breathe.

Amazing Body Facts

Autocontrol of Cardiopulmonary System

The cardiovascular and pulmonary systems function without any conscious effort on your part. You probably didn't realize it, but as you read the previous paragraph and these last two sentences, your heart beat approximately 70 times and pumped approximately 5 liters of blood around your body. During that same time, you breathed approximately 12 times, moving over 6,000 milliliters of air.

When the cells use oxygen, they produce the gaseous waste **carbon dioxide (CO_2)**. If allowed to build up in the body, carbon dioxide would become toxic, so the bloodstream carries the carbon dioxide to the lungs to be exhaled and eliminated from the body. The **respiratory system's** primary role, therefore, is to bring oxygen from the atmosphere into the bloodstream and to remove the gaseous waste by-product, carbon dioxide. The respiratory system, also called the **pulmonary system,** is closely connected with the heart and circulatory system. Due to their close relationship, these two systems are often grouped together in medicine to form the **cardiopulmonary system.**

The respiratory system consists of the following major components:

* Two lungs, the vital organs of the respiratory system
* Upper and lower airways that conduct gas in and out of the system
* Terminal air sacs called alveoli surrounded by a network of capillaries that provide for gas exchange
* A thoracic cage that houses, protects, and facilitates function for the system
* Muscles of breathing that include the main muscle, the diaphragm, and accessory muscles

Please take a few minutes to look at **FIGURE 13-1** ▲. We will explore each of these components as we travel through the respiratory system.

carbon dioxide (CO_2) A colorless gas heavier than air and produced in the combustion or decomposition of carbon or its compounds.

respiratory system The organs involved in the interchange of gases between an organism and the atmosphere. In humans, this system consists of the air passageways and organs (nasal cavities, pharynx, larynx, trachea, and lungs, including bronchi, bronchioles, alveolar ducts, and alveoli) and the respiratory muscles.

pulmonary system Another term for respiratory system.

cardiopulmonary system Body system that includes the heart, blood, arteries, veins, capillaries, lungs, and associated structures.

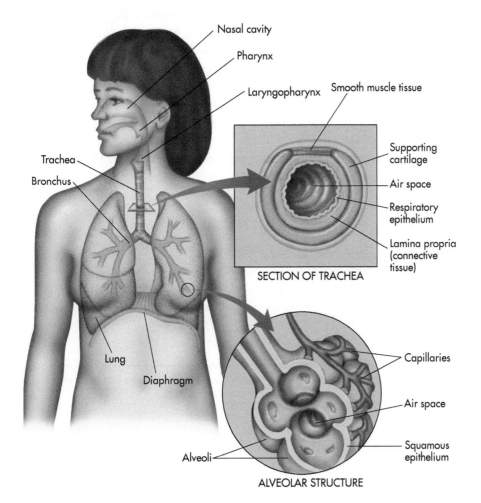

FIGURE 13-1 ▲ The various components of the respiratory system.

Ventilation versus Respiration

Before beginning our journey, it is important to pave the way with a solid understanding of some commonly confused concepts. The air we breathe is a mixture of several gases, listed in TABLE 13-1 ■. The predominant gas is nitrogen (N_2), but this is an inert gas, which means it does not interact in the body. Even though nitrogen travels into the respiratory system and comes out virtually unchanged, it is vitally important as a support gas that keeps the lungs open with its constant volume and pressure. The next greatest concentrated gas is oxygen, and it is very physiologically active within our bodies. You'll notice that carbon dioxide is in low concentration in the air we inhale; however, it is in much higher concentration in the air we exhale.

The respiratory system contains a very intricate set of tubes that conducts gas from the atmosphere to deep within the lungs. This movement of gas is accomplished by breathing. However, a more precise look at the process of breathing shows that it is actually two separate processes. The first is **ventilation**, which is the bulk movement of the air into and out of the lungs. Ventilation moves fresh air down into the terminal end of the lungs, where the gas exchange will take place. The second is **respiration**, the gas exchange process, in which oxygen is added to the blood and carbon dioxide is removed. When an individual breathes, inspiration (breathing in) and expiration (breathing out) occurs, otherwise known as the ventilation process. The measurement of these ventilations per minute is typically referred to as the respiration rate and is approximately 14 to 20 respirations per minute. However, keep in mind respiration is the process of gas exchange.

Because the gas exchange in the lungs occurs between the blood and the air in the external atmosphere, it is more precisely called **external respiration**. The oxygenated blood is transported internally via the cardiovascular system to the cells and tissues, where gas exchange is now termed **internal respiration**, and oxygen moves into the cells as carbon dioxide is removed. Ventilation, therefore, is not the same thing as respiration. When you watch a television show that says place the patient on a respirator, it is incorrect, and the person should say "a ventilator" because the machine is only moving the gas mixture (ventilating), not causing gas exchange. See FIGURE 13-2 ▲, which contrasts these important processes.

ventilation *(ven tih LAY shun)* The bulk movement of gas into and out of the lungs.

respiration *(ress pire AY shun)* The process of gas exchange. Oxygen and carbon dioxide are exchanged in the alveoli during external respiration. Oxygen and carbon dioxide are exchanged at the cellular level during internal respiration.

external respiration Process of gas exchange between the atmosphere and the lungs.

internal respiration Process of gas exchange at the cells and tissue level.

TABLE 13-1 ■ GASES IN THE ATMOSPHERE

GAS	% OF ATMOSPHERE
Nitrogen (N_2)	78.08
Oxygen (O_2)	20.95
Carbon dioxide (CO_2)	.03
Argon	.93

Note: The atmosphere also contains trace gases such as neon and krypton.

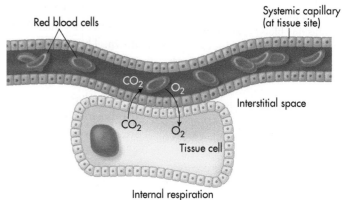

VENTILATION

Diaphragm contracts and flattens during inhalation

Diaphragm relaxes during exhalation

Alveolus

Oxygen (O_2)

Pulmonary capillary (at lung site)

Carbon dioxide (CO_2)

Interstitial space

CO_2 O_2

Red blood cells

External respiration in the lungs

Red blood cells

Systemic capillary (at tissue site)

CO_2 O_2

Interstitial space

CO_2 O_2

Tissue cell

Internal respiration

FIGURE 13-2 ▲ Contrast of ventilation and external and internal respiration.

RESPIRATION

APPLIED SCIENCE

Gas Exchange in Plants

Fortunately for the earth's ecosystem, plant physiology of gas exchange is exactly opposite that of humans. Plants take in the CO_2 in the atmosphere and utilize it to help create energy, and then they release oxygen into our atmosphere. The earth's largest source of oxygen released is the Amazon rainforest, which is unfortunately being destroyed at a high rate every day. We truly need a green earth to survive, so thank the next plant you see.

bronchi *(BRONG kye)* Tubular air passages that branch off the trachea to the right and left and enter each lung. They carry inhaled and exhaled air to and from the lungs.

bronchioles *(BRONG kee ohlz)* Small tubular air passageways that branch off the bronchi. They carry inhaled and exhaled air to and from the alveoli.

alveoli *(al VEE oh lye)* Hollow spheres of cells in the lungs where oxygen and carbon dioxide are exchanged.

capillaries *(KAP ih LAIR eez)* The smallest blood vessels in the body, connecting blood vessels between arterioles and venules. The exchange of oxygen and carbon dioxide takes place in the capillaries.

alveolar-capillary membrane *(al VEE oh lar KAP uh ler ee MEM breyn)* Site of the connection between the respiratory and cardiovascular system where gas exchange occurs.

nostrils See nares.

nares *(NAY reez)* The paired external openings of the nasal cavity.

vocal cords Connective tissue bands in the larynx that vibrate and produce sounds for speaking and singing.

olfaction *(ol FAK shun)* Sense of smell.

phonation *(foh NAY shun)* Producing sounds.

THE RESPIRATORY SYSTEM

The respiratory system is responsible for providing all the body's oxygen needs and removing carbon dioxide. Unlike cars that have large gas tanks for fuel storage, the human body has a very small reserve of oxygen. In fact, its oxygen reserve lasts only about 4 to 6 minutes. If that reserve is used up and additional oxygen is unavailable, then death is the obvious outcome. Therefore, the body must continually replenish its oxygen by bringing in the oxygen molecules from the atmosphere. Again, this process is called ventilation. We now begin our breathtaking journey through the internal structures of the respiratory system by following the path oxygen molecules take.

The Airways and The Lungs

In a general sense, the respiratory system is a series of branching tubes called **bronchi** and **bronchioles** that transport the atmospheric gas deep within our lungs to the small air sacs called **alveoli,** which represent the terminal end of the respiratory system. The tissue of the lung is light, porous, and spongy. It floats if placed in water because of the air in the alveoli.

To better visualize this system, consider the shape of a stalk of broccoli held upside down. The stalk and its branchings represent the airways, and the green bumpy stuff on the end is like the terminal alveoli. See, not only is broccoli good for you, but it can also be a learning tool.

Each alveolus is surrounded by a network of small blood vessels called **capillaries**. This combination of the alveolus and the capillary is called the **alveolar-capillary membrane** (respiratory membrane) and represents the connection between the respiratory and cardiovascular systems. This is where the vital process of gas exchange takes place. Before getting in depth into this process, let's trace the journey that oxygen molecules must take to arrive at the alveolar-capillary membrane.

The Upper Airway of the Respiratory Tract

The upper airway, which starts at the nose, is responsible for initially conditioning the inhaled air. The upper airway consists of the nose, mouth, pharynx, and larynx and performs several other important functions.

Upper Airway Functions

The upper airways begin at the two openings of the nose, called **nostrils** or **nares,** and end at the **vocal cords** (see FIGURE 13-3 ▲). The functions of the upper airway include

- Heating or cooling inspired (inhaled) gases to body temperature (37 degrees Celsius)
- Filtering particles from the inspired gases
- Humidifying inspired gases to a relative humidity of 100%
- Providing for the sense of smell, or **olfaction**
- Producing sounds, or **phonation**
- Ventilating, or conducting, the gas down to the lower airways

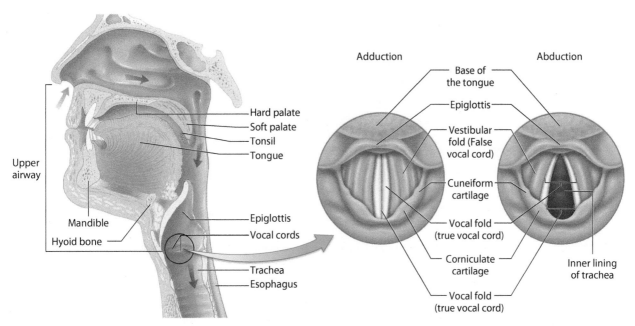

FIGURE 13-3 ▲ The upper airway and vocal cords.

The Nose

Although some people do breathe in through their mouths, under normal circumstances we were meant to breathe in through our noses, for reasons that will become clear. The nose is a rigid structure made of cartilage and bone. The **nasal cavity** is the space behind the nose and consists of three main regions: vestibular, olfactory, and respiratory. The two nasal cavities are separated by a wall called the **septal cartilage,** or **nasal septum,** which divides the nose into right and left sides. Please see FIGURE 13-4 ▲.

The **vestibular region** is located inside the nostrils and contains the coarse nasal hairs that act as the first line of defense for the respiratory system. These hairs, called **vibrissae,** are covered with sebum, a greasy substance secreted by the sebaceous glands of the nose. Sebum helps to trap large particles and also keeps the nose hairs soft and pliable. Those unwanted nose hairs really do have a role as a gross particle filter. *Gross* in this case means large. The vestibular region helps to filter out large particles so they do not enter the lungs, where they could irritate and clog the airways. You may also sneeze after inhaling particles, such as dust or allergens. Sneezing forces air quickly through the nose, to clear the upper respiratory tract.

The **olfactory region** is strategically placed on the roof of the nasal cavity. The advantage to this is that sniffing inspired gas into this region keeps it there and does not

nasal cavity Hollow area inside the nose that is lined with mucosa or mucous membrane.

septal cartilage See nasal septum.

nasal septum Cartilaginous wall that separates the nose into right and left sides.

vestibular region Region of the nose located just inside the nostrils that contains nasal hairs that act as the first line of defense for the respiratory system.

vibrissae *(vye BRISS ee)* Coarse nasal hairs used to trap large particulate matter.

olfactory region Region of the roof of the nasal cavity where sense of smell originates.

Amazing Body Facts

Breath Test May Detect Cancer

In the past, people have reported dogs that were able to sniff out cancerous (malignant) growths. Recent research by Israeli scientists is proving that this is not so far-fetched. They are developing an electronic sensor that samples the breath and can detect lung, breast, bowel, and prostrate cancers by chemical variations related to the specific tumors.

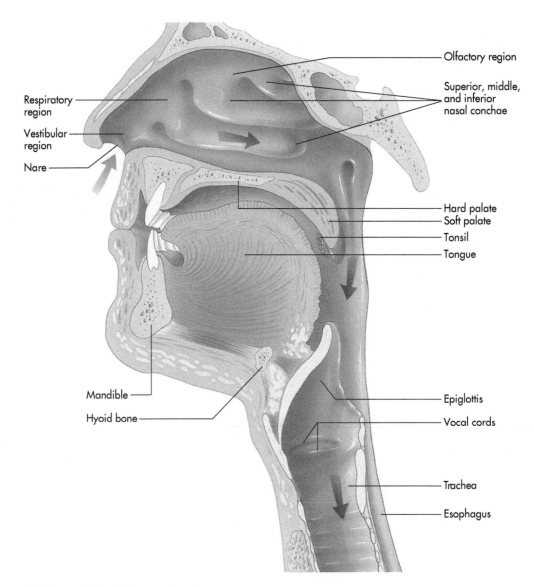

FIGURE 13-4 ▲ The nasal regions.

allow the gas to reach deeper into your lungs. This is a relatively safe way to sample a potentially noxious or dangerous gas without taking a deep breath into the lungs, where it could cause severe damage. Only four molecules of a substance are required for the olfactory senses to detect a gas. It is interesting to note that your ability to taste is related to your sense of smell. If you ever had a nasty head cold and could not taste your food as well, now you know why.

The air from the atmosphere must be warmed to body temperature and must also be moistened so the airways and the lungs do not dry out. This is a job for the **respiratory region** of the nose. Even though it is called the respiratory region, no respiration or gas exchange takes place here. Keep in mind that the respiratory region resides in the nasal cavity, which is lined with mucous membranes that are richly supplied with blood. The respiratory region possesses three scroll-like bones known as **turbinates**, or **conchae** (again see Figure 13-4). These split up the gas into three channels, thereby providing more surface area for incoming air to make contact with the nasal mucosa. Although the

respiratory region Region of nose that contains turbinates that allow for warning and moistening of inspired air.

turbinates *(TER bih nayts)* Three long projections (superior, middle, inferior) of the ethmoid bone that jut into the nasal cavity. They break up the stream of air as it enters the nose. Also known as the nasal conchae.

conchae *(KONG kay)* Shell-like structures inside the nasal cavity.

Amazing Body Facts

Why Do We Breathe Through Our Mouth?

You may have seen your favorite football player wearing an odd-looking strip of plastic across the nose. This is to help make breathing easier by increasing the diameter of the nostrils. The nose is responsible for one-half to two-thirds of the total airway resistance in breathing. Airway resistance represents the work required to move the gas down the tube. The larger the tube, the less resistance and thus less work involved in breathing. Therefore, mouth breathing predominates during stress and exercise because it is easier for the gas (less resistant) to travel through the larger oral opening. Of course, when you get a head cold and your nasal passages become blocked by secretions, it becomes necessary to breathe through the easier or open route of the mouth. On your journey, you must always be ready for detours.

respiratory region has a small volume of 20 milliliters, if you could unfold the turbinates, you would have a surface area of 106 square centimeters (about the size of a postcard)!

Because the nasal cavity is not a straight passageway, the air current becomes turbulent so more air makes contact with these richly vascularized mucous membranes that transmit heat and moisture to the inspired gas. Incredibly, these moist mucous membranes add 650 to 1000 milliliters of water *each day* to moisten inspired air to 80% relative humidity within the respiratory region of the nose. In such a short distance, this is a pretty impressive humidification process. When the furnace in your house turns on in cold weather, this may dry the inspired air significantly and make it harder for your respiratory region to work. Therefore, humidifying this dry gas with water, such as from a room humidifier, may keep added stress off your body's natural humidification system.

Pathology Connection

THE NOSE

Often the nose can indicate the body's sensitivity to certain airborne allergens such as seasonal pollens from grass or ragweed. **Allergic rhinitis** occurs when allergens trigger the nasal mucosa to secrete excessive mucus, causing the infamous runny nose. Because the release of histamine is often the culprit, antihistamines can be used to treat many cases. Some individuals can also take allergy injections to desensitize their reaction to the specific allergen. (For more on allergies, see Chapter 14, "The Immune System.")

Nasal polyps are noncancerous growths within the nasal cavity. The exact cause is unknown but it is believed that they occur due to chronic inflammation. If they become large enough, they can obstruct the nasal passageway and make breathing difficult. In these cases, surgical removal is necessary.

allergic rhinitis *(rye NY tiss)*
Condition of excessive nasal secretions (runny nose) due to irritations caused by allergic agents.

nasal polyps Painless, noncancerous, rubbery tissue growth that projects from the nasal mucosa.

TEST YOUR KNOWLEDGE 13-1

Choose the best answer:

1. Which gas is found in the atmosphere?
   a. oxygen
   b. nitrogen
   c. carbon dioxide
   d. all the above

2. The process of moving gas into and out of the respiratory system is:
   a. ventilation
   b. external respiration
   c. internal respiration
   d. diffusion

3. The process of gas exchange at the tissue sites is called:
   a. ventilation
   b. external respiration
   c. internal respiration
   d. osmosis

4. Gas exchange takes place across the:
   a. bronchi
   b. bronchioles
   c. alveolar-capillary membrane
   d. heart

5. The bones in the respiratory region of the nose are called:
   a. sinuses
   b. turbinates
   c. tetonic plates
   d. bronchioles

Complete the following:

6. Noncancerous nasal growths are called _____, and seasonal _____ can occur with the release of airborne pollens.

Clinical Application

EXCESSIVE MUCUS PRODUCTION

Some diseases, such as chronic bronchitis and cystic fibrosis, cause excess mucus to be produced, which must be expectorated (spit out) or swallowed. The color of the expectorant is clinically useful. In general, yellow and green sputum indicate an infection, but also indicate that the immune system is helping to fight an infection because the mucus becomes green when enzymes (from the defense cells) that fight bacteria are activated. Red or brown mucus indicates that bleeding has occurred, which is seen in lung cancer or advanced tuberculosis. Cystic fibrosis causes the exocrine glands to secrete very thick mucus. This blocks the airways and increases the susceptibility to bacterial infections.

pseudostratified ciliated columnar epithelium *(SOO doh STRAT ih fide SILL ee ate ed)* Specialized cells found throughout the respiratory region of the nose and most of the airways.

epithelium The layer of cells forming the epidermis of the skin and the surface layer of mucous and serous membranes.

Going to Ride the Mucociliary Escalator

The epithelial lining of the respiratory region of the nose plays a very important role in keeping this region of the nose clean and free of debris buildup. Cells in the epithelial layer (or respiratory mucosa) are called **pseudostratified ciliated columnar epithelium** and are found not only in the respiratory region of the nose but also throughout most of the airways. See FIGURE 13-5 ▲. The **epithelium** is a single layer of tall, columnlike cells with nuclei located at different heights, giving the false appearance of two or more layers of cells when in fact there is only one—hence the term *pseudostratified columnar.* Each columnar cell has 200 to 250 **cilia** on its surface.

Goblet cells and submucosal glands are interspersed in the respiratory mucosa and produce about 100 milliliters (approximately 1/4 pint) of mucus per day. The mucus actually forms in two layers. The cilia reside in the **sol layer,** which contains thin, watery fluid that allows them to beat freely. The **gel layer** is on top of the sol layer; as its name suggests, it is more viscous or gelatinous in nature. This sticky gel layer traps small particles, such as dust or pathogens, on the mucus blanket, much like fly paper. Once debris is trapped on the mucus blanket, it must be removed from the lung.

So how does this mucus layer actually work? The microscopic, hairlike cilia act as tiny "oars," and in Figure 13-5, you can see that these oars rest in the watery sol layer. They beat at an incredible rate of 1,000 to 1,500 times per minute and propel the gel layer and its trapped debris onward and upward about 1 inch per minute to be expelled from the body. When this process occurs in the nose, the debris-laden secretions are pushed toward the front of the nasal cavity to be expelled through the nose. The pseudostratified ciliated columnar epithelium, located in the airways of the lungs, propels the gel layer toward the oral cavity to be either expectorated with a cough or swallowed into the stomach. Some texts refer to this epithelial layer as the *mucociliary escalator,* which gives a better picture of what it does. This escalator works 24/7—that is, unless something paralyzes it, such as smoking.

The Sinuses

Have you ever heard of someone being called an airhead? Technically, we are *all* airheads because the skull contains air-filled cavities (commonly called **sinuses**) that connect with the nasal cavity via small ducts (passageways). Because these are located around the nose, they are called **paranasal sinuses.** (*Para* means "around;" *sinus* means "hollow cavity.") They are lined with respiratory mucosa (mucous membranes) that continually drain their secretions into the nasal cavity, warming and moistening the air passing through the nasal cavity. The sinuses are named for the specific facial bones in which they are located. (See **FIGURE 13-6** ▲.)

cilia *(SILL ee ah)* Small hairs that flow in waves to move foreign particles away from the lungs toward the nose and the throat where they can be expelled. Also found inside the fallopian tube to propel an ovum toward the uterus.

sol layer The thin, watery layer of mucus in the airways of the lungs.

gel layer The top layer of the mucociliary blanket that entraps inhaled particles.

sinus *(SIGHnus)* Hollow cavity within a bone of the cranium.

paranasal sinuses Hollow areas of the skull located around the nose.

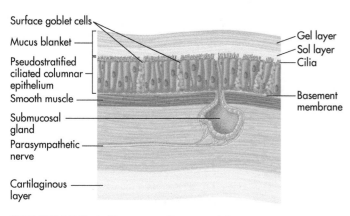

FIGURE 13-5 ▲ The mucociliary escalator.

FIGURE 13-6 ▲ The paranasal sinuses.

pharynx *(FAR inks)* The throat; contains the passageways for food and for inhaled and exhaled air.

nasopharynx *(NAY zoh FAR inks)* Uppermost portion of the throat where the posterior nares unite. The nasopharynx contains the opening for the eustachian tubes and the adenoids.

adenoid *(AD eh noid)* Lymphoid tissue in the superior part of the nasopharynx. Also known as the pharyngeal tonsils.

eustachian tube *(yoo STAY she ehn)* Tube that connects the middle ear to the nasopharynx and equalizes the air pressure in the middle ear.

oropharynx *(OR oh FAR inks)* Middle portion of the throat just behind the oral cavity. It begins at the level of the soft palate and ends at the epiglottis.

palatine tonsils *(PAL ah tine)* Lymphoid tissue on either side of the throat where the soft palate arches downward in the oropharynx.

lingual tonsils Patches of lymphoid tissue found at the back of the tongue.

These cavities of air in the bones of the cranium are believed to help prolong and intensify sound produced by the voice. If you ever shouted inside a cave, you noticed a more resonant quality to the sound. In addition, it is theorized that the air-filled sinuses help to lighten your head. Imagine how heavy your head would be if those facial bones were solid!

Sinuses do not exist at birth, but develop as you grow. Facial changes are influenced by the sinuses as you mature. Sinuses also provide further warming and moisturizing of inhaled air.

The Pharynx

The **pharynx** is a hollow, muscular structure, about 2 1/2" long, lined with epithelial tissues. It serves as a common passageway for both air and food. The pharynx begins behind the nasal cavities and is divided into the following three sections, as shown in FIGURE 13-7 ▲.

- Nasopharynx
- Oropharynx
- Laryngopharynx

The **nasopharynx** is the uppermost section of the pharynx and begins right behind the nasal cavities. Air that is breathed through the nose passes through the nasopharynx. This section also contains lymphatic tissue of the immune system, called the **adenoids**, and passageways to the middle ear, called **eustachian tubes.** You can understand how an infection located in the nasal cavities can lead to an ear infection, and vice versa.

The **oropharynx** is the next structure, located right behind the oral or buccal cavity. The oropharynx conducts not only atmospheric gas but also food and liquid. Air breathed through both the nose and the mouth passes through here, as does anything that is swallowed.

The oral entrance is a strategic area to place "guardians" for the immune system because this is where pathogens can easily enter the body. Lymphoid tissue such as the **palatine tonsils** are located in this area. Another set of tonsils, the **lingual tonsils,** are found at the back of the tongue. During the process of swallowing, the uvula and soft palate move in a posterior and superior position to prevent the nasopharynx and nasal cavity from allowing food or liquid to enter the respiratory system. Swallow and feel this happening within your

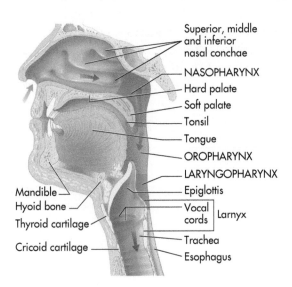

FIGURE 13-7 ▲ The nasopharynx, oropharynx, and laryngophaynx and related structures.

oral cavity. This protection can be overcome by forceful laughter, and that is why when you laugh with liquid or food in your mouth, the food or liquid can sometimes come up through your nose.

The **laryngopharynx** is the lowermost portion of the pharynx; an older term for it was the hypopharynx because of its inferior position. Air that is breathed and anything that is swallowed passes through the laryngopharynx. Swallowed materials pass through the **esophagus** to get to the stomach, and air travels through the larynx (the next part of the respiratory system) and then the trachea on its way to the lungs. What directs the flow of "traffic" (air to the lungs and food and liquid to the stomach)? Is it a tiny highway worker directing traffic? No, it is directed by the swallowing reflex to be discussed soon.

The Larynx

The **larynx,** located in the neck, is a triangular chamber below the laryngopharynx that houses the important structures needed for speech. Commonly known as the voice box, the larynx is a semirigid structure composed of cartilage plates connected by muscles and ligaments that provide for movement of the vocal cords to control speech. The "Adam's apple" is the largest of the cartilages found in the larynx and is more prominent in males than females. This cartilage is also anatomically known as the **thyroid cartilage,** beneath which is the **cricoid cartilage.** Both cartilages in the exposed areas of airways found in the neck are necessary to provide structure and support for airways so they do not collapse and block the flow of air in and out of the lungs.

laryngopharynx *(lah RING goh FAR inks)* The most inferior portion of the pharynx.

esophagus *(eh SOFF ah gus)* Flexible, muscular tube that moves food from the pharynx to the stomach.

larynx *(LAR inks)* Triangular-shaped structure in the anterior neck (visible as the laryngeal prominence or Adam's apple) that contains the vocal cords and is a passageway for inhaled and exhaled air. Also known as the voice box.

thyroid cartilage Large, protective cartilage found in the neck and part of the larynx; also known as the "Adam's Apple."

cricoid cartilage *(CRY koid CAR tih lij)* Ring shaped cartilage found inferior to the thyroid cartilage within the neck, providing structure and support for the airway.

Clinical Application

KEEPING THE VITAL AIRWAY OPEN

Just like any vital highway, the airway needs to remain open to a flow of traffic, or the oxygen molecules will cease to flow into the alveoli and therefore not get into the bloodstream to supply the tissues. While a traffic jam can last for hours, oxygen flow can be disrupted for only a few minutes without tragic results. For example, if the upper airway swells shut from a severe allergic reaction to a bee sting, an emergency airway must be established. Referring back to Figure 13-7, you see a space between the thyroid and cricoid cartilages, and this is where an emergency cricoidthyroidotomy is performed. This space has few blood vessels or nerves, which makes it ideal in an emergency situation to place a temporary breathing tube.

Sometimes a longer-term breathing tube must be inserted into the lungs via a technique called **intubation.** This tube passes through the vocal cords and sits about 2.5 cm above the juncture (carina) between the right and left lung. A machine called a ventilator can move air into and out of the damaged lungs at this juncture. The tube has an inflatable cuff to seal the airway once it is in place. Knowledge that the vocal cords open and close during breathing becomes clinically significant. Adduction during expiration partially seals the vocal cords, whereas abduction during inspiration opens the cords, increasing the size of the glottic opening. If the patient is breathing, it is better to pass the tube with the deflated cuff through the narrow opening of the vocal cords during an inhalation, when the cords are most open. Conversely, when removing the tube (**extubation**), the health care professional must always remember to deflate the cuff so it doesn't damage the cords as the tube is pulled back through them. It should go without saying (no pun intended) that a patient cannot talk when intubated because the vocal cords cannot function properly. If you ever see a TV soap opera or movie where someone is talking with a tube going down his or her mouth into the lungs, you will know it is impossible. More permanent airways, called **tracheostomy tubes,** can be placed in the anterior portion of the neck.

intubation Technique of inserting a breathing tube past the vocal cords and into the trachea to facilitate breathing.

extubation The technique of removing a breathing tube.

tracheostomy tubes *(TRAY kee AWS toh mee)* A long-term breathing tube surgically placed through the anterior portion of the neck below the vocal chords.

rima glottis *(RYE mah GLOT iss)* Space between the vocal cords.

glottis *(GLOT iss)* V-shaped structure of mucous membranes and vocal cords within the larynx.

epiglottis *(EP ih GLAW tiss)* Lid-like structure that seals off the larynx, so that swallowed food goes into the esophagus.

glottic See sphincter.

sphincter *(SFINGK ter)* Muscular ring around a tube; a valve.

vocal cords Connective tissue bands in the larynx that vibrate and produce sounds for speaking and singing.

common cold Usually a communicable viral infection of the upper airways that can spread to other areas of the respiratory tract.

sinusitis *(SIGH nus EYE tiss)* Inflammation of the sinus.

tonsillitis An inflammation of the tonsil or tonsils.

pharyngitis *(FAR in JIGH tiss)* Bacterial or viral infection of the throat. When the bacteria group betahemolytic streptococcus causes the infection, it is known as strep throat.

strep throat Inflammation of the throat caused by streptococcus bacteria.

laryngitis *(lar in JIGH tiss)* Hoarseness or complete loss of the voice, difficulty swallowing, and cough due to swelling and inflammation of the larynx.

The space between the vocal cords is called the **rima glottis,** or simply the **glottis.** The glottis is the opening that leads into the larynx and eventually the lungs. There is a leaf-shaped, flaplike fibrocartilage, located above the glottis, called the **epiglottis.** The epiglottis closes over the opening to the larynx when you swallow and opens up when you breathe, as part of swallowing reflex. This selective closure is called the **glottic** or **sphincter** mechanism. It facilitates the closing of the epiglottis over the glottic opening during swallowing, sealing it so food does not enter the lungs.

Therefore, the lungs are closed to traffic when swallowing. As you swallow, the food and liquid travel down the only open tube or route, which is the esophagus, leading into the stomach. When you breathe in, the gas preferentially travels into the lungs through a process that actually draws it into the lungs because of pressure differences. More on this soon.

The **vocal cords** are the area of division between the upper and lower airways, representing the point of transition to the lower airways. The lower airways start below the vocal cords, and we soon continue our journey down the lower airways all the way down to the end point, or alveoli.

Pathology Connection

THE UPPER AIRWAY

The major pathologies of the upper airway are infections or allergies of the sinuses, nose, or throat. The **common cold** is familiar to everyone and is caused by over 200 different strains of viruses. A cold is a contagious disease with an acute inflammation of the mucous membranes of the upper airway, which causes swelling and congestion. You may become more susceptible to the cold virus if your immune system has been weakened by lack of sleep, poor nutrition, stress, or fatigue. Exposure to cigarette smoke can also make you more susceptible. There is no cure for the common cold, but the symptoms can be treated. The best way to prevent the spread of a cold is to wash your hands and cover your mouth when you sneeze or cough. Often colds, allergies, and the flu are confused and can lead to misdiagnosis and therefore mistreatment. See TABLE 13-2 ■, which compares and contrasts the differences.

Sinusitis is an infection of the sinus cavities by viruses or bacteria with subsequent inflammation of the mucous membrane linings. Allergies can also affect the sinuses and cause inflammation. This inflammation causes pressure, pain, and often a headache. The tonsils, pharynx, and larynx can also be infected with viruses and bacteria and even other microorganisms such as yeast. Again, the resulting inflammation can lead to swelling, redness, and pain. **Tonsillitis** causes the tonsils to swell and become painful, especially when swallowing. If severe, a tonsillectomy may be needed. **Pharyngitis** (sore throat) can cause discomfort, especially when swallowing. **Strep throat** is caused by the streptococcus bacteria and causes a red, purulent (forming pus), and painful throat. **Laryngitis,** or an inflamed voice box, is characterized by hoarseness and loss of speech. Laryngitis can also be caused by excessive use of the voice such as in prolonged singing. Please see FIGURE 13-8 ▲ for examples of locations of these infections. If bacteria are known to be the cause of any of these infections, an antibiotic can be used. However, if no bacterial infection is involved, the symptoms should be treated until the infection or allergy symptoms run their course.

Acute epiglottitis is a potential airway emergency in which the bacteria *Haemophilus influenzae type B* (often abbreviated *H. influenzae type B* or *Hib*) causes acute swelling of the epiglottis which, if

Pathology Connection

it swells large enough, can totally block the airway leading to the lungs. Its onset is rapid, with fever and sore throat usually the first symptoms. Acute epiglottitis is most prevalent in children ages 2 to 6 and requires rapid recognition and treatment. Since the introduction of the universal Hib vaccine, the incidences have been decreasing. Airway maintenance is the mainstay of treatment, with antibiotic therapy selective against *H. influenzae type B,* although other pathogens can still cause the disease.

Laryngotracheobronchitis (LTB) is different from epiglottitis but also results from an infection of the laryngeal area. It too can cause airway obstruction and is characterized by noisy breathing, especially on inspiration. LTB can be viral or bacterial, and the clinical presentation is that of a barking cough and inspiratory stridor (a high-pitched harsh sound often heard without a stethoscope).

Croup was the former confusing term used for both LTB and acute epiglottitis, but it is clinically important to differentiate the two because of the life-threatening nature of acute epiglottitis.

Sleep apnea is a condition in which breathing stops during sleep. Sleep apnea is most commonly caused by soft tissue at the back of the throat relaxing and blocking the airway. This condition is called *obstructive* sleep apnea. A rarer form of sleep apnea is caused by failure of the brain to communicate with muscles involved in breathing so there is no attempt to breathe. This form is known as *central* sleep apnea. When a sleeping person stops breathing, the brain briefly wakes him or her up to trigger restored breathing. A person with sleep apnea may awaken briefly many times during the night but not remember waking up. This interrupted sleep can cause fatigue during the day. Long-term, undiagnosed sleep apnea can cause other health problems, such as high blood pressure, weight gain, and headaches. Sleep apnea can be diagnosed during a sleep study, where the patient is monitored while sleeping. Mild obstructive sleep apnea may be treated with special pillows and positioning the patient that help to keep the airway open. Weight loss may reduce the severity of sleep apnea. More severe obstructive sleep apnea may be treated with oral appliances, breathing devices, or surgery. Central sleep apnea often requires pharmacologic treatment.

acute epiglottitis
(EP ih glawt EYE tiss)
Inflammation of the epiglottis due to infection.

laryngotracheo-bronchitis (LTB)
(lah RING goh TRAY kee oh brong KIGH tiss) A bacterial or viral infection that causes a barking cough and inspiratory stridor.

sleep apnea A condition of abnormal cessation of breathing during sleep.

TABLE 13-2 ■ COMPARISON OF ALLERGY, COLD, AND INFLUENZA

SYMPTON/SIGN	ALLERGY	COLD	FLU
Onset	Response to allergen	Slow	Fast
Duration	> 1+ weeks	1 week	1–3 weeks
Season	Spring/Summer/Fall	Fall/Winter	Fall/Winter
Fever	None	Rare, < 100	102–104; lasts 3–4 days
Fatigue, weakness	Mild; varies	Quite mild	May last 2–3 weeks
Extreme exhaustion	Rare	Never	Early and prominent
General aches, pains	Varies	Slight	Usual; often severe
Headache	Usual	Rare	Prominent
Sneezing	Usual	Usual	Sometimes
Sore throat	Sometimes	Common	Sometimes
Stuffy nose	Common	Common	Sometimes
Nasal discharge	Clear	Yellow/greenish	Varies
Chest discomfort	Sometimes	Mild to moderate	Common; can be severe
Cough	None; dry	Yes	Yes; dry hacking
Vomit and/or diarrhea	Rare; varies	Rare	Common

FIGURE 13-8 ▲ The upper airway and related infections.

LEARNING HINT

Epiglottitis

Respiratory distress, drooling, dysphagia, and dysphonia are the four Ds that are signs of epiglottitis.

TEST YOUR KNOWLEDGE 13-2

Choose the best answer:

1. The hairlike structures that propel mucus in the airways are:
   a. the sol layer
   b. the gel layer
   c. pathogens
   d. cilia

2. Which of the following is *not* true about the sinuses?
   a. They are air-filled cavities.
   b. They are located in the skull and around the nose.
   c. They help to lighten the head.
   d. Gas exchange occurs there.

3. Food is prevented from entering the _____ when eating by the closure of the _____.
   a. esophagus; glottis
   b. esophagus; epiglottis
   c. trachea; epiglottis
   d. epiglottis; glottis

4. The vocal cords are found in the:
   a. nasal cavity
   b. nasopharynx
   c. nasal cavity
   d. larynx

Match the disease

1. _____ Common cold
2. _____ Sinusitis
3. _____ Pharyngitis
4. _____ Laryngitis
5. _____ Acute epiglottitis
6. _____ LTB

a. sore throat will cause discomfort especially when swallowing
b. characterized by hoarseness and loss of speech
c. caused by over 200 different strains of viruses
d. airway emergency distress, drooling, dysphagia, and dysphonia
e. infection causing pressure, pain, and often a headache
f. noisy breathing, barking cough, and inspiratory stridor

THE LOWER RESPIRATORY TRACT

The airway that leads to the lungs and then branches out into the various lung segments resembles an upside-down tree and is sometimes called the tracheobronchial tree. See FIGURE 13-9 ▲. On leaving the vocal cords in the larynx, the inspired air enters the **trachea,** also known as the windpipe, a 4 1/2″ long tube lined with ciliated mucous membrane. Any dust or mucus that also enters the trachea can be removed by expectoration. During expectoration, deep breaths followed by forceful air expulsion (coughing) moves substances out of the lower respiratory tract and into the mouth, where they can be spit out or swallowed. The trachea extends from the cricoid cartilage of the larynx to the sixth thoracic vertebrae (approximately to the midpoint of the chest). The cartilage found in the trachea is in the form of C-shaped structures in the anterior portion of the trachea to provide rigidity and protection for the exposed airway in the neck. This C shape also serves another important purpose: the esophagus lies in the area where the C opens up posteriorly. Without the cartilage, there is some "give" in the posterior aspect of the larynx and trachea, so there is room for the esophagus to expand when you swallow larger chunks of food.

The trachea is the largest bronchus and can be thought of as the trunk of the tracheobronchial tree. Once the trachea reaches the center of the chest, it begins its first branching, or bifurcation, into two bronchi (*bronchus* is the singular form), the **right mainstem** and the **left mainstem**. The site of bifurcation is called the **carina** (again, see Figure 13-9). One bronchus goes to the right lung, and the other bronchus goes to the left lung. The mainstem

trachea *(TRAY kee ah)* Rigid tubular air pipe between the larynx and the bronchi that is a passageway for inhaled and exhaled air.

right mainstem Largest bronchus leading into right lung.

left mainstem Largest bronchus leading into the left lung.

carina *(kuh RYE nuh)* A structure with a projecting central ridge such as occurs at the bifurcation of the mainstem bronchi in the lung.

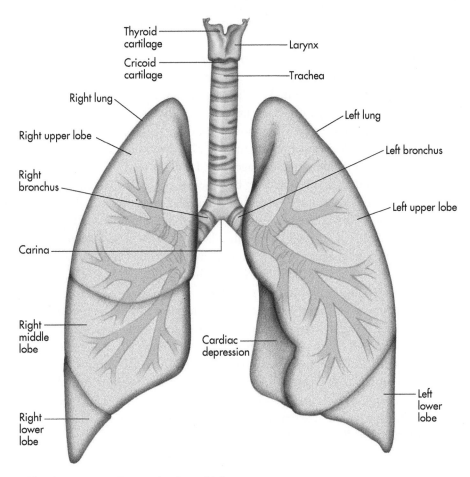

FIGURE 13-9 ▲ The tracheobronchial tree.

Clinical Application

THE ANGLE MAKES A DIFFERENCE

The angle of branching is not the same for both sides of the tracheobronchial tree. The right mainstem branches off at a 20- to 30-degree angle from the midline of the chest. The left mainstem branches off at a more pronounced 40- to 60-degree angle. This is important because the lesser angle of the right mainstem branching allows foreign bodies that are accidentally breathed in to more often lodge in the right lung. This is nice to know if a child has aspirated (taken into the lung) an object and the physician must enter the lung with a bronchoscope to remove the object. Time may be critical, and it may make a difference if the search is begun immediately in the right lung because its anatomic structure increases the probability that the object has lodged there. In addition, an endotracheal tube (breathing tube) may be placed too far into the lung, and instead of sitting above the carina so both lungs are ventilated, the tube will most likely pass into and ventilate only the right lung. This is why an x-ray for proper tube placement is so important.

primary bronchi *(BRONG kye)* Older term for main stem bronchi.

lobar bronchi Airway leading into specific lobe of lungs.

segmental bronchi Airways leading into specific lung segments.

bronchioles *(BRONG kee ohlz)* Small tubular air passageways that branch off the bronchi. They carry inhaled and exhaled air to and from the alveoli.

terminal bronchioles Last, very small airways that lead to the respiratory zone of the lung.

respiratory bronchioles *(ress PIRE eh toh ree brong kee ohls)* Very small airways where the first part of gas exchange begins.

simple squamous pneumocytes *(SKWAY mus NEW moh sites)* Flat, pancake-like cells that comprise most of the alveolus and are where gas exchange takes place.

alveolar sacs *(al VEE oh lar saks)* Grape bunch–like structures composed of several alveoli.

bronchi are sometimes also referred to as the **primary bronchi**. Now the bronchi must branch into the five **lobar bronchi** that correspond to the five lobes of the lungs.

Each lung lobe is further divided into specific segments, and the next branching of bronchi is called the **segmental bronchi**. At the point from the trachea down to the segmental bronchi, the tissue layers of the bronchi are all the same, only smaller, as they branch downward. The first layer is the epithelial layer, which contains the mucociliary escalator—or pseudostratified ciliated columnar cells—that keeps the area clean of debris. A middle lamina propria layer contains smooth muscle, lymph, and nerve tracts. The third layer is the protective and supportive cartilaginous layer (see **FIGURE 13-10** ▲).

The branching becomes more numerous with tiny *subsegmental bronchi* that branch deep within each lung segment. The diameter of subsegmental bronchi ranges from 1 to 6 millimeters. Cartilaginous rings are now irregular pieces of cartilage and will soon fade away completely. Notice as we move toward the gas exchange regions that the airways simplify to make it easier for gas molecules to pass through. Next are the very tiny airways called **bronchioles** that average only 1 millimeter in diameter. They have no cartilage layer, and the epithelial lining becomes ciliated cuboidal cells (short squat cells as opposed to large columns). The cilia, goblet cells, and submucosal gland are almost all gone by this point. There is no gas exchange yet, just simple conduction of the gas mixture containing the oxygen molecules down the tree. The **terminal bronchioles,** which have an average diameter of 0.5 millimeters, no goblet cells, no cartilage, no cilia, and no submucosal glands, mark the end of the conducting areas. Finally, we journey into the gas exchange or respiratory zone of the lung.

The next airway beyond the terminal bronchiole is called the **respiratory bronchiole** because a small portion of gas exchange takes place here. The epithelial lining consists of simple cuboidal cells interspersed with actual alveoli-type cells, which are flat, pancake-like cells called **simple squamous pneumocytes**. Alveolar ducts originate from the respiratory bronchioles, wherein the walls of the alveolar ducts are completely made up of simple squamous cells arranged in a tubular configuration. The alveolar ducts give way to the grape bunch–like structures of several connected alveoli, better known as the **alveolar sacs**. See **FIGURE 13-11** ▲.

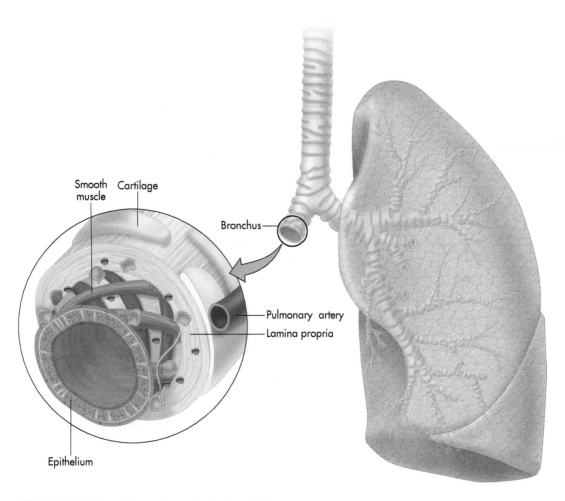

Smooth muscle   Cartilage

Bronchus

Pulmonary artery

Lamina propria

Epithelium

FIGURE 13-10 ▲ Tissue layers in the bronchi.

Clinical Application

THERAPEUTIC OXYGEN

Often, a distressed respiratory system and sometimes the cardiac system needs supplemental oxygen to assist its function and meet its needs. There are many ways to deliver an enriched oxygen supply to the lungs, including various oxygen masks, nasal cannula (tube), and specialized devices to deliver both oxygen and extra humidity to the lungs to assist their function.

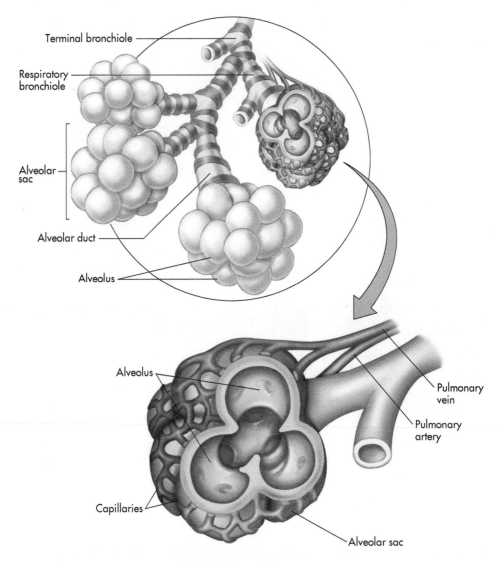

Terminal bronchiole

Respiratory bronchiole

Alveolar sac

Alveolar duct

Alveolus

Alveolus

Capillaries

Pulmonary vein

Pulmonary artery

Alveolar sac

STRUCTURES OF THE LUNGS		GENERATIONS (BRANCHES)	
Conducting zone	Trachea	0	Cartilaginous airways
	Main stem bronchi	1	
	Lobar bronchi	2	
	Segmental bronchi	3	
	Subsegmental bronchi	4-9	
	Bronchioles	10-15	Noncartilaginous airways
	Terminal bronchioles	16-19	
Respiratory zone	Respiratory bronchioles	20-23	Gas exchange region
	Alveolar ducts	24-27	
	Alveolar sacs	28	

FIGURE 13-11 ▲ Conduction and gas exchange structures and functions.

Alveolar Capillary Membrane: Where the Action Is

alveolar capillary membrane *(al VEE oh lar KAP uh ler ee MEM breyn)* Site of the connection between the respiratory and cardiovascular system where gas exchange occurs.

The alveoli are the terminal air sacs that are surrounded by numerous pulmonary capillaries and together make up the functional unit of the lung known as the **alveolar capillary membrane.** The average number of alveoli in an adult lung ranges from 300 million to 600 million. This gives a total 80 square meters (m^2) surface area for the oxygen molecules to diffuse across (about the size of a tennis court!) into the surrounding pulmonary capillaries, which have about the same cross-sectional area (70 m²). The blood entering the pulmonary capillaries comes from the right side of the heart and is low in oxygen and high in carbon dioxide because it just came from the body tissues. Gas exchange or external respiration takes place, and the blood leaving the pulmonary capillaries is high in oxygen and travels to the left side of the heart to be pumped around to the tissues. Conversely, carbon dioxide molecules are in high concentration in the blood in the pulmonary capillaries and very low in the lung (remember, there is little CO_2 in the atmosphere), so CO_2 leaves the blood and enters the lung to be exhaled.

On closer inspection of the alveolar capillary membrane, you will see four distinct components. The first layer is the liquid **surfactant** layer that lines the alveoli. This *phospholipid* helps lower the surface tension in these very tiny spheres (alveoli) that would otherwise collapse due to the high surface tension.

The second component is the actual tissue layer, or alveolar epithelium, comprised of simple squamous cells of two types. The main type (95%) comprising the alveolar

surfactant *(sir FACK tent)* Protein–fat compound that creates surface tension and keeps the walls of the alveolus from collapsing inward with each inhalation.

erythrocyte *(eh RITH roh sight)* A red blood cell. Erythrocytes contain hemoglobin and carry oxygen and carbon dioxide to and from the lungs and cells of the body.

hemoglobin *(HEE moh GLOH bin)* Substance in an erythrocyte that binds to oxygen and carbon dioxide. Its globin chains give it a round shape. When it is bound to oxygen, it forms the compound oxyhemoglobin.

erythropoiesis *(eh RITH roh poy EE sis)* Formation of red blood cells.

erythropoietin *(eh RITH roh poy EE tin)* In the body, a hormone secreted by the kidneys when the number of red blood cells decreases. It stimulates the bone marrow to make more red blood cells. As a drug, erythropoietin does the same.

Clinical Application

WHAT CAN GO WRONG WITH GAS EXCHANGE?

The membrane between the alveoli and the capillaries is quite thin. In fact, it is only 0.004 millimeters thick! The thinness of this membrane aids in the diffusion of the gases between the lungs and the blood. Anything that would act as a barrier to oxygen molecules getting to or through this barrier would decrease the amount of oxygen that gets into the blood. For example, excessive secretions and fluid such as in pneumonia act as a barrier and reduce the oxygen levels in the blood, which can be measured by sampling arterial blood and analyzing the amount of each gas dissolved in it. This is called an arterial blood gas, or ABG. In the case of severe pneumonia, the level of oxygen known as the PaO_2 goes down because less oxygen can get into the blood, and the $PaCO_2$ in the arterial blood goes up because less CO_2 crosses into the lungs to be exhaled.

Changes in the bloodstream can also affect blood gases. Red blood cells, or **erythrocytes,** are responsible for the bulk of the transportation of oxygen and carbon dioxide in the blood via a protein- and iron-containing molecule called **hemoglobin,** which performs the actual transportation. It is estimated that there are about 280 million hemoglobin molecules found in *each* erythrocyte!

In general, if the hemoglobin is carrying large amounts of oxygen, the blood will be bright red. If there is less oxygen and more carbon dioxide being carried, then the blood will be darker in color or may have a "bluish" tint. An obvious example of this can be seen when you look at the veins in your arm. Venous blood has lower levels of oxygen and higher levels of carbon dioxide. As a result, venous blood has a dark red tint. Low levels of red blood cells or anemia would limit the number of hemoglobin molecules that could transport oxygen and thus greatly reduce the amount in the blood available for the tissues. Therefore, the number of red blood cells and the amount of hemoglobin in your blood (both of which can be measured) are important in oxygen delivery to your tissues.

Your body can attempt to respond to low hemoglobin levels by producing more red blood cells by a process called **erythropoiesis.** (*Poiesis* means "to make.") This process begins once the kidneys detect low levels of oxygen coming to them from the blood. The kidneys release into the bloodstream a hormone called **erythropoietin.** This substance travels through the blood and eventually reaches specialized cells found in the red bone marrow. Once stimulated, these specialized cells begin to increase their production of erythrocytes until demand is met. Having too little iron in the body can also affect oxygen delivery because the iron in the hemoglobin is what holds onto the oxygen molecules. The terms *iron-poor* blood and *tired* blood come from the fact that a patient with low levels of iron tires easily due to low oxygen levels.

squamous pneumocyte (*SKWAY mus NEW moh sites*) Flat, pancake-like cells that comprise most of the alveolus and are where gas exchange takes place.

granular pneumocytes (*GRAN yuh ler NOO moh SITE*) Plump type II cell that produces surfactant and aids in cellular repair.

wandering macrophage (*MACK roh feyj*) Mobile cell moving throughout the alveoli, ingesting foreign particles.

pores of Kohn Small opening between alveoli that allow for the movement of gas and macrophages.

interstitial space The area that separates the basement membrane of alveolar epithelium from the capillary endothelium.

capillary endothelium (*KAP ih LAIR ee en doh THEE lee uhm*) Known as simple squamous endothelium and forms the wall of the capillary.

simple squamous epithelium See capillary endothelium.

surface is a flat, pancakelike cell called a **squamous pneumocyte** or Type I cell. This is where the gas molecules can easily pass through in the process of gas exchange. The alveoli also need to produce the valuable surfactant, and this is where the plump Type II, or **granular pneumocytes**, come in. These highly metabolic cells not only produce surfactant but also aid in cellular repair responsibilities.

In addition, this area needs to be free of debris that would act as barriers to the vital process of gas exchange. The "cleanup" cells called Type III cells or **wandering macrophages**, ingest foreign particles as the macrophages wander throughout the alveoli. There are even small holes between the alveoli called **pores of Kohn** that allow for gases and the macrophages to move from one alveolus to another.

The third component of the alveolar capillary membrane is the **interstitial space**. This is the area that separates the basement membrane of alveolar epithelium from the basement membrane of the capillary endothelium and contains interstitial fluid. This space is so small that the membranes of the alveoli and capillary appear fused. However, if too much fluid gets into this space (interstitial edema), the membranes separate, which makes it harder for gas exchange to occur because the gas has to travel a greater distance and through a congested, fluid-filled space.

The fourth component is the **capillary endothelium** (also known as the **simple squamous epithelium**) that forms the wall of the capillary. The capillary contains the blood with the red blood cells that carry the precious gas cargo to its destination.

Pulmonary Function Testing

Lung function can be measured in terms of volumes and flows using pulmonary function testing (PFTs). First, the various volumes can be measured by having the patient breathe normally and then take a maximum deep breath followed by a maximum exhalation. The tracing is recorded as in FIGURE 13-12 ▲. For example, tidal volume (V_T) is the amount of air moved into or out of the lungs at rest during a single breath. The normal tidal volume is 500 mL, although there is considerable variation depending on age, sex, height, and general fitness. Your inspiratory reserve volume (IRV) is what you can breathe in beyond a normal inspiration. Likewise, your expiratory reserve volume (ERV) is what you can exhale beyond a normal exhalation. You can never totally exhale all the air out of your lungs; your residual volume (RV) prevents total lung collapse. We can combine these volumes to get various lung capacities as shown in Figure 13-12:

- Function residual capacity (FRC)—the volume of air remaining in the lungs at the end of a normal expiration
- Inspiratory reserve volume (IRV)—the amount of air that can be forcefully inhaled after a normal inspiration
- Expiratory reserve volume (ERV)—the amount of air that can be forcefully exhaled after a normal expiration
- Residual volume (RV)—the volume of air remaining in the lungs after a maximum expiration
- Vital capacity (VC)—the maximum amount of air that can be moved into and out of the respiratory system in a single respiratory cycle

APPLIED SCIENCE

The Amazing Surfactant

When the alveoli are small (during end-expiration), the surfactant layer lowers the surface tension, thereby preventing alveoli collapse. However, when you take a deep breath (end-inspiration), your alveoli get larger and the surfactant layer thins and becomes less effective, its surface tension increasing because of its thinning. This prevents overexpansion or rupture of the alveoli. Lack of surfactant can cause "stiff" lungs that resist expansion. Surfactant develops late in fetal development, and premature babies therefore may not have sufficient levels. Without immediate intervention, their tiny lungs would collapse (**atelectasis**) and thus prevent the movement of air into and out of the lung and vital gas exchange. If they are given too much volume to reexpand their stiff lungs, the alveoli may rupture, again because surfactant is not there to prevent over-expansion. Surfactant also has an antibacterial property that helps to fight harmful pathogens. Fortunately, medical science has developed surfactant replacement therapy that can instill surfactant into the lungs to maintain their function until babies have matured and can produce it on their own.

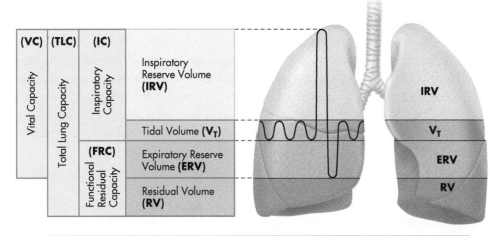

atelectasis *(AT eh LEK tah sis)* Incomplete expansion or collapse of part or all of a lung due to mucus, tumor, monotonous breathing, or a foreign body that blocks the bronchus. The lung is said to be atelectatic.

Lung volume measurements	Male (in milliliters)	Female (in milliliters)
Tidal Volume (V$_T$): The volume of gas in and out of the lungs during one normal breath	500	400-500
Inspiratory Reserve Volume (IRV): The volume of air forcefully inspired beyond a normal inspiration	3100	1900
Expiratory Reserve Volume (ERV): Volume of gas forcefully exhaled beyond a normal expiration	1200	800
Residual Volume (RV): The volume of gas still remaining in the lungs after a forced expiration.	1200	1100
Lung Capacities (combination of two or more volumes)		
Vital Capacity (VC): VC = IRV + V$_T$ + ERV	4800	3200
Inspiratory Capacity (IC): IC = V$_T$ + IRV	3600	2400
Functional Residual Capacity (FRC): FRC = ERV + RV	2400	1800
Total Lung Capacity (TLC): TLC = IRV + V$_T$ + ERV + RV	6000	4200

FIGURE 13-12 ▲ Normal lung volumes and capacities.

Pathology Connection

THE LOWER AIRWAYS

Respiratory disease is one of the most common diseases seen in health care settings. The following sections review some of these.

Atelectasis and Pneumonia

Atelectasis, commonly found in the hospital setting, is a condition in which the air sacs of the lungs are either partially or totally collapsed. Atelectasis can occur in patients who cannot or will not take deep breaths to fully expand the lungs, stimulate surfactant production, and keep the air passageways open. Surgery, pain, or an injury of the **thoracic** cage (such as broken ribs) often makes deep breathing painful. Taking periodic deep breaths is important not only to expand the lungs but also to stimulate the production of surfactant, which helps to keep the small alveolar sacs open between breaths.

Patients with large amounts of secretions who cannot cough them up are also at risk for atelectasis because the secretions block airways and lead to areas of collapse. Quite often, if atelectasis is not corrected and secretions are retained, **pneumonia** can develop within 72 hours. Pneumonia is a lung infection that can be caused by a virus, fungus, bacterium, aspiration, or chemical inhalation. Inflammation occurs in the infected areas, with an accumulation of cell debris and thick fluid in the alveoli. In certain pneumonias, lung tissue is destroyed. Pneumonias, if severe enough, can lead to death. It is interesting to note that secondary pneumonia is what often kills people following a flu illness and not the actual flu attack. Pneumonias can also be classified according to their location as illustrated in FIGURE 13-13 ▲.

Tuberculosis

Tuberculosis (TB) is a bacterial infection that has seen a recent rise in occurrence. Tuberculosis thrives in areas of the body that have high oxygen content such as in the lungs. A healthy immune system can destroy tuberculosis bacteria or encase the bacteria in nodules called **tubercles**. Tubercles (lesions) form in the lungs. Within a tubercle, the bacteria remain inactive. Tuberculosis can lay dormant in the body for years. However, if the immune system weakens, tubercles can burst, and the bacteria can multiply. If the bacteria's spread is unchecked, vast lung damage can occur. There has been recent concern about a form of tuberculosis that is very resistant to the drugs normally used to treat TB and has a high mortality rate. Someone with tuberculosis will have a cough, low-grade fever in the afternoon, weight loss, and night sweats.

Chronic Obstructive Pulmonary Disease (COPD)

Obstructive pulmonary disease is a general term used to describe abnormal pulmonary conditions associated with cough, sputum production, dyspnea, airflow obstruction, and impaired gas exchange. It is the fourth leading cause of death in the United States. **Chronic obstructive pulmonary disease (COPD)** is a group of diseases in which patients have difficulty getting all the air out of their lungs and often have large amounts of secretions and lung damage. COPD refers to one of or a combination of emphysema and chronic bronchitis. Asthma used to be included in

thoracic Pertaining to the chest or thorax.

pneumonia *(noo MOH nee uh)* Infectious lung disease characterized by fever, excessive secretions, shortness of breath, lethargy, and cough.

tuberculosis (TB) *(too BER kew LOH sis)* Lung infection caused by the bacterium mycobacterium tuberculosis and spread by airborne droplets expelled by coughing.

tubercles *(TOO ber kulz)* Nodules formed as a result of tuberculosis.

obstructive pulmonary disease A general term used to describe abnormal pulmonary conditions associated with cough, sputum production, dyspnea, airflow obstruction, and impaired gas exchange.

Pathology Connection (continued)

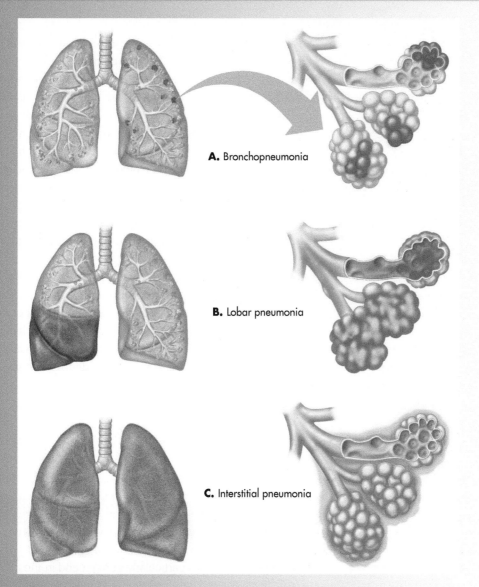

A. Bronchopneumonia

B. Lobar pneumonia

C. Interstitial pneumonia

FIGURE 13-13 ▲ General locations for pneumonias.

the COPD category but has become separate because it is distinguished by having reversible airway narrowing and airway hyperreactivity; it is most commonly characterized as an inflammatory process. **Emphysema** is characterized anatomically as the permanent, abnormal enlargement of distal airway spaces and destruction of the alveolar walls. **Chronic bronchitis** is associated with a productive cough, enlargement of mucous glands, and hypertrophy of the airway smooth muscle. Acute bronchitis is a temporary and very common lung condition that can affect people of any age. It differs from chronic bronchitis in that it is reversible and there are no permanent structural changes. All these illnesses share features of airway obstruction and therefore share some similar treatments. However, asthma is typically treated as a separate disease from COPD because of its greater reversibility. TABLE 13-3 ■ summarizes each of the COPD-associated diseases, each of which is discussed in greater detail later in this chapter.

chronic obstructive pulmonary disease (COPD) A group of progressive, debilitating, and often fatal lung diseases that exhibit difficulty with air movement into and out of the lungs, prolonged expiratory periods, and the loss of normal lung elasticity. COPD includes emphysema and chronic bronchitis.

emphysema *(EM fih SEE mah)* Chronic pulmonary disease resulting in destruction of air spaces distal to the terminal bronchiole.

chronic bronchitis *(brong KYE tiss)* Chronic inflammation or infection of the bronchi. Inflammation of the bronchi can be due to pollution or smoking.

(continued)

asthma *(AZ mah)*
Sudden onset of hyperreactivity of the bronchi and bronchioles with bronchospasm (contraction of the smooth muscle). Inflammation and swelling severely narrow the lumen of the airways.

bronchospasm An abnormal narrowing of the bronchi, due to spasms of the airway's smooth muscle, creating partial obstructions of the lumen, often accompanied by coughing and wheezing.

gas trapping A condition in which exhalation of air is impaired, leading to stale air remaining in the lung.

Pathology Connection (continued)

Asthma

Asthma is a chronic inflammatory illness of the airways affecting nearly 25 million people in the United States, including 6.2 million children. Asthma is the most common chronic disease of childhood and younger adults, with about 80% of cases developing before the age of 45. It is a potentially life-threatening lung condition in which the airways of the lungs constrict (**bronchospasm**), often in reaction to an allergy. See FIGURE 13-14 ▲. It is difficult to get air in and even more difficult to get air out of the lungs. The inability to get air out of the lungs is known as **gas trapping**. As a result of gas trapping, fresh air cannot get into the lungs, so the victim breathes the same air over and over. This lowers the amount of oxygen in the blood and increases the blood levels of carbon dioxide. Asthma can be controlled with the use of medication. The most common symptoms of asthma include episodic wheezing, shortness of breath, cough, and chest tightness. These symptoms are often worse at nighttime or in the early morning due to diurnal variations in muscle tone of the airways. (For more information about the relationship between asthma and allergies see Chapter 14, "The Immune System.")

Persons with asthma develop bronchospasm on exposure to specific sensitizing substances usually described as "triggers." Common triggers include allergens, inhalants, viruses, cold air, and exercise. TABLE 13-4 ■ provides a more complete list of asthma triggers. Asthma is a chronic disease, even though certain disease triggers may wax and wane leading to episodic attacks. Therefore, patients and their caregivers need to understand the chronic nature of asthma and the underlying inflammatory process. It is important that patients be able to identify and control their exposure to environmental allergens or other types of triggers.

TABLE 13-3 ■ ASTHMA AND COPD DISEASES

DISEASE	DESCRIPTION
Asthma	A chronic inflammatory disorder of the airways in which many cells and cellular elements play a role. In susceptible individuals, this inflammation causes recurrent episodes of wheezing, breathlessness, chest tightness, and cough, particularly at night and in the early morning. These episodes are usually associated with widespread but variable airflow obstruction that is often reversible either spontaneously or with treatment.
Chronic bronchitis	Usually defined in clinical terms as the presence of productive cough during 3 months of the year for 2 consecutive years, provided that other causes of chronic sputum production, such as tuberculosis, are excluded. Airway hyperreactivity may be present, but airflow limitation is not fully reversible.
Emphysema	A pathologic diagnosis marked by destruction of alveolar walls, with resultant loss of elastic recoil in the lung. Dyspnea on exertion is the predominant clinical feature, and airway hyperreactivity may also be present.

(continued)

Pathology Connection (continued)

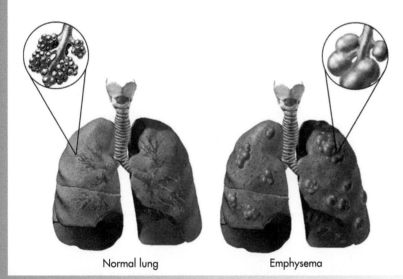

Normal lung   Emphysema

FIGURE 13-14 ▲ Asthma and emphysema.

TABLE 13-4 ■ TRIGGERS FOR ASTHMATIC ATTACKS

Allergens

Animal dander (pets with fur or feathers)	House dust mites (in mattresses, pillows, upholstered furniture, carpets)
Pollen (grass, trees, weeds)	Mold
	Cockroaches

Inhaled Irritants

Tobacco smoke	Strong odors or sprays (perfumes, paint fumes, pesticides, hair
Wood smoke	sprays, cleaning agents)
Sulfur dioxide	Occupational inhalants
Air Pollution	

(continued)

Pathology Connection (continued)

TABLE 13-4 ■ TRIGGERS FOR ASTHMATIC ATTACKS (continued)

Viral Respiratory Infections (Rhinovirus, Influenza, Parainfluenza, Corona Virus, RSV)

Cold Air

Exercise

Strong Emotions

Menses

Drugs

Aspirin	Methacholine (used to provoke bronchoconstriction during diagnostic testing)
NSAIDs	
Beta-adrenergic blockers (oral or ophthalmic)	Histamine (alternative agent to provoke bronchoconstriction during testing)
Preservatives (sulfites and benzalkonium chloride)	

Other Factors

Allergic rhinitis	Gastroesophageal reflux (GERD)
Rhinosinusitis	

emphysema *(EM fih SEE mah)* Chronic pulmonary disease resulting in destruction of air spaces distal to the terminal bronchiole.

Emphysema

Emphysema is a nonreversible lung condition in which the alveolar air sacs are destroyed and the lung itself becomes "floppy" (again see Figure 13-14), much like a balloon that has been inflated and deflated many times. As the alveoli are destroyed, it becomes more difficult for gases to diffuse between the lungs and the blood. The lung tissue becomes fragile and can easily rupture (again, much like a worn tire), causing air to escape into the thoracic cavity and further inhibit gas exchange.

The work of breathing for the severely emphysemic patient expends energy similar to the energy spent jogging. They must continually work to maintain airway pressure in their abnormally large airspaces and must maintain a rapid respiratory rate. Weight loss is typical with severe emphysema. Think how much weight you'd lose if you ran a marathon each day!

About 2 million persons in the United States are estimated to have emphysema. The majority of cases were caused by smoking. However, 60,000 to 100,000 have a genetic deficiency of alpha$_1$-antitrypsin (α_1-AT) as their underlying etiology. α_1-AT is a glycoprotein that is essential in protecting the lungs against naturally occurring proteases that have the ability to destroy lung tissue. Patients with this deficiency tend to develop emphysema at a younger age (in their 40s or

(continued)

Pathology Connection

50s) than do patients with emphysema from other causes. Most persons with α_1-AT deficiency are Caucasians of northern European descent.

Smoking further accelerates the process. Manifestations of severe α_1-AT deficiency involve the lungs, liver, and skin, and the major clinical feature is emphysema. The disorder is detected by a decreased level of α_1-AT to below a so-called protective value of 80 mg/dL. This is in comparison to normal serum levels of 150 to 350 mg/dL.

Chronic Bronchitis

Chronic bronchitis is lung disease in which there are inflamed airways and large amounts of sputum produced. As inflammation occurs, the airways swell, and the inner diameter of the airways get smaller. As they get smaller, it becomes difficult to move air in and out, which increases the work of breathing. Because of this increased work level, more oxygen is used and more carbon dioxide is produced.

Chronic bronchitis is more common than emphysema, with a prevalence of over 9 million persons in the United States. Cigarette smoking is the major causative factor in up to 90% of cases. Patients with chronic bronchitis have an increase in size and number of the mucus-secreting glands, narrowing and inflammation of the small airways, obstruction of airways caused by narrowing and mucus hypersecretion, and bacterial colonization of the airways. Acute episodes are usually brought on by a respiratory tract infection. The usual clinical presentation of chronic bronchitis begins with morning cough productive of sputum. The patient may report a decline in exercise tolerance, although he or she may not have appreciated this decline until questioned. Wheezes may be present, and an increase in the anterior-posterior diameter of the chest (the classic "barrel chest") may be present in both emphysema and chronic bronchitis as a result of excessive accessory muscle use. The patient who has predominantly chronic bronchitis symptoms may undergo repeated episodes of respiratory failure and frequently develop right-sided heart failure.

chronic bronchitis *(brong KYE tiss)* Chronic inflammation or infection of the bronchi. Inflammation of the bronchi can be due to pollution or smoking.

Amazing Body Facts

Smoking Kills

The major preventable cause of many of the respiratory diseases is smoking. It has been estimated that smoking kills more people than road accidents, suicides, and AIDS combined. This is the equivalent of one person dying every 15 minutes from a smoking-related illness.

Clinical Application

FAMILY HISTORY AND ASTHMA

The patient's history can be very helpful, as many asthmatic patients will have a family history of allergies such as asthma, eczema, or hay fever. Usually, the patient or their parents will be able to identify exposures or circumstances that trigger the patient's symptoms. According to a 2009 Center for Disease Control and Prevention (CDC) survey, nearly 25 million people suffer with asthma, which is approximately 8% of the U.S. population.

Clinical Application

COPD DEMOGRAPHICS

Men have a higher incidence of COPD than women; however, women are catching up because more women are smoking in recent years.

Clinical Application

SMOKING HISTORY

Smoking history is a very important initial screening procedure the clinician can perform, as it can help to clinically determine how much a person has actually smoked in their lifetime as well as estimate how much damage smoking has caused. A 10- to 20-pack-year history will cause changes in PFT findings. A 70-pack-year history of smoking or greater has been described as a specific finding suggestive of COPD. Pack-year history is calculated by multiplying the number of packs smoked per day by the number of years smoked.

Besides volumes and capacities, we can also measure the flow rates coming out of the lung at various points during a forced (maximum patient effort) vital capacity (FVC). For example we can measure the forced expiratory volume in 1 second (FEV_1) and peak expiratory flow rate (PEFR). Normally one can exhale 75 to 85% of their FVC in 1 second. However, someone with an obstructive disease would take longer to exhale and get less than 70% of their total FVC out in 1 second and therefore have a reduced FEV_1.

Another test that helps to establish whether the airways have become "narrower" than normal (as would be seen in an asthma episode) is the peak expiratory flow rate, or PEFR, which is the maximum flow rate or speed of air a person can rapidly expel after taking the deepest possible breath. PEFR is measured in liters per minute and should be within a predicted range. This a good test to reflect how the larger airways are functioning and monitor diseases such as asthma that affect these airways.

The primary etiology for COPD is exposure to tobacco smoke. Smokers have higher death rates from both chronic bronchitis and emphysema. Smokers also have more lung-function abnormalities, show more respiratory symptoms, and experience all forms of COPD at a much higher rate than nonsmokers. Age of starting, total pack-years, puff volume, and current smoking status are predictive of COPD mortality. Passive smoking (the exposure of nonsmokers to cigarette smoke) also seems to increase the risk of COPD-related disease. Children of parents who smoke have a higher prevalence of respiratory symptoms and ear infections than children of nonsmokers. Exposure to smoke at an early age may impair lung maturation and the attainment of maximal lung function in adult life. Air pollution, occupational exposure, asthma, and nonspecific airway hyperresponsiveness may all play a role in the development of COPD.

TABLE 13-5 ■ lists the differential diagnostic markers for COPD and asthma. No one marker is conclusive, so the entire clinical picture must be assessed for correct diagnosis and treatment.

TABLE 13-5 ■ DIAGNOSTIC MARKERS TO DIFFERENTIATE COPD AND ASTHMA

DIAGNOSTIC MARKERS	COPD	ASTHMA
Age of patient when diagnosed	Typically over 40	Often child or young adult
Smoking history	Smokers and ex-smokers	No direct correlation between smoking and asthma, although smoke will trigger attack
Dyspnea	Shortness of breath, especially on exertion	Episodic attacks, especially on exposure to allergen/ irritant/exercise
Cough	Productive cough, typically in the morning	Cough typically precedes an episode
Triggers (allergens, exercise)	None usually identified for attacks	Exposure leads to attacks temperature, humidity, etc.
Spirometry	FEV_1/FVC ratio < 70%	FEV_1/FVC ratio low during attacks only
Daily variation in peak expiratory	Little	Morning dip and day-to-day variability flow rate (PEFR)
Effect of corticosteroid trial	Inconclusive (< 20% of patients are successful)	Improvement
Eosinophilia (increased number of eosinophils)	No	In allergic reaction forms of asthma
Chest x-ray	Overinflation	Overinflation during attacks

TEST YOUR KNOWLEDGE 13-3

Choose the best answer:

1. The largest bronchus or trunk of the tracheobronchial tree is the:
   a. right mainstem bronchus
   b. left mainstem bronchus
   c. bronchiole
   d. trachea

2. The site of bifurcation of the right and left lungs is called the:
   a. alveoli
   b. carina
   c. trachea
   d. capillary

3. If an object is aspirated into the airways, it is most likely to go to:
   a. the right lung
   b. the left lung
   c. the stomach
   d. the oropharynx

4. The first portion of the airway where gas exchange begins is the:
   a. terminal bronchiole
   b. trachea
   c. mainstem bronchus
   d. respiratory bronchiole

5. The alveolar layer that lowers surface tension to keep the alveoli expanded is the:
   a. surfactant layer
   b. capillary layer
   c. epithelium layer
   d. macrophage layer

6. The alveolar cell that allows for gas exchange is the:
   a. squamous cell
   b. granular cell
   c. macrophage cell
   d. Kohn cell

The Housing of the Lungs and Related Structures

mediastinum *(ME dee as TYE num)* Central area within the thoracic cavity. It contains the trachea, esophagus, heart, and other structures.

visceral pleura *(VISS er al PLOO rah)* One of the two membranes of the pleura. It covers the surface of the lung.

parietal pleura *(pah RYE eh tal PLOO rah)* One of the two layers of the pleura. It lines the thoracic cavity.

pleural fluid Slippery liquid found within the space between the visceral and parietal pleura of the thoracic cavity.

The lungs reside in the thoracic cavity and are separated by a region called the **mediastinum,** which contains the esophagus, heart, great vessels (superior and inferior vena cava, pulmonary vein, pulmonary artery, and aorta), and trachea (see **FIGURE 13-15** ▲).

Breathing in and out causes the lungs to move within the thoracic cavity. Over time, an irritation could occur as the lungs rub the inside of the thoracic cage. To prevent such damage, each lung is wrapped in a sac, or serous membrane (see Chapter 4), called the **visceral pleura.** The thoracic cavity and the upper side of the diaphragm are lined with a continuation of this membrane called the **parietal pleura.** Between these two pleural layers is an intrapleural space (pleural cavity) that contains a slippery liquid called **pleural fluid.** This fluid greatly reduces the friction as an individual breathes.

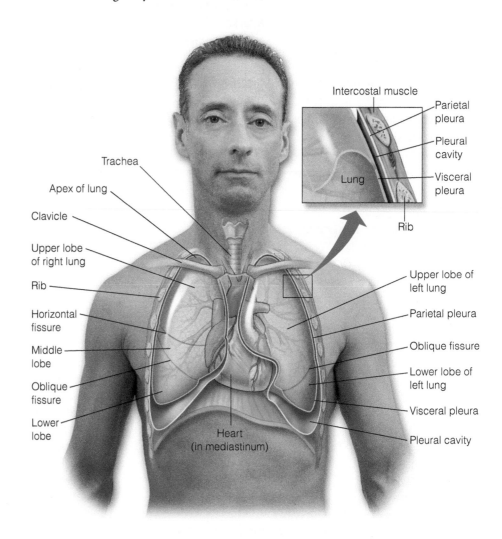

FIGURE 13-15 ▲ Structures of the thoracic cavity.

Pathology Connection

PLEURAL SPACE PROBLEMS

Trauma or certain disease states can interfere with the structure and therefore the function of the thoracic cavity. A **pneumothorax** is a condition in which there is air inside the thoracic cavity and outside the lungs. Air can enter the thoracic cavity from two directions. See **FIGURE 13-16** △. A stab wound or gunshot wound to the chest would allow air to rush into the thoracic cavity from the outside. Alternately, the lung might develop a leak as a result of either a structural deformity or a disease process (such as in emphysema). In this situation, air would enter the thoracic cavity from the lung as air is breathed in. In either case, if the gas cannot escape, it will continue to fill a space in the thoracic cavity and provide less space for the lung

pneumothorax *(NOO moh THOH raks)* Large volume of air that forms in the pleural space and progressively separates the two pleural membranes.

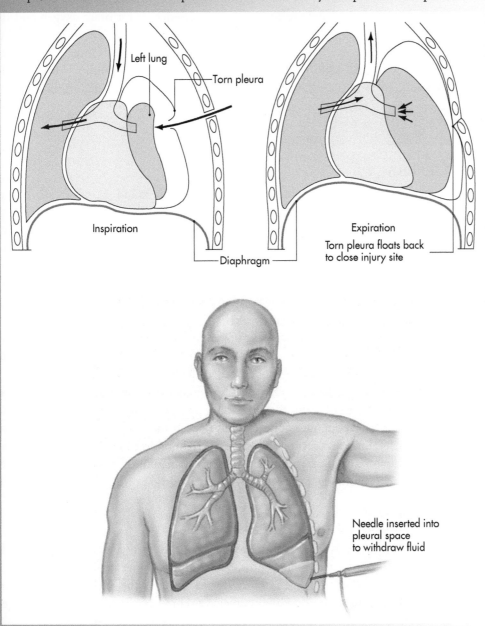

FIGURE 13-16 △ Pneumothorax (sucking chest wound) and technique for performing thoracentesis.

(continued)

pleural effusion
(PLOO ral eh FYOO zhun) Accumulation of fluid within the pleural space due to inflammation or infection of the pleura and lungs.

empyema *(EM pye EE mah)* Localized collection of purulent material (pus) in the thoracic cavity from an infection in the lungs. Also known as pyothorax.

hydrothorax A form of pleural effusion in which blood serum is found in the intrapleural space.

hemothorax
(HE moh THOH raks) Presence of blood in the thoracic cavity, usually from trauma.

apex The rounded top of each lung.

cardiac impression The concave cavity found in the medial surface of the left lung that houses the heart.

hilum *(HIGH lim)* Indentation on the medial side of each lung where the bronchus, pulmonary artery, pulmonary vein, and nerves enter the lung.

horizontal fissure The fissure that divides the upper and middle lobes of the right lung.

oblique fissure A line that divides the upper and lower lobes of the left lung and the middle and lower lobes of the right lung.

lingula The region of the left lung that corresponds with the right middle lobe.

bony thorax The portion of the skeleton, including the sternum, rib cage, and vertebrae, that protects the heart, lungs, and great vessels.

Pathology Connection (continued)

or lungs to expand when breathing. If the lungs are too greatly restricted to expand and begin to collapse, a life-threatening situation may occur.

A **pleural effusion** is a condition in which there is an excessive buildup of fluid in the pleural space between the parietal and the visceral pleura. This fluid may be pus (in which case it is known as **empyema**), serum from the blood (called a **hydrothorax**), or blood (called a **hemothorax**). Because fluids are affected by gravity, pleural effusions tend to move to the lowest point in the pleural space. If a pleural effusion is large enough, it can have the same effect as a large pneumothorax. It can restrict the amount of expansion of a lung or lungs and lead to lung collapse. Because less air can flow in and out of the lungs, the patient has to work harder by breathing in and out more rapidly to meet the body's demands for more oxygen and the removal of carbon dioxide. This additional work of breathing may exhaust an individual to the point that he or she can no longer breathe without intervention. This intervention often includes a chest tube inserted into the pleura space to allow drainage of fluid. This will allow for the lung to reexpand. Again, see FIGURE 13-16 ▲ for illustrations of a sucking chest wound and how to perform a thoracentesis to remove pleural fluid.

The Lungs

The right and left lungs are conical-shaped organs; the rounded peak is called the **apex** of the lung. The apices of the lung extend 1 to 2 inches above the clavicle. The bases of the lungs rest on the right and left hemidiaphragm. The right lung base is a little higher than the left to accommodate the large liver lying underneath. The medial surface of the lung has a deep, concave cavity that contains the heart and therefore is called the **cardiac impression**; it is deeper on the left side. The **hilum** is the area where the root of each lung is attached. Each root contains the mainstem bronchus, pulmonary artery and vein, nerve tracts, and lymph vessels.

The right lung has three lobes—the upper, middle, and lower lobes—that are divided by the **horizontal** and **oblique fissures**. The left lung has only one fissure—the oblique fissure—and therefore only two lobes, called the left upper and left lower lobes. Why only two lobes in the left, you may ask? Remember that the heart is located in the left anterior area of the chest and therefore takes up some space of the left lung. The right lung is larger, and about 60% of gas exchange occurs there. The term **lingula** refers to the area of the left lung that corresponds with the right middle lobe. The lobes are even further divided into specific segments related to their anatomical position. For example, the apical segment of the right upper lobe is the top portion or tip of the right upper lobe.

The Protective Bony Thorax

The lungs, heart, and great vessels are all protected by the **bony thorax**. This bony and cartilaginous frame provides protection and also movement of the thoracic cage to accommodate breathing. The bony thorax includes the rib cage, the sternum or breastbone, and the corresponding thoracic vertebrae to which the ribs attach (see FIGURE 13-17 ▲).

The **sternum,** or breastbone, is centrally located at the anterior portion of the thoracic cage and is comprised of the manubrium, body, and xiphoid process. This anatomical

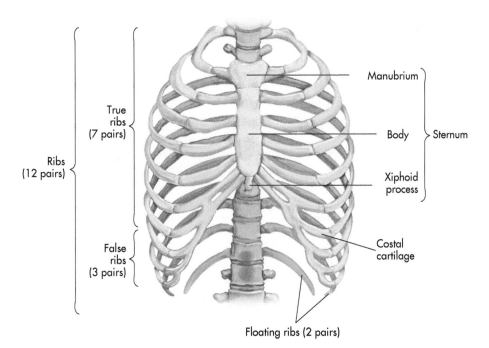

True
ribs
(7 pairs)

Ribs
(12 pairs)

False
ribs
(3 pairs)

Manubrium

Body ⟩ Sternum

Xiphoid
process

Costal
cartilage

Floating ribs (2 pairs)

FIGURE 13-17 ▲ The thoracic cage.

landmark is very important for proper hand placement in CPR. The hand is placed over the body of the sternum where compressions squeeze the heart between the body of the sternum and the thoracic vertebrae. If the hand placement is too low on the xiphoid process, it can break off and lacerate the internal organs.

The **thoracic cage** consists of 12 pairs of elastic arches of bone called ribs. The ribs are attached by cartilage to allow for their movement while breathing. The true ribs are pairs 1 through 7 and are called **vertebrosternal** because they connect anteriorly to the sternum and posteriorly to the thoracic vertebrae of the spinal column. Pairs 8, 9, and 10 are called the false ribs, or **vertebrocostal** because they connect to the costal cartilage of the superior rib and again posterior to the thoracic vertebrae. Rib pairs 11 and 12 are called the floating ribs because they have no anterior attachment and only attach to the vertebral column.

How We Breathe

The control center that tells us to breathe is located in the brain in an area known as the **medulla oblongata**. Inspiration is an active process of ventilation in which the main breathing muscle, the **diaphragm** (a dome-shaped muscle when at rest), is sent a signal via the **phrenic nerve** and contracts and flattens downward, thereby increasing the space in the thoracic cavity (see **FIGURE 13-18 ▲**). The increase in volume in the thoracic cavity causes a decrease in pressure because volume and pressure are inversely related. This creates a lower than atmospheric pressure in the lungs, allowing air to rush into the lungs. The external intercostal muscles also assist by moving the sternum and ribs up and outward during inspiration to increase the total volume in the thoracic cavity. By the way, a hiccup happens when your diaphragm muscle has an involuntary spasm that causes the glottis to close suddenly. As you probably know, these spasms can last for awhile, and it might be hard to figure out how to stop them.

sternum *(STER num)* Vertical bone of the anterior thorax to which the clavicle and ribs are attached. Also known as the breastbone.

thoracic cage *(tho RASS ick)* The portion of the skeleton that includes the ribs, sternum, and thoracic vertebrae that house and protect the lungs, heart, and great vessels.

vertebrosternal *(VER teh broh STIR null)* Referring to the true rib pairs 1–7 and their points of attachment.

vertebrocostal *(VER teh broh KOSS tul)* Referring to the false rib pairs 8–10 and their points of attachment.

medulla oblongata *(meh DULL lah ob long GAW tah)* Most inferior part of the brain stem that joins to the spinal cord. It relays nerve impulses from the cerebrum to the cerebellum. It contains the respiratory center. Cranial nerves IX through XII originate there.

diaphragm *(DYE ah fram)* Muscular sheet that divides the thoracic cavity from the abdominal cavity. Most important ventilation muscle.

phrenic nerve *(FRIN ick)* Nerve that innervates the diaphragm that controls breathing.

Boyle's Law

The process of ventilation takes place because there is an inverse relationship between pressure and volume, which means that if there is a decrease in the volume of a gas, the pressure will rise; if you increase the volume of a gas, its pressure will fall. This was first recognised by Robert Boyle in the 1600s and is now called Boyle's law.

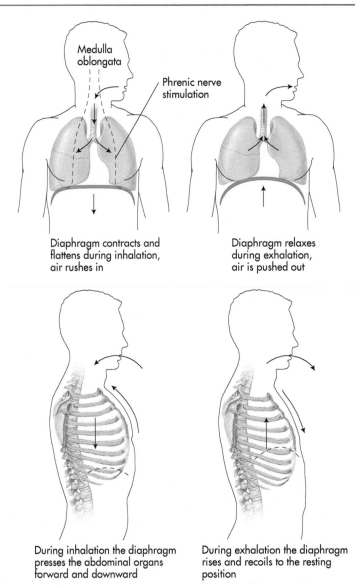

Diaphragm contracts and flattens during inhalation, air rushes in

Diaphragm relaxes during exhalation, air is pushed out

During inhalation the diaphragm presses the abdominal organs forward and downward

During exhalation the diaphragm rises and recoils to the resting position

FIGURE 13-18 ▲ How we breathe.

PH and Ventilation

CO_2 levels are directly related to hydrogen ion concentration. When CO_2 levels rise, so does hydrogen ion concentration. Consequently, pH falls; that is, blood becomes more acidic. Because of this relationship, your body interprets any decrease in blood pH, no matter the cause, as if it were due to increased CO_2, and ventilation increases. For example, when Maria's diabetes is poorly controlled, she might have lower blood pH (increased hydrogen ion concentration) due to metabolic acidosis. In an attempt to bring her blood pH back to normal, her ventilation rate would increase.

To achieve changes in volume and pressure, the diaphragm flattens and thereby increases the volume of the thoracic cavity. At the same time, the ribs move upward and outward via the external intercostal muscles, which also increases the thoracic volume. Because the lungs adhere to the pleural membranes, they are moved upward and outward. This increases the volume of the lungs and decreases their internal pressure. Air then flows from the relative high pressure of the atmosphere, down the trachea, and into the low pressure of the alveoli. Because air is a gas, it will fill all the available alveoli and therefore facilitate gas exchange.

The ease by which ventilation occurs is referred to as **compliance**. Low compliance means that it is more difficult to expand the lungs, whereas high compliance means that less effort is required to expand the lungs. This becomes clinically significant when assessing people who have asthma, emphysema, chronic bronchitis, or any other lung disease. In emphysema, the bronchioles become damaged and wider, allowing air into the lungs, increasing compliance but making it much more difficult to breathe out.

compliance Relates to the flexibility of the lungs and the ease with which ventilation occurs.

Exhalation, on the other hand, is usually a passive act. As the diaphragm relaxes, it forms a dome shape, which decreases the amount of space in the thoracic cavity. As a result, pressure in the lungs becomes greater than the atmospheric pressure, and the air is pushed out of the lungs. The fact that the lungs are elastic tissue that is stretched during inspiration also aids in expiration because this elastic tissue now wants to return to rest, much like a stretched rubber band that is released.

What makes the brain tell the lungs how quickly or slowly to breathe? Although we can consciously speed up or slow down our breathing, our breathing rate is normally controlled by the level of carbon dioxide in our blood. If carbon dioxide levels rise, it means that not enough CO_2 is being ventilated. When this occurs, chemoreceptors in the medulla oblongata send signals to the respiratory muscles to increase the rate and depth of breathing. Chemoreceptors in the carotid arteries and aortic arch are also sensitive to high CO_2 levels and low blood pH and can trigger increased ventilation.

Amazing Body Facts

Exhaled CO_2 and Mosquitoes

Because mosquitoes are too small to carry flashlights, how do they find you in the dark? They do it by using carbon dioxide sensors to locate increased concentrations of CO_2 emitted by—you guessed it—your exhaled breath. Once they detect your exhaled CO_2, they use their heat sensors to find an area of skin on which to begin their banquet!

Another amazing carbon dioxide fact is that many people believe swimmers hyperventilate to get more oxygen in their systems before a sustained underwater dive. In reality, they are "blowing off" CO_2 to get their levels low. Because higher levels of CO_2 cause us to want to breathe, the body is fooled into believing it doesn't need to for a while longer, so swimmers can remain underwater longer. Unfortunately, the body still uses up its oxygen at a regular rate and sometimes uses enough of the reserve that swimmers risk losing consciousness.

COPD patients over time adjust to having a higher-than-normal level of CO_2 in their blood. As a result these individuals rely on levels of oxygen in their blood to determine when to breathe. When these patients have an exacerbation and are erroneously placed on too much oxygen, the higher levels of oxygen in their blood can actually trigger a slowdown in their breathing. Thus, a thorough patient history is imperative.

TEST YOUR KNOWLEDGE 13-4

Choose the best answer:

1. The _____ pleura lines the thoracic cavity.
   a. visceral
   b. parietal
   c. mediastinum
   d. chest

2. The portion of the sternum where CPR is performed is the:
   a. xiphoid process
   b. ribs
   c. manubrium
   d. body

3. The _____ nerve innervates the main breathing muscle, called the _____.
   a. thoracic; internal intercostals
   b. thoracic; diaphragm
   c. phrenic; external intercostals
   d. phrenic; diaphragm

4. Rib pairs 1 to 7 are attached to:
   a. the vertebral column only
   b. the vertebral column and the sternum
   c. the sternum only
   d. are free floating

5. Fill in the blank for the following diseases:
   a. _____ is a condition in which air leaks out of the lung into the thoracic cavity.
   b. _____ is a disease in which there is excessive airway secretions often as the result of smoking.
   c. _____ is a condition that leads to wheezing and shortness of breath, often allergic related.

Other factors can change breathing rate as well. Our breathing rate changes as we grow and mature into adults. A developing newborn has a breathing rate of 40 to 60 breaths/minute. This slows to 14 to 20 breaths/minute in adulthood. When we sleep, our breathing rate slows down because body cells are using less oxygen and producing less carbon dioxide. Breath rate increases with exercise, when body cells are rapidly producing carbon dioxide. It can also increase when we feel strong emotions. We may yawn when we are tired and need more oxygen. Yawning is a deep breath that fills the lungs and brings oxygen to the blood.

Sometimes the body needs help to breathe beyond resting or normal breathing. For example, during increased physical activity or in disease states in which more oxygen is required, **accessory muscles** are used to help pull up your rib cage to make an even larger space in the thoracic cavity. The accessory muscles used are the scalene muscles in the neck, the sternocleidomastoid, and pectoralis major and pectoralis minor muscles of the chest.

Although exhalation is a passive process, there are times, especially with certain disease states, when exhalation may need to be assisted. Again, the body has accessory muscles of exhalation that assist in a more forceful and active exhalation by increasing abdominal pressure. The main accessory muscles of exhalation are the various abdominal muscles that push up the diaphragm or the back muscles that pull down and thus compress the thoracic cage. See **FIGURE 13-19** ▲ for the specific accessory muscles of exhalation.

accessory muscles Muscles in the neck, chest, and abdomen that can be used, if necessary, to help expand the thoracic cavity on inspiration.

FIGURE 13-19 ▲ The accessory muscles of exhalation.

A QUICK TRIP THROUGH THE DISEASES OF THE RESPIRATORY SYSTEM

DISEASE	ETIOLOGY	SIGNS AND SYMPTOMS	DIAGNOSTIC TEST(S)	TREATMENTS
Lung cancer	Cause not known but linked to smoking and inhalation of carcinogens.	Obstruction of airways interfering with ventilation, weight loss, weakness, cough, or change in cough	Bronchoscopy, imaging studies, biopsy, sputum exam, patient exam, and history.	Radiation, chemotherapy, surgery.
Asbestosis	Prolonged exposure to airborne asbestos particles	Dyspnea, chest pain, productive cough in smokers, decreased lung inflation.	Chest x-rays fine irregular linear infiltrates. May have a honeycomb appearance on x-ray. Decreased pulmonary function tests and hypoxemia.	No cure, and the goal is to relieve symptoms and treat any complications such as infections.
Infections:				
Acute bronchitis	Viral or bacterial.	Inflamed mucous membranes of trachea and bronchi; expectorating or dry cough, shortness of breath, fever, rales (raspy sound).	Physical exam.	Antibiotics if bacterial.

(continued)

A QUICK TRIP *(continued)*

DISEASE	ETIOLOGY	SIGNS AND SYMPTOMS	DIAGNOSTIC TEST(S)	TREATMENTS
Common cold	Viral.	Upper airway congestion, cough, sore throat.	History and physical exam.	Treat symptoms, pain meds, bed rest, drink fluids, proper nutrition.
Pharyngitis	Viral or bacterial.	Red, sore swollen throat, pus.	History and physical exam, throat culture.	If bacterial use antibiotics, antiseptic gargle.
Laryngitis	Viral or bacterial, allergies, over-use of voice.	Dysphonia, sore throat, trouble swallowing.	History and physical exam.	Rest voice.
Tonsillitis	Viral or bacterial.	Sore throat, swollen tonsils, and dysphagia.	History and physical exam, culture.	Antibiotics for bacterial, surgery if needed.
Influenza	Viral.	Fever, cough, body aches, and headaches.	History and physical exam.	Rest, fluids, pain meds. Treat symptoms.
Pneumonia	Viral, bacterial, or fungal.	Productive cough, chest pain, weakness, malaise, dyspnea.	Imaging, blood work, sputum culture.	Antibiotics if confirmed bacterial infection. Antifungal drugs if confirmed fungal infection.
Pulmonary tuberculosis	Bacterial.	Primary, may be asymptomatic. Secondary, cough (may be blood tinged), fever (night sweats), weight loss.	Imaging, TB skin test, sputum test.	Antibiotic agents.

Inflammations and allergies:

Seasonal allergic rhinitis (hay fever)	Allergic agents.	Upper airway congestion, watery nose and eyes, sneezing.	History and physical exam, allergy testing.	Antihistamines, preventative allergy shots.

(continued)

DISEASE	ETIOLOGY	SIGNS AND SYMPTOMS	DIAGNOSTIC TEST(S)	TREATMENTS
Asthma	Many triggers such as allergens, food, exercise, cold air, inhaled irritants, smoking.	Dyspnea, wheezing, productive cough, hypoxia.	History and physical exam, lung function tests.	Bronchodilators, steroids, and anti-asthmatic agents. Oxygen if needed.

COPD:

DISEASE	ETIOLOGY	SIGNS AND SYMPTOMS	DIAGNOSTIC TEST(S)	TREATMENTS
Chronic bronchitis	Cigarette smoking and long-term exposure to air pollutants, middle or old age.	Dyspnea, wheezing, productive cough, hypoxia.	History and physical exam, lung function tests.	Antibiotics if bacterial, bronchodilators, oxygen if needed.
Emphysema	Cause not fully known but associated mostly with smoking and also associated with one genetic form from alpha 1-antitrypsin deficiency.	Dyspnea, tachypnea, wheezing, productive cough, hypoxia.	History and physical exam, lung function tests.	Oxygen therapy, bronchodilators, alpha 1-antitrypsin replacement.

Other respiratory diseases

DISEASE	ETIOLOGY	SIGNS AND SYMPTOMS	DIAGNOSTIC TEST(S)	TREATMENTS
Acute respiratory distress syndrome (ARDS)	Form of pulmonary edema that has a high mortality rate and very noncompliant (stiff) lungs. Many causes but most often caused by shock, sepsis, and trauma.	Rapid shallow breathing with dyspnea. Hypoxemia and fluid accumulation in lungs with rhonchi and crackles.	Arterial blood gases showing respiratory acidosis and severe hypoxemia, bilateral infiltrates on x-rays with white outs in lung fields.	Intubation and mechanical ventilation. Sedatives and diuretics and in some cases high doses of corticosteroids.
Cystic fibrosis	Hereditary disease transmitted via a recessive gene.	Excessive thick mucus secretion, repeated infections, large salt losses, difficult digestion.	Sweat test, genetic testing.	Respiratory hygiene therapy, mucus thinning agents, antibiotics, pancreatic enzyme supplements.

Pharmacology Corner

Although oxygen is often not thought of as a drug, it is the major drug used in treating respiratory diseases as well as cardiac disease. The basic purpose is to reduce the work of breathing, increase the oxygen content of the blood, and reduce the work of the heart. Oxygen therapy comes in various forms of delivery.

Problems with the airway are usually due to inflammatory processes that narrow the airways, making it difficult to breathe. For rapid relief of an acute situation of airway narrowing, aerosolized bronchodilators can be given. For long-term treatment of chronic airway inflammation, inhaled steroids have been used because they have less systemic effects than oral or injectable steroids.

The only method known to prevent or slow the progression of COPD is to stop smoking or eliminate the occupational source. All patients who smoke need to be regularly encouraged to stop. Cigarette smoking kills nearly 450,000 Americans each year and debilitates nearly one-half of all long-term smokers. Tobacco dependence is a powerful addiction and one that is extremely difficult to break, often requiring four to six attempts. Even after quitting, patients sometimes have a lifelong craving that does decrease with time. Some patients will be successful on their own, but most will require behavioral counseling and encouragement in addition to pharmacological therapy. This treatment usually consists of nicotine replacement therapy in the form of gum, skin patches, or inhaled forms. In addition, drugs can be given to decrease the desire such as Chantix™ or Wellbutrin™.

In many cases premature infants have underdeveloped lungs that do not have adequate surfactant maturation to breathe on their own. Natural and synthetic surfactant forms have been developed that can be instilled into the lungs. This can buy time until the infant develops adequate amounts on his or her own.

Bacterial lung infections can be treated with systemic antibiotics. Although not related to lung disease, new research has allowed for the development of aerosolized insulin that can be inhaled for the treatment of diabetes. Many antiviral medications are available to reduce the length and severity of a viral infection such as the cold or flu. The possibility of developing the flu is greatly reduced through the use of annual flu vaccinations. See FIGURE 13-20 ▲ for an illustration of drugs used to treat the respiratory system.

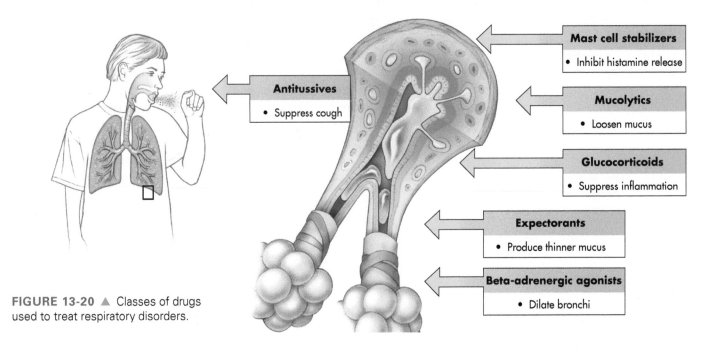

FIGURE 13-20 ▲ Classes of drugs used to treat respiratory disorders.

SUMMARY

Snapshots from the Journey

- Moving approximately 12,000 quarts of air each day, the respiratory system is responsible for providing oxygen for the blood to take to the body's tissues and removing carbon dioxide, one of the waste products of cellular metabolism.

- Ventilation is the movement of gases in and out of the lungs; during respiration oxygen is added to the blood and carbon dioxide is removed.

- The lungs contain continually branching airways called bronchi and bronchioles.

- At the end of bronchioles are alveolar sacs.

- Each alveolar sac is surrounded by a capillary network where gas exchange occurs with the blood.

- The purpose of the upper airways is to see change, and moisten inhaled air for its journey to the lungs.

- In addition, the upper airways provides for *olfaction* (sense of smell) and *phonation* (speech).

- The mucociliary escalator captures foreign particles, and the hairlike cilia constantly move a layer of mucus up to the upper airways to be swallowed or expelled.

- Adenoids and tonsils aid in preventing pathogens from entering the body.

- Because activities of breathing and swallowing share a common pathway, the epiglottis protects the airway to the lungs from accidental aspiration of food and liquids.

- Vocal cords are the gateway between the upper and lower airways.

- The tracheobronchial tree is like an upside-down tree with ever-branching airways, where the trunk of the tree is represented by the trachea and the leaves by the alveoli.

- The alveolar capillary membrane is where external respiration or gas exchange occurs.

- The bony thorax provides support and protection for the respiratory system.

- The main muscle of breathing is the diaphragm, and accessory muscles assist in times of need such as exercise and disease.

- The medulla oblongata in the brain is the control center for breathing and sends impulses via the phrenic nerve to the diaphragm.

RAY'S STORY

Ray, a quadriplegic, was brought into the emergency room with thick secretions and a fever. His heart rate and blood pressure are increased, and his lungs do not sound clear on examination. The carbon dioxide levels in his blood are greatly increased, and the oxygen levels are well below normal, even given his dependence on a ventilator.

a. What possible respiratory diseases or conditions could he have?

_____

_____

b. What are some recommended treatments for this patient?

_____

_____

REVIEW QUESTIONS

Multiple Choice

1. The process of gas exchange between the alveolar area and capillary is:
   a. external ventilation
   b. internal ventilation
   c. internal respiration
   d. external respiration

2. The bulk movement of gas into and out of the lung is called:
   a. internal respiration
   b. ventilation
   c. diffusion
   d. gas exchange

3. Which of the following is *not* a function of the upper airway?
   a. humidification
   b. gas exchange
   c. filtration
   d. heating or cooling gases

4. The largest cartilage in the upper airway is the:
   a. cricoid
   b. eustachian
   c. mega cartilage
   d. thyroid

5. Which structure controls the opening to the trachea?
   a. esophagus
   b. hypoglottis
   c. epiglottis
   d. hyperglottis

Fill in the Blank

1. Small bronchi are called _____.

2. The sense of smell is termed _____, and the act of speech is called _____.

3. The hairlike projections called _____ beat within the _____ layer and propel the _____ layer toward the oral cavity to be expectorated.

REVIEW

4. The _____ are thought to lighten the head and provide resonance for the voice.

5. The _____ and the _____ are part of the immune system and are found in the nasopharynx and oropharynx.

Matching

1. _____ Asthma
2. _____ Chronic bronchitis
3. _____ Laryngitis
4. _____ Emphysema
5. _____ Cystic fibrosis

    a. An inherited disease transmitted by a recessive gene, causing excessive mucus production
    b. Causes permanent destruction of alveolar walls and surrounding capillaries
    c. Has many triggers that include pet dander, food allergies, and cold air
    d. Caused by bacteria or viruses and will affect your voice
    e. Cigarette smoking causes large amounts of secretions and inflamed airways

Short Answer

1. Describe the tissue layers in the bronchi.

_____
_____

2. Explain how gas exchange takes place in the lungs.

_____
_____

3. Discuss the importance of surfactant.

_____
_____

4. Describe the process of normal breathing, beginning with the brain.

_____
_____

Suggested Activities

1. Research the effects of secondhand smoking and smokeless tobacco, and share results with the class or develop posters on these subjects.

2. Working as a group, research occupational causes of lung diseases and see how long a list you can develop.

CAREER CONNECTIONS

Now that you have read this chapter, here is a list of related professions you may be interested in investigating for a future career:

- Respiratory Therapist

- Perfusionist

Research each profession and report on the following:

1. Profession description to include job responsibilities
2. Educational requirements
3. Job opportunities
4. Opportunities outside of the hospital setting
5. Salary range
6. Licensure and continuing education requirements

ANATOMY, PHYSIOLOGY, AND DISEASE IN ACTION

Materials:
Balloon
Metric tape measure

Note: If any students have breathing problems, such as asthma, this exercise should be modified to accommodate the condition.

Stretch or blow up a balloon several times. Taking a normal breath, exhale normally into the balloon. Seal off the balloon. Measure the circumference in centimeters. Using the following formula: Circumference = 2π x radius, calculate the radius. Next, using the value of the radius, calculate the volume of air in the balloon using the following formula: Volume of a sphere = $4/3\pi\ r^3$. This is the **tidal volume**. Next, determine the number of breaths taken in a minute. The pulmonary ventilation or minute volume is determined by multiplying the number of breaths per minute by the tidal volume. Collect the data from the class and record on a chart.

Student	Tidal Volume	Breaths/Minute	Ventilations

Do any of the students have similar ventilation values but different tidal volumes and breaths per minute? What could be some of the factors that would lead to these results and other differences in the class?

Next, breath normally then exhale as much air as possible into the balloon. Seal the balloon and determine the volume as previously done. This is the **Expiratory Reserve Volume**. Blow the balloon as large as possible, seal the balloon, and determine the volume of air in the balloon. Resume breathing normally, then inhale as much air as possible from the balloon after a normal breath. Measure the volume of air in the balloon. The difference between the maximum volume of air and the volume of air left in the balloon after inhalation is the **Inspiratory Reserve Volume**. Record the values on the table that follows to calculate the **Vital Capacity**.

Tidal Volume			
Inspiratory Reserve Volume			
Expiratory Reserve Volume			
Vital Capacity			

How do these values compare with the normal values listed in Figure 13-12 of the text?

The Lymphatic and Immune Systems
Your Defense Systems

So far in our travels, we have visited control systems, transport systems, and infrastructure, to name just a few. We have seen how each separate system works together to allow the body to function as an integrated unit. Like all cities, the body must be protected. Cities have police and fire departments. On a larger scale, countries have armies and bases. Similarly, your body has the immune and lymphatic systems with a variety of protective mechanisms and cells each performing specific duties. These systems help to protect the body from pathogens that can produce disease. Without your immune and lymphatic systems, your journey would be a very short one—the first exposure to a potential pathogenic organism would wreak havoc in your body and literally stop the journey before it began.

LEARNING OUTCOMES

Upon completion of your journey through this chapter, you will be able to:

- List and describe the major components of the lymphatic and immune system and their functions
- Explain the antigen–antibody relationship
- Name and describe the functions of the blood cells responsible for protecting the body from invasion
- Discuss how inflammatory responses and fevers relate to infection
- Compare innate immunity to adaptive immunity
- Describe the function of T and B lymphocytes in the immune response
- List and describe several common diseases of the immune system

Pronunciation Guide

Correct pronunciation is important in any journey so that you and others are completely understood. Here is a "see and say" Pronunciation Guide for the more difficult terms to pronounce in this chapter. Please note that pronunciations given are referenced to medical dictionaries, and regional variations may exist.

antigen (AN tih jenn)
cytokines (SIGH tow kynz)
cytotoxic T cells (SIGH tow TOX ick)
dendritic cells (den DRID ick)
histamine (HISS tah meen)
interferon (in ter FEAR on)
interleukins (IN ter LOO kinz)
leukocytes (LOO koh sights)
lymph (LIMF)
lymphatic (lim FAT ick)
lymphatic fluid (lim FAT ick)
lymphatic vessels (lim FAT ick)

lymph capillaries (LIMF KAP ih LAIR eez)
lymph nodes (LIMF nohdz)
macrophages (MACK roh fage ez)
myelogenous (my eh LOH jen us)
neutrophils (NOO troh filz)
pathogen (PATH oh jenn)
plasma cells (PLAZ mah)
T lymphocytes (T LIMF oh sights)
thoracic duct (thoh RASS ick)
thymus (THIGH mus)
tumor necrosis factor (neh KROH sis)

THE DEFENSE ZONE

Although war may seem a harsh analogy to use, it is the reality of what happens when a potentially dangerous threat invades the body. Suppose that a nasty army of pathogens attempts to invade your body. First, it must get past your barriers. Many invaders will be repelled simply by your intact skin or the secretions of your mucous membranes. If the invader does get inside your body, it is recognized as *not* belonging in your body. This recognition stimulates a series of responses to neutralize the foreign invader. Weapons in the form of specialized cells are engaged by the immune and lymphatic systems to fend off the pathogens. In addition, the immune and lymphatic systems release powerful chemicals to help to fight off the invaders.

These chemicals also stimulate the inflammatory response and leave a chemical mess to clean up. The "war" also leaves behind an area of neutralized pathogens and excessive debris and fluid that has collected around the battlefield and must be cleaned up. This again is accomplished by the combined and integrated efforts of the immune and lymphatic systems until the danger is over and your body can return to normal functioning. Let's begin the discussion with the lymphatic system, then bring in the immune system, and finally show how the two work in concert to keep your body healthy.

THE LYMPHATIC SYSTEM

The **lymphatic system** is both the transport system and barracks of your immune system. It is a unique circulatory system parallel to the cardiovascular system. As you will soon see, it works closely with the cardiovascular system, and their close proximity is needed for mutual benefit.

The lymphatic system has the following four functions:

- Recycling fluids lost from the cardiovascular system
- Transporting **pathogens** to the lymph nodes where they can be destroyed

lymphatic system *(lim FAA tick)*
Body system that includes lymphatic vessels, lymph nodes, lymphatic fluid, and lymphoid tissues (tonsils and adenoids, appendix, Peyer's patches), lymphoid organs (spleen and thymus), and the blood cells, lymphocytes, and macrophages.

pathogen *(PATH oh jenn)*
Microorganism that causes a disease. Pathogens include bacteria, viruses, protozoa, and other microorganisms, as well as plant cells like fungi or yeast.

- Storing and maturing some types of white blood cells
- Absorbing glycerol and fatty acids from food (see Chapter 15, "The Gastrointestinal System," for details)

Given that the lymphatic system is intimately connected to the function of the cardiovascular system, it should come as no surprise that the smallest pipes of the lymphatic system, called **lymph capillaries,** run parallel to blood capillaries. Lymph capillaries, tubes that form a network between the cells of connective tissues, are so named because they are structurally similar to blood capillaries, but unlike blood capillaries, lymph capillaries are open ended. Proteins and fluids are lost from cardiovascular capillaries and enter the interstitial space. This interstitial fluid lies between the cells and is returned to the blood by way of the lymphatic system. Once this fluid enters the lymph capillaries, it is known as **lymphatic fluid,** or simply **lymph.** Lymph is a straw-colored, clear fluid that is similar to blood plasma. The primary component of lymph is water. It also contains digested nutrients, such as fats, gases such as oxygen, proteins, and white blood cells called lymphocytes and macrophages. You will learn more about these white blood cells later in the chapter. For a map of the lymphatic system, see **FIGURE 14-1 ▲**.

lymph capillaries Smallest vessels of the lymphatic system which run parallel to blood capillaries.

lymphatic fluid *(lim FAA tick FLOO id)* Clear and colorless fluid of the lymphatic system.

lymph *(LIMF)* Fluid that flows through the lymphatic system.

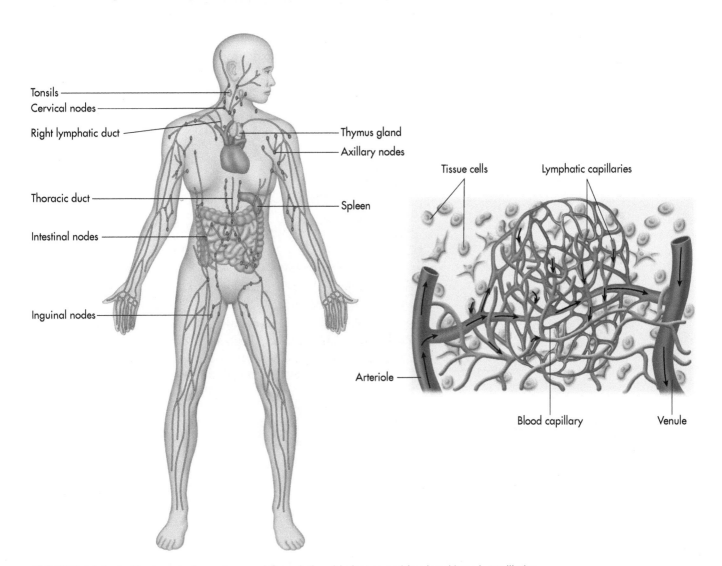

FIGURE 14-1 ▲ The lymphatic system and the relationship between blood and lymph capillaries.

lymphatic vessels *(lim FAA tick)* Vessels that begin as capillaries carrying lymph, continue through lymph nodes, and empty into the right lymphatic duct and the thoracic duct.

lymph nodes Small, encapsulated pieces of lymphoid tissue located along the lymphatic vessels. Lymph nodes filter and destroy invading microorganisms and cancerous cells present in the lymph.

lymphocytes *(LIM foh SIGHTS)* Specialized, infection-fighting white blood cells produced by the lymphatic system.

lymphatic sinuses Portion of the lymph node that is filled with lymphatic fluid.

Several lymph capillary networks empty into **lymphatic vessels**, which are structurally similar to veins, including having valves that prevent backward flow. Lymphatic vessels are located in almost all tissues and organs that have blood vessels. Body movement (e.g., contraction of skeletal muscle around the vessels) and contraction of smooth muscle in the vessel walls propel lymph through the system. Small lymphatic vessels empty into larger lymphatic vessels. Larger lymphatic vessels empty into **lymph nodes**. Ranging in size from a pinhead to an olive, and existing either individually or in groups, the lymph nodes can be thought of as filters strategically placed all along the pathways or vessels of the lymphatic system. Think about a water filtration system for a city where a system of pipes (vessels) bring the dirty water into a plant with a filtration system (node) that then recycles clean water back into the system. Lymphatic fluid carries digested food, oxygen, and hormones to cells, and then carries waste back to capillaries for excretion.

Lymph nodes are small, encapsulated bodies divided into sections (see FIGURE 14-2 ▲). Inside the nodes are sections of lymphatic tissue containing white blood cells known as **lymphocytes**. The lymphatic tissue is surrounded by **lymphatic sinuses** filled with lymph fluid. A number of lymphatic vessels enter or exit each lymph node. This ensures that all lymph fluid must pass through a lymph node for filtration and destruction of pathogens by the white blood cells, and it also ensures that the flow slows enough to allow the lymphocytes and macrophages to destroy pathogens.

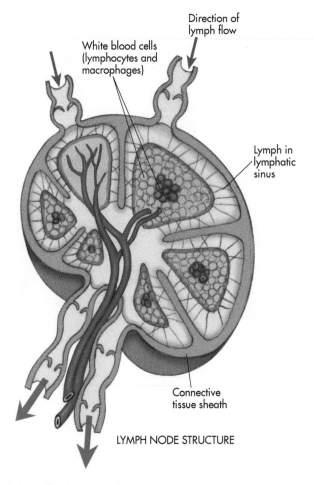

Direction of lymph flow

White blood cells (lymphocytes and macrophages)

Lymph in lymphatic sinus

Connective tissue sheath

LYMPH NODE STRUCTURE

FIGURE 14-2 ▲ The lymph node structure.

Pathology Connection

TONSILLITIS

Tonsillitis is an inflammation of the tonsils, usually caused by a bacterial or viral infection. The symptoms of tonsillitis include sore throat, difficulty swallowing, swollen tonsils, fever, upper respiratory symptoms, swollen lymph nodes, visible coating or spots on the tonsils, and even upset stomach. Tonsillitis is diagnosed by a physical examination noting inflamed tonsils. It is important, however, to distinguish between viral and bacterial causes of tonsillitis. Viral tonsillitis is generally characterized by a low-grade fever and the presence of upper respiratory symptoms resembling the common cold. Bacterial tonsillitis, generally caused by infection with *Streptococcus* bacteria (which also causes strep throat), is characterized by higher fever and lack of upper respiratory coldlike symptoms. Bacterial tonsillitis can be diagnosed, or ruled out, by the use of a throat culture that tests for the presence of strep throat. A negative throat culture indicates the absence of a bacterial infection. Bacterial tonsillitis must be treated with antibiotics to combat the bacterial infection. Viral tonsillitis, like all viral infections, does not respond to antibiotics and will usually go away by itself. Treatment of symptoms, rest, fluids, and an analgesic like Tylenol™ is recommended until symptoms subside. In the past, many children had their tonsils removed after even a single bout of tonsillitis. Today tonsillectomies are performed only if the tonsillitis has become chronic or the tonsils are so enlarged that they obstruct the patient's airway.

Lymph nodes are concentrated in several areas around the body and are identified by their regional location: cervical, axillary, inguinal, pelvic, abdominal, thoracic, and supratrochlear. Notice that the lymph nodes are concentrated to catch pathogens where they are most likely to enter the body, such as in the lungs, digestive system, and reproductive system.

Tonsils are masses of lymphocyte-producing lymphatic tissue located in the rear of the pharynx, or throat. The three sets of tonsils include the **palatine tonsils**, located on either side of the oropharynx (the posterior mouth); the pharyngeal tonsils (**adenoids),** located at the posterior of the nasopharynx (the superior part of the throat); and the **lingual tonsils,** located at the base of the tongue.

Lymphatic vessels exiting lymph nodes empty into one of several **lymphatic trunks**. These trunks, named for their location, are the lumbar, intestinal, intercostal, bronchomediastinal, subclavian, and jugular. Lymphatic trunks empty into one of two collecting ducts. The lumbar, intestinal, and intercostal trunks all empty into the **thoracic duct,** which is the largest lymph vessel. The thoracic duct runs from the abdomen up through the diaphragm and into the left subclavian vein. More than two-thirds of the lymphatic system drains into the thoracic duct. The bronchomediastinal, subclavian, and jugular trunks empty into the **right lymphatic duct,** a smaller duct within the right thorax that empties into the right subclavian vein (see FIGURE 14-3 ▲).

tonsil A mass of lymphoid tissue in the mucous membranes of the pharynx and base of the tongue.

palatine tonsils *(PAL ah tine)* Lymphoid tissue on either side of the throat where the soft palate arches downward in the oropharynx.

adenoid *(AD eh noid)* Lymphoid tissue in the superior part of the nasopharynx. Also known as the pharyngeal tonsils.

lingual tonsils Patches of lymphoid tissue found at the back of the tongue.

lymphatic trunks Large lymphatic vessels found throughout the body which empty into collecting ducts.

thoracic duct *(thoh RASS ick)* The main lymph duct of the body.

right lymphatic duct *(lim FAT ick)* The duct that collects lymphatic fluid from the bronchomediastinal, subclavian, and jugular trunks.

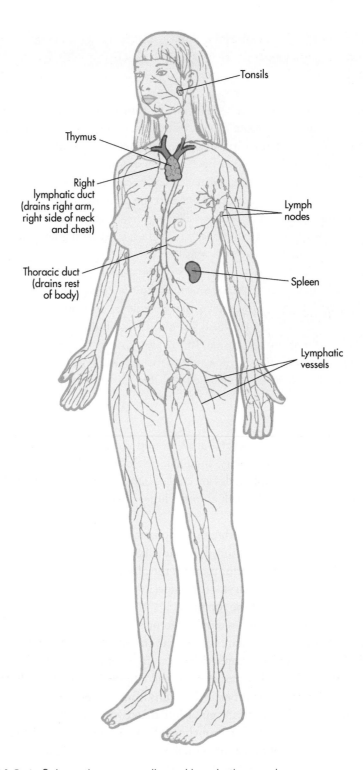

FIGURE 14-3 ▲ Spleen, thymus, tonsils, and lymphatic vessels.

Lymphatic fluid flows in only one direction: from the body tissues and organs to the heart. The circulation of lymphatic fluid follows this path: from blood to tissue to lymphatic capillaries to lymphatic vessels to lymph nodes to lymphatic vessels (exiting nodes) to lymphatic trunks to collecting ducts to subclavian veins and then back to the blood. The fluid that moves from blood capillaries into tissues is filtered through the white blood cells in the lymph nodes, where pathogens are removed and destroyed and recycled back to the cardiovascular system. If a substance cannot be destroyed, the node becomes enlarged and inflamed.

Lymph Organs

As previously mentioned, there are two larger collections of lymphatic tissue, known as lymph organs. These lymph organs are the thymus and the spleen. Although they are not strictly lymph nodes and are not part of lymph circulation, they are so similar to lymph nodes that they are classified as part of the lymph system.

The **spleen** (again see Figure 14-3) is a spongy saclike mass of lymphatic tissue in the upper left quadrant of the abdomen. It is structurally similar to lymph nodes but instead of having lymphatic sinuses, the spleen has blood sinuses. The blood sinuses surround islands of white pulp containing lymphocytes and islands of red pulp containing both red blood cells and white blood cells. One of the functions of the spleen is to remove and destroy old, damaged, or fragile red blood cells. Can you guess the second function of the spleen, given its anatomy? Because it is similar to a lymph node, the spleen also filters pathogens from the bloodstream and destroys them in the same way that lymph nodes filter pathogens from lymph.

Even though the spleen is a very important organ, it is not vital, and in some cases, such as trauma, it may need to be surgically removed. Because of the spleen's rich supply of blood vessels, injury to the spleen can often cause internal bleeding. Its removal in children can severely compromise their ability to ward off disease, whereas the effects of the spleen's removal in an adult is more subtle. As we age, the body becomes better at fighting off infections that it has seen in the past, but new invaders present more of a challenge when we are first exposed to them as children. However, in adults there is an increased risk of septicemia if the entire spleen is removed. To decrease this risk every effort is made to leave at least some of the spleen intact if possible when surgery is needed.

The **thymus** is a soft organ located between the aortic arch and the sternum (again, see Figure 14-3). The thymus is very large in children because it must defend against many new infections. It gets smaller, but continues to have some activity in adults as the immune system fully matures in its ability to fight infection. The thymus produces lymphocytes that mature into a type of white blood cell called a **T lymphocyte**. The thymus also secretes a hormone that stimulates the maturation of T lymphocytes in lymph nodes.

spleen Lymphoid organ located in the abdominal cavity posterior to the stomach. The spleen destroys old erythrocytes, breaking their hemoglobin into heme and globins. It also acts as a storage area for whole blood. Its white pulp is lymphoid tissue that contains B and T lymphocytes.

thymus *(THIGH mus)* Lymphoid organ in the thoracic cavity. As an endocrine gland, it releases hormones known as thymosins. Thymosin causes lymphoblasts in the thymus to mature into T lymphocytes.

T lymphocytes *(T LIMF oh sights)* White blood cells involved in adaptive immunity. There are four types of T lymphocytes: helper T cells, cytotoxic T cells, memory T cells, and regulatory T cells.

Pathology Connection

LYMPHATIC DISORDERS

Lymphadenitis is a disorder of the lymphatic system in which lymph nodes swell. Lymphadenitis may be localized, affecting only a few lymph nodes in a small area, or generalized, affecting several lymph nodes over a larger area. Lymphadenitis is usually the result of bacterial infection, but viruses, parasites, and fungi can cause lymphadenitis.

Initial symptoms of lymphadenitis include swelling of lymph nodes due to fluid buildup and increased production of white blood cells. More advanced symptoms include fever, chills, excessive sweating, rapid pulse, and weakness. Treatment includes infection-specific medication, such as antibacterial or antiviral medication, and rest of the affected area. Hot moist compresses can also be used.

Mononucleosis is a viral infection that typically affects children and young adults. Caused by the Epstein-Barr virus, mononucleosis symptoms are usually milder in younger children than they are in teens and young adults. The disease is often referred to as the "kissing disease" because the virus can be transmitted through oral contact and exchange of saliva. The effects of the disease continue from 2 or 3 weeks to 2 months after infection. Symptoms include fatigue, sore throat, fever, lymphadenitis, and an increased number of lymphocytes. Mononucleosis does not have specific treatment. The patient is told to get plenty of bed rest. Antibiotics may be prescribed to treat secondary infections.

Hodgkin's disease, or **Hodgkin's lymphoma,** is a relatively rare cancer that affects the lymphatic system. Early symptoms include swollen lymph nodes, unexplained fevers, night sweats, and fatigue. The disease may also be characterized by weight loss and itchy skin. The cause of Hodgkin's disease is unknown, but factors such as Epstein-Barr infection and being male can contribute to the likelihood of developing the disease. If caught early, the disease can be treated successfully by chemotherapy, radiation, or a combination of both.

Pathology Connection

CANCER STAGES AND THE LYMPHATIC SYSTEM

When patients are diagnosed with cancer, they are often told they have a certain "stage" of cancer. Cancer is staged and prognosis is determined by the amount of metastasis (spread), type of tumor, and lymph node involvement. The lymphatic system is amazingly efficient at capturing and transporting pathogens from connective tissue to lymph nodes for destruction. Unfortunately, this ability can also be a liability when cancerous cells develop in one part of the body and use the lymphatic system to hitch a ride to distant areas of the body. Once the cancerous cells make their way from their point of origin into lymphatic capillaries, and if the lymphocytes in the lymph nodes do not overpower the tumor cells, cancer cells can easily move around the body, invading many different areas simultaneously.

Cancers that are diagnosed after they have already spread are much more likely to be fatal than cancers that are treated before cells have a chance to spread. This is why screening for certain types of cancer is so important and often why lymph nodes are removed for study around surgical sites of cancer. The earlier a patient is diagnosed, the better his or her chances

(continued)

lymphadenitis *(lim FAD in EYE tiss)* An inflammation of lymph nodes, which results from the responsive actions of lymphocytes and phagocytes to invading microorganisms, or cancer cells.

mononucleosis *(MON oh NEW klee OH sis)* The presence of a higher-than-normal number of mononuclear leukocytes in the blood, and can be a result of an acute infection of the Epstein Barr virus.

Hodgkin's disease *(HAWJ kinz)* A malignant lymphoma in which the early stages of the disease present with no symptoms other than a painless lump or enlarged gland in the neck or armpit. Some patients may develop fevers/night sweats and loss of appetite/weight.

Hodgkin's lymphoma See Hodgkin's disease.

Pathology Connection (continued)

of beating the disease. In the last several years, specific staging criteria have been developed for many cancers, making staging the disease much more accurate. However, cancer stages generally include a pattern similar to this:

- Stage 1, no spread from origin
- Stage 2, spread to nearby tissues
- Stage 3, spread to nearby lymph nodes
- Stage 4, spread to distant tissues and organs

Stage 4 cancers are often terminal.

TEST YOUR KNOWLEDGE 14-1

Choose the best answer:

1. Any organism that invades your body and causes disease is known as a:
   a. bacteria
   b. fungus
   c. virus
   d. pathogen

2. Which of the following areas do *not* have large number of lymph nodes?
   a. cervical
   b. axillary
   c. abdominal
   d. adrenal

3. Cancer that has entered the lymph nodes is in this stage:
   a. first
   b. second
   c. third
   d. center

4. Which cells are housed in lymph nodes?
   a. red blood cells
   b. white blood cells
   c. platelets
   d. lymph nodules

5. The thoracic duct of the lymphatic system empties into this blood vessel:
   a. right subclavian vein
   b. left subclavian vein
   c. aorta
   d. hepatic portal vein

6. The function of the thymus is to:
   a. remove pathogens from blood
   b. destroy damaged red blood cells
   c. both a and b
   d. none of the above

7. The recommended treatment for uncomplicated viral tonsillitis is:
   a. antibiotics
   b. fluids and pain relievers
   c. tonsillectomy
   d. all of the above

THE IMMUNE SYSTEM

If the lymphatic system can be considered a transport and storage system for the body's defense systems, then the components of the **immune system** are the weapons and the actual troops. Much like the National Guard, the immune system can be called in to protect a city in times of extreme need. The immune system is a series of cells, chemicals, and barriers that protect the body from invasion by pathogens. Some of the weapons are active, and some are passive; some are inborn, and some change with experience. Together they form a system that is remarkably good at keeping the body free of infection.

Antigens and Antibodies

As you should remember from our discussion of blood types in Chapter 12, cells have molecules on the outer surface of their membranes to distinguish whether they are friend or foe. These molecules are called **antigens**. Each human being has his or her own unique cell surface antigens, as do all other living things, including bacteria, viruses, animals, and plants. The presence of these unique markers or antigens allows the immune system to distinguish between cells that are naturally yours and cells that are not. This ability, called **self-recognition** and **non-self-recognition**, is at the heart of immune system function.

Antigens are like the identity codes sent out by airplanes. Air traffic controllers and fighter jets on patrol over a no-fly zone depend on the identity codes to tell which aircraft are friendly. Antigens do the same for your immune system. A well-functioning immune system tolerates the body's own antigens (self) and attacks other antigens (non-self). We discuss this in more depth later in this chapter.

As part of its defense system, the body can make proteins that bind to antigens, eventually leading to their destruction. Can you remember these proteins from the discussion of blood types? You got it! They are **antibodies,** one of the most potent weapons in the body's defensive arsenal. Antibodies are called into action when a foreign antigen invades the body.

Innate versus Adaptive Immunity

The immune system defends the body on two fronts: by innate immunity and adaptive immunity. **Innate (natural) immunity** is the first line of defense against invasion. Innate immunity, as the name suggests, is the body's inborn ability to fight infection. It is inborn, a part of our physiology, not affected by our environment, and is permanent. Innate immunity prevents invasion, or if pathogens do get inside, innate immunity recognizes the invasion and takes steps to stop the infection from spreading. However, innate immunity can only recognize that something is not native to the body; it can't identify the invaders. Innate immunity cannot improve with experience, and because it does not recognize specific pathogens, it cannot "remember" an infection that the body has encountered before.

Innate immunity consists of a collection of relatively crude mechanisms for defending the body from infection, sort of like building a wall around a city or having metal detectors at the airport. Keep in mind that metal detectors can't tell car keys from a pocket knife. Other parts of innate immunity are like weapons of mass destruction, indiscriminately killing pathogens and healthy tissue alike.

Innate immunity is backed up by a platoon of mechanisms that specifically target invaders, can remember invaders from previous encounters (and therefore prepare for future

---

immune system The lymphatic tissues, organs, and physiological processes that identify an antigen as abnormal or foreign and prevent it from harming the body.

antigens *(AN tih jennz)* Substance that causes a formation of antibodies. Cell surface markers that help the immune system identify cells.

self vs. non-self recognition The ability of the immune system to distinguish between the body's cells and cells that do not belong in the body.

antibody *(AN teh bahd ee)* Proteins secreted by B lymphocytes (plasma cells) that attack infected cells.

innate (natural) immunity The defense against pathogens that you are born with and that does not improve with experience or remember specific pathogens. The first line of defense.

invasions), and can improve responses with experience. These mechanisms are known as **adaptive immunity,** or **acquired immunity** because the mechanisms "learn" and change each time they are engaged. The components of adaptive immunity can be trained as an elite fighting force for particular pathogens. Their goals are "surgical strikes" targeting particular invaders and sparing as much of the healthy body tissue as possible.

It is tempting to think of these two parts of immunity as separate entities. However, the two work closely together. Innate immunity prepares the way for adaptive immunity, weakening some pathogens and stimulating components of adaptive immunity. Adaptive immunity in turn further stimulates innate immunity. It is through the mutual cooperation of both innate and adaptive immunity attacking the pathogen on two fronts that invaders can be removed from the body.

adaptive immunity Immune mechanisms that "learn" to deal with specific invaders.

acquired immunity See adaptive immunity.

TEST YOUR KNOWLEDGE 14-2

Choose the best answer:

1. Cell surface molecules that can be used to identify cells are called:
   a. antibodies
   b. antigens
   c. antihistamines
   d. antibiotics

2. Proteins that bind to antigens are called:
   a. binding proteins
   b. receptors
   c. hormones
   d. antibodies

3. This type of immunity has no memory and is not specific:
   a. adaptive
   b. acquired
   c. innate
   d. nonspecific

Components of the Immune System

We often think the immune system begins in the blood with the white blood cells. However, physical barriers exist to act as a first line of defense to attempt to stop the infective agents from getting into the body in the first place. This is much like concrete traffic barriers you see in front of public buildings.

Barriers

Anything that prevents invaders from getting inside your body prevents infection. Therefore, your body has many barriers located in the places where invaders are most likely to gain entrance. Physical barriers include skin and the mucous membranes of the eyes, digestive system, respiratory system, and reproductive system. Not only are these surfaces difficult to penetrate, but they are also packed with white blood cells and lymph capillaries to trap any invaders that might get through. The fluids associated with these physical barriers contain chemicals that act as chemical barriers. These chemicals are contained in tears, saliva, urine, mucous secretions, and sweat. One example is the antibacterial properties of the oil secreted by the sebaceous glands of your integumentary system. These barriers, both chemical and physical, prevent some invaders from ever getting inside the body. They are the "fortress" of the body, part of your innate immunity. After reading this information, can you see why wounds are frequent sources of infection?

Cells

leukocytes *(LOO koh sights)* White blood cells. There are five different types of mature leukocytes: neutrophils, eosinophils, basophils, lymphocytes, and monocytes.

If an invader has an opportunity to enter the body, white blood cells (**leukocytes**) are responsible for defending the body against invaders. You learned about red blood cells and platelets in Chapter 12. Red blood cells are responsible for carrying oxygen throughout the body, and platelets are responsible for blood's ability to clot. White blood cells, on the other hand, are the mobile units of the immune system. White blood cells, which form in the bone marrow like red blood cells and platelets, often move to other parts of the body to grow and mature until they are needed during an invasion. They are generally not released into the bloodstream in large numbers unless an infection is present. FIGURE 14-4 ▲ shows the major white blood cells found in the plasma.

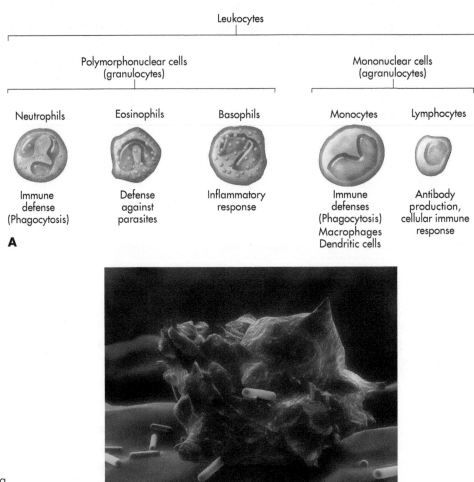

FIGURE 14-4 ▲ **A.** Major leukocytes. **B.** Enhanced color photograph from a scanning electron microscope of a macrophage ingesting rod-shaped bacteria. (Source: Sebastian Kaulitzki/Shutterstock.com.)

Types of White Blood Cells

In a police department of a large city, several types of jobs are needed for the entire department to function: traffic control officers, homicide detectives, forensic crime scene technicians, evidence control officers, internal affairs investigators, and more. Each has a specific duty and is called on as needed, but in essence they all have the same goal—fighting crime. Similarly, the body has various types of white blood cells that are required to protect the body in varying circumstances. TABLE 14-1 ■ lists the major white blood cells in the blood and the additional specialized white blood cells of the lymphatic system.

Pathology Connection

LEUKEMIA

Leukemia is a cancer of the bone marrow and blood, characterized by the overproduction of white blood cells. In some forms of leukemia, the cells are immature or nonfunctional. There are several different types of leukemia, differentiated by the type of white blood cells involved and the nature of the symptoms. They include acute myelogenous leukemia, chronic myelogenous leukemia, acute lymphocytic leukemia, and chronic lymphocytic leukemia. (There are also some rarer types of leukemia that will not be discussed here.)

In myelogenous leukemia, blood stem cells divide out of control. In lymphocytic leukemia, lymphocytes are the culprit. Both myelogenous and lymphocytic leukemia can be either acute or chronic. In acute leukemias, there is a rapid onset of symptoms caused by the overproduction of immature, nonfunctional cells. In chronic leukemias, symptoms develop slowly, and patients may even be symptom free in the early stages of the disease because the white blood cells, though overproduced, are functional. The causes of leukemia are not known, though some types are more common in children and/or older adults. Chronic myelogenous leukemia is known to be caused by a particular chromosomal abnormality (the Philadelphia chromosome), and Down syndrome patients are known to be at higher risk for acute myelogenous leukemia.

Symptoms of leukemia are caused by decreased *function* of white blood cells (if cells are immature) and decreased *numbers* of red blood cells and platelets, which are crowded out by the excessive numbers of white blood cells. Thus, symptoms may include anemia, shortness of breath, fatigue, repeated infections, enlarged lymph nodes, weight loss, muscle aches, excessive bruising, and bleeding. Leukemia is diagnosed mainly by laboratory tests, including complete blood count, bone marrow, and genetic testing.

Treatments and success rates differ among the types of leukemia. Chemotherapy (to kill the abnormal cells), antibody treatments, and stem cell or bone marrow transplants may be useful in treating the disease. In some cases, such as with chronic lymphocytic leukemia, there is no cure. The disease and its symptoms may be managed for years. Acute lymphocytic leukemia, a common childhood leukemia, has a very high rate of successful treatment.

leukemia *(loo KEE mee uh)* Cancer of leukocytes (white blood cells), including mature lymphocytes, immature lymphoblasts, as well as myeloblasts and myelocytes that mature into neutrophils, eosinophils, or basophils. The malignant leukocytes crowd out the production of other cells in the bone marrow. Leukemia is named according to the type of leukocyte that is the most prevalent and whether the onset of symptoms is acute or chronic. Types of leukemia include acute myelogenous leukemia (AML), chronic myelogenous leukemia (CML), acute lymphocytic leukemia (ALL), and chronic lymphocytic leukemia (CLL).

myelogenous leukemia A hematological malignancy in which neoplastic cells develop from myeloid, monocytic, erythrocytic, or megakaryocytic precursors. Neoplastic cells replace normal bone marrow.

lymphocytic leukemia A hematological malignancy marked by the unchecked multiplication of immature lymphoid cells in the bone marrow, blood, and body tissues.

acute Having rapid onset, severe symptoms, and a short course.

chronic Of long duration; long-lasting.

TABLE 14-1 ■ WHITE BLOOD CELLS INVOLVED IN IMMUNE RESPONSE

CELL TYPE	FUNCTION	INNATE OR ADAPTIVE
Neutrophils	Phagocytosis early in infection.	Innate.
Macrophages	Phagocytosis later in infection, stimulate immune system, antigen presenting cell (APC).	Innate but stimulate adaptive immunity.
Basophils and mast cells	Release inflammatory chemicals. Basophils are mobile; mast cells are found in connective tissue.	Innate.
Eosinophils	Fight parasites and contributes to allergic reactions.	Innate.
Dendritic cells	Antigen presenting cells, weakly phagocytic.	Innate but stimulate adaptive immunity.
Natural killer cells	Kill cells displaying foreign antigens.	Innate.
T cells (lymphocytes)	Kill pathogens directly, regulate immune response, activate other lymphocytes, remember past infections.	Adaptive.
B cells (lymphocytes)	Release antibodies to foreign antigens, remember past infections.	Adaptive.

cytokines *(SIGH tow kines)* Chemicals released by injured body tissues that summon leukocytes and cause them to move to the area.

interferon *(in ter FEAR on)* Substance released by macrophages that have engulfed a virus. Interferon stimulates body cells to produce an antiviral substance that keeps a virus from entering a cell and reproducing.

tumor necrosis factor (TNF) *(neh KROH sis)* Released by macrophages, this chemical destroys endotoxins produced by certain bacteria. It also destroys cancer cells.

interleukin *(in ter LOO kin)* Released by macrophages, it stimulates B cell and T lymphocytes and activates NK cells. It also produces the fever associated with inflammation and infection.

complement cascade A series of chemical reactions triggered by infection that leads to the destruction of a pathogen.

lysis *(LYE sis)* Destruction or breakdown.

inflammation *(in flah MAY shun)* Tissue reaction to injury that includes swelling and reddening due to increased blood flow to the area.

Chemicals

Not only do blood cells fight invaders, but chemicals found in the body can also assist in neutralizing and destroying invaders. **Cytokines** are proteins produced by damaged tissues and white blood cells that stimulate immune response in a variety of ways, including increasing inflammation, stimulating lymphocytes, and enhancing phagocytosis. Cytokines are involved in both innate and adaptive immunity. **Interferons** are cytokines produced by cells infected by a virus. Interferon binds to neighboring, uninfected cells and stimulates them to produce chemicals that may protect these cells from viruses. Interferons have also had some success as anticancer drugs, but are still considered experimental. **Tumor necrosis factor** (TNF), another cytokine, stimulates macrophages and also causes cell death in cancer cells. Many cytokines are types of molecules called **interleukins**. There are at least 10 different interleukins. They are involved in nearly every aspect of innate and adaptive immunity. Interleukins also have been used with moderate success in treating some forms of cancer.

Complement cascade is a complex series of reactions that activate a series of plasma proteins that are usually inactive in the blood unless activated by a pathogen invasion. When these proteins are activated, they have a variety of effects, including **lysis** of bacterial cell membranes, stimulation of phagocytosis, and attraction of white blood cells to the site of infection. (Lysis means "to break down or destroy.") Complement cascade is part of both innate and adaptive immunity.

Inflammation

Inflammation, or the inflammatory response, is one of the most familiar weapons in the body's arsenal. Nearly everyone has experienced the swelling, pain, heat, and redness associated with inflammation at one time or another. Think back several chapters to the example of hitting your thumb with a hammer. What would happen to your thumb within a few minutes of injury? It would swell, turn red, get hot to the touch, and hurt for some time after the injury. What about an infected cut? Or a sore throat when you have a cold or the flu? Again, the symptoms are the same: redness, heat, swelling, and pain. This reaction is a deliberate action of your body in response to tissue damage, whether a mechanical injury, like hitting your thumb with a hammer, or damage due to the invasion of a pathogen, as in a wound infection or a strep throat. Part of this response helps to wall off the infected area to prevent further spread and allow the battle to focus at this site. This process is called **margination** and is an attempt to isolate the problem.

margination Walling off of an infected area to prevent further spread and allow the body to focus at the specific site.

Pathology Connection

INFLAMATION, A TWO-DEGED SWORD

Inflammation, like many of the body's weapons, has a positive feedback loop. Once inflammation starts, it continues until turned off. This kind of runaway positive feedback can cause problems if localized swelling increases pressure, causing more tissue damage. One of the reasons you "ice" a sprained ankle is to decrease inflammation to prevent further damage. Inflammation is a particular problem in enclosed or small spaces like the brain, spinal cord, respiratory system, and extremities, where a small buildup of pressure can cause serious damage. Remember Ray? Some of the damage to his spinal cord was due to postinjury inflammation. Even more dangerous is inflammation that becomes systemic, spreading throughout the whole body. This type of inflammation, called **anaphylaxis,** often causes blood pressure to plummet due to widespread vasodilation. Some people who are allergic to insect stings, nuts, or shellfish may experience this kind of inflammation. Anaphylaxis can be fatal unless treated by a medical professional immediately. People prone to anaphylaxis usually carry injectable epinephrine (adrenaline) to treat acute reactions. They should also wear medic alert bracelets to inform medical personnel of their allergies in the event of an emergency. Inflammation can be treated with several medications, such as nonsteroidal anti-inflammatory drugs (NSAIDs), including ibuprofen and naproxen sodium, steroids, and/or antihistamines (especially for allergic reactions).

anaphylaxis *(AN ah fih LAK sis)* An immediate, usually allergic response characterized by smooth muscle contraction and dilation of capillaries due to various chemical releases by the body that may lead to rapid decrease in blood pressure.

Fever

During an infection, tissues and components of the immune system release a number of cytokines that promote inflammation and immune responses. These cytokines circulate through the bloodstream and often reach distant targets, including the brain. One of the cytokine targets in the brain is the hypothalamus, which is responsible for setting and maintaining body temperature. Under the stimulation of cytokines, the hypothalamus raises the body's temperature set point. You feel cold and put on more clothes, huddle under more blankets, and shiver. Eventually, body temperature rises to the new set point, and a fever results. Although unpleasant, this rise in body temperature is a deliberate attempt by the immune system to destroy the pathogens that have invaded the body. Like the rest of the innate response system, fever is a crude weapon against invaders. It might help fight off the infection, but it also causes overall discomfort.

histamine *(HISS tah meen)* A chemical released by basophils. Histamine dilates blood vessels and increases blood flow to damaged tissue. Allows protein molecules to leak out of blood vessels into the surrounding tissue. This produces redness and swelling.

When tissue is damaged, the cells send out chemicals such as **histamine,** an inflammation modulator, which have several effects. These chemicals attract white blood cells to the site of injury, increase the permeability of capillaries, and cause local vasodilation. Extra fluid moves from the capillaries into the damaged tissue, causing swelling. More blood comes to the site, increasing the temperature of the tissue. White blood cells enter the area, destroying pathogens and clearing away dead and dying cells. The increase in fluid and cells coming to the area increases the pressure and is part of the reason the area remains painful even as the damage is being repaired. Inflammation is an innate immune mechanism, but it is also an important player in adaptive immunity. There are several causes and consequences of an inflammatory response. Please see **FIGURE 14-5** ▲.

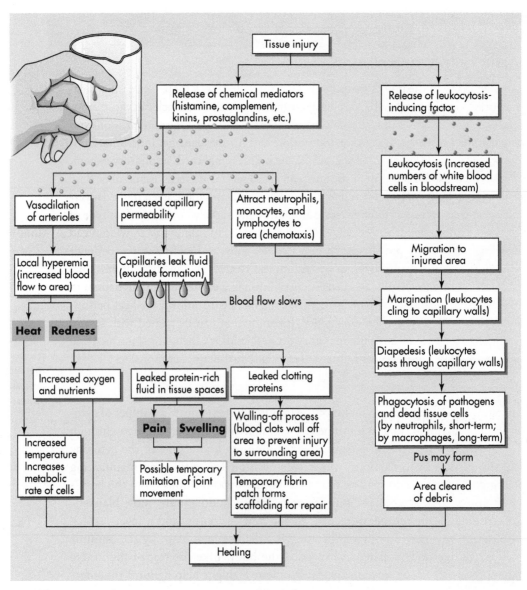

FIGURE 14-5 ▲ Causes and consequences of the inflammatory response.

TEST YOUR KNOWLEDGE 14-3

Choose the best answer:

1. Which of the following is *not* a function of complement cascade?
   a. lysis of bacterial cell membrane
   b. stimulation of macrophages
   c. alteration of viral structures
   d. swelling

2. These chemicals may protect the body against viruses and some cancers:
   a. complement
   b. histamine
   c. interferons
   d. immunoglobulins

3. B cells (lymphocytes) are directly responsible for:
   a. killing cells directly
   b. inflammation
   c. complement cascade
   d. none of the above

4. Neutrophils and macrophages aid the innate immune system by doing this:
   a. secreting cytokines
   b. phagocytosis
   c. stimulating immune response
   d. all of the above

5. Redness, heat, swelling, and pain are all symptoms of:
   a. complement
   b. fever
   c. inflammation
   d. shock

6. _____ is a rapidly growing cancer of blood stem cells.
   a. Acute myelogenous leukemia
   b. Acute lymphocytic leukemia
   c. Chronic myelogenous leukemia
   d. Chronic lymphocyte leukemia

HOW THE IMMUNE SYSTEM WORKS

Think back to when you were in grade school and remember all the colds and sore throats you and your friends suffered through, not to mention chicken pox and measles for you older students. Compare that to the frequency of colds and sore throats you get as an adult. Chances are the number is much lower. What has happened?

Innate Immunity

As we have seen, for a pathogen to successfully invade your body, it must first get past your physical and chemical barriers. (Think of your body as a castle and the barriers of innate immunity as the alligator-filled moat protecting the castle from the marauding hoards.) Most of the millions of pathogens you encounter each day are kept out by these barriers. However, some pathogens—influenza or the cold virus, for example—are very good at getting past barriers.

When a pathogen does get past the barriers, the more active portions of innate immunity are activated. The presence of a foreign antigen is detected by **neutrophils**. Neutrophils ingest the foreign antigen, destroying it, and release chemicals (cytokines, for example) that attract other white blood cells to the site of infection and stimulate inflammation. (Continuing our castle analogy, the neutrophils are the guards who greet any marauders who manage to survive the alligators.)

The release of cytokines and stimulation of inflammation attract **macrophages** and **natural killer (NK)** cells to the infection site. Macrophages destroy more infected cells by phagocytosis. NK cells use chemicals to destroy infected cells. Both cells release

neutrophil *(NOO troh fill)* A type of leukocyte that performs nonspecific phagocytosis.

macrophages *(MACK roh FAGE ez)* Cells that take fragments of the pathogen they have eaten and present them to a B cell (lymphocyte). This stimulates the B cell to become a plasma cell and make antibodies against that specific pathogen. Macrophages also activate helper T cells in this way. Macrophages also produce special immune response chemicals: interferon, interleukin, and tumor necrosis factor.

natural killer (NK) cell Type of lymphocyte that matures in the red marrow and is the body's first cellular defense against invading microorganisms. An NK cell recognizes non-self by the antigens on the cell wall and releases chemicals that penetrate and destroy it.

chemicals that further stimulate inflammation, activate more immune cells, and trigger the complement cascade. (The castle guards sound the alarm that the castle has been breached, summoning more troops to fight the invaders.)

At this point, the infected cells, or the pathogens themselves, are under attack on several fronts: phagocytosis, noxious chemicals, membrane rupture, clumping, and even alteration of their molecular structure. Chemicals have signaled your hypothalamus to raise your body temperature, and you run a fever. There is no question in your mind that you are ill. (Even though the guards are protecting the castle, the castle will be damaged.)

You would think this would be enough to fight off most pathogens. But keep in mind that this is crude warfare. Innate immunity simply destroys anything non-self. It does not use surgical strikes or specific weapons. Innate immunity lays waste to the infected area with almost indiscriminate attacks. Defending the castle is warfare in the crudest sense—no specialized weapons, just desperate attempts to defeat the invaders. Healthy cells can be destroyed in the process.

The activities of innate immunity stimulate adaptive immunity. Chemicals released by NK cells, neutrophils, and other cells help activate adaptive immunity. When phagocytic cells ingest pathogens, they display the foreign antigen on their cell membranes. This ability to display foreign antigens without being infected is absolutely necessary for activation of B and T cells.

Adaptive Immunity

Fighting specific pathogens is the job of adaptive immunity. This part of the immune system has memory, "learns" with experience, and recognizes specific pathogens. It is because of adaptive immunity that people get the chicken pox only once. (Thank goodness for that!) It is because of adaptive immunity that immunizations are able to prevent illness. When was the last time you heard of somebody in the United States getting polio? Just 60 years ago, polio was an epidemic in the United States. Keep in mind that innate and adaptive immunity work hand in hand. One cannot do its job without the other.

Lymphocyte Selection

positive selection During lymphocyte development, only those lymphocytes that can actually react to antigens will survive.

negative selection The destruction of lymphocytes, which destroy "self" antigens. These lymphocytes must be deleted to prevent autoimmunity.

To function, lymphocytes must be able to recognize pathogens and ignore the body's own tissues. Think of these cells as members of the local fire company. They have a very specific job—putting out fires. Like any professional firefighter, lymphocytes must be *selected*. To work in your body, lymphocytes must recognize self-antigens, but not destroy them. During **positive selection,** T lymphocytes that recognize self-antigens are allowed to survive. T lymphocytes that do not recognize self-antigens are neglected and die, much like a firefighter who cannot carry a hose or climb a ladder will not become part of the company. Unfortunately, some of the selected T lymphocytes will destroy self-antigens. These lymphocytes must be deactivated or they will attack and destroy your own tissues. The destruction or deactivation of self-destroying lymphocytes is known as **negative selection**. Both positive and negative selection must work for your immune system to function appropriately. You must have lymphocytes that attack invaders but that don't attack you.

Pathology Connection

AUTOIMMUNE DISORDERS

Autoimmune disorders occur when the immune system attacks some part of the body. For some reason, the body fails to recognize "self" and destroys its own tissue as if it were an invader. There are literally hundreds of autoimmune disorders. Any part of the body can come under attack by mistake. Some of the more common disorders (and what they attack) are as follows:

- Rheumatoid arthritis (joint linings)
- Multiple sclerosis (myelin sheath in central nervous system; see Chapter 9)
- Lupus erythematosis (every tissue, perhaps DNA)
- Type 1 diabetes (beta cells in pancreas; discussed several times)
- Myasthenia gravis (acetylcholine receptors in skeletal muscle; see Chapter 7)
- Graves' disease (thyroid gland; see Chapter 10)
- Addison's disease (adrenal gland; see Chapter 10)

Just this short list illustrates how devastating an autoimmune disorder can be. Imagine the full power of your immune system turning against your thyroid gland or myelin sheath. The effects are devastating. Most autoimmune disorders can be treated with immunosuppressant drugs, but treatment may not be spectacularly successful, and side effects are often severe.

Rheumatoid Arthritis (RA)

Rheumatoid arthritis (RA) is an autoimmune disorder in which the immune system attacks the synovial membrane of a patient's joints. The damage to the synovial membrane leads to destruction of bone and cartilage, leading to weakening of the soft tissue supporting the joints. Joints eventually collapse, bones fuse, and tendons shorten, causing disfigurement particularly of the hands and feet. The bone damage happens very early in untreated disease. The destruction of joint tissue itself causes increased inflammation, which causes more destruction in a massive positive feedback loop. Symptoms of RA include joint stiffness, particularly in the morning, symmetrical joint damage, fatigue, and fever. Because RA is a systemic disorder, patients may also have anemia; dry eyes; osteoporosis; lung, pericardial, and blood vessel inflammation; and increased risk of heart attack. Like in any chronic disease, many patients also have problems with depression or anxiety. RA may be moderate or severe, chronic or flaring. Many patients show a relapsing and remitting pattern. There are both juvenile and adult forms of the disease. Interestingly, pregnancy may improve RA symptoms in some patients. The cause of RA is unknown but seems to be caused by a combination of genetics and some environmental trigger, such as a virus, a bacterium, or hormonal changes. There are approximately 2 million RA patients in the United States, and women are two to three times more likely than men to have RA.

There is no definitive test for RA. Medical history and physical examination can be used to diagnose the disorder, as can imaging and lab tests including leukocyte counts, erythrocyte sedimentation rates, and a test for the presence of rheumatoid factor. Treatment is long-term and often difficult. Drugs to treat RA include **disease modifying anti-rheumatic drugs (DMARDs)** such as injected gold, methotrexate (a cancer drug), or plaquinil (a malaria drug). For patients who have used DMARDs unsuccessfully or for whom DMARDs have stopped working, there is a newer class of drugs called **biological response modifiers (BRMs;** aka biologics) that includes Humira™, Enbrel™, Orencia™, Kineret™, and Remicade™. These medications suppress the immune system by decreasing immune-enhancing chemicals or inhibiting immune cells. In the past, **non-steroidal anti-inflammatory drugs (NSAIDs)** like ibuprofen and naproxen were initially prescribed for RA,

autoimmune disorders A disorder in which the immune system attacks some part of the body, when the body fails to recognize itself.

rheumatoid arthritis *(ROO meh toyd awr THRIGH tiss)* A chronic, systemic condition affecting synovial joints. Women are three times more affected than men. A common complaint is morning joint stiffness rather than after physical activities.

disease modifying anti-rheumatic drugs (DMARDs) Drugs used to treat rheumatoid arthritis such as injected gold, methotrexate, or plaquinil.

biological response modifiers (BRMs) A newer class of drugs for the treatment of rheumatoid arthritis that suppress the immune system.

non-steroidal anti-inflammatory drugs (NSAIDs) An older class of drugs such as ibuprofen and naproxen.

(continued)

Pathology Connection (continued)

but NSAIDs are ineffective in halting the progression of joint damage. Patients are also counseled to make lifestyle changes including reducing stress, increasing moderate exercise, and eating healthy. Assistive devices or surgery are often necessary for severe cases of RA.

Systemic Lupus Erythematosis

systemic lupus erythematosus (SLE) *(LOO pus ER ih theh mat OHS is)* A chronic, autoimmune, inflammatory condition that involves multiple organ systems. There are periodic acute episodes of this disease. There is a characteristic "butterfly" rash over the patient's nose and cheeks resembling a wolf's snout.

Systemic lupus erythematosis (SLE) is an autoimmune disorder in which the immune system attacks a variety of structures in the body. The immune system appears to attack connective tissue in general. Nearly every part of the body may be attacked, including joints, skin, kidney, heart, lungs, blood vessels, and the brain. Symptoms include fatigue, joint pain and stiffness, fever, rashes (particularly butterfly-shaped on the face), and kidney disease. Pregnancy may worsen lupus symptoms or even bring on a flare-up. Patients may experience chest pain, hair loss, swollen glands, anemia, heart problems, atherosclerosis, and depression or anxiety. Lupus may be moderate to severe and may be chronic or show a relapsing and remitting pattern. The cause of lupus is unknown but both genetic predisposition and an environmental trigger is probably necessary for the onset of the disease.

Diagnosis is difficult because symptoms vary so much from patient to patient. There is no definitive test, but some patients test positive for antinuclear (anti-DNA) antibodies. Medical history, tissue biopsies, blood counts, urinalysis, erythrocyte sedimentation rate, complement levels, and imaging studies may be used to diagnose the disorder. Treatment is complicated because of the nature of the disease. Drug treatments include NSAIDs, DMARDs, steroids, and immunosuppressants. Several BRMs that have been successful in treating other autoimmune disorders are being investigated as treatments for lupus.

Lymphocyte Activation

Lymphocytes develop and mature when you are a baby or a very young child. Just like you, they begin as undifferentiated cells, meaning they have the potential to become anything. They must undergo a maturation process to become **differentiated**—in other words, to grow up to be a specialized cell with a specialized function. Undifferentiated lymphocytes are produced in the bone marrow, but some migrate to the thymus and are destined to become T cells. Others stay, develop, and mature in the bone marrow to become B cells.

differentiated The maturing of certain cells to allow them to become specialized with specialized functions.

After they are specialized, the lymphocytes hang out in the lymph nodes waiting for a pathogen to come along that they recognize. The lymphocytes can go into suspended animation for the duration. For the lymphocytes to fight off the pathogen, they must have a wake-up call. Picture the fire company sleeping in the middle of the night and the alarm going off. This wake-up call is called **lymphocyte activation**. It causes lymphocytes to circulate continuously in the bloodstream and activates the immune system to combat the pathogen.

lymphocyte activation Stimulation of lymphocytes, "waking them up" to fight a pathogen.

Let's go back to innate immune response for a minute. When a pathogen invades your tissues, your innate immunity mounts a response to the pathogen. One part of innate immunity is the phagocytosis of infected cells or bits of pathogen. When these cells— macrophages, **dendritic cells,** and others—eat the pathogen, the pathogen's antigens are displayed on the outside of the phagocytic cells, kind of like little wanted posters. These cells then prowl the lymph nodes, displaying these tiny bits of pathogen, searching for the lymphocytes that can recognize the pathogen bits. When the right lymphocytes meet the

dendritic cells *(den DRIT ick)* One of several types of antigen-presenting cells that stimulate adaptive immunity.

right antigen display, the lymphocytes are activated (their wake-up call for battle). This activation is the beginning of adaptive immunity. Remember, water doesn't come out of a fire hose until the hose is turned on. See **FIGURE 14-6** ▲ to see how the immune system activates and differentiates lymphocytes.

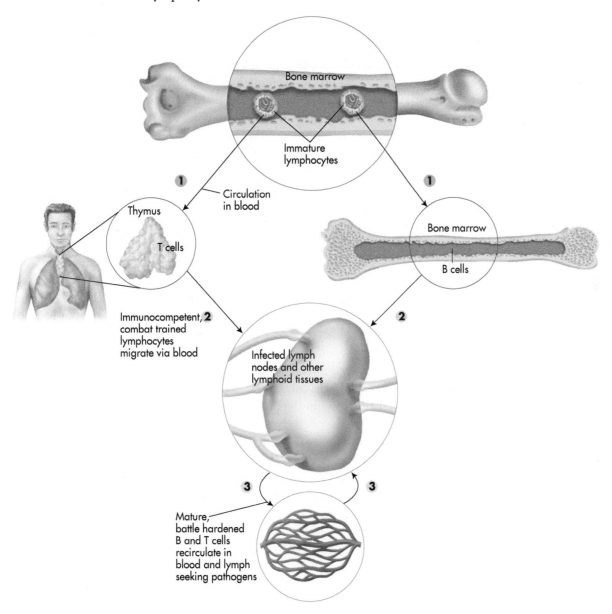

KEY:

❶ Site of lymphocyte origin: Some lymphocytes are sent to the thymus where they become T cells, while others remain in the bone marrow to become B cells. These cells are now much like soldiers in boot camp that have learned their combat training but have yet to face the real enemy.

❷ Sites of development of immunocompetence as B or T cells: An infection occurs and these cells are now given their marching orders to travel to the site of need. This is usually in the lymphoid tissue where the antigen challenge (the enemy has arrived) and the lymphocytes get placed into actual battle.

❸ Site of antigen challenge and final differentiation to mature B and T cells: Now the battle-hardened lymphocytes can competently patrol the rest of the body through the blood and lymph system, seeking out the enemy.

FIGURE 14-6 ▲
Lymphocyte differentiation and activation.

Lymphocyte Proliferation

The body has only a few lymphocytes that recognize each invader to which it has been exposed. But to fight off an infection, hundreds of thousands of lymphocytes are needed to attack the infection. Simple activation of lymphocytes is not enough. The activated lymphocytes must make thousands of copies of themselves to fight off the thousands of pathogens reproducing in the body. This reproduction of lymphocytes is called **lymphocyte proliferation** (see FIGURE 14-7 ▲).

Just like one platoon would not be enough to repel a full-scale invasion of a country, or one fire company enough to save a city block from burning down, a few lymphocytes are not enough to defend the entire body.

When you first met lymphocytes, earlier in our tour of the troops, you discovered that B cells and T cells have different roles in the defense of the body. Whereas activation and selection is, for our purposes, the same for both B and T cells, proliferation is different depending on the type of lymphocyte that is being reproduced.

There are two types of proliferation: proliferation of effector T cells (helper and cytotoxic T cells) and proliferation of all other types of lymphocytes. The job of helper T cells is to help other lymphocytes. There must be lots of helper T cells before any other lymphocytes (except cytotoxic T cells) can be activated. Helper T cells are stimulated to divide by binding to antigen-displaying cells (from innate immunity) and by stimulation by cytokines. The helper T cells continue to divide, producing more helper T cells, and then help (hence their name) in the proliferation of B cells and other types of T cells (again, see Figure 14-7).

Helper T cells are absolutely necessary for the reproduction of B cells and several other types of T cells. This is why HIV, the virus that causes AIDS, is so devastating to the immune system. HIV targets helper T cells specifically. To understand the role of the helper T cells, imagine a huge game of tag in which no lymphocytes can be activated or reproduced until they have been tagged by a helper T cell.

lymphocyte proliferation
(LIM foh SIGHT pruh lif uh REY shun) Reproduction of activated lymphocytes so there are many copies.

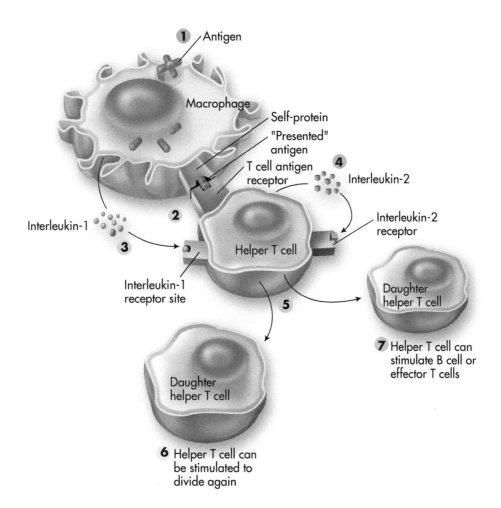

1 Antigen

Macrophage

Self-protein

"Presented" antigen

T cell antigen receptor

4 Interleukin-2

Interleukin-1

2

Interleukin-2 receptor

3

Helper T cell

Interleukin-1 receptor site

5

Daughter helper T cell

7 Helper T cell can stimulate B cell or effector T cells

Daughter helper T cell

6 Helper T cell can be stimulated to divide again

KEY:

1 Antigen processing cell such as a macrophage ingests a pathogen and displays its antigen on the macrophage's cell membrane.

2 Presented antigen is recognized by helper T cell.

3 The macrophage secretes a cytokine called interleukin-1.

4 Interleukin-1 stimulates the helper T cell to secrete interleukin-2 which combines with interleukin receptors.

5 When interleukin-2 binds to the receptor site the helper T cell divides.

6 The daughter cell produced can divide again if exposed to the same antigen. This greatly increases the number of helper T cells which can even further divide proportionate to the antigen exposure.

7 As helper T cells continue to divide they can stimulate B cell activation and produce effector T cells.

FIGURE 14-7 ▲ Activation and proliferation of helper T cells.

Pathology Connection

acquired immune deficiency syndrome (AIDS) An immune deficiency disorder caused by the human immunodeficiency virus (HIV).

human immunodeficiency virus (HIV) A virus that leads to decreased immune function and kills off helper T cells.

AIDS–related complex (ARC) Symptoms may include enlarged lymph nodes, fatigue, night sweats, weight loss, and diarrhea.

Acquired immune deficiency syndrome (AIDS) is an immune deficiency disorder caused by infection with the **human immunodeficiency virus (HIV)**. It is characterized by a severe decrease in immune function, particularly helper T cells (a group called CD4). HIV causes AIDS by directly killing helper T cells, by destroying lymph nodes through their chronic infection, and by decreasing the amount of immune-enhancing chemicals in the body. HIV is most commonly contracted during sexual contact with an infected person or by sharing IV needles with an infected drug user. HIV can also be passed via use of blood products (rare in the United States today), from mother to fetus *in utero* and in breast milk, and via accidental exposure to infected body fluids (rare). It cannot be spread by casual contact, coughing, sneezing, shaking hands, or sharing eating utensils.

Symptoms of HIV infection may appear approximately four weeks after infection and may include flulike symptoms due to the body's attempt to fight off the infection. In some cases the immune system fights the disease for up to 10 to 12 years after infection before symptoms appear. Some people who are infected remain asymptomatic. Others may have **AIDS-related complex (ARC)** or full-blown AIDS. Symptoms of ARC include enlarged lymph nodes, fatigue, night sweats, weight loss, and diarrhea. Symptoms of full-blown AIDS include the symptoms of ARC plus opportunistic infections (such as Kaposi's sarcoma, *Pneumocystis jiroveci,* previously known as *Pneumocystis carinii* pneumonia, and toxoplasmosis), CNS dysfunction, and some forms of cancer. Patients with AIDS catch infections that are virtually unknown in humans or become very ill from viruses, fungi, and bacteria that are typically mild in patients with normal immune systems. HIV entered the United States in the late 1970s. In 2010 more than 1,000,000 patients had AIDS, and 40,000 new cases were diagnosed in 2009. To date more than 500,000 patients have died from AIDS in the United States since 1978. Worldwide totals are in the tens of millions.

HIV is diagnosed by medical history and by a blood test that detects very low helper T cell count of less than 200 cells/μl. Treatment is complicated. Patients positive for HIV or in full-blown AIDS are treated with one of a number of drug "cocktails" consisting of combinations of drugs. These drugs may block viral reproduction, keep the virus from assembling new viruses, or block the entrance of the virus into cells. These cocktails, although effective, are complicated and have severe side effects. Infections are treated appropriately. Advances in treatment in the last 10 years have greatly improved the prognosis of patients who are HIV positive. Many patients have survived for years postinfection without developing full-blown AIDS. HIV infection is not necessarily a death sentence. Education is one of the most important methods of preventing HIV/AIDS.

TEST YOUR KNOWLEDGE 14-4

Choose the best answer:

1. To be activated, B and T cells must bind with:
   a. an antigen-displaying cell
   b. a pathogen
   c. a damaged cell
   d. all of the above

2. Selection for immune-competent cells is called:
   a. negative selection
   b. positive selection
   c. immune selection
   d. make a selection

3. After a lymphocyte is activated, what must it do before it can fight off a pathogen?
   a. die
   b. agglutinate
   c. proliferate
   d. congregate

4. The primary function of these cells is the activation of other lymphocytes:
   a. cytotoxic T cells
   b. helper T cells
   c. memory T cells
   d. regulatory T cells

5. HIV targets these cells:
   a. cytotoxic T cells
   b. helper T cells
   c. memory T cells
   d. B cells

6. The best treatment for HIV infection today is:
   a. wait for full-blown AIDS to treat patient
   b. use cocktail of drugs to prevent AIDS from developing
   c. practice safe sex
   d. there is no treatment

B and T Cell Action

So, let's get back to the body's response to invasion. The innate immune system has been attacking the pathogen or cells infected with the pathogen on a number of fronts, using phagocytic cells, NK cells, fever, and a variety of noxious chemicals. A number of the body's own cells have been destroyed in the process, but the pathogen has not been defeated. However, while innate immunity has been holding down the fort, **antigen-presenting cells (APCs)**, formerly known as antigen-displaying cells (ADC's) have sent out a signal calling on the weapons of adaptive immunity, B cells and T cells.

B Cells

B cells are responsible for a type of adaptive immunity known as **antibody mediated immunity**. B cells fight pathogens by making and releasing antibodies to attack a specific pathogen. B cells develop into **plasma cells** and **memory B cells**. Plasma cells make antibodies and release them into the bloodstream. Antibodies bind to the antigens of infected cells or the antigens on the surface of freely floating pathogens. They are missiles programmed to home in on a specific target. Antibodies destroy pathogens using several methods, including inactivating the antigen (neutralization), causing antigens to clump together (agglutination), activating complement cascade, causing the release of chemicals to stimulate the immune system, and enhancing phagocytosis. This response to the pathogen is called the **primary response**.

All these antibody-mediated mechanisms not only destroy pathogens specifically, but they also further stimulate both adaptive and innate immune response, continually increasing response to the pathogen. Remember that immune response is a positive

antigen-presenting cells (APCs) Cells that engulf antigens and display them as markers.

antibody mediated immunity Immunity that results from a formation of antibodies in response to antigens.

plasma cell A cell derived from a B lymphocyte that has been sensitized to a specific foreign antigen and produces antibodies to that particular antigen.

memory B cells Antibody-producing cells that are produced when a pathogen is encountered the first time. Memory B cells are stored until the pathogen comes again. They are responsible for secondary response.

primary response The reaction the body conducts to destroy a pathogen which may include antigen neutralization and antigen agglutination, activating complement cascade.

secondary response Increased immune response mediated by memory cells when meeting a pathogen that they recognize.

cytotoxic T cells *(sigh tow TOX ick)* Type of T lymphocyte that matures in the thymus. Cytotoxic T cells destroy all types of pathogens as well as body cells infected with viruses.

cell-mediated immunity Destruction of pathogens by T lymphocytes. T lymphocytes directly attack infected cells, destroying them.

perforin *(PUR fuh rinn)* Chemical secreted by cytotoxic T cells, which makes holes in the cell membranes of pathogens or infected cells, killing them.

regulatory T cells Type of T cell that shuts down immune response.

memory T cells Memory cells responsible for cell mediated immunity. They are produced when a pathogen is encountered the first time. Memory T cells are stored until the pathogen comes again. They are responsible for secondary response.

feedback loop that must be deliberately turned off. It will not stop on its own. This makes sense if you think in terms of protection. Your protective systems should not give up until the danger is past. Smoke alarms keep wailing until there is no more smoke.

Other B cells, memory B cells, are stored in lymph nodes until they are needed at some future date. If the body is exposed to the same pathogen in the future, memory cells allow it to mount a much faster response to the invasion. This response is known as **secondary response** and is responsible for the ability of adaptive immunity to improve with experience (see FIGURE 14-8 ▲).

T Cells

There are at least four types of T cells: helper T cells and cytotoxic T cells (collectively known as effector T cells), regulatory T cells (formerly known as suppressor T cells), and memory T cells. We have already seen the action of helper T cells. Helper T cells are responsible for activation of B and some T cells.

Cytotoxic T cells are responsible for a part of adaptive immune response known as **cell-mediated immunity,** so called because the cytotoxic T cells are directly responsible for the death of pathogens or pathogen-infected cells. Cytotoxic T cells release a cytokine called **perforin,** which causes infected cells to develop holes in their membranes and die. Cytotoxic T cells also release other cytokines that stimulate both innate and adaptive immunity, especially attracting macrophages to the site of infection to dispose of cellular debris. The response of cytotoxic T cells is the primary response of cell-mediated immunity.

Regulatory T cells are the off-switch for the immune system. Immunity is controlled largely by positive feedback. Tissue damage causes the release of stimulatory chemicals that cause inflammation and increased immune response. Increased immune response results in the release of more chemicals, which causes more stimulation, which causes more chemicals to be released, and so on. Something must actively work to turn off the response when the threat is over or the immune response could become rampant and out of control and thus cause damage. This is the job of the regulatory T cells.

Some T cells give rise to **memory T cells.** Like memory B cells, memory T cells are responsible for secondary response, storing the recognition of the pathogen until the next encounter (see FIGURE 14-9 ▲).

FIGURE 14-8 ▲ The primary response causes B cells to produce memory B cells and a few antibodies. The second exposure causes the secondary response to produce more memory B cells and even more antibodies to fight the invaders. Now that the body has antibodies and more memory B cells, the secondary response begins more rapidly after exposure, produces more antibodies, and lasts a longer time.

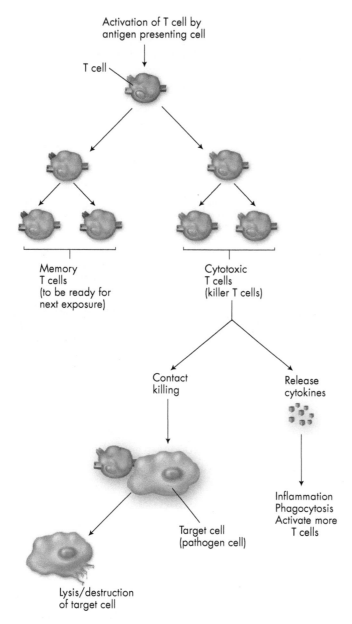

Activation of T cell by
antigen presenting cell

T cell

Memory
T cells
(to be ready for
next exposure)

Cytotoxic
T cells
(killer T cells)

Contact
killing

Release
cytokines

Inflammation
Phagocytosis
Activate more
T cells

Target cell
(pathogen cell)

Lysis/destruction
of target cell

FIGURE 14-9 ▲ Cell-mediated immunity, primary, and secondary response.

You can acquire immunity in several different ways. **Natural active immunity** is acquired in the course of daily life. When you catch a virus or a bacterium, your immune system fights it off, and memory cells are created for the next meeting. Anybody old enough to have had the chicken pox as a child (before the vaccine became available) is usually protected from a second round of chicken pox. **Artificial active immunity** is acquired during vaccinations. Getting a measles shot exposes you to small amounts of weakened virus, not enough to make you sick, but enough for your immune system to create memory cells. If you meet the virus later in life, you will be able to fight it off. Babies acquire **natural passive immunity** to many pathogens via antibodies passed across the placenta or during breast feeding. These antibodies, which babies can't yet make, protect them from infection for several months after birth. **Artificial passive immunity** is acquired when antibodies from one person are injected into another to help fight infection. An example is the HRIG shots that people get right after they are exposed to rabies. These shots are given before the actual rabies vaccine, which confers artificial active immunity. Passive acquired immunity lasts only a few weeks; active acquired immunity lasts longer. See **FIGURE 14-10** ▲.

natural active immunity
Antibodies developed due to exposure to a pathogen.

artificial active immunity
Vaccination. Intentional exposure to pathogens so patient makes own antibodies.

natural passive immunity
Immunity due to the passage of antibodies from mother to child across the placenta or in breast milk.

artificial passive immunity
Injection of antibodies to help patient fight infection.

FIGURE 14-10 ▲ Types of immunities.

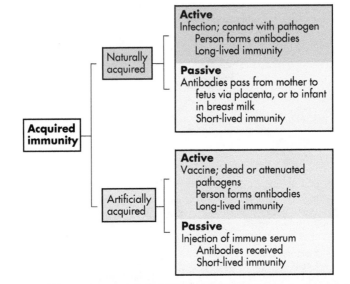

immunization Techniques such as vaccinations that train the immune system by creating memory cells to destroy a specific pathogen.

Clinical Application

HOW YOU ACQUIRE IMMUNITY TO PATHOGENS

Your adaptive immune system is able to acquire immunity to new pathogens by creating memory cells each time you meet a pathogen. This process, called **immunization,** whether natural or done by medical procedures such as vaccinations, trains your immune system by creating memory cells for a pathogen. When you are exposed to the pathogen a second time, you do not get ill. Your immune system fights off the pathogen very quickly. In active acquired immunity, *you make* antibodies to fight the pathogens. In passive acquired immunity, antibodies *are introduced* to your body and therefore you don't make your own.

TEST YOUR KNOWLEDGE 14-5

Choose the best answer:

1. B cells, once activated, can become two different kinds of cells: memory B cells and:
   a. cytotoxic T cells
   b. natural killers
   c. plasma cells
   d. macrophages

2. Secondary response is mediated by:
   a. cytotoxic T cells
   b. macrophages
   c. memory cells
   d. all of the above

3. _____ cells are responsible for antibody-mediated immunity, whereas cell-mediated immunity is performed by _____ cells.
   a. B cells; cytotoxic T cells
   b. B cells; RBCs
   c. B cells; plasma cells
   d. plasma cells; memory cells

4. These cells, which were only discovered recently, are part of the "off-switch" for the immune system:
   a. cytotoxic T cells
   b. memory T cells
   c. regulatory T Cells
   d. helper T cells

5. As a new EMT, Cindy is required to have the Hepatitis B vaccine series. She will gain this type of immunity:
   a. natural active immunity
   b. artificial active immunity
   c. natural passive immunity
   d. artificial passive immunity

THE BIG PICTURE

At this point we have talked about the lymphatic system, innate immunity, and adaptive immunity as separate means to the same end: ridding the body of invading pathogens. We have mentioned repeatedly that the divisions are *not* separate but are intimately connected. Now that we have inspected them separately, it is time to put the entire defense system back together as a single, integrated fighting force (see **FIGURE 14-11** ▲).

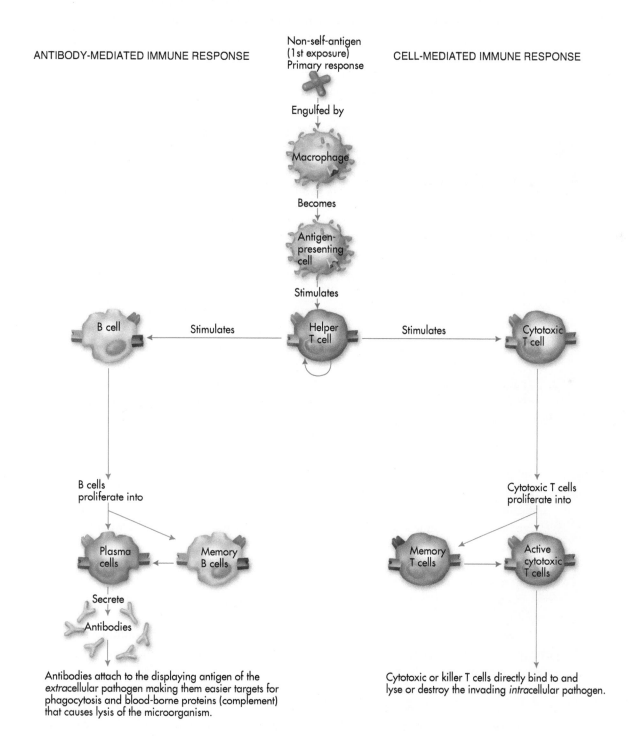

FIGURE 14-11 ▲ The battle plan of the body's defenses.

anaphylaxis *(AN ah fih LAK sis)* An immediate, usually allergic response characterized by smooth muscle contraction and dilation of capillaries due to various chemical releases by the body that may lead to rapid decrease in blood pressure.

atopic march A condition in patients in which early exposure to an allergen may cause an initial skin reaction while later exposures lead to allergic rhinitis, asthma, or even anaphylaxis.

A nasty army of pathogens attempts to invade your body. First, they must get past your barriers. Many invaders will be repelled simply by your intact skin or the secretions of your mucous membranes. If the invader gets inside your body, a series of weapons are stimulated by the introduction of a non-self-antigen. Cells (neutrophils, macrophages, basophils, etc.) are stimulated. Chemicals (cytokines) are also released that stimulate inflammation and phagocytosis.

Macrophages and other cells, having ingested some of the invaders and now wearing the foreign antigens, move to the lymphatic system and search the lymph nodes, looking for the T and B cells that will recognize the intruder. Helper T cells activate and cause the proliferation of B cells and other T cells, as well as release chemicals that further stimulate the phagocytic cells and inflammation. Cytotoxic T cells are activated and proliferate. B cells produce antibodies that destroy the invaders and

Pathology Connection

HYPERSENSITIVITY REACTIONS

During a hypersensitivity reaction, more commonly known as an allergy, the immune system mounts a hyperactive response to a foreign antigen, often treating a harmless antigen, like grass or mold or insect bite, as an invading pathogen. Hypersensitivity reactions, like hay fever (allergic rhinitis), hives (urticaria), skin rashes, and asthma, are generally mild and not life threatening. (Asthma is an obvious exception because it interferes with ventilation.) Millions of people in the United States have asthma, allergic rhinitis, or both.

In contrast, systemic hypersensitivity reactions, known as **anaphylaxis,** are life threatening. During anaphylaxis, mast cells and basophils release immune-stimulating chemicals throughout the body. The chemicals cause widespread vasodilation, which leads to dangerously low blood pressure and heart failure. Hives and respiratory distress may also accompany an anaphylactic reaction. FIGURE 14-12 ▲ shows stimulation of the mast cells within the nose due to an allergen, which causes allergic rhinitis (runny nose). Note that mast cells are found throughout the body. If overstimulated in the eyes, mast cells cause red and runny eyes; if overstimulated in the lungs, they cause allergic asthma. In addition to mast cells, other immune cells also get involved in allergic reactions, including basophils, B cells, eosinophils, and macrophages. The activation of these cells lead to increased inflammation and release of immune stimulating chemicals. For many people, one type of allergy may be complicated by another or a mild allergy may progress to a more severe form. For example, many patients with asthma also have hay fever. Other patients may experience what is called **atopic march.** In these patients, early exposure to an allergen may cause a skin reaction, for example, whereas later exposures cause allergic rhinitis and later exposures cause asthma or even anaphylaxis. That's why a bee sting may cause a minor reaction in a child and a much more severe reaction when that person is stung again as an adult. For many people the worsening of their allergies is predictable.

Allergies are often difficult to diagnose. Blood tests may show increased immune activity but pinpointing the allergen is often difficult. Exposing the patient's skin or a blood sample to suspected allergens may help find the allergen but these are often inconclusive.

The best way to treat an allergy is to avoid coming in contact with whatever causes the problem. That, however is almost impossible if a patient is allergic to grass, mold, or pollen. If the culprit is unavoidable, several treatments are possible and will be elaborated on in the upcoming Pharmacology Corner.

further stimulate immune response. Cytotoxic T cells destroy invaders directly and release chemicals that further stimulate immune response.

Immune response, both innate and adaptive, will continue to be stimulated until the feedback loop is stopped, at least in part by regulatory T cells. Memory B cells and T cells will be stored in the lymph nodes for later use, in case another army of those same type of pathogens attempts another invasion. Macrophages and other phagocytic cells will clean up the debris left by the warfare waged by your immune system. Once the danger has passed, your body will return to normal.

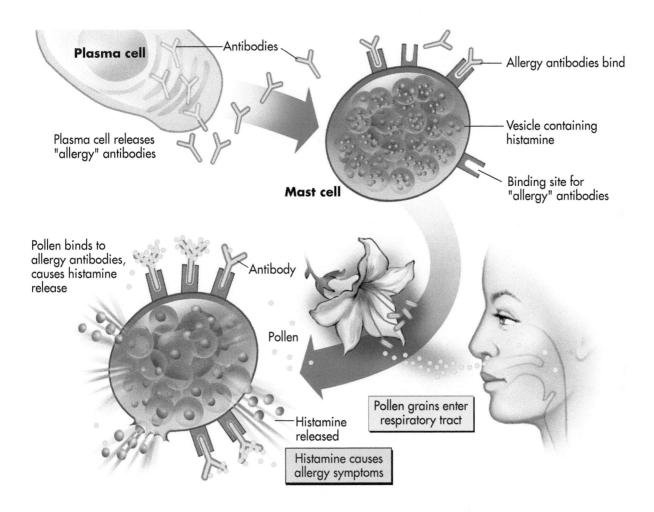

Plasma cell
Antibodies
Allergy antibodies bind

Plasma cell releases "allergy" antibodies
Vesicle containing histamine

Mast cell
Binding site for "allergy" antibodies

Pollen binds to allergy antibodies, causes histamine release
Antibody
Pollen
Pollen grains enter respiratory tract

Histamine released
Histamine causes allergy symptoms

FIGURE 14-12 ▲ Allergic rhinitis.

A QUICK TRIP THROUGH SOME DISEASES OF THE IMMUNE SYSTEM

DISEASE	ETIOLOGY	SIGNS AND SYMPTOMS	DIAGNOSTIC TEST(S)	TREATMENT
Lymphoma	Uncontrolled proliferation of lymphocytes (30 diffferent types).	Enlarged lymph nodes, fever, weight loss, other vague symptoms.	Biopsy, imaging, bone marrow tests.	Chemotherapy, radiation, antibody therapy, stem cell or bone marrow transplant.
Tonsillitis	Inflammation of the tonsils due to bacterial or viral infection.	Sore throat, swollen tonsils, fever, upper respiratory symptoms, swollen lymph nodes, visible coating or spots on the tonsils, upset stomach.	Examination showing inflamed tonsils, rule out bacterial infection.	If bacterial, treat with antibiotics. If viral, rest and fluids until virus runs its course. If swollen tonsils impair breathing, tonsillectomy may be necessary.
Leukemia	Excess production of white blood cells, causes decreased function of WBCs, RBCs, and platelets.	Increased infection, anemia, bleeding, bruising, fatigue, weight loss.	CBC, genetic testing, bone marrow biopsy.	Depending on the type of leukemia, chemotherapy, stem cells, bone marrow transplant.
Hodgkin's disease	Cancer of lymph nodes, effecting white blood cells—most common in people 5–35 years of age; a type of lymphoma.	Painless swelling of lymph node is early symptom (often in neck), fever, night sweats, weight loss, weakness, fatigue, and itching. Respiratory symptoms may occur with chest involvement.	Biopsy, various types of x-rays, ultrasound and lymphangiograms.	Possibly chemotherapy and radiation depending on age and stage.
RA	Joints.	Swollen painful joints, fatigue, anemia, cardiovascular abnormalities.	Blood tests, imaging studies.	DMARDs, BRMs, and lifestyle changes. Difficult to treat effectively.
Lupus	Many different tissues.	Swollen painful joints, fatigue, anemia, cardiovascular abnormalities.	Blood tests, imaging studies.	DMARDs, BRMs, and life style changes. Difficult to treat effectively.
HIV/AIDS	Infection of helper T cells by HIV causing decreased numbers of T cells, eventually leading to severe immune deficiency.	Flu-like symptoms in early stages, opportunistic infections and some forms of cancer in full-blown AIDS.	Medical history, very low helper T-cell counts. AIDS diagnosis made when helper T cells counts are less than 200/µl.	Drug cocktails designed to prevent infection from progressing to full-blown AIDS, treatment of opportunistic infections when they develop.

(continued)

A QUICK TRIP (continued)

DISEASE	ETIOLOGY	SIGNS AND SYMPTOMS	DIAGNOSTIC TEST(S)	TREATMENT
Severe combined immune deficiency (SCID)	Severe decreased T cell production (and sometimes other cells) caused by a number of different genetic defects.	Repeated opportunistic or severe infections in babies, fatal if untreated.	Genetic testing.	Depending on the underlying genetic problem: enzyme replacement, complete sterile environment, bone marrow transplant, stem cells, gene therapy. Most types difficult to treat.
Allergies	Overreaction of the immune system to typically harmless antigens, such as mold, pollen, or animals.	Depending on severity: upper respiratory symptoms, asthma, skin rashes, anaphylaxis.	Medical history, elimination of suspected culprits, skin tests, blood tests.	Avoidance, antihistamines, allergy shots, steroids, epinephrine.

Pharmacology Corner

Most drugs that are given to control the immune system are immune suppressants of some sort. They are prescribed to decrease the activity of an overactive immune system. The first class of drugs is the anti-inflammatory drugs. Anti-inflammatory drugs specifically decrease inflammation though many have other effects. Most of you are familiar with the nonsteroidal anti-inflammatory drugs (NSAIDs), including aspirin, naproxen (Aleve™), ibuprofen (Advil™), celecoxib (Celebrex™), and many others. NSAIDs relieve pain and inflammation by inhibiting a group of hormones called **prostaglandins**. NSAIDs are also notorious for other, less desirable effects, like the formation of stomach ulcers. All NSAIDs inhibit prostaglandins, but they each work in a different way, so one NSAID may work well for one person but not for another.

Another class of anti-inflammatory drugs is the steroids, like prednisone and cortisone. These drugs are powerful anti-inflammatories, but when given systematically (orally or by injection) they may have dangerous side effects when used for long periods. Topical steroids, applied to the skin or nasal passages, are quite effective for treating skin inflammation and upper respiratory symptoms due to allergies. Inhaled steroids are used to control asthma symptoms. Topical and inhaled steroids do not have the severe side effects associated with oral or injected steroids.

Allergies are treated with specialized drugs, like antihistamines. Traditional antihistamines, which decrease mast cell activation, have long been prescribed or available over the counter. They work well but cause severe drowsiness. Newer antihistamines that do not cause drowsiness have proven to be safe and effective, but do not decrease congestion or

prostaglandins *(PROSS teh GLAN dinz)* A group of hormones that can lead to vasodilation, bronchoconstriction, platelet aggregation, and stimulate pain receptors.

(continued)

Pharmacology Corner

inflammation. More specific drugs that block cytokines are currently available, as are drugs that block the antibodies that mediate allergies. Experimental medications that block B cells, TNF, and complement are currently being tested. Steroids may often be effective in treating asthma and severe allergies, but long-term use of oral steroids can produce nasty side effects. Topical steroids, either inhaled or administered as nasal sprays, work well for many people. Patients with anaphylactic reactions to common allergens may be required to carry an EpiPen for emergencies. A shot of epinephrine constricts blood vessels, stimulates the heart, and opens air passages, decreasing the effects of anaphylactic reactions and giving a patient time to get to medical care.

Autoimmune disorders like RA and lupus used to be treated with NSAIDs and steroids, but those drugs proved ineffective for many disorders. Today, autoimmune disorders are more likely to be treated with **disease modifying antirheumatic drugs (DMARDs)**. DMARDs are confusing pharmacologically. It is not well understood how they work, and they are highly toxic. DMARDs include immunosuppressants (Cyclosporine, an antirejection drug used after organ transplants), gold shots, methotrexate (a chemotherapy drug), and antimalarial medications.

For patients who have used DMARDS unsuccessfully or for whom DMARDS have stopped working, there is a newer class of drugs called **biological response modifiers (BRMs)**. Three BRMs on the market—etanercept (Enbrel™), infliximab (Remicade™), and adalimumab (Humira™)—inhibit tumor necrosis factor (TNF), a cytokine. Another, anakinra (Kineret™), inhibits interleukin-1, another cytokine, and still another, rituximab (Rituxan™), inhibits B cells. These medications suppress the immune system because they decrease immune-enhancing chemicals or inhibit the proliferation of cells. Side effects include increased risk of infection and some forms of cancer, but the drugs are less toxic than most DMARDs. In addition, BRMs seem to do a better job at decreasing fatigue in RA patients than the DMARDs.

disease modifying anti-rheumatic drugs (DMARDs) Drugs used to treat rheumatoid arthritis such as injected gold, methotrexate, or plaquinil.

biological response modifiers (BRMs) A newer class of drugs for the treatment of rheumatoid arthritis that suppress the immune system.

SUMMARY

Snapshots from the Journey

- The lymphatic system is the transport system for the immune system and houses the lymphocytes. It consists of lymph capillaries, vessels, trunks, and ducts containing lymphatic fluid and lymph nodes, which house white blood cells.

- Lymph nodes are concentrated in several regions of the body: cervical, axillary, inguinal, pelvic, abdominal, thoracic, and supratrochlear. These patches are in areas where pathogens are most likely to enter. Tonsils, adenoids, spleen, and thymus all contain lymphatic tissue.

SUMMARY

- Fluid leaking from blood capillaries enters tissue fluid and flows into lymph capillaries. The fluid is carried through lymph capillaries to lymph vessels to lymph nodes. In the nodes, any pathogens are destroyed by white blood cells. Fluid then flows from nodes to vessels to lymphatic trunks to collecting ducts and into either the right or left subclavian vein, returning the fluid to the bloodstream. Cancer cells may use this "highway" to spread to other parts of the body.

- The thymus and spleen are lymphatic organs. The spleen contains blood sinuses and removes dead and dying red blood cells as well as pathogens. The thymus is where T lymphocytes mature.

- Immune system function is based on its ability to recognize cell surface molecules called antigens. The immune system must tolerate self-antigens (the body's antigens) and destroy non-self-antigens (foreign cells).

- The immune system is divided into two separate but extremely interdependent parts, innate immunity and adaptive immunity. Innate immunity is nonspecific, has no memory, and cannot improve performance with experience. Adaptive immunity is specific, has memory, and can improve performance with experience.

- Barriers prevent pathogens from getting into the body. Barriers can be either physical or chemical. Skin and tears are examples of barriers.

- The immune system uses a dozen or more different types of cells to combat pathogens. All these cells are leukocytes or modified leukocytes. Some are part of innate immunity, and some are part of adaptive immunity. Their functions range from phagocytosis, chemical stimulation of other cells, and antigen display to antibody secretion and direct destruction of pathogens. Cancer of these cells, which leads to excessive production in the bone marrow, is known as leukemia.

- Immune response is stimulated by a variety of chemicals, including the cytokines and complement.

- Inflammation, the familiar redness, heat, swelling, and pain associated with infection, is a powerful tool in the immune system's arsenal. During inflammation, white blood cells are stimulated and attracted to the site of infection to destroy pathogens and clean up cellular debris. Inflammation is, like much of immune response, a two-edged sword. Too much inflammation may be more damaging than the infection itself.

- Fever, like inflammation, is a deliberate attempt by the body to destroy a pathogen. Chemicals trick the hypothalamus into raising the temperature set point in an attempt to make body temperature too hot for pathogens.

SUMMARY

- Innate immune mechanisms are triggered by the presence of foreign antigens in the body. These mechanisms hold off the infection and stimulate adaptive immune mechanisms.

- Adaptive immunity uses T and B lymphocytes to fight specific pathogens. Lymphocytes must be selected during development to recognize foreign antigens but to ignore the body's own antigens. To fight a pathogen, lymphocytes must be activated by binding with antigen-presenting cells. Once activated, lymphocytes must proliferate, making thousands of copies of themselves. Helper T cells are required for activation of most types of lymphocytes. If lymphocytes continue to respond to body tissues, an autoimmune disorder may result.

- Rheumatoid arthritis (RA) is an autoimmune disorder in which the immune system attacks the lining of synovial joints. RA is a systemic illness that involves many joints at once and may also cause damage to the heart, eyes, and lungs. Systemic lupus erythematosis (SLE) is a more generalized autoimmune disorder in which the immune system attacks connective tissue, and even DNA. Lupus is also a systemic illness causing joint, heart, and kidney damage.

- HIV, the virus which causes AIDS, infects and destroys helper T cells. When HIV infection progresses to full-blown AIDS, helper T cell numbers drop so low that activation and proliferation of T and B cells is negatively affected. Adaptive immunity ceases to function, and patients are at increased risk of rare infections or may become seriously ill from infections that are not usually dangerous in people with healthy immune systems.

- B cells are mediators of antibody-mediated immunity. B cells are activated by binding to antigen-presenting cells and helper T cells. Once B cells begin to proliferate, they become either plasma cells or memory B cells. Plasma cells secrete antibodies during primary response. Antibodies help destroy pathogens by binding to antigens on infected cells. Memory B cells are stored for the next time the pathogen is encountered. They mediate secondary response.

- Cytotoxic T cells mediate cell-mediated immunity by directly killing infected cells. This is the primary T cell response. Like B cells, T cells are activated by helper T cells. Some T cells become memory T cells and mediate secondary response if the pathogen is encountered again.

- Regulatory T cells are one of the off-switches for the immune system. We don't know very much about how these cells work because they were only discovered in the last 10 years.

- Keep in mind that innate and adaptive immunity do not work separately. They work together. One stimulates the other in a huge positive feedback loop. If either innate or adaptive immunity stops working, the whole system breaks down.

RAY'S STORY

Remember Ray, the daredevil who broke his neck in the pool and injured his spinal cord? Several years ago, he would have been treated with steroids as soon as he entered the hospital. The evidence that steroids are helpful is not convincing, so he may not be given steroids today.

a. What benefit did physcians hope steroids would have for spinal cord injury patients?

_____

_____

_____

b. Since the time Ray was injured, doctors have begun experimenting with treating injuries like Ray's by inducing hypothermia. How might making Ray's body very cold have helped treat his injury?

_____

_____

_____

MARIA'S STORY

Maria was diagnosed with diabetes mellitus when she was 12 years old. After not taking care of herself in her teen years, she had been doing much better until recently. Though she is following all her doctor's advice, her diabetes is currently not well controlled.

What is the cause of her diabetes?

_____

_____

b. How is the immune system involved?

_____

_____

_____

c. It has been suggested that Maria have a pancreas transplant to relieve her symptoms. If she accepts this treatment option, how might her immune system continue to be a problem?

_____

_____

_____

d. What kind of drugs may she have to take after the transplant to prevent problems?

_____

_____

_____

REVIEW QUESTIONS

Multiple Choice

1. Lymphocytes are selected for their ability to:
   a. recognize self-antigens
   b. tolerate self-antigens
   c. produce T-cells
   d. both a and b

2. Mounting an excessive immune response to a harmless antigen is called a(n):
   a. autoimmune disorder
   b. allergy
   c. immunodeficiency
   d. AIDS infection

3. Which of the following is an innate immune cell?
   a. neutrophil
   b. memory cell
   c. helper T cell
   d. plasma cell

4. Lymphocytes are activated by binding with antigens on:
   a. bacteria
   b. antigen-displaying cells
   c. viruses
   d. lymph nodes

5. Innate immunity is not stimulated by foreign antigens.
   a. true
   b. false
   c. it depends
   d. all of the above

6. Fever and inflammation are both part of what kind of immunity?
   a. auto
   b. adaptive
   c. acquired
   d. innate

7. Which of the following is an autoimmune disorder?
   a. leukemia
   b. AIDS
   c. lupus
   d. allergies

8. Which of the following drugs are not useful in treating rheumatoid arthritis even though they are anti-inflammatory?
   a. DMARDs
   b. BRMs
   c. NSAIDs
   d. chemotherapy

9. Which of the following is not a symptom of leukemia?
   a. bruising
   b. anemia
   c. weight gain
   d. increased infections

Short Answer

1. List the regions of the body containing many lymph nodes.

   _____

   _____

   _____

2. Trace the circulation of lymph from the cardiovascular system through the lymphatic system and back to the cardiovascular system.

   _____

   _____

   _____

REVIEW QUESTIONS

3. List four types of cells and their functions in immunity.

_____

_____

_____

4. Explain the differences between innate and adaptive immunity.

_____

_____

_____

5. What is atopic march? Why is it so dangerous?

_____

_____

_____

6. HIV is not the same as AIDS. Explain.

_____

_____

_____

7. Explain the categories of leukemia.

_____

_____

_____

Suggested Activities

1. Draw a flowchart of innate and adaptive immunity and their interactions.

2. Form a group of students and role-play parts of the immune system. Assign some to be macrophages, others to be NK cells, and others to be B and T lymphocytes. Describe the process of fighting off a pathogen as per your role.

3. Using the Internet, do a search of autoimmune disorders. How many can you find? What tissues can be attacked by your immune system?

CAREER CONNECTIONS

Now that you have read this chapter, here is a list of related professions you may be interested in investigating for a future career:

- Nuclear Medicine

- Pharmacy

Research each profession and report on the following:

1. Profession description to include job responsibilities
2. Educational requirements
3. Job opportunities
4. Opportunities outside of the hospital setting
5. Salary range
6. Licensure and continuing education requirements

ANATOMY, PHYSIOLOGY, AND DISEASE IN ACTION

Working in groups of four, enlarge the diagram of the inflammatory process (Figure 14-5) on tag board or chart paper. Use pictures/images taken from magazines and/or the Internet to illustrate the steps of the complex inflammatory process. Explain the rationale for the choice of picture or image.

15

The Gastrointestinal System
Fuel for the Trip

So far, we have discussed a variety of body systems and learned how they are put together and how they function. All these systems need to function together to create a smooth-running machine. But just like a Ferrari, no matter how well it is designed nor how precisely it is put together, the body cannot function without fuel. This chapter focuses on the digestive, or **gastrointestinal (GI)**, system and how it:

- Takes in (ingests) raw material
- Breaks it down (digests) both physically and chemically to usable elements
- Absorbs those elements
- Eliminates what isn't usable

These processes are accomplished through an amazing array of main and accessory organs and substances. Here is a concept to ponder as we journey through the digestive system: The food that enters your mouth, travels through your digestive system, and is eventually eliminated is never once *inside* your body! It remains in a tubelike "highway," with materials contained within the food exiting the highway ramps in specific areas!

gastrointestinal (GI) system Body system that includes the oral cavity, pharynx, stomach, esophagus, small and large intestines, and the accessory organs of the liver, gallbladder, and pancreas. Its function is to digest food and remove undigested food from the body. Also known as the gastrointestinal tract, digestive system, or digestive tract.

LEARNING OUTCOMES

Upon completion of your journey through this chapter, you will be able to:

- Locate and describe the functions of the organs of the digestive system
- Locate and describe the functions of the accessory organs for digestion
- Differentiate between ingestion and digestion and between chemical and mechanical processing of food
- Describe the journey of a bolus of food from the mouth to the anus
- Discuss the structure of the tooth
- Describe the various enzymes and chemicals needed for digestion
- Describe common disorders of the gastrointestinal system

Pronunciation Guide

Correct pronunciation is important in any journey so that you and others are completely understood. Here is a "see and say" Pronunciation Guide for the more difficult terms to pronounce in this chapter. Please note that pronunciations given are referenced to medical dictionaries, and regional variations may exist.

adventitia (ADD ven TISH ee ah)
alimentary tract (AL ah MEN tair ee)
anus (AY nus)
appendicitis (ah PEN dih SIGH tiss)
appendix (ah PEN dicks)
bolus (BOW lus)
cecum (SEE kum)
cementum (see MEN tum)
cheilitis (kye LYE tiss)
cholecystitis (KOH lee siss TYE tiss)
cholecystokinin (KOH lee SISS toh KINE en)
cholelithiasis (KOH lee lih THIGH ah sus)
chyle (KILE)
chyme (KIME)
deciduous (dee SID you us)
defecation (def eh KAY shun)
duodenum (DOO oh DEE num)
emulsification (ee MULL sih fih KAY shun)
epiglottis (ep ih GLOT iss)
esophagus (eh SOFF ah gus)
frenulum (FREN you lum)
fundus (FUN dus)
gastrin (GAS trin)
gingivae (JIN jih vah)
hepatic duct (heh PAA tic)
ilium (ILL ee um)
jejunum (jee JOO num)

labia (LAY bee ah)
lacteal (LACK tee al)
leukoplakia (loo coe PLAY kee ah)
mastication (MASS tih CAY shun)
palates (PAL ats)
pancreas (PAN kree ass)
pancreatitis (PAN kree ah TYE tiss)
parotid salivary gland (pah RAH tid SAL ih vair ee)
periodontal (PER ee oh DON tal)
peristalsis (per ih STALL sis)
pharyngoesophageal sphincter
  (fair ING goh es SOFF uh jeel)
pharynx (FAIR inks)
plicae circulares (PLY kay sir cue LAIR es)
ptyalin (TIE uh lin)
pyloric sphincter (pye LOR ik SFINK ter)
pylorus (pye LOR us)
rugae (ROO gay)
serosa (seh ROSE ah)
sublingual salivary glands
  (sub LIN gwall SAL ih VAIR ee)
submandibular salivary glands
  (SUB man dib you lar SAL ih VAIR ee)
uvula (YEW view lah)
villi (VILL eye)

SYSTEM OVERVIEW

alimentary tract *(al ah MEN tar ee)* Alternate name for the gastrointestinal system.

alimentary canal Alternate name for the gastrointestinal system.

GI tract Alternate name for the gastrointestinal system.

anus *(AYE nus)* External opening of rectum, located between the buttocks. The external anal sphincter is under voluntary control. The perianal area is around the anus.

The digestive tract (often called the **alimentary tract, alimentary canal,** or **GI tract**) is an approximately 30-foot muscular tube or tunnel-like structure that contains the organs of the digestive system. This tube begins at the mouth and ends at the **anus.** Between these two points are the pharynx, esophagus, stomach, and small and large intestines. In addition, accessory organs (such as teeth, tongue, salivary glands, liver, pancreas, and gallbladder) are necessary for processing materials into usable substances. Refer to **FIGURE 15-1** ▲ as we journey through the digestive system.

The components of the digestive system work together to perform the following general steps:

1. Ingestion
2. Mastication
3. Digestion
4. Secretion
5. Absorption
6. Excretion (defecation)

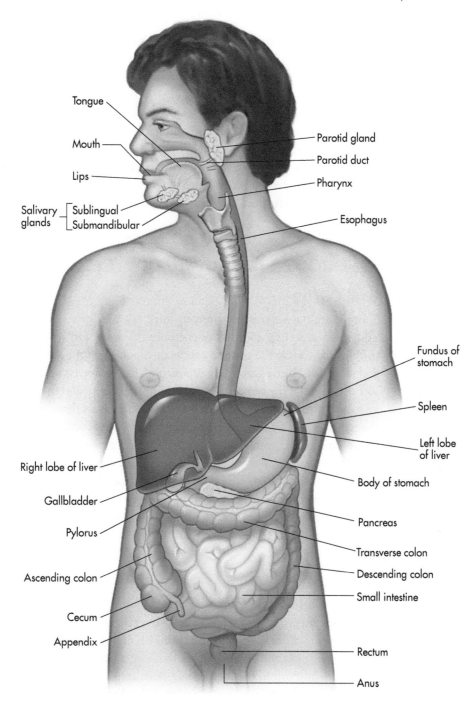

FIGURE 15-1 ▲ The digestive system.

Food first enters the mouth, an activity called **ingestion**. Once food is ingested, the tongue and teeth work together to mechanically process the food by physically breaking it down. The chewing action is called **mastication**.

ingestion Process of taking in material (particularly food).

mastication *(MASS tih CAY shun)* Process of chewing, during which the teeth and tongue together tear, crush, and grind food. This is part of the process of mechanical digestion.

digestion Process of mechanically and chemically breaking food down into nutrients that can be used by the body.

defecation *(def eh CAY shun)* Process by which undigested food fiber and water are removed from the body in the act of a bowel movement.

buccal cavity *(BUCK al)* Alternate name for mouth (oral cavity).

labia *(LAY bee ah)* Alternate name for lips.

hard palate The anterior part of the palate (the roof of the mouth) supported by the maxillary and palatine bones.

soft palate A musculomembranous fold that partly separates the mouth and the pharynx; the posterior roof of the mouth. It is elevated during swallowing to block the nasopharynx.

tongue Large muscle that fills the oral cavity and assists with eating and talking. It contains taste buds and receptors for the sense of taste.

uvula *(YOO vyuh luh)* Soft lymphoid structure dangling from the soft palate that acts as a boundary between the oral cavity and pharynx.

pharynx *(FAR inks)* The throat; contains the passageways for food and for inhaled and exhaled air.

ingest To take in material (particularly food).

bolus *(BOW lus)* A mass of masticated food.

frenulum *(FREN you lum)* Structure that attaches the lower side of the tongue to the gum.

parotid salivary gland *(pah RAH tid SAL ih vair ee)* Gland that secretes saliva that helps to lubricate food so that it is easier to chew and swallow.

This mechanical mixing process also continues in the muscular motions of the digestive tract, as you will soon see. **Digestion** is the chemical process of breaking down food into small molecules. This is necessary so nutrients can be absorbed by the lining of the digestive tract.

The *secretion* of acids, buffers, enzymes, and water aids in the breakdown of food. Once the food is broken down both physically and chemically in the intestine, it is ready for absorption into the blood and lymph. Finally, waste products and unusable materials are prepared for *excretion* and are eliminated by the body through **defecation**.

Now that you have a general idea of what's going on, let's begin the journey through the digestive system from beginning to end as if we were a slice of double cheese, pepperoni pizza!

THE MOUTH AND ORAL CAVITY

Oral Cavity

Your mouth (oral cavity) is a mucous-lined opening, also called the **buccal cavity**. Your lips, or **labia,** act as a door to this chamber. The **hard** and **soft palates** create the roof of the chamber, while the **tongue** acts as the floor. The tongue's base (area of attachment) and the **uvula** ("little grape"), that punching bag–shaped object dangling down from the soft palate, act as the boundary between the oral cavity and the next part of the digestive system, the **pharynx.** As we discovered in our travels through the respiratory system, the uvula aids in swallowing because it helps direct food toward the pharynx and helps block food from coming out your nose! There is a pair of lingual tonsils back there too. Although they aren't important for digestion, the tonsils help in fighting infection as part of the lymphatic system. The sides of the cavity are created by your cheeks. Your mouth and oral cavity region receive, or **ingest,** food. The food is tasted, mechanically broken down into smaller pieces, and chemically broken down to some degree. Liquid is added to make it easier to swallow. See **FIGURE 15-2** ▲ to view the oral cavity.

Tongue

Would you believe your tongue is actually a skeletal muscle that performs many duties? It provides taste stimuli to your brain via the taste buds on its surface, senses temperature and texture (as does the rest of your mouth), manipulates food while chewing, and aids in swallowing. As the tongue moves the food around in the oral cavity, saliva is added to moisten and soften the food, while teeth continue to crush the food until it reaches the right consistency. The tongue pushes the food into a ball-like mass called a **bolus** so it can be passed on to the pharynx. If you can push that bolus into the pharynx with your tongue, why don't you swallow your tongue too? A membrane under your tongue, called the lingual (pertains to tongue) **frenulum,** which you can see when you lift up your tongue, prevents this from happening. Not only is the frenulum important for swallowing, but it also aids in proper speaking. An abnormally short frenulum prevents clear speech—hence the term "tongue-tied!"

Salivary Glands

As you can see in **FIGURE 15-3** ▲, there are three pairs of salivary glands, all controlled by the autonomic nervous system. A large **parotid salivary gland** is found slightly inferior and anterior to each ear. These are the ones that swell up and make you look

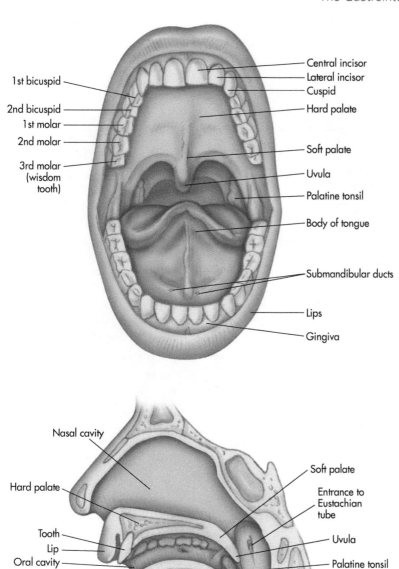

1st bicuspid

2nd bicuspid

1st molar

2nd molar

3rd molar (wisdom tooth)

Central incisor

Lateral incisor

Cuspid

Hard palate

Soft palate

Uvula

Palatine tonsil

Body of tongue

Submandibular ducts

Lips

Gingiva

Nasal cavity

Hard palate

Tooth

Lip

Oral cavity

Tongue

Tooth

Gingiva

Root of tongue

Soft palate

Entrance to Eustachian tube

Uvula

Palatine tonsil

Pharynx

Lingual tonsil

FIGURE 15-2 ▲ The mouth and oral cavity.

like a chipmunk when you get the mumps. Mumps were widespread occurrences when the authors were youngsters before vaccination for it was required. However, recent small outbreaks in the United States are believed to be a result of children not being vaccinated against the mumps. The ducts from these glands empty into the upper portion of the oral cavity. The smallest of the salivary glands, the **sublingual salivary glands,** are located under the tongue. The **submandibular salivary glands** are located on both sides along the inner surfaces of the mandible, or lower jaw.

sublingual salivary glands
(sub LING will SAL eh vair ee)
Smallest of the salivary glands, found between the tongue and the mandible, one on each side.

submandibular salivary glands
(sub MAN dib you lair SAL eh vair ee)
Salivary glands beneath the mandible or jaw.

FIGURE 15-3 ▲
The salivary glands.

enzyme *(IN zyme)* Molecules that speed up the rate of chemical reactions in cells. Enzymes are particularly important in the breakdown and synthesis of biological molecules.

amylase *(AM ih lace)* Salivary enzyme that begins the breakdown of carbohydrates such as starches.

ptyalin *(TYE ih lin)* A specific salivary amylase that converts starches to simple sugars.

deciduous teeth *(dee SID you us)* Teeth that erupt during childhood from age 6 months to 2 years. Also called the milk teeth, baby teeth, or primary teeth.

primary teeth See deciduous teeth.

On average, these glands collectively produce *1 to 1.5 liters of saliva daily!* Small amounts of saliva are continuously produced to keep your mouth moist, but once you start eating or even think about eating, look out! The flood gates open! Although saliva is almost totally water (99.4%), it also contains some antibodies, buffers, ions, waste products, and **enzymes.** (Remember enzymes from Chapter 3?) Enzymes are formed by cells. They are biological catalysts whose job is to speed up chemical reactions. Salivary **amylase** is a general term for the digestive enzymes that speed up the chemical activity that breaks down carbohydrates, such as starches, into smaller molecules, such as glucose, that are more easily absorbed by the digestive tract once they get there. So, before you even swallow a bite of pizza, amylase is breaking down the starch in the crust for digestion. **Ptyalin** is a specific salivary amylase that converts starches to simple sugars. Saliva plays an important role even *after* you eat. As the saliva is continuously secreted in small amounts, it cleans the oral surfaces and also aids in reducing the amount of bacteria that grows in your mouth. Just remember, that action is *not* a substitute for brushing your teeth!

Teeth

The final important components of the mechanical aspect of digestion in the oral cavity are the teeth. It is unfortunate that we get only two sets of them in a lifetime.

The first set of teeth is called baby teeth, or more properly, **deciduous** or **primary** teeth. Like the leaves on a deciduous tree, they fall away in time. Beginning at around 6 months of age, they start to appear, beginning with the lower central incisors, and all 20 are usually in place by 2 1/2 years of age. Between the ages of 6 and 12 years the Tooth Fairy is kept busy as these teeth are pushed out and replaced by the 32 larger **permanent teeth.** The exception to this is the **wisdom teeth,** the four molars in the back, which may not appear until an individual is as old as 21 years.

Not all teeth are the same, as you can see by their shapes and locations. Each has special responsibilities. Look at **FIGURE 15-4** ▲ as we discuss the various types of teeth. The first tooth type is the **incisor,** located at the front of your mouth. Incisors are blade-shaped teeth used to cut food. **Canine teeth** are for holding, tearing, or slashing food. Canine teeth are also known as eyeteeth, or **cuspids,** and are located next to the incisors. Next in line are the **bicuspids,** or premolars, which are transitional teeth. **Molars** are the final type of teeth and have flattened tops. Both the bicuspids and molars are responsible for crushing and grinding.

Regardless of its type, the structure of each tooth is pretty much the same. As you can see in Figure 15-4, each tooth has a **crown, neck,** and **root.** The *crown* is the visible part of the tooth. It is covered by the hardest biologically manufactured substance in the body, **enamel.** The neck is a transitional section that leads to the root.

Internally, most teeth are made up of a mineralized, bonelike substance called **dentin.** The next internal layer is a connective tissue called **pulp,** which is located in the **pulp cavity.** The pulp cavity also contains blood vessels and nerves that provide nutrients and sensations. The nerves and blood vessels get to the pulp cavity via the infamous root canal.

The root is nestled in a bony socket and is held in place by fibers of the **periodontal ligament.** In addition, **cementum** (a soft version of bone) covers the dentin of the root, aiding in securing the periodontal ligament. Healthy gums, or **gingiva,** also help to hold the teeth in place. Epithelial cells form a tight seal around the tooth to prevent bacteria from coming into contact with the tooth's cementum.

Clinical Application

SUBLINGUAL MEDICATION

Go to a mirror and open your mouth. Lift your tongue, and you will notice that there are blood vessels everywhere just barely underneath the surface. This sublingual (under the tongue) blood vessel network can readily absorb certain drugs. Rapid absorption into the blood system is vital in some cases, such as for those patients who need the drug nitroglycerin to treat angina quickly. Angina is caused by insufficient blood flow to the heart and consequently not enough oxygen to coronary tissues. Nitroglycerin improves coronary blood flow and in most cases temporarily relieves angina.

permanent teeth The 32 teeth that develop as the second dentition and replace the deciduous teeth.

wisdom teeth The last four molars that appear usually in the late teens.

incisors (*in SIGH zers*) Chisel-shaped teeth in the middle of the dental arch that cut and tear food on their incisal surface. There are eight incisors, four in the maxilla, and four in the mandible.

canine teeth Long, pointed teeth located between the incisors and the premolars. The canines sink deeply into food to hold it. There are four canines: two in the maxilla and two in the mandible. Also known as cuspids (because they have one large, pointed cusp) or eyeteeth.

cuspids (*KUS pidz*) Canine teeth.

bicuspid tooth (*by KUS pid*) A permanent, premolar tooth. There are eight premolars, two in each quadrant (four in each jaw) between the canines and molars. Premolars have two or three cusps on the occlusal surface.

molars The largest teeth, located posterior to the premolars. They crush and grind food on their large, flat, occlusal surfaces.

crown White part of the tooth that is visible above the gum line.

neck The constricted area that connects the crown of a tooth to the root of a tooth.

root Part of the tooth that is hidden below the gum line. The premolars have one or more roots. The molars have multiple roots.

enamel Glossy, thick white layer that covers the crown of the tooth. Enamel is the hardest substance in the body.

dentin Hard layer of tooth just beneath the enamel layer.

pulp The internal layer of connective tissue located in the pulp cavity of a tooth.

pulp cavity Cavity that contains pulp, blood vessels, and nerves that provide nutrients and sensations.

periodontal ligament Fibers that hold the root of the tooth in place.

cementum (*see MEN tum*) Continuous layer of bonelike connective tissue that covers the dentin layer of the tooth and roots below the gum line. It begins at the gum line where the enamel stops. It anchors one side of the periodontal ligaments.

Deciduous (baby) teeth

Central incisors (7.5 mo)
Lateral incisor (9 mo)
Cuspid (18 mo)
Primary 1st molar (14 mo)
Primary 2nd molar (24 mo)
Upper teeth

Primary 2nd molar (20 mo)
Lower teeth
Primary 1st molar (12 mo)
Cuspid (16 mo)
Lateral incisor (7 mo)
Central incisor (6 mo)

Permanent (adult) teeth

Central incisor (7–8 yr)
Lateral incisor (8–9 yr)
Cuspid (11–12 yr)
1st Premolar (10–11 yr)
2nd Premolar (10–12 yr)
1st Molar (6–7 yr)
Hard palate
2nd Molar (12–13 yr)
Upper dental arch
3rd Molar or wisdom tooth (17–21 yr)

3rd Molar or wisdom tooth (17-21 yr)
2nd Molar (11–13 yr)
Lower dental arch
1st Molar (6–7 yr)
2nd Premolar (11–12 yr)
1st Premolar (10–12 yr)
Cuspid (9–10 yr)
Lateral incisor (7–8 yr)
Central incisor (6–7 yr)

Enamel
Dentin
Pulp cavity
Crown
Gingiva
Neck
Periodontal ligament
Cementum
Root
Root canal
Apical foramen
Branches of blood vessels and nerve

Upper jaw

Lower jaw

Incisors Cuspids (canines) Bicuspids (premolars) Molars

FIGURE 15-4 ▲ Types, location, and structures of teeth.

Pathology Connection

ORAL DISORDERS

We have all experienced some form of gastrointestinal (GI) disorder at some time in our lives. In fact, GI problems are some of the most common problems in the health care field. That is because the causes of these disorders are so varied. These conditions may have etiologies based on inherited traits, behavioral issues, structural abnormalities, eating habits, lifestyles, or even prescribed medications used to treat other problems! Let's begin at the entrance of the GI system, your mouth.

Dental caries (cavities) are a result of microorganisms attacking tooth enamel. Bacteria, diets rich in carbohydrates, poor dental hygiene, and the lack of regular visits to the dentist all work together to create a soft sticky substance called **dental plaque,** which is a great hideout for the bacteria that create the acid that attacks the surface of teeth. Once a cavity forms, it must be cleaned out and filled to protect the tooth. If the cavity is ignored, further destruction of the tooth will occur, with potentially major problems that may require tooth removal or surgical intervention, produce systemic infection, or even damage heart valves. Proper dental care and fluoride (found in most municipal water systems and toothpaste) aid tremendously in cavity prevention.

Periodontal disease is a wider problem attributed to the same causative agents as dental caries and sometimes to an inadequate diet. Not only can the teeth be affected, but gums and the supportive structures for your teeth can also be involved. Periodontal disease is the major cause of tooth loss in the adult population. As the plaque builds up at the gum line, the gums become inflamed, causing a condition called **gingivitis** that can cause bleeding at the affected site(s).

Your lips and oral region are also susceptible to cancer. The main causative agents are tobacco products and excessive sun exposure. Consumption of alcohol with tobacco products appears to raise the chances of the development of cancer, not only in the oral region but the throat, stomach, and bladder as well. It is believed that alcohol acts as a solvent to dissolve the carcinogenic substances in tobacco, which are more readily absorbed by the highly vascularized tissues in the mouth. **Leukoplakia** is a precancerous condition usually attributed to the use of chewing tobacco or snuff. The affected areas exhibit a white patch of tissue. The use of chewing tobacco can also increase the incidence of cavities due to the amount of sugar normally used in the processing of chewing tobacco. Not all sores or ulcers in the mouth are cancerous. Poor-fitting dentures can lead to a condition known as **stomatitis** that inflames areas of oral mucosa. **Canker sores (aphthous stomatitis)** are small ulcers in your mouth and are sometimes caused by eating certain foods, although their cause is often unknown. **Cheilitis,** which is cracking and associated inflammation of the lips and corners of the mouth, is not caused by cancer, but rather can be traced to infections, allergies, or even nutritional deficiency.

gingiva The tissue that surrounds the necks of the teeth and covers the alveolar processes of the maxilla and mandible; the gums.

dental caries Holes or cavities created by bacteria due to poor oral hygiene.

dental plaque A biofilm that accumulates and grows on the crowns of teeth.

periodontal disease Gum disease.

gingivitis Inflammation of the gums characterized by redness, swelling, and tendency to bleed.

leukoplakia *(LOO koh PLAY kee ah)* White patches in the mouth commonly seen in snuff and chewing tobacco users that is a precursor to oral cancer.

stomatitis *(STOH mah TYE tis)* An inflammation of the mouth that can include the lips, tongue, and mucous membranes.

canker sores (aphthous stomatitis) An ulcer of the oral mucosa, usually less than 0.5 cm in diameter.

cheilitis *(ky LIE tiss)* Inflammation of the lips that includes redness and fissures.

nasopharynx *(NAY zoh FAR inks)* Uppermost portion of the throat where the posterior nares unite. The nasopharynx contains the opening for the eustachian tubes and the adenoids.

oropharynx *(OR oh FAR inks)* Middle portion of the throat just behind the oral cavity. It begins at the level of the soft palate and ends at the epiglottis.

PHARYNX

The pharynx brings us to the next part of the journey. It is a common passageway not only for food but also for water and air. It has three parts: the nasopharynx, the oropharynx, and the laryngopharynx. The **nasopharynx** is primarily part of the respiratory system. The **oropharynx** and the **laryngopharynx** serve double duty as a passageway for food and water and for air. During swallowing, passageways to the nasal and respiratory regions are protected from the accidental introduction of food and liquids. The nasopharynx is blocked by the soft palate, and a flap of tissue called the **epiglottis,** a part of the larynx, covers the airway to the lungs as the larynx rises during swallowing. These actions force the food to enter the only possible route, the esophagus.

laryngopharynx *(lah RING goh FAR inks)* The most inferior portion of the pharynx.

epiglottis *(EP ih GLAW tiss)* Lid-like structure that seals off the larynx, so that swallowed food goes into the esophagus.

esophagus *(eh SOFF ah gus)* Flexible, muscular tube that moves food from the pharynx to the stomach.

pharyngoesophageal sphincter *(fah RING go ee SOFF eh JEE al)* Muscular ring at the beginning of the esophagus.

peristalsis *(per ih STALL sis)* Contractions of the smooth muscle of the gastrointestinal tract that propel food through it.

ESOPHAGUS

The **esophagus** is approximately 10 inches (25 centimeters) long and is responsible for transporting food from the pharynx to the stomach. It extends from the pharynx, through the thoracic cavity and diaphragm, to the stomach, which is located in the peritoneal cavity (see **FIGURE 15-5** ▲).

The esophagus is normally a collapsed tube, much like a deflated balloon, until a bolus of food is swallowed. As this bolus moves to the esophagus, a muscular ring at the beginning of this structure, known as the **pharyngoesophageal sphincter,** relaxes. This is like opening the door to the esophagus so food can enter. We can't rely on gravity to move food through the esophagus, so the muscles of the esophagus begin rhythmic contractions that work the food down to the stomach. This rhythmic wavelike muscular contraction is known as **peristalsis**. Once the bolus reaches the end of the esophagus, a

FIGURE 15-5 ▲ The movement of a bolus of food from the mouth to the stomach via the esophagus.

second door must be opened to allow entry to the stomach. This is the **lower esophageal sphincter,** or **LES,** also known as the **cardiac sphincter.** It relaxes to let food into the stomach and then closes to prevent acidic gastric juices from squirting up into the esophagus. Heartburn (pyrosis) occurs if that door inadvertently opens. Heartburn is the term used, even though it has nothing to do with the heart, but the pain caused by this condition appears to many to be coming from the region where the heart is located.

The esophagus also helps move the bolus by excreting mucus so its walls are slippery. The esophageal walls are lined with stratified squamous epithelium, which makes the esophagus resistant to abrasion, temperature extremes, and irritation by chemicals.

The whole process of swallowing food takes about 9 seconds on average. Dry or "sticky" food may take longer with repeated attempts to work it down. (Ever try to swallow too large a bite of a peanut butter sandwich and have it stick, pounding on the LES door?) Fluids take only a few seconds to get to the stomach.

THE WALLS OF THE ALIMENTARY CANAL

It is interesting to note that the same four basic tissue types form the wall of the entire alimentary canal from the esophagus onward (see FIGURE 15-6 ▲). The innermost layer that lines the lumen of the canal is the **mucosa** (a mucous membrane just like in the respiratory system). This layer is composed mostly of stratified squamous epithelium with some connective tissue and a thin smooth muscle layer surrounding it. The mucosa also possesses cells that secrete digestive enzymes to break down foodstuffs and **goblet cells** that secrete mucus for lubrication.

The **submucosa** is the next layer and is composed of connective tissue. This layer contains blood and lymph vessels, lymph nodes (called **Peyer's patches,** similar to tonsils), and nerve endings. The next layer is the **muscularis externa** and is composed of two layers of smooth muscle. The innermost layer encircles the canal, whereas the outer layer is longitudinal in nature so it lies in the direction of the canal. There is an additional third layer of oblique smooth muscle, but it is found only surrounding the stomach.

The outermost layer is the **serosa,** composed of a single thin layer of flat, serous, fluid-producing cells supported by connective tissue. For most of the canal, the serosa is the **visceral peritoneum.** The peritoneum is a serous membrane in the abdominopelvic cavity. Like all serous membranes, it has two layers. The visceral peritoneum covers the organs, and the parietal peritoneum lines the wall of the abdominopelvic cavity. Between the layers is a fluid-filled potential space called the **peritoneal cavity.** This fluid is important both for keeping the outer surface of the organs moist and allowing friction-free movement of the digestive organs against the abdomenopelvic cavity. Some abdominopelvic organs such as the urinary bladder and the duodenum are not surrounded by peritoneum and are called **retroperitoneal organs.** The esophagus differs in that it possesses only a loose layer of connective tissue called the **adventitia.** (This shouldn't come as any great shock because the esophagus is not in the abdominopelvic cavity!)

lower esophageal sphincter (LES) *(eh SOFF eh JEE al SFINGK ter)* Ringed muscle leading into the stomach.

cardiac sphincter *(SFINGK ter)* Ring-shaped muscle also known as the lower esophageal sphincter (LES) that allows food into the stomach.

mucosa *(myoo KOH suh)* Lining throughout the gastrointestinal system that consists of a mucous membrane that produces mucus and an underlying smooth muscle layer that contracts to move food.

goblet cells Specialized cells that secrete mucus.

submucosa *(SUB myoo KOH suh)* Layer of connective tissue under a mucous membrane.

Peyer's patches *(PIE erz)* Lymph nodes found in the submucosa of the alimentary canal.

muscularis externa The outside muscular layer of an organ or tubule.

serosa *(see ROH sah)* A serous membrane.

visceral peritoneum *(VIS er al PAIR ih TOE nee um)* Serous membrane lining the abdominal cavity.

peritoneal cavity The potential space between the parietal peritoneum, which lines the abdominal wall, and the visceral peritoneum, which forms the surface layer of the visceral organs. It contains serous fluid.

retroperitoneal organs Organs behind the peritoneum and outside the peritoneal cavity.

adventitia *(add ven TISH ah)* The outermost covering of a structure or organ.

FIGURE 15-6 ▲
Basic tissue types of the alimentary canal.

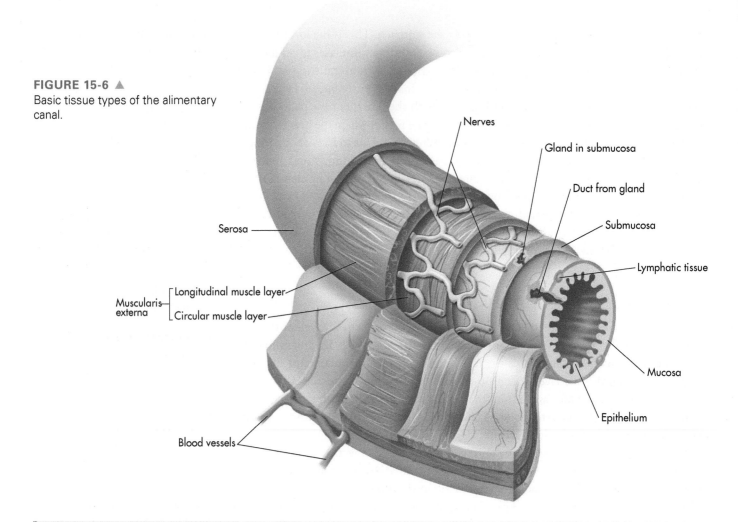

TEST YOUR KNOWLEDGE 15-1

Choose the best answer:

1. The digestive tract is also called the:
   a. elementary canal
   b. integumentary canal
   c. alimentary canal
   d. panama canal

2. A ball-like mass of food is called a:
   a. bolus
   b. wad
   c. chyme
   d. mastion

3. What is the punching bag–shaped object dangling from the soft palate?
   a. tonsil
   b. uvula
   c. labia
   d. incisor

4. Which of the following is *not* a salivary gland?
   a. parotid
   b. sublingual
   c. submandibular
   d. substernal

Complete the following:

5. Externally, the three main structural parts of a tooth are the _____, _____, and _____.

6. _____ are a result of microorganisms attacking tooth enamel.

7. The consumption of _____ and _____ products appears to increase the chances of oral, throat, and stomach cancers.

STOMACH

The stomach is located in the left central region of the abdominal cavity under the diaphragm. This organ is approximately 10 inches (25 centimeters) long with a diameter that varies, depending on how much you eat at any given time. Although the stomach can hold up to 4 liters (about a gallon) when totally filled, it can expand or decrease in diameter thanks to deep, mucous-coated folds in the stomach wall called **rugae** that allow for these size changes. As the stomach receives food from the esophagus, it performs several functions:

- Acts as a temporary holding area for the received food
- Secretes gastric acid and enzymes, which it mixes with the food, causing chemical digestion
- Regulates the rate at which the now partially digested food (a thick, heavy, creamlike liquid—semisolid mixture of food and gastric juices—called **chyme**) enters the small intestine
- Absorbs small amounts of water and substances on a very limited basis (although the stomach does absorb alcohol)

It takes about 4 hours for the stomach to empty after a meal. Liquids and carbohydrates pass through fairly quickly. Protein takes a little more time, and fats take even longer, usually from 4 to 6 hours.

The stomach is divided into four regions. Located near the heart, the **cardiac region** surrounds the lower esophageal sphincter, sometimes referred to as the cardiac sphincter. This location is the reason why indigestion is sometimes referred to as heartburn (see FIGURE 15-7 ▲). The **fundus,** which is lateral and slightly superior to the cardiac region, temporarily holds the food as it first enters the stomach. The **body** is the midportion and largest region of the stomach. The funnel-shaped, terminal end of the stomach is called the **pylorus.** Most of the digestive work of the stomach is performed in the pyloric region. This is also the region where chyme must pass through another door, the **pyloric sphincter,** to travel on to the small intestine. Two other points of interest are the concave curve called the **lesser curvature** and the larger convex curve to the left of the lesser curve called the **greater curvature.**

The muscular action of the stomach works much like a cement mixer and is achieved by the three layers of muscle found in its walls. One layer is longitudinal, one is circular, and the third is oblique in orientation. This arrangement of muscles enables the stomach to churn food as it mixes with gastric juices excreted by **gastric glands** from gastric pits in the columnar epithelial lining of the stomach as well as to work the food toward the pyloric sphincter through the muscle activity, peristalsis. With the combined efforts of muscle and gastric juices, both physical and chemical digestion occur in the stomach.

Gastric juice is a general term for a combination of hydrochloric acid (HCl), pepsinogen, and mucus. The gastric glands produce about 1,500 milliliters of gastric juice each day. Pepsinogen is secreted by the **chief cells,** and HCl is secreted by **parietal cells.** These two cell types have a special relationship in that once pepsinogen makes contact with HCl, the chief digestive enzyme, **pepsin,** is formed. Pepsin is needed to break down proteins (like the ones found in pepperoni). Even though it doesn't actually digest food by itself, HCl does break down connective tissue in meat. The HCl must be very

rugae *(ROO gay)* Deep folds in the gastric mucosa.

chyme *(KIME)* Mixed food and digestive juices in the stomach and small intestine.

cardiac region Region of the stomach where the lower esophageal sphincter also known as the cardiac sphincter is located.

fundus *(FUN dus)* A larger part, base, or body of a hollow organ such as the rounded, most superior part of the stomach.

body Mid point and largest region of the stomach.

pylorus *(pye LOR us)* Narrowing canal of the stomach just before it joins the duodenum. It contains the pyloric sphincter.

pyloric sphincter *(pye LOR ick SFINK ter)* Muscular ring that keeps food in the stomach from entering the duodenum.

lesser curvature The concave curve of the stomach.

greater curvature The large convex curve of the stomach.

gastric glands Located in the stomach, these excrete gastric juices for digestion.

chief cells Specialized cells that secrete pepsinogen.

parietal cells *(pah RYE eh tal)* Specialized cells that secrete hydrochloric acid.

pepsin *(PEP sin)* Digestive enzyme produced by the stomach that breaks down food protein into smaller protein molecules.

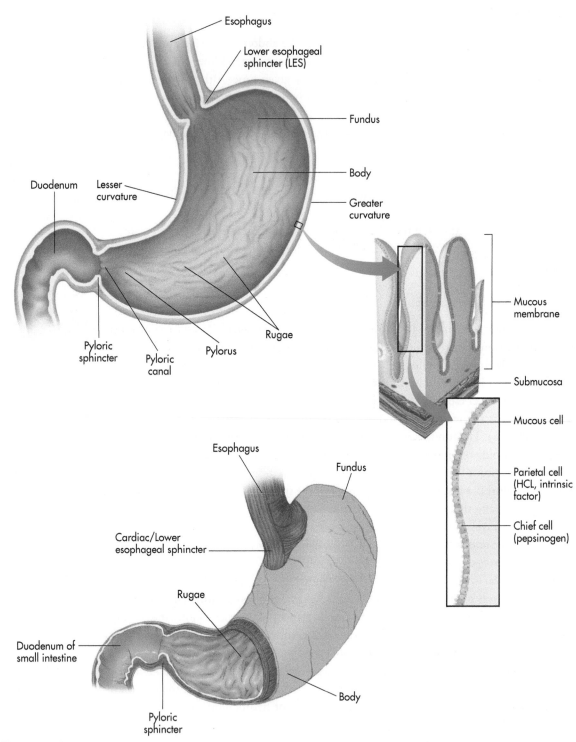

FIGURE 15-7 ▲ The stomach.

strongly acidic to work. Normally, it has a pH of 1.5 to 2. This highly acidic environment plays another important role: killing off most pathogens that enter the stomach.

You may wonder why the stomach doesn't digest itself. A healthy stomach is protected by mucous cells that generate a thick layer of mucus to shield the stomach lining from the effects of HCl. Other specialized cells secrete what is known as **intrinsic factor,** which is needed for absorption of vitamin B$_{12}$. **TABLE 15-1** ■ describes gastric glands and their functions.

intrinsic factor Specialized substance that is needed for the absorption of vitamin B12.

TABLE 15-1 ■ GASTRIC GLANDS AND THEIR FUNCTIONS

DIGESTIVE CELLS	SECRETION TYPE	FUNCTION
Chief cells	Pepsinogen	Begins digestion of protein
Parietal cells	HCl, intrinsic factor	Kills pathogens, activates pepsinogen, breaks down connective tissue in meat
Mucous cells	Alkaline mucus	Protects stomach lining
Endocrine cells	The hormone gastrin	Stimulates gastric gland secretion

The stomach's activity is controlled by the parasympathetic nervous system, particularly the **vagus nerve.** Once the vagus nerve is stimulated, the stomach's motility (churning action) increases, as does the secretory rates of the gastric glands.

The three phases of gastric juice production are illustrated in FIGURE 15-8 ▲. The **cephalic phase** occurs as a result of sensory stimulation such as the sight or smell of food. This sensory input stimulates the parasympathetic nervous system (via the medulla oblongata), and the release of the hormone **gastrin** is increased. Once gastrin travels through the blood and reaches the stomach, gastric gland activity is increased. So, the sight or smell of that pizza literally does get your gastric juices flowing.

This leads us to the **gastric phase,** in which over two-thirds of the gastric juices are secreted as the food moves into the stomach. As the food moves in, the stomach begins to distend. As the stomach distends, it sends signals back to the brain, which fires a reply to the gastric glands to step up their work. As chyme is formed, peristalsis pushes it through the pyloric sphincter to the first part of the small intestine, the **duodenum**.

The entry of the food into the duodenum begins the **intestinal phase** of gastric juice regulation. As the duodenum distends and senses the acidity of chyme, intestinal hormones are released that cause the gastric glands in the stomach to decrease gastric juice production. The brain is also signaled and sends a message to inhibit gastric juice secretion because it is no longer needed now that the food bolus (now called chyme) has left the stomach. Once the chyme begins its movement through the duodenum and on to the rest of the small intestine, those inhibitory responses are halted so gastric juice production can continue once again when a new bolus of food enters the stomach.

The rate of the movement of chyme is very important. If it moves too slowly through the stomach, the rate of nutrient digestion and absorption is decreased, and the acidity of the chyme may cause erosion of the stomach lining. If chyme passes too quickly through the stomach, the food particles may not be sufficiently mixed with gastric juices, leading to insufficient digestion. Chyme that is not given time to be neutralized may cause acidic erosion of the intestinal lining.

vagus nerve *(VAY gus)* Cranial nerve X. Sensation and movement of the throat. Sensory and motor for thoracic and abdominal organs.

cephalic phase The first phase of gastric juice production that is stimulated by the sight or smell of food.

gastrin *(GAS trin)* Hormone produced by the stomach that stimulates the release of hydrochloric acid and pepsinogen in the stomach.

gastric phase The second phase of gastric juice production in which over two thirds of the gastric juices are secreted as the food moves into the stomach.

duodenum *(doo ODD eh num)* First part of the small intestine. It secretes cholecystokinin, a hormone that stimulates the gallbladder and pancreas to release bile and digestive enzymes.

intestinal phase The final phase of gastric juice production in which the production of gastric juice diminishes.

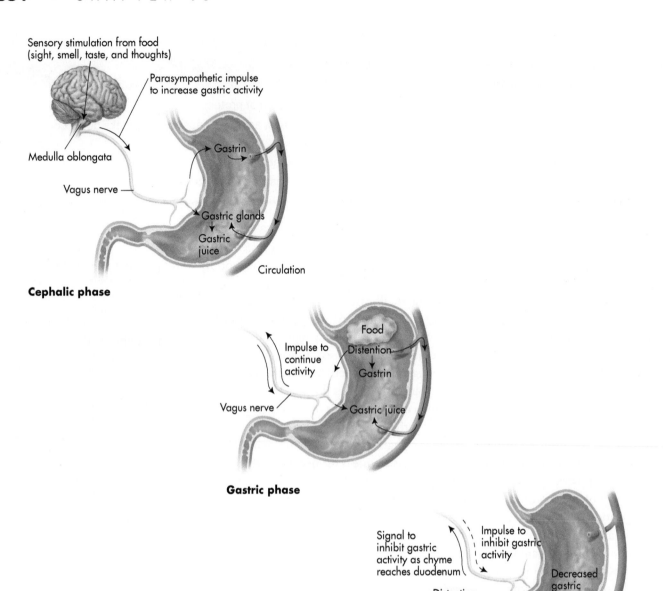

Cephalic phase

Sensory stimulation from food
(sight, smell, taste, and thoughts)

Parasympathetic impulse
to increase gastric activity

Medulla oblongata

Vagus nerve

Gastrin

Gastric glands

Gastric juice

Circulation

Gastric phase

Impulse to
continue
activity

Food

Distention

Gastrin

Vagus nerve

Gastric juice

Intestinal phase

Signal to
inhibit gastric
activity as chyme
reaches duodenum

Impulse to
inhibit gastric
activity

Distention

Chyme

Intestinal hormones

Decreased
gastric
secretions

Inhibit
gastric
activity

FIGURE 15-8 ▲ Phases of gastric secretions.

Clinical Application

PEG TUBE

Patients who are unable to consume nutrients via the normal oral route often
have a permanent feeding tube implanted called a PEG tube (percutaneous endoscopic gastrostomy). This tube is attached at the abdominal wall and the stomach
wall and allows nutrients to be directly injected to the stomach.

Pathology Connection

STOMACH ACID DISORDERS

Of growing concern over the past several years is the condition known as **gastroesophageal reflux disease** (GERD). The lay term for this is heartburn. GERD occurs when acidic stomach contents "squirt" back (acid reflux) through the lower esophageal sphincter and into the esophagus. Because the esophagus does not have the protective mucus barrier like the stomach, repeated episodes of acid reflux can cause inflammation and eventually ulceration of the affected area. Scar tissue can eventually form, causing a narrowing of the esophagus that may impede peristalsis. If left untreated, GERD can lead to esophageal cancer. The reason that GERD has become a major concern recently is due to our society's diet and exercise habits. As a nation, we overeat consistently, making sure that we get our money's worth at every buffet. Instead of walking after stuffing ourselves, we flop down on the sofa or easy chair complaining about "how stuffed" we are. Smoking also may aggravate GERD. So how do we deal with GERD? The quick fix for the burning sensation is the use of antacids and medications that decrease acid production. More important, lifestyle changes may prevent GERD. Changes in diet, including limiting fats, alcohol, caffeine, and chocolate, may be helpful. Lying down after eating should be avoided for approximately 4 hours. This will give the stomach time to empty. Sleeping with your head elevated and avoiding sleeping on your right side also helps to decrease GERD. If you are obese, lose weight. The pressure from abdominal fat helps to push on stomach contents, increasing the chance of acid reflux occurring. Another rapidly spreading, obesity-related disease called metabolic syndrome is covered with diabetes in Chapter 10, "The Endocrine System."

Peptic ulcers are the result of a breakdown of the mucosal membrane found in the esophagus, stomach, or small intestine. About 80% of the peptic ulcers are located in the duodenum and the bulk of the remaining peptic ulcers located in the stomach are called *gastric ulcers*. It was once thought that a high-stress lifestyle was the main cause of ulcer development. Stress is a factor in some cases, but the major offender appears to be the *Helicobacter pylori* (*H. pylori*.) bacterium, which causes the initial erosion of the mucosal lining and leads to the inflammation called **gastritis**. See FIGURE 15-9 ▲.

Other contributing agents can include smoking, heavy and chronic consumption of alcohol, aspirin and other NSAIDs, caffeine, corticosteroids, and other medications.

Duodenal ulcers may also be associated with *H. pylori,* but patients with duodenal ulcers appear to overproduce stomach acid and pepsin. In addition, they seem to respond more to the stimuli of acid secretion as well as have a more rapid rate of gastric emptying. This speeded up process may expose the duodenum to greater acidity. Interestingly, patients with gastric (stomach area) ulcers have lower than normal gastric acid. It appears that stomach ulcers are either a result of defective gastric mucosa or of a weakened pyloric sphincter that allows bile to squirt back into the stomach.

Please see Figure 15-9, which shows the pathophysiologic causes of GERD and peptic ulcer disease (PUD).

(continued)

gastroesophageal reflux disease (GERD) *(GAS troh ee SAWF ah JEE al)* A combination of symptoms caused by a backflow of gastric contents into the esophagus.

peptic ulcer An ulcer occurring in the lower end of the esophagus, in the stomach, or in the duodenum.

gastritis *(gas TRY tis)* An acute or chronic inflammation of the stomach's lining.

duodenal ulcers An open ulcer on the mucosa of the first portion of the duodenum, most often the result of infection with Helicobacter pylori. It is the most common form of peptic ulcer.

Pathology Connection (continued)

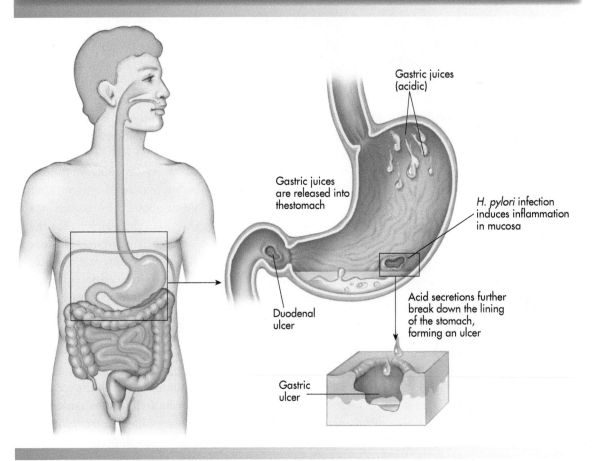

Gastric juices (acidic)

Gastric juices are released into the stomach

H. pylori infection induces inflammation in mucosa

Duodenal ulcer

Acid secretions further break down the lining of the stomach, forming an ulcer

Gastric ulcer

FIGURE 15-9 ▲
Mechanisms of peptic ulcers and GERD.
(Source: Juan Gaertner/ Shutterstock.com.)

Peptic ulcer

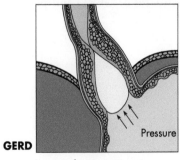

GERD

Pressure

Increased intragastric pressure

Incompetent lower esophageal sphincter

Reflux bolus

Transient lower esophageal sphincter relaxation

SMALL INTESTINE

The small intestine, located in the central and lower abdominal cavity between the stomach and large intestine, is *the* major organ of digestion. It is where most food is digested (see **FIGURE 15-10** ▲). The small intestine is small in diameter, but not in length. Beginning at the pyloric sphincter, the small intestine is the longest section of the alimentary canal, with a length up to 20 feet (up to 6 meters) and a diameter ranging from 4 centimeters where it connects with the stomach to 2.5 centimeters where it meets the large intestine.

The walls of the small intestine secrete several digestive enzymes important for the final stages of chemical digestion and two hormones that stimulate the pancreas and gallbladder to act and that control stomach activity.

In the small intestine, almost 80% of the absorption of usable nutrients takes place when chyme comes in contact with the mucosal walls. Amino acids, fatty acids, ions, simple sugars, vitamins, and water are all absorbed from here into the bloodstream and then on to the body's cells. Some of the remaining 20% was already absorbed by the stomach, with the rest being absorbed by the large intestine. Any residue that cannot be utilized is sent on to the large intestine for removal from the body.

There are three regions of the small intestine. The **duodenum** is approximately 25 to 30 centimeters (10 to 12 inches) long and is located near the head of the **pancreas**. The duodenum gets its name from *duo* (two), and *denum* (ten), which equal 12, the number of finger widths long that this organ is (10 inches)!

The **jejunum** is the middle section and is approximately 2.5 meters (8 feet) long.

The terminal end of the small intestine is the **ileum**. This section (6–12 feet long) attaches to the large intestine at the **ileocecal valve**. (Here is one place where spelling counts. The *ileum* is part of your small intestine. The *ilium* is part of your pelvic girdle. You don't want to get them mixed up!)

duodenum *(doo ODD eh num)* First part of the small intestine. It secretes cholecystokinin, a hormone that stimulates the gallbladder and pancreas to release bile and digestive enzymes.

pancreas *(PAN kree ass)* A digestive and endocrine organ located in the abdominal cavity that produces digestive enzymes (amylase, lipase, protease, peptidase) and releases them into the duodenum. It also contains the islets of Langerhans (alpha, beta, and delta cells) that produce and secrete the hormones glucagon, insulin, and somatostatin.

jejunum *(jee JOO num)* Second part of the small intestine.

ileum *(ILL ee um)* Third portion of small intestine which is attached to the large intestine.

ileocecal valve The valve that attaches the ileum to the large intestine.

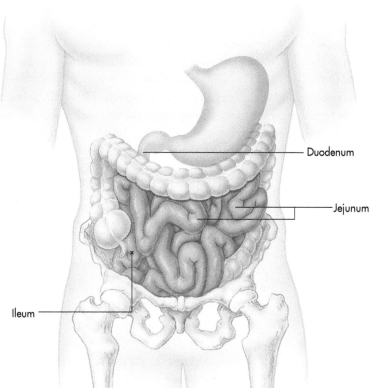

Duodenum

Jejunum

Ileum

FIGURE 15-10 ▲
The small intestine.

gallbladder Small organ that provides bile for digestion.

bile Substance, produced by the liver and stored in the gallbladder, that emulsifies fat.

biliverdin *(bill ih VER din)* Green bile pigment.

bilirubin *(bill ih ROO bin)* A yellow bile pigment formed from the breakdown of old worn out red blood cells.

cholecystokinin (CCK) *(KOH lee SIS toh KINE in)* Hormone released by the duodenum when it receives food from the stomach. It causes the gallbladder to release bile and the pancreas to release its digestive enzymes.

secretin A hormone secreted by the duodenal mucosa that stimulates sodium bicarbonate secretion by the pancreas and bile secretion by the liver. It decreases gastrointestinal peristalsis and motility.

segmentation Division into similar parts.

lactase Enzyme needed for the digestion of double sugars.

maltase Enzyme needed for the digestion of double sugars.

sucrase *(SOO krace)* Enzyme needed for the digestion of double sugars.

disaccharides *(die SAK uh rides)* Two monosaccharides linked together.

The pyloric valve is important in allowing small portions of chyme to enter the first part of the small intestine (duodenum) because the small intestine can process only small amounts of food at a time. At the duodenum, additional secretions are added from the pancreas and gallbladder. The pancreas provides pancreatic juices. The **gallbladder,** a small green organ located on the inferior surface of the liver, provides bile. **Bile,** produced by the liver and stored in the gallbladder, is yellow-brown or yellow-green and contains acids, mucus, fluids, and two pigments, **biliverdin** (verd/o = green) and **bilirubin** (yellow, rubin/o = red). Whoa! If rubin/o = red, why is the pigment yellow? "Rubin" refers to the fact that bilirubin is formed from the breakdown of old, worn-out red blood cells. Bile emulsifies fat—that is, it makes fat able to disperse in water—making the fat found in the cheese of the pizza easier to break down. Pancreatic juice contains enzymes and sodium bicarbonate, which neutralizes the acidic chyme. As chyme enters the duodenum, your gallbladder contracts, sending bile down the cystic duct and into the common bile duct to the duodenum. Gallbladder activity is caused by the hormone **cholecystokinin,** also known as **CCK,** which is also produced by the small intestine. The pancreas is stimulated to secrete as a result of the hormone **secretin,** which is produced by the small intestine. Two types of muscular action occur in the small intestine. **Segmentation** is the muscle action that mixes chyme and digestive juices, working much like a cement mixer. Peristalsis also occurs, moving undigested food remains toward the large intestine. See TABLE 15-2 ■ for the hormones active in the digestive process.

As previously stated, the small intestine also produces digestive enzymes that are needed to complete chemical digestion. These enzymes (and mucus) are produced by exocrine cells. **Lactase, maltase,** and **sucrase** are needed for the digestion of double sugars called **disaccharides** that are contained in starches (such as in the pizza crust). **Peptidase** is needed to digest portions of the protein structure called peptides. **Lipase** is needed for digestion of certain fats. It is interesting to note that the secretion of these substances is mainly due to the presence of chyme in the small intestine. Because of the acidity of chyme, both chemical and mechanical irritation occur. This irritation plus the distention of the intestinal wall causes the localized reflex action that results in the release of the enzymes and the two hormones.

The structure of the wall of the small intestine is rather interesting. The wall possesses circular folds called **plicae circulares** and fingerlike protrusions into the lumen called **villi** (see FIGURE 15-11 ▲). The villi also have outer layers of columnar epithelial cells, which possess microscopic extensions known as **microvilli.** These villi are tightly packed, giving a velvety texture and appearance. The purpose of the microvilli, villi, and circular folds is to provide an incredible increase in the surface area of the small intestine. This area, almost the surface area of a tennis court, increases the efficiency of the absorption of nutrients.

Each villus (singular form of villi) contains a network of capillaries and a lymphatic capillary called a **lacteal.** Intestinal glands are located between villi. The capillaries absorb and transport sugars (the result of carbohydrate digestion) and amino acids (the result of protein

TABLE 15-2 ■ HORMONES IN THE DIGESTIVE PROCESS

HORMONE	SECRETING ORGAN	ACTION
Gastrin	Stomach	Stimulates release of gastric juice
Secretin	Duodenum	Stimulates release of bicarbonate and water from pancreas and bile from liver; slows stomach activity
Cholecystokinin (CCK)	Duodenum	Stimulates digestive enzyme release from pancreas and bile release from gallbladder; slows stomach activity

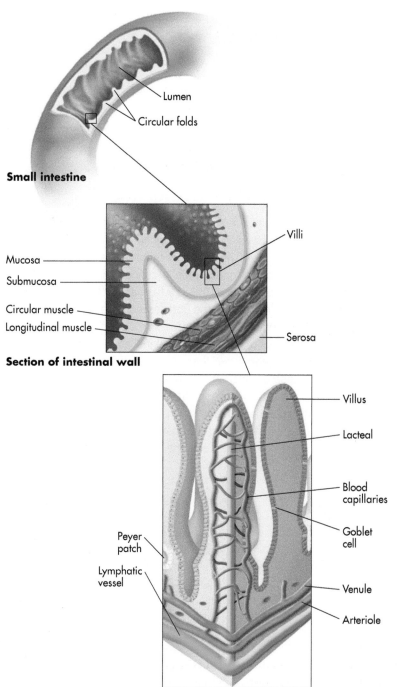

Small intestine

Lumen
Circular folds

Mucosa
Submucosa
Circular muscle
Longitudinal muscle
Villi
Serosa

Section of intestinal wall

Villus
Lacteal
Blood capillaries
Goblet cell
Venule
Arteriole
Peyer patch
Lymphatic vessel

peptidase *(PEP tih dace)* Enzyme needed to digest portions of the protein structure called peptides.

lipase Enzyme needed for the digestion of certain fats.

plicae circulares *(PLY kay)* One of the transverse folds in the small intestine.

villi *(VILL eye)* Microscopic projections of the mucosa within the lumen of the small intestine.

microvilli Microscopic extensions from the wall of the small intestine that absorb nutrients.

lacteal *(LACK tee al)* The lymph vessel associated with villi in the small intestine. It is involved in absorption of nutrients from the small intestine.

chyle *(KILE)* Milklike substance formed from digested and absorbed fats.

FIGURE 15-11 ▲ Villi.

digestion) to the liver for further processing before they are sent throughout the body. Glycerol and fatty acids (obtained from the digestion of fat) are absorbed by the villi and converted into a lipoprotein that travels on to the lacteal, where it is now a white, milky substance called **chyle**. Chyle goes directly to the lymphatic vessels, to the cisterna chyli, and then onto the thoracic duct. From there it goes to the subclavian vein and into the bloodstream.

LEARNING HINT

The Ending Ase

Enzymes end in *"ase"* and break substances down.

LEARNING HINT

Emulsifiers

Think about what a bottle of Italian salad dressing is like before you shake it. Emulsifiers allow the oil, water, and vinegar to blend together.

Clinical Application

LACTOSE INTOLERANCE

This unfortunate condition is the inability to digest the sugar (lactose) found in milk and dairy products such as cheese and ice cream. A person with lactose intolerance has a deficiency of lactase, an intestinal enzyme. As a result, lactose is not sufficiently digested. Normal bacteria found in the intestine utilize those undigested sugars with gas production as a by-product. This is what causes that "bloated feeling" you see on TV advertisements. In addition, the undigested lactose prevents normal water absorption by the small intestine, so diarrhea is formed. So the cheese pizza in our example would not be the meal of choice for these individuals who are lactose intolerant.

Interestingly, it seems that there is a genetic basis for this condition. In some populations, lactase production continues throughout their entire lives. Approximately 15% of the Caucasian population develops lactose intolerance, whereas 80 to 90% of the African-American and Asian populations develop this condition to some degree. To avoid this situation, individuals must either avoid milk and other dairy products or take an oral form of the enzyme lactase before consuming such products.

TEST YOUR KNOWLEDGE 15-2

Choose the best answer:

1. The deep folds of the stomach wall that allow for size changes of the stomach are called:
   a. rugby
   b. sphincter
   c. rugae
   d. glottal folds

2. The final "door" of the stomach that needs to open for chyme to travel to the small intestine is located at the end of the:
   a. fundus
   b. pylorus
   c. epiglottis
   d. adventitia

3. This chief digestive enzyme is needed to break down protein:
   a. guaifenesin
   b. pepsin
   c. pylorin
   d. rugelin

4. A full two-thirds of the gastric juices secreted in the stomach happen as food passes through this gastric juice production phase:
   a. cephalic phase
   b. intestinal phase
   c. gastric phase
   d. pharyngeal phase

Complete the following:

5. _____ _____ is a genetic condition in which an individual cannot digest a sugar found in milk and dairy products.

LARGE INTESTINE

Beginning at the junction with the end of the small intestine (the **ileocecal orifice**) and extending to the **anus**, the **large intestine** almost totally borders the small intestine (see FIGURE 15-12 ▲). The large intestine is responsible for:

- Water reabsorption
- Absorption of vitamins produced by normal bacteria in the large intestine
- Packaging and compacting waste products for elimination from the body

Because there are no villi in the walls of the large intestine, little nutrient absorption occurs here.

ileocecal orifice *(ILL ee oh SEE kuhl OR ih FIS)* Opening at the end of the small intestine.

anus *(AYE nuss)* External opening of rectum, located between the buttocks. The external anal sphincter is under voluntary control. The perianal area is around the anus.

large intestine Organ of absorption between the small intestine and the anal opening to the outside of the body. The large intestine includes the cecum, appendix, colon, rectum, and anus. Also known as the large bowel.

FIGURE 15-12 ▲ The large intestine.

cecum *(SEE kum)* First part of the large intestine; a short, pouchlike area. The appendix is attached to its wall.

colon *(KOH lon)* The longest part of the large intestine. It has four parts: the ascending colon, the transverse colon, the descending colon, and the S-shaped sigmoid colon.

rectum Final part of the large intestine. It is a short, straight segment that lies between the sigmoid colon and the outside of the body.

appendix *(ah PEN dicks)* Long, thin pouch on the exterior wall of the cecum. It does not play a role in digestion. It contains lymphatic tissue.

vermiform appendix See appendix.

appendicitis *(ah pen dih SIGH tiss)* Inflammation and infection of the appendix.

appendectomy Surgical removal of the vermiform appendix.

ascending colon The portion of the colon located on the right side of the patient and initially receives materials from small intestine.

transverse colon Upper portion of the colon that transverses the abdominal region

descending colon Located on left side of the patient, the last portion of the colon before it connects to the rectum.

sigmoid colon *(SIG moyd)* The s-shaped portion of the colon that extends to the rectum.

flatulence A condition of gas production as a result of bacteria action in the large intestine.

Approximately 1.5 meters (5 feet) long and 7.5 centimeters (2.5 inches) in diameter, the large intestine is divided into three main regions: the **cecum, colon,** and **rectum.** The large intestine is large in diameter, but not in length.

A pouch-shaped structure, the cecum receives any undigested food (such as cellulose) and water from the ileum of the small intestine. The infamous **appendix** is attached to the cecum. About 9 centimeters (3 inches) long, the appendix is a slender, hollow, dead-end tube lined with lymphatic tissue. Because it is wormlike in appearance, it is often called the **vermiform** appendix. In the past, it was thought that there was no reason why we have an appendix. It was considered a *vestigial organ*—an organ whose size and function seem to have been reduced as humans evolved. Recent belief, however, is that it serves as a reservoir for useful bacteria to replace bacteria lost in the intestines as a result of diseases such as cholera. Researchers also feel that because it possesses lymphatic tissue, it somehow fights infection. Ironically, if the appendix becomes blocked, inflammation can occur, causing **appendicitis.** Treatment for appendicitis is normally surgical removal of the appendix (an **appendectomy**); however, in some cases medical personnel may first attempt antibiotics.

Some of the water (used in digestion) and electrolytes are reabsorbed by the cecum and the ascending colon, which we will discuss momentarily. Although this is a relatively small amount of water reabsorption, it is crucial in maintaining the proper fluid balance in the body.

The colon can further be divided into four sections: ascending, transverse, descending, and sigmoid. The **ascending** colon travels up the right side of the body to the level of the liver. The **transverse** colon travels across the abdomen just below the liver and the stomach. Bending downward near the spleen, the **descending** colon goes down the left side, where it becomes the **sigmoid** colon. The sigmoid ("S" shaped) colon extends to the rectum. The rectum opens to the anal canal, which leads to the anus that relaxes and opens to allow the passage of solid waste (feces).

Peristalsis also occurs in the large intestine, but at a slower rate. As these slower, intermittent waves move fecal matter toward the rectum, water is removed, turning feces from a watery soup to a semisolid mass. As the rectum fills with feces, a defecation reflex occurs, which causes rectal muscles to contract and the anal sphincters to relax. If fecal material moves through the large intestine too rapidly, not enough water is removed, and diarrhea occurs. Conversely, if fecal matter remains too long in the large intestine, too much water is removed, and constipation occurs.

Bacteria found in the large intestine play two important roles. They help to further break down indigestible materials, and they produce B complex vitamins, as well as most of the vitamin K that we need for proper blood clotting. Another by-product of bacterial action in the large intestine is **flatulence,** or the production of gas.

Here is a case where bacteria in the right place keep us healthy. If those same bacteria left the intestinal wall and entered the bloodstream, it could be fatal.

Clinical Application

COLOSTOMY

Sometimes a portion of the colon must be bypassed because of disease to allow for healing and/or surgical repair. A new opening needs to be made, and this procedure is called a colostomy. A colostomy can be temporary or permanent depending on the condition. The sites where this procedure is formed are shown in **FIGURE 15-13** ▲.

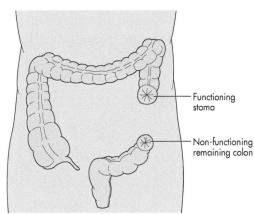

FIGURE 15-13 ▲
Colostomy sites.

Pathology Connection

DISORDERS OF THE LOWER GASTROINTESTINAL TRACT

What exactly are hemorrhoids? Interestingly, they are varicose veins caused by increased hydrostatic pressure that weakens the fibromuscular attachments of the blood vessels. Some people have a genetic predisposition for them, whereas others develop them due to chronic straining during bowel movements (either due to constipation or diarrhea), or from the pressures caused by pregnancy. Hemorrhoids can be either internal (located above the anorectal line) or external (which can actually be seen but are covered by modified anal skin). Bleeding from internal hemorrhoids can produce bright red blood that can merely streak the stool or can reach significant volumes that can occur even when not defecating. Hemorrhoids are often treated with medication, but surgical intervention may be necessary if they become severe.

A very common and potentially lethal condition, **colorectal cancer,** claims over 65,000 lives in the United States annually but is readily cured if detected early enough. Although the development of this disease has some genetic predisposition, it appears to be affected more by environmental influences such as:

- A diet rich in animal fat
- A diet lacking inappropriate amounts of fiber and calcium
- Tobacco usage and excessive alcohol consumption
- Higher-than-normal levels of serum cholesterol (the "bad" form)
- A sedentary lifestyle

A simple colonoscopy is the main diagnostic modality of choice. A barium enema with imaging studies is a less-accurate alternative.

Diverticulitis is an infection and inflammation of diverticula or sacs in the intestinal tract, especially in the colon. This is caused by lodged stool and may cause swelling and rupture of the

colorectal cancer
A malignancy of the colon or rectum.

diverticulitis *(DYE ver tik yuh LYE tiss)* An inflammatory condition of the diverticulum of the intestinal tract, especially in the colon, that can lead to pain, fever, and weight loss.

diverticulosis
Diverticula in the colon without inflammation or symptoms. Only a small percentage of persons with diverticulosis develop diverticulitis.

peritonitis
(per ih tone EYE tiss)
Inflammation of the peritoneal cavity.

Pathology Connection (continued)

diverticula. **Diverticulosis** is a condition in which there are diverticula in the intestinal tract, especially the colon, that are not inflamed or produce any symptoms. See **FIGURE 15-14** ▲, which shows examples of hemorrhoids and diverticulitis.

As noted earlier, appendicitis is an inflammation of the appendix that's caused by a blockage. Symptoms of appendicitis include abdominal pain in the right lower quadrant, nausea, vomiting, and rebound tenderness. Additional symptoms include increased white blood cells, fever, diarrhea or constipation, loss of appetite, and abdominal swelling. In some cases, the appendix ruptures, causing **peritonitis** or abscesses. The most common sign of rupture is initial pain relief followed by extremely high fever and pain. Peritonitis is an infection that occurs when bacteria and the contents of the appendix enter the peritoneal (abdominal) cavity.

FIGURE 15-14 ▲ Examples of diverticulitis and the locations of internal and external hemorrhoids.

ACCESSORY ORGANS

In addition to the salivary glands of the mouth, other accessory organs are necessary for digestion: the liver, gallbladder, and pancreas.

Liver

Weighing in at approximately 1.5 kilograms (3.3 pounds) and located below the diaphragm in the upper-right quadrant, the liver is the largest glandular organ in the body *and* the largest organ in the abdominopelvic cavity. This organ performs many functions that are vital for survival. As you can see in **FIGURE 15-15** ▲, the liver is divided into a larger right side and a smaller left lobe. (Remember, this is from the patient's perspective.) The right side has an anterior lobe and two smaller, inferior lobes.

hepatic duct *(heh PAA tic)*
Pertaining to the liver.

The liver receives about 1.5 quarts of blood *every minute* from the **hepatic** portal vein (carrying blood full of the end products of digestion) and hepatic artery (providing oxygen-rich blood).

Although this chapter is about the digestive system and the liver plays a central role in regulating the metabolism of the body, it is important to understand *all* the functions that this amazing organ performs. Here is a list of what the liver does:

- Detoxifies (removes poisons from) the body, removing harmful substances such as certain drugs and alcohol.
- Creates body heat.

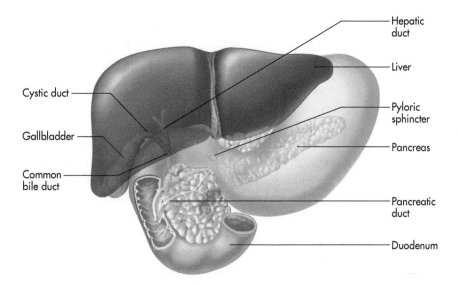

FIGURE 15-15 ▲ The liver.

- Destroys old blood cells and recycles their usable parts while eliminating unneeded parts such as bilirubin. Bilirubin is eliminated in bile and gives feces its distinctive color.
- Forms blood plasma proteins such as albumin and globulins.
- Produces the clotting factors fibrinogen and prothrombin.
- Creates the anticoagulant heparin.
- Manufactures bile, which is needed for the digestion of fats.
- Stores and modifies fats for more efficient usage by the body's cells.
- Synthesizes urea, a by-product of protein metabolism, so it can be eliminated by the body.
- Stores the simple sugar glucose as glycogen. When the blood sugar level falls below normal, the liver reconverts glycogen to glucose and releases enough of it into the bloodstream to bring blood sugar back to an acceptable concentration. (Remember the job of the hormones glucagon and insulin from Chapter 10?)
- Stores iron and vitamins A, B_{12}, D, E, and K.
- Produces cholesterol, which is necessary in the building of cell walls in your body, making of bile acids to aid digestion, and for forming certain hormones.

Stimulated into action by the duodenum's secretion of the hormone **secretin**, bile production is a critical liver digestive function. The salts found in bile act like a detergent to break up fat into tiny droplets that make the work of digestive enzymes easier. Once again, this action of breaking up fat into smaller particles is called **emulsification**, and it provides more surface area for the enzymes to do their job of chemically digesting fat.

In addition, bile helps in the absorption of fat from the small intestine and transports bilirubin and excess cholesterol to the intestines for elimination. Once produced by the liver's cells, bile leaves the liver via the **hepatic duct** and travels through the cystic duct to the gallbladder, where it is stored until needed by the small intestine.

Gallbladder

The **gallbladder** is a sac-shaped organ approximately 7.5 to 10 centimeters (3 to 4 inches) long, located right under the liver's right lobe. Again, please refer to Figure 15-15. While it is storing the bile, your gallbladder also concentrates it by reabsorbing much of its water content. This makes the bile 6 to 10 times more concentrated than it was in the liver. This is a bit of a balancing act: if too much water is reabsorbed and the bile is constantly too concentrated, bile salts may solidify into gallstones.

secretin A hormone secreted by the duodenal mucosa that stimulates sodium bicarbonate secretion by the pancreas and bile secretion by the liver. It decreases gastrointestinal peristalsis and motility.

emulsification *(ee MULL sih fih KAY shun)* Process performed by bile of breaking down large fat droplets into smaller droplets with more surface area.

hepatic duct *(heh PAA tick)* Duct that carries bile from the liver.

gallbladder Small organ that provides bile for digestion.

When fatty foods enter the duodenum, the duodenum releases the hormone CCK (cholecystokinin). This release causes the smooth muscle walls of the gallbladder to contract and squeeze bile into the cystic duct and on through the common bile duct and then into the duodenum.

Pancreas

carbohydrases One of a group of enzymes (such as amylase and lactase) that hydrolyze carbohydrates.

lipase Enzyme needed for the digestion of certain fats.

proteinases *(PROH tee in ACES)* Enzymes that break down proteins.

nucleases Enzymes that break down nucleic acids.

Although discussed in the endocrine chapter, your pancreas also plays an extremely important role in digestion. This 15-centimeter (6- to 9-inch) organ is located posterior to the stomach and extends laterally from the duodenum to the spleen (see **FIGURE 15-16** ▲). The exocrine portion of this organ secretes buffers and digestive enzymes through the pancreatic duct to the duodenum. The buffers are needed to neutralize the acidity of the chyme in the small intestine. With a pH ranging from 7.5 to 8.8, the chyme is neutralized, saving the intestinal wall from damage. This secretory action is activated by the release of hormones by the duodenum.

The general digestive enzymes excreted by the pancreas are **carbohydrases** that work on sugars and starches, **lipases** that work on lipids (fats), **proteinases** that break down proteins, and **nucleases** that break down nucleic acids.

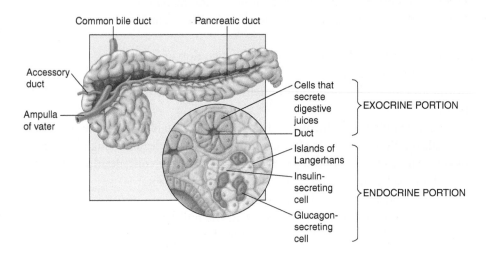

FIGURE 15-16 ▲ **A.** The pancreas: An endocrine and exocrine gland. **B.** Relationship between the pancreas and the digestive system.

A

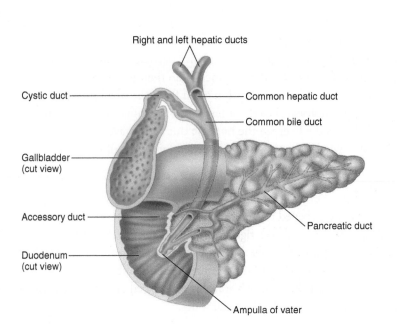

B

Pathology Connection

CHOLECYSTITIS, PANCREATITIS, AND HEPATITIS

As we previously discussed, stones can form from substances in the bile while it is stored in the gallbladder (see FIGURE 15-17 ▲). This condition is called **cholelithiasis**. (Chole means "gall;" lith means "stone.") These stones, which are most often formed from cholesterol, can range in size from grains of sand to marble-size and larger. A person can often pass the small stones, but larger ones need to be removed surgically. This condition can worsen if the stones lodge in the bile ducts, causing extreme pain, which, surprisingly, often radiates to the right shoulder. (This is a good example of referred pain.) If inflammation develops, the condition is called **cholecystitis**. (Cyst means "bladder;" itis means "inflammation.") The surgical removal of the gallbladder is called **cholecystectomy**.

If the bile backs up into the liver, the disease **obstructive jaundice** can occur. In this scenario, bilirubin is reabsorbed back into the blood, giving the victim a yellowish tint to the skin and eyes.

The problem must be resolved by unblocking the bile ducts. This can be done by dissolving the stone through medication, using shock waves to smash the stones (**lithotripsy**), or surgically removing them.

Problems can also occur with the pancreas when the bile duct becomes blocked. In some cases, the pancreatic enzymes back up into the pancreas. As a result, those enzymes begin to inflame and destroy the pancreas. This condition is known as **pancreatitis** and can be caused by excessive alcohol consumption, gallbladder disease, or some irritation that causes an abnormally high rate of pancreatic enzyme activation. If this situation is not stopped, death can eventually occur.

Hepatitis is an inflammation of the liver usually caused by an exposure to an infectious agent, a toxin, or certain drugs. Viruses cause infectious hepatitis. There are several types of infectious hepatitis. Hepatitis A virus (HAV) is the most common type of hepatitis infection worldwide. HAV is spread by food or water that has been contaminated with infected fecal matter. The disease is an acute disease, and the symptoms are typically mild and short lived, requiring only bed rest for treatment.

Infection by the Hepatitis B virus (HBV) causes more serious symptoms than HAV infection causes. HBV is a blood-borne virus that usually causes acute illness, but in a small percentage of cases it develops into a chronic illness that causes permanent liver damage. HBV is transmitted during sexual intercourse, during intravenous drug use, and during organ transplants or blood transfusions. Health care workers are especially at risk of HBV infection due to accidental needle

FIGURE 15-17 ▲ Cutaway view of actual gallbladder containing gallstones. (Source: Delalande/Photo Researchers, Inc.)

cholelithiasis *(KOH lee lih THIGH ah siss)* One or more gallstones in the gallbladder.

cholecystitis *(KOH lee siss TYE tiss)* Acute or chronic inflammation of the gallbladder usually because of gallstones.

cholecystectomy *(KOH lee sis TEK toh mee)* Surgical removal of the gall bladder.

obstructive jaundice Condition in which bile backs up into the liver and bilirubin is reabsorbed into the blood.

lithotripsy *(LITH oh TRIP see)* Medical or surgical procedure that uses sound waves to break up a kidney stone.

pancreatitis *(PAN kree ah TYE tiss)* Inflammation or infection of the pancreas.

hepatitis Inflammation of the liver most commonly caused by an exposure to an infectious agent, or excessive exposure to drugs (such as acetaminophen) or toxins (such as alcohol).

cirrhosis *(si ROH sis)* A chronic liver disease that exhibits liver scarring, loss of normal liver architecture and function, often caused by alcoholism and chronic viral hepatitis.

Pathology Connection (continued)

sticks, and all health care workers should be vaccinated against HBV. They should also practice Standard Precautions.

Alcoholism is an example of toxic hepatitis. Some drugs are toxic to the liver in small doses, whereas others, such as acetaminophen in large doses, can cause liver damage. Chronic liver disease is detected by the elevation of liver enzymes. Acute liver disease can cause jaundice, hepatomegaly (enlarged liver), altered mental status, and possible multisystem failure. Alcohol and drug abuse also contribute to **cirrhosis,** a liver disease in which healthy tissue is replaced by fibrous connective tissue.

COMMON SYMPTOMS OF DIGESTIVE SYSTEM DISORDERS

Symptoms of digestive disorders generally include one or more of the following:

- Vomiting
- Constipation
- Diarrhea
- Pain

vomiting Ejection through the mouth of the contents of the gastrointestinal tract.

Vomiting is a protective means of ridding the digestive tract of an irritant or overload of food. Sensory fibers are stimulated by the irritant or overdistension and send signals to the vomiting center (yes, you have a vomiting center) in the brain. Motor impulses are then sent to the diaphragm and abdominal muscles to contract, which squeezes the sphincter at the esophageal opening, and the contents are regurgitated.

diarrhea Defecation of liquid feces.

Diarrhea results when the fluid contents in the small intestine are rushed through the large intestine before they can adequately reabsorb the water. (*Dia* means "through;" *rrhea* means "flow.") Proper absorption of electrolytes and nutrients is also prevented, which can cause serious problems. Diarrhea is characterized by frequent loose and watery bowel movements. It is caused by a number of factors, including infection, poor diet, toxins, food allergies or irritants, and stress.

Constipation is the opposite of diarrhea. There are several possible causative factors:

constipation Decrease in the frequency of defecation accompanied by difficult or incomplete passage of stool.

- The feces may travel so slowly through a colon that too much water gets reabsorbed and the stool becomes hard, dry, and difficult to push through the system.
- There may be an overstimulation of the musculature of the intestine, creating a more narrow passage for the material.
- The musculature has become flaccid or slow, as is often the case in bedridden geriatric patients.

Dietary changes with more liquid and more roughage (such as high-fiber cereals, fruits, and vegetables), reestablishment of regular bowel habits, avoidance of stress/tension, and moderate exercise all can contribute to improving the patient's condition. Chronic use of laxatives and enemas should be avoided and may, in fact, aggravate existing conditions (such as hemorrhoids) or create new ones (such as injury to the mucous membrane of the intestinal lining).

GI pain can be sharp, dull, localized, diffuse, radiating, occasional, or constant. The severity of the pain does not always indicate the severity of the disease. Large amounts of flatus (gas) can be extremely painful, but once that wretched cloud is released, all is well (except for the innocent bystanders). Stomach cancer, on the other hand, may initially present with a relatively mild form of indigestion. Any pain from the GI tract should be investigated.

A QUICK TRIP THROUGH SOME DISEASES OF THE GASTROINTESTINAL SYSTEM

DISEASE	ETIOLOGY	SIGNS AND SYMPTOMS	DIAGNOSTIC TEST(S)	TREATMENT
Upper GI Region				
Anorexia nervosa	Eating disorder characterized by refusal to eat, classified as a psychiatric disorder.	Patients limit the intake of food until starvation occurs but at the same time consider themselves fat. Emaciated appearance.	Physical exam and history.	Counseling, reversal of the malnourished status.
Bulimia nervosa	Eating disorder characterized by recurrent binge eating and purging of the food with laxatives and vomiting; classified as a psychiatric disorder.	Erosion of dental enamel, esophageal ulceration.	Physical exam and history.	Counseling, reversal of malnourished status, dental repair.
Caries	Also known as dental cavities, the gradual decay of teeth; can cause inflamed tissue.	Destruction of tooth enamel, pain, may lead to abscesses and even heart disease.	Visual inspection, x-rays.	Evacuation and filling of cavity, proper dental hygiene, proper diet.
Cleft lip	Congenital anomaly in which the upper lip fails to come together, often seen along with a cleft palate.	Obvious structural deformity making nursing difficult.	Physical examination.	Surgical correction.
Cleft palate	Congenital anomaly in which the roof of the mouth has a split or fissure.	Obvious structural deformity making nursing difficult, allowing milk to be aspirated into the lungs from the nasal cavity.	Physical examination, imaging studies.	Surgical correction.
Esophageal stricture	Narrowing of the esophagus that makes the flow of fluids and food difficult. May be due to GERD.	Difficulty swallowing, indigestion, pain, feeling of fullness in the throat.	Patient history, physical exam, imaging studies.	Surgical repair or dilation.

A QUICK TRIP *(continued)*

DISEASE	ETIOLOGY	SIGNS AND SYMPTOMS	DIAGNOSTIC TEST(S)	TREATMENT
Gastroesophageal reflux disease (GERD)	Erosion of the esophageal lining by acid reflux, often due to a weakened lower esophageal sphincter. Other causative agents: overeating, reclining too soon after eating, obesity, overconsumption of alcohol, caffeine, or chocolate.	Heartburn, especially following a meal, often while reclining.	Patient history, examination, gastroscopy, barium studies.	Treat causative agents, medications such as antacids and those reducing stomach acid production, changes in the timing of eating and the types of food consumed, such as avoidance of chocolate, peppermint, coffee, citrus, fried or fatty foods, and tomato products. Stop smoking and don't lie down 2–4 hours after eating.
Gingivitis (gum disease)	Inflammation of the gums, leading to tooth loss; generally due to poor dental hygiene.	Sore, bleeding gums, receding gum line.	Physical examination.	Proper diet/dental hygiene.
Hiatal hernia	Protrusion of the stomach through the diaphragm and extending into the thoracic cavity; reflux is a common symptom. More common in women, incidence increases with age.	May be asymptomatic, heartburn within 1–4 hours following eating, esophageal reflux.	Patient history and exam, radiologic studies.	Similar to GERD: Frequent, small meals, loss of excess weight, elevation of head of bed, cough suppressants, smoking cessation, antacids, avoid sleeping on right side.
Impacted wisdom tooth	Wisdom tooth that is tightly wedged into the jawbone so that it is unable to erupt.	Pain, discomfort, realignment of normal teeth. May become infected, producing pus.	Oral examination, radiographic study.	Removal.
Leukoplakia	Thick, white patches of tissue of the mucosal membranes in the mouth where there is chronic physical contact with tobacco.	White patches of tissue, which are considered to be precancerous.	Visual examination.	Quit using snuff/chewing tobacco.

(continued)

DISEASE	ETIOLOGY	SIGNS AND SYMPTOMS	DIAGNOSTIC TEST(S)	TREATMENT
Periodontal disease	Disease of the supporting structures of the teeth, including the gums and bones. Approximately 80% of tooth loss in individuals age 45 and older can be attributed to periodontal disease.	Destruction of gum tissue and supporting bone structure, tooth loss.	Visual examination, radiologic studies.	Correct causative agents, improve dental hygiene.
Pyorrhea	Discharge of purulent material from dental tissue.	Pain, offensive odor.	Oral exam, radiographic studies, culture of discharge.	Correct source of the discharge, antibiotics (if a bacterial source), maintain proper oral care.

Mid GI Region

DISEASE	ETIOLOGY	SIGNS AND SYMPTOMS	DIAGNOSTIC TEST(S)	TREATMENT
Cholecystitis	An acute or chronic inflammation due to gallstones (cholelithiasis) blocking ducts in the gallbladder.	Sudden severe pain, fever, nausea, vomiting, tenderness in the right upper quadrant of the abdomen.	Patient history, physical exam, imaging studies.	Avoid fatty foods, surgical removal.
Cholelithiasis	Formation or presence of stones or calculi in the gallbladder or common bile duct. Incidence increases with age. Common in men, women following multiple pregnancies, the obese, diabetics, and patients who have had rapid weight loss.	Asymptomatic or mild discomfort to extreme pain, often preceded by ingestion of fatty or greasy foods. Pain is usually steady, lasting from 15–30 minutes up to several hours with a spontaneous resolution. Nausea, vomiting, bloating, flatulence, abdominal tenderness. Acute cholecystitis includes low-grade fever, well-localized right upper quadrant tenderness.	Physical exam, patient history, radiologic studies, ultrasound, oral cholescintigraphy, blood work with a rise in leukocyte count during acute cholecystitis (although other values usually within normal range).	Changes in diet, observation, surgical removal if deemed severe enough.

A QUICK TRIP (continued)

DISEASE	ETIOLOGY	SIGNS AND SYMPTOMS	DIAGNOSTIC TEST(S)	TREATMENT
Cirrhosis	Chronic fibrosis of the liver, leading to irreversible scarring and destruction of active liver tissue. Seventy-five percent of cases caused by heavy/chronic alcohol consumption. Other causes include overuse of prescription medications, viral hepatitis, or chronic obstruction of the bile ducts. Cause sometimes is unknown.	Enlargement of the liver (hepatomegaly) with normal tissue being replaced by fibrous tissue. This causes a decrease in its function, along with nausea, vomiting, weakness, jaundice, swollen ankles, loss of weight, loss of body hair, massive hematemesis, coma, and death.	Patient exam and history, blood results.	Cessation of causative agent.
Gastritis	Acute or chronic inflammation of the stomach due to infection, spicy foods, excess acid production, stress, alcohol, aspirin consumption, heavy smoking.	Pain, tenderness, nausea, and vomiting.	Patient history, imaging studies, endoscopy, gastric biopsy.	Antacids, antibiotics (if a bacterial infection).
Gastroenteritis	Infection and/or inflammation of the stomach and small intestines due to a virus or bacterium. Source may also be chemical in nature.	Abdominal pain, nausea, vomiting, diarrhea. Dehydration may also result as a complication.	Patient history, imaging studies, identification of offending agent.	Antibiotics (if bacterial infection), antiemetics, antidiarrheal drugs.
Hepatitis, viral	Inflammation of the liver; the most common chronic liver disease. Caused by a virus. Several types of hepatitis (A [food- or water-borne], B [blood-borne or sexually transmitted], C, D, E) with varying severity and outcomes.	Jaundice, fever, nausea, anorexia, weakness, arthralgia, enlarged and tender liver, dark urine. Oddly, an aversion to food and cigarette smoking can occur. May lead to chronic hepatitis and cirrhosis.	Patient history and physical examination, blood work, liver biopsy, stool samples, immunodiagnostics.	Preventative vaccine (for hepatitis type B), preventative infection control practices, immunoglobulin injections, antiviral drugs, rest, hydration. Health care workers at risk should be offered vaccine.

(continued)

DISEASE	ETIOLOGY	SIGNS AND SYMPTOMS	DIAGNOSTIC TEST(S)	TREATMENT
Peptic ulcer	Ulcer occurring in the lower portion of the esophagus, stomach, and duodenum caused by the breakdown of the mucosal membrane by the acid of gastric juices and pepsin. Causative agents can include *H. pylori* bacterium, stress, excessive consumption of alcohol, tobacco, aspirin/NASIDs, caffeine, corticosteroids, and other drugs.	Heartburn, indigestion, sharp localized pain, often relieved by eating, only to return again within 2 to 4 hours, possible back pain, possible diarrhea, bleeding a possibility.	Patient history and examination, barium/radiologic studies, biopsy.	Remove causative agent(s), reduce stress, utilize medications such as antacids/antibiotics, or H2 blockers (drugs) that block release of histamine, surgery only in extreme cases.
Reflux esophagitis	Acid from the stomach backs up into the esophagus, causing inflammation and pain.	Heartburn, continued erosion of the tissue of the esophagus can lead to scar, stricture, difficulty swallowing.	Patient history, radiologic studies, visual examination.	Reduce reflux through smaller meals, stop eating approximately 4 hours before going to bed, smoking cessation, avoid alcohol, caffeine, chocolate, elevate head of bed, avoid sleeping on right side, utilize medications that decrease gastric acidity, surgery only in extreme cases.

Lower GI Region

DISEASE	ETIOLOGY	SIGNS AND SYMPTOMS	DIAGNOSTIC TEST(S)	TREATMENT
Celiac sprue (gluten-induced enteropathy)	A chronic condition in which wheat glutens (or equivalent substances in barley, oats, or rye) cause damage to the mucosa of the small intestine, creating a malabsorption situation. Disease more common in white European groups, especially western Ireland.	Malabsorption, diarrhea, weight loss, flatulence, distended abdomen, anemia, back pain, hypoproteinemia, impotence, osteopenic bone disease, and other nutritional deficiency manifestations may occur. Death may occur in severe cases.	Patient history and physical exam, radiologic studies, intestinal biopsy, blood studies for specific antibodies.	Gluten-free diet, anti-inflammatory medication.

A QUICK TRIP *(continued)*

DISEASE	ETIOLOGY	SIGNS AND SYMPTOMS	DIAGNOSTIC TEST(S)	TREATMENT
Crohn's disease	Form of chronic inflammatory bowel disease affecting the ileum and/or colon. Also called regional ileitis/enteritis.	Pain, cramps, diarrhea, bloating, weight loss.	Physical exam and history, radiologic studies.	Anti-inflammatory medications, such as prednisone, surgical intervention if severe.
Diverticulitis	Infection and inflammation of a diverticulum or sac in the intestinal tract, especially in the colon.	Bleeding, abdominal pain, fever, hyperactive bowel sounds, muscular hypertrophy/shortening of the colon due to muscular hyperactivity, inflammation, pelvic abscess.	Patient history and physical exam, blood work, radiographic studies, endoscopy.	High-fiber diets, stool softeners, antibiotics, surgical intervention.
Hemorrhoids	Varicose veins in the rectum.	Pain, itching, burning sensation, bleeding.	Proctoscopy, stool sample examination.	Dietary changes (more fiber and water), stool softeners, medication to relieve discomfort.
Inguinal hernia	Hernia or outpouching of intestines into the inguinal region of the body.	Visual bulging, pain, discomfort, possible adhesions, incarceration of intestinal loop, strangulation.	Patient history, physical examination.	May be reduced in the early stages, binding, surgical repair.
Irritable bowel syndrome (IBS)	Disturbance in the functions of the intestine from unknown causes; often seen in young to middle-age females. May be stress related; may also be due to laxative abuse or irritating foods.	Symptoms generally include abdominal discomfort/pain, bloating, and an alteration in bowel activity (diarrhea, constipation).	Patient exam and history, radiologic studies, stool sample examination.	Lifestyle alterations, dietary considerations, medication.
Intussusception	Result of the intestine slipping or telescoping into another section of intestine just below it, often in the ileocecal region; more common in children.	Pain.	Radiographic studies.	Surgery.

(continued)

DISEASE	ETIOLOGY	SIGNS AND SYMPTOMS	DIAGNOSTIC TEST(S)	TREATMENT
Malabsorption syndrome	Inadequate absorption of nutrients from the intestinal tract; caused by a variety of diseases and disorders of the pancreas or gallbladder.	Malnourishment, "failure to thrive," failure to absorb fats or other nutrients, abnormal stools (black/tarry, pale/floating), foul odor.	Patient examination and history, stool samples, blood work, radiographic studies.	Treat offending disease, dietary adjustments, supplemental vitamins/minerals.
Peritonitis	An infectious and/or inflammatory process of the peritoneum; may be due to leakage of contents from the gallbladder, appendix, duodenal ulcer, penetrating injuries, or the result of a cancerous tumor.	Pain, fever, malaise, shock, abscesses.	Patient history, physical examination, blood work.	Correction of cause, surgical intervention, antibiotics.
Polyposis	Small tumors that contain a pedicle or footlike attachment in the mucous membranes of the large intestine (colon).	Discomfort, bleeding.	Endoscopic studies.	Surgical removal.
Ulcerative colitis	Ulceration of the mucous membranes of the colon; cause is unknown, but UC tends to run in families; belongs to a group of conditions known as inflammatory bowel disease (IBD).	Inflammation of the region, lesions, decreased flexibility of the bowel, fistulas, abdominal pain, diarrhea, fever, weight loss, bleeding, anemia, malabsorption of nutrients; may lead to carcinoma.	Patient history, radiographic studies, endoscopic studies, colonoscopy, blood work.	Anti-inflammatories, such as prednisone, immunomodulators, biologic therapies, or surgery.
Volvulus	This is a condition as a result of a congenital deformity or a foreign body in which the bowel twists on itself and causes an obstruction. Painful and requires immediate surgery.	Pain. Symptoms generally include abdominal discomfort and an alteration in bowel activity.	Radiologic studies.	Surgery.

Pharmacology Corner

We previously discussed the damage caused by stomach acid in conditions such as GERD and GI ulcers. So how can we decrease the amount or acidity of gastric juices? This can be done in several ways. Antacids directly decrease the acidity of gastric juices by providing an alkaline (base) substance to the stomach. Proton pump inhibitors decrease the production of gastric juices in the stomach.

Diarrhea and vomiting are common symptoms of a variety of GI disorders. Antidiarrheal agents basically slow the movement of digestive particles through the system to allow for more water absorption back into the body. Sometimes vomiting is something you want to encourage as in the case of certain poisonings. Syrup of ipecac was commonly used to induce vomiting. However, ingestion of activated charcoal to absorb the poison and whole bowel irrigation is more commonly used.

The nausea associated with sea or motion sickness can be treated by medications that depress the CNS and parasympathetic nervous system as well as provide mild sedation. Scopolamine is an example in this category and can be used as a transdermal patch or pill to prevent motion sickness. This can also be used to treat vertigo.

SUMMARY

Snapshots from the Journey

■ The digestive tract is a hollow tube extending from the mouth to the anus. It contains a variety of structures that allow the digestion of food and the absorption of nutrients necessary for life.

■ Food is processed mechanically and chemically to efficiently break it down to usable substances.

■ The following are some of the main components of the digestive systems and their functions:

ORGAN	DIGESTIVE ACTIVITY	SUBSTANCE DIGESTED	REQUIRED DIGESTIVE SECRETIONS
Mouth, or oral cavity	Chews food and mixes it with saliva; forms food into a bolus, and swallows; sense of taste	Starch	Salivary amylase and ptyalin
Esophagus	Moves bolus to the stomach through peristalsis	Not applicable	Not applicable
Stomach	Stores food, also churns food while mixing in digestive juices	Proteins	Hydrochloric acid, pepsin
Small intestine	Secretes enzymes, receives secretions from the pancreas and liver, neutralizes the acidity in chyme, absorbs nutrients into the bloodstream and lymphatic system	Carbohydrates, fats, nucleic acid, proteins	Intestinal and pancreatic enzymes, bile from the liver
Large intestine	Creates and absorbs fat-soluble vitamins, reabsorbs water, forms and eliminates feces	Vitamins B_{12} and K	Not applicable

- Enzymes are formed by special cells and act as a catalyst that speeds up chemical reactions.

- The bulk of the digestive process and the absorption of most nutrients occur in the small intestine.

- Although not directly a part of the alimentary canal, the accessory organs (liver, gallbladder, and pancreas) are needed for proper and efficient functioning of the digestive process.

- The rate of speed that food travels through the gastrointestinal system affects the acidity of the digesting food, the absorption of nutrients, and the quality of the feces.

- Diseases of the gastrointestinal system can be a result of heredity, the type and amount of food consumed, substance abuse, or emotions.

RAY'S STORY

Eating was always important to Ray as he considered himself somewhat of a chef. However, since his accident the natural act of eating we take for granted has now become a difficult process. Considering Ray's situation as a quadriplegic, research the best way(s) to deliver his food.

a. How effective would a PEG tube be as opposed to a tube utilizing the nasogastric route?

_____

_____

_____

_____

b. What are the potential hazards that Ray may encounter?

_____

_____

_____

_____

c. Are there any special nutritional considerations for patients in Ray's situation?

_____

_____

_____

_____

REVIEW QUESTIONS

Multiple Choice

1. Which of the following is not a responsibility of the large intestine?
   a. production of vitamin K
   b. absorption of water
   c. digestion of carbohydrates
   d. elimination of feces

2. Starches begin to be digested in the:
   a. oral cavity
   b. esophagus
   c. stomach
   d. large intestine

3. This structure prevents food and liquid from entering the lungs:
   a. larynx
   b. pharynx
   c. epiglottis
   d. glottis

4. The liver receives approximately this much blood every minute:
   a. 500 milliliters
   b. 1 gallon
   c. 2 units
   d. 1.5 quarts

REVIEW QUESTIONS

5. Which of the following is *not* a colon segment?
   a. transverse
   b. ascending
   c. descending
   d. absorbing

6. A condition that includes the cracking with associated inflammation of the lips and corners of the mouth is called:
   a. chelation
   b. cheilitis
   c. condrosite
   d. leukoplakia

Fill in the Blank

1. _____ is the muscle action that mixes chyme with digestive juices, whereas _____ is the muscular action that moves food through the digestive system.

2. This vermiform structure is attached to the large intestine and is considered a vestigial organ: _____.

3. The exocrine portion of this important organ secretes buffers needed to neutralize the acidity of chyme and also secretes several digestive enzymes: _____.

4. _____ is the breaking up of fat into smaller particles that can more readily be acted on by digestive enzymes.

5. The end result of fecal matter remaining in the large intestine too long, with too much water being removed from it, is _____.

6. _____ is a precancerous condition creating white patches in the oral region and is associated with the chronic use of snuff and chewing tobacco.

REVIEW QUESTIONS

Short Answer

1. Explain the difference between *chyme* and *chyle*.

_____

_____

_____

_____

_____

2. Explain the importance of bacteria in the large intestine.

_____

_____

_____

_____

_____

3. Discuss the importance of the liver in the digestive process.

_____

_____

_____

_____

_____

4. Could you live without a gallbladder? Defend your answer.

_____

_____

_____

_____

REVIEW QUESTIONS

5. Describe GERD and ways to treat/prevent this condition.

_____

_____

_____

_____

_____

Suggested Activities

1. Nutrition is a very important consideration when planning a healthy lifestyle. Research the different food groups and the daily recommended amounts that you should consume. List your daily consumption of food for a week and compare what you eat to what you should eat. List suggestions for changes that you should make in your diet, if any.

2. Although it is felt that most stomach ulcers are a result of bacteria, research ways that you can help to prevent their formation.

CAREER CONNECTIONS

Now that you have read this chapter, here is a list of related professions you may be interested in investigating for a future career:

- Dental Assistants and Hygienists

- Dietician

Research each profession and report on the following:

1. Profession description to include job responsibilities
2. Educational requirements
3. Job opportunities
4. Opportunities outside of the hospital setting
5. Salary range
6. Licensure and continuing education requirements

ANATOMY, PHYSIOLOGY, AND DISEASE IN ACTION

Materials:
Chart paper
Colored markers

Nutrition is the taking in of nutrients and changing them to a usable form. After eating a meal of meat (protein), noodles (starch) with butter (fat), and iceberg lettuce (cellulose), trace the macromolecules through the digestive process and tract, their journey into the blood, and finally into the cell where they are converted into cellular components such as enzymes, energy, cell membrane, etc. Choose complementary colors for each organic nutrient group and its digestive product such as red and pink, orange and yellow, dark green and lime green, etc. Determine the digestive products in the chart below:

Organic Nutrient	Digestive Product
Carbohydrates	
Lipids (fats)	
Proteins	

Graph the different forms of the nutrient as it passes from ingestion to the cell using the following graph (y-axis is volume).

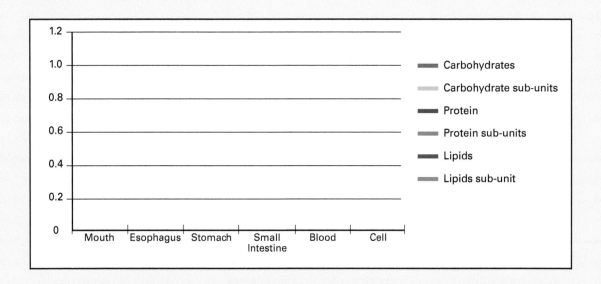

What happens to cellulose?

The Urinary System
Filtration and Fluid Balance

A city must have a safe, reliable water supply, usually obtained by pumping water from a reservoir or diverting a river. Sometimes cities have a series of wells to supply drinkable water. In desert areas, there are even special water treatment plants to remove salt from seawater to make fresh water for human consumption. In any case, there must be a way to clean the water. Water purification plants remove chemicals and debris and disinfect the water before it ever gets to your faucet. You are completely unaware of the activities of your city's water purification plant, but if it stopped working, you would be extremely unhappy. Imagine a glass full of muddy, bacteria-laden water. Yum!

Your body also must have a purification plant for its fluid—blood. Your liver does some of the purification, but your urinary system is responsible for controlling the electrolyte (ion) and fluid balance of your body. The kidneys filter blood, reabsorb and secrete ions, and produce urine. Without them, fluid and ion imbalance, blood pressure irregularities, and nitrogen waste buildup could cause death in a matter of days.

LEARNING OUTCOMES

Upon completion of your journey through this chapter, you will be able to:

- Present an overview of the organs and functions of the urinary system
- Describe the internal and external anatomy and physiology of the kidneys
- Discuss the importance of renal blood flow
- Describe the process of urine formation
- Trace the pathway of reabsorption or secretion of vital substances
- List and discuss the importance of hormones for proper kidney function
- Explain the relationship between kidney function and hypertension
- Describe the anatomy and physiology of the bladder and urination
- Discuss several common disorders of the urinary system

Pronunciation Guide

Correct pronunciation is important in any journey so that you and others are completely understood. Here is a "see and say" Pronunciation Guide for the more difficult terms to pronounce in this chapter. Please note that pronunciations given are referenced to medical dictionaries, and regional variations may exist.

afferent arterioles (AFF er ent ahr TEE ree ohlz)
aldosterone (al DOSS ter ohn)
antidiuretic hormone (ADH) (AN tye dye you RET ick)
atrial natriuretic peptide
(AY tree al NAY tree your ET ick PEP tide)
calyx, calyces (KAY licks, KAY leh seez)
efferent arterioles (EFF er ent ahr TEE ree ohlz)
external urethral sphincter
(EKS ter nal yoo REE thral SFINK ter)
glomerular capsule (gloh MAIR you ler CAP sell)
glomerular filtrate (gloh MAIR you ler FILL trate)
glomerulonephritis
(gloh MAIR you loh neh FRY tiss)
glomerulosclerosis
(gloh MAIR you loh skleh ROW sis)
glomerulus (gloh MAIR yoo lus)
hematuria (HE mah TOO ree ah)
internal urethral sphincter (IN ter nal yoo REE thral SFINK ter)

juxtaglomerular cells (JUX tah gloh MAIR you ler)
lithotripsy (LITH oh TRIP see)
nephron (NEFF rahn)
nephropathy (neh FROP ah thee)
peritubular (per ee TUBE you ler)
renal capsule (REE nal CAP sell)
renal corpuscle (REE nal KOR pus el)
renal cortex (REE nal CORE tex)
renal hilum (REE nal HIGH lum)
renal medulla (REE nal meh DULL lah)
renal pelvis (REE nal PELL vis)
renin-angiotensin-aldosterone
(REE nen-an gee oh TEN sen-al DOSS ter ohn)
urea (you REE ah)
uremia (you REEM ee ah)
ureter (yoo REE ter)
urethra (yoo REE thrah)

kidney Organ of the urinary system that filters blood and produces urine, controlling fluid and electrolyte balance.

ureter *(yoo REE ter)* Tube that connects the pelvis of the kidney to the bladder.

urinary bladder A holding receptacle for urine before it is expelled (voided) from the body.

urethra *(yoo REE thrah)* Tube that connects the bladder to the outside of the body.

filtration Process in which water and substances in the blood are pushed through the pores of the glomerulus. The resulting fluid is known as filtrate.

reabsorption Process by which water and substances in the filtrate move out of the renal tubule and into the blood in a nearby capillary.

SYSTEM OVERVIEW

The urinary system (see **FIGURE 16-1** ▲) consists of two **kidneys**, bean-shaped organs located in the superior dorsal abdominal cavity between the peritoneum and the back muscles, and several accessory structures. They are retroperitoneal as shown in Figure 16-1. The kidneys filter blood and make urine. A **ureter** is a tube of smooth muscle, lined with a mucous membrane, that carries urine from each kidney to the single **urinary bladder,** located in the inferior ventral pelvic cavity. The urinary bladder is basically an expandable sac that holds the urine. The **urethra** is the tubing that transports urine from the bladder to the outside of the body.

The job of the urinary system is to make urine, thereby controlling the body's fluid and electrolyte (ion) balance, eliminating waste products, and removing nitrogen-containing wastes, certain salts, and excess water from blood through excretion. (The kidney also is instrumental in controlling blood pressure, as you will see later in this chapter.) To make urine, three processes are necessary: **filtration, reabsorption, and secretion.** Filtration involves passing substances in the blood through pores to create a filtrate (what has passed through the filter). This filtrate, which contains various substances, can then be either reabsorbed into the bloodstream or secreted into the urine and removed from the body. Keep in mind the part of the filtrate that is reabsorbed is conserved and placed back into the bloodstream, whereas the part that is secreted is eliminated from the body. You'll learn how these processes occur as you travel through this chapter.

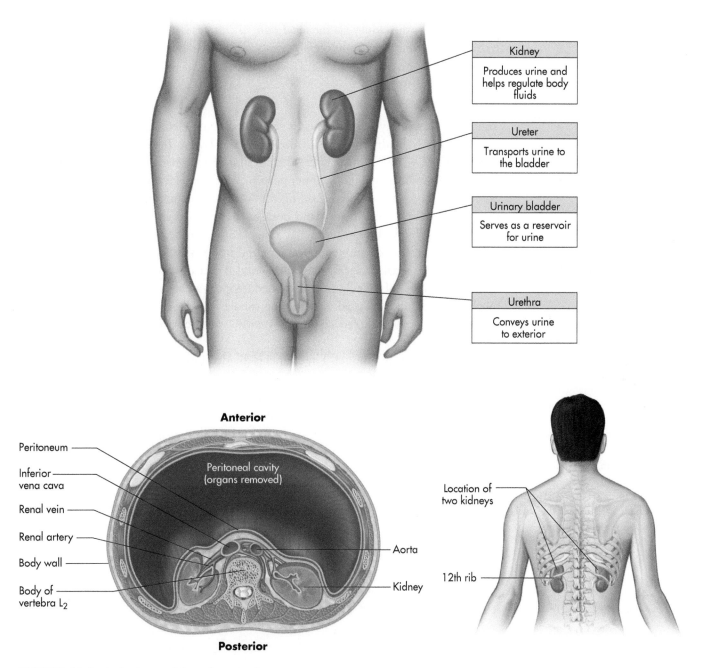

Kidney
Produces urine and helps regulate body fluids

Ureter
Transports urine to the bladder

Urinary bladder
Serves as a reservoir for urine

Urethra
Conveys urine to exterior

Anterior

Peritoneum
Inferior vena cava
Renal vein
Renal artery
Body wall
Body of vertebra L₂

Peritoneal cavity (organs removed)

Aorta
Kidney

Posterior

Location of two kidneys
12th rib

FIGURE 16-1 ▲ Anatomy of the urinary system.

THE ANATOMY OF THE KIDNEY

The kidney is a very intricate filtration system. Though you have two kidneys, you can actually function well with only one healthy kidney. That is why someone can donate a kidney while he or she is alive.

External Anatomy

The external anatomy of the kidney is relatively simple. The kidney is covered by a fibrous layer of connective tissue called the **renal capsule**. The indentation that gives the kidney its bean-shaped appearance is called the **renal hilum**. (Hilum means "root.") At the hilum, renal arteries bring blood into the kidneys to be filtered. Once filtered,

secretion *(seh CREE shun)* The movement of substances from the renal tubules into the nephron. Secreted substances end up in urine and leave the body.

renal capsule The fibrous membrane on the outer surface of a kidney, which is in turn enclosed by adipose tissue that cushions the kidney.

renal hilum *(REE nal HIGH luhm)* The indentation that gives the kidney its bean-shaped appearance.

the blood leaves the kidney via the renal vein. The ureter is also attached at the hilum to transport the urine away from the kidney to the bladder (see **FIGURE 16-2** ▲).

Internal Anatomy

The internal anatomy of the kidney is considerably more complicated than the external anatomy. The kidney can be divided into three layers. The outer layer is the **renal cortex** (cortex = rind or outer layer, like the rind of a watermelon), the middle region is the **renal medulla** (medulla = inner portion), and the innermost region is the **renal pelvis** (pelvis = basin-shaped). Adding the word *renal* is important here. Remember that the brain and the adrenal gland both have a medulla and a cortex. Also keep in mind that the body also has more than one pelvis, as in the bony pelvis.

The renal cortex is grainy in appearance and has very little obvious structure to the naked eye. The renal cortex is where the blood is actually filtered. The renal medulla contains a number of triangle-shaped striated (striped) areas called **renal pyramids**. The renal pyramids are composed of collecting tubules for the urine that is formed in the kidney. Adjacent pyramids are separated by narrow **renal columns,** which are extensions of the cortical tissue.

The renal pelvis is a funnel. The funnel is divided into two or three large collecting tubes called **major calyces.** Each major **calyx** is divided into several **minor calyces.** (Calyx means "cup or cup shaped.") The calyces form cup-shaped areas around the tips of the pyramids to collect the urine that continually drains through the pyramids. The kidney is essentially a combination of a filtration and collection system. The blood is filtered by millions of tiny filters in the cortex, the filtered material flows through tiny tubes in the medulla, and the resulting urine is collected in the renal pelvis. The renal pelvis, which is simply the enlarged proximal portion of the ureter, empties into the tube of the ureter. Through peristalsis, the ureter then carries the

renal cortex Tissue layer of kidney just beneath the renal capsule.

renal medulla *(REE nal meh DULL uh)* The middle layer of the kidney.

renal pelvis *(REE nal PELL viss)* Funnel-shaped part of the kidney that collects urine.

renal pyramids Triangle-shaped, striated areas composed of collecting tubules for the urine that is formed in the kidney.

renal columns Narrow structures that separate adjacent renal pyramids.

major calyx, minor calyces *(KAY licks, KAY leh seez)* Tubes in the kidney that carry urine from the nephrons to the renal pelvis.

calyx A cuplike extension of the renal pelvis that encloses the papilla of a renal pyramid; urine from the papillary duct is emptied into it.

Pyramid in renal medulla

Renal capsule

Renal cortex

Hilum of kidney

Renal artery

Renal vein

Renal pelvis

Renal column

Ureter

Calyx

FIGURE 16-2 ▲ The internal anatomy of the kidney.

urine to the urinary bladder, where it is stored and eventually eliminated from the body. (Again, see Figure 16-2.)

Blood Vessels

Because the kidney's job is to filter blood, the blood must reach every part of the kidney. To accomplish this filtration process there is a network of blood vessels throughout the kidney. A single **renal artery** enters each kidney at the hilum (see FIGURE 16-3 ▲). The renal artery then branches into five **segmental arteries**, and the segmental arteries in turn branch into **lobar arteries**. The lobar arteries branch into **interlobar arteries**, which pass through the renal columns. **Arcuate arteries** originate from the interlobar arteries. The arcuate arteries are so named because they arch around the base of the pyramids in the renal medulla. Many **cortical radiate arteries** branch from the arcuate arteries, supplying blood to the renal cortex. These cortical radiate arteries give rise to numerous **afferent arterioles**.

Each afferent arteriole leads to a ball of capillaries called a **glomerulus**. **Efferent arterioles** then leave from the glomerulus and travel to a specialized series of capillaries called the **peritubular capillaries** and on to the **vasa recta** (straight blood vessels) that are associated with the **renal nephron,** the functional unit of the kidney. The peritubular capillaries wrap around the tubules of the nephron. You have seen a situation like this in the lungs, where the pulmonary capillaries surround the alveoli. Having blood vessels close to the nephron allows efficient movement of ions between blood

renal artery *(REE nal AHR ter ee)* Major artery that carries blood to the kidney.

segmental arteries Branches formed from the renal artery.

lobar arteries Further branching of the segmental arteries in the kidney.

interlobar arteries *(in TUR LOH bar AHR tu hrees)* Branches of the lobar arteries which pass through the renal columns.

arcuate arteries *(ARE koo ate)* Branches of interlobar arteries that arch around the base of the renal pyramids.

cortical radiate arteries Arteries branching from arcuate arteries that supply blood to renal cortex.

afferent arterioles *(AFF er ent ahr TEE ree ohlz)* Small arteries traveling toward an organ.

glomerulus *(glow MAIR yoo lus)* Network of intertwining capillaries within Bowman's capsule in the nephron. Filtration takes place in the glomerulus.

efferent arterioles *(EFF er ent ahr TEE ree ohlz)* Small blood vessels that carry blood away from the glomeruli of the kidney.

peritubular capillaries *(per ih TUBE you ler)* Capillaries surrounding the renal tubules.

vasa recta Straight blood vessels associated with the renal nephron.

renal nephron *(REE nal NEF ron)* Fundamental functional unit of the kidney, consists of the renal corpuscle and renal tubule.

Renal artery → Segmental arteries → Lobar arteries → Interlobar arteries → Arcuate arteries → Interlobular arteries → Afferent arterioles → Glomerulus → Efferent arterioles → Peritubular capillaries → Interlobular veins → Arcuate veins → Interlobar veins → Lobar veins → Renal vein

FIGURE 16-3 ▲ Renal blood vessels and the pathway of blood through the renal system.

renal vein Major blood vessel that carries blood away from the kidneys.

and the fluid in the nephron, just as having pulmonary capillaries near the alveoli allows efficient diffusion of respiratory gases between the alveoli and the bloodstream.

From each set of peritubular capillaries, blood flows out the cortical radiate veins. From there, the blood flows out a series of veins that are the direct reverse pattern of the arteries, with one exception. There are no segmental veins. The blood finally leaves the kidney via the **renal vein**. Please see Figure 16-3 again for a diagram of the renal blood vessels.

nephron *(NEFF rahn)* Microscopic functional unit of the kidney.

LEARNING HINT

Visualizing the Peritubular System

Think of the peritubular capillaries as blue yarn wrapped around plastic pipe, which represents the actual renal tubular system. You will soon learn that the filtrate that stays in the pipe eventually becomes urine, and the filtrate that is reabsorbed into the blue yarn (peritubular capillaries) is brought back into the bloodstream.

---

renal corpuscle *(REE nal KOR pus el)* The filtration apparatus of the kidney, consists of the glomerulus and the glomerular capsule.

renal tubule Network of convoluted tubules found within the kidneys.

glomerulus *(glow MAIR yoo lus)* Network of intertwining capillaries within Bowman's capsule in the nephron. Filtration takes place in the glomerulus.

glomerular capsule *(glow MAIR you ler)* A double layered membrane surrounding the glomerulus.

Bowman's capsule See glomerular capsule.

visceral layer Inner layer of glomerular capsule.

podocytes Specialized squamous cells that compose the visceral layer of the glomerular capsule.

glomerular filtrate *(glow MAIR you ler FILL trate)* The filtered fluid within the glomerulus.

renal tubule Network of convoluted tubules found within the kidneys.

proximal tubule *(PROK sim al TOO byool)* The part of the renal tubule closest to the glomerulus. Many substances are secreted or absorbed in this part of the renal tubule.

Microscopic Anatomy of the Kidney: The Nephron

So far we have looked at an overview of the kidney's structure and function. Now let's take a closer look at what actually happens within the kidneys. The business end of the kidney, the part that performs the real functions of the kidney, consists of millions of microscopic funnels and tubules. These fundamental functional units of the kidney are called **nephrons** (see FIGURE 16-4 ▲). The nephron is divided into two distinct parts: the **renal corpuscle** and the **renal tubule**. The renal corpuscle is a filter, much like a window screen or coffee filter.

Blood enters the renal corpuscle via the **glomerulus,** a capillary ball. Surrounding the glomerulus is a double-layered membrane called the **glomerular capsule** (or **Bowman's capsule**). The layers of the glomerular capsule are similar to the layers of a serous membrane like the pleura or pericardium. The inner layer of the glomerular capsule, the **visceral layer,** surrounds the glomerular capillaries. The visceral layer is made of specialized squamous epithelial cells called **podocytes**. The combination of podocytes and the simple squamous epithelium making up the walls of the glomerular capillaries makes a very effective filter.

The outer or parietal layer of the glomerular capsule is simple squamous epithelium and completes the container for the filter. Blood flows into the glomerulus, and everything *but* blood cells and a few large molecules, mainly proteins, are pushed from the capillaries across the filter and into the glomerular capsule. The material filtered from the blood into the glomerular capsule is called **glomerular filtrate**. Can you see why blood cells or excessive protein found in urine may indicate a kidney filtration problem?

The rest of the nephron is series of tubes known as the **renal tubule,** sort of like a Habitrail system for a gerbil or hamster (see FIGURE 16-5 ▲). Just like the water filtration system in our towns and cities, the water (glomerular filtrate) travels through a network of pipes (tubules) where the impurities remain in the pipes to be discharged while the filtered water is collected (peritubular capillaries) and recycled back into the city's water supply.

Now back to the kidney. Glomerular filtrate flows from the glomerular capsule into the first part of the renal tubule, the **proximal tubule** (sometimes called the proximal *convoluted* tubule). The wall of the proximal tubule is made of cuboidal epithelium

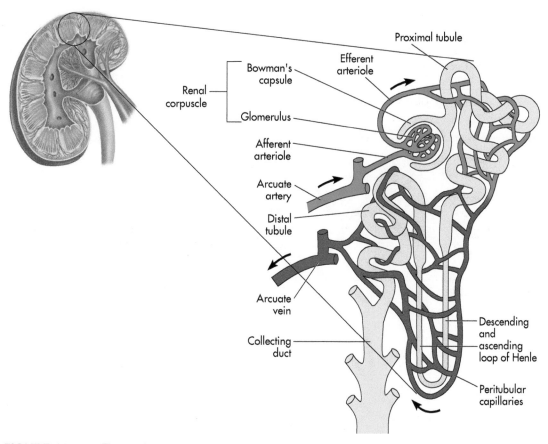

FIGURE 16-4 ▲ The nephron.

with microvilli. From the proximal tubule, glomerular filtrate flows into the **nephron loop** (also called the **loop of Henle**). The nephron loop consists of two segments, the **descending loop,** with a structure similar to the proximal tubule, and the **ascending loop,** with a wall made of simple cuboidal epithelium without microvilli. From the nephron loop, the glomerular filtrate flows into the **distal tubule** (a.k.a. the distal convoluted tubule). The wall of the distal tubule is like that of the ascending branch of the nephron loop.

From the distal tubule, glomerular filtrate flows into one of several **collecting ducts,** also made of cuboidal epithelium. The collecting ducts lead to the minor calyces, then to the major calyces, renal pelvis, and ureter. At this point, the glomerular filtrate is urine. Again, if you refer to our previous learning hint, what stays in the tubular system (plastic pipe) eventually gets eliminated as urine.

nephron loop Structure composed of the descending and ascending loop of the renal tubular system.

loop of Henle See nephron loop.

descending loop Portion of nephron loop with similar structure to the proximal tubule.

ascending loop Portion of nephron loop with a wall made up of simple cuboidal epithelium.

distal tubule Tubule of the nephron that begins at the loop of Henle. It empties into the collecting duct. Reabsorption takes place there.

collecting duct Common passageway that collects fluid from many nephrons. The final step of reabsorption takes place there, and the fluid is known as urine after it leaves this duct.

Glomerular Filtration

Blood from the renal artery is filtered in the glomerulus. The filtered product which contains water, salts, nutrients, and waste products is called the glomerular filtrate.

Tubular Reabsorption

Nutrients and salts are actively reabsorbed and transported to the peritubular capillary network and some water is passively reabsorbed into the peritubular capillaries.

Tubular Secretion

Some substances are actively secreted from the peritubular capillaries into the distal tubule for removal from the body.

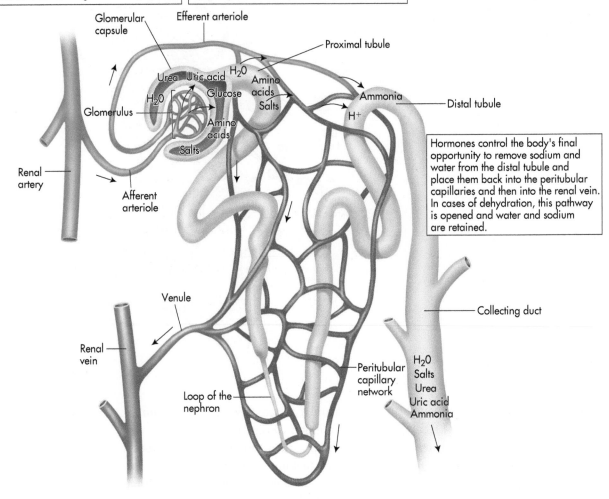

Hormones control the body's final opportunity to remove sodium and water from the distal tubule and place them back into the peritubular capillaries and then into the renal vein. In cases of dehydration, this pathway is opened and water and sodium are retained.

FIGURE 16-5 ▲ A functional renal unit.

Pathology Connection

KIDNEY STONES AND POLYCYSTIC KIDNEY DISEASE (PKD)

kidney stones
Stones formed by many substances such as calcium or uric acid or may be a result of an infection that can block proper function.

Kidney stones are exactly what their name implies: hard bodies (stones) in the kidney. Kidney stones result when substances in the urine crystallize in the renal tubule, often because the concentration of that substance is higher than normal in the renal tubule. However, sometimes the cause of kidney stones is a mystery. Kidney stones are quite common. As many as 10% of people in North America will have a kidney stone in their lifetime. Stones are more common in men than women. Patients with kidney disease, who have had bariatric (weight control) surgery, or who have bone disease are at a higher risk of kidney stones.

Stones can be made of many different substances, including calcium (70% of stones) or uric acid (10% of stones), or can be caused by kidney infection. Some individuals appear to

Pathology Connection (continued)

be more susceptible to stones than others, and once you have had a kidney stone, you are more susceptible to more kidney stones in the future. Many kidney stones pass through the kidney unnoticed. However, larger or irregular-shaped stones may lodge in the kidney tubules, obstructing flow and irritating nearby tissues. Most patients diagnosed with kidney stones are driven to seek treatment because of blood in their urine (**hematuria**) or excruciating back pain. Some patients may have fever, nausea, and urinary urgency. Patients with kidney stones often describe the pain as the worst they have ever felt. Kidney stones are diagnosed using medical exam and patient history, urinalysis, ultrasound, capture and analysis of the stone, and imaging studies. Metabolic analysis may help pinpoint the cause of the stones and thus determine long-term treatment to prevent recurrence.

Treatment for kidney stones depends on the number, size, location, and composition of the stones. Many patients are treated for pain and sent home with instructions to drink lots of water and wait for the stone to pass. (Often, they are asked to save the stone as it passes so it can be sent for chemical analysis.) Some patients are prescribed medication (usually corticosteroids and alpha-blockers) to increase the chance of passing the stones. If the stone is large or is obstructing urine flow, several less-invasive techniques are available that may enable patients to avoid surgery. **Extracorporeal shock wave lithotripsy,** an outpatient procedure, uses shock waves applied to the outside of the body to break up the stone so it is small enough to pass through the kidney. During **ureteroscopy,** a fiberoptic endoscope is threaded up the urethra, through to bladder, and into the ureter. An instrument attached to the endoscope shatters the stone and captures the pieces. **Percutaneous nephrolithotomy** uses an endoscope and a small incision to remove large stones. See FIGURE 16-6 ▲, which shows two different methods of lithotripsy.

Recurrence is often a problem, with as many as 50% of patients who have had a kidney stone developing another stone. Many patients are advised to adhere to a diet to prevent their particular type of stone or are prescribed medication to decrease the likelihood that they will develop another kidney stone. Long-term treatment depends on stone composition.

Polycystic kidney disease (PKD) is a genetic disorder in which large cysts (made mainly of epithelial cells) form in the kidneys and liver. It is the most common genetic cause of kidney disease in the United States. Patients with PKD are also at higher risk for aneurysms and heart abnormalities. One form of PKD is so serious that patients die in infancy. The more common form (1 in 1000 adults in the United States) is an adult-onset disorder characterized by decreasing kidney function as normal nephrons are displaced by cysts. Few cysts develop in people under the age of 30. As more and more cysts develop, kidneys get very large. One polycystic kidney weighed 22 pounds! Symptoms of PKD are variable but include hypertension, impaired renal function, urinary tract infections, dilute urine, liver cysts, cerebral hemorrhage, decreased kidney perfusion, pain, hematuria and hormone abnormalities, particularly increased erythropoietin and increased activity of the renin-angiotensin-aldosterone system (RAS). PKD is diagnosed by ultrasound and genetic testing. There is no cure for PKD except kidney transplantation. Patients generally progress to renal failure in their late 40s, 50s, or early 60s. Patients are treated for complications of kidney disease, such as hypertension. Several medications are being investigated that may be helpful, including angiotensin-converting enzyme (ACE) inhibitors, statin drugs, and immunosuppressants. For PKD patients who develop end-stage renal disease, either kidney dialysis or kidney transplant is necessary.

hematuria *(HEE mah TOO ree ah)* Blood in the urine.

extracorporeal shock wave lithotripsy *(EKS trah core POOR ee al LITH oh TRIP see)* An outpatient procedure utilizing shock waves applied to the outside of the body to shatter a kidney stone so it is small enough to excrete.

ureteroscopy A procedure in which a fiberoptic endoscope is threaded up the urethra to view the ureter.

percutaneous nephrolithotomy *(PUR kyoo TAY nee uhs nef roh lih THOT oh mee)* The use of an endoscope to create a small incision to remove large kidney stones.

polycystic kidney disease (PKD) Several inherited disorders causing cysts to form in the kidneys and other organs leading to destroyed kidney tissue and function.

(continued)

Pathology Connection (continued)

FIGURE 16-6 ▲ Two methods of lithotripsy. **A.** Percutaneous ultrasonic lithotripsy. A nephroscope is inserted into the renal pelvis, and ultrasound waves are used to fragment the stones. The fragments are then removed through the nephroscope. **B.** Water immersion lithotripsy.

Clinical Application

TRAUMA, ISCHEMIA, AND KIDNEY DAMAGE

The kidney is obviously very well vascularized. Each nephron is literally surrounded by blood vessels, and the flow of blood around the nephron is controlled by flow through the afferent arteriole. **Ischemia** is a condition of tissue injury resulting from too little oxygen delivery to tissues, usually caused by decreased blood flow. When blood flow to the nephrons decreases for a period of time, oxygen delivery to the nephron decreases, and ischemia can result. Decreased blood flow to the kidney results from anything that causes prolonged constriction of the afferent arterioles.

For example, a young boy runs into a storm door, shattering the glass and in the process punctures his femoral artery, which begins to bleed profusely. As his blood volume falls, so does his blood pressure. His body fights desperately to bring his blood pressure back to normal, causing widespread vasoconstriction. The afferent arterioles, under the influence of sympathetic hormones and other vasoconstrictors, get smaller and smaller, greatly decreasing blood supply to the nephrons. If the situation continues long enough, the tissues will become ischemic and eventually begin to die. Even if the boy survives the initial blood loss from the wound, his kidneys may be damaged, resulting in temporary or permanent renal failure. It is not uncommon for trauma patients to survive the initial trauma only to become the victim of organ damage due to ischemia. Kidney failure will be discussed in more detail later in the chapter.

ischemia *(iss KEE mee ah)* Tissue injury due to a decrease in blood flow.

TEST YOUR KNOWLEDGE 16-1

Choose the best answer:

1. What carries urine from the kidneys to the bladder?
   a. urethra
   b. ureter
   c. vagina
   d. all of the above

2. The renal _____ is the outer region of the kidney.
   a. medulla
   b. pelvis
   c. hilum
   d. cortex

3. These vessels carry blood into the glomerulus:
   a. peritubular capillaries
   b. afferent arterioles
   c. segmental arteries
   d. none of the above

4. The fundamental functional unit of the kidney is the:
   a. renal corpuscle
   b. renal pelvis
   c. nephron
   d. pyramid

5. Glomerular filtrate flows from the _____ into the _____.
   a. proximal tubule; distal tubule
   b. ascending loop; descending loop
   c. glomerular capsule; proximal tubule
   d. proximal tubule; collecting duct

6. Kidney stones are most often made of this material:
   a. bacteria
   b. uric acid
   c. calcium
   d. nickel

URINE FORMATION

As the body's water purification system, the job of the kidneys is to control fluid and electrolyte balance by carefully controlling urine volume and composition. The kidneys also remove nitrogen-containing waste, excess water, certain salts, and other impurities from blood. To form urine, the nephron must perform three processes: **glomerular filtration, tubular reabsorption,** and **tubular secretion**. Please see FIGURE 16-7 ▲ for a diagram of these three processes.

During glomerular filtration, the first step in urine formation, blood from the renal artery enters the glomerulus. Fluid and molecules pass from the glomerular capillaries into the glomerular capsule (also called Bowman's capsule), across a filter composed of the wall of the capillaries and the podocytes of the glomerular capsule. The filtrate flows into the renal tubule, where the composition of the filtrate is controlled by reabsorption and secretion.

Substances are either reabsorbed by the body or secreted. The substances that are reabsorbed pass from the renal tubule into the peritubular capillaries and stay within the body. The body uses secretion and reabsorption to regulate its supply of a variety of chemicals. Substances that are secreted pass from the peritubular capillaries into the renal tubule and eventually leave the body via the urine. For example, hydrogen ions (H^+) are selectively secreted to maintain the body's acid–base balance. If blood levels of certain substances are high, such as glucose, amino acids, vitamins, or sodium, those substances will not be completely reabsorbed.

The combination of all three processes is necessary for the formation of urine. Filtration moves fluid and chemicals into the nephron from blood, whereas reabsorption and secretion control the concentration of chemicals and volume of urine. Glomerular filtrate is chemically similar to blood, whereas urine is chemically very different. Some substances, like glucose, are normally completely reabsorbed, and other substances, like the metabolic waste products **urea** and **creatinine,** are secreted such that urea and creatinine are much more concentrated in urine than in blood. See TABLE 16-1 ■ for a comparison of plasma, glomerular filtrate, and urine chemistry.

Control of Filtration

Think for a moment about filters you are familiar with. What controls these filters? What force drives filtration? What determines whether a substance passes through the filter or stays on one side? The example you are probably most familiar with is a window screen. Why do you have window screens in your windows? To keep out the bugs. Without

glomerular filtrate *(glow MAIR you ler FILL trate)* The filtered fluid within the glomerulus.

tubular reabsorption Movement of substances out of the renal tubule and back into the blood. The substances will be retained in the body.

tubular secretion Movement of substances from the blood into the renal tubule. These substances will leave the body in the urine.

urea The main nitrogenous substance found in urine. The amount excreted in urine is directly related to the amount of protein consumed.

creatinine *(kree AT in in)* A waste product produced by muscle metabolism that is normally eliminated by the kidney.

TABLE 16-1 ■ KIDNEY FLUID CHEMISTRY

SUBSTANCE	PLASMA	GLOMERULAR FILTRATE	URINE
Protein	3,900–5,000 mg/100 mL	None	None
Glucose	100 mg/100 mL	100 mg/100 mL	None
Sodium	142 mg/100 mL	142 mg/100 mL	128 mg/100 mL
Potassium	5 mg/100 mL	5 mg/100 mL	60 mg/100 mL
Urea	26 mg/100 mL	26 mg/100 mL	1,820 mg/100 mL
Creatinine	1.1 mg/100 mL	1.1 mg/100 mL	140 mg/100 mL

Afferent arterioles

Glomerulus

Efferent arterioles

Glomerular capsule

Rest of renal tubule

Peritubular capillaries

To cortical radiate veins

Urine

Key

A → Filtration

B → Reabsorption

C → Secretion

Schematic view of the three stages of urine production: (A) filtration; (B) reabsorption; and (C) secretion.

FIGURE 16-7 ▲ The processes involved in urine formation.

screens, every insect in the neighborhood would be in your bedroom eating you alive, right? So what determines whether something gets through the screen? The most obvious answer is the size of the mesh in the screen. Dust gets through the screen, but most bugs don't. Imagine a screen with holes twice the size of a typical screen. You would spend all night swatting mosquitoes! The screens would be pretty much useless. Filter size determines what gets through the filter. All filters are *selective:* Only some substances pass through, mainly depending on the size of the openings in the filter (see **FIGURE 16-8** ▲).

Can you think of a situation where something might get through a window screen? Leaving behind the bugs, let's think about a screened-in porch. During a gentle snowstorm, snow doesn't come through the screen. But in a high wind, the floor of the porch becomes covered in snow. The high winds force the snow through the screen. Substances are moved through a filter by differences in pressure across the filter. Pressure pushes stuff through the holes. The higher the pressure on one side of the filter compared to the other side, the faster substances are passed through the filter.

This combination works great in coffeemakers. The filters have holes too small to let any but the tiniest coffee grounds pass through. The pressure of the water on top of the filter pushes the water and the substances in coffee grounds that make drinkable coffee through the filter, as the grounds stay on the other side.

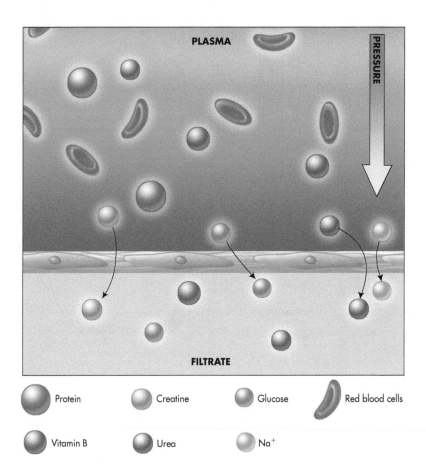

FIGURE 16-8 ▲ Filter selectivity.

- ⬤ Protein
- ⬤ Creatine
- ⬤ Glucose
- 🔴 Red blood cells
- ⬤ Vitamin B
- ⬤ Urea
- ⬤ Na⁺

The glomerulus and glomerular capsule work in much the same way. Like most filters, the podocytes and capillary walls of the renal corpuscle create a filter with fixed openings. Plasma and many of the substances dissolved in plasma pass through the filter, but red and white blood cells, platelets, and some large molecules, like proteins, do not pass through the filter in a healthy kidney but remain in the bloodstream. What passes through the filter is predetermined by the size of the openings. This explains why protein in urine is a sign of kidney damage. Under normal circumstances, protein molecules are too large to fit through the glomerular filter, so proteins do not get into the renal tubule or into the urine. Only when the filter is damaged can protein pass into the filtrate and then into the urine (see **FIGURE 16-9** ▲).

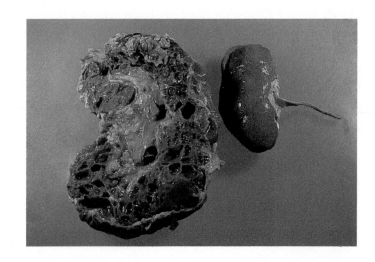

FIGURE 16-9 ▲ Comparison of damaged and healthy kidneys. (Source: A. Glauberman/Photo Researchers/Science Source)

Clinical Application

TESTING FOR URINARY HEALTH

Problems in the urinary system are indicated by abnormalities in urine composition or rate of urine formation, so tests center around concentration of waste in the blood (because if waste is in the blood, it hasn't been removed by the kidneys) and urine composition. Blood tests that are most useful for assessing kidney health are creatinine levels and **blood urea nitrogen (BUN)** tests. **Creatinine** is a waste product produced by muscle metabolism that should be largely eliminated by the kidney. High blood creatinine levels indicate decreased filtration. (A test for serum creatinine is a stand-in for a test of the glomerular filtration rate, which is incredibly difficult to measure directly.) A BUN test measures the amount of urea in the blood. Urea is the chief waste product formed from protein metabolism. High BUN in the blood suggests decreased urea secretion by the kidneys.

Urinalysis is a routine part of any physical examination because abnormalities of urine chemistry can often signal problems in the urinary system before patients have any symptoms. Urine should be clear and nearly colorless. The presence of certain cells, casts (masses of red blood cells, white blood cells, or kidney cells molded by renal tubules), dark color, pus, or crystals indicates a possible problem. Urinalysis also tests for chemicals such as bilirubin, glucose, protein, blood, ketones, ions, and urine pH. Protein in the urine is often an early indication of filtration problems in the urinary system.

In addition, imaging tests such as x-rays, ultrasound, CT scan, and MRI can show structural abnormalities in the kidney, and hormone tests can be used to rule out some causes of kidney malfunction. See Chapter 18 for more information.

blood urea nitrogen (BUN) Nitrogen in the blood in the form of urea, the metabolic product of the breakdown of amino acids used for energy production. The normal concentration is about 8 to 18 mg/dL. The level of urea in the blood provides a rough estimate of kidney function.

creatinine *(kree AT in in)* A waste product produced by muscle metabolism that is normally eliminated by the kidney.

Amazing **Body Facts**

Urine

In a healthy renal system, the urine produced is sterile. The urea found in urine is the same substance that is used to melt ice in the winter. Urea is also a component in plant fertilizer: Although nitrogen is a waste product for humans, it is an essential product for plant growth.

Filtration Rate

Filtration rate can be controlled by changing the pressure difference across the filter. The most obvious way to control the pressure is to change the pressure of the blood in the glomerular capillaries. Higher pressure in the glomerulus will increase filtration, and lower pressure will decrease filtration. You might think that every minor change in systemic blood pressure would affect glomerular filtration rate. That would be the logical conclusion. However, the glomerulus is protected from minor changes in blood pressure by a mechanism called **autoregulation**. As systemic blood pressure increases, the afferent arterioles leading into the glomerulus constrict, decreasing the amount of blood getting into the glomerulus. If less blood gets into the glomerulus, the pressure doesn't rise. Autoregulation protects the delicate filter from repeated rapid changes in blood pressure caused, for example, by walking up steps.

autoregulation Renal mechanism to insure glomerular filtration is unaffected by changes in blood pressure.

Amazing **Body Facts**

Glomerular Filtration

The millions of tiny filters in your kidneys perform a truly Herculean task. Average glomerular filtration rate is 110 milliliters per minute, or 160 liters per day. That's more than 40 gallons filtered every 24 hours!

Autoregulation can be overridden in situations when blood pressure must be regulated. Because the kidney controls fluid volume, it is often part of mechanisms, along with the cardiovascular system, that regulate systemic blood pressure. For example, if there is a decrease in systemic blood pressure or volume, such as during severe blood loss, glomerular filtration decreases dramatically in an attempt to conserve fluid volume by producing less urine.

Remember that the fight-or-flight response includes decreased urine production. The sympathetic nervous system and the hormones of the adrenal medulla—epinephrine and norepinephrine—decrease glomerular filtration by causing dramatic vasoconstriction of the afferent arterioles. This prevents blood from flowing to the glomerulus, decreasing glomerular filtration rate. Small changes in systemic blood pressure do not affect glomerular filtration because autoregulation keeps glomerular pressure relatively constant, but during shock, for example, glomerular filtration decreases significantly. This is one of the reasons why urine output is monitored in trauma and surgery patients. As you learned earlier when we discussed renal blood vessels, one serious complication of severe blood loss is permanent kidney damage due to decreased blood flow and subsequent death of kidney tissue.

nephropathy Disease of the kidney.

diabetes mellitus (DM) Condition resulting from too little secretion of insulin leading to increased levels of blood glucose.

The reverse is also true: If blood volume is elevated, sympathetic output to the afferent arterioles decreases, the arterioles dilate, and glomerular filtration rate increases, allowing the kidneys to get rid of excess fluid.

Pathology Connection

NEPHROPATHY

Nephropathy is a general term for kidney disease, particularly damage to the filtering apparatus of the nephrons. Nephropathy is generally progressive, but in the early stages some types of nephropathy can be reversed with treatment. There are many different causes of nephropathy. Symptoms include proteinuria, hematuria, and hypertension, but the onset, type, and severity of symptoms differ depending on the cause and the severity of the nephropathy. Nephropathy is diagnosed using urinalysis and blood tests. Treatments include corticosteroids, immunosuppressants, blood pressure medications, diet, and in cases that progress to end-stage renal disease, kidney dialysis or transplant.

Diabetes mellitus is a condition characterized by abnormally high blood glucose. This hyperglycemia, caused by production of too little insulin or by insensitivity to insulin, wreaks havoc with blood chemistry, including osmotic balance. One of the functions of your kidney is to remove all that extra glucose from your blood. When the blood glucose is high, the kidneys must work that much harder to remove it. Patients with elevated glucose produce a much greater volume of urine than do patients with healthy levels of blood glucose because their kidneys try to excrete the excess blood glucose.

Pathology Connection (continued)

Prolonged high blood glucose causes a type of kidney damage known as **diabetic nephropathy**. 40% of diabetic patients will develop diabetic nephropathy. It begins with a thickening of the filter surface of the glomerular capsule and eventually leads to a complete breakdown of that tissue. Once the tissue is damaged, the selectivity of the filter is destroyed. Substances that usually would not pass through the filter and into glomerular filtrate, like proteins and blood cells, begin to appear in urine. The efficiency of filtration is compromised, and kidney function begins to deteriorate. Protein and blood cells in the urine are early indicators of renal failure. In the early stages, characterized by increased filtration and even small amounts of protein in the urine (microalbuminuria), diabetic nephropathy can be reversed by strict glycemic control and ACE inhibitors (even if blood pressure is normal). Diabetics can help prevent the onset of kidney damage by keeping blood sugar levels as tightly controlled as possible, preventing high blood pressure, and reducing blood cholesterol to safe levels. Diabetic nephropathy is the leading cause of kidney failure in the United States. One-third of patients on dialysis have diabetes mellitus. Death from diabetic nephropathy usually occurs 5 to 10 years after large amounts of protein begin to show up in the urine (macroalbuminuria).

Many prescription drugs or chemicals can cause nephropathy either by direct toxicity, allergy-induced damage to the kidney, or crystallization in the kidney. Analgesic nephropathy is caused by the use of some pain relievers, such as the nonsteroidal anti-inflammatory drugs (NSAIDs) ibuprofen and naproxyn, particularly in people with renal disease or other risk factors. Even some patients without renal disease have transient decreases in kidney function while on postopterative doses of NSAIDs for pain relief. Antibiotics may also cause nephropathy, mainly due to allergic reactions. Immunosuppressants, like those used after kidney transplant, also increase the risk of drug-induced nephropathy. Contrast dye used during imaging studies causes nephropathy by causing severe vasospasm in the afferent arterioles and is the third-leading cause of kidney failure in hospitalized patients. People with diabetes mellitus, dehydration, or kidney disease or people who are on diuretics or have congestive heart failure are at higher risk for kidney damage caused by contrast dyes. As many as 30% of patients are left with permanent kidney damage.

Nephritis is a general term that refers to an inflammation of the kidney. Nephritis may affect the glomerulus, tubules, or interstitial tissue within the kidney. It may cause permanent kidney damage if not diagnosed and treated. Acute nephritis, which comes on suddenly, often occurs as an allergic reaction or hypersensitivity to drugs. Chronic nephritis may be caused by drug hypersensitivity, infection, high blood pressure, urinary blockage, or an autoimmune reaction. Hypercalcemia and other metabolic disorders can also cause chronic nephritis.

Glomerulonephritis is a type of nephritis that results in inflammation of the glomerulus. **Glomerulosclerosis** is scarring of the glomerulus. Both cause damage to the delicate filter apparatus. When the filter is damaged, blood cells and blood proteins enter the filtrate and eventually appear in the urine. Removal of waste products is decreased, and electrolyte balance is generally abnormal because of the change in urine chemistry. Glomerulosclerosis and glomerulonephritis may be primary, without any obvious cause, or secondary, due to another condition that causes kidney damage. There are many secondary causes of glomerulonephritis and glomerulosclerosis, including bacterial infection, drug toxicity, diabetes mellitus, systemic lupus erythematosus, and genetic disorders such as Alport's syndrome and Goodpasture's syndrome.

diabetic nephropathy *(neh FROP eh thee)* Damage to the kidneys as a result of prolonged levels of high blood glucose.

nephritis *(nef RYE tiss)* A general term referring to inflammation of the kidney.

glomerulonephritis *(glow MAIR you loh neh FRY tiss)* The inflammatory disease of the glomerular capsular membranes of the kidneys.

glomerulosclerosis *(glow MAIR you loh sklee ROW sis)* Fibrotic or scarring changes of the kidney.

Control of Tubular Reabsorption and Secretion

Glomerular filtration controls the rate of urine formation. Tubular reabsorption and secretion control the chemistry and volume of the urine. Substances that are reabsorbed move from the tubule back to the bloodstream via the peritubular capillaries and stay in the body. Substances that are secreted stay in the tubule and eventually leave the body via the urine. Thus, anything that affects reabsorption and secretion affects urine chemistry and/or volume.

The first thing that affects tubular reabsorption and secretion is tubule permeability. Each portion of the tubule can reabsorb and secrete different substances. Remember that molecules can move across membranes via several different methods. **Diffusion** is the movement of molecules from high to low concentration. **Osmosis** is the movement of water across a semipermeable membrane. Some molecules can only move across membranes by being carried across by proteins. This type of movement can be either active or passive. Differences in tubule permeability result in dramatic differences in which molecules are reabsorbed or secreted in each part of the tubule. See TABLE 16-2 ■ for a list of substances reabsorbed or secreted in each part of the tubule.

The second factor that affects tubular reabsorption and secretion is a special type of circulation around the nephron loop, called **countercurrent circulation**. When ions move across cell membranes, they move from areas of high to low concentration. They are said to move down their concentration gradient. In a solution, if there is a lot of solvent (water), there is less solute (dissolved substances), and vice versa, so you would expect that solute and solvent would move in opposite directions down their concentration gradients (FIGURE 16-10 ▲).

Because of the tendency for water and ions to move in opposite directions, the kidneys could not reabsorb both ions and water without the special selective environment around the nephron loop. One would be reabsorbed and one would be secreted if it weren't for selected areas of the nephron being impermeable to one or the other. The characteristics of the nephron that make the countercurrent circulation work include the concentration gradient in the fluid surrounding the nephron, with low ion concentration at the beginning of the descending loop and high concentration at the tip of the loop, and the differences in permeability between the descending loop (permeable to water) and ascending loop (permeable to ions).

diffusion Process of movement of a substance from high concentration to low concentration.

osmosis The passage of the solvent through a semipermeable membrane to equalize concentrations.

countercurrent circulation Exchange of substances between two streams on either side of a membrane. Helps control concentration of fluids as in the nephron loop.

TABLE 16-2 ■ INDIVIDUAL TUBULE FUNCTIONS

TUBULE	SUBSTANCES REABSORBED OR SECRETED
Proximal tubule	Potassium, chloride, sodium (80% of sodium is normally reabsorbed in the proximal tubule), magnesium, bicarbonate, phosphate, amino acids, glucose, fructose, galactose, lactate, citric acid, water, hydrogen (H^+), neurotransmitters, bile, uric acid, drugs, toxins, ammonia, urea
Descending loop	Water (90% of the water is normally reabsorbed in the descending loop), urea
Ascending loop	Sodium, potassium, chloride, urea
Distal tubule	Sodium, potassium, chloride, hydrogen (H^+), water
Collecting duct	Sodium, potassium, chloride, water, urea

Side A   **Side B**

FIGURE 16-10 ▲ Movement of solute (ions) and solvent (water) down their concentration gradient.

As filtrate flows into the descending loop, *water* is reabsorbed, and the concentration of ions in the loop increases as water leaves the tubule. As the filtrate turns the corner and enters the ascending loop, much of the water has left, and the fluid is extremely concentrated. The ascending loop is permeable only to ions, so *ions* are reabsorbed from the ascending loop. Water and ions that leave the renal tubule enter the capillaries and go back to the bloodstream (see **FIGURE 16-11** ▲).

The third set of factors that affect reabsorption and secretion are several hormones that regulate blood pressure. It should come as no surprise that these mechanisms affect kidney function because the kidneys control ion and fluid balance. The hormones that affect the kidneys perform a variety of functions. You met some of these hormones during your visit to the cardiovascular and endocrine systems.

- **Antidiuretic hormone (ADH)** is made by the hypothalamus and secreted from the posterior pituitary when blood pressure decreases or blood ionic concentration increases. ADH increases the permeability of the distal tubule and the collecting duct so that more water is reabsorbed, thereby increasing the blood volume and blood pressure and diluting the ionic concentration. Less urine is produced as more water is reabsorbed, hence the name antidiuretic. Alcohol inhibits ADH from working and thus prevents the distal tubules and collecting ducts from becoming permeable to water. The water then stays in the collecting ducts and is sent to the bladder, thereby increasing urination. The more beverages containing alcohol that you drink, the more dehydrated you become.
- **Aldosterone** is an adrenocorticosteroid, a steroid secreted by the adrenal cortex. Aldosterone is secreted when plasma sodium decreases or plasma potassium increases. It increases the reabsorption of sodium ions (thus bringing more back into the blood)

antidiuretic hormone (ADH) *(AN tye dye yoo RET ik)* Hormone secreted by the posterior pituitary gland. It stimulates the kidneys to move water back into the blood to increase the volume of blood.

aldosterone *(al DOSS ter ohn)* Most abundant and biologically active of the mineralocorticoid hormones secreted by the adrenal cortex. It regulates the balance of electrolytes, keeping sodium (and water) in the blood while excreting potassium in the urine.

FIGURE 16-11 ▲ Sites of tubular reabsorption and secretion.

atrial natriuretic peptide (ANP) *(AY tree al NAY tree your ET ick PEP tide)* Hormone released by the atria when blood pressure rises. Causes increased excretion of water by the kidney, thereby decreasing blood pressure.

renin-angiotensin-aldosterone system *(RIN in-an gee oh TEN sen-al DOSS ter ohn)* A complex hormone system that regulates blood volume and blood pressure. The system is triggered when blood flow to the kidney decreases.

juxtaglomerular apparatus *(JUKS tah glow MAIR you lair)* A special group of cells near the glomerulus that secrete renin into the bloodstream.

angiotensinogen *(AN jee oh ten SIN oh jin)* A protein produced by the liver.

and secretion of potassium ions (thus decreasing the plasma levels) by the distal tubule and ascending limb of the nephron loop. Because sodium is reabsorbed back into the bloodstream, so is more water, and urine volume therefore decreases under the influence of aldosterone.

- **Atrial natriuretic peptide (ANP)** is secreted by the atria of the heart when blood volume increases. As blood flow into the right atrium increases, the right atrium stretches and releases ANP. ANP decreases sodium reabsorption and therefore increases urination. Does this make sense? If blood volume has increased dramatically, how would you keep blood pressure constant? Would you get rid of water or keep more water?

- The **renin-angiotensin-aldosterone system** is a series of chemical reactions that regulate blood pressure in several different ways. When there is a decrease in blood flow to the kidneys, a special group of cells near the glomerulus called the **juxtaglomerular apparatus** secretes renin into the bloodstream. Renin converts **angiotensinogen,** a protein made by the liver, into angiotensin I. Another enzyme made by the lungs, angiotensin converting enzyme (ACE), converts angiotensin I to angiotensin II. Angiotensin II (active angiotensin) has several effects. It increases thirst, increases aldosterone secretion, and causes vasoconstriction. Blood pressure is therefore increased either by increased fluid volume due to higher water intake or decreased urination caused by increased levels of aldosterone. Notice how the kidneys, lungs, and liver work together to regulate blood pressure. Many patients with high blood pressure may be given an ACE inhibitor, which inhibits the renin-angiotensin-aldosterone system and therefore lowers blood pressure.

Amazing Body Facts

Tubular Reabsorption

You already know about the amazing ability of your kidneys to filter blood. However, the ability of your renal tubule to reabsorb the fluid filtered by the glomerulus is just as incredible. Your kidneys filter 160 liters (40 gallons) per day, yet you produce only about 1500 milliliters (less than 1 gallon) of urine per day!

APPLIED SCIENCE

Electrolytes and Acid Base Balance

The kidneys maintain electrolyte balance by selectively excreting or reabsorbing the electrolytes within the tubular system. One very important interaction is the relationship of hydrogen ions (H^+) and bicarbonate ions (HCO_3^-). The relationship between these ions determines the blood's **pH** (level of acidity or alkalinity). This is referred to as the **acid–base relationship.** If too much acid is present in the blood, H^+, which causes increased acidity (pH decrease), will be excreted to a greater level in the urine. At the same time, more bicarbonate ions (which neutralize acids) will be reabsorbed back into the acidic blood to bring the pH value back toward normal. The respiratory system also plays a role in maintaining the acid–base relationship by increasing ventilation to "blow off" more acid in the form of exhaled carbon dioxide (carbonic acid) if the blood is too acidic.

Pathology Connection

UREMIA AND RENAL FAILURE

Uremia is a blood condition that accompanies kidney disease but cannot be explained by problems with volume, ion concentration, or hormonal abnormalities. The disorder appears to be due to the accumulation of organic wastes in the bloodstream (**azotemia**). The symptoms of uremia include fatigue, seizures, lack of appetite, decreased sense of smell and taste, cramps, mental confusion, metabolic disorders, insulin resistance, itching, hiccups, anemia, clotting abnormalities, and systemic inflammation. Uremia is very difficult to treat. A low-protein diet and kidney replacement therapy (dialysis or transplant) are the only treatments.

A transplant involves acquiring a donor organ from someone with a similar immune system, so finding a compatible transplant donor can take time. In the interim, kidney dialysis serves as a substitute kidney by externally performing the functions of a kidney upon the blood. Dialysis leads to partially treated uremia, prolonging the life of patients but not treating the condition fully. In 2007 more than 300,000 people were on kidney dialysis. Currently, the 5-year survival rate for patients on dialysis is approximately only 40%. Kidney transplant is the only effective treatment. See **FIGURE 16-12** ▲ on the location of a transplanted kidney within the body.

Hemolytic uremic syndrome is a disorder caused by an infection with the bacteria *E. coli,* typically from eating undercooked meat. The bacteria infect the digestive tract and release toxins that destroy red blood cells. The damaged red blood cells lodge in the blood vessels in the kidneys, blocking them and preventing blood flow to the nephrons. Without treatment, permanent kidney damage may result.

(continued)

pH A test to determine how acidic or alkaline a substance is.

acid-base relationship The relationship between the hydrogen ion and bicarbonate ions within the body to determine blood pH.

uremia *(yoo REE mee uh)* Blood found in urine as a result of a pathologic process.

azotemia (uremia) *(AZ oh TEE mee uh)* Condition of increased amounts of nitrogenous waste products in the blood.

hemolytic uremic syndrome An acute condition consisting of acute nephropathy, thrombocytopenia, and microangiopathic hemolytic anemia and is caused by eating contaminated or raw meats (esp. hamburger) containing *E. coli* *0157:H7.*

Pathology Connection (continued)

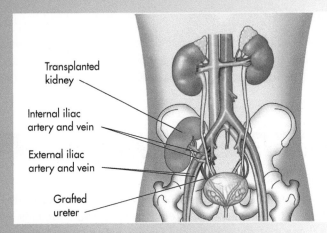

FIGURE 16-12 ▲ Placement of transplanted kidney.

kidney disease
Impaired functioning of the kidneys leading to a buildup of toxic waste products and fluids in the body.

renal disease See kidney disease.

kidney failure See kidney disease.

acute renal failure
Rapid decrease in kidney function as measured by blood urea and creatinine levels.

chronic kidney disease Ongoing progressive kidney disease lasting three or more months.

Kidney disease (also known as **renal disease** or **kidney failure**) is a spectrum of disorders including acute renal failure, chronic kidney disease, and end-stage kidney disease (kidney failure). Diabetes and hypertension are the number one and two causes of kidney failure. Fortunately, both conditions are largely preventable through proper diet, exercise, and weight control. Even if either one of these conditions develops, kidney failure can usually be prevented through early detection and the use of proper medication. There are many other risk factors for renal failure, including injury, ischemia, nephrotoxic medications, hypovolemia, hypotension, liver disease, lupus, infections, urinary tract obstruction, immune system malfunctions, PKD, and cardiovascular disease. Symptoms of renal failure include decreased urine output, uremia, fluid retention, anorexia, fatigue, hiccups, nausea, mental confusion, clotting disorders, and seizures. Staging of kidney disease is often determined by glomerular filtration rate. In the early stages of kidney disease, symptoms are vague and mild. As kidney function worsens, symptoms increase in severity and number.

Acute renal failure is a rapid decrease in kidney function, as measured by blood urea and creatinine levels, which develops over minutes or days. Acute renal failure can be caused by hypoperfusion (decreased blood supply) to the kidney, urinary tract abnormalities, crushing injuries or injury to renal blood vessels or other renal tissues. Decreased blood supply to the kidney due to decreased blood pressure leads to tissue damage, which leads to decreased renal function. It is also possible for local kidney damage to occur even in the range of normal blood pressure. Acute renal failure is exacerbated by the presence of any risk factors for kidney disease, including diabetes mellitus, heart disease, or existing kidney disease. In addition, the use of NSAIDs or contrast dyes increases the likelihood that acute renal failure will develop. Acute renal failure is treated by treating the cause, replacing fluid volume, normalizing BP, decreasing nephrotoxic drugs, and treating any infections. Some patients may require kidney dialysis or transplant therapy. If no structural changes occur in the kidney, patients can recover from acute renal failure in 1 or 2 days if the cause of the failure is treated; however, if the kidneys are permanently damaged, patients may develop chronic renal failure.

Chronic kidney disease (chronic renal failure) is defined as an ongoing, progressive kidney disease lasting 3 months or more. In the United States 8 million adults have moderate or severe chronic kidney disease, and that number is on the rise. In the early stages, chronic renal failure

Pathology Connection (continued)

is often asymptomatic. In later stages symptoms increase in severity and number as kidney function deteriorates. The most common risk factor for chronic kidney disease is diabetes mellitus (45%), followed by hypertension (20%), cardiovascular disease, age, obesity, ethnicity (African Americans, Latinos, and Native Americans are at higher risk), nephrotoxic drugs, polycystic kidney disease, lupus, and structural damage to the kidneys. Often, the progression can be controlled by treating the underlying cause of the damage or controlling blood pressure and blood cholesterol. Screening for and treating risk factors for kidney disease may delay or even prevent the development of the disease. For patients who already have kidney disease, treatment consists of treating the underlying cause, decreasing progression, and preparing patients for kidney replacement. Treatments include angiotensin-converting enzyme (ACE) inhibitors, angiotensin receptor blockers, statin drugs, smoking cessation, and good blood sugar control. As the disease progresses, patients may need kidney replacement.

Eventually, chronic kidney failure may lead to **end-stage renal failure**; however, most chronic kidney disease patients do not reach end-stage disease. Instead, most patients with kidney disease die of cardiovascular disease, often in early stages of kidney disease. Thus many of the treatments for chronic kidney disease focus on decreasing cardiovascular risk factors that accompany loss of kidney function. End-stage renal failure is the final stage of renal failure. Nearly half a million patients in the United States have end-stage renal failure. Patients in end-stage renal failure can be treated only with kidney dialysis or transplantation.

end stage renal failure Final stage of chronic kidney failure that can be only treated by kidney dialysis or kidney transplantation.

Clinical Application

KIDNEY DISEASE AND HYPERTENSION

It should be pretty clear now that blood pressure and the kidneys are intimately connected. One of the most important risk factors for kidney disease is hypertension. If blood pressure is high all the time, that pressure damages the delicate blood vessels of the nephron, leading eventually to chronic kidney disease. However, decreased blood flow to the kidneys also causes kidney damage due to ischemia. In addition, the kidneys are an integral part of blood pressure control mechanisms. The connection between kidney function and blood pressure can set up a vicious cycle that exacerbates kidney injuries (positive feedback). For example, in kidneys damaged by nephropathy, blood flow to the kidneys decreases, causing a decrease in glomerular filtration rate. To compensate, the kidneys release renin to raise blood pressure. Systemic blood pressure (BP) rises. However, because the kidneys are damaged, the increased blood pressure does not improve circulation in the kidneys. The kidneys increase blood pressure more, but kidney function does not improve. However, pressure in the renal blood vessels rises with systemic BP, causing more damage to the kidney. If the rise in BP is not stopped, the damage will progress as BP rises. Hypertension causes kidney damage and damaged kidneys work to increase blood pressure, causing hypertension. It's a classic runaway positive feedback loop. In addition, damage to the kidney also causes abnormalities in regulation of sodium balance, which exacerbates the problem. That's why in early nephropathy, ACE inhibitors and other medications that lower BP may reverse or at least slow down the progression of kidney damage, and why people with hypertension are often told to decrease their salt intake.

TEST YOUR KNOWLEDGE 16-2

Choose the best answer:

1. Glomerular filtrate is most similar in composition to:
   a. blood
   b. lymph
   c. urine
   d. none of the above

2. When substances move from the tubule into the bloodstream, this is known as:
   a. secretion
   b. reabsorption
   c. filtration
   d. all of the above

3. Which of the following is usually completely reabsorbed in the proximal tubule?
   a. sodium
   b. urea
   c. glucose
   d. water

4. The descending nephron loop is permeable to _____, whereas the ascending is permeable to _____.
   a. water; ions
   b. ions; water
   c. water; water
   d. ions; ions

5. If blood pressure increases beyond normal range, what happens to glomerular filtration rate?
   a. It increases.
   b. It decreases.
   c. It stays the same.
   d. None of the above.

6. Which of the following is not typically found in urine?
   a. glucose
   b. protein
   c. blood cells
   d. all of the above

7. Renin is released by the kidney when:
   a. blood glucose increases
   b. blood flow to the kidney decreases
   c. blood pressure rises
   d. angiotensin is in short supply

8. Which of the following is a symptom of renal disease?
   a. high blood pressure
   b. proteinuria
   c. high serum creatinine
   d. all may be symptoms

9. Which of the following is the most common cause of nephropathy and chronic kidney failure?
   a. urinary tract infections
   b. systemic lupus erythematosis
   c. diabetes mellitus
   d. kidney dialysis

Pathology Connection

DIALYSIS OR KIDNEY TRANSPLANT THERAPY

For patients in end-stage renal failure, the only treatment is kidney replacement therapy. Kidney replacement therapy consists of either kidney dialysis, in which the patient's blood is filtered by an artificial or biological filter, or kidney transplant, the surgical replacement of the damaged kidney with a donor kidney.

There are two types of kidney dialysis, **hemodialysis** and **peritoneal dialysis**. During hemodialysis, blood is removed from the patient via a needle and IV line and circulated through a dialysis machine. In the machine, blood is passed through a semipermeable membrane that removes fluid, electrolytes, and wastes. The blood is then returned to the patient through another IV line. Hemodialysis must be performed about two to three times a week, usually at a dialysis center. Some patients may also do home dialysis. It usually takes about 2 to 4 hours each time.

During peritoneal dialysis, dialysis fluid is pumped into the peritoneal cavity. Waste from body fluids is filtered across the peritoneum and into the dialysis fluid. After several hours, the dialysis fluid is removed. The peritoneum acts as a biological filter. Peritoneal dialysis is more convenient for patients because it can be done while patients are sleeping and requires less equipment when traveling. However, the downside is the patient must do multiple exchanges each day, and it is typically done each day because it is not as efficient as hemodialysis.

Kidney dialysis is only a partial treatment for patients in end-stage renal failure. Dialysis does not work as well as functional kidneys and does a particularly bad job at treating uremia. In addition, dialysis has many side effects, including low BP, nausea, cramps, headaches, fatigue, infection, fluid overload, and clotting abnormalities. Outpatient dialysis is also inconvenient because patients must be near the dialysis center. See FIGURE 16-13 ▲ for illustrations of peritoneal and hemodialysis.

hemodialysis *(HEE moh dye AL ih sis)* The use of an artificial kidney to clear waste products, toxins, and excess fluid from the blood.

peritoneal dialysis *(per ih TONE ee al dye AL eh sis)* A form of dialysis, in which the lining of the peritoneal cavity is used as the dialyzing membrane.

FIGURE 16-13 ▲ Peritoneal dialysis and hemodialysis.

(continued)

> ### *Pathology Connection (continued)*
>
> Kidney transplant, the replacement of a damaged kidney with a donor kidney, is the only real cure for end-stage renal disease. There are three types of transplants: cadaver transplants, living related-donor transplants, and living unrelated-donor transplants. Kidney transplants are the second most common organ transplant in the United States (with corneal transplants being the most common), with 9,000 kidneys transplanted each year. Kidney transplants are also quite successful. One year posttransplant, 90% of patients still survive; at 3 years the figure is 80%. Even after 10 years, 50% of kidney transplant recipients still survive. There are several possible complications of kidney transplant, including the typical complications from surgery and the possibility of organ rejection. Kidney transplant recipients must take immunosuppressant drugs after transplant, usually for the rest of their lives. Ironically, some of the best antirejection drugs are also nephrotoxic. There are never enough kidneys to go around. Every year thousands of patients die waiting for donor kidneys.

The Urinary Bladder and Urination Reflex

Glomerular filtrate flows out the collecting ducts into the minor calyces and then into the major calyces that form the renal pelvis. Once the glomerular filtrate leaves the collecting ducts, its concentration cannot be changed. At this point, filtrate is urine. Urine collects in the renal pelvis and flows down the ureters to the urinary bladder, where it is stored.

The urinary bladder is a small, hollow organ lined with transitional epithelium, the only epithelium stretchy enough to expand as the bladder fills. The stretchiness of the bladder is enhanced by a series of pleats called **rugae**, similar to the rugae that allow for stomach expansion. The bladder has a muscular wall consisting of circular and longitudinal smooth muscle and is covered by connective tissue and parietal peritoneum (see FIGURE 16-14 ▲). The muscle layer is known as the **detrusor muscle**.

As urine accumulates, the bladder fills and stretches and can hold approximately 500 mL of fluid. At some point, this stretch triggers urination, also know as micturation or voiding—the emptying of the bladder. For years, urination was thought to be a spinal cord reflex, influenced but not controlled by the brain. New research, however, suggests that the brain actually controls urination. When the bladder is full, signals are sent from the bladder to the spinal cord and then to the pons. The pons sends parasympathetic signals down the spinal cord that cause contraction of the muscular walls of the bladder, and the bladder empties. The "urge to go," caused by bladder contractions, is involuntary.

Urine leaves the bladder via the **urethra**, a thin muscular tube lined with several different types of epithelium along its length. The urine travels from the bladder through the urethra to the final opening, called the **urethral meatus**. (For details on the anatomy of the urethra, including sexual differences, see Chapter 17.) Parts of the brain can inhibit urination by controlling the **internal urethral sphincter**, a valve at the junction of the bladder and the urethra, and the **external urethral sphincter**, a valve that is part of the muscles of the pelvic floor. Sympathetic stimulation of these sphincters prevents urine from leaving the body (see FIGURE 16-15 ▲). Fortunately, although you have little control over contractions of the bladder wall, you have very good voluntary control over the sphincters.

rugae *(ROO gay)* Folds in the mucosa of the bladder that disappear as the bladder fills with urine.

detrusor muscle The three-layered muscular wall of the urinary bladder.

urethra *(yoo REE thrah)* Tube that connects the bladder to the outside of the body.

urethral meatus *(yoo REE thrall mee AY tus)* The final opening of the urethra.

internal urethral sphincter *(yoo REE thruhl SFINGK ter)* Valve at the junction of the bladder and urethra.

external urethral sphincter *(yoo REE thral SFINK ter)* One of two valves, made of circular muscle, that allows voluntary control of urination.

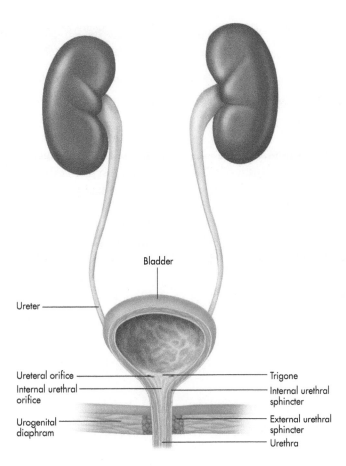

Bladder

Ureter

Ureteral orifice

Internal urethral orifice

Urogenital diaphram

Trigone

Internal urethral sphincter

External urethral sphincter

Urethra

FIGURE 16-14 ▲ The urinary bladder.

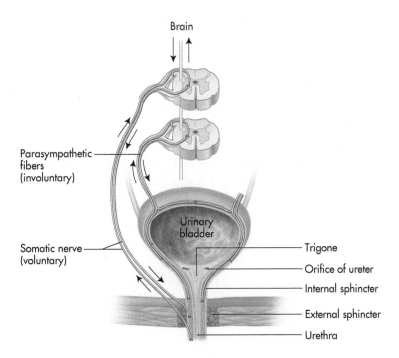

Brain

Parasympathetic fibers (involuntary)

Somatic nerve (voluntary)

Urinary bladder

Trigone

Orifice of ureter

Internal sphincter

External sphincter

Urethra

FIGURE 16-15 ▲ Control of urination.

Pathology Connection

INCONTINENCE AND URINARY TRACT INFECTION (UTI)

incontinence
(in KAHNT in ins)
Condition of involuntary urination and defecation.

Incontinence is the inability to control urination. Often incontinence is accompanied by urinary urgency, urinary frequency, and nighttime urination. There are many causes of incontinence, including overactive bladder, urinary tract infection, and benign prostatic hypertrophy (BPH). (See Chapter 17 for information about the closely related reproduction system.)

urinary tract infection (UTI) or cystitis A general term for an infection involving the kidney(s), ureter(s), or bladder.

Urinary tract infection (UTI) or cystitis is most often caused by the movement of fecal bacteria into the urinary tract, infecting the urethra or urinary bladder. Symptoms include frequent, painful urination often with very small volume, nighttime urination, urine cloudiness, foul smell, and hematuria. Women are 50 times more likely than men to develop urinary tract infections, probably because women's urethras are shorter than men's. Also at risk are elderly hospitalized patients, patients requiring catheters, pregnant women, postmenopausal women, patients with structural abnormalities of the urinary tract, and men with BPH. UTIs are diagnosed via urinalysis (hematuria, bacteria in urine) and bacterial culture of the urine. Urinary tract infections must be treated promptly because they can cause damage to the kidneys if the infection moves from the bladder up the ureters and into the kidneys. Untreated UTIs may develop into pyelonephritis, an infection of the kidneys. Symptoms include pain, fever, chills, nausea, fatigue, mental confusion, and UTI symptoms. In the elderly, mental confusion may be the *only* symptom of kidney infection. Treatment for UTI includes antibiotics and increased fluids.

interstitial cystitis Chronic form of urinary tract infection.

Many patients with UTI develop more chronic conditions, including recurrent UTI or **interstitial cystitis**. Interstitial cystitis is a disorder with bladder, pelvic, vaginal, or abdominal pain; hematuria; and chronic UTI symptoms including urinary frequency, urgency, and nighttime urination. These symptoms may overlap with endometriosis. Some patients with interstitial cystitis have a history of UTIs. Treatment for chronic UTI or interstitial cystitis includes preventative antibiotics and adequate hydration. An experimental treatment, the addition of hyaluronic acid into the bladder as a protective barrier, has shown some promise for preventing chronic UTIs and treating interstitial cystitis. The home remedy of consumption of cranberry juice or cranberry extract for treatment of UTI has shown little promise. In studies, the doses necessary to prevent UTI caused unpleasant side effects, including acid reflux and nausea.

overactive bladder Bladder condition leading to increased urge to urinate.

Overactive bladder is a common (33 million people in the United States) condition with symptoms of urinary urgency, nighttime urination, and urinary frequency with or without incontinence, but without pain or obvious urinary pathology such as hematuria or UTI. Though overactive bladder does not involve infection or progressive degenerative illness as do other renal disorders, patients with untreated overactive bladder experience significant decrease in quality of life, increased stress from dependence on restroom availability, and fatigue from interrupted sleep. Overactive bladder is more common in women than men and much more common in people after age 40. The cause of overactive bladder is unknown, but it is thought to be caused either by abnormalities of the bladder muscles, the nerves innervating the bladder, or the stretch receptors in the bladder wall. The cause is probably different in different patients. Diagnosis of overactive bladder is made mainly by ruling out other disorders using medical history, physical exam, and urinalysis. Treatment is difficult. The most common and effective nonpharmaceutical treatment is bladder training, designed to decrease the sensitivity of the bladder to fullness and to increase bladder control. The most effective drug treatments are anticholinergic drugs and alpha adrenergic agonists, which block parasympathetic stimulation or increase sympathetic activity. These drugs have side effects including dry mouth and anxiety. These drugs may be dangerous

Pathology Connection (continued)

for patients with heart disease or high blood pressure. The combination of training and drugs is more effective than either treatment alone, but nearly 50% of patients are not cured. Many patients make lifestyle changes such as drinking fewer fluids and avoiding situations in which frequent trips to the restroom could be problematic. Medications, including antidepressants, nerve blockers, and botulinum toxin, are also used with varying degrees of effectiveness.

There are a variety of other conditions associated with urination. Some of these conditions are related to production of urine or frequency of urination. **Nocturia** is frequent urination at night. It can be caused by a variety of conditions, including diabetes mellitus, urinary tract infection, or congestive heart failure. Nocturia can also result from drinking too much fluid before bedtime. **Polyuria** is the production of large amounts of urine. Polyuria is often a symptom of untreated diabetes mellitus. Nocturnal **enuresis** is a condition in which the person, usually a child, wets the bed during sleep. Enuresis can be caused by poor muscle control, neurological disease, sleep disorders, or disorders of the urinary tract and can happen any time. **Anuria** is a condition in which *no* urine is produced. Anuria may be caused by an obstruction, such as a kidney stone or tumor, in the ureter or urethra. **Oliguria** is diminished production of urine and can be an early sign of acute renal failure.

Sometimes, conditions related to urination can help a physician to diagnose disease. **Glycosuria** is the secretion of sugar in urine. It is usually a sign of untreated diabetes mellitus. **Pyuria** is the secretion of pus in urine. It can be a sign of a urinary tract infection. **Dysuria** is painful urination. It is also often related to bacterial infection in the urinary tract.

nocturia *(nawk TOO ree ah)* Frequent urination at night.

polyuria *(PAUL ee YOOR ee uh)* Production of large amounts of urine.

enuresis *(IN yoo REE sis)* A condition of involuntary urine discharge after the age at which bladder function comes under an individual's conscious control.

anuria *(an YOO ree ah)* Condition where no urine is produced.

oliguria Diminished production of urine.

glycosuria *(GLY koh SHOO ree ah)* Condition of sugar in the urine.

pyuria *(pye YOU ree uh)* Pus in the urine.

dysuria *(dis YOO ree ah)* Painful urination.

A QUICK TRIP THROUGH DISORDERS OF THE URINARY SYSTEM

DISORDER	ETIOLOGY	SIGNS AND SYMPTOMS	DIAGNOSTIC TEST(S)	TREATMENTS
Kidney stones	Increased urine concentration, infection, kidney disease. Stones are composed of calcium and uric acid crystals. They get larger and can block ureters.	Severe pain, hematuria, fever, chills, nausea, urinary urgency.	Symptoms, imaging, urinalysis, patient history.	Pain relief, extracorporeal shock wave lithotripsy, ureteroscopy, percutaneous nephrolithotomy.
Polycystic kidney disease	Genetic disorder causing large cysts to form in kidney.	Enlarged, cystic kidneys, hypertension, UTI, dilute urine, liver cysts, pain, hematuria, aneurysm.	Imaging, genetic tests.	Medication, kidney replacement, no cure.

(continued)

A QUICK TRIP *(continued)*

DISORDER	ETIOLOGY	SIGNS AND SYMPTOMS	DIAGNOSTIC TEST(S)	TREATMENTS
Ischemic nephropathy	Decreased blood flow to kidneys.	Kidney failure, uremia, hypertension or hypotension, decreased urine output, increased serum creatinine and urea.	Urinalysis, blood tests.	Treat underlying cause and symptoms, kidney replacement if needed.
Diabetic nephropathy	Diabetes mellitus.	Early stages: increased glomerular filtration, protein in urine. Later: uremia, hypertension, pain, and loss of sensation in the extremities.	Blood tests, urinalysis.	Tight glycemic control, blood pressure medications, lipid control, diet, kidney replacement.
Drug-induced nephropathy	Drugs toxic to kidney tissue, especially contrast dye and NSAIDs.	Same as for ischemic nephrothpathy.	Same as for ischemic nephropathy.	Stop drugs, do not use contrast dyes for patients with known risk factors, keep patients well hydrated when using contrast dyes.
Glomerulonephritis and glomerulosclerosis	Inflammation and scarring of the glomerulus.	Same as for ischemic nephrothpathy.	Same as for ischemic nephropathy.	Depends on cause. Treating underlying cause may decrease progression.
Uremia	Buildup of organic waste products in blood due to renal insufficiency.	Fatigue, neuropathy, seizures, lack of appetite, decreased smell and taste, mental confusion, insulin resistance, itching, inflammation, clotting.	Blood tests.	Difficult to treat. Dialysis only partial treatment. Transplant only cure.
Diabetes insipidus	ADH deficiency.	Copious, dilute urine.	Rule out diabetes mellitus, ADH levels.	Tumor removal, pre- and postoperative medication
Renal failure (kidney disease)	Either acute or progressive damage to the kidneys from many different causes.	Decreased urine output, uremia, fluid retention, loss of appetite, fatigue, hiccups, nausea, mental confusion, clotting disorders, seizures.	Blood test, urinalysis, imaging.	Blood pressure medication, glucose control, diet, treatment of underlying condition, prevention of cardiovascular disease, kidney replacement when progresses to end stage disease.

DISORDER	ETIOLOGY	SIGNS AND SYMPTOMS	DIAGNOSTIC TEST(S)	TREATMENTS
Urinary tract infection (UTI)	Bacterial infection of urinary tract, usually bladder.	Painful urination, urinary frequency, nighttime urination, foul smell, cloudy urine.	Urinalysis.	Antibiotics, prevention of recurrence is difficult.
Overactive bladder	Unknown, may be abnormalities in nervous or muscle control of bladder.	Frequent urination without pain or infection.	Rule out UTI.	Bladder training, sympathetic drugs.
Hemolytic uremic syndrome	Bacterial infection with certain strains of *E. coli,* toxins destroy red blood cells, which damages kidneys.	Fever, abdominal pain, pallor, fatigue, bruising, decreased urination, swelling.	Blood tests, history.	Blood transfusion, kidney dialysis.

Pharmacology Corner

High blood pressure is a common condition that can affect the kidneys. In addition, kidney disease can also lead to high blood pressure, and therefore treatment of high blood pressure is critical. One way of treating high blood pressure is to decrease blood volume by decreasing overall fluid volume. This can be accomplished via the use of diuretics, which will increase urine output. Lasix™ is an older drug that still is used and works by not allowing sodium and thus water to be reabsorbed; therefore more is excreted. Another way of controlling blood pressure is through the use of ACE inhibitors. ACE inhibitors decrease blood levels of angiotensin II, which leads to systemic vasodilation. The relaxation of the vessel walls will decrease overall blood pressure.

In cases of severe hypotension (cardiac and septic shock), renal perfusion may be severely decreased, which can lead to renal damage. In these cases, dopamine can be administered to increase blood flow to the renal vessels. Dopamine is very dosage dependent and must be given in low dosages to achieve this affect.

Kidney transplants are becoming more common and successful due to technological advancements. One reason for their long-term success is the use of immunosuppressant drugs that reduce the chance of organ rejection.

Because the kidneys act as a filter for all blood, drugs found in the bloodstream may lead to nephrotoxicity. A variety of prescription and OTC drugs can cause damage by direct toxicity, allergy-induced damage to the kidney, or crystallization in the kidney. The overuse of pain medications, like the nonsteroidal anti-inflammatory drugs (NSAIDs) ibuprofen and naproxyn, can also lead to renal damage. Antibiotics may also cause nephropathy, mainly due to allergic reactions.

UTIs are very common infections that can be treated with antibiotics and increased fluids. Two common antibiotics used are Bactrim® and Cipro®. The most effective drug treatments for incontinence are anticholinergic drugs, which block the parasympathetic stimulation to empty your bladder. These drugs have side effects, including dry mouth and anxiety, and may be dangerous for patients with heart disease or high blood pressure. Therefore, bladder training may be preferred when possible.

SUMMARY

Snapshots from the Journey

- The urinary system consists of paired kidneys and paired ureters, which carry urine to the single urinary bladder. The urethra transports urine from the bladder to outside the body. The function of the urinary system is control of fluid and electrolyte balance and elimination of nitrogen-containing waste.

- A kidney is bean shaped and covered in a capsule. It has an indentation known as the renal hilum and an interior cavity known as the renal sinus. The kidney can be divided into three layers: renal cortex, renal medulla, and renal pelvis. The renal pelvis is a funnel that is divided into large pipes, the major calyces. Each major calyx is divided into several minor calyces. The renal pelvis empties into the ureter.

- The kidney is very well vascularized. Blood is supplied to each kidney by a renal artery. The blood vessels split into smaller and smaller branches until there are millions of tiny arterioles, the afferent arterioles. The afferent arterioles supply millions of nephrons, the functional unit of the kidney, with blood. Blood leaves the kidney by a series of veins and ultimately returns to circulation via the renal vein.

- The nephron is the functional unit of the kidney. There are millions of nephrons in each kidney. The nephron is divided into two parts. The renal corpuscle, consisting of the glomerulus (capillaries) and the glomerular capsule, filters blood and produces glomerular filtrate. The renal tubule, consisting of the proximal tubule, nephron loop, distal tubule, and collecting ducts, controls the concentration and volume of urine by reabsorbing and secreting water, electrolytes, and other molecules. The walls of the nephron are made of epithelium. The type of epithelium changes depending on the specific function of each part of the nephron.

- Urine is formed by a combination of three processes: glomerular filtration, tubular reabsorption, and tubular secretion. The selectivity of the glomerular filter is determined by the size of the openings in the filter and the difference between the blood pressure of the glomerulus and the pressure in the glomerular capsule. The size of the filter does not change unless the glomerulus is damaged. Protein, for example, cannot pass through the filter. However, the filtration rate will change if the pressure in the glomerulus changes. Most of the time, autoregulation, control of the diameter of the afferent arteriole, keeps glomerular pressure and glomerular filtration rate constant. However, sympathetic stimulation can regulate (in this case decrease) glomerular filtration and urine output due to constriction of afferent arterioles.

- Tubular reabsorption and secretion is controlled by differences in tubular permeability. The proximal tubule is the most versatile, reabsorbing dozens of different molecules. The nephron loop is part of an elaborate countercurrent mechanism, with the descending loop permeable to water and ascending loop permeable to ions. The distal tubule and collecting ducts reabsorb water. The permeability of the renal tubule can be regulated by a number of hormones that control blood pressure. These hormones, aldosterone, ADH, atrial natriuretic peptide, and others, regulate blood pressure by regulating urine volume and ion secretion. Changes in urine volume change total body fluid volume and thereby change blood pressure.

SUMMARY

- The urinary bladder is a collecting and storage device for urine and is located in the pelvic cavity. It has a muscular wall. Contractions of the muscle result in voiding (urination), emptying the bladder. Urination is a reflex controlled by parasympathetic neurons in the pons. Signals from a full bladder reach the pons. The neurons in the pons then send signals for the bladder to contract. Sympathetic neurons control two valves, the internal and external urethral sphincters, which allow significant conscious control of the urination reflex.

- The symptoms of renal disease are common no matter what the cause of the kidney dysfunction. They include blood in the urine, decreased removal of wastes from the blood (increased BUN and serum creatinine), and hypertension. Treatment of kidney disease usually involves treating the underlying cause of the disorder, by decreasing blood pressure, tightening blood sugar control, changing lifestyle, and decreasing cardiovascular disease risk factors. Most people with kidney disease do not die from uremia caused by end-stage renal failure, but from cardiovascular disease caused in part by kidney dysfunction. The only cure for kidney disease is kidney transplant, but many patients can be helped by kidney dialysis.

MARIA'S STORY

During a recent trip to the doctor's office, Maria had a standard urinalysis. The results worry her doctor. In her urine there was a tiny amount of protein. The doctor orders more extensive tests.

a. Why is Maria's doctor concerned? It's only a little protein.

_____

_____

b. What other tests should the doctor order?

_____

_____

c. When the tests come back, the doctor tells Maria she needs to go on an ACE inhibitor, even though her blood pressure is normal. What is the diagnosis?

_____

_____

RAY'S STORY

Ray, paralyzed from the neck down after a swimming pool accident, has been doing pretty well except for one thing. He keeps having urinary tract infections.

a. Why is Ray so susceptible to urinary tract infections?

_____

_____

REVIEW QUESTIONS

Multiple Choice

1. The function of this part of the renal tubule is filtration of blood:
   a. renal calyx
   b. renal corpuscle
   c. renal cortex
   d. renal colums

2. The collecting ducts are found in this part of the kidney:
   a. renal cortex
   b. renal capsule
   c. renal pelvis
   d. renal pyramids

3. This tube leads from the urinary bladder to the outside:
   a. collecting ducts
   b. distal tubule
   c. ureter
   d. none of the above

4. The ion responsible for causing acidic blood is:
   a. Na^+
   b. H^+
   c. K^+
   d. HCO_3^-

5. The renal hormone secreted by the hypothalamus when blood pressure decreases to promote the reabsorption of water is:
   a. aldosterone
   b. atrial natriuretic peptide
   c. antidiuretic hormone
   d. epinephrine

6. The most common genetic disorder of the kidney is:
   a. diabetes mellitus
   b. nephropathy
   c. polycystic kidney disease
   d. overactive bladder

7. BUN is:
   a. blood glucose
   b. nitrogen wastes in blood
   c. blood pressure
   d. where you put a hamburger

8. This disorder appears to be caused by the buildup of organic waste in blood:
   a. nephropathy
   b. diabetes mellitus
   c. uremia
   d. hypertension

9. Why are UTIs more common in women than men?
   a. men have better hygiene
   b. women go through menopause
   c. women have shorter urethras than men
   d. autoimmune disorders are often more common in women

10. The only cure for kidney disease is:
    a. prevention
    b. dialysis
    c. transplant
    d. there is no cure

Fill in the Blank

1. Most substances are reabsorbed or secreted in this part of the renal tubule: _____.

2. This part of the renal tubule has an elaborate countercurrent mechanism for reabsorption of sodium and water: _____.

3. This hormone is released by the heart when fluid volume increases: _____.

REVIEW QUESTIONS

4. Blood in the urine is called _____.

5. List two substances that should not be found in urine: _____ and _____.

Short Answer

1. List and explain the activity of three regulators of kidney function.

_____

_____

2. Explain the three processes that are necessary for urine formation. In which part of the nephron are these functions performed?

_____

_____

3. Describe the structure of the wall of the urinary bladder.

_____

_____

4. Explain the control of urination reflex.

_____

_____

5. List the symptoms of kidney failure.

_____

_____

6. Explain the relationship between blood pressure and kidney disease.

_____

_____

7. Explain the difference between overactive bladder and UTI.

_____

_____

Suggested Activities

1. Select a partner and trace the flow of a particular substance from blood through the kidney. What happens to hydrogen ions or vitamin C? Use the Internet to help you find the answers.

2. Quiz yourself. Do you know what happens in each part of the nephron? Do you know the difference between plasma, glomerular filtrate, and urine chemistry?

3. There are many different disorders that affect the kidneys. Use the Internet to research one of these diseases. How does it cause the changes in kidney function?

CAREER CONNECTIONS

Now that you have read this chapter, here is a list of related professions you may be interested in investigating for a future career:

• Ultrasound Technician

Research each profession and report on the following:

1. Profession description to include job responsibilities
2. Educational requirements
3. Job opportunities
4. Opportunities outside of the hospital setting
5. Salary range
6. Licensure and continuing education requirements

ANATOMY, PHYSIOLOGY, AND DISEASE IN ACTION

Materials:
Paper cup
Paper towel/wrapping paper roll
Scissors
Salt
Red hot candies/cinnamon imperials used for cake decorating
Two different colored sprinkles/ sugar crystals
Glue
Small ball of thick yarn

1. Cut paper cup and paper towel roll in half length-wise
2. In the bottom of the cup cut a slit just large enough and in the shape of the paper towel roll.
3. Inert the towel roll into the bottom of the cup. This represents Bowman's capsule and renal tubule (see Figure 16-7 in the text).
4. Place the small ball of yarn in the paper cup. This represents the glomerulus. Cut the yarn in two places and pull the pieces out of the cup to represent the afferent and efferent arterioles. The efferent should be long enough to extend down and wrap around the paper towel roll. This represents the peritubular capillaries.
5. Using the red hot candies as red blood cells, salt as sodium ions, one color of sprinkles to represent glucose and another color to represent urea, trace their journey from the afferent arteriole.
6. Glue each item to the yarn, paper cup, and paper towel roll to trace its path at each step through filtration, reabsorption, and secretion.

17

The Reproductive System
Replacement and Repair

For a city to run smoothly, it must have an infrastructure, buildings, roads, playgrounds, schools, and more. All these structures must be repaired on a regular basis, or if damaged beyond repair, they must be replaced. As a city grows along with its population, it needs the resources and means to expand. The same is true of your body. Cells and tissues are damaged or simply wear out. Damaged or worn-out cells and tissues must be repaired or replaced. Asexual reproduction, or mitosis, the process by which cells make exact copies of themselves, is absolutely necessary to maintain a healthy body. Mitosis was discussed in Chapter 4. Ultimately, cellular reproduction is needed for the complicated process by which humans produce new humans: sexual reproduction. Without this ability, the human species would die out, and the journey would end for the human race. Thankfully, all the splendid diversity of the human race is passed on for generations to come, who will also get to enjoy this amazing journey called "life."

LEARNING OUTCOMES

Upon completion of your journey through this chapter, you will be able to:

- Differentiate mitosis from meiosis
- Locate and describe the male and female reproductive organs
- Describe the function of the male and female reproductive organs
- Discuss the phases of the menstrual cycle
- Discuss the effects of hormonal control on the male and female reproductive systems
- Describe the stages of labor and delivery
- Explain the common disorders of the male and female reproductive systems

Pronunciation Guide

Pro·nun·ci·a·tion
Definitions/Parts

Correct pronunciation is important in any journey so that you and others are completely understood. Here is a "see and say" Pronunciation Guide for the more difficult terms to pronounce in this chapter. Please note that pronunciations given are referenced to medical dictionaries, and regional variations may exist.

amenorrhea (ah MEN oh REE ah)
bulbourethral gland (BUHL boh you REE thral)
cervix (SER viks)
clitoris (KLIT oh ris)
corpus luteum (CORE pus LOO tee uhm)
cryptorchidism (kript OR kid izm)
dysmenorrhea (DISS men oh REE ah)
endometriosis (EHN doh MEE tree OH sis)
endometrium (EHN doh MEE tree um)
epididymis (EP ih DID ih miss)
eukaryotic cell (you CARE ee AH tic)
fimbria (FIM bree ah)
follicle-stimulating hormone
   (FALL ih kul STIM you LAY ting HOR mohn)
follicular (fa LICK you lair)
gametes (GAM eets)
genitalia (jen ih TALE ee uh)
gonad (GO nad)
gonadotropin-releasing hormone
   (GOH nuh doh TROH pin)
human chorionic gonadotropin (HUE man core ee
   AH nik GOH nuh doh TROH pin)
hydrocele (HIGH droh seel)
labia majora (LAY bee ah mah JOR ah)
labia minora (LAY bee ah mih NOR ah)
luteal phase (LOO tee al faze)
luteinizing hormone (LOO tee en IZE ing)
mammary glands (MAM ah ree)
meiosis (my OH sis)
menses (MEN seez)
menstrual cycle (MEN stroo al)
menstruation (MEN stroo AY shun)
mesosalpinx (MESS oh SAL pinks)

mitosis (my TOE sis)
myometrium (MY oh MEE tree um)
oocyte (OH oh site)
oogenesis (OH oh JENN eh sis)
ovarian cycle (oh VAIR ee an)
ovary, ovaries (OH vah ree, OH vah reez)
ovulation (OV you LAY shun)
perimetrium (pair ee MEE tree um)
prepuce (PREE pewce)
primordial follicles (pry MORE dee all FALL ih kulz)
progesterone (proh JESS ter ohn)
proliferative (pro LIFF er ah TIV)
pudendal cleft (PEW den dall cleft)
semen (SEE men)
seminal vesicles (SEM ih nal VESS ih kulz)
seminiferous tubules
   (SEM ih NIF er uss TOO byoolz)
sertoli cells (sir TOW lee)
spermatids (SPER mat ids)
spermatocytes (sper MAT oh sites)
spermatogonia (sper MAT oh GO nee ah)
spermatozoa (sper MAT oh ZOE ah)
testicles (TESS tih kulz)
testis, testes (TESS tiss, TESS teez)
testosterone (tess TOSS ter ohn)
urethra (you REE thrah)
uterine cycle (YOU ter in)
uterus (YOU ter us)
vagina (vah JYE nah)
vaginitis (vaj ih NYE tiss)
vas deferens (VAS DEFF er enz)
vulva (VULL vah)
zygote (ZIGH goht)

TISSUE GROWTH AND REPLACEMENT

Although mitosis was discussed in Chapter 4, we will briefly review that form of cellular reproduction in this chapter. Cellular reproduction is the basis for all more complex reproduction, so this is a good starting point.

cellular reproduction See cell division.

cell division The process of cellular replication.

Mitosis

Cellular reproduction is the process of making a new cell. It is also known as **cell division** because one cell divides into two cells when it reproduces. Cells can only come from other cells. When cells make *identical* copies of themselves *without the involvement of* *another cell,* the process is called **asexual reproduction.** (Remember *a* means "without.") Most cells can reproduce themselves asexually, whether they are animal cells, plant cells, or bacteria.

The cells that make up the human body are a type of cell known as a **eukaryotic cell.** Eukaryotic cells have a nucleus, cellular organelles, and usually several chromosomes in the nucleus. (Reminder: The genetic material of the cell, DNA, is bundled into "packages" of chromatin known as chromosomes.) Because chromosomes carry all the instructions for the cells, all cells must have a complete set after reproduction. These instructions include how the cell is to function within the body and blueprints for reproduction. No matter whether a cell has one chromosome, like bacteria (not eukaryotic), or 46 chromosomes, like humans, all the chromosomes must be copied before the cell can divide.

Now let's go to the more complex form of cellular reproduction. Eukaryotic cells, like yours, must go through a more complicated set of maneuvers in order to reproduce. Not only do your cells have to duplicate all 46 of their chromosomes, but they have to make sure that each cell gets all the chromosomes and all the right organelles. The process of sorting the chromosomes so that each new cell gets the right number of copies of all the genetic material is called **mitosis.** Mitosis is the only way that eukaryotic cells can reproduce asexually. For a quick review of mitosis, go back to Chapter 4.

Mitosis in the Body

Mitosis, asexual cellular reproduction, serves many purposes in your body. Any time your cells must be replaced, mitosis is the method used to replace them. Many of your tissues, such as bone, epithelium, skin, and blood cells, are replaced on a regular basis. Repair and regeneration of damaged tissue is accomplished by mitosis as well. If you cut your hand, the skin is replaced, first by collagen, but eventually by the original tissue. Mitosis increases in cells near the injury so that the damaged or destroyed cells can be replaced. A broken bone is replaced in much the same way.

Growth is also accomplished by mitosis. Lengthening of bones as you grow, increases in muscle mass due to exercise, indeed, most ways that tissue gets bigger, are due to mitosis of cells in the tissues or organs. Without mitosis, your body would not be able to grow or replace old or damaged cells.

SEXUAL REPRODUCTION

Thus far we have discussed cell division for growth and repair, but we must also be able to perpetuate the species. This requires sexual reproduction.

Reduction Division: Meiosis

Many animals reproduce sexually; that is, they produce, with the aid of another individual, offspring that are not exactly identical to themselves. Sexual reproduction involves the union of a cell from one organism with a cell from another organism of the same species. In animals, females produce **eggs (ova),** and males produce **sperm** for the purpose of reproducing sexually. These special cells are known as **gametes.**

asexual reproduction Reproduction in which sex cells are not utilized.

eukaryotic cell *(yoo CARE ee awt ick)* The cells that make up the human body, possessing a nucleus, organelles, and several chromosomes.

mitosis Asexual cellular reproduction that produces exact copies of the original cell.

eggs (ova) Female sexual cells.

sperm Male reproductive cells possessing motility.

gametes *(GAM eets)* General term for reproductive cells of female or male origin.

meiosis *(mye OH sis)* Form of cellular division that produces gametes.

reduction division See meiosis.

Gametes are produced by a specialized type of cell division known as **meiosis,** or **reduction division.** Meiosis is called reduction division because the *daughter* cells produced at the end of meiosis have half as many chromosomes as the original *mother* cell. (Note: The cells are called mother cells and daughter cells even when we are talking about the process in males.) These daughter cells must have half as many chromosomes because they will fuse together during sexual reproduction. In humans, the total number of chromosomes in a cell is 46. If the gametes did not lose half of their chromosomes somewhere along the way, then the cell that resulted from sexual reproduction would have twice as many chromosomes (92 chromosomes) as a normal human cell. It is absolutely necessary to control the number of chromosomes in a cell. Cells with too few or too many chromosomes often die.

The fact that you were produced by the fusion of an egg from your mother and a sperm from your father means that your 46 chromosomes can be thought of as being 23 *pairs* of chromosomes. Each pair of chromosomes consists of one chromosome from your father and one from your mother. They can be thought of as pairs because they can be matched based on size, shape, and the genes they carry. For example, you get a chromosome 1 from your father and a chromosome 1 from your mother, the same for chromosomes 2, 3, 4, and up to 22.

Clinical Application

DOWN SYNDROME

Down syndrome is a relatively common birth defect that causes short stature, heart defects, and mental retardation. Down syndrome is caused by the presence of an extra chromosome 21 in a person's cells, hence the name *Trisomy 21.* Sometime during meiosis, usually in the mother, chromosomes fail to separate, leaving some daughter cells without a chromosome 21 and others with two copies of chromosome 21. If the egg with the extra chromosome is fertilized, the resulting fetus will have three copies of chromosome 21 instead of two.

The possibility of having a baby with Down syndrome increases dramatically in women over 35 years old. Down syndrome is one of very few disorders resulting from abnormal chromosome numbers, probably because most fertilized eggs with abnormal numbers of chromosomes do not develop normally enough to survive.

Historically, babies with Down syndrome were assumed to be severely intellectually disabled and were often institutionalized. More recently, it has been recognized that Down syndrome patients have a wide variety of intellectual abilities. With early intervention and accommodation to meet their needs, many people with Down syndrome can even live independently as adults.

The 23rd "pair" of chromosomes is a set of sex chromosomes. These are called sex chromosomes because their identity determines the sex of a baby. XX is female, and XY is male (see **FIGURE 17-1** ▲). The female parent always contributes an X, but the male parent can contribute either an X or Y chromosome. The male actually determines the sex of the baby by either contributing an X chromosome for a girl or a Y chromosome for a boy.

FIGURE 17-1 ▲ Photo of human chromosome profile known as a karotype: Both an X and a Y chromosome appear in the image; this is therefore a male sample. (Source: CNRI/SPL, Photo Researchers, Inc.)

THE HUMAN LIFE CYCLE

Both mitosis and meiosis are absolutely necessary parts of human life. Without them, cells could not be replaced, injuries could not be repaired, and new humans could not be produced. The relationship between mitosis and meiosis and their importance can be easily explained by looking at human life as a cycle (see **FIGURE 17-2** ▲). Eggs and sperm, with only half as many chromosomes as other cells, are produced by meiosis in specialized organs known as the **gonads**. The male gonads are called **testes**. The female gonads are the **ovaries**. During sexual reproduction, the gametes (egg and sperm) unite and combine their genetic material. This union and combination of genetic material is called **fertilization**. The fertilized egg is known as a **zygote**. Unlike gametes, which have only 23 chromosomes, the zygote has the typical number of chromosomes for a human cell, 46. The zygote undergoes millions of rounds of mitosis and development within the female to change into an **embryo**. The embryo then develops into a **fetus**. The fetus will continue to develop in the uterus until birth, after which the fetus is a newborn infant. The rest of this chapter is devoted to describing sexual reproduction in humans.

gonads Specialized organs for reproduction; testes in males and ovaries in females.

testes *(TESS teez)* Small, egg-shaped glands in the scrotum. Also known as the testicles. They contain interstitial cells that secrete testosterone. They also contain the seminiferous tubules that produce spermatozoa.

ovaries Female gonads that contain eggs.

fertilization Union and combination of genetic material.

zygote *(ZYE goat)* Fertilized egg possessing 46 chromosomes.

embryo A maturing zygote usually requiring seven days to reach this stage of development.

fetus Further development of the embryo after the two month point; the fetus now resembles a human.

Mitosis (each cell has 46 chromosomes)

4-cell stage

8-cell stage

2-cell stage

Week 3
(embryo)

Fallopian
tube

Sperm cell
nucleus (with
23 chromosomes)

Zygote

Ovary

Fertilization

Egg cell
nucleus (with
23 chromosomes)

Ovulation

Implantation

Week 10
(fetus)

Placenta

Umbilical chord

Umbilical cord

3 months
(fetus)

5 months
(fetus)

9 months
(infant)

FIGURE 17-2 ▲ The early stages of the human life cycle.

TEST YOUR KNOWLEDGE 17-1

Choose the best answer:

1. Cells with half the number of chromosomes used for sexual reproduction are known as:
   a. zygotes
   b. daughter cells
   c. gametes
   d. half cells

2. Organs that produce sperm and egg are called:
   a. gametes
   b. gonads
   c. zygotes
   d. chromosomes

3. After _____, the egg is called a _____ and has 46 chromosomes.
   a. reproduction; gamete
   b. meiosis; daughter cell
   c. mitosis; zygote
   d. fertilization; zygote

THE HUMAN REPRODUCTIVE SYSTEM

Reproductive organs are called **genitalia**. The general term for primary genitalia of both male and female is the gonads, which produce the gametes. The accessory genitalia are all the other structures that aid in the reproductive process. In this section, we will first discuss female anatomy and physiology and then male anatomy and physiology.

Female Anatomy

In females, the primary genitalia are called the ovaries. The accessory genitalia are the **uterine tubes** (also known as **oviducts** or **fallopian tubes**), the **uterus**, the **vagina**, and the external genitalia, called the **vulva**.

The Ovary

The ovaries are paired structures, about 3 centimeters long, in the peritoneal cavity (in the lower part of the abdominal cavity). There is one ovary on each side of the uterus. Several ligaments suspend or anchor each ovary. The **mesovarium** suspends the ovary, the **suspensory ligament** attaches the ovary to the lateral pelvic wall, and the **ovarian ligament** anchors the ovary to the uterine wall. Blood vessels, the ovarian artery, and the ovarian branch of the uterine artery all travel through the mesovarium and suspensory ligament, supplying the ovary with oxygenated blood. Each ovary contains thousands of microscopic sacs, or follicles. Please see FIGURE 17-3 ▲ for a diagram of internal reproductive anatomy.

The ovary is covered by a fibrous capsule called the **tunica albuginea** made of cuboidal epithelium. The interior of the ovary is divided into the cortex, which contains the eggs, and the medulla, which contains blood vessels, nerves, and lymphatic tissue surrounded by loose connective tissue.

The anatomy of the cortex is relatively complicated and will be described during our discussion of physiology. Ovaries produce eggs, or ova (female gametes; singular, ovum), and manufacture the female hormones estrogen and progesterone. Ova production and hormone level fluctuations usually occur as a result of specific reproductive cycles—the menstrual cycle, ovarian cycle, and uterine cycles—which you will learn about later in the chapter.

genitalia General term for reproductive organs.

uterine tubes Also known as fallopian tubes or oviducts; the tubes allow the passage of the egg from the ovary to the uterus.

oviducts *(OH vih ducts)* See uterine tubes.

fallopian tubes See uterine tubes.

uterus Thick walled, pear shaped structure which houses a developing embryo.

vagina The female structure that serves as a birth canal and allows passage of menstrual fluid.

vulva External female genitalia.

mesovarium *(MESS oh VAY ree um)* Structure that connects the anterior border of the ovary to the posterior layer of the broad ligament.

suspensory ligament A ligament extending from the tubal end of the ovary laterally to the pelvic wall. It lies in the layers of the broad ligament in which the ovarian artery is found.

ovarian ligament Ligaments used to keep the ovaries in proper position.

tunica albuginea A layer of firm white fibrous tissue forming the sheath of an organ or part, as of the eye, testicle, ovary, or spleen.

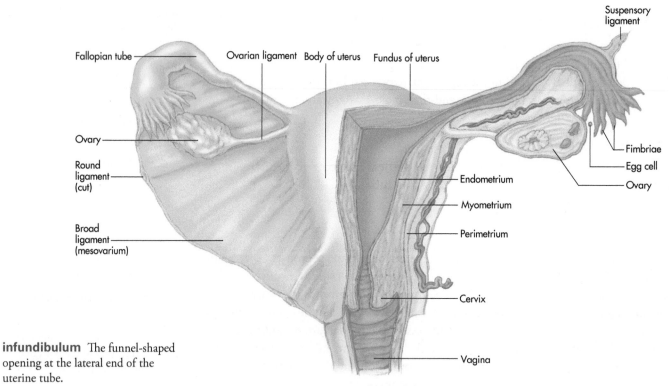

infundibulum The funnel-shaped opening at the lateral end of the uterine tube.

fimbria The longest fringelike extremity of a fallopian tube, extending from the infundibulum close to the ovary.

ampulla The dilated distal end of a uterine tube terminating in a funnel-like infundibulum.

isthmus Narrow inferior part of the uterus.

FIGURE 17-3 ▲ Internal female reproductive organs.

The Uterine Tubes

The uterine tubes, also known as oviducts or fallopian tubes, are the passageway for the egg to get to the uterus (see Figure 17-3). The uterine tubes, which are about 4 inches long and not attached to the ovaries, begin as a large funnel, the **infundibulum,** surrounded by ciliated projections, the **fimbria.** The infundibulum leads to a widened area, the **ampulla,** followed by a longer, narrower portion known as the **isthmus.** The uterine tubes are connected to the superior portion of the uterus. The tube is constructed of sheets of smooth muscle lined with highly folded, ciliated, simple columnar epithelium that help propel the ova to the uterus. The outside of the tube is covered by the visceral peritoneum and suspended by a mesentery known as the **mesosalpinx**. Again, see Figure 17-3.

The Uterus

The thick-walled and pear-shaped uterus is in the pelvic cavity, posterior and superior to the urinary bladder and anterior to the rectum. The major portion of the uterus is called the **body**. The rounded superior portion between the uterine tubes is the **fundus**, and the narrow inferior part is the **isthmus**. The **cervix** is a valvelike portion of the uterus that protrudes into the vagina, whereas the **cervical canal** connects with the vagina. Like the ovaries, the uterus is suspended and anchored by a series of ligaments. The **mesometrium** attaches the uterus to the lateral pelvic walls. (The combination of the mesometrium and mesovarium is called the **broad ligament**.) The lateral cervical ligaments attach the cervix and vagina to the lateral pelvic walls. The uterus is anchored to the anterior wall of the pelvic cavity by the **round ligaments**.

Like most of the hollow organs or tubes we have visited, the walls of the uterus consist of three layers. The **perimetrium**, the outermost layer, is also the **visceral peritoneum**, just like the outermost layer of the heart is the visceral pericardium. The middle layer, the **myometrium**, consists of smooth muscle. The **endometrium**, or inner lining, is a mucosa layer of columnar epithelium and secretory cells. The mucosa has two divisions: the basal layer and the functional layer. The **basal layer** is responsible for regenerating the uterine lining each month. The **functional layer** sheds about every 28 days when a woman has her period.

The endometrium is highly vascular. (This is no big surprise to any woman of child-bearing age.) Blood is supplied by the **uterine arteries** that branch from the internal iliac arteries on each side. The uterine arteries split into *arcuate arteries,* which supply the myometrium, and *radial arteries,* which supply blood to the endometrium. As you might expect, because the endometrium has two separate divisions, there are two different types of radial arteries. *Straight radial arteries* supply the basal layer. *Spiral radial arteries* supply the functional layer. The spiral arteries actually decay and regenerate every month as part of the menstrual cycle and undergo spasms that contribute to the shedding of the endometrium each month. (For more on control of the menstrual cycle, see the section "Hormonal Control" later in this chapter.) Blood returns to circulation via a network of venous sinuses.

Clinical Application

PAP TEST

A Pap test (name after George Papanicolaou) is taken from the cervix to examine scrapings from the cervical cells to detect the presence of cancer. Regular Pap tests allow for early cancer detection, which increases the likelihood of successful treatment. The human papilloma virus (HPV) has been directly linked as a cause for cervical cancer. It is also a cause of genital warts, which is a sexually transmitted disease. This originally caused controversy because of Guardisil®, the new vaccine for HPV. Guardisil® was originally recommended as a mandatory vaccination to be given to girls ages 12 to 13 to prevent some types of cervical cancer. It is now also recommended for boys, who may become infected with the virus and can pass it to their sexual partners.

mesosalpinx *(mess oh SAL pinks)* Support band of the uterine tubes.

body The large central portion of the uterus.

fundus *(FUN dus)* A larger part, base, or body of a hollow organ such as the uterus above the fallopian tubes.

isthmus Narrow inferior part of the uterus.

cervix Valvelike portion of the uterus that protrudes into the vagina.

cervical canal Connects the cervix to the vagina.

mesometrium The broad ligament below the mesovarium.

broad ligaments Support structures of the uterus that are a combination of the mesometrium and the mesovarium.

round ligaments Structures that anchor the uterus to the anterior wall of the pelvic cavity.

perimetrium *(per ih MEE tree um)* The serous layer of the uterus.

visceral peritoneum *(VIS er al PAIR ih TOE nee um)* Serous membrane lining the abdominal cavity.

myometrium *(MY oh MEE tree um)* Muscle layer in the uterus.

endometrium *(IN doh MEE tree um)* The mucous membrane lining the uterus.

basal layer Part of the uterus that is responsible for generating the uterine lining each month.

functional layer The layer of the uterus that is shed every 28 days.

uterine arteries Branches of the anterior division of the internal iliac artery; they supply blood to the upper vagina, cervix, uterus, and fallopian tubes.

Pathology Connection

ENDOMETRIOSIS

Each month, women of child-bearing age shed and replace the endometrium, the lining of the uterus. In many women, this endometrial tissue escapes the uterus and implants in the abdominal and pelvic cavities. There, the tissue responds to the woman's hormonal cycles, continuing to build up and decay each month. Unfortunately, the continued proliferation and decay and bleeding of endometrial tissue in the abdominal and pelvic cavities can cause scarring and damage to the organs. This condition is called **endometriosis**.

As many as 6 million women in the United States alone have endometriosis. Many women who have endometriosis have no noticeable symptoms, whereas other women experience severe abdominal and back pain around the time of their period, painful intercourse, chronic pelvic pain, painful urination, and painful bowel movements, especially during their periods. Some women even have symptoms that mimic a bladder infection. Untreated endometriosis can cause *adhesions* on the intestines and urinary bladder. This holding together of two parts or surfaces can be extremely painful and must be removed surgically. Endometriosis is among the top three causes of infertility. The scar tissue may block the uterine tubes and therefore block the journey of the egg through the tubes, in addition to scarring the ovaries and uterus. Some women are diagnosed with endometriosis only when they are being treated for infertility.

Endometriosis is diagnosed after a detailed medical history and exam. Ultrasound may be helpful in finding large implants of endometrial tissue outside the uterus. However, the only way to diagnose endometriosis with certainty is to perform a laparoscopic examination of the woman's pelvic cavity. Suspected endometrial implants are removed for biopsy. A biopsy is the only sure way to identify that the tissue is actually endometrial tissue.

The cause of endometriosis is unknown, so treating the disease is often difficult. Many women find relief of symptoms during treatment only to have their symptoms recur after treatement has ended. Endometrial implants often reoccur. Endometrial pain can be treated successfully using NSAIDs, but endometrial implants will continue to progress. To halt progression of the disease, implants must either be removed surgically or suppressed using hormones. Surgery typically involves removing the implants and scar tissue during laproscopic examination of the pelvic cavity. Severe or intractible cases may require laparotomy (open surgery) or even hysterectomy (including removal of the ovaries). Hormonal treatment includes the use of contraceptives (combined estrogen and progesterone), GnRH agonists, and synthetic androgens (male hormones). Most hormonal treatments have side effects, and many cannot be used for longer than a few months and cannot be used at all in adolescents or in women who are trying to get pregnant. Infertility is treated with a number of fertility drugs. For further discussion of hormone treatment drugs see the Pharmacology Corner at the end of the chapter. See FIGURE 17-4 ▲ for locations of endometriosis outside the uterus.

endometriosis
(IN doh mee tree OH sis) An inflammation of the mucous membrane lining the uterus.

The Vagina

vagina The female structure that serves as a birth canal and allows passage of menstrual fluid.

hymen The perforated membrane that covers the external opening of the vagina.

The **vagina** is a smooth muscle tube with a mucous membrane lining, approximately 10 centimeters long, which runs from the uterus to the outside of the body. Its purpose is to receive the penis during intercourse and to allow for the passage of menstrual fluid out of the uterus. The vagina is also known as the birth canal because its primary function is to allow the movement of a baby out of the uterus during childbirth. The external opening of the vagina may be covered by a perforated membrane called the **hymen**. A torn hymen was once thought to "prove" that a woman had had intercourse. However, many hymens are highly perforated and easily ruptured by day-to-day activities

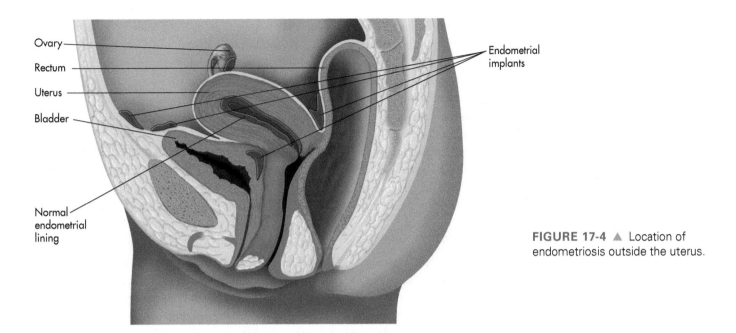

Ovary

Rectum

Uterus

Bladder

Normal endometrial lining

Endometrial implants

FIGURE 17-4 ▲ Location of endometriosis outside the uterus.

such as riding a bicycle or jogging. An intact hymen is no longer considered a litmus test for virginity; however, some cultures still hold this erroneous belief to be true.

The External Genitalia

The external genitalia (**FIGURE 17-5** ▲), collectively known as the **vulva**, although not perhaps as obvious as the male external genitalia, are a complex and important part of reproduction. The vulva is surrounded on each side by two prominences called the **labia majora**. The labia majora are rounded fat deposits that surround the entrance to the vagina; they protect the rest of the external genitalia. The labia majora meet anteriorly to form the mons pubis. Both the mons pubis and the labia majora are covered by pubic hair. The **perineum** is the area between the vagina and the anus.

vulva External female genitalia.

labia majora *(LAY bee ah)* The two folds of skin and adipose tissue on either side of the labia minora and vaginal opening that form the lateral borders of the vulva.

perineum *(per ih NEE uhm)* The region between the vagina and rectum.

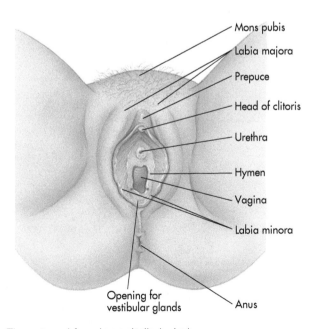

Mons pubis

Labia majora

Prepuce

Head of clitoris

Urethra

Hymen

Vagina

Labia minora

Opening for vestibular glands

Anus

FIGURE 17-5 ▲ The external female genitalia (vulva).

pudendal cleft *(PEW den dall)* Opening between two halves of the labia majora.

vestibule An almond-shaped space between the lines of attachment of the labia minora.

labia minora The two thin folds of integument that lie between the labia majora. They enclose the vestibule.

prepuce *(PREE pewce)* Foreskin.

clitoris *(klih TORE iss)* Small erectile structure that becomes engorged during sexual arousal in females.

mammary glands External female accessory organs that produce milk.

alveoli *(al VEE oh lye)* Glandular structures arranged in clusters throughout the breast and the site of milk synthesis.

Between the two halves of the labia majora is an opening known as the **pudendal cleft**. Within the pudendal cleft lies the **vestibule**, a space into which the urethra (anterior) and vagina (posterior) empty. (Unlike the male reproductive system, the female urinary system is completely separate from the reproductive system.) The lateral border of the vestibule is formed by the thin **labia minora**, which meet anteriorly to form the **prepuce**. Several glands, such as Bartholin's gland, surround the vestibule, helping to keep it moist.

Just posterior to the prepuce, and anterior to the vestibule, is the **clitoris**. The clitoris is a small erectile structure. Like the penis (see "Male Anatomy" in this chapter), the clitoris has a shaft, or body, and a glans (tip), and it becomes engorged with blood during sexual arousal. However, the clitoris increases in diameter, not in length.

Mammary Glands

Another set of external accessory sexual organs in the female, far removed from the pubic area, is the **mammary glands**. The mammary glands are milk production glands housed in the breasts (see **FIGURE 17-6** ▲). In young children, mammary tissue is virtually identical in boys and girls. At puberty, estrogen and progesterone stimulate breast development in girls. In adult females, the breasts consist of 15 to 20 lobes, which are glandular, and lots of adipose tissue. Each lobe is divided into smaller lobules, which house milk-secreting sacs called **alveoli**, when a woman is lactating (producing milk). Milk, made in the alveoli, travels through a series of ducts and sinuses, eventually reaching the nipple. The areola is the darkened area that surrounds the nipple. Milk production is controlled by the hormone prolactin.

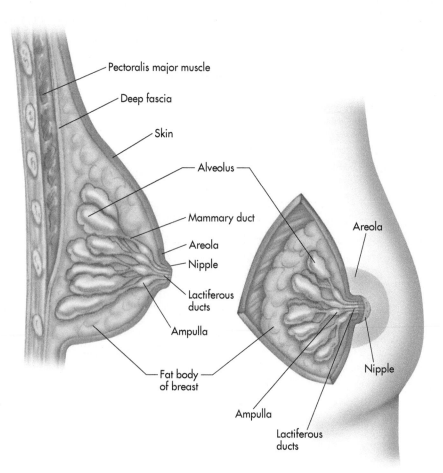

FIGURE 17-6 ▲ The mammary glands.

TEST YOUR KNOWLEDGE 17-2

Choose the best answer:

1. The _____ is also known as the birth canal.
   a. ovary
   b. uterus
   c. uterine tubes
   d. vagina

2. The inner lining of the uterus that is shed each month is the:
   a. perimetrium
   b. endometrium
   c. myometrium
   d. all of the above

3. This part of the female reproductive system is erectile:
   a. ovary
   b. labia majora
   c. clitoris
   d. penis

4. Which of the following is *not* a symptom of endometriosis?
   a. pain
   b. infertility
   c. hot flashes
   d. painful intercourse

REPRODUCTIVE PHYSIOLOGY: FEMALE

The female reproductive physiology is closely tied to a regulated cycle. This cycle is normally regulated by hormonal control.

The Menstrual Cycle

Female reproduction is organized around an approximately 28-day cycle known as the **menstrual cycle**. This cycle can range from 25 to 35 days in duration. This cycle involves the ovaries, the uterus, the pituitary gland, and the hypothalamus. The **ovarian cycle** involves the monthly maturation and release of eggs from the ovary. The **uterine cycle** consists of the monthly buildup, decay, and shedding of the uterine lining. The cycles begin by a woman's teen years at the beginning of puberty, with **menarche,** or the first menstrual cycle, and end usually during her 40s or 50s, with the end of **menopause,** which is the cessation of menstruation and is characterized by symptoms such as hot flashes, dizziness, headaches, and emotional changes. The ultimate goal of the cycle is to release an egg that might be fertilized and to prepare the uterus to receive and nourish the fertilized egg should pregnancy result. If pregnancy does not occur, the uterine lining sheds, and the cycle begins again.

The menstrual cycle is divided into four stages, usually over 28 days. During the **follicle stage,** which usually lasts about 10 days, a hormone called **follicle-stimulating hormone (FSH)** is released by the pituitary gland. At the ovary, FSH stimulates the follicle and ovum to mature, resulting in a release of estrogen and preparation of the uterine lining. In the next stage, the **ovulation stage,** the pituitary stops producing FSH and starts producing another hormone, **luteinizing hormone (LH).** At day 14, the follicle ruptures, and the ovum is released. During the third stage, the **corpus luteum stage,** the corpus luteum (described in detail later in the chapter) secretes progesterone and continues to do so if the egg is fertilized, preventing further ovulation and maintaining the uterine lining. This stage lasts about 14 days. The final stage is the **menstruation stage,** which occurs if the egg

menstrual cycle The female reproductive cycle based on approximately 28 days.

ovarian cycle The monthly maturation and release of eggs from the ovary.

uterine cycle The monthly build-up, decay, and shedding of the uterine lining.

menarche *(men ARE kee)* The onset of the first menstruation.

menopause The permanent cessation of menses, menstrual activity, usually occurring between ages 45 and 58.

follicle stage The first 10 days of the menstrual cycle during which the hormone FSH is released.

follicle-stimulating hormone (FSH) Hormone released by the pituitary gland as part of the menstrual cycle that initiates the development of primary follicles each month.

ovulation stage The stage of the menstrual cycle where the egg (ovum) is released.

luteinizing hormone (LH) *(LOO tee in EYE zing)* A hormone that is released by the pituitary gland during the menstrual cycle that triggers ovulation.

corpus luteum stage *(CORE pus LOO tee uhm)* Stage of the menstrual cycle in which the corpus luteum secretes progesterone to prevent further ovulation and to maintain the uterine lining.

menstruation stage Final stage of the menstrual cycle that occurs if the egg is not fertilized.

menses *(MEN seez)* The monthly flow of bloody fluid from the uterus.

menstruation *(MEN stroo AY shun)* The cyclic hormonal shedding of the uterine endometrium.

ovulation *(OV yoo LAY shun)* Periodic maturation and expulsion of eggs from the ovary.

oocyte *(OH oh site)* An immature stage of the female sex egg.

follicular phase The time between menses and ovulation.

proliferative phase See follicular phase.

follicle *(FALL ih kul)* Mass of cells with a hollow center. It holds an oocyte before puberty and a maturing ovum after puberty. The follicle ruptures at the time of ovulation and becomes the corpus luteum.

luteal phase See secretory phase.

secretory phase The time between ovulation and menses; also known as the luteal phase.

oogenesis *(oh oh JEN eh sis)* The process by which eggs are produced.

oogonia *(oh oh GOH nee uh)* Egg stem cells found in the ovary.

primary oocyte *(OH oh site)* Oogonia egg cells undergoing mitosis and thus reproducing.

granulosa cell One of the many cuboidal cells that surround and nurture the maturing oocyte.

primordial follicles Primary oocytes that are surround by granulosa (helper) cells which stay dormant until puberty.

is not fertilized. The corpus luteum diminishes progesterone production, and the uterine lining is broken down and discharged over the course of 3 to 6 days. You will learn more about these stages and the structures and hormones involved as you read this chapter.

The menstrual cycle, occurring approximately every 28 days in sexually mature women who are not pregnant, begins with the first day of **menses**. Menses is the time period when the uterine lining is shed. You are probably more familiar with the term **menstruation**. Menstruation is the actual shedding of the endometrium, whereas menses is the time during which a woman is menstruating. In more common terms, menses is the time during which a woman is having her "period," and menstruation is the "period" itself. Menses typically lasts 4 to 5 days but can be longer or shorter in different women and can even vary from month to month in the same woman.

Once menses is over, the endometrium begins to proliferate, or build up, readying itself for the egg that is about to be released from the ovary during **ovulation**. From day 1 to day 14, the ovary is also busy. In the ovary, an egg cell, or **oocyte,** is undergoing a number of developmental changes getting ready for ovulation on day 14 (can vary from day 11–21). The time between the end of menses and ovulation is known as the **follicular** or **proliferative phase** because the endometrium is proliferating, and the follicles are maturing in the ovary. **Follicle** is the term used to refer to an egg and associated helper cells. Ovulation is the release of a mature egg from the ovary. The egg travels from the ovary to the uterus, which has been getting ready to receive the egg, by way of the fallopian tube. The time between ovulation and menses is known as the **luteal phase**, or **secretory phase**, because of the development of the **corpus luteum** in the ovary and the beginning of secretion in the uterus. If the oocyte has been fertilized by a sperm, it will implant in the thickened endometrium. If the egg does not implant within a few days, the endometrium will begin to decay, and menstruation will occur about 2 weeks after ovulation.

Sounds simple enough, right? The cycle is deceptively simple when described without details or information about control of the cycle. Now that you understand the cycle itself, let's get down to the nitty-gritty. Just how does an egg mature, and how is the cycle controlled?

Oogenesis, Follicle Development, and Ovulation

The process by which eggs are produced is called **oogenesis**. Oogenesis begins with the birth of **oogonia**, or egg stem cells, in the ovary. The oogonia undergo mitosis, producing millions of **primary oocytes**. This happens very early in a woman's life. Millions of primary oocytes are produced in a fetus. That's right: Women have all the eggs they will ever have 5 months before they are born!

Primary oocytes, because they are born via mitosis, still have all 46 chromosomes. To become gametes, they must undergo meiosis to cut their chromosome number to 23. Remember, gametes must have only 23 chromosomes for fertilization (successful combining of sperm and egg) to produce a cell with the normal number of 46 chromosomes. So, primary oocytes begin meiosis. However, they do not fully complete meiosis. The primary oocytes stay in a kind of suspended animation until puberty when they finish one round of meiosis at ovulation. (That's at least 10 years!)

These primary oocytes eventually are surrounded by helper cells, called **granulosa cells**. Once surrounded by granulosa cells, the primary oocyte and surrounding cells are known as **primordial follicles**. These primordial follicles stay dormant until puberty. Hormonal signals during puberty cause some primordial follicles to enlarge and increase the number of granulosa cells. These enlarged cells are then called **primary follicles** and represent thousands of microscopic sacs within the ovary.

Once a girl reaches puberty, one primary follicle will become a **secondary follicle**. The secondary follicle will not complete meiosis unless it is ovulated and fertilized. Just before ovulation, the secondary follicle matures, fills with fluid, and moves toward the surface of the ovary, where it forms a visible lump. The mature follicle in its sac is sometimes called a **graafian follicle**. The fimbriae of the uterine tubes brush the surface of the ovary, causing the follicle to rupture. When the follicle ruptures, the egg (now an oocyte) is released into the peritoneal cavity. The fimbriae then pulls the egg toward the funnel, drawing it into the uterine tube (see FIGURE 17-7 ▲).

As the egg travels down the uterine tube (also called the **oviduct** or **fallopian tube**), it either will or will not be fertilized. If sperm are present in the uterine tube and all the conditions are right, the sperm will penetrate the egg, fertilizing it and triggering the rest of meiosis. The successfully fertilized egg has 46 chromosomes and is called a **zygote**. The zygote starts out as a single cell, but the cell divides, and subsequent cell divisions multiply the number of cells in the zygote as it travels down the fallopian tube to implant in the uterus. When the zygote enters the uterus, the newly proliferated endometrium is ready for it. If the zygote successfully implants in the uterus, pregnancy will result, and the woman will not menstruate. The ruptured follicle left behind in the ovary during ovulation will become the **corpus luteum** (remember the luteal phase?) and secrete hormones to help maintain the thickened endometrium, which will serve to nourish the growing fetus.

If there are no sperm in the uterine tube, conditions are not right, or something goes wrong after fertilization, the zygote will not implant in the uterus. If there is no implantation within a few days, the uterine lining will begin to degenerate, and the woman will have her period. The corpus luteum will become a corpus albicans and eventually disappear (see FIGURE 17-8 ▲).

primary follicles The result of primordial follicles that have received hormonal signals to enlarge and increase the number of granulosa cells.

secondary follicle Further development of a primary follicle once a female reaches puberty; the secondary follicle will not complete its full development unless it is ovulated and fertilized.

graafian follicle *(GRAFF ee an FALL eh kul)* Mature follicle surrounded by a sac.

oviducts *(OH vih ducts)* See uterine tubes.

fallopian tubes See uterine tubes.

zygote *(ZYE goat)* Fertilized egg possessing 46 chromosomes.

corpus luteum *(CORE pus LOO tee uhm)* Structure that secretes progesterone and continues to do so if an egg is fertilized, thus preventing further ovulation.

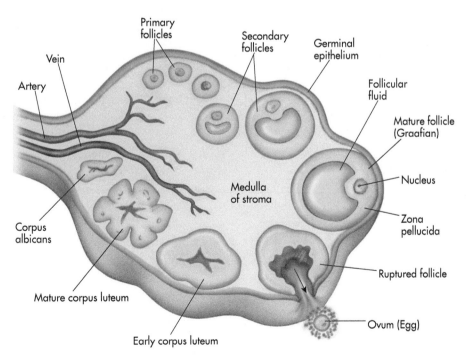

FIGURE 17-7 ▲ Maturation of follicle and release of egg.

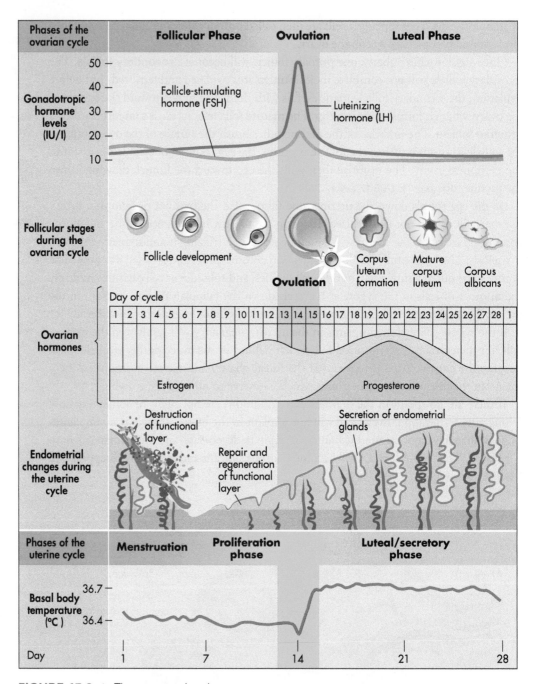

FIGURE 17-8 ▲ The menstrual cycle.

TEST YOUR KNOWLEDGE 17-3

Choose the best answer:

1. The time from the end of menses to ovulation is what phase?
   a. luteal phase
   b. follicular phase
   c. mitotic phase
   d. ovarian phase

2. The union of an egg and a sperm is called:
   a. sex
   b. fertilization
   c. oogenesis
   d. ovulation

3. The act of the egg being expelled from the ovary is called:
   a. oogenesis
   b. ovulation
   c. puberty
   d. pregnancy

4. If _____ does not occur, the endometrium will decay and a woman will menstruate.
   a. sex
   b. ovulation
   c. fertilization
   d. oogenesis

Hormonal Control

It seems obvious that something must control the complex cyclic changes in the female reproductive system. The control system that keeps the uterus and ovaries in synch is the endocrine system, specifically hypothalamic, pituitary, and ovarian hormones.

Remember that hormones are chemical signals released by one organ into the bloodstream to control another organ or tissue some distance away. Hormone levels are generally controlled by negative feedback. As hormone levels rise, the organ releasing the hormone decreases the amount of hormone released. Hormones are often released as part of a hierarchy, with the hypothalamus releasing a hormone that controls the pituitary, which then releases a hormone that controls another organ.

The hormones controlling female reproduction are no exception. The menstrual cycle is controlled by a combination of four hormones: **estrogen** and **progesterone** from the ovaries and **luteinizing hormone (LH)** and **follicle-stimulating hormone (FSH)** from the pituitary gland. At the beginning of puberty, estrogen and progesterone secretion from the ovaries increases greatly, increasing the secretion of LH and FSH.

The release of **gonadotropin-releasing hormone (GnRH)** from the hypothalamus causes an increase in the secretion of LH and FSH from the pituitary. FSH initiates the development of primary follicles each month, and LH triggers ovulation. During this part of the cycle (the follicular or proliferative phase), estrogen levels continue to rise as more and more is secreted by the developing follicle. Estrogen exerts a positive influence on the hypothalamus, increasing secretion of GnRH and thus increasing LH and FSH secretion. This positive feedback loop increases the levels of LH and FSH, stimulating follicle development and triggering ovulation. Rising estrogen levels also stimulate proliferation of the uterine lining (endometrium).

Once ovulation occurs, the feedback loop actually reverses itself! The leftover ruptured follicle, now the corpus luteum, begins to secrete progesterone and secretes a little estrogen. Under the influence of progesterone, estrogen exerts negative feedback on the hypothalamus and pituitary, decreasing GnRH, LH, and FSH secretion. Progesterone also exerts negative feedback on the hypothalamus and pituitary. Thus, during the luteal

estrogen Hormone secreted by the corpus luteum that stimulates uterine lining and mammary gland development.

progesterone *(proh JES teh rohn)* Hormone secreted by corpus luteum that helps to maintain the build-up of the endometrium and decrease uterine contraction.

luteinizing hormone (LH) *(LOO tee in EYE zing)* A hormone that is released by the pituitary gland during the menstrual cycle that triggers ovulation.

follicle-stimulating hormone (FSH) Hormone released by the pituitary gland as part of the menstrual cycle that initiates the development of primary follicles each month.

gonadotropin-releasing hormone (GnRH) *(GOHN ad doh TROH pin)* Released by the hypothalamus and causes the increase in the secretion of LH and FSH from the pituitary gland.

human chorionic gonadotropin (HCG) *(KOH ree on ick GOHN ah doh TROH pin)* Hormone released by fertilized egg that stimulates the corpus luteum to keep secreting progesterone and a small amount of estrogen to maintain the uterine lining.

premenstrual syndrome (PMS) Syndrome of physical and psychological changes that occur before menstruation in many women.

premenstrual dysphoric disorder (PMDD) Disorder characterized by severe depression, marked anxiety, and decreased interest in activity.

or secretory phase, LH, FSH, and estrogen levels drop while progesterone levels rise. These hormonal changes prevent another egg from maturing.

For about 10 days after ovulation, progesterone levels remain high as the corpus luteum continues to secrete the hormone. Progesterone's effect on the uterus is to *maintain* the buildup of the endometrium and to decrease uterine contractions. If no pregnancy results, then the corpus luteum will degenerate and stop producing progesterone. Decreased progesterone causes degeneration of the endometrium, followed by menstruation. Decreased progesterone also releases the hypothalamus and pituitary from inhibition. FSH and LH levels rise and the cycle begins again (again see Figure 17-8).

If pregnancy does result, the implanted fertilized egg secretes a hormone called **human chorionic gonadotropin (HCG)**. HCG stimulates the corpus luteum, which keeps secreting progesterone and a little estrogen to maintain the uterine lining. At about 3 months' gestation (pregnancy), the placenta begins to secrete its own progesterone and estrogen, thereby becoming an endocrine organ. For a list of hormones and functions related to pregnancy, please see TABLE 17-1 ■.

Pathology Connection

MENSTRUAL DISORDERS

Most women (as high as 90%) have some symptoms a few days before their period; 20 to 40% say the symptoms are problematic, and 1% of women experience debilitating symptoms that severely interfere with daily activities. When the symptoms are severe enough to affect quality of life, women may be diagnosed with **premenstrual syndrome (PMS)** or **premenstrual dysphoric disorder (PMDD)**.

PMS is characterized by predictable cognitive, physical, emotional, and behavioral symptoms associated with the luteal phase of a women's reproductive cycle. The symptoms begin approximately 5 days before the onset of menses and end within a few days after. There is no definitive criteria for diagnosis because symptoms vary dramatically not just from woman to woman, but even from month to month in the same woman. There are no tests that can be taken, and to date no differences in hormone levels have been found between women with diagnosed PMS or PMDD and women who do not have the disorders. Currently, PMS is diagnosed if a woman has one affective (psychological) and one physical symptom from the following list:

- **Affective/Psychological:** depression, anger, irritability, anxiety, confusion, and withdrawal
- **Physical:** breast tenderness, bloating, swelling extremities, and headache

For a diagnosis of PMS, the symptoms must begin 5 days prior to menses, cease 4 days into menses, and not recur until day 12 of the woman's cycle. This pattern must have been repeated for the last three cycles. Other conditions must be ruled out. A woman is diagnosed with PMDD if she has five of the criteria, in the same pattern as for PMS, for most of her cycles in the previous year. One of the symptoms must be affective. In addition, the woman must not have an underlying condition, such as depression or anxiety. These chronic conditions are usually worsened by hormonal changes during the menstrual cycle, making it impossible to tell whether the patient has PMDD itself, or just increased symptoms of an ongoing chronic condition.

Treatment for PMS and PMDD varies depending on the severity of the disease. Mild/moderate PMS/PMDD is treated by lifestyle changes, including good nutrition, regular exercise, complex carbohydrates, and calcium supplements. NSAIDs or hormonal suppression may be used if more conservative treatments do not work effectively. If affective symptoms are severe, SSRIs or

(continued)

TABLE 17-1 ■ HORMONES CONTROLLING PREGNANCY

HORMONE	WHERE SECRETED	CAUSES
Human chorionic gonadotropin	Implanted fertilized egg	Maintains the function of corpus luteum; this is what gives a positive pregnancy test
Estrogen and progesterone	Corpus luteum for first 2 months of pregnancy; then by the placenta	Both stimulate development of uterine lining and mammary glands; progesterone prohibits uterine contractions during pregnancy; estrogen relaxes the pelvic joints; once labor begins, estrogen negates the effects of progesterone on uterine contractions and makes the myometrium sensitive to oxytocin
Prolactin	Anterior pituitary gland	Stimulates milk production by breasts
Oxytocin	Posterior pituitary gland	Uterine contractions to begin labor; stimulates the release of milk from the breasts (see FIGURE 17-9 ▲)

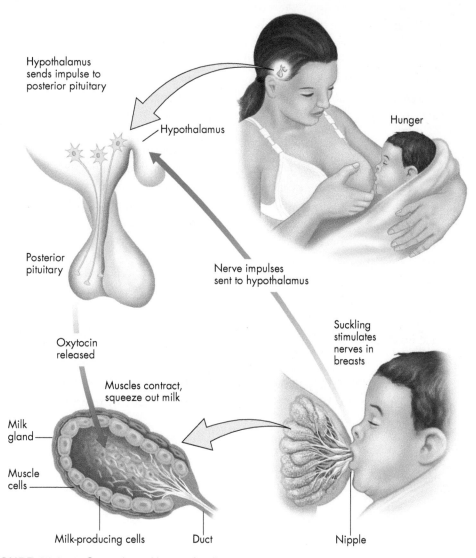

Hypothalamus sends impulse to posterior pituitary

Hypothalamus

Hunger

Posterior pituitary

Nerve impulses sent to hypothalamus

Oxytocin released

Suckling stimulates nerves in breasts

Muscles contract, squeeze out milk

Milk gland

Muscle cells

Milk-producing cells

Duct

Nipple

FIGURE 17-9 ▲ Oxytocin and breast feeding.

Pathology Connection (continued)

anti-anxiety medications are the next step. If symptoms do not respond to lifestyle changes and mood elevators, then GnRH agonists may be used. The cause of PMS/PMDD and the relationship between the two disorders remains a mystery.

Amenorrhea is the absence of menstruation and can be the result of pregnancy, menopause, or other factors such as distress, extreme dieting, or poor health. **Dysmenorrhea** is difficult menstruation and usually results in painful cramping. (*Dys* means "difficult.")

Toxic Shock Syndrome (TSS) is an inflammatory disease that occurs in menstruating women, often as a result of tampon misuse. It can also be seen in men and children, but not as a result of tampon misuse. TSS is the result of a bacterial infection, usually *Staphylococcus aureus* and *Streptococcus pyogenes* infection. The bacteria produce a toxin that causes symptoms including high fever, headache, vomiting, diarrhea, sore throat, rash, and irritability. In more severe cases, people experience abdominal tenderness, hypotension, shock, respiratory distress, and renal failure. Treatment includes antibiotics and other prescription medications to control symptoms, rest, and hydration.

Polycystic Ovarian Syndrome (PCOS) is a disorder characterized by the formation of multiple cysts on the ovaries, hormonal abnormalities, infertility, obesity, and insulin resistance. The ovaries make too much testosterone and estrogen, but too little progesterone. The result is that women may fail to ovulate and have excess facial hair, male-pattern baldness, and irregular menstrual cycles. In addition, women with PCOS are more likely to be overweight, be insulin resistant (even if they are not overweight), and to have hypertension and hyperlipidemia. Many women with PCOS develop metabolic syndrome and Type II diabetes (regardless of body weight).

PCOS is diagnosed using imaging and blood work. Large ovaries (> 10 cm^3) with 12 or more large follicles (2–3 cm diameter) are characteristic of PCOS. Women with PCOS also have increased blood levels of LH, testosterone, prolactin, and insulin.

Because the cause of PCOS is unknown, treatment is mainly symptom relief. First and foremost is weight control. Losing weight causes a decrease in severity of most other symptoms, including infertility. Birth control pills can regulate a woman's menstrual cycle. Drugs can treat hyperlipidemia and hyperinsulinemia. Infertility can be treated by fertility drugs and/or by surgery to repair the damaged ovaries.

Surgery for PCOS and other uterine disorders may involve a procedure known as laparoscopy. During laparoscopy, a tube is inserted through an incision in the abdominal wall. The tube is equipped with a scope or a camera and a fiber-optic light source. The tube allows doctors to observe internal structures for defects and to more precisely guide instruments during surgeries. Laparoscopy is a less-invasive procedure than traditional surgery, resulting in smaller incisions, shorter recovery time, and less patient discomfort.

Vaginitis is the inflammation of the vagina that is usually caused by a microorganism such as a bacteria or yeast. Vaginitis is not always a result of sexually transmitted diseases. For coverage of sexually transmitted diseases, please see Chapter 19.

---

amenorrhea
(ah MEN oh REE ah) The absence or lack of menstruation.

dysmenorrhea
(DISS men oh REE ah) Difficult menstruation.

toxic shock syndrome (TSS) Inflammatory disease that occurs in menstruating woman often as a result of improper tampon use.

polycystic ovarian syndrome (PCOS) Formation of multiple cysts on the ovary.

vaginitis
(VAJ ih NYE tiss) An inflammatory process involving the vagina.

TEST YOUR KNOWLEDGE 17-4

Choose the best answer:

1. At puberty, the ovaries begin to secrete:
   a. FSH
   b. LH
   c. estrogen
   d. all of the above

2. These hormones stimulate follicle maturation and ovulation:
   a. estrogen and progesterone
   b. estrogen and GnRH
   c. LH and FSH
   d. FSH and progesterone

3. Before ovulation, estrogen _____ the secretion of FSH and LH.
   a. decreases
   b. increases
   c. stabilizes
   d. there is no relationship between estrogen, FSH, and LH

4. The role of progesterone is:
   a. to promote ovulation
   b. to keep the endometrium from shedding
   c. to enhance fertilization
   d. to increase FSH and LH levels

5. Symptoms of PMS generally end:
   a. just before a woman's period
   b. just after her period begins
   c. at ovulation
   d. there is no pattern

6. PCOS symptoms most closely resemble this endocrine disorder:
   a. hyperthyroidism
   b. Addison's
   c. Cushing's
   d. none of the above

Male Anatomy

Like the female reproductive system, the male reproductive system has a pair of primary genitalia, or gonads, called the **testes**. The testes produce the male gamete or sperm that must travel along its journey to find the egg. Unlike in the female, the male primary genitalia are external. In addition, the male has many accessory genitalia—the **penis**, an external sperm-delivery organ; several sperm ducts; the **epididymis**; the **vas deferens**; and the **urethra**. The urethra performs dual roles, as a channel for both excreting urine and expelling semen. Males also have several accessory glands: the **prostate gland**, the **seminal vesicles,** and the **bulbourethral glands**. Please see FIGURE 17-10 ▲ for the anatomy of the male reproductive system.

The Testes (Testicles)

The primary genitalia, the testes (or testicles), are paired glands suspended in a sac called the **scrotum**. The testicles form in the abdomen during the last three months of embryonic development and migrate into the scrotum. The testicles are external genitalia, one hanging on either side of the penis. The failure of the testes to descend into the scrotal sac is termed **cryptorchidism** and may require surgical intervention. If the testes remain undescended, the male may become sterile because of the body heat destroying the sperm. (Viable sperm cannot be made at normal human body temperature.) Another pathologic condition of the testes is **hydrocele,** which is an abnormal collection of fluid within the testes.

testes *(TESS teez)* Small, egg-shaped glands in the scrotum. Also known as the testicles. They contain interstitial cells that secrete testosterone. They also contain the seminiferous tubules that produce spermatozoa.

penis External genitalia in males that delivers the sperm.

epididymis *(EP ih DID ih miss)* A comma-shaped duct on the posterior and lateral part of the testes where sperm mature.

vas deferens *(VAS DEF er inz)* The 45-cm-long tube running from the scrotum to the penis through which sperm travels.

urethra *(yoo REE thrah)* Tube that connects the bladder to the outside of the body.

prostate gland A chestnut-size gland that secretes a slightly alkaline fluid that forms part of the seminal fluid.

FIGURE 17-10 ▲ Male reproductive anatomy.

seminal vesicles Highly coiled glands posterior to the bladder.

bulbourethral glands *(BUL boh yoo REE thral)* Pea sized glands inferior to the prostate.

scrotum Sac that contains the testes.

cryptorchidism *(kript OR kid izm)* The failure of the testes to descend into the scrotal sac.

hydrocele *(HIGH droh seel)* An abnormal collection of fluid within the testis.

tunica vaginalis A serous membrane that surrounds each testis.

lobules Pyramidal divisions separated from each other by incomplete partitions called septa. Each consists of one to three coiled seminiferous tubules.

seminiferous tubules *(SEM ee NIF er us TOO byoolz)* Tubules located in the testes that contain sperm cells and sperm helper cells (also known as Sertoli or nurse cells).

sertoli cells Sperm helper cells.

penis External genitalia in males that delivers the sperm.

root A portion of an organ implanted in tissues.

shaft The principal portion of any cylindrical body.

body See shaft.

glans penis The cone-shaped head of the penis that contains the urethral orifice. It is covered with a movable hood known as the foreskin or prepuce, under which is secreted the substance called smegma.

foreskin Loose section of skin that covers the glands penis.

urethra *(yoo REE thrah)* Tube that connects the bladder to the outside of the body.

epididymis *(EP ih DID ih miss)* A comma-shaped duct on the posterior and lateral part of the testes where sperm mature.

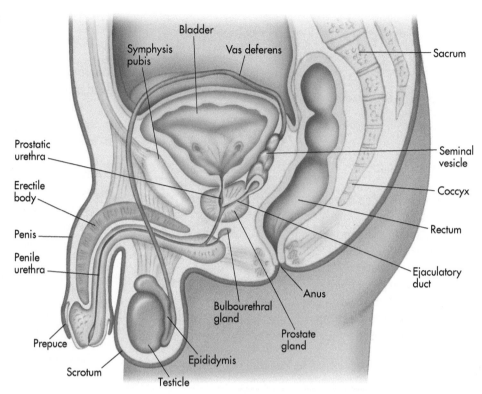

Each small walnut-shaped testis is surrounded by a serous membrane called the **tunica vaginalis,** which originates from the peritoneum. The inside of the testes are divided into 250 to 300 wedges called **lobules,** each of which contains one to four **seminiferous tubules.** The seminiferous tubules, which are made of epithelium and areolar tissue, contain sperm stem cells and sperm helper cells (**sertoli cells** or nurse cells).

The Penis

The other part of the external genitalia in males is the **penis.** The penis, from the Latin word for "tail," is a sperm-delivery organ that transfers sperm to the outside of the body. The attached portion of the penis is called the **root,** and the freely moving portion is the **shaft** or **body.** The tip of the penis, the **glans penis,** is covered by a loose section of skin called the **foreskin,** unless a man has been circumcised. Internally, the penis contains the **urethra,** which is a transport passage for both sperm and urine. (But not at the same time!) In addition, the penis has three erectile bodies, or tubes with a spongelike network of blood sinuses.

The Epididymis

There are several ducts in the male reproductive system. The **epididymis** is a comma-shaped duct on the posterior and lateral part of the testes. (It looks something like a stocking cap for each gonad.) Its highly coiled tubes connect the testes to the vas deferens. If unraveled, the epididymis would be 6 meters long! It is made of pseudostratified ciliated epithelium and smooth muscle. Sperm mature here.

The Vas Deferens

The **vas deferens** is a 45-centimeter-long tube. It is lined with ciliated pseudostratified epithelium, like the epididymis, but has a thick smooth muscle layer and is surrounded by

Amazing Body Facts

Boxers or Briefs?

Normal human body temperature is too warm for healthy sperm development. The testes are on the outside of the body because sperm development is extremely temperature sensitive, and sperm could not develop normally inside the pelvic cavity. Indeed, there is some speculation that very tight clothing might contribute to male infertility by holding the gonads too close to the body and raising their temperature.

a connective tissue layer called the **adventitia**. The vas deferens runs from the scrotum to the penis via a relatively complicated pathway. It runs from the epididymis as a pair of tubes, one on each side, into the abdominal wall (through the inguinal canal) and pelvic cavity, medially over the urethra and along the posterior bladder wall. Posterior to the bladder, the vas deferens joins the seminal vesicles to form the **ejaculatory duct**. The ejaculatory duct then passes through the prostate gland and empties into the urethra. (Remember, the urethra carries both sperm and urine in males.) Between the scrotum and the inguinal canal, the vas deferens runs through a tube, with blood vessels and nerves, collectively called the **spermatic cord**.

Accessory Glands

There are three accessory glands in the male reproductive system. The **seminal vesicles** are highly coiled glands posterior to the bladder, made of pseudostratified epithelium, smooth muscle, and connective tissue. The **prostate gland** is a chestnut-size gland surrounding the urethra just inferior to the bladder. It is a dense mass of connective tissue and smooth muscle with embedded glands. The **bulbourethral glands** are pea-size glands inferior to the prostate.

vas deferens *(VAS DEF er inz)* The 45-cm-long tube running from the scrotum to the penis through which sperm travels.

adventitia *(add ven TISH ah)* The outermost covering of a structure or organ.

ejaculatory duct The passageway formed by the vas deferens and seminal vesicles to eject sperm.

spermatic cord Term used for the combination of the vas deferens and surrounding blood vessels and nerves.

seminal vesicles Highly coiled glands posterior to the bladder.

prostate gland A chestnut-size gland that secretes a slightly alkaline fluid that forms part of the seminal fluid.

bulbourethral glands *(BUL boh yoo REE thral)* Pea sized glands inferior to the prostate.

benign prostatic hyperplasia (BPH) *(bee NINE pro STAT ik HIGH per PLAY zhuh)* The noncancerous enlargement of the prostate gland that often interferes with urine flow.

Pathology Connection

MALE REPRODUCTIVE DISEASES

Benign Prostatic Hyperplasia (BPH), the noncancerous enlargement of the prostate, is the most common cause of lower urinary tract symptoms in men. It is common in men ages 60 and older, and as many as 70% of men will have some enlargement of their prostate by the age of 70. The cause of BPH is not known but may be due to age-related hormonal changes. Symptoms of BPH, due to the enlargement of the prostate impinging on the urethra and bladder, include urinary urgency and frequency, nighttime urination, weak urine stream, and incomplete voiding. For many men, the problems are serious enough to have significant impact on quality of life. Diagnosis is made by taking a detailed history and performing a physical exam, including examining the prostate. Prostate-specific antigen (PSA) blood levels should be tested to rule out prostate cancer. Other urinary conditions such as UTI, diabetes mellitus, and overactive bladder must also be ruled out. Treatment for BPH has changed in the last 20 years, from primarily surgical

(continued)

Pathology Connection (continued)

intervention (prostatectomy) to primarily hormonal treatment. In mild cases, a "watch and wait" strategy is used with changes in lifestyle to decrease symptoms. Drug treatments include 5-alpha-reductase inhibitors, which decrease testosterone (and shrink the prostate) and alpha blockers, which cause smooth muscle to relax (improving urine stream). Other interventions include minimally invasive laser or microwave ablation, surgical removal of partial or whole prostate, and the placement of a stent in the urethra. See **FIGURE 17-11** ▲ for an illustration of BPH.

prostate cancer
Cancerous condition of the prostate gland.

Prostate cancer is the most common nonskin form of cancer that affects American men. In fact, over 32,000 men die each year from prostate cancer, many of whom could have been saved with early detection. A common blood test called the prostate-specific antigen (PSA) can be used to help detect this disease. It is recommended this test be done at age 50 or earlier if there is a family history of prostate cancer.

Urinary bladder

Hypertrophied tissue

True prostate tissue

Narrowed urethra

FIGURE 17-11 ▲ Benign prostatic hypertrophy.

TEST YOUR KNOWLEDGE 17-5

Choose the best answer:

1. The _____ are the gonads, where sperm are made.
   a. vas deferens
   b. testes
   c. scrotum
   d. penis

2. After passing the seminal vesicles, the vas deferens becomes the:
   a. prostate gland
   b. urethra
   c. penis
   d. none of the above

3. Sperm mature in the:
   a. epidiymis
   b. testes
   c. scrotum
   d. penis

4. _____ has the same symptoms as UTI and overactive bladder.
   a. PCOS
   b. ED
   c. BPH
   d. PMS

REPRODUCTIVE PHYSIOLOGY: MALE

Unlike female reproduction, male reproductive physiology is not organized around a tightly controlled monthly cycle. Let's explore the physiologic processes of the male reproductive system.

Spermatogenesis

Sperm production, in the testes, is a continuous process beginning when a boy reaches puberty and usually continuing until death. As such, the control of spermatogenesis, sperm production, is much less complicated than control of oogenesis. Spermatogenesis occurs in the seminiferous tubules.

The **spermatogonia**, sperm stem cells, undergo mitosis to form **primary spermatocytes**. Unlike primary oocytes, the primary spermatocytes do not wait to go through meiosis. Primary spermatocytes form two **secondary spermatocytes**. Secondary spermatocytes complete meiosis to form **spermatids**, and spermatids go through a period of development to form immature **spermatozoa (sperm)**. All this takes place in the testes inside the seminiferous tubules. The distribution of the different stages of sperm development is predictable. Spermatogonia line up against the walls of the tubules, and mature sperm cluster near the lumen of the tubules (see FIGURE 17-12 ▲). Sperm then travel from the seminiferous tubules to the epididymis, where the sperm spend about 2 weeks maturing and gaining the ability to swim.

Hormonal Control of Male Reproduction

Testosterone is arguably the most important male sex hormone. Before birth, **human chorionic gonadotropin (HCG)** secreted by the placenta causes the embryonic (still developing) testes to secrete testosterone, masculinizing the fetus. (Fetuses not exposed to testosterone or insensitive to testosterone look female.) After birth, there is little testosterone secreted until puberty. At puberty, two hormonal changes occur that signal the beginning of sexual maturity. First, testosterone secretion by the testes increases dramatically. Second, there is a change in the relationship between testosterone and GnRH, LH, and FSH. (Yes, the same hormones that control female reproduction control male reproduction!) Before puberty, the small amount of testosterone that is secreted by the testes inhibits GnRH secretion. After puberty, testosterone does not inhibit GnRH secretion. So after puberty, GnRH, and therefore FSH and LH, secretion increases. In addition, FSH and LH also enhance testosterone secretion in a major positive feedback loop, but only after the onset of puberty. Testosterone secretion at puberty is also responsible for the obvious physical changes of the male secondary sexual characteristics, including body, facial, and pubic hair growth; deepening of the voice; and increased muscle and bone mass.

LH and FSH affect males exactly as they do females. They stimulate gamete development. They are controlled in the same way in males as in females. GnRH is released from the hypothalamus, which stimulates LH and FSH secretion from the pituitary.

Erection and Ejaculation

When a man is sexually aroused, the erectile tissue in the penis becomes engorged with blood, stiffening and expanding the penis. The change in shape of the penis is called an **erection**.

For sperm to leave the male reproductive system, ejaculation must occur. **Ejaculation** is the expulsion of **semen** (sperm and assorted chemicals) from the urethra. Smooth

---

spermatogonia *(sper MAT oh GOH nee ah)* Large, unspecialized germ cells that form primary spermatocytes by mitosis.

primary spermatocytes A cell formed by mitosis of a spermatogonium.

secondary spermatocytes A cell formed by meiosis of a primary spermatocyte. It undergoes a second meiotic division to form two spermatids, each with the haploid number of chromosomes.

spermatids *(SPER mah tidz)* Cells that are the result of the division of a secondary spermatocyte.

spermatozoa *(sper MAT oh ZOE ah)* The plural form of spermatozoon, the mature male sex cell.

testosterone Main male sex hormone that provides masculine characteristics.

human chorionic gonadotropin (HCG) *(KOH ree on ick GOHN ah doh TROH pin)* Hormone released by fertilized egg that stimulates the corpus luteum to keep secreting progesterone and a small amount of estrogen to maintain the uterine lining.

erection The stiffening of the penis due to increased blood flow.

ejaculation Sudden discharge of semen from the body.

semen *(SEE men)* A sperm-containing, thick secretion produced by males.

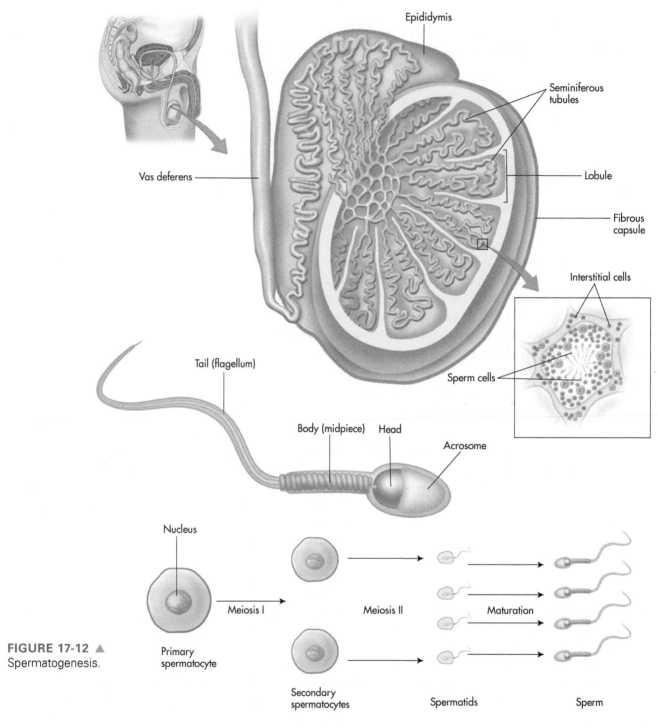

FIGURE 17-12 ▲
Spermatogenesis.

impotence The inability of a male to achieve or maintain an erection. The cause of this condition may be a vascular, neurological, or psychological dysfunction.

erectile dysfunction (ED) An inability to develop a full erection. May be physiological or psychological.

muscle contracts throughout the ducts and glands of the male reproductive system and propels the sperm from the epididymis into the vas deferens, which then carries the sperm into the pelvic cavity. As the sperm passes the seminal vesicles, sugar and chemicals are added to the sperm. The sperm and chemicals then enter the ejaculatory duct. As the ejaculatory duct passes through the prostate gland, prostatic fluid is added, liquefying the semen. The semen then passes by the bulbourethral glands, which add mucus to the semen and protect sperm from the acid environment of the vagina by the secretion of an alkaline substance. The semen then enters the urethra and is carried outside the body. A sexual dysfunction called **impotence,** now commonaly referred to as **erectile dysfunction (ED),** often interferes with the process of ejaculation because the penis does not become or will not stay erect. Impotence can result from physical or

Clinical Application

ANDROGEN INSENSITIVITY SYNDROME

Testosterone secretion *in utero* is important for masculinizing a male fetus. Males who are not sensitive to testosterone will not respond to the masculinizing effects and will not develop normal male reproductive systems. Androgen insensitivity is a genetic disorder that can result in a broad range of malfunctions of the male reproductive system, from complete lack of external or internal male genitalia (testicular feminization—individuals look female though they are genetically male) to patients with ambiguous genitalia to patients who have typical male genitalia but are sterile. Treatment for the disorder depends on genital anatomy.

Amazing Body Facts

Hormones

Did you know that females have some natural testosterone and males have natural estrogen? It's true. The balance between the hormones—not the presence or absence of the hormones—is what is important.

psychological problems, including alcoholism, endocrine disease, anxiety, depression, stress, poor blood circulation, or prostate disease.

If a man is engaged in sexual intercourse with a woman and ejaculates, the sperm enter the vagina and make their way to the uterus and into the uterine tubes. The female reproductive system is not particularly hospitable to sperm, and many sperm do not survive the journey to the uterine tubes. If there is an egg waiting to be fertilized in one of the uterine tubes, sperm will find the egg and attempt to penetrate it and fertilize it. New research suggests that the egg is not a passive participant in fertilization, but may actually engulf the sperm and even choose which sperm to allow inside. One sperm and only one sperm will fertilize the egg. If the egg is fertilized, and all other conditions are met, a pregnancy will result.

Pathology Connection

ERECTILE DYSFUNCTION (ED)

Erectile dysfunction (ED) is the long-term (3 months or more) inability to maintain an erection. ED increases with age and is relatively common, with 50% of men between the ages of 40 and 70 having some degree of ED. ED has many different causes, which can be grouped into organic (caused by an underlying endocrine, neurological, anatomical, or vascular condition) or psychogenic (having an underlying emotional cause) or mixed (a combination of organic and psychogenic causes). ED is diagnosed via medical history and specially designed questionnaires. Physical exam and blood work including PSA and testosterone levels as well as blood glucose and cholesterol levels can help determine the underlying cause of ED. Treatment of ED depends on the underlying cause. Improvement of underlying conditions often improves erectile function. In addition, several drugs improve the symptoms of ED, including Phosphodiesterase type 5 inhibitors, apomorphine, prostaglandins, and androgens. (For more information on medications to treat ED see the pharmacology section at the end of this chapter.) If drugs do not solve the problem or cannot be tolerated, penile prosthetics may restore function.

TEST YOUR KNOWLEDGE 17-6

Choose the best answer:

1. The stiffening and expanding of the penis is known as:
   a. ejaculation
   b. erection
   c. emulsification
   d. erectile dysfunction

2. The combination of sperm, sugars, chemicals, and mucus is:
   a. semen
   b. urine
   c. spermatozoa
   d. all of the above

3. Male secondary sexual characteristics, masculinization of the body, and enhancement of FSH and LH levels are caused by:
   a. LH
   b. FSH
   c. estrogen
   d. testosterone

4. ED is always caused by psychological problems.
   a. true
   b. false

PREGNANCY

Pregnancy occurs when an egg is fertilized by the sperm and implants in the female reproductive system. The period of time during which the developing baby grows within the uterus is called the gestation period, approximately 40 weeks. A baby born before 37 weeks gestation period is termed a premature infant. Occasionally, miscarriages occur during pregnancy. A miscarriage is a spontaneous abortion, or expulsion of the fetus, that may be the result of an inherited defect in the fetus, infectious disease, physical injury, or endocrine disorder. Often the cause is a mystery. Many women who miscarry during one pregnancy go on to have subsequent successful pregnancies.

Fertilization occurs at conception when sperm and egg unite forming a zygote. The following is an explanation of the embryological development of systems. The blastocyst (as the zygote is so called until two weeks after conception) is a grouping of two cell types, outer cells, which will become the placenta, and inner cells, which will become the fetus. At week four, the blastocyst will implant into the mother's uterus. Week five of gestation is referred to as the embryonic period as this is when the growing embryo is now developing structures of organs and organ systems. Cells of the blood, heart, and liver begin to develop and organ systems like the nervous system can be seen. The developing embryo is growing the external structures, like arms and eyes. Between the 4th and 6th months of development, the fetus also begins to move. It isn't until weeks 6-7 that arm and leg buds can be seen. These organs and systems continue to grow rapidly. Beyond the 8-week period until the birth, the developing infant is called a fetus. The fetus has distinct facial features and the gastrointestinal system is beginning to develop. Between weeks 11 and 14 genitals will form. By week 20, the fetus can hear because the external ear has developed and the nervous system is now capable of processing sounds. By week 25, the bone marrow has developed and the fetus can make red blood cells. By week 30, the lungs are immature but are able to "breathe" by moving with a rhythm. By 40 weeks, the fetus has been in gestation for 38 weeks and may be born any day. FIGURE 17-13 ▲ shows the stages in utero of human development

The growing fetus is nourished by a spongy structure called the **placenta,** which is attached to the fetus via the umbilical cord. The fetus is encased in a membranous sac called the **amnion,** which contains the amniotic fluid in which the fetus floats.

placenta *(pluh SEN tuh)* A spongy structure attached to the fetus via the umbilical cord that provides nourishment.

amnion *(AM nee on)* The membranous sac that encases the fetus.

Pathology Connection

INFERTILITY

Infertility, or a failure to conceive offspring, can be caused by numerous factors, some of which are medically treatable. Infertility can be primary or secondary. Couples with primary infertility have never been able to conceive a child together. Couples with secondary infertility have conceived a child in the past but are currently unable to do so.

Some women are infertile because their ovaries do not produce and release eggs. This can sometimes be corrected with injections or oral medications that stimulate follicles in the ovaries or adjust hormone levels (for example, for women who are infertile due to metabolic syndrome or PCOS). Women with damaged uterine tubes may be able to have surgery to repair the damage. In women with thyroid or adrenal abnormalities or diabetes, treating those conditions may help with the ability to conceive.

In males, the primary cause of infertility is insufficient sperm production, which can be caused by hormone imbalance, illness, or injury. Some drugs that treat common problems like high blood pressure and arthritis can cause low sperm count, for example. A fertility specialist can work with a couple to diagnose the root cause of the infertility and suggest medication and lifestyle changes that may improve the odds.

Clinical Application

CONTRACEPTION

The prevention of pregnancy is termed **contraception** ("against conception") and can be accomplished by a number of means such as intrauterine devices (IUDs), spermicidal agents, birth control pills, or shields such as a condom.

Sterilization of the male can be accomplished through a **vasectomy,** in which part of the vas deferens is removed or blocked to prevent the sperm from traveling out of the penis during sexual intercourse. Females may be sterilized via **tubal ligation,** in which the fallopian tubes are cut or tied shut to prevent the egg from traveling from the ovary to the uterus.

Labor is the actual process whereby the fetus is delivered from the uterus through the vagina and into the outside world.

The amniotic fluid can be tested through a procedure called an **amniocentesis,** which punctures the amniotic sac and withdraws a fluid sample. The fluid can be sampled to test for chromosomal abnormalities leading to birth defects. In addition, biochemical disorders can be detected. See **FIGURE 17-14** ▲, which demonstrates this procedure.

Labor consists of three stages. In the **dilation stage,** the uterine smooth muscle begins to contract, thereby moving the fetus down the uterus and causing the cervix to begin to dilate. When the cervix is completely dilated (10 centimeters), the **expulsion stage** begins, during which the baby is actually delivered. Generally, the head presents first, which is called **crowning.** At this time the baby's mouth should be suctioned before the baby takes its first breath to prevent aspiration of fluid into the baby's lung.

infertility A condition of diminished fertility or an inability to produce offspring. It does not necessarily imply sterility.

contraception The prevention of fertilization.

vasectomy *(vas ECK toh mee)* Form of male sterilization in which the vas deferens is removed or blocked to prevent the travel of sperm.

tubal ligation Form of female sterilization in which the fallopian tubes are cut or tied shut to prevent the passage of the egg.

labor The actual process of fetal delivery from the uterus to the vagina to the outside world.

amniocentesis *(AM nee oh sen TEE sis)* A diagnostic test in which a needle and syringe is utilized to withdraw amniotic fluid that is chemically and cytologically studied for any genetic or biochemical disorders of the fetus. This is usually performed no earlier than 14 weeks gestation.

dilation stage The first stage of labor in which uterine smooth muscle begins to contract and move the fetus down the uterus causing the cervix to dilate.

expulsion stage When the cervix dilates to 10 centimeters and the baby is delivered.

crowning Occurring during delivery, it is the visible presentation of the fetal head as it comes out of the vaginal opening.

A

B

FIGURE 17-13 ▲ **A.** The stages in utero of human development. **B.** Actual photo of fetus at week 9. (Source: Claude Edelmann/Photo Researchers, Inc.)

placental stage The last stage of labor in which the placenta is delivered as a result of final uterine contractions.

Sometimes, the baby is turned the wrong way, and the buttocks appear first in a breech presentation, which makes the delivery difficult. The last stage of labor is the **placental stage,** in which the placenta or afterbirth is delivered due to final uterine contractions (see FIGURE 17-15 ▲).

Amazing **Body Facts**

A Million to One Shot

The adult male produces 200 million sperm daily, but it takes only one sperm to fertilize the egg.

90°

Skin

Fascia

Uterine wall

Amniotic cavity

Empty bladder

FIGURE 17-14 ▲ Amniocentesis. The woman is usually scanned by ultrasound to determine the placental site and to locate a pocket of fluid. As the needle is inserted, three levels of resistance are felt when the needle penetrates the skin, the fascia, and the uterine wall. When the needle is placed within the amniotic cavity, amniotic fluid is withdrawn.

Amazing Body Facts

Fertilization to Newborn

Fertilization occurs at conception when sperm and egg unite forming a zygote. The blastocyst (as the zygote is so called until two weeks after conception) is a grouping of two cell types, outer cells which will become the placenta and inner cells which will become the fetus. At week four the blastocyst will implant into the mothers uterus. Week five of gestation is referred to as the embryonic period as this is when the growing embryo is now developing structures of organs and organ systems. Cells of the blood, heart and liver begin to develop and organ systems like the nervous system can be seen. The developing embryo is growing the external structures, like arms and eyes. It isn't until weeks 6-7 that arm and leg buds can be seen. These organs and systems continue to grow rapidly. Week 10 is a milestone in development; this is the week that the embryo is now called a fetus. The fetus has distinct facial features and the gastrointestinal system is beginning to develop. Between weeks 11 and 14 genitals will form. By week 20 the fetus can hear because the external ear has developed and the nervous system is now capable of processing sounds. By week 25 the bone marrow has developed and the fetus can make red blood cells. By week 30 the lungs are immature but are able to "breathe" by moving with a rhythm. By 40 weeks the fetus has been in gestation for 38 weeks and may be born any day!

DILATION STAGE:
First uterine contraction to dilation of cervix

FIGURE 17-15 ▲
Stages of labor.

EXPULSION STAGE:
Birth of baby or expulsion

PLACENTAL STAGE:
Delivery of placenta

Pathology Connection

BREAST HEALTH

mastitis
(mass TYE tiss)
Inflammation or
infection of the
breast.

breast cancer
Malignant tumors
located in the breast
tissue. Most common
malignancy in
American women.

After birth, the baby is often fed with breast milk. One of the complications is **mastitis,** which
is an inflammation of the breast. Mastitis can occur at any age in both males and females, but is
usually associated with lactating females. It is caused by bacteria that can enter through a break
in the tissue of the nipple, causing localized breast pain, redness, and swelling, with difficulty in
getting the milk to flow. Treatment is usually local application of heat, analgesics, and—if severe
enough—antibiotics and anti-inflammatory drugs.

Breast cancer is one of the leading causes of death in women between the ages of 32 and 52,
killing approximately 40,000 women per year. Men can also develop breast cancer, but at a much
lower rate.

The earlier breast cancer is detected, the greater the chance for survival. It is often detected by
a mammogram, which is an x-ray of the breast. Annual mammograms are typically recommended
for women over age 40, or for women under 40 who have a strong family history of breast cancer.
Recently, recommendations to decrease the number of screening mammograms for women under 50
created a lengthy public debate about the cost of large-scale screening tests, like mammograms, and
their worth in discovering early cancers. Although adherence to the new recommendations would
decrease false positives (more common in younger women) and save money due to decreased use of

Pathology Connection (continued)

mammograms, many groups argued that cancers in women under 50 would not be detected until they were advanced.

Treatment for breast cancer may include chemotherapy, radiation therapy, or partial or full mastectomy (surgical removal of the breast). Women who have a family history may elect to have a mastectomy before any cancer symptoms occur. This is somewhat controversial. One of the most important procedures to detect cancer at an early, more treatable stage is regular breast self-examination. See FIGURE 17-16 ▲ for how to perform a breast self-examination (BSE).

WHY DO THE BREAST SELF-EXAM?

There are many good reasons for doing a breast self-exam each month. One reason is that it is easy to do and the more you do it, the better you will get at it. When you get to know how your breasts normally feel, you will quickly be able to feel any change, and early detection is the key to successful treatment and cure.

REMEMBER: A breast self-exam could save your breast—and save your life. Most breast lumps are found by women themselves, but in fact, most lumps in the breast are not cancer. Be safe, be sure.

WHEN TO DO BREAST SELF-EXAM

The best time to do breast self-exam is right after your period, when breasts are not tender or swollen. If you do not have regular periods or sometimes skip a month, do it on the same day every month.

NOW, HOW TO DO BREAST SELF-EXAM

1. Lie down and put a pillow under your right shoulder. Place your right arm behind your head.

2. Use the finger pads of your three middle fingers on your left hand to feel for lumps or thickening. Your finger pads are the top third of each finger.

3. Press firmly enough to know how your breast feels. If you're not sure how hard to press, ask your health care provider. Or try to copy the way your health care provider uses the finger pads during a breast exam. Learn what your breast feels like most of the time. A firm ridge in the lower curve of each breast is normal.

4. Move around the breast in a set way. You can choose either the circle (A), the up and down line (B), or the wedge (C). Do it the same way every time. It will help you to make sure that you've gone over the entire breast area, and to remember how your breast feels.

5. Now examine your left breast using your right hand finger pads.

6. If you find any changes, see your doctor right away.

FOR ADDED SAFETY:

You should also check your breasts while standing in front of a mirror right after you do your breast self-exam each month. See if there are any changes in the way your breasts look: dimpling of the skin, changes in the nipple, or redness or swelling.

You might also want to do a breast self-exam while you're in the shower. Your soapy hands will glide over the wet skin, making it easy to check how your breasts feel.

FIGURE 17-16 ▲ Breast self-examination (BSE).

A QUICK TRIP THROUGH SOME DISEASES OF THE REPRODUCTIVE SYSTEM

DISEASE	ETIOLOGY	SIGNS & SYMPTOMS	DIAGNOSITIC TEST(S)	TREATMENTS
Female				
Amenorrhea/ dysmenorrhea	Absent or painful menstruation; may be due to many different causes.	Lack of menstrual period/ pain during period.	Physical exam, hormone levels, imaging, exploratory surgery.	Hormones, NSAIDS, surgery, treat underlying conditions.
Premenstrual syndrome/ premenstrual dysphoric disorder	Exact cause not determined; may be due to irregular levels of estrogen or progesterone.	Constipation, nausea, headache, backache, edema, malaise, irritability, mental confusion, depression.	Currently, PMS is diagnosed if a woman has one affective (psychological) and one physical symptom. A woman is diagnosed with PMDD if she has five of the criteria.	Treat symptoms; proper nutrition, complex carbohydrates, anti-depressants, analgesics, and hormone therapy.
Endometriosis	Cause unknown.	Hematuria, dysuria, painful intercourse, and excessive menstrual bleeding; increasing painful periods; lower back, vaginal, and abdominal pain.	Patient history and exam, laparoscopic exam.	Early diagnosis is critical, use of oral contraceptives and other hormones appear to delay onset; analgesics for relief of discomfort; surgery for severe cases.
Polycystic ovarian syndrome	The ovaries produce too much testosterone and estrogen, but too little progesterone.	Multiple cysts on the ovaries, hormonal abnormalities, infertility, obesity, and insulin resistance; failure to ovulate, excess facial hair, and irregular menstrual cycles.	Imaging and blood work; increased blood levels of LH, testosterone, prolactin, and insulin.	Mainly symptom relief; weight control. Birth control pills to regulate a woman's menstrual cycle. Treat hyperlipidemia and hyperinsulinemia if present.
Breast cancer	Most common malignancy of American women and leading cause of death between ages 40 and 55. Uncontrolled growth of breast tissue; family history.	Bloody, brown, or serous nipple discharge, noticeable lump, changes in breast tissue.	Mammogram, imaging, biopsy.	Lumpectomy, mastectomy, chemotherapy, radiation, etc.

(continued)

A QUICK TRIP *(continued)*

DISEASE	ETIOLOGY	SIGNS & SYMPTOMS	DIAGNOSITIC TEST(S)	TREATMENTS
Cervical cancer	Current research shows connection with human papilloma virus and early and frequent sexual activity; may be genetic predisposition; most common in woman between 30 and 50.	Early stages are asymptomatic; watery vaginal discharge; occasional spotting of blood; later stages foul smelling vaginal discharge.	PAP test with microscopic examination, patient history, and exam.	Cryotherapy (freezing) or laser surgery; hysterectomy (removal of uterus); radiation.
Vaginitis	Inflammation of the vagina (infection, irritation, menopause).	Discharge, itching, pain.	Pelvic exam, lab tests, patient history.	Depending on cause: antibiotics, antifungals, vaginal creams, avoid irritant.
Abruptio placenta	Placenta separates from uterus.	Bleeding, pain, preterm labor.	Ultrasound.	Depends on severity: ranges from nothing to emergency cesarian.
Placenta previa	Placenta grows over cervix; causes unknown.	Bleeding late in pregnancy, pain.	Ultrasound.	Transfusions, medication, cesarian.
Ectopic (tubal) pregnancy (embryo implants in uterine tube)	Scarring, endometriosis.	Bleeding, abdominal pain, nausea, unconsciousness, and shock if tube ruptures.	Ultrasound, exploratory surgery, blood tests, pregnancy test.	Termination of pregnancy, treatment of symptoms.
Postpartum depression	Changes in hormone levels after pregnancy.	Fatigue, anxiety, feelings of worthlessness.	Exam.	Counseling, medication.

Male

DISEASE	ETIOLOGY	SIGNS & SYMPTOMS	DIAGNOSITIC TEST(S)	TREATMENTS
Erectile dysfunction disorder	Many underlying physical and/or psychological causes.	Inability to maintain erection (problem lasts 3 months or more).	Exam, blood work.	Medication, counseling, prosthetics.
Benign prostatic hyperplasia	Unknown, age-related hormone changes perhaps.	Lower urinary tract symptoms similar to UTI or overactive bladder.	Exam, blood work, rule out other causes.	Medication, surgery.
Prostate cancer	Uncontrolled growth of prostate cells which can spread.	Same as for BPH.	Same as for BPH.	Prostatectomy, chemotherapy, etc.

Pharmacology Corner

Pharmacology Corner

Many drugs are used to treat reproductive disorders. First we will discuss drugs that are prescribed to women and then those that are prescribed to men.

Oral contraceptives, otherwise known as birth control pills, are used to prevent pregnancy and to regulate the menstrual cycle. These pills, generally combinations of estrogen and progesterone, work by preventing ovulation and decreasing menstruation. Side effects include irregular bleeding, weight gain, increased appetite, depression, and headaches.

Progestins (synthetic progesterone such as Depo-provera®), may also be administered to regulate the menstrual cycle, either orally or by injection. The progestins, like the combination estrogen and progesterone medications, prevent ovulation and decrease menstruation. Side effects are the same as for oral contraceptives.

Gonadotropin releasing hormone (GnRH) agonists (such as Lupron®) are a newer class of hormones that can be administered by injection or as a nasal spray. These medications inhibit estrogen production and are often used in combination with low-dose estrogen and progesterone. GnRH agonists are the current best hormonal therapy for endometriosis. Side effects are the same as for menopause, including hot flashes and bone loss. Prior to the development of GnRH agonists, the synthetic androgen Danazol® was the treatment of choice for endometriosis. (It is only rarely prescribed today.) The addition of androgens and the subsequent decrease in natural estrogens stopped ovulation and menstruation, which relieved endometriosis symptoms. The side effects, however, were severe and sometimes permanent, including voice deepening, excess facial and body hair growth, acne, hyperlipidemia, decreased sex drive, and weight gain. Many women could not continue treatment because of the side effects.

Drugs prescribed to men are generally used for treatment of BPH or ED. For BPH treatment is via 5-alpha-reductase inhibitors or alpha blockers. The 5-alpha-reductase inhibitors, administered orally, decrease testosterone levels, preventing further enlargement of the prostate and even shrinking the enlarged gland. Side effects include decreased sex drive, ED, breast enlargement, and decreased sperm count. Alpha blockers cause smooth muscle in the urethra to relax, increasing the urine stream. Side effects include headache, dizziness, decreased blood pressure, and fatigue. Most practitioners suggest combination therapy with 5-alpha-reductase inhibitors and alpha-blockers. To treat ED, the most common (and becoming even more common) medications are phosphodiesterase type 5 inhibitors. These medications (for example, Viagra®, Levitra®, and Cialis®) increase blood accumulation in erectile tissue, increasing the likelihood of erection. The side effects for each of these medications are different for each medication but can include visual disturbances, headache, dizziness, and flushing. These are the first-line medications for treating ED of any cause.

oral contraceptives Drugs taken orally to prevent pregnancy and regulate the menstrual cycle.

progestins Class of drugs that act like estrogen and progesterone which prevent ovulation and or decrease menstruation.

gonadotropin-releasing hormone (GnRH) agonists Newer class of hormones that can be administered either by injection or nasal spray that inhibit estrogen production.

SUMMARY

Snapshots from the Journey

■ Tissues grow, are replaced, and are repaired by asexual reproduction. Cells make identical copies of themselves. Asexual reproduction takes place all over the body as tissues grow or are repaired. Some tissues, like epidermis, blood, and bone, replace themselves continually, always by asexual reproduction.

■ Asexual reproduction in eukaryotic cells is accomplished by a relatively complex process called mitosis.

■ If an organism is going to reproduce sexually, it must use specialized cells called gametes with only half the typical number of chromosomes for that organism. (The gametes must have half as many chromosomes because, during fertilization, the gametes will fuse and combine their genetic material.)

■ In humans, the gametes are eggs and sperm. Eggs and sperm are produced by a special type of cell division called meiosis, or reduction division. Reduction division produces four daughter cells, each with only 23 chromosomes. These cells are not identical to each other or to the mother cell.

■ Cells undergoing meiosis go through two divisions. The chief difference between mitosis and meiosis is the pairing of homologous chromosomes (alike in size, shape, and genetic content) during meiosis.

■ Human reproduction can be described as a cycle, known as the human life cycle. Adult humans have specialized organs called gonads (ovaries and testes), which produce gametes via meiosis. Gametes get together during sexual reproduction in a process known as fertilization. The fertilized egg is called a zygote. The zygote undergoes many rounds of mitosis, eventually becoming an embryo, a fetus, a baby, a child, and finally an adult.

■ The female reproductive system consists of several internal genitalia. The gonads (ovaries) produce eggs (gametes). The uterine tubes provide a passageway for the egg to get to the uterus. The uterus is an incubator for the fertilized eggs. The vagina is the birth canal, connecting the uterus with the outside world. The external genitalia include the external opening of the vagina and several protective structures.

■ Female reproductive physiology is relatively complicated, organized around a monthly cycle of changes in both the ovaries and the uterus, collectively known as the menstrual cycle. The cycle begins with menstruation, the shedding of the uterine lining. After the lining, the endometrium, has finished shedding, it begins to build up again in a process called proliferation. As the endometrium is proliferating, an egg (follicle) is maturing in the ovary. Eventually, the follicle will be released from the ovary (ovulation) and travel to the uterus. If fertilization occurs, then the fertilized egg will implant in the thickened endometrium, and pregnancy will result. If the egg is not fertilized, the endometrium will degenerate and menstruation will occur.

SUMMARY

- Control of the menstrual cycle is accomplished by four hormones: estrogen, progesterone, follicle-stimulating hormone (FSH), and luteinizing hormone (LH). During puberty, the ovaries begin to secrete larger amounts of estrogen and progesterone, which cause the development of female secondary sexual characteristics and set the cycle in motion.

- The cycle works this way: The hypothalamus releases gonadotropin-releasing hormone (GnRH) that causes the pituitary to increase secretion of FSH and LH. FSH and LH cause follicles to develop and eventually trigger ovulation. Estrogen levels continue to rise as the developing follicles secrete more and more estrogen. Estrogen causes positive feedback to the hypothalamus and pituitary, which increases the levels of FSH and LH. This positive feedback loop continues right up until ovulation.

- At ovulation, the ruptured follicle (left behind after ovulation) begins to secrete progesterone and backs off on estrogen secretion. Under the influence of progesterone, the feedback loop between estrogen and the hypothalamus and pituitary reverses itself, becoming a negative feedback loop. Thus, LH and FSH levels drop. Progesterone levels continue to rise, maintaining the thickened endometrium in case fertilization occurs. If fertilization does not occur, progesterone decreases, the endometrium decays, and the cycle begins all over again.

- The male reproductive system has somewhat more obvious external genitalia, the penis, and the testes. Internal genitalia include a series of ducts, the vas deferens, ejaculatory duct and urethra, and a series of glands, the seminal vesicles, prostate, and bulbourethral glands.

- Male reproductive physiology is not cyclic and is therefore a bit less complicated than female reproduction. Sperm, like eggs, develop via meiosis under the control of LH and FSH in the testes. Sperm mature in the epididymis. The penis is the organ of copulation. When a man is sexually aroused, the penis becomes engorged with blood, and an erection occurs. If arousal continues, ejaculation, the movement of sperm from the testes to the penis and out of the man's body, may occur. During ejaculation, sperm move from the epididymis through the vas deferens, ejaculatory duct, and out the urethra. Along the journey, the seminal vesicles, prostate, and bulbourethral glands add sugar, chemicals, and mucus to the sperm to form semen.

- Testosterone is the chief male hormone. It is secreted by the testes and is responsible for masculinizing male fetuses, triggering LH and FSH production, and the development of male secondary sexual characteristics.

MARIA'S STORY

Maria has always wanted to have children, but she has read horror stories about diabetes and pregnancy. Her doctor has told her that if she is healthy, she could try to get pregnant when the time is right. There are significant risks, however, including a high birth weight baby.

a. What characteristic of diabetes mellitus would contribute to increased birth weight?

_____

_____

_____

_____

b. How can the condition be prevented?

_____

_____

_____

_____

c. What other conditions might Maria need to take care to prevent?

_____

_____

_____

_____

REVIEW QUESTIONS

Multiple Choice

1. In each lobule of the testes are several _____, tubes in which the sperm are made and develop.
   a. seminal vesicles
   b. seminiferous tubules
   c. bulbourethral glands
   d. all of the above

2. The female primary genitalia are the:
   a. ovaries
   b. uterus
   c. vagina
   d. testes

3. This division of the endometrium sheds each month:
   a. horny layer
   b. basal layer
   c. menstrual layer
   d. none of the above

4. This hormone stimulates ovulation:
   a. estrogen
   b. progesterone
   c. LH
   d. FSH

REVIEW QUESTIONS

5. Which of the following is not a function of asexual reproduction (mitosis)?
   a. making gametes
   b. tissue growth
   c. tissue repair
   d. all are functions of asexual reproduction

6. Danazol®, a synthetic testosterone, has which of the following side effects when prescribed to women to treat endometriosis?
   a. facial hair growth
   b. bone loss
   c. increased ovulation
   d. all of the above

7. Which hormone is inhibited during treatment for BPH?
   a. estrogen
   b. progestin
   c. testosterone
   d. GnRH

Fill in the Blank

1. The stiffening of the penis is known as _____, and the actual movement of sperm out of the penis is _____.

2. In the male reproductive system the _____ is posterior to the bladder, and the _____ gland is inferior to the bladder.

3. _____ is the type of cell division that produces egg and sperm.

4. After ovulation, estrogen and progesterone send _____ (positive or negative) feedback to the pituitary and hypothalamus.

5. The union of sperm and egg is called _____.

6. Oral contraceptives are typically a combination of these two hormones _____ and _____.

Short Answer

1. Trace the journey of a sperm from its birth through fertilization.

_____

_____

_____

_____

REVIEW QUESTIONS

2. Explain the role of hormones in controlling the female reproductive cycle.

_____

_____

_____

_____

3. Contrast mitosis and meiosis.

_____

_____

_____

_____

4. Distinguish between PMS and PMDD.

_____

_____

_____

_____

5. Explain the treatment strategies for benign prostatic hyperplasia.

_____

_____

_____

_____

Suggested Activities

1. List all the hormones involved in reproduction. Describe what they do.

2. Describe the human life cycle in detail. How much do you know about your own reproductive system?

3. With a partner, list the similarities and differences between male and female reproduction. How many can you list?

4. Describe the differences between a blastocyst, embryo and fetus. How do they differ from a baby?

CAREER CONNECTIONS

Now that you have read this chapter, here is a list of related professions you may be interested in investigating for a future career:

- Doula or Midwife

Research each profession and report on the following:

1. Profession description to include job responsibilities
2. Educational requirements
3. Job opportunities
4. Opportunities outside of the hospital setting
5. Salary range
6. Licensure and continuing education requirements

ANATOMY, PHYSIOLOGY, AND DISEASE IN ACTION

Case I

The following case history was reported at labmed.ascpjournals.org/content/40/4/215.full.pdf.

Clinical History
Patient: 1-month-old male
History: Features suggestive of Down's syndrome
Family history: Parents 43 and 45, 3 healthy sons, 39 weeks gestation, 6 lb. oz. 19 inches at birth
Physical Examination: Low set and malformed ears, protruding tongue, open mouth, hypotonia, short broad hand. The child was born also with cryptorchidism but normal penis size.

Laboratory Results

48,XXY,+21
Double trisomy (Down's Syndrome & Klinefelter's Syndrome)   Karyotype

- Identify the chromosome that indicates the abnormal condition/syndrome.
- How could these abnormalities arise?
- What is Klinefelter's Syndrome? What signs and symptom might be found associated with this syndrome? How might this be treated?

(continued)

ANATOMY, PHYSIOLOGY, AND DISEASE IN ACTION

Case II

This case history was reported at: www.meddean.luc.edu/lumen/MedEd/genetics/diseases/turner.htm.

Clinical History

A 7-year-old female goes for a school physical. She is noted to be below the 5th percentile for height, 25% for weight. She is doing well in school. The mother is 5' 3", father is 5' 9". (This is part of the family history to indicate the parents were of normal size.). The patient has one brother, age 9. He is at 50% for height on the chart for his age. Her younger sister is 4. She is the same height as the patient. On physical exam she was noted to have a low hairline and wide-spaced nipples. Blood chromosomes indicate 45, X.

- Is there a risk of this disorder to her siblings?
- What is the name of the syndrome?
- What are the other signs and symptoms expected to be found associated with this case?
- How could the short stature be treated?
- What additional treatments should be employed?
- Will she be able to become pregnant?

Basic Diagnostic Tests
What Do the Tests Tell Us?

Sometimes a general map just isn't enough to understand and enjoy various parts of your trip. City maps, dining guides, tourist highlights, and brochures on geologic/historic points of interest are all important tools that help you zero in on specific areas of interest. The same thing can be said about diagnostic tests, which help to provide us with a more accurate view of the patient's overall condition and disease state, including diagnosis, progression, or improvement. To make sure we have a trouble-free journey, we need a reliable means of transportation. A quick check of our car (oil, gas, or windshield washer fluid) can be compared to a general physical examination, but there are times when we may need to check the more involved car systems that require special equipment such as the transmission, brakes, or engine compression. Medical diagnostics are like those more advanced diagnostics for your car. These tests can be used to verify the obvious or to discover where the signs and symptoms are pointing. In this chapter, we will provide you with an overview of some of the common diagnostic tests used in health care, including quick reference tables and lists of possible causes for abnormal test results of some common clinical tests.

LEARNING OUTCOMES

At the end of your journey through this chapter, you will be able to:

- List and describe common diagnostic tests often used in clinical settings
- Determine which diagnostic test(s) should be chosen to determine a patient's suspected disease state
- Recognize abnormal findings of several basic diagnostic tests
- Determine conditions that may produce abnormal test results

Pronunciation Guide

Correct pronunciation is important in any journey so that you and the others are completely understood. Here is a "see and say" Pronunciation Guide for the more difficult terms to pronounce in this chapter. Please note that pronunciations given are referenced to medical dictionaries, and regional variations may exist.

alkaptonuria (AL cap toh NEW ree ah)
anemia (uh NEE me uh)
dyspnea (DISP nee uh)
endoscope (EN doh skope)
endoscopy (en DOS koh pee)
eosinophil (EE oh SIN oh fill)
erythrocytes (eh RITH roh sites)
hemoglobin (HEE moh GLOH bin)
ketonuria (kee toh NEW ree ah)
leukocytes (LOO koh sites)
leukocytosis (LOO koh sigh TOE sis)

leukopenia (LOO koh PEE nee uh)
occult (uh KULT)
polycythemia (PAUL ee sigh THEE me uh)
polymorphonuclear
  (PAUL ee MORE foh NEW klee air)
polysomnography (PAUL ee sahm NAH gra fee)
thrombocytes (THROM boh sites)
thrombocytopenia
  (THROM boh SIGH toe PEE nee ah)
urea (you REE ah)

OVERVIEW OF DIAGNOSTIC TESTING

Although a good physical examination with a solid patient history (including family/occupational information) and review of current medications are very important, they aren't always enough to make a correct diagnosis. A headache can be caused by infected sinuses, stress, tumors, eyestrain, medication side effects, and so on. **Dyspnea** (difficulty breathing) can be caused by asthma, heart problems, stress, anxiety, smoking or inhalation of other toxic substances, or tumors, to name just a few. To help determine the specific cause of various signs or symptoms, appropriate medical testing comes into play. Another aspect of diagnostic testing is to confirm the effectiveness of a prescribed treatment or medication.

To thoroughly cover all the types of diagnostic testing available, you need a textbook much larger than this one. This chapter provides an overview of a variety of common diagnostic tests that aid in determining a patient's disease state. In addition, each system chapter of this textbook has more information on "system-specific" diagnostic tests. Not only will this information aid in your understanding of these tests, but it will also help you to explain to your patient the "whys and hows" of their ordered tests, when appropriate. Note that the normal values listed in this chapter for the various tests may sometimes vary slightly from other reference sources. Different hospital labs utilize different *but similar* test values, and that is okay. These values are all within acceptable ranges for making a correct diagnosis.

One major caution: *A diagnosis is based on the patient, not solely on the test numbers!* As you spend more time in the clinical setting, you will see a variety of exceptions to the rules. Each patient is different. Here's one more very important caution: *One*

dyspnea *(DISP nee uh)* Difficulty in breathing.

abnormal test result alone does not make a diagnosis. Though we struggle daily to maintain homeostasis, there are occasions when our own diagnostic test values may be abnormal, even when we are healthy!

BLOOD TESTING

The one type of test that most of us have had at some time in our lives is the common blood test. Blood is a vital fluid that communicates with all parts of our bodies. Therefore, the information gained from analyzing the various components of blood can greatly aid in diagnosis and treatment.

Blood Basics

Blood is composed of a liquid portion called **plasma** (which is about 90% water and originates from the intestines and organs) and a variety of cells (which are mainly produced by bone marrow) called **red blood cells** (**erythrocytes**), **white blood cells** (**leukocytes**), and **platelets** (**thrombocytes**). These cell types are not of a uniform size. Leukocytes are the largest, thrombocytes are the smallest, and erythrocytes are in the middle. Their numbers also vary, normally, with one leukocyte for every 30 thrombocytes and every 500 erythrocytes.

Each of these three main blood cell types has distinct responsibilities. Red blood cells have the main responsibility of transporting oxygen from the lungs to all the body's cells. White blood cells are our protectors against infection. Platelets help blood to clot so we don't bleed to death from minor cuts and abrasions. **FIGURE 18-1** ▲ shows the major cell types found in the blood.

Blood samples are usually obtained from the veins, which are the vessels you see in your skin that have a bluish tint to them. A *venipuncture* is performed when a needle is inserted usually into an arm vein in the anticubital space and then is attached to a sealed tube (called a Vacutainer) that has a vacuum in it. The vacuum allows for blood that is under low pressure in the vein to easily rush in and fill the tube. The tube size varies depending on how much blood is needed to do a specific test. These vacuum tubes also have different colored tops. The color of the top indicates which test(s) are to be done with that collected blood specimen. If multiple blood tests have been ordered, the same needle can remain in the vein while the tubes are replaced as they fill up. The order in which the tubes are filled is specific. This is to prevent contamination to the next blood sample and tube, as in cases where there may be a particular additive in the tube of the

plasma *(PLAZ mah)* Clear, straw-colored fluid portion of the blood that carries blood cells and contains dissolved substances like proteins, glucose, minerals, electrolytes, clotting factors, complement proteins, hormones, bilirubin, urea, and creatinine.

red blood cells (erythrocytes) *(eh RITH roh sight)* A red blood cell. Erythrocytes contain hemoglobin and carry oxygen and carbon dioxide to and from the lungs and cells of the body.

white blood cells (leukocytes) *(LOO koh sights)* White blood cells. There are five different types of mature leukocytes: neutrophils, eosinophils, basophils, lymphocytes, and monocytes.

platelets (thrombocytes) *(THROM boh sight)* Cell fragment that is flat and does not have a nucleus. It is active in the blood-clotting process. Thrombocytes are also known as blood platelets.

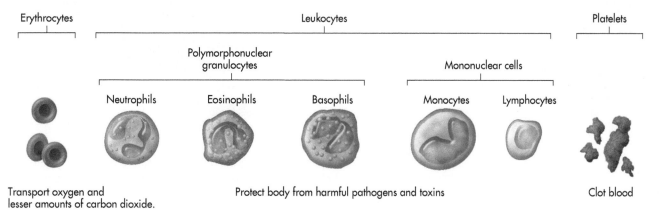

| Erythrocytes | Leukocytes | | | | | Platelets |

Polymorphonuclear granulocytes — Neutrophils, Eosinophils, Basophils

Mononuclear cells — Monocytes, Lymphocytes

Transport oxygen and lesser amounts of carbon dioxide.   Protect body from harmful pathogens and toxins   Clot blood

FIGURE 18-1 ▲ Major blood cell types.

patient who is suspected of having bacterial colonization on the skin. See TABLE 18-1 ■ for the order of the draw and FIGURE 18-2 ▲, which shows examples of the various colored vacutainers.

Another way to obtain a blood sample is from a pinprick of your skin, usually on the fingertip. Diabetics often do this when they are measuring their blood glucose (sugar) levels. See FIGURE 18-3 ▲ for an example of a device that measures blood glucose in this manner. For special testing to determine the amount of oxygen you have in your body, or how well you are breathing, blood samples are taken from your arteries, usually the ones in your arms. You can't see arteries because they are deeper than veins, but you can feel them. As a result, it takes special skill to obtain an arterial blood sample.

TABLE 18-1 ■ THE ORDER OF BLOOD DRAW, SPECIFIC VACUUM TUBES, AND THEIR TESTS

ORDER OF DRAW	VACUUM TUBE TOP COLOR	TEST ORDERED
1	Yellow	Blood Culture
2	Light Blue	Blood Coagulation
3	Red	Serum Testing/Blood Bank, Serology/Blood Chemistry
4	Red Marbled	Serum Testing
5	Green	Blood Chemistry (whole blood)/plasma tests
6	Light Green	Plasma Determination
7	Lavender	Hematology (such as CBC/glycosylated hemoglobin)
8	White, Pink, or Royal Blue	Chemistry for Trace Elements
9	Gray	Glucose Tolerance Test/Alcohol Level/Chemistry Tests
10	Dark Blue	Clot/Embolus Status

FIGURE 18-2 ▲ Examples of the various colored vacutainers. (Source: Cmpost/Fotolia)

FIGURE 18-3 ▲ After the patient pricks his or her skin a droplet of blood is placed on the absorbent test strip, which is then inserted into the monitor. The patient's blood glucose level is then numerically displayed. (Source: Arka38/Shutterstock.com.)

General Blood Disorders

Numerous potential blood disorders can be categorized by *blood cell type* and by the *numbers* of those major blood cell types. Red blood cell disorders can be classified as either **anemias** (*an* means "without") or **polycythemias** (*poly* means "many;" *cyt/o* means "cells;" *hemia* means "blood").

In cases of *anemia,* there are fewer than normal amounts of erythrocytes for a given volume of blood. This could be a result of blood loss caused by a bleeding injury, lower-than-normal production of red blood cells, or some disorder that is destroying erythrocytes at a higher than normal rate. *Polycythemia,* on the other hand, is a condition in which there is a higher-than-normal amount of erythrocytes for a given blood volume. In Chapter 13, "The Respiratory System," you learned that a form of polycythemia can be caused by chronically insufficient amounts of oxygen in your blood.

Problems with white blood cells can also be determined through testing. **Leukocytosis** occurs when there is a higher-than-normal number of white blood cells. This can occur when there is an infection or your patient has leukemia, for example. **Leukopenia** is a situation in which there are lower-than-normal amounts of white blood cells. In an interesting twist, this can occur if an individual has a long-term (*chronic*) infection and the body just can't keep up with sufficient white blood cell production. Of course, there are other reasons why a patient may have leukopenia, as you have seen in other chapters.

Thrombocytopenia is a condition in which the number of platelets is below normal. This can lead to a decreased blood clotting ability. Patients with thrombocytopenia are in danger of experiencing massive bleeding.

anemias *(ah NEE mee ah)* Any condition in which the number of erythrocytes in the blood is decreased.

polycythemias *(PAUL ee sigh THEE mee ah)* Increased number of erythrocytes due to uncontrolled production by the red marrow. The viscosity of the blood increases; it becomes viscous (thick), and the total blood volume is increased.

leukocytosis *(LOO koh sigh TOH sis)* Increase in the number of white blood cells above normal.

leukopenia Abnormal decrease of white blood cells.

thrombocytopenia *(THROM boh SIGH toh PEE nee ah)* Deficiency in the number of thrombocytes. This can be due to exposure to radiation or toxic chemicals or drugs that damage the stem cells in the bone marrow.

Amazing Body Facts

The weight of the normal blood volume of an adult is approximately 1/13 of his or her total body weight!

Specific Blood Tests

When venous blood is withdrawn, it is placed in a tube that is centrifuged (spun around) at a very high speed. This separates the blood into two major components, as shown in FIGURE 18-4 ▲. The heavier cells are forced to the bottom of the tube and are referred to as the **formed elements**. The upper level, which is lighter in weight and color, is the plasma, or liquid portion of the blood, containing numerous dissolved substances. Please refer back to Figure 18-4 as you read through the upcoming sections.

formed elements Cellular parts of the blood including red and white blood cells and platelets.

Complete Blood Count (CBC)

This is one of the most commonly ordered tests. Due to the number of things that this test looks at, it is useful in determining a patient's diagnosis, their prognosis, their response to medication or treatment, or if they have recovered from the diagnosed disease. Among other things, a typical CBC looks at the following:

- RBC (red blood cell count)
- Hct (hematocrit)
- Hgb (hemoglobin)
- WBC (white blood cell count)
- DIFF (differential white blood cell count)
- Platelet count

FIGURE 18-4 ▲ As blood is spun around in a centrifuge, the heavier cells (RBCs, WBCs, and platelets) form the bottom layer with plasma remaining as the top layer.

hemoglobin *(HEE moh GLOH bin)* Substance in an erythrocyte that binds to oxygen and carbon dioxide. Its globin chains give it a round shape. When it is bound to oxygen, it forms the compound oxyhemoglobin.

RBC (red blood cell count) Whereas white blood cells (WBCs) are mostly involved with protecting us from infection, erythrocytes are mainly responsible for transporting oxygen from the lungs and depositing it into body tissue. This is accomplished by a substance found in red blood cells (RBCs) called **hemoglobin**. RBCs are manufactured in the red bone marrow and are shaped like a biconcave, or hollow on both sides, disk. Some RBCs are also manufactured in the yellow marrow. RBCs are flexible to better fit through tiny capillaries when necessary.

Normally, millions of RBCs die each day, so millions have to be created daily to replace them. RBCs are measured by the number of them contained in a cubic millimeter (mm^3) of blood. The normal amount found in that mm^3 varies between males and females:

> **Normal RBC Values**
> Men: $4.6–6.2 \times 10^6$ / mm^3
> Women: $4.2–5.4 \times 10^6$ / mm^3

Anemia is a condition in which there is a decrease in the normal RBC amount. It is *not* a disease, but rather a sign of some disease or cause such as:

- Blood loss
- Dietary insufficiency (iron, some vitamins, folic acid)
- Decreased RBC production
- Increased RBC destruction

anemia *(ah NEE mee ah)* Any condition in which the number of erythrocytes in the blood is decreased.

As stated before, polycythemia is a general term for an excess of RBCs in the blood. Some of the causative agents of this condition are:

- Dehydration
- Diarrhea (severe)
- High altitude living
- Overproduction by bone marrow

Hct (Hematocrit) This test is used to determine the amount of red blood cells packed in a specific volume of blood. A tube two-thirds full of blood is spun in a centrifuge so the RBCs are separated from the rest of the blood. The height of the packed RBCs at the bottom of the tube is measured and recorded in terms of the volume of RBCs in 100 mL of blood. Again, please see Figure 18-4. This result is written as a percentage of the total amount of blood that was centrifuged.

> **Normal Hct Values**
> Men = 40–54%
> Women = 38–47%

Higher-than-normal percentages of Hct can be caused by:

- Severe dehydration (loss of fluid concentrates the cells)
- Shock

Lower-than-predicted values can be a result of:

- **Hemolytic** reactions (incompatible blood transfusions and infections) (*Hem/o* means "blood;" *lytic* means "breakdown.")
- Acute massive hemorrhage (blood loss)

hemolytic *(HEE moh LIT ik)* The destruction of blood and blood particles.

Amazing **Body Facts**

Red blood cells make up approximately half of your blood's volume!

hemoglobin *(HEE moh GLOH bin)* Substance in an erythrocyte that binds to oxygen and carbon dioxide. Its globin chains give it a round shape. When it is bound to oxygen, it forms the compound oxyhemoglobin.

Hgb (Hemoglobin) Erythrocytes contain a substance called **hemoglobin** that is needed to transport oxygen from the lungs to all the tissues in the body. Normally, every gram of hemoglobin can carry 1.34 mL of oxygen. Hemoglobin also acts as a buffer to help maintain the acid–base balance of the blood. Hemoglobin levels are measured in grams per deciliter, or g/dL, to determine if the individual is anemic or not.

Normal Hgb Values
Women: 12–16 g/dL
Men: 13.5–17.5 g/dL
Newborn: 14–16 g/dL

Decreases in the level of hemoglobin can be caused by:

- Anemia
- Excessive fluid intake
- Hemorrhage (severe)
- Pregnancy

An increased level of hemoglobin can be a result of:

- Chronic obstructive pulmonary disease
- High altitude living

WBC (White Blood Cells) Several types of leukocytes (white blood cells) help to protect us from infection. They can be divided into two main groups. The first group is called **granulocytes** because they possess granules in their cytoplasm. They also have multilobed nuclei, and because of this are also known as **polymorphonuclear leukocytes,** or—more commonly—PMNs. This group consists of *basophils, eosinophils,* and *neutrophils.* The second group is comprised of **agranulocytes** that includes *monocytes* and *lymphocytes.*

Finding out the number of *total* WBCs in the blood is important when looking for a diagnosis or prognosis for your patient. As you will see in a little while, increases or decreases of *specific* types of WBCs can aid us in determining a *specific* disease.

granulocytes *(GRAN yoo loh SITE)* A specific group of white blood cells that possess granules in their cytoplasm.

polymorphonuclear leukocyte *(PAUL ee MORE foh NEW klee er)* A white blood cell with a nucleus made of two or more lobes, i.e., the granular leukocytes: neutrophils, eosinophils, or basophils.

agranulocyte A nongranular, mononuclear white blood cell (a lymphocyte or a monocyte).

leukocytosis *(LOO koh sigh TOH sis)* Increase in the number of white blood cells above normal.

Normal WBC Values
Men: 4.5–11 $\times$ 10^3 / mm^3
Women: 4.5–11 $\times$ 10^3 / mm^3

Leukocytosis is diagnosed when the total WBC count is greater than 10,000/mm^3. It is usually a result of one type of WBC increasing in number. Leukocytosis can occur when there is an acute infection, but sometimes it occurs with no clinical disease. Other potential causes include but are not limited to:

- Circulatory disease
- Coma
- Hemorrhage
- Leukemia
- Malignancy (especially in the gastrointestinal tract, bone/liver)
- Menstruation
- Steroid therapy
- Stress (pain/excitement)

Leukopenia is diagnosed when the total number of WBCs falls below 4,000/mm³. Some possible causes can be:

leukopenia Abnormal decrease of white blood cells.

- Alcoholism
- Viral infections
- Drugs (such as epinephrine)
- Fever
- Severe electric shock
- Tissue necrosis
- Toxins
- Trauma/tissue injury

As previously stated, leukopenia can occur in a patient with chronic infection(s) and whose body is so "worn out" that it just can't produce enough WBCs anymore. A WBC count less than 500 is a panic value requiring immediate attention.

DIFF (Differential Leukocyte Count) It is important to remember that several different types of WBCs circulate through the body in varying amounts.

Each of these types performs a special function and will increase in percentage if the following situations exist:

Neutrophils: Combat bacterial infection, inflammation, stress
Lymphocytes: Fight viral infections including measles, chicken pox, infectious mononucleosis
Eosinophils: Respond to asthma, allergic conditions, parasitic invasions
Monocytes: Respond to severe and chronic infections
Basophils: Respond to inflammation and blood disorders

Normal DIFF Values
Neutrophils make up about 60–70% of all circulating WBCs
Lymphocytes comprise about 20–40%
Eosinophils are around 1–4%
Monocytes are 2–6%
Basophils are 0.5–1%

By monitoring the varying amounts of the specific types of WBCs and comparing that to the total amount of WBCs we may see which type of disorder is causing the problem—one more piece of the puzzle. For example, an **eosinophil** count above 4% may indicate an allergic reaction.

eosinophil *(EE oh SIN oh fill)* Type of leukocyte. It is classified as a granulocyte because it has granules in the cytoplasm. The nucleus has two lobes. Eosinophils are involved in allergic reactions and defense against parasites.

TEST YOUR KNOWLEDGE 18-1

Choose the best answer:

1. The largest of the blood cells are:
   a. leukocytes
   b. touristcytes
   c. erythrocytes
   d. thrombocytes

2. The general blood cell type that aids in fighting infection is:
   a. WBC
   b. CBC
   c. RBC
   d. NBC

3. A disorder involving fewer-than-normal red blood cells per a given volume of blood:
   a. analogue
   b. leukopenia
   c. anemia
   d. RBC

4. An increase in hemoglobin levels can be caused by:
   a. excessive fluid intake
   b. anemia
   c. severe hemorrhage
   d. high altitude living

5. This type of blood cell is responsible for the transportation of oxygen to the cells of the body:
   a. WBC
   b. CBC
   c. RBC
   d. NBC

platelets *(PLATE lets)* Another term for thrombocytes which help blood to clot.

Platelet Count Also known as thrombocytes, **platelets** are the smallest of the formed elements in your blood. They can be disk shaped, oval, flattened, or round. They are important in helping blood to clot and maintaining vascular integrity. They can also pick up, store, and release certain vasoactive substances. In normal situations, two-thirds of all your platelets circulate in the blood, whereas one-third are found in the spleen. A platelet count is important to help see how well anticoagulant therapy is working, if there is bone marrow failure (as in leukemia), if a patient has thrombocytopenia, and to diagnose a variety of conditions such as a bleeding disorder due to liver disease.

Normal Platelet Values
150,000–350,000/mm^3

Situations in which there are higher-than-normal numbers of platelets can include:

- Cancer/heart disease
- High-altitude living
- Iron deficiency
- Splenectomy
- Trauma
- Tuberculosis
- Vitamin K deficiency
- Vomiting
- Excessive sweating
- Fever

Conditions that can lead to a decrease in platelet numbers include:

- Blood transfusions
- Bone marrow lesions
- Cancer chemotherapy
- Infections/pneumonia

PT (Prothrombin Time or Pro Time)

Pro Time is a timed test to measure the blood's ability to clot. This is an indicator of levels of prothrombin, a protein produced by the liver that converts to thrombin during the clotting process. A body needs vitamin K to produce prothrombin. Because prothrombin is produced by the liver, low blood levels of this substance may be indicative of liver disease.

> Normal PT: 10–14 seconds

Increases in PT indicate that the blood will not clot as quickly as normal. For example, individuals on anticoagulant therapy such as Coumadin® will have an increased PT. Most cardiac patients are kept at a PT time that's 2 to 2 1/2 times normal to inhibit clots from forming in the cardiovascular system.

Decreases in PT indicate an increase in the blood's ability to clot. This can be a result of consumption of excessive amounts of green, leafy vegetables, which increases the absorption of vitamin K, thus increasing the amount of prothrombin. Drugs, depending on which type, can either increase or decrease PT.

PTT (Partial Thromboplastin Time)

PTT is another test for the ability of blood to clot. This one looks at the intrinsic thromboplastin system and is often used to monitor the effectiveness of heparin (an anticoagulation drug) therapy. Conditions that cause changes to PTT are similar to the ones that cause changes to PT.

> Normal PTT: 30–45 seconds

TABLE 18-2 ■ provides a quick reference to blood test abnormalities and their possible causative conditions or situations.

Blood Chemistry

In addition to the blood cells we have discussed, there are also numerous chemicals in the blood. Looking back at Figure 18-4, note the plasma portion of the centrifuged blood. That is where you will find these numerous chemicals. Disease processes can alter the amounts of many of these chemicals. Measuring their values can aid us in making a diagnosis. So many substances can be measured in the blood that it would be impossible to discuss them all in this chapter. The following are common ones often found in the results of a physician-ordered patient's blood chemistry.

BUN (Blood Urea Nitrogen) No, BUN isn't something you eat but rather an important blood chemistry measurement. **Urea** is formed by the liver and is a very significant nonprotein nitrogenous end waste product of protein catabolism in the body. Once urea is produced, it is transported to the kidneys via the blood for eventual excretion in the urine. Although this is a diagnostic test often used to determine renal function, **TABLE 18-3 ■** shows that there are other causes for abnormal BUN levels.

> Normal BUN Values: 7–18 mg/dL or 2.5–6.3 mmol/L

Pro Time The time it takes for clotting to occur after thromboplastin and calcium are added to decalcified plasma. The test is used to assess levels of anticoagulation in patients taking warfarin, to determine the cause of unexplained bleeding (as in patients with hemophilia), or to assess the ability of the liver to synthesize blood-clotting proteins.

urea The main nitrogenous substance found in urine. The amount excreted in urine is directly related to the amount of protein consumed.

TABLE 18-2 ■ BLOOD TESTING RESULTS

ABNORMAL TEST RESULT(S)	POSSIBLE CAUSATIVE CONDITIONS/SITUATIONS
WBCs, decreased	Alcoholism, bone marrow depression, viral infections
WBCs, increased	Circulatory disease, coma, drugs (such as anesthetics and quinine), fever, hemorrhage, leukemia, malignancy, menstruation, moderate physical activity, newborns, serum sickness, severe electric shock, steroid therapy, stress (pain/excitement), tissue necrosis, toxins, trauma/tissue injury, uremia, allergies
RBCs, decreased	Blood loss, dietary insufficiency, decreased RBC production, increased RBC destruction, Hodgkin's disease, leukemia, multiple myeloma, pernicious anemia, rheumatic fever, Addison's disease
RBCs, increased	Dehydration, diarrhea (severe), exercise, high altitude, poisoning (acute), secondary polycythemia, pulmonary fibrosis
Hct, decreased	Anemia, cirrhosis, hemolytic reactions (incompatible transfusions, infections, drugs/chemicals, burns), hyperthyroidism, leukemia, massive hemorrhage
Hct, increased	Erythrocytosis, dehydration (severe), polycythemia, shock
Hgb, decreased	Anemia, cirrhosis of the liver, excessive fluid intake, hemolytic reactions, hemorrhage (severe), hyperthyroidism, pregnancy
Hgb, increased	Chronic obstructive pulmonary disease (COPD), congestive heart failure, high-altitude living, conditions of hyperconcentration of blood
Platelet count, decreased	Allergic conditions, anemia, blood transfusions, bone marrow lesions, cancer chemotherapy, chemical exposures, toxic drug effects, infections, pneumonia
Platelet count, increased	Asphyxiation, anemia (posthemorrhagic), cancer, cirrhosis, exercise/excitement, heart disease, high-altitude living, iron deficiency, polycythemia vera, rheumatoid arthritis, splenectomy, trauma, tuberculosis, Winter (!).

TABLE 18-3 ■ BUN TESTING RESULTS

ABNORMAL TEST RESULT(S)	POSSIBLE CAUSATIVE CONDITIONS/SITUATIONS	SIGNS/SYMPTOMS (S/S)
Increased BUN	Acute myocardial infarction, chronic gout, dehydration, diabetes, drugs, excessive protein consumption/protein catabolism, GI hemorrhage, infection, pregnancy (late stage), renal function impairment, shock, tissue trauma (severe)	Confusion, convulsions, disorientation, many more
Decreased BUN	Diet (low protein/high carbohydrate), drugs, fluid overload (as in intravenous therapy), liver failure, malnutrition, kidney disease, overhydration	Edema, many more that are disease specific

Electrolytes Electrolytes are crucial for proper cellular function throughout the body. As a result, the body must maintain normal concentrations of the various electrolytes. In severe imbalances, life-threatening heart arrhythmias can occur. The amount of water in the body (too much or too little) can affect electrolyte concentrations. In the clinical setting we have patients with conditions that will affect their fluid balances, and thus their electrolyte balances. Dehydration may result from not drinking enough water, from diarrhea, or from vomiting, whereas excessive intravenous (IV) therapy may add too much water to the patient. TABLE 18-4 ■ shows the possible causes of abnormal values of some common electrolytes.

Normal Electrolyte Values

Calcium (Ca^{2+}): 4.5.–5.4 mEq/L

Chloride (Cl^-): 95–103 mEq/L

Potassium (K^+): 3.8–5.0 mEq/L

Sodium (Na^+): 136–142 mEq/L

TABLE 18-4 ■ ELECTROLYTE TESTING RESULTS

ABNORMAL TEST RESULT(S)	POSSIBLE CAUSATIVE CONDITIONS/SITUATIONS	SIGNS/SYMPTOMS (S/S)
Calcium increased	Diuretic therapy, excessive consumption of antacids or milk, hyperparathyroidism, malignant tumors, vitamin D intoxication	Anorexia, constipation, hyporeflexia, lethargy, mental deterioration, renal stones, weakness
Calcium decreased	Pregnancy, hypoparathyroidism, vitamin D deficiency	Convulsions, cramping of muscles, mental disturbances, paresthesia
Chloride increased	Renal tubular acidosis	Breathing rapid and deep, disorientation, weakness
Chloride decreased	Excessive vomiting	Breathing depressed, muscle hypertonicity, tetanus
Potassium increased	Muscle tissue damage, renal failure	Diarrhea, irritability, nausea, ventricular fibrillation, weakness
Potassium decreased	Chronic stress, diuretic therapy, diarrhea, endocrine disorder	Cardiac arrhythmias, hypotension, malaise, muscle weakness
Sodium increased	Dehydration	Dry mucous membranes, dry tongue, flushed skin, intense thirst
Sodium decreased	Burns, excessive water intake, loss of gastrointestinal secretions, excessive sweating	Abdominal cramping, confusion, muscle twitching, perfusion decrease, seizures, vasomotor collapse

Enzymes Enzymes are complex proteins that create changes, often speeding up changes or processes, without changing themselves. They can be found in the majority of the body's cells. Because of this, the levels of certain enzymes are often noted in the blood when they are released following an injury to or the death of cells. This fact is particularly useful in the case of heart attacks. Cardiac tissue death is a common result of a heart attack. As a result, particular enzymes are released over a specific period of time. These enzyme levels can be measured through a series of blood tests. This was discussed in more detail in Chapter 12, "The Cardiovascular System."

TEST YOUR KNOWLEDGE 18-2

Choose the best answer:

1. Situations that can lead to higher-than-normal numbers of platelets include all *except:*
   a. high-altitude living
   b. Vitamin K deficiency
   c. exercise
   d. massive blood transfusions

2. Platelets can be found in all the following shapes *except:*
   a. oval
   b. disk-shaped
   c. rhomboid
   d. round

3. A severe imbalance of this blood chemistry value can lead to potential life-threatening cardiac arrhythmias:
   a. BUN
   b. electrolytes
   c. platelets
   d. PTT

4. An increased BUN can be caused by all the following *except:*
   a. fluid overload
   b. acute myocardial infarction
   c. shock
   d. protein catabolism

5. These values are often measured over time to determine if the patient had a heart attack (often a sign of tissue injury or death):
   a. erythrocytes
   b. enzymes
   c. leukocytes
   d. erythropoietin

URINE TESTING

Although it is 95% water, urine is a complex fluid containing thousands of dissolved substances. Keep in mind that urine is the end product of metabolism, with all its waste products, that is performed by *trillions* of cells in your body! As a result of this activity and the body's need to maintain proper fluid balance, you produce approximately 1 to 1 1/2 liters of urine daily.

The chief excretory systems of the body are the skin, lungs, and kidneys, with the kidneys being responsible for urine production. This is a very important job. Kidneys regulate the dilution or concentration of urine and regulate the excretion of sodium, among other substances.

Most of the substances found in urine are also found in your blood, but in different amounts. Some blood substances, such as glucose, will "spill" over into your urine once the substance reaches a certain concentration in the blood. This is why diabetics like Maria sometimes have glucose in their urine. If your kidneys couldn't function properly, death could occur in a matter of days. And yes, normal urine is sterile. You *can* (ugh) drink it. Urine testing can also be utilized to screen for infection, drug usage, or pregnancy.

In general, it is best to use urine that is freshly voided in the morning for testing purposes. This urine usually is more concentrated (sort of like adding extra packets of drink mix to a pitcher of water), so it should show more abnormalities. A *clean catch* method of urine specimen collection is the recommended procedure for routine urinalysis requests. The basic steps for this type of collection are as follows:

- Wash hands.
- Wash the urethal opening and surrounding area.
- Void a small amount of urine into the toilet.
- Void the remainder of the urine into a sterile container until it is properly filled without touching the inside of the container with any body part (this is why this method of collection is often called a *clean-catch midstream urine specimen, or CCMS*).
- Place and secure a lid on the container.

A *24-hour urine specimen* is used to determine the rate of glomular filtration of the kidneys, specific hormone levels, or any other metabolic abnormalities. This type of collection typically begins *after* the patient voids for the first time in the morning. From that point, *all* urine is collected for 24 hours, including the first voided urine of the next morning.

The following are some of the urine tests you might see.

Dipsticks

More than a name you call someone or a device to measure the amount of motor oil in your engine, a dipstick is an important tool in urinalysis. Performing a **dipstick test** doesn't require the skills of an accredited laboratory technologist and often can be "read" at home by the patient. A dipstick looks a lot like a strip of blotter paper and is impregnated with different types of reactive chemicals, depending on the type of test. Either the tip of the dipstick changes color, or the color just changes shades, depending on the concentration of the substance that is being measured. See FIGURE 18-5 ▲ for an example of a dipstick and how it is read.

Different dipsticks can quickly determine the presence of the following properties of urine:

> Bilirubin
> Glucose
> Hemoglobin
> Ketones
> Leukocyte esterase
> Nitrite
> pH protein

dipstick test A general term for a test that involves the application of urine to a chemical impregnated paper for the purpose of analysis. The results are usually read as color changes to the paper.

FIGURE 18-5 ▲ Once a fresh urine sample is passed over and absorbed by the dipstick, color changes will occur. By matching the dipstick colors to the reference chart, various substances found in the sample can be determined. (Source: Andy Crawford © Dorling Kindersley.)

Specific Urine Tests

A urine sample can yield a variety of valuable diagnostic information.

Specific Gravity (SG) A specific gravity (SG) test looks at the kidneys' ability to concentrate urine. The weight of a given amount of urine is compared to a weight of distilled water (which has a weight of 1.000). As we said before, urine is composed of water *plus* minerals, salts, and a variety of other compounds that would make it heavier than 1.000.

Normal Specific Gravity Values
1.003–1.035 (usually 1.010–1.025)
1.025–1.030+ (if urine is concentrated)
1.001–1.010 (if urine is diluted)

Specific gravity of urine depends on how well or poorly the patient is hydrated, the volume of urine being excreted, or the amount of solids mixed in the urine. The results can be a reflection of how well the kidneys are functioning.

Concentration If there is suspicion of renal disease, a concentration analysis is often performed because it measures the kidneys' ability to concentrate urine when liquid is withheld from the patient for several hours. Healthy kidneys can produce urine that has a greater than 1.020 concentration in this situation. Any concentration less than this indicates renal failure. However, a normal finding does not always indicate healthy kidneys.

Normal Concentration 1.020–1.025 (Depending on the test performed)

Patients who take diuretics before their urine concentration is measured can create a false reading that wouldn't provide a true picture of the kidneys' function. There are also numerous other factors that can interfere with these test results, including:

Acute renal disease
Bone disease
Chronic liver disease
Hypercalcemia
Hyperparathyroidism
Potassium deficiency
Low salt or protein diets

Urine Color Normally, a color range from straw to amber is acceptable and is usually due to the pigments in food that is consumed or from the metabolism of bile. Abnormal pigments (often a result of disease) can change the color of urine. Although clinically there are many colors and shades of color in urine, some of the major ones can be found in TABLE 18-5 ■.

Urine Odor Odor from fresh, normal urine is a result of volatile acids and isn't offensive. Certain foods, such as asparagus, create a distinctive odor. An ammonia scent usually comes from stale urine that has bacterial activity and the decomposition of urea. Infected urine has a very disagreeable odor, depending on how intense the infection is. A sweet smell is usually indicative of diabetic ketosis; however, an amino acid metabolic disorder in some infants produces a smell much like maple syrup.

Urine pH The acidity of your urine is mainly controlled by your kidneys in their attempt to maintain a homeostatic pH in your body.

> Normal pH range 4.6–8 (Average: 6, which is slightly acidic)

An individual with lung disease in which CO_2 is retained in the lungs and blood, a condition called **respiratory acidosis,** will have excessively acidic urine. Ray, our quadriplegic, may have problems with respiratory acidosis due to the paralysis of his diaphragm. Carbon dioxide acts as an acid, so acid has to be excreted through the urine to maintain homeostasis in the body. Other potential causes of excessive acidic urine can include:

respiratory acidosis *(ress PIRE eh toh ree)* Condition where the respiratory system is retaining carbon dioxide and thus causing acidity in the arterial blood.

Dehydration
Diabetes (uncontrolled)
Diarrhea
High-protein diets
Sleep disorders that affect breathing
Starvation

TABLE 18-5 ■ URINE TESTING RESULTS

ABNORMAL TEST RESULT(S)	POSSIBLE CAUSATIVE CONDITIONS/SITUATIONS
Color	**Straw:** Normal with specific gravity less than 1.010 except in diabetics with a higher specific gravity due to high glucose levels
	Yellow: Normal with a specific gravity of 1.011–1.019 with an output of 1–1.5 liters
	Amber: Normal but indicates a higher specific gravity greater than 1.020 with an output of less than 1 liter
	Black: Alkaptonuria, hemoglobin, melanin, Lysol poisoning
	Brown: Addison's disease, blood/hemoglobin, bilirubin, drugs, rhubarb ingestion, drugs (phenolic class), possible melanotic tumor
	Clear/nearly clear: Alcohol ingestion, chronic interstitial nephritis, diabetes insipidus, diuretics, large fluid intake, nervousness/excitement, reduced perspiration, untreated diabetes mellitus
	Orange: Concentrated urine, decreased fluid intake, drugs (e.g., Pyridium®), excessive sweating, fever
	Red: Beets, blood/hemoglobin, drugs (e.g., certain laxatives, Dilantin®, Pyridium®), methemoglobin, and oxyhemoglobin
Concentration, decreased	Kidney failure, overhydration (IV overload)
Concentration, increased	Dehydration, excessive sweating ketone bodies (acetone), anorexia, diabetes, diarrhea, drugs (e.g., ether, insulin, isopropyl alcohol)
pH, acidic, more than normal	Dehydration, diabetes (uncontrolled), diarrhea, high-protein diets, pulmonary diseases with retained CO_2 (causes respiratory acidosis forming acidic urine), starvation
pH, alkaline	Chronic liver failure, pulmonary diseases with hyperventilation, pyloric obstruction, renal tubular acidosis, salicylate intoxication, urinary tract infection (UTI)
Protein (albumin), increased	Temporary increase: Bathing or swimming in cold water, high-protein diet, severe emotional stress, strenuous exercise
	Chronic increase: Abdominal tumors, acute infections, anemia (severe) ascites, cancer of the kidney, cardiac disease, convulsive disorders, fever, hyperthyroidism, intestinal obstruction, kidney stones, liver disease, poisoning (e.g., lead, mercury, opiates, turpentine), nephritis, polycystic kidney, trauma, tuberculosis of the kidney
Specific gravity, decreased	Overhydration
Specific gravity, increased	Dehydration
Sugar, increased	Diabetes, emotional stress, diet, low reabsorption rate of kidneys
Turbidity (increased)	Foods (e.g., fat/greasy), precipitates (rapidly cooled specimens), vaginal contamination

hyperventilation *(HIGH per ven tih LAY shun)* The process of excessive ventilation in which carbon dioxide levels are lowered below normal.

Urine that is alkaline in nature (pH greater than 7) can be caused by pulmonary diseases that cause **hyperventilation,** a condition in which too much CO_2 is lost, leaving too little acid in the body. As a result, the body holds on to as much acid as possible, trying to bring itself back to homeostasis. Other potential causes of alkaline urine include:

Chronic renal failure
Renal tubular acidosis
Salicylate (aspirin) intoxication
Urinary tract infections (UTI)

Turbidity

If urine appears cloudy it could be an indicator of the presence of bacteria, pus, or red (sometimes white) blood cells. However, normal urine can be cloudy due to rapid cooling, which allows for the formation of precipitates, ingestion of some foods (especially greasy/fatty foods), or vaginal contamination from samples taken from women (a rather common occurrence). See **FIGURE 18-6** ▲ for examples of colors of urine and examples of turbidity.

Normal Turbidity: clear to slightly hazy

Sugar (Glucose)

This glucose test can be used to detect diabetes, confirm the diagnosis of diabetes, or determine the effectiveness of the treatment for diabetes. Note that sugar in urine, known as glucosuria or glycosuria, is not always abnormal. Situations of emotional stress, diet, or a low reabsorption rate by the kidneys with normal blood levels of glucose may cause high readings. You will find that in most cases, sugar in the urine of your patient is a result of diabetes mellitus.

Normal Urine Glucose: < 0.5 mg/dL

Protein (Albumin)

Healthy patients pass, at most, only trace amounts of protein in their urine. If there is *continual* excretion of protein (which is a rather large molecule) in the urine, that is often indicative of renal disease. Maria's kidney disease may have been detected by the presence of protein in her urine. It's kind of like trying to throw a rock through a screen door; the only way it will get through is if the screen becomes damaged (Assuming you just don't open the door and throw it in!).

Normal Urine Protein Amount: 50–80 mg/24 hrs.

A   **B**

FIGURE 18-6 ▲ **A.** Examples of colors of urine. **B.** Examples of urine turbidity.

Some situations that can lead to a temporary proteinuria can include:

Bathing or swimming in cold water
Eating large amounts of protein
Severe emotional stress
Violent/intense exercise

Renal diseases that can lead to chronic proteinuria include:

Kidney stones
Nephritis/nephrosis
Polycystic kidney
Tuberculosis or cancer of the kidney
Kidney failure
Diabetic Nephropathy

Ketone Bodies (Acetone)

This is an important test, especially with the continued popularity of high fat and protein/low carbohydrate diets. Ketones are released as a result of the metabolism of fat and fatty acids. Normally, ketones are produced by the liver and are completely metabolized so only minute amounts would be in urine.

Normal Urine Ketone Bodies: Negative

ketonuria *(kee toh NOOR ee uh)*
A condition of excessive acetone bodies in the urine.

If the body runs out of carbohydrates to burn, it switches to fats. **Ketonuria** is usually associated with diabetes, but consider the effects of diet on your patients as well as the following:

Anorexia
Diarrhea
Drugs (i.e., insulin)
Fasting
Fever
Postanesthesia
Prolonged vomiting
Starvation
Very low carbohydrate/high fat/high protein diets

Bacteria

Even small numbers of bacteria may indicate a urinary tract infection (UTI), which when untreated may lead to serious kidney disease. Patients with abnormal bladder function or who need a urinary catheter to empty their bladder, like Ray the quadriplegic patient, are at high risk for developing UTIs.

Normal Urine Bacteria: Negative

Sediment Examination

Usually, healthy urine contains a small number of cells and other formed elements. By examining the sediment of urine, a diagnosis or prognosis can be made without the need for a biopsy/surgery, in some cases. See Table 18-5 for a summary of urine testing results.

FECAL TESTING

The examination of feces (also known as *stool*) aids in the detection of bleeding or obstruction of the gastrointestinal system, parasites, ulcerative colitis, gallstones, and a variety of other gastrointestinal disorders. A stool examination looks at consistency, color, odor, pH, shape, size, and the presence or absence of the following: blood, bacteria, food residue, mucus, parasites (and their eggs), pus, and tissue particles.

Let's look at some aspects of a fecal examination.

Amount, Consistency, Form, and Shape

Stool consistency is dependent on diet but normally is malleable and soft with a definite shape—usually the same diameter as the colonic lumen. Depending on diet, there may be indigestible seeds and vegetable/fruit skin fragments present. A pasty stool is often associated with high fat content. Patients with cystic fibrosis have a greasy, tarlike/buttery texture stool. A bulky, frothy stool is often related to celiac disease and a condition called sprue. Diarrhea is watery due to its rapid passage through the intestine before water can be reabsorbed.

Shape can be changed to a narrow, ribbonlike structure possibly due to spastic bowel, decreased elasticity, rectal narrowing or stricture, or a partial obstruction. Small, ball-like stools are often a result of chronic moderate constipation, whereas excessively hard stools are often a result of excessive fluid absorption due to slow movement through the colon.

Normal Amount of Stool Produced : 100–200 g/day

Stool pH

Normal pH is neutral or slightly alkaline and is dependent on diet and bacterial fermentation. Carbohydrates tend to cause an acidic pH, whereas proteins tend to cause an alkaline pH.

Stool Color

Normal stool color is brown. After eliminating dietary or food dye as a cause for abnormal color, changes in color may be indicative of a disease process or drug intake. Color changes with some of their possible causative factors are as follows:

Yellow/yellow-green: Severe diarrhea, breast-fed infant, bowel sterilization due to antibiotics

Green: Severe diarrhea, antibiotic therapy, ingestion of chlorophyll-rich vegetables

Tan/clay-colored: Common bile duct blockage, pancreatic insufficiency, excessive fat intake

Black: Usually due to upper GI bleeding, high meat diet, ingestion of iron, charcoal, or bismuth

Red: Bleeding from the lower GI tract. If streaking is on the outer surface, consider hemorrhoids or anal pathology; if blood is throughout the stool, consider a problem higher up the GI tract

Blood in Stool

occult Not readily seen, as in blood in the stool.

A healthy individual passes 2.0 to 2.5 mL of blood daily into the gastrointestinal, or GI, tract. If an individual passes more than 2.8 mL of blood into their GI tract over a given 24-hour period, that is indicative of some form of GI pathology. The most common causes for this are hemorrhoids and anal fissures. If there is **occult** blood (blood that is hidden) in the feces, that may be a result of bleeding somewhere in the upper GI region. A gastric ulcer would cause this, for example. Testing for blood in the feces is also one of the ways to detect colon cancer. A false reading of this test can be a result of the ingestion of red meat, large doses of vitamin C, or inorganic iron. Some drugs, such as aspirin or steroids, can cause greater-than-normal blood loss to the GI tract.

Conditions that can lead to blood in the stool include:

Cancer (e.g., colon, gastric)
Colitis (ulcerative)
Diverticulitis
Gastric ulcers
Gastritis

Mucus in Stool

Normally there is no mucus in the stool. Mucus is secreted as a result of parasympathetic stimulation. Mucus that is translucent and gelatinous can be a result of:

Emotional excitation
Excessive straining during bowel movements
Mucus colitis
Spastic constipation

Mucus with blood may indicate:

Inflammation of the rectal canal
Neoplasm (in some cases, up to 3–4 liters of
mucus/24 hrs.)

Mucus with a blood/pus mixture may indicate:

Cancer of the colon (ulcerative)
Colonitis (ulcerative)
Diverticulitis (acute, in rare cases)
Dysentery (bacterial)
Tuberculosis (intestinal, in rare cases)

TEST YOUR KNOWLEDGE 18-3

Choose the best answer:

1. Urine turbidity can be a result of all of these *except:*
   a. rapid cooling
   b. bacteria
   c. bacon ingestion
   d. overhydration

2. This measuring device is impregnated with reactive chemicals that cause either a color change or a change in color shade when exposed to a substance.
   a. dipstick
   b. needle gauge
   c. test tube
   d. blotter paper

3. Which of the following is *not* a normal color of urine:
   a. straw
   b. yellow
   c. amber
   d. orange

4. Starvation will change urine's pH to be more:
   a. acidic
   b. alkaline
   c. neutral
   d. no change

5. Tan or clay-colored feces can be indicative of:
   a. severe diarrhea
   b. upper GI bleed
   c. excessive fat intake
   d. hemorrhoids

CEREBRAL SPINAL FLUID (CSF) TESTING

This fluid is found in the ventricles of the brain and the central canal of the spinal cord. Cerebral spinal fluid serves many purposes that include acting as a shock absorber, helping to regulate intracranial pressure that can affect the transporting of nutrients and waste produces in the brain, and influencing brain functions, such as regulating glucose levels, leading to hunger sensations and eating behaviors. CSF is generally collected for testing via a lumbar puncture (for details see Chapter 9). CSF can be tested for the different types and amounts of cells found in the sample, pathogens, substances such as protein, sugar, and chloride along with their concentration, as well as its general appearance and consistency.

Normal CSF Values

Normal Daily Production: 500 mL

Normal Circulation Around Brain and Spinal Cord: 150–200 mL

CSF Color

Normally, CSF fluid is clear and colorless, like water. Appearance changes can be due to:

Hemorrhage/inflammatory disease (e.g., meningitis)
Microorganisms (e.g., bacteria, yeast)
Trauma (like Ray's injury)
Tumors

CSF Cell Counts

Normal CSF does not contain white blood cells. If there are white blood cells present, the percentage of each WBC type is counted and compared to the total number of WBCs found.

> Normal CSF Cell Counts: 0–5/μL

Usually, increased numbers of white blood cells are a result of an inflammatory disease, hemorrhage, neoplasms, or trauma. If WBCs reach above 500 (mostly neutrophils), then expect a purulent (pus) infection.

High numbers of neutrophils in CSF can be associated with:

Cerebral abscess
Emboli (bacterial endocarditis)
Meningitis (bacterial, early viral, aseptic, mycotic)
Syphilis
Tuberculosis (early)

If there are high numbers of mononuclear cells, it could be indicative of:

Guillain-Barré syndrome
Multiple sclerosis
Syphilis of the central nervous system
Tuberculosis meningitis
Tumor/abscess
Viral infection (e.g., poliomyelitis)

CULTURE AND SENSITIVITY (C&S) TESTING

We fight bacterial infections through the use of antibiotics. Fungi are dealt with through the use of antifungal agents. Remember, not all pathogens are the same, and not all antibiotics or antifungal agents are the same. Some antibiotics are labeled as "broad-spectrum" drugs, which means that they do a pretty good job of killing off a wide variety of bacteria. Due to the ever-increasing problem of drug-resistant bacteria, the ideal objective is to first determine the specific organism by growing it (culturing) and then find the best drug (or several acceptable ones) for a specific pathogen—one that will kill it most effectively with as little toxic effect to the patient as possible.

culture and sensitivity (C&S) test The growth of bacteria and exposing it to a variety of antibiotics to see which drug is most effective.

To perform a **culture and sensitivity (C&S) test,** a patient sample is first taken from the suspected infected area. Areas of interest can include the lungs, wounds, throat, eyes, ears, blood, urine, stool, and so forth. The sample is then placed in a nutrient growth medium and allowed to grow over a period of time so colonies of that organism can increase. Certain types of organisms can grow certain shaped or colored colonies. Some of these organisms are subjected to a staining agent applied by a laboratory technologist. Some types of organisms will accept the stain, whereas others are resistant to staining. Then a microscopic examination is made to further determine the type of organism. These are some of the ways to help determine the identity of the organism.

To determine a pathogen's sensitivity to a variety of antibiotics, that organism is placed on a growth medium and allowed to colonize. What makes this different from just culturing is that small discs of several types of antibiotic (or antifungal) drugs are placed throughout the culture medium (see **FIGURE 18-7** ▲). The "weakest" drug for

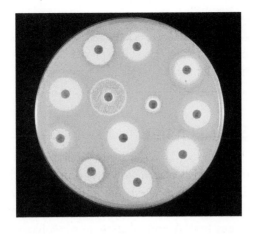

FIGURE 18-7 ▲ Note the different sizes of the ring around each disc that was placed in the bacterial growth medium. The larger the ring of nongrowth, the more effective that drug is against that specific pathogen. (Source: Birn/Custom Medical Stock Photo, Inc.)

that pathogen can be identified by observing how close the organism colonizes near it. In some cases, the colony grows right over a disc, indicating no effect against that pathogen. The most powerful drug disc(s) in that nutrient medium won't allow any colonization to occur near them at all. Those are the ones you consider when determining which drugs are best for getting rid of an infection.

Here are some things to consider. Normal flora may grow in these colonies. Make sure the specimen that is comprised of normal flora came from where that organism is normally found. For example, the organism *E. coli* is part of the normal flora in your intestinal tract. But if it is found in a blood sample, that is indicative of a potentially fatal situation. Also, verify whether the patient may be on some form of antibiotic treatment before a C&S test is performed. That may alter findings.

CARDIAC DIAGNOSTICS

Due to the importance of the heart, several tests can be done to determine its level of function. Malfunctioning of the heart can affect all the body systems.

Electrocardiogram (ECG/EKG)

In Chapter 12 you learned that the heart is a muscle, so it needs electrical impulses for it to correctly contract allowing blood to be efficiently pumped. We can monitor how these electrical impulses travel through the heart with the use of an **electrocardiogram (ECG/EKG)**. Electrical wires, known as *leads,* are attached at specific locations on a patient's torso and extremities to detect any electrical activity occurring in the heart. That electrical activity is converted to either an image seen on the screen of an ECG monitor or as a tracing on a strip of paper.

electrocardiogram (ECG / EKG) The graphic record created by electrocardiography.

Holter Monitor

Sometimes heart irregularities don't occur all day long, or occur only during certain activities. A simple ECG taken in a doctor's office or in the clinical setting may miss that abnormal cardiac event. A **Holter monitor,** which attaches to a belt or shoulder strap and utilizes ECG leads, is used to record all cardiac activity, usually during a 24-hour period (although it may even be a longer time). The patient also keeps a written diary that includes a list of activities plus the time the activities were done. Clinicians then compare the activities to the tracings provided by the Holter monitor to determine any cardiac pathology.

Holter monitor A portable device used to record cardiac activity usually during a 24-hour period that may show cardiac arrhythmias that would not be revealed during a regular ECG or stress test.

Stress Testing

stress test A diagnostic test that either uses physical activity or a drug to cause the heart to work harder to reveal any possible coronary artery blockage. Commonly called an exercise tolerance test.

Patients may develop heart disease that is not recognizable in its early stages. If the individual is placed in a situation where there is physical exertion, symptoms of the disease (such as chest discomfort/pain, shortness of breath, or lightheadedness) may exhibit themselves. This situation can be created in a controlled environment during a **stress test**. A normal stress test involves walking on a treadmill at varying speeds and inclines over a given period of time. The patient is monitored by an ECG to determine any arrhythmias, and blood pressures are taken throughout the test. Radioactive dyes may also be injected into the bloodstream and followed via a monitor to determine if there is sufficient blood perfusing the heart muscle. Decreased blood flow through cardiac muscle may indicate clogged cardiac arteries that may need to be opened (balloon angioplasty) or replaced (coronary artery grafting or bypass). In cases when the patient is unable to walk, a drug is injected intravenously to cause the heart to beat rapidly, mimicking exercise.

"SCOPES"

endoscope A lit tubular device that is inserted into a region of the body for therapeutic and diagnostic purposes.

endoscopy The inspection of various body organs, structures, and cavities by the use of an endoscope.

otoscope A device used to examine the external ear canal and eardrum.

bronchoscope *(BRONG koh skohp)* An endoscope utilized to visually examine the airways of the body.

Technological advances such as fiber optics not only revolutionized communication systems, but also led to great advances in medicine such as the development of flexible fiber optic scopes that can see inside the various body openings for both diagnosis and therapeutic treatment.

"Scope" is a general clinical term incorrectly used to describe a procedure in which a lit, tubular device, usually with a magnifying lens, is inserted into a region of the body to obtain a better view. **Endoscope** is the correct general term for the device used, and to be correct, "scope" is replaced with "scopy" when referring to the actual procedure. (*Endo* means "within;" *scope* means "to examine.") So an endoscope is used to perform an **endoscopy**. There are a variety of specialized scopes in the health field. Here is a sampling of some of them.

A common one that most of us have had utilized on us, especially as children, is the **otoscope**. An otoscope is often used to examine the external ear canal (auditory canal) and the eardrum (tympanic membrane) when there is a suspicion of an inner ear infection or a ruptured eardrum. If done properly, it is a painless procedure.

A flexible **bronchoscope** is comprised of a magnifying lens (often called a "head") and a tube approximately the thickness of a pencil. There are several channels within this tube. These channels provide for a light source, the instillation of fluids such as saline or drugs, suctioning of airway secretions/fluids, and little forceps that can take a small tissue sample. This is a somewhat uncomfortable procedure, so the patient is usually mildly sedated, and numbing agents are administered.

The **gastroscope** is used to examine the interior of the stomach. Because this is somewhat uncomfortable, the patient is mildly sedated.

A **laparoscope** is used to examine the abdominal region and has revolutionized surgery. Laparoscopic surgery allows for much smaller incisions and quicker patient recovery time. Because this is a surgical procedure, a higher level of sedation and anesthesia is used.

If you look at **FIGURE 18-8** ▲ you will see a **cystoscope**. This scope is used for viewing the internal anatomy of the bladder.

Colonoscopy is the term for visual examination of the colon. Often used to look for sources of bleeding, growths, or cancerous tumors, this procedure requires a level of sedation that is less than laparoscopic surgery.

gastroscope *(GAS troh skohp)* A lit tubular device used to examine the interior of the stomach.

laparoscope *(LAP eh roh skohp)* A lit tubular device used to internally examine the abdominal region.

cystoscope *(SIS toh skohp)* A lit tubular device used to view the internal anatomy of the bladder.

colonoscopy The visualization of the lower gastrointestinal tract through the use of an endoscope.

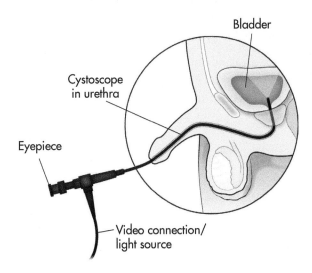

FIGURE 18-8 ▲ A cystoscope is utilized to view the internal anatomy of a bladder. Note that it is a flexible tube with a light providing illumination.

PULMONARY FUNCTION TESTING (PFT)

A basic **pulmonary function test (PFT)** looks at the flow and volume of air going both into and out of your lungs to determine if there is a pathologic occurrence. Lower-than-normal inhaled volumes may be indicative of a restrictive problem. Lower-than-normal flows may indicate an obstructive disease.

Basic PFTs are regularly used to determine the degree of lung involvement in several diseases such as asthma, emphysema, chronic bronchitis, and cystic fibrosis as well as determining the severity of neuromuscular diseases.

More complex PFTs involve the inhalation of gases to see how effective lungs are at transferring gases to the blood system.

Often the success and accurate results of PFTs are dependent on the effort made by the patient to breathe as instructed. That is why good explanations and coaching are important when conducting the test.

pulmonary function test (PFT) A diagnostic exam of the lungs that measures flow and volumes and compares to predicted values.

POLYSOMNOGRAPHY

polysomnography *(PAUL ee sahm NOG grah fee)* The study of sleep patterns and pathology.

Polysomnography, or sleep studies, is an area of rapid growth in the clinical setting. Sleep disorders can be a result of certain patient conditions such as stress or depression. They can also be a causative agent in a variety of conditions such as heart disease, memory difficulties, and personality changes and can be a major factor in automobile and industrial accidents.

A basic polysomnographic study looks at several things while a person is asleep:

- The flow of air into and out of the nose/mouth
- Eye movement to determine the stage of sleep
- Movements of muscles needed to breathe
- Monitoring of brain waves to determine the stage of sleep
- ECG to monitor heart rate and any irregularities
- Monitoring of oxygen levels in the blood

By monitoring these areas, it can be determined if there is a structural problem in the airway that blocks the flow of air as a person sleeps or if there is a problem with the brain telling the body to breathe during periods of sleep.

TEST YOUR KNOWLEDGE 18-4

Choose the best answer:

1. White blood cell counts are important when determining:
   a. infection
   b. age
   c. coronary artery blockage
   d. race

2. This test is used to determine a specific pathogenic organism and the drug(s) most effective in combating it:
   a. PTT
   b. BUN
   c. C&S
   d. PT

3. A testing device used to record heart activities during a 24-hour period is a(n):
   a. EMG
   b. Holter monitor
   c. Hanasen monitor
   d. GMC

4. This device has revolutionized abdominal surgery in that a large incision isn't needed, and as a result, recovery time is shortened:
   a. bronchoscope
   b. endoscope
   c. otoscope
   d. laparoscope

5. This patient effort dependent test measures flows and volumes of air breathed into and out of the lungs to determine the degrees of obstruction and/or restriction:
   a. LSMFT
   b. PFT
   c. STD
   d. C&S

SUMMARY

Snapshots from the Journey

■ Diagnostic tests help to provide a better picture of your patient's overall condition.

■ These tests help to determine the diagnosis, prognosis, and improvement of a disease condition as well as aid in determining the effectiveness of a treatment.

■ Usually, it is best to not base a diagnosis solely on one abnormal diagnostic test.

■ Even healthy individuals can occasionally produce an abnormal test result.

■ Blood is composed of a liquid portion called plasma, a variety of specialized cells such as leukocytes, erythrocytes, and platelets, and a variety of other substances, all of which can be analyzed to determine your patient's condition.

■ Excessive or lower-than-normal levels of the various blood cell types can be indicative of disease.

■ A complete blood count (CBC) is a common diagnostic test.

■ White blood cell analysis can provide evidence of infection.

■ Urine is 95% water but also contains thousands of dissolved substances that can be analyzed.

■ The best urine samples are obtained in the morning on awakening due to its high concentration.

■ Fecal examination is important in the determination of gastrointestinal bleeding.

■ Cerebral spinal fluid (CSF) regulates intracranial pressure, transports nutrients and waste in the brain, influences brain function, and acts as a shock absorber.

■ Culture and sensitivity (C&S) testing identifies the specific organism and the drug (or drugs) that is most effective against it.

■ Diagnostic tools that are valuable for cardiac assessment include electrocardiogram (EKG/ECG), Holter monitor, and stress testing.

■ A variety of scoping devices play important roles in diagnostics and surgical procedures such as the otoscope, endoscope, bronchoscope, and laparoscope.

■ Pulmonary function testing (PFT) is utilized as an aid in determining lung function and disease.

■ Polysomnography testing monitors several parameters during sleep to determine if a sleep disorder is present.

RAY AND MARIA'S STORY

Given that our common cases in this textbook deal with a diabetic and a quadriplegic patient, select two diagnostic tests that could assess and monitor their conditions. Also list and discuss associated problems along with a justification for each test and what results you might expect.

Maria, diabetic patient

Diagnostic test 1 _____

Justification _____

Expected results _____

Diagnostic test 2 _____

Justification _____

Expected results _____

Ray, quadriplegic patient

Diagnostic test 1 _____

Justification _____

Expected results _____

Diagnostic test 2 _____

Justification _____

Expected results _____

REVIEW QUESTIONS

Multiple Choice

1. Polysomnography is a diagnostic test used to determine:
   a. sleep disorders
   b. blood chemistry
   c. many bacteria
   d. cell counts

2. Mucus found in a fecal sample may be a result of:
   a. a normal finding
   b. emotional excitement
   c. gelatin ingestion
   d. runny nose

3. A value measured to determine the effectiveness of heparin therapy is:
   a. PTT
   b. MRI
   c. BUN
   d. DOG

4. A specific gravity test looks at the kidneys' ability to concentrate:
   a. RBCs
   b. enzymes
   c. urine
   d. bacteria

REVIEW QUESTIONS

5. This test is used to determine the extent of lung damage from diseases such as emphysema, chronic bronchitis, or cystic fibrosis:
   a. BUN
   b. EKG
   c. C&S
   d. PFT

6. High-protein diets or dehydration can cause urine to be more:
   a. acidic
   b. alkaline
   c. neutral
   d. thin

Fill in the Blank

1. _____ is the term used for a condition of excess RBCs in the blood.

2. A group of blood chemistry values used to determine if a patient had a heart attack is the _____ levels.

3. The body organ(s) chiefly responsible for the regulation of the excretion of sodium and the concentration of urine is(are) the _____.

4. A(n) _____ is a diagnostic tool used to quickly determine the level of glucose in a patient's urine.

5. A(n) _____ is utilized to place physical exertion on the heart and is often helpful in determining early stages of heart disease.

Short Answer

1. List the things that basic polysomnography looks at to determine if there is a possible sleep disorder.

_____

2. Explain why diagnostic tests are important when diagnosing a patient's condition.

_____

3. Explain why it is important not to treat a patient based solely on diagnostic test values.

_____

Suggested Activities

1. Contact your local hospital to arrange a tour of their clinical laboratory.

2. Do a Web search to discover the effects of the overuse of antibiotics in humans.

3. Do a Web search on the usage and possible effects of antibiotics administered to animals that we consume.

4. Scopes are a technology that can be used for both diagnosis and therapeutic treatment. Some have the capability to be flexible and go deep within the body, such as the flexible bronchoscope that can travel within the branching of the airways. Investigate different types of scopes and other therapeutic technologies used in medicine and write a report on their use for diagnostic and therapeutic treatment. Present your findings to a partner or to the class.

5. Working with a partner, research the embryological development of systems such as the nervous or circulatory systems. Create a presentation and present your findings to the class.

CAREER CONNECTIONS

Now that you have read this chapter, here is a list of related professions you may be interested in investigating for a future career:

- Physician Assistant

Research each profession and report on the following:

1. Profession description to include job responsibilities

2. Educational requirements

3. Job opportunities

4. Opportunities outside of the hospital setting

5. Salary range

6. Licensure and continuing education requirements

ANATOMY, PHYSIOLOGY, AND DISEASE IN ACTION

What possible disease conditions are suggested by the following laboratory results?

Case I

Laboratory Test	Significance
Hyperkalemia (See Appendix A)	
Increased BUN	
Increased CK-MB	
Normal ECG	

Diagnosis:

Case II

	Significance
Purple and red- topped tube	
Thrombocytopenia	
Hypokalemia	
Urine acidosis	
Ketonuria	

Diagnosis:

19

Anatomy and Physiology and the Scientific Method

When a patient presents with unusual signs and symptoms, their doctor may develop a prediction (initial diagnosis) of the underlying cause or condition. To diagnose the patient, the doctor and health care team must then perform tests to either confirm or reject the doctor's prediction. This procedure of formulating predictions and testing them is the basis of the scientific method. In this chapter, we will explore the scientific method and its use in diagnosing patients and conducting research.

Chapter Author: Luis A. Bonachea, PhD

LEARNING OUTCOMES

At the end of your journey through this chapter, you will be able to:

- Distinguish a scientific approach from other patterns of knowing and describe its limitations
- Explain how scientific hypotheses become incorporated into theories
- Collect, analyze, and interpret scientific data
- Compare the benefits and limitations of science

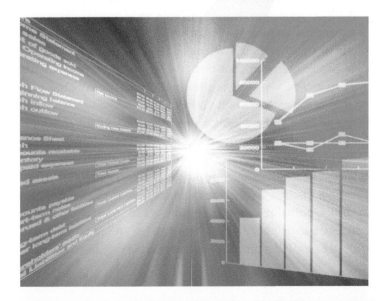

HISTORY OF SCIENCE AND AN OVERVIEW OF THE SCIENTIFIC METHOD

The history of science explores the development of both science and scientific knowledge. Research shows that science and scientists have made important contributions to civilization and the accumulation of general knowledge. Scientific developments date back thousands of years, but some of the most historic discoveries have occurred more recently. Following is a list that describes some important historic events and contributions since the late 18th century:

- The development of the Small Pox vaccine in the late 1790s by Edward Jenner in England.
- The development of Germ Theory in 1854 when John Snow linked an outbreak of cholera to a specific water pump in London.
- The refinement of anesthesia in the late 19th Century that enabled its use in surgery.
- The discovery of Penicillin by Alexander Fleming in 1928.
- The first isolation of Insulin by scientists at the University of Toronto in 1921.
- The development of in-vitro fertilization, first developed in the 1950s, that led to the birth of the first test tube baby in 1978.
- The discovery of the DNA molecule by Cambridge University scientists Francis Crick and James Watson in 1953.

Although the scientific method was formulated in Ancient Greece, Sir Francis Bacon (1561-1626) is considered the modern father of the Scientific method. Bacon advocated always having a specific plan for any scientific investigation.

Patterns of Knowing

patterns of knowing Methods of acquiring knowledge to make decisions, answer questions, or explain phenomena.

Imagine for a moment that a patient in your care has just been declared "brain dead" (usually this means they no longer have a response to pain and all cranial nerve reflexes are absent). Brain death is a legally defensible criterion for declaring a patient dead, but ultimately the patients' family needs to make the decision to remove the patient from life support or not. They may look to you for advice. How does anyone make a difficult decision like this? The knowledge we need to make decisions can be obtained in a number of ways.

empirical knowledge Factual knowledge gained by testing or measurement.

In some cases, we may look to factual knowledge that can be obtained by measurement, observation, and testing. This **empirical** or scientific approach might tell you that the patient has no measurable activity in the cerebrum and that patients in this condition do not recover. You may empathize with the patient, using **personal knowledge** or an understanding of your own feelings to understand that the patient's family may have a hard time letting go of their loved one and may need a few days to say goodbye. You may perceive that, in this current situation, the patient's family have really already made a decision and are just looking to you to reassure them it is the right one. In that moment, the **aesthetic** pattern of knowing might come into play. You may have deep religious or moral feelings that pulling someone off life support is wrong, relying on your personal **ethics** to help them make the decision you feel is right.

personal knowledge Knowledge gained by understanding ones own feelings or empathizing with those of others.

aesthetic knowledge Knowledge obtained from an understanding of the current circumstances or situation.

ethics Knowledge gained from your own religious or moral beliefs.

In 1978, Barbara Carper, then a professor in the College of Nursing at Texas Women's University, formalized these different ways of gaining knowledge to address a problem as the four patterns of knowing (TABLE 19-1 ■). All four patterns of knowledge have their own place in solving problems and answering questions in life.

TABLE 19-1 ■ CARPER'S PATTERNS OF KNOWING

NAME	DESCRIPTION
Empirical (Scientific)	Factual knowledge gained by testing or measurement
Personal Knowledge	Knowledge obtained by understanding your own feelings and empathizing with others
Aesthetics	Knowledge obtained from an understanding of the current circumstances or situation
Ethics	Knowledge gained from your own religious or moral beliefs

The empirical approach described by Carper is the center of the **scientific method**, an approach used by researchers, engineers, and health professionals to solve a variety of problems.

scientific method An approach to answering questions based on observations of natural or physical phenomena.

The Scientific Method

The scientific method is an approach to answering questions and explaining phenomena that relies on formulating hypotheses and using direct or indirect observations and experimentation to test those hypotheses. Scientific hypotheses, by definition, can only invoke observable or testable natural and physical explanations. By relying on empirical observations, the scientific method produces the most objective knowledge and information possible, less subjective and subject to individual belief or experience than the other three patterns of knowing.

The scientific method consists of five steps or parts:

- *Question* - Formulating and researching a question
- *Hypothesis* - Developing one or more testable hypotheses
- *Methods* - Choosing a methodology or designing an experiment to test the hypothesis
- *Results* - Collecting data and making observations
- *Conclusions* - Drawing inferences or conclusions about the validity of the hypothesis

The five steps of the scientific method are repeated in a cycle, rejecting false hypotheses and further refining those hypotheses that stand up to scrutiny.

FIGURE 19-1 ▲ Scientists use the scientific method to test hypotheses.

Formulating Questions

Formulating research questions can be the easiest or most difficult part of the scientific method. Good research is typically the result of a healthy sense of scientific curiosity. While reading scientific literature or making your own observations of the world, questions will come up.

A good research question will have a few key features. First, the question should be narrow enough that it can be tested readily within an appropriate amount of time and effort. Second, it should typically not be overly similar to questions asked by other researchers. Demonstrating that a result can be replicated is an important part of science, but repeating the same studies over and over again may be less useful than exploring new directions and avenues of research. Third, research is a human endeavor that will require a great deal of effort on your part. It may be challenging and frustrating at times. A good research question will be something that interests you enough to make the struggle worth it!

Hypotheses and Theories

hypothesis An educated guess used to explain a phenomenon or answer a question, based on natural or physical explanations.

In science, a **hypothesis** is an "educated guess" used to explain a phenomenon or answer a question. A good hypothesis must be directly testable, meaning that one could collect data to either support or reject it. A good hypothesis should also be developed by carefully studying previously published research and data.

For instance, if you learned that a newly discovered type of lung cancer caused symptoms consistent with Cushing's Syndrome (see Chapter 10), you could read through published journal articles and case studies to develop a hypothesis about why. In your research, you might find references that found other types of tumors can produce ACTH, the hormone released by the anterior pituitary that causes the adrenal cortex to produce cortisol. An appropriate hypothesis would be that this new lung cancer works using the same mechanism. This hypothesis meets our earlier criteria for good scientific hypotheses. This hypothesis can be readily rejected or supported by testing patients with the tumor and Cushing's-like symptoms for their ACTH (adrenocorticotropic hormone) levels. You observe high ACTH levels, supporting your initial hypothesis. If you had observed normal or low ACTH levels, you instead reject your hypothesis.

One important feature of hypotheses is that they can never be proven true, only supported or rejected. Even when a hypothesis is supported by one experiment or study, it may be rejected later on. This is because new experiments, tests, or methodologies might suggest a different answer in subsequent studies.

Imagine that another researcher isolates the lung cancer cells and grows them in a culture. Following up on your hypothesis, they might expect the isolated tumor to produce ACTH. To their surprise, no ACTH is produced. Instead, the tumor produced CRH (corticotropin releasing hormone). Your hypothesis is now soundly rejected, but why did your previous experiment support your hypothesis if it was wrong? Recall from Chapter 10 that the hypothalamus releases CRH to direct the release of ACTH from the anterior pituitary. IF the tumor produces CRH, it makes sense that the patients would have elevated ACTH levels as well. Hypotheses are tentative in this sense. Since a hypothesis can never be definitively proven true, they must be tested repeatedly by multiple, independent researchers for us to be confident in their validity. Even then, they may one day be disproven using new technologies or approaches.

Hypotheses that stand up to repeated testing and evaluation become incorporated into larger, more detailed explanations know as **scientific theories**. Like hypotheses, theories use observable, natural and physical processes to answer questions or explain phenomena. Also like hypotheses, a scientific theory must be capable of rejection. The main difference between theories and hypotheses is how well supported they are. Scientific theories are robust hypotheses that have been tested over and over and are very well supported. Theories may be modified over time in light of new data, but their core remains the same.

scientific theories Larger scientific explanations that have withstood rigorous testing by multiple, independent researchers.

TEST YOUR KNOWLEDGE 19-1

Choose the best answer:

1. If a patient does not want a blood transfusion due to their religious beliefs, they are making their decision using the _____ pattern of knowing.
   a. empirical
   b. personal knowledge
   c. aesthetic
   d. ethics

2. Which of the following terms would be a synonym for the word inference?
   a. hypothesis
   b. data
   c. question
   d. conclusion

3. Which of the following is a feature of a good scientific hypothesis?
   a. It is based on observable, natural or physical phenomena
   b. It can be supported or rejected using rigorous testing methods
   c. It is developed by carefully examining previously published research and data
   d. All of these.

Answer the following:

4. What distinguishes hypotheses from theories?

   _____

   _____

   _____

Testing Hypotheses

Scientific hypotheses can be tested either through **direct** or **indirect testing**. Direct methods involve making measurements and observations of the test subjects, experiment, or patient. Indirect methods are typically used when direct methods are not possible. This may be because the phenomenon you wish to study cannot be directly observed, or because it occurred sometime in the past. In these cases, hypotheses are typically tested by making predictions and measuring indirect evidence to either verify or disprove those predictions.

For example, imagine that an astronomer observes a dark area of space with their telescope and suspects a black hole might be present there. It would be difficult to directly observe the black hole because they do not emit visible light. However, that researcher might be able support their hypothesis about the presence of a black hole by making predictions about how the black hole would affect light from nearby stars. Similarly, a paleontologist might come up with a hypothesis that an asteroid striking the Earth caused climate change, leading to the extinction of the non-avian dinosaurs. This event cannot be directly observed because it already happened. Instead, the researcher would have to test several predictions. Somewhere on Earth, there should be a sufficiently large crater that dates to the time when these dinosaurs went extinct. There should be a layer of iridium dust in rock strata around the same time. Iridium is rare on Earth, but common in many objects in space. There should be evidence of rock deformations and cracking consistent with a period of rapid cooling around the same time. As with direct testing, finding evidence verifying these predictions would not prove your hypothesis correct, only add support for it.

Types of Investigations

Regardless of whether a direct or indirect testing method is necessary, researchers can conduct three basic types of investigations. These types of investigations differ in the goals of the researcher and the methodologies used to collect relevant data.

Regardless of what type of investigation is used, it is important to note that ethical practices must guide the investigation. Often a review board will determine the ethical validity of your research methods. In addition to ethics, all types of investigation must follow safety and environmental protection guidelines.

Descriptive investigations involve making observations to describe a natural phenomenon, species, or condition without necessarily testing a specific hypothesis. For example, a researcher interested in determining if prostate cancer is more prevalent in certain age or racial groups might start by looking through hospital records and calculating incidence rates.

Comparative investigations involve comparing different groups of people or other organisms to each other to test hypotheses. For example, to test the hypothesis that hematocrit levels in freshwater fish relate to dissolved oxygen content in the water around them, a researcher might visit different streams containing the same species of fish and compare hematocrit across those populations and the dissolved oxygen content in the water at the same locations.

Experimental investigations involve testing hypotheses by manipulating one or more experimental variables, called factors or **independent variables**. By measuring **dependent variables**, or responses, the researchers can determine cause and effect relationships.

---

direct testing Testing hypotheses by directly observing or measuring the subject or phenomenon.

indirect testing Testing hypotheses when direct observation or measurement is impossible by generating predictions as testing them instead.

descriptive investigations Use of observation to describe a system without testing a specific hypothesis.

comparative investigations Comparing different organisms or groups of the same organism to test for relationships between variables.

independent variables Values that allowed by researchers to vary among experimental groups. Independent variables are thought to cause changes in other variables.

dependent variables The measured response(s) in an experiment. Changes in the dependent variable are inferred to be caused by the independent variable.

In order to ensure that a result is caused by the intended independent variable, researchers must carefully identify other potential factors that could influence the outcome. These factors must be accounted for using carefully designed **control group**. A control group is that sample that is compared to the experimental group and should be as close to identical to the experimental group as possible. The only difference should be the independent variable. For example, if you wanted to test for an effect of 20 minutes of aerobic exercise on blood glucose level, your experimental group and control group should only differ in that one group did exercise and the other did not. Other factors like the biographical features of the participants (sex, age, or race), their diet, their physical condition, and how strenuously they exercise should all be as similar as possible. Otherwise, any of these factors could cause undesirable effects on the study.

control group In an experiment, the control should be identical to the treatment group in every way except in the independent variables of the study.

Selecting Equipment and Technology

As with any other task or project, selecting the right tool for the job is important for conducting quality research. When choosing equipment or technologies, consider the following factors:

- Does this tool produce data relevant to your question?
- Is using this tool possible within budget or facility constraints?
- Do you know how to use this tool or is there training help available?
- Are there safer or more ethical alternatives?

A good way to determine what equipment or technologies to use is to look at previous studies. Using background research to develop your hypotheses, take note of the methods other researchers have used to answer similar questions.

Safety and Disposal

When designing and implementing experiments, laboratory safety is paramount. Research activities can expose participants and researchers to a variety of different hazardous conditions. **Physical hazards** include sources of mechanical or physical injury, such as sharp instruments or tools, machinery with moving parts, very hot or very cold surfaces, and sources of electric shock. **Chemical hazards** are risks that come from contact with chemicals. Chemical agents in the lab may be toxic if ingested, irritate sensitive mucous membranes if inhaled, or cause corrosive burns if they get on the skin or eyes. **Biohazards** are risks related to infectious pathogens that may be used directly in research or may be present in body fluids and tissues.

physical hazards Sources of mechanical or physical injury.

chemical hazards Risks of injury from exposure to chemicals including irritants, toxins, or corrosives.

biohazards Risks of injury from contact with infectious agents, body fluids, or tissues.

While completely eliminating the possibility of injury is nearly impossible, taking a few steps can dramatically reduce the risk to researchers, patients, or subjects.

- Follow instructions and protocols carefully. Using devices, tools, or reagents in a manner different from their intended uses can increase risk of injury.
- Be mindful of potential hazards and establish a set of safety procedures to be enacted in the event of an accident.
- Wear appropriate personal protective equipment (PPE) such as lab coats or gowns, gloves, goggles, and respirators or face masks.
- Dispose of wastes in appropriate containers. Biohazardous waste and sharps like dissecting tool, pipettes, or broken glassware should not be thrown away in the trash. Doing so subjects janitorial or housekeeping staff to unnecessary risk. Similarly, chemical waste should not be poured down the sink. Water treatment procedures may not remove

these chemical from the water, causing them to stay in the water supply or enter the environment.

• Whenver possible, utilize recycling procedures for conservation of resoruces and environmental protection.

Even after the study is completed, waste from the study can continue to present risks to researchers and staff. As a result, studies should be designed to generate as little waste as possible. Waste minimizing practices not only reduce the likelihood of exposing people to hazardous materials, but can also significantly reduce costs. Waste disposal can be a significant portion of a research institution or hospital's annual costs. Chemical reagents and animals used in research can be very expensive as well, so minimizing their use can lead to significant cost savings.

FIGURE 19-2 ▲ Biohazardous waste.

FIGURE 19-3 ▲ Personal Protective Equipment: gloves, goggles, and a respirator.

TOXIC

HARMFUL

CORROSIVE

IRRITANT

OXIDISING

EXTREMELY
FLAMMABLE

FIGURE 19-4 ▲ Hazardous chemicals should be labeled with appropriate warnings.

Clinical Application

Just as in scientific research, medical procedures and therapies can generate waste that is potentially hazardous and could transmit infectious agents to health care professionals and other patients. Body fluids, tissue, and soiled materials must typically be disposed of in designated Biohazard waste containers. A 2010 survey of 114 hospitals by Practice Greenhealth found that an average of 34 pounds of waste was generated per patient daily. Of this, 15% is estimated to be biohazardous waste. Some surgical supplies, like stainless steel tools and instruments are reused to cut down on waste by autoclaving them.

Making Measurements

Once a type of investigation has been chosen and the methods of the study laid out, the next step is to collect data, or the measurements that will be used to either support or reject the hypothesis. Data can either be **quantitative** or **qualitative**. Qualitative measurements are descriptive observations that cannot be measured numerically. For example, a doctor might observe a patient and look for indications that the patient might be in pain. They might note that the patient is moving less than normal, is frowning or wincing, and looks pale. These are important observations, even if they cannot be directly quantified. Quantitative measurements are numerical measurements made using tools such as rulers, probes, or balances. Quantitative measurements, when taken correctly, are more objective and easier to compare between different subjects or researchers. Good quantitative measurements have two features: **accuracy** and **precision.**

quantitative Numerical measurements made using tools such as rulers, probes, or balances.

qualitative Descriptive observations that cannot be measured numerically.

accuracy The degree to which a measured value matches the correct value.

precision The degree to which a set of measurements of the same object or subject match each other.

FIGURE 19-5 ▲ To use glassware accurately, always measure from the lowest point or meniscus.

FIGURE 19-6 ▲ Graphing calculators are programmed with a number of functions to analyze and plot data.

Imagine that a doctor wants to measure a patient's blood pressure. They have two sphygmomanometers (blood pressure cuffs). They measure the patient's systolic blood pressure five times and get slightly different numbers. They then try the other sphygmomanometers and are surprised to find how different they are (TABLE 19-2 ■).

TABLE 19-2 ■ SYSTOLIC BLOOD PRESSURE OF THE SAME PATIENT USING TWO DIFFERENT SPHYGMOMANOMETERS.

SPHYGMOMANOMETER A	SPHYGMOMANOMETER B
125	149
120	149
122	155
125	160
121	153

The two sphygmomanometers give very different answers. The first gives several similar values in the 120s. The second gives much higher numbers and they are also more variable. Let's assume the patient's actual systolic pressure was 152. Sphygmomanometer B gave values much closer to the patient's actual value. For this reason, this sphygmomanometer would be considered more accurate. However, sphygmomanometer A's readings were much closer together. For this reason, it would be considered more precise. Good measurements are both accurate and precise.

Amazing **Body Facts**

Repeatedly measuring a patient's blood pressure can be uncomfortable or even painful. This can cause an elevation in blood pressure. While taking multiple readings can help improve accuracy, give the patient at least 1-3 minutes between readings from the same arm.

Even with the best tools, measurements of different individuals in a sample, let alone multiple measurements of the same individual, are rarely perfectly precise. Instead, they tend to be variable. As such, finding a way to describe a typical or average value within the sample is important. From a set of numbers, three values can be used to describe the average value: the **mode, median,** and **mean.**

The mode of a set of numbers is the number that is repeated the most. From Table 19-2, we can see that the mode of measurements made using sphygmomanometer A would be 125, as it is the only number repeated in the set. Similarly, the mode for sphygmomanometer B would be 149.

The median of a sample is the value that splits the data set into an upper and lower half. To find the median, rank all the values from smallest to largest. For sphygmomanometer A, we would rank the values as 120-121-122-125-125. The median would be 122 because that value separates the two largest values from the two smallest. Calculating a median is slightly trickier when the sample contains an even number of values. Imagine that the doctor only took four measurements: 120-121-122-125. In this case, 121 and 122 are in the middle. The median is calculating by adding the tow middle numbers and dividing by two. (121+122)/2 = 121.5. What is the median for the measurements taken using sphygmomanometer B?

The mean, or weighted average, of a sample is calculated by adding up all the values in a sample dividing by the total number of values in the sample. For sphygmomanometer A, we would add up the values 120+121+122+125+125 and divide the answer by 5 because there are 5 values. In this case, the mean would be 122.6. What is the mean for the measurements taken using sphygmomanometer B?

mode The value in a set of numbers that is repeated the most.

median The value that separates a set of numbers into upper and lower halves.

mean The weighted average of a set of number. Calculated by adding up all the values and dividing the sum by the number of values.

FIGURE 19-7 ▲ When arranged in order, the median is the value that separates the upper an lower half of a set of numbers.

TEST YOUR KNOWLEDGE 19-2

Choose the best answer:

1. Which of the following would be an example of a descriptive investigation?
   a. Collecting height measurements from your classmates to describe the average height of your class.
   b. Comparing the weight of house cats to feral cats to see if housecats get more to eat.
   c. Adding nitrogen to the soil of one group of plants while using a control group to eliminate other factors while testing for the effect of nitrogen.
   d. All of these.

2. When selecting a piece of equipment or technology for research, one should consider...
   a. the type of data that can be collected with it
   b. the budget for the study and the cost of the equipment
   c. the researcher's familiarity or training with the equipment
   d. all of these.

3. Coming into contact with blood potentially containing the HIV virus would be an example of a _____.
   a. physical hazard
   b. chemical hazard
   c. biohazard
   d. corrosive hazard

Answer the following:

4. Explain how you would measure height using qualitative and quantitative measurements.

   _____

   _____

   _____

5. Compute the mode, median, and mean of the following numbers:

   10   5   8   10   14

   _____

   _____

   _____

Presenting and Data

The old adage "a picture is worth a thousand words" is just as true in science. Depending on the type of data collected, a table or figure is chosen as a means of visually presenting data. While the diversity of types of graphs and tables is staggering, the three most common types are the **bar graph**, the **scatter plot**, and the **summary table**. Every figure and table should be accompanied by a descriptive **caption**. The caption should provide enough information that a reader could understand the basic idea of the study from the figure/table and caption alone.

bar graph A graph that displays means for one or more samples.

scatter plot A graph that displays a series of points comparing two continuous variables.

summary table A table that displays numerical data or compares two or more categorical variables.

caption A formal description that accompanies a figure or table and summarizes it for the reader.

FIGURE 19-8 ▲ Graphing data by hand with graph paper and straight edge.

Bar Graphs

This type of graph is typically chosen when you have an independent variable that is **categorical** (comes in discrete states or categories, i.e. placebo vs. drug, none-low-medium-high, etc.) and a dependent variable that is **continuous** (measured on a numerical scale). By convention, the independent variable is always plotted on the horizontal or **X-axis**. The dependent variable is then plotted on the vertical or **Y-axis** as the mean of your sample. A good bar graph usually has **error bars**. Error bars are used to communicate how much variation there is in a sample or how confident we should be in the measured mean. There are many types of error bars, but the most commonly used error bars report

categorical variable A variable that is measured in discrete states.

continuous variable A variable that is measured on a numerical scale.

X-axis The horizontal axis of a graph. By convention, the independent variable is plotted on the x-axis of a graph.

Y-axis The vertical axis of a graph. By convention, the dependent variable is plotted on the y-axis of a graph.

error bars Bars used to show uncertainty or variability in a sample around a measurement, often the mean.

standard deviation A measure of the variability within a set of numbers.

the **standard deviation**. The standard deviation of a sample is a good measure of precision. Big standard deviations are usually a bad thing. Calculating a standard deviation by hand is somewhat tedious, but most statistical or spreadsheet software can calculate it easily.

Regardless of what type of error bar you choose, always include the type of error bar in your figure caption. FIGURE 19-9 ▲ has an example of a good bar graph. Notice the detailed caption accompanying the figure.

FIGURE 19-9 ▲ Average heart rates (beats/min) of mice injected with a placebo, low dose, medium dose, or high dose of atropine. Error bars are +/- 1 standard deviation.

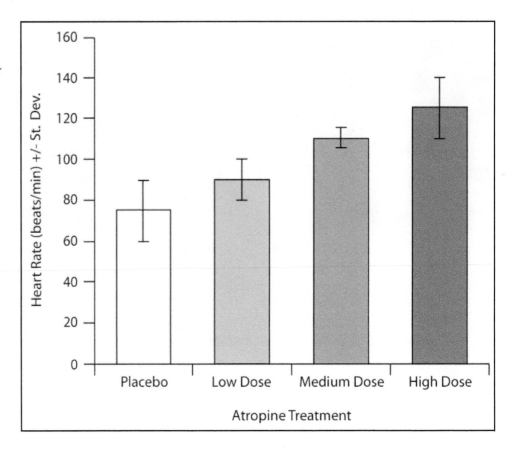

Scatter Plots

When plotting results consisting of two continuous variables, the graph of choice is a scatter plot. Using an X-Y axis grid, each data point is plotted according to its value of X (independent variable) and Y (dependent variable). Depending on the type of data you've collected, it may be appropriate to either connect the data points with lines or add a best fit line. If data points on your graph are related to each other, connecting them with straight lines is appropriate. In FIGURE 19-10 ▲, the researchers continually measured the heart rate of a koala as the ambient temperature was increased. Every data point in this data set is taken from the same koala, so it would be appropriate to connect them. If on the other hand, we had koalas in trees, measured the temperature where they were and measured their heart rates, each data point would come from a different subject. They would be independent. It would not appropriate to connect the dots in that case.

Quick note: Always connect data points with straight lines when making a graph by hand. Curved lines are used when a computer mathematically calculates the probable value of y for all the x-values between your data points. This is impossible to do by hand.

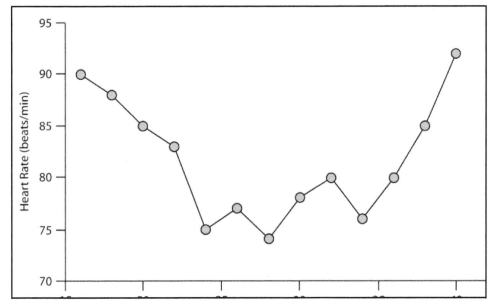

FIGURE 19-10 ▲ Heart rate (beats/min) of a koala as ambient temperature was increased from 16 to 40°C in 2 degree intervals.

For independent data points, it is not uncommon to include a **best-fit line** or curve. These lines are used to represent the likely mathematical relationship between your x and y variables. A technique called linear regression has been used to determine a simple linear relationship between height and weight in **FIGURE 19-11** ▲. Note: Calculating a best-fit line is also impossible* to do by hand.

best-fit line A model used to show a general trend in a data set graphed as a scatter plot.

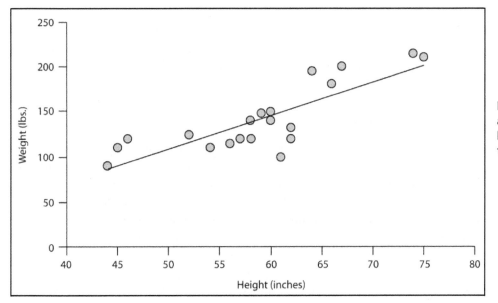

FIGURE 19-11 ▲ Height (inches) and weight (lbs) for 20 students in a biology class. Best-fit line determined through a simple linear regression.

Summary Tables

Tables are typically used to summarize large amounts of data. For our purposes, choose this type of figure when your dependent variable is categorical. For example, TABLE 19-3 ■ summarizes qualitative results of a titration experiment. Notice that, unlike figures, the caption for a table is placed before the table.

TABLE 19-3 ■ RESULTS OF A COLORIMETRIC TEST FOR BLOOD CALCIUM LEVELS.

VOLUME OF TITRATANT (ML) ADDED	COLOR OF SOLUTION
2.5	Purple
3	Purple
3.5	Purple
4	Red
4.5	Red
5	Red

Common Graphing Errors

The most common errors in graphing have to do with labeling. Make sure every table or figure has a caption accompanying it. Make sure all axes are labeled. If your figure includes multiple series, make sure a legend is included. Make sure to include units on axes labels.

Drawing Inferences

With data in hand, the next step in testing a hypothesis is analyzing the data to draw inferences, or conclusions. Conclusions about hypotheses are made by determining if the data are consistent with the hypothesis or not. If a chemical is hypothesized to lower blood pressure, than patients on the drug should have a lower mean blood pressure than patients in the control group. If both groups had similar blood pressures, we would have to reject this hypothesis.

For example, imagine that two competing drug companies have produced two similar drugs to reduce circulating cholesterol levels. In their marketing materials to doctors, they provide data on cholesterol levels of patients on the drug and control group subjects. FIGURE 19-12 ▲ shows their relative effects on cholesterol. Notice that the mean cholesterol levels for both groups are much lower than the control group. This data would support the hypothesis that both drugs lower cholesterol levels.

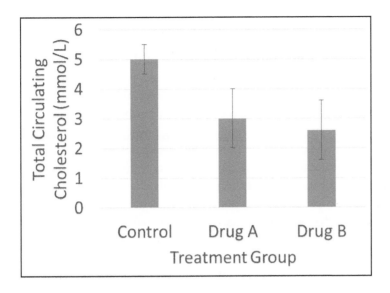

FIGURE 19-12 ▲ Circulating cholesterol levels of patients taking one of two competing drugs and a control group.

The company that produces Drug B boasts that it has a stronger effect on lowering cholesterol levels than Drug A. While Drug B seems to do a slightly better job, the error bars show us that both samples have a great deal of variation. This slightly lower mean is likely not significant. This data would most likely lead us to reject the drug company's claim.

Ultimately, comparing results requires more objective methods than simply looking at figures or comparing means qualitatively. In most cases, scientists use one of many **statistical tests** to objectively decide whether or not a hypothesis should be rejected. Ultimately, statistical tests work by estimating the probability that a result is a **false positive**, meaning that it appears to be true, but it is in fact not. Most often, a hypothesis will only be supported if there is a less than 5% chance that it is a false positive. While more strict values can be used, doing so dramatically increases the probability of a **false negative**, or saying there is no effect when in fact there is.

Even with statistical testing, making analyzing data more objective, researchers may disagree with how to interpret results. While peer-review greatly improves the validity of scientific research, not all reviewers may agree on the quality of methods used in a study. Different studies may produce conflicting results. For all these reasons, interpreting scientific results and information requires looking at all the evidence. In many cases, conflicting results may need to be resolved by conducting new studies and more research.

statistical tests Objective methods to decide whether or not to reject a hypothesis, typically by estimating the likelihood of a false positive.

false positive Supporting a hypothesis that is actually false.

false negative Rejecting a hypothesis that is actually true.

Evaluating and Using Models

One important way that data is used to make inferences is constructing **models**. Models are simple mathematical equations or figures that are constructed to describe trends in a data set. For example, a best fit line is a very simple model used to describe the relationship between two variables as a straight line. Models have two basic purposes: 1) to describe relationships between variables in a sample, and 2) to make predictions about data points that are not in a sample. Using models to explain biological data and make predictions has several important limitations.

First, models describe an average relationship. Within any sample, there is typically variation around the average. A model that predicts resting hear rate based on weight may on average be good, but it would be unlikely to predict every value perfectly.

models Mathematical equations or figures used to explain relationships in a data set or make predictions about values not included in the original sample.

Second, models are often based on a sample of data that may be small in comparison to the population the model describes, risking that the sample is not representative of the population. A model predicting colon cancer risk based on meat consumption may only include data on a few dozen patients, but the results would be interesting to millions or more. If all the patients included in the study were American men aged 45-75, how applicable would the model be to a teenage girl in southern India?

Last, models are typically only useful in making predictions within the range of values seen in the data set. Making predictions about data parts far out requires making some assumptions, most notably that the relationship stays the same. Climate scientists have created a number of models to try to predict how changes in ocean temperature will affect weather, food production, and animal populations, but these models are always treated cautiously. Because the average ocean temperature is rising to levels higher than climate scientists have ever observed, the models may not take into account processes that only occur at very high temperatures.

Consider the data on height and weight of students given in **FIGURE 19-11** ▲. The best-fit line not only summarizes the data for the students in the sample, it also allows us to make predictions for students that weren't include. Imagine that Jose was absent that day. Jose is a star member of the basketball team at a whopping 6'8", or 80 inches, tall. Assuming the relationship between height and weight was typical, we could extend the best fit line out to 80 inches and see where on the y-axis that line would be, about 215 pounds. In reality, Jose is only 200 pounds. Why did the model give the incorrect weight for him?

Models are, by design, simplified versions of reality. They are used to describe the average or expected value. Looking at the **FIGURE 19-11** ▲ again, notice that very few of the data points actually fall perfectly on the line. It is not surprising that Jose's actual weight is not perfectly predicted. If we used the model to predict the weight of several students, we would only expect the model to describe their average weight well. Jose, being an athlete, may also be in better condition than the class as a whole. A model based off of other athletes might have produced a better prediction. Also notice that Jose is taller than everyone else in the class. Maybe the relationship between height and weight changes after 6 feet.

To improve the accuracy of this model, we could incorporate more students, especially athletes and other tall students. We could also measure and incorporate more variables: diet, exercise, parents' weights, etc. Including more variables however makes models harder to use and less applicable to a wide range of values.

Communicating Scientific Results

Once inferences have been made and a hypothesis either rejected or supported, the next step is to communicate those results to other scientists and the general public. Scientists communicate results to other scientists in a variety of forms. The most common form is an article in a **scientific journal**. Journals are monthly or quarterly publications in specific areas of research. Journal articles are peer-reviewed, meaning that other scientists read them prior to publication and scrutinize the validity of their claims. Occasionally, large bodies of work are reviewed and condensed in the form of book. Many college level textbooks used by upperclassmen are essentially collections of journal articles. As in many professions, scientists also hold meeting or symposia where researchers from all over the world can come together to share results and discuss ideas. At these meetings, scientists often communicate their results using posters and short lectures.

scientific journal A peer-reviewed publication of scientific societies that contains articles by researchers reporting on recent studies.

To communicate scientific results to the general population, reporters or science writers typically read through scientific articles and distill the results down into a form that non-scientists can understand. In doing so, errors are sometimes introduced. Imagine that a researcher has just found that cervical cancer cells grown in a petri dish with a chemical found in hand soap causes the tumor cells to grow and reproduce. The researchers might publish a journal article detailing this result and suggest that the chemical influences growth of this type of tumor. A reporter might write an article for a news website that says the chemical in hand soap caused tumors to grow, perhaps without mentioning that these tumor cells were not in an actual patient. It might not mention that the researchers exposed the cells to only the chemical (not hand soap) and at concentrations 1000 times higher than are found in hand soap. By the time the nightly news picks up the story, they might be saying that scientists have "proven" using hand soap will give you cancer. Recall from earlier discussions, that nothing can be proven true in science. With this in mind, try to count how many times a day you hear a statement like this. This story might seem silly, but this is a shockingly common occurrence. The best source for finding scientific information is to read the initial journal articles. When getting scientific information from other sources, always carefully consider the validity of the information and the reputation of the source.

Limitations of the Scientific Method

The scientific method has been an invaluable driving force in driving technological and societal advancement. Research has lengthened the human lifespan, provided us with the means of sending people into space and other worlds, and improved our understanding of the world around us. As a way of acquiring knowledge, the scientific method is a very powerful tool for acquiring knowledge. However, it does have two potential limitations. First, scientific explanations can never be proven definitively true; they change over time in light of new tests and data. The inherent skepticism of scientists and the tentative nature of scientific explanations lead to a constantly changing and improving body of knowledge. However, these same features can be a source of confusion and distrust among non-scientists.

Second, scientific explanations and answers, by definition, can only rely on naturalistic or physical phenomena. Explanations that require invoking supernatural forces or breaking laws of nature cannot be tested or considered using the scientific method. The scientific method could never be used to disprove the existence of ghosts for example, if ghosts are defined as being able to break laws of physics or change experimental results at their whim. To some people, this is considered a limitation of science. People who would seek to use supernatural forces to answer questions or explain phenomena in the world may not agree with the fact that these types of explanations can not be considered when using a scientific approach.

SUMMARY

Snapshots from the Journey

- The scientific method is a way of gathering empirical knowledge, facts and observations of natural and physical phenomena.

- The scientific method consists of identifying research questions, formulating hypotheses, and testing them.

- Scientific hypotheses must rely on natural or physical explanation and must be refutable given sufficient evidence.

- Hypotheses are never proven true, only rejected or supported.

- Scientific theories are the result of rigorous experimentation and investigation by multiple, independent researchers. They are very well supported by existing data, but may one day be disproven in light of new data.

- Collecting data to test hypotheses requires careful consideration of the methodologies used, necessary controls, and safety concerns.

- While both qualitative and quantitative measurements can be used to test hypotheses, the best quantitative measurements are both accurate and precise.

- Figures can be great ways to report data, be they bar graphs, scatter plots, or summary tables.

- Although science has been crucial in shaping our modern world, it is not the only pattern of knowledge and it has its limitations.

REVIEW QUESTIONS

Multiple Choice

1. Which of the following is not true of a scientific hypothesis?
   a. hypotheses can be proven true
   b. hypotheses are tentative and must be refutable given sufficient data
   c. hypotheses can only invoke natural or physical phenomena
   d. well supported hypotheses can be incorporated into scientific theories

2. Which of the following would be a qualitative measurement?
   a. height measured in inches
   b. mass measured in grams
   c. pain measured on a scale of 1-10
   d. color measured as red, blue, or green

3. What type of graph should be used when the independent variable is categorical and the dependent variable is continuous?
   a. a bar graph
   b. a scatter plot
   c. a line graph
   d. a summary table

4. A scientist studies a group of men from Tobago and creates a model to predict the likelihood that they have prostate cancer based on the level of a specific compound in the blood. The model predicts that a man from Georgia named John has an 83% chance of prostate cancer. Tests reveal he is cancer free. Why was the model incorrect?
   a. The model may have been made using too small of a sample
   b. The compound might have a different relationship with prostate cancer in men from Tobago than it does for men in the US
   c. The model only predicts average risk. It is not 100% effective in predicting any one value.
   d. All of these.

REVIEW QUESTIONS

Fill in the Blank

1. _____ knowledge is acquired by considering your own feelings or empathizing with those of others.

2. A false _____ is when a hypothesis is supported, even though it is false.

3. Minimizing the amount of _____ generated by a study can significantly reduce safety risks, conserve resources, and reduce operating costs.

4. The _____ of a sample is the value that is repeated the most.

5. A _____ is an inference drawn about a hypothesis by carefully considering the results of a study or experiment.

Short Answer

1. What distinguishes a scientific hypothesis from a theory?

2. Briefly explain why science cannot be used to disprove the existence of ghosts.

3. Design an experimental investigation to test the hypothesis that drinking caffeine increases heart rate. List all the factors that you would need to control for.

4. List and describe three types of hazards that might be encountered when do research.

5. A drug company publishes results of an in house study on a new cancer drug. They took a group of patients that had recently had pituitary tumors removed and gave them a new drug. None of the patients had a recurrence in the five years following treatment, despite published figures of a 20% recurrence rate. The paper says they have proven the drug prevents recurrence. Discuss all the possible reasons why the drug company is or might be wrong.

6. A research study on the number of teens who smoke cigarettes in Europe shows the following:

   Year 1: -.02%; **Year 2:** -.04%; **Year 3:** -.06%; **Year 4:** -.08%

   Based on the data, predict the trends for Years 5 and 6. Explain your answer.

ANATOMY, PHYSIOLOGY, AND DISEASE IN ACTION

I. History of the Scientific Method

Choose one of the following historical figures and research their contributions to the development of the modern scientific method. Present your findings in class using a brochure or poster.

- Aristotle
- Epicurus
- Ibn al-Haytham
- Roger Bacon
- René Descartes

II. Accuracy and Precision

Materials:
Small object of known mass
Digital balance
Triple beam balance
Calculator
Graph paper

Group up with 2-3 students and take turns measuring a small object using the digital balance and the triple beam balance. Once you have your measurements, use the calculator to determine the mode, median, and mean of each set of measurements. As a group, look at the data and come to a conclusion about which method was more precise. Next, ask your teacher to tell you the actual mass of the object. Use this information to determine which method was more accurate.

Using graph paper, construct a bar graph to show the difference in the means of your two sets of measurements. Don't forget to label your axes! Present your results to the rest of the class. Discuss proper safe practices during field research.

III. Lab and Field Research Safety

Materials:
Poster boards
Markers and colored pencils

As a class, discuss proper lab safety and develop a series of safety procedures to use in the event of an accident. Make posters of each procedure and hang them around the room as reminders.

IV. Reading News about Science

Find several newspaper, magazine, or web articles about a new discovery in medicine or science. Read the articles carefully and see if you can find places where the authors of the articles might have overstated or misrepresented the results of the study. Try to find the original research articles and discuss the results with a classmate or your teacher.

Create a poster about the discovery you've researched and present it to the class. Make sure that you don't add any of your own inferences!

V. Comparative Investigative Methods

Working in groups, develop and implement a research design for a comparative investigation that includes formulating a testable hypothesis with appropriate questions.

VI. History of Science Timeline

Working with a partner, create a report, presentation, or timeline that explores the history of science. Include information on the important contributions that scientists have made. Present your findings to the class. Be sure that you communicate what you've learned in a clear and effective manner.

The Journey's End:
Now What?

For any of you who have ever taken a memorable journey or have lived through a significant event, you know that you have been changed to some degree forever. We hope that this book in some positive way has also changed you.

Your study of anatomy, physiology, and disease has only just begun. The basics that you have learned will act as a foundation of understanding for many things that you will encounter in your life. So go forth and make your mark in the world! The following topics are just a small sampling of how anatomy and physiology and pathology play an important role in many areas. We have added a whole section of Amazing Facts so you can impress friends and family. Enjoy the chapter!

LEARNING OUTCOMES

Upon completion of your journey through this chapter, you will be able to:

- Discuss the relationship between forensic science and anatomy, physiology, and pathology
- Relate anatomy and physiology changes to the process of aging
- Describe the concept of wellness and personal choices
- List and describe wellness concepts for each body system
- Discuss cancer prevention and treatment
- Dazzle your friends with amazing anatomy, physiology, and pathology facts

Pronunciation Guide

Pro·nun·ci·a·tion
Definitions/Parts

Correct pronunciation is important in any journey so that you and others are completely understood. Here is a "see and say" Pronunciation Guide for the more difficult terms to pronounce in this chapter. Please note that pronunciations given are referenced to medical dictionaries, and regional variations may exist.

anhidrosis (an high DROH sis)
bacilli (bah SILL eye)
chlamydia trachomatis
  (klah MID ee ah tray KOH mah tiss)
forensic science (for IN sick)
geriatric (JAIR ee AT rick)
herpes simplex virus 2 (HER peez)
human papilloma virus (pap ih LOW ma)

incontinence (in KAH tih nens)
neisseria gonorrhea
  (nye SEE ree ah gon oh REE ah)
spina bifida (SPY nah BIFF ih dah)
thallium (THAL ee um)
treponema pallidum
  (TREP oh NEE mah PAL ih dum)

FORENSIC SCIENCE

forensic science The application of science and medicine to law.

We've all watched movies or TV shows featuring super-sleuths solving such crimes as murders or disappearances using some amazing scientific technology. Some of the methods used seem pretty far-fetched, as though invented just for entertainment purposes. Actually, much of the **forensic science** we see on TV is very close, if not "dead on," to the actual technologies that are applied to solve crimes. However, it is important to note that this kind of investigation can be extremely tedious and expensive and take longer than a 46-minute TV show to solve a crime. Most forensic scientists don't look like supermodels or drive $50,000 SUVs either. This section deals with just a sampling of how anatomy and physiology and an understanding of pathology are used to help solve crimes and explain historical mysteries.

So what exactly is forensic science? Simply put, forensic science is the application of science to crime and law. A forensic scientist often searches for and examines physical traces that can be useful in establishing or excluding some association between a victim and an individual or individuals suspected of committing a crime. It is interesting to

(Source: Joe Belanger/Shutterstock.com.)

note that both natural science and social science are used when solving crime. The natural sciences of anatomy, physiology, and pathology often play a key role in solving a crime or identifying the remains of a victim. The pathologist also often plays a vital role in his or her autopsy findings.

APPLIED SCIENCE

Forensics and History

DNA fingerprinting techniques are used extensively to clear up mysteries. For example, it is now standard to use this technology to solve rape and murder cases. DNA fingerprinting also helped determine that Thomas Jefferson most likely fathered some children of his slave Sally Hemings. It was also used to identify many of the victims of the World Trade Center, Pentagon, and Flight 93 in Shanksville, Pennsylvania, after 9/11.

Disease Detection

Forensic science has unlocked ancient mysteries and allowed us to learn something about the health of ancient people. Proof that the ancient Egyptians were stricken with tuberculosis was discovered by examining their skeletons. We normally think of tuberculosis as a lung disease, but tuberculosis thrives in areas of the body that possess high levels of oxygen. These include the lungs, brain, kidneys, and *the ends of long bones!* Because the organs were long ago decomposed, the only thing left to examine were the skeletal remains, particularly the ends of the long bones such as the femur. On examination of these bones, bone scouring that is typically caused by tuberculosis was discovered. Bone scouring is the destruction of the smooth bone surface as a result of colonization by the tuberculosis **bacilli**.

bacilli Plural of bacillus, which is a rod-shaped microorganism.

Primitive Surgery

Forensic scientists have discovered evidence of primitive surgery. A skull fragment found in a 400-year-old trash dump at the site of the Jamestown, Virginia, settlement provided evidence that skull surgery had been performed on a patient. The circular marks on the fragment indicated that there was an attempt to drill a hole in the skull, probably to relieve pressure on the brain due to a skull fracture that may have been caused by an accident or a war club blow to the head. Scientists analyzing the fragment were able to determine that the patient was a European male on the basis of the fragment's shape and thickness *and* because the bone contained traces of lead that was absorbed by the body from using lead-glazed pottery and/or eating from pewter plates!

APPLIED SCIENCE

Tomatoes Were Once Thought to be Poisonous

For several hundreds of years, it was believed that tomatoes were poisonous. This erroneous fact occurred because during the Middle Ages, the wealthier people ate from pewter plates that contained high levels of lead. The acidic tomatoes leached out the lead, which was consumed and resulted in lead poisoning. Even in modern times the threat of lead poisoning exists—but not from tomatoes.

Remains Identification

Nazi Josef Mengele, the "Angel of Death," was responsible for the death of at least 400,000 people during World War II. As the war ended, Mengele escaped to South America and avoided capture. There were numerous reported sightings throughout the years, but none produced the war criminal. Then, in 1979, an elderly man named Wolfgang Gerhard drowned and was buried in a Brazilian cemetery. Suspicions that he was Mengele prompted the Brazilian government to exhume the body. Analysis of the bones revealed a right-handed male Caucasian between 60 and 70 years old with a height approximated within a half centimeter of Mengele's. Having a pile of bones, a shattered skull, and no current medical information or dental records, the forensic anthropologists turned to a technique called video skull–face superimposition. After reconstructing the shattered skull, the experts marked it with pins at 30 specific structural landmarks. The same thing was done with a picture of Mengele that was scaled to match the size of the skull. Compared side by side, the pins matched up. Photo images of the skull and picture were then superimposed and the points matched up. They had their man. Later, when his old dental records were found, it was again a match, as was a later DNA analysis. More recently, an updated similar procedure was used to determine the actual facial structure of Tutankhamen (King Tut), the Boy Pharaoh of Egypt.

Murder Most Foul!

Although it possesses no vocal chords, your hair speaks volumes about your health and your habits. Hair can reveal the race of an individual, whether the hair was cut or pulled out from the body, or if it was dyed. If the hair shaft has its follicle still attached, genetic information such as DNA or blood type can also be discerned. Hair samples can place an individual at the scene of a crime.

Even though hair is technically dead, just like your fingernails and toenails, it acts like a library (as do your nails), storing information about substances you have been exposed to or ingested. Because hair grows relatively slowly, it can contain a *timeline* of substances that an individual ingested or was exposed to. In an interesting case of thallium poisoning, a man's wife was convicted of murder partially on the basis of hair samples of the victim. The victim's hair was long enough that it provided a record of ingestion of thallium for approximately 330 days. During that period of time, the spikes in concentration of thallium in sections of his hair matched the times the victim was with his wife. Drops in the level of thallium in other sections of his hair coincided with the times he was away from his wife or in the hospital for other illnesses. There was a massive spike in thallium concentration a few days before he died, which was indicative of premeditated poisoning. In a plea bargain, it was revealed that the victim's wife had been feeding him rat poison that contained thallium to collect on a life insurance policy!

APPLIED SCIENCE

If Bones Could Speak

Skeletal remains can also assist in telling the sex of an individual. The female pelvis is shaped like a basin and is wider than the male pelvis to allow for the larger birth canal. In general, it is broader and lighter than the male pelvis, and the pubic angle is 90 degrees or greater (see **FIGURE 20-1** ▲). The male pelvis is heavier, stronger, and more funnel shaped, with a pubic angle of 90 degrees or less.

Male
Pelvis

90°
or less

Female
Pelvis

90°
or more

FIGURE 20-1 ▲ The male pelvis and female pelvis.

Fingerprints

Even with all the new advances, fingerprints are still a time-honored crime-solving method (see **FIGURE 20-2** ▲). Like snowflakes, no two prints are exactly alike. Fingerprints are **friction ridges** that form a pattern on the anterior surface of the hands and also on the plantar surface of the feet. As the name applies, the friction ridges help prevent slippage when grasping or holding objects. They are especially prominent on the skin covering the tips of the fingers and toes. Fingerprints are made inside the

friction ridges Irregular patterns found on the anterior surface of hands and the plantar surface of feet that decrease slippage and also form the unique patterns of fingerprints and footprints.

FIGURE 20-2 ▲ A fingerprint.
(Source: © Dorling Kindersley.)

womb in response to the pull of the elastic fibers in the dermal papillary layer on the epidermis. Because fingerprints are not wholly determined by DNA, identical twins do not have identical fingerprints.

Interest in fingerprint analysis has been around for a long time. The uniqueness of fingerprints was discovered in the 1600s. They were described and studied for many years, and then in 1880, Dr. Henry Faulds wrote the first article suggesting that fingerprints may be used to solve crimes. In 1886, he began trying to convince Scotland Yard to adopt a fingerprinting identification system.

DNA Fingerprinting

Forensic scientists may also use DNA, the molecule found in the nucleus of our cells, to identify unknown individuals. DNA can be sampled at a crime scene from body fluids, such as blood or semen, or can be extracted from skeletal or even very tiny soft tissue remains. During the process of DNA fingerprinting (which has nothing to do with actual fingerprints), DNA molecules are split into pieces and separated using electrical currents. These pieces can be compared to pieces of a known DNA sample from a relative of a victim, from hair samples off a comb, or from mouth cells from a toothbrush, or can be compared to a suspect in a criminal case.

TEST YOUR KNOWLEDGE 20-1

Choose the best answer:

1. This part of your body acts as a library and provides a timeline to record substances that you have ingested or have been exposed to:
   a. heart
   b. lungs
   c. hair
   d. spinal cord

2. This metal has been detected in the bones of medieval skeletons and can be traced to eating from pewter plates:
   a. silver
   b. gold
   c. kryptonite
   d. lead

3. Proof that ancient Egyptians had tuberculosis was discovered by examining their:
   a. tombs
   b. bones
   c. hair
   d. mommies

4. The difference between male and female skeletal remains can be determined by examining the angle of the:
   a. skull
   b. vertebrae
   c. sternum
   d. pelvis

GERIATRICS

Many regions in the United States are exhibiting a major change in patient demographics. In general, we are seeing an older population due to safer workplaces, healthier lifestyles, effective vaccines and medications, and opportunities to access health care. As a result, you probably will deal with a high number of **geriatric** patients in the health care profession that you choose. (Even the maternity departments may have 50- to 60-year-old mothers in the future, as witnessed by several recent news reports!)

Geriatric patients differ in many ways from other patient age groups, so it is important to recognize these differences to provide the best health care possible for this patient population. Here are some general tidbits to get you started.

The general use of the term *elderly* when describing patients is somewhat misleading. Currently, some experts divide this patient group into the following classifications.

- Age 65 to 75: younger old
- Age 76 to 84: older old
- Age 85 and older: elite old

Using the vague term *aging* as a way to generally describe a patient is a misnomer in that an individual's body does not age uniformly. For example, an individual may

geriatric A general term applied to older adult patients.

look older due to aging skin but may have a cardiovascular system of a person 10 to 15 years younger than his or her chronological age. With that said, there is the general "1% rule" in which we see a 1% decrease in the function of most body systems each year beginning around the age of 30.

So what general characteristics or tendencies do we see in an aging patient? The hallmark sign of aging is a decrease in the ability to maintain homeostasis. These individuals may have normal baselines but begin exhibiting a decrease in the ability to adapt to stressors. Often, disease processes along with aging will accelerate the loss of body reserves that younger patients take for granted, such as recovery time or complications following an accident or surgery. In addition, you may have increased difficulties in evaluating these patients because of decreases in their vision, hearing, and possibly their mental abilities.

Amazing Body Facts

You're Not Getting Older, You're Getting Smarter

There are a lot of misconceptions about the brain and aging. In the absence of disease, your brain continues to mature up to the age of 50. Interestingly, we have better overall brain function and decision-making skills at age 60 than at age 30! Even though an older patient may lose up to 1,000 neurons a day, we all start out with several billion, so percentagewise, a loss of 1,000 a day is minor. This is why you may not begin to see a decrease in brain function until around the age of 75.

General Body Changes

Let's take a general look at the aging process of the body. There is a decrease in the total body water for both males and females. The clinical significance of this is that older people have a tendency to dehydrate more rapidly, which can potentially affect the excretion rate of medications they are on.

From ages 20 to 70, we see a loss of lean body mass due to an up to 30% loss in the number of muscle cells, atrophy of remaining muscle cells, and a general decrease in muscle strength. Conversely, we see an increase in total body fat, which slowly increases between the ages of 25 and 45. However, this trend can continue up to age 70. The fat accumulated is a "deeper" fat, meaning that it is abdominal fat and found more in the viscera than subcutaneously.

Bone density usually reaches its greatest peak around age 35. Contrary to what you see on TV, loss of bone mass occurs both in women *and* men. For women, during the first 5 years after menopause, 1 to 2% bone loss per year can occur. Interestingly, women with osteoporosis are almost three times as likely to lose a tooth compared to those without that condition. Why, you may ask? Remember that teeth are anchored to the jaw, so the loss of mandibular bone integrity translates to potential tooth loss. In general, we see a 1% bone loss per year between the ages of 55 and 70. After that, it is approximately 0.5% per year.

In general, as an individual ages, that person loses muscle mass, gains fat, and loses bone density. This varies among individuals and can be affected by lifestyle choices. Later in this chapter, we discuss steps that can be taken to slow (or even reverse) this process.

Gustatory Changes

Sensory changes can also occur in this patient group. The senses of taste and smell begin to deteriorate as a natural process of aging. The number of taste buds decreases by about 50% as the body reaches the geriatric stage. Sweet versus bitter tastes becomes less discernable. The acuity of salt and bitter tastes decline. Orange juice may taste metallic. Patients on oxygen via a nasal cannula may have a decrease in their ability to taste. These changes are clinically significant because they may make it more difficult to ensure a properly balanced diet for good health. This is also a concern coupled with the additional functional and physiologic difficulties affecting grocery shopping and food preparation. It is estimated that 33% of this patient group lives alone. These and other sensory impairments affect activities of daily living (ADLs), and as a result, we see approximately 5 to 15% of this population exhibiting protein and calorie malnutrition.

Additional barriers to proper nutrition include tooth loss, difficulty swallowing, and decreased saliva. In addition, there are decreases in digestive juice acidity and secretion, nutrient absorption, and bowel function.

The Brain and Nervous System

One main problem with the aging process and the nervous system is the slower reaction time that occurs. As a result, there are increased chances for motor vehicle accidents, falls, burns, and so forth.

Pain is something usually associated with the aging process. Even though the authors of this book are young in spirit, vibrant, and good looking, they have occasional creaking joints and stiff, sore muscles! Untreated pain can lead to an overall decrease in the quality of a person's life, including impaired sleep, a decrease in socialization, confusion, depression, malnutrition, polypharmacy (use of multiple medications), and impaired ambulation. If any of these conditions were occurring before the pain was introduced, the pain may cause these conditions to worsen.

Often, geriatric patients are undermedicated for pain. This may be because patients who are debilitated, are cognitively impaired, or have a history of substance abuse are sometimes unable to effectively relate how they feel. Sometimes, it is a result of the ignorance of health care professionals who cannot recognize indicators of pain.

Clinically, these are some of the potential behavioral changes related to pain:

- Changes in personality such as becoming agitated, quiet, withdrawn, sad, confused, depressed, grumpy
- Loss of appetite
- Screaming, swearing, name calling, grunting, noisy breathing
- Crying, rocking, fidgeting
- Splinting or rubbing a sore area, wincing
- Cold, clammy, and pale skin

The Cardiovascular System

Within the cardiovascular system, we see changes such as calcification of the heart valves, which decreases their efficiency. We also see a lessening in the flexibility of the blood vessels. This makes vessels less able to respond to blood pressure changes, so increased blood pressure is common. There is also a decrease in cardiac output and an approximate 25% decrease in the maximum heart rate.

What do you think are some of the benefits of regular exercise? (Source: Monkey Business Images/Shutterstock.com.)

Genitourinary System

Between ages of 20 and 80, we lose up to approximately 50% of our renal function. This is clinically significant when you consider the amount of drugs used by the geriatric population that are excreted by the kidneys. Therefore, a drug taken by someone with impaired renal (and/or liver) function can lead to the drug not being metabolized at the expected rate. This can lead to an accumulation of the drug in the body at harmful or toxic levels. There is also an increase in **incontinence** (loss of bladder control) in this group.

incontinence *(in KAHNT in ins)* Condition of involuntary urination and defecation.

Integumentary System

Here we see a loss in skin elasticity, increased skin delicacy, multiple skin lesions, and increases in skin cancer. Although many of these problems could have been reduced by limiting sun exposure and not smoking earlier in their lives, the use of medications such as systemic corticosteroids does accelerate many of these conditions.

Polypharmacy

Polypharmacy, the administration of many drugs at the same time, is a major concern for this patient group. Contributing factors to this problem include the fact that these patients typically see several specialists for a variety of diseases, often with one doctor not knowing what the other is prescribing. These multiple diseases have competing therapeutic needs, and the combinations of utilized drugs can cause life-threatening situations. Aging also can affect the rates of drug absorption, drug distribution throughout the body, metabolism of the drugs, as well as their excretion from the body.

As a result, here are some clinical considerations. Review the drugs that the individual is taking, looking for possible drug interactions or medications that are no longer needed. Look at your patient's liver and kidney functions. They will affect the rate of removal of medications from the body and resultant drug blood levels. When medicating with opioids, dose by age, not by body weight. Remember, opioids slow the gastrointestinal tract. In general, when considering an *equal* dose given to a geriatric patient compared to a middle-aged patient, analgesics are stronger and last longer in elderly patients. Start low and go slow.

It is important that patients tell all their doctors what medications they are taking. If you work in a physician's office or do home care, you can help your patients relay this information more effectively by reminding them to bring all the drugs they're taking to each appointment. It is also important to instruct them to keep an updated list of their drugs and dosages in case they have to make a trip to the emergency department.

TEST YOUR KNOWLEDGE 20-2

Choose the best answer:

1. There is a _____ decrease in the function of most body systems each year beginning around the age of 30.
   a. 10%
   b. 20%
   c. 5%
   d. 1%

2. The hallmark sign of aging is the decrease in the ability to maintain:
   a. cardiac enzymes
   b. exercise potential
   c. homeostasis
   d. sense of humor

3. _____ is a term used for the administration of many drugs at the same time.
   a. Addiction
   b. Polypharmacy
   c. Multimeds
   d. Overdose

4. In the absence of disease, your brain continues to mature up to the age of:
   a. 50
   b. 35
   c. 75
   d. 10

WELLNESS

One of the most important personal choices you will ever make will be the decision of what kind of lifestyle you want to live. Choices you make now may have a *profound* effect on your future health and life span. Will you eat properly, exercise within reason, smoke, do drugs and/or alcohol, live or work in a dangerous environment, and/or engage in risky behaviors?

Individual accountability and *informed choices* are two key concepts in deciding your lifestyle. It is amazing that individuals have sued fast-food companies for making their food too appealing and, as a result, making the "victim" get fat. People don't force other people to smoke cigarettes. In each of these cases, the individual made a conscious choice to eat more than necessary and to begin smoking.

Yes, peer pressure is real, but it is too often looked at from the negative side. What about peers and influential people who promote good, healthy lifestyles? Think about it. Do you know people or have friends who do healthy things? Once again, it is a conscious choice to surround yourself with the type of friends you want.

Read and critically analyze what you read. Utilize multiple reliable sources. Even though the Internet is a wonderful source of information, there is a lot of "junk" science that is more opinion than fact.

Let's take a quick review of the body systems that we covered and briefly discuss some ways to improve your health. Although there are always some controversial issues in wellness, we have chosen the more commonly held beliefs to discuss here.

Nervous System

Stress is a natural part of life. Stress is also good and necessary: It is a motivator, and it helps you protect yourself. The problem occurs when stress becomes chronic and you can no longer effectively deal with it. The high cost of stress is that it can affect some or all of your body's various systems to varying degrees. A poor stress response can lead to an assortment of disorders such as eating and digestive disorders, decreased immune response, decreased memory and work capacities, sleep problems, joint and muscle aches, heart problems, and personality changes. Some of these problems can be life threatening. For an extensive review of a healthful stress management system, consult the Study Companion Guide found in the back of your textbook.

Often, when dealing with a patient, we focus specifically on the presenting illness and fail to realize we should look at the whole person. The "whole person" includes not only other systems of the body but also the mental and spiritual aspects of the person. Too often in the past, dealing with mental health has had a negative image. We don't hide the fact that we have the flu or a broken arm, so why should we hide the fact that we may be sad for long periods of time (depression) and need help to resolve that condition?

Skeletal System

Diet is extremely important in the growth and protection of your bones. A diet rich in calcium and vitamins helps to maintain good bone growth and development. Weight-bearing exercise has also been shown to be beneficial in maintaining healthy bones over a lifetime.

One common occupational condition related to repetitive motion, such as typing on a keyboard, playing a piano, or hammering, is known as **carpal tunnel syndrome**. Although this syndrome is caused by damage to the median nerve, it is the result of the *skeletal* structure of the wrist being too restrictive during extended periods when the wrist is kept in an upward bent position. See **FIGURE 20-3** ▲, which illustrates the structures that affect this repetitive syndrome.

carpal tunnel syndrome A condition affecting the median nerve distribution of the hand leading to pain and/or numbness. Repetitive motion is the most common cause of this condition.

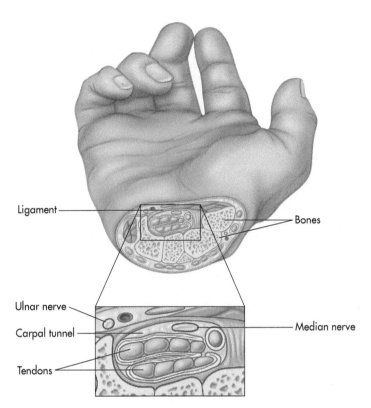

FIGURE 20-3 ▲ Anatomical structures affecting carpal tunnel syndrome.

Muscular System

Again, proper exercise and diet will help to develop and maintain properly functioning muscles. Although there are many types of muscle-training programs, you need to investigate which type is best for you depending on your needs or desired outcomes. See **FIGURE 20-4** ▲, which presents the Activity Pyramid as a possible guide.

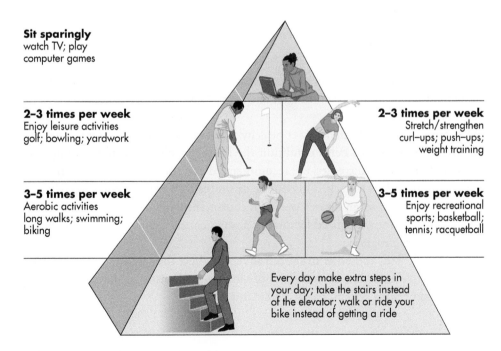

Sit sparingly
watch TV; play computer games

2–3 times per week
Enjoy leisure activities
golf; bowling; yardwork

2–3 times per week
Stretch/strengthen
curl–ups; push–ups;
weight training

3–5 times per week
Aerobic activities
long walks; swimming;
biking

3–5 times per week
Enjoy recreational
sports; basketball;
tennis; racquetball

Every day make extra steps in your day; take the stairs instead of the elevator; walk or ride your bike instead of getting a ride

FIGURE 20-4 ▲ The Activity Pyramid.

Integumentary System

Proper diet and hydration is important for the functioning of the integumentary system. This is why it is important to drink enough fluids to meet your hydration needs. Other fluids such as caffeinated coffee and alcohol are diuretics and can cause a net water loss. Smoking also affects this system by causing premature aging of the skin.

Although sun exposure is important for the production of vitamin D in your body, limiting the amount of sun exposure to prevent skin cancer is equally important. Some forms of skin cancer are treatable, but others can be lethal. The effect of the sun is cumulative, and severe sun burns as a child can have severe consequences in adulthood. There are several ways to prevent excessive sun exposure. Minimize your time in the sun between 10 a.m. and 4 p.m. because this is when the sun's rays are most intense. Wear long-sleeved shirts when possible, brimmed hats, sunglasses (preferably wraparounds), and of course, sunscreen.

An example of skin cancer. (Courtesy of National Cancer Institute [NCI])

Cardiovascular System

A heart-healthy diet low in saturated fats (remember, we all need some fat for proper function) and high in fiber, rich in fruit and vegetables will help maintain an optimal cardiovascular system.

Diet alone is not sufficient for a healthy heart, however. The proper level and regularity of exercise also helps condition the heart for maximum functioning. The newest guidelines have increased the recommended exercise level to 30 to 45 minutes of activity, 5 to 7 days a week. This can be as simple as walking briskly for 30 to 45 minutes a day, five to seven times a week. Of course, the level of your exercise program depends on many individualized factors. As always, consult your doctor before beginning any exercise program.

Smoking, alcohol, and other drugs can adversely affect the cardiovascular and other systems. For an illustration of the effects of chronic alcoholism on the cardiovascular, digestive, and nervous system, please see **FIGURE 20-5** ▲.

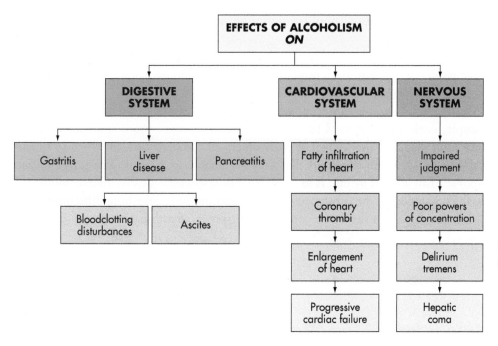

FIGURE 20-5 ▲ The effects of alcoholism on the body systems.

The Financial Importance of Cardiovascular Health

Cardiovascular disease is the number one cause of death in the United States. It is projected that the costs incurred in treating heart disease will triple from now until the year 2030 to over 800 *billion* dollars annually! The condition that will take the biggest chunk of these costs (approximately 389 billion by 2030) will be for the treatment of high blood pressure and the related diseases it affects such as kidney failure and stroke.

The projection for the increase in incidences of heart disease is 10%. This translates to a total of about 40% of adults in the United States (116 million people) having one or more form of cardiovascular disease by 2030.

The frustrating part for health care workers, hospitals, and health insurance companies is that most heart disease is preventable. Healthy diets, reasonable exercise, smoking cessation, and a generally healthy lifestyle coupled with regular check-ups and properly taking prescribed cardiovascular medications would go a long way in reducing the number of individuals suffering with heart disease. Something as simple as reducing salt intake by 3 grams per day could potentially reduce the number of new cases of heart disease, heart attacks, and strokes by one half! While it is never too late to begin living healthy, it is imperative that a healthy lifestyle be developed as a child and continues through adulthood.

Respiratory System

Smoking is the number one preventable cause of respiratory diseases. Smoking can lead to damage of lung tissue and chronic diseases such as bronchitis, emphysema, and asthma. In addition, smoking increases the occurrence of lung infections and colds as well as sinus infections. Approximately 80% of all lung cancers can be traced to smoking. Smoking also affects the heart by reducing the availability of oxygen to the heart muscle.

Smoking, along with alcohol consumption, leads to an increase in stomach and mouth cancers.

What we breathe in, depending on where we live or work, can also affect the health of the respiratory system. Both outdoor and indoor pollution can lead to a number of respiratory problems.

Occupational hazards can occur when workers are exposed to dust or vapors. For example, coalminers exposed to coal dust without proper protection can develop **black lung disease,** also known as coalworkers' pneumoconiosis, in which so much coal dust builds up in the lungs that they are unable to expel it. The lung's initial response to an inhaled irritant is to close down or restrict the airway, thereby minimizing the inhalation of the substance. This can lead to severe breathing difficulties. See FIGURE 20-6 ▲, which shows the constricted airway in an asthma attack.

black lung disease Also known as coal workers pneumoconiosis, this lung disease is a result of the chronic inhalation and retention of coal dust.

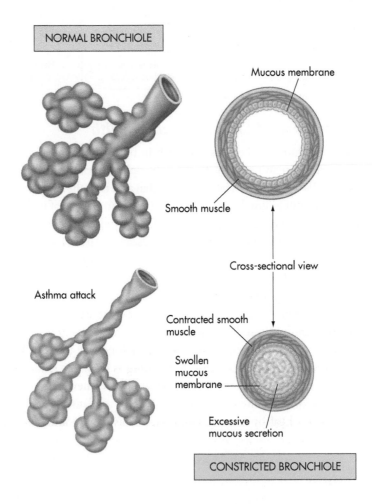

FIGURE 20-6 ▲ The normal and constricted airway.

Gastrointestinal System

A proper diet is critical for growth, development, and health in general. Lack of a proper diet, which leads to undernourishment, can affect all the systems, as can be seen in FIGURE 20-7 ▲. Although most experts agree that the best source of vitamins and minerals comes from natural food sources, the responsible use of supplemental vitamins and minerals can play an important role in health. For example, excessive dosages of fat-soluble vitamins (A, D, E, and K) can actually harm the body because they can build up to toxic levels. See TABLE 20-1 ■ for more information about vitamins and what they do.

Clinical Application

AGE- AND ACTIVITY-RELATED DIETS AND NUTRITIONAL NEEDS

At some time in our educational careers, we have seen the old food pyramid, which told us what portion of our diet should be dairy, what portion of our diet should be vegetables, and so forth. One of the problems with this pyramid was that it was designed to fit *everyone*. Unfortunately, not everyone is the same sex, height, shape, or age, nor has the same level of activity. Enter MyPyramid.gov, created in 2005 as the USDA's newest spin on the food pyramid that took into account your age, sex, and activity level when determining the best diet for you. However, in 2011, the USDA unveiled myplate.gov, which is meant to be a teaching tool for young children but also serves for adults to give a general recommendation for the amounts of the various food groups to consume with each meal.

TABLE 20-1 ■ VITAMINS AND THE BODY SYSTEMS

VITAMIN	DESCRIPTION
Vitamin A	Proper night vision; proper development of bones and teeth; mucous membrane and epithelial cell integrity; helps resist infection
Vitamin B	B_2 promotes healthy muscular growth; B_{12} is needed for healthy blood cell development and to treat pernicious anemia; B_1 and B_{12} promote healthy function of nervous tissue; B_1 aids in carbohydrate metabolism, normal digestion, and appetite; niacin is necessary for fat synthesis and cellular respiration
Vitamin C	Aids in absorption of iron; promotes healing of fractures, development of teeth and bone matrix, and wound healing; ensures capillary integrity; bolsters immune system
Vitamin D	Promotes strong bones and teeth, regulates skeletal calcium reabsorption; aids in absorption of calcium and phosphorus from the intestinal tract; D_3 helps regulate release of parathyroid hormone
Vitamin E	Promotes muscle growth; E_1 necessary for hemolytic resistance of red blood cell membranes; helps prevent anemia for proper reproductive system functioning; current research shows that consumption from natural sources may reduce the risk of Parkinson's disease; further investigation is needed
Vitamin K	Needed for proper blood clotting

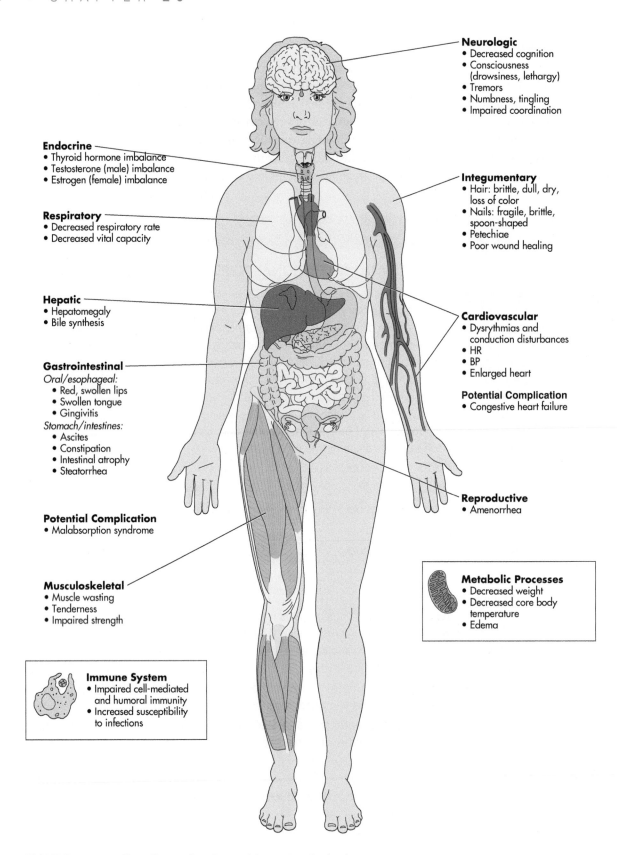

Neurologic
- Decreased cognition
- Consciousness (drowsiness, lethargy)
- Tremors
- Numbness, tingling
- Impaired coordination

Endocrine
- Thyroid hormone imbalance
- Testosterone (male) imbalance
- Estrogen (female) imbalance

Integumentary
- Hair: brittle, dull, dry, loss of color
- Nails: fragile, brittle, spoon-shaped
- Petechiae
- Poor wound healing

Respiratory
- Decreased respiratory rate
- Decreased vital capacity

Hepatic
- Hepatomegaly
- Bile synthesis

Cardiovascular
- Dysrythmias and conduction disturbances
- HR
- BP
- Enlarged heart

Potential Complication
- Congestive heart failure

Gastrointestinal
Oral/esophageal:
- Red, swollen lips
- Swollen tongue
- Gingivitis

Stomach/intestines:
- Ascites
- Constipation
- Intestinal atrophy
- Steatorrhea

Potential Complication
- Malabsorption syndrome

Reproductive
- Amenorrhea

Musculoskeletal
- Muscle wasting
- Tenderness
- Impaired strength

Metabolic Processes
- Decreased weight
- Decreased core body temperature
- Edema

Immune System
- Impaired cell-mediated and humoral immunity
- Increased susceptibility to infections

FIGURE 20-7 ▲ The effects of undernourishment on the body systems.

Endocrine System

Proper diet and exercise also assist the endocrine system. One of the areas of concern, in professional and even high school sports, is the use of performance-enhancing substances. For example, anabolic steroids are used to increase strength and endurance rapidly and to build muscle mass. Anabolic steroids are closely related to the male hormone testosterone. However, these steroids have *serious* side effects that include kidney damage, liver damage, increased risk of heart disease, irritability, and aggressive behavior. Woman taking steroids can develop facial hair and deeper voices. In men, these substances diminish sperm production. Some of these effects can be permanent even after ceasing the use of the drugs. The use of anabolic steroids is banned and is tested for in sports.

Sensory System

Care of the sensory system includes proper diet, wearing hearing and sight protective devices when necessary, and periodic examination of the eyes and ears. Wearing hearing protection during activities that produce high levels of noise will greatly extend the functional life of your hearing. Damage to the ear is cumulative, so there is no better time to start than right now. In addition, protective eyewear should be worn any time that the risk of eye injury can occur, such as in certain occupations, hobbies, and sports. FIGURE 20-8 ▲ shows the Snellen Eye chart for determining visual acuity.

FIGURE 20-8 ▲ The Snellen Eye Chart.

Immune System

Proper diet and exercise are needed for optimal functioning of the immune system. In addition, other factors can assist your immune system. One of the simplest and most effective ways to protect not only yourself but also your patients is hand-washing. Always wash your hands before and after working with each of your patients. Even though you are a staff member in a hospital or health care institution, and not a patient, you may still be a carrier of infectious organisms. In addition, you could be susceptible to becoming infected by hospital pathogens. Correct washing of your hands goes a long way toward stopping the spread of infection.

However, there is also another way to protect yourself and others from the spread of pathogens via body fluids: follow the Standard Precaution Guidelines (refer to Figure 1-6 in Chapter 1). These guidelines are standard precautions that are to be followed for every patient that you treat.

Having current immunizations is important to assist the immune system in being prepared for certain pathogens. Immunization schedules are recommended by the Centers for Disease Control and Prevention (CDC), the American Academy of Pediatrics (AAP), and the American Academy of Family Physicians (AAFP). Many individuals mistakenly believe immunizations only occur in childhood. The influenza vaccine is just one example of an important immunization for the geriatric population.

A big issue is when and when not to take antibiotics. The body handles most infections using its own immune system in a few days, so antibiotics are in most cases not required. Further, the overuse of antibiotics has led to several critical health issues. First, many viral infections are mistakenly treated with antibacterial agents, which do nothing to the virus and cause harm to normal bacteria such as those in the intestinal system. Second, overuse does not allow the immune system of a child to properly develop and respond to future infections; this can cause related disorders such as asthma. Finally, many patients do not properly take their antibiotics. For example, they do not take the full dose for the full length of time but discontinue when they "feel better." However, often there are still surviving bacteria that are left that represent a stronger, drug-resistant strain, and they are now free to reproduce stronger drug-resistant offspring. This has led to limited epidemics of drug-resistant infections.

APPLIED SCIENCE

Antibiotics

The term *antibiotic* means "against life" and technically includes medications that inhibit or destroy any microorganism, including bacteria, viruses, and fungi. However, *antibiotic* in medicine has become associated only with antibacterial agents.

Reproductive System

Don't smoke! Smoking mothers tend to have babies of lower birth weights, tendency toward premature births, and a higher rate of SIDS (sudden infant death syndrome). And while we're talking about babies and children, don't forget about the hazards of secondhand smoke in the home. In homes that have at least one smoking parent, kids have slower than normal lung development and are predisposed to increased incidences of bronchitis, asthma, and ear infections (otitis media).

Diet

As the old saying goes, when you are pregnant you are now eating for two! This doesn't mean that mom should pig out at every chance she gets, however. What it means is that diets should be followed that provide important vitamins, minerals, and nutrients for the developing fetus and to maintain the health of the mother. Think about it. If the diet is lacking in calcium, where does the fetus get calcium for bone development? It has to take it from the bones and teeth of the mother, thus decreasing the integrity of her system. The congenital condition of **spina bifida** can be prevented by a dietary supplement of folic acid, a member of the vitamin B complex. The elimination of alcohol during pregnancy is also important to ensure the best chances of normal spinal cord and nervous system development.

spina bifida (SPY nah BIF ih duh) A congenital defect in which the vertebral arches fail to form properly. This leads to varying levels of disability.

Sexually Transmitted Diseases (STDs)

STDs, also known as sexually transmitted infections (STIs), are a growing problem and can have serious effects on the reproductive system and lethal effects on the body. Various types of diseases and organisms can be transmitted through unprotected sex (including oral sex). Please see TABLE 20-2 ■ for a list of sexually transmitted diseases.

TABLE 20-2 ■ SEXUALLY TRANSMITTED DISEASES

DISEASE	ORGANISM	SYMPTOMS
Herpes	Herpes simplex virus 2	Male: fluid-filled vesicles on penis
		Female: blisters in and around vagina
Gonorrhea	Neisseria gonorrhoeae	Male: purulent discharge from urethra, dysuria, and urinary frequency
		Female: purulent vaginal discharge, dysuria, urinary frequency, abnormal menstrual bleeding, abdominal tenderness; can lead to sterility
Chlamydia	Chlamydia trachomatis	May be asymptomatic
		Male: mucopurulent discharge from penis, burning and itching in genital area, dysuria, swollen testes; can lead to sterility
		Female: mucopurulent discharge from vagina, inflamed bladder, pelvic pain, inflamed cervix; can lead to sterility
Syphilis	Treponema pallidum	Systemic disease that can lead to lesions, lymph node enlargement, nervous system degradation, chancre sores
Genital Warts	Human papilloma virus (HPV)	Cauliflower-like growths on penis and vagina

CANCER PREVENTION AND TREATMENT

All the body systems can be ravaged by cancer. Cancer is the runaway reproduction and spreading of abnormal cells and is a very complicated disorder. Each type of cancer, named for the location or the type of cells that are running amok (for example, colon cancer, prostate cancer, squamous cell carcinoma) has its own unique characteristics. However, in the past few years, medical science has learned a number of things about cancer that have resulted in great improvements in cancer prevention and treatment.

Any number of triggers can make a cell cancerous, including genes, radiation, sunlight exposure, smoking, fatty foods, viruses, and chemical exposure. Some of these triggers, like genes or some viruses, are difficult to avoid. But others, like smoking, sunlight, radiation exposure, and fatty foods, can be pretty easily avoided by eating right, avoiding smoking, and wearing sunscreen. Many types of cancer can be prevented or managed with a healthy diet and exercise. Even genetic susceptibility to cancer does not make cancer unavoidable. Testing, such as mammograms (for breast cancer), colonoscopy (for colon cancer), and Pap tests (for cervical cancer), can improve survival by catching cancers early, before they have spread, or even allowing the removal of abnormal cells before they become cancerous. See **TABLE 20-3** ■ for testing suggestions for various cancers.

Treatments for cancer typically involve surgical removal of the cancerous cells, if possible, and some form of treatment to kill any cells remaining in the body. **Chemotherapy** is the treatment of cancer with chemicals that kill rapidly dividing cells. Radiation uses energy waves to shrink tumors. Biological agents or immunotherapy targets the cancer by manipulating the immune system to hunt down and kill the cancer cells. New treatments are constantly under development to treat cancers that are difficult to fight.

Melanoma is one of the most deadly forms of skin cancer. It is formed by the runaway reproduction of melanocytes, the pigment-forming cells of the skin. People at the highest risk of melanoma are those with fair skin and light eyes or hair who have been exposed to lots of sun during their lifetime. However, new evidence indicates that even people who tan easily may develop melanoma if they get enough sun exposure. Melanoma risk is higher for those living near the equator, but people in the northern parts of the United States are not without risk. Exposure to sunlight, particularly sunburns, even as an adult, is the key risk factor for melanoma. Genetic factors are involved in some cases of melanoma.

Melanoma can be easily prevented by decreasing exposure to UV light. Aside from staying indoors all the time, which isn't very practical, limited exposure and the use of sunscreen is the best way to protect yourself from melanoma. Individuals at risk should have a skin screening on a regular basis.

Standard treatment for melanoma in early stages (stage I, no spread) has been the "watch and wait" approach. The melanoma is removed, and the patient is monitored

chemotherapy The use of chemical substances or drugs to treat a disease, usually used in reference to cancer treatment.

for several years. Patients with more advanced melanomas often have lymph nodes sampled and removed to prevent further spread. This more extensive surgery was deemed unnecessary for patients in very early-stage disease. However, a 2005 study has shown that even patients with no obvious spread of their cancer benefit from having lymph nodes sampled and removed if they contain cancer cells. Patients who had the procedure, called a sentinel lymph node mapping and biopsy, were 26% less likely to have their cancer return within 5 years than patients who only had the tumor removed. See FIGURE 20-9 ▲ for the possible causes and warning signs of cancer.

TABLE 20-3 ■ SUMMARY OF AMERICAN CANCER SOCIETY RECOMMENDATIONS FOR EARLY DETECTION OF CANCER IN ASYMPTOMATIC PEOPLE

SITE	RECOMMENDATION
Breast	Annual mammography for women over 40
	Annual breast exam
	Monthly self-breast examination
Colon and rectum	Beginning at age 50:
	Fecal occult blood test every year or
	Flexible sigmoidoscopy every 5 years or
	Annual fecal occult blood test and flexible sigmoidoscopy every 5 years
	A double contrast barium enema every 5 to 10 years
	A colonoscopy every 10 years
	Combined testing is preferred over annual tests every 5 years; people at moderate or high risk should talk with doctor about a different testing schedule
Prostate	Prostate-specific antigen test and digital rectal exam should be offered annually beginning at age 50; men at risk should start testing at age 45
Uterus	Cervix: All women should start getting regular Pap tests at age 21 or within 3 years of the first time having sexual intercourse.
	Endometrium: all women should be informed about the risks and symptoms of endometrial cancer
Cancer-related checkup	A cancer-related check up is recommended every 3 years for people aged 20 to 39 years and every year for people 40 and older; exam should include health counseling and, depending on a person's age, examinations for cancers of the thyroid, oral cavity, skin, lymph nodes, testes, and ovaries, as well as for some nonmalignant diseases

Source: American Cancer Society

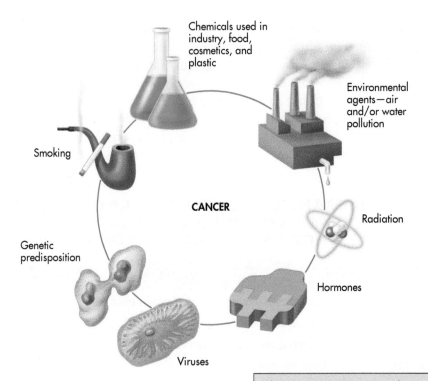

Chemicals used in industry, food, cosmetics, and plastic

Environmental agents—air and/or water pollution

Smoking

CANCER

Radiation

Genetic predisposition

Hormones

Viruses

FIGURE 20-9 ▲ Possible causes and warning signs of cancer.

The American Cancer Society lists several signs of cancer, the first letter of each word spelling the acronym,

CAUTION.

Change in bowel or bladder habits
A sore that does not heal
Unusual bleeding or discharge
Thickening or lump in breast or elsewhere
Indigestion or difficulty in swallowing
Obvious change in wart or mole
Nagging cough or hoarseness

TEST YOUR KNOWLEDGE 20-3

Choose the best answer:

1. This vitamin is needed for proper blood clotting:
   a. A
   b. B
   c. C
   d. K

2. The abuse of this substance can have side effects such as facial hair and deeper voices in women, kidney and liver damage, and aggressive behavior.
   a. antidepressants
   b. aspirin
   c. anabolic steroids
   d. chocolate

3. The _____ eye chart is used to determine normal vision.
   a. Snellen
   b. Seymour
   c. See Clear
   d. Optical

4. The guidelines that help prevent the spread of disease by contact with body fluids are the:
   a. Barrier reef
   b. Splash guard
   c. Standard Precautions
   d. Body shield

MORE AMAZING FACTS

Remember those amazing facts we promised you at the beginning of the chapter? True to our word, here is a list of a few to amaze your friends and family.

- Senior citizens are more prone to food poisoning not only because of decreases in their senses of smell and taste but also because their digestive juices are not as acidic as they used to be and so cannot always efficiently destroy all of the food-borne pathogens they ingest.
- Nerve impulses can travel up to 426 feet per second!
- Approximately 450,000 people die in the United States annually because of smoking-related diseases. That is about equivalent to a jumbo jet full of passengers crashing *each day with no survivors.*
- On average, a healthy kidney filters about 180 quarts of fluid every day. What makes this amazing is that the kidney is only about 4 inches long, 2 inches wide, and 1 inch thick!
- Hair grows about a quarter inch each month and grows faster during the day than at night. Hair also grows faster in the summer than in the winter.
- You use a little over a half pint of oxygen each minute when you are at rest.
- Everyone has one nare (nostril) that is larger than the other. If you don't believe it, take a look at people next time you go out to the mall or out to eat.
- Talk about a busy worker! Your heart beats over 36 million times a year!
- You possess over 16,000 miles of capillaries!
- Because viruses are continuously mutating, your immunity to influenza will not last a lifetime.
- More hair facts! You have from 110,000 to 150,000 hairs just on your head! Each strand of hair can support approximately 100 grams of weight, so, at least in theory, a full head of hair could support the weight of two African elephants!
- Research appears to indicate that vitamins and minerals from natural food sources are better utilized than synthetic pills. But the pills are better than nothing!
- The horns of a bull are composed of the same material that makes up your fingernails and toenails.
- You have about a quarter million sweat glands on your feet.
- Based on current research of fibroblasts' doubling ability before they can no longer accurately divide, human bodies have the *potential* to live to 120 years of age.
- Your eyes can see approximately 7 million shades of color.
- The ability to roll your tongue into a tube is inherited; not everyone can do it (or cares to do it).
- Cavities and poor oral hygiene can lead to diabetes and heart attacks. In fact some health experts believe that daily flossing can add 6.4 years to your life! That's because bacteria that grows in the mouth of an individual with poor oral hygiene can escape into the bloodstream and travel throughout the body, causing problems. As a result, in worst-case scenarios, that individual may be at a 4 times greater risk for stroke and at a 14 times greater risk for heart attack. The risk for diabetes is also increased.
- Current research indicates that stomach cancer, which affects 24,000 Americans annually, may originate from bone marrow cells that enter the stomach to repair damage to the stomach lining.
- Walking uphill or downhill may make a difference in your desired health outcomes. A recent study showed that individuals who walked uphill cleared fats (especially triglycerides) from their blood faster, whereas downhill hiking reduced blood sugars more readily and improved glucose tolerance. Hiking either way removed LDL, or bad cholesterol. This information may be applicable for exercise regimens for diabetics who may have trouble with aerobic exercises.

anhidrosis *(AN hy DROH sis)* A genetic- or disease-related condition of diminished or complete absence of sweat. It can be temporary or permanent, depending on the causative agent.

- CIPA (congenital insensitivity to pain with **anhidrosis**) is a rare genetic disorder that affects the development of the small nerve fibers that transmit the sensations of pain, heat, and cold to the brain. There are only 17 cases known in the United States. Patients with this untreatable condition receive bruises without knowing they are hurt. Because these patients can't sense extreme cold or heat, they don't sweat! Biting through their tongue while eating is a distinct possibility.

SOME THINGS TO PONDER AND SOME THINGS TO KEEP YOU UP AT NIGHT

We hope you enjoyed your journey through our book and that you learned a thing or two! As with any textbook, it is virtually impossible to put everything you want in a book of a given size. Not only that, but with the speed of technologic advancements, what the author or authors consider "the latest" may be old news by the time you, the student, read it in your textbooks. So here are a few things that are developing as we put this book to bed. Some are amusing, some a little scary.

- New research may shed light on the purpose of the appendix! It may be the producer and storage area for the good bacteria your GI tract needs for the proper digestion of food. If a situation occurs where your normal digestive tract bacteria die out or are greatly reduced (such as from amoebic dysentery or cholera), the appendix can "reseed" the GI tract with the normal flora that you previously had!

- Lung cancer, one of our deadliest cancers, can exist and metastasize in a patient for years before it is detected. Patient screening using computed tomography appears to find lung cancer at early, more treatable stages. Does this increase the survivability rate in these patients? Will this become a standard screening routine for patients believed at risk? Time will tell.

- Global warming with brain-eating amoebas! The *Naegleria fowleri* amoeba thrives in the bottom sediment of warm, slow-moving waters such as lakes, hot springs, and in rare cases, swimming pools. If water containing this amoeba gets splashed up an individual's nose, the amoeba can attach to the olfactory nerve and eat its way up to the brain, with almost always fatal results. The initial symptoms are headache, stiff neck, and fever that can be attributed to an incredible number of health conditions. Later stages include hallucinations and changes in behavior. The complete clinical scenario from initial exposure to death normally occurs within 2 weeks.

nitric oxide Gaseous substance present in the body that causes vasodilation.

- A recent problem has been uncovered by doctors that relates to the increased incidence of heart attacks and strokes in people who have received blood transfusions. It appears that stored blood loses a valuable component called **nitric oxide** even after the first day of storage. Nitric oxide is important because it causes blood vessel walls to relax and open up, allowing an easier flow of red blood cells, which carry oxygen, to the body's tissues. Current research indicates that adding nitric oxide to stored blood before transfusing it will once again allow the opening up of blood vessels for more effective oxygen delivery and, thus, a decrease in heart attacks and strokes.

- Think that all hunger impulses and cravings are in your head? A small study has found that certain individuals who crave chocolate daily have different bacteria in their GI tract than others! When measuring metabolic by-products in the blood and urine of the chocolate cravers, higher levels of the amino acid glycine and lower levels of the "bad" cholesterol, LDL were found. This may open up new areas of research where cravings for various foods dictated by the gut and different bacteria may affect weight loss outcomes in patients.

SUMMARY

Snapshots from the Journey

- Forensic science is the application of science to crime. Natural sciences (including anatomy, physiology, and pathology) and social sciences are used when solving crimes.

- Forensic science has been used to solve not only current mysteries but ancient mysteries as well.

- The uniqueness of fingerprints was written about as early as the 1600s.

- DNA fingerprinting is a form of identifying individuals from small samples of body fluids or tissues.

- The geriatric population is the fastest-growing population in the United States.

- The hallmark sign of aging is the decreased ability to maintain homeostasis.

- Our bodies don't age evenly, and certain systems age more rapidly than others.

- The loss of mental capacities is not directly related to aging until around age 75, when it is still minimal unless disease is present.

- Due to changes in the gastrointestinal, renal, and hepatic systems, geriatric patients respond differently to many medications.

- Polypharmacy is the use of many drugs at the same time and often is the result of seeing many specialists at the same time.

- The most important personal choice you will make is a healthy lifestyle.

- To maintain a healthy lifestyle, it is important to eat properly, exercise, manage stress, and avoid bad habits.

- Some cancers, such as skin and lung cancer, can be highly preventable. Limiting the amount and intensity of sunlight exposure and not smoking are two ways that can help prevent cancer.

RAY AND MARIA'S STORY

Now that we have followed Ray, a quadriplegic, and Maria, a diabetic's, trials and tribulations throughout this text, let's think about the systemic problems that may befall them as they age.

a. What research can you find that may help or reverse their initial medical conditions (spinal cord injuries and diabetes) in the near future?

_____

_____

_____

_____

b. What can be done proactively to prevent some of the potential problems that come with aging, especially in their individual cases?

_____

_____

_____

REVIEW QUESTIONS

Multiple Choice

1. The pelvic angle of the female is:
   a. less than 90 degrees
   b. 90 degrees or greater
   c. 75 degrees
   d. greater than 180 degrees

2. From ages 20 to 70, there is up to a
   _____ % loss of lean body mass:
   a. 10
   b. 20
   c. 30
   d. 50

3. This vitamin is needed for strong bones and teeth and calcium absorption:
   a. A
   b. B
   c. C
   d. D

4. The overuse of this classification of drugs has caused drug-resistant strains of bacteria:
   a. steroids
   b. antibiotics
   c. diuretics
   d. pain killers

5. The congenital condition of spina bifida can be prevented by the addition of what vitamin during pregnancy?
   a. A
   b. folic acid
   c. niacin
   d. K

REVIEW QUESTIONS

Fill in the Blank

1. The new food pyramid takes into account your _____, _____, and _____ when determining the best diet for you.

2. The fat soluble vitamins are _____, _____, _____, and _____.

3. Cauliflower-like growths on the penis and vagina are _____.

4. The test for cervical cancer is called the _____.

Short Answer

1. Discuss various ways to prevent skin cancer.

_____

_____

_____

2. List and discuss way to prevent STDs.

_____

_____

_____

3. Discuss ways to protect yourself and your patient from the spread of infection.

_____

_____

_____

4. Discuss ways that forensic science can be used in solving crimes.

_____

_____

_____

REVIEW QUESTIONS

Suggested Activities

1. Discuss the various aging processes you have seen in your parents and grandparents.

2. Be old for a day by changing your senses. This can be experienced by covering your eyes or your glasses with clear plastic wrap. Wear thin cotton gloves or surgical gloves (if you are not allergic to latex). Gently plug your ears with cotton balls (not cotton swabs). During the next class period, discuss the difficulties you had doing simple, everyday activities.

3. List the foods you've eaten for 3 days. Share the list with your classmates and determine whether or not it is a healthy diet. Discuss ways to improve it.

4. Make poster presentations on one of the following topics or choose your own: STDs, passive smoking, hazards of smoking, healthy lifestyles, forensic science, aging process, proper diet, or healthy pregnancy.

ANATOMY, PHYSIOLOGY, AND DISEASE IN ACTION

Materials:
Simulation geriatric glasses
Blind fold
Cotton balls
Foam rubber
Knee braces
Gloves or mittens
Additional resource:
http://fcs.tamu.edu/families/aging/vision/index.php

Have students experience the infirmities of old age.

Sight: Wearing the goggles that simulate glaucoma, macular degeneration, cataracts, and blindness. Have students research the etiology of each condition and write of their experiences wearing the glasses when trying to read a book or walk around the room.

Hearing: (1) Students can place cotton in their ears and try to hear and interpret a conversation. Use students who have different frequencies to speak to the individual. Were some frequencies easier to hear? What are some of the methods used to compensate for hearing loss? (2) Have three students give different directions to another student. Have the student repeat the directions given.

Dexterity: (1) Have students put on gloves or mittens and try to tie their shoes and pick up small items such as paper clips. Explain any difficulties. (2) Tape two fingers together to represent stiffened joints and try to repeat the above processes.

Mobility and Balance: (1) Tape foam rubber to one shoe and have students walk the length of the room. (2) Wear an ace bandage or knee brace and have students get out of a chair with arms and walk the length of the room.

In all cases, have students write of the difficulties they experienced, feelings they might have had, and methods they might have used to compensate for their deficiencies. How can these disabling conditions be delayed in many of the aging?

Health Care:
Careers and Career Planning

When you consider an occupation in a health care field, it is important to focus on your interests, values, and abilities. When you understand yourself, it is easier to select the right occupation. There are many different career opportunities in the health care field. Researching several careers will help you choose the right career for you. Learning how to use the resources for researching occupations will make it easier for you to choose a career.

LEARNING OUTCOMES

Upon completion of your journey through this chapter, you will be able to:

- Identify Interests, Values, and Abilities
- Understand Health Care Education and Resources
- Discuss Jobs and Professions
- List and Describe Professional and Personal Characteristics
- Understand Ethical Roles and Responsibilities of a Health Care Worker
- Explore Job Seeking Skills, a Career Plan, and Volunteer Opportunities

INTERESTS

Your interests tell what you like to do and what you do not like to do. Recognizing your interests helps you make a good career choice. Do you prefer to problem solve as part of a team, or would you prefer to work on your own? For instance, if you like to work alone, a career in direct patient/client care probably is not right for you. Working in one of the computer areas might be better. When you know your interests early in your career search, you can identify careers that use those interests. If you discover that many of the tasks listed in an occupation are not interesting to you, reconsider your choice, and research careers that match your interests.

VALUES

A value is the importance that you place on various elements in your life. Money might be more important to you than leisure time. Working with people might be more important to you than what shift you work. Knowing what values you feel most strongly about helps you avoid compromising the things that are most important to you. Recognizing your values also helps you prioritize your work-related values, such as job security, leisure time, wages, recognition, creativity, advancement, working environment, home life, responsibility, and management. Ask yourself the following questions.

- **Job security.** Is it important that you find a job immediately upon the completion of your training program? How important is job availability?
- **Leisure time.** Is it important for you to have extra time for leisure activities?
- **Wages.** Is an average wage acceptable if you like your work, or is a very high wage necessary?
- **Recognition.** Is it important that the job you choose is respected by the people in your community?
- **Creativity.** Do you like to come up with new ideas to solve problems, or do you prefer a job in which there is exactly one way to do things?
- **Advancement.** Do you want a career that provides opportunities for promotion? Working environment. Do you prefer to work indoors or outdoors?
- **Home life.** Do you want to work a daytime schedule (9 to 5) with some overtime and with weekends and holidays off, or are you willing to do shift work (all hours, any day of the week)?
- **Responsibility.** Do you want a job that requires you to make a number of decisions?
- **Management.** Do you want to be responsible for supervising the work of other people or for organizing many tasks at once?

All of these factors affect your job choice. Make a list of these work values and put them in order of their importance to you. When you research an occupation, refer to your list so you do not choose a job that conflicts with many of your values.

ABILITIES

An ability is something you do well. You have many abilities. For example, you may work well with your hands, or you may be very good at mathematics. It is much more pleasant to work in an occupation that uses your abilities. If you choose an occupation that is too far below your ability level, you will be bored. If it is too far above your ability level, you will be frustrated. It is important to evaluate your abilities during your career search. List your abilities, and use the list when researching an occupation. Match your abilities to the job description.

HEALTH CARE EDUCATION

When you have decided to become a health care professional, it is important to choose a quality health care education program that fits your interests. Technical, community, or four-year colleges in your area may have accredited health care programs. These programs offer a variety of degrees, including:

- **Certification**, where a person is certified as being able to competently complete a job, usually by the passing of an examination.
- **Associates degree**, usually awarded after completion of a two-year program.
- **Bachelor's degree**, usually awarded after completion of a four-year program.
- **Master's degree**, a post-graduate degree awarded after completion of a one- to six-year program.
- **Doctoral degree**, the highest certificate of membership in the academic community.

Visit the Web sites of these schools, to see which program is most appealing to you. Visit each college and talk to students before you enroll. You may also want to talk to health professionals in local clinics or hospitals, to see where they received their education.

After enrolling in a health care program, be sure to work hard at your studies. Health care information can be complicated and detailed. It is important for you to learn all procedures correctly, so you can pro- vide the best treatment to patients.

Health care procedures and knowledge change all the time. Even after you are employed as a health care professional, it is important for you to continue your education. Take any training sessions that are provided by your health care facility. Read professional journals to learn about new health breakthroughs. Discuss procedures with other health care professionals in your facility, to make sure you are all providing the most up-to-date treatment. Continuing education credits, or CEUs, are required for maintenance of certification or advancement in many positions. This is to insure that health care professionals stay current on developments in their fields in order to provide the best patient care.

RESOURCES FOR OCCUPATIONAL RESEARCH

There are many resources you can use in your research. Two of them are the *Dictionary of Occupational Titles* (http://www.occupationalinfo.org/), which lists job titles, tasks, and duties for 20,000 occupations, and the *Occupational Outlook Handbook* (http://www.bls.gov/oco/), which discusses the nature of the work, employment outlook, training and qualification requirements, earnings, and working conditions for a variety of occupations. *Work Briefs* by Science Research Associates, the Career Exploratory Kit, the *Encyclopedia of Careers*, and computer programs are also good resources. In addition, check career-related pamphlets, microfilm, and videos. You can find all of these resources in libraries and career centers. Interview individuals who are already working in health care occupations, as well as looking at written materials.

By conducting occupational research, you learn about the tasks performed, the job outlook, the education required, the working environment, and many other things. It requires time and effort to research the occupations that interest you and to prepare for a specific career. If possible, find a mentor who performs this occupation. Spend time following them on the job site. Remember, your efforts allow you to find a job that gives you satisfaction.

JOBS AND PROFESSIONS

There are hundreds of job opportunities in the health care field. Population growth, the increase of middle-aged and elderly people, new medical technology, and the need for more rehabilitation and long-term care make a health care occupation a very good choice for the future. The focus on preventative medicine and health status maintenance has also promoted the use of a variety of health care workers with different educational backgrounds, skills, and licensing. Listed below are descriptions of some of health care careers.

AUDIOLOGIST

An audiologist is healthcare professional who specializes in the diagnosis and treatment of disorders of the auditory and vestibular system portions of the ear. Audiologists also screen newborns for hearing problems, conduct hearing tests for school children, and help certain industries design safety programs to help prevent hearing loss.

Audiologists must complete a doctoral degree (Au.D. or Ph.D.) in audiology from an accredited university graduate or professional and a license to practice.

ANESTHESIOLOGIST

An anesthesiologist is a doctor trained to administer anesthesia before surgery and other procedures. Anesthesia is used so that patients do not experience pain during surgery and other procedures.

Anesthesiologists must complete a four-year undergraduate college degree, including pre-medical requirements. After the undergraduate degree they must complete four years of medical school. Then they must complete an internship and three years of residency; however, they do get paid during residency.

BIOMEDICAL ENGINEER

A biomedical engineer uses a combination of biology, medicine, and engineering to help solve medical and health-related problems. Biomedical engineers design equipment and supplies, such as MRI machines and microscopes to use in surgery; they develop prostheses; and they evaluate the use of artificial organs. Biomedical engineers must be scientific, technical, and be able to pay close attention to detail. Most biomedical engineers are employed in medical equipment and supplies manufacturing.

You will need at least a four-year degree in order to become a biomedical engineer. Some schools offer undergraduate degrees in biomedical engineering. Most biomedical engineer's hold advanced degrees in this area.

CARDIOLOGIST

Cardiologists are medical doctors who diagnose, treat, and try to prevent problems in the cardiovascular system. The cardiovascular system includes the heart and blood vessels. Patients are usually referred to a cardiologist by their primary care physicians. If a problem is suspected, the cardiologist checks the medical records, discusses signs and symptoms, conducts tests, and recommends a course of treatment. This may involve medication, lifestyle changes, or surgery. In the case of surgery, patients are sent to a cardiovascular surgeon.

Cardiologists typically work in clinics and hospitals. Some choose to specialize their practice, such as pediatric or adult cardiology. To become a cardiologist, you must graduate from college and then medical school. You must complete a residency and become certified in internal medicine. Then, you must complete another residency and become certified in cardiology. Further specialization requires another residency and certification.

CARDIOPULMONARY TECHNICIAN

A cardiopulmonary technician, also called a perfusionist, is someone who operates a heart-and-lung machine. This life-supporting equipment replaces the function of the heart and lungs when they must be temporarily stopped, such as during cardiac surgery. Cardiopulmonary technicians must pay extremely close attention to detail. They must notice even the slightest change in heart or lung function during surgery, as any change could indicate a problem.

Cardiopulmonary technicians may work for hospitals, surgeons, or in a group practice. Some are independent contractors who work for one or more different employers. There are several different routes to this profession. In general, though, you must have a four-year college degree with an emphasis on medical terminology, respiratory therapy, or nursing. You must then complete a training program that can last anywhere from one to four years. This will result in either a certificate or a master's degree, depending upon the type of program completed. Finally, you pass a test to become certified by the American Board of Cardiovascular Perfusion.

CHIROPRACTOR

Chiropractors treat patients with musculoskeletal system problems and the effects these problems may have on the patient's general health. Most chiropractors focus on the spine, using natural, nonsurgical manipulations to realign the spine. Chiropractors may recognize that other factors—such as diet, stress, and exercise—may affect a patient's general health and encourage patients to keep their lifestyles in check.

Chiropractors must complete two to four years of undergraduate education and a four-year chiropractic college course, and pass and state examinations.

CLINICAL LABORATORY TECHNOLOGISTS AND TECHNICIANS

These are the people who examine and analyze body fluids, and they play an important role in detection, diagnosis, and treatment of disease. These technologists and technicians prepare specimens for examinations; look for abnormal cells in blood and body fluids; and look for bacteria, parasites, and other microorganisms. They use microscopes, cell counters, and other sophisticated equipment. Most jobs are in hospitals.

Clinical laboratory technologists usually have a bachelor's degree with a major in medical technology or in one of the life sciences; clinical laboratory technicians generally need either an associate degree or a certificate.

DENTAL HYGIENIST

Dental hygienists remove soft and hard deposits from teeth, teach patients how to practice good oral hygiene, and provide other preventive dental care. They examine patients' teeth and gums, recording the presence of diseases or abnormalities.

Dental hygienists must graduate from an accredited dental hygienist program in a two-year community college, a four-year bachelor's degree program, or a five-year master's degree program. They must pass written and clinical exams and be licensed in the state of employment.

DENTIST

A dentist is a healthcare professional who specializes in the diagnosis, prevention, and treatment of diseases of the teeth and gums. Other oral health professionals include dental hygienists, dental assistants, and dental technicians.

Dentists must complete at least four years of postgraduate study and have two years of clinical experience working with patients.

DIALYSIS TECHNICIAN

A dialysis technician is the primary caregiver for patients who are undergoing dialysis, which is a process through which waste products are filtered from the blood when the kidneys are not functioning properly. Although the dialysis technician performs the actual dialysis treatment, a nurse is responsible for overall patient care.

The dialysis technician works under the supervision of that nurse. On-the-job duties include assembling supplies, preparing the machine for use, obtaining patient vital signs, administering local anesthetics and drugs under supervision, and closely monitoring the patient before, during, and after dialysis treatment.

Dialysis technicians work in hospitals, out-patient facilities, and home dialysis programs. To become a dialysis technician, you must have a high school diploma. A dialysis technician may be trained on the job, through an employer-sponsored training program, or at a vocational school or community college.

DIAGNOSTIC SERVICES

Diagnostic service workers help with the diagnosis of illness and disease. Some diagnostic service workers have direct contact with the patient/client, whereas others do not. They plan services and prepare and perform tests accurately. They also understand quality control and report results in a timely manner.

DIETARY AIDE

A dietary aide prepares and delivers food trays to patients in hospitals or facilities such as nursing homes. Duties may include: reading menu cards to determine which items to place on a tray; placing items on trays; helping the cook prepare food items; preparing foods for soft or liquid diets; pushing a food cart; serving meals to patients; collecting dirty dishes; washing dishes; and recording the amount and type of special foods served to patients. To become a dietary aide, you must have a high school diploma.

DIETICIAN

Dieticians plan food and nutrition programs that help treat or prevent disease. They are often part of a medical team in a hospital, private practice, or other health care facility. Dieticians promote healthy eating habits, evaluate clients' diets, and suggest modifications. Some dieticians specialize in the management of overweight or critically ill patients.

Because they help identify and treat health ailments, a detailed knowledge of growth and development, metabolism, and biochemistry of nutrients and food components is required.

To become a registered dietician, you must have at least a bachelor's degree in nutrition or dietetics and complete a six- to twelve-month internship at a health care facility, food service company, or nonprofit agency. You must also pass an exam given by the Commission on Dietetic Registration.

DERMATOLOGIST

A dermatologist is a physician trained to treat conditions and diseases of the skin, hair, and nails. This may involve skin allergies, cancer, melanomas, moles, acne, or even some sexually transmitted diseases. Dermatologists must be able to perform various types of dermatologic surgery and be able to analyze and interpret cultures. They must also have a broad base of knowledge that includes things such as allergies and immunology, environmental and industrial medicine, radiology, microbiology, and surgery.

To become a dermatologist, you must complete college and medical school. Following medical school, all dermatologists must complete one year of clinical training. Next, they spend three to four years as a resident specializing in dermatology. Those who choose to specialize must train for one more year in that area.

ECG/EKG TECHNICIAN

ECG/EKG technicians perform tests, such as electrocardiograms (ECGs/EKGs) and stress tests, that help physicians diagnose and treat problems with the heart and blood vessels. These tests record and monitor the electrical impulses transmitted by the heart. Tracking these impulses can identify any irregularities and potential problems. ECG/EKG technicians work in hospitals and physicians' offices. Community colleges and vocational/technical schools offer training in this area, but most ECG/EKG technicians are trained on the job by an EKG supervisor or a cardiologist. Not all ECG/EKG technicians are certified, but there is a growing trend in that direction.

ECHOCARDIOGRAM TECHNICIAN

Echocardiogram technicians use ultrasound equipment to perform specialized tests called echocardiograms. During these tests, high-frequency sounds waves are transmitted into the heart chambers, valves, and blood vessels to create an image. The technician checks the image on screen for any abnormalities, photographs or videotapes the image, and sends the images and a report to the patient's physician for evaluation.

Nearly three-fourths of all echocardiogram technicians work in cardiology departments in hospitals. Others are employed in physicians' offices or diagnostic laboratories. Although some are trained on the job, most have completed a two- or four-year program in this specialty. Professional certification is available.

ENDOCRINOLOGIST

An endocrinologist is a physician who specializes in the endocrine system. These doctors treat conditions that affect your glands. This may include diabetes, thyroid diseases, metabolic disorders, osteoporosis, hypertension, lack of growth, infertility, or cancer.

Endocrinologists treat these hormone problems and try to restore a normal balance of hormones in their patients. Endocrinologists also do research to learn how glands work and to find the best treatments for patients with glandular problems.

Like many other specialties, to become an endocrinologist you must first complete medical school and then complete a two- to three-year residency to become certified in internal medicine. Following that, you must then spend two or three more years studying the endocrine system. It takes more than 10 years to become trained as an endocrinologist.

EMT (EMERGENCY MEDICAL TECHNICIAN)

EMTs are providers of pre-hospital medical care in an emergency. A heart attack, unscheduled birth, automobile accident, or near drowning all require immediate attention. The EMT administers basic life support and transports sick and injured people to medical facilities. EMT workers have many career opportunities and may work in rescue, police, and fire departments, ski patrols, hospital emergency departments, and private ambulance services.

Training to be an EMT occurs at the community college level. There are various levels of EMTs. The level of expertise wanted will determine the amount of training needed.

EPIDEMIOLOGIST

Epidemiologists study the occurrence and frequency of disease in large populations and determine the source and cause of infectious disease epidemics. For example, epidemiologists might study childhood obesity, avian influenza, or AIDS.

Most epidemiologists are physicians and work in the community, universities, hospitals, and government agencies such as the Centers for Disease Control.

FAMILY PRACTITIONER

A family practitioner is a doctor who provides primary care, which includes preventative care, diagnosis and treatment of illness, and health education. For many people, the family practitioner is the first point of contact for people seeking health care. The family practitioner will refer patients to a specialist as needed.

A family practitioner must complete four years of undergraduate school, four years of medical school, and three to eight years of internship and residency, depending on the specialty selected. All states require licensing. They must also complete a postgraduate year of training, more commonly called a rotating internship.

FORENSIC SCIENTIST

Forensic scientists help solve crimes by collecting and analyzing physical evidence and other facts found at the scene of the crime. They analyze evidence such as fingerprints, blood, semen, firearms, and saliva. They may also reconstruct skeletal bones. Very often forensic scientists need to testify in court to help prove a person's guilt or innocence in a crime.

To become a forensic scientist, you must complete a four-year degree in physics, biology, microbiology, chemistry, medical technology, or genetics.

GASTROENTEROLOGIST

A gastroenterologist is a physician who specializes in the digestive system. A gastroenterologist treats diseases of the gastrointestinal tract, which includes the esophagus, stomach, small intestine, colon and rectum, pancreas, gallbladder, bile ducts, and liver. A gastroenterologist treats conditions including colon polyps, cancer, hepatitis, gastroesophageal reflux (heartburn), and irritable bowel syndrome.

Gastroenterologists are trained in endoscopy, which is the use of narrow, lighted tubes with built-in cameras. By utilizing these instruments, one can see the inside of the intestinal tract.

To become a gastroenterologist, you must complete medical school followed by a three-year residency in internal medicine. Then you must complete additional specialized training in gastroenterology, which lasts two to three years.

GENE THERAPIST

A gene therapist treats disease by replacing, altering, or supplementing a gene that is absent or abnormal and whose absence or abnormality is responsible for the disease. Gene therapists may use DNA, the genetic material itself, as the means of the treatment.

You must have a graduate degree, such as a Master of Science in Human Genetics or a Ph.D. in Genetics and Complex Diseases, in order to become a gene therapist. Some undergraduate programs are available, including a Bachelor of Science in Genomics and Molecular Genetics, which prepares students for graduate study or entry-level research positions.

GYNECOLOGIST

Gynecologists are physicians who specialize in the female organs and reproductive system. They manage hormonal disorders, treat infections, perform routine pap smears, diagnose cancers of the reproductive system, and perform operations such as hysterectomies. Much of a gynecologists work is to perform routine check-ups so that serious problems do not occur. Some gynecologists specialize in a specific area such as critical care medicine, gynecologic oncology, or reproductive endocrinology.

To become a gynecologist, you must graduate from college and medical school. You must then complete a four-year gynecology residency and two years of clinical practice. One to three additional years of training is required if you decide to pursue a specialty area. All gynecologists must pass an exam to become certified before practicing medicine.

HEMATOLOGIST

A hematologist is a physician that specializes in the study of blood, blood-forming organs, and the treatment and prevention of blood diseases. Hematologists may also run hematology laboratories.

A hematologist must complete four years of undergraduate school, four years of medical school, and three to eight years of internship and residency. All states require licensing.

HEPATOLOGIST

A hepatologist is a physician who specializes in treatment of the liver. As a hepatologist, you might deal with hepatitis, cirrhosis, genetic or metabolic liver diseases, liver cancer, liver transplants, or metabolic or immunologic issues related to the liver. To become a hepatologist, you must first be trained as a gastroenterologist.

To become a certified gastroenterologist, you must complete college, medical school, a three-year residency in internal medicine, and a two- to three-year fellowship in gastroenterology. To become a hepatologist, you must complete another one-year fellowship in which you will receive both clinical and research training specific to hepatology. Once this training is complete, you must pass an exam to become certified in this field.

IMMUNOLOGIST

An immunologist is someone who studies and/or treats the immune system. An immunologist may be a research scientist who works in a laboratory. The scientist investigates the components needed for a healthy immune system or the diseases that disrupt the immune system.

An immunologist can also be a doctor who treats people with immune system disorders including allergies or autoimmune disease. Some immunologists perform both duties and combine research with patient care.

Immunologists who conduct independent research usually have an advanced degree such as a Ph.D. or MD, although some jobs only require a master's degree. Training must include a combination of course- work, laboratory research, and a thesis or dissertation, followed by two to four years in a postdoctoral training fellowship. Physicians who work as immunologists typically go to medical school, complete a residency in internal medicine, pediatrics, or a medicine-pediatrics program, and then spend more two years specializing in allergies/immunology.

INTERNIST

An internist is a physician who may provide either primary or long-term comprehensive care. They also may specialize in fields such as cardiology, critical care, infectious disease, or pulmonology. Internists, as the name implies, focus on the health of internal organs. They generally treat illnesses such as high blood pressure or diabetes, which do not require surgery. The majority of an internist's patients are adults.

Internists must complete medical school followed by a three-year residency in which they receive training focused on internal medicine. In order to specialize in a particular area, internists must complete another one to three years of training. Between 20% and 25% of all physicians are internists.

LICENSED PRACTICAL AND LICENSED VOCATIONAL NURSE

A licensed practical nurse (LPN), or licensed vocational nurse (LVN) as they are called in Texas and California, provides basic bedside care for patients. Responsibilities are limited as all duties are conducted under the direct supervision of a physician or registered nurse.

A common task for a LPN/LVN is to take a patient's vital signs, which includes temperature, blood pressure, pulse, and respiration. LPN/LVNs also give injections and enemas, monitor catheters, collect samples, and conduct routine laboratory tests. LPN/LVNs also apply dressings, treat bedsores, and give alcohol rubs and massages. They observe patients and report any adverse reactions to medications or treatment. They also help patients with personal hygiene and ensure that patients are comfortable.

People wishing to become a LPN/LVN can attend a one-year program at a vocational or technical school. They then must pass a licensing examination regulated by the state. Many LPN/LVNs work in hospitals and nursing-care facilities. Others work in physicians' offices, outpatient-care facilities, or for pubic healthcare agencies.

MEDICAL DOCTOR (MD)

A medical doctor (MD) is a licensed physician who is responsible for comprehensive patient care. An MD promotes, maintains health, and treats both injuries and disease. Duties include, but are not limited to: examining patients; obtaining medical histories; ordering, performing, and interpreting diagnostic tests; counseling patients on health-related issues; and prescribing medicines. Many physicians with an MD go on to specialize in other areas.

In general, MDs complete four years of undergraduate school, four years of medical school, and three to eight years of internship and residency, depending upon the specialty pursued. All candidates must also pass a licensing exam, and they must continue to study throughout their careers to keep up with advances in medical technology.

MIDWIFE

Midwives are trained medical professionals who care for and support women throughout normal pregnancies. This care extends from the onset of pregnancy to just after delivery. Midwives stress communication with the mother and provide individualized health care information, emotional and social support, and continuous hands-on assistance during labor and delivery. If any problems arise, the midwife does not deliver the baby but calls for an obstetrician.

There are two types of midwives in the United States: direct-entry midwives and nurse-midwives. Direct-entry midwives are not nurses. However, they have at least a bachelor's degree, have completed specific health science courses, have graduated from an accredited midwifery education program, and have passed a national exam to become a certified midwife. Nurse-midwives are registered nurses who have completed an accredited midwifery program and passed an exam to become certified in this area.

NEPHROLOGIST

A nephrologist, also called a renal physician, is someone who specializes in the treatment of patients with kidney diseases. This includes patients with diabetes, polycystic kidney disease, and chronic kidney failure. Many patients must receive dialysis therapy and some will require kidney transplants.

Nephrologists are trained in internal medicine. They do not perform surgery. However, they may do a kidney biopsy in order to obtain a sample of kidney tissue. Their goal is to find ways to preserve patients' remaining kidney function. To become a nephrologist, you must graduate from medical school, complete an internal medicine residency program, and complete a two- to three-year fellowship in nephrology. You must also take an exam to become certified in this field.

NEUROLOGIST

A neurologist is a physician who specializes in nervous system disorders. This includes diseases of the brain, spinal cord, nerves, muscles, and the blood vessels that relate to these structures. Neurologists examine the nerves of the head or neck and test muscle strength and movement. They see how well you move and balance. They test your reflexes. They also examine your sense of sensation, your memory, speech, language, and other cognitive abilities. They do many tests to complete these assessments, including CAT scans, MRIs, and spinal taps.

To become a neurologist, you must complete medical school followed by a one-year internship. At least eight months of that internship must be spent in internal medicine. Then, you must complete a three-year residency in neurology and pass an exam to become a certified neurologist. If you choose to pursue a specialty area, such as child neurology, clinical neurophysiology, or pain medicine, you must complete one to three years of additional training.

NURSING ASSISTANT

Nursing assistants (NAs) work under the direct supervision of a nurse. They have extensive daily contact with patients and are the caregivers who help patients perform day-to-day tasks such as bathing, feeding, and dressing. They help patients walk and go to the bathroom. They transport patients, take vital signs, make beds, and set up equipment. NAs assist patients with activities of daily living and works as part of a collaborative team in the delivery of health care. Because of the physical requirements of the jobs, good physical conditioning is a plus.

NAs work in hospitals, physicians' offices, home health agencies, nursing homes, private homes, and mental health institutions. To become a NA, you need at least a high school diploma followed by 120 hours of training. Some employers offer on-site training. Courses are also offered through high school allied health science programs and community and state colleges. Once training is complete, the NA may have the opportunity to be certified as a nursing assistant.

NURSE PRACTITIONER

A nurse practitioner (NP) is a registered nurse who has received additional education and clinical training in the diagnosis and treatment of illness. Most NPs have completed a two- or three-year master's degree program. Some have a doctorate degree in their specialty. These specialties include acute care; adult or family health; gerontology health; neonatal health; oncology; pediatric/child health; psychiatric/mental health; and women's health. NPs may further specialize in everything from allergy and immunology to urology.

Nurse practitioners work in a variety of settings. They can be found everywhere from clinics, hospitals, and private practices to nursing homes, schools, and public health departments. On the job, they order, perform, and interpret diagnostic tests, diagnose and treat common acute illnesses and injuries, prescribe medications and therapies, perform procedures, and educate patients and their families on living a healthy lifestyle.

OBSTETRICIAN

An obstetrician is a physician who cares for women throughout childbirth. Some of their patients are women who are having complications during pregnancy. Obstetricians closely monitor the mother's health and diagnose any abnormalities or health issues in the developing fetus. If an issue does arise, the obstetrician may refer the mother to a specialist for treatment.

Many doctors who become obstetricians also train as gynecologists. To become an obstetrician, you must complete college and medical school. You must also complete a four-year residency specializing in obstetrics and gynecology and two more years of clinical practice. One to three more years of training is required for those who pursue an area of specialization. All obstetricians must also pass a national examination to become certified to practice in this field.

OCCUPATIONAL THERAPIST

An occupational therapist works with disabled people to help them maximize their abilities to perform the tasks of daily life. These therapists serve people who have mentally, physically, developmentally, or emotionally disabling conditions. OTs help their patients improve their basic motor functions, or, in cases where there is a permanent loss of function, they help the patient physically compensate for that loss.

Occupational therapists must complete a master's degree in occupational therapy, have 6 months of supervised fieldwork, and pass national and State examinations. Occupational therapists must be licensed.

ONCOLOGIST

An oncologist is a physician who diagnosis and treats cancer. Oncologists typically specialize in a particular form or cancer. Oncologists work closely with pathologists to assess the biological nature of the tumor being treated. Treatments include chemotherapy and radiotherapy, or surgery to remove the entire tumor.

Oncologists must complete four years of undergraduate school, four years of medical school, and three to eight years of internship and residency, depending upon the specialty pursued. All candidates must also pass a licensing exam, and they must continue to study throughout their careers to keep up with advances in medical technology.

OPTHALMOLOGIST

An opthalmologist is a medical doctor who specializes in the eye and the visual system. Their job is to diagnose and treat eye disease. They also treat eye injuries. This may entail routine eye exams, diagnosis and treatment of eye disorders or diseases, prescribing eyeglasses or contact lenses, surgery, or managing problems caused by systemic illness.

To become an opthalmologist, you must complete college and medical school. That is followed by a one-year clinical internship and at least three years as a hospital resident in opthalmology. To specialize in a specific area, such as a disease, an eye part, or pediatrics, you must complete one or two years of addition- al training. Once training is complete, opthalmologists must pass an exam to become certified in this profession.

OPTOMETRIST

Optometrists provide vision care by examining the eyes for diseases such as glaucoma, nearsightedness and farsightedness, and depth and color perception. Optometrists prescribe eyeglasses and contact lenses. Optometrists do not perform surgery.

Optometrist must complete a four-year program at an accredited optometry school, preceded by at least three years of pre-optometric study at an accredited college or university. All states require optometrists to be licensed.

ORTHOPEDIST

An orthopedist, also called an orthopedic surgeon, is a physician who specializes in treating disorders of the musculoskeletal system. The musculoskeletal system is comprised of bones, joints, muscles, tendons, ligaments, nerves, skin, and any of the structures related to these body parts. Orthopedists use casts to repair broken bones, prescribe exercise and medication for musculoskeletal injury or disease, and perform surgeries such as implanting artificial joints or reconstructing damaged limbs. Although historically orthopedists primarily worked with children, modern orthopedists have patients of all ages. Some orthopedists specialize in one area, such as sports injuries, but most treat a wide variety of conditions.

To become an orthopedist, you must first become a physician. That means four years of medical school and passing an exam to get a medical license. Then, you must complete one year of general surgery training followed by four years of orthopedic surgery training and two years in clinical practice. At this point, you must take an exam to become certified. Another year of training is needed to practice in a subspecialty area such as pediatric orthopedics or orthopedic sports medicine. Once certified, orthopedic surgeons must continue to take medical courses to keep their knowledge and skills up to date.

OTOLARYNGOLOGIST

An otolaryngologist, also called an ENT (for "ear, nose, and throat" specialist), is a doctor who specializes in the diagnosis and treatment of ear, nose, throat, head, and neck disorders.

Otolaryngologists must complete four years of undergraduate school, four years of medical school, and at least five years of surgical residency training, including one year in general surgical training and four years in otolaryngology and in head and neck surgery. All otolaryngologist must be licensed in the state in which they practice.

OTOLOGIST

An otologist, also known as a neurotologist, is a physician who specializes in conditions affecting the ears. These conditions include problems with balance and dizziness, all types of hearing loss, noises in the ear, facial nerve disorders, persistent infections, congenital malformations of the ear, and tumors of the ear. Trained as a surgeon, an otologist performs surgical procedures such as the repair of eardrum perforations, hearing reconstruction, and tumor removal.

To become an otologist, you must attend medical school and then become a trained otorhinolaryngologist. Then to specialize as an otologist, you must complete another residency in that area. All otologists must pass an exam in order to become board certified before practicing medicine.

PATHOLOGIST

A pathologist is a doctor who diagnosis disease through the study of organs, tissues, cells, and bodily fluids. Pathologists take tissue samples, called biopsies, and other specimens for analysis. Pathologists don't actually see patients directly, but work with other doctors as consultants. For example, pathologists work closely with oncologists sample and analyze tumors. Pathologists may also conduct autopsies to determine cause of death.

Pathologist must complete four years of undergraduate school, four years of medical school, and three to eight years of internship and residency. All candidates must also be licensed in the state that they practice.

PEDIATRICIAN

Pediatricians study and treat the care and health of infants, children, teenagers, and young adults. Like other doctors a pediatrician is a licensed physician who is responsible for comprehensive patient care. Pediatrician promotes, maintains health, and treats both injuries and disease.

Pediatricians must complete four years of undergraduate school, four years of medical school, and three to eight years of internship and residency. All candidates must also pass a licensing exam, and they must continue to study throughout their careers to keep up with advances in medical technology.

PHARMACY TECHNICIAN

Pharmacy technicians work with licensed Pharmacists to provide medication to patients. Pharmacy technicians have many administrative responsibilities, such as filing, helping customers, answering the phones, stocking the shelves. They may also be responsible for counting tablets and labeling bottles. Technicians who are employed in retail may also work the cash register. Technicians employed in a hospital, may also be responsible for reading the patient's chart and preparing the medication, which would then be checked by the pharmacist. The pharmacy technician always refers any questions or problems to the pharmacist.

Currently, there are few State and no Federal requirements for formal training or certification. Most training is done on-the-job.

PLASTIC SURGEON

A plastic surgeon is a doctor who uses surgical techniques to correct or enhance the look or function of a person's body. Plastic surgery is used for reconstructive surgery, such as breast reconstruction for women who have had mastectomies, correction of congenital abnormalities, such as cleft palates and cleft palates, and skin grafts for burn victims. The term "cosmetic surgery" is typically used when the procedure is done strictly for cosmetic reasons.

Surgeons are required to complete four years of undergraduate school, four years of medical school, and three to eight years of internship and residency, depending on the specialty selected. All states require licensing.

PHARMACIST

A pharmacist prepares and dispenses medications prescribed by physicians, podiatrists, dentists, and other health care professionals. They provide information to health care professionals and to the public about medicines. Another important task is to review the medicines that patients/clients are taking. This reduces the chance that the patient/client will have a drug interaction that can cause illness or an allergic reaction.

A pharmacist must complete five years in an accredited pharmacy program, one year of pharmacy internship, and be licensed in state of employment.

PHYSICIAN'S ASSISTANT

A physician assistant practices medicine under the supervision of a physician or surgeon. Duties include, but are not limited to, providing preventive care services, diagnostic services, and therapeutic services as delegated by the physician. PAs may also be responsible for taking and maintaining the patient's medical history, ordering and reviewing laboratory tests and X-rays, and treating minor injuries.

Physician assistants programs usually last at least two years; physician assistants must complete an accredited education program and pass a national exam in order to obtain a license.

PHYSICAL THERAPIST

Physical therapists (PTs) work with accident victims and people who suffer from disabling conditions such as lower back pain, fractures, heart disease, and cerebral palsy. They help these patients restore function, improve mobility, relieve pain, and prevent or limit permanent physical disabilities. PTs test and measure everything from a patient's strength and range of motion to their balance and coordination. They develop individualized treatment plans that may include things such as electrical stimulation, hot packs and cold compresses, ultrasound, traction, or deep-tissue massage.

To become a physical therapist, you must graduate from an accredited physical therapy program. The minimum requirement is a B.S. degree. Many have a master's or doctoral degree.

PODIATRIST

Podiatrists diagnose and treat diseases and injuries of the foot including corns, calluses, bunions, skin and nail infections, and deformities. Podiatrists also create orthotics, which are corrective shoe inserts. Problems with the feet may indicate more a more serious condition, such as arthritis, diabetes, or a heart condition.

Podiatrists must complete three to four years of undergraduate education, a four-year podiatric college program, and passing scores on national and state examinations. All podiatrists need to be licensed.

PROCTOLOGIST

A proctologist, also referred to as a colorectal surgeon, is a doctor who specializes in diseases of the colon, rectum, and anus. A proctologist diagnosis and treats a variety of conditions, including cancers of the colon and rectum, severe constipation, and hemorrhoids. Proctologists often work closely with urologists, doctors of the urogenital tract in males and urinary tract of women.

Proctologists must complete four years of undergraduate school, four years of medical school, and three to eight years of internship and residency. All candidates must also pass a licensing exam, and they must continue to study throughout their careers to keep up with advances in medical technology.

PSYCHIATRIST

A psychiatrist is a doctor who specializes in the diagnosis and treatment of mental illness. Mental health problems may be treated with non-medical treatments (such as psychotherapy and psychoanalysis) in which the doctor helps the patient work through their problems. If necessary, medication is used to correct chemical imbal-ances. Hospitalization may also be required.

A psychiatrist must complete four years of undergraduate school, four years of medical school, and three to eight years of internship and residency, depending on the specialty selected. All states require licensing.

PSYCHOLOGIST

Psychologists study human behavior and the human mind. There are many different fields of psychology including clinical, educational, and research. The majority of psychologists are clinical psychologists. They provide mental and emotional health care for people in crisis. Clinical psychologists are typically not allowed to prescribe medication. They can consult with a physiatrist when treatment requires medication. Other types of psychologists include school psychologists, who work with students, teachers, and families, and counseling psychologists.

A psychologist must complete a master's or doctoral degree, and a license is required. To have an independent practice, a doctoral degree is required.

PULMONOLOGIST

Pulmonologists are physicians who are specially trained to treat diseases and conditions of the chest. These conditions, which affect the lungs and bronchial tubes, include such things as pneumonia, asthma, tuberculosis, and emphysema. Pulmonologists do not perform major surgical procedures, but they do often obtain samples from the lining of a lung or the chest wall for diagnostic testing.

Pulmonology is a subspecialty of internal medicine. This means that in order to become a pulmonologist, you must first become certified in internal medicine. It takes at least seven years to accomplish this. Once this is completed, you must continue your studies for two or three more years focusing on conditions specifically related to the respiratory system.

RADIOLOGIST

A radiologist is a doctor who uses medical imaging techniques to diagnosis and treat disease. A variety of tools are used, including X-rays; fluoroscopy, which provides real-time images of the internal organs; magnetic resonance imaging (MRI); and ultrasound. The radiologic technologist (see below) is typically the person who acquires the images and then the radiologist analysis and evaluates the images.

A radiologist must graduate from an accredited medical school, be licensed to practice medicine in the state of employment, complete three years of special training in radiology, and be recognized and by the board and by the Council on Medical Education and Hospitals of the American Medical Association.

RADIOLOGIC TECHNICIAN/TECHNOLOGIST

Radiologic technicians operate X-ray equipment to take pictures of the internal parts of the body. The X- rays provide information for the diagnosis and treatment of patients. For example, X-rays of the chest help detect lung diseases such as lung cancer and tuberculosis. Some of the diseases or injuries that X-rays help diagnose or treat include ulcers, blood clots, cancer, and fractures. The use of imaging techniques like ultra- sound and magnetic resonance imaging (MRI) is growing. The term diagnostic imaging includes these procedures as well as X-ray techniques.

A radiologic technologist must graduation from an accredited program, have a bachelor's degree in radiologic technology, experience in two or more radiologic disciplines (such as nuclear medicine or radiation therapy), and be registered as a radiologic technologist through the American Registry of Radiologic Technologies (ARRT).

REGISTERED NURSE

Registered nurses (RNs) are involved in every aspect of patient care. Some RNs treat patients. They per- form diagnostic tests and analyze the results. They give treatment and medication, and they closely observe patients and record their progress as well as any reactions. Other medical professionals use this detailed record as a basis for proper patient care. RNs also help with patient follow-up and rehabilitation.

Some RNs work with the public rather than individual patients. They educate the public on warning signs and symptoms of various conditions and tell them where to get help. Some RNs run immunization clinics and blood drives. Some are trained in grief counseling. RNs account for the largest health-care occupation. Although they may work in a variety of settings, roughly three out of every five RNs works in a hospital.

To become an RN, one must graduate from an approved nursing program and pass a national licensing exam. There are three main ways to become an RN. One option is to get a Bachelor of Science degree in nursing (BSN) through a four-year program at a college or university. A second option is an associate's degree in nursing (ADN) through a two- or three-year program at a community or junior college.

The third option is to go through a three-year diploma program at a hospital. Advancement opportunities are usually broader for those who complete a BSN program. A master's degree is usually required to work in administration or teaching.

RESPIRATORY THERAPIST

Respiratory therapists work with patients who have breathing or other cardiopulmonary disorders. Working under the direction of a physician, these specialists evaluate, treat, and care for patients and are primarily responsible for all respiratory care therapeutic treatments and diagnostic procedures. They also supervise respiratory care technicians, who perform many of these same functions.

Many respiratory therapists work in hospitals. Some work for home health care agencies and travel to patients' homes. Many programs at colleges, universities, medical schools, and vocational/technical schools offer programs in respiratory therapy.

Some programs offer associate's degrees, which would prepare you for an entry-level position. Others offer bachelor's degrees, which would prepare you for an advanced position in this field. Graduates must then pass a test and become either a Registered Respiratory Therapist or a Certified Respiratory Therapist.

SURGEON

A surgeon is a medical doctor who performs surgery. Surgeons also correct physical deformities and repair bone and tissue after injuries. A patient must be under anesthesia before surgery is performed. Most surgeons specialize in a specific type of surgery, such as cardiovascular surgery, neurological surgery, orthopedic surgery, or plastic surgery.

Surgeons are required to complete four years of undergraduate school, four years of medical school, and three to eight years of internship and residency, depending on the specialty selected. All states require licensing.

SURGICAL TECHNOLOGIST

These are the people who help prepare the operating room before surgery. Surgical technologists set up the surgical instruments and equipment, sterile drapes, and sterile solutions. They assemble equipment, and check and adjust it to ensure that it is working properly during surgery.

In order to become a surgical technologist, you need an undergraduate degree in this area. You can also obtain certification in this field by attending a CAAHEP-accredited program and passing a national certification examination.

UROLOGIST

Urologists specialize in issues related to the male and female urinary tracts and the male reproductive organs. People see urologists for issues ranging from discomfort while urinating to male infertility. Urologists look for such things as signs of infection, blood in the urine, or excess sugars or protein, which could indicate diabetes or other kidney problems. Because urologists encounter such a wide variety of issues, they must have a broad knowledge of internal medicine, pediatrics, gynecology, and other specialties.

Urologists must graduate from medical school and then complete an accredited urology residency pro- gram. This program can last up to five years and involves a combination of surgical and clinical training.

Urologists can specialize in a variety of areas, including urologic oncology, male infertility, female urology, or pediatric urology. To practice as a pediatric urologist, one more year of training is required. All urologists must also pass an exam to become certified in this field.

VETERINARIAN

A veterinarian is a doctor for animals. Veterinarians take care of sick and injured animals; provide preventative services; perform surgery as needed; and provide offer all other diagnostic and treatment services for animals. Some veterinarians may focus on animal production practices to make sure that animal diseases are not spread to humans.

A veterinarian must completion of three–four years of pre-veterinary college, graduate from an accredited veterinary college, and receive a Doctor of Veterinary Medicine degree. Veterinarians must also be licensed in the state of employment.

PROFESSIONAL AND PERSONAL CHARACTERISTICS

Health care workers must maintain a professional appearance and practice professional behavior. They must also safeguard the confidentiality of patient information. You must keep in mind all of these standards of appearance and behavior as you become a health care worker.

STANDARDS OF APPEARANCE

A professional appearance makes a statement about your commitment to patient care. A well-groomed and well-dressed staff signals that everyone in the facility is interested in the welfare of the patient. A clean appearance reassures patients who may be anxious and sick that the staff is efficient, professional, and capable of providing necessary medical service. The following are recommendations for maintaining a well-groomed, professional appearance.

- Dress according to your facility's dress code. This usually means that clothes will be clean, neat, and in good repair. They should not be of extreme fashion.
- Wear your name badge every day, in view of patients/clients. People need to be able to relate to you, and to call you if they need you. It also helps them identify who is assisting them.
- Wear clean and appropriate shoes every day.
- Keep your hair clean.
- Follow rules of good hygiene:
  - Brush your teeth at least twice a day.
  - Floss daily.
  - Use mouthwash or breath mints.
  - Bathe daily.
  - Use unscented deodorant. Remember that odors can be offensive to patients that are ill and nauseated and some patients may be allergic to perfumes and scented deodorants.
  - Wear your hair up and off your collar. You do not want your hair to fall on a patient when working with them, nor do you want to block their view.

FEMALE

- Undergarments should match the body color, so as not to "show." When wearing a skirt, wear full-length hose without runs.
- Keep makeup conservative (e.g., no dark, heavy makeup).
- Keep jewelry to a minimum (e.g., watch, stud earrings, and a ring). Jewelry can cause injury to the patient and the professional (if the patient grabs on to it), as well as transmit germs. Body piercings do not indicate a professional appearance, and can cause infections.

- Do not use perfume or cologne, for the same reason as you would use unscented deodorant.
- Keep nails short, clean, and bare, or only use light-colored nail polish. Long nails can scratch a patient. Polish can cover up dirt and can chip and contaminate a patient's wound or dressing. No acrylic or artificial nails are allowed.

MALE

- Do not use cologne or strong aftershave, for the same reason as you would use unscented deodorant.
- Keep your beard or mustache neatly trimmed.
- Shave daily. No stubble!

STANDARDS OF BEHAVIOR

As a health care worker, you should always behave professionally. By practicing the following set of behaviors, you show respect for patients and your fellow health care workers.

- Maintain a calm, courteous manner.
- Listen carefully when patients or other health care workers are speaking with you.
- Monitor patients appropriately, in order to ensure their safety.
- Perform tasks efficiently and carefully.
- Do not gossip about patients or other health care workers.
- Do not use coarse or offensive language.
- Do not practice horseplay or other dangerous behaviors.
- Watch for hazardous situations and correct any hazards that you see.
- Follow all safety procedures that are required by your health care facility.

PERSONAL CHARACTERISTICS

In addition to professional behavior, health care workers who exhibit the following personal characteristics will be more involved and interested in the welfare of their patients and in being a critical part of the medical team.

- **Empathy:** being sensitive to and experiencing the feelings, thoughts, and experiences of another
- **Honesty:** being fair, truthful, and morally upright
- **Dependability:** being reliable or trustworthy
- **Willingness to learn:** having the openness to admit that you don't know the answer or that you can be helped to understand a situation more fully
- **Patience:** having the ability to put up with waiting, delay, or provocation without becoming annoyed or upset, or to act calmly when faced with difficulties
- **Acceptance of criticism:** having the ability to deal with disapproval or a suggestion that something can be improved
- **Enthusiasm:** showing excited interest in or eagerness to do something
- **Self-motivation:** being energetic, ambitious and able to get things done without being directed by others
- **Tact:** avoiding giving offense; having an intuitive sense of what is right or appropriate
- **Competence:** having the ability to do something well, measured against a standard, especially ability acquired through experience or training
- **Responsibility:** accountability; the state of being accountable to somebody or for something

- **Discretion:** showing tact; the good judgment and sensitivity needed to avoid embarrassing or upsetting others
- **Teamwork:** working cooperatively with other people, subordinating personal interests in order to achieve a common goal

COMMUNICATING IN THE WORKPLACE

Knowing how to use communication skills to manage workplace conflict will help you earn the respect of your supervisor and co-workers. It will make you a valuable member of your work team.

The steps for effective communication include:

- **Be clear.** Use words and body language that the other person can understand, and that send a clear message.
- **Be personal.** Address the other person by his or her name or title. Use "I" statements to show that you take responsibility for your role in the conflict.
- **Be positive.** State your message in positive terms directed at how to achieve your common goal.
- **Get to the point.** Explain why you feel or think this way.
- **Use active listening.** Be sure you hear the response.
- **Think before you respond.** Use critical thinking instead of emotions.
- **Recognize any potential communication barriers,** such as language barriers, cultural barriers, or value/belief barriers. Think about ways you can overcome these barriers—both when you listen and when you speak.

Good interpersonal relationships are fostered through positive attitudes toward each other. Interpersonal competency comes from being self-aware and using that self-awareness to relate to others. Respecting and valuing the input of your team members creates an environment in which each person gives individually to make a better whole. Practicing positive interactions encourages each team member to focus on team goals and quality outcomes.

DIFFERENT TYPES OF VERBAL COMMUNICATION

Just as you use different types of verbal communication when speaking to your friends and your parents, you use different types of verbal communication when speaking to people with whom you relate on the job, such as your boss, your co-workers, your customers, and your subordinates—the people you supervise.

- Your boss has a higher rank in the company than you do and has control over your job. When communicating with a boss, you usually use a formal style of verbal communication. You show deference—courteous regard or respect—by using his or her title and refraining from jokes or casual remarks you might use with a friend. You must also recognize that your boss has the final say on most matters, and so you must know when to agree with his or her decisions, even if you disagree with them personally.
- Your co-workers, or colleagues, have the same rank in the company that you do. This does not mean that you should joke around with them as you do with your friends. It also does not mean you should use the same style of verbal communication you would use with your boss. You can speak to them more casually.
- Your customers are the source of your business. When communicating with customers, remember the old saying, "the customer is always right." This means that in order to be successful, you must respect your customers and speak with them positively. You may also interact with "internal customers." If one department within a company

supplies another department with goods or services, then the department being supplied is the "internal customer." What would happen if customer expectations for good communication and service are unmet? How should you go about identifying customers?

- If you supervise others in the company, you communicate with them using the respect that is due to any worker. You can also use an assertive or positive style of verbal communication, so that they know exactly what is expected of them.

DIFFERENT TYPES OF NON-VERBAL COMMUNICATION

Non-verbal communication helps puts words into context. This includes sign language and body language. You can communicate everything you would with speech using sign language, without saying a word. This enables people with an inability to use their voices to communicate. Using sign language requires that all parties in the conversation know how to understand the various signs. This problem is often solved using sign language interpreters who sign as someone is speaking to deliver spoken messages to those who cannot hear them, and translate the signed communication for those who cannot understand sign language.

Body language includes facial expressions, posture, gestures, and tone. A smile indicates friendliness or happiness. Rolling your eyes or slouching shows disrespect. Crossed arms indicate defensiveness. Body language can be either positive or negative. It can show you are confident and prepared or that you are unsure or afraid.
Finally, one other way to communicate without speaking or writing is to use visual aids—pictures, graphs, charts, or anything without words that conveys your ideas. Visual aids can often deliver a clearer or more easily understood message than written or verbal communication.

Be cognizant of the non-verbal communications that you utilize both with patients and with colleagues. By using the above techniques, you can clearly demonstrate non-verbal communication in a clear, concise, and effective manner. This will help you in your overall communications as a health professional.

MAINTAINING CONFIDENTIALITY

Maintaining the confidentiality of medical records is critical. Medical records contain private information that must not be shared with people who are not involved in the patient's health care. If some private information gets into the wrong hands, it may be used to damage the patient's personal reputation or financial well-being.

Each patient signs a confidentiality form before receiving treatment. This form is a legally binding document that promises that the medical facility will protect patient information. Any health care worker who does not follow procedures to ensure patient confidentiality may be reprimanded.

As a health care worker, you should learn your health care facility's policies and procedures related to confidentiality. Carefully follow these procedures to protect patient privacy.

ETHICAL ROLES AND RESPONSIBILITIES OF A HEALTH CARE WORKER

Members of the health care team must be aware of their ethical roles and responsibilities. This awareness protects them, the patients, their co-workers, and the facility where they work. Ethical behavior ensures quality patient care, positive work relationships, and a well-managed workplace environment.

Ethics is a code of conduct representing ideal behavior for a group of people. A health care worker observes the following code of ethics.

RECOGNIZING AND REPORTING ILLEGAL AND UNETHICAL BEHAVIOR

Health care workers must be aware of their ethical responsibilities for the protection of their patients/clients, their co-workers, their employers, and themselves. One of a health care worker's main responsibilities is to recognize and report unsafe, illegal, or unethical behaviors occurring in their work environment. How can you recognize reportable incidents? A reportable incident is any event that can adversely affect the health, safety, or welfare of students, clients, or co-workers. There are countless ways someone's behavior can negatively affect the people in the hospital.

There is no set list of reportable behaviors. Rather, it is required and expected that every employee will:

* Obey the laws of the city, state, and federal government.
* Fulfill his or her job requirements to the best of his or her ability, including following a code of ethics and respecting others.
* Treat everyone in the hospital environment with care, dignity, and respect.

If you or anyone fails to fulfill these obligations, that behavior must be reported.

Reporting an illegal or unethical incident helps ensure the health, safety, and welfare of everyone in the hospital environment. If you even suspect an incident might be illegal or unethical, report it at once. Follow your employer's policy regarding how you report illegal and unethical incidents.

Your employee manual should explain clearly how you should report illegal and unethical conduct. In most cases, your manager should be able to help you report illegal and unethical behavior. If you have any doubt about how to report an incident, contact your human resources department.

MEETINGS IN THE WORKPLACE

Meetings are important in the workplace. There are different types of meetings: a team meeting for co-workers to communicate about team duties; a staff meeting for supervisors and managers to communicate information to a group about topics such as policies and schedules; a status meeting for team members to report on procedures, schedules, and so forth.

Meetings are a way for teams to communicate. Effective meetings requires specific leadership:

* **Set goals.** These goals are based on topics that need to be covered.
* **Schedule.** Set a time and location for the meeting. Be firm about attendance. Prepare an agenda to share objective(s) before, or at the start of, the meeting.
* **Maintain control.** Begin on time. Assign a note-taker. Introduce each topic, guiding the team to focus and make decisions. If something cannot be resolved, set a time to address the issue. In concluding, all attendees should be aware of resulting duties.
* **Follow up.** After the meeting, send a memo with a brief summary. List action steps and a timeline for the team to achieve required follow-up.

SAFETY IN THE WORKPLACE

In 1970, the federal government passed a law called the **Occupational Safety and Health Act**. This law requires all employers to provide a safe and healthful workplace. Workers must be provided with safe equipment, protective clothing when needed, and education about safety practices. **The Occupational Safety and Health Administration (OSHA)** was formed to inspect companies and enforce safety laws. Even so, more than 5,000 Americans die from on-the-job accidents every year. As a worker under the Occupational Safety and Health Act, you have the following rights and responsibilities:

- **Right to know.** You have the right to know about hazards in your workplace, as well as the right to training to learn how to identify workplace hazards and what to do if there is an incident.
- **Right to refuse unsafe work.** If you have reasonable grounds to believe the work you do or the piece of equipment you use is unsafe, you can stop work immediately. You cannot be laid off, suspended, or penalized for refusing unsafe work if you follow the proper procedures.
- **Responsibility to follow safety rules.** It is your employer's responsibility to teach you the safety rules; it is your responsibility to follow the rules.
- **Responsibility to ask for training.** If you feel that you need more training than your employer provides, it is your responsibility to ask for it.
- **Responsibility to speak up.** It is your responsibility to report incidents and unsafe work practices as well as unsafe conditions.

Part of your responsibility as a worker is to make sure that you keep your work environment safe for yourself and for others. You have to take some responsibility for your own safety. If you are a new worker, enroll in any safety classes offered by the company. If you work around chemicals, poisons, or dangerous machinery, ask how they can be handled safely. If a company offers you hard hats or other safety equipment, use them. Read your manuals and handbook, and don't take shortcuts if it means endangering your safety or the safety of customers or co-workers. Remember—failure to follow safety guidelines is cause for dis- missal. What are some of the safety issues you might encounter in a selected career?

JOB-SEEKING SKILLS

Before you apply the skills you have learned, you must find a job and be hired as an employee. It is important to learn the skills needed to find a job and to keep a job. These skills will enable you to practice the career you worked so hard to learn about.

DEVELOPING YOUR PORTFOLIO

As time approaches to begin your search for a job, review your portfolio notebook. Obtain a new cover and section dividers, so your finished portfolio has a clean, crisp look. A portfolio is a collection of materials that show the knowledge, abilities, skills, and insights you gain in your search for a career. The purpose in developing a portfolio is to show your mastery of vocational requirements to an employer, a college, or a higher-level training program. You also see your own growth and accomplishments over time. Identify the items that best reflect your knowledge level, skills, and personality. When you complete your résumé and other portfolio requirements, place them in the appropriate section of your new portfolio.

TABLE 1 Common Abbreviations

ABBREVIATION	MEANING
appl.	applicant
asst.	assistant
cert.	certified
exp.	experience
FT	full time
immed.	immediately
incl.	included
lic.	licensed
N.A.	nurse aide
PT	part time

PLACES TO SEEK EMPLOYMENT

There are many potential sources of job information. Some of them include the following:

- **Newspaper ads.** Jobs in health care careers appear in newspaper ads. When you look for a job in the newspaper, turn to the classified ads and look under "Help Wanted." Some papers list all health care positions under "Medical." Others list them under a particular job. You also need to become familiar with the abbreviations used by newspapers. Table 1 provides some of these.
- **Directly to the employer.** If you are looking for a position in a laboratory, you might apply directly to a medical laboratory. If you want to work in a hospital, you go to the Personnel department.
- **Friends and relatives.** You may know of someone working in the health care field who can suggest a place to apply or who can introduce you to a possible employer.
- **School counselors.** Many schools have career counselors and/or work experience counselors. They are a good resource for the types of jobs available in your community.
- **School bulletin boards.** If you have a career center or a bulletin board where jobs are listed, be sure to check it daily.
- **Employment agencies.** There are both public and private employment agencies. Employers call these agencies to list the job openings that they have. A public agency does not charge a fee; however, a private agency charges either the employer or the person seeking a position.
- **Internet.** If you have access to a computer that is connected to the Internet, go to Search and type in the words "*job search*" or "*job link*." You can find job referrals, workshops, placement activities, and tips on writing a resume or interviewing.

YOUR CAREER PLAN

A career plan is a strategy for a person's growth as a professional. Many employers require employees to create a career plan that shows how their career will change and grow over the next few years. The plan shows the responsibilities that the employee should take on and the skills he or she should learn to advance to the next stage of his or her career. Employees should review their career plan annually with a supervisor who can help adjust or revise the plan as needed.

During the annual review and evaluation conference, the employee and the employer will evaluate the employee's success at meeting the goals set up for the past term. If any problems are identified the employee should expect the scheduling of frequent sessions until any problems identified are corrected. This is a joint effort and should reflect the goal of the organization to provide quality care and support the employee's growth in the job role.

As you grow professionally, your career plan needs to be updated annually. With a supervisor or men- tor, review any professional development experiences you have had over the past year, and evaluate those experiences. Next, make a new set of learning goals for the coming year, and find concrete ways to achieve those learning goals. Discuss specific work opportunities that can help you learn and apply what you need to know.

CAREER SELF-ASSESSMENT

A career self-assessment is a process by which you learn more about your career-related skills, interests, values, and abilities. To perform a career self-assessment, you examine your strengths and weaknesses honestly and objectively.

CHANGING CAREERS

When you review your career plan, you might find that you are growing in a different direction than you expected. For example, you might discover that you really enjoyed training people in a new skill, and so make training and teaching a focus of your career.

People change careers for other reasons, too. For example:

- Some people get tired, and simply need a change.
- Some careers become out-dated, and replaced.
- Some people decide that they have a better chance of advancing professionally in another career.

If you decide you would like to change careers, use the same process to investigate your new career that you used to find your first one. You can research on your own, as well as seek the help of career counselors and career centers, such as those at colleges and universities.

REASONS TO GROW AS A PROFESSIONAL

Why should a health science professional always learn and grow? There are many reasons, such as:

- **Ethical behavior demands it.** If you are to provide the best, and most up-to-date service to your patients and clients, you need to learn the latest developments in your field. It would be unethical to offer out-dated, sub- standard care. In fact, many licensed professionals, such as doctors, nurses, and EMTs, must participate in a specific number of hours of continuing education each year to maintain their license.
- **Technology changes.** Technology in the health science industry changes rapidly. Diagnostic equipment that was unavailable a generation ago is part of routine medical care now. Computers and software programs continue to be more powerful and useful in all aspects of health care. Each of these changes in technology enables professionals to provide new services and better care to patients and clients, but only if professionals learn to use the technology effectively.
- **Client needs change.** The population you serve as a health science professional is dynamic. An increase in the number of older people means you need to learn more about the health care needs of seniors. If you are a nurse, and a new disease or pathogen emerges and affects your patients, you need to learn how to treat patients with the new disease as best you can.
- **Responsibilities increase.** You probably want to advance in your career. As you advance, you will have new responsibilities at every stage. You need new skills to manage these responsibilities. For example, your position might grow and you might need you to know how to make a budget. If you have never have made a budget before, you need to learn how to make one.
- **Become more flexible.** By learning skills outside your own job, you are able to help your coworkers when they need it. You may learn that you like your new skills enough to move your career in a new direction.

RESOURCES FOR PROFESSIONAL DEVELOPMENT

Where can you get professional development? There are many resources available for the professional development of people working in the health sciences:

- **Associations** Many professional associations provide meetings, courses, workshops, and other opportunities for professional development.

- **Employer training courses** Many employers offer training courses that help develop employees. Employer programs often include workshops to improve management and communication skills and courses to help employees use new equipment and software.
- **Colleges and Universities** Many colleges and universities offer classes that can help you learn more about your profession.
- **Journals** Professional journals help alert people to the latest developments in their fields.
- **Job Shadowing** Spending a period of time with a experienced worker, observing everything that he or she does that is related to the job responsibilities.

CAREER AND TECHNICAL STUDENT ORGANIZATIONS

Career and technical student organizations (CTSOs) are groups of students who are enrolled in a career and technical education program that engages in career and technical activities as part of the curriculum. There are different CTSOs for different career and technical programs; students join the organization related to the CTE program in which they are enrolled.

CTSOs provide members with a range of individual and group programs and activities. They promote career education and training and provide opportunities for leadership, teamwork, competition, and citizenship. CTSOs offer a unique program of career and leadership development, motivation, and recognition for students in grades 6 through 12.

Members benefit from:

- Belonging to a positive and supportive group of their peers
- Examining firsthand the relationship between academics and the world of work
- Identifying career opportunities
- Building confidence and knowledge through competition
- Exercising leadership and teamwork skills
- Practicing personal skills for success
- Developing employability skills
- Recognizing and developing interests and abilities that align with career goals

The National CTSOs supported by educators in most states include the following:

- Health Occupations Students of America (HOSA) for students in health services programs (www.hosa.org)
- SkillsUSA for students in technical, skills, and service programs (www.skillsusa.org)

VOLUNTEERING

Volunteering—in other words, doing work without pay—is a great way to contribute to the communities you care about and gain valuable work experience.

Many types of organizations welcome volunteers, including schools, environmental protection groups, social services organizations, and political action groups. All of these thrive on the work of many volunteers and are likely to have well-established programs set up that make it easy to contribute your time. Some organizations have restrictions on volunteer work because of insurance liability, laws, or medical privacy issues. For example, some medical facilities may require that everyone who provides care to patients be paid employees, so there may be limits on the things you can do for residents there. When you go through volunteer orientation/training at such facilities, the limits will be explained to you. Think of ways that you can get involved in your community.

SUGGESTED ACTIVITIES

1. When you want to achieve something quickly, you set short-term goals. Typically you need to accomplish your short-term goals before you accomplish long-term goals—something you want to achieve in the more distant future. Describe self-motivation techniques, and make a list of ways to pursue short-term and long-term goals.

2. Prepare a presentation on a career that interests you. Find out the educational requirements, job responsibilities, average starting salaries, and more. Present your findings to your class.

3. Take turns role playing a job interview with a classmate. Take turns being the interviewer and the interviewee. List specific examples of effective, clear, and concise verbal and non-verbal communication that occurred during the mock interviews.

4. Select and research a business in your community. If possible, obtain an application form from the business. Identify the different parts of the application, and practice completing the form.

5. Managing your time is a key skill. For a week, keep track of how you spend your time—how much time you spend socializing with friends, doing homework, spending time with your family, etc. Write a short paragraph on ways in which you can improve your time-management skills.

6. Select a professional journal and prepare a presentation describing the target audience for the journal, the content, and the format of the journal.

7. Attend a meeting in your community. Report to your class what you learned about meeting procedures and rules. Take turns role-playing meeting skills.

8. Working with a partner, brainstorm the roles and responsibilities of a manager or supervisor.

The Study Success Companion
The Key to Your Successful Journey

WHY USE THIS STUDY SUCCESS COMPANION?

On any journey, a well-written travel guide can make the experience positive, less stressful, and more productive. This is the main reason for including this guide along with your textbook.

Anatomy, physiology, and pathology can be tough topics to navigate, and it might feel like a very long and arduous journey. It is also a fascinating journey, though, for the human body is the vehicle in which we will all travel through life.

This guide provides effective study strategies, along with a simple and effective stress management system to help you through the rough parts of this journey and even throughout the rest of your life. In addition, this guide helps with "need to know" concepts such as the metric system that are usually not covered in an A&P/Pathology course due to time constraints. Knowing the metric system is critical because it is the mathematical language of anatomy and physiology and of medicine in general.

The *Study Success Companion* covers the following areas:

- Study Skills
- Stress Management
- The Metric System

"The difference between ordinary and extraordinary is that little extra."

Author unknown

STUDY SKILLS

Although you may have had courses on study skills, it can never hurt to review the fundamentals. We have chosen the top three general study skills we feel are critical, not just for this course, but for all the current and future courses you will ever take. And the top three choices are

1. Select a Good Time and Place to Study

As with any trip, there is *no* substitute for good planning and preparation. Successful preparation includes developing a daily schedule that includes proper study time. Don't be discouraged if your first few schedules don't work well; just make sure to build in some flexibility. Be sure to schedule relaxation and recreational time, as these are important. Studies show that you learn more in three 30-minute sessions than in one marathon 2-hour session. Therefore, studying notes over shorter periods of time at more frequent intervals is more effective than long cramming sessions. We suggest using 30 to 45 minutes as your *maximum* study time without a break. A good way to check if you are studying efficiently is to periodically ask yourself questions about what you have just read. If you can't answer these questions, you probably are losing interest and need to take a short break and become more focused.

The time of day you choose to study is very important. It may not be the same time for everyone. Some people are "morning people," and others are not. The message for now is to schedule study times when you are most alert and focused.

The place you choose to study is also very important. Ideally, it should be the same place each time so you "connect" this place to studying and consequently become focused. It should have minimal or no distractions and good lighting. The table or desk should have the needed study tools such as pen, paper, calculator, computer, etc.

Clinical Application

CLASSICAL CONDITIONING

Throughout the textbook you will notice instances of the mind–body connection. The psychological term classical conditioning illustrates this concept and actually has impact on study skills. The term came from an experiment performed on dogs by the Russian scientist Ivan Pavlov. In this experiment, a bell was rung, and dogs were then fed meat. The meat stimulated the dogs to salivate in anticipation of beginning the digestive process. Repeatedly, experimenters would ring a bell and feed the dogs. The dogs soon learned to connect the ringing of the bell to the arrival of meat. Eventually, the scientists only had to ring a bell, and the dogs would salivate like crazy, even if they didn't receive meat.

So what's the purpose of telling you this story other than making you hungry or grossing you out? When you study in bed and then go to sleep repeatedly, you soon connect studying to sleeping. Every time you begin to study (even in midafternoon), you may begin to yawn and feel unfocused. You are conditioning yourself to connect studying to sleeping. Simply avoid studying in bed because you will be less focused and therefore less effective. Besides, studying in bed may interfere with your ability to get a good night's sleep. Classical conditioning can also be used to your advantage in health care. Repeated, positive interactions and therapies with clients will "classically condition" them to feel good each time they see you.

TEST YOUR KNOWLEDGE 1

Assess your current place of study by answering the following questions. Be critical and honestly circle the response that best answers the question.

1. Do you have a dedicated study area?
   a. Sometimes
   b. Always
   c. Rarely

2. Is it quiet where you study?
   a. Sometimes
   b. Always
   c. Rarely

3. Are the conditions and lighting comfortable?
   a. Sometimes
   b. Always
   c. Rarely

4. Do you have all the tools (pencils, paper, electronic tools, etc.) you need to study at this place?
   a. Sometimes
   b. Always
   c. Rarely

How well did you do? For now, it doesn't matter as long as you were honest. Remember, this is an assessment of where you are now. Your eventual goal should be to have all your responses be "Always." If they are now—great! If not, you need to develop an action plan to make all the responses "Always" in the near future.

2. Use Good Study Habits

Take good, accurate, legible notes. Remember that the purpose of taking notes is to get key points from textbooks and lectures and not to write down every word that is said or written. Instead of highlighting the chapter, outline your chapters so you can make the connection from your brain to the pencil. This is what you'll need to do on the test. Outlining may *initially* take longer than highlighting, but you will learn the material better. Outlining will actually save you studying time in the long run. Review your lecture and outline notes frequently.

Also, make diagrams and pictures to help visualize concepts within your outline. The more you can "see it" the better you can understand relationships or how it all fits together.

Anatomy, physiology, and pathology are great subjects to study with a friend or study group. An excellent method to help truly learn the material is to explain concepts to each other. Each time you explain something, the oral recitation reinforces your understanding. *You'll soon learn that there is no better way to learn something than to teach it to someone else.*

Other good study habits include taking personal responsibility for your success. Go to class and read the assigned readings *prior* to class. This will also help you to begin to develop professional responsibility skills that are crucial in health care. Good study habits will greatly reduce the test anxiety you may feel because you will have properly prepared. However, it is normal to have some anxiety about taking an exam no matter how well you have prepared.

Here are some other hints on test taking that may help to further reduce the anxiety and increase your performance. Know what type of test you are taking. With an

APPLIED SCIENCE

How We Learn

A quick generalization of learning theory is as follows:

We learn:

10% of what we read
20% of what we hear
30% of what we see
50% of what we both see and hear
70% of what is discussed with others
80% of what we experience
95% of what we TEACH to someone else

Although some may argue the percentages, the general concepts are true to what the research on learning has shown. The more senses you can get involved in the learning process, the more internalized the learning becomes. Therefore, the text illustrations enhance the learning process. Lab experiences and interactive games and exercises will also increase learning. Group or study discussions are highly beneficial, and if you have to teach the group your concept, you will really learn what it is all about.

Clinical Application

AIDING YOUR MEMORY

To succeed, it is important to truly "learn" the material and use critical thinking and problem-solving skills. One who knows how to obtain information and understand it is much better off than someone who merely memorizes for short-term storage.

Say, for example, you memorize the steps to cardiopulmonary resuscitation (CPR) but you truly don't understand *why* you need to establish an open airway, or even *how* to actually do it. You may be able to repeat the steps on a pen-and-paper test and receive a good grade, but what if, in 6 months, you are in a situation where you need to perform CPR on an individual in need? You don't want to say, "I had that 6 months ago and I really didn't learn the material."

While the purpose of education is to encourage thinking skills rather than memorization, memory is vital. Memory is used as an index of success because most of the techniques used to measure learning rely on it. Therefore, a good memory is an asset that you should definitely develop. Try to memorize only when you are well rested, and use memorization techniques such as mnemonics. **Mnemonics** are words, rhymes, or formulas that aid your memory. Acronyms are one type of mnemonic. An **acronym** is a word made from the first letters of other words. For example, the ABCs of CPR remind you that **A** = establish **A**irway, **B** = rescue **B**reathing, and **C** = establish **C**irculation. This helps you to better remember the steps and their proper order in a critical situation.

You can also use rhymes or formulas to assist your memory. For example, "Spring forward, Fall back" helps us to adjust our clocks accordingly for Daylight Savings Time. You can also make up silly stories to help remember facts. In fact, the sillier the story, the easier it often is to remember.

mnemonics Anything intended to aid memory.

acronym Memory aid by using first letters of words to make a unique word.

objective exam (multiple choice, true/false) be sure you understand all directions first. With objective exams, usually your first idea about the answer is your best. If it is an essay exam (short answer), survey the questions, plan your time, and give time to questions in proportion to their value.

Some people develop their own test-taking strategies. For example, they may do all the easy questions first and then return to the more difficult ones. Make sure you mark the questions you skipped or you may forget to return to them. Finally, do not destroy your old exams—keep them and learn from them!

3. Take Care of Yourself

Learning requires a healthy mind, body, and attitude. It is important to exercise your brain to stay mentally fit, but it is also important to stay physically fit. A poor physical condition can distract the mind and minimize your mental focus. Eating right, exercising several times a week, and staying free of drugs will make you feel better and enhance your ability to learn. There may be times you must study when sick or tired. Begin these study sessions with slow rhythmic breathing. This can help you relax and, in turn, your concentration may improve. Remember to get sufficient rest, especially before exams. Learning to manage your stress level is so important to both your mental and physical fitness that the next section is devoted to this topic. Taking time for hobbies, music, or doing things you like to do is important to help refresh your mind.

TEST YOUR KNOWLEDGE 2

A portion of Chapter 19 is devoted to proper exercise, nutrition, and healthy living habits. Circle the answer to the following general questions and make an action plan for each "yes" answer.

1. Do you feel tired during the day when studying?
   a. Yes
   b. No

2. Do you feel stressed out when you start your study session?
   a. Yes
   b. No

3. Do you skip your exercise sessions during the week?
   a. Yes
   b. No

4. Do you eat a diet that is heavy in fats and "junk food"?
   a. Yes
   b. No

STRESS MANAGEMENT

Managing your stress is critical to your academic and personal success. Let's learn more about the concept of stress to better manage the stress in a positive manner.

Stress Misconceptions

The major misconception about stress is that all stress is bad for you. This is certainly not true. As you are reading this text, your body is probably in a room that is between 20 and 25 degrees Celsius. This may feel comfortable to you, but it is actually causing stress within your body. To survive, the body must react to this stress and make needed physiologic changes to maintain a core temperature of around 36 degrees Celsius, and therefore it is continually working at a level we are not consciously aware of to sense and adapt to an externally stressful environment. This response is vital and needed for our survival.

Here is another example of good stress: in Chapter 9, "The Nervous System" you learned about the sympathetic system and the fight-or-flight response. Picture for a moment the first time you are called on to do CPR on a cardiac arrest victim. This is going to be a stressful event in your life and may stimulate your sympathetic nervous system. Even though you practiced and trained hard, you are still uncertain of how it will be in a real life-and-death situation. This is normal. Your physical and psychological symptoms may include

- Increased adrenalin levels for more energy to perform better
- Faster heart rate (*tachycardia*) to supply more oxygen to muscles
- Increased blood pressure to get more blood flow to the brain
- Pupil dilation to bring in more light to see better
- Faster breathing (*tachypnea*) to bring in more oxygen
- Heightened state of awareness to focus on the job at hand
- Mild level of anxiety to keep you sharp and not take the situation too lightly

These can all be helpful reactions that enhance your performance. However, they can go too far and lead to a "bad stress" situation where you can't perform at your peak level. Therefore, you can have "good stress" and "bad stress." The key, again, is balance or moderation. A little stress will get you "up" for the task at hand. However, if you let stress get out of hand and panic, you have bad stress and your anxiety level rises to the point where you perform poorly or maybe even not at all.

What Causes Physical and Emotional Stress?

To be able to manage and harness stress to your advantage, you must first understand what stress is all about. First, it is important to realize that no situation or event by itself causes us stress. Rather, it is how we *perceive* a situation that causes stress. It is our learned, internal response to external stimuli.

For example, two individuals can volunteer to give blood. They will both undergo the same procedure with the same technician in the same environment. Yet one individual may not feel any stress or anxiety and the other may be highly stressed at the thought of giving blood. Stress occurs as a result of how we *interpret* and *react* to a situation or event. It can be either positive or negative, depending on our reaction.

Stress can have many definitions. For now, we will define the *stress reaction* as "how our mind and body react to an environment that is largely shaped by our perceptions of an event or situation." Notice the mind/body connection. Have you ever heard any of the following sayings?

I lost my breath.
My heart was pounding.
My stomach was twisted in knots.

Stress can also relate to time. We all have temporary stressors in our lives. However, when a stressor becomes constant and negative, it has serious effects upon our body and mind. Continual or constant negative stress can lead to:

- High blood pressure, heart attack, or stroke
- Stomach ulcers
- Lack of sleep, or insomnia
- Decreased immune system functioning
- Depression and personality changes
- Poor academic and job performance

However, good or positive stress can actually help us to perform better. Indeed, any time you try something new or meet a new challenge, stress can be a powerful friend. This is how we grow and develop. Continual uncontrolled negative stress will exact a price on our minds and bodies. So the key is learning how to maintain good stress in your life and avoid bad stress.

APPLIED SCIENCE

Test Yourself—How Many Stress Signals Do You Have?

How many of the following signals do you have on a regular basis (once every week or two)? If you checked two or fewer signals, you're doing pretty good and need minor improvement. Three or more means you need to work harder on how you're handling stress.

_____ Headaches
_____ Shortness of breath
_____ Fast or irregular pulse
_____ Nausea
_____ Insomnia
_____ Difficulty eating
_____ Sadness
_____ Chronic fatigue
_____ Irritability
_____ Diarrhea
_____ Feeling overwhelmed
_____ Difficulty concentrating
_____ Neck or back pain

Clinical Application

SADNESS VERSUS DEPRESSION

It's important to differentiate between depression and sadness. If someone is sad following a painful disappointment or the loss of a loved one, this is a normal part of the grieving process. However, if the sadness remains for a prolonged period of time and interferes with the ability to go about your daily business, it becomes depression.

A Stress Management System

The first step in treating a patient is good assessment. This is also the first step in a good personal stress management system. First, recognizing your own stressors and the symptoms they cause can help you determine when your stress is out of balance or, in other words, when you have entered your bad stress zone. These signals can be valuable to your good health and positive attitude. They represent a "wake up call" that says you need to cope with what's going on in your life before it overtakes you.

As already stated, a certain amount of stress is normal. We need it to develop and grow. This good stress can make you feel energized, focused, and "up" for the event: so you can ace your course exams, for example. However, going beyond your good stress zone and "losing it" by entering your bad stress zone can be harmful. You need to determine when you are losing balance. The best way is to look for physical and emotional signs or indicators that the stress is too much. See TABLE 1 ■ for some physical and emotional changes that signal too much stress.

Looking at the list of stress signs should paint a pretty good visual picture of what high levels of stress can cause. It's no wonder that individuals who can't handle stress have more accidents, have poorer attendance, and are unable to study and learn.

Effective Coping Strategies

Remember, the most important aspect of stress is that it is individually determined. Its meaning lies within us. Therefore, we are the ones to determine what is stressful and whether we are going to use stress to our advantage or let it use us. It should logically follow, if *we* determine the level of stress, *we* should be able to control it.

Someone once said you don't get ulcers from what you eat, but rather from what's eating you. It's important to cope with stress before you suffer from stress overload or burnout. There are two basic ways you can cope with stress. The first is to effectively cope with the emotional side of stress. The second way is to deal with its physical side. Keep in mind the key is to recognize when you are stressed out and intervene as early as possible.

TABLE 1 ■ PHYSICAL AND EMOTIONAL SIGNS OF STRESS

PHYSICAL CHANGES	EMOTIONAL CHANGES
Headaches	Lack of concentration
Shortness of breath	Irritability
Increased pulse rate (tachycardia)	Hopeless feelings
Nausea	Mood swings
Insomnia	Overreaction
Fatigue	Depression
Neck or back pain	Eating disorders
Dermatological problems (acne)	Anxiety
Chronic constipation/diarrhea	Low self-image

Effective Physical Strategies

You can't separate the mind and body. If we mentally feel bad, it affects our physical well-being. If we don't take care of our physical bodies, we lack energy and focus, can't sleep, and do not reach our full intellectual potential. Therefore, you must balance emotional and physical strategies. Indeed, you'll see that some of these techniques help both our physical and emotional health.

Let's discuss some of the major points you should consider in reducing physical stress. Handling stress "physically" can be broken down into the following four areas:

* Rest and leisure
* Exercise
* Nutrition
* Relaxation techniques

Rest and Leisure

Adequate sleep is a must for us to function at our peak and handle stress. Research has shown that lack of sleep (sleep deprivation) makes you more susceptible to illness. Of course, lack of sleep also makes you more irritable and less able to focus. Experts recommend that most adults get between 7 and 9 hours of sleep a night.

Clinical Application

PREVENTIVE MEDICINE AND EARLY INTERVENTION

In recent years preventive medicine has gained much focus versus the traditional disease model in which we *waited* until the individual got sick and then treated them. The signals in Table 1 are all late signals that mean you have been in your bad stress zone for quite some time. If you can pick up earlier signals and perform a healthy intervention, you can prevent many of these from happening. One hint is that nervous habits such as biting fingernails, pulling your hair, shaking your leg, clicking your pen, etc. are early signs you have just entered your bad stress zone. If you intervene then and there, you can prevent more serious problems. This awareness is often difficult because many of these habits are so automatic that we aren't aware of them. So, if you catch yourself shaking your leg and intervene, you can prevent the subsequent muscle tightness, upset stomach, and headache from occurring.

Taking leisure time for yourself can also help restore your ability to deal with stress. Even if that leisure time is only 15 minutes, it can help greatly. Sometimes the more you focus on a major problem, the more stress it causes. When this happens it is good to take a break and get away from the problem by doing something else. In many cases, the solution will then just come to you as if by magic. It's not magic, just your subconscious mind working for you.

Exercise

Physical exercise and sports are a great way to work off the tensions of everyday life. If done properly they help you to gain both a physical and mental focus. Any type of aerobic activity that gets your heart beating will exercise your muscles and relieve mental tension. Vigorous walking, jogging, running, bicycling, and lifting weights are all things you can do by yourself. Of course, you can find a good workout partner or play team sports also. Vigorous exercise also releases a group of hormones known as *endorphins.* These are our body's natural painkillers. They also are mood-elevating chemicals that give us a healthy, natural high.

Remember to properly warm up and stretch before any vigorous exercise. This not only helps prevent injuries, but stretching also helps to relieve muscular tension and lower blood pressure. Never rush through the stretches by bouncing or using fast, jerky movements that could strain or tear muscles. Stretch slowly until you feel mild tension and then hold the position for 10 to 30 seconds.

Nutrition

Good nutrition is a must for growth and development. It also aids in fighting off stress and disease. In addition, it is a good idea to drink plenty of water. Water makes up the majority of the body. Water aids in digestion, absorption of nutrients, and removal of waste products.

Cut down on caffeine, which is found in coffee, tea, and many sodas. Caffeine is a potent central nervous system stimulant. Large amounts can make you anxious, nervous, and unable to get a good night's sleep. Eating a well-balanced diet in moderation is important in maintaining nutritional health.

Relaxation Techniques

Practicing relaxation techniques will help to clear your mind and make you sharper. Most people will find a million excuses why they can't take the time to relax. Do you see the illogical thinking? If they are *that busy,* then they need to take the time to relax and restore the body and mind. This time also allows you to listen to your body. Two types of relaxation techniques that are very effective are breathing relaxation and meditation.

Slow, deep breathing serves several purposes. First, it increases oxygen to your brain and your body. It also slows down your thinking to help clear your head and relax your muscles.

Finally, don't forget to have a good laugh. Laughter helps bring you back in to perspective, and besides, it feels good. Laughter also helps you physically by lowering blood pressure, releasing endorphins, and stimulating the pleasure centers of the brain. TABLE 2 ■ lists some do's and don'ts to follow when stress is getting the better of you.

TABLE 2 ■ THE DO'S AND DON'TS OF STRESS MANAGEMENT

DO	DON'T
Appropriately confront a problem	Think it will resolve itself
Discuss calmly	Fight or yell
Exercise	Be a couch potato
Accept responsibility	Blame others
Use relaxation techniques	Use alcohol or drugs
Accept/learn from your mistakes	Be perfectionistic
Follow good nutrition	Over- or undereat
Be concerned and take action	Worry and do nothing
Live in the present	Agonize over past or future
Help others	Avoid people

THE MATHEMATICAL LANGUAGE OF MEDICINE
Why Learn the Metric System?

Whereas medical terminology represents the written and spoken language for understanding anatomy, physiology, and pathology, the metric system is the "mathematical language" of medicine. For example, blood pressure is measured in millimeters of mercury (mm Hg), and organ size is usually measured in centimeters (cm). Medications and fluids are given in milliliters (mL) or cubic centimeters (cc), and weight is often measured in kilograms (kg). What exactly does it mean when you are taught that normal cardiac output is 6 liters per minute? You can now see why one must be familiar with the metric system to truly understand A&P and medicine.

In addition, you must be able to perform calculations to properly treat patients. For example, a particular drug may be ordered to be given at 5 milligrams/kilogram of body weight. To find the right amount to administer, you must first be able to convert the patient's body weight in pounds to kilograms. Although it may seem complicated, it really isn't if you have a basic understanding of exponential powers of 10 and systems of measurement, particularly the metric system.

LEARNING HINT

Metric versus English

Try to visualize the physical comparison between the metric and English system. For example, a meter is a little more than a yard, and a liter is a little more than a quart. So a normal cardiac output of 6 liters per minute means that the heart is pumping out approximately 6 quarts of blood every minute.

Exponential Powers of 10

Understanding the powers of 10 gives us a thorough knowledge of the base on which the metric system is built.

To understand the powers of 10, we need to review some terminology. Consider the expression b^n, where *b* is called the *base* and *n* the *exponent*. The **n** represents the number of times that **b** is multiplied by itself. See FIGURE 1 ▲.

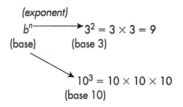

$$b^n \longrightarrow 3^2 = 3 \times 3 = 9$$

(exponent)

(base)   (base 3)

$$10^3 = 10 \times 10 \times 10$$

(base 10)

FIGURE 1 ▲ The Exponential Expression

If we use 10 as the base, we can develop an exponential representation of the powers of 10 as follows:

$10^0 = 1$ (mathematically, any number that has an exponent of $0 = 1$)

$10^1 = 10$

$10^2 = 10 \times 10 = 100$

$10^3 = 10 \times 10 \times 10 = 1,000$

$10^4 = 10 \times 10 \times 10 \times 10 = 10,000$

$10^5 = 10 \times 10 \times 10 \times 10 \times 10 = 100,000$

$10^6 = 10 \times 10 \times 10 \times 10 \times 10 \times 10 = 1,000,000$

Thus far, we have discussed positive exponents, which result in numbers equal to or greater than 1. However, numbers that are less than one can also be represented in exponential notation, using negative exponents. A negative exponent can be thought of as a fraction. For example,

$10^{-1} = 1/10 = .1$

$10^{-2} = 1/10 \times 1/10 = .01$

$10^{-3} = 1/10 \times 1/10 \times 1/10 = .001$

$10^{-4} = 1/10 \times 1/10 \times 1/10 \times 1/10 = .0001$

$10^{-5} = 1/10 \times 1/10 \times 1/10 \times 1/10 \times 1/10 = .00001$

$10^{-6} = 1/10 \times 1/10 \times 1/10 \times 1/10 \times 1/10 \times 1/10 = .000001$

Systems of Measurement

There are two major systems of measurement in our world today. The U.S. Customary System (USCS) is used in the United States and Myanmar (formerly Burma), and the System International (SI) is used everywhere else and especially in health care. The SI system is

APPLIED SCIENCE

Scientific Notation—This is Not the Scribblings of Albert Einstein

In medicine we often use extremely large numbers (for example, there are about 25,000,000,000 blood cells circulating in an adult's body) and extremely small numbers (for example, 0.0000005 meters is the size of some microscopic organisms). It is often useful to write these numbers in more convenient (or shorthand) form based on their power of 10. This abbreviated form is known as *scientific notation*. The basic rule is to move the decimal point to have one integer to the left of the decimal point and multiply by the appropriate power of 10 (the number of places you moved the decimal point). So 25,000,000,000 becomes 2.5×10^{10}. The number 0.0000005 would become 5.0×10^{-7}. Notice that because this number is less than one, the exponent must be a negative number. In simpler terms, movements of the decimal point to the right are negative values, and movements to the left are positive values.

APPLIED SCIENCE

The Apothecary System

The Apothecary System developed in the 1700s still has measurements used today. For example, the pint, quart, and gallon were derived from this system. Apothecary measurements for calculating liquid doses of drugs include the minim and fluid dram. Solids are measured in grams, scruples, drams, ounces, and pounds. Two unique features of the apothecary system are the use of Roman numerals and placement of the unit of measure before the Roman numeral. However, the metric system is now used to calculate drug dosages because the apothecary system is less precise.

also known as the International or **metric system.** The metric system is also the system used by drug manufacturers.

The USCS system is based on the British Imperial System and uses several different designations for the basic units of length, weight, and volume. We commonly call this the **English system.** For example, in the English system volumes can be expressed as ounces, pints, quarts, gallons, pecks, bushels, or cubic feet. Distance can be expressed in inches, feet, yards, and miles. Weights are measured in ounces, pounds, and tons. This may be the system you are most familiar with, but it is not the system of choice used throughout the world nor within the medical profession. The reason is the English system is very cumbersome to use because it has no common base. It is very difficult to know the relationship between each of these units because they are not based, in an orderly fashion, according to the powers of 10 as in the metric system. For example, how many pecks are in a gallon? Just what is a peck? How many inches are in a mile? These all require extensive calculations and memorization of certain equivalent values, whereas in the metric system you simply move the decimal point the appropriate power of 10.

Most scientific and medical measurements utilize what is commonly referred to as the metric system. The metric system utilizes three basic units of measure for lengths, volume, and mass and these are the *meter, liter,* and *gram,* respectively. Although the term *mass* is commonly used for weight, weight is actually the force exerted on a body by gravity. In space, or zero gravity, all objects have mass but are indeed weightless. Because current health care is confined to earthly gravitational forces, we will use the term *weight.* TABLE 3 ■ gives you the metric designation for the three basic units of measure, along with an approximate English system comparison.

Again, notice that there are only three basic types of measures (meter, liter, and gram), and the metric system has only one base unit per measure. Because the metric system is a

TABLE 3 ■ METRIC AND ENGLISH SYSTEM COMPARISON

TYPE	UNIT	ENGLISH SYSTEM COMPARISON (APPROXIMATE SIZE)
Length	Meter	Slightly more than a yard
Volume	Liter	Slightly more than 1 quart
Mass/weight	Gram	About 1/40 of an ounce

base 10 system, prefixes are used to indicate different powers of 10. Conversion within the metric system is done by simply moving the decimal point in the appropriate direction by the power of ten according to the prefix before the unit of measure. For example, the prefix kilo means 1,000× or 10^3. Therefore, one kilogram is equal to 1,000 grams. See TABLE 4 ■ for the common prefixes and their respective powers of 10.

It can be seen from Table 4 that a kilometer would be 1,000 or 10^3 meters. A centigram would be (.01) one-hundredth or 10^{-2} of a gram. Working with the metric system is easy because to change from one prefix to another you simply move the decimal point to the correct place. In other words, to convert within the system, simply move the decimal point for each power of 10 as indicated in the prefix.

TABLE 4 ■ COMMON PREFIXES OF THE METRIC SYSTEM

THOUSANDS	HUNDREDS	TENS	BASE UNITS	TENTH	HUNDREDTH	THOUSANDTH
kilo	hecto	deca	liter, meter, or gram	deci	centi	milli
(K)	(H)	(Da)	(l) (m) (g)	(d)	(c)	(m)
10^3	10^2	10^1	10^0 or 1	10^{-1}	10^{-2}	10^{-3}

Example Calculation 1

In drug dosage calculations you often need to convert between grams and milligrams and liters and milliliters. A common conversion requirement might be something like: 500 milliliters is equal to how many liters? We know from Table 2 that 500 milliliters (mL) would be equal to 0.5 liters because you would simply move the decimal point three spaces (powers of 10) to the left for the equivalent value because you are starting with milliliters and going to the base unit of liters.

LEARNING HINT

Metric Prefixes

Deci is associated with decade meaning 10 years; centi is associated with cents or a hundred cents in a dollar; and milli is associated with a millipede with a thousand legs. Biological note: A millipede doesn't actually have a thousand legs, it just looks like it.

Example Calculation 2

How many grams are equal to 50 kilograms? Start at kilograms on Table 4 and move to the unit you want to convert to, in this case grams. You would need to move the decimal point three places (powers of ten) to the right to give an equivalent answer of 50,000 grams.

This knowledge of the metric system will prove invaluable to you as you work within the medical profession and even if you travel outside the United States. That is, of course, unless you go to Myanmar.

One final note before leaving this part of the discussion on the metric system: It has been determined that one cubic centimeter (cc) would hold the approximate volume of one milliliter (ml). Therefore, 1 cc = 1 mL. See **FIGURE 2** ▲. You may hear someone say you have 500 cc of an intravenous (IV) solution on hand, whereas someone else may say you have 500 mL of solution; either way, they are both saying the same thing. Efforts are being made to standardize between cubic centimeters and milliliters, making milliliters the preferred choice. However, you will see and hear both used in health care settings.

You will also note in the health care setting that decimals are always preceded by a zero if they are less than one. For example, if you need one-half of a milligram, then it is written 0.5 mg. On the other hand, zeros are never used after whole numbers. For example, if you need five milligrams, then it is written 5 mg. This is part of the effort to reduce the number of medication errors.

Being able to convert temperatures from Fahrenheit to Celsius and from Celsius to Fahrenheit is another important conversion to know. Following is the formula to use.

Fahrenheit to Celsius
(F–32) × 5/9
Celsius to Fahrenheit
(C × 9/5) + 32

LEARNING HINT

Check Your Work

Always check your answer to see if it makes sense. For example, a common mistake is moving the decimal point in the wrong direction. If you had done that in example calculation 1, you may have erroneously said that 500 milliliters is equal to 500,000 liters. If you visualize this, you would know that 500 comparatively very small units (milliliters) in no way can equal 500,000 comparatively larger units (liters).

FIGURE 2 ▲ 1 cc = 1 mL

TEST YOUR KNOWLEDGE 3

Choose the best answer:

1. The metric system is based on the exponential power of:
   a. 100
   b. 10
   c. 2
   d. 15

2. Which of the following is *not* a basic unit of measure in the metric system?
   a. liter
   b. gram
   c. pound
   d. meter

Complete the following:

3. A cubic centimeter (cc) is equal to:

4. 500 grams is equal to how many kilograms?

5. 200 meters is equal to how many centimeters?

Conversion of Units

You should now be able to work comfortably within the metric system, but what if you need to take an English unit and convert it to a metric unit? For example, in the introduction of this Study Success Guide, we said that a certain drug order read to give a patient 5 milligrams per kilogram of body weight. You would need to know the relationship between pounds in the English system and kilograms in the metric system to properly treat this patient.

The following is a method for changing units or converting between the English and metric system. This method is sometimes referred to as the *Factor-Label Method* or *Fraction Method.* This method allows your starting units to cancel or divide out until you reach your desired unit. There are two basic steps:

Step One: Write down your starting value with units over one. This places it in the form of a fraction, but because the number one is in the denominator, it does not change the numerical value.

Step Two: Place the starting unit in the denominator of the next fraction to divide or cancel out and place the desired unit in the numerator along with the corresponding equivalent values. Because the values are equivalent, this is the same as multiplication by 1, which does not change the value of the quantity. This allows you to treat the units as in the multiplication of fractions and "cancel" the units. Notice that by carefully placing the units so that canceling is possible, the units can be converted.

The following problem shows an example of this conversion.

Example Calculation 3

How many inches are there in one mile?

First, put down what value is given as a fraction over 1.

$$\frac{1\ \text{mile}}{1}$$

Next, put miles in the denominator and the desired unit in the numerator with equivalent values. You know that 1 mile = 5,280 feet so:

$$1\ \cancel{\text{mile}} \times \frac{5{,}280\ \text{ft}}{1\ \cancel{\text{mile}}}$$

You've cancelled out miles, but need to go to inches. Just carry the process out until you reach your desired unit.

$$1\ \cancel{\text{mile}} \times \frac{5{,}280\ \cancel{\text{ft}}}{1\ \cancel{\text{mile}}} \times \frac{12\ \text{inches}}{1\ \cancel{\text{ft}}} = 63{,}360\ \text{inches}$$

Example Calculation 4

How many seconds are there in 8 hours?

Step One: $\dfrac{8\ \text{hours}}{1}$

Step Two: $\dfrac{8\ \cancel{\text{hours}}}{1} \times \dfrac{60\ \cancel{\text{minutes}}}{1\ \cancel{\text{hour}}} \times \dfrac{60\ \text{seconds}}{1\ \cancel{\text{minute}}} = \dfrac{28{,}800}{\text{seconds}}$

TEST YOUR KNOWLEDGE 4

Complete the following:

1. How many days in 3 years? _____

2. How many inches in 4.5 yards? _____

3. How many quarts in 10.5 gallons? _____

Clinical Application

BODY SURFACE AREA

A six-foot man who weighs 240 lbs. may require a different dosage than a six-foot man weighing 150 lbs. This is especially true with highly toxic agents such as those used in cancer chemotherapy. A method to determine the total body surface area (BSA) combines both height and weight in a single measurement to determine the true overall body size. Comparisons like this are called nomograms. See **FIGURE 3** ▲ for a nomogram used in determining BSA. Simply mark the patient's corresponding height and weight on the respective scale and either draw a straight line or use a ruler to find the intersection point to get the body surface area. Due to America's poor eating habits, the importance of BSA in relationship to the development of a form of diabetes is very important. Often that form of diabetes may improve with simple weight loss.

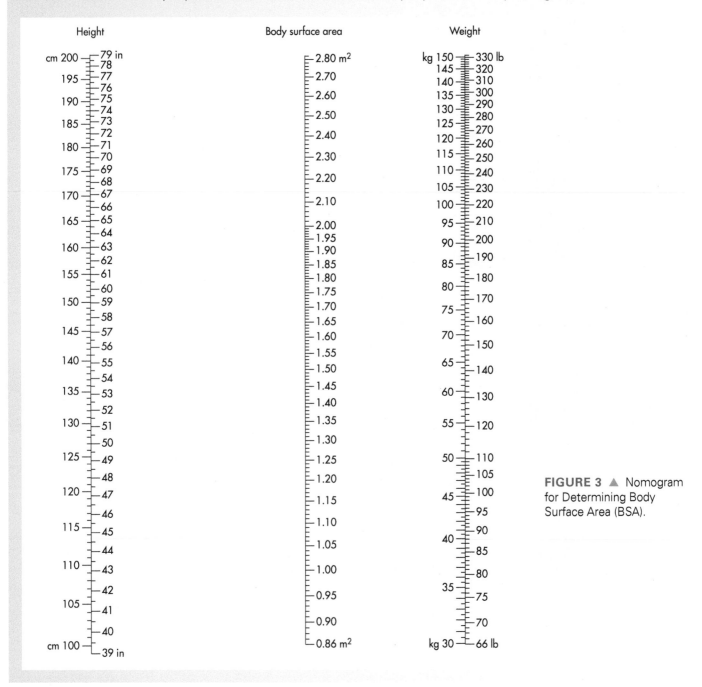

FIGURE 3 ▲ Nomogram for Determining Body Surface Area (BSA).

Using the Factor Label Method for Conversion Between Systems

One can attempt to memorize the hundreds of conversions between the English and metric systems, but that would be nearly impossible. All that is needed is to memorize one conversion in each of the three units of measure. This will allow a "bridging of the systems." These conversions are

1 inch = 2.54 cm	used for units of lengths
2.2 lbs = 1 kg	used for units of mass or weights
1.06 qt = 1 L	used for units of volume

Example Calculation 5

If an individual weighs 150 pounds, how many kilograms does the patient weigh? First, you must change pounds to kilograms; therefore, write the given weight as a fraction over 1. Then place the unit you want to cancel (pounds) in the denominator and the unit you want to convert to (kilograms) in the numerator of the next fraction.

$$\frac{150 \text{ pounds}}{1} \times \frac{1 \text{ kilogram}}{2.2 \text{ pounds}} = 68.18 \text{ kilorams}$$

Example Calculation 6

The conversion will not always be as direct as in the previous example, but it is no problem if you simply follow the system. For example, 1 foot is equal to how many centimeters? There is an equivalency somewhere for feet and centimeters, but you don't need to know that using the Factor Label Method and the conversion for distance.

Now, answer the question of how many centimeters are there in 1 foot. Remember, your unit conversion for length is 1 inch = 2.54 cm.

$$\frac{1 \text{ foot}}{1} \times \frac{12 \text{ inches}}{1 \text{ foot}} \times \frac{2.54 \text{ cm}}{1 \text{ inch}} = 30.48 \text{ cm}$$

TEST YOUR KNOWLEDGE 5

Choose the best answer:

1. The Body Surface nomogram compares what two units of measure?
   a. weight and sex
   b. height and sex
   c. surface area and length
   d. height and weight

Complete the following:

2. A quart of blood is equal to how many milliliters (mL)? _____

3. If a patient voids (passes) 3.2 liters of urine in a day, what is the amount in milliliters? _____

4. Convert 175 lbs to kilograms. _____

APPENDICES

Appendix A: Medical Terminology, Words Parts, and Singular and Plural Endings

Appendix B: Clinical Abbreviations and "Do Not Use" List

Appendix C: Infectious Diseases and Their Pathogens

Appendix D: Laboratory Reference Values

Appendix E: Multisystem Effects of Various Diseases and Conditions

Appendix F: Vitamins and Minerals: Sources, Functions, and Effects of Deficiency and Toxicity

Appendix G: Standard and Transmission-Based Precautions

Appendix H: Health Care Careers and Career Planning

Medical Terminology, Word Parts, and Singular and Plural Endings

Word Parts Arranged Alphabetically and Defined

The word parts that have been presented in this textbook, and additional terms you may encounter, are summarized with their definitions for quick reference.

PREFIX	DEFINITION
a-	without, absence of
ab-	away from
ad-	toward
an-	without, absence of
ana-	up, toward, apart
ante-	before
anti-	against, opposing
aut-	self, same
bi-	two
bin-	two
brady-	slow
circum-	around, about
contra-	in contrast; against
di-	two
dia-	around, passing through
diplo-	double
dys-	bad, abnormal
ecto-	on outer side, situated on
en-	within, upon, on, over
endo-	within, inner, absorbing
ep-	upon, on, over
epi-	upon
eu-	normal, good
ex-	outside, away from
exo-	outside, away from
hemi-	one-half
homo-	same
hydro-	water
hyper-	excessive
hypo-	under, below normal
im-	not

PREFIX	DEFINITION
inter-	between
intra-	within
later-	side
lipo-	fat
macro-	large
mal-	bad
mega-	large
meta-	after, change
micro-	small
mono-	single
multi-	many
my-	muscle
myo-	muscle
neo-	new
nulli-	none
ortho-	straight, normal
pan-	all, entire
para-	near, alongside; departure from normal
per-	through
peri-	around, about, surrounding
poly-	many
post-	after
pre-	before
pro-	forward, preceding
pseudo-	false
quad-	four
re-	back
retro-	backward, located behind
semi-	half
sub-	beneath

PREFIX	DEFINITION
sym-	together, joined
syn-	together, joined
tachy-	rapid, fast
tele-	distant
tetra-	four
trans-	through, across, beyond
ultra-	beyond, in excess
uni-	one

COMBINING FORM	DEFINITION
abdomin/o	abdomen, abdominal cavity
acou/o	hearing
acoust/o	hearing
acr/o	extremity, extreme
aden/o	gland
adren/o	adrenal gland
aer/o	air or gas
albumin/o	albumin
alveol/o	alveolus (air sac)
amni/o	amnion, amniotic fluid
amnion/o	amnion, amniotic fluid
an/o	anus
andr/o	male
angi/o	blood vessel
ankyl/o	crooked
anter/o	front
aort/o	aorta
appendic/o	to hang onto, appendix
aque/o	water
arche/o	first, beginning
arter/o	artery
arteri/o	artery
arthr/o	joint
astheni/o	weakness
atel/o	imperfect, incomplete
ather/o	fat
atri/o	atrium
aud/o	hearing
audi/o	hearing
aur/i	ear
aut/o	self
azot/o	urea, nitrogen
bacter/o	bacteria

COMBINING FORM	DEFINITION
balan/o	glans penis
bi/o	life
bil/i	bile
blast/o	germ, bud
blephar/o	eyelid
bronch/i	bronchus (airway)
bronch/o	bronchus (airway)
burs/o	purse or sac; bursa
calc/i	calcium
cancer/o	cancer
carcin/o	cancer
card/o	heart
cardi/o	heart
carp/o	wrist
cartil/o	gristle, cartilage
caud/o	tail
cec/o	blind intestine, cecum
cel/o	hernia, protrusion
celi/o	abdomen, abdominal cavity
cephal/o	head
cerebell/o	cerebellum (little brain)
cerebr/o	cerebrum (brain)
cerumin/o	wax
cervic/o	cervix, neck
cheil/o	lip
chem	chemistry, drug
chir/o	hand
chol/e	bile, gall
choledoch/o	common bile duct
chondr/o	cartilage
chori/o	membrane, chorion
chromat/o	color
clon/o	spasm
col/o	colon
colp/o	vagina
conjunctiv/o	to bind together, conjunctiva
cor/o	pupil
core/o	pupil
corne/o	horny, cornea
coron/o	crown, circle
cortic/o	tree bark, outer covering, cortex

COMBINING FORM	DEFINITION
cost/o	rib
cran/o	skull, cranium
crani/o	skull, cranium
crin/o	to secrete
crypt/o	hidden
cutane/o	skin
cyan/o	blue
cyes/i	pregnancy
cyes/o	pregnancy
cyst/o	bladder, sac
cyt/o	cell
dacry/o	tear
dent/i	teeth
derm/o	skin
dermat/o	skin
diaphragmat/o	diaphragm
dipl/o	double
dips/o	thirst
dist/o	away
diverticul/o	small blind pouch, diverticulum
dors/o	back
duct/o	lead, move
duoden/o	twelve, duodenum
dur/o	hard
ech/o	sound
electr/o	electricity
embol/o	plug
embry/o	embryo
encephal/o	brain
endocrin/o	endocrine
enter/o	small intestine
epididym/o	epididymis
epiglott/o	epiglottis
episi/o	vulva
eryth/o	red
erythr/o	red
esophag/o	gullet, esophagus
esthesi/o	sensation
eti/o	cause (of disease)
fasci/o	fascia
femor/o	thigh
fet/i	fetus

COMBINING FORM	DEFINITION
fet/o	fetus
fibr/o	fiber
fibul/o	clasp of buckle, fibula
fovea/o	small pit
gangli/o	ganglion
gastr/o	stomach
gen/o	formation, cause, produce
ger/o	old age
geront/o	old age
gingiv/o	gums
gli/o	glue, neuroglia
glomerul/o	little ball, glomerulus
gloss/o	tongue
gluc/o	glucose, sugar
glut/o	buttock
glyc/o	glycogen, sugar
glycos/o	sugar
gravid/o	pregnancy
gravidar/o	pregnancy
gyn/o	woman
gynec/o	woman
halat/o	breath
hem/o	blood
hemat/o	blood
hepat/o	liver
hern/o	protrusion, hernia
herni/o	protrusion, hernia
heter/o	other
hidr/o	sweat
hist/o	tissue
hom/o	sameness, unchanging
hormon/o	to set in motion
hydr/o	water
hymen/o	hymen
hyster/o	uterus
iatr/o	physician
idi/o	person, self
ile/o	ileum of small intestine, to roll
ili/o	flank, groin, ilium of the pelvis
immun/o	exempt; immunity
infect/o	to enter, invade
infer/o	below
inguin/o	groin

COMBINING FORM	DEFINITION
ir/o	rainbow, iris
irid/o	rainbow, iris
isch/o	to hold back, deficiency, blockage
ischi/o	haunch, hip joint, ischium
jejun/o	empty, jejunum
kal/i	potassium
kerat/o	hard, horny; cornea
ket/o	ketone bodies
keton/o	ketone bodies
kinesi/o	motion
kyph/o	hump
labyrinth/o	labyrinth, internal ear
lacrim/o	tear
lact/o	milk
lamin/o	thin, lamina
lapar/o	abdomen, abdominal cavity
laryng/o	larynx
later/o	side
lei/o	smooth
leuk/o	white
lingu/o	tongue
lip/o	fat, lipid
lith/o	stone
lob/o	lobe
lord/o	bent forward
lumb/o	loin, lower back
lymph/o	clear water or fluid
lys/o	dissolution
mal/o	bad
mamm/o	breast
mast/o	breast
meat/o	opening
medi/o	middle
megal/o	abnormally large
melan/o	dark, black
men/o	month, menstruation
menstru/o	month, menstruation
mening/o	meninges, membrane
menisc/o	crescent-shaped moon, meniscus membrane
ment/o	mind
metr/o	uterus

COMBINING FORM	DEFINITION
mon/o	one
muc/o	mucus
my/o	muscle
myc/o	fungus
myel/o	bone marrow; spinal cord; medulla; myelin
myelon/o	bone marrow; spinal cord; medulla; myelin
myos/o	muscle
myring/o	membrane; eardrum
myx/o	mucus
nas/o	nose
nat/o	birth
natr/o	sodium
necr/o	death
nephr/o	kidney
neur/o	sinew or cord, nerve, fascia
noct/i	night
nucl/o	kernel, nucleus
nyct/o	night, nocturnal
nyctal/o	night, nocturnal
obstetr/o	midwife, prenatal development
ocul/o	eye
odont	of or pertaining to teeth
olig/o	few in number
omphal/o	umbilicus (navel)
onc/o	tumor
onych/o	nail
oophor/o	ovary
opt/o	eye, vision
opthalm/o	eye
or/o	mouth
orch/o	testis or testicle
orchi/o	testis or testicle
orchid/o	testis or testicle
organ/o	tool
orth/o	straight
oste/o	bone
ot/o	ear
ov/i	egg
ov/o	egg
ovari/o	ovary
ox/o	oxygen

COMBINING FORM	DEFINITION	COMBINING FORM	DEFINITION
pachy/o	thick	pub/o	grown up
palat/o	roof of mouth, palate	puerper/o	childbirth
pancreat/o	pancreas	pulmon/o	lung
par/o	parturition or labor	py/o	pus
parathyroid/o	parathyroid	pyel/o	pelvis (renal)
pariet/o	wall	pylor/o	pylorus
part/o	parturition or labor	quad/o	four
patell/o	small pan, patella	quadr/i	four
path/o	disease	rachi/o	spine
pector/o	chest	radi/o	spoke of a wheel, radius
ped/o	child	radic/o	nerve root
pediatr/o	child	radicul/o	nerve root
pelv/l	basin, pelvis	rect/o	straight, erect, rectum
pen/o	penis	ren/o	kidney
peps/o	digestion	retin/o	net, retina
perine/o	perineum	rhabd/o	rod
peritone/o	to stretch over, peritoneum	rhin/o	nose
petr/o	stone	rhytid/o	wrinkles
phac/o	lens	sacr/o	sacred, sacrum
phag/o	eat, swallow	salping/o	tube: fallopian tube
phak/o	lens	sarc/o	flesh, muscle
phalang/o	bones of fingers and toes	scler/o	thick, hard; sclera
pharyng/o	pharynx (throat)	scoli/o	curved
phas/o	speech	seb/o	sebum, oil
phleb/o	vein	semin/o	seed
phot/o	light	sept/o	wall, partition
physi/o	nature	sial/o	saliva, salivary gland
physis/o	growth	sigm/o	sigmoid colon, the letter "s"
plegi/o	paralysis	sinus/o	cavity
pleur/o	pleura	somat/o	body
pneum/o	lung or air	somn/o	sleep
pneumat/o	lung or air	son/o	sound
pod/o	foot	sperm/o	seed
poikil/o	irregular	spermat/o	seed
polyp/o	polyp	sphygm/o	pulse
poster/o	back	spin/o	spine or thorn
presby/o	old age	spir/o	breathe
prim/i	first	splen/o	spleen
proct/o	anus	spondyl/o	vertebra
prostat/o	prostate gland	staped/o	stapes
proxim/o	near	staphyl/o	grapelike clusters (bacterium)
pseud/o	false	stasis/o	standing still
psych/o	mind	steat/o	fat

COMBINING FORM	DEFINITION
sten/o	narrowness, constriction
stern/o	chest, sternum
steth/o	chest
stigmat/o	point
stomat/o	mouth
strept/o	twisted or gnarled (bacterium)
super/o	above
synov/o	synovial fluid
synovi/o	synovial fluid
syndesm/o	binding together
tars/o	flat surface
taxi/o	reaction to a stimulus
ten/o	to stretch out; tendon
tend/o	to stretch out; tendon
tendin/o	to stretch out; tendon
test/o	testis, testicle
testicul/o	small testis, testicle
thalam/o	thalamus
thel/o	nipple
therm/o	heat
thorac/o	thorax (chest)
thromb/o	clot
thym/o	wartlike, thymus gland
thyr/o	shield, thyroid
toc/o	birth, labor
tom/o	cut, section
ton/o	tone, tension, pressure
toxic/o	poison
trache/o	trachea
trachel/o	neck, cervix
trich/o	hair
tubercul/o	little mass of swelling
tympan/o	eardrum
umbilic/o	navel
ur/o	urine
ureter/o	ureter
urethr/o	urethra
urin/o	urine
uter/o	womb, uterus
uvul/o	grape, uvula
vagin/o	sheath, vagina
valvul/o	little valve
varic/o	dilated vein

COMBINING FORM	DEFINITION
vas/o	blood vessel; duct
vascul/o	little blood vessel
ven/o	vein
ventr/o	front, belly
ventricul/o	little belly or cavity, ventricle
vers/o	turn
vertebr/o	joint, vertebra
vesic/o	bladder, sac
vesicul/o	vesicle (seminal vesicle)
vitr/o	glassy
vitre/o	glassy
vulv/o	vulva
xanth/o	yellow
xer/o	dry

SUFFIX	DEFINITION
-a	singular
-ac	pertaining to
-acusis	hearing condition
-ad	toward
-al	pertaining to
-algesia	pain
-algia	pain
-apheresis	removal
-ar	pertaining to
-ary	pertaining to
-ase	enzyme
-asthenia	weakness
-atresia	closure; absence of a normal body opening
-capnia	carbon dioxide
-cele	hernia, swelling, protrusion
-cente	100
-centesis	surgical puncture
-centre	center
-cide	causing death or destruction
-clasia	break apart
-clasis	break apart
-clast	break apart
-crit	separate
-cusis	hearing condition
-cyte	cell
-desis	surgical fixation, fusion

SUFFIX	DEFINITION
-dipsia	thirst
-drome	run, running
-dynia	pain
-eal	pertaining to
-ectasis	expansion, dilation
-ectomy	excision
-elle	small
-emesis	vomiting
-emetic	vomiting
-emia	blood (condition of)
-esthesia	sensation
-gen	formation, cause, produce
-genesis	origin, cause
-genic	pertaining to formation, causing, producing
-gram	recording
-graph	instrument for recording
-graphy	recording process
-hemia	blood (condition of)
-ia	diseased state (condition of)
-ial	pertaining to
-iasis	condition of
-iatry	treatment, specialty
-ic	pertaining to
-ion	pertaining to
-ior	pertaining to
-is	pertaining to
-ism	condition or disease
-ist	one who practices
-itis	inflammation
-lepsy	seizure
-logist	one who studies
-logy	study of
-lytic, -lysis	to loosen, dissolve
-malacia	softening
-meter	measuring instrument
-metry	measurement
-oid	resemblance to
-oma	abnormal swelling, tumor
-opia	vision
-opsy	view of
-orrhagia	bursting forth

SUFFIX	DEFINITION
-orrhea	flow
-osis	process or condition that is usually abnormal
-otomy	cutting into, excision
-ous	pertaining to
-oxia	oxygen
-paresis	paralysis (minor)
-pathy	disease
-penia	abnormal reduction in number, deficiency
-pepsia	digestion
-pexy	surgical fixation, suspension
-phagia	eating or swallowing
-phasia	speaking
-phil	loving, affinity for
-philia	loving, affinity for
-phobia	fear
-phonia	sound or voice
-phylaxis	protection
-physis	growth
-plasia	shape, formation
-plasm	something shaped
-plasty	surgical repair
-plegia	paralysis (major)
-pnea	breathing
-poiesis	formation
-practic	one who practices
-ptosis	falling downward (condition of)
-ptysis	spit out a fluid
-rrhagia	bleeding, hemorrhage
-rrhaphy	suturing
-rrhea	excessive discharge
-rrhexis	rupture
-salpinx	trumpet, fallopian tube
-sarcoma	malignant tumor
-schisis	split, fissure
-sclerosis	hardening
-scope	viewing instrument
-scopy	process of viewing
-sis	state of
-some	body

SUFFIX	DEFINITION
-spasm	sudden, involuntary muscle contraction
-stasis	standing still
-stenosis	narrowing, constriction
-stomy	surgical creation of an opening
-tic	pertaining to
-tocia	birth, labor
-tome	cutting instrument
-tomy	incision
-toxic	toxin, poison
-tripsy	surgical crushing
-trophy	nourishment, development
-um	pertaining to
-uria	urine, urination
-y	process of

Endings in Medical Terminology

Plural endings. The following list provides a summary of plural endings that are in common use with medical terms. Examples are provided to demonstrate how these endings are applied.

ENDINGS SINGULAR	PLURAL
-a	-ae
-ax	-aces
-ex	-ices
-is	-es
-ix	-ices
-ma	-mata
-on	-a
-um	-a
-us	-i
-y	-ies

EXAMPLES SINGULAR	PLURAL
fistula	fistulae
hemothorax	hemothoraces
cortex	cortices
mastoiditis	mastoidites
cicatrix	cicatrices
fibroma	fibromata
contusion	contusia
bacterium	bacteria
fungus	fungi
episiotomy	episiotomies

Adjective endings. The following list provides a summary of suffixes that mean "pertaining to" and form an adjective (a description of a noun) when combined with a root.

ENDING	EXAMPLE	DEFINITION
-ac	cardiac	pertaining to the heart
-al	endotracheal	pertaining to within the trachea
-ar	submandibular	pertaining to below the mandible
-ary	pulmonary	pertaining to a lung
-eal	esophageal	pertaining to the esophagus
-ic	leukemic	pertaining to leukemia
-ous	fibrous	pertaining to fiber
-tic	cyanotic	pertaining to cyanotic (blue)

Diminutive endings. The endings listed here provide the meaning of "small" to the word of origin.

ENDING	EXAMPLE	DEFINITION
-icle	ossicle	small bone
-ole	bronchiole	small bronchus (airway)
-ula	macula	small macule (spot)
-ule	pustule	small pimple

Diagnostic endings. The endings in this list summarize the suffixes that are in common use to indicate measurements, treatments, and procedures.

ENDING	MEANING	EXAMPLE	DEFINITION
-gram	record	bronchogram	recording of bronchus image
-graph	recording instrument	sonograph	ultrasound instrument
-graphy	process of recording	echocardiography	procedure of heart recording
-iatrics	treatment	pediatrics	treatment of children
-iatry	treatment	psychiatry	treatment of the mind
-logy	study of	oncology	study of cancer
-logist	one who studies	audiologist	one who studies hearing
-ist	one who specializes	optometrist	specialist in eye measurement
-meter	instrument of measure	spirometer	instrument measuring breathing
-metry	process of measuring	spirometry	process of measuring breathing
-scope	instrument for exam	endoscope	instrument for examination within
-scopy	examination	endoscopy	examination within

Clinical Abbreviations and "Do Not Use" List

Listed here are the currently acceptable abbreviations to use; however, different health care facilities may use others as well. The Joint Commission, which accredits and certifies over 15,000 health care organizations and programs in the United States, has created a list of abbreviations that should not be used because in handwritten documents or forms they may cause confusion or problems. Those are also included. It is important that health care employees follow their facility policy regarding the use of medical abbreviations.

ABBREVIATION	MEANING
ABGs	arterial blood gases
ac	before meals
ACAT	automated computerized axial tomography
Acc	accommodation
ACL	anterior cruciate ligament
ACTH	adrenocorticotropic hormone
AD	right ear, Alzheimer's disease
ad lib	as desired
ADD	attention deficit disorder
ADH	antidiuretic hormone
ADHD	attention-deficit-hyperactivity disorder
ADL	activities of daily living
AE	above elbow
AF	atrial fibrillation
AGN	acute glomerulonephritis
AHF	antihemophilic factor
AI	artificial insemination
AIDS	acquired immunodeficiency syndrome
AK	above knee
ALL	acute lymphocytic leukemia
ALS	amyotrophic lateral sclerosis
ALT	alanine transaminase
am, AM	morning
AMI	acute myocardial infarction
AML	acute myelogenous leukemia
amt	amount

ABBREVIATION	MEANING
Angio	angiography
ANS	autonomic nervous system
ante	before
AP	anteroposterior
APAP	acetaminophen (Tylenol®)
aq	aqueous (water)
ARC	AIDS-related complex
ARD	acute respiratory disease
ARDS	adult respiratory distress syndrome
ARF	acute respiratory failure, acute renal failure
ARMD	age-related macular degeneration
AROM	active range of motion
AS	aortic stenosis, arteriosclerosis, left ear
ASA	aspirin
ASCVD	arteriosclerotic cardiovascular disease
ASD	atrial septal defect
ASHD	arteriosclerotic heart disease
ASL	American Sign Language
AST	aspartate transaminase
Astigm.	astigmatism
ATN	acute tubular necrosis
AU	both ears
AuD	doctor of audiology
AV, A-V	atrioventricular

ABBREVIATION	MEANING
Ba	Barium
BaE	barium enema
basos	basophil
BBB	bundle branch block (L for left; R for right)
BC	bone conduction
BCC	basal cell carcinoma
BDT	bone density testing
BE	barium enema, below elbow
bid	twice a day
BK	below knee
BM	bowel movement
BMR	basal metabolic rate
BMT	bone marrow transplant
BNO	bladder neck obstruction
BP	blood pressure
BPD	bipolar disorder
BPH	benign prostatic hypertrophy
bpm	beats per minute
Bronch	bronchoscopy
BS	bowel sounds
BSE	breast self-examination
BSN	bachelor of science in nursing
BUN	blood urea nitrogen
BX, bx	biopsy
$\bar{c}$	with
C	100
C1, C2, etc.	first cervical vertebra, second cervical vertebra, etc.
Ca^{2+}	calcium
CA	cancer, chronological age
CABG	coronary artery bypass graft
CAD	coronary artery disease
cap(s)	capsule(s)
CAPD	continuous ambulatory peritoneal dialysis
CAT	computerized axial tomography
cath	catheterization
CBC	complete blood count
CBD	common bile duct
CC	clean catch urine specimen, cardiac catheterization, chief complaint

ABBREVIATION	MEANING
CCS	certified coding specialist
CCU	cardiac care unit, coronary care unit
CD4	protein on helper T-cell lymphocyte
CDH	congenital dislocation of the hip
c.gl.	correction with glasses
CGL	chronic granulocytic leukemia
chemo	chemotherapy
CHF	congestive heart failure
chol	cholesterol
Ci	Curie
CIS	carcinoma in situ
Cl^-	chloride
CLL	chronic lymphocytic leukemia
CLS	clinical laboratory scientist
CLT	clinical laboratory technician
CMA	certified medical assistant
CML	chronic myelogenous leukemia
CNA	certified nurse aide
CNIM	certification in neurophysiologic intraoperative monitoring
CNS	central nervous system
CO_2	carbon dioxide
CoA	coarctation of the aorta
COLD	chronic obstructive lung disease
COPD	chronic obstructive pulmonary disease
COTA	certified occupational therapy assistant
CP	cerebral palsy, chest pain
CPD	cephalopelvic disproportion
CPK	creatine phosphokinase
CPR	cardiopulmonary resuscitation
CRF	chronic renal failure
crit	hematocrit
CRT	certified respiratory therapist
C&S	culture and sensitivity test
CS, C-section	Cesarean section
CSD	congenital septal defect
CSF	cerebrospinal fluid

ABBREVIATION	MEANING
CT	computerized tomography, cytotechnologist
CTA	clear to auscultation
CTS	carpal tunnel syndrome
CUC	chronic ulcerative colitis
CV	cardiovascular
CVA	cerebrovascular accident
CVD	cerebrovascular disease
CVS	chorionic villus biopsy
Cx	cervix
CXR	chest X-ray
cyl lens	cylindrical lens
cysto	cystoscopic exam
D	diopter (lens strength)
D & C	dilation and curettage
D/C, d/c	discontinue
dB	decibel
DC	doctor of chiropractic
DDM	doctor of dental medicine
DDS	doctor of dental surgery
DEA	Drug Enforcement Agency
decub	lying down, decubitus ulcer
Derm, derm	dermatology
DI	diabetes insipidus, diagnostic imaging
diff	differential
dil	dilute
disc	discontinue
disp	dispense
DJD	degenerative joint disease
DM	diabetes mellitus
DO	doctor of osteopathy
DOB	date of birth
DOE	dyspnea on exertion
DPT	diphtheria, pertussis, tetanus; doctor of physical therapy
dr	dram
DRE	digital rectal exam
DSA	digital subtraction angiography
DSM-IV	*Diagnostic and Statistical Manual for Mental Disorders, Fourth Edition*

ABBREVIATION	MEANING
DTR	deep tendon reflex; dietetic technician, registered
DUB	dysfunctional uterine bleeding
DVA	distance visual acuity
DVT	deep vein thrombosis
Dx	diagnosis
E. coli	*Escherichia coli*
EAU	exam under anesthesia
EBV	Epstein-Barr virus
ECC	endocervical curettage, extracorporeal circulation
ECCE	extracapsular cataract extraction
ECG	electrocardiogram
Echo	echocardiogram
ECT	electroconvulsive therapy
ED	emergency department; erectile dysfunction
EDC	estimated date of confinement
EEG	electroencephalogram, electroencephalography
EENT	eyes, ears, nose, throat
EGD	esophagogastroduodenoscopy
EKG	electrocardiogram
ELISA	enzyme-linked immunosorbent assay
elix	elixir
EM	emmetropia (normal vision)
EMB	endometrial biopsy
EMG	electromyogram
EMT-B	emergency medical technician-basic
EMT-I	emergency medical technician-intermediate
EMT-P	emergency medical technician-paramedic
emul	emulsion
Endo	endoscopy
ENT	ear, nose, throat
EOM	extraocular movement
eosins, eos	eosinophil
ER	emergency room
ERCP	endoscopic retrograde cholangiopancreatography

ABBREVIATION	MEANING
ERT	estrogen replacement therapy
ERV	expiratory reserve volume
ESR	erythrocyte sedimentation rate
ESRD	end-stage renal disease
e-stim	electrical stimulation
ESWL	extracorporeal shock-wave lithotripsy
et	and
ET	endotracheal
FBS	fasting blood sugar
FDA	Food and Drug Administration
Fe	iron
FEF	forced expiratory flow
FEKG	fetal electrocardiogram
FEV	forced expiratory volume
FHR	fetal heart rate
FHT	fetal heart tone
fl	fluid
FOBT	fecal occult blood test
FRC	functional residual capacity
FS	frozen section
FSH	follicle-stimulating hormone
FTND	full-term normal delivery
FVC	forced vital capacity
Fx, FX	fracture
G_1	first pregnancy
Ga	gallium
GA	general anesthesia
GB	gallbladder
GC	gonorrhea
GERD	gastroesophageal reflux disease
GH	growth hormone
GI	gastrointestinal
gm	gram
GOT	glutamic oxaloacetic transaminase
gr	grain
grav I	first pregnancy
gt	drop
gtt	drops
GTT	glucose tolerance test
GU	genitourinary

ABBREVIATION	MEANING
GVHD	graft vs. host disease
GYN, gyn	gynecology
H_2O	water
HA	headache
HAV	hepatitis A virus
Hb	hemoglobin
HBOT	hyperbaric oxygen therapy
HBV	hepatitis B virus
HCG, hCG	human chorionic gonadotropin
HCO_3^-	bicarbonate
HCT, Hct	hematocrit
HCV	hepatitis C virus
HD	Hodgkin's disease
HDL	high-density lipoproteins
HDN	hemolytic disease of the newborn
HEENT	head, ears, eyes, nose, throat
HF	heart failure
Hgb, HGB	hemoglobin
HIV	human immunodeficiency virus
HMD	hyaline membrane disease
HNP	herniated nucleus pulposus
HPV	human papilloma virus
HRT	hormone replacement therapy
hs	hour of sleep
HSG	hysterosalpingography
HSV	*Herpes simplex* virus
HTN	Hypertension
HZ	hertz
IBD	inflammatory bowel disease
IBS	irritable bowel syndrome
IC	inspiratory capacity
ICCE	intracapsular cataract cryoextraction
ICP	intracranial pressure
ICU	intensive care unit
I & D	incision and drainage
ID	Intradermal
IDDM	insulin-dependent diabetes mellitus
Ig	immunoglobins (IgA, IgD, IgE, IgG, IgM)

ABBREVIATION	MEANING
i	one
ii	two
iii	three
IM	intramuscular
inj	injection
I & O	intake and output
IOL	intraocular lens
IOP	intraocular pressure
IPD	intermittent peritoneal dialysis
IPPB	intermittent positive pressure breathing
IRDS	infant respiratory distress syndrome
IRV	inspiratory reserve volume
IUD	intrauterine device
IV	intravenous
IVC	intravenous cholangiogram
IVF	*in vitro* fertilization
IVP	intravenous pyelogram
JRA	juvenile rheumatoid arthritis
JVP	jugular venous pulse
K+	potassium
kg	kilogram
KS	Kaposi's sarcoma
KUB	kidney, ureter, bladder
L	left, liter
L1, L2, etc.	first lumbar vertebra, second lumbar vertebra, etc.
LASIK	laser-assisted in-situ keratomileusis
LAT, lat	lateral
LAVH	laparoscopic-assisted vaginal hysterectomy
LBW	low birth weight
LDH	lactate dehydrogenase
LDL	low-density lipoproteins
LE	lower extremity
LGI	lower gastrointestinal series
LH	luteinizing hormone
liq	liquid
LL	left lateral
LLE	left lower extremity
LLL	left lower lobe

ABBREVIATION	MEANING
LLQ	left lower quadrant
LMP	last menstrual period
LP	lumbar puncture
LPN	licensed practical nurse
LUE	left upper extremity
LUL	left upper lobe
LUQ	left upper quadrant
LVAD	left ventricular assist device
LVH	left ventricular hypertrophy
lymphs	lymphocyte
LVN	licensed vocational nurse
mA	milliampere
MA	mental age
MAO	monoamine oxidase
mcg	microgram
mCi	millicurie
MCV	mean corpuscular volume
MD	doctor of medicine, muscular dystrophy
mEq	milliequivalent
mets	metastases
mg	milligram
MH	marital history
MI	myocardial infarction, mitral insufficiency
mL	milliliter
MLT	medical laboratory technician
mm	millimeter
MM	malignant melanoma
mm Hg	millimeters of mercury
MMPI	Minnesota Multiphasic Personality Inventory
Mono	mononucleosis
monos	monocyte
MR	mitral regurgitation
MRA	magnetic resonance angiography
MRI	magnetic resonance imaging
MRSA	methicillin-resistant *Staphylococcus Aureus*
MS	mitral stenosis, multiple sclerosis, musculoskeletal
MSH	melanocyte-stimulating hormone

ABBREVIATION	MEANING
MSN	master of science in nursing
MT	medical technologist
MTX	methotrexate
MUA	manipulation under anesthesia
MV	minute volume
MVP	mitral valve prolapse
n & v	nausea and vomiting
Na^+	sodium
NB	newborn
NG	nasogastric (tube)
NGU	nongonococcal urethritis
NHL	non-Hodgkin's lymphoma
NIDDM	non-insulin-dependent diabetes mellitus
NK	natural killer cells
NMR	nuclear magnetic resonance
no sub	no substitute
noc	night
non rep	do not repeat
NP	nurse practitioner
NPDL	nodular, poorly differentiated lymphocytes
NPH	neutral protamine Hagedorn (insulin)
npo	nothing by mouth
NS	normal saline
NSAID	nonsteroidal anti-inflammatory drug
NSR	normal sinus rhythm
O_2	oxygen
OA	osteoarthritis
OB	obstetrics
OCD	obsessive-compulsive disorder
OCPs	oral contraceptive pills
OD	overdose, right eye, doctor of optometry
oint.	ointment
OM	otitis media
O & P	ova and parasites
Ophth.	ophthalmology
OR	operating room
ORIF	open reduction-internal fixation
Orth, ortho	orthopedics

ABBREVIATION	MEANING
OS	left eye
OT	occupational therapy
OTC	over the counter
Oto	otology
OTR	occupational therapist
OU	each eye
oz	ounce
$\bar{p}$	after
P	pulse
PI	first delivery
PA	posteroanterior, physician assistant, pernicious anemia
PAC	premature atrial contraction
PAP	Papanicolaou test, pulmonary arterial pressure
para I	first delivery
PARR	postanesthetic recovery room
PBI	protein-bound iodine
pc	after meals
PCA	patient-controlled administration
PCV	packed cell volume
PDA	patent ductus arteriosus
PDR	*Physician's Desk Reference*
PE tube	polyethylene tube placed in the eardrum
PEG	pneumoencephalogram, percutaneous endoscopic gastrostomy
per	with
PERRLA	pupils equal, round, react to light and accommodation
PET	positron emission tomography
PFT	pulmonary function test
pH	acidity or alkalinity
PharmD	doctor of pharmacy
PID	pelvic inflammatory disease
PKU	phenylketonuria
PM, pm	evening
PMN	polymorphonuclear neutrophil
PMP	previous menstrual period
PMS	premenstrual syndrome
PND	paroxysmal nocturnal dyspnea, postnasal drip

ABBREVIATION	MEANING
PNS	peripheral nervous system
po	phone order, by mouth
polys	polymorphonuclear neutrophil
PORP	partial ossicular replacement prosthesis
pp	postprandial (after meals)
PPD	purified protein derivative (tuberculin test)
preop, pre-op	preoperative
prep	preparation, prepared
PRK	photo refractive keratectomy
PRL	prolactin
prn	as needed
Pro-time	prothrombin time
PROM	passive range of motion
prot	protocol
PSA	prostate specific antigen
pt	pint
PT	prothrombin time, physical therapy, physical therapist
PTA	physical therapy assistant
PTC	percutaneous transhepatic cholangiography
PTCA	percutaneous transluminal coronary angioplasty
PTH	parathyroid hormone
PUD	peptic ulcer disease
PVC	premature ventricular contraction
q	every
qam	every morning
qh	every hour
qhs	every night; during hours of sleep
qs	quantity sufficient
R	respiration, right, roentgen
Ra	radium
RA	rheumatoid arthritis
rad	radiation absorbed dose
RAI	radioactive iodine
RAIU	radioactive iodine uptake
RBC	red blood cell
RD	respiratory disease, registered dietitian

ABBREVIATION	MEANING
RDA	recommended daily allowance
RDH	registered dental hygienist
RDS	respiratory distress syndrome
REEGT	registered electroencephalography technologist
REM	rapid eye movement
REPT	registered evoked potential technologist
Rh-	Rh-negative
Rh+	Rh-positive
RHIA	registered health information administrator
RHIT	registered health information technician
RIA	radioimmunoassay
RL	right lateral
RLE	right lower extremity
RLL	right lower lobe
RLQ	right lower quadrant
RML	right mediolateral, right middle lobe
RN	registered nurse
ROM	range of motion
RP	retrograde pyelogram
RPh	registered pharmacist
RPR	rapid plasma reagin (test for syphilis)
RPSGT	registered polysomnographic technologist
RRT	registered radiologic technologist, registered respiratory therapist
RUE	right upper extremity
RUL	right upper lobe
RUQ	right upper quadrant
RV	reserve volume
Rx	take
$\overline{s}$	without
S1	first heart sound
S2	second heart sound
SA, S-A	sinoatrial
SAD	seasonal affective disorder
SAH	subarachnoid hemorrhage

ABBREVIATION	MEANING
SBFT	small bowel follow-through
SC, sc	subcutaneous
SCC	squamous cell carcinoma
SCI	spinal cord injury
SCIDS	severe combined immunodeficiency syndrome
Sed-rate	erythrocyte sedimentation rate
SEE-2	Signing Exact English
SG	skin graft, specific gravity
s.gl.	without correction or glasses
SGOT	serum glutamic oxaloacetic transaminase
SIDS	sudden infant death syndrome
Sig	label as follows/directions
SK	streptokinase
sl	under the tongue
SLE	systemic lupus erythematosus
SMAC	sequential multiple analyzer computer
SMD	senile macular degeneration
SOB	shortness of breath
sol	solution
SOM	serous otitis media
SPP	suprapubic prostatectomy
SR	erythrocyte sedimentation rate
ss	one-half
st	stage
ST	skin test
stat, STAT	at once, immediately
STD	skin test done, sexually transmitted disease
STSG	split-thickness skin graft
subcu	subcutaneous
subq	subcutaneous
supp.	suppository
suppos	suppository
susp	suspension
syr	syrup
T	tablespoon
t	teaspoon
T & A	tonsillectomy and adenoidectomy

ABBREVIATION	MEANING
T1, T2, etc.	first thoracic vertebra, second thoracic vertebra, etc.
T_3	triiodothyronine
T_4	thyroxine
T_7	free thyroxine index
tab	tablet
TAH-BSO	total abdominal hysterectomy-bilateral salpingo-oophorectomy
TB	tuberculosis
tbsp	tablespoon
TENS	transcutaneous electrical nerve stimulation
TFT	thyroid function test
THA	total hip arthroplasty
THR	total hip replacement
TIA	transient ischemic attack
tid	three times a day
tinc	tincture
TKA	total knee arthroplasty
TKR	total knee replacement
TLC	total lung capacity
TMJ	temporomandibular joint
TNM	tumor, nodes, metastases
TO	telephone order
top	apply topically
TORP	total ossicular replacement prothesis
tPA	tissue-type plasminogen activator
TPN	total parenteral nutrition
TPR	temperature, pulse, and respiration
tr	tincture
TSH	thyroid-stimulating hormone
tsp	teaspoon
TSS	toxic shock syndrome
TUR	transurethral resection
TURP	transurethral resection of prostate
TX, Tx	traction, treatment
U/A, UA	urinalysis
UC	uterine contractions, urine culture

ABBREVIATION	MEANING
UE	upper extremity
UGI	upper gastrointestinal, upper gastrointestinal series
ung	ointment
URI	upper respiratory infection
US	ultrasound
UTI	urinary tract infection
UV	ultraviolet
VA	visual acuity
VC	vital capacity
VCUG	voiding cystourethrography
VD	venereal disease
VF	visual field

ABBREVIATION	MEANING
VFib	ventricular fibrillation
VLDL	very low density lipoproteins
VO	verbal order
VRE	Vancomycin-resistant enterococcus
VS	vital signs
VSD	ventricular septal defect
V_T	tidal volume
VT	ventricular tachycardia
WBC	white blood cell
wt	weight
X	times

Official "Do Not Use" List[1]

DO NOT USE	POTENTIAL PROBLEM	USE INSTEAD
U (unit)	Mistaken for "0" (zero), the number "4" (four) or "cc"	Write "unit"
IU (International Unit)	Mistaken for IV (intravenous) or the number 10 (ten)	Write "International Unit"
Q.D., QD, q.d., qd (daily)	Mistaken for each other	Write "daily"
Q.O.D., QOD, q.o.d, qod (every other day)	Period after the Q mistaken for "I" and the "O" mistaken for "I"	Write "every other day"
Trailing zero (X.0 mg)*	Decimal point is missed	Write X mg
Lack of leading zero (.X mg)	Decimal point is missed	Write 0.X mg
MS	Can mean morphine sulfate or magnesium sulfate	Write "morphine sulfate"
MSO_4 and $MgSO_4$	Confused for one another	Write "magnesium sulfate"

[1]Applies to all orders and all medication-related documentation that is handwritten (including free-text computer entry) or on preprinted forms.

*Exception: A "trailing zero" may be used only where required to demonstrate the level of precision of the value being reported, such as for laboratory results, imaging studies that report size of lesions, or catheter/tube sizes. It may not be used in medication orders or other medication-related documentation.

Additional Abbreviations, Acronyms, and Symbols
(For possible future inclusion in the official "Do Not Use" list)

DO NOT USE	POTENTIAL PROBLEM	USE INSTEAD
> (greater than)	Misinterpreted as the number "7" (seven) or the letter "L"	Write "greater than"
< (less than)	Confused for one another	Write "less than"
Abbreviations for drug names	Misinterpreted due to similar abbreviations for multiple drugs	Write drug names in full
Apothecary units	Unfamiliar to many practitioners Confused with metric units	Use metric units
@	Mistaken for the number "2" (two)	Write "at"
cc	Mistaken for U (units) when poorly written	Write "mL" or "milliliters"
μg	Mistaken for mg (milligrams) resulting in one thousand-fold overdose	Write "mcg" or "micrograms"

© The Joint Commission, 2008. Reprinted with permission.

Infectious Diseases and Their Pathogens

Viral Conditions

DISEASE	VIRUS
Acquired immunodeficiency syndrome (AIDS)	*Human immunodeficiency virus (HIV)*
Chickenpox (varicella) and shingles (herpes zoster)	*Varicella zoster virus (VZV)*
Common cold and upper respiratory infections (URIs)	*Rhinoviruses*
Fever blisters and herpes	*Herpes simplex 1 and 2*
Hantavirus pulmonary syndrome	*Hantavirus*
Hepatitis (infectious)	*Hepatitis A virus*
Hepatitis (serum)	*Hepatitis B virus*
Hepatitis (non A; non B)	*Hepatitis C virus*
Infectious mononucleosis	*Epstein-Barr virus (EBV)*
Influenza	*Influenza A, B, C, etc.*
Measles	*Rubeola virus*
Mumps	*Paramyxovirus*
Poliomyelitis	*Poliovirus 1, 2, and 3*
Rabies	*Rabies virus*
Rubella (German measles)	*Rubella virus*
Viral encephalitis	*(many)*
Warts, genital warts, and cervical cancer	*Human papilloma viruses (HPV)*

Bacterial Conditions

DISEASE	ORGANISM
Acute bacterial conjunctivitis	*Staphylococcus, Haemophilus, Proteus*, and other organisms
Anthrax	*Bacillus anthracis*
Botulism	*Clostridium botulinum* (bacillus)
Brucellosis	*Brucella species* (bacilli)
Cholera	*Vibrio cholerae* (curved)
Dental caries	*Streptococcus mutans* (coccus) and other organisms
Diarrhea	*Campylobacter jejuni*
Diphtheria	*Corynebacterium diphtheriae* (bacillus)
Epiglottitis	*Haemophilus influenzae*
External otitis (swimmer's ear)	*Pseudomonas aeruginosa, Staphylococcus aureus, Streptococcus pyogenes*, etc.
Gonorrhea	*Neisseria gonorrhoeae* (coccus)

DISEASE	ORGANISM
Legionnaires' disease	*Legionella pneumophila* (bacillus)
Lyme disease	*Borrelia burgdorferi* (spirochete)
Meningitis	*Streptococcus pneumoniae, Neisseria meningitidis, Haemophilus influenzae*, and other organisms
Parrot fever (psittacosis)	*Chlamydia psittaci*
Pelvic inflammatory disease (PID)	*Neisseria gonorrhoeae* (coccus), *Mycoplasma hominis*, and other organisms
Peptic ulcer	*Helicobacter pylori*
Pertussis (whooping cough)	*Bordetella pertussis* (bacillus)
Pharyngitis (strep throat)	*Streptococcus pyogenes*
Pneumonia	*Streptococcus pneumoniae, Pseudomonas aeruginosa*, and other organisms
Rheumatic fever	*Group A beta-hemolytic streptococci* (cocci)
Rocky Mountain spotted fever (RMSF)	*Rickettsia rickettsii*
Salmonellosis	*Salmonella* species (bacilli)
Shigellosis (Shigella dysentery and bacillary dysentery)	*Shigella* species (bacilli)
Skin infections	*Staphylococcus* species (cocci)
Syphilis	*Treponema pallidum* (spirochete)
Tetanus	*Clostridium tetani* (bacillus)
Toxic shock syndrome (TSS)	*Staphylococcus aureus* strains (cocci)
Trachoma (chlamydial conjunctivitis)	*Chlamydia trachomatis*
Tuberculosis	*Mycobacterium tuberculosis*
Typhoid fever	*Salmonella typhi* (bacillus)
Urinary tract infections	*Pseudomonas aeruginosa, E. coli*

Note: Although the organisms listed are the most common causes of these diseases, other organisms may also be causative agents.

Mycotic (Fungal) Conditions

DISEASE	ORGANISM
Aspergillosis	*Aspergillus* species
Blastomycosis	*Blastomyces dermatitidis*
Candidiasis (thrush)	*Candida albicans* and other species
Coccidioidomycosis (San Joaquin fever)	*Coccidioides immitis*
Histoplasmosis	*Histoplasma capsulatum*
Tinea (includes athlete's foot and jock itch)	*Epidermophyton, Microsporum*, and *Trichophyton* species

Conditions Caused by Protozoa

DISEASE	ORGANISM
Amebiasis and amebic dysentery	*Entamoeba histolytica, Entamoeba polecki,* and other organisms (ameba)
Giardiasis (traveler's diarrhea)	*Giardia lamblia* (flagellate)
Isosporiasis	*Isospora belli* (sporozoan)
Malaria	*Plasmodium* species (sporozoa)
Pneumonia associated with AIDS	*Pneumocystis jiroveci*
Toxoplasmosis	*Toxoplasma gondii* (sporozoan)
Trichomoniasis	*Trichomonas vaginalis* (flagellate)

Laboratory Reference Values

Abbreviations Used in Reporting Laboratory Values

ABBREVIATION	MEANING
cm^3	cubic centimeter
cu μ	cubic microns
dL	deciliter
fL	femtoliter
g	gram
g/dL	grams per deciliter
kg	kilogram
L	liter
mol (M)	mole
mEq	milliequivalent
mg	milligram
mg/dL	milligram per deciliter
mm	millimeter
mmol	millimole
mm^3	cubic millimeter
mm Hg	millimeter of mercury
ng	nanogram
ng/dL	nanogram per deciliter
ng/mL	nanogram per milliliter
pg	picogram
U/L	units per liter
uIU/mL	units International Unit per milliliter

Hematology Tests: Normal Ranges*

Erythrocytes–Red blood cells (RBC)	Females 4.2–5.4 million/mm^3 Males 4.6–6.2 million/mm^3 Children 4.5–5.1 million/mm^3
Hemoglobin (HGB, Hgb)	Females 12.0–14.0 g/dL Males 14.0–16.0 g/dL
Hematocrit (HCT)	37.0–54% Females 37–47% Males 40–54%
Leukocytes–White blood cells (WBC)	4500–11,000/mm^3

Hematology Tests: Normal Ranges* (*continued*)

Differential (WBCs)	Neutrophils 54–62%
	Lymphocytes 20–40%
	Monocytes 2–10%
	Eosinophils 1–2%
	Basophils 0–1%
Thrombocytes– Platelets	200,000–400,000/mm^3

*These values may vary between hospital laboratories.

Hematology Tests: Coagulation Tests

Bleeding time	2.75–8.0 min
Prothrombin time (PT)	12–14 sec
Partial thromboplastin time (PTT)	30–45 sec

Blood Chemistries: Normal Ranges

A/G ratio	0.7–2.0 g/dL
Alanine aminotransferase (ALT)	5–30 U/L
Albumin	3.5–5.5 g/dL
Alkaline phosphatase (ALP)	20–90 U/L
Anion gap	10–17 mEq/L
Aspartate aminotransferase (AST)	10–30 U/L
Bilirubin	0.3–1.1 mg/dL
Blood urea nitrogen (BUN)	8–20 mg/dL
Calcium (Ca)	9.0–11.0 mg/dL
Chloride (Cl)	100–108 mmol/L
Cholesterol	< 200 mg/dL
High-density lipoprotein (HDL)	> 60 mg/dL
Low-density lipoprotein (LDL)	< 100 mg/dL
Creatine phosphokinase (CPK)	Females 30–135 U/L
	Males 55–170 U/L
Creatinine	0.9–1.5 mg/dL
Free T$_4$	0.8–1.8 ng/dL
Globulin	1.4–4.8 g/dL
Glucose (fasting)	70–115 mg/dL
Lactate dehydrogenase (LDH)	100–190 U/L
Phosphate (PO$_4$)	3.0–4.5 mg/dL
Potassium (K)	3.5–5.0 mEq/L
Prostate specific antigen (PSA) Male	0.0–4.0 ng/mL
Sodium (Na)	136–145 mEq/L
Testosterone	241–827 ng/dL

Thyroid stimulating hormone (TSH)	0.5–6.0 uIU/mL
Thyroxine (T$_4$)	4.4–9.9 µg/dL
Triglycerides	< 150 mg/dL
Uric acid	Females 1.5–7.0 mg/dL
	Males 2.5–8.0 mg/dL

Urinalysis: Normal Ranges

Color	Yellow to amber
Turbidity (appearance)	Clear to slightly hazy
Specific gravity	1.003–1.030
Reaction (pH)	5.0–7.0
Odor	Faintly aromatic
Output	1–1.5 liters per day
Protein	Negative
Glucose	Negative
Ketones	Negative
Bilirubin	Negative
Blood	Negative
Urobilinogen	0.1–1.0
Nitrite	Negative
Leukocytes	Negative

Normal Values of Arterial Blood Gases*

pH	7.35–7.45
PaO$_2$	80–100 mm Hg
PaCO$_2$	35–45 mm Hg
HCO$_3^-$	22–26 mEq/L
O$_2$ saturation	95–98%

*Some normal values will vary according to the kind of test carried out in the laboratory.

Common Blood Chemistries and Examples of Disorders They Indicate

TEST			EXAMPLES OF POSSIBLE DIAGNOSIS	
	ABBREVIATION	NORMAL RANGE	RESULTS INCREASED	RESULTS DECREASED
Alkaline phosphate	ALP	30–115 mU/mL	Liver disease, bone disease, mononucleosis	Malnutrition hypothyroidism, chronic nephritis
Blood urea nitrogen	BUN	8–25 mg/dL	Kidney disease, dehydration, GI bleeding	Liver failure, malnutrition
Calcium	Ca	8.5–10.5 mg/dL	Hypercalcemia, bone metastases, Hodgkin's disease	Hypocalcemia, renal failure, pancreatitis

TEST			EXAMPLES OF POSSIBLE DIAGNOSIS	
	ABBREVIATION	NORMAL RANGE	RESULTS INCREASED	RESULTS DECREASED
Chloride	Cl	96–11 mEq/L	Dehydration, eclampsia, anemia	Ulcerative colitis, burns, heat exhaustion
Cholesterol	CHOL	120–200 mg/dL	Atherosclerosis, nephrosis, obstructive jaundice	Malabsorption, liver disease, hyperthyroidism
Creatinine	Creat	0.4–1.5 mg/dL	Chronic nephritis, muscle disease, obstruction of urinary tract	Muscular dystrophy
Globulin	Glob	1.0–3.5 g/dL	Brucellosis, rheumatoid arthritis, hepatic carcinoma	Severe burns
Glucose fasting blood sugar	FBS	70–110 mg/100 mL	Diabetes mellitus	Excess insulin
Two-hour postprandial glucose	2-hr PPBS	140 mg/dL	Cushing syndrome, brain damage	Addison's disease, CA of pancreas
Lactic acid	LDH	100–225 mU/mL	Acute MI, acute leukemia, hepatic disease	
Potassium	K	3.5–5.5 mEq/L	Renal failure, acidosis, cell damage	Malabsorption, severe burn, diarrhea
Serum glutamic-oxaloacetic	SGOT	0–41 mU/mL	MI, liver disease, pancreatitis	Uncontrolled diabetes mellitus with acidosis
Serum glutamic pyruvic transaminase	SGPT	0–45 mU/mL	Active cirrhosis, pancreatitis, obstructive jaundice	
Sodium	Na	135–145 mEq/L	Diabetes insipidus, coma, Cushing syndrome	Severe diarrhea, severe nephritis, vomiting, SIADH
Free thyroxine	T4	1–2.3 mg/dL	Thyroiditis, hyperthyroidism, Graves' disease	Goiter, myxedema, hypothyroidism
Total bilirubin	TB	0.1–1.2 mg/dL	Liver disease, hemolytic anemia, lupus erythremia	
Triglycerides	TRIG	40–170 mg/dL	Liver disease, atherosclerosis, pancreatitis	Malnutrition
Uric acid	UA	2.2–9.0 mg/dL	Renal failure, gout, leukemia, eclampsia	

Multisystem Effects of Various Diseases and Conditions

Diabetes Mellitus

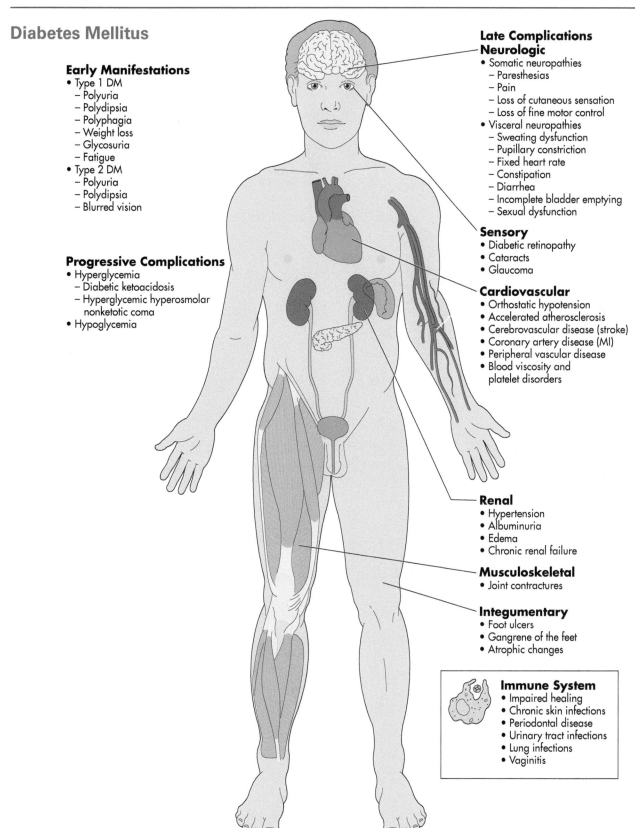

Early Manifestations
- Type 1 DM
  - Polyuria
  - Polydipsia
  - Polyphagia
  - Weight loss
  - Glycosuria
  - Fatigue
- Type 2 DM
  - Polyuria
  - Polydipsia
  - Blurred vision

Progressive Complications
- Hyperglycemia
  - Diabetic ketoacidosis
  - Hyperglycemic hyperosmolar nonketotic coma
- Hypoglycemia

Late Complications
Neurologic
- Somatic neuropathies
  - Paresthesias
  - Pain
  - Loss of cutaneous sensation
  - Loss of fine motor control
- Visceral neuropathies
  - Sweating dysfunction
  - Pupillary constriction
  - Fixed heart rate
  - Constipation
  - Diarrhea
  - Incomplete bladder emptying
  - Sexual dysfunction

Sensory
- Diabetic retinopathy
- Cataracts
- Glaucoma

Cardiovascular
- Orthostatic hypotension
- Accelerated atherosclerosis
- Cerebrovascular disease (stroke)
- Coronary artery disease (MI)
- Peripheral vascular disease
- Blood viscosity and platelet disorders

Renal
- Hypertension
- Albuminuria
- Edema
- Chronic renal failure

Musculoskeletal
- Joint contractures

Integumentary
- Foot ulcers
- Gangrene of the feet
- Atrophic changes

Immune System
- Impaired healing
- Chronic skin infections
- Periodontal disease
- Urinary tract infections
- Lung infections
- Vaginitis

Heart Failure

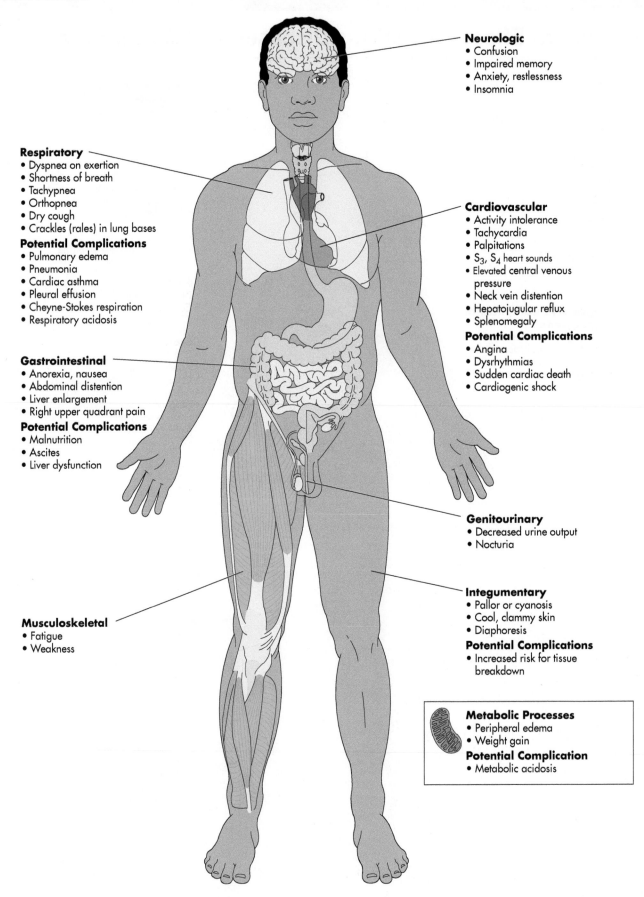

Neurologic
- Confusion
- Impaired memory
- Anxiety, restlessness
- Insomnia

Respiratory
- Dyspnea on exertion
- Shortness of breath
- Tachypnea
- Orthopnea
- Dry cough
- Crackles (rales) in lung bases

Potential Complications
- Pulmonary edema
- Pneumonia
- Cardiac asthma
- Pleural effusion
- Cheyne-Stokes respiration
- Respiratory acidosis

Cardiovascular
- Activity intolerance
- Tachycardia
- Palpitations
- S_3, S_4 heart sounds
- Elevated central venous pressure
- Neck vein distention
- Hepatojugular reflux
- Splenomegaly

Potential Complications
- Angina
- Dysrhythmias
- Sudden cardiac death
- Cardiogenic shock

Gastrointestinal
- Anorexia, nausea
- Abdominal distention
- Liver enlargement
- Right upper quadrant pain

Potential Complications
- Malnutrition
- Ascites
- Liver dysfunction

Genitourinary
- Decreased urine output
- Nocturia

Integumentary
- Pallor or cyanosis
- Cool, clammy skin
- Diaphoresis

Potential Complications
- Increased risk for tissue breakdown

Musculoskeletal
- Fatigue
- Weakness

Metabolic Processes
- Peripheral edema
- Weight gain

Potential Complication
- Metabolic acidosis

Hyperthyroidism

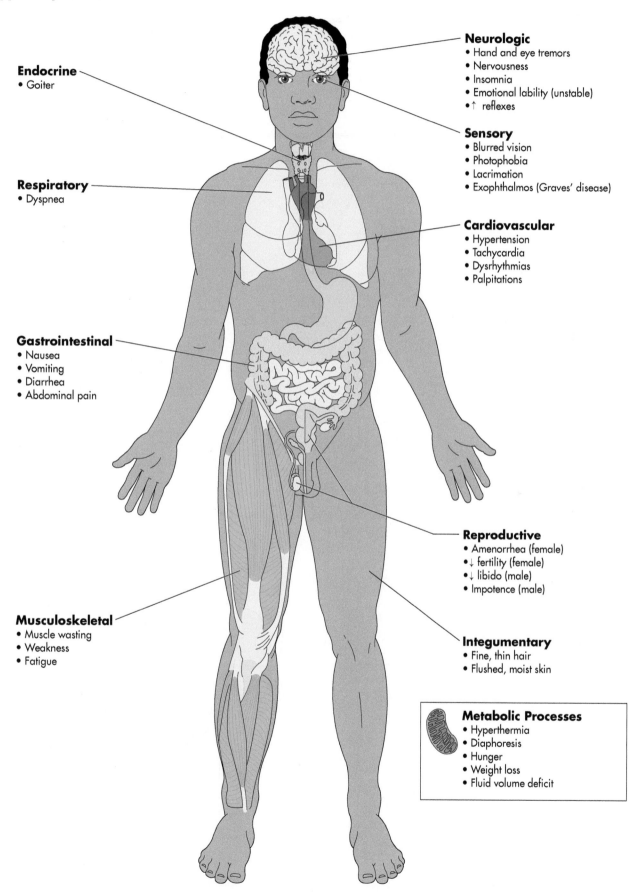

Endocrine
• Goiter

Respiratory
• Dyspnea

Gastrointestinal
• Nausea
• Vomiting
• Diarrhea
• Abdominal pain

Musculoskeletal
• Muscle wasting
• Weakness
• Fatigue

Neurologic
• Hand and eye tremors
• Nervousness
• Insomnia
• Emotional lability (unstable)
• ↑ reflexes

Sensory
• Blurred vision
• Photophobia
• Lacrimation
• Exophthalmos (Graves' disease)

Cardiovascular
• Hypertension
• Tachycardia
• Dysrhythmias
• Palpitations

Reproductive
• Amenorrhea (female)
• ↓ fertility (female)
• ↓ libido (male)
• Impotence (male)

Integumentary
• Fine, thin hair
• Flushed, moist skin

Metabolic Processes
• Hyperthermia
• Diaphoresis
• Hunger
• Weight loss
• Fluid volume deficit

Hypothyroidism

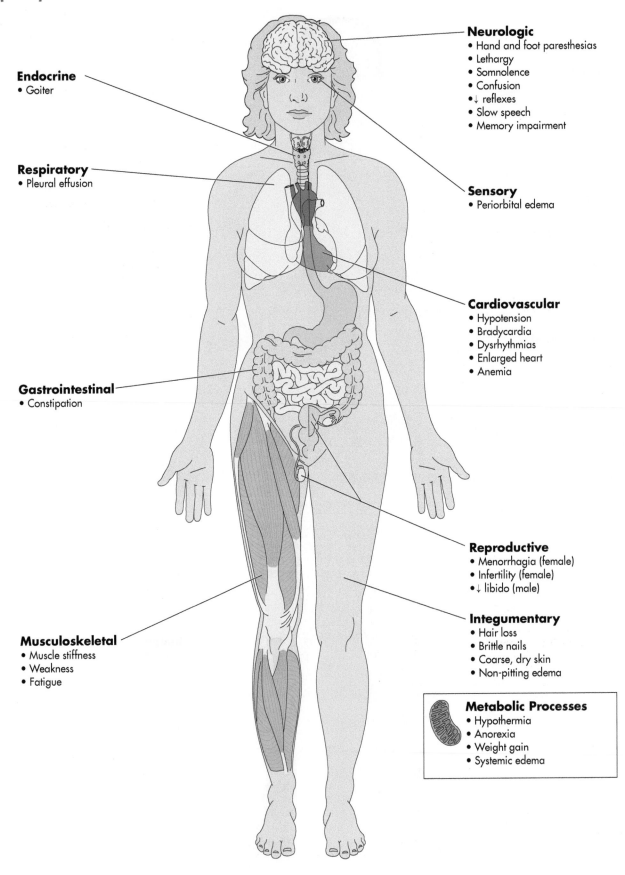

Endocrine
• Goiter

Respiratory
• Pleural effusion

Gastrointestinal
• Constipation

Musculoskeletal
• Muscle stiffness
• Weakness
• Fatigue

Neurologic
• Hand and foot paresthesias
• Lethargy
• Somnolence
• Confusion
• ↓ reflexes
• Slow speech
• Memory impairment

Sensory
• Periorbital edema

Cardiovascular
• Hypotension
• Bradycardia
• Dysrhythmias
• Enlarged heart
• Anemia

Reproductive
• Menorrhagia (female)
• Infertility (female)
• ↓ libido (male)

Integumentary
• Hair loss
• Brittle nails
• Coarse, dry skin
• Non-pitting edema

Metabolic Processes
• Hypothermia
• Anorexia
• Weight gain
• Systemic edema

Leukemia

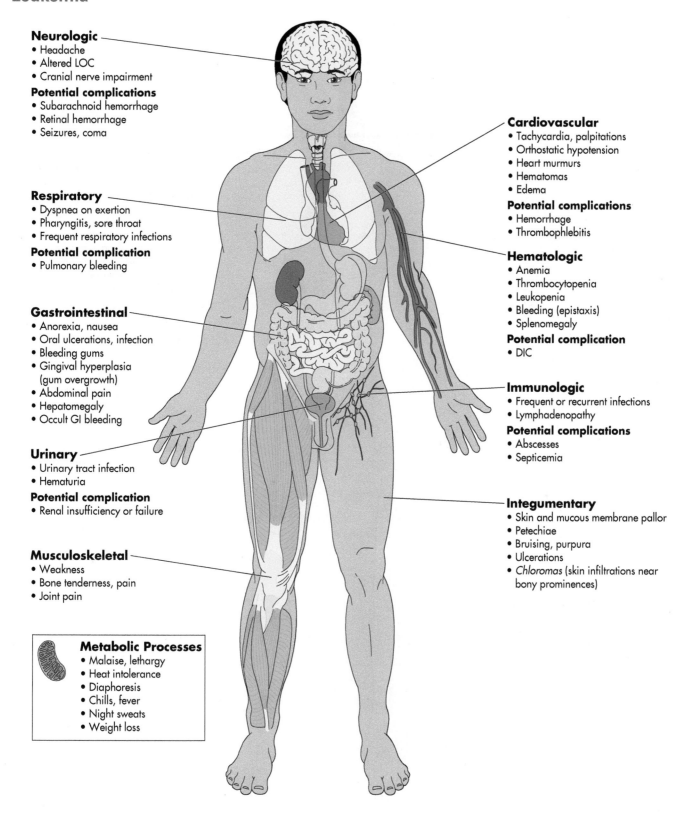

Neurologic
- Headache
- Altered LOC
- Cranial nerve impairment

Potential complications
- Subarachnoid hemorrhage
- Retinal hemorrhage
- Seizures, coma

Respiratory
- Dyspnea on exertion
- Pharyngitis, sore throat
- Frequent respiratory infections

Potential complication
- Pulmonary bleeding

Gastrointestinal
- Anorexia, nausea
- Oral ulcerations, infection
- Bleeding gums
- Gingival hyperplasia
  (gum overgrowth)
- Abdominal pain
- Hepatomegaly
- Occult GI bleeding

Urinary
- Urinary tract infection
- Hematuria

Potential complication
- Renal insufficiency or failure

Musculoskeletal
- Weakness
- Bone tenderness, pain
- Joint pain

Metabolic Processes
- Malaise, lethargy
- Heat intolerance
- Diaphoresis
- Chills, fever
- Night sweats
- Weight loss

Cardiovascular
- Tachycardia, palpitations
- Orthostatic hypotension
- Heart murmurs
- Hematomas
- Edema

Potential complications
- Hemorrhage
- Thrombophlebitis

Hematologic
- Anemia
- Thrombocytopenia
- Leukopenia
- Bleeding (epistaxis)
- Splenomegaly

Potential complication
- DIC

Immunologic
- Frequent or recurrent infections
- Lymphadenopathy

Potential complications
- Abscesses
- Septicemia

Integumentary
- Skin and mucous membrane pallor
- Petechiae
- Bruising, purpura
- Ulcerations
- *Chloromas* (skin infiltrations near bony prominences)

Lung Cancer

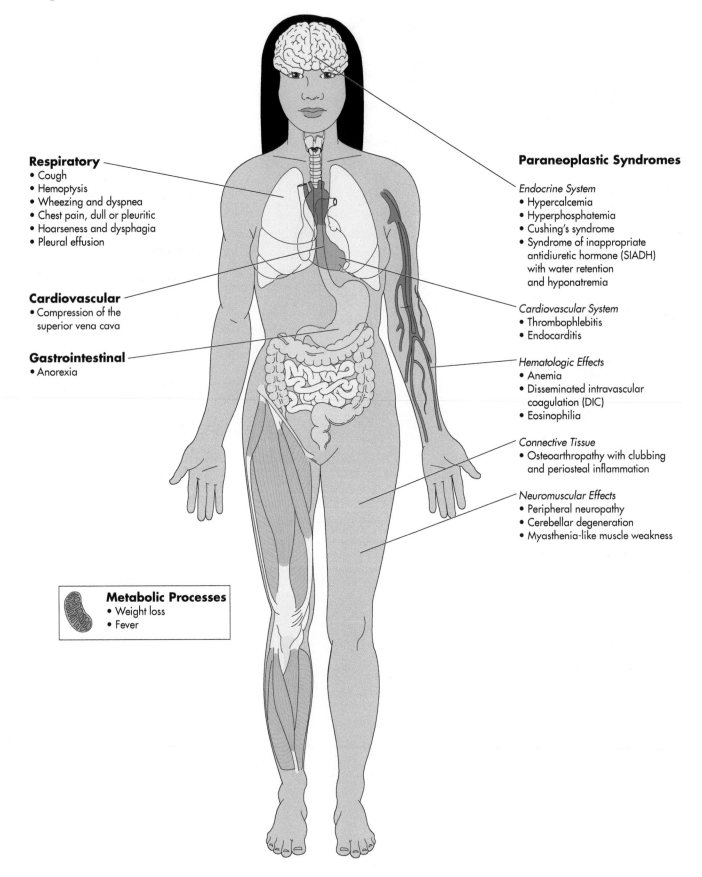

Respiratory
- Cough
- Hemoptysis
- Wheezing and dyspnea
- Chest pain, dull or pleuritic
- Hoarseness and dysphagia
- Pleural effusion

Cardiovascular
- Compression of the superior vena cava

Gastrointestinal
- Anorexia

Metabolic Processes
- Weight loss
- Fever

Paraneoplastic Syndromes

Endocrine System
- Hypercalcemia
- Hyperphosphatemia
- Cushing's syndrome
- Syndrome of inappropriate antidiuretic hormone (SIADH) with water retention and hyponatremia

Cardiovascular System
- Thrombophlebitis
- Endocarditis

Hematologic Effects
- Anemia
- Disseminated intravascular coagulation (DIC)
- Eosinophilia

Connective Tissue
- Osteoarthropathy with clubbing and periosteal inflammation

Neuromuscular Effects
- Peripheral neuropathy
- Cerebellar degeneration
- Myasthenia-like muscle weakness

Multiple Sclerosis

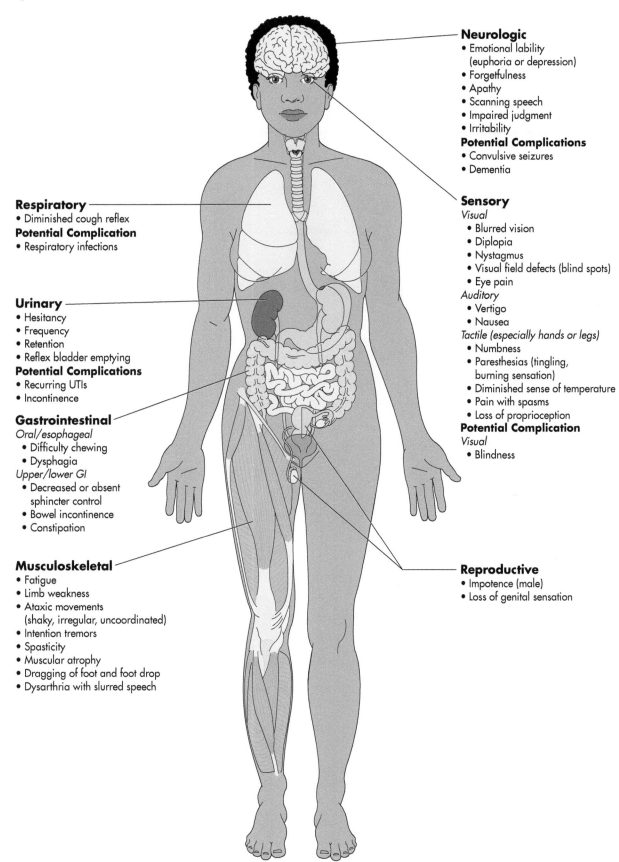

Neurologic
- Emotional lability (euphoria or depression)
- Forgetfulness
- Apathy
- Scanning speech
- Impaired judgment
- Irritability

Potential Complications
- Convulsive seizures
- Dementia

Sensory

Visual
- Blurred vision
- Diplopia
- Nystagmus
- Visual field defects (blind spots)
- Eye pain

Auditory
- Vertigo
- Nausea

Tactile (especially hands or legs)
- Numbness
- Paresthesias (tingling, burning sensation)
- Diminished sense of temperature
- Pain with spasms
- Loss of proprioception

Potential Complication

Visual
- Blindness

Respiratory
- Diminished cough reflex

Potential Complication
- Respiratory infections

Urinary
- Hesitancy
- Frequency
- Retention
- Reflex bladder emptying

Potential Complications
- Recurring UTIs
- Incontinence

Gastrointestinal

Oral/esophageal
- Difficulty chewing
- Dysphagia

Upper/lower GI
- Decreased or absent sphincter control
- Bowel incontinence
- Constipation

Musculoskeletal
- Fatigue
- Limb weakness
- Ataxic movements (shaky, irregular, uncoordinated)
- Intention tremors
- Spasticity
- Muscular atrophy
- Dragging of foot and foot drop
- Dysarthria with slurred speech

Reproductive
- Impotence (male)
- Loss of genital sensation

Premenstrual Syndrome

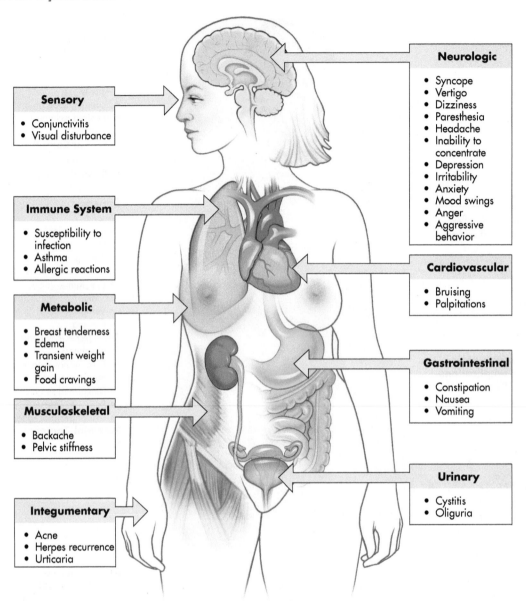

Sensory
- Conjunctivitis
- Visual disturbance

Immune System
- Susceptibility to infection
- Asthma
- Allergic reactions

Metabolic
- Breast tenderness
- Edema
- Transient weight gain
- Food cravings

Musculoskeletal
- Backache
- Pelvic stiffness

Integumentary
- Acne
- Herpes recurrence
- Urticaria

Neurologic
- Syncope
- Vertigo
- Dizziness
- Paresthesia
- Headache
- Inability to concentrate
- Depression
- Irritability
- Anxiety
- Mood swings
- Anger
- Aggressive behavior

Cardiovascular
- Bruising
- Palpitations

Gastrointestinal
- Constipation
- Nausea
- Vomiting

Urinary
- Cystitis
- Oliguria

Rheumatoid Arthritis

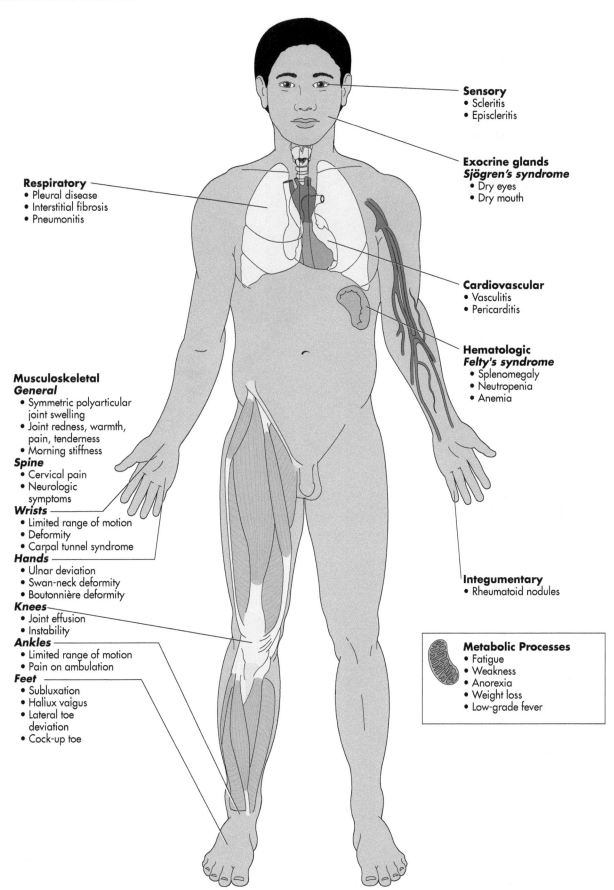

Sensory
- Scleritis
- Episcleritis

Exocrine glands
Sjögren's syndrome
- Dry eyes
- Dry mouth

Respiratory
- Pleural disease
- Interstitial fibrosis
- Pneumonitis

Cardiovascular
- Vasculitis
- Pericarditis

Hematologic
Felty's syndrome
- Splenomegaly
- Neutropenia
- Anemia

Musculoskeletal
General
- Symmetric polyarticular joint swelling
- Joint redness, warmth, pain, tenderness
- Morning stiffness

Spine
- Cervical pain
- Neurologic symptoms

Wrists
- Limited range of motion
- Deformity
- Carpal tunnel syndrome

Hands
- Ulnar deviation
- Swan-neck deformity
- Boutonnière deformity

Knees
- Joint effusion
- Instability

Ankles
- Limited range of motion
- Pain on ambulation

Feet
- Subluxation
- Haliux valgus
- Lateral toe deviation
- Cock-up toe

Integumentary
- Rheumatoid nodules

Metabolic Processes
- Fatigue
- Weakness
- Anorexia
- Weight loss
- Low-grade fever

Shock

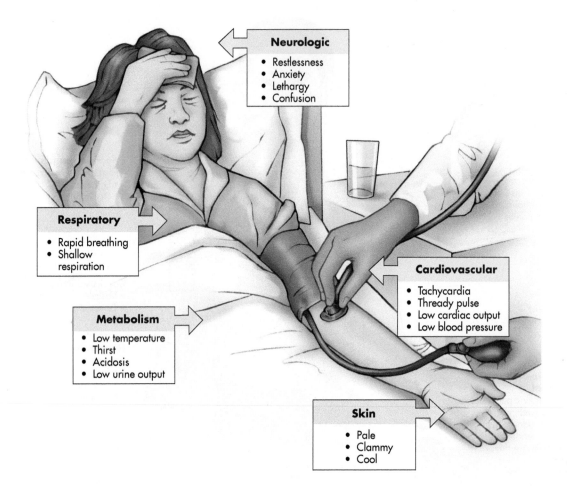

Neurologic
- Restlessness
- Anxiety
- Lethargy
- Confusion

Respiratory
- Rapid breathing
- Shallow respiration

Metabolism
- Low temperature
- Thirst
- Acidosis
- Low urine output

Cardiovascular
- Tachycardia
- Thready pulse
- Low cardiac output
- Low blood pressure

Skin
- Pale
- Clammy
- Cool

Uremia

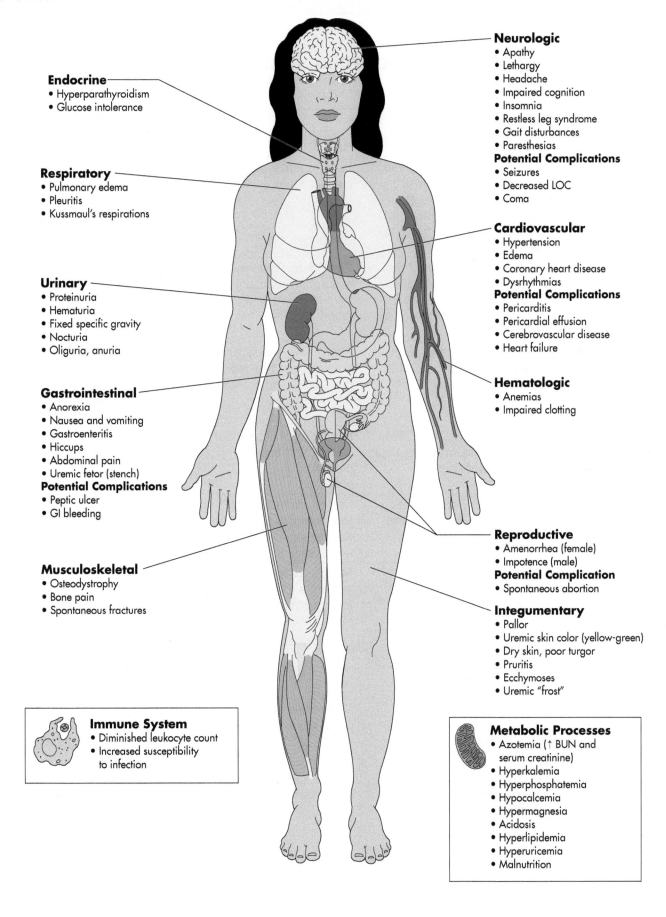

Endocrine
- Hyperparathyroidism
- Glucose intolerance

Respiratory
- Pulmonary edema
- Pleuritis
- Kussmaul's respirations

Urinary
- Proteinuria
- Hematuria
- Fixed specific gravity
- Nocturia
- Oliguria, anuria

Gastrointestinal
- Anorexia
- Nausea and vomiting
- Gastroenteritis
- Hiccups
- Abdominal pain
- Uremic fetor (stench)
Potential Complications
- Peptic ulcer
- GI bleeding

Musculoskeletal
- Osteodystrophy
- Bone pain
- Spontaneous fractures

Neurologic
- Apathy
- Lethargy
- Headache
- Impaired cognition
- Insomnia
- Restless leg syndrome
- Gait disturbances
- Paresthesias
Potential Complications
- Seizures
- Decreased LOC
- Coma

Cardiovascular
- Hypertension
- Edema
- Coronary heart disease
- Dysrhythmias
Potential Complications
- Pericarditis
- Pericardial effusion
- Cerebrovascular disease
- Heart failure

Hematologic
- Anemias
- Impaired clotting

Reproductive
- Amenorrhea (female)
- Impotence (male)
Potential Complication
- Spontaneous abortion

Integumentary
- Pallor
- Uremic skin color (yellow-green)
- Dry skin, poor turgor
- Pruritis
- Ecchymoses
- Uremic "frost"

Immune System
- Diminished leukocyte count
- Increased susceptibility to infection

Metabolic Processes
- Azotemia (↑ BUN and serum creatinine)
- Hyperkalemia
- Hyperphosphatemia
- Hypocalcemia
- Hypermagnesia
- Acidosis
- Hyperlipidemia
- Hyperuricemia
- Malnutrition

Vitamins and Minerals: Sources, Function, and Effects of Deficiency and Toxicity

NUTRIENT	PRINCIPLE SOURCES	FUNCTIONS	EFFECTS OF DEFICIENCY AND TOXICITY
Vitamin A (retinol)	Fish liver oils, liver, egg yolk, butter, cream, vitamin A-fortified margarine; as carotenoids: dark green, leafy vegetables; yellow fruits; red palm oil	Photoreceptor mechanism of retina, integrity of skin	**Deficiency:** night blindness, keratomalacia, increased morbidity and mortality in young children **Toxicity:** headache, peeling of skin
Vitamin D (cholecalciferol, ergocalciferol)	Ultraviolet irradiation of the skin (main source); fortified milk (main dietary source), fish liver oils, butter, egg yolk, liver	Calcium and phosphorus absorption; reabsorption mineralization, and maturation of bone	**Deficiency:** rickets (sometimes with tetany), osteomalacia **Toxicity:** anorexia, renal failure
Vitamin E group (α-tocopherol and other tocopherols)	Vegetable oil, wheat germ, leafy vegetables, egg yolk, margarine, legumes	Intracellular antioxidant, scavenger of free radicals in biologic membranes	**Deficiency:** RBC hemolysis or rupture of red blood cells, neurologic damage **Toxicity:** interference with enzymes
Vitamin K group (phylloquinone and menaquinones)	Leafy vegetables, pork, liver, vegetable oils, intestinal flora after newborn period	Formation of coagulation factors, and bone proteins	**Deficiency:** hemorrhage from deficiency of coagulation factors
Thiamine (vitamin B_1)	Dried yeast, whole grains, meat (especially pork, liver), enriched cereal products, nuts, legumes, potatoes	Carbohydrate metabolism, central and peripheral nerve cell function, heart function	**Deficiency:** beriberi peripheral nerve degeneration, heart failure, Wernicke Korsakoff syndrome
Riboflavin (vitamin B_2)	Milk, cheese, liver, meat, eggs, enriched cereal products	Many aspects of energy and protein metabolism, integrity of mucous membranes	**Deficiency:** dry lips, mouth sores, dermatitis
Niacin (nicotinic acid, niacinamide)	Dried yeast, liver, meat, fish, legumes, whole-grain enriched cereal products	Carbohydrate metabolism	**Deficiency:** pellagra (dermatitis, swelling of the tongue, gastrointestinal and nervous system disturbance)
Vitamin B_6 group (pyridoxine, pyridoxal, pyridoxamine)	Dried yeast, liver, organ meats, whole-grain cereals, fish, legumes	Many aspects of protein metabolism	**Deficiency:** convulsions, nervous system disturbance **Toxicity:** peripheral degeneration of nervous tissue
Folic acid	Fresh green leafy vegetables, fruits, organ meats, liver, dried yeast	Maturation of red blood cells	**Deficiency:** anemia, neural tube defects

NUTRIENT	PRINCIPLE SOURCES	FUNCTIONS	EFFECTS OF DEFICIENCY AND TOXICITY
Vitamin B$_{12}$ (cobalamins)	Liver, meats (especially beef, pork, organ meats), eggs, milk and milk products	Maturation of red blood cells, neural function, DNA synthesis	**Deficiency:** pernicious anemia, megaloblastic anemia
Biotin	Liver, kidney, egg yolk, yeast, cauliflower, nuts, legumes	Amino acid and fatty acid metabolism	**Deficiency:** dermatitis, swelling of the tongue
Vitamin C (ascorbic acid)	Citrus fruits, tomatoes, potatoes, cabbage, green peppers	Essential to bone tissue, collagen formation, vascular function, tissue oxygenation, and wound healing	**Deficiency:** scurvy (hemorrhages, loose teeth, gingivitis, bone disease)
Sodium	Wide distribution—beef, pork, sardines, cheese, green olives, corn bread, potato chips, sauerkraut	Acid–base balance, fluid balance, blood acidity, muscle contractility, nerve transmission	**Deficiency:** confusion, coma **Toxicity:** confusion, coma
Chloride	Wide distribution—mainly animal products but some vegetables; similar to sodium	Acid–base balance, fluid balance, blood acidity, kidney function	**Deficiency:** failure to thrive in infants hypertension **Toxicity:** increase in extracellular volume
Potassium	Wide distribution—whole and skim milk, bananas, prunes, raisins, meats	Muscle activity, nerve transmission, intracellular acid–base balance and water retention	**Deficiency:** paralysis, cardiac disturbances **Toxicity:** paralysis, cardiac disturbances
Calcium	Milk and milk products, meat, fish, eggs, cereal products, beans, fruits, vegetables	Bone and tooth formation, blood coagulation, neuromuscular irritability, muscle contractility, myocardial conduction	**Deficiency:** long term: osteoporosis tetany, neuromuscular hyperexcitability **Toxicity:** gastrointestinal paralysis, kidney failure, psychosis
Phosphorus	Milk, cheese, meat, poultry, fish, cereals, nuts, legumes	Bone and tooth formation, acid–base balance, component of nucleic acids, energy production	**Deficiency:** irritability, weakness, blood cell disorders, gastrointestinal tract and kidney dysfunction **Toxicity:** accumulation in kidney disease
Magnesium	Green leaves, nuts, cereal grains, seafood	Bone and tooth formation, nerve conduction, muscle contraction, enzyme activation	**Deficiency:** neuromuscular irritability **Toxicity:** hypotension, respiratory failure, cardiac disturbances
Iron	Wide distribution (except dairy products)—soybean flour, beef, kidney, liver, beans, clams, peaches Heme iron in meat well absorbed (10–30%); nonheme iron in vegetables poorly absorbed (1–10%)	Hemoglobin and myoglobin formation, cytochrome enzymes, iron-sulfur proteins	**Deficiency:** anemia, decreased work performance, impaired learning ability **Toxicity:** nausea, vomiting, diarrhea, gastrointestinal damage; fatal in children
Iodine	Seafood, iodized salt, eggs, dairy products, drinking water in varying amounts	Synthesis of thyroid hormones	**Deficiency:** hypothyroidism, impaired fetal growth and brain development **Toxicity:** hyperthyroidism

NUTRIENT	PRINCIPLE SOURCES	FUNCTIONS	EFFECTS OF DEFICIENCY AND TOXICITY
Fluorine	Seafood, vegetables, grains, tea, coffee, fluoridated water (sodium fluoride 1.0–2.0 ppm)	Bone and tooth formation	**Deficiency:** predisposition to dental caries, osteoporosis **Toxicity:** mottling and pitting of permanent teeth
Zinc	Meat, liver, eggs, oysters, peanuts, whole grains	Component of enzymes; skin integrity, wound healing, growth	**Deficiency:** growth retardation, small reproductive gland (testes) acrodermatitis enteropathica causes zinc deficiency
Copper	Organ meats, oysters, nuts, dried legumes, whole-grain cereals	Enzyme component, red blood cell synthesis, bone formation	**Deficiency:** anemia in malnourished children **Toxicity:** nausea, vomiting, diarrhea, brain damage
Chromium	Brewer's yeast, liver, processed meats, whole-grain cereals, spices	Promotion of glucose tolerance	**Deficiency:** impaired glucose tolerance in malnourished children, some diabetics, and some elderly persons
Selenium	Wide distribution—meats and other animal products	Functions as an antioxidant with vitamin E	**Deficiency:** rare; muscle weakness **Toxicity:** loss of hair and nails, nausea, dermatitis, polyneuritis
Manganese	Whole-grain cereals, green leafy vegetables, nuts, tea	Component of enzymes	**Primary Deficiency:** rare **Toxicity:** Rare due to occupational exposure
Molybdenum	Milk, beans, breads, cereals	Component of coenzyme	**Deficiency:** tachycardia, headache, nausea, disorientation

Source: Modified from Merck Manual, 2009.

Standard and Transmission-Based Precautions

Transmission of infectious agents requires three elements: (1) a source of infectious agents; (2) a susceptible host with a source of entry receptive to the agent; and (3) a mode of transmission for the agent. All blood, body fluids, secretions, excretions (except sweat), nonintact skin, and mucous membranes may contain contagious infectious agents. As discussed in Chapter 1, because of the risk of transmitting these infectious agents, a set of Standard and Transmission-Based Precautions were developed. The guidelines, *The Guideline for Isolation Precautions: Preventing Transmission of Infectious Agents in Healthcare Settings 2007,* were updated in 2007 by the Centers for Disease Control and Prevention (CDC). Go to http://www.cdc .gov for the complete text of the 2007 CDC Standard Precautions as well as any updates to the guidelines.

Standard Precautions serve as the basis for preventing the transmission of infectious agents in all health care settings. Transmission-Based Precautions should be implemented until the origin of the infection is known. These guidelines include practices that apply to all health care providers, patients, visitors, and family members. Hand hygiene is the single-most effective way to prevent the spread of infections and is a critical element in Standard Precautions. Other safe practices may involve the use of gloves, goggles, face shield, and/or a gown when there is a risk of splashing or spray of blood or body fluids. Safe handling of soiled linens also reduces the risks of spreading infectious agents. Listed here are procedures to follow to minimize the risk of spreading infectious agents.

HAND HYGIENE

Hand hygiene includes effective hand washing with plain or antiseptic-containing soap and water or the use of alcohol-based products that do not require the use of water. You should wash your hands:

- Between patient contacts.
- After removing protective gloves.
- After contact with body fluids, even if gloves have been worn.

Hand-Washing Procedure

1. Stand at sink. Avoid contact of your uniform with the sink. Roll a paper towel out to have ready to use after washing your hands.

2. Turn on water and adjust water temperature.
3. Wet the hands and wrists thoroughly. Keep hands lower than elbows.
4. Apply skin cleanser or soap to hands.
5. Using friction, wash the palms, backs of the hands, fingers, between the fingers, knuckles, wrists, and forearms. Clean nails. If no nail brush is available, rub nails across palms of hands.
6. Continue washing for at least 15 seconds.
7. Rinse thoroughly all surfaces of wrists, hands, and fingers, keeping hands lower than the elbows and the fingertips down.
8. Dry hands thoroughly using a clean, dry paper towel.
9. Use a clean, dry paper towel to turn off faucets. Do not touch inside of sink at any time.
10. Dispose of used paper towel(s) in wastebasket immediately after shutting off faucet.

RESPIRATORY HYGIENE/COUGH ETIQUETTE

It is essential that sneezes and coughs are covered so that the air is not contaminated with respiratory secretions. This may include placing a mask on a coughing patient. Respiratory hygiene/cough etiquette procedures should be used for all patients with respiratory symptoms (e.g., coughing and sneezing). The elements of cough etiquette are listed next:

1. Education of health care facility staff, patients, and visitors
2. Posted signs, in language(s) appropriate to the population served, with instructions to patients and accompanying family members or friends
3. Source control measures (e.g., covering the mouth/ nose with a tissue when coughing and prompt disposal of used tissues, using surgical masks on the coughing person when tolerated and appropriate)
4. Hand hygiene after contact with respiratory secretions
5. Spatial separation, ideally greater than 3 feet, of persons with respiratory infections in common waiting areas when possible

PERSONAL PROTECTIVE EQUIPMENT

Personal protective equipment (PPE) includes a variety of barriers and respirators used alone or in combination to protect mucous membranes, airways, skin, and clothing from contact with infectious agents. It can include gowns, masks, gloves, and so on. The PPE items chosen should be based on how you will be interacting with the patient. First, determine the expected level of exposure. Then refer to the CDC guidelines for the use of personal protective equipment to determine the appropriate PPE equipment to use. Always practice safe work practices, which include

- Keep hands away from face.
- Work from clean to dirty.
- Limit surfaces touched.
- Change when torn or heavily contaminated.
- Perform hand hygiene.

Procedures

Note: When using personal protective equipment, don in the order the procedures are given.

Prior to donning protective equipment:

1. Remove your watch or push it well up your arm.
2. Wash your hands.

Gown

Isolation gowns are usually worn to protect the employee's arms and exposed body areas and clothing from blood and body fluids and are used in combination with gloves and other PPE as necessary.

Gown Procedures

1. Pick up gown and unfold.
2. Facing the back opening of the gown, place arms through each sleeve.
3. Fasten the neck opening.
4. Secure gown at waist making sure that back of clothing is covered by gown (as much as possible).
5. Put on gloves (see gloving procedure). Cuffs of gloves overlap cuffs of gown.
6. Prior to removing gown, with one gloved hand, grasp the other glove at the palm, and pull glove off.
7. Slip fingers from ungloved hand underneath cuff of remaining glove at wrist, and remove glove, turning it inside out as it is removed.

8. Dispose of gloves into designated waste container/ waste container without contaminating self.
9. Unfasten gown at neck after removing gloves.
10. Remove gown without touching outside of gown.
11. While removing gown, hold gown away from body, turn gown inward and keep it inside out, and dispose of in appropriate receptacle.

Mask

Surgical masks are used to cover the nose and mouth and provide protection from contact with large infectious droplets (over 5 mm in size). For protection from inhalation of small particles or droplet nuclei, particulate respirators are recommended. The health care worker must be fitted for these masks prior to use to maintain appropriate seal and protection. The Infection Control Department staff will do fit testing for the employee during the employee's orientation period. Masks may be used with goggles to protect the mouth, nose, and eyes.

Mask Procedures

1. Determine the appropriate type of face mask to be used.
2. Place the mask snugly over your nose and mouth. Secure the mask by tying the strings behind your head or placing the loops around your ears.
3. If the mask has a metal strip, squeeze it to fit your nose firmly.
4. If you wear eyeglasses, tuck the mask under their lower edge.
5. Front of mask is contaminated—DO NOT TOUCH!
6. To remove, grasp ONLY bottom then top ties/elastics and remove.
7. Discard in waste container.
8. Wash hands.

Goggles/Face Shield

Goggles or face shield should be worn when there is a risk of contaminating the eyes. The eye protection chosen for specific work situations (e.g., goggles or face shield) depends on the circumstances of exposure, other PPE used, and personal vision needs. Note that personal eyeglasses and contact lenses are not considered appropriate eye protection. Safe removal of a face shield, goggles, and mask should be performed after gloves have been removed and hand hygiene performed.

The front of a mask, goggles, and face shield are considered contaminated. The ties, earpieces, and/or headband used to secure the equipment to the head are considered clean to touch with bare hands.

Goggles/Face Shield Procedures

1. Determine whether to use face shield or goggles.
2. Put on face and adjust to fit.
3. Once used, the outside of goggles or face shield are contaminated.
4. To remove, handle by "clean" head band or earpieces.
5. Place in designated receptacle for reprocessing or in waste container.
6. Wash hands.

Gloves

Gloves should be worn when there is risk of touching blood or body fluids. Gloves are worn only once and are discarded according to agency policy. Some care activities for an individual patient may require changing gloves more than once. Hands should be thoroughly washed after gloves are removed.

Gloves Procedures

1. Use clean, disposable gloves.
2. Select a glove that provides appropriate fit.
3. Place the gloves on the hands so that the gloves extend to cover the wrist of the isolation gown. Note: Once used, the outside of gloves are contaminated.
4. When removing, grasp outside of glove with opposite gloved hand; peel off.
5. Hold removed glove in gloved hand.
6. Slide fingers of ungloved hand under remaining glove at wrist, peeling off while capturing other contaminated glove.
7. Dispose of in appropriate waste receptacle.
8. Wash hands.

Removing Personal Protective Equipment

The order or sequence used for removing personal protective equipment is very important. Remember that the outside surfaces of your personal protective equipment are contaminated. The CDC recommends removing PPE at the doorway to the patient's room, or anteroom (if applicable). Practice hand hygiene immediately after removing the PPE. The following procedure summarizes the correct removal of gown, gloves, and mask/eye protection.

Removing Personal Protective Equipment Procedures

1. While wearing gloves, untie the gown's waist strings.
2. With your gloved left hand, remove the right glove by pulling on the cuff, turning the glove inside out as you pull.
3. Remove the left glove by placing two fingers in the glove and pulling it off, turning it inside out as you remove it. Discard. Wash your hands.
4. Untie the neck strings of your gown. Grasp the outside of the gown at the back of the shoulders and pull the gown down over your arms, turning it inside out as you remove it.
5. Holding the gown well away from your uniform, fold it inside out. Discard it in the laundry hamper.
6. Wash your hands. Turn off the faucet using a paper towel, and discard the towel in trash container.
7. Remove the mask/goggles to avoid contaminating your face or hair in the process. Untie your mask and/or remove your goggles by holding only the strings/strap. Discard.
8. Wash your hands and forearms with soap or antiseptic after leaving the room.

Mouthpieces, Resuscitation Bags, and Other Ventilation Devices

Use a ventilation device, which provides protection for the caregiver from oral contact, as an alternative to mouth-to-mouth resuscitation. Using a ventilation device prevents the health care provider from being exposed to oral and respiratory fluids during the procedure.

CARING FOR SOILED LINENS

The hospital laundry uses water temperature and cleaning products capable of destroying any pathogens that might be present in patient's bed linens. Before you care for soiled linens, wash your hands and don disposable gloves.

Caring for Soiled Linens Procedures

1. Fold the soiled bed linens inward on themselves when removing them from the bed.
2. Hold the linens away from your uniform when removing from room.
3. Place in the nearest hamper.
4. Should the outside surface of the linen hamper bag become soiled, it should be placed in a clean outer bag prior to pickup by the laundry staff.

DISPOSING OF SHARPS

Because of the danger inherent in handling sharp objects or contaminated needles, the health care industry has moved toward needleless systems whenever possible. However, when a needleless system cannot be provided, needles will have a protective sheath used to cover before and after use. There is no longer any need to recap used needles. Be sure to select the safest method of using sharps, using a needleless system whenever possible. Before you handle the sharp items, be sure to wash your hands and don disposable gloves. Locate the closest sharps container to the area in which you will be working.

Note: Gloves are not meant to protect the caregiver from needle stick or sharps injuries.

Disposing of Sharps Procedures

1. After the use of any needle, place the protective sheath on the needle before leaving the patient area.
2. If sharps are used during a procedure, carefully separate them from other items on the tray and cover them with the procedure tray cover.
3. Place any disposable sharps items in the closest sharps container.
4. Place nondisposable sharps items in the designated area of the closest dirty utility room.
5. Remove and discard disposable gloves.
6. Wash hands.

COMMUNICABLE DISEASES

A communicable disease, also called an infectious disease, is any type of disease that can be transmitted from one person to another. Transmission of the disease can occur through one or more ways, including body fluids, airborne inhalation, food, or physical contact with an infected individual.

HIV

The first cases of AIDS (acquired immune deficiency syndrome) were reported in the 1980s. AIDS is a chronic life-threatening condition caused by the human immunodeficiency virus (HIV). HIV destroys the cells of your immune system, which affects your body's ability to fight bacteria, fungi, and viruses. This makes the body more susceptible to certain types of cancers and to opportunistic infections your body would normally resist, such as pneumonia, Kaposi's sarcoma, and tuberculosis. When AIDS was first discovered, there was rampant fear of anyone with HIV or AIDS. People avoided contact with anyone diagnosed with HIV or AIDS.

Even some health care workers devoted to the care of the ill refused to care for these patients.

On a positive note, the recognition of this disease was instrumental in the creation of Standard Precautions and the continuing revision of *Precautions for Occupational Health and Bloodborne Pathogens*. Education about the causes and treatment of HIV and AIDS has progressed to the point that health care workers and the general public are more accepting and much less fearful of those infected.

Things to Do When Treating HIV-Positive or AIDS Patients

- Educate yourself and the patient.
- Help the patient understand options for treatment.
- Be supportive.
- Promote the patient's role as an individual and a member of the community.

Things not to Do When Treating HIV-Positive or AIDS Patients

- Avoid personal contact.
- Isolate patient from human contact.
- Exhibit personal prejudices.

There is no need to wear protective gloves when directly interacting with these patients. Use gloves only when there is a danger of contact with blood or body fluids, mucous membrane, or nonintact skin. As with any other patient, practicing good hand-washing techniques is always appropriate and in the caregiver's and patient's best interests.

MRSA (Methicillin-Resistant Staphylococcus Aureus)

MRSA causes an infection that is resistant to many types of antibiotics. MRSA infections are caused by *Staphylococcus aureus* bacteria—often called "staph." The organism is often subcategorized as community-associated MRSA (CA-MRSA) or hospital-associated MRSA (HA-MRSA), depending how the disease is acquired; the two forms of MRSA are distinct strains of the bacterial species. The key to stopping MRSA in hospitals is to practice infection control. CA-MRSA, which is mainly transmitted through close skin-to-skin contact, can be prevented by practicing good hygiene, keeping cuts and scrapes healed and covered, and avoiding sharing personal items, such as towels or washcloths. MRSA infections can be fatal.

MRSA was first discovered in England in 1961, but it is now found worldwide. In recent years the number of MRSA infections in the United States has increased considerably. A 2007 report by the CDC estimated that the number of MRSA infections treated in hospitals doubled nationwide, from approximately 127,000 in 1999 to 278,000 in 2005, and the number of deaths increased from 11,000 to more than 17,000.

SARS (Severe Acute Respiratory Syndrome)

SARS is a highly contagious and sometimes fatal respiratory disease. SARS coronavirus, the same family of virus that causes the common cold, is the virus that causes SARS.

SARS first appeared in China in 2002. Within 6 weeks, the virus had spread worldwide. During that outbreak, 8,000 people were infected, and 800 died of the disease. In part, the CDC saw the need to develop Respiratory Hygiene/Cough Etiquette as a result of the SARS outbreak.

Patients who can contaminate the area with known communicable diseases should be in a private room or isolated from other patients. There will be a list of diseases that are communicable and the precautions that should be taken available on the patient unit. The Infection Control Department will monitor all admissions and advise staff of any additional precautions that need to be taken.

A

abdominopelvic cavity *(ab DOM ih noh PELL vik)* Continuous cavity within the abdomen and pelvis that contains the largest organs of the gastrointestinal system.

abduction *(ahb DUK shun)* Moving a body part away from the midline of the body.

abscess *(AB ses)* A collection of pus in an enclosed body space.

absorption *(ab SORP shun)* Process by which nutrients move through villi of the small intestine into the bloodstream or substances move from the kidney tubules into the bloodstream.

accessory muscles Muscles in the neck, chest, and abdomen that can be used, if necessary, to help expand the thoracic cavity on inspiration.

accommodation The change in size of the pupil and lens curvature to allow for proper focusing on the retina.

acoustic nerve See vestibulocochlear nerve.

acetylcholine *(AS eh till KOH leen)* Neurotransmitter between neurons in the brain and spinal cord or between a neuron and a voluntary skeletal muscle.

acetylcholinesterase *(AS eh till KOH lin ehs tur ace)* The enzyme that stops the action of acetylcholine.

acid–base relationship The relationship between the hydrogen ion and bicarbonate ions within the body to determine blood pH.

acquired immune deficiency syndrome (AIDS) An immune deficiency disorder caused by the human immunodeficiency virus (HIV).

acquired immunity *See* adaptive immunity.

acromegaly *(ACK row MEG ah lee)* A hormonal condition of gradual coarsening and enlargement of bones and facial features.

acronym Memory aid by using first letters of words to make a unique word.

actin *(ak TIN)* One of the two proteins in muscle fibers needed for contraction.

action potential The change of the electrical charge of a nerve or muscle fiber when stimulated. Action potentials are all or none.

active transport The movement of cellular material that requires energy.

active transport pumps (also called carrier mediated active transport) The movement of substances across cell membranes at the expense of adenosine triphosphate.

acute Having rapid onset, severe symptoms, and a short course.

acute epiglottitis *(EP ih glawt EYE tiss)* Inflammation of the epiglottis due to infection.

acute renal failure Rapid decrease in kidney function as measured by blood urea and creatinine levels.

adaptation The adjustment of an organism to changing environments.

adaptive immunity Immune mechanisms that "learn" to deal with specific invaders.

adduction *(ah DUCK shun)* Moving a body part toward the midline of the body.

adenoid *(AD eh noid)* Lymphoid tissue in the superior part of the nasopharynx. Also known as the *pharyngeal tonsils*.

adenosine diphosphate (ADP) *(ah DEN oh seen die FOSS fate)* The compound that can be converted to ATP for energy storage. When ATP is broken down to ADP, energy is released that can be used for cellular energy.

adenosine triphosphate (ATP) *(ah DEN oh seen try FOSS fate)* Energy storage molecule used to power muscle contraction and other cellular reactions.

adipose tissue *(AD ih pose)* Fatty tissue.

adrenal *(ad REE nal)* Referring to the adrenal gland.

adrenal cortex *(ad REE nal KOR teks)* Outermost part of the adrenal gland. It produces and secretes three groups of hormones: mineralocorticoids (aldosterone), glucocorticoids (cortisol), and some androgens (male hormones).

adrenal medulla   *(ad REE nal meh DULL lah)* Innermost part of the adrenal gland. It produces and secretes the hormones epinephrine and norepinephrine.

adrenaline   *(ah DREN ah lin)* Also known as epinephrine, secreted by the adrenal medulla.

adrenocorticosteroids   *(ad REE noh KORE tih koh STEER oydz)* Collective term for numerous hormones secreted by the adrenal cortex.

adventitia   *(add ven TISH ah)* The outermost covering of a structure or organ.

afferent arterioles   *(AFF er ent ahr TEE ree ohlz)* Small arteries traveling toward an organ.

agglutinate   *(ah GLUE tin ate)* To clump.

agonist   *(AG on ist)* The most important muscle that causes a movement, the prime mover.

agranulocyte   A nongranular, mononuclear white blood cell (a lymphocyte or a monocyte).

AIDS–related complex (ARC)   Symptoms may include enlarged lymph nodes, fatigue, night sweats, weight loss, and diarrhea.

airborne transmission   The spread of infectious agents through the air, often the result of sneezing or coughing.

albumin   *(AL byoo men)* Most abundant plasma protein.

aldosterone   *(al DOSS ter ohn)* Most abundant and biologically active of the mineralocorticoid hormones secreted by the adrenal cortex. It regulates the balance of electrolytes, keeping sodium (and water) in the blood while excreting potassium in the urine.

alimentary canal   Alternate name for the gastrointestinal system.

alimentary tract   *(al ah MEN tar ee)* Alternate name for the gastrointestinal system.

allergic reaction   Relating to any body response stimulated by an allergen.

allergic rhinitis   *(rye NY tis)* Condition of excessive nasal secretions (runny nose) due to irritations caused by allergic agents.

alopecia   *(AL oh PEE she ah)* Absence or loss of hair.

alveolar capillary membrane   *(al VEE oh lar KAP uh ler ee MEM breyn)* Site of the connection between the respiratory and cardiovascular system where gas exchange occurs.

alveolar sacs   *(al VEE oh lar)* Grape bunch–like structures composed of several alveoli.

alveoli   *(al VEE oh lye)* Hollow spheres of cells in the lungs where oxygen and carbon dioxide are exchanged; Glandular structures arranged in clusters throughout the breast and the site of milk synthesis.

Alzheimer's disease   *(ALTS high merz)* A progressive, degenerative disease of the brain that is the most common cause of dementia in individuals 65 or older.

amblyopia   *(am blee OH pee ah)* Reduction or dimness of vision. Also known as *lazy eye*.

amenorrhea   *(ah MEN oh REE ah)* The absence or lack of menstruation.

amino acids   Building blocks of proteins.

amniocentesis   *(AM nee oh sen TEE sis)* A diagnostic test in which a needle and syringe is utilized to withdraw amniotic fluid that is chemically and cytologically studied for any genetic or biochemical disorders of the fetus. This is usually performed no earlier than 14 weeks gestation.

amnion   *(AM nee on)* The membranous sac that encases the fetus.

ampulla   The dilated distal end of a uterine tube terminating in a funnellike infundibulum.

amylase   *(AM ih lace)* Salivary enzyme that begins the breakdown of carbohydrates such as starches.

amyotrophic lateral sclerosis (ALS)   *(AA mee o TROF ic)* Neuromuscular disease that destroys both upper and lower motor neurons that leads to a loss of muscle control.

anabolic steroids   *(an ah BALL ick)* A class of steroids that cause large increases in muscle mass with many side effects.

anabolism   *(ah NAB oh lizm)* Assembly of new molecules in the body.

anaphase   Third step in mitosis in which chromosomes split and spindles pull them apart.

anaphylaxis   *(AN ah fih LAK sis)* An immediate, usually allergic response characterized by smooth muscle contraction and dilation of capillaries due to various chemical releases by the body that may lead to rapid decrease in blood pressure.

anastomosis   *(ah NASS te MOE sis)* The suturing of one blood vessel to another.

anatomical position   *(an ah TOM ih kal)* This is a standard position in which the body is standing erect, the head is up with the eyes looking forward, the arms are by the sides with the palms facing forward, and the legs are straight with the toes pointing forward.

anatomy *(ah NAT oh mee)* The study of the structures of the human body.

anemia *(ah NEE mee ah)* Any condition in which the number of erythrocytes in the blood is decreased.

anesthesia *(an ess THEE zee ah)* Condition in which sensation of any type, including touch, pressure, proprioception, or pain, has been completely lost.

aneurysm *(AN yoo rizm)* Area of dilation and weakness in the wall of an artery. This can be congenital or where arteriosclerosis has damaged the artery. With each heartbeat, the weakened artery wall balloons outward. Aneurysms can rupture without warning. A dissecting aneurysm is one that is enlarging by tunneling between the layers of the artery wall.

angina pectoris *(AN jih nah PEK tor iss)* A constricting pain or uncomfortable heaviness in the chest often radiating to the shoulder and down the left arm due to cardiac muscle ischemia related to coronary disease.

angiogram *(AN jee oh gram)* A radiographic recording of the size, shape, and location of the heart and its blood vessels following the injection of a radiopaque medium.

angiotensinogen *(AN jee oh ten SIN oh jin)* A protein produced by the liver.

anhidrosis *(AN hy DROH sis)* A genetic- or disease-related condition of diminished or complete absence of sweat. It can be temporary or permanent, depending on the causative agent.

anorexia nervosa *(an oh REK see ah ner VOH sah)* An eating disorder exhibiting an unrealistic body image, fear of weight gain, weight loss, and emaciation.

antagonist The muscle that does the opposite of the agonist.

antebrachial *(AN tee BREY kee uhl)* The area of the forearm.

antecubital *(AN tee KYOO bi tl)* The area in front of the elbow.

anterior *(an TEER ee or)* The front of the body.

anterior commissure *(an TEER ee or KAH mih sure)* A nerve pathway in the anterior part of the brain that allows communication between the right and left halves of the cerebrum.

anterior pituitary *(an TEER ee or pih TOO eh TAIR ee)* A gland controlled by the hypothalamus but also secretes a number of hormones.

anteroposterior (AP) *(AN ter oh paws TEE ree or)* A view from the front to the back as in an AP chest x-ray.

antibiotics *(AN teh by OT icks)* Natural or synthetic substances that either destroy a bacterial microorganism or inhibit its growth.

antibody *(AN teh bahd ee)* Proteins secreted by B lymphocytes (plasma cells) that attack infected cells.

antibody mediated immunity Immunity that results from a formation of antibodies in response to antigens.

antidiuretic hormone (ADH) *(AN tye dye yoo RET ik)* Hormone secreted by the posterior pituitary gland. It stimulates the kidneys to move water back into the blood to increase the volume of blood.

antigen presenting cells (APC) Cells that engulf antigens and display them as markers.

antigens *(AN tih jennz)* Substance that causes a formation of antibodies. Cell surface markers that help the immune system identify cells.

antiseptic A substance capable of destroying microorganisms.

anuria *(an YOO ree ah)* Condition where no urine is produced.

anus *(AYE nuss)* External opening of rectum, located between the buttocks. The external anal sphincter is under voluntary control. The perianal area is around the anus.

anvil One of the three small bones in the ear.

apex The rounded top of each lung and the gently rounded lower tip of the outer surface of the heart.

apocrine glands *(APP oh krin)* Sweat glands found in the pubic and axillary regions which open into the hair follicles.

aponeurosis *(AP oh nyoo ROH sis)* Broad sheet of connective tissue that serves as a muscle attachment.

appendectomy Surgical removal of the vermiform appendix.

appendicitis *(ah pen dih SIGH tiss)* Inflammation and infection of the appendix.

appendicular skeleton *(app en DIK yoo lahr SKELL eh ton)* The bones of the shoulders, arms, hips, and legs.

appendix *(ah PEN dicks)* Long, thin pouch on the exterior wall of the cecum. It does not play a role in digestion. It contains lymphatic tissue.

aphthous stomatitis *(AFF thouse stow meh TIGHT es)* Inflammation of the mouth that results in an ulcer.

aqueous humor *(AY kwee us HYOO mer)* Clear, watery fluid of the eye produced by the ciliary body. It circulates through the posterior and anterior chambers and takes nutrients and oxygen to the cornea and lens.

arachnoid mater *(ah RAK noyd MAY ter)* Weblike connective tissues that attach to the pia mater. The space under the arachnoid mater (subarachnoid space) contains cerebral spinal fluid.

arachnoid villi *(vill EYE)* Folds of the arachnoid layer of the cranial meninges that project through the inner layer of dura mater into the superior sagittal sinus and other venous sinuses of the brain. Through them, cerebrospinal fluid re-enters the bloodstream.

arbor vitae *(ARE ber VAHY tee)* The white matter center of the cerebellum known as the "tree of life."

arcuate arteries *(ARE koo ate)* Branches of interlobar arteries that arch around the base of the renal pyramids.

areolar tissue Delicate webs of loosely connected tissue.

arrector pili *(are ek tor pil eye)* Muscle used to straighten hair when one becomes chilled or frightened.

arrhythmia *(ah RITH mee ah)* An irregularity or loss of rhythm in the cardiac conduction system.

arteries Blood vessels that carry blood away from the heart.

arteriole *(ahr TEE ree ohl)* Smallest branch of an artery.

arteriosclerosis *(ar TEE ree oh skleh ROH sis)* Progressive degenerative changes that produce a narrowed, hardened artery.

arthritis *(ahr THRYE tiss)* Inflammation of the joints.

arthroscope An instrument used to view a joint.

arthroscopy *(ar THROSS koh pee)* The endoscopic examination of the interior region of the joint.

articular cartilage Cartilage located on the ends of bones that acts as a shock absorber.

articulation *(AHR tick you LAY shun)* A joint where two bones come together and join or articulate.

artificial active immunity Vaccination. Intentional exposure to pathogens so patient makes own antibodies.

artificial passive immunity Injection of antibodies to help patient fight infection.

atrophic A decrease in size of an organ or tissue; wasting.

ascending colon The first portion of the colon that travels up the right side of the body to the level of the liver.

ascending loop Portion of nephron loop with a wall made up of simple cuboidal epithelium.

asexual reproduction Reproduction in which sex cells are not utilized.

association neuron Neurons that mediate impulses between a sensory and motor neuron.

asthma *(AZ mah)* Sudden onset of hyperreactivity of the bronchi and bronchioles with bronchospasm (contraction of the smooth muscle). Inflammation and swelling severely narrow the lumen of the airways.

astrocyte *(ASS troh SITE)* Star-shaped cell that provides structural support for neurons, connects them to capillaries, and forms the blood–brain barrier.

ataxia *(ah TAK see ah)* Lack of coordination of the muscles during movement, particularly the gait. Caused by diseases of the brain or spinal cord, cerebral palsy, or an adverse reaction to a drug.

atelectasis *(AT eh LEK tah sis)* Incomplete expansion or collapse of part or all of a lung due to mucus, tumor, monotonous breathing, or a foreign body that blocks the bronchus. The lung is said to be atelectatic.

atherosclerosis *(ATH er oh skleh ROH sis)* The most common form of arteriosclerosis, marked by cholesterol-lipid-calcium deposits in the walls of arteries that may restrict blood flow.

atom Smallest part of an element that still retains its properties.

atopic march A condition in patients in which early exposure to an allergen may cause an initial skin reaction while later exposures lead to allergic rhinitis, asthma, or even anaphylaxis.

atrial natriuretic peptide *(AY tree al NAY tree your ET ick PEP tide)* Hormone released by the atria when blood pressure rises. Causes increased excretion of water by the kidney, thereby decreasing blood pressure.

atrioventricular node *(AY tree oh vehn TRIK yoo lahr)* Small knot of tissue located between the right atrium and right ventricle. The AV node is part of the conduction system of the heart and receives electrical impulses from the SA node.

atrioventricular valve *(AY tree oh vehn TRIK yoo lahr)* The valve situated between the atrium and the ventricle.

atrium (atria) *(AY tree um, AY tree ah)* Two upper chambers of the heart. Intra-atrial structures are located within the atria.

atrophy *(AT roh fee)* Loss of muscle bulk in one or more muscles. It can be caused by malnutrition or can occur in any part of the body that is paralyzed and the muscles receive no electrical impulse from the nerves.

auditory canal One of two canals that lead to the ear.

auricle *(AW rih kul)* The visible external ear. Also known as the *pinna*.

autografting The use of one's own skin to replace burnt/damaged tissue.

autoimmune disorders A disorder in which the immune system attacks some part of the body, when the body fails to recognize itself.

autonomic nervous system Division of the peripheral nervous system that carries nerve impulses to the heart, involuntary smooth muscles, and glands. It includes the parasympathetic nervous system (active during sleep and light activity) and the sympathetic nervous system (active during increased activity, danger, and stress).

autoregulation 1. The ability to self control a cardiac impulse. 2. Renal mechanism to insure glomerular filtration is unaffected by changes in blood pressure.

autorhythmicity *(AW tow rith MIH sih tee)* The heart's ability to generate its own stimulus.

avascular *(ay VASS cue ler)* Without blood vessels.

AV bundle See bundle of His.

AV node See atrioventricular node.

AV valve See atrioventricular valve.

axial skeleton *(AK see al)* The bones of the head, chest, and back.

axillary Pertaining to the area of the armpit.

axon *(AK son)* Part of the neuron that is a single, elongated branch at the opposite end from the dendrites. It receives an electrical impulse and releases neurotransmitters into the synapse. Axons are covered by an insulating layer of myelin.

axon terminal The end point of a neuron.

azotemia (uremia) *(AZ oh TEE mee uh)* Condition of increased amounts of nitrogenous waste products in the blood.

B

B lymphocytes *(B LIMF oh sights)* White blood cells that make antibodies to destroy specific pathogens.

bacilli Plural of bacillus, which is a rod-shaped microorganism.

bacteria Asexually reproducing cell capable of creating an infection.

basal layer Part of the uterus that is responsible for generating the uterine lining each month. Also the stem cell layer of the epidermis.

basal nuclei *(BAY sal NOO klee eye)* Clusters of cells (nuclei) deep in the diencephalon, midbrain, and cerebrum that help fine-tune voluntary movements.

base The bottom of each lung.

basophil *(BAY soh fill)* Least numerous of the leukocytes. It is classified as a granulocyte because granules in its cytoplasm stain dark blue to purple with basic dye. It releases histamine and heparin at the site of tissue damage.

benign *(bee NINE)* Not progressive, nonmalignant.

benign prostatic hyperplasia (BPH) *(bee NINE pro STAT ik HIGH per PLAY zhuh)* The noncancerous enlargement of the prostate gland that often interferes with urine flow.

bicuspid *(by KUS pid)* A two-leafed structure, as in the bicuspid valve of the heart.

bicuspid tooth *(by KUS pid)* A permanent, premolar tooth. There are eight premolars, two in each quadrant (four in each jaw) between the canines and molars. Premolars have two or three cusps on the occlusal surface.

bifocals Corrective lenses with two points of focus, used to treat presbyopia.

bile Substance, produced by the liver and stored in the gall bladder, that emulsifies fat.

bilirubin *(bill ih ROO bin)* A yellow bile pigment formed from the breakdown of old worn out red blood cells.

biliverdin *(bill ih VER din)* Green bile pigment.

binary fission Asexual reproduction in prokaryotic cells in which the cell enlarges, duplicates its chromosomes, and creates a transverse septum, forming two identical daughter cells.

biological agent An agent derived from or made of living tissues or cells and used in health care.

biological molecules Molecules that make up the composition of your body and contain mainly carbon, hydrogen, oxygen, nitrogen, sulfur, and phosphorous.

biological response modifiers (BRMs) A newer class of drugs for the treatment of rheumatoid arthritis that suppress the immune system.

biological vector   An animal vector which carries internally a disease-causing organism.

biopsy   Obtaining of tissue samples for microscopic examination to help determine a diagnosis.

black lung disease   Also known as coal workers pneumoconiosis, this lung disease is a result of the chronic inhalation and retention of coal dust.

blind spot   An area of the retina where no vision occurs due to a lack of rods and cones.

blood   The cell-containing connective tissue fluid that circulates through the heart, arteries, veins, and capillaries, carrying nourishment, electrolytes, hormones, vitamins, antibodies, heat, and oxygen to the tissues and taking away waste matter and carbon dioxide.

blood–brain barrier   A structural and functional barrier that prevents some substances from diffusing from the blood to the brain tissue.

blood platelets   Blood cells responsible for clotting. Also known as *thrombocytes*.

blood urea nitrogen (BUN)   Nitrogen in the blood in the form of urea, the metabolic product of the breakdown of amino acids used for energy production. The normal concentration is about 8 to 18 mg/dL. The level of urea in the blood provides a rough estimate of kidney function.

blood vessels   The veins, arteries, and capillaries.

body   The large central portion of the uterus.

body lice   Inhabits the seams of clothing worn next to the body and feeds on regions of the body covered by that clothing. Eggs are attached to fibers of the clothing. This organism causes human illnesses including pediculosis corporis and trench fever.

body of stomach   Mid portion and largest region of the stomach.

bolus   *(BOW lus)* A mass of masticated food.

bone conduction   The process of the middle ear amplifying the sound through respective ossicles.

bony thorax   *(BOH nee THAWR aks)* The portion of the skeleton, including the sternum, rib cage, and vertebrae, that protects the heart, lungs, and great vessels.

BP (blood pressure)   The tension exerted on the walls of arteries by: the strength of the contraction of the heart; the resistance of arterioles and capillaries; the elasticity of blood vessels; the blood volume; and blood viscosity.

Bowman's capsule   *See* glomerular capsule.

brachial artery   *(BRAY kee uhl AHR tur ee)* Major artery that carries blood to the upper arm.

brain stem   Most inferior part of the brain that joins with the spinal cord. It is composed of the midbrain, pons, and medulla oblongata.

breast cancer   Malignant tumors located in the breast tissue. Most common malignancy in American women.

broad ligaments   Support structures of the uterus that are a combination of the mesometrium and the mesovarium.

Broca's area   *(BROH kas)* Area of brain that controls movements associated with speech.

bronchi   *(BRONG kye)* Tubular air passages that branch off the trachea to the right and left and enter each lung. They carry inhaled and exhaled air to and from the lungs.

bronchioles   *(BRONG kee ohlz)* Small tubular air passageways that branch off the bronchi. They carry inhaled and exhaled air to and from the alveoli.

bronchoscope   *(BRONG koh skohp)* An endoscope utilized to visually examine the airways of the body.

bronchospasm   An abnormal narrowing of the bronchi, due to spasms of the airway's smooth muscle, creating partial obstructions of the lumen, often accompanied by coughing and wheezing.

buccal   *(BUCK al)* Pertaining to cheek or mouth region.

buccal cavity   *(BUCK al)* Alternate name for mouth (oral cavity).

bulbourethral glands   *(BUL boh yoo REE thral)* Pea sized glands inferior to the prostrate.

bulimia   *(boo LIM ee uh)* An eating disorder marked by recurring episodes of binge eating, self-induced vomiting and diarrhea, and other attempts to reduce weight such as excessive exercising, dieting, and/or fasting; individual exhibits excessive and unrealistic concerns about body image.

bundle of His   *(HISS)* Section of the conduction system of the heart after the AV node. It splits into the right and left bundle branches.

bursa   *(BUR sah)* Fluid-filled sac that decreases friction where a tendon rubs against a bone near a synovial joint.

bursitis   *(bur SIGH tiss)* Inflammation of the bursa, resulting in joint swelling and pain.

C

calcitonin   A hormone produced by the human thyroid gland that is important for maintaining a dense, strong bone matrix and regulating the blood calcium level.

calcium (Ca)   Important for blood clotting, enzyme activation, and acid-base balance. It gives firmness and rigidity to bones and teeth. It is essential for lactation, the function of nerves and muscles (including heart muscle), and maintenance of membrane permeability.

calcium ion channels   Pathways that allow calcium ions to pass through the cell membrane.

cancellous bone   *(CAN cell us)* Spongy bone found in the epiphyses of long bones. Its spaces are filled with red bone marrow that makes blood cells.

canine teeth   Long, pointed teeth located between the incisors and the premolars. The canines sink deeply into food to hold it. There are four canines: two in the maxilla and two in the mandible. Also known as *cuspids* (because they have one large, pointed cusp) or *eyeteeth*.

canker sores (aphthous stomatitis)   An ulcer of the oral mucosa, usually less than 0.5 cm in diameter.

capillaries   *(KAP ih LAIR eez)* The smallest blood vessels in the body, connecting blood vessels between arterioles and venules. The exchange of oxygen and carbon dioxide takes place in the capillaries.

capillary bed   A network of capillaries.

capillary endothelium   *(KAP ih LAIR ee en doh THEE lee uhm)* Known as simple squamous endothelium and forms the wall of the capillary.

capsid   *(KAP sid)* The protein covering around a virus particle.

carbon dioxide (CO$_2$)   A colorless gas heavier than air and produced in the combustion or decomposition of carbon or its compounds.

carbohydrases   One of a group of enzymes (such as amylase and lactase) that hydrolyze carbohydrates.

carbohydrates   Sugars and starches used as energy sources and to provide structure.

cardiac   Pertaining to the heart.

cardiac arrhythmias   *(ah RITH mee uhs)* Abnormal conductive and contraction rhythms of the heart.

cardiac cycle   The movement of the heart in which it contracts to pump blood (systolic phase) and relaxes to allow the chambers to fill with blood (diastolic phase).

cardiac impression   The concave cavity found in the medial surface of the left lung that houses the heart.

cardiac muscle   One of three types of muscle in the body. It is found only in the heart and cannot be controlled consciously.

cardiac output (CO)   The amount of blood discharged from the left or right ventricle per minute.

cardiac region   Region of the stomach where the lower esophageal sphincter also known as the cardiac sphincter is located.

cardiac sphincter   *(SFINGK ter)* Ring-shaped muscle also known as the lower esophageal sphincter (LES) that allows food into the stomach.

cardiology   Study of the structure, function, and pathology of the cardiac system.

cardiopulmonary   Pertaining to the heart and lungs.

cardiopulmonary circulation   The process of circulating blood through the lungs to pick up oxygen and drop off carbon dioxide to be exhaled into the atmosphere.

cardiopulmonary resuscitation (CPR)   The actions (both through cardiac compressions and assisted breathing) to create normal heart function in an individual who has cardiac arrest.

cardiovascular system   Body system that includes the heart, arteries, veins, and capillaries. It distributes blood throughout the body.

carina   *(kuh RYE nuh)* A structure with a projecting central ridge such as occurs at the bifurcation of the mainstem bronchi in the lung.

carotene   *(CARE eh teen)* A yellow pigment found in plant and animal tissue. The precursor of vitamin A.

carpal bones   The eight small bones of the wrist joint.

carpal tunnel syndrome   A condition affecting the median nerve distribution of the hand leading to pain and/or numbness. Repetitive motion is the most common cause of this condition.

carrier   An individual who is infected by a disease and can potentially spread the disease.

carrier mediated passive transport   Also known as facilitated diffusion where a substance is helped across the cell membrane without the use of ATP.

cartilage   *(KAR tih lij)* Smooth, firm, but flexible connective tissue.

cartilaginous   *(KAR tih LAJ ih nus)* Referring to cartilage.

cartilaginous joint A joint with cartilage between the bones.

catabolism *(ka TAB oh lizm)* Breaking down of molecules in the body.

cataract *(KAT ah rakt)* Clouding of the lens. Protein molecules in the lens begin to clump together. Caused by aging, sun exposure, eye trauma, smoking, and some medications.

caudal *(KAWD al)* Toward the tailbone, feet, or lower part of the body.

cauda equina *(KAW dah ee KWYE nah)* A bundle of spinal nerves dangling at the end of the spinal cord similar to a horse's tail.

calyx A cuplike extension of the renal pelvis that encloses the papilla of a renal pyramid; urine from the papillary duct is emptied into it.

cecum *(SEE kum)* First part of the large intestine; a short, pouchlike area. The appendix is attached to its wall.

cell cycle The life cycle of the cell, including normal activity (interphase) and cell division (mitotic phase).

cell division The process of cellular replication.

cell-mediated immunity Destruction of pathogens by T lymphocytes. T lymphocytes directly attack infected cells, destroying them.

cell membrane Semipermeable barrier that surrounds a cell and holds in the cytoplasm. It allows water and some nutrients to enter and waste products to leave the cell.

cells The basic unit of life.

cellular reproduction See cell division.

cellular respiration The cellular process in which oxygen is used to break down glucose and other nutrients for energy needed for cellular activity.

cellulitis *(SELL you LIE tis)* Bacterial infection of skin and subcutaneous tissues.

cementum *(see MEN tum)* Continuous layer of bonelike connective tissue that covers the dentin layer of the tooth and roots below the gum line. It begins at the gum line where the enamel stops. It anchors one side of the periodontal ligaments.

central Located in the middle or equidistant from multiple points.

central nervous system (CNS) Division of the nervous system that includes the brain and the spinal cord.

centriole *(SEN tree ohl)* An organelle that precedes mitosis.

centrosome *(SEN truh sohm)* Region of cytoplasm usually near the nucleus that contains 1–2 centrioles.

cephalic *(seh FAL ik)* Toward the head of the body.

cephalic phase The first phase of gastric juice production that is stimulated by the sight or smell of food.

cerebellum *(ser eh BELL um)* Small rounded section that is the most posterior part of the brain. Monitors muscle tone and position and coordinates new muscle movements.

cerebral palsy A general term for a nonprogressive motor impairment due to lesions or abnormalities of the brain that occurred during early stages of its development.

cerebrospinal fluid (CSF) *(SER eh broh SPY nal FLOO id)* The fluid cushion that protects the brain and spinal cord from shock.

cerebrovascular accident (CVA; Stroke) *(SER eh broh VAS kyuh ler)* A sudden loss of neurological function caused by some vascular injury to the brain, either through hemorrhage or blockage of blood flow to the brain.

cerebrum *(SER eh brum)* The largest and most visible part of the brain. Its surface contains gyri and sulci and is divided into two hemispheres.

cerumen *(seh ROO men)* Sticky wax that traps dirt in the external auditory canal.

ceruminous gland *(seh ROO men us)* Gland that produces the waxlike substance in the ear.

cervical Pertaining to the region of the neck and the cervix.

cervical canal Connects the cervix to the vagina.

cervix Valvelike portion of the uterus that protrudes into the vagina.

chain of infection A process of infection that must have the following links in sequential order for an infection to occur: infecting agent, reservoir, portal of entry, mode of transmission, susceptible host.

cheilitis *(ky LIE tiss)* Inflammation of the lips that includes redness and fissures.

chemical synapse *(KEH mih cull SIN aps)* Site of communication between neurons and other excitable cells. Neurotransmitters are released from the neuron (presynaptic cell) and travel to a muscle or gland cell (the postsynaptic cell), allowing communication between the two cells.

chemotherapy The use of chemical substances or drugs to treat a disease, usually used in reference to cancer treatment.

chickenpox (Varicella) An acute, contagious disease found usually in children, caused by the Varicella Zoster virus, exhibiting papules that become vesicles, and then pustules.

chief cells Specialized cells that secrete pepsinogen.

chief complaint The main sign or symptom that caused an individual to seek healthcare.

cholecystectomy *(KOH lee sis TEK toh mee)* Surgical removal of the gall bladder.

cholecystitis *(KOH lee siss TYE tiss)* Acute or chronic inflammation of the gallbladder usually because of gallstones.

cholecystokinin (CCK) *(KOH lee SIS toh KINE in)* Hormone released by the duodenum when it receives food from the stomach. It causes the gallbladder to release bile and the pancreas to release its digestive enzymes.

cholelithiasis *(KOH lee lih THIGH ah siss)* One or more gallstones in the gallbladder.

cholesterol Lipid molecule that is a component of bile (from the gallbladder), sex hormones, neurotransmitters, and cell membranes.

chondrosarcoma *(KON droe sar KOE ma)* Cancer of the cartilage.

choroid *(KOH royd)* Spongy membrane of blood vessels that begins at the iris and continues around the eye. In the posterior cavity, it is the middle layer between the sclera and the retina.

choroid plexus Small, tufted projections into the third, fourth, and lateral ventricles of the brain that are made of blood vessels of the pia mater covered by a thin coat of ependymal cells. These projections secrete cerebrospinal fluid.

chromatin Genetic material found in the nucleus of a cell.

chronic Of long duration; long-lasting.

chronic bronchitis *(brong KYE tiss)* Chronic inflammation or infection of the bronchi. Inflammation of the bronchi can be due to pollution or smoking.

chronic kidney disease Ongoing progressive kidney disease lasting three or more months.

chronic obstructive pulmonary disease (COPD) A group of progressive, debilitating, and often fatal lung diseases that exhibit difficulty with air movement into and out of the lungs, prolonged expiratory periods, and the loss of normal lung elasticity. COPD includes emphysema and chronic bronchitis.

chyle *(KILE)* Milklike substance formed from digested and absorbed fats.

chyme *(KIME)* Mixed food and digestive juices in the stomach and small intestine.

cilia *(SILL ee ah)* Small hairs that flow in waves to move foreign particles away from the lungs toward the nose and the throat where they can be expelled. Also found inside the fallopian tube to propel an ovum toward the uterus.

ciliary muscle *(SILL ee AIR ee)* Smooth muscle that alters the lens of the eye to accommodate for near vision.

circumduction The combination of movements to create a circular arm movement similar to a softball pitch.

cirrhosis *(si ROH sis)* A chronic liver disease that exhibits liver scarring, loss of normal liver architecture and function, often caused by alcoholism and chronic viral hepatitis.

clitoris *(klih TORE iss)* Small erectile structure that becomes engorged during sexual arousal in females.

closed reduction The setting of a bone into proper alignment without opening the skin.

clot A thrombus or coagulated blood.

coagulation The formation of a blood clot by platelets and the clotting factors.

coccyx *(KAWK siks)* The final 3–5 small bones at the inferior end of the spinal column; also called tailbone.

cochlea *(COCK lee ah)* Structure of the inner ear that is associated with the sense of hearing. It relays information to the brain via the cochlear branch of the vestibulocochlear nerve.

collecting duct Common passageway that collects fluid from many nephrons. The final step of reabsorption takes place there, and the fluid is known as urine after it leaves this duct.

colon *(KOH lon)* The longest part of the large intestine. It has four parts: the ascending colon, the transverse colon, the descending colon, and the S-shaped sigmoid colon.

colonoscopy The visualization of the lower gastrointestinal tract through the use of an endoscope.

colorectal cancer A malignancy of the colon or rectum.

columnar cells Column-shaped epithelial cells.

columns The white matter found in the spinal cord that acts as nerve tracts and pathways.

coma A state of unconsciousness in which the patient cannot be aroused, even following stimulation.

comminuted fracture *(KOM uh noot ed)* Fracture that is a result of a bone being crushed.

commissures *(KAHM ih shurz)* Transverse bands of nerve fibers; carry information from one side of the nervous system to the other.

common cold Usually a communicable viral infection of the upper airways that can spread to other areas of the respiratory tract.

common vehicle transmission The transmission of infectious agents via consumable goods such as blood or ground meat.

common wart Also known as verruca vulgaris, usually found on the backs of the hands and fingers; however, it may occur on any area of the skin.

communicable While communicable and contagious may sound like the same thing, there is a fine difference. A communicable disease has the potential to be spread by a variety of ways such as person to person or insect to person. A contagious disease is one that is readily transmitted from one person to another such as the common cold.

compact bone Hard or dense bone forming the superficial layer of all bones.

complement cascade A series of chemical reactions triggered by infection that leads to the destruction of a pathogen.

compliance Relates to the flexibility of the lungs and the ease with which ventilation occurs.

compound fracture Also called an open fracture, where the bone is pushed through the skin.

computed tomography (CT) Imaging diagnostic tool that combines a series of x-rays to give a three-dimensional view.

concentration The amount of solute dissolved in a solvent.

concentration gradient The difference between solute concentrations of two solutions.

conchae *(KONG kay)* Shelflike structures inside the nasal cavity.

concussion A brain injury resulting from an impact with an object.

cones Light-sensitive cells in the retina that detect colored light. There are three types of cones, each of which responds to either red, green, or blue light.

congenital hypothyroidism Hypothyroidism present at birth.

conjunctiva *(kon JUNK tih vah)* Delicate, transparent mucous membrane that covers the inside of the eyelids and the anterior surface of the eye. It produces clear, watery mucus.

conjunctivitis *(kon JUNK tih VYE tiss)* Inflamed, reddened, and swollen conjunctivae with dilated blood vessels on the sclera. Caused by a foreign substance in the eye or an infection.

constipation Decrease in the frequency of defecation accompanied by difficult or incomplete passage of stool.

contact transmission General term for the spread of infectious agents by touch.

contagious disease Any disease readily transmitted from one person to another.

contraception The prevention of fertilization.

contractile muscle Muscle that has the ability to shorten and relax, thus causing movement.

contralateral Term describing the left side of the body being controlled by the right side of the brain and vice versa.

contusion A bruise.

conus medularis *(KOH nuss med you LAIR iss)* A pointed structure at the posterior end of the spinal cord.

convolutions Folds found on the surface of the cerebrum.

cor pulmonale *(CORE pull mah NAIL ee)* Failure of the pumping ability of the right ventricle.

corium *(CORE ee um)* Layer of skin immediately under the epidermis. Also known as the *true skin* or *dermis*.

cornea *(CORE nee uh)* Transparent layer over the anterior part of the eye. It is a continuation of the white sclera.

coronal plane *(kor ROW nal)* Also called *frontal plane;* an imaginary vertical plane that divides the entire body into front and back sections. The coronal plane is named for the coronal suture where the anterior and posterior skull bones meet.

coronary arteries Blood vessels that provide oxygen enriched blood to the heart.

coronary thrombosis *(throm BOH sis)* A blood clot in the coronary artery, which is the most common cause of a myocardial infarction.

corpus callosum *(CORE pus kah LOH sum)* Thick white band of nerve fibers that connects the two hemispheres of the cerebrum and allows them to communicate and coordinate their activities.

corpus luteum *(CORE pus LOO tee uhm)* Structure that secretes progesterone and continues to do so if an egg is fertilized, thus preventing further ovulation.

cortex The outer layer of a structure, as a hair or the lens of the eye; In the brain, a surface sheet of layered or laminated gray matter, as in the outermost sector of the cerebral and cerebellar hemispheres.

cortical radiate arteries Arteries branching from arcuate arteries that supply blood to renal cortex.

corticobulbar tract *(CORE tih coh BUL bar)* Spinal cord tract that carries impulses to the brainstem from the motor cortex. Carries orders for voluntary movements.

corticospinal tract *(CORE tih coh SPY nal)* Pertaining to the tract between the cerebral cortex and spinal cord. Carries orders for voluntary movements.

countercurrent circulation Exchange of substances between two streams on either side of a membrane. Helps control concentration of fluids as in the nephron loop.

covalent bond Bond formed by sharing of electrons in the outer shells.

cramp Spasmodic muscle contraction.

cranial *(KRAY nee al)* Pertaining to the skull.

cranial cavity Body cavity, located in the skull, that houses the brain.

cranial nerves Twelve pairs of nerves that originate in the brain. Carry sensory nerve impulses to the brain from the nose, eyes, ears, and tongue for the senses of smell, vision, hearing, and taste. Also carry sensory nerve impulses to the brain from the skin of the face. Also carry motor nerve impulses from the brain to the muscles of the face, mouth, and throat; eye; and salivary glands.

craniosacral The brainstem and sacral spinal cord, origin of parasympathetic preganglionic neurons.

creatinine *(kree AT in in)* A waste product produced by muscle metabolism that is normally eliminated by the kidney.

cricoid cartilage *(CRY koid CAR tih lij)* Ring shaped cartilage found inferior to the thyroid cartilage within the neck, providing structure and support for the airway.

cross-sectioning Making slices of a sample for examination purposes.

crown White part of the tooth that is visible above the gum line.

crowning Occurring during delivery, it is the visible presentation of the fetal head as it comes out of the vaginal opening.

crural *(KROO rall)* Pertaining to the leg or thigh.

cryptorchidism *(kript OR kid izm)* The failure of the testes to descend into the scrotal sac.

cuboidal cells *(KYOO boid al)* Cube-shaped epithelial cells.

culture and sensitivity test The growing of bacteria and exposing it to a variety of antibiotics to see which drug is most effective.

Cushing's syndrome A condition usually the result of the usage of higher levels of corticosteroids in which the patient develops physical features that can include buffalo hump, a rounded face (moon face), weight gain, and increased fragility of the skin.

cuspids *(KUS pidz)* Canine teeth.

cutaneous membranes *(cue TAY nee us)* Membranes of the skin.

cutaneous senses Result from receptors on the skin that include touch, heat, cold, pressure, and pain.

cuticle Layer of dead skin that arises from the epidermis around the proximal end of the nail. It keeps microorganisms from the nail root.

cyanosis *(sigh ah NOH sis)* Bluish-gray discoloration of the skin from abnormally low levels of oxygen and often abnormally high levels of carbon dioxide in the tissues.

cystic fibrosis *(SIS tik fy BROH sis)* An inherited disease involving abnormal high sweat chloride levels, pancreatic insufficiency, and pus-producing pulmonary disease with high levels of thick tenacious mucus.

cystoscope *(SIS toh skohp)* A lit tubular device used to view the internal anatomy of the bladder.

cytokines *(SIGH tow kines)* Chemicals released by injured body tissues that summon leukocytes and cause them to move to the area.

cytokinesis *(SIGH tow ki NEE sis)* The division of cytoplasm during cellular division.

cytoplasm *(SIGH toh plazm)* Gel-like intracellular substance. Organelles are embedded in it.

cytoskeleton *(SIGH toe SKEL ih ten)* The framework of a cell.

cytotoxic T cells *(sigh tow TOX ick)* Type of T lymphocyte that matures in the thymus. Cytotoxic T cells destroy all types of pathogens as well as body cells infected with viruses.

D

deciduous teeth *(dee SID you us)* Teeth that erupt during childhood from age 6 months to 2 years. Also called the *milk teeth, baby teeth*, or *primary teeth*.

decubitus *(dee KYOO bih tus)* Lying down position; on the back.

deep Located underneath or further from a surface.

defecation *(def eh CAY shun)* Process by which undigested food fiber and water are removed from the body in the form of a bowel movement.

defibrillator An external or internal electronic device used to shock the patient's heart in an attempt to bring it back to a normal rhythm.

dehydration synthesis *(dee high DREY shuhn SIN thuh sis)* An anabolic reaction that involves the removal of water to combine larger biological molecules.

dendrite *(DEN dright)* Multiple branches at the end of a neuron that carry information to the cell body.

dendritic cells *(den DRIT ick)* One of several types of antigen-displaying cells that stimulate adaptive immunity.

dental caries Holes or cavities created by bacteria due to poor oral hygiene.

dental plaque A biofilm that accumulates and grows on the crowns of teeth.

dentin Hard layer of tooth just beneath the enamel layer.

deoxyribonucleic acid (DNA) *(dee AWK see RYE boh new KLEE ick)* Sequenced pairs of nucleotides that form a double helix. A segment of DNA makes up a gene.

depolarization Changing of the permeability of the cell membrane of any excitable cell, for example cardiac muscle or a neuron, that leads to a change in charge across the cell membrane.

dermis *(DER miss)* Layer of skin under the epidermis. It is composed of collagen and elastic fibers. It contains arteries, veins, nerves, sebaceous glands, sweat glands, and hair follicles.

descending colon Portion of the colon that travels down the left side of the abdominal cavity eventually becoming the sigmoid colon.

descending loop Portion of nephron loop with similar structure to the proximal tubule.

detrusor muscle The three-layered muscular wall of the urinary bladder.

diabetes *(DYE eh BEE teez)* A general term for a group of diseases that are marked by excessive urination.

diabetes insipidus A condition in which there is excessive urination due to either inadequate antidiuretic hormone or an inability of the kidney to respond to the available antidiuretic hormone.

diabetes mellitus (DM) Condition resulting from too little secretion of insulin leading to increased levels of blood glucose.

diabetic nephropathy *(neh FROP eh thee)* Damage to the kidneys as a result of prolonged levels of high blood glucose.

diagnosis *(dye egg NOH sis)* A determination as to the cause of the patient's symptoms and signs.

diapedesis *(dahy uh pi DEE sis)* The degradation of a capillary wall that allows neutrophils to escape into surrounding tissue to provide an immune system response.

diaphragm *(DYE ah fram)* Muscular sheet that divides the thoracic cavity from the abdominal cavity. Most important ventilation muscle.

diaphysis *(dye AFF ih sis)* The straight shaft of a long bone.

diarrhea Defecation of liquid feces.

diastole *(dye ASS toe lee)* Resting period between contractions. It is when the heart fills with blood.

diencephalon *(dye en SEFF ah lon)* Central part of the brain that contains the thalamus and hypothalamus.

differentiated The maturing of certain cells to allow them to become specialized with specialized functions.

differentiation Process by which embryonic cells assume different shapes and functions in different parts of the body.

diffusion Process of movement of a substance from high concentration to low concentration.

digestion Process of mechanically and chemically breaking food down into nutrients that can be used by the body.

digestive system The alimentary canal (oral cavity, pharynx, esophagus, stomach, small and large intestines) and the accessory organs (teeth, tongue, salivary glands, liver, and pancreas).

digital Pertaining to the fingers or toes.

dilation stage The first stage of labor in which uterine smooth muscle begins to contract and move the fetus down the uterus causing the cervix to dilate.

diplopia Brain receives two images and the person has double vision.

dipstick test A general term for a test that involves the application of urine to a chemical impregnated paper for the purpose of analysis. The results are usually read as color changes to the paper.

direct contact The spread of infectious agents by directly touching a contaminated surface.

disaccharides *(die SAK uh rides)* Two monosaccharides linked together.

disease *(dih ZEEZ)* Any change in the normal structure or function of the body.

disease modifying anti-rheumatic drugs (DMARDs) Drugs used to treat rheumatoid arthritis such as injected gold, methotrexate, or plaquinil.

distal *(DISS tall)* Moving from the body toward the end of a limb (arm or leg).

distal tubule *(DISS tall TOO byool)* Tubule of the nephron that begins at the loop of Henle. It empties into the collecting duct. Reabsorption takes place there.

diverticulitis *(DYE ver tik yuh LYE tiss)* An inflammatory condition of the diverticulum of the intestinal tract, especially in the colon, that can lead to pain, fever, and weight loss.

dorsal *(DOR sal)* Pertaining to the posterior of the body, particularly the back.

dorsal column tract Spinal cord pathway that carries fine touch sensation from the spinal cord to the brain.

dorsal root The radix dorsalis or sensory root of each spinal nerve.

dorsal root ganglion *(DOR sal ROOT GANG lee on)* A collection of sensory neurons on the dorsal roots of the spinal cord.

dorsiflexion *(DOR seh FLEK shun)* Movement occurring when the foot is bent up toward the leg.

Duchenne's muscular dystrophy (DMD) Pseudohypertrophic muscular dystrophy marked by weakness and pseudohypertrophy of the affected muscles. It is caused by mutation of the gene responsible for producing the protein dystrophin. The disease begins in childhood, is progressive, and affects the shoulder and pelvic girdle muscles. The disease, mostly affecting males, is transmitted as a sex-linked recessive trait.

duodenal ulcers An open ulcer on the mucosa of the first portion of the duodenum, most often the result of infection with Helicobacter pylori. It is the most common form of peptic ulcer.

duodenum *(doo ODD eh num)* First part of the small intestine. It secretes cholecystokinin, a hormone that stimulates the gallbladder and pancreas to release bile and digestive enzymes.

dural sinuses Any of several large endothelia-lined collecting channels into which veins of the brain and inner skull empty and which then empty into the internal jugular vein. These venous sinuses are found between the two layers (periosteal and meningeal) of the dura mater. Their walls have no muscle, and they have no valves to give direction to the blood flow. The venous sinuses in the skull include the superior sagittal, inferior sagittal, straight, transverse, and cavernous sinuses.

dura mater *(DOO ra MAY ter)* Tough, outermost layer of the meninges. The dura mater lies just under the bones of the cranium and vertebrae.

dwarfism A condition of being abnormally undersized. May be due to an endocrine condition, heredity, nutritional deficiency, diseases of the skeleton, or others.

dysmenorrhea *(DISS men oh REE ah)* Difficult menstruation.

dysplasia *(dis FAY jee ah)* Abnormal development of tissue.

dyspnea *(DISP nee uh)* Difficulty in breathing.

dysrhythmia *(dis RITH mee ah) See* arrhythmia.

dysuria *(dis YOO ree ah)* Painful urination.

E

eardrum Also known as the tympanic membrane; found in the middle ear.

ecchymosis *(eck ih MOH sis)* Superficial bruising under the skin or mucous membrane due to bleeding.

eccrine glands *(ECK rin)* Sweat glands that cover the entire skin surface.

echocardiography *(ECK oh CAR dee AWG rah fee)* A non-invasive diagnostic procedure using sound waves to visualize cardiac structure and function.

efferent arterioles *(EFF er ent ahr TEE ree ohlz)* Small blood vessels that carry blood away from the glomeruli of the kidney.

eggs Female sexual cells.

ejaculation Sudden discharge of semen from the body.

ejaculatory duct The passageway formed by the vas deferens and seminal vesicles to eject sperm.

elastic laminae *(LAM eh nee)* Sheets of elastic tissue found in the middle walls of larger arteries.

electrical synapse Gap or junction between two neurons involving electrical charges.

electrocardiogram The graphic record created by electrocardiography.

electrocardiograph A device for recording changes in the electrical energy produced by the action of heart muscles.

electrolyte *(ee LEK troh lite)* Chemical element that carries a positive or negative charge and conducts electricity when dissolved in a solution: Examples include sodium (Na^+), potassium (K^+), chloride (Cl^-), calcium (Ca^{++}), and bicarbonate (HCO_3^-). Electrolytes are carried in the plasma. Excess amounts in the blood are removed by the kidneys.

electromyogram (EMG) *(ee LEC troh MY oh gram)* A recording or tracing of the muscular activity as a result of electrical stimulation.

electromyography (EMG) *(ee LEK troh my AWG rah fee)* Diagnostic procedure to diagnose muscle disease or nerve damage. A needle electrode inserted into a muscle records electrical activity as the muscle contracts and relaxes. The electrical activity is displayed as waveforms on an oscilloscope screen and permanently recorded on paper as an electromyogram.

electron Negatively charged particle that circles the nucleus of the atom.

element A substance that cannot be further divided without losing its unique properties.

emboli *(EM boh lie)* Plural of embolus.

embolism A sudden obstruction of a blood vessel by debris.

embolus *(EM boh lus)* Mass of undissolved matter present in the blood or lymphatic vessels that was brought there by the blood or lymph current.

embryo A maturing zygote usually requiring seven days to reach this stage of development.

emphysema *(EM fih SEE mah)* Chronic pulmonary disease resulting in destruction of air spaces distal to the terminal bronchiole.

empyema *(EM pye EE mah)* Localized collection of purulent material (pus) in the thoracic cavity from an infection in the lungs. Also known as *pyothorax*.

emulsification *(ee MULL sih fih KAY shun)* Process performed by bile of breaking down large fat droplets into smaller droplets with more surface area.

enamel Glossy, thick white layer that covers the crown of the tooth. Enamel is the hardest substance in the body.

end stage renal failure Final stage of chronic kidney failure that can be only treated by kidney dialysis or kidney transplantation.

endemic A condition or disease related to a specific population or region of the world.

endocardium *(IN doh KAR dee um)* Innermost layer of the heart. It covers the inside of the heart chambers and valves.

endochondral *(IN doh KON druhl)* Within a cartilage.

endocrine glands Ductless glands that secrete macromolecules, called hormones, directly into the bloodstream, and such glands are richly supplied by blood capillaries. The endocrine glands include the adrenals, the parathyroids, the pineal, the pituitary, and the thyroid.

endocrine system *(IN doh krin)* Body system that includes the testes, ovaries, pancreas, adrenal glands, thymus, thyroid gland, parathyroid glands, pituitary gland, and pineal gland. It produces and releases hormones into the blood to direct the activities of other body organs.

endocrinology *(IN doh krin ALL oh jee)* The study of the endocrine system and related disorders.

endocytosis *(IN doh sigh TOH sis)* Ingestion of substances by a cell. Substances are taken into the cells after being surrounded by vesicles.

endolymph *(IN doe limf)* Fluid within the labyrinth of the ear.

endometriosis *(IN doh mee tree OH sis)* An inflammation of the mucous membrane lining the uterus.

endometrium *(IN doh MEE tree um)* The mucous membrane lining the uterus.

endomysium   A thin sheath of connective tissue, consisting principally of reticular fibers, that invests each striated muscle fiber and binds the fibers together within a fasciculus.

endoplasmic reticulum   *(IN doh PLAS mik reh TIK yoo lum)* Organelle that consists of a network of channels that transport materials within the cell. Also the site of protein, fat, and glycogen synthesis.

endoscope   A lit tubular device that is inserted into a region of the body for therapeutic and diagnostic purposes.

endoscopy   The inspection of various body organs, structures, and cavities by the use of an endoscope.

endosteum   *(in DOS tee uhm)* Lining of the spongy bone similar to periosteum.

English system   The weights and measuring system commonly used in the United States.

enuresis   *(IN yoo REE sis)* A condition of involuntary urine discharge after the age at which bladder function comes under an individual's conscious control.

enzyme   *(IN zyme)* Molecules that speed up the rate of chemical reactions in cells. Enzymes are particularly important in the breakdown and synthesis of biological molecules.

eosinophil   *(EE oh SIN oh fill)* Type of leukocyte. It is classified as a granulocyte because it has granules in the cytoplasm. The nucleus has two lobes. Eosinophils are involved in allergic reactions and defense against parasites.

ependymal cells   *(ep IN dih mal)* Specialized cells that line the walls of the ventricles and spinal canal and produce cerebrospinal fluid.

epicardium   *(EP ih KAR dee um)* Another name for the visceral pericardium.

epidemic   An outbreak of a disease that suddenly affects a large group of people in a geographical region or a defined population group.

epidemiology   *(EP ih dee mee OL oh jee)* The study of the origin, distribution, and determinants of diseases.

epidermis   *(EP ih DER miss)* Thin, outermost layer of skin. The most superficial part of the epidermis consists of dead cells filled with keratin. The deepest part (basal layer) contains constantly dividing cells and melanocytes.

epididymis   *(EP ih DID ih miss)* A comma-shaped duct on the posterior and lateral part of the testes where sperm mature.

epidural   Located either over or on the dura; an injection of anesthetic into the peridural space to produce epidural anesthesia.

epidural space   *(ep ih DURE all)* Area between the dura mater and the vertebral body.

epigastric   *(EP ih GAS trik)* Above the stomach.

epiglottis   *(EP ih GLAW tis)* Lid-like structure that seals off the larynx, so that swallowed food goes into the esophagus.

epimysium   *(EP ih MIZ ee uhm)* The outermost sheath of connective tissue that surrounds skeletal muscle.

epinephrine   *(EP ih NEFF rinn)* Hormone secreted by the adrenal medulla in response to stimulation by nerves of the sympathetic nervous system.

epiphyseal plate   *(eh piff ih SEE al)* The growth plate.

epiphysis   *(eh PIFF ih sis)* The widened ends of a long bone. Each end contains the epiphysial plate where bone growth takes place.

epithelial membrane   *(EP ih THEE lee al)* Comprised of epithelial and connective tissues that serves as linings and coverings for various body structures.

epithelial tissue   *(EP ih THEE lee al)* Layers of cells that form the epidermis of the skin as well as the surface layer of mucous and serous membranes.

epithelium   The layer of cells forming the epidermis of the skin and the surface layer of mucous and serous membranes.

erectile dysfunction (ED)   An inability to develop a full erection. May be physiological or psychological.

erection   The stiffening of the penis due to increased blood flow.

erythrocyte   *(eh RITH roh sight)* A red blood cell. Erythrocytes contain hemoglobin and carry oxygen and carbon dioxide to and from the lungs and cells of the body.

erythropoiesis   *(eh RITH roh poy EE sis)* Formation of red blood cells.

erythropoietin   *(eh RITH roh poy EH tin)* In the body, a hormone secreted by the kidneys when the number of red blood cells decreases. It stimulates the bone marrow to make more red blood cells. As a drug, erythropoietin does the same.

esophagus   *(eh SOFF ah guss)* Flexible, muscular tube that moves food from the pharynx to the stomach.

estrogen   Hormone secreted by the corpus luteum that stimulates uterine lining and mammary gland development.

etiology   *(ee tee ALL oh jee)* The cause or origin of a disease.

eukaryotic cell *(yoo CARE ee awt ick)* An organism in which the cell nucleus is surrounded by a cell membrane; the cells that make up the human body, possessing a nucleus, organelles, and several chromosomes.

eustachian tube *(yoo STAY she ehn)* Tube that connects the middle ear to the nasopharynx and equalizes the air pressure in the middle ear.

eversion Turning outward of the feet so the toes point away.

exacerbation *(eks AS er BAY shun)* A worsening or flare up of a disease process.

excitable cell Cell that carries an electrical charge when stimulated.

excretion *(eks KREE shun)* Removal of waste matter from the body.

exocrine Glands and organs that excrete through a duct.

exocytosis Secretion. The expulsion of material from a cell using vesicles.

expulsion stage When the cervix dilates to 10 centimeters and the baby is delivered.

extension *(eks TEN shun)* Straightening a joint to increase the angle between two bones or body parts.

extensor muscle Muscle that produces extension when it contracts.

external Near or on the outside surface of the body or an organ.

external auditory meatus *(AW dih tor ee mee AY tuss)* Opening at the entrance to the external auditory canal where sound waves enter.

external ear A portion of the ear we see that includes the auricle (pinna), ear lobe, and external auditory canal.

external otitis *(oh TYE tiss)* An inflammation of the outer ear.

external respiration Process of gas exchange between the atmosphere and the lungs.

external urethral sphincter *(yoo REE thral SFINK ter)* One of two valves, made of circular muscle, that allows voluntary control of urination.

extracorporeal shock wave lithotripsy *(EKS trah core POOR ee al LITH oh TRIP see)* An outpatient procedure utilizing shock waves applied to the outside of the body to shatter a kidney stone so it is small enough to excrete.

exudative Pathological oozing of fluids, usually the result of inflammation.

extubation The technique of removing a breathing tube.

eyeball The globe of the eye.

eyelash A stiff hair on the margin of the eyelid.

eyelid One of two movable protective folds that cover the anterior surface of the eyeball when closed.

F

facilitated diffusion Also known as *carrier mediated passive transport;* the movement of substances into cells via carrier proteins.

fallopian tubes *See* uterine tubes.

familial hypercholesterolemia *(HIGH per koh LESS ter ol EE mee uh)* A condition in which the low-density lipoproteins are not being removed from the blood properly by the lipoprotein receptors in the liver.

femoral artery Major artery that carries blood to the upper leg.

fermentation The oxidative decomposition, under anaerobic conditions, of complex substances through the action of enzymes or ferments, produced by microorganisms. Bacteria, molds, and yeasts are the principal groups of organisms involved.

fertilization Union and combination of genetic material.

fetus Further development of the embryo after the two month point; the fetus now resembles a human.

fibrillations *(FIB rih LAY shuns)* Rapid erratic abnormal heart beats.

fibrin *(FYE brin)* Fiber strands that are formed by the activation of clotting factors. Fibrin traps erythrocytes and this forms a blood clot.

fibrinogen *(fye BRINN oh jenn)* Blood clotting factor.

fibroblasts Any cell from which connective tissue is created.

fibromyalgia *(FYE bro my AL je uh)* Pain located at specific, small trigger points along the neck, back, and hips. The trigger points are very tender to the touch and feel firm.

fibrous joints *(FYE brus)* Joints located on your skull that allow for minimal flexing.

filtration Process in which water and substances in the blood are pushed through the pores of the glomerulus. The resulting fluid is known as filtrate.

fimbria The longest fringelike extremity of a fallopian tube, extending from the infundibulum close to the ovary.

first-degree burn A superficial burn in which damage is limited to the outer layer of the epidermis and is marked by redness, tenderness, and mild pain. Blisters do not form, and the burn heals without scar formation. A common example is sunburn.

fissure *(FISH er)* Deep division on the surface of the brain and spinal cord.

flaccid *(FLAH sid)* Limp or without muscle tone.

flagella *(fluh JEL uh)* Hairlike processes on bacteria or protozoa that cause movement.

flatulence A condition of gas production as a result of bacteria action in the large intestine.

flexion *(FLEK shun)* Bending of a joint to decrease the angle between two bones or body parts. Opposite of extension.

flexor muscle Muscle that produces flexion when it contracts.

floating ribs Rib pairs 11 and 12 that have no anterior attachment.

flora *(FLOOR ah)* Microbial life that has adapted to live in the human body. Also can be plant life occurring in a specific environment.

flutter An abnormal, rapid heartbeat of up to 300 coordinated contractions per minute.

follicle *(FALL ih kul)* 1. Mass of cells with a hollow center. It holds an oocyte before puberty and a maturing ovum after puberty. The follicle ruptures at the time of ovulation and becomes the corpus luteum. 2. Also a site where a hair is formed. The follicle is located in the dermis.

follicle stage The first 10 days of the menstrual cycle during which the hormone FSH is released.

follicle-stimulating hormone (FSH) Hormone released by the pituitary gland as part of the menstrual cycle that initiates the development of primary follicles each month.

follicular phase The time between menses and ovulation.

fontanels *(FAWN tah NELZ)* "Soft spots" found in newborn skulls.

forensic science The application of science and medicine to law.

foreskin Loose section of skin that covers the glands penis.

formed elements Cellular parts of the blood including red and white blood cells and platelets.

fornix *(FOR niks)* 1. Tract of nerves that joins all the parts of the limbic system. 2. Area of the superior part of the vagina that lies behind and around the cervix.

fourth degree burn A full thickness burn that penetrates to the bone.

Fowler's position A semisitting position with the torso at a 45- to 60-degree angle.

fracture A break in the bone.

frenulum *(FREN you lum)* Structure that attaches the lower side of the tongue to the gum.

friction ridges Irregular patterns found on the anterior surface of hands and the plantar surface of feet that decrease slippage and also form the unique patterns of fingerprints and footprints.

frontal lobe Lobe of the cerebrum that is responsible for motor activities, conscious thought, and speech.

frontal plane An imaginary plane parallel with the long axis of the body that divides the body into an anterior and posterior section.

full-thickness burn An assessment of the severity of a burn in which the burn has penetrated through all three of the skin layers.

functional layer The layer of the uterus that is shed every 28 days.

fundus *(FUN dus)* A larger part, base, or body of a hollow organ such as the dome-shaped top of the bladder, uterus above the fallopian tubes, or rounded, most superior part of the stomach.

fungi *(FUN jie)* A plantlike organism (includes mold and yeasts).

furuncle *(FOO rung kul)* A boil.

G

gallbladder Small organ that provides bile for digestion.

gametes *(GAM eets)* General term for reproductive cells of female or male origin.

ganglion *(GANG lee on)* Mass of nervous tissue composed mostly of nerve cell bodies and lying outside the brain and spinal cord.

gap junction A special connection found in electrical synapses.

gas trapping A condition in which exhalation of air is impaired, leading to stale air remaining in the lung.

gastric glands Located in the stomach, these excrete gastric juices for digestion.

gastric phase The second phase of gastric juice production in which over two thirds of the gastric juices are secreted as the food moves into the stomach.

gastrin *(GAS trin)* Hormone produced by the stomach that stimulates the release of hydrochloric acid and pepsinogen in the stomach.

gastritis *(gas TRY tis)* An acute or chronic inflammation of the stomach's lining.

gastroenterology *(GAS troh en ter ALL oh jee)* The study of diseases related to the gastrointestinal tract.

gastroesophageal reflux disease (GERD) *(GAS troh ee SAWF ah JEE al)* A combination of symptoms caused by a backflow of gastric contents into the esophagus.

gastrointestinal (GI) system Body system that includes the oral cavity, pharynx, stomach, esophagus, small and large intestines, and the accessory organs of the liver, gallbladder, and pancreas. Its function is to digest food and remove undigested food from the body. Also known as the *gastrointestinal tract, digestive system,* or *digestive tract.*

gastroscope *(GAS troh skohp)* A lit tubular device used to examine the interior of the stomach.

gel layer The top layer of the mucociliary blanket that entraps inhaled particles.

gene An area on a chromosome that contains all the DNA information needed to produce one type of protein molecule.

general senses Senses that are scattered throughout the various regions of the body that include sensations of heat, cold, pain, nausea, hunger, thirst, and pressure or touch.

genitalia General term for reproductive organs.

genital wart A wart of the genitalia, caused by strains of human papillomavirus (HPV), some of which are transmitted by sexual contact.

genitourinary system *(JEN ih toe YOUR ih nair ee)* Combination of two closely related body systems: the female and male genitalia and the urinary system. Also known as the *urogenital system.*

geriatric A general term applied to older adult patients.

gigantism (giantism) *(jy GAN tizm)* An excessive development of a body or body part often as a result of an abnormal hormone level.

gingiva The tissue that surrounds the necks of the teeth and covers the alveolar processes of the maxilla and mandible; the gums.

gingival *(jin jih VAL)* Referring to the gum.

gingivitis Inflammation of the gums characterized by redness, swelling, and tendency to bleed.

GI tract Alternate name for the gastrointestinal system.

glans penis The cone-shaped head of the penis that contains the urethral orifice. It is covered with a movable hood known as the foreskin or prepuce, under which is secreted the substance called smegma.

glaucoma *(glaw KOH mah)* Increased intraocular pressure (IOP) because aqueous humor cannot circulate freely. In open-angle glaucoma, the angle where the edges of the iris and cornea touch is normal and open, but the trabecular meshwork is blocked. Open-angle glaucoma is painless but destroys peripheral vision, leaving the patient with tunnel vision. In closed-angle glaucoma, the angle is too small and blocks the aqueous humor. Closed-angle glaucoma causes severe pain, blurred vision, and photophobia. Glaucoma can progress to blindness.

glia *(GLEE ah)* Nonnervous or supporting tissue found in the brain and spinal cord; made of glial cells.

glial cells *(GLEE all)* Cells that include astrocytes, oligodendrocytes, ependymal cells, microglia cells, Schwann cells, and satellite cells.

globulins *(GLOB yuh linz)* Protein antibodies that protect against infection.

glomerular capsule *(glow MAIR you ler)* A double layered membrane surrounding the glomerulus.

glomerular filtrate *(glow MAIR you ler FILL trate)* The filtered fluid within the glomerulus.

glomerulonephritis *(glow MAIR you loh neh FRY tiss)* The inflammatory disease of the glomerular capsular membranes of the kidneys.

glomerulosclerosis *(glow MAIR you loh sklee ROW sis)* Fibrotic or scarring changes of the kidney.

glomerulus *(glow MAIR yoo lus)* Network of intertwining capillaries within Bowman's capsule in the nephron. Filtration takes place in the glomerulus.

glottic See sphincter.

glottis *(GLOT is)* V-shaped structure of mucous membranes and vocal cords within the larynx.

glucagon *(GLOO kah gawn)* Hormone secreted by the pancreas that increases the blood glucose by stimulating the liver to change stored glycogen to glucose.

glucocorticoids *(GLOO koh CORE tih koidz)* Hormones produced by the adrenal cortex that regulate blood sugar.

glucose *(GLOO kohs)* 1. A simple sugar found in foods and also the sugar in the blood. 2. Glucose is not normally found in the urine. Its presence (glycosuria) indicates uncontrolled diabetes mellitus with excess glucose in the blood "spilling" over into the urine.

gluteal *(GLOO tee al)* Pertaining to buttocks.

glycerol *(GLIS uh rall)* Portion of the fat molecule.

glycogen *(GLIE coh jin)* The form that glucose (sugar) takes when it is stored in the liver and skeletal muscles.

glycosuria *(GLY koh SHOO ree ah)* Condition of sugar in the urine.

goblet cells Specialized cells that secrete mucus.

goiter *(GOY ter)* Enlargement of the thyroid gland.

golgi apparatus *(GOAL jee ap uh RAT uhs)* Organelle of the cell that packages cellular material for transport.

gonadotropin-releasing hormone (GnRH) *(GOHN ad doh TROH pin)* Released by the hypothalamus and causes the increase in the secretion of LH and FSH from the pituitary gland.

gonadotropin-releasing hormone agonists Newer class of hormones that can be administered either by injection or nasal spray that inhibit estrogen production.

gonads Specialized organs for reproduction; testes in males and ovaries in females.

gout Disease caused by excessive uric acid in the blood that is deposited in the joints, producing inflammation and pain.

graafian follicle *(GRAFF ee an FALL eh kul)* Mature follicle surrounded by a sac.

granular pneumocyte *(GRAN yuh ler NOO moh SITE)* Plump type II cell that produces surfactant and aids in cellular repair.

granulocytes *(GRAN yoo loh SITE)* A specific group of white blood cells that possess granules in their cytoplasm.

granulosa cell One of the many cuboidal cells that surround and nurture the maturing oocyte.

Graves' disease A distinct form of hyperthyroidism that includes an enlarged thyroid gland and various ocular findings such as proptosis (downward displacement), stare, and lid lag.

greater curvature The large convex curve of the stomach.

greenstick fracture An incomplete bone break, usually found in children who have softer more pliable bones.

Guillain-Barré syndrome (GBS) *(gee YAH bar RAY)* A neuromuscular disease that usually leads to ascending flaccid paralysis.

gustatory sense *(GUSS ta tore ee)* Sense of taste.

gynecology *(guy neh KOL oh jee)* The study and treatment of female diseases.

gyri *(JYE rye)* Convolutions of the cerebral hemispheres of the brain.

H

hairline fracture A fine bone fracture that resembles a hair on the x-ray.

hammer One of the three small bones of the ear, also known as the *malleus*.

hard palate The anterior part of the palate (the roof of the mouth) supported by the maxillary and palatine bones.

Hashimoto's thyroiditis *(HAH shee MOH tohs THIGH roy DYE tiss)* An autoimmune disease involving inflammation, then destruction and fibrosis of the thyroid gland, which leads to hypothyroidism.

head lice Lives in the fine hair of the head, including the beard and eyebrows. Its eggs, commonly called nits, may be found glued to hairs. They form nests in the vicinity of the ears. This organism is the cause of pediculosis capitis.

heart A hollow, muscular organ, the pump of the circulatory system.

heart block A blockage of the normal cardiac conduction system pathways.

heart failure (HF) Inability of the heart to pump sufficient amounts of blood. Caused by chronic coronary artery disease or hypertension.

helper T cell Cell that stimulates the production of some T cells and B cells. Also known as *CD4 cells*.

hematology *(hee mah TALL oh jee)* The study of blood-related diseases and conditions.

hematoma *(HEE mah TOH mah)* A swelling as a result of a break in a blood vessel(s) usually confined to a specific area (tissue, organ, or space) in the body.

hematuria *(HEE mah TOO ree ah)* Blood in the urine.

hemisphere One-half of the cerebrum, either the right hemisphere or the left hemisphere. The right hemisphere recognizes patterns and three-dimensional structures (including faces) and the emotions of words. The left hemisphere performs mathematical and logical reasoning, analysis, and interpreting sights, sounds, and sensations. The left hemisphere is also active in reading, writing, and speaking.

hemodialysis *(HEE moh dye AL ih sis)* The use of an artificial kidney to clear waste products, toxins, and excess fluid from the blood.

hemoglobin *(HEE moh GLOH bin)* Substance in an erythrocyte that binds to oxygen and carbon dioxide. Its globin chains give it a round shape. When it is bound to oxygen, it forms the compound oxyhemoglobin.

hemolytic *(HEE moh LIT ik)* The destruction of blood and blood particles.

hemolytic uremic syndrome An acute condition consisting of acute nephropathy, thrombocytopenia, and microangiopathic hemolytic anemia and is caused by eating contaminated or raw meats (esp. hamburger) containing *E. coli 0157:H7*.

hemophilia *(HEE moh FILL ee ah)* Inherited genetic abnormality of a gene on the X chromosome that causes an absence or deficiency of a specific clotting factor. When injured, hemophiliac patients cannot easily form a blood clot and continue to bleed for long periods of time.

hemopoiesis *(HEE moh poy EE sus)* Formation of blood cells.

hemorrhoid *(HEM oh royd)* Varicose veins in the rectum.

hemostasis *(HEE moh STAY siss)* The cessation of bleeding after the formation of a blood clot.

hemothorax *(HE moh THOH raks)* Presence of blood in the thoracic cavity, usually from trauma.

heparin Substance that inhibits coagulation of blood.

hepatic duct *(hepp ah TIC)* Duct that carries bile from the liver.

hepatitis Inflammation of the liver most commonly caused by an exposure to an infectious agent, or excessive exposure to drugs (such as acetaminophen) or toxins (such as alcohol).

hernia A weakness in the muscles of the abdominal wall that allows loops of intestine to balloon outward.

herniated disk Common disorder in older patients where the soft central portion of the invertebral disk is forced through its outer covering.

herpes simplex type 1 Herpes caused by herpes simplex virus 1. The infections are categorized by the site of infection.

herpes simplex type 2 Herpes caused by herpes simplex virus 2. The infections are categorized by the site of infection.

herpes Viral infection that can cause a variety of skin conditions to include cold sores and shingles.

heterografting The use of donor tissue to repair burnt skin.

hilum *(HIGH lim)* 1. Indentation on the medial side of each lung where the bronchus, pulmonary artery, pulmonary vein, and nerves enter the lung. 2. Indentation on the medial side of each kidney where the renal artery enters and the renal vein and the ureter leave.

histamine *(HISS tah meen)* A chemical released by basophils. Histamine dilates blood vessels and increases blood flow to damaged tissue. Allows protein molecules to leak out of blood vessels into the surrounding tissue. This produces redness and swelling.

Hodgkin's disease *(HAWJ kinz)* A malignant lymphoma in which the early stages of the disease present with no symptoms other than a painless lump or enlarged gland in the neck or armpit. Some patients may develop fevers/night sweats and loss of appetite/weight.

Hodgkin's lymphoma See Hodgkin's disease.

Holter monitor A portable device used to record cardiac activity usually during a 24-hour period that may show cardiac arrhythmias that would not be revealed during a regular ECG or stress test.

homeostasis *(HOH mee oh STAY sis)* State of equilibrium of the internal environment of the body, including fluid balance, acid–base balance, temperature, metabolism, and so forth, to keep all the body systems functioning optimally.

hordeolum See stye.

horizontal fissure The fissure that divides the upper and middle lobes of the right lung.

horizontal plane Another name for the transverse plane.

hormonal control Hormone levels controlled by other hormones.

hormone *(HOR mohn)* Chemical messenger of the endocrine system that is released by a gland or organ and travels through the blood.

horns Grey matter in spinal cord that contain neuron cell bodies and are involved in sensory, motor, and autonomic functions.

human chorionic gonadotropin (HCG) *(KOH ree on ick GOHN ah doh TROH pin)* Hormone released by fertilized egg that stimulates the corpus luteum to keep secreting progesterone and a small amount of estrogen to maintain the uterine lining.

human immunodeficiency virus (HIV) A virus that leads to decreased immune function and kills off helper T cells.

humoral control Hormone levels controlled by body fluids such as blood.

hydrocele *(HIGH droh seel)* An abnormal collection of fluid within the testis.

hydrocephalus *(HIGH droh SEF uh luhs)* A general term for the accumulation of excessive amounts of cerebrospinal fluid within the brain's ventricles.

hydrogen bond The bond between hydrogen molecules.

hydrolysis A catabolic reaction in which water is added to break apart large molecules.

hydrophilic Water loving.

hydrophobic Water fearing.

hydrothorax A form of pleural effusion in which blood serum is found in the intrapleural space.

hymen The perforated membrane that covers the external opening of the vagina.

hypercholesterolemia *(HIGH per koh LESS tur ul EE me ah)* High levels of cholesterol in the blood.

hyperextension The forced straightening of a joint beyond its normal limits.

hyperopia *(HIGH per OH pee ah)* Farsightedness. Light rays from a far object focus correctly on the retina, creating a sharp image. However, light rays from a near object come into focus posterior to the retina, creating a blurred image.

hyperplasia *(HIGH per PLAY zee uh)* Excessive growth of normal cells.

hyperpolarized The charge across the cell membrane is more negative than resting.

hyperthyroidism The overproduction of thyroid hormones, often resulting in increased metabolic rate, weight loss, and nervous irritability.

hypertrophy *(high PER troh fee)* Greater than normal growth.

hyperventilation *(HIGH per ven tih LAY shun)* The process of excessive ventilation in which carbon dioxide levels are lowered below normal.

hypochondriac Name of two of the abdominal regions left and right, under the ribs. Also, a person who complains of imaginary conditions or diseases.

hypodermis The fatty tissue layer below the dermis of the skin.

hypogastric Inferior to the stomach.

hypopituitarism *(HIGH poh pih TOO ih TAIR izm)* A condition caused by a less than normal secretion of pituitary hormones.

hypothalamus *(HGH poh THAL ah mus)* Endocrine gland located in the brain just below the thalamus. It produces (but does not secrete) antidiuretic hormone (ADH) and oxytocin. The hypothalamus is in the center of the brain and coordinates the activities of the pons and medulla oblongata. It also controls heart rate, blood pressure, respiratory rate, body temperature, sensations of hunger and thirst, and the circadian rhythm. It also produces hormones as part of the endocrine system. In addition, the hypothalamus helps control emotions (pleasure, excitement, fear, anger, sexual arousal) and bodily responses to emotions; regulates the sex drive; contains the feeding and satiety centers; and functions as part of the "fight-or-flight" response of the sympathetic nervous system.

hypothyroidism The underproduction of thyroid hormones, resulting in low metabolism, excessive weight gain, lethargy, and depression.

I

idiopathic A condition with an uncertain or not yet determined cause.

ileocecal orifice *(ILL ee oh SEE kuhl OR ih FIS)* Opening at the end of the small intestine.

ileocecal valve The valve that attaches the ileum to the large intestine.

ileum *(ILL ee um)* Third portion of small intestine which is attached to the large intestine.

ilium *(ILL ee um)* Most superior hip bone. Bony landmarks include the iliac crest and the anterior-superior iliac spine (ASIS). Posteriorly, each ilium joins one side of the sacrum.

immune response The series of body reactions to a pathogenic organism.

immune system The lymphatic tissues, organs, and physiological processes that identify an antigen as abnormal or foreign and prevent it from harming the body.

immunization Techniques such as vaccinations that train the immune system by creating memory cells to destroy a specific pathogen.

immunology *(IM yoo NALL oh jee)* The study of diseases and conditions of the immune system.

immunotherapy The use of natural and synthetic substances to stimulate or suppress the immune response (as in patients with anaphylaxis or severe allergies), to treat deficits, or to interfere with the growth of malignant neoplasms.

impotence The inability of a male to achieve or maintain an erection. The cause of this condition may be a vascular, neurological, or psychological dysfunction.

impulse conduction The propagation of an electrical impulse through the nervous system.

in situ keratomileusis (LASIK) surgery *(in SIT oo KER ah toh mih LOO sis)* The use of laser to reshape corneal tissue to improve vision.

incisors *(in SIGH zers)* Chisel-shaped teeth in the middle of the dental arch that cut and tear food on their incisal surface. There are eight incisors, four in the maxilla, and four in the mandible.

incontinence *(in KAHNT in ins)* Condition of involuntary urination and defecation.

incus *(ING cuss)* Second bone of the middle ear. It is attached to the malleus on one end and the stapes on the other end. Also known as the *anvil*.

indirect contact Spread of an infectious agent by touching a contaminated surface and then transmitting it to another individual.

infarct *(IN farkt)* Cellular death due to lack of blood flow (perfusion).

inferior Pertaining to the lower half of the body or a position below an organ or structure.

inferior vena cava The vena cava is the largest vein in the body. The inferior vena cava receives blood from the abdomen, pelvis, and lower extremities and takes it to the heart.

infertility A condition of diminished fertility or an inability to produce offspring. It does not necessarily imply sterility.

inflammation *(in flah MAY shun)* Tissue reaction to injury that includes swelling and reddening due to increased blood flow to the area.

inflammatory response The defensive series of actions/events that the body performs in reaction to trauma or infection.

infundibulum The funnel-shaped opening at the lateral end of the uterine tube.

ingestion Process of taking in material (particularly food).

inguinal region *(ING gwuh nal)* The groin; the term *inguinal* means referring to groin.

innate immunity The defense against pathogens that you are born with and that does not improve with experience or remember specific pathogens. The first line of defense.

inner ear Region of ear that contains the cochlea, vestibule chamber, and the semicircular canals.

inotropism *(EYE no TROPE izm)* An influence on the force of muscular contraction.

insula *(IN soo luh)* The deep lobes of the cerebral hemispheres.

insulin Hormone secreted by the pancreas that allows for glucose to be utilized for cellular respiration.

integumentary system *(in TEG you men tah ree)* The skin and its accessory components of hair, nails, and associated glands.

interatrial septum *(IN ter AY tree al)* The wall that separates the right and left atria.

intercalated discs *(in ter KUH late ed)* Structures that connect heart tissue cells to facilitate a smooth contraction.

interferon *(in ter FEAR on)* Substance released by macrophages that have engulfed a virus. Interferon stimulates body cells to produce an antiviral substance that keeps a virus from entering a cell and reproducing.

interleukin *(in ter LOO kin)* Released by macrophages, it stimulates B cell and T lymphocytes and activates NK cells. It also produces the fever associated with inflammation and infection.

interlobar arteries *(in TUR LOH bar AHR tuh rees)* Branches of the lobar arteries which pass through the renal columns.

internal Structures deep within the body or an organ.

internal medicine Specialization in the study of function, relationships, and treatment of body systems.

internal respiration Process of gas exchange at the cells and tissue level.

internal urethral sphincter *(yoo REE thruhl SFINGK ter)* Valve at the junction of the bladder and urethra.

interneurons *(in ter NEW ronz)* Neurons that facilitate communication between neurons.

interphase The stage of a cell between mitotic divisions during which DNA replication takes place.

interstitial cystitis Chronic form of urinary tract infection.

interstitial space The area that separates the basement membrane of alveolar epithelium from the capillary endothelium.

interventricular septum *(in TUR ven TRIK yuh ler SEP tum)* The wall that separates the right and left ventricles.

intestinal phase The final phase of gastric juice production in which the production of gastric juice diminishes.

intradermally Into the skin.

intramembranous ossification *(os uh fih KAY shun)* Bone development between two sheets composed of fibrous connective tissue such as found in the skull.

intrinsic factor Specialized substance that is needed for the absorption of vitamin B_{12}.

intubation Technique of inserting a breathing tube past the vocal cords and into the trachea to facilitate breathing.

inversion The movement of the sole of a foot toward the other foot.

invertebral disks Cartilage pads that separate vertebrae.

involuntary muscle Muscle that is not under conscious control.

ion An atom or group of atoms that have lost one or more electrons giving it a positive charge or has gained one or more electrons giving it a negative charge.

ionic bond Bond formed by transfer of electrons.

iris *(EYE riss)* Colored ring of tissue whose muscles contract or relax to change the size of the pupil in the center of the iris.

ischemia *(iss KEE mee ah)* Tissue injury due to a decrease in blood flow.

Islet of Langerhans *(EYE let , LAN gur hanz)* Specialized group of cells in pancreatic tissue that produce insulin and glucagon.

isthmus Narrow inferior part of the uterus.

J

jaundice *(JAWN dis)* A general term for the yellow staining of body tissues and fluids due to an excessive amount of bilirubin in the blood. There are various causes of jaundice.

jejunum *(jee JOO num)* Second part of the small intestine.

joint Area where two bones come together.

joint dislocation The movement of the joint out of its normal position.

jugular venous distension (JVD) The enlargement of the jugular veins due to venous engorgement.

juxtaglomerular apparatus *(JUKS tah glow MAIR you lair)* A special group of cells near the glomerulus that secrete renin into the bloodstream.

K

keloid *(KEE loid)* An unusually thick and fibrous scar on the skin.

keratin *(KER ah tin)* Hard protein found in the cells of the outermost part of the epidermis and in the nails.

keratinization *(KER ah tin eye ZAY shun)* The process of forming a horny growth such as fingernails.

keratinized To become hard.

ketonuria *(kee toh NOOR ee uh)* A condition of excessive acetone bodies in the urine.

kidney disease Impaired functioning of the kidneys leading to a buildup of toxic waste products and fluids in the body.

kidney failure See kidney disease.

kidney Organ of the urinary system that filters blood and produces urine, controlling fluid and electrolyte balance.

kidney stones Stones formed by many substances such as calcium or uric acid or may be a result of an infection that can block proper function.

kyphosis *(kigh FOH sis)* An exaggerated posterior curvature of the thoracic spine, also known as humpback, hunchback, or Pott's curvature.

L

labia *(LAY bee ah)* An outer pair of vertical fleshy lips covered with pubic hair (the labia majora) and a smaller, thinner, inner pair of lips (the labia minora) that partially cover the clitoris, and urethral and vaginal openings. Part of the external female genitalia; alternate name for lips.

labia majora *(LAY bee ah)* The two folds of skin and adipose tissue on either side of the labia minora and vaginal opening that form the lateral borders of the vulva.

labia minora The two thin folds of integument that lie between the labia majora. They enclose the vestibule.

labor The actual process of fetal delivery from the uterus to the vagina to the outside world.

labyrinth *(LAB ih rinth)* Intricate communicating passage of the inner ear essential for maintaining equilibrium.

labyrinthitis *(LAB ih rinn THIGH tiss)* Bacterial or viral infection of the semicircular canals of the inner ear, causing severe vertigo.

lacrimal apparatus *(LACK rim al app ah RA tuss)* Structures involved with the secretion and production of tears.

lacrimal gland The gland that secretes tears.

lactase Enzyme needed for the digestion of double sugars.

lacteal *(LACK tee al)* The lymph vessel associated with villi in the small intestine. It is involved in absorption of nutrients from the small intestine.

lactic acid Acid that builds up due to anaerobic metabolism.

laparoscope *(LAP eh roh skohp)* A lit tubular device used to internally examine the abdominal region.

large intestine Organ of absorption between the small intestine and the anal opening to the outside of the body. The large intestine includes the cecum, appendix, colon, rectum, and anus. Also known as the *large bowel*.

laryngitis *(lar in JIGH tis)* Hoarseness or complete loss of the voice, difficulty swallowing, and cough due to swelling and inflammation of the larynx.

laryngopharynx *(lah RING goh FAR inks)* The most inferior portion of the pharynx.

laryngotracheobronchitis (LTB) *(lah RING goh TRAY kee oh brong KIGH tiss)* A bacterial or viral infection that causes a barking cough and inspiratory stridor.

larynx *(LAR inks)* Triangular-shaped structure in the anterior neck (visible as the laryngeal prominence or Adam's apple) that contains the vocal cords and is a passageway for inhaled and exhaled air. Also known as the *voice box*.

lateral *(LAT er al)* Pertaining to the side of the body or the side of an organ or structure.

left atrium The chamber of the heart that receives oxygenated blood from the lungs.

left bundle branch An atrioventricular bundle of "electrical wiring" that spreads across the inner surface of the left ventricle allowing for a smooth and effective heart contraction.

left main stem Largest bronchus leading into the left lung.

left ventricle Chamber of the heart that pumps the oxygenated blood through the body.

lens Clear, hard disk in the internal eye. The muscles and ligaments of the ciliary body change its shape to focus light rays on the retina.

lesion *(LEE zhun)* General category for any area of visible damage on the skin, whether it is from disease or injury.

lesser curvature The concave curve of the stomach.

leukemia *(loo KEE mee uh)* Cancer of leukocytes (white blood cells), including mature lymphocytes, immature lymphoblasts, as well as myeloblasts and myelocytes that mature into neutrophils, eosinophils, or basophils. The malignant leukocytes crowd out the production of other cells in the bone marrow. Leukemia is named according to the type of leukocyte that is the most prevalent and whether the onset of symptoms is acute or chronic. Types of leukemia include acute myelogenous leukemia (AML), chronic myelogenous leukemia (CML), acute lymphocytic leukemia (ALL), and chronic lymphocytic leukemia (CLL).

leukocytes *(LOO koh sights)* White blood cells. There are five different types of mature leukocytes: neutrophils, eosinophils, basophils, lymphocytes, and monocytes.

leukocytosis *(LOO koh sigh TOH sis)* Increase in the number of white blood cells above normal.

leukopenia Abnormal decrease of white blood cells.

leukoplakia *(LOO koh PLAY kee ah)* White patches in the mouth commonly seen in snuff and chewing tobacco users that is a precursor to oral cancer.

ligament Fibrous band that holds two bones together.

ligand gated The opening and closing of a cellular channel when a molecule binds to a receptor.

limbic system *(LIM bick)* Processes memories and controls emotions, mood, motivation, and behavior. Links the conscious to the unconscious mind. Limbic system consists of the thalamus, hypothalamus, hippocampus, amygdaloid bodies, and fornix.

lingual *(LING gwal)* Pertaining to the tongue.

lingual tonsils Patches of lymphoid tissue found at the back of the tongue.

lingula The region of the left lung that corresponds with the right middle lobe.

lipase Enzyme needed for the digestion of certain fats.

lipids Biological molecules consisting mostly of carbon and hydrogen.

lipocyte Cell in the subcutaneous layer that stores fat.

lithotripsy *(LITH oh TRIP see)* Medical or surgical procedure that uses sound waves to break up a kidney stone.

lobar arteries Further branching of the segmental arteries in the kidney.

lobar bronchi Airway leading into specific lobe of lungs.

lobes 1. Large divisions of the lung, visible on the outer surface. 2. Large area of the hemisphere of the cerebrum. Each lobe is named for the bone of the skull that is next to it: frontal lobe, parietal lobe, temporal lobe, and occipital lobe.

lobules Pyramidal divisions separated from each other by incomplete partitions called septa. Each consists of one to three coiled seminiferous tubules.

local potential Change in the electrical charge across a cell membrane that is proportional to the size of the stimulus.

Loop of Henle *See* nephron loop.

lordosis *(lore DOH sis)* An anteroposterior curvature of the spine (backward bending).

lower esophageal sphincter (LES) *(eh SOFF eh JEE al SFINGK ter)* Ringed muscle leading into the stomach.

lumbar Pertaining to the loins (the part of the back between the thorax and pelvis).

lumbar puncture Technique used to sample cerebral spinal fluid (CSF); also known as a spinal tap.

lumbar region Two of the nine regions of the abdominopelvic area. The right and left lumbar regions are inferior to the right and left hypochondriac regions. Also refers to the lower back, spinal cord, and spinal column.

lumen *(LOO men)* Opening in the center of a large tube, for example the center of the tubes in the digestive and respiratory systems and the blood vessels.

lunula *(LOO new lah)* Whitish half-moon visible under the proximal portion of the nail plate. It is the visible tip of the nail root.

luteal *(LOO tee al)* Pertaining to the corpus luteum.

luteal phase See secretory phase.

luteinizing hormone (LH) *(LOO tee in EYE zing)* A hormone that is released by the pituitary gland during the menstrual cycle that triggers ovulation.

Lyme disease Named after the town of Lyme, Connecticut, it is the number one vector-borne disease in the United States. A multisystem disorder caused by the spirochete, *Borrelia burgdorferi*, it is spread by deer tick bites causing a bull's-eye rash at the bite site.

lymph *(LIMF)* Fluid that flows through the lymphatic system.

lymph capillaries Smallest vessels of the lymphatic system which run parallel to blood capillaries.

lymph nodes Small, encapsulated pieces of lymphoid tissue located along the lymphatic vessels. Lymph nodes filter and destroy invading microorganisms and cancerous cells present in the lymph.

lymphadenitis *(lim FAD in EYE tiss)* An inflammation of lymph nodes, which results from the responsive actions of lymphocytes and phagocytes to invading microorganisms, or cancer cells.

lymphatic fluid *(lim FAA tick FLOO id)* Clear and colorless fluid of the lymphatic system.

lymphatic sinuses Portion of the lymph node that is filled with lymphatic fluid.

lymphatic system *(lim FAA tick)* Body system that includes lymphatic vessels, lymph nodes, lymphatic fluid, and lymphoid tissues (tonsils and adenoids, appendix, Peyer's patches), lymphoid organs (spleen and thymus), and the blood cells, lymphocytes, and macrophages.

lymphatic trunks Large lymphatic vessels found throughout the body which empty into collecting ducts.

lymphatic vessels *(lim FAA tick)* Vessels that begin as capillaries carrying lymph, continue through lymph nodes, and empty into the right lymphatic duct and the thoracic duct.

lymphocyte activation Stimulation of lymphocytes, "waking them up" to fight a pathogen.

lymphocyte proliferation *(LIM foh SIGHT pruh lif uh REY shun)* Reproduction of activated lymphocytes so there are many copies.

lymphocytes *(LIM foh SIGHTS)* Specialized, infection-fighting white blood cells produced by the lymphatic system.

lymphocytic leukemia A hematological malignancy marked by the unchecked multiplication of immature lymphoid cells in the bone marrow, blood, and body tissues.

lysis *(LYE sis)* Destruction or breakdown.

lysosome *(LIE so soam)* Organelle that consists of a small sac with digestive enzymes in it. These destroy pathogens that invade the cell.

M

macrophages *(MACK roh FAGE ez)* Cells that take fragments of the pathogen they have eaten and present them to a B cell (lymphocyte). This stimulates the B cell to become a plasma cell and make antibodies against that specific pathogen. Macrophages also activate helper T cells in this way. Macrophages also produce special immune response chemicals: interferon, interleukin, and tumor necrosis factor.

macroscopic anatomy *(MAK roh SCOP ick ah NAH toh mee)* Study of large structures of the body.

macular degeneration Progressive deterioration of the macula lutea of the retina leading to vision loss.

magnetic resonance imaging (MRI) Imaging technique utilizing high-intensity magnetism to produce high-quality body images for diagnostic purposes.

major calyx, minor calyces *(KAY licks, KAY leh seez)* Tubes in the kidney that carry urine from the nephrons to the renal pelvis.

malignant *(mah LIG nant)* Cancerous, able to spread to distant parts of the body.

malleus *(MALL ee us)* First bone of the middle ear. It is attached to the tympanic membrane on one end and to the incus on the other end. Also known as the *hammer*.

maltase Enzyme needed for the digestion of double sugars.

mammary glands External female accessory organs that produce milk.

manubrium *(mah NOO bree um)* The superior portion of the sternum.

margination Walling off of an infected area to prevent further spread and allow the body to focus at the specific site.

mast cells Connective tissue cells that are important in cellular defense and contain heparin and histamine.

mastication *(MASS tih CAY shun)* Process of chewing, during which the teeth and tongue together tear, crush, and grind food. This is part of the process of mechanical digestion.

mastitis *(mass TYE tiss)* Inflammation or infection of the breasts.

mastoiditis *(mass toy DYE tiss)* Inflammation of the mastoid sinuses, usually as a result of the spread of infection from acute otitis media.

mechanical vector A vector where the infectious agent exists on the exterior of the insect or arthropod.

medial *(MEE dee al)* Pertaining to the middle of the body or the middle of an organ or structure.

median plane Imaginary division of the body from top to bottom dividing it into right and left sections.

mediastinum *(ME dee as TYE num)* Central area within the thoracic cavity. It contains the trachea, esophagus, heart, and other structures.

medulla The central axis of a hair.

medulla oblongata *(meh DULL lah ob long GAW tah)* Most inferior part of the brain stem that joins to the spinal cord. It relays nerve impulses from the cerebrum to the cerebellum. It contains the respiratory center. Cranial nerves IX through XII originate there.

medullary canal *See* medullary cavity.

medullary cavity Hollow region in the bone that stores bone marrow.

megakaryocytes Large bone marrow cells with large or multiple nuclei from which platelets are derived.

meibomian glands *(mye BOH me an)* Also known as tarsal glands; specialized form of sebaceous glands located at the rim of the eyelids.

meiosis *(mye OH sis)* Form of cellular division that produces gametes.

melanin *(MELL an in)* Dark brown or black pigment that gives color to the skin and hair.

melanocytes *(mell AN oh sights)* Cells that produce melanin.

melanoma A malignant pigmented mole or tumor.

melatonin *(MELL ah TOH ninn)* Hormone secreted by the pineal body. It maintains the 24-hour wake–sleep cycle known as the circadian rhythm.

membrane A thin soft pliable layer of tissue that can line a cavity or cover an organ or structure.

memory B cells Antibody-producing cells that are produced when a pathogen is encountered the first time. Memory B cells are stored until the pathogen comes again. They are responsible for secondary response.

memory T cells Memory cells responsible for cell mediated immunity. They are produced when a pathogen is encountered the first time. Memory T cells are stored until the pathogen comes again. They are responsible for secondary response.

menarche *(men ARE kee)* The onset of the first menstruation.

Ménière's disease *(MAIN ee AIRZ)* Recurring and progressive disease that includes progressive deafness, ringing ears, dizziness, and the feeling of fullness in the ears.

meninges *(men IN jeez)* Three separate membranes that envelope and protect the entire brain and spinal cord. The meninges include the dura mater, arachnoid, and pia mater.

meningitis *(men in JYE tiss)* Inflammation of the meninges of the brain or spinal cord by a bacterial or viral infection. Initial symptoms include fever, headache, nuchal rigidity (stiff neck) lethargy, vomiting, irritability, and photophobia.

menopause The permanent cessation of menses, menstrual activity, usually occurring between ages 45 and 58.

menses *(MEN seez)* The monthly flow of bloody fluid from the uterus.

menstrual cycle The female reproductive cycle based on approximately 28 days.

menstruation *(MEN stroo AY shun)* The cyclic hormonal shedding of the uterine endometrium.

menstruation stage Final stage of the menstrual cycle that occurs if the egg is not fertilized.

mesentery *(MEZ in tare ee)* Membranous sheet of peritoneum that supports the jejunum and ileum.

mesometrium The broad ligament below the mesovarium.

mesosalpinx *(mess oh SAL pinks)* Support band of the uterine tubes.

mesovarium *(MESS oh VAY ree um)* Structure that connects the anterior border of the ovary to the posterior layer of the broad ligament.

metabolism *(me TAH bow lizm)* Process of using oxygen and glucose to produce energy for cells. Metabolism also produces by-products like carbon dioxide and other waste products. The ongoing cycle of anabolism and catabolism.

metaphase Second step in mitosis where chromosomes line up in the center of the cell.

metaplasia Conversion of one kind of tissue into a form that is not normal for that tissue.

metastasis *(meh TASS tah sis)* Process by which cancerous cells break off from a tumor and move through the blood vessels or lymphatic vessels to other sites in the body.

metastasize To spread throughout the body to distant sites.

metric system System of measurement based on the power of 10.

microglia *(MYE crow GLEE ah)* Cells that move, engulf, and destroy pathogens anywhere in the central nervous system.

microscopic anatomy Study of structures that require the aid of magnification.

microvilli Microscopic extensions from the wall of the small intestine that absorb nutrients.

midbrain An area that connects the pons and the cerebellum with the hemispheres of the cerebrum.

middle ear Region of the ear that includes the ear drum, malleus, incus and stapes, oval window, and eustachian tubes.

midsagittal plane *(mid SAJ ih tal)* An imaginary vertical plane that divides the entire body into right and left sides and creates a midline. The midsagittal plane is named for the sagittal suture of the skull.

mineralcorticoids *(MIN er al CORE teh koydz)* Hormones secreted by the adrenal cortex that regulate electrolytes, salts, and fluid balance.

miotic agents Class of drugs that constrict the pupil.

mitochondria *(MYE toh KON dree uh)* The energy organelle of the cell.

mitosis Asexual cellular reproduction that produces exact copies of the original cell.

mitotic phase The phase devoted to actual cell division.

mitral *(MYE tral)* Pertaining to the bicuspid or mitral valve of the heart.

mixed nerve A nerve that carries both sensory and motor information.

mnemonics   Anything intended to aid memory.

MODS   Multiple organ dysfunction syndrome.

molars   The largest teeth, located posterior to the premolars. They crush and grind food on their large, flat, occlusal surfaces.

molecule   An electrically neutral collection of atoms held together and forming a unique substance.

monocytes   Mononuclear white blood cells commonly found in high numbers in chronic infections.

mononuclear agranulocytes   A nongranular white blood cell having one nucleus, (a lymphocyte or a monocyte).

mononucleosis   *(MON oh NEW klee OH sis)*   The presence of a higher-than-normal number of mononuclear leukocytes in the blood, and can be a result of an acute infection of the Epstein Barr virus.

monosaccharides   *(MON oh SACK uh ridez)*   Simple sugars with five or six carbons.

morbidity   The level of disability/ dysfunction caused by a specific disease.

morphology   The science of structure and form of organisms.

mortality   Condition of being dead or the number of deaths in a given population.

motor coordination loop   A complicated relationship between the thalamus, basal nuclei, and the cerebellum that allows for fine tuned movement.

motor neuron   Neuron that innervates muscle tissue.

motor system   The system responsible for movement.

motor unit   Motor neuron and all the muscle fibers it stimulates.

mouth   The cavity within the cheeks, containing the tongue and teeth, and communicating with the pharynx.

mucosa   *(myoo KOH suh)*   1. Lining throughout the gastrointestinal system that consists of a mucous membrane that produces mucus and an underlying smooth muscle layer that contracts to move food. 2. Mucous membrane that lines the respiratory tract. It warms and humidifies incoming air. It produces mucus to trap foreign particles. 3. Mucous membrane lining the inside of the bladder. 4. Mucous membranes lining the nasal cavity that warm and moisturize the incoming air. They also produce mucus to trap foreign particles.

mucous   Pertaining to mucus.

multiple sclerosis   *(sklih ROH sis)*   A chronic disease of the central nervous system involving the destruction of myelin and the nerve axons in various regions of the brain and the spinal cord at different times. This leads to temporary (sometimes sustained) but repetitive episodes of disrupted nerve impulse conduction.

murmur   An abnormal heart sound that may or may not be a result of heart disease.

muscle   Many muscle fascicles grouped together and surrounded by fascia. Contractile tissue.

muscular dystrophy   *(DISS troh fee)*   Genetic disease due to a mutation of the gene that makes the muscle protein dystrophin. Without dystrophin, the muscles weaken and then atrophy. Symptoms appear in early childhood as weakness, first in the lower extremities and then in the upper extremities. The most common and most severe form is Duchenne's muscular dystrophy; Becker's muscular dystrophy is a milder form.

muscularis externa   The outside muscular layer of an organ or tubule.

myalgia   *(my AL jee ah)*   Pain in one or more muscles due to injury or muscle disease. Polymyalgia is pain in several muscle groups.

myasthenia gravis   *(MY ass THEE nee ah)*   Abnormal and rapid fatigue of the muscles, particularly evident in the muscles of the face; there is ptosis of the eyelids. Symptoms worsen during the day and can be relieved by rest. The body produces antibodies against its own acetylcholine receptors located on muscle fibers. The antibodies destroy many of the receptors. There are normal levels of acetylcholine, but too few receptors remain to produce sustained muscle contractions.

mycelia   *(my SEE lee uh)*   Cellular filaments as seen in fungal bodies.

mydriatic agents   *(mid ree AT ik)*   Drugs that dilate the pupil.

myelin sheath   Layers of the cell membrane of Schwann cells (peripheral nervous system) or oligodendrocytes (central nervous system) that wrap nerve fibers, providing electrical insulation and increasing the velocity of impulse transmission.

myelogenous leukemia   A hematological malignancy in which neoplastic cells develop from myeloid, monocytic, erythrocytic, or megakaryocytic precursors. Neoplastic cells replace normal bone marrow.

myelin *(MY eh lin)* Fatty sheath around the axon of a neuron. It speeds up impulse conduction. Myelin around the axons of the brain and spinal cord is produced by oligodendrocytes. Myelin around axons of the cranial and spinal nerves is produced by Schwann cells. An axon with myelin is said to be myelinated.

myelin sheath Layers of the cell membrane of Schwann cells (peripheral nervous system) or oligodendrocytes (central nervous system) that wrap nerve fibers, providing electrical insulation and increasing the velocity of impulse transmission.

myelogenous leukemia A hematological malignancy in which neoplastic cells develop from myeloid, monocytic, erythrocytic, or megakaryocytic precursors. Neoplastic cells replace normal bone marrow.

myocardial infarction (MI) The disruption of blood flow to the heart leading to cardiac tissue damage and decreased function, commonly referred to as a heart attack.

myocardium *(MY oh CAR dee uhm)* Middle layer of the heart wall composed of cardiac muscle.

myofibril *(my oh FYE bril)* Cylinder containg the thin filament (actin) and thick filament (myosin) within the muscle fiber that give it its characteristic striated appearance.

myofilament *(MY oh FILL uh mints)* A filament within the myofibril of muscle cells.

myometrium *(MY oh MEE tree um)* Muscle layer in the uterus.

myopathy *(my OP uh thee)* A general term for muscle disease.

myopia *(my OH pee ah)* Nearsightedness. Light rays from a near object focus correctly on the retina, creating a sharp image. However, light rays from a far object come into focus anterior to the retina, creating a blurred image.

myosin *(MY oh sin)* The thick protein filament found in muscle fibers.

myringotomy *(mir in GOT oh mee)* A surgical procedure in which tiny tubes are inserted through the tympanic membrane to relieve pressure in cases of recurrent or chronic otitis media.

N

nail bed Pink portion under the fingernail that is part of the epidermis.

nail body The visible portion of the nail.

nail root Also known as the germinal matrix; where nails begin their growth.

nares *(NAY reez)* The paired external openings of the nasal cavity.

nasal Pertaining to the nose.

nasal cavity Hollow area inside the nose that is lined with mucosa or mucous membrane.

nasal polyp Painless, noncancerous, rubbery tissue growth that projects from the nasal mucosa.

nasal septum Cartilaginous wall that separates the nose into right and left sides.

nasopharynx *(NAY zoh FAR inks)* Uppermost portion of the throat where the posterior nares unite. The nasopharynx contains the opening for the eustachian tubes and the adenoids.

natural active immunity Antibodies developed due to exposure to a pathogen.

natural killer (NK) cell Type of lymphocyte that matures in the red marrow and is the body's first cellular defense against invading microorganisms. An NK cell recognizes non-self by the antigens on the cell wall and releases chemicals that penetrate and destroy it.

natural passive immunity Immunity due to the passage of antibodies from mother to child across the placenta or in breast milk.

neck of tooth Transitional area between the root and crown where the tooth becomes narrower. The neck of the tooth is located just above and below the gum line.

necrosis *(neh KROH sis)* Gray-to-black discoloration of the skin in areas where the tissue has died.

negative feedback loop Physiological process that works against the trend. Most often brings a variable back to set point. For example, as blood pressure rises, heart rate may decrease to bring blood pressure back to "normal."

negative selection The destruction of lymphocytes, which destroy "self" antigens. These lymphocytes must be deleted to prevent autoimmunity.

nephritis *(nef RYE tiss)* A general term referring to inflammation of the kidney.

nephrology *(neh FRALL oh jee)* The study of the structure, function, and pathology of the renal system.

nephron *(NEFF rahn)* Microscopic functional unit of the kidney.

nephron loop Structure composed of the descending and ascending loop of the renal tubular system.

nephropathy *(neff ROPP ah thee)* General word for any disease process involving the kidney. Diabetic nephropathy involves progressive damage to the glomeruli because of diabetes mellitus. The tiny arteries of the glomerulus harden (glomerulosclerosis) because of accelerated arteriosclerosis throughout the body.

nerves Bundles of individual axons.

nervous system Body system that includes the brain, cranial nerves, spinal cord, spinal nerves, and neurons. It receives signals from parts of the body and interprets them as pain, touch, temperature, body position, taste, sight, smell, and hearing. It coordinates body movement. It maintains and interprets memory and emotion.

neural control The nervous system control of hormone levels.

neuroglia *(new ROG lee ah)* Cells that hold neurons in place and perform specialized tasks. Includes astrocytes, ependymal cells, microglia, oligodendrocytes, satellite cells, and Schwann cells. Also called *glial cells.*

neuromuscular *(noor oh MUHS kyuh ler)* Pertaining to the nervous and muscular system.

neuromuscular junction *(noor oh MUHS kyuh ler JUHNGK shuhn)* Area on a single muscle fiber where a nerve connects.

neuron *(NEW ron)* An individual nerve cell. The functional part of the nervous system.

neuron cell body The part of cell containing the nucleus but not the axon or dendrite.

neurotransmitter *(NEW roh TRANS mitt er)* Chemical messenger that travels across the synapse between a neuron and another neuron, muscle fiber, or gland.

neutron A noncharged or neutral particle of the atom.

neutrophil *(NOO troh fill)* A type of leukocyte that performs nonspecific phagocytosis.

nitric oxide Gaseous substance present in the body that causes vasodilation.

nociceptors *(NOH see SEP torz)* Free nerve endings that are receptors of pain stimuli (pain receptors).

nocturia *(nawk TOO ree ah)* Frequent urination at night.

nodal cells Pacemaker cells that create an electrical impulse at a regular interval causing the heart to contract.

nodes of Ranvier Constriction of the myelin sheath on a myelinated nerve fiber that facilitates nodal transmission of the impulse.

non-steroidal anti-inflammatory drugs (NSAIDs) An older class of drugs such as ibuprofen and naproxen.

norepinephrine *(NOR ep ih NEFF rinn)* 1. Neurotransmitter for the sympathetic nervous system. It moves between neurons and an involuntary muscle, organ, or gland. Controls the fight-or-flight response. 2. Hormone secreted by the adrenal medulla in response to stimulation by nerves of the sympathetic nervous system.

normal flora *(FLOOR ah)* The normal microorganisms found in a particular body region.

nosocomial *(NO suh KOH mee all)* An infection acquired by a patient while at a hospital, nursing home, or any health care facility. Nosocome was a 17th-century word for "hospital." Newer term is HAI (hospital acquired infection).

nostrils See nares.

nucleases Enzymes that break down nucleic acids.

nuclei In the central nervous system, a group of neuronal cell bodies that are clustered together and form a coherent demarcated mass in stained brain sections.

nucleic acids RNA and DNA that control activities of cells and contain genetic codes for reproduction.

nucleolus Round, central region within the nucleus. It makes ribosomes.

nucleus The control center or "brain" of the cell.

nyctalopia *(nick tah LOW pee ah)* The inability to see in dim light, night blindness.

O

oblique fissure A line that divides the upper and lower lobes of the left lung and the middle and lower lobes of the right lung.

obstetrics *(ob STET ricks)* Branch of medicine concerning managing pregnancy and childbirth.

obstructive jaundice Condition in which bile backs up into the liver and bilirubin is reabsorbed into the blood.

obstructive pulmonary disease A general term used to describe abnormal pulmonary conditions associated with cough, sputum production, dyspnea, airflow obstruction, and impaired gas exchange.

occipital lobe *(awk SIP eh tal)* Lobe of the cerebrum that receives sensory information from the eyes. Contains the visual cortex for the sense of sight.

occult Not readily seen, as in blood in the stool.

olfaction *(ol FAK shun)* Sense of smell.

olfactory region Region of the roof of the nasal cavity where sense of smell originates.

oligodendrocytes *(ALL ih go DEN droh sites)* Neuroglial cells, which produce myelin in the CNS.

oliguria Diminished production of urine.

oocyte *(OH oh site)* An immature stage of the female sex egg.

oogenesis *(oh oh JEN eh sis)* The process by which eggs are produced.

oogonia *(oh oh GOH nee uh)* Egg stem cells found in the ovary.

ophthalmologist *(off thal MALL oh jist)* A doctor who specializes in the eyes.

ophthalmology *(off thal MALL oh jee)* The study and treatment of visual conditions.

optic disk Area where neurons of the optic nerve exit the retina.

optic nerve Cranial nerve II which carries information to the brain for interpretation of vision.

oral Pertaining to the mouth.

oral cavity The space inside the teeth and gums that is filled by the tongue when the mouth is closed and relaxed.

oral contraceptives Drugs taken orally to prevent pregnancy and regulate the menstrual cycle.

orbit Bony socket in the skull that surrounds all but the anterior part of the eyeball.

orbital cavity See orbit.

organ A part of the body, comprised of tissues, that has a specialized function.

Organ of Corti Structure that possesses tiny hair-like receptors that pick up vibrations whose signals are sent to the brain for interpretation.

organelles *(OR guh NELLZ)* Small structures in the cytoplasm that have various specialized functions. Organelles include mitochondria, ribosomes, the endoplasmic reticulum, the Golgi apparatus, and lysosomes.

organism An individual living thing.

oropharynx *(OR oh FAR inks)* Middle portion of the throat just behind the oral cavity. It begins at the level of the soft palate and ends at the epiglottis.

orthopedics *(OR thoh PEE diks)* The medical science that deals with structures of the skeleton, joints, muscles, ligaments, and cartilage that create movement.

orthopnea *(or THOP nee uh)* Labored breathing when lying flat and which improves when sitting up or standing.

orthostatic hypotension *(OR thoh STAT ick HIGH poh TEN shun)* An abnormal decrease in blood pressure as a result of changing position (such as quickly standing up).

osmosis The passage of the solvent through a semipermeable membrane to equalize concentrations.

osmotic pressure The pressure that develops when there are two solutions of varying concentrations that are separated by a semipermeable membrane.

osseous tissue *(AH see us)* Bone, a type of connective tissue.

ossicles *(AH sih kulz)* Three tiny bones in the middle ear that function in the process of hearing: malleus, incus, and stapes.

ossification *(AH siff ih KAY shun)* Process by which cartilaginous tissue is changed into bone from infancy through puberty. Also known as *osteogenesis*.

osteoarthritis *(OSS tee oh ahr THRYE tiss)* Chronic inflammatory disease of the joints, particularly the large weight-bearing joints of the knees and hips, although it often occurs in the joints that move repeatedly like the shoulders, neck, and hands.

osteoblasts *(OSS tee oh blasts)* Osteocytes that form new bone.

osteoclasts *(OSS tee oh klasts)* Osteocytes that break down old or damaged areas of bone.

osteocytes *(OSS tee oh sites)* Mature bone cells surrounded by bone matrix. They maintain the matrix in mature bone.

osteomalacia *(OSS tee oh mah LAY she ah)* Abnormal softening of the bones due to a deficiency of vitamin D. Chondromalacia is abnormal softening of the cartilage, specifically of the patella.

osteons *(OSS tee ons)* Microscopic unit of compact bone.

osteoporosis *(OSS tee oh por OH sis)* Condition of increased bone porosity that weakens the bones, usually seen in the elderly.

osteoprogenitor *(OSS tee oh proh JEN ih ter)* Nonspecialized cells that can become specialized (differentiate) when needed.

osteosclerosis *(OSS tee oh sklih ROH sis)* Progressive chronic middle ear disorder characterized by excessive bone growth of the middle ear.

otitis media *(oh TYE tiss ME dee ah)* Acute or chronic bacterial infection of the middle ear.

otolaryngology *(OH toh LAIR ing GALL oh jee)* The study of the structure, function, and diseases of the ears and throat.

otorhinolaryngology *(OH toh RYE noh lair ing GALL oh jee)* The study of the structure, function, and diseases of the ears, nose, and throat.

otosclerosis Chronic progressive deafness, especially for low tones. It is caused by the formation of spongy bone, especially around the oval window.

otoscope A device used to examine the external ear canal and eardrum.

oval window Opening in the temporal bone between the middle ear and the vestibule of the inner ear. The opening is covered by the end of the stapes.

ovarian cycle The monthly maturation and release of eggs from the ovary.

ovarian ligament Ligaments used to keep the ovaries in proper position.

ovaries Female gonads that contain eggs.

overactive bladder Bladder condition leading to increased urge to urinate.

oviducts *(OH vih ducts)* See uterine tubes.

ovulation *(OV yoo LAY shun)* Periodic maturation and expulsion of eggs from the ovary.

ovulation stage The stage of the menstrual cycle where the egg (ovum) is released.

oxygen (O_2) A colorless, odorless, tasteless, gaseous chemical element. It occurs free in the atmosphere and makes up approximately 21% of the volume of the atmosphere.

oxygen debt The amount of extra oxygen that is required by muscle tissue during its recovery from strenuous exercise.

oxytocin *(AWK see TOH sin)* Hormone secreted by the posterior pituitary gland. It stimulates the uterus to contract and begin labor. It stimulates the "let-down reflex" to get milk flowing for breastfeeding.

P

pacemaker cells Cells or groups of cells that automatically generate electrical impulses.

palate *(PAL at)* Roof of the mouth.

palatine tonsils *(PAL ah tine)* Lymphoid tissue on either side of the throat where the soft palate arches downward in the oropharynx.

pancreas *(PAN kree ass)* A digestive and endocrine organ located in the abdominal cavity that produces digestive enzymes (amylase, lipase, protease, peptidase) and releases them into the duodenum. It also contains the islets of Langerhans (alpha, beta, and delta cells) that produce and secrete the hormones glucagon, insulin, and somatostatin.

pancreatitis *(PAN kree ah TYE tiss)* Inflammation or infection of the pancreas.

pandemic Disease or condition that affects many people worldwide.

papillary muscles *(PAP uh LAIR ee)* Specialized muscles that are attached to the valves of the heart.

paralysis *(puh RAL uh sis)* Temporary or permanent loss of muscle function.

paranasal sinuses Hollow areas of the skull located around the nose.

paraplegia *(par uh PLEE jee uh)* Paralysis of the lower body and of both legs.

parasympathetic nervous system *(PAIR uh SIM peh THET ik)* Division of the autonomic nervous system that uses the neurotransmitter acetylcholine and carries nerve impulses to the heart, involuntary smooth muscles, and glands while the body is at rest.

parathyroid glands *(PAIR ah THIGH royd)* Endocrine glands, four of them, on the posterior lobes of the thyroid gland. They produce and secrete parathyroid hormone.

parathyroxide hormone (PTH) Hormone secreted by the parathyroid glands that regulates levels of calcium in the bloodstream.

paravertebral ganglia *(PAIR ah VUR teh brawl GANG glee uh)* Ganglia of the sympathetic nervous system that form a chain-like structure that runs parallel to the spinal cord.

parietal cells *(pah RYE eh tal)* Specialized cells that secrete hydrochloric acid.

parietal layer The middle layer of the pericardial sac, a serous membrane lining the fibrous pericardium.

parietal lobe *(pah RYE eh tal)* Lobe of the cerebrum that receives sensory information about temperature, touch, pressure, vibration, and pain from the skin and internal organs.

parietal pleura *(pah RYE eh tal PLOO rah)* One of the two layers of the pleura. It lines the thoracic cavity.

Parkinson's disease A chronic degenerative disease of the central nervous system that causes impaired movement and changes in mood and cognition. Usually found in individuals older than 65.

parotid salivary gland *(pah RAH tid SAL ih vair ee gland)* Gland that secretes saliva that helps to lubricate food so that it is easier to chew and swallow.

partial-thickness burn A classification of the severity of a burn. This level of burn damage includes the entire depth of the epidermis and a portion of the dermis.

passive transport The general term for the transportation of cellular material without the use of energy.

patellar *(peh TELL are)* Pertaining to the kneecap.

pathogen *(PATH oh jenn)* Microorganism that causes a disease. Pathogens include bacteria, viruses, protozoa, and other microorganisms, as well as plant cells like fungi or yeast.

pathology *(path ALL oh jee)* The study of disease.

pedal Pertaining to the foot or feet.

pediculosis *(pee DICK you LOH sis)* A condition of lice infestation.

penis External genitalia in males that delivers the sperm.

pepsin *(PEP sin)* Digestive enzyme produced by the stomach that breaks down food protein into smaller protein molecules.

peptic ulcer An ulcer occurring in the lower end of the esophagus, in the stomach, or in the duodenum.

peptidase *(PEP tih days)* Enzyme needed to digest portions of the protein structure called peptides.

percutaneous nephrolithotomy *(PUR kyoo TAY nee uhs nef roh lih THOT oh mee)* The use of an endoscope to create a small incision to remove large kidney stones.

perforin *(PUR fuh rinn)* Chemical secreted by cytotoxic T cells, which makes holes in the cell membranes of pathogens or infected cells, killing them.

perfusion Blood flow to a particular region.

pericardial cavity The potential cavity between the parietal and visceral layers of the pericardium.

pericardium *(per ih CAR dee uhm)* The serous membrane that surrounds the heart.

perilymph *(per ih LIMF)* Pale lymph fluid found in the labyrinth of the inner ear.

perimetrium *(per ih MEE tree um)* The serous layer of the uterus.

perimysium *(per ih MISS ee uhm)* The connective tissue sheath that surrounds each primary bundle of muscle fibers.

perinatal *(per ih NAY tall)* At or near the time of birth.

perineum *(per ih NEE uhm)* The region between the vagina and rectum.

periodontal *(perr ee oh DAHN til)* Literally means "around the teeth" and may refer to the area of the gum.

periodontal disease Gum disease.

periodontal ligament Fibers that hold the root of the tooth in place.

periosteum *(per ee OSS tee um)* Thick, fibrous membrane that goes around and covers the outside of a bone.

peripheral *(per IF er uhl)* Referring to "away from center" or the extremities.

peripheral nervous system (PNS) Division of the nervous system that includes the cranial nerves and the spinal nerves.

peripheral neuropathy Condition of the peripheral nerves resulting in pain and dysfunction of these nerves. Often related to diabetes.

peripheral resistance The resistance of the arterial vascular system, especially the arterioles and capillaries, to the flow of blood.

peripheral vascular disease (PVD) *(per IF er uhl VAS kyuh ler)* Condition of reduced blood flow to the extremities.

peristalsis *(per ih STALL siss)* Contractions of the smooth muscle of the gastrointestinal tract that propel food through it. Can also be the process of smooth muscle contractions that propel urine through the ureter.

peritoneal cavity The potential space between the parietal peritoneum, which lines the abdominal wall, and the visceral peritoneum, which forms the surface layer of the visceral organs. It contains serous fluid.

peritoneal dialysis *(per ih TONE ee al dye AL eh sis)* A form of dialysis, in which the lining of the peritoneal cavity is used as the dialyzing membrane.

peritonitis *(per ih tone EYE tiss)* Inflammation of the peritoneal cavity.

peritubular capillaries (*per ih TUBE you ler*) Capillaries surrounding the renal tubules.

permanent teeth The 32 teeth that develop as the second dentition and replace the deciduous teeth.

persistent vegetative state A continuous condition of complete unawareness of the environment with either complete or partial hypothalamic and autonomic brain stem functions. Sleep–wake cycles also exist. This condition may be caused by brain trauma, degenerative disease, metabolic disorders, or developmental defects.

personal protective equipment (PPE) Items such as gowns, gloves, and masks used to prevent the spread of infectious agents.

Peyer's patches (*PIE erz*) Lymph nodes found in the submucosa of the alimentary canal.

pH A test to determine how acidic or alkaline a substance is.

phagocytosis (*FAG oh sigh TOH sis*) The process by which a phagocyte destroys a foreign cell or cellular debris; a type of endocytosis.

phalanges (*fuh LAN jeez*) Bones of the fingers.

phantom pain A sensation that an amputated limb is still present and is exhibiting pain.

pharyngitis (*FAR in JIGH tiss*) Bacterial or viral infection of the throat. When the bacteria group *beta-hemolytic streptococcus* causes the infection, it is known as strep throat.

pharyngoesophageal sphincter (*fah RING go ee SOFF eh JEE al*) Muscular ring at the beginning of the esophagus.

pharynx (*FAR inks*) The throat; contains the passageways for food and for inhaled and exhaled air.

phenylketonuria (PKU) (*FIN ill KEY toh NEW ree uh*) Inherited disease characterized by the excess of phenylketone in the urine due to an accumulation of phenylalanine in the tissues that may lead to brain injury or death.

phonation (*foh NAY shun*) Producing sounds.

phospholipid (*FOSS foh LIP id*) Key molecules for structure and function of cell membranes composed of two fatty acid tails and a phosphate head.

photopigments (*FOE toe PIG mints*) Chemicals in retinal cells that have light sensitivity.

phrenic nerve (*FRIN ick*) Nerve that innervates the diaphragm that controls breathing.

physiology (*FIZ ee ALL oh jee*) The study of the function of the body's structures.

pia mater (*PEE ah MAY ter*) Thin, delicate, innermost layer of the meninges that covers the surface of the brain and spinal cord. It contains many small blood vessels.

pineal gland (*PIN ee al*) Endocrine gland in the brain that lies posterior to the pituitary gland. It secretes the hormone melatonin.

pink eye Also known as conjunctivitis; it is an inflammation of the membrane that lines the eye.

pinna (*PINN ah*) The auricle of the exterior ear that collects sound waves.

pinocytosis (*PIE noh sigh TOH sis*) Process in which a cell absorbs fluid material.

pituitary gland (*pih TOO ih tair ee*) Endocrine gland in the brain that is connected by a stalk of tissue to the hypothalamus. Also known as the *hypophysis*. It is known as the master gland of the body. It consists of the anterior and the posterior pituitary gland.

placenta (*pluh SEN tuh*) A spongy structure attached to the fetus via the umbilical cord that provides nourishment.

placental stage The last stage of labor in which the placenta is delivered as a result of final uterine contractions.

plane A flat surface formed by making an imaginary cut through the body or a portion of it.

plantar Referring to the sole of the foot.

plantar flexion Movement of the foot away from the leg as a ballerina who dances on her toes.

plantar wart A wart on a pressure bearing area, especially the sole of the foot.

plaque (*plak*) A patch on skin or mucous surface often caused by lipids or calcium. Can build up in atherosclerotic heart disease and block blood vessels.

plasma (*PLAZ mah*) Clear, straw-colored fluid portion of the blood that carries blood cells and contains dissolved substances like proteins, glucose, minerals, electrolytes, clotting factors, complement proteins, hormones, bilirubin, urea, and creatinine.

plasma cell A cell derived from a B lymphocyte that has been sensitized to a specific foreign antigen and produces antibodies to that particular antigen.

plasma exchange The therapeutic removal of diseased blood and subsequent replacement with fresh healthy blood.

plasma proteins *(PLAZ mah)* Protein molecules in the plasma. An important one is albumin.

platelets *(PLATE lets)* Another term for thrombocytes which help blood to clot.

pleural cavity *(PLOO ral)* The space between the parietal and visceral layers of the pleura.

pleural effusion *(PLOO ral eh FYOO zhun)* Accumulation of fluid within the pleural space due to inflammation or infection of the pleura and lungs.

pleural fluid Slippery liquid found within the space between the visceral and parietal pleura of the thoracic cavity.

plexus *(PLECK sus)* A network of nerves or vessels.

plicae circulares *(PLY kay)* One of the transverse folds in the small intestine.

pneumonia *(noo MOH nee uh)* Infectious lung disease characterized by fever, excessive secretions, shortness of breath, lethargy, and cough.

pneumothorax *(NOO moh THOH raks)* Large volume of air that forms in the pleural space and progressively separates the two pleural membranes.

podocytes Specialized squamous cells that compose the visceral layer of the glomerular capsule.

point of insertion Muscle end that is attached to a moving bone.

point of origin End of the muscle that is attached to stationary bone.

polar Having a charge at one end of a molecule.

polar covalent bond Unequal sharing of one or more electrons that result in a slight charge as in the water molecule.

polarized Cell that has a difference in charge across its membrane so it is more negative on the inside than on the outside of the membrane.

polycystic kidney disease Several inherited disorders causing cysts to form in the kidneys and other organs leading to destroyed kidney tissue and function.

polycystic ovarian syndrome (PCOS) Formation of multiple cysts on the ovary.

polycythemia *(PAUL ee sigh THEE mee ah)* Increased number of erythrocytes due to uncontrolled production by the red marrow. The viscosity of the blood increases; it becomes viscous (thick), and the total blood volume is increased.

polymorphonuclear leukocyte *(PAUL ee MORE foh NEW klee er)* A white blood cell with a nucleus made of two or more lobes, i.e., the granular leukocytes: neutrophils, eosinophils, or basophils.

polymorphonuclear granulocytes White blood cells with a nucleus made of two or more lobes, i.e., the granular leukocytes: neutrophils, eosinophils, or basophils, and whose cytoplasm contains granules.

polysomnography *(PAUL ee sahm NOG grah fee)* The study of sleep patterns and pathology.

polyuria *(PAUL ee YOOR ee uh)* Production of large amounts of urine.

pons Area of the brain stem that relays nerve impulses from the body to the cerebellum and back to the body. Area where nerve tracts cross from one side of the body to the opposite side of the cerebrum. Cranial nerves V through VIII originate there.

Pores of Kohn Small opening between alveoli that allow for the movement of gas and macrophages.

positive feedback "Vicious cycle." During positive feedback, physiological processes send body chemistry or other attributes further and further away from equilibrium (set point). The trend will continue until something breaks the cycle.

positive selection During lymphocyte development, only those lymphocytes that can actually react to antigens will survive.

postcentral gyrus *(JYE russ)* Ridge on the surface of the cerebrum posterior to the central sulcus in each hemisphere. The postcentral gyrus contains the primary somatic sensory area for your sense of touch.

posterior The back of the body.

posterior pituitary *(poh STEER ee er pih TOO ih tair ee)* An extension of the hypothalamus that secretes oxytocin and ADH.

posteroanterior (PA) *(pohs tee roh an TEE ree or)* View from the back to the front such as a PA x-ray.

postganglionic neuron *(post GANG lee ON ick NEW ron)* Autonomic neuron that connects to a smooth muscle or a gland.

pre-capillary sphincters Smooth muscle structures that direct the flow of blood before entering the capillary bed.

precentral gyrus *(JYE russ)* Ridge on the surface of the cerebrum anterior to the central sulcus in each hemisphere. The precentral gyrus contains the primary motor cortex for voluntary movements.

preganglionic neuron *(pre GANG lee ON ick NEW ron)* Found in the autonomic system, it uses ACh as the neurotransmitter and junctions with post-ganglionic neurons.

premenstrual dysphoric disorder (PMDD) Disorder characterized by severe depression, marked anxiety, and decreased interest in activity.

premenstrual syndrome (PMS) Syndrome of physical and psychological changes that occur before menstruation in many women.

prepuce *(PREE pewce)* Foreskin.

presbycusis Progressive loss of hearing with aging, typically resulting from sensorineural hearing loss.

presbyopia *(PRESS bee OH pee ah)* Loss of flexibility of the lens with blurry near vision and loss of accommodation.

primary bronchi *(BRONG kye)* Older term for main stem bronchi.

primary follicles The result of primordial follicles that have received hormonal signals to enlarge and increase the number of granulosa cells.

primary motor cortex Located in the precentral gyrus, this portion of the brain contains a map of the body to control motor function.

primary movers Muscles or muscle groups that cause movement. Also known as *agonists*.

primary oocyte *(OH oh site)* Oogonia egg cells undergoing mitosis and thus reproducing.

primary ossification center *(oss ih fih KAY shun)* A region where osteoblasts congregate to create spongy bone.

primary polycythemia An abnormally high amount of erythrocytes in the blood that can be a result of bone cancer.

primary response The reaction the body conducts to destroy a pathogen which may include antigen neutralization and antigen agglutination, activating complement cascade.

primary somatic sensory cortex Area of the cerebral cortex that allows for understanding and interpretation of somatic sensory information.

primary spermatocytes A cell formed by mitosis of a spermatogonium.

primary teeth See deciduous teeth.

primordial follicles Primary oocytes that are surround by granulosa (helper) cells which stay dormant until puberty.

proctology *(prok TALL oh jee)* The specialization of medicine dealing with the treatment of diseases of the colon, rectum, and anus.

progesterone *(proh JES teh rohn)* Hormone secreted by corpus luteum that helps to maintain the build-up of the endometrium and decrease uterine contraction.

progestins Class of drugs that act like estrogen and progesterone which prevent ovulation and or decrease menstruation.

prognosis *(prog NOH sis)* The predicted outcome of a disease.

prokaryotic Cells that do not have a nucleus or organelles as in bacterial cells.

prolactin *(proh LAK tinn)* Hormone secreted by the anterior pituitary gland. It stimulates milk glands of the breasts to develop during puberty and to produce milk during pregnancy.

proliferate *(pro LIFF er ate)* To increase by rapid reproduction.

proliferative phase See follicular phase.

pronation Turning of the hand so the palm faces downward.

prone position Lying with the anterior section of the body down.

prophase The first step in mitosis where the nucleus disappears, chromosomes become visible and act as anchor lines, and centrioles move toward the sides of the cell.

proprioception *(PROH pree oh SEP shun)* The sensation of movement and position of the body.

prostaglandins *(PROSS teh GLAN dinz)* A group of hormones that can lead to vasodilation, bronchoconstriction, platelet aggregation, and stimulate pain receptors.

prostate cancer Cancerous condition of the prostate gland.

prostate gland A chestnut-size gland that secretes a slightly alkaline fluid that forms part of the seminal fluid.

proteinases *(PROH tee in ACES)* Enzymes that break down proteins.

proteins Versatile molecules made of long chains of amino acids.

prothrombin *(pro THROM bin)* Blood clotting factor that is activated just before the thrombus is formed.

Pro Time   The time it takes for clotting to occur after thromboplastin and calcium are added to decalcified plasma. The test is used to assess levels of anticoagulation in patients taking warfarin, to determine the cause of unexplained bleeding (as in patients with hemophilia), or to assess the ability of the liver to synthesize bloodclotting proteins.

proton   Positively charged particle in the nucleus of the atom.

protozoa   *(PROH teh ZOH uh)* Unicellular organisms.

protraction   Movement of a body part forward.

proximal   *(PROK sim al)* Referring to "near" a reference point.

proximal tubule   *(PROK sim al TOO byool)* The part of the renal tubule closest to the glomerulus. Many substances are secreted or absorbed in this part of the renal tubule.

pseudostratified   Apparently composed of layers.

pseudostratified ciliated columnar epithelium   *(SOO doh STRAT ih fide SILL ee ate ed)* Specialized cells found throughout the respiratory region of the nose and most of the airways.

ptyalin   *(TYE ih lin)* A specific salivary amylase that converts starches to simple sugars.

pubic lice   Also known as crab lice, which infests human pubic hair. It is transmitted by direct contact and through bedding or shared towels.

pudendal cleft   *(PEW den dall)* Opening between two halves of the labia majora.

pulmonary artery   Artery that carries blood from the heart to the lungs. The pulmonary artery is the only artery in the body that carries blood that has low levels of oxygen.

pulmonary circulation   Movement of blood from right ventricle to lungs and then back to left atrium.

pulmonary edema   *(eh DEE mah)* A potentially life-threatening condition in which there is an accumulation of fluid in the interstitium and the alveoli of the lungs that can block the exchange of oxygen and carbon dioxide.

pulmonary function test (PFT)   A diagnostic exam of the lungs that measures flow and volumes and compares to predicted values.

pulmonary semi-lunar valve   Valve located between the right ventricle and pulmonary trunk.

pulmonary system   Another term for respiratory system.

pulmonology   *(PULL mon ALL oh jee)* The branch of medicine that studies the treatment of lung disorders.

pulp   The internal layer of connective tissue located in the pulp cavity of a tooth.

pulp cavity   Cavity that contains pulp, blood vessels, and nerves that provide nutrients and sensations.

pulse   What is felt when an artery is palpated and the heart contracts.

pupil   *(PYOO pill)* Round opening in the iris that allows light rays to enter the internal eye.

Purkinje fibers   *(per KIN jee)* Specialized cells that carry the impulse to the contractile muscle cells of the ventricle.

pus   Yellow or whitish yellow substance that is a by-product of phagocytosis.

pustule   *(PUS tyool)* A small elevation of skin filled with lymph or pus.

P wave   The first wave on an electrocardiogram and represents the depolarization of the atria, whose electrical changes in turn cause atrial contraction.

pyloric sphincter   *(pye LOR ick SFINK ter)* Muscular ring that keeps food in the stomach from entering the duodenum.

pylorus   *(pye LOR us)* Narrowing canal of the stomach just before it joins the duodenum. It contains the pyloric sphincter.

pyrexia   *(pie REK see uh)* Fever produced as part of the body's immune response to infection and disease.

pyuria   *(pye YOU ree uh)* Pus in the urine.

Q

QRS Complex   Electrical tracing found on an electrocardiogram that represents the depolarization of the ventricles.

quadriplegia   *(kwad reh PLEE jee uh)* Paralysis of all four limbs.

quadriplegic   *(kwad reh PLEE jik)* One who has paralysis of all four limbs.

R

radial keratotomy   *(ker eh TOT oh mee)* Vision surgery that makes incision around the cornea to improve sight.

radiation therapy   The use of energy from man-made ionizing radiation or from the radioactive decay of atomic nuclei to destroy diseased tissues, especially cancers.

radiocontrast agent A dye placed into the blood to make it contrast its surroundings on an x-ray.

radiolucent *(RAY dee oh LOO sent)* Property of being partly or wholly penetrable by x-rays, giving a darker or black appearance.

radiopaque *(RAY dee oh PAYK)* Impenetrable to x-rays making the image lighter or white.

rapid eye movement (REM) The dream stage of sleep.

reabsorption Process by which water and substances in the filtrate move out of the renal tubule and into the blood in a nearby capillary.

rectum Final part of the large intestine. It is a short, straight segment that lies between the sigmoid colon and the outside of the body.

red blood cells (RBCs) See erythrocytes.

red marrow A form of bone marrow that creates blood cells.

reduction division *See* meiosis.

referred pain A perceived pain site other than the actual site of the trauma or disease.

reflex Involuntary muscle reaction that is controlled by the spinal cord. In response to pain, the spinal cord immediately sends a command to the muscles of the body to move. All of this takes place without conscious thought or processing by the brain. The entire circuit is also known as a *reflex arc.*

refractive eye surgery A surgical procedure that alters the eye to improve vision.

refractory period Short period of time when an excitable cell, like a neuron or cardiac muscle cell, is resting and unresponsive to electrical impulses.

regulatory T cells Type of T cell that shuts down immune response.

relapse A reoccurrence of a disease or symptoms after an apparent recovery.

remission A lessening of severity or disappearance of symptoms.

renal artery *(REE nal AHR ter ee)* Major artery that carries blood to the kidney.

renal capsule The fibrous membrane on the outer surface of a kidney, which is in turn enclosed by adipose tissue that cushions the kidney.

renal columns Narrow structures that separate adjacent renal pyramids.

renal corpuscle *(REE nal KOR pus el)* The filtration apparatus of the kidney, consists of the glomerulus and the glomerular capsule.

renal cortex Tissue layer of kidney just beneath the renal capsule.

renal disease See kidney disease.

renal failure Impaired functioning of the kidneys leading to a buildup of toxic waste products and fluids in the body.

renal hilum *(REE nal HIGH luhm)* The indentation that gives the kidney its bean-shaped appearance.

renal medulla *(REE nal meh DULL uh)* The middle layer of the kidney.

renal nephron *(REE nal NEF ron)* Fundamental functional unit of the kidney, consists of the renal corpuscle and renal tubule.

renal pelvis *(REE nal PELL viss)* Funnel-shaped part of the kidney that collects urine.

renal pyramids Triangle-shaped, striated areas composed of collecting tubules for the urine that is formed in the kidney.

renal tubule Network of convoluted tubules found within the kidneys.

renal vein Major blood vessel that carries blood away from the kidneys.

renin-angiotensin-aldosterone *(RIN in-an gee oh TEN sen-al DOSS ter ohn)* A complex hormone system that regulates blood volume and blood pressure. The system is triggered when blood flow to the kidney decreases.

repolarization The return of membrane potential toward resting.

respiration *(ress pire AY shun)* The process of gas exchange at the lungs or tissue sites. Oxygen and carbon dioxide are exchanged in the alveoli during external respiration. Oxygen and carbon dioxide are exchanged at the cellular level during internal respiration. Also the use of glucose and oxygen by cells to produce ATP.

respiratory acidosis Condition where the respiratory system is retaining carbon dioxide and thus causing acidity in the arterial blood.

respiratory bronchioles *(brong kee ohls)* Very small airways where the first part of gas exchange begins.

respiratory region Region of nose that contains turbinates that allow for warning and moistening of inspired air.

respiratory system   The organs involved in the interchange of gases between an organism and the atmosphere. In humans, this system consists of the air passageways and organs (nasal cavities, pharynx, larynx, trachea, and lungs, including bronchi, bronchioles, alveolar ducts, and alveoli) and the respiratory muscles.

resting cell   Nervous cell that is neither stimulated nor excited.

reticular system   Diffuse network of neurons in the brainstem that "wakes up" the cerebral cortex thus providing awareness of one's surroundings.

reticulospinal tract   *(reh TIK yoo loh SPY nal)* One of several descending spinal motor pathways that carry information to help coordinate movements.

retina   *(RET ih nah)* The innermost membrane lining the eye. It contains rods and cones. Landmarks include the optic disk and macula.

retinopathy   *(ret ih NAH path ee)* Disease of the retina caused by hypertension or diabetes.

retraction   Drawing backward of a body part.

retroperitoneal organs   Organs behind the peritoneum and outside the peritoneal cavity.

Rh factor   A blood group discovered on the surface of erythrocytes of Rhesus monkeys and found to a variable degree in humans. Can be Rh-negative or Rh-positive.

rheumatoid arthritis   *(ROO meh toyd awr THRIGH tiss)* A chronic, systemic condition affecting synovial joints. Women are three times more affected than men. A common complaint is morning joint stiffness rather than after physical activities.

rheumatology   *(ROO meh TALL oh jee)* Division of medicine concerned with rheumatic (inflammation, pain, stiffness in muscles and joints) diseases.

rhinitis   *(rye NIGH tiss)* An acute, temporary, seasonal or year-round inflammation of the nasal mucosa with nasal congestion and increased mucus production.

rhinoplasty   *(RYE noh plass tee)* Surgical procedure that uses plastic surgery to change the size or shape of the nose.

ribonucleic acid (RNA)   Molecule contained in ribosomes and necessary for making proteins.

ribosome   Granular organelle located throughout the cytoplasm and on the endoplasmic reticulum. Ribosomes contain RNA and proteins and are the site of protein synthesis.

right atrium   Chamber that collects blood that is returning from the venous system of the body.

right bundle branch   An atrioventricular bundle of "electrical wiring" that spreads across the inner surface of the right ventricle allowing for a smooth and effective heart contraction.

right lymphatic duct   *(lim FAT ick)* The duct that collects lymphatic fluid from the bronchomediastinal, subclavian, and jugular trunks.

right main stem   Largest bronchus leading into right lung.

right ventricle   Chamber of the heart that pumps blood to the lungs for gas exchange.

rigor mortis   *(RIG er MORE tiss)* A stiffness that occurs in dead bodies as a result of retained calcium and decreased ATP.

rima glottis   *(RYE mah GLOT is)* Space between the vocal cords.

rods   Light-sensitive cells in the retina. They detect black and white and function in daytime and nighttime vision.

root   1. Part of the tooth that is hidden below the gum line. The premolars have one or more roots. The molars have multiple roots; 2. A portion of an organ implanted in tissues.

rotation   Occurs when a bone spins on its axis.

round ligaments   Structures that anchor the uterus to the anterior wall of the pelvic cavity.

rubrospinal tract   One of several descending spinal motor pathways that carry information to help coordinate movements.

rugae   *(ROO gay)* 1. Deep folds in the gastric mucosa. 2. Folds in the mucosa of the bladder that disappear as the bladder fills with urine.

S

sacral   *(SEY kral)* Referring to the five fused vertebra in the mid-buttock region.

SA node   See sinoatrial node.

sarcolemma   *(sahr kuh LEM uh)* The cell membrane of a muscle cell.

sarcomeres   *(SAR koh meerz)* Portion of striated muscle fibril that lies between the two adjacent dark lines.

sarcoplasmic reticulum   *(SAR koh PLAZZ mic re TICK you lum)* Storage space within muscle for calcium.

satellite cells   Neuroglia cells that enclose the cell bodies of neurons in the spinal ganglia.

scabies   A contagious skin condition caused by the itch mite, *Sarcoptes scabiei.*

Schwann cell   *(SHWAN sell)* Cell that forms the myelin sheaths around axons of the cranial and spinal nerves.

sclera   *(SKLAIR ah)* White, tough, fibrous connective tissue that forms the outer layer around most of the eye. Also known as the *white of the eye.*

scoliosis   *(SKOH lee OH sis)* Lateral curvature of the spine.

scrotum   Sac that contains the testes.

sebaceous glands   *(seh BAY shus)* An exocrine gland of the skin that secretes sebum. Sebaceous glands are located in the dermis. Their ducts join with a hair and sebum coats the hair shaft as it moves toward the surface of the skin. Also known as *oil glands.*

sebum   *(SEE bum)* Oily substance secreted by sebaceous glands.

second degree burn   A partial thickness burn that involves the entire depth of the epidermis and a portion of the dermis.

secondary follicle   Further development of a primary follicle once a female reaches puberty; the secondary follicle will not complete its full development unless it is ovulated and fertilized.

secondary polycythemia   Condition of abnormally high numbers of erythrocytes in the blood due to chronic low levels of oxygen.

secondary response   Increased immune response mediated by memory cells when meeting a pathogen that they recognize.

secondary spermatocytes   A cell formed by meiosis of a primary spermatocyte. It undergoes a second meiotic division to form two spermatids, each with the haploid number of chromosomes.

secretin   A hormone secreted by the duodenal mucosa that stimulates sodium bicarbonate secretion by the pancreas and bile secretion by the liver. It decreases gastrointestinal peristalsis and motility.

secretion   *(seh CREE shun)* The movement of a chemical out of a cell or gland. Also the movement of substances from the renal tubules into the nephron. Secreted substances end up in urine and leave the body.

secretory phase   The time between ovulation and menses; also known as the luteal phase.

segmental arteries   Branches formed from the renal artery.

segmental bronchi   Airways leading into specific lung segments.

segmentation   Division into similar parts.

self vs. non-self recognition   The ability of the immune system to distinguish between the body's cells and cells that do not belong in the body.

semen   *(SEE men)* A sperm-containing, thick secretion produced by males.

semicircular canals   *(SEM ee SIR kyoo lar)* Three canals in the inner ear that are oriented in different planes (horizontally, vertically, obliquely) that help the body keep its balance. They relay information to the brain via the vestibular branch of the vestibulocochlear nerve.

seminal vesicles   Highly coiled glands posterior to the bladder.

seminiferous tubules   *(SEM ee NIF er us TOO byoolz)* Tubules located in the testes that contain sperm cells and sperm helper cells (also known as Sertoli or nurse cells).

sensation   A feeling or awareness as a result of the stimulation of sensory receptors.

sensorineural conduction   *(SEN soh ree NEW ral)* The process of sending nerve impulses to the temporal lobe of the brain where it is interpreted as sound.

sensory neuron   Input neurons also known as afferent neurons.

sensory system   Portion of nervous system that receives input.

septal cartilage   *See* nasal septum.

septic arthritis   A form of joint inflammation due to infection.

septicemia   *(SEP teh SEE me uh)* Infection by pathogenic organisms in the blood.

septum   *(SEP tum)* 1. Wall of cartilage and bone that divides the nasal cavity into right and left sides. 2. Partitioning wall that divides the right atrium from the left atrium (interatrial septum) and the right ventricle from the left ventricle (interventricular septum).

serosa   *(see ROH sah)* A serous membrane.

serotonin   A vasoconstrictor found in platelets.

serous membrane *(SEER us)* Double-layered membrane lining a serous cavity. The parietal layer lines the wall of the cavity, and the visceral layer covers the organs in the cavity. There is a fluid-filled potential space between the layers.

serous pericardium A flattened sac formed of a single layer of cells and connective tissue.

sertoli cells Sperm helper cells.

serum Blood plasma without fibrinogen and other clotting agents.

set (reduced) The act of putting fractured bones in alignment so the ends meet.

set point The normal physiologic range (as in body temperature and blood pressure) to maintain homeostasis.

shaft The principal portion of any cylindrical body.

shin splints A common running-induced injury of the extensor muscles and surrounding tissues of the lower leg.

shingles The common name for the skin rash caused by *herpes zoster*.

shunt Diversion of fluids from their normal pathway.

sigmoid colon *(SIG moyd)* The s-shaped portion of the colon that extends to the rectum.

sign A measurable, quantifiable indicator of body function.

silent MI A myocardial infarction that does not exhibit the classic signs of a heart attack, such as chest pain radiating from the left shoulder down the arm.

simple cells Epithelial cells that are arranged in a single layer and are of the same type.

simple fracture Also called a closed fracture; it is a bone break without a puncture to the skin.

simple squamous epithelium See capillary endothelium.

simple squamous pneumocytes *(SKWAY mus NEW moh sites)* Flat, pancake-like cells that comprise most of the alveolus and are where gas exchange takes place.

sinoatrial node *(sigh noh AY tree al)* Pacemaker of the heart. Small knot of tissue located in the posterior wall of the right atrium in a shallow channel near the entrance of the superior vena cava. The SA node dictates the heart rate at 70–80 beats per minute when the body is at rest. It generates the electrical impulse for the entire conduction system of the heart.

sinus *(SIGH nus)* Hollow cavity within a bone of the cranium.

sinusitis *(SIGH nus EYE tis)* Inflammation of the sinus.

skeletal muscle *(SKELL eh tal)* One of three types of muscles in the body, but the only muscle that is under voluntary, conscious control. Under the microscope, skeletal muscle has a striated appearance.

sleep apnea A condition of abnormal cessation of breathing during sleep.

smooth muscle One of three types of body muscles that is involuntarily controlled and found in the lining of the airways, blood vessels, and uterus.

sodium ion channels Pathways for sodium ions to exist and enter the cell.

soft palate A musculomembranous fold that partly separates the mouth and the pharynx; the posterior roof of the mouth. It is elevated during swallowing to block the nasopharynx.

sol layer The thin, watery layer of mucus in the airways of the lungs.

solute The substance dissolved in a solution.

solution The combination of one or more substances dissolved in another.

solvent The substance that dissolves the solute, usually water.

somatic nervous system *(so MAT ick)* Division of the peripheral nervous system that uses the neurotransmitter acetylcholine and carries nerve impulses to the voluntary skeletal muscles.

somatic sensation The sense of touch.

somatic sensory association area An area of parietal lobe needed for understanding and interpretation of somatic sensory information.

somatic sensory system The portion of the nervous system that provides sensory input for the sense of touch.

sound conduction The process in which sound waves enter the external canal and vibrate the eardrum.

spasm Involuntary contraction of a muscle.

spastic Characterized by increased muscle tone and overactive reflexes.

special senses Senses that include sight, hearing and balance, taste, and smell.

specific immune response A targeted immune response to a specific pathogenic organism.

sperm Male reproductive cells possessing motility.

spermatic cord Term used for the combination of the vas deferens and surrounding blood vessels and nerves.

spermatids *(SPER mah tidz)* Cells that are the result of the division of a secondary spermatocyte.

spermatocytes *(sper MAT oh sites)* Cells from the spermatogonium that divide to form spermatids.

spermatogonia *(sper MAT oh GOH nee ah)* Large, unspecialized germ cells that form primary spermatocytes by mitosis.

spermatozoa *(sper MAT oh ZOE ah)* The plural form of spermatozoon, the mature male sex cell.

sphincter *(SFINGK ter)* Muscular ring around a tube; a valve.

spina bifida *(SPY nah BIF ih duh)* A congenital defect in which the vertebral arches fail to form properly. This leads to varying levels of disability.

spinal block An obstruction of the flow of cerebrospinal fluid through the spinal subarachnoid space. This term is commonly (though inaccurately) used to refer to spinal anesthesia.

spinal cavity *(SPY nal)* The spinal cavity lies within, and is protected by, the bones (vertebrae) of the spinal column. The spinal cavity contains the spinal cord, the spinal nerves, and spinal fluid.

spinal column A series of connected vertebrae that protect the spinal cord.

spinal cord Part of the central nervous system. Continuous with the medulla oblongata of the brain and extends down the back in the spinal cavity. Ends at L2 and separates into individual nerves (cauda equina).

spinal nerves Thirty-one pairs of nerves. Each pair comes out from the spinal cord between two vertebrae. An individual spinal nerve consists of dorsal nerve roots and ventral nerve roots.

spinal roots Axon bundles attached to each spinal cord segment. The dorsal roots are sensory, and the ventral roots are motor. The dorsal and ventral roots join to form the spinal nerves.

spinal tap *See* lumbar puncture.

spinocerebellar tract *(SPY no SAIR eh BELL ar)* Sensory pathway from the spinal cord to the cerebellum.

spinothalamic tract *(SPY no THAL ah mick)* Sensory pathway from the spinal cord to the thalamus and eventually the primary somatic sensory cortex. Contains pain and crude touch information.

spiral fracture Bone break caused by a severe twist.

spleen Lymphoid organ located in the abdominal cavity posterior to the stomach. The spleen destroys old erythrocytes, breaking their hemoglobin into heme and globins. It also acts as a storage area for whole blood. Its white pulp is lymphoid tissue that contains B and T lymphocytes.

spongy bone A form of bone that makes bones lighter and provides a space for red bone marrow.

spores Cells that have a protective barrier to allow for future reproduction in a hostile environment.

sprain Overstretching or tearing of a ligament.

squamous cells *(SKWAY mus)* Flat, scaly epithelial cells.

Standard Precautions Guidelines recommended by the Centers for Disease Control and Prevention to reduce the risk of the spread of infection in hospitals. These precautions (e.g., handwashing and wearing personal protective equipment such as gloves, mask, eye protection, gown) apply to blood, all body fluids, secretions, excretions (except sweat), nonintact skin, and mucous membranes of all patients and are the primary strategy for successful hospital acquired (nosocomial) infection control.

stapedectomy *(STAY pee DECK toh mee)* A surgical procedure in which the stapes of the ear is removed and replaced with a plastic or wire substitute.

stapes *(STAY peez)* Third bone of the middle ear. It is attached to the incus on one end and the oval window on the other end. Also known as the *stirrup*.

startle reflex A reflex seen in infants in response to stimuli, such as that produced by suddenly striking the surface on which the infant rests. The infant responds by rapid abduction and extension of the arms followed by an embracing motion (adduction) of the arms.

stenosis Narrowing of a passage or an orifice.

stenotic The constriction or narrowing of a passage or orifice.

stents Screen-like cylinders that are inserted into coronary vessels to hold them open, thus increasing blood flow.

sterile matrix The proximal layer of cells that help the nail body stick to the nail bed.

sternal Pertaining to the sternum.

sternum *(STER num)* Vertical bone of the anterior thorax to which the clavicle and ribs are attached. Also known as the *breastbone*.

steroids   Ringed lipids that function as extremely powerful hormones.

stirrup   One of the three small bones in the ear, also known as the stapes.

stomatitis   *(STOH mah TYE tis)* An inflammation of the mouth that can include the lips, tongue, and mucous membranes.

strabismus   *(struh BIZ muhs)* Condition of eyes crossing due to inability to coordinate muscles of both eyes.

strain   Overstretching of a muscle or tendon, often due to physical overexertion. This causes inflammation, pain, swelling, and bruising as the capillaries in the muscle tear. There can be small tears in the muscle itself. Also known as a *pulled muscle*.

stratified   *(STRAT eh fied)* Having more than one layer.

stratum basale   The stem cell layer of the epidermis.

stratum corneum   *(STRAY tum CORE nee um)* The outermost, horny layer of the epidermis.

strep throat   Inflammation of the throat caused by *streptococcus* bacteria.

stress response   A general term for an individual's physical, physiological, and psychological reaction to stressors.

stress test   A diagnostic test that either uses physical activity or a drug to cause the heart to work harder to reveal any possible coronary artery blockage. Commonly called an exercise tolerance test.

striated   *(STRY ate ed)* Striped.

striated muscle   *(STRY ate ed)* Skeletal muscle or cardiac muscle.

stroke (CVA)   A condition of sudden neurological function brought about by vascular injury to the brain. Can be caused by a blood blockage due to a clot or by hemorrhage.

stroke volume (SV)   The amount of blood ejected by the left ventricle at each heartbeat.

stupor   *(STOO per)* A brief period of impaired consciousness.

stye   Also known as hordeolum, this is an abscess that forms at the base of an eyelash due to infection of a sebaceous gland.

subarachnoid space   *(SUB ah RACK noyd)* Space beneath the arachnoid layer of the meninges. It is filled with cerebrospinal fluid.

subcutaneous fascia   *(sub kyoo TAY nee us FAY she ah)* Connective tissue layer beneath the skin.

subcutaneously   *(sub kyoo TAY nee us lee)* Under the skin.

subdural space   *(sub DOO ral)* The space between the arachnoid and dura mater.

sublingual salivary glands   *(sub LING will SAL eh vair ee)* Smallest of the salivary glands, found between the tongue and the mandible, one on each side.

sublingually   Under the tongue.

submandibular salivary glands   *(sub MAN dib you lair SAL eh vair ee)* Salivary glands beneath the mandible or jaw.

submucosa   *(SUB myoo KOH suh)* Layer of connective tissue under a mucous membrane.

substrate   The substance upon which an enzyme acts.

sucrase   *(SOO krays)* Enzyme needed for the digestion of double sugars.

sulcus   *(SULL cuss)* One of many shallow grooves between the gyri in the cerebrum and cerebellum. Plural: sulci.

superficial   Related to, or located near, the surface.

superior   Pertaining to the upper half of the body or a position above an organ or structure.

superior vena cava   *(VEE nah KAY vah)* Largest vein that drains venous blood from the upper portions of the body into the right atrium.

supination   The turning of the hand so the palm faces upward.

supine position   *(sue PINE)* Position of lying on the posterior part of the body. Also known as the *dorsal supine position*.

surfactant   *(sir FACK tent)* Protein–fat compound that creates surface tension and keeps the walls of the alveolus from collapsing inward with each inhalation.

surgery   The branch of medicine dealing with manual and operative procedures to correct deformities and defects, repair injuries, and diagnose and cure certain diseases.

surgical or open reduction   A more complex setting of bone that may require pins, screws, plates, or other hardware to fix the bone fragments in place.

suspensory ligament   A ligament extending from the tubal end of the ovary laterally to the pelvic wall. It lies in the layers of the broad ligament in which the ovarian artery is found.

suture   Fibrous connective tissue joints of the skull.

sympathetic nervous system   Division of the autonomic nervous system that uses the neurotransmitter norepinephrine and carries nerve impulses to the heart, involuntary muscles, and glands during times of increased activity, danger, or stress.

symptom   Any change in the body or its function as subjectively perceived by the patient.

synapse   *(SIN aps)* Space between the axon of one neuron and the dendrites of the next neuron.

syndrome   *(SIN drohm)* A set of symptoms and signs associated with, and characteristic of, one particular disease.

syndrome of inappropriate antidiuretic hormone (SIADH)   A condition characterized by severe hyponatremia (low blood sodium), usually due to overproduction of ADH regardless of blood osmolarity.

synergistic   *(sin er GIS tick)* A cooperating action of certain muscles.

synovial fluids   *(sin OH vee al)* Clear, lubricating fluid that is secreted by the synovial membrane.

synovial joints   *(sin OH vee al)* Joints, such as the knee, that have synovial fluid as a lubricant.

synovial membrane   *(sin OH vee al)* The membrane lining a capsule of the joint.

systemic circulation   Movement of blood from the left ventricle throughout the body and back to the right atrium.

systemic lupus erythematosus   *(LOO pus ER ih theh mat OHS is)* A chronic, autoimmune, inflammatory condition that involves multiple organ systems. There are periodic acute episodes of this disease. There is a characteristic "butterfly" rash over the patient's nose and cheeks resembling a wolf's snout.

systems   An organized grouping of related structures or parts that perform specific functions.

systole   *(SISS toh lee)* Combined contractions of the atria and the ventricles.

T

T lymphocytes   *(T LIMF oh sights)* White blood cells involved in adaptive immunity. There are four types of T lymphocytes: helper T cells, cytotoxic T cells, memory T cells, and regulatory T cells.

T wave   Electrical tracing found on electrocardiogram that represents the repolarization of the ventricles.

tachycardia   *(TAK ih KAR dee ah)* A more rapid than normal heart rate (greater than 100 beats per minute in adults).

tactile corpuscles   *(TAK tile KOR pus elz)* Elongated bodies found in nerve ends that act as receptors for slight pressure or touch.

taste buds   Sensory end organs that provide us with a sense of taste.

telophase   Fourth step in mitosis in which chromosomes migrate to ends of cell, spindles disappear, and the nuclei reappear.

temporal lobe   Lobe in the cerebrum that contains neurons for processing auditory and olfactory information.

tendinosis (tendinitis)   Chronic tendon injury.

tendon   Cordlike, white band of nonelastic fibrous connective tissue that attaches a muscle to a bone.

tendonitis   Inflammation of any tendon from injury or overuse.

tinea corporis   Tinea of the body. It begins with red, slightly elevated scaly patches that on examination reveal minute vesicles or papules. New patches spring from the periphery while the central portion clears. There is often considerable itching.

tinea cruris   A fungal skin disease of surfaces of contact in the scrotal, crural, anal, and genital areas.

tinea pedis   Also known as athlete's foot. A scaling, cracked, or macerated rash typically found between the toes and occasionally on the sole of the foot or the heels.

tinea unguium   Also known as onychomycosis. A fungal infection of the nails usually caused by Trichophyton and Tinea species and occasionally by Candida or other fungi. The hallmarks of the disease are thickening, scaling, and discoloration of the nailbed.

terminal bronchioles   Last, very small airways that lead to the respiratory zone of the lung.

terminal illness   A fatal illness.

testes   *(TESS teez)* Small, egg-shaped glands in the scrotum. Also known as the *testicles*. They contain interstitial cells that secrete testosterone. They also contain the seminiferous tubules that produce spermatozoa.

testosterone   Main male sex hormone that provides masculine characteristics.

tetanus   *(TET ah nus)* An acute, infectious disease caused by a bacterium that can lead to severe spasms of voluntary muscles.

tetany   Rigid paralysis.

thalamus   *(THAL ah mus)* Relay station in the brain that receives sensory nerve impulses from the optic nerves and sends them to the visual centers in the occipital lobes of the brain.

third-degree burn   A burn that extends through the full thickness of the skin and subcutaneous tissues beneath the dermis. The burn leaves skin with a pale, brown, gray, or blackened appearance. The burn is painless because it destroys nerves in the skin. Scar formation and contractures are likely complications.

thoracic   Pertaining to the chest or thorax.

thoracic cage   *(tho RASS ick)* The portion of the skeleton that includes the ribs, sternum, and thoracic vertebrae that house and protect the lungs, heart, and great vessels.

thoracic cavity   *(thoh RASS ick)* Hollow space within the thorax that is filled with the lungs, heart, and related structures in the mediastinum.

thoracic duct   *(thoh RASS ick)* The main lymph duct of the body.

thoracic surgery   *(thoh RASS ick)* Manual or operative procedures involving structures or organs located in the thoracic region of the body.

thoracolumbar   Pertaining to the thoracic and lumbar parts of the spinal cord; denoting their ganglia and the fibers of the sympathetic nervous system.

thrombin   *(THROM bin)* An enzyme that reacts with fibrinogen, converting it to fibrin, which forms a clot.

thrombocyte   *(THROM boh sight)* Cell fragment that is flat and does not have a nucleus. It is active in the blood-clotting process. Thrombocytes are also known as *blood platelets*.

thrombocytopenia   *(THROM boh SIGH toh PEE nee ah)* Deficiency in the number of thrombocytes. This can be due to exposure to radiation or toxic chemicals or drugs that damage the stem cells in the bone marrow.

thrombosis   See thrombus.

thrombus   *(THROM bus)* A blood clot.

thymosin   *(thigh MOH sin)* Hormone secreted by the thymus gland that helps white blood cells mature during childhood.

thymus   *(THIGH mus)* Lymphoid organ in the thoracic cavity. As an endocrine gland, it releases hormones known as thymosins. Thymosin causes lymphoblasts in the thymus to mature into T lymphocytes.

thyroid cartilage   Large, protective cartilage found in the neck and part of the larynx; also known as the "Adam's Apple."

thyroid gland   *(THIGH royd)* Endocrine gland in the neck that produces and secretes the hormones T_3, T_4, and calcitonin. Its two lobes and narrow connecting bridge (isthmus) give it a shieldlike shape.

thyroid storm   A rare but potentially life-threatening result of untreated hyperthyroidism that can cause cardiac arrhythmias, congestive heart failure, and shock.

thyroxine   Hormone T_4 secreted by the thyroid gland.

tinea   Any fungal infection found on the body.

tinnitus   *(tinn EYE tus)* Sounds (buzzing, ringing, hissing, or roaring) that are heard constantly or intermittently in one or both ears, even in a quiet environment.

tissues   Collection of similar cells that form a particular function.

tongue   Large muscle that fills the oral cavity and assists with eating and talking. It contains taste buds and receptors for the sense of taste.

tonsil   A mass of lymphoid tissue in the mucous membranes of the pharynx and base of the tongue.

tonsillitis   An inflammation of the tonsil or tonsils.

tonus   *(TONE us)* A partial, steady contraction of a muscle; firmness.

torn rotator cuff   Tear or inflammation of the rotator cuff tendons in the shoulder.

toxic shock syndrome   Inflammatory disease that occurs in menstruating woman often as a result of improper tampon use.

trabecula   *(tra BECK you la)* A thin bone strip used as a support structure in spongy bone.

trachea   *(TRAY kee ah)* Rigid tubular air pipe between the larynx and the bronchi that is a passageway for inhaled and exhaled air.

tracheostomy tube   *(TRAY kee AWS toh mee)* A long-term breathing tube surgically placed through the anterior portion of the neck below the vocal chords.

trachoma   *(tray KOH mah)* A chronic form of conjunctivitis that is highly contagious.

traction   Use of weights to hold broken bones in place for proper healing.

transdermal patches   A form of drug delivery that allows drug absorption through the skin from a patch, containing the medication, that adheres to the skin.

transient ischemic attack (TIA) *(is KEE mick)* A "mini-stroke" that causes minor symptoms that are temporary in nature.

transitional *(tran ZISH on al)* Moving from one state to another.

transitional cells *(tran ZISH on al)* Stretchable epithelial cells.

transverse colon A portion of the colon that travels across the abdomen just below the liver and stomach.

transverse plane *(tranz VERS)* Plane that divides the body into top and bottom sections, superior and inferior.

traumatic brain injury (TBI) Severe brain injury that may leave residual impairment.

Trendelenburg *(trin DELL in berg)* A patient position in which the head is lower than the body and legs.

tricuspid *(try KUS pid)* Having three cusps or points as in the tricuspid valve of the right heart.

triiodothyronine *(TRY eye oh doh THYE roh nin)* Hormone T_3 secreted by the thyroid gland.

true capillaries The actual blood vessels where gas and nutrient exchange occurs.

tubal ligation Form of female sterilization in which the fallopian tubes are cut or tied shut to prevent the passage of the egg.

tubercles *(TOO ber kulz)* Lump-like structures formed as a result of tuberculosis.

tuberculosis (TB) *(too BER kew LOH sis)* Lung infection caused by the bacterium *mycobacterium tuberculosis* and spread by airborne droplets expelled by coughing.

tubular reabsorption Movement of substances out of the renal tubule and back into the blood. The substances will be retained in the body.

tubular secretion Movement of substances from the blood into the renal tubule. These substances will leave the body in the urine.

tumor necrosis factor (TNF) *(neh KROH sis)* Released by macrophages, this chemical destroys endotoxins produced by certain bacteria. It also destroys cancer cells.

tunica albuginea A layer of firm white fibrous tissue forming the sheath of an organ or part, as of the eye, testicle, ovary, or spleen.

tunica externa *(TOO nee kah ex TERN ah)* The outer layer of a blood vessel.

tunica interna *(TOO nee kah in TERN ah)* The inner lining of a blood vessel.

tunica media *(TOO nee kah mee DEE ah)* The middle muscular layer of a blood vessel.

tunica vaginalis A serous membrane that surrounds each testis.

turbinates *(TER bih nayts)* Three long projections (superior, middle, inferior) of the ethmoid bone that jut into the nasal cavity. They break up the stream of air as it enters the nose. Also known as the *nasal conchae*.

T wave The portion of the electrical activity of the heart that reflects repolarization of the ventricles.

tympanic cavity See middle ear.

tympanic membrane *(tihm PAN ik)* Membrane that divides the external ear from the middle ear. Also known as the *eardrum*.

U

umami *(oo MAM ee)* Japanese for savory or delicious and one of our tastes.

umbilical *(uhm BIL ih kuhl)* Pertaining to the umbilicus ("belly button").

universal donor A person who has a form of type O blood, which can be transfused to any individual of the ABO blood groups.

universal recipient A person who has type AB blood and therefore can receive blood from any of the ABO blood groups.

upper respiratory infection (URI) Bacterial or viral infection of the nose that can spread to the throat and ears. Also known as a *common cold* or *head cold*.

urea The main nitrogenous substance found in urine. The amount excreted in urine is directly related to the amount of protein consumed.

uremia *(yoo REE mee uh)* Blood found in urine as a result of a pathologic process.

ureter *(yoo REE ter)* Tube that connects the pelvis of the kidney to the bladder.

ureteroscopy A procedure in which a fiberoptic endoscope is threaded up the urethra to view the ureter.

urethra *(yoo REE thrah)* Tube that connects the bladder to the outside of the body.

urethral meatus *(yoo REE thrall mee AY tus)* The final opening of the urethra.

urinary bladder A holding receptacle for urine before it is expelled (voided) from the body.

urinary system The organ system that includes the kidneys, ureters, bladder, and urethra. The kidneys form urine from blood plasma by filtration, reabsorption, and secretion. The formation of urine includes the excretion of waste products, but the kidneys also regulate the water and mineral content and the acid-base balance of the blood and all other body fluids. The other organs of the system are concerned with the elimination of urine after it has been formed.

urinary tract infection (UTI) A general term for an infection involving the kidney(s), ureter(s), or bladder.

urology *(yoo RALL oh jee)* A branch of medicine involving the urinary tract of both males and females and the male genital tract.

uterine arteries Branches of the anterior division of the internal iliac artery; they supply blood to the upper vagina, cervix, uterus, and fallopian tubes.

uterine cycle The monthly build-up, decay, and shedding of the uterine lining.

uterine tubes Also known as fallopian tubes or oviducts; the tubes allow the passage of the egg from the ovary to the uterus.

uterus Thick walled, pear shaped structure which houses a developing embryo.

UTI Urinary tract infection.

uvula *(YOO vyuh luh)* Soft lymphoid structure dangling from the soft palate that acts as a boundary between the oral cavity and pharynx.

V

vagina The female structure that serves as a birth canal and allows passage of menstrual fluid.

vaginitis *(VAJ ih NYE tiss)* An inflammatory process involving the vagina.

vagus nerve *(VAY gus)* Cranial nerve X. Sensation and movement of the throat. Sensory and motor for thoracic and abdominal organs.

valvular insufficiency A pathologic condition in which the valve(s) of the heart do not function normally.

vas deferens *(VAS DEF er inz)* The 45-cm-long tube running from the scrotum to the penis through which sperm travels.

vasa recta Straight blood vessels associated with the renal nephron.

vascular shunt *(VAS kyuh ler shuhnt)* In a capillary bed, it is the main pathway connecting the arteriole to the venule.

vasculature Network of blood vessels in a particular organ.

vasectomy *(vas ECK toh mee)* Form of male sterilization in which the vas deferens is removed or blocked to prevent the travel of sperm.

vasoconstriction *(VAY zoh kon STRIK shun)* Constriction of the smooth muscle in the artery wall which causes the artery to become smaller in diameter.

vasodilation *(VAY zoh dye LAY shun)* Relaxation of the smooth muscle in the artery wall, causing the artery to become larger in diameter.

vector borne An infective agent or disease carried by an insect or arthropod.

vegetative state Situation in which an individual has no response to surroundings.

vein Blood vessel that carries oxygen-poor blood as well as carbon dioxide and waste products of cellular metabolism away from the cells and back to the heart. Veins have one-way valves that keep blood from flowing backward, away from the heart. The exception is the pulmonary vein, which carries oxygenated blood from the lungs to the heart.

ventilation *(ven tih LAY shun)* The bulk movement of gas into and out of the lungs.

ventral Pertaining to the anterior of the body, particularly the abdomen.

ventral root Spinal root that carries motor information.

ventricles *(VEN trih kulz)* 1. Two lower chambers of the heart. Intraventricular structures are located in the ventricles. 2. Four hollow chambers within the brain that contain cerebrospinal fluid. The two lateral ventricles are within the right and left hemispheres of the cerebrum. The third ventricle is small and connects the lateral ventricles to the fourth ventricle, which is at the level of the pons and medulla oblongata.

venules *(VIN yulz)* Smallest branches of a vein.

vermiform appendix See appendix.

verruca *(vur ROO kuh)* A wart.

vertebrae *(VER teh bray)* One of 33 irregularly shaped bony segments of the spinal column.

vertebrocostal *(VER teh broh KOSS tul)* referring to the false rib pairs 8–10 and their points of attachment.

vertebrosternal *(VER teh broh STIR null)* Referring to the true rib pairs 1–7 and their points of attachment.

vertigo *(VER tih goh)* Sensation of being off balance when the body is not moving. Caused by upper respiratory infection, middle or inner ear infection, head trauma, or degenerative changes of the semicircular canals.

vesicle *(VESS ih kul)* A small bladder or blister; a membrane-bound storage sac inside a cell.

vestibular reflex A reaction that stabilizes the position of the head according to sensory information from the labyrinth of the ear and the nerves in the neck.

vestibular region Region of the nose located just inside the nostrils that contains nasal hairs that act as the first line of defense for the respiratory system.

vestibule An almond-shaped space between the lines of attachment of the labia minora.

vestibule chamber *(VESS tih byool)* A small cavity or space at the beginning of a canal.

vestibulocochlear nerve *(VESS tih byoo loh KOHK lee are)* The eighth cranial nerve responsible for hearing and balance. Sometimes called the *acoustic nerve.*

vibrissae *(vye BRISS ee)* Coarse nasal hairs used to trap large particulate matter.

villi *(VILL eye)* Microscopic projections of the mucosa within the lumen of the small intestine.

virus A parasitic microorganism that depends on other cells for its metabolic and reproductive needs.

visceral *(VISS er al)* Pertaining to organs.

visceral layer The side of the sac attached to the external surface of the heart.

Visceral muscle See smooth muscle.

visceral peritoneum *(VIS er al PAIR ih TOE nee um)* Serous membrane lining the abdominal cavity.

visceral pleura *(VISS er al PLOO rah)* One of the two membranes of the pleura. It covers the surface of the lung.

visceral senses Senses that include nausea, hunger, thirst, and the need to urinate and defecate.

vital signs Medical assessment during a physical examination in which the temperature, pulse, and respirations (TPR), as well as the blood pressure, are measured.

vitreous humor *(VITT ree us HYOO mer)* Clear, gel-like substance that fills the posterior cavity of the eye.

vocal cords Connective tissue bands in the larynx that vibrate and produce sounds for speaking and singing.

voluntary muscle Muscle under conscious control.

vomiting Ejection through the mouth of the contents of the gastrointestinal tract.

vulva External female genitalia.

W

wandering macrophage *(MACK roh feyj)* Mobile cell moving throughout the alveoli, ingesting foreign particles.

warts Raised, cutaneous elevations. Also called verruca.

Wernicke's area *(VER nih KEEZ)* Found in parietal lobe, this region controls the understanding of language.

white blood cells (WBCs) Leukocytes; responsible for the immune response.

wisdom teeth The last four molars that appear usually in the late teens.

withdrawal reflex Flexion of a body part in response to a painful stimulus.

X

xiphoid *(ZYE foyd)* The inferior portion of the sternum.

x-ray An electromagnetic radiation utilized to form a two dimensional image of the body for diagnostic purposes.

Y

yellow marrow A form of marrow that has high fat content and can produce blood cells.

Z

z lines Lines visible on the surface of skeletal muscle that mark the ends of each sarcomere.

zygote *(ZYE goat)* Fertilized egg possessing 46 chromosomes.

INDEX

A

Abbreviations, 9
Abdominal quadrants, 43, 44
Abdominal region, divisions in, 41, 42
Abdominopelvic cavity, 41
Abducens nerve, 290
Abduction, 156, 194
Abrasion, 238
Abruptio placenta, 635
Abscess, 402
Accessory glands in male reproductive system, 623
Accessory muscles, 468–469
Accessory nerve, 290
Accessory organs, 543–547
Accommodation, in eyes, 348
Accuracy, quantitative data, 685–686
ACE inhibitors, 595
Acetone test, 664
Acetylcholine (ACh), 200, 263, 264
Acetylcholinesterase (AChE), 200, 263
ACh. See Acetylcholine (ACh)
AChE. See Acetylcholinesterase (AChE)
Acid-base relationship, 585
Acids, 58–60
Acne, 219, 238, 243
Acoustic nerve, 359
Acquired immune deficiency syndrome (AIDS), 502, 510
Acquired immunity, 489
Acromegaly, 323, 338
Acronyms, 733
ACTH. See Adrenocorticotropic hormone (ACTH)
Actin, 197
Action potentials, 258, 259
Activation, lymphocyte, 498–499
Active transport, 79, 84–86
Active transport pumps, 84, 85, 86
Activity Pyramid, 711
Acute bronchitis, 469
Acute epiglottitis, 444–445, 446
Acute leukemias, 491
Acute renal failure, 586
Acute respiratory distress syndrome (ARDS), 471
Adaptation, 364
Adaptive immunity, 488–489, 496, 498–501
Addison's disease, 334, 339
Adduction, 156, 194
Adenoids, 442, 483
Adenosine diphosphate (ADP). See ADP (Adenosine diphosphate)
Adenosine triphosphate (ATP). See ATP (Adenosine triphosphate)
ADH. See Antidiuretic hormone (ADH)
Adipose tissue, 115
ADP (Adenosine diphosphate), 68, 69, 92
Adrenal cortex, 329, 330–331
Adrenal glands, 128, 313, 317, 329
Adrenaline, 329
Adrenal medulla, 329–330
Adrenocorticosteroids, 330
Adrenocorticotropic hormone (ACTH), 321
Adventitia, 529, 623
Aesthetic pattern of knowing, 678
Afferent arterioles, 569
Age, bone building and, 150
Agglutinate, 404

Agonists, 192, 193
Agranulocytes, 652
AIDS. See Acquired immune deficiency syndrome (AIDS)
AIDS-related complex (ARC), 502
Airborne transmission, 19
Airway, 436, 443
Albinism, 218
Albumin, 400
Albumin test, 662, 663–664
Alcohol, 322, 548, 712, 713
Aldosterone, 583–584
Alimentary canal, 520, 529–530. See also Gastrointestinal (GI) system
Alimentary tract, 520. See also Gastrointestinal (GI) system
Allergic reaction, 18
Allergic rhinitis, 439, 470, 509
Allergies, 445, 493, 508, 511–512
Alopecia, 233
ALS. See Amyotrophic lateral sclerosis (ALS)
Alveolar-capillary membrane, 436, 450–452
Alveolar sacs, 448
Alveoli, 131, 436, 612
Alzheimer's disease, 288, 289, 304
Amblyopia, 352, 368
Amenorrhea, 620, 634
Amino acids, 65
Amniocentesis, 628, 630
Amnion, 628
Amoebas, 724
Ampulla, 608
Amylase, 523
Amyotrophic lateral sclerosis (ALS), 296–297, 304
Anabolic steroids, 335, 717
Anabolism, 12, 67
Anaphase, 96, 97
Anaphylaxis, 493, 508
Anastomoses, 385
Anatomical position, 32
Anatomy
    definition of, 2
    fine, 2
    gross, 2
    macroscopic, 2
    microscopic, 2
Androgen insensitivity syndrome, 627
Anemia, 3, 406, 420, 649, 651
Anesthesia, 366
Aneurysm, 414, 417
Angina, 417, 525
Angina pectoris, 387–388
Angiogram, 384
Angiotensinogen, 584
Anhidrosis, 724
Anorexia nervosa, 134, 549
ANP. See Atrial natriuretic peptide (ANP)
Antacids, 556
Antagonists, 194
Antebrachial, 45
Antecubital, 45
Anterior, 36, 45
Anterior pituitary glands, 320, 321, 322, 323
Anteroposterior (AP) view, 47
Antibiotics, 103, 105, 718
Antibodies, 399, 403, 488

Antibody mediated immunity, 503
Antidiuretic hormone (ADH), 321, 322, 583
Antigen-presenting cells (APCs), 503
Antigens, 403, 488
Antihistamines, 511
Anti-inflammatory drugs, 511
Antiseptic, 348
Antitussives, 472
Antivert, 370
Anuria, 593
Anus, 520, 541
Anvil, 358
Aorta, 383, 389, 407
APCs. See Antigen-presenting cells (APCs)
Apex, 464
Aphthous stomatitis, 527
Aplastic anemia, 406
Apocrine glands, 220
Aponeurosis, 185
Apothecary system, 742
Appendectomy, 542
Appendicitis, 45, 542
Appendicular skeleton, 160
Appendix, 45, 542, 543, 724
AP view. See Anteroposterior (AP) view
Aqueous humor, 348
Arachnoid mater, 266
Arachnoid villi, 288
Arbor vitae, 287
ARC. See AIDS-related complex (ARC)
Arcuate arteries, 569, 609
ARDS. See Acute respiratory distress syndrome (ARDS)
Areola, 612
Areolar tissue, 115
Arm, skeletal muscles in, 190
Arrector pili, 236
Arteries, 129, 378, 380, 381, 404, 408
Arterioles, 378, 379, 407
Arteriosclerosis, 389, 417
Arthritis, 154, 158, 171
Arthroscope, 159
Arthroscopy, 159
Articular cartilage, 153
Articulation, 154
Artificial active immunity, 505
Artificial blood, 407
Artificial passive immunity, 505
Asbestosis, 469
Ascending colon, 542
Ascending loop, 571, 582
Asexual reproduction, 95, 97, 602–603
Association neurons, 257
Asthma, 456, 457–458, 459, 461, 471, 714
Astigmatism, 368
Astrocytes, 255
Ataxia, 194
Atelectasis, 453, 454
Atherosclerosis, 119, 389, 390, 418
Athlete's foot, 223, 242
Atmospheric gases, 434
Atoms, 57–58, 76
Atopic march, 508
ATP (Adenosine triphosphate)
    active transport and, 84
    definition of, 68

energy and, 68, 69, 92
  in muscle movement, 198
Atria, 381
Atrial natriuretic peptide (ANP), 584
Atrioventricular node, 393, 394
Atrioventricular valve, 381
Atrophic macular degeneration, 351
Atrophy, 98, 184
Auditory canal, 357, 359
Auricle, 357, 359
Autografting, 228
Autoimmune disorders, 497, 512
Autoregulation, 579–580
Autorhythmicity, 393
Avascular, 217
AV bundle, 396
AV node, 393, 394
AV valve, 381
Axial skeleton, 160
Axillary, 45
Axons, 117, 256
Axon terminal, 257
Azotemia, 585

B

Bacilli, 701
Bacteria
  and disease, 103, 104–105
  general discussion, 99, 100
  infections, 96
  resistance to antibiotics, 105
  urinalysis, 664
Bacterial meningitis, 119, 279
Bacterial tonsillitis, 483
Ball-and-socket joints, 154, 155
Balloon angioplasty, 390
Bar graphs, 689–690
Barriers, body, 18
Basal cell carcinoma, 238
Basal layer, 609
Basal nuclei, 279
Bases, 58–60
Basophils, 401, 402, 492
B cells, 492, 500, 503–504
Becker's muscular dystrophy (BMD), 199
Bed sores, 238
Benign prostatic hyperplasia (BPH), 623–624, 635
Benign tumors, 98
Beta-adrenergic agonists, 472
Biceps brachii, 193
Bicuspids, 525, 526
Bicuspid valve, 382, 383
Bifocals, 351–352
Bile, 538
Bilirubin, 219, 538
Biliverdin, 538
Binary fission, 95
Biochemistry
  acids and bases, 58–60
  atoms, 56–58
  biological molecules, 63–66
  bonding, 60–61
  elements, 56–58
  enzymes, 67–69
  ions, 56–58
  metabolism, 67
  periodic table, 58
  solutions, 62

water, 61–62
Biohazards, 683–685
Biological, 98
Biological molecules, 63–66
Biological response modifiers (BRMs), 497, 512
Biological vector, 19
Biopsy, 98
Bioterrorism, 264
Blackheads, 219
Black lung disease, 714
Blepharitis, 368
Blind spot, 354
Blood
  artificial, 407
  clotting, 411–414
  color-coding of, 380
  composition of, 399–401
  conditions, 406
  as connective tissue, 115
  definition of, 378
  disorders, 420–422
  inflammation, 402
  red blood cells, 401
  septicemia, 130
  in stool, 666
  thrombocytes, 403
  transfusions, 403–405, 724
  types, 403–405, 407
  white blood cells, 401–402
Blood-brain barrier, 279, 304
Blood chemistry, 655–658
Blood circulation
  cardiopulmonary, 382
  coronary, 385
  pulmonary, 384
  systemic, 385
Blood clots, 37, 168, 411–414
Blood poisoning, 130
Blood pressure (BP)
  definition of, 407
  hypertension, 418
  kidney disease and, 587, 595
  measurement of, 410
  in orthostatic hypotension, 34
  regulation of, 203, 204, 409
Blood testing
  basics, 647–648
  blood chemistry, 655–658
  blood urea nitrogen, 655, 656
  complete blood count, 649–650
  differential leukocyte count, 653
  electrolytes, 657
  enzymes, 658
  general blood disorders, 649
  hematocrit, 651
  hemoglobin, 652
  partial thromboplastin time, 655
  platelet count, 654–655
  prothrombin time, 655
  red blood cell count, 650–651
  sampling, 647–648
  white blood cells, 647, 652–653
Blood urea nitrogen (BUN), 579, 655, 656
Blood vessels
  blood clotting, 411–414
  capillaries, 129, 231, 378, 379, 411
  definition of, 379
  function of, 129, 407–408
  in kidney, 569–570
  problems associated with, 414, 417–419
  structure of, 407–408

veins, 34, 129, 378, 379, 381, 408–409
BMD. *See* Becker's muscular dystrophy (BMD)
Body, human
  cavities, 40, 41
  directional terms, 35–37, 38
  map, 32–45
  planes, 35–37
  positions, 32–34
  regions, 41–45
Body(ies)
  of penis, 622
  of sternum, 163
  of stomach, 531
  of uterus, 609
Body lice, 234
Body temperature
  adaptation, 364–365
  homeostasis and, 12–14
  integumentary regulation of, 235–236
  muscles and, 202
Boils, 238
Bolus, 522, 528
Bonds
  covalent, 60, 61
  general discussion, 60–61
  hydrogen, 62
  ionic, 60, 61
  polar covalent, 60–61
Bone
  aging and, 150
  anatomy, 145
  cartilage, 153–154
  classification, 144–145
  compact, 147
  diseases, 155
  disorders, 170
  flat, 144
  forensic science and, 701, 703
  fractures, 168–169
  growth, 149
  health, 169–170
  irregular, 144–145
  joints, 154–155
  ligaments, 154–155
  long, 144
  movement classification, 156–157
  osteoporosis, 151
  repair, 149
  short, 144
  skeleton, 160–166
  spongy, 147
  surface structure, 148
  tissue, 147
Bone conduction of sound, 359
Bone marrow
  red, 145, 146
  yellow, 145
Bony thorax, 163, 464–465
Botox injection, 205
Botulism, 205
Bowman's capsule, 570
Boxers versus briefs, 623
Boyle's Law, 466
BP. *See* Blood pressure (BP)
BPH. *See* Benign prostatic hyperplasia (BPH)
Brachial, 45
Brachial arteries, 383
Bradycardia, 419
Brain
  aging and, 706
  cerebrospinal fluid, 288

cranial nerves, 288–290
external anatomy, 276–279
in geriatric patients, 707
injuries, 280–283
internal anatomy, 279, 284–287
in nervous system, 127
overview, 276
surface of, 278
vesicles, 288
Brain dead, 678
Brain stem, 276, 278
Breaking fevers, 14
Breastbone, 163, 464–465
Breast cancer, 632–633, 634, 721
Breast feeding, 619
Breast health, 632–633
Breast self-examination (BSE), 633
Breathing, 194, 195, 439, 465–469
Breath test for cancer, 437
Briefs versus boxers, 623
BRMs. *See* Biological response modifiers (BRMs)
Broad ligament, 609
Broca's area, 284
Bronchi, 131, 436, 447–449, 450
Bronchioles, 436, 448, 450
Bronchitis
acute, 469
chronic, 455, 456, 459, 471
Bronchoscope, 670
Bronchoscopy, 670
Bronchospasm, 456
Bruises, 239, 414
BSE. *See* Breast self-examination (BSE)
Buccal, 41, 45
Buccal cavity, 522
Bulbourethral glands, 621, 622, 623
Bulimia, 134, 549
BUN. *See* Blood urea nitrogen (BUN)
Bundle of His, 396
Burns, 227–229, 239, 243
Bursa, 154
Bursitis, 158, 172

C

C&S test. *See* Culture and sensitivity (C&S) test
CAD. *See* Coronary artery disease (CAD)
Caffeine, 739
Calcitonin, 325
Calcium, 169, 175, 198, 657
Calyces, 568
Cancellous bone, 147
Cancer
breast, 632–633, 634, 721
breath test for, 437
CAUTION acronym, 722
cervical, 635
colon, 721
colorectal, 543
leukemia, 405, 406, 422, 491, 510
lung, 469, 724
lymphatic system and, 486–487
lymphoma, 510
melanoma, 121, 720–721
mitosis and, 98
prevention of, 720–722
prostate, 624, 635, 721
rectum, 721
skin, 712
stages, 487

stomach, 723
treatment, 720–722
uterine, 721
Canine teeth, 525, 526
Canker sores, 527
Capillary(ies)
bed, 411
definition of, 378, 379
endothelium, 452
function of, 129
general discussion, 411
lung, 436
lymph, 481
peritubular, 569
refill assessment, 231
Capsid, 100
Carbohydrases, 546
Carbohydrates, 63
Carbon dioxide, 60, 61, 433, 467
Cardiac arrhythmias, 395
Cardiac cycle, 382–386, 393–396
Cardiac enzymes, 392
Cardiac impression, 464
Cardiac muscle, 117, 182, 183, 204–205, 385
Cardiac output (CO), 409
Cardiac region of stomach, 531
Cardiac sphincter, 529
Cardiac tamponade, 415
Cardiac tests, 395, 669–670
Cardiology, 6
Cardiopulmonary circulation, 382
Cardiopulmonary resuscitation (CPR), 163, 396, 733
Cardiopulmonary system, 433
Cardiovascular system. *See also* Heart
definition of, 378
diseases of, 415–422
drugs for, 423
general discussion, 129–130
in geriatric patients, 707
hematology, 399–407
organs in, 122
overview, 377–380
vascular system, 407–415
wellness, 712–713
Caries, 527, 549, 723
Carina, 447
Carotene, 218
Carotid arteries, 383
Carpal, 45
Carpal tunnel syndrome (CTS), 275, 710, 711
Carper, Barbara, 678–679
Carrier mediated active transport, 84
Carrier mediated passive transport, 82
Carriers of disease, 118
Cartilage
articular, 153
cricoid, 443
flexibility of, 154
general discussion, 153–154
septal, 437
thyroid, 443
Cartilaginous joint, 154
Catabolism, 12, 67
Cataract, 351, 367, 368
Cauda equina, 265
Caudal, 36
CAUTION acronym, 722
Cavities, body, 40, 41
Cavities, dental, 527, 549, 723
CBC. *See* Complete blood count (CBC)

CC. *See* Chief complaint/concern (CC)
CCK. *See* Cholecystokinin (CCK)
CCMS. *See* Clean-catch midstream urine specimen (CCMS)
Cecum, 542
Celiac sprue, 553
Cell division, 95, 602–603
Cell-mediated immunity, 504, 505
Cell(s)
cancer, 98
components, 78
cycle, 96–98
division, 602–603
eukaryotic, 95
in immune system, 489–492
membrane, 78–79, 88
microorganisms, 99–105
overview, 75–76
prokaryotic, 95
structure, 77–78
transport methods, 79–95
types of, 77
cellular reproduction, 95
Cellular reproduction, 602
Cellular respiration, 68, 92, 432
Cellulitis, 224, 239
Cementum, 525
Central, 37, 38
Central cyanosis, 38
Central nervous system (CNS), 127, 253, 293
Centrioles, 89
Centrosomes, 88, 89
Cephalic, 36
Cephalic phase, 533, 534
Cerebellum, 276, 277, 287, 295
Cerebral cortex, 294
Cerebral palsy (CP), 296, 297, 303
Cerebrospinal fluid (CSF), 265, 272, 288, 289, 291
Cerebrospinal fluid (CSF) testing, 667–668
Cerebrovascular accident (CVA), 280–281, 282
Cerebrum, 276, 277, 284–287
Cerumen, 357
Ceruminous glands, 357
Cervical, 45
Cervical canal, 609
Cervical cancer, 635
Cervical vertebrae, 43, 164
Cervix, 609
Chain of infection, 21
Charcot-Marie-Tooth disorder, 302
Cheilitis, 527
Chemical hazards, 683, 685
Chemicals, in immune system, 492
Chemical synapse, 262–263
Chemotherapy, 98, 720
Chickenpox, 101, 221–222
Chief cells, 531, 533
Chief complaint/concern (CC), 16, 17
Childbirth, positive feedback in, 14, 318
Chlamydia, 719
Chloride, 657
Cholecystectomy, 547
Cholecystitis, 547, 551
Cholecystokinin (CCK), 538
Cholelithiasis, 547, 551
Cholesterol, 64, 86, 389
Choroid, 348, 350
Choroid plexus, 288
Chromatin, 88
Chromosomes, 604–605
Chronic bronchitis, 455, 456, 459, 471

Chronic kidney disease, 586–587
Chronic leukemias, 491
Chronic obstructive pulmonary disease (COPD), 92, 454, 455, 456, 460, 461, 467, 471
Chronic stress, 339
Chyle, 539
Chyme, 531
Cigarettes, effect on lung cilia, 92
Cilia, 91, 92, 441
Ciliary muscle, 348
CIPA. *See* Congenital insensitivity to pain with anhidrosis (CIPA)
Circulation
    cardiopulmonary, 382
    coronary, 385
    pulmonary, 384
    systemic, 385
Circulatory system. *See* cardiovascular system
Circumduction, 157
Cirrhosis, 548, 552
Clean-catch midstream urine specimen (CCMS), 659
Cleft lip, 549
Cleft palate, 549
Clitoris, 136, 612
Closed fracture, 168
Closed reduction, 159, 168
Clotting, 37, 168, 411–414
CNS. *See* Central nervous system (CNS)
CO. *See* Cardiac output (CO)
Coalworkers' pneumoconiosis, 714
Coccyx, 43, 164
Cochlea, 358, 359
Coconut juice, 407
Colds, 444, 445, 470
Cold sores, 221, 222
Cold therapy, 365
Collecting duct, 571, 582
Colon, 542
Colon cancer, 721
Colonoscopy, 671
Color
    of cerebral spinal fluid, 667
    of stool, 665–666
    of urine, 661, 662, 663
Color blindness, 352, 354, 368
Colorectal cancer, 543
Colostomy, 543
Columnar cells, 112
Columns, 267
Coma, 280
Combining forms, 6, 8
Comminuted fracture, 168, 169
Commissures, 269
Common cold, 444, 470
Common vehicle transmission, 19
Common warts, 222, 242
Communicable disease, 4
Compact bone, 147
Comparative investigations, 682
Complement cascade, 492
Complete blood count (CBC), 649–650
Compliance, 467
Compound fracture, 168
Computed tomography (CT) scanning, 46, 48
Concentration, 62
Concentration analysis, 660–661, 662
Concentration gradient, 79–80
Conchae, 438
Concussion, 280
Condyle, 148

Condyloid joints, 155
Cones, 354
Congenital disorders, 170
Congenital hypothyroidism, 326, 337, 338
Congenital insensitivity to pain with anhidrosis (CIPA), 724
Congestive heart failure, 387, 388, 415, 416
Conjunctiva, 347, 350
Conjunctival hemorrhage, 367
Conjunctivitis, 351, 367, 368
Connective tissue, 115–116
Consistency of stool, 665
Constipation, 548
Contact
    direct, 19
    indirect, 19
Contact dermatitis, 239, 243
Contact transmission, 19
Contagious disease, 4
Contraception, 629
Contractile tissue, 182
Contractions, muscle, 192, 194, 200
Contralateral, 277
Contusion, 239, 280
Conus medullaris, 265
Conversion of units, 745–748
Convolutions, 277
COPD. *See* Chronic obstructive pulmonary disease (COPD)
Coping strategies for stress, 737
Copper, 56
Corium, 218
Cornea, 348
Coronal plane, 36, 37
Coronary arteries, 385
Coronary artery disease (CAD), 418
Coronary thrombosis, 388
Corpus callosum, 287
Corpus luteum, 613, 615
Cortex
    adrenal, 329, 330–331
    cerebral, 279, 294
    of hair, 232
    primary motor, 284, 286
    primary somatic sensory, 284, 286
    renal, 568
Cortical radiate arteries, 569
Corticobulbar tract, 268, 269, 295
Corticospinal tract, 268, 295
Corticotropin-releasing hormone (CRH), 321
Cortisol, 335–336
Cortisol busters, 336
Countercurrent circulation, 582
Covalent bonds, 60, 61
CP. *See* Cerebral palsy (CP)
CPR. *See* Cardiopulmonary resuscitation (CPR)
Cramps, muscle, 206
Cranial, 36
Cranial cavity, 41
Cranial nerves, 288–290
Craniosacral, 300
Cravings, food, 724
Creatinine, 576, 579
Crest, 148
CRH. *See* Corticotropin-releasing hormone (CRH)
Cricoid cartilage, 443
Crohn's disease, 554
Cross-sectioning, 35
Crowning, 629

Crown, of tooth, 525
Cruciate ligament tears, 172
Crust, 237
Cryptorchidism, 621, 622
CSF. *See* Cerebrospinal fluid (CSF)
CSF testing. *See* Cerebrospinal fluid (CSF) testing
CTS. *See* Carpal tunnel syndrome (CTS)
CT scanning. *See* Computed tomography (CT) scanning
Cuboidal cells, 112
Culture and sensitivity (C&S) test, 668–669
Cupric, 56
Cushing's syndrome, 334, 337, 339
Cuspids, 525, 526
Cutaneous membranes, 114
Cutaneous senses, 347
Cuticle, 230, 232
CVA. *See* Cerebrovascular accident (CVA)
Cyanosis, central versus peripheral, 38
Cystic fibrosis, 82, 471
Cystitis, 592
Cystoscope, 671
Cystoscopy, 671
Cytokines, 492
Cytokinesis, 96
Cytoplasm, 87, 88
Cytoskeleton, 91
Cytotoxic T cells, 504

D

Data collection, 685–687
Data presentation, 689–692
Deciduous teeth, 524–525, 526
Decubitus, 238
Deep, 37, 38
Defecation, 522
Defibrillator, 398
Degenerative disorders
    in bones, 170
    in joints, 170
Dehydration synthesis, 67
Deltoid, 193
Dendrites, 117, 256
Dendritic cells, 492, 498
Dental caries, 527, 549, 723
Dental plaque, 527
Dentin, 525
Deoxyribonucleic acid (DNA). *See* DNA (deoxyribonucleic acid)
Dependent variables, experimental investigations, 682
Depolarization, 258, 259
Depression, 736
Dermatitis, 239
Dermis, 126, 217, 218–219
Descending colon, 542
Descending loop, 571, 582
Descriptive investigations, 682
Detrusor muscle, 590
Diabetes insipidus (DI), 322, 338, 594
Diabetes mellitus (DM)
    cellular respiration and, 93
    cerebrovascular disease in, 333
    definition of, 83
    facilitated diffusion and, 82–83
    general discussion, 331–333, 338
    kidneys and, 580–581
    nephropathy, 333, 580–581, 594
    retinopathy in, 333, 369

tissue damage from, 119
type 1, 93, 331, 332
type 2, 93, 331, 332
Diabetic nephropathy, 333, 580–581, 594
Diagnosis, 16
Diagnostic testing
  blood
    basics, 647–648
    blood chemistry, 655–658
    blood urea nitrogen, 655, 656
    complete blood count, 649–650
    differential leukocyte count, 653
    electrolytes, 657
    enzymes, 658
    general blood disorders, 649
    hematocrit, 651
    hemoglobin, 652
    partial thromboplastin time, 655
    platelet count, 654–655
    prothrombin time, 655
    red blood cell count, 650–651
    white blood cells, 647, 652–653
  blood pressure, 410
  breath test for cancer, 437
  bronchoscopy, 670
  cardiac, 669–670
  cerebral spinal fluid, 667–668
  colonoscopy, 671
  culture and sensitivity, 668–669
  cystoscopy, 671
  electrocardiogram, 395
  endoscopy, 670
  fecal, 665–666
  gastroscopy, 671
  laparoscopy, 671
  otoscopy, 670
  polysomnography, 672
  pulmonary function, 671
  sleep studies, 672
  urinalysis
    acetone, 664
    albumin, 663–664
    bacteria, 664
    color, 661
    concentration, 660–661
    dipstick test, 659
    general discussion, 658–659
    glucose, 663
    ketone bodies, 664
    odor, 661
    pH, 661, 662–663
    protein, 663–664
    sediment examination, 665
    specific gravity, 660
    sugar, 663
    turbidity, 663
Dialysis, 585, 589
Diapedesis, 401
Diaphragm, 34, 193, 194, 195, 465
Diaphysis, 145
Diarrhea, 548, 556
Diastole, 382, 383
Diencephalon, 287
Diet, 712, 715, 716, 719, 739
Differential leukocyte count (DIFF), 653
Differentiation, lymphocyte, 498, 499
Diffusion, 79, 80, 86, 582
Digestion, 522
Digestive enzymes, 538, 546
Digestive system. *See* Gastrointestinal (GI) system
Digital, 45

Dilation stage, 628, 631
Diplopia, 352
Dipstick test, 659
Direct contact, 19
Directional terms, 35–37, 38
Direct testing, 682
Disaccharides, 63, 538
Disease
  carriers, 118
  communicable, 4
  concepts, 15–17
  contagious, 4
  definition of, 4
  diagnosis, 16
  endemic, 4
  epidemic, 4
  etiology, 17
  exacerbation, 17
  forensic science and detection of, 701
  fungi and, 103–104
  idiopathic, 4
  morbidity, 17
  mortality, 17
  pandemic, 4
  pathogens associated with, 104–105
  prognosis, 17
  protozoan infections, 104
  relapse, 17
  remission, 17
  signs of, 15
  symptoms of, 15
  terminal, 17
  viruses and, 103
Disease modifying anti-rheumatic drugs
    (DMARDs), 497, 512
Dislocation, joint, 159
Distal, 37, 38
Distal tubule, 571, 582
Diverticulitis, 543–544, 554
Diverticulosis, 544
DM. *See* Diabetes mellitus (DM)
DMARDs. *See* Disease modifying anti-rheumatic
    drugs (DMARDs)
DMD. *See* Duchenne's muscular dystrophy (DMD)
DNA (deoxyribonucleic acid)
  fingerprinting, 701, 704–705
  in nucleus, 88
Dorsal, 37
Dorsal column, 293
Dorsal column tract, 268
Dorsal root, 269
Dorsal root ganglion, 269
Dorsiflexion, 156
Down syndrome, 604
Drug abuse, 548
Drug-induced nephropathy, 594
Dry eye syndrome, 369
Duchenne's muscular dystrophy (DMD), 199, 206
Ductus deferens, 136
Duodenal ulcers, 535
Duodenum, 533, 537
Dural sinuses, 288, 289
Dura mater, 266
Dwarfism, 323, 338
Dysmenorrhea, 620, 634
Dysplasia, 98
Dyspnea, 646
Dysrhythmias, 395
Dysuria, 593

E
Eardrum, 357, 359
Ear(s)
  diseases of, 360–361, 369–370
  drugs for, 370
  external, 356, 357
  hearing, 356–361, 717
  inner, 356, 358–359, 361
  middle, 356, 357–358
  overview, 356
  sound conduction, 357
Ecchymosis, 219
Eccrine glands, 220
ECG, 395, 669
Echocardiography, 389
E. coli (Escherichia coli), 18
Ectopic pregnancy, 635
Eczema, 240
ED. *See* Erectile dysfunction (ED)
Efferent arterioles, 569
Eggs, 603
Ejaculation, 625–626
Ejaculatory duct, 623
EKG, 395, 669
Elastic laminae, 408
Electrical synapses, 264
Electrocardiogram (ECG/EKG), 395, 669
Electrocardiograph, 395
Electrolytes, 58, 399, 585, 657
Electromyogram (EMG), 199
Electrons, 57
Elements, 56–58
Ellipsoidal joints, 155
Embolism, 37, 418
Embolus, 413, 414
Embryo, 605
EMG, 199
Emphysema, 455, 456, 457, 458–459, 471
Empirical method. *See* Scientific method
Empyema, 464
Emulsification, 545
Emulsifiers, 540
Enamel, 525
Endemic disease, 4
Endocarditis, 415
Endocardium, 380
Endochondral ossification, 150, 151
Endocrine cells, 533
Endocrine glands, 128
Endocrine system
  adrenal glands, 329
  control of hormone activity in, 315–318
  cortisol and stress response, 335–336
  diseases of, 338–339
  drugs for, 339
  general discussion, 128–129
  gonads, 336
  hormones in, 313–315
  hypothalamus, 319
  organization of, 312–315
  organs in, 122, 312–313
  overview, 311
  pancreas, 325, 329
  pineal gland, 325
  pituitary, 320–323
  prostaglandins, 337
  thymus gland, 325
  thyroid gland, 324–325, 326–328
  wellness, 717
Endocytosis, 84, 86
Endolymph, 359

Endometriosis, 610, 611, 634
Endometrium, 609
Endomysium, 196
Endoplasmic reticulum
    general discussion, 90
    rough, 90
    smooth, 90
Endorphins, 264
Endoscope, 670
Endoscopy, 670
Endosteum, 147
End-stage renal failure, 587
English system, 11, 740, 742–746
Enuresis, 593
Enzymes
    in blood testing, 658
    cardiac, 392
    digestive, 523, 538, 546
    phenylketonuria and, 94
    in reactions, 67–69, 94
Eosinophils, 401, 402, 492, 653
Ependymal cells, 255
Epicardium, 380
Epicondyle, 148
Epidemic, 4
Epidemiology, 4
Epidermis, 126, 217–218
Epididymis, 136, 621, 622
Epidural, 272
Epidural space, 267
Epigastric region, 41, 42
Epiglottis, 444–445, 527
Epilepsy, 261
Epimysium, 196
Epinephrine, 264, 300, 329
EpiPen, 509, 512
Epiphyseal plate, 151
Epiphysis, 145
Epithelial membranes, 112–113
Epithelial tissue
    columnar cells, 112
    cuboidal cells, 112
    general discussion, 112–113
    melanoma and, 121
    pseudostratified, 112
    simple, 112
    squamous cells, 112
    stratified, 112
    transitional cells, 112
    types and locations of, 113
Epithelium, 440–441
Erectile dysfunction (ED), 626–627, 635
Erection, 625–626
Erosion, 237
Erythema infectiosum, 243
Erythrocytes. *See* Red blood cells (RBCs)
Erythrocytopenia, 421
Erythrocytosis, 421
Erythropoiesis, 401, 451
Erythropoietin, 451
Esophageal stricture, 549
Esophagus, 133, 443, 528–529
ESP. *See* Extrasensory perception (ESP)
Estrogen, 336, 617, 619
Ethical pattern of knowing, 678
Etiology, 4
etiology, 17
Eukaryotic cell, 95, 603
Eustachian tubes, 358, 359, 442
Eversion, 157
Exacerbation, 17

Excitable cells, 257–258
Exercise, 169, 711, 723, 739
Exocrine, 312
Exocytosis, 85, 86
Expectorants, 472
Experimental investigations, 682–683
Expulsion stage, 629, 631
Extensibility, 183
Extension, 156, 194, 195
Extensor muscle, 194
External, 37, 38
External auditory meatus, 357, 359
External ear, 356, 357, 359
External genitalia, 136, 611–612
External intercostal, 193
External otitis, 360, 369
External respiration, 434, 435
External urethral sphincter, 590
Extracorporeal shock wave lithotripsy, 573, 574
Extrasensory perception (ESP), 347
Extubation, 443
Exudative macular degeneration, 351
Eyeball, 347, 350
Eyelashes, 347
Eyelids, 347, 350
Eye muscles, 350
Eye(s)
    disorders of, 350–354, 367, 368–369
    dominance, 355
    drugs for, 370
    external structures of, 347–348, 349, 350
    injuries, 350–354
    internal structures of, 348–349, 350
    refractive surgery, 355
    sight, 347–355, 717

F

Facet, 148
Facial muscles, 189
Facial nerve, 290
Facilitated diffusion, 82–83, 86
Factor-label method, 745–748
Fallopian tubes, 607, 608–609, 615
False negatives, statistical testing, 693
False positives, statistical testing, 693
Familial hypercholesterolemia, 86
Fats, 64
Fecal testing, 665–666
Feedback
    negative, 13
    positive, 14
Female reproductive system
    anatomy of, 607–612
    physiology of, 613–620
    pregnancy, 628–632
Femoral, 45
Femoral arteries, 384
Femur, 144, 169
Fermentation, 202
Ferrous, 56
Fertilization, 605
Fetus, 605
Fever, 14, 493
Fever blisters, 221, 222
Fibrillations, 397, 419
Fibrin, 412
Fibrinogen, 400, 412
Fibroblasts, 226
Fibromyalgia syndrome (FMS), 192, 206

Fibrous joints, 154
Fifth disease, 243
Fight-or-flight response, 254, 580
Filtration, 81–82, 86, 566
Filtration, in urinary system, 576–578, 579–580
Fimbria, 608
Fine anatomy, 2
Fingernails, 230–231
fingerprinting, 701, 704–705
Fingerprinting, DNA, 701, 704–705
Fingerprints, 703–704
First-degree burn, 227, 229
Fissures
    in central nervous system, 267
    horizontal, 464
    oblique, 464
    in skin, 237
Flaccid, 184
Flaccid paralysis, 297
Flagella, 91
Flat bones, 144
Flexibility of cartilage, 154
Flexion, 156, 194, 195
Flexor muscle, 194
Floating ribs, 163
Flossing, 723
Fluorine, 57
Flutter, 397, 420
FMS. *See* Fibromyalgia syndrome (FMS)
Follicle, 232, 614
Follicle stage, 613
Follicle-stimulating hormone (FSH), 321, 613, 617
Follicular phase, 614
Folliculitis, 219, 240
Fontanels, 153
Food cravings, 724
Food poisoning, 723
Food pyramid, 715
Foramen, 148
Forensic science
    bones in, 703
    definition of, 700
    disease detection with, 701
    DNA fingerprinting, 701, 704–705
    fingerprints in, 703–704
    and hair, 233
    history and, 701
    murder in, 702
    overview, 700–701
    primitive surgery in, 701
    remains identification with, 702
Foreskin, 622
Formed elements, 399, 400, 649, 650
Fossa, 148
Fourth-degree burns, 228
Fowler's position, 33
Fraction method, 745–748
Fractures
    closed, 168
    comminuted, 168, 169
    compound, 168
    general discussion, 168–169
    greenstick, 168
    hairline, 168
    open, 168, 169
    reduction of, 168
    simple, 168, 169
    spiral, 168
Free nerve endings, 365

Frenulum, 522
Friction ridges, 703
Frontal lobe, 277, 278
Frontal plane, 36, 37
FSH. *See* Follicle-stimulating hormone (FSH)
Fugu, 259
Full-thickness burns, 228, 229
Functional layer, 609
Functional unit of muscle, 196–198
Fundus
  of stomach, 531
  of uterus, 609
Fungal infections, 223, 242
Fungi, 101, 102, 103–104
Furuncle, 238

G

Gallbladder, 133, 538, 545–546, 547
Gallstones, 547, 551
Gametes, 603
Ganglion, 298
Gap junction, 264
Gases, atmospheric, 434
Gas exchange
  disorders, 451
  in lungs, 434–435
  in plants, 435
Gas trapping, 456
Gastric gland, 531, 533
Gastric phase, 533, 534
Gastric ulcers, 535
Gastrin, 533, 538
Gastritis, 535, 552
Gastrocnemius, 193
Gastroenteritis, 552
Gastroesophageal reflux disease (GERD), 533, 535, 536, 550
Gastrointestinal (GI) system
  accessory organs, 543–547
  diseases of, 549–555
  drugs for, 556
  esophagus, 528–529
  general discussion, 132–133
  large intestine, 541–543
  mouth and oral cavity, 522–527
  organs in, 123
  overview, 519–522
  pharynx, 527
  small intestine, 537–540
  stomach, 531–536
  symptoms of digestive disorders, 548
  walls of alimentary canal, 529–530
  wellness, 715–716
Gastroscope, 671
Gastroscopy, 671
GBS. *See* Guillain-Barré syndrome (GBS)
Gel layer, 441
General senses, 346–347
Genes, 88
Genitalia, 607
Genital warts, 223, 242, 719
Genitourinary system, 136, 708
GERD. *See* Gastroesophageal reflux disease (GERD)
Geriatric patients
  body changes in, 706
  brain function in, 706, 707
  cardiovascular system in, 707
  genitourinary system in, 708

gustatory changes in, 707
  integumentary system in, 708
  nervous system in, 707
  overview, 705–706
  polypharmacy in, 708–709
  special considerations with, 19
Germinal matrix, 230
GH. *See* Growth hormone (GH)
GHIH. *See* Growth hormone-inhibiting hormone (GHIH)
GHRH. *See* Growth hormone-releasing hormone (GHRH)
GI. *See* Gastrointestinal (GI) system
Giantism, 323
Giardia, 104
Gigantism, 323, 337, 338
Gingiva, 525
Gingivitis, 527, 550
GI tract, 520. *See also* Gastrointestinal (GI) system
Glans penis, 622
Glasgow Coma Scale, 281
Glaucoma, 351
Glia, 117, 118
Glial cells, 255
Gliding joints, 155
Globulins, 400
Glomerular capsule, 570
Glomerular filtrate, 570
Glomerular filtration, 572, 576–578, 579–580
Glomerulonephritis, 581, 594
Glomerulosclerosis, 581, 594
Glomerulus, 569, 570
Glossopharyngeal nerve, 290
Glottic mechanism, 444
Glottis, 444
Glucagon, 329
Glucocorticoids, 331, 472
Glucophage, 339
Glucose
  in cellular respiration, 92
  in diabetes, 93
  humoral control of, 318
  muscles and, 202
  pancreas and, 329, 330
Glucose test, 662, 663
Gluteal, 45
Gluten-induced enteropathy, 553
Gluteus maximus, 193
Glycerol, 64
Glycogen, 63, 202, 329
Glycosuria, 593
GnRH. *See* Gonadotropin-releasing hormone (GnRH)
GnRH agonists. *See* Gonadotropin releasing hormone (GnRH) agonists
Goblet cells, 529
Goiter, 327, 328
Golgi apparatus, 90–91
Gonadotropin-releasing hormone (GnRH), 321, 617
Gonadotropin releasing hormone (GnRH) agonists, 636
Gonads, 128, 336, 605
Gonorrhea, 719
Gout, 158, 172
Graafian follicle, 615
Grafting, for burns, 228
Granular pneumocytes, 452
Granulocytes, 652
Granulosa cells, 614, 615
Graphing data

bar graphs, 689–690
  common errors, 692
  scatter plots, 690–691
  summary tables, 692
Graves' disease, 326–327, 328, 338
Greater curvature, 531
Greenstick fracture, 168
GRH. *See* Gonadotropin-releasing hormone (GnRH)
Gross anatomy, 2
Growth, bone, 149
Growth hormone (GH), 321, 323
Growth hormone-inhibiting hormone (GHIH), 321
Growth hormone-releasing hormone (GHRH), 321
Growth plate, 151
Guardisil, 609
Guillain-Barré syndrome (GBS), 262, 302
Gum disease, 550
Gustatory sense, 362, 707
Gyri, 277

H

Hair, 126, 232–234, 702, 723
Hair follicles, 126
Hairline fracture, 168
Hammer, 358
Hamstrings, 193
Hand(s)
  fingerprints, 703–704
  nails, 230–231
  skeletal muscles in, 190
  washing, 718
Hard palate, 522
Hashimoto's thyroiditis, 326, 338
Haversian system, 147
Hay fever, 470
HCG. *See* Human chorionic gonadotropin (HCG)
Hct. *See* Hematocrit (Hct)
Head injuries, 280–283
Head lice, 234
Head of bone, 148
Health, maintaining. *See* Wellness
Hearing, 356–361, 717
Heart
  arrhythmias, 395
  cardiac cycle, 382–386, 393–396
  cardiac muscle, 117, 182, 183, 204–205, 385
  conduction system of, 394
  definition of, 378
  diagnostic tests, 669–670
  electrical conduction problems, 419–420
  electrical disturbances, 397–398
  electric pathway in, 393–396
  enzymes in, 392
  fibrillations, 397, 419
  flutter, 397, 420
  function of, 129, 380–381
  jugular venous distension, 34
  murmur, 417
  overview, 380
  pacemakers, 397
  pulse, 383–384
  pump problems, 387–389
  structure of, 380–381
  vessel problems, 389–391
  wellness, 712–713
Heart attacks, 398, 419, 423
Heart block, 397, 420

Heartburn, 535
Heart failure, 387, 388, 415, 416
Heat therapy, 365
Helium, 57
Hematocrit (Hct), 651, 656
Hematology
    blood composition, 399–401
    blood types, 403–405, 407
    inflammation, 402
    overview, 399
    problems related to, 420–422
    red blood cells, 401
    thrombocytes, 403
    transfusions, 403–405
    white blood cells, 401–402
Hematoma, 168, 281, 415
Hematuria, 573
Hemispheres, brain, 277
Hemodialysis, 589
Hemoglobin (Hgb), 401, 451, 650, 652, 656
Hemolytic, 651
Hemolytic uremic syndrome, 585, 594
Hemophilia, 413, 421
Hemopoiesis, 146
Hemorrhoids, 543, 554
Hemostasis, 412
Hemothorax, 464
Henle, loop of, 571
Heparin, 401, 402
Hepatic duct, 545
Hepatic portal vein, 544
Hepatitis, 547, 552
Hernias, 42, 550, 554
Herniated disk, 165
Herpes, 221, 240, 243, 719
Herpes simplex type 1, 222
Herpes simplex type 2, 222
Herpes varicella, 221–222
Herpes zoster, 101, 222
Heterografting, 228
Hgb. *See* Hemoglobin (Hgb)
Hiatal hernia, 550
Hilum, 464
Hinge joints, 155
Hip, skeletal muscles in, 191
Histamine, 364, 494
Hives, 240, 243
HIV (Human immunodeficiency virus), 502, 510
Hodgkin's disease, 486, 510
Hodgkin's lymphoma, 486
Holter monitor, 669
Homeostasis
    blood and, 399
    body temperature and, 12–14
    definition of, 12
    endocrine system and, 315–317
    negative feedback, 12, 315–317
    positive feedback, 14, 316–317
Homunculus, 286
Hordeolum, 350–351
Horizontal fissures, 464
Horizontal plane, 35
Hormonal control, 317
Hormones
    control of levels of, 315–318
    definition of, 312
    in digestive process, 538
    endocrine system, 128
    in endocrine system, 313–315
    in female reproductive system, 617–618

kidneys and, 583–584
    in male reproductive system, 625
    names of, 319
    neurotransmitters versus, 314
    during pregnancy, 619
Horns, in nervous system, 267–268
HPV. *See* Human papilloma virus (HPV)
Human chorionic gonadotropin (HCG), 618, 619, 625
Human immunodeficiency virus (HIV), 502, 510
Human life cycle, 605–606
Human papilloma virus (HPV), 609
Humoral control, 317, 318
Huntington's disease, 304
Hydrocele, 621, 622
Hydrocephalus, 291, 303
Hydrochloric acid, 59
Hydrocortisone, 339
Hydrogen, 57, 59
Hydrogen bonds, 62
Hydrolysis reactions, 67
Hydrophilic, 61
Hydrophobic, 62
Hydrostatic pressure, 392
Hydrothorax, 464
Hymen, 610–611
Hypercholesterolemia, 86, 326
Hyperextension, 156
Hyperlipidemia, 421
Hyperopia, 351, 352, 353
Hyperpituitarism, 323
Hyperplasia, 98
Hyperpolarization, 258
Hypersensitivity reaction, 18, 508
Hypertension, 418, 587
Hyperthyroidism, 326–327
Hypertrophy, 98, 184
Hyperventilation, 662
Hypochondriac region, 41, 42
Hypodermis, 217, 221
Hypogastric region, 41, 42
Hypoglossal nerve, 290
Hypoglycemia, 332
Hypopituitarism, 323
Hypotension, 34
Hypothalamus
    fevers, 14
    function of, 128, 313
    general discussion, 287, 319
    homeostasis, 13
    hormones, 321
    targets and associated hormones, 320
Hypotheses
    overview, 680–681
    testing, 682–685
Hypothyroidism, 326, 327, 337

I
IBS. *See* Irritable bowel syndrome (IBS)
IDDM. *See* Insulin-dependent diabetes mellitus (IDDM)
Identification, of remains, 701
Idiopathic disease, 4
Ileocecal orifice, 541
Ileocecal valve, 537
Ileum, 537
Immune response, 18
Immune system
    antibodies, 488

antigens, 488
    components of, 489–494
    in defense system, 507–509
    diseases of, 510–511
    drugs for, 511–512
    function of, 495–506
    general discussion, 131–132
    innate versus adaptive immunity, 488–489
    organs in, 123
    overview, 488
    wellness, 718
Immunity
    acquired, 489
    adaptive, 488–489, 496, 498–501
    antibody mediated, 503
    artificial active, 505
    artificial passive, 505
    cell-mediated, 504, 505
    innate, 488–489, 495–496
    natural active, 505
    natural passive, 505
Immunization, 506, 718
Immunotherapy, 98
Impacted wisdom tooth, 550
Impotence, 626–627
Impulse conduction, 258, 259–260
Incisors, 525, 526
Incontinence, 592, 595, 708
Incus, 358
Independent variables, experimental investigations, 682
Indirect contact, 19
Indirect testing, hypotheses, 682
Infarct, 388
Infection
    bacterial, 96
    in bones, 170
    chain of, 21
    fungal, 103–104
    in joints, 170
    nosocomial, 4
    protozoan, 104
    of skin, 221–224
    viral, 103
Infectious hepatitis, 547–548
Inferences, drawing, 692–695
Inferior, 35
Inferior vena cava, 381
Infertility, 629
Inflammation, 170, 402, 492–494
Inflammatory response, 18, 492–494
Influenza, 445, 470
Infundibulum, 608
Ingestion, 521, 522
Inguinal hernia, 42, 554
Inguinal region, 41, 42
Injections, 230
Innate immunity, 488–489, 495–496
Inner ear, 356, 357, 358–359, 361
Inotropism, 394
Insertion, point of, 192, 193
In situ keratomileusis (LASIK) surgery, 355
Insula, 277, 278
Insulin, 83, 329, 339
Insulin-dependent diabetes mellitus (IDDM), 93
Integumentary system
    definition of, 216
    diseases of, 238–242
    drugs for, 244
    functions, 216
    general discussion, 126

in geriatric patients, 708
hair, 232–234
medicine delivery via, 230
nails, 230–231
organs in, 122
overview, 215
skin, 217–229
temperature regulation, 235–236
wellness, 712
Interatrial septum, 381
Intercalated disc, 204, 205, 385
Interferons, 492
Interleukins, 492
Interlobar arteries, 569
Internal, 37, 38
Internal intercostal, 193
Internal respiration, 434, 435
Internal urethral sphincter, 590
Interneurons, 257
Interphase, 96
Interstitial cystitis, 592
Interstitial space, 452
Interventricular septum, 381
Intervertebral disks, 165
Intestinal phase, 533, 534
Intestine
    large, 541–543
    small, 537–540
Intracoronary stent, 391
Intradermally, 230
Intramembranous ossification, 149
Intrinsic factor, 532
Intubation, 443
Intussusception, 554
Inversion, 157
Investigations
    comparative, 682
    descriptive, 682
    experimental, 682–683
Involuntary muscle, 125, 183
Iodine, 57
Ionic bonds, 60, 61
Ions, 56–58
Iris, 348, 350
Iron, 56
Iron-deficiency anemia, 406
Irregular bones, 144–145
Irritable bowel syndrome (IBS), 554
Ischemia, 387, 575
Ischemic nephropathy, 594
Islets of Langerhans, 329
Isthmus, 608, 609

J

Jaundice, 219
Jejunum, 537
Jock itch, 223, 242
Joint(s)
    ball-and-socket, 154, 155
    cartilaginous, 154
    condyloid, 155
    dislocation, 159
    disorders, 158–159, 170
    ellipsoidal, 155
    fibrous, 154
    general discussion, 154–155
    gliding, 155
    hinge, 155
    movement of, 156–157

pain in, 175
pivot, 154, 155
saddle, 155
synovial, 116, 153, 154
Jugular venous distension (JVD), 34
Junction, 257
Juxtaglomerular apparatus, 584
JVD. *See* Jugular venous distension (JVD)

K

Keloids, 227, 240
Keratin, 218, 232
Keratinized, 230
Ketone bodies test, 664
Ketonuria, 664
Kidney disease, 586–587, 594
Kidneys
    damage to, 575, 578
    definition of, 566
    dialysis, 585, 589
    electrolyte balance, 585
    external anatomy, 567–568
    failure of, 585–587, 594
    fluid chemistry, 576
    function of, 570–571, 723
    in geriatric patients, 708
    internal anatomy, 568–570
    nephrons, 570–571
    polycystic kidney disease (PKD), 573
    transplants, 585, 586, 590
    in urinary system, 135
Kidney stones, 547, 572–573, 574, 593
Kinesiology, 196
Knee-jerk reflex, 274
Kyphosis, 165, 166, 173

L

Labia, 136, 522
Labia majora, 611
Labia minora, 612
Labor, 628, 629, 631
Laboratory testing. *See* Diagnostic testing
Labyrinth, 356, 359
Labyrinthitis, 361, 369
Lacrimal apparatus, 347, 350
Lacrimal gland, 347
Lactase, 538, 540
Lacteal, 538, 539
Lactic acid, 202
Lactose intolerance, 540
Language
    abbreviations, 9
    combining forms, 6, 8
    importance of, 1
    medical terminology, 6–8
    metric system, 11
    overview, 5
    prefixes, 7, 8
    suffixes, 7, 8
Laparoscope, 671
Laparoscopy, 671
Large intestine, 133, 541–543
Laryngitis, 444, 470
Laryngopharynx, 443, 527
Laryngotracheobronchitis (LTB), 445
Larynx, 131, 443–444
LASIK surgery, 355

Lasix, 595
Lateral, 36, 38
Lateral view, 47
Laughter, 739
Lazy eye, 352, 368
LDL. *See* Low-density lipoprotein (LDL)
Lead poisoning, 701
Leads, electrocardiogram, 669
Learning theory, 733
Left, 38
Left atrium, 382
Left bundle branch, 396
Left lower quadrant (LLQ), 44
Left main stem, 447
Left upper quadrant (LUQ), 44
Left ventricle, 382, 383
Leg, skeletal muscles in, 191
Leisure time, for stress management, 738
Lens, eye, 348, 350
LES. *See* Lower esophageal sphincter (LES)
Lesions, skin, 237
Lesser curvature, 531
Leukemia, 405, 406, 422, 491, 510
Leukocytes. *See* White blood cells (WBCs)
Leukocytopenia, 422
Leukocytosis, 406, 422, 649, 652–653
Leukopenia, 404, 406, 649, 653
Leukoplakia, 527, 550
LH. *See* Luteinizing hormone (LH)
Lice, 234, 241
Ligaments, 154–155, 185
Ligand gated, 200
Limbic system, 279
Lingual tonsils, 442, 483
Lingula, 464
Lipase, 538, 546
Lipids, 63, 64
Lipocytes, 221
Lithium, 57
Lithotripsy, 547, 574
Liver, 133, 545, 547
LLQ. *See* Left lower quadrant (LLQ)
Lobar arteries, 569
Lobar bronchi, 448
Lobes, cerebral, 277, 278
Lobules, 622
Local potential, 258–259
Lockjaw, 201, 206
Long bones, 144
Loop of Henle, 571
Lordosis, 165, 166
Lou Gehrig's disease, 296–297
Low-density lipoprotein (LDL), 86
Lower esophageal sphincter (LES), 529
Lower extremities, 165, 166
Lower respiratory tract
    alveolar capillary membrane, 450–452
    bony thorax, 464–465
    breathing, 465–469
    diseases of, 454–460
    general discussion, 447–450
    housing of lungs and related structures, 462–463
    lungs, 464
    pulmonary function testing, 452–453, 460
LTB. *See* Laryngotracheobronchitis (LTB)
Lumbar puncture, 272
Lumbar region, 41, 42, 45
Lumbar vertebrae, 43, 164
Lumen, 409
Lungs
    cancer, 469, 724

cigarettes, effect on lung cilia, 92
diseases of, 454–460
function of, 131
general discussion, 464
lower respiratory tract, 447–453
overview, 436
pleural space problems, 463–464
pulmonary function testing, 452–453, 460, 671–672
volumes and capacities, 453
wellness, 713–714
Lunula, 230
Lupus, 498, 510
LUQ. *See* Left upper quadrant (LUQ)
Luteal phase, 614
Luteinizing hormone (LH), 321, 613, 617
Lyme disease, 224, 241
Lymph, 115, 481
Lymphadenitis, 486
Lymphatic duct, right, 483
Lymphatic fluid, 481, 485
Lymphatic sinuses, 482
Lymphatic system
    cancer stages and, 486–487
    in defense system, 507–509
    disorders, 486
    general discussion, 131–132, 480–485
    organs in, 123, 485
Lymphatic trunks, 483
Lymphatic vessels, 132, 482, 484
Lymph capillaries, 481
Lymph nodes, 131, 132, 482
Lymphocytes
    activation, 498–499
    in blood, 401, 402
    differentiation, 498, 499
    in immune response, 492
    in lymph nodes, 131, 482
    proliferation, 500–501
    selection, 496
Lymphocytic leukemia, 491
Lymphoma, 510
Lysis, 492
Lysosomes, 91, 92, 401, 402

M

Macrophages, 492, 495
Macroscopic anatomy, 2
Macular degeneration, 351
Macule, 237
Magnetic resonance imaging (MRI), 46, 48
Major calyces, 568
Malabsorption syndrome, 555
Malaria, 104
Male reproductive system
    anatomy of, 621–624
    diseases of, 623–624
    physiology of, 625–627
Malignant melanoma, 241, 243
Malignant tumors, 98
Malleus, 358
Maltase, 538
Mammary glands, 136, 612
Mammograms, 632–633
Manganese, 57
Manubrium, 163
Margination, 493
Massage therapists, 203
Masseter, 193

Mast cells, 492
Mast cell stabilizers, 472
Mastication, 521
Mastitis, 632
Mastoiditis, 361
Mathematics, 740–748
MCS. *See* Minimally conscious state (MCS)
Mean value, 687
Measurement
    apothecary system, 742
    conversion of units, 745–748
    English system, 11, 740, 742–746
    mathematics, 740–748
    metric system, 11, 740, 742–746
    systems of, 741–744
Meatus, 148
Mechanical vector, 19
Medial, 36, 38
Median plane, 36
Median value, 687
Mediastinum, 462
Medical terminology, 6–8
Medulla, 232
Medulla oblongata, 278, 465
Medullary canal, 145
Medullary cavity, 145
Megakaryocytes, 403
Meibomian glands, 221
Meiosis, 97, 99, 603–604
Melanin, 218, 233
Melanocytes, 218
Melanoma, 121, 720–721
Melatonin, 325
Membrane(s)
    alveolar-capillary, 436, 450–452
    cell, 78–79, 88
    cutaneous, 114
    epithelial, 113–114
    mucous, 114
    parietal, 114
    serous, 114
    synovial, 114
    visceral, 114
Memory aids, 733
Memory B cells, 503
Memory T cells, 504
Menarche, 613
Mengele, Josef, 702
Ménière's disease, 361, 370
Meninges, 266–267, 278–279
Meningitis, 118–119, 279
Menopause, 613
Menses, 614
Menstral disorders, 618, 620
Menstrual cycle, 613–620
Menstruation, 614
Menstruation stage, 613
Mesometrium, 609
Mesosalpinx, 609
Mesovarium, 607
Metabolic syndrome, 12
Metabolism
    anabolism, 67
    catabolism, 12, 67
    definition of, 12
    dehydration synthesis, 67
    general discussion, 67
    hydrolysis reactions, 67
Metaphase, 96, 97
Metaplasia, 98

Metastasis, 98
Metric system, 11, 740, 742–746
MG. *See* Myasthenia gravis (MG)
MI. *See* Myocardial infarction (MI)
Microglia, 255
Microorganisms
    bacteria, 99, 100, 104–105
    and disease, 103–104
    fungi, 101, 102
    protozoa, 101, 102
    viruses, 100–101
Microscopic anatomy, 2
Microvilli, 538, 539
Midbrain, 278
Middle ear, 356, 357–358, 359
Midsagittal plane, 36
Military time, 14
Mineralocorticoids, 331
Minimally conscious state (MCS), 278
Minor calyces, 568
Miotic agents, 370
Mitochondria, 89
Mitochondrial myopathy, 206
Mitosis, 95
    in body, 97
    cancer and, 98
    general discussion, 95, 602–603
    versus meiosis, 99, 604
    phases in, 96–97
Mitotane, 339
Mitotic phase, 96
Mitral valve, 382, 383
Mixed nerves, 269
Mnemonics, 290, 733
Mode value, 687
MODS. *See* Multiple organ dysfunction syndrome (MODS)
Molars, 525, 526
Molecules
    biological, 63–66
    definition of, 56
Monocytes, 149, 401, 402
Mononuclear agranulocytes, 401
Mononucleosis, 486
Monosaccharides, 63
Morbidity, 17
Morphology, definition of, 3
Mortality, 17
Mosquitoes, 467
Motor coordination loop, 295
Motor neurons, 257
Motor system, 254, 294–295
Motor unit, 200
Mouth
    breathing through, 439
    in GI system, 522–527
    sense of taste, 362–363
    in skull, 161
Movement
    bone, 156–157
    of joints, 156–157
    skeletal muscle, 192–195, 196–198
MRI. *See* Magnetic resonance imaging (MRI)
MS. *See* Multiple sclerosis (MS)
Mucociliary escalator, 440–441
Mucolytics, 472
Mucosa, 529
Mucous cells, 533
Mucous membranes, 114, 116
Mucus
    excessive, 440

mucous versus, 116
in stool, 666
Multiple organ dysfunction syndrome (MODS), 130
Multiple sclerosis (MS), 261, 302
Mumps, 523
Murder, 702
Murmur, heart, 388–389, 417
Muscle(s)
  accessory, 468–469
  body temperature and, 202
  cardiac, 117, 182, 183, 204–205, 385
  contraction, 192, 194, 200
  diseases and conditions of, 205–206
  drugs for, 207
  extensor, 194
  eye, 350
  flexor, 194
  fuel for, 202
  functional unit of, 196–198
  involuntary, 125, 183
  movement, 192–195, 196–198
  names, 189
  point of insertion, 192, 193
  point of origin, 192, 193
  pulled, 185
  relaxation, 192, 194
  skeletal, 116, 182, 183, 185–191
  smooth, 117, 182, 183, 203–204
  strains, 185, 188, 205
  striated, 182
  synergistic, 192
  tears, 185, 188, 205
  tissue, 116–117
  tonus, 184
  types of, 182–183
  visceral, 125, 183, 203–204
  voluntary, 125, 182
Muscular dystrophy
  Becker's, 199
  Duchenne's, 199, 206
Muscularis externa, 529
Muscular system. See also Muscle(s)
  diseases and conditions of, 205–206
  general discussion, 182–191
  nervous system and, 200
  overview, 125, 181
  wellness, 711
Musculoskeletal system, 122
Myalgia, 192
Myasthenia gravis (MG), 199, 206, 302
Mycelia, 101
Mydriatic agents, 370
Myelin, 255
Myelin sheath, 118
Myelogenous leukemia, 491
Myocardial infarction (MI), 387–388, 419, 423
Myocardium, 380
Myofibrils, 196–197
Myofilament, 197
Myometrium, 609
Myopathy, 184
Myopia, 352, 353
Myosin, 197
Myplate.gov, 715
MyPyramid.gov, 715
Myringotomy, 360–361

N

Nail bed, 230
Nail body, 230
Nail root, 230
Nails, 126, 230–231
Nares, 436
Nasal, 45
Nasal cavity, 131, 437
Nasal polyps, 439
Nasal septum, 437
Nasopharynx, 442, 527
Natural active immunity, 505
Natural immunity, 488
Natural killer cells, 492, 495
Natural passive immunity, 505
Neck, of tooth, 525
Negative feedback loop, 12
Negative selection, 496
Nephritis, 581
Nephron loop, 571
Nephrons, 570–571
Nephropathy, 333, 580–581, 594
Nerves. See also Neurons
  cranial, 288–290, 291
  peripheral neuropathy, 272
  phrenic, 272, 273
  spinal, 265, 269
Nervous system. See also Brain
  autonomic, 254, 298–301, 394
  basic operation of, 252–254
  central, 253
  diseases of, 302–304
  drugs for, 304
  general discussion, 127
  in geriatric patients, 707
  motor pathologies, 296–297
  motor system, 294–295
  muscular system and, 200
  nervous tissue, 255–257
  neurons, 257–264
  organs in, 123
  overview, 251
  paralysis, 297
  parasympathetic, 254, 298, 300–301
  parts of, 252–254
  peripheral, 253
  somatic, 254, 292–294
  speed of, 254
  spinal cord and spinal nerves, 265–273
  sympathetic, 254, 298, 299–300, 301
  wellness, 710
Nervous tissue, 117–120
Neural control, 317
Neuroglia, 117, 118, 255
Neuromuscular synapse, 257
Neuron cell body, 256
Neurons
  action potentials, 258
  association, 257
  excitable cells, 257–258
  function of, 256–257
  impulse conduction, 259–260
  local potential, 258–259
  motor, 257
  in nervous tissue, 117, 118
  postganglionic, 299
  preganglionic, 299
  sensory, 257
  synapses, 262–264
Neurotransmitters, 262, 264, 314
Neutrons, 57

Neutrophils, 401, 492, 495
NIDDM. See Non-insulin-dependent diabetes mellitus (NIDDM)
Nitric oxide, 724
Nitroglycerin, 525
NK. See Natural killer cells
Nociceptors, 365
Nocturia, 593
Nodal cells, 393
Nodes of Ranvier, 259
Nodule, 237
Non-insulin-dependent diabetes mellitus (NIDDM), 93
Non-self-recognition, 488
Nonsteroidal anti-inflammatory drugs (NSAIDs), 497–498, 511
Norepinephrine, 264, 300, 329
Normal flora, 100
Nose
  in respiratory tract, 437–441
  rhinoplasty, 9
  sense of smell, 363–364
Nosocomial infection, 4
Nostrils, 436
NSAIDs. See Nonsteroidal anti-inflammatory drugs (NSAIDs)
Nuclear medicine, 487
Nucleases, 546
Nuclei, 279
Nucleic acids, 63, 65, 66
Nucleolus, 88
Nucleus, 87–88
Nurse cells, 622
Nutrition, 712, 715, 716, 719, 739
Nutritional disorders, 170
Nyctalopia, 352

O

Oblique fissures, 464
Obstructive jaundice, 547
Obstructive pulmonary disease, 454
Occipital lobes, 277, 278
Occult blood, 666
Occupational therapists, 203
Oculomotor nerve, 290
Odor of urine, 661
Olfaction, 436
Olfactory nerve, 290
Olfactory region, 437
Oligodendrocytes, 255, 259
Oliguria, 593
Oocyte, 614
Oogenesis, 614
Oogonia, 614
Open fracture, 168, 169
Open reduction, 168
Optic disk, 350, 354
Optic nerve, 290, 354
Oral, 45
Oral cavity, 161, 522–527
Oral contraceptives, 636
Oral disorders, 527
Oral hygiene, 723
Orbicularis oculi, 193
Orbit, 347, 350
Orbital, 45
Orbital cavity, 347
Organelles, 67, 75, 92
Organisms, 111

Organ of Corti, 359
Organ(s)
    definition of, 121
    overview, 111, 121
    systems, 122–136
    vital, 121
Origin, point of, 192, 193
Oropharynx, 442, 527
Orthopnea, 34
Orthostatic hypotension, 34
Osmosis, 81, 86, 582
Osmotic pressure, 81, 392
Ossicles, 357–358, 359
Ossification
    definition of, 149
    endochondral, 150, 151
    intramembranous, 149
Osteoarthritis, 154, 158, 171
Osteoblasts, 149
Osteoclasts, 149
Osteocytes, 147, 149
Osteogenesis, 149
Osteomalacia, 173
Osteomyelitis, 173
Osteons, 147
Osteoporosis, 151, 174
Osteoprogenitor cells, 149
Otitis media, 360–361, 369
Otosclerosis, 361
Otoscope, 670
Otoscopy, 670
Ova, 603
Oval window, 358
Ovarian cycle, 613, 616
Ovarian ligament, 607
Ovaries, 128, 136, 313, 336, 605, 607
Overactive bladder, 592–593, 594
overview, 579
Oviducts, 607, 608–609, 615
Ovulation, 614–615, 616
Ovulation stage, 613
Oxygen, 39, 432, 449
Oxygen debt, 202
Oxygen therapy, 472
Oxytocin, 14, 318, 321, 322, 619

P

Pacemaker, artificial, 397
Pacemaker cells, 393
Pain
    in geriatric patients, 707
    in joints, 175
    phantom, 365
    referred, 365
    sense of, 365–366
    symptom of disease, 15
Palatine tonsils, 442, 483
Palpitation, 420
Pancreas
    in endocrine system, 128, 313, 325, 329
    in gastrointestinal system, 133, 537, 546
Pancreatitis, 547
Pandemic, 4
Papillary muscles, 389
Pap test, 609
Papule, 237
Paralysis, 297
Paranasal sinuses, 441
Paraplegia, 272, 273

Parasympathetic division, 394
Parasympathetic nervous system, 254, 298, 299,
    300–301
Parathyroid gland, 128, 313, 325, 327
Parathyroid hormone (PTH), 327
Paravertebral ganglia, 300
Parietal cells, 531, 533
Parietal layer, 380
Parietal lobes, 277, 278
Parietal membrane, 114
Parietal pleura, 462
Parkinson's disease (PD), 296, 297, 303
Parotid salivary gland, 522–523
Partial-thickness burn, 227, 229
Partial thromboplastin time (PTT), 655
Passive transport, 79–82, 86
Patellar, 45
Patellar reflex, 274
Pathogens, 18, 99, 104–105, 480
Pathology, 4
Patterns of knowing, 678–679, 693–694
PA view. See Posteroanterior (PA) view
PCOS. See Polycystic ovarian syndrome (PCOS)
PD. See Parkinson's disease (PD)
Pectoralis major, 193
Pedal, 45
Pedal arteries, 384
Pediculosis, 234, 241
PEG tube, 534
Pelvis, 703
Penicillin, 105
Penis, 136, 621, 622
Pepsin, 531
Peptic ulcers, 535, 536, 553
Peptidase, 538
Percutaneous nephrolithotomy, 573, 574
Perforin, 504
Pericardial cavity, 41, 380
Pericarditis, 415
Pericardium, 380
Perilymph, 358
Perimetrium, 609
Perimysium, 196
Perinatal, 296, 297
Perineum, 611
Periodic table, 58
Periodontal disease, 527, 551
Periodontal ligament, 525
Periosteum, 145
Peripheral, 37, 38
Peripheral cyanosis, 38
Peripheral nervous system (PNS), 127, 253, 293
Peripheral neuropathy, 272, 303
Peripheral perfusion, assessing, 231
Peripheral resistance, 409
Peripheral vascular disease (PVD), 231, 415, 419
Peristalsis, 528
Peritoneal cavity, 529
Peritoneal dialysis, 589
Peritonitis, 544, 555
Peritubular capillaries, 569
Permanent teeth, 525, 526
Persistent vegetative state (PVS), 278, 280
Personal knowledge pattern of knowing, 678
Personal protective equipment (PPE), 21
Peyer's patches, 529
PFT. See Pulmonary function test (PFT)
PH
    acid-base relationship, 585
    blood and, 399
    of stool, 665

    urinalysis, 661, 662–663
    ventilation and, 466
Phagocytosis, 84, 85, 86, 401, 402
Phalanges, 160
Phantom pain, 365
Pharyngitis, 444, 470
Pharyngoesophageal sphincter, 528
Pharynx, 131, 133, 442–443, 522, 527
Phenylketonuria (PKU), 94
Phonation, 436
Phospholipid, 64
Photopigments, 354
Phrenic nerve, 272, 273, 465
PH scale, 59
Physical hazards, 683
Physical strategies for stress management, 738
Physical therapists, 203
Physiology, definition of, 3
Pia mater, 266
Pimples, 219
Pineal body, 287
Pineal gland, 313, 325
Pinkeye, 351, 367, 368
Pinna, 357, 359
Pinocytosis, 84, 85, 86
Pituitary gland, 128, 287, 313, 320–323
Pivot joints, 154, 155
PKD. See Polycystic kidney disease (PKD)
PKU. See Phenylketonuria (PKU)
Placenta, 628
Placental stage, 629, 631
Placenta previa, 635
Planes, of body, 35–37
Plantar, 45
Plantar fasciitis, 174
Plantar flexion, 156
Plantar warts, 222, 223, 242
Plants, gas exchange in, 435
Plaque
    in arteries, 389
    dental, 527
Plasma, 379, 399, 400, 647, 649, 650
Plasma cells, 503
Plasma membrane, 78–79
Plasma proteins, 400
Platelet count, 654–655, 656
Platelets, 400, 401, 403, 647
Pleural effusion, 464
Pleural fluid, 462
Plexuses, 269, 270
Plicae circulares, 538, 539
PMDD. See Premenstrual dysphoric disorder
    (PMDD)
PMS. See Premenstrual syndrome (PMS)
Pneumonia, 454, 455, 470
Pneumothorax, 463–464
PNS. See Peripheral nervous system (PNS)
Podocytes, 570
Point of insertion, 192, 193
Point of origin, 192, 193
Poison ivy, 243
Polar covalent bonds, 60–61
Polar ions, 58
Polarization, 258, 259
Polio, 271, 302
Polycystic kidney disease (PKD), 573, 593
Polycystic ovarian syndrome (PCOS), 620, 634
Polycythemia, 387, 422, 649
Polymorphonuclear granulocytes, 401
Polymorphonuclear leukocytes, 652
Polypharmacy, in geriatric patients, 708–709

Polyposis, 555
Polysomnography, 672
Polyuria, 593
Pons, 278
Popliteal arteries, 384
Pores of Kohn, 452
Position(s)
    anatomical, 32
    anatomic and physiologic changes and, 34
    body, 32–34
    Fowler's, 33
    prone, 33
    supine, 33
    Trendelenburg, 33
Positive feedback, 14, 315
Positive selection, 496
Postcentral gyrus, 284
Posterior, 37, 45
Posterior association area, 284
Posterior pituitary glands, 320, 321–322
Posteroanterior (PA) view, 47
Postganglionic neuron, 298, 299
Postpartum depression, 635
Post-polio syndrome (PPS), 271, 302
Potassium, 657
Powers of 10, 740–742
PPE. See Personal protective equipment (PPE)
PPS. See Post-polio syndrome (PPS)
Precapillary sphincters, 411
Precentral gyrus, 284
Precision, quantitative data, 685–686
Prednisone, 334–335, 339
Prefixes, 7, 8
Preganglionic neurons, 299
Pregnancy, 619, 628–632
Premature contraction, 420
Premenstrual dysphoric disorder (PMDD), 618,
    620, 634
Premenstrual syndrome (PMS), 618, 634
Prepuce, 612
Presbycusis, 361
Presbyopia, 351, 352
Pressure
    blood, in orthostatic hypotension, 34
    hydrostatic, 392
    osmotic, 392
Pressure points, 414, 416
Pressure ulcers, 238
Prevention, cancer, 720–722
Preventive medicine, 738
Primary bronchi, 448
Primary follicles, 615
Primary motor cortex, 284, 286
Primary movers, 192
Primary oocyte, 614
Primary ossification center, 151
Primary polycythemia, 406
Primary response, 503, 505
Primary somatic sensory cortex, 284, 286
Primary spermatocytes, 625
Primary teeth, 524–525
Primitive surgery, 701
Primordial follicles, 614, 615
Process, 148
Progesterone, 336, 617, 619
Progestins, 636
Prognosis, 17
Prokaryotic cells, 95
Prolactin, 319, 321, 619
Prolapse, 417
Proliferation, lymphocyte, 500–501

Proliferative phase, 614
Pronation, 157
Prone position, 33
Prophase, 96, 97
Proprioception, 366
Prostaglandins, 337, 511
Prostate, 136, 621, 623
Prostate cancer, 624, 635, 721
Proteinases, 546
Proteins, 63, 65
Protein test, 662, 663–664
Proteinuria, 664
Prothrombin, 401, 412
Prothrombin time (PT), 655
Pro time, 655
Protons, 57
Protozoa, 101, 102, 104
Protraction, 157
Proximal, 37, 38
Proximal tubule, 570–571, 582
Pseudostratified ciliated columnar epithelium,
    440–441
Pseudostratified columnar epithelium, 112
Psoas test, 44
Psoriasis, 241
PT. See Prothrombin time (PT)
PTH. See Parathyroid hormone (PTH)
PTT. See Partial thromboplastin time (PTT)
Ptyalin, 523
Pubic, 45
Pubic lice, 234
Pudendal cleft, 612
Puffer fish, 259
Pulled muscles, 185
Pulmonary arteries, 382
Pulmonary circulation, 384
Pulmonary edema, 387
Pulmonary function test (PFT), 452–453, 460, 671
Pulmonary semi-lunar valve, 382
Pulmonary system. See Respiratory system
Pulmonary tuberculosis, 470
Pulp, 525
Pulp cavity, 525
Pulse, 16, 383–384
Pupil, 348, 350, 370
Purkinje fibers, 396
Pus, 402
Pustules, 219, 234, 237
PVD. See Peripheral vascular disease (PVD)
PVS. See Persistent vegetative state (PVS)
P wave, 395
Pyloric sphincter, 531
Pylorus, 531
Pyorrhea, 551
Pyrexia, 402
Pyuria, 593

Q
QRS complex, 395
Quadriceps, 193
Quadriplegics, 272, 273
Qualitative data, 685
Quantitative data, 685–686

R
RA. See Rheumatoid arthritis (RA)
Radial arteries, 609

Radial keratotomy (RK), 355
Radial pulse, 384
Radiation therapy, 98
Radiocontrast agent, 384
Radiographs, 46–47
Radiology, 46–49
Radiolucent, 46
Radiopaque, 46
RBC. See Red blood cell count (RBC)
RBCs. See Red blood cells (RBCs)
Reabsorption, 566
Reaction(s)
    enzymes in, 67–69, 94
    hydrolysis, 67
    hypersensitivity, 18, 508
Rectum, 542
Rectum cancer, 721
Red blood cell count (RBC), 650–651, 656
Red blood cells (RBCs)
    in blood, 400, 401
    blood testing and, 647
    disorders, 406
    formed in bone marrow, 145, 146
    in sickle-cell anemia, morphology of, 3
Red bone marrow, 145, 146
Reduction division, 604
Reduction of bone, 168
Referred pain, 365
Reflexes, 270, 274
Reflux esophagitis, 553
Refractive eye surgery, 355
Refractory period, 258
Regions, of body, 41–45
Regulatory T cells, 504
Relapse, 17
Relaxation, muscle, 192, 194
Relaxation techniques, for stress management, 739
Remains identification, 701
Remission, 17
Renal artery, 569
Renal capsule, 567
Renal columns, 568
Renal corpuscle, 570
Renal cortex, 568
Renal disease, 586–587
Renal failure, 585–587, 594
Renal hilum, 567–568
Renal medulla, 568
Renal nephron, 569
Renal pelvis, 568
Renal pyramids, 568
Renal tubule, 570
Renal vein, 570
Renin-angiotensin-aldosterone system, 584
Repair, bone, 149
Repolarization, 258, 259
Reproduction
    asexual, 95, 97, 602–603
    cellular, 95, 602
    sexual, 97, 603–605
Reproductive system
    diseases of, 634–635
    drugs for, 636
    female anatomy, 607–612
    female reproductive physiology, 613–620
    general discussion, 136
    human life cycle, 605–606
    male anatomy, 621–624
    male reproductive physiology, 625–627
    organs in, 123

overview, 601
pregnancy, 628–632
sexual reproduction, 603–605
tissue growth and replacement, 602–603
wellness, 718–719
Respiration
cellular, 432
external, 434, 435
internal, 434, 435
ventilation versus, 434–435
Respiratory acidosis, 661
Respiratory bronchioles, 448
Respiratory region, 438–439
Respiratory system
airway and lungs, 436, 443
alveolar capillary membrane, 450–452
bony thorax, 464–465
breathing, 465–469
components of, 433
diseases of, 454–460, 469–471
drugs for, 472
elimination of carbon dioxide, 60
general discussion, 130–131
housing of lungs and related structures, 462–463
infections, 469–470, 472
larynx, 443–444
lower respiratory tract, 447–469
lungs, 464
organs in, 123
overview, 431–433
pharynx, 442–443
pulmonary function testing, 452–453, 460
sinuses, 441–442
upper airway, 436–441, 444–445
ventilation versus respiration, 434–435
wellness, 713–714
Rest, for stress management, 738
Resting cell, 258, 259
Reticular system, 278
Reticulospinal tract, 268, 269
Retina, 348, 350
Retinopathy, 351, 352, 369
Retraction, 157
Retroperitoneal organs, 529
Rheumatoid arthritis (RA), 158, 171, 497–498, 510, 512
Rh factor, 404
Rhinitis, 364
Rhinoplasty, 9
Rh-negative, 404
Rh-positive, 404
Ribonucleic acid (RNA), 88, 105
Ribosomes, 88
Ribs
bony thorax, 464–465
floating, 163
vertebrocostal, 163, 465
vertebrosternal, 163, 465
RICE sprain treatment, 159, 188
Rickets, 174
Right, 38
Right atrium, 381
Right bundle branch, 396
Right lower quadrant (RLQ), 43, 44
Right lymphatic duct, 483
Right main stem, 447
Right upper quadrant (RUQ), 43, 44
Right ventricle, 381
Rigor mortis, 201
Rima glottis, 444
Ringworm, 223, 224, 242

RK. See Radial keratotomy (RK)
RLQ. See Right lower quadrant (RLQ)
RNA. See Ribonucleic acid (RNA)
Rods, 354
Roentgenograms, 46–47
Root, of penis, 622
Root, of tooth, 525
Rotation, 157, 194
Rotator cuff tear, 159
Rough endoplasmic reticulum, 90
Round ligaments, 609
Routes of transmission, 19
Rubrospinal tract, 268, 269
Rugae, 531, 590
Rule of nines, 228, 229
RUQ. See Right upper quadrant (RUQ)

S
Sacral vertebrae, 43, 164
Sacrum, 43
Saddle joints, 155
Sadness versus depression, 736
Salivary glands, 133, 522–524
SA node, 393, 394
Sarcolemma, 198
Sarcomeres, 197–198
Sarcoplasmic reticulum (SR), 198
Sarin, 264
Satellite cells, 255
Scabies, 234, 242
Scale, 237
Scapular, 45
Scars, 227
Scatter plots, 690–691
Schwann cells, 255, 259
SCID. See Severe combined immune deficiency (SCID)
Scientific journals, 694–695
Scientific method
data collection, 685–687
data presentation, 689–692
drawing inferences, 692–695
formulating question, 680
hypotheses, 680–681
limitations of, 695
overview, 679
patterns of knowing, 678–679
testing hypotheses, 682–685
theories, 681
Scientific notation, 740–742
Sclera, 348, 350
Scoliosis, 165, 166, 175
Scrotum, 136, 621, 622
Seasonal allergic rhinitis, 470
Sebaceous glands, 126, 220–221, 233
Seborrheic keratosis, 242
Sebum, 220–221
Secondary disorders
in bones, 170
in joints, 170
Secondary follicle, 615
Secondary polycythemia, 406
Secondary response, 504, 505
Secondary spermatocytes, 625
Second-degree burns, 227, 229, 243
Secretin, 538, 545
Secretion, 566, 567
Secretory phase, 614
Sediment examination, 665

Segmental arteries, 569
Segmental bronchi, 448
Segmentation, 538
Selection, lymphocyte, 496
Selective serotonin reuptake inhibitors (SSRIs), 263
Self-recognition, 488
Semen, 625
Semicircular canals, 358, 359
Seminal vesicles, 136, 621, 622, 623
Seminiferous tubules, 622
Sensations, 127
Senses
cutaneous, 347
diseases, 368–370
drugs for, 370
general, 346–347
hearing, 356–361
organs in, 123
overview, 345–347
sight, 347–355
smell, 363–364
special, 346
taste, 362–363
touch, 364–366
visceral, 347
Sensorineural conduction, 359
Sensory neurons, 257
Sensory receptors, 126
Sensory system, 253, 717
Sepsis, 130
Septal cartilage, 437
Septic arthritis, 158, 171
Septicemia, 130
Serosa, 529
Serotonin, 264, 403
Serous membranes, 114
Serous pericardium, 380
Sertoli cells, 622
Serum, 401
Set point, 315
Setting bones, 168
Severe combined immune deficiency (SCID), 511
Sex chromosomes, 605
Sexually transmitted diseases (STDs), 719
Sexual reproduction, 97, 603–605
SG test. See Specific gravity (SG) test
Shaft, of penis, 622
Shape of stool, 665
Shingles, 101, 221, 222
Shin splints, 188, 206
Short bones, 144
Shoulder, skeletal muscles in, 190
Shunt, 291
SIADH. See Syndrome of inappropriate antidiuretic hormone (SIADH)
Sickle-cell anemia, 3, 406
Sight, 347–355, 717
Signals of stress, 736, 737
Signs, definition of, 15
Silent myocardial infarction, 398
Simple cells, 112
Simple fracture, 168, 169
Simple squamous epithelium, 452
Simple squamous pneumocytes, 448
Sinoatrial node, 393
Sinuses, 441–442
Sinuses, lymphatic, 482
Sinusitis, 444
Sinus of bone, 148
Skeletal muscle
anterior and posterior view of, 186–187, 190

of arm and shoulder, 190
drugs for, 207
facial, 189
general discussion, 185–188
movement, 192–195
overview, 116, 182, 183
Skeletal system. *See also* Bone
bones in, 124
diseases of, 171–175
general discussion, 124
overview, 143, 160
special regions of, 160–166
wellness, 710
Skeleton, 160–166
Skin
burns, 227–229
cleaning, 219
color and disease, 219
dermis, 218–219
epidermis, 217–218
function of, 126
healing, 225–227
infections of, 221–224
lesions, 237
medicine delivery via, 230
melanoma, 121
overview, 217
subcutaneous fascia, 221
sweat and sebaceous glands, 220–221
vitamin production and, 113
Skin cancer, 712
Skull, 161–162, 701
SLE. *See* Systemic lupus erythematosis (SLE)
Sleep apnea, 445
Sleep studies, 672
Small intestine, 133, 537–540
Smell, 363–364, 707
Smoking
and bone health, 169
effect on lung cilia, 92
history, 460
mortality, 723
quitting, 472
reproductive system and, 718
respiratory diseases and, 459, 713
Smooth endoplasmic reticulum, 90
Smooth muscle, 117, 182, 183, 203–204
Snellen eye chart, 355, 717
Sodium, 657
Sodium chloride, 58
Sodium ion channels, 198
Soft palate, 522
Sol layer, 441
Solute, 62, 81
Solutions, 62
Solvent, 62
Somatic nervous system, 254
Somatic sensation, 292
Somatic sensory association area, 284
Somatic sensory system, 292–294
Somatostatin, 339
Sonography, 48
Sound conduction, 357, 359
Spasms, muscle, 206
Spastic paralysis, 297
Special senses, 346
Specific gravity (SG) test, 660, 662
Sperm, 603, 625
Spermatic cord, 623
Spermatids, 625
Spermatogenesis, 625–627

Spermatogonia, 625
Spermatozoa, 625
Sphincters
cardiac, 529
in digestive system, 203–204
external urethral, 590
internal urethral, 590
lower esophageal, 529
pharyngoesophageal, 528
precapillary, 411
pyloric, 531
in respiratory system, 444
Sphygmomanometers, 686–687
Spina bifida, 719
Spinal blocks, 271–272
Spinal cavity, 41
Spinal column
abnormalities, 165, 166
general discussion, 164
as landmark, 43
Spinal cord
directional terms, 266
external anatomy of, 265–267
injury to, 272–273, 302
internal anatomy of, 267–269
knee-jerk reflex, 274
in nervous system, 127
pathways, 295
reflexes, 270
somatic sensory system, 292–293
spinal blocks, 271–272
spinal nerves, 269
Spinal nerves, 265, 269
Spinal roots, 269
Spinal tap, 272
Spine of bone, 148
Spinocerebellar tract, 293
Spinothalamic tract, 268, 293
Spiral fracture, 168
Spleen, 132, 484, 485
Spongy bone, 147
Spores, 101
Sprain, 159
Squamous carcinoma, 242
Squamous cells, 112
Squamous pneumocyte, 452
SR. *See* Sarcoplasmic reticulum (SR)
SSRIs. *See* Selective serotonin reuptake inhibitors (SSRIs)
Standard precautions, 20, 21
Stapedectomy, 361
Stapes, 358
Startle reflex, 270
Statistical testing, 693
STDs. *See* Sexually transmitted diseases (STDs)
Stenosis, 417
Stenotic, 388
Stents, 391
Sterile matrix, 230
Sternal, 45
Sternocleidomastoid, 193
Sternum, 144, 163, 464–465
Steroids, 64, 315, 334–335, 511, 717
Stirrup, 358
Stomach, 133, 531–536
Stomach acid disorders, 535
Stomach cancer, 723
Stomatitis, 527
Stool testing, 665–666
Strabismus, 352
Strains, 185, 188, 205

Stratified cells, 112
Stratum basale, 217
Stratum corneum, 218
Strep throat, 444
Stress
causes of, 735–736
chronic, 339
coping strategies, 737
depression, 736
exercise for, 739
leisure time for, 738
management, 734–740
misconceptions about, 734–735
nutrition and, 739
physical strategies for, 738
relaxation techniques for, 739
response, 335–336, 710
rest for, 738
signals of, 736, 737
Stress test, 670
Striated muscle, 116, 182
Stroke, 280–281
Stroke volume (SV), 409
Study skills, 731–734
Stupor, 280
Stye, 350–351, 367
Subarachnoid, 281
Subarachnoid space, 267, 288
Subcortical structures, 295
Subcutaneous, 230
Subcutaneous fascia, 217, 221
Subdural, 281
Subdural space, 267
Sublingually, 230
Sublingual medication, 525
Sublingual salivary glands, 523
Submandibular salivary glands, 523
Submucosa, 529
Subsegmental bronchi, 448
Substrates, 68
Sucrase, 538
Suffixes, 7, 8
Sugar test, 662, 663
Sulcus, 267, 277
Summary tables, 692
Sun exposure, 712
Superficial, 37, 38
Superior, 35
Superior vena cava, 381
Supination, 157
Supine position, 33
Surfactant, 451, 453
Surgery
for cancer, 98
LASIK, 355
primitive, 701
Surgical reduction, 168
Suspensory ligament, 607
Suture lines, 161
SV. *See* Stroke volume (SV)
Sweat glands, 126, 220–221
Swimmer's ear, 360, 369
Sympathetic division, 394
Sympathetic nervous system, 254, 298, 299–300, 301
Symptoms, definition of, 15
Synapses, 257, 262–264
Syndrome, 16
Syndrome of inappropriate antidiuretic hormone (SIADH), 322, 338
Syndrome X, 12

Synergistic muscles, 194
Synovial fluids, 154
Synovial joint, 116, 153, 154
Synovial membrane, 114
Synthroid, 339
Syphilis, 719
Systemic circulation, 385
Systemic lupus erythematosis (SLE), 498
Systems, 111
Systole, 382

T

Tachycardia, 6, 420
Tactile corpuscles, 364
Tailbone, 164
Tarsal glands, 221
Taste, 362–363, 707
Taste buds, 362
Tay-Sachs, 92
TB. *See* Tuberculosis (TB)
TBI. *See* Traumatic brain injury (TBI)
T cells, 492, 500–501, 504–505
Tears, muscle, 205
Teeth, 524–527
Telophase, 96, 97
Temperature, body
    adaptation, 364–365
    homeostasis and, 12–14
    integumentary regulation of, 235–236
    muscles and, 202
Temporal lobes, 277, 278
Tendinitis, 188, 205
Tendinosis, 188, 205
Tendonitis, 158, 175, 188
Tendons, 154, 185
Terminal bronchioles, 448
Terminal illness, 17
Testes, 128, 136, 313, 336, 605, 621–622
Testicles, 621–622
Testing, diagnostic. *See* Diagnostic testing
Testosterone, 336, 625, 627
Tetanus, 201, 206
Tetany, 327
Thalamus, 287
Thallium poisoning, 702
Theories, scientific, 681
Therapeutic oxygen, 449
Therapeutic steroids, 334–335
Third-degree burns, 228, 229
Thoracic, 45
Thoracic cage, 454, 465
Thoracic cavity, 41, 462
Thoracic duct, 483
Thoracic vertebrae, 43, 164
Thoracolumbar, 299
Thrombin, 412
Thrombocytes, 401, 403, 647
Thrombocytopenia, 413, 422, 649
Thrombosis, 413
Thrombus, 37, 413
Thymosin, 325
Thymus, 128, 132, 484, 485
Thymus gland, 313, 325
Thyroid cartilage, 443
Thyroid gland, 128, 313, 324–325, 326–328
Thyroid-stimulating hormone (TSH), 321, 324
Thyroid storm, 326
Thyrotropin-releasing hormone (TRH), 321, 324
Thyroxine, 324–325

TIAs. *See* Transient ischemic attacks (TIAs)
Tibialis anterior, 193
Time, 14
Tinea, 223
Tinea barbae, 242
Tinea capitis, 242
Tinea corporis, 224, 242
Tinea cruris, 223, 242
Tinea pedis, 223, 242
Tinea unguium, 224, 242
Tinnitus, 361, 370
Tissue(s)
    adipose, 115
    areolar, 115
    bone, 147
    connective, 115–116
    damage from diabetes, 119
    epithelial, 112–113
    growth and replacement, 602–603
    membranes, 113–114
    muscle, 116–117
    nervous, 117–120, 255–257
    overview, 111
    types of, 112–120
T lymphocytes, 485
TNF. *See* Tumor necrosis factor (TNF)
Tomatoes, 701
Tongue, 522
Tonsillitis, 444, 470, 483, 510
Tonsils, 483, 484
Tonus, 184
Topical creams, 244
Torn rotator cuff, 159
Touch, 292–293, 364–366
Toxic Shock Syndrome (TSS), 620
Trabecula, 147
Trachea, 131, 447
Tracheobronchial tree, 447, 448
Tracheostomy tubes, 443
Trachoma, 351
Traction, 168
Transdermal patches, 230, 244
Transfusions, blood, 403–405, 724
Transient ischemic attacks (TIAs), 281
Transitional cells, 112
Transmission
    airborne, 19
    common vehicle, 19
    contact, 19
    routes of, 19
    vector-borne, 19
Transplants, kidney, 585, 586, 590
Transport
    active, 79, 84–86
    in cells, 79–86
    passive, 79–82
Transverse colon, 542
Transverse plane, 35
Trauma
    in bones, 170
    in joints, 170
Traumatic brain injury (TBI), 280, 303
Trendelenburg position, 33
TRH. *See* Thyrotropin-releasing hormone (TRH)
Triceps brachii, 193
Tricuspid valve, 381
Trigeminal nerve, 290
Triglyceride, 64
Triiodothyronine, 324–325
Trochanter, 148
Trochlear nerve, 290

True capillaries, 411
TSH. *See* Thyroid-stimulating hormone (TSH)
TSS. *See* Toxic Shock Syndrome (TSS)
Tubal ligation, 629
Tubal pregnancy, 635
Tubercle, 148, 454
Tuberculosis (TB), 454
Tubular reabsorption, 572, 576, 577, 582–584, 585
Tubular secretion, 572, 576, 577, 582–584
Tumor necrosis factor (TNF), 492
Tumors
    benign, 98
    in bones, 170
    malignant, 98
Tunica albuginea, 607
Tunica externa, 407
Tunica interna, 407
Tunica media, 407
Tunica vaginalis, 622
Turbidity, urine, 662, 663
Turbinates, 438
T wave, 395
24-hour urine specimen, 659
Tympanic cavity, 356
Tympanic membrane, 357, 359
Types of blood, 403–405, 407

U

Ulcer
    duodenal, 535
    gastric, 535
    peptic, 535, 536, 553
Ulcerative colitis, 555
Ultrasound, 48
Umami, 362–363
Umbilical cord blood, 405
Umbilical hernia, 42
Umbilical region, 41, 42
Undernourishment, 716
Units, conversion of, 745–748
Universal donor, 404
Universal recipient, 404
Upper airway, 436–441, 444–445
Upper extremities, 165, 166
Urea, 576, 579, 655
Uremia, 585, 594
Ureter, 135, 566
Ureteroscopy, 573
Urethra
    definition of, 566, 590
    female, 135, 136, 612
    male, 135, 136, 621, 622
Urethral meatus, 590
Urinalysis, 579
    acetone, 664
    albumin, 663–664
    bacteria, 664
    color, 661
    concentration, 660–661
    dipstick test, 659
    general discussion, 658–659
    glucose, 663
    ketone bodies, 664
    odor, 661
    pH, 661, 662–663
    protein, 663–664
    sediment examination, 665
    specific gravity, 660
    sugar, 663

turbidity, 663
Urinary bladder, 135, 566, 590–591
Urinary system
    disorders of, 593–595
    drugs for, 595
    general discussion, 135
    kidneys in, 567–575
    organs in, 123
    overview, 565–567
    regulation of electrolyte balance, 58
    testing, 579
    urine formation in, 576–584, 590–591
Urinary tract infection (UTI), 592, 594, 595
Urination reflex, 590–591
Urine formation, 576–584, 590–591
Urticaria, 240, 243
Uterine arteries, 609
Uterine cancer, 721
Uterine contractions, as positive feedback, 14, 318
Uterine cycle, 613, 616
Uterine tubes, 136, 607, 608–609, 615
Uterus, 136, 607, 609
UTI. *See* Urinary tract infection (UTI)
Uvula, 522

V

Vaccinations
    chickenpox, 221–222
    meningitis, 118–119
    tetanus, 201
Vagina, 136, 607, 610–611
Vaginitis, 620, 635
Vagus nerve, 290, 394, 533
Valvular insufficiency, 388
Varicose veins, 419
Vasa recta, 569
Vascular shunt, 411
Vascular system, 407–415
Vas deferens, 621, 622–623
Vasectomy, 629
Vasoconstriction, 203, 235–236, 407, 409
Vasodilation, 203, 235, 407, 409
Vasopressin, 321
Vector
    biological, 19
    mechanical, 19
Vector-borne transmission, 19
Vegetative state, 280
Veins
    arteries versus, 380
    definition of, 378, 379
    function of, 129, 407
    general discussion, 408–409
    jugular venous distension, 34
    locations of major, 408
    varicose, 419

Venipuncture, 647
Ventilation, 434–435, 465–467
Ventral, 36
Ventral root, 269
Ventricles, 288, 381
Venules, 378, 379, 407
Vermiform appendix, 542
Verruca, 222
Vertebrae
    cervical, 43, 164
    coccyx, 43, 164
    as irregular bones, 145
    lumbar, 43, 164
    number of, 165
    sacral, 164
    sacrum, 43
    tailbone, 164
    thoracic, 43, 164
Vertebral column, 164
Vertebrocostal ribs, 163, 465
Vertebrosternal ribs, 163, 465
Vertigo, 361
Vesicles, 84, 221, 237, 262
Vestibular reflex, 270
Vestibular region, 437
Vestibule, 612
Vestibule chamber, 358
Vestibulocochlear nerve, 290, 359
Vibrissae, 437
Video skull-face superimposition, 702
Villi, 538, 539
Viral hepatitis, 552
Viral meningitis, 279
Viral tonsillitis, 483
Viruses, 100–101, 103
viruses, 105
Visceral layer, 380, 570
Visceral membrane, 114
Visceral muscle, 125, 183, 203–204
Visceral peritoneum, 529, 609
Visceral pleura, 462
Visceral senses, 347
Vision, 347–355, 717
Vital organs, 121
Vital signs, 15, 16
Vitamin A, 352, 715
Vitamin B, 715
Vitamin C, 715
Vitamin D, 113, 175, 715
Vitamin E, 715
Vitamin K, 715
Vitamins, 715
Vitreous humor, 348
Vocal cords, 436, 437, 444
Voluntary muscle, 125, 182
Volvulus, 555
Vomiting, 548, 556
Vulva, 607, 611–612

W

Walls of alimentary canal, 529–530
Wandering macrophages, 452
Warts, 222, 242
Waste disposal, 683–685
Water, 59, 61–62
Water immersion lithotripsy, 574
Waxes, 64
WBCs. *See* White blood cells (WBCs)
Weight loss, 336
Wellness
    cardiovascular system, 712–713
    endocrine system, 717
    gastrointestinal system, 715–716
    immune system, 718
    integumentary system, 712
    muscular system, 711
    nervous system, 710
    overview, 709–710
    reproductive system, 718–719
    respiratory system, 713–714
    sensory system, 717
    skeletal system, 710
Wernicke's area, 284
Wheal, 237
White blood cell count, 652–653, 656
White blood cells (WBCs)
    in blood, 399, 400, 647
    in cerebral spinal fluid, 668
    disorders, 406
    general discussion, 401–402
    in immune system, 489–492
Wisdom teeth, 525, 550
Withdrawal reflex, 270
Wound repair, 225–227

X

Xiphoid, 163
X-rays, 46–47, 48, 49

Y

Yellow bone marrow, 145

Z

Zinc, 56
Z lines, 197
Zygomatic arch, 162
Zygomatic bone, 161, 162
Zygote, 605